BUSINESS STUDIES

DAVE HALL · ROB JONES · CARLO RAFFO
EDITED BY IAN CHAMBERS AND DAVE GRAY

Second Edition

CAUSEWAY PRESS LTD

CPL

Dedication

To Elaine, Holly, Caitlin, Amanda Jane, Kath, Sandra, Georgina, Rebecca, Jan and Natalie for all their love and support in the writing of this book.

Cover design by Dave Weston
Graphics by Caroline Waring-Collins, Elaine Marie-Anne Cox and Chris Collins
Photography by Andrew Allen and Dave Gray
Typing by Ingrid Hamer and Pauline Groome

Acknowledgements

The publishers would like to thank the following for the use of photographs. Other copyright material is acknowledged at source. Arjo Wiggins Appleton 60; Ben Taggart Modelmaking 6; Berisford plc 392; Bonnet 452; British Airways 32; Cadbury Schweppes 383, 393; Capital Radio 397; Carpetright 376; Coates Viyella 479; Corel 165, 209, 219, 241, 287, 343; Drew Scientific Group 458; Digital Stock 2, 57, 140, 206, 289, 320, 355, 370, 375, 395, 407, 447, 477, 486, 511, 512, 533, 571, 585, 613, 649; Digital Vision 63, 265, 379; Ford Motor Company 147; Greenalls Group plc 263; Hattersley Newman Hender 377, Harris Tweed Authority 106; House of Fraser 494; HSBC 307; Mike Gibbons 3; Kingfisher 83; Lego 327; Leyland Trucks 520; Ian McAnulty 200; Marks & Spencer 36; Merseyside Tec/APR 557; Monk Cotton Group 106; National Power 406; Nestlé 266; Nissan 686; Hugh Nutt 600; Oasis 461; Nick On 295; Photobiz 306, 496; Photodisc 3, 7, 22, 24, 27, 38, 39, 45, 70, 89, 90, 112, 127, 132, 141, 146, 156, 192, 280, 286, 301, 311, 349, 350, 357, 360, 362, 363, 387, 394, 395, 401, 407, 409, 412, 416, 430, 434, 435, 439, 443, 444, 449, 469, 475, 478, 490, 533, 539, 545, 552, 565, 568, 569, 580, 585, 592, 596, 634, 649, 664, 680, 688; Pilkington Glass 645; PizzaExpress 425; Precoat International 375, Railtrack Group PLC 28; Reckitt & Colman 331; Rex Features Ltd 117, 191, 243, 289, 316, 351, 382, 538, 560, 589, 618, 656, 709, 711; Richer Sounds 654; Rover Group 262, 504; Sefton Photo Library 694; Shell 516; Stagecoach 398, 615; Stakis 84; Tate & Lyle 197; Topham Picturepoint 42, 63, 134, 151, 179, 382, 623, 711, 728; Twinbridge Precision Engineers 3; Unigate PLC 20, 61; United Norwest 43.

Office for National Statistics material is Crown Copyright, reproduced here with the permission of Her Majesty's Stationery Office.

British Library Cataloguing in Publication Data
A catalogue record for this book is available from the British Library.

ISBN 1-873929-90-0

Causeway Press Limited
PO Box 13, Ormskirk, Lancs, L39 5HP
© Dave Hall, Rob Jones, Carlo Raffo, Ian Chambers, Dave Gray
1st impression, 1993, reprinted eight times
2nd impression 1999, reprinted 2000

Typesetting by Waring-Collins Partnership
Printed and bound by Legoprint, Italy.

Contents

(iii)

Preface

Business Studies does not provide a step-by-step guide to how to be 'good at business'. There is no simple set of rules that can be applied at all times which will always be successful. However, by being analytical, rigorous and critical it may be possible to develop skills and approaches which can be useful, at certain times and in certain situations, when making business decisions. It is possible that different approaches will be used by different people in business and there may be disagreement as to which approach to take.

Business Studies is integrated and different areas of business are interdependent. There are links, for example, between:
● what is being produced and the funds available to pay for it (production and finance);
● the selling of the product and ethical considerations (marketing and ethics);
● the type of business and many aspects of its operation.

Being aware of these aspects of business will help us to understand how and why business decisions are made, and how they affect a variety of people, both within and outside the business. The aim of **Business Studies (Second Edition)** is to help those studying Business to understand business decisions and to be analytical, rigorous and critical in their business thinking. A number of features are included in the book which we believe will help this task.

Comprehensive course coverage The book contains material which should meet the demands of a wide range of courses. These include AS/A level, Higher Grade, Advanced GNVQ/Vocational A Levels, higher education and professional courses. The second edition has been completely rewritten for the new AS/A level Business Studies specifications and the new Higher Grade course in Business Management. The book is organised into 104 units across six sections:
● objectives, strategy and the business environment;
● external influences;
● marketing;
● accounting and finance;
● people in organisations;
● operations management.
In addition there are two units on study skills and assessment at the end. There is a development in the units contained in each section which reflects progress throughout a course and the requirements of new courses.

Guidance is given on exactly how the book can be used for specific courses in **Business Studies Teachers' Guide (Second Edition)**. To allow flexibility in course construction and teaching **Business Studies AS Level** is also available. It provides the AS Level units in a seperate book.

Flexible unit structure The unit structure allows the lecturer or teacher greater freedom to devise the course. Business Studies teachers and lecturers often teach different aspects of the course in different orders. So, whilst there is a logical order to the book, it has been written on the assumption that teachers or lecturers and students will piece the units together to suit their own teaching and learning needs and the requirements of the course being taught.

Cross referencing has been used in many of the units. This helps the teacher, lecturer or student to follow the course as they want. It will also be useful for modular courses and courses where Business Studies is only one part of the total course. The units in the book which relate to specific aspects of business, such as marketing or accounting, can be used in specialist courses or provide a short course in that area. Cross referencing also helps to stress the integrated nature of Business Studies and the interdependence and possible conflict that may exist in many areas.

Accessibility The book has been written in a clear and logical style which should make it accessible to all readers. Each unit is divided into short, easily manageable sections.

A workbook The text is interspersed with a large number of questions. The questions which appear as part of the units mostly refer to preceding information. Answers in most cases are expected to be relatively short. Questions are based on a variety of case studies, data, articles, photographs, etc. They should allow the student and teacher/lecturer to assess whether the information has been understood. One longer question appears at the end of each unit. This is either a data response, problem solving, report writing or case study question. It draws on information contained in the whole unit and answers are expected to reflect this.

Business Studies Teachers' Guide (Second Edition) provides suggested answers and mark schemes for the activities and questions that appear in this book. The questions at the end of each unit are designed to reflect the level of understanding, application, analysis and evaluation required at different stages of courses. Summary questions provide a means of revising each unit.

Use of business examples, case studies and data Modern technology has allowed much of the book to proceed from manuscript to book form in a very short period. This has meant that we have been able to use the latest statistics and business examples available. Materials used have been chosen to demonstrate appropriate arguments and theories. They should, therefore, allow students to answer questions which require knowledge of what has happened 'in recent years' or 'over the past decade', as well as questions which deal with current debates.

Study skills and assessment The last two units in the book provide guidance on how to study and the methods of assessment used in Business Studies. They are presented in the form of a manual and are designed to be used at various stages throughout the course.

Key terms Many units contain a key terms section. Each section defines new concepts, which appear in capitals in the text of the unit. Taken together, they provide a comprehensive dictionary of business terms.

Presentation Great care has been taken with how the book has been presented. It is hoped that the layout of the book, the use of colour and the use of diagrams will help learning.

We would like to thank the following for their efforts in the preparation of this book: Richard Dunill, for keeping the debate sharp and yet accessible; Mike Kidson and Lisa Fabry for the unenviable task of proof reading; Ingrid Hamer for her long hours of typing; Nigel Lewis; Michael J. Forshaw for bringing a 'real' accountant's view to the book; all staff and students at Bolton Sixth Form College, King George V College, Loreto College, and Manchester University School of Education; Diane Wallace and Steve Robertson for working on the early development of the book; Alain Anderton for sharing his style ideas.

Dave Hall   Rob Jones   Carlo Raffo
Ian Chambers   Dave Gray

What is business activity?

A few years ago, Helena Houtris and her two children Barry and Mary opened a Greek restaurant in Coronation Walk, Southport. They had all previously worked in the restaurant trade, but wanted to run their own business. They invested about £10,000 of their own money to set up The Ledra, a restaurant specialising in Cypriot cuisine. Before they could begin trading they had to:

- obtain a five year lease on a property;
- convert the premises which had previously been a ladies' hair salon;
- line the kitchen with aluminium panels to conform with health regulations;
- obtain a fire certificate and a license to sell alcohol;
- acquire furniture, kitchen equipment and stocks for the bar;
- recruit part time staff to help out;
- advertise the restaurant in a local newspaper.

Each person had a role to play in the running of the business. Helena concentrated on the preparation of the food. Barry acted as the restaurant manager and was also responsible for purchasing. Mary's role was as an assistant to both Barry and Helena, which gave the business a great deal of flexibility. Barry and his mother also handled the financial side together. The part time staff were employed to wait on tables, wash up and work in the bar.

The business flourished very quickly. The Ledra was the only authentic Greek restaurant in North Merseyside and developed a reputation for quality food and a friendly service. The Houtris family worked long hours to make the business successful and were rewarded as the number of customers returning on a regular basis grew over time.

The above case illustrates many features of business activity.

- Business activity produces an **output** - a good or service. A specialist restaurant service is provided by the Houtris family.
- Goods and services are **consumed**. Restaurant customers consumed the service provided by The Ledra.
- **Resources** are used up. Money, food and drinks, furniture, staff and electricity are just a few examples of resources used by The Ledra.
- A number of business **functions** may be carried out. Administration, managing staff (human resources) and decisions about marketing, finance and production are some examples.
- Businesses can be affected by **external factors**. The lack of competition from other Greek restaurants in the area may have contributed to the success of The Ledra.

Figure 1.1 shows a diagram which illustrates the nature of business activity. All types of business may be represented by this diagram - a building society, a window cleaner, a multinational chemical company, a shoe manufacturer or the BBC.

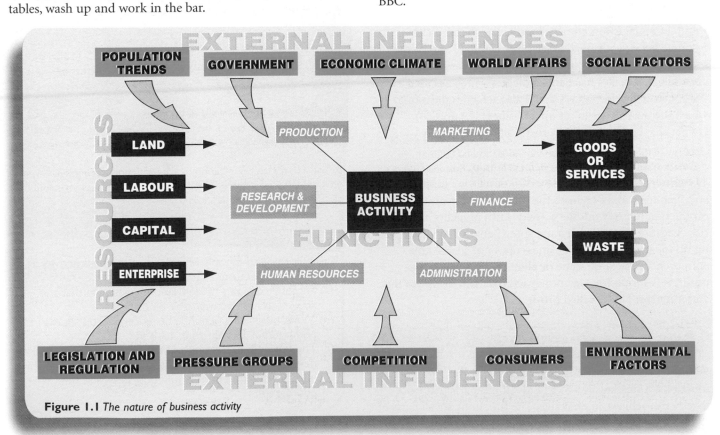

Figure 1.1 *The nature of business activity*

Business resources

Businesses use resources or FACTORS OF PRODUCTION in business activity. These are usually divided into four groups.

Land Land is not just a 'plot of land' where business premises might be located. It also includes natural resources, such as coal, diamonds, forests, rivers and fertile soil. The owners of land receive **rent** from those who use it.

Business activity uses both **renewable** and **non-renewable** resources. Renewable resources are those like fish, forests and water which nature replaces. Examples of non-renewable land resources are mineral deposits like coal and diamonds, which once used are never replaced. There has been concern in recent years about the rate at which renewable resources are being used. For example, overfishing has led to a decline in North Sea cod stocks from around 1 million tonnes in 1971 to around one-third of this amount by the year 2000.

Labour Labour is the workforce of business. Manual workers, skilled workers and management are all members of the workforce. They are paid **wages** or **salaries** for their services. The quality of individual workers will vary considerably. Each worker is unique, possessing a different set of characteristics, skills, knowledge, intelligence and emotions.

It is possible to improve the quality of **human resources** through training and education. Human resources become more productive if money is invested by business or government in training and education.

Capital Capital is sometimes described as the **artificial** resource because it is made by labour. Capital refers to the tools, machinery and equipment which businesses use. For example, JCB makes mechanical diggers which are used by the construction industry. Capital also refers to the money which the owners use to set up a business (☞ unit 56). Owners of capital receive **interest** if others borrow it.

Enterprise Enterprise has a special role in business activity. The **entrepreneur** or businessperson develops a business idea and then hires and organises the other three factors of production to carry out the activity. Entrepreneurs also take risks because they will often use some personal money to help set up the business. If the business does not succeed the entrepreneur may lose some or all of that money. If the business is successful, any money left over will belong to the entrepreneur. This is called **profit**.

Business functions

Figure 1.1 showed that business activity involves a number of functions. A business is a SYSTEM - it has parts that work together to achieve an objective. The functions are all parts of the system. A business is also part of other systems such as the economic and political systems (☞ unit 8). What functions does a business carry out?

- **Production** involves changing natural resources into a product or the supply of a service. Most business resources are used up in the production process. Examples of production can be seen on a building site where houses are constructed, in a dental surgery where dental treatment is given and in a coal mine where coal is extracted.
- **Marketing** has become very important in recent years due to an increase in competition in business. It is concerned with identifying consumer needs and satisfying them. Examples of marketing activities are market research, advertising, packaging, promotion, distribution and pricing.
- The **finance** department is responsible for the control of money in a business. It has a number of important duties. This includes recording transactions, producing documents to illustrate the performance of the business and its financial position and controlling the flow of money in the business.
- Dealing with enquiries, communicating messages and producing documents for the workforce are all examples of **administrative** tasks.

Question 1

Look at the photograph which shows business activity at a clothing manufacturer's factory.
(a) Suggest examples of land, labour or capital that the above business activity may be using.
(b) What business function is being carried out in the photograph? Explain your answer.
(c) The business in the photograph decides to advertise a new range of products. Suggest two ways in which this might affect the business function shown in the photograph.

The **human resources** function involves the management of people. The personnel department looks after the welfare of the workforce, and is responsible for such things as recruitment, selection, training, appraisal, health and safety, equal opportunities, payment systems and worker disputes.

Research and development (R&D) involves technical research, for example, research into a new medicine or a new production technique. R&D can be very expensive. Consequently, many businesses do not have a R&D department but rely on adapting new products and new technology developed by other companies.

In a large business these functions should be easy to identify. However, a self-employed window cleaner will also carry out these functions.

- Production - cleaning windows.
- Marketing - distributing business cards to potential customers.
- Administration - dealing with enquiries from potential customers and recording their personal details in preparation for a first visit.
- Human resources management - recruiting and supervising part time helpers during busy periods.
- Finance - keeping records of all financial transactions.

Business activity is highly **integrated**. For example, production is heavily influenced by marketing activities. If marketing is effective and more of the product is sold, then more will have to be produced. Also, the finance department, for example, will carefully watch the amount of money used by other departments.

What does business activity produce?

All business activity results in the production of a good or a service. CONSUMER GOODS are those which are sold to the general public. They fall into two categories.

- **Durable goods** such as cookers, televisions, books, cars and furniture can be used repeatedly for a long period of time.
- **Non-durable goods** such as food, confectionery, newspapers and shoe polish are used very soon after they are purchased. Some of these goods are called **fast moving consumer goods**, such as soap, crisps and cornflakes.

CAPITAL GOODS are those goods purchased by businesses and used to produce other goods. Tools, equipment and machinery are examples of capital goods.

The supply of **services** has grown in recent years. Banking, insurance, hairdressing, car valeting and gardening are examples of this type of business activity.

Business activity also results in the production of waste materials. Most waste is useless and some waste, like radioactive nuclear waste, is very dangerous and expensive to dispose of. Some production techniques result in **by-products** (☞ unit 97) which can be sold. For example, the brewing process generates yeast which is sold to the producers of Marmite.

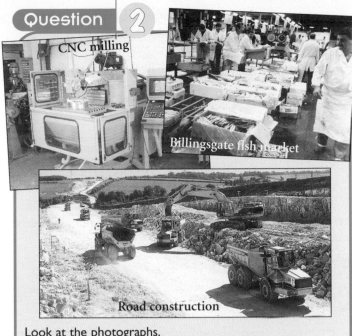

Question ②

CNC milling

Billingsgate fish market

Road construction

Look at the photographs.
(a) Which of the above are examples of: (i) consumer goods; (ii) capital goods; (iii) services?
(b) Suggest two examples of waste that a road construction company might generate.
(c) Explain how a personal computer might be classified as both a consumer good and a capital good.

External factors

Business activity is affected by a number of external forces, some of which are shown in the diagram in Figure 1.1. These are beyond the control of the individual business. In some cases they constrain a firm's decisions and may prevent its growth and development.

- **The government** has a great deal of influence over business activity. In most countries the government will be in favour of business development. A **legal framework**, where all individuals abide by the law and offenders are punished, will help this. A country also needs an **infrastructure** including roads, railways, telecommunications, schools and hospitals. Some of these items may be provided by the state (☞ unit 6). Government policy can also influence business. For example, profits and many goods and services which businesses produce are taxed.
- The **economic climate** can have a tremendous impact on business activity. For example, in the early 1990s the UK suffered from a recession and a falling demand for goods and services. This resulted in considerable hardship for many firms - approximately 73,000 individuals and companies were forced out of business in 1992. By 1997 this had fallen to around 40,000 as trading conditions improved.
- **World events** can influence business activity. Every few years the El Niño weather phenomenon occurs in the Pacific Ocean. This involves an increase in the sea water

temperature of the Eastern Pacific. The 1997 and 1998 El Niño resulted in abnormal levels of rainfall and flooding in South America and drought in South East Asia. Indonesia, the world's third largest coffee producer, experienced a crop reduction of 25 per cent. The drought and low rainfall also led to a 15 per cent fall in production for rice producers in the Philippines and sugar cane producers in Thailand.

● Some individuals form **pressure groups** (☞ unit 27) in order to influence businesses. For example, in 1995 pressure on Shell from Greenpeace prevented the oil company from sinking the Brent Spar oil storage platform at sea. In 1998 Shell announced the platform was to be dismantled and parts used to build a ferry quay near Stavanger in Norway. The cost of the recycling was £26 million.

● Most businesses face **competition** from other firms. Rivals' activities often have an influence on their operations. Following the introduction of the National Lottery a number of firms in the gaming industry, such as Littlewoods the pools company and Ladbrokes the betting shop chain, suffered reductions in turnover.

● **Consumers' tastes** change. The mid-1990s saw styles of clothes and music that had not been fashionable since the 1970s become popular again. Greater awareness of health issues has led to growing sales of products such as bottled water and low fat meals. In 1971, 28 per cent of males read the *Daily Express*. By 1998 this had fallen to 6 per cent.

● **Social factors** may influence business activity from time to time. For example, the roles of women in society have changed considerably in recent years. This has meant that more women have become involved in business management and business ownership. Some businesses have also been prepared to offer creche facilities as women have returned to work.

● **Environmental factors** have had a major effect on businesses in recent years. Some now use recycled materials in their manufacturing processes to reduce costs. Certain businesses have tried to manufacture products which are environmentally friendly in order to boost sales.

● **Legislation** and **regulation** may influence business activity. This may be in the form of government imposed laws, EU regulations, independent bodies set up by government to regulate industry or industry self-regulation.

● Changes in **population** can affect the demand for products and the supply of workers. The falling numbers of men aged 60-64 in work have been replaced by increasing numbers of women aged 16-59. This trend is predicted to continue until the year 2006.

Satisfying needs and wants

The success of a business activity depends on many factors. The most important is to supply a product that consumers want to buy. Businesses must satisfy consumers' NEEDS and WANTS to be successful. People's needs are limited. They

Question 3

Carr Meats Ltd is a family meat wholesaling business in Witney, Oxfordshire. It was set up in the 1980s and employs 30 staff. It sells a range of meat products (mainly beef) to butchers and general retailers in the area. Since the company began, sales turnover and profits had risen steadily. Turnover in 1995 was around £10 million. In late 1995 the family needed funds for expansion. EU regulations regarding the handling of meat products meant that their premises had to be upgraded. They also decided to build a new slaughterhouse in preparation for an export drive. They hoped to increase sales in new markets abroad. The cost of this investment was around £3 million.

There was no shortage of lenders for what was expected to be a profitable investment project. In 1995, beef exports were worth £520 million to UK businesses. However, in 1996 the BSE (mad cow disease) crisis had a devastating effect on the business. The EU banned all beef exports from Britain. As a result, most of the potential lenders withdrew their interest. Demand for the business's products fell as a result.
Source: adapted from company information.

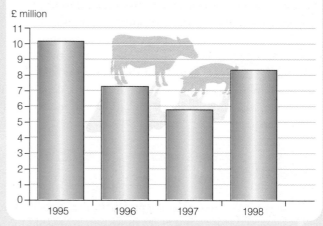

Figure 1.2 *Sales turnover of Carr Meats Ltd over the period 1995-98*

(a) What two external factors might have influenced the activities of Carr Meats in 1995?
(b) Describe the problems that Carr Meats faced as a result of the BSE scare.
(c) Explain what happened to turnover after the BSE scare.

include things which are needed to survive, such as food, warmth, shelter and security. Humans also have psychological and emotional needs such as recognition and love. Wants, however are infinite. People constantly aim for a better quality of life, which might include better housing, better health care, better education, longer holidays, and more friends. Unit 8 deals with the way in which an economy attempts to satisfy people's needs.

Markets

The **goods** and **services** produced by businesses are sold in MARKETS. A market exists when buyers and sellers communicate in order to exchange goods and services. In some cases buyers and sellers might meet at an agreed place to carry out the exchange. For example, many villages and towns have regular open air markets where buyers and sellers exchange goods and services. Also, buying and selling can be carried out over the telephone. For example, the First Direct banking facility allows customers to conduct nearly all of their banking business over the telephone. Buying and selling can also take place in shopping centres, in newspapers and magazines, through mail order, and more recently, through television and through the internet.

The goods and services of most businesses are bought by CUSTOMERS and used by CONSUMERS to satisfy their wants and needs. A business may be interested in some of the following markets.

● Consumer goods markets - where products like food, cosmetics and magazines are sold in large quantities.
● Markets for services - these are varied and could include services for individuals, such as banking, or services for industry, such as cleaning.
● Capital goods markets - where items used by other businesses are bought and sold, such as machinery.
● Labour markets - where people are hired for their services.
● The housing market - where people buy and sell properties.
● Money markets - where people and institutions borrow and lend money, such as commercial banks.
● Commodity markets - where raw materials, such as copper and coffee are bought, mainly by business.

Specialisation

One feature of modern businesses is SPECIALISATION. This is the production of a limited range of goods by an individual, firm, region or country. Specialisation can take place between firms. For example, McDonald's supplies a limited range of fast foods, Ford manufactures cars, Heinz processes food products and MFI supplys furniture products. Examples of regional specialisation might be Kidderminster, which specialises in carpet production, Stoke-on-Trent, which produces pottery and Kent, which is one of the country's main hop growers. Different countries also specialise. For example, Scotland specialises in the distilling of whisky, Saudi Arabia in oil extraction and South Africa in the supply of gold.

Specialisation within a firm is an important part of production. Departments specialise in different activities, such as marketing, purchasing, personnel and finance. People specialise in different tasks and skills. This is called the DIVISION OF LABOUR and allows people to concentrate on the task or skill at which they are best. In business, production is divided amongst workers, who each concentrate on a limited range of tasks. For example, the building of a house involves an architect to draw up the plans, a bricklayer to build the structure, a joiner to undertake woodwork, a roofer to lay the tiles etc. It is argued that the division of labour raises the productivity and efficiency of business and the economy. There is a number of reasons for this.

● Workers can concentrate on the tasks that they do best, leaving other tasks to more specialist workers.
● People's skills are improved by carrying out tasks over a long period of time. It is also possible to develop a brand new skill.
● Time is saved because workers are not constantly changing tasks, moving from one area to another or collecting new tools.
● The organisation of production becomes easier and more effective.

Specialisation, however, does have disadvantages.

● Work can become tedious and boring. This can result in poor worker motivation with the likelihood of a higher rate of absenteeism and increased staff turnover.
● Problems can also occur when one stage of production depends on another stage. If one stage breaks down, production might be halted.
● Over-specialisation can pose problems when there is a change in demand. If people are only competent in one skill they may have to retrain, causing delays in

Question 4

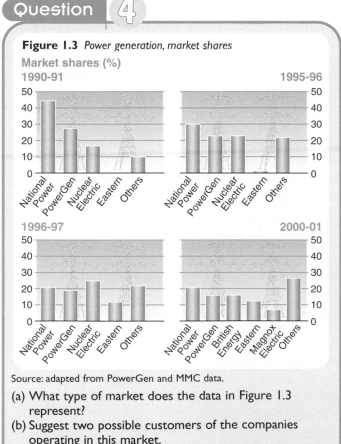

Figure 1.3 *Power generation, market shares*

Source: adapted from PowerGen and MMC data.

(a) What type of market does the data in Figure 1.3 represent?
(b) Suggest two possible customers of the companies operating in this market.
(c) Describe the changes which have taken place between 1990-1996 and those which are expected to take place between 1997-2001.

production. Some are not able to retrain and become unemployed.

Question 5

Ben Taggart is a former 'specialist effects' painter and decorator who worked on designs for television programmes and films. Having worked for a model maker, he set up his own business designing and making accurate scale models of buildings and property facades. Typically the process involves:
- a visit to the customer to discuss their needs;
- measuring and calculating the size of the property;
- taking photographs;
- drawing a plan and elevation of the model to the required scale;
- making the model.

Each model is built from medium density fibreboard and takes around 3-4 weeks to complete. The price of each model will vary, but a typical Victorian terraced house facade will cost around £950.

Source: adapted from Ben Taggart Modelmaking.

(a) Explain why Ben Taggart 'specialises' in model making.
(b) It has been suggested that Ben could employ part time workers. Each worker could specialise in a task involved in the design and production process. Explain: (i) two advantages; and (ii) two disadvantages to Ben Taggart of employing part time workers and the division of labour.
(c) Is it likely that the business would benefit from the division of labour given the nature of its activities? Explain your answer.

The importance of money

MONEY is anything which is generally accepted as a means of exchange. It is essential for the smooth exchange of goods and services in markets and helps specialisation.

Without money goods have to be exchanged using a BARTER SYSTEM. This involves swapping goods directly, which is inefficient. It is necessary for the wants of individuals to be perfectly matched. Searching for the perfect match in a barter deal can be very time consuming. It is also difficult to value different goods without money. In addition, giving change can be a problem when the values of the goods being exchanged do not match exactly. Money also has a

number of other functions. It:
- allows individuals to save some of their income and buy goods and services at a later date;
- enables all goods and services to be valued in common units, for example, a house which costs £60,000 is worth exactly 10 times more than a car which is valued at £6,000;
- allows payments to be deferred, ie goods can be bought and payment made at a later date.

There is no single definition of the money supply. No financial asset has all the characteristics or fulfils all the functions of money perfectly. In the UK, two measures tend to be used by the government. M0 is a 'narrow' measure. It includes notes and coins in circulation, cash in banks' tills and cash held for operational reasons at the Bank of England. M4 is a 'broad' measure. It includes M0 plus a wider range of financial assets. These include money held in bank accounts by the private sector and building society deposits. Cheques, debit cards and credit cards are not money. They are a means of transferring money from one account to another.

Classification of business activity

Business activity is often classed by the type of production that takes place.

PRIMARY production includes activity which takes the natural resources from the earth, ie the extraction of raw materials and the growing of food. Mining, fishing, farming and forestry are examples of primary business activity. SECONDARY production involves manufacturing, processing and construction which transform raw materials into goods. Car production, distilling, baking, shipbuilding and office construction are examples of secondary sector activity. TERTIARY production includes the provision of services. Hairdressing, distribution, security, banking, theatre and tourism are all examples of business activity in this area. Other methods of classifying business include by:
- size (☞ unit 93);
- geographical area (☞ unit 100);
- sector (☞ units 5 and 6);
- ownership (☞ unit 5).

Trends in business activity

Business activity does not follow a constant pattern. Different industries grow and decline over time. In the UK some major changes have occurred in the structure of the economy. Before the Industrial Revolution most of the UK's resources were used for primary production. This included industries such as agriculture and mining. During the nineteenth century, secondary production expanded rapidly. The Industrial Revolution resulted in a growing quantity of resources being employed in manufacturing.

Since around 1960 tertiary production has grown at the

expense of secondary production. The decline in manufacturing is often called DE-INDUSTRIALISATION. The process of de-industrialisation has resulted in the decline of some once prosperous industries, such as shipbuilding, textiles, steel and engineering. Certain reasons have been put forward to explain the decline which include:

● changes in consumer demand;
● a lack of competitiveness amongst UK manufacturers;
● increasing competition from overseas manufacturers;
● a lack of investment in manufacturing;
● trade union restrictive practices;
● unhelpful government policy.

In contrast, service industries now employ around 70 per cent of the UK's workforce. Financial services, personal services, household services and the leisure industry are just some growth areas. For example, in 1996 and 1997 the profile of the football industry was raised significantly. A number of clubs floated on the stock exchange and the amount of money flowing into the industry rose. Media interest

increased, attendances at matches in the Premier League were high and commercial activities began to flourish.

The way in which activity in different industries may fluctuate is shown in Figure 1.4. The graph illustrates growth in two areas - business, financial and telecom services and manufacturing, distribution, construction and public services - between 1987 and 1997. Both declined between 1987 and 1992 and then expanded afterwards. However, since 1995 service industry has grown more sharply than manufacturing.

The overall trend in business activity suggests a growth in services at the expense of primary and secondary production. Care needs to be taken when identifying trends from figures. For example, output in one particular service industry may be growing but employment figures may be falling. This could be because businesses in the industry are replacing workers with technology or are reorganising to reduce the workforce. However, employment figures do show clearly the changing patterns of business activity.

Question 6

(a) Which of the categories of employment in Table 1.1 fall into (i) primary industry; (ii) secondary industry; (iii) tertiary industry?
(b) Explain what is meant by the term 'All manufacturing' used in Table 1.1.
(c) Describe briefly two trends which have taken place between 1990 and 1998.
(d) Suggest one reason to account for each trend you have identified in your answer to the previous question.
(e) What effects might the trends in employment shown in Table 1.1 have on: (i) a skilled construction worker; (ii) a business providing equipment for the banking industry?

Table 1.1 *Employment in selected UK industries*

		000s
	1990	1998
All industries	22,920	23,237
Selected industries		
Mining and quarrying	163	80
Energy and water supplies	404	222
Construction	1,143	1,003
Manufacture of office machinery and computers	65	48
All manufacturing	4,708	4,076
Retailing	2,131	2,450
Hotels and restaurants	1,262	1,316
Financial intermediation	1,059	1,064
Health and social work	2,317	2,582
Service industries	16,350	17,664

Source: adapted from *Annual Abstract of Statistics*, 1999, Office for National Statistics.

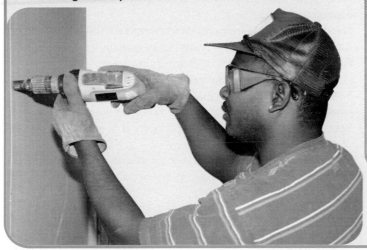

Summary

1. What are the 4 factors of production?
2. What is the financial reward paid to each factor of production?
3. Why is capital said to be an artificial resource?
4. Describe 6 functions involved in business activity.
5. Why is business activity highly integrated?
6. Explain the difference between needs and wants.
7. What is the difference between capital and consumer goods?
8. What is meant by specialisation in business?
9. State 3:
   (a) advantages;
   (b) disadvantages; of specialisation.
10. Briefly describe the role of money in business.
11. List 10 business activities in your local town. State which of these are examples of:
    (a) primary production;
    (b) secondary production;
    (c) tertiary production.
12. What are the possible causes of de-industrialisation?

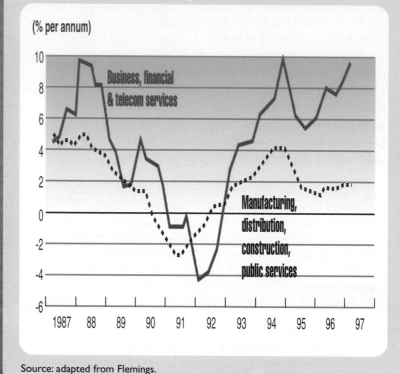

Figure 1.4 *Output growth in two different areas, 1987-1997*

(% per annum)

Business, financial & telecom services

Manufacturing, distribution, construction, public services

Source: adapted from Flemings.

Key terms

Barter - a system of exchange which involves the swapping of goods between individuals.

Capital goods - goods used to produce other goods, such as tools, equipment and machinery.

Consumers - individuals who use or 'consume' goods and services to satisfy their needs and wants.

Consumer goods - goods produced for general use by the public. They can be durable and non-durable.

Customers - individuals who buy goods and services supplied by businesses.

De-industrialisation - the decline in manufacturing.

Division of labour - specialisation in specific tasks or skills by individuals.

Factors of production - resources used by business to produce goods and services.

Market - anywhere that buyers and sellers communicate to exchange goods and services.

Money - any substance which is generally accepted as a means of exchange.

Needs - human requirements which must be satisfied for survival.

Primary production - activities which involve the extraction of raw materials from the earth and the growing of food.

Secondary production - activities such as manufacturing which transform raw materials into finished goods.

Specialisation - in business, the production of a limited range of goods.

System - parts that work together to achieve an objective; a system can be a communications system, a business, an economic or a political system.

Tertiary production - activities which involve the provision of services.

Wants - human desires which are unlimited.

Case study

Diesel

Diesel, the hip Italian clothing company, owns 30 stores and sells clothes in over 80 countries. The president of Diesel is 43 year old Renzo Rosso. His first job was as production manager for Moltex, a Venetian jean making factory. However, his heart was not in working for someone else. After two years he became bored and lazy, despite a passion for the fashion industry. He was eventually sacked, but persuaded the owner, Adriano Goldschmied, to give him one more chance. The owner was going to close the whole production line managed by Rosso, but was persuaded to keep it open. Rosso negotiated a three month trial period on the condition that his salary was linked to productivity. Rosso motivated his staff by sharing his own wages with them if they reached production targets. Within two months he raised his own salary from £100 to £1,300 per week.

This experience made Rosso realise that he had the expertise and inspirational skills to set up his own business. Although Rosso had reached his goal at Moltex, he was eager for more demanding objectives. In 1978 he bought 40 per cent of Goldschmied's business with £2,500 cash borrowed from his father. This enabled him to use the factory's facilities to make jeans according to his own designs. He produced unusual designs and called his brand Diesel.

He started by making small numbers of jeans, 100 or 200 pairs. He found two agents, one in Germany, the other in Sicily, who approached retailers to stock them. From day one he was unable to keep up with demand and made a profit. Rosso was quick to expand and in 1982 he opened a factory-outlet store. By 1985 he had increased staff from 28 to 40, his profit had reached £500,000 and he decided to buy Goldschmied's share of the business. He then expanded his range into other casual wear and focused the business on retailing.

In 1998 he employed 1,100 staff and made a profit in 1997 of £18 million. The success of Diesel jeans can be attributed to a number of factors. They have been described as 'cool', 'ironic' and artfully distressed'. Some have commented that Diesel could argue convincingly to have started the revival of 70s/kitsch trends. Denim has had to find other markets in the 1990s. Younger buyers have

rebelled against the trend for older people to wear jeans. However, sales to the fashionable line dancing crowd continue. Diesel also faces competition from a growing number of sources. Traditional jean manufacturers such as Wrangler and Levis have been joined by own brand manufacturers such as Next and Marks and Spencer. Even the fashion houses of Armani and Calvin Klein are represented in high streets and shopping centres.

Competing in such a competitive market is not without its difficulties. Certain Diesel advertisements have been criticised. In July 1998 the Advertising Standards Authority (ASA) told Diesel that it must stop using a poster of four young women dressed as nuns from the waist up wearing jeans and holding rosaries under the headline 'superior denim'. The ASA is a body which oversees complaints against advertising and attempts to ensure the advertisers follow a code of advertising practice.

Source: adapted from *The Sunday Times*, 11.10.98, *The Times* 12.8.1998, *The Guardian*, 17.1.1998, 4.2.1998, 10.6.1998.

(a) **What classification of business activity would Diesel fall into? Explain your answer.**

(b) **Suggest examples of land, labour and capital that might be used by Diesel.**

(c) **Explain why Rosso could be said to have been an entrepreneur when setting up his business.**

(d) **Explain the types of specialisation suggested in the article.**

(e) (i) **What external factors in the article might have influenced Diesel's activities?**

   (ii) **Explain how these external factors may have affected Diesel's business.**

② Setting up in Business

Why set up?

What do ICI, Virgin, Prontaprint, your nearest newsagent and the local window cleaner all have in common? At some time in the past, these businesses have been set up by their owners. Many, though not all, began as small operations. They are often started by entrepreneurs (☞ unit 3) working in a small shop or factory, or from home. Alan Sugar, the businessman behind Amstrad, started by convincing customers they really were buying the last television he had left in his flat! The Body Shop began as one retail outlet opened in 1976 in Brighton by Anita Roddick, having previously sold her own cosmetics in the 1960s. According to the NatWest Start-up Index, around 330,000 businesses were expected to start up in 1998. In the UK in the late 1990s there were around 2.7 million organisations. Small firms were 97 per cent of all employers. In the EU there were around 16 million businesses. 93 per cent of these employed less than 10 people.

Why do people set up in business?

● Independence. Some people prefer to make their own decisions and take responsibility rather than being told what to do.

Question 1

Jason Olim is chief executive of the worlds' largest internet music store, CDnow. Olim turned his passion into a business. He had tried to find a copy of a Kind of

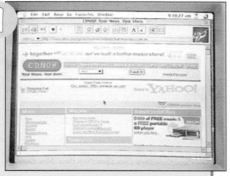

Blue by Miles Davis in his local record store without success. He thought that: 'A music store needs to give guidance to help you find what you are looking for.' At the time he was studying for a computer science degree. He came up with the idea of a database of all available albums and combining this with a database of all the books and reviews he could find. In 1994, working as a software engineer, he decided to put all the databases on the internet as a kind of music store. By 1998 the business had a music library of 300,000 CDs, 10 times that of a record store. Customers can log on, review the information and buy the CD. He said: 'I'm a music lover and I'm a pop musician. But if I can't create music myself I may as well help people find it.'

Source: adapted from *The Observer*, 1998.

(a) Identify the factors that may have influenced Jason Olim to set up his business.
(b) Explain two possible risks that he may have faced when setting up the business.

● To increase rewards. People setting up their own business often believe that they will earn more than if they were working for an employer.

● As a result of redundancy. Some businesses start when an employee is made redundant and decides to use her skills in her own venture. **Redundancy payments** can be used to fund the business.

● Commitment to a product. A business may be set up to sell a new invention or because of commitment to a product. For example, James Dyson took five years and 5,127 prototypes before creating a working model of the best selling vacuum cleaner. 10 years later, after rejection by many companies, he produced the product under his own name.

● Sometimes people extend their hobbies into a business. A stamp collector may set up a small stall at local markets, for example.

● To satisfy creative needs. A worker on a production line packing biscuits may be artistic. Setting up a business to paint portraits may allow the individual to satisfy these needs.

● A person may want to work in a particular job, but can't find employment. Someone who has trained as a hairdresser or joiner may find that setting up their own business is the only alternative to being unemployed.

● An employee may be dissatisfied with their job. Setting up in business is one alternative to looking for a job with another firm.

Implications

What faces a person setting up their own business? He or she will come up against many problems and challenges. The way in which the entrepreneur works will probably be different to that of an employee. Take an example of a chef who has decided to 'go it alone' and open a cafe specialising in crepes and pancakes. At first, the chef would be uncertain about whether there is demand for this type of meal. Arguably this risk never goes away, but it is likely to be far greater at first until regular customers visit the cafe. The earnings of the chef are also likely to vary, depending on sales. Working for an employer, he would have earned a regular wage or salary.

The responsibility for the business would fall onto the owner. This means problems, from the non-delivery of ingredients to the placing of local adverts, will fall onto the chef. Even if employees are hired, the responsibility falls onto the owner. Many business people find that great personal commitment is needed. They must also be able to come up with new ideas and 'keep going' even if things get tough. This means the person must be single minded and self-sufficient.

Organisation of time is very important. He must decide

what is to be done and place tasks in order of priority. He must also decide if the task can be done by someone else, ie what to **delegate.** Many people who set up in business talk about the lack of time to get things done. Working from 6am until midnight every night of the week is likely in the early stages. This places great stress on their personal and social life and their family and friends.

The entrepreneur must also consider the skills they have and whether they are enough. Working for an employer may demand skill as a chef. This technical skill will be important to the cafe. However, the chef will also need management skills. These range from making sure that correct materials and equipment are available to having effective stock control. As workers are hired, the entrepreneur must develop personnel skills to control, motivate and organise the workforce. The owner will also need to sell himself and the company, a skill that is unlikely to be part of his role as an employee. Most people find that their technical skills are much greater than their managerial skills. It is often this lack of managerial skills which leads to problems. If a skill is needed which the entrepreneur does not have, he can:

● retrain, although there may be little time to attend a course and available courses are not always designed for specific needs;
● hire full time employees with the necessary skills;
● employ a specialist, such as an accountant, designer or market research agency, ideally for 'one off' tasks so that they do not become a full time cost;
● find a partner or take over another business. This is dealt with later.

Setting up

Whatever the reasons people want to set up in business, they must have a **business idea** before they can begin. It might be a specialist shop selling items for dolls houses, a door to door hairdressing service or a company producing computers. The idea can come from many places. It might be based on the skills or experience of the entrepreneur. It might be an idea from a colleague or advice from an independent. Often the idea is simply the same as other businesses, and the entrepreneur feels she can do it better. It might just be inspiration!

The next stage is to **consider** whether the business is likely to be a success. This can depend on many factors, some of which are dealt with in the next section of this unit. If the entrepreneur is sure that the business will be a success and is prepared to take the risk, then she is likely to go ahead. Setting up the business without careful **planning** can lead to problems. It is advisable to plan the business and take advice before finally setting up, to avoid these problems.

One final decision that the entrepreneur must make is **how to set up** the company. She may set up on her own, with a partner, or by buying an existing business.

The process involved in setting up the business is shown in Figure 2.2.

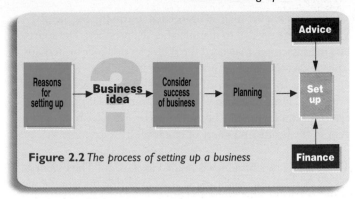

Figure 2.2 *The process of setting up a business*

The chances of success

Many businesses that are set up fail within a few years. The Department for Trade and Industry has estimated that a quarter of all business start-ups fail within the first eighteen months and 35 per cent fail after five years. If a business is going to be a success, the entrepreneur must consider a number of factors. Any one of these factors may be important. The Showering family made fine cider at a good profit in Somerset. When they produced a high quality drink from pears, in a champagne-like bottle, and called it Babycham, they became millionaires.

Take an example of someone aiming to produce and sell training shoes. There is a number of questions that may help to make this idea into a success.

The basic business idea What business is the person entering and what will be sold? It may be better to sell 'high quality and performance sports shoes' rather than just 'trainers'. Who are the customers? It may be possible to target an audience, such as 25-35 year olds in a certain income bracket. How is the product used? The shoes could be designed to be hard wearing for sports, or with fashion in mind.

The market How many products exist already? Customers may prefer other types of shoes for fashion wear or a different type of design. What are the strengths and weaknesses of the competition? It may be possible to find a gap in the market, such as trainers that can be used for hiking, water sports or with a special design feature, such as a cut away back with flexible material.

Marketing What price can be charged? It may be possible to undercut competitors' prices or sell initially at less than unit cost (☞ unit 52) until the product begins to sell well. Can the business compete in some other way, such as advertising? American advertisers argue that every product has a **unique selling proposition** (USP) (☞ unit 37). The business could identify this and promote it. For example, the trainers may be 'comfortable, but robust'. How will the product be sold? The producer may sell through a retailer, representative or direct to the public, for example.

People What are the main skills needed to run the business? What skills are needed to manufacture the product? The sports shoe manufacturer may need the skills of a designer or perhaps a sports scientist before production can begin. How workers can be attracted and retained in the business must also be considered. How much do you know about legislation regarding employment? The entrepreneur will have to take into account the health and safety of employees, for example.

Finance How much money is needed to start up? The business person will need to work out the costs of setting up, eg rent and rates, wages, machinery, sales and distribution costs and professional fees. How much is available to invest? The business person may have savings or insurance policies which can be used. According to HSBC only 50 per cent of businesses borrow from a bank. Many people use redundancy cheques or sell their house to raise finance. Over and above the initial investment, how much more will be required before cash flows into the business? The sports shoe manufacturer may have orders but no cash flowing in until goods are sold. In the meantime, bills must still be paid. Often an overdraft is negotiated with the bank to see the business through this period. What other sources of finance can be used? If the entrepreneur approaches a third party to fund start up costs, control may be lost.

The product or service offered Is the product or service ready for sale? If not, how far has it been developed? It is unlikely that the sports shoe manufacturer will find a backer for the business if the idea has not yet been developed. Is the product idea safe? It may be possible to protect the idea by patent (☞ unit 99) or copyright before production takes place.

Is production cost effective? The manufacturer may want to consider the way the shoe is produced, the location of production, how production is organised and the materials used. Each of these will affect the cost and speed of production.

Risk, timescale and cost What are the main risks involved in the venture? How can they be reduced? The producer may try the product on a small scale basis before trading or work part time while still employed to reduce risk.

Planning

Although there are examples of businesses that just 'set up and prosper', these are limited. Most firms must plan carefully what they aim to achieve and how to do it. Answering the questions in the last section will help the business to produce a BUSINESS PLAN. This is a statement that outlines the way that the business will achieve its objectives (☞ unit 4).

An established business may produce a business plan to show how it will obtain the funds to pay back a loan for a new piece of machinery. For a business starting up, a business plan is vital. It can be used to:
- give a clear idea of its direction and operation;
- show a bank or other institution its likely position and its ability to pay back a loan;
- identify problems that may occur to allow the business to deal with them before they can become a problem;

Question 2

Peachey's is a furniture, interiors and garden ornament shop. It was set up by Caroline Peachey in the former piggery of the farm run by her and her husband. She had previously worked in an estate agency and retail outlets. Caroline said: 'We had a spare building and saw an opportunity to turn it into something. I'd seen a gap in the furniture market between the very expensive and the very cheap. There was nowhere selling unusual but affordable pieces. When we opened we got a lot of editorial in local papers. But then trade dropped off. I had to learn other ways of keeping up interest - a visitors book for a mailing list, postcards of the shop ...' The biggest mistake was when Caroline printed 1,000 leaflets and put them on car windscreens. It brought no extra trade at all. The shop has grown. 'People love the personal service and the prices ... they love coming to the farm. We're still farmers; it just happens that a shop selling furniture and candlesticks is part of the farm business'.

Source: adapted from *You* magazine, *The Mail on Sunday*, 25.4.1999.

(a) Identify the factors that may have influenced the success of Caroline's business.

Question 3

Look at Figure 2.1 which shows part of a business plan of a small business selling signed and numbered limited edition artists' etchings, greetings cards and picture frames.

Figure 2.1

> **c Major competitors - their prices, strengths and weaknesses:**
> Major competition is from 'Anystore' which has a well-known prints department, but this helps more often than not, as customers are drawn to the area and the small print gallery is cheaper.
> Other competition is from all of the other shops selling gift items, but again they draw custom into the area.
> Strengths of the small print gallery are:
> Something for everyone at any price level. Once it is bought people cannot tell how much it costs.
> Numbered handmade prints are exclusive and special, and possibly an investment for the future.
> Weaknesses of the competition are that they are more expensive and less flexible. Jewellers, for instance have nothing under £18.00.

Source: *The Business Start-up Guide*, NatWest Bank.

(a) Explain how competition can:
   (i) help;
   (ii) harm;
   the business.
(b) If the business was applying for a loan, why might a bank manager be interested in this information?

Table 2.1

Features	What is included	Examples

The business	Name and address of
	  the business
	What the business
	  aims to achieve
	Type of organisation
		Cross-Hatchard
		Partnership

The product or service	What is being produced What quantities will be produced The proposed price	Specialist cycles Average price £300

The market	Results of research or testing
	The size of the market
	If the market is growing or not
	Who will buy the product
	Competition and their strengths
	  and weaknesses
	Methods of promotion and
	  advertising
		Growing demand
		for mountain cycles,
		racing cycles etc.
		Advertising in trade
		journals.

Personnel	Who is involved in the business What experience and skills people have	Former Raleigh workers
Buying and production	Likely costs of production Who the main suppliers are What benefits suppliers have	Production costs £30,000
Premises and equipment	The type of premises Location of premises and cost Age, style and value of machinery Replacement cost of machinery How to cope with expansion	Produced on industrial estate site

Profit	Likely profit based on:
	  * turnover (price x sales)
	  * costs
	Break even point. This is the
	  quantity sold where turnover is
	  equal to costs
		Total costs = £55,000
		At £300 need to sell
		  183 to break even

Cash flow	When cash will come in When cash will go out If payments will be cash or credit Difference between cash in and cash out each month	Payment by cash and credit

Finance	How much cash owners will put in
	How much will have to
	  be borrowed
	What money is needed for
	How much borrowing will cost
	What assets can be used as security
	How long borrowing will be for
	  and when it will be paid back
		£5,000 put in
		by each of
		the partners

● highlight its strengths and weaknesses.

What is included in a business plan? Table 2.1 shows the details that might appear in the plan of a business aiming to produce and sell specialist cycle equipment.

Who can help and in what way?

There is a variety of organisations that provide help and advice for new businesses. They range from those set up by government or private organisations to individuals with certain skills. Advice may be in the form of:
● a telephone number of a specialist who can help;
● a detailed discussion on the best way to run a business;
● telephone numbers of organisations providing funds;
● training videos or seminars;
● specialist information on markets and types of business.
Where can an entrepreneur obtain help?

Individuals It may be possible to get advice from people who have started their own business and have been through the process of setting up. They may be able to point out what they did right or wrong and how they might do things differently. Advice about specific skills needed for running a business might come from:
● an accountant - who can give advice on accounts, book-keeping, taxation;
● a solicitor - who can give advice on the legal requirements of the business;
● an insurance adviser - who can give advice on how to protect and cover such things as equipment and employees.

Banks All of the main commercial banks provide advice for potential business people. This ranges from information about sources of finance to helping to draw up a business plan. For example, the NatWest Start-up Service allows people to talk to a small business adviser at a local branch. The adviser can help to find out whether the business is entitled to a government or EU grant. Many banks produce folders or publications with details and guidance on setting up in business.

Training and Enterprise Councils (TECS) These are government-funded organisations which provide support and advice for businesses. In 1998 they were responsible for nearly 17,000 business start-ups in the UK. TECs run Business Start-up schemes. These schemes provide training and advice for businesses that are setting up, such as writing a suitable business plan and applying for funding. They also provide short term finance for start-ups. They are funded from government, for example from the Single Regeneration Budget. After 2001 it was suggested that the work of TECS could be carried out by Learning and Skills Councils and the small business service.

Business Links and chambers and commerce In the late 1990s, TECs had started to merge with other independent organisations that help business, such as chambers of commerce. They had also started to merge and work together with Business Links. The National Federation of Business Links offers a variety of help to businesses, such as technical assistance. It is an independent body. Local Business Links have been particularly successful in obtaining funds for businesses.

Enterprise agencies These were created specially by the government to help small businesses. Most offer free advice on how to start up and run a business, training courses, contacts and information on potential investors. Local authorities often help in their setting up.

Other organisations Other organisations can offer help and advice.
● The Department of Trade and Industry runs, amongst other things, roadshows to areas of the country where consultants are available to help with business problems and a small business service offering advice on marketing,

exporting etc. It also produces *A Guide to help Small Firms.*
- Trade associations, such as The Wool Marketing Board, The Association of British Travel Agents or the Booksellers Association, can provide advice about certain types of business or industry. The Consumers Association, publishers of *Which?*, produces *The Which? Guide to Starting your own Business.*
- The Federation for Small Business produce a 'Be Your Own Boss' starter pack.
- The Prince's Youth Business Trust gives training, advice and sometimes funds to young people starting a business.
- LiveWIRE is a scheme started by Shell to encourage entrepreneurs between the ages of 16 and 25.
- Information on internet websites.

Business clubs These are regional organisations found all over the UK. They are made up of businesses in the area and are particularly useful for new firms. Often speakers from the Inland Revenue or insurance companies are invited to speak on tax, VAT, grants etc. A list of members is available and businesses provide information and advice to each other. A certain amount of inter-trading also takes place. This helps new firms to make contacts and removes some of the risk when first trading.

Getting finance

Where do new businesses find the finance that is needed to buy materials, pay wages etc? Funds can come from a number of sources.
- Personal savings or past earnings. A person aiming to set up a business in the future may have saved for some years or a redundant employee can use payments made when they became unemployed.
- Funds from partners or investors. A partnership can obtain finance from all partners, even if some are not actively involved in the business. Limited companies can raise large amounts of finance. Investors buy a 'share' of the company by purchasing shares. This is then used to finance business activity and the shareholders are paid with a dividend as a reward.
- It is possible to buy machinery and equipment and pay for it at a later date or over a period of time. Businesses may allow components or materials to be bought on CREDIT SALE or HIRE PURCHASE, where the goods are used and the cost is paid over time, plus interest. Businesses often sell goods and are paid at a later date (30, 60 or 90 days). This is known as trade credit.
- A business may decide to lease or hire equipment from a hire company. A small construction firm, for example, may hire scaffolding for a large building rather than buy their own which they might not use all the time.
- Banks or other financial institutions. Banks offer loan and overdraft facilities and charge interest. Services such as business accounts, insurance and salary payments are also

available. They may be free for a time if the firm remains in credit. Banks often ask for security against a loan. This can be any assets owned by the business or perhaps the house of the owner. Banks also need convincing that the loan is secure. They will ask for a business plan, references or proof of trading in the past. Loans can be in many forms. Some allow only the interest to be paid off in the first one or two years. It may also be possible to use a mortgage to buy premises.
- Help from organisations. Businesses starting up have been able to obtain funds from various organisations, as explained in the previous section.
- Government funds. Government funds are available for businesses locating in particular areas of the country (☞ unit 100). The government also runs a Small firms loan guarantee scheme. This allows small firms starting up or which do not have a track record to borrow. Banks lend the money and government guarantees part of the loan. In the late 1990s a new Enterprise Fund was suggested to replace this. **Venture capitalists** (☞ unit 57) would invest in businesses and the government would provide insurance against business failure.
- EU funds. A variety of funds is available from the European Union, particularly for businesses setting up in areas with

Question

If it's edible, Stephen Taylor will wrap it, box it and put a message on it. His company, Sweet Concepts, is the UK's leading supplier of corporate confectionery. It manufactures chocolates, mints, lollipops and popcorn for businesses to give to clients. The company began with £2,500 of Stephen Taylor's savings. He worked from home, persuading businesses to buy mints with the message 'Thank you'. Eventually he sold them all and was able to repay the factory that ran off a trial batch on credit. In 1998 the company hoped to turn over £2 million.

Stephen Taylor is proud of the fact that he has never borrowed a penny. Growth has been financed out of earnings and all profits have been ploughed back into the business. Starting with limited capital restricted the range of products. However, it did mean that the business didn't have money to 'blow'. Stephen said: 'I would definitely have misallocated money and wasted it on promotional material and advertisements. Because you have to make every penny count, you think carefully about promotion. You start with a one colour leaflet, then move to two colours.' A study by BDO Stoy Hayward, an accountancy firm, showed that more than 70 per cent of successful start ups in the UK raised their initial finance from personal funds and most combined them with a loan or overdraft.

Source: adapted from *The Observer*, 11.1.1999 and *The Sunday Times*, 25.10.1998.

(a) Identify the sources of finance used by Stephen Taylor.
(b) Suggest reasons to explain why he might have chosen these sources of finance.

problems (☞ unit 100). Grants are available in areas such as job creation, investment, energy conservation, new buildings, research into new markets and innovation.
● Business angels (☞ unit 57). These are businesses or individuals who invest between £10,000 -£100,000, mainly in new business start-ups.
● Certain industries can sometimes offer funds for businesses. Examples have included British Coal Enterprise giving low-interest loans to firms thinking of locating in coal mining areas and similar offers from the British Steel Industry.

How to set up

A business person must decide what form the new business will take. What alternatives are available?

Setting up a new business alone Perhaps the simplest way of starting a business is to set up alone. There are certain advantages and problems of being a sole trader (☞ unit 5). There are few legal requirements and trading can begin straight away. However, the owner will have to take all the responsibility and bear all costs.

Setting up with others One way of avoiding the problems of a sole trader is to set up with others. A partnership would allow the business person to share the load of running the business and to raise more finance, without the demands of becoming a limited company. It is, of course, possible to start business as a limited company. This may be likely if a business is to be run as a family concern (a private limited company), or if a great deal of finances were needed because of the scale of the operation (a public limited company). Limited companies are dealt with in unit 5.

Buying a business A potential business person may be able to buy an existing business. There are many examples of this. An electrician made redundant from a large public limited company may 'buy out' a local retailer selling electrical goods who wants to retire. Managers, shareholders or directors may wish to leave one company and buy out the interests of another. In some cases the managers of a company may try to buy the business from the shareholders because they feel the company can be run better. This is an example of a management buy-out (☞ unit 3). It is also possible for a worker buy out to take place, where workers buy out the shareholders of a business.

Buying a franchise If a person wants independence, but is better at carrying out or improving someone else's ideas than their own, franchising might be the ideal solution. FRANCHISING has grown steadily. It was estimated that annual turnover of franchises in the UK was around £7 billion in the late 1990s. There were 568 business format franchises in 1999. 92 per cent of franchisees reported that they were trading profitably.

There are many examples of franchises in the UK. They include names such as Wimpy, Dyno-rod, Body Shop, Holiday Inn and the British School of Motoring. What types of franchise exist?
● Dealer franchises. These are used by petrol companies, breweries and vehicle and computer producers. The companies (the **franchisors**) agree that other businesses (the **franchisees**) can sell their products. A written agreement between the two will cover areas such as the back up service of the franchisor, maintaining the image of the franchisor, sales targets, stock levels and the 'territory' of the franchisee. For example, Ford Motor Company does not allow dealers more than 5 dealerships or advertising outside the allocated 'area'. Ford does not charge a fee. It earns revenue by a mark up on sales to the dealer.
● Brand franchising. This is designed to allow an inexperienced franchisee to set up from scratch. It is used by firms such as Wimpy and McDonald's. The franchisor will already have a reputation for a product or service. It 'sells' the rights of these branded products to the franchisee. The intention is that a consumer will know they are buying the same product whether in London or Edinburgh. It is important that franchisees are monitored to make sure that the standard is maintained. To buy the franchise a business will pay between £15,000-£20,000 and a percentage of turnover (a royalty of usually 10 per cent). Often publicity, marketing and support services are carried out by the franchisor.
The benefits to the franchisor might be:
● using the specialist skills of a franchisee (as in the case of Ford dealers' retailing skills);
● the market is increased without expanding the firm;
● a fairly reliable amount of revenue (because royalties are based on turnover not profits, money is guaranteed even if a loss is made by the franchisee);
● risks and uncertainty are shared.
The advantages to franchisees might be:
● the franchisor might advertise and promote the product nationally;
● they are selling a recognised product so the chance of failure is reduced;
● services such as training and administration may be carried out by the franchisor.
Franchising is not without its problems. The royalty must be paid even if a loss is made. Also franchisees may be simply 'branch managers', rather than running their own businesses, because of restrictions in the agreement. The franchisor has the power to withdraw the agreement and in some cases, prevent the franchisee from using the premises in future.

Licensing This is similar to franchising. It is where a business sells the rights to use its copyright or patent on a product to another business. It may allow a business to produce its product. For example, Dyson earned 5 per cent for allowing USA producers to manufacture its vacuum cleaners under the names Fantom, Fury and Lightning. A business may also allow others to use its company name and logo. Coca-Cola does this in many countries worldwide, for example. This allows a business to earn revenue, without any any extra cost. A problem might be if the license is given to a poor producer or poor selling product which could affect the reputation of the business selling the licence.

Running a business

When a business is set up, there are legal and operational tasks that must be carried out.

Keeping records All transactions which take place must be recorded. This includes all sales of goods or services, the purchase of all materials, equipment and the payment of all bills for heating, lighting, wages, transport etc. This information can be used to show how well the business is performing. There are also certain records that some businesses must keep by law. For example, a business must produce a profit and loss account (☞ unit 55).

The use of documents When goods and services are bought and sold, a number of documents are used. They provide evidence and records of the transactions that have taken place. Some documents that might be used include:
● an invoice - a document sent with goods sold on trade credit, informing the purchaser that payment is due on a certain date;
● a cash receipt - a proof of purchase given when something is paid for in cash;
● a credit note - a document issued to a purchaser when they have overpaid, allowing 'credit' on future payments;
● proof of delivery - proof that items have been delivered and received at a certain destination.

If a business person employs workers, they will be given a contract of employment (☞ unit 78). This shows the terms under which the employee is hired and with which they must conform. Employees also need to be provided with wages or salary slips, showing their total earnings and any deductions.

The larger the business becomes, the more documents it is likely to use. Examples of documents that may be used internally include memos from, say, the production manager to the marketing manager, or agendas for meetings to discuss a new promotional campaign.

Tax and insurance Part of any revenue earned by a business must be paid to the government.
● Taxation. Profits made by a business are liable for tax. Government policy (☞ unit 26) has tried to reduce the corporation tax and income tax paid by businesses in the last decade to encourage growth and development. Businesses can claim allowances, which will reduce the amount of tax paid.
● Value Added Tax (VAT). Businesses must pay VAT on any goods they sell. Usually, they add this on to the price of a good or service. Some products in the UK are exempt from VAT. In the early 1990s, these included children's clothing, food and books. A business will have VAT placed onto the cost of materials, components and other items they buy.
● National Insurance contributions. Employers must make NATIONAL INSURANCE contributions to the government and must also remove employees' contributions from their wages.
● Businesses will pay Business Rates to the local authority. This is a tax on the percentage value on any building owned by the business.
● Insurance. It is sensible for an entrepreneur to insure against damages and theft. If production ceases for any reason, this could be a major problem for a new business. Revenue will not be earned and there may be cash flow problems (☞ unit 59) or the business may not be able to afford the immediate cost of repairing or replacing a piece of machinery. Some insurance is required by law. All businesses must have public liability, in case a customer or visitor to the premises is injured and makes a claim.

Question

The idea of franchising has seen a rebirth as the world economy grows and retailing becomes increasingly international. Because of the reduction in financial exposure for the franchisor, franchising has become a favoured strategy for cross border business. Retailers that have set up in foreign countries have often experienced problems. K-Mart, the US retailer, was forced to withdraw from Slovakia and the Czech Republic. Franchising may take the form of products being sold by other businesses, often used for petrol and soft drinks, or licensing, used by Benetton and Doc Martens. Business format franchising, which is designed to allow the franchisee to replicate all of the franchisor's operations, products and standards, is still the most popular method. It is suggested that, faced with increasing demand for variety, businesses can now operate in unfamiliar markets more easily. Sales from business format franchises were expected to reach $510 million worldwide in 1998. Even companies that had not previously considered franchising within a country, such as the Early Learning Centre, were considering franchising abroad.

Source: adapted from *en*, June 1997.

(a) Identify the methods of franchising explained in the article.
(b) Explain why franchising might be a popular method of setting up in business for:
  (i) a franchisor setting up in the Czech Republic;
  (ii) a franchisee setting up in the Czech Republic.
(c) A business in the UK is setting up in an Eastern European country. Using evidence from the article, suggest the most suitable method of franchising.

Key terms

Business plan - a statement made by a business, outlining the way it will attempt to achieve its objectives.

Franchise - an agreement where a business (the franchisor) sells rights to other businesses (the franchisees) allowing them to sell products or use the company name.

Hire purchase/credit sale - methods used to buy goods now and pay off the balance over a period of time. In the case of the former, the goods only belong to the buyer when the final payment is made.

National Insurance contributions - payments made by employees and employers to the government as a form of insurance premium.

Summary

1. Give 6 reasons why people set up in business.
2. Briefly explain the likely changes an employee may find in their work if they become a business owner.
3. Where might a business idea come from?
4. What questions about:
   (a) the market;
   (b) finance;
   might a business person ask when starting a business?
5. How might a small business use a business plan?
6. List 6 aspects of a business plan.
7. What help and finance might:
   (a) Business Link;
   (b) The Department of Trade and Industry;
   (c) a commercial bank;
   provide for a small business?
8. Why might a business club be particularly useful for a small new business?
9. What is the Business Start-up Scheme?
10. 'A franchise allows the franchisee and franchisor to do what they do best.' Explain this statement.
11. What problems might a small business setting up as a franchisee face?
12. Why might a business need to use documents?

Case study

A lot of bottle

William Record is MD of Braebourne Spring. It is a supplier of cooled mineral water to offices. In 1998 it was expected to turn over £7 million and make a £1.6 million profit. He started the company after taking an economics and politics degree at Southampton University. Within three years he had £3.5 million backing from investment capitalist 3i. Its finance increased as the business grew. Record said: 'I nearly went down the tubes a few times, but I was determined to make it work. My father was an entrepreneur ... and it's been useful having his guidance when it all looked like going belly up'.

The idea came from a visit to America in 1989 where every hotel had an ice machine and every office mineral water. The UK did not have the same 'convenience culture', however, and people were cynical about bottled water. The average person in the UK consumed around 8 litres a year compared to 100 in Italy. The business benefited at the start from two scorching summers in a row and concern over the purity of tap water.

Initially distribution was Record driving a van to a spring in Dorset, filling 30 bottles, and driving back to London to sell it. He even transferred two tonnes of water by hand when a van broke down! His first coolers were bought with £10,000 from the family, which was matched by Lloyds TSB Bank. He rented them to offices in London for £11 a month

plus 33p per litre of water consumed. Lloyds TSB were so impressed they lent a further £100,000.

At the start marketing consisted of ringing firms from *Yellow Pages* and a few mail shots. The money dried up until 3i came up with £106,000. 3 years later the company had declared profits of £20,000 and was in the black. Initially Record had been concerned about venture capitalists because he thought they would want more of the business than he was prepared to give.

The company hoped to grow in future, mainly by acquisition. The business had 80 competitors in 1998. The company was still predominantly London based, but hoped to branch out into Europe eventually.

Source: adapted from *The Guardian*, 1998.

(a) **Describe the help that the business has received.**
(b) **What problems did the business face when it was first set up?**
(c) **Explain the factors that may have led William Record to be a successful business person.**
(d) **Examine the reasons for the methods of finance used by the business.**
(e) **Advise the business on a possible method of setting up in Europe.**

Who is involved in business activity?

Various groups of people have an interest in business. Such groups are referred to as STAKEHOLDERS. The interest each stakeholder has in a business will vary according to the nature of their 'stake'. Figure 3.1 shows possible stakeholders that can be identified in business activity. They include:

● owners or shareholders;
● managers;
● employees;
● customers;
● government;
● suppliers;
● the community.

It could be argued that owners, managers and employees are internal stakeholders as members of the business organisation. The remainder could be seen as external stakeholders because they are not part of the business.

However, there are likely to be exceptions to this. For example, some members of the community may be employees or shareholders.

Some stakeholders may have more than one interest in the business. An employee might also be a shareholder. Managers will be employees of the business. A customer might be a member of the local community.

Stakeholders in business will usually benefit from their involvement with the organisation. Employees will earn money which they can spend on goods and services. Customers will consume the goods and services supplied by the business and the government will collect tax from the organisation.

Owners

A business is the property of its owner or owners. The owner of a van can use it to earn income by hiring it out. The owner of jewellery can wait for its value to increase and then sell it. It is possible for the owners of a business to do these things as well.

Not all owners are the same. The owner of a small business, such as a small retail outlet selling watches, may be the only person in the business. The owner would make all of the decisions, possibly use personal finance to start the firm and carry out all tasks, such as selling, ordering stock and recording transactions. In very large companies there can be thousands of joint owners. They all own **shares** (☞ units 5 and 57) in the company. This entitles them to a share in the profit, known as a DIVIDEND and a vote each year to elect the DIRECTORS of the company. Examples of shareholders might be the Moores family owning shares in Littlewoods, or the people all over the UK who own shares in British Telecom or ICI. The involvement of shareholders in the business will depend, perhaps, on their position in the business and the amount of money invested in it. Figure 3.2 shows a summary of the different types of business owner.

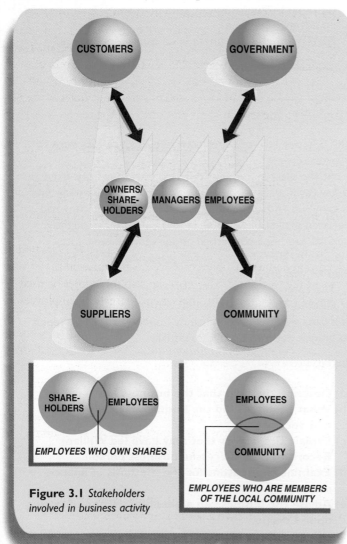

Figure 3.1 *Stakeholders involved in business activity*

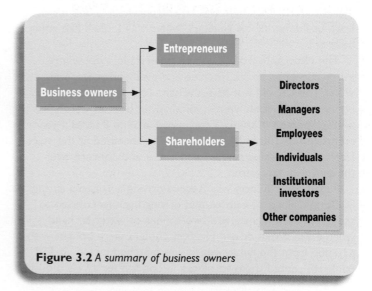

Figure 3.2 *A summary of business owners*

The entrepreneur

Unit 1 showed that **enterprise** was a **factor of production.** Arguably, it is the most important. Without an entrepreneur to organise the land, labour and capital, business activity would not take place. What is an entrepreneur? People who have this role usually perform three functions in business.

Innovation Business activity usually begins with the entrepreneur having a business idea. The entrepreneur could be said to be innovative. He or she is forming a new business where one did not exist before. When Anita Roddick opened the first Body Shop in March 1976 in Brighton, she created a new business idea of her own. This was to sell toiletries and cosmetics with conservation, the environment and animal rights in mind. Even when ideas are copied or adapted, it could be argued that the entrepreneur is being innovative. The creation of a business producing a vacuum cleaner which does not use dust bags by James Dyson may be said to be innovative. The British inventor Trevor Baylis was arguably innovative in creating a clockwork radio which could be wound-up to work, rather than using electricity.

Organisation Land, labour and capital are hired by the entrepreneur and organised to produce goods or services. Decisions about the location of the premises, the method of production, product design, prices and wages are often made by the entrepreneur. If the firm grows, it is likely that some of these tasks may be passed down to others.

Risk taking Setting up a business is risky. Money has to be paid out in advance to buy materials, business premises, equipment and pay wages. The entrepreneur may use some personal money to meet these costs. There is no guarantee that the final product or service will be sold. If goods are unsold then the entrepreneur will have to suffer this loss. It is not possible to insure against **unquantifiable** risks, such as these, so the entrepreneur bears all the costs of failure.

The type of people who become entrepreneurs is extremely varied. Some, like Richard Branson, start businesses when they are young and help them to grow. Some people extend their hobbies to a business situation, some leave their jobs voluntarily to start a business, some use redundancy money to set up and some inherit businesses.

Entrepreneurs often tend to be associated with small firms. This is because the entrepreneur will face risk and will control all aspects of the business activity. Many small businesses do become large businesses and thus the role of the entrepreneur may well change. In large business organisations many people bear the risk, are innovative and are responsible for control. Someone such as Rupert Murdoch, the owner of The Sun and The Times and BSkyB, is arguably an example of an entrepreneur in a large company.

Question 1

In January 1999, Rahila Ahmed decided to leave her job as a systems analyst at a computer manufacturer. She had built up a fund of £25,000 to set up in business as a computer programmer. Rahila bought £20,000 worth of computer equipment. She designed computer software for children with learning difficulties. She selected this specialism because a friend's daughter had quite serious learning difficulties and Rahila had designed a number of programs to help her read, count and spell. Because there was a desperate lack of software in this area Rahila very quickly sold her programs. Within six months she had generated £55,000 worth of sales and had employed a salesperson and a secretary.

(a) In what way is Rahila an entrepreneur?
(b) What risks did Rahila face when deciding to become an entrepreneur?
(c) If the business continued to grow, how might Rahila's role as an entrepreneur change? Explain your answer.

Type of shareholder

Certain types of business do not have shareholders, such as sole traders and partnerships. Limited companies can raise money by issuing shares (☞ unit 5). Shareholders become the 'joint owners' of the business. The shareholder or group of shareholders with the majority of shares, ie 51 per cent, will be the majority shareholder in the business. Examples of these shareholders are shown in Figure 3.2.

Directors Directors are elected by the shareholders each year and are responsible for running the business. They do not have to hold shares in the companies they run, but generally they do. Some directors have quite large shareholdings, sometimes large enough to exert control, such as in a family business. Some businesses have **worker directors**. In Germany and in some UK companies worker directors are workers that are co-opted onto the board of directors to represent the views of the workforce. The term can also sometimes be used to describe workers in a business owned largely by employees with shares, that also run the business.

Managers Managers are usually appointed by directors and are actively involved in running the business. Some managers own shares in their companies, but they do not have to. Sometimes they are allowed to buy shares or are given shares as a bonus. It is argued that if managers own shares in the company it might motivate them to perform well in their jobs. This is because if they perform well, profits may be higher and higher dividends can then be paid to shareholders like themselves.

Employees In the 1980s and 1990s an increasing number of employees began to own shares in companies. The government at that time encouraged wider share ownership. Shares in privatised industries (☞ unit 6) were made available to the workforce and the public as previously state owned industries became part of the private sector. In 1999, 93 out of the FTSE 100 companies offered share as you earn schemes (☞ unit 72). Companies have also offered shares to employees as bonuses. Sainsbury's is an example of one company which has done this. It is unlikely that employees will own enough shares to have any control in the running of the business. However, it may motivate (☞ unit 71) workers to take an interest in the company.

Individuals It is possible for individuals to own shares in companies. Any member of the public is allowed to buy shares in any **public limited company** (☞ unit 5). One common way of buying them is through a **stockbroker.** Individuals generally buy shares because they want to earn dividends. Buying shares is an alternative to other methods of saving, for example putting money in a building society account. Such people play no role in running the business. Also, they rarely have any control since they own only a small fraction of the total number of shares. If individuals are not happy with the performance of the company they may sell their shares.

Institutional investors These are financial institutions (☞ unit 57) such as insurance companies, pension funds and unit trusts who buy shares to earn income. They buy and sell very large numbers of shares, but rarely participate in the running of the companies. Their aim is to hold those shares which they think will generate the most return. In some cases they may exert control, since they own such large blocks of shares.

Other companies Some firms hold shares to earn income, some to control other companies and some to build up stakes in other companies with a view to taking them over in the future (☞ unit 101).

Managers

Firms of all sizes employ managers. A MANAGER may be defined as an individual who is accountable for more work than he could undertake alone. In a small firm the owner is likely to be responsible for all managerial tasks. When a business grows the responsibility for some decision making is often **delegated** (☞ unit 73) to others since it is not possible for one person to carry the whole burden.

There is a number of common functions of managers in business.

Organising and decision making Businesses are often divided into departments. A smaller business may have production, marketing, finance and administration departments. The owners may appoint one manager to control each department. The manager will have responsibility for all activities and employees in the

department. For example, he may have helped to recruit employees, must make decisions about how the department should be run and ensure that department objectives are met. Employees in the department will look to the manager for leadership, to solve problems, to communicate information to them, settle disputes, motivate them and represent the department at meetings.

Question 2

Unigate is a European food and distribution group. Part of the group is the fresh food and dairy product manufacturers St.Ivel and Unigate Dairies, the processor and distributor of fresh milk. In 1997 Unigate had 23,906 shareholders. Between them they owned 238,440,103 shares.

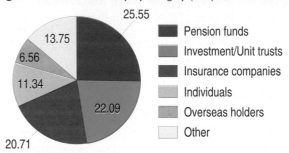

Figure 3.3 Share ownership by category (% of all issued shares)

- Pension funds: 25.55
- Investment/Unit trusts: 22.09
- Insurance companies: 20.71
- Individuals: 11.34
- Overseas holders: 6.56
- Other: 13.75

Table 3.1 Shareholders by size of holding

Size of shareholdings	Holders	Shares	% of shares
up to 1,000	14,245	6,960,970	2.92
1,001-10,000	8,915	21,029,764	8.82
10,001-100,000	483	15,819,240	6.63
100,001-250,000	104	16,751,950	7.03
above 250,000	159	177,878,179	74.60
	23,906	238,440,103	100.0

Source: adapted from Unigate PLC, *Annual Report and Accounts.*

(a) (i) What is the most common size of shareholding?
   (ii) What percentage of shares is owned by this group?
(b) At the end of the financial year Unigate paid its shareholders 20.2 pence per share. Calculate the total dividend payment made by the company.
(c) To what extent might:
   (i) pension funds;
   (ii) all shareholders other than pension funds
   be able to exert any control over the company?

Planning and control Managers are also likely to contribute to the overall planning of company activities along with the owner and other managers. They also have a controlling role in the business. This may involve control of finance, equipment, time and people, for example. In larger business organisations managers become more specialist and concentrate on a narrower aspect of management.

Accountability Managers are accountable to the owners. If the production department does not achieve a satisfactory level of output, the manager may have to 'shoulder the blame'. This might mean a loss of a bonus payment.

Entrepreneurial role Although managers may not risk their own money, they might risk their job. A manager might make a decision to install some revolutionary new machinery. This could be successful and the manager might be promoted. However, if the machinery is unsuccessful, leading to heavy losses, the manager may be sacked. In carrying out this task, the manager is innovating and risk taking.

Employees

The role of employees in business is to follow the instructions of employers. Employees are hired by firms to help business activity. A business needs people with a range of skills and knowledge. Many provide a training programme for new employees to familiarise them with the firm's policies and working practices. Employees will be more productive if they are taught good working practices from the time they start at a new company. Note that managers of the business are usually employees.

Employees normally sign **contracts of employment** (☞ unit 78) agreeing to follow all reasonable instructions related to their job. In return for their time and effort they receive a payment, ie a **wage** or **salary**. The amount workers are paid depends on a wide range of factors such as age, experience, qualifications, the type of industry, the nature of the job (full time or part time) and the level of skill required.

The role of employees in business has begun to change in recent years.

● They have had to cope with the introduction of new technology.
● They have been encouraged by some companies to participate more in problem solving and decision making, perhaps in teams.
● They have become more flexible and have adapted to the introduction of new working practices. For example, many employees are trained in a number of tasks and are expected to be able to change from one job to another.
● Increased emphasis has been placed on training and learning new skills. For example, departmental managers have been encouraged to develop personnel skills.

Customers

Customers are not 'members' of businesses, but they are vital to their survival. Customers buy the goods and services that businesses supply. Most customers are consumers who use or 'consume' products. Spending by customers generates income for businesses. Customers may be individuals, but could also be other businesses. For example, Sage PLC manufactures computer software for accounting systems. Most of its customers are other businesses.

It is important for businesses to understand the needs of their customers. Customers dictate the pattern of business activity, as firms will only produce goods and services which customers will buy. Firms that produce unwanted goods or services will struggle and fail. The McPloughman's, a cheese, pickle and salad sandwich launched by McDonald's in the 1990s to compete in the cold sandwich market, was quickly withdrawn after poor customer reaction in London. Lifestyle and business magazines produced by Manchester Evening News failed as a result of being launched into an already saturated market. Flavoured crisps produced by Spuddles Ltd, a subsidiary of Park Food, failed to take off, leading to losses for the year to March 1998 of £3 million.

Customers and consumers have many different relationships with businesses.

● Contact between businesses and customers takes place when goods or services are bought. This can vary. When services are bought there is usually a personal contact between the two groups, as there would be when a client makes an appointment to see a solicitor. In the case of water supply, the contact for many customers is limited, ie through the post when the quarterly bill arrives.
● Businesses need to communicate with consumers to find out what they want. **Marketing research** (☞ unit 37) helps a business to collect information about its potential customers.
● As well as collecting information from consumers, businesses also pass on information about the nature of products, the price charged, how products work and where they might be bought. **Advertising** (☞ unit 44) is often used to do this.
● Consumers are more aware today about products that are available, prices, channels of complaint and product performance. Consumers have more income than ever before, and much greater expectations of products. Businesses must take these expectations into account when designing, manufacturing and marketing products. For example, 25 years ago, a radio in a new car would have been an 'extra'. Today, a complete 'sound system' in a car is virtually a necessity.
● Businesses operate in a world where consumers have increasing rights and protection. This is dealt with in unit 22.

Because of increased consumer expectations and awareness, improved consumer rights and fiercer competition in business, the vast majority of companies work hard at promoting good customer relations. Indeed, more and more firms are happy to give consumers a lot more than their strict legal rights. Most high street stores will accept returned goods and reimburse customers without too much investigation. Free after sales service is common and sales staff receive a lot more 'customer care' training.

Suppliers

Suppliers are businesses that provide resources which allow other businesses to produce goods and services. Resources might include raw materials, components, equipment, energy and services. It is important for good relations to exist between businesses and suppliers because they rely heavily on each other. Generally, businesses require suppliers to provide good quality resources at reasonable prices. They also need suppliers to be reliable and flexible. In return suppliers want businesses to provide a constant flow of profitable orders and to pay on time.

The relationship between suppliers and producers has become more important in recent years. The main reason for this is because modern production techniques often require businesses to cooperate. A business can only operate just-in-time manufacturing (☞ unit 92), for example, if suppliers are prepared to deliver quickly and at short notice.

Government

The government can influence business in a number of ways. A certain amount of legislation is aimed at business in order to protect stakeholders. Health and safety regulations are designed to protect employees in the workplace. Environmental legislation aims to protect the community and the environment from business activity. For example, the 1996 landfill tax on the disposal of waste may encourage greater recycling.

The government can also affect businesses through its economic policies (☞ unit 26). An increase in interest rates will raise the cost of borrowing for business. In addition, some government activity attempts to help business. The Private Finance Initiative encourages business to build roads, hospitals etc. and charge for them, such as the Skye Road Bridge. More direct help may come from European Union (☞ unit 30) funds to set up in a particular area.

The government will want businesses to flourish because they provide jobs and generate wealth. If businesses are successful the government will also benefit. Tax revenues will rise, providing the government with extra funds.

Community

Many communities have a major stake in local businesses. A business is likely to provide employment and training for local people. Certain businesses, particularly small ones, draw most of their customers from the local area. Indeed, in some remote areas residents may rely almost entirely upon the goods and services supplied by local firms such as shops. Some businesses even become involved in community life. They might sponsor local social or sporting events or help raise money for local charities.

Unfortunately the existence of business in local communities can also have drawbacks. Some businesses, particularly manufacturers located in residential areas, might create noise, congestion and air pollution. Their factories may be unsightly. As a result the local community might try to exert pressure on the owners to reduce the costs borne by the community or to relocate.

Interdependence

There is a significant degree of interdependence within business. In large firms the owners are dependent upon the skill and ability of the management team. If managers perform well then the business is likely to make more profit which will benefit the owner. Managers rely on business owners for their jobs and to support their decisions.

Managers and other employees are also dependent upon each other. Employees rely on the **leadership** of management in order to do their jobs. Management depend on workers to produce output according to their instructions. Management will be accountable to the owners of the business if workers are inefficient.

Businesses are dependent on consumers. Business activity would not take place if consumers did not buy goods or services. However, consumers can only purchase these goods and services if they have income. They may earn this income from employment in business. Thus, business owners are dependent upon consumers for their income, and consumers, in their role as employees and managers, are dependent upon business owners for their income.

Objectives and conflict

Conflict can occur in business when STAKEHOLDER OBJECTIVES are different. Each type of stakeholder is likely to have a set of goals which they want to achieve. It could be argued that:
- shareholders want regular, secure and high returns and a say in the goals of the business (☞ unit 4);
- managers want responsibility, high rewards and a lack of interference in their actions;
- employees want high earnings, an interesting job and secure employment;
- customers want quality products at low prices and a good service;
- suppliers want secure, regular and profitable orders;
- government wants to achieve a large number of goals including growth in the economy and low inflation;
- the local community wants thriving local businesses which do not cause problems.

Conflict can exist between many different groups of stakeholders.

Employees and owners What might lead to conflict between the employees and the owners of a business?
- Levels of pay. In most businesses, rates of pay are negotiated every year. Bargaining (☞ unit 85) takes place between employees and owners or managers. It is common for the two sides to disagree on new wage levels. This is because workers generally want more than the owners or managers are prepared to pay.
- Working conditions. Conflict may arise if, for example, the working environment is too cold for employees to do their jobs.
- Changing practices. In recent years a number of new working practices have been introduced in business. Disputes have occurred when employees have been asked to perform new tasks or change the way they undertake existing tasks. Employees often feel that they are being asked to do more work.
- Redundancy. When employees are faced with the threat of losing their jobs, quite naturally they react. In the early 1980s and early 1990s there were a very large number of redundancies. Workers are often angry when their jobs are replaced by machines.

Owners and managers In some businesses the management team may become powerful and influential. When this happens they may pursue their own interests rather than those of the owners. This might involve paying themselves high salaries or organising their time to suit their own needs, whilst achieving satisfactory levels of profit rather than high levels of profit. This would go against the interests of owners who benefit more from higher profits. Such conflict may result in some owners selling their shares. This is often referred to as a **divorce of ownership and control** (☞ unit 5).

It is in everyone's interests to settle conflict as quickly as possible. Conflict can lead to lower levels of output and loss of profits for the owners. Managers and other employees may suffer from poor motivation, a lack of job security and loss of wages.

Customers and business What might lead to conflict between consumers and business?
- Price. Owners may wish to maximise their profit which might involve charging the highest possible price. However, consumers want to buy goods as cheaply as possible. If competition exists in the market (☞ unit 18) consumers will generally benefit. However, if there is a lack of competition, as there is in the water supply industry for example, consumers do not have a choice, except to go without.
- Quality. Consumers may be dissatisfied with the quality of the products they have bought. If consumers return goods then businesses lose income, so disagreements often occur as to whether a firm should accept returned goods.
- Delivery time. Customers are often keen to receive the goods which they have ordered as quickly as possible. A dispute would occur if, for example, a business cannot deliver a wedding dress promised for the day of a wedding.
- After sales service. Consumers may be upset by poor after sales service. For example, if a person buys a hi-fi system,

and finds that it does not work, a dispute might emerge if the business refused to investigate the problem.

Suppliers and managers 'New' production methods have led to a closer relationship between suppliers and managers. However, conflict does still exist. Some suppliers, particularly small firms supplying larger businesses, have criticised the customers' managers or owners for taking too long to pay for products. Late payment can cause severe hardship for smaller suppliers. This issue was addressed to some extent by the government. It acknowledged that some managers were causing hardship to suppliers by delaying payments for unreasonable amounts of time. However, the government did not pass any legislation such as forcing creditors to pay interest on debts owed. Instead it suggested that managers should be more responsible and understand the importance of smaller suppliers.

Question

Henley Garden Centre is owned by Sandra Thompson who is retired and lives in Venice. She employs a manager who has an assistant to help run the business. The manager concentrates on finance and administration while his assistant is responsible for production, selling and staff. Thirty staff are employed in the large garden centre and they have just been offered a 4 per cent wage increase. They had requested a 13 per cent pay rise on the grounds that in the previous two years they had agreed to a pay freeze. The staff are very angry with this final offer and they have all agreed not to work at weekends. The management have always been unpopular with the employees because they feel that they are being exploited. For example, the manager and the assistant manager both drive company BMWs and take it in turns to take time off to play golf three times a week. However, since the owner lives abroad, is reasonably satisfied with the profit made by the company and is not entirely aware of the circumstances, the situation is unlikely to change.

(a) Identify possible sources of conflict between the management and the employees.
(b) How might the conflict between the management and employees affect the business?
(c) Explain whether there might be a conflict in this case between the owner and management.
(d) Which stakeholder would have the most to lose if the business were to collapse? Explain your answer.

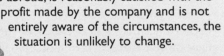

Owners and the community Conflict can arise between owners and the community when the quality of life enjoyed by local residents is threatened by business activity. The most likely causes of conflict are businesses disturbing the local community or polluting the nearby environment. An example of such conflict was the opposition of residents in South Manchester to the construction of a new runway at Manchester Airport. They argued that noise pollution resulting from extra traffic would be intolerable.

In the 1990s an increasing amount of business activity has been located away from residential areas. Popular sites on the edges of towns have developed. Industrial parks have been set up and some businesses have chosen to operate on greenfield sites (☞ unit 100). This trend would help to reduce conflict between business owners and local communities.

Management buy-outs

A MANAGEMENT BUY-OUT is where the ownership of a business is transferred to the current management team. The team is likely to buy shares from the existing owners. Funds for the buy-out might be provided by members of the management team itself or financial institutions, such as banks or venture capitalists. Venture capitalists, such as CinVen, 3i and Schroder Ventures, are specialists who are prepared to take the risk of investing directly in a business.

Table 3.2 *UK management buy-outs and buy-ins*

Year	Buy-out			Buy-in		
	Number	Value (£m)	Average (£m)	Number	Value (£m)	Average (£m)
1979	18	14	0.8	1	0	0.5
1980	36	28	0.8		.	.
1981	145	180	1.2	6	24	4.0
1982	237	346	1.5	9	317	35.2
1983	235	366	1.6	10	9	0.9
1984	242	408	1.7	6	5	0.8
1985	261	1,135	4.3	30	40	1.3
1986	316	1,181	3.7	53	321	6.1
1987	343	3,132	9.1	91	307	3.4
1988	379	3,795	10.0	114	1,214	10.6
1989	378	3,889	10.3	147	3,599	24.5
1990	490	2,447	5.0	112	658	5.9
1991	451	2,164	4.8	122	717	5.9
1992	455	2,550	5.6	136	712	5.2
1993	393	2,165	5.5	99	701	7.1
1994	403	2,513	6.2	148	1,103	7.5
1995	377	2,831	7.5	215	2,639	12.3
1996	434	3,653	8.4	208	4,172	20.1
1997	445	4,458	10.0	243	6,038	24.8
1998 (to June)	201	2,230	11.1	112	5,357	47.8

Source: adapted from CMBOR, Barclays Private Equity, Deloitte & Touch.

The capital they provide is sometimes called risk capital. Some buy-outs involve these venture capitalists taking complete control. This is known as a LEVERAGED BUY-OUT.

The number of management buy-outs grew after 1979 as shown in Table 3.2. The average value of buy-outs between 1979 and 1997 was generally less than £10 million. There was some fluctuation in the value of buy-outs over the period. For example, in 1989 the value hit a peak of £3,889 million and then fell during the early 1990s, before rising again to another peak in 1997. Both the number and the value of buy-outs was expected to break all records in 1998, according to the Centre for Management Buy-out Research.

What might account for the popularity of management buy-outs?

● Many buy-outs occur when large companies restructure their operations. They sell off parts of the business which do not fit into their future plans. For example, in 1997 Greenalls, one of Britain's biggest pub groups, sold off its 460 chain of off-licenses, including Cellar 5, for £56 million. Greenalls planned to focus on its pubs and restaurants business. The deal was backed by CVC Capital Partners and NatWest Ventures.

● As part of the privatisation programme (☞ unit 6) the UK government has sold businesses to management buy-out teams. For example, in 1996 two rail leasing

companies, Porterbrook and Eversholt, were sold to management buy-out teams. So was the British Rail heavy maintenance depot at Eastleigh in Hampshire, for around £10 million.

● It is an alternative to full or part closure of a family business or its subsidiary. In the early 1990s, BSM, the driving school business, was sold to a management team.

● To resurrect all or part of a company that has been struggling or has gone into receivership. In 1997 Country Casuals sold the loss-making Elvi, the large sized women's wear retailer, and Lerose, a clothes manufacturer, for small sums to management teams.

What might be the advantages of a management buy-out? From the sellers' point of view it lets them raise finance for a possibly ailing firm or subsidiary, which might otherwise have closed down. From the managers' and employees' point of view it would enable them to keep their jobs in the same occupation and area as they had before. It is also argued that the efficiency of the business would be improved by a buy out. This is perhaps because there is an increased incentive for managers to perform well. Following a buy-out the management team will benefit financially from any profit made by the company, so there is an incentive to keep costs down and motivate the workforce, for example. In addition, the potential for conflict between the owners and the managers is reduced because after a buy-out the owners are the managers.

Generally, it seems that buy-outs are successful as they keep the business going. A study by the Warwick Business School reported that management buy-outs outperformed their industry average for the first three years. However, after that, they tended to underperform. Other, longer term, studies have suggested that performance after the first three years continued to be better than the industry average.

Management buy-ins

MANAGEMENT BUY-INS are where an outside management team takes over a business. They have grown since 1979, as shown in Table 3.2. In the late 1990s the total and average value of management buy-ins were greater than those of buy-outs. In 1997, Whitbread sold Pizza Piazza for £11.25 million to a management buy-in team led by Ivan Taylor, the former Pizzaland managing director. The deal was funded by venture capitalists 3i.

Deals of this type are becoming more complex.

● Investor buy-outs (IBOs) are where the seller negotiates more closely with the fund provider rather than the management team.

● Buy-in management buy-outs (bimbos) are when an external management team, combined with the existing management team, buy the business from its owner. In

---

Question 6

In 1998, UK Safety, a maker of army boots and industrial footwear, accepted a £1 million takeover offer from a management buy-out team. The company was enduring severe financial difficulties. Indeed, UK Safety was so short of cash that it was not able to afford redundancies which were needed to help the company survive. In the previous financial year the company lost £900,000 and was in very serious debt. It had managed to survive thanks to the Royal Bank of Scotland, which was owed £11 million. The bank threatened to call in the loans if the current shareholders did not accept the buy-out bid. One of the main shareholders was Schroder Ventures, who owned 26 per cent of the company.

The management team was being backed by Alchemy Partners, which provided £7.5 million for the deal. However, the team faced a difficult future. There was a sharp fall in the number of soldiers and miners that wear its boots. In addition, its factory, which employed 430 people, was located in Bristol and the company would find it difficult to fight off foreign competition.

Source: adapted from The Times, 21.3.1998.

(a) Who is funding the management buy-out of UK Safety?
(b) Explain why the company is being sold to the management team.
(c) How might the employees be affected by the buy-out?

1997, Phildrew, one of Britain's largest venture capital firms, put together a bimbo. GWS Group, a privately owned shopfitting company that kits out Sainsbury's Homebase stores, agreed a £18.5 million cash injection. A new executive chairman was appointed with a 10 per cent stake, while the founders remained joint managing directors with a 20 per cent stake.

Question (7)

In 1997, Bass, the giant brewer and leisure company, sold its Gala bingo chain to a management buy-in team for £279 million. The team was led by John Kelly, the former head of Mecca's bingo division. The deal was backed by PPM Ventures, the venture capital arm of the Prudential. Mr Kelly became chief executive of Gala and Nat Solomon, the current chairman of Crown Leisure, became the non-executive chairman. The £279 million price included £43 million to cover cash balances. Bass said it would make a £12 million profit from the deal and would use the proceeds to reduce debt.

Profits in the bingo industry had fallen recently partly as a result of interest in the National Lottery. However, venture capitalists said that it was recovering, encouraged by government deregulation of advertising and new edge-of-town sites, attracting younger players.

Source: adapted from *The Times*, 16.12.1997.

(a) Explain the difference between a management buy-out and a management buy-in.
(b) Why do you think Bass wanted to sell the Gala bingo chain?
(c) How might customers benefit from the new management team taking control of Gala?

Key terms

Directors - people elected by shareholders to run companies.
Dividend - a proportion of a company's profits paid to owners of shares in that company.
Leveraged buy-out - a situation where a group of financial institutions takes control of a company.
Manager - an individual who is accountable for more work than he or she could undertake alone.
Management buy-in - the sale of a business to an outside management team.
Management buy-out - the sale of a business to the existing management team.
Stakeholders - groups who have an interest in business activity.
Stakeholder objectives - the goals of people with interests in the business. What stakeholders want to achieve.

Summary

1. Describe the interest that each internal stakeholder has in a business.
2. List 3 functions of an entrepreneur.
3. Why are entrepreneurs often associated with small businesses?
4. List 5 possible groups of shareholders.
5. Briefly explain 4 roles of management.
6. 'The role of employees in business is changing.' Explain this statement using an example.
7. Briefly explain 3 ways in which businesses and consumers are related.
8. Why are owners, managers and employees interdependent?
9. Explain one source of conflict between:
   (a) owners and managers; (b) managers and employees; (c) businesses and consumers.
10. Explain how management buy-outs might benefit the buy-out team.

Case study

The Furniture Club

Julia Collins set up a furniture design business in 1994 after completing a design and textiles course at university. The business collapsed after 9 months because she was unable to find any buyers for her designs. However, Julia was convinced that her furniture would be popular if only manufacturers would use her designs and market the products effectively. Fortunately Julia was able to secure substantial financial backing from her grandparents and set up her own manufacturing company, The Furniture Club. Julia would own 40 per cent of the shares, with each of her grandparents owning 30 per cent. However, she was not experienced in several aspects of business so she employed a production manager, Mark Wallwork, and asked a friend of hers, Caitlin Davis, to manage the marketing of her products.

After a hesitant start the business began to flourish. Julia was right about her designs and found that there was quite a demand for her furniture, particularly in the South East. She sold her furniture range to retailers in the London area and also to the national market through mail order. In 1998 the company turned over £890,000 and made a gross profit of £320, 400. This was the profit before overheads, such as wages and marketing costs, tax and directors' dividends had been taken away. Julia was extremely pleased for a number of reasons:

● she was right about her designs;
● Mark Wallwork proved to be highly skilled and reliable;
● Julia's marketing friend, Caitlin, had been a revelation. It was her idea to market the furniture through mail order. Initially Julia was not keen on the idea because of the high advertising costs;
● Julia had paid back half of the money borrowed from her grandmother and was beginning to grow quite wealthy.

At the end of 1998 Julia was confronted by Mark and Caitlin. During one of the weekly managers' meetings it became obvious that they had both grown a little jealous of Julia's success. Although Mark and Caitlin were grateful for the opportunities given to them by Julia, they felt that the financial rewards generated by the business had not been shared fairly. Both Mark and Caitlin were being paid £27,000 a year. However, in light of the profit made in 1998 they thought that their contribution deserved rather more. They proposed that their salaries should be raised to £40,000 per year or that they should be given the chance to buy shares in the company so that they could enjoy some of the dividends.

At about the same time Julia was confronted by another problem. Some of her best customers from the retailers in London had discovered that The Furniture Club was selling products through mail order. The problem was that the mail order prices were lower than they were charging in their retail outlets. Furthermore, some shoppers had returned furniture to the stores after they had learnt about the cheaper, mail order method of purchase.

The pressures of being an entrepreneur were beginning to take their toll on Julia. She wondered whether it was time to sell the business. She consulted her grandparents who agreed that they would also be prepared to sell their share of the business. One option was to set up a management buy-out, allowing Mark and Caitlin to buy the business from the current shareholders.

(a) (i) Describe the features of Julia's role as an entrepreneur.
(ii) What is meant by the phrase 'the pressures of being an entrepreneur'?
(b) How might a management buy-out be funded if Mark and Caitlin are not able to raise the finance themselves?
(c) What might be the disadvantages to Julia of allowing Mark and Caitlin to buy shares in her business?
(d) Explain two examples of conflict between the stakeholders of The Furniture Club.
(e) In what way does this business illustrate interdependence between different stakeholders?
(f) If a management buy-out was organised, what might be the advantages to:
(i) Julia;
(ii) Mark and Caitlin;
(iii) employees?
(g) In your view, who has the most influence in The Furniture Club?

What are business objectives?

All businesses have objectives. These are the **goals** of the business - what the business wants to achieve. For example, the efforts of a small self-employed carpenter may be directed towards increasing the number of products that he sells. His goal may therefore be to increase sales by 10 per cent over the next year.

The objectives of business organisations will be shaped by various stakeholders (☞ unit 3) in the business. Those with most influence will tend to set the objectives. If the owners are the most dominant stakeholders then making a profit is likely to be an important goal. If employees have great influence then job security, good working conditions and suitable rewards could be important. In practice, business objectives are likely to be determined by negotiation between various stakeholders.

It is important for a business to have well defined objectives. These will help the business to be clear about what it wants to achieve. The performance of a business could be assessed by how effectively it achieves its objectives. For example, if a company's objective is to survive a poor period of sales or a recession, then it will have been successful if it is still trading when conditions improve.

Mission statements

Businesses are increasingly issuing MISSION STATEMENTS (☞ unit 15). These are descriptions of the overall aims of the business and its short term and long term objectives. They tend to be aimed at all stakeholders and may be printed in the Annual Report and Accounts. However, they often focus on meeting the needs of customers, identifying the specific service to be provided. They usually express objectives in 'qualitative' terms and may emphasise the desire of a business to become 'the best' in its field.

Mission statements may be displayed in places such as reception areas, where they can be viewed by employees, customers and suppliers. They show what the business is striving to achieve. Mission statements also remind staff of their general purpose. They are usually brief so that the goals and purpose of the business can easily be remembered.

Survival

From time to time all businesses, regardless of their size and status, will consider survival important.

Early stages of trading Most firms begin on a small scale, establish themselves and then grow. The owners of a new firm will probably be happy to see the firm survive in its first few months (or even years) of trading. Firms may encounter a number of problems when they first begin trading including:

● a lack of experience;
● a lack of resources;
● competition from established firms;
● unforeseen problems such as unexpected costs;
● limited recognition by customers.

Also, in the early stages decision makers might make mistakes. As a result of this uncertainty the most important business objective might be to survive in the initial stages of trading.

Railtrack is the heart of Britain's railway – the tracks, signals, bridges, tunnels and stations – and we are committed to delivering the world-class network our customers, the passenger and freight train operating companies, want for the 21st century.

We provide access to our tracks and stations, manage timetabling and operate signalling, and have responsibility for maintaining, renewing and upgrading the rail infrastructure.

Railtrack's aim is to achieve continuous improvement in every aspect of the business; to develop efficient solutions to the needs of our customers; to provide growing returns for our shareholders; to work in partnership with our maintenance contractors and to act responsibly with regard to the community and the environment.

We are revitalising our organisation to rise to the challenges of the next decade of a major national asset.

Source: Railtrack Group PLC, *Annual Report and Accounts*, 1998
Figure 4.1 *Mission statement of Railtrack*

When trading becomes difficult During a recession (☞ unit 21), for example, a business could face falling demand, bad debts and low confidence. In the UK recession of 1990-92 many well known companies ceased trading. In 1992 around 73,000 businesses collapsed. Improved trading conditions in the 1990s reduced this figure to around 44,000 in 1995 and 40,000 in 1998. Individual businesses or industries may face difficulties due to competition from rivals, falling demand for their products or the effects of poor decisions. Arguably the objective of Apple, the computer manufacturer, in allowing Microsoft, a rival, to take a stake in its operation in 1997 was to protect the company during a difficult period.

Threat of takeover Firms sometimes become targets for other firms to take over (☞ unit 101). When this happens the survival of the firm in its existing form may be the main objective. One way to achieve this is to persuade the owners (the shareholders) not to sell shares to the person or company bidding for them.

In the long term it is unlikely that survival would remain the only objective, except perhaps for small businesses. Business owners tend to be ambitious and so pursue other objectives.

Question 1

Due to an increase in overseas competition the UK's shipbuilding industry has been devastated in recent decades. One company which has struggled to survive in the 1990s is Swan Hunter. The Swan Hunter shipyard was rescued by the Dutch company, THC, in 1995. The company went into receivership in 1993 when it failed to win a helicopter carrier contract from the Royal Navy. The Wallsend-based shipyard employed 2,400 staff when it went into receivership. By 1995 it employed only a permanent core staff of 20.

In 1996 Swan Hunter won a £50 million contract for finishing the world's largest pipe laying vessel, Solitaire. Local trade union leaders said that the new contract, awarded in preference to German, French and Italian builders, signalled the re-emergence of the 136-year-old shipyard 'like a phoenix rising from the ashes'. The new contract required Swan Hunter to recruit about 1,200 new staff. However, it was stressed that the jobs would be on a contract basis, with the bulk of the work being completed by the end of the year. Around 4,000 Tynesiders had applied for the jobs and unions hoped that the company would consider seriously the skills and talents of former Swan Hunter workers.

Source: adapted from *The Guardian*, 7.3.1996.

(a) What would you say was Swan Hunter's main business objective over the period 1993-1995? Explain your answer.

(b) Explain why the new workers were being recruited on short contract terms in 1996.

Profit maximisation

It is often argued that the main aim of private sector businesses (☞ unit 5) is to MAXIMISE their profits. This is achieved where the difference between the total revenue earned by the business from selling its products and the total costs of those products is the greatest. The manufacturer in Table 4.1 would produce 3,000 units as this is the output where its profit is highest.

Table 4.1 *Profit maximising position*

			£000
Output	Total costs	Total revenue	Profit
2,000	10	20	10
3,000	15	30	15
4,000	30	35	5

It may be reasonable to assume that firms aim for as much profit as possible. In practice a business is more likely to have a satisfactory level of profit as an objective. This is known as SATISFICING. Why is this likely to be a more reasonable objective?

Objectives of small firms Owners of small firms may not want to expand their output to a point where their profits are maximised. This may be because:
● it involves employing more workers, making more decisions and working longer hours;
● they may want to keep their turnover below the VAT threshold, avoiding the need to charge their customers VAT and filling in VAT returns;
● they are happy with a satisfactory profit level and their current lifestyle.

Information In practice it may be difficult to identify precisely the level of output that will maximise profits. For a business to do this it must be able to measure all of its costs at every possible level of production. It must also be able to estimate accurately the prices it can charge and predict the likely demand at these prices.

Other objectives A business might sacrifice short term profit maximisation for long term profits. This might explain why a firm lowers its price initially to build a market share and then increases price when competitors have left the market. It might also account for firms operating in the short term at a loss. In this case, the owners may be optimistic that in the future sales will pick up.

Growth

Many businesses pursue growth as their main objective. Business people argue that firms must grow in order to survive.

Question 2

Webster's Ltd manufactures horse saddles. It is a small company which employs 3 skilled craft workers in a factory in Devon. The owner of the business is Wendy Webster. She enjoys running the business but the profit at the current level of output is only £15,000 p.a. Wendy is a talented horsewoman and spends 3 days a week eventing. Although this is a hobby, Wendy is able to generate some business through contacts which she makes during these events. Wendy knows that she could make a lot more profit by producing and selling more saddles, but she prefers not to expand output. The diagram in Figure 4.2 shows the total costs and total revenue for Webster's Ltd. The current level of output which generates £15,000 profit is 200 saddles.

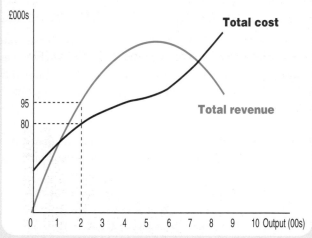

Figure 4.2 *The total costs and total revenue of Webster's Ltd*

(a) Estimate (to the nearest hundred) the level of output that would maximise profit for Webster's from Figure 4.2.
(b) Explain why Wendy might not wish to maximise profits.
(c) Suggest why a large plc might seek to maximise profits.

Failure to grow might result in a loss of competitiveness, a decline in demand and eventual closure. If a firm is able to grow and dominate the market, in the future it may be able to enjoy some monopoly power and raise its price. By growing, a firm can diversify and reduce the risk of business enterprise. It can sell to alternative markets and introduce new products. If one market or product fails it will have a range of others to fall back on. Firms can exploit economies of scale if they grow large enough. This will enable them to be more efficient and enjoy lower costs. Motives for growth are dealt with in unit 93.

A number of people involved in business activity might benefit from growth.

● Employees may find their jobs will be more secure (although this might not always be the case if growth involves purchasing more machinery).
● Managers and directors will tend to have more power and status. For example, a director of BP Amoco is likely to

Question 3

Meyer International PLC is a timber and buildings merchant operating in the UK, Holland and the USA. Part of the company includes the builders merchants Jewson. Its Annual Report and Accounts showed the following data.

Meyer International is the **largest** timber and building materials merchant in the UK and Holland and a **leading** distributor of laminate and specialist timber products in the UK and North America. In 1997/98 we have made **significant** progress in reshaping the Group for future **growth** through a major acquisition and disposal programme.

Table 4.2 *Meyer International in 1997*

The Year in brief

April 1997
● *Acquisition of three builders merchants' branches on the Isle of Wight, trading as Moreys.*

October 1997
● *Announcement of acquisition of 201 Harcros branches - to create the largest chain of builders merchants in the UK.*
● *1 for 4 rights issue launched to raise £112.2 million, net of expenses.*
● *Intention to sell the UK softwood and panel product businesses also announced.*

November 1997
● *Acquisition of 22 tool and catering equipment hire branches, trading as Torex Hire.*

December 1997
● *Harcros acquisition completed.*
● *Specialist Products division acquired CIP, a laminates distributor with four branches in the UK.*
● *Sale of Bouwvaria, the Dutch DIY business.*

Figure 4.3 *Meyer International PLC turnover and fixed assets, 1994 to 1998*

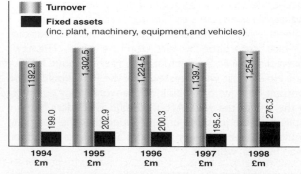

Source: adapted from Meyer International PLC, *Annual Report and Accounts, 1998.*

(a) What evidence is there to support the view that one of Meyer's key business objectives is growth?
(b) How has the business prepared itself for growth in future?

enjoy more power and recognition than the director of a small manufacturer.

● The salaries of directors and the chairperson are often linked to the size of the firm.

● The owners of companies might have mixed feelings about growth. On the one hand, growth often means that current profits have to be invested to fund the expansion. However, growth might generate much higher profits in the future which will benefit the owners.

Managerial objectives

Sometimes the managers of a firm are able to pursue their own objectives. For this to happen there must be some divorce of ownership and control. In other words the owners of the company do not necessarily control the day to day running of it. This may be possible when there is a very large number of joint owners as in a public limited company. Each owner has such a small part of the firm that he or she is able to exert little control over its running. As a result management take control and run the company according to their own objectives. These vary depending on individual managers. Some common examples might be to:

● maximise personal salary;
● maximise their departmental budgets;
● improve their status and recognition;
● maximise the number of employees in their charge;
● maximise their leisure time;
● delegate as much as work as possible;
● maximise fringe benefits, such as expense accounts for entertaining or company cars.

If managers are seen by owners to be abusing their power they are likely to be fired. To protect their positions managers often pacify owners by ensuring that the business generates enough profit to keep them satisfied. Profit may also be important to managers if their salaries are linked to profit levels.

Sales revenue maximisation

SALES REVENUE MAXIMISATION was put forward by William Baumol in the 1950s. He argued that an objective of firms may be to gain the highest possible sales revenue. This objective will be favoured by those employees whose salaries are linked to sales. Managers and sales staff are examples of staff paid according to the sales revenue which they generate. Sales revenue maximisation is not the same as profit maximisation. In Table 4.1, the business maximised profits at an output of 3,000 units. Producing 4,000 units would have maximised sales revenue (£35,000).

Image and social responsibility

In recent years firms have started to appreciate how important their image is. Many have also seen the benefit of

Question 4

Geoffrey Horrocks is the chief executive of Arnold Carrington Associates, a family civil engineering business specialising in the construction of tower blocks. He has been with the company for 7 years and guided it from a position of insecurity in the early 1990s to one of growing prosperity in 1998. The company now employs 18 people and Geoffrey's role has changed significantly. Initially he was very much involved on the engineering side, but now he deals with clients and new business. Geoffrey has delegated a great deal of responsibility to his assistant and other members of the management team. He has seen his own salary rise from £12,500 in 1991 to £110,000 in 1998. Geoffrey is a valued member of the company, but the owners, who retired to Sardinia in 1994, have lost touch with the day to day running of the business. In addition, the Carrington family are extremely wealthy and the profit from this business represents less than 5 per cent of their annual income.

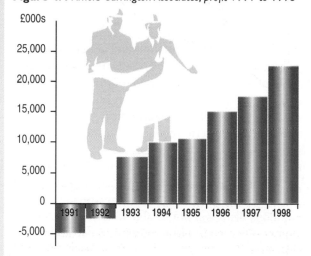

Figure 4.4 *Arnold Carrington Associates, profit 1991 to 1998*

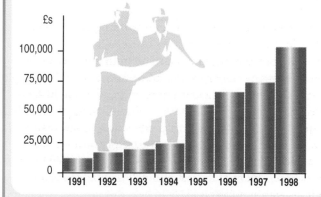

Figure 4.5 *Geoffrey Horrocks, annual salary 1991 to 1998*

(a) What evidence is there in the case to suggest that Geoffrey Horrocks might be pursuing managerial objectives?

(b) Explain how it is possible for management to pursue its own objectives in this business.

(c) Examine the factors that might lead to a change in the objectives of this company.

showing responsibility to a wider range of stakeholders, such as customers, employees and suppliers. Why has this happened?

● Legislation has been passed which favours consumers.
● There have been changes in social attitudes.
● Competitive pressure has forced businesses to take into account the needs of others.

Customers Companies with household names such as Heinz, Kellogg's, Ford, Cadbury's and Sainsbury's would not wish the general public to think badly of them. Some companies have made serious efforts in recent years to improve their image. For example, Skoda, the car manufacturer has in the past had an image as a producer of 'budget', 'downmarket' or 'unfashionable' cars. It has tried to shake off this image by exploiting its new owner's name, VW.

Faced with competition, firms are likely to lose sales if they don't take into account the needs of customers. Increasingly, firms are giving free after sales service, replacing unwanted goods without question and training their staff to deal with the public.

Employees Government legislation and arguably trade unions have influenced how businesses treat employees. A number of laws have been passed to protect workers (☞ units 81 and 82). An example of legislation which affects workers is the **Disability Discrimination Act, 1996.** This is designed to reduce discrimination by businesses against disabled workers.

One effect of legislation is that it protects companies with high standards of responsibility from those competitors who have little regard for health and safety at work. Unscrupulous firms will not be able to lower costs by neglecting health and safety because they will have to keep within the law.

Trade unions have argued for the rights of the workforce for many years (☞ units 85-87). They have aimed to improve social facilities, wages and working conditions.

Suppliers Some firms have benefited from good relations with suppliers of raw materials and components. One example is in manufacturing, where companies are adopting **Just-in-time** manufacturing (☞ unit 92). This means that firms only produce when they have an order and stocks of raw materials and components are delivered to the factory only when they are needed. Reliable and efficient suppliers are needed by firms if they order stocks 'at the last minute'. Maintaining good relations with suppliers is likely to help this process. Examples of good relations might be prompt payment to suppliers or regular meetings to discuss each other's needs.

Behavioural theories

BEHAVIOURAL THEORIES assume that business objectives are not determined by owners and managers alone. They

Question 5

In 1997 British Airways invited more than 50 artists to help the company revolutionise its image. Artists were asked to submit designs that would turn the BA fleet into flying works of largely abstract art. The change would involve BA scrapping its traditional Union Jack motif on planes, replacing the grey and dark blue livery with bright colours, replacing the 'speedwing' arrow logo with a curvy abstract design and making staff uniforms softer and more colourful. On Concorde the sleek lines would be broken by bright blue triangles, circles and shapes painted over the rear fuselage.

BA was attempting to shed its British image and become a global airline. It also aimed to become more open, youthful, cosmopolitan and friendly. Research showed that the company was seen as aloof by many customers, mainly because of its British origins. BA even considered dropping 'British' from its name, but decided against this. The redesign was seen as essential to BA's ambition to increase the number of passengers it carried by 70 per cent, to 51 million, by 2005. The cost of the new look was expected to be around £60 million. Every plane in the fleet and thousands of ground vehicles would need repainting, as airport signs, check-in desks and stationery would have to be changed.

Some experts warned that BA had a large number of loyal customers who might feel alienated if the airline went too far. One design consultant said: 'The fact that they have kept red, white and blue colours somewhere in the design shows that they are worried that they could drive people away. They don't want to lose their British roots'. David Barrie, director of the National Art Collections Fund asked: ' Are BA seriously proposing to run all these at the same time? Some of the individual designs are attractive and striking, like the eagle woodcarving. Others seem to be pretty corny, like the tartan for Scotland. Overall it seems extravagant and confusing'.

Source: adapted from *The Sunday Times*, 1.6.1997.

(a) Explain why BA decided to change its corporate image.
(b) Explain the potential: (i) advantages; and
    (ii) disadvantages to BA of changing its image.

suggest that other stakeholders, such as the government, consumers and pressure groups, may affect the firm's objectives. The objective a company has will depend on the power of these groups to influence decisions. It is argued that groups inside and outside the business have certain minimum goals.

● The owners will require a certain level of profit to retain their interest in the business.
● Workers will demand a minimum level of pay and acceptable working conditions if they are to be retained in

employment.

- Suppliers will want regular contracts, reasonable lead times and prompt payment.
- Managers will insist on enough resources to carry out their tasks (this might include an appropriate expense allowance, for example).
- The government will require the company to obey laws and pay taxes.
- Customers will demand quality products at reasonable prices.
- Pressure groups, such as environmentalists, will try to protect their interests, eg avoiding pollution.

In practice, the group with the most influence will achieve its objectives. In the 1990s animal rights pressure groups, such as Lynx, persuaded customers to buy fewer fur products. Some businesses saw sales reduced as a result and others switched to the manufacture of synthetic fur clothing. Also in the 1990s managers and owners of large businesses often pursued a policy of delayering or downsizing - reducing the number of tiers in the business hierarchy (☞ unit 70). They were convinced that such measures would make their businesses more efficient and reduce costs. This resulted in many employees losing their jobs.

The dominant group may change over time. In the 1970s trade unions were powerful in many industries. They gained large wage increases, sometimes resulting in lower profits for owners. Government legislation over the period 1979-96 restricted their ability to take industrial action and push for unreasonable wage increases. As a result the position of the employer strengthened.

Sometimes groups will compromise. Figure 4.6 illustrates the total costs, total revenue and profit of a business. If it is dominated by the directors, they might have growth as an objective. This would be achieved at output level Q_1, where output is pushed to the limit before the firm makes a loss. However, the owners may prefer the business to produce a level of output Q_2 where profits are greatest. A compromise might be at Q_3, where a minimum level of profit is made for the owners, but output is high enough for some growth.

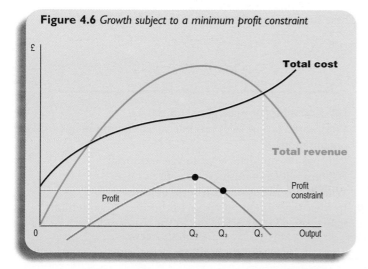

Figure 4.6 *Growth subject to a minimum profit constraint*

What determines business objectives?

Behavioural theories suggest that the stakeholder which dominates the business will determine the objectives. If the owners are in control they are likely to aim for profit. However, there are other factors that influence the choice of objective.

- The size and status of the firm. For example, many small businesses may be content with profit satisficing or survival. Larger companies may aim for growth and market domination.
- The age of the business. Businesses starting off may be content with survival. Later, when they are established, they may pursue other objectives.
- Whether a business is in the public or private sector. In the past, organisations in the public sector were set up to provide a service, whereas firms in the private sector pursued other objectives such as making a profit.
- Long term business objectives may differ from those in the short term. In the long term businesses will want to make a profit. In the short run they may be prepared to break even (☞ unit 54) or even make a loss. For example, British Biotechnology PLC, the pharmaceuticals company started in 1986 had still not made a profit by 1998. Such companies often invest large amounts at the start and do not expect to make a profit for some time.
- External pressures. New environmental legislation, for example, may force a business to change its behaviour and take into account the effect of its activities on the environment. A landfill tax, which would increase the cost of waste disposal, may encourage greater recycling. Changing market trends can affect goals. Increasing demand for products may force a business to grow and expand into new areas of production.
- Internal pressures. The appointment of a new chairperson, for example, might result in a completely new set of goals for a business.
- Risk. Pursuing some objectives might involve taking risks. For example, trying to achieve growth by entering new and unknown markets will be risky for a business. Some businesses are happy to take risks because the potential rewards outweigh the costs involved. Other businesses are risk averse. It could be argued that the move by Virgin into the operation of a rail franchise in 1996 was risky as the firm had no previous experience in running trains.
- Business culture. The values and norms of behaviour developed by a business over time are likely to influence its objectives (☞ unit 14). A business with a caring culture is likely to have different objectives to one with a competitive culture.

Objectives in the public sector

As a result of government policy in the last two decades of the twentieth century, public sector organisations

(☞ unit 6) changed their objectives. Historically, the main objective of public sector businesses was to supply a public service. For example, previously state owned organisations, such as British Rail and British Gas, had to supply services in isolated regions which were unprofitable. Profit was not really a motive for public sector organisations. Many made losses.

In the 1990s public sector organisations aimed to offer their services in a more 'business like' way. The government expected them to operate efficiently and produce a cost effective and quality service. Some had fairly substantial 'surpluses', part of which are paid to the Treasury. Public sector organisations adopted many private sector business techniques, such as marketing, business planning, budgeting and investment appraisal. For example, many schools, colleges and hospital trusts actively marketed their services. Service providers were encouraged to compete for customers. Examples might be colleges trying to attract students to obtain government funds or NHS trusts competing to sell services to fund holding GPs.

For some public sector organisations performance targets were set to ensure that a 'good' standard of service was supplied. For example, hospitals aimed to reduce waiting lists for beds and operations. Councils had their budgets cut to ensure that waste is minimised. Sixth form colleges were instructed to improve efficiency in the delivery of their education services. The performance rates of many public sector organisations are widely published. National league tables are compiled for crime and detection rates, exam results and truancy rates. Such tables are designed to introduce an element of competition in the public sector and inform the public of performance.

Business planning and strategy

Once a business has decided upon its objectives it needs to **plan** how to achieve them and decide on the most suitable **strategies** to use.

When planning its strategy, a business will first analyse its current position. This will give it a variety of information about factors that could affect its plans including:
- its position in relation to its competitors, for example

whether its product has a well known brand name which will be recognised over those of its rivals;
- any factors that might affect its plans, such as new legislation which may affect how much it pays its employees;
- the amount of competition it faces, which is likely to affect its prices for example;
- the influence of other businesses such as suppliers;
- whether product sales are likely to rise or fall in future;
- the costs of the business and how they are likely to change.

There are certain methods that a business might use to analyse its current position. These methods are discussed in detail in unit 15. One that many find useful is SWOT analysis. This is where the business identifies its:
- Strengths, such as the quality of its products compared to those of others;
- Weaknesses, such as its high costs relative to those of rivals;
- Opportunities, such as a growing market in another country;
- Threats, such as new smaller companies charging lower prices.

The business must then decide on the most suitable strategy to use in order to achieve its objectives. Strategies can take a number of forms.
- Operational strategies tend to be methods used to improve the efficiency of the business (☞ unit 96). For example, a business may find ways to improve the response time to customer complaints.
- Generic strategies affect the whole business. They are used to gain a **competitive advantage** over rivals (☞ unit 16). An example might be where a business no longer produces certain products to concentrate on its 'core' or most important markets.
- Corporate strategies aimed at the long term position of the business. An example might be a company aiming to double in size in the next ten years by merging with other businesses.
- Global strategies. For example, a business may set up factories in other countries in order to supply products more easily to those countries.

These strategies are discussed in more detail in unit 16.

Summary

1. Under what circumstances might survival be an important objective?
2. Why might a successful business still not survive in its existing form?
3. What is the difference between short term and long term profit maximisation?
4. Why might a business pursue growth as an objective?
5. Which stakeholders involved in the business are likely to want business growth? Explain why.
6. List 5 examples of managerial objectives.
7. Who would favour sales revenue maximisation in an organisation?
8. Why has the importance of image and social responsibility as a business objective grown?
9. What factors determine business objectives?
10. In what ways might public sector business organisations have changed their objectives in the last decade?

Key terms

Behavioural theories - theories which state that business objectives are determined jointly by groups of interested parties.

Mission statement - a brief summary of a firm's aims and objectives.

Profit maximisation - producing a level of output which generates the most profit for a business.

Sales revenue maximisation - producing a level of output where sales revenue is greatest.

Satisficing - generating sufficient profit to satisfy the owners, not necessarily at an output which gives greatest profit.

Question

Sefton Council seeks to provide high quality and effective public services and aims to continually improve its performance. In the 1997/8 financial year Sefton improved services in a number of areas. For example it:
- improved the levels of rent collection;
- reduced the cost of refuse collection;
- increased the amount of rubbish it recycled;
- speeded up and reduced the cost of processing benefit claims and collecting council tax.

For the last five years councils have been required to publish performance indicators. The performance of councils is monitored by the Audit Commission. Table 4.3 shows some performance indicators for the provision of housing by Sefton Council.

(a) Describe the objectives of Sefton Council.
(b) Describe some similarities between Sefton Council's objectives and those which might exist in the private sector.
(c) What evidence is there in Table 4.3 to suggest that Sefton Council improved the quality of its housing provision?

Table 4.3 *Performance indicators for housing provision by Sefton Council*

HOUSING	97/98	96/97
Allocating and letting housing		
The % of lettings to new tenants arranged by the Council to:		
(i) homeless households	4%	10%
(ii) others	96%	90%
The % of homes that are empty and ready for new tenants	1.7%	1.5%
The % of houses that are empty because of major repairs to be done	0.9%	0.4%
The average time taken to get a new tenant into an empty Council home	7.9 weeks	7 weeks
Does the Council follow the Commission for Racial Equality's code of practice in rented housing?	Yes	No
Repairing council homes		
The % of all repairs requested by tenants completed within the Council's target times	83%	90%
Collecting rent		
The % of council house rents which the Council collected	97.4%	97.1%
The % of tenants who owed more than 13 weeks' rent on 31st March 1997 (except those who owed less than £250)	6.2%	7.7%
Rent and costs		
Average weekly costs for each home, broken down as follows:		
Management	£7.08	£7.26
Repairs	£15.71	£14.24
Rent rebates	£26.89	£26.86
Capital charges and other items	£13.76	£16.66
Government subsidy	-£24.10	-£26.41
Total (average rent)	£39.34	£38.61
Average amount the Council spent on major repairs and improvements per home	£411.70	£253.55

Source: adapted from a Sefton Council publication, 1998.

Case study

Marks & Spencer

Marks & Spencer is a company well known for taking its responsibility to society seriously. It claims to be a 'good corporate citizen' that shares its success with charities and community organisations. It runs its business with concern for human health, safety and the effect its operations have on the environment.

Each year Marks & Spencer receives some 10,000 requests for help and support. In 1996 the company offered assistance to over 1,200 projects. Its social responsibility programme covers community development and environmental projects, health and care projects, and arts and heritage initiatives. Marks & Spencer tends to focus its support on those projects which help young and elderly people, those with special needs and the vulnerable. During 1998 the company contributed more than £10 million to the communities in which it operated. More than 260 staff were seconded to support projects, either on part time projects or longer term assignments. The company also raises further funds through charity fashion shows and the sale of charity Christmas cards.

One aspect of Marks & Spencer's programme is working to combat deprivation. Marks & Spencer supports the Prince's Trust Volunteers, which mixes employed and unemployed young people in training programmes to raise confidence and develop skills. A Marks & Spencer personnel manager runs The Safety Centre in Milton Keynes. The Safety Centre co-ordinates volunteers from the emergency services who help to foster personal safety and responsible behaviour amongst children.

Marks & Spencer is also active in the promotion of concern for the mentally ill. It works with a number of medical and voluntary organisations and supports a wide range of social welfare and health needs. For example, it supported the National Schizophrenia Fellowship to help people with severe mental illness. Other beneficiaries in this field are the Samaritans and the London Collection, a charity which aids young, homeless and mentally ill people.

Some of Marks & Spencer's financial support is channelled into the arts at the grassroots level. For example, organisations such as Live Music Now, which helps young musicians gain experience of live audiences, and Learning Through Landscape which works with schools in design and creative projects, have received help from the company. Marks & Spencer is also sensitive to green issues. It has reduced its costs by introducing environmentally friendly methods in its operations. For example:

● waste disposal costs have been reduced by half since 1991 through minimising and recycling waste;
● the volume of waste sent to landfill has fallen from 18,000 tonnes to 1,000 tonnes between 1992 and 1997;
● 25,000 tonnes of cardboard for transporting food has been saved each year due to cuts and recycling;
● a £1 million investment in energy-saving equipment was made in 1997;
● 40 million plastic hangers were collected in stores in 1995
● recycling of technology in 1998 meant that for every £1 spent on recycling, £3 was saved in equipment and disposal costs.

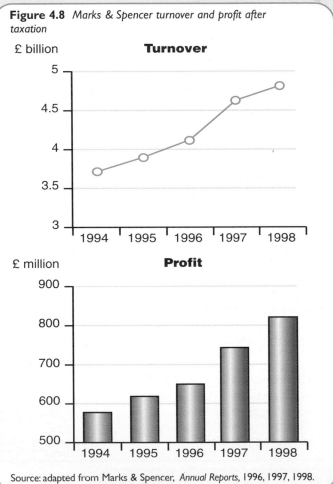

Figure 4.8 *Marks & Spencer turnover and profit after taxation*

Source: adapted from Marks & Spencer, *Annual Reports*, 1996, 1997, 1998.

(a) **What is meant by social responsibility as a business objective?**

(b) **(i) Suggest two other objectives that the business might have had over the period 1994-98.**
  (ii) Why might the business have had these objectives?

(c) **Suggest how:**
  (i) people in the community;
  (ii) Marks & Spencer;
  might benefit from the approach of the business to social responsibility.

(d) **Explain the factors that might affect the degree to which the company is socially responsible.**

(e) **Evaluate the strengths of Marks & Spencer from the information and data presented.**

What is a business organisation?

Businesses are often referred to as organisations. An ORGANISATION is a body that is set up to meet needs. For example, the St. John's Ambulance organisation was originally set up by volunteers to train the public in life saving measures.

Business organisations satisfy needs by providing people with goods and services. All organisations will:
- try to achieve objectives (☞ unit 4);
- use resources;
- need to be directed;
- have to be accountable;
- have to meet legal requirements;
- have a formal structure (☞ unit 7).

Private sector business organisations

Unit 1 showed the different methods of classifying business. One of these methods was by sector. The PRIVATE SECTOR includes all those businesses which are set up by individuals or groups of individuals. Most business activity is undertaken in the private sector. The types of business in the private sector can vary considerably. Some are small retailers with a single owner. Others are large multinational companies (☞ unit 32), such as BP Amoco and Cadbury Schweppes. Businesses will vary according to the legal form they take and their ownership.

- Unincorporated businesses. These are businesses where there is no legal difference between the owners and the business. Everything is carried out in the name of the owner or owners. These firms tend to be small, owned either by one person or a few partners.

- Incorporated businesses. An incorporated body is one which has a separate legal identity from its owners. In other words, the business can be sued, can be taken over and can be liquidated.

Figure 5.1 shows the different types of business organisation in the private sector, their legal status and their ownership. These are examined in the rest of this unit.

The sole trader

The simplest and most common form of private sector business is a SOLE TRADER or SOLE PROPRIETOR. This type of business is owned by just one person. The owner runs the business and may employ any number of people to help.

Sole traders can be found in different types of production. In the primary sector many farmers and fishermen operate like this. In the secondary sector there are small scale manufacturers, builders and construction firms. The tertiary sector probably contains the largest number of sole traders. They supply a wide range of services, such as hairdressing, retailing, restaurants, gardening and other household services. Many sole traders exist in retailing and construction where a very large number of shops and small construction companies are each owned by one person. Although there are many more sole traders than any other type of business, the amount they contribute to total output in the UK is relatively small.

Setting up as a sole trader is straightforward. There are no legal formalities needed. However, sole traders or self-employed dealers do have some legal responsibilities once they become established. In addition, some types of business need to obtain special permission before trading.
- Once turnover reaches a certain level sole traders must register for VAT.
- They must pay income tax and National Insurance contributions.

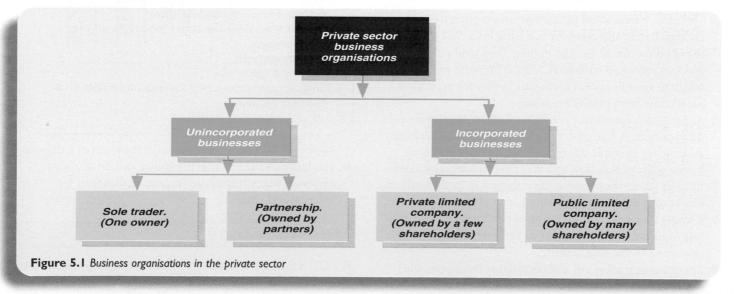

Figure 5.1 *Business organisations in the private sector*

- Some types of business activity need a licence, such as the sale of alcohol or supplying a taxi service or public transport.
- Sometimes planning permission is needed in certain locations. For example, a person may have to apply to the local authority for planning permission to run a fish and chip shop in premises which had not been used for this activity before.
- Sole traders must comply with legislation aimed at business practice. For example, legally they must provide healthy and safe working conditions for their employees (☞ unit 81).

Advantages of sole traders

- The lack of legal restrictions. The sole trader will not face a lengthy setting up period or incur expensive administration costs.
- Any profit made after tax is kept by the owner.
- The owner is in complete control and is free to make decisions without interference. For many sole traders independence is one of the main reasons why they choose to set up in business.
- The owner has flexibility to choose the hours of work he or she wants and to take holidays. Customers may also benefit. Sole traders can take individual customer's needs into account, stocking a particular brand of a good or making changes to a standard design, for example.
- Because of their small size, sole traders can offer a personal service to their customers. Some people prefer to deal directly with the owner and are prepared to pay a higher price for doing so.
- Such businesses may be entitled to government support (☞ unit 2).

Disadvantages of sole traders

- Sole traders have UNLIMITED LIABILITY. This means that if the business has debts, the owner is personally liable. A sole trader may be forced to sell personal possessions or use personal savings to meet these debts.
- The money used to set up the business is often the owner's savings. It may also come from a bank loan. Sole traders may find it difficult to raise money. They tend to be small and lack sufficient **collateral**, such as property or land, on which to raise finance. This means money for expansion must come from profits or savings.
- Although independence is an advantage, it can also be a disadvantage. A sole trader might prefer to share decision making, for example. Many sole traders work very long hours, without holidays, and may have to learn new skills.
- In cases where the owner is the only person in the business, illness can stop business activity taking place. For example, if a sole trader is a mobile hairdresser, illness will lead to a loss of income in the short term, and even a loss of customers in the long term.
- Because sole traders are unincorporated businesses, the

Question 1

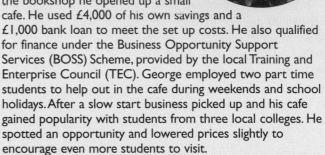

George Saunders had worked for a national newspaper but was made redundant. He spent seven months searching for another reporting job, but eventually gave up and decided to set up his own business. He had always enjoyed books and opened up a second-hand book shop in Blackpool. In a room above the bookshop he opened up a small cafe. He used £4,000 of his own savings and a £1,000 bank loan to meet the set up costs. He also qualified for finance under the Business Opportunity Support Services (BOSS) Scheme, provided by the local Training and Enterprise Council (TEC). George employed two part time students to help out in the cafe during weekends and school holidays. After a slow start business picked up and his cafe gained popularity with students from three local colleges. He spotted an opportunity and lowered prices slightly to encourage even more students to visit.

After one year he extended his bank loan to £2,000 and bought some more kitchen equipment to provide substantial lunch time meals. Again he kept prices low and targeted the student market. The business expanded and George was beginning to enjoy good profits. The book shop only made a small contribution to turnover, but George felt that it helped the image of the cafe which attracted his customers.

One morning when he was opening, a local authority representative arrived unannounced to inspect the business premises. After a two hour investigation the inspector left saying that George would hear from the authority the next day. A letter from them informed George that his kitchen must conform to a long list of health regulations. George estimated that the cost would be £3,000. He arranged a meeting with the bank that same afternoon. Unfortunately they could only lend him half the amount. George was eventually forced to borrow from a private loan company, paying high rates of interest.

(a) What features of a sole trader does the example of George Saunders' business show?
(b) In what ways does the above case highlight the:
  (i) advantages;
  (ii) disadvantages;
  of being a sole trader?
(c) Suggest two reasons why George might take on a business partner.

owner can be sued by customers in the event of a dispute.
- The business may rely on the ability and drive of one person. If that person loses interest or dies then the business will cease.

Partnerships

A PARTNERSHIP is defined in **The Partnership Act, 1890** as the 'relation which subsists between persons carrying on business with common view to profit'. Put simply, a partnership has more than one owner. The 'joint' owners will share responsibility for running the business and also share the profits. Partnerships are often found in the professions, such as accountants, doctors, estate agents, solicitors and veterinary surgeons. After sole traders, partnerships are the most common type of business organisation. It is usual for partners to specialise. A firm of chartered accountants with five partners might find that each partner specialises in one aspect of finance, such as tax law, investments or VAT returns.

There are no legal formalities to complete when a partnership is formed. However, partners may draw up a DEED OF PARTNERSHIP. This is a legal document which states partners' rights in the event of a dispute. It covers issues such as:
- how much capital each partner will contribute;
- how profits (and losses) will be shared amongst the partners;
- the procedure for ending the partnership;
- how much control each partner has;
- rules for taking on new partners.

If no deed of partnership is drawn up the arrangements between partners will be subject to the Partnership Act. For example, if there was a dispute regarding the share of profits, the Act states that profits are shared equally amongst the partners.

Advantages of partnerships
- There are no legal formalities to complete when setting up the business.
- Each partner can specialise. This may improve the running of the business, as partners can carry out the tasks they do best.
- Since there is more than one owner, more finance can be raised than if the firm was a sole trader.
- Partners can share the workload. They will be able to cover each other for holidays and illness. They can also exchange ideas and opinions when making key decisions. Also, the success of the business will not depend upon the ability of one person, as is the case with a sole trader.
- Since this type of business tends to be larger than the sole trader, it is in a stronger position to raise more money from outside the business.

Disadvantages of partnerships
- The individual partners have unlimited liability. Under the Partnership Act, each partner is equally liable for debts.
- Profits have to be shared amongst more owners.
- Partners may disagree. For example, they might differ in their views on whether to hire a new employee or about the amount of profit to retain for investment.
- The size of a partnership is limited to a maximum of 20 partners. This limits the amount of money that can be

introduced from owners.
- The partnership ends when one of the partners dies. The partnership must be wound up so that the partner's family can retrieve money invested in the business. It is normal for the remaining partners to form a new partnership quickly afterwards.
- Any decision made by one partner on behalf of the company is legally binding on all other partners. For example, if one partner agreed to buy four new company cars for the business, all partners must honour this.
- Partnerships have unincorporated status, so partners can be sued by customers.

Limited partnerships The **Limited Partnerships Act 1907** allows a business to become a LIMITED PARTNERSHIP, although this is rare. This is where some partners provide capital but take no part in the management of the business. Such a partner will have LIMITED LIABILITY - the partner can only lose the original amount of money invested. She can

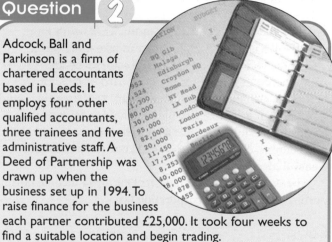

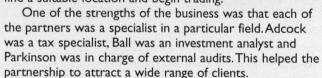

Question **2**

Adcock, Ball and Parkinson is a firm of chartered accountants based in Leeds. It employs four other qualified accountants, three trainees and five administrative staff. A Deed of Partnership was drawn up when the business set up in 1994. To raise finance for the business each partner contributed £25,000. It took four weeks to find a suitable location and begin trading.

One of the strengths of the business was that each of the partners was a specialist in a particular field. Adcock was a tax specialist, Ball was an investment analyst and Parkinson was in charge of external audits. This helped the partnership to attract a wide range of clients.

In 1998 the partners decided to expand. They needed to raise £40,000 to obtain more office space and to buy a new computer system. They did think about inviting a sleeping partner to contribute some capital or invite the other accountants to become partners. In the end, however, they borrowed all the money from a bank.

(a) Why do you think Adcock, Ball and Parkinson drew up a Deed of Partnership?
(b) In what ways does the case illustrate the advantages of a partnership?
(c) Suggest reasons why Adcock, Ball and Parkinson decided against inviting:
   (i) a sleeping partner;
   (ii) other accountants;
   to join the partnership.

not be made to sell personal possessions to meet any other business debts. This type of partner is called a **sleeping partner**. Even with a limited partnership there must always be at least one partner with **unlimited liability**. The Act also allows this type of partnership to have more than 20 partners.

Companies

There are many examples of LIMITED COMPANIES in the UK. They range from Garrick Engineering, a small family business, to British Airways which has many thousands of shareholders. One feature is that they all have a separate legal identity from their owners. This means that they can own assets, form contracts, employ people, sue and be sued in their own right. Another feature is that the owners all have **limited liability**. If a limited company has debts, the owners can only lose the money they have invested in the firm. They cannot be forced to use their own money, like sole traders and partners, to pay business debts.

The **capital** of a limited company is divided into **shares**. Each member or **shareholder** (☞ unit 3) owns a number of these shares. They are the joint owners of the company and can vote and take a share of the profit. Those with more shares will have more control and can take more profit.

Limited companies are run by **directors** who are appointed by the shareholders. The board of directors, headed by a **chairperson**, is accountable to shareholders and should run the company as the shareholders wish. If the company's performance does not to live up to shareholders' expectations, directors can be 'voted out' at an **Annual General Meeting (AGM)**.

Whereas sole traders and partnerships pay income tax on profits, companies pay corporation tax.

Forming a limited company

How do shareholders set up a limited company? Limited companies must produce two documents - the **Memorandum of Association** and **Articles of Association**. The Memorandum sets out the constitution and gives details about the company. The **Companies Act 1985** states that the following details must be included.

- The name of the company.
- The name and address of the company's registered office.
- The objectives of the company, and the scope of its activities.
- The liability of its members.
- The amount of capital to be raised and the number of shares to be issued.

A limited company must have a minimum of two members, but there is no upper limit.

The Articles of Association deal with the internal running of the company. They include details such as:

- the rights of shareholders depending on the type of share they hold;

- the procedures for appointing directors and the scope of their powers;
- the length of time directors should serve before re-election;
- the timing and frequency of company meetings;
- the arrangements for auditing company accounts.

These two documents, along with a statement indicating the names of the directors, will be sent to the Registrar of Companies. If they are acceptable, the company's application will be successful. It will be awarded a **Certificate of Incorporation** which allows it to trade. The registrar keeps these documents on file and they can be inspected at any time by the general public for a fee. A limited company must also submit a copy of its annual accounts to the Registrar each year. Finally, the shareholders have a legal right to attend the AGM and should be told of the date and venue in writing well in advance.

Private limited companies

Private limited companies are one type of limited company. They tend to be relatively smaller businesses, although certain well known companies, such as C&J Clarke and Littlewoods, were privately owned through the 1990s. Their business name ends in Limited or Ltd. Shares can only be transferred 'privately' and all shareholders must agree on the transfer. They cannot be advertised for general sale. Private limited companies are often family businesses owned by members of the family or close friends. The directors of these firms tend to be shareholders and are involved in the running of the business. Many manufacturing firms are private limited companies rather than sole traders or partnerships.

Advantages

- Shareholders have limited liability. As a result more people are prepared to risk their money than in, say, a partnership.
- More capital can be raised as there is no limit on the number of shareholders.
- Control of the company cannot be lost to outsiders. Shares can only be sold to new members if all shareholders agree.
- The business will continue even if one of the owners dies. In this case shares will be transferred to another owner.

Disadvantages

- Profits have to be shared out amongst a much larger number of members.
- There is a legal procedure to set up the business. This takes time and also costs money.
- Firms are not allowed to sell shares to the public. This restricts the amount of capital that can be raised.
- Financial information filed with the Registrar can be inspected by any member of the public. Competitors could use this to their advantage.

● If one shareholder decides to sell shares it may take time to find a buyer.

Question 3

Falcon Marketing Services Ltd was incorporated in December 1998 as a private limited company. The registered office of the company, which is also its principal place of business, is at 112 Mornington Parade, Westcliffe, Devon. The main objectives of Falcon Marketing Services Ltd, as set out in clause 4 of its Memorandum of Association, are to act as a provider of marketing services and enter into financial and commercial transactions of all kinds.

The company, whose chairman is Richard Collins, made a profit of £180,000 in its first year of trading and looks set to be the largest marketing agency in the South West by the end of the millennium. The company's other shareholders are all members of the Collins family. Between the 5 of them they contributed £40,000 of share capital when the company was formed.

(a) Explain the main purpose of the Memorandum of Association.
(b) State two other pieces of information required by the Registrar of Companies when forming a limited company.
(c) Describe the possible disadvantages to Falcon Marketing Services Ltd of being a private limited company.
(d) One family member has suggested that a friend who has worked for a marketing agency in London could become a shareholder and contribute extra capital. Discuss whether this is a good idea for the business.

Public limited companies

The second type of limited company tends to be larger and is called a **public limited company**. This company name ends in plc. There are around 1.2 million registered limited companies in the UK, but only around 1 per cent of them are public limited companies. However, they contribute far more to national output and employ far more people than private limited companies. The shares of these companies can be bought and sold by the public on the stock exchange (☞ unit 57).

To become a public limited company, a Memorandum of Association, Articles of Association and a **Statutory Declaration** must be provided. This is a document which states that the requirements of all the Company Acts have been met. When the company has been issued with a **Certificate of Incorporation**, it is common to publish a **Prospectus**. This is a document which advertises the company to potential investors and invites them to buy shares before a FLOTATION. Some examples of companies which have 'gone public' in the latter part of the 1990s are Railtrack, the company which owns the railway infrastructure in the UK, and Orange, the mobile phone and communications operator.

'Going public' is expensive. This is because:

● the company needs lawyers to ensure that the prospectus is 'legally' correct;
● a large number of 'glossy' publications have to be made available;
● the company may use a financial institution to process share applications;
● the share issue has to be **underwritten** (which means that the company must insure against the possibility of some shares remaining unsold) and a fee is paid to an underwriter who must buy any unsold shares;
● the company will have advertising and administrative expenses;
● it must have a minimum of £50,000 share capital.

A public limited company cannot begin trading until it has completed these tasks and has received at least a 25 per cent payment for the value of shares. It will then receive a Trading Certificate and can begin operating, and the shares will be quoted on the Stock Exchange or the Alternative Investment Market (AIM) (☞ unit 57).

The stock exchange is a market where second hand shares are bought and sold. A full stock exchange listing means that the company must comply with the rules and regulations laid down by the stock exchange. Many of these rules are to protect shareholders from fraud. The AIM is designed for companies which want to avoid some of the high costs of a full listing. However, shareholders with shares quoted on the AIM do not have the same protection as those with 'fully' quoted shares.

Advantages

Some of the advantages are the same as those of private limited companies. For example, all members have limited liability, the firm continues to trade if one of the owners dies and more power is enjoyed due to their larger size. Others are as follows.

● Huge amounts of money can be raised from the sale of shares to the public.
● Production costs may be lower as firms may gain economies of scale (☞ unit 93).
● Because of their size, plcs can often dominate the market.
● It becomes easier to raise finance as financial institutions are more willing to lend to plcs.

Disadvantages

● The setting up costs can be very expensive - running into millions of pounds in some cases.
● Since anyone can buy their shares, it is possible for an outside interest to take control of the company.
● All of the company's accounts can be inspected by members of the public. Competitors may be able to use some of this information to their advantage. They have to publish more information than private limited companies.
● Because of their size they are not able to deal with their customers at a personal level.
● The way they operate is controlled by various Company

Acts which aim to protect shareholders.
● There may be a divorce of ownership and control
(☞ unit 5) which might lead to the interests of the owners
being ignored to some extent.
● It is argued that many of these companies are inflexible
due to their size. For example, they find change difficult to
cope with.

Some public limited companies are very large indeed. They
have millions of shareholders and a wide variety of business
interests situated all over the world. They are known as
multinationals, (☞ unit 32) which means that they have
production plants in a number of different countries. For
example, Kellogg's is an American based multinational company
with a production plant and head office situated in Battle Creek,
USA. Kellogg's has also had factories in Manchester, Wrexham,
Bremen, Barcelona and Brescia near Milan.

Holding companies

Some public limited companies operate as HOLDING
COMPANIES. This means that they are not only a company
in their own right, but also have enough shares in numerous
other public limited companies to exert control. This type of
company tends to have a very diversified range of business
activities. For example, the Kingfisher group owns a number
of companies including Woolworth's, B & Q, Superdrug,
Comet and a property arm, Chartwell.

The main advantage of this type of company is that it
tends to have a diverse range of business activities. This helps
protect it when one of its markets fails. Also, because it is so
large, it can often gain financial economies of scale. The main
disadvantage is that the holding company may see the
businesses it owns only as a financial asset. It may have no
long term interest in the businesses or its development.

Co-operatives

The UK Co-operative Movement grew from the activities of
28 workers in Rochdale, Lancashire. In 1844 they set up a
retail co-operative society - The Rochdale Equitable Pioneers
Society. With capital of just £28 they bought food from
wholesalers and opened a shop, selling 'wholesome food at
reasonable prices'. The surplus (or profit) made was returned
to members of the society in the form of a 'dividend'. The
dividend was in proportion to how much each member had
spent. The principles of the society were:
● voluntary and open membership;
● democratic ownership - one member, one vote;
● the surplus allocated according to spending (the dividend);
● educational facilities for members and workers.

The principles of the modern Co-op are similar. Co-
operatives are organised on a regional basis, for example the
West Midlands Co-operative Society and United Norwest.
Members can purchase shares and each member has one vote
at the Annual General Meeting, no matter how many shares

In March 1996, Chelsea became the sixth football club to
be 'floated'. It joined Manchester United, Tottenham
Hotspur, Preston North End and two Scottish clubs.
Chelsea Village, the company which owns Chelsea, was
floated on the Alternative Investment Market with a value
of £58 million. Unusually, no new shares were issued and
no new money was raised. Rather, 9 million of the 105
million shares were made available to the public at a price
of 55p.

Under the terms of the flotation Ken Bates, the chairman,
and his assistant retained a combined 54 per cent of the
shares. Bates's aim was to make Chelsea the number one
club in England. Trading as a public limited company would
allow it to raise large amounts of money to redevelop the
ground and enhance the playing staff. Plans included a
hotel, flats, underground parking and an underground
station. In the summer of 1996 the club signed the Italian
Gianluca Vialli, who took over as manager in 1997. Other
international players bought by the club which was dubbed
the 'Foreign Legion' included Roberto Di Matteo,
Gianfranco Zola and Frank Leboeuf. In October 1998
shares were trading at 70.0p, having achieved a high of
125.5p. In 1998, 19 football clubs in England and Scotland
had a share quotation.

Source: adapted from articles in *The Guardian* and the *Financial Times*,
1996-98.

(a) State two advantages of Chelsea becoming a public
limited company.
(b) Explain why the chairman and his assistant retained 54
per cent of shares after the flotation.
(c) Why is it do you think that only a few football clubs
have become public limited companies?

are owned. Members elect a board of directors who appoint
managers to run day to day business. The Co-operative is run
in the interests of its customers and part of any surplus is
distributed to members as a dividend. In 1997 the Members'
dividend from all Co-operative Retail Societies was £28
million. Shares are not sold on the stock exchange, which
limits the amount of money that can be raised.

The UK Co-operative Movement is organised into a
number of areas.

Retail co-operatives Perhaps the most familiar activity is the

Co-op retail store, which has traditionally sold food products. Over the years RETAIL CO-OPERATIVES have faced increasing competition from supermarket chains. In the late 1990s they had only 6 per cent of the UK grocery trade they once dominated. As a result of competition a number of Co-operative retail societies merged. There are now less than 50 in the UK. The largest is the CRS (Co-operative Retail Society) based in Manchester. Another response to competition from supermarket chains was to open large Co-op superstores and hypermarkets. These sold everything from food and furniture to garden equipment and DIY products. However, this strategy proved unsuccessful and in recent years Co-operative societies have developed medium sized supermarkets and convenience stores geared to the needs of the local community.

The Co-operative Wholesale Society To ensure delivery of products to retailers the Co-operative Wholesale Society (CWS) was set up in 1863. Retail societies are the shareholders. It acts as a manufacturer and wholesaler for retail societies. 60 per cent of products sold by retailers are 'own brand', as they are manufactured by the CWS. The CWS is also Britain's largest commercial farmer. Other activities include tea and coffee blending and packaging.

Other activities There is a variety of other business activities carried out by the Co-op. The Co-operative Insurance Society continues to retain a relatively large market share of the insurance market. The Co-operative Bank is noted for its ethical investment policy and was the first to introduce interest bearing current accounts and all day opening. The funeral directing side of the Co-operative operations continues to be successful. Other business activity includes Co-operative travel, opticians and chemists.

Worker co-operatives

Another form of co-operation in the UK with common ownership is a WORKER CO-OPERATIVE. This is where a business is jointly owned by its employees. A worker co-operative is an example of a producer co-operative - where people work together to produce a good or service. Examples might be a wine growing co-operative or a co-operative of farmers producing milk.

In a worker co-operative employees are likely to:
● contribute to production;
● be involved in decision making;
● share in the profit (usually on an equal basis);
● provide some capital when buying a share in the business.

In 1998 there were over 1,000 worker co-operatives in the UK. Examples have ranged from Tower Colliery in South Wales to Delta-T Devices, a manufacturer of environmental monitoring equipment. One advantage of a worker co-operative is that all employees, as owners of the business, are likely to be motivated. Conflict will also tend to be reduced as

Question 5

In 1997 the Co-operative retail societies and the CWS faced takeover pressure from Mr Andrew Regan and his investment companies Lanica Trust and Galileo. He hoped to buy them and then sell off their assets. Sara Parkin, the Director of the Forum for the Future, and a resident of Islay, a Hebridean Island with a population of 4,000, argued that any takeover would be a disaster for the Island as the local Co-op would be bound to close. 'How many branches of Asda or Sainsbury's would serve such a small catchment area?', she argued. The Co-op can provide a personalised service and cares about its clients. This perhaps means that it is not as economically efficient as it could be in pure accounting terms. However, she suggests that: 'if a proper value is placed on the social benefits of the local shop then the cost of the inefficiency is cheap at twice the price'. The takeover bid eventually collapsed and the bidders were investigated for illegal dealings.

Source: adapted from *The Guardian*, 26.4.1997.

In 1997 there were conflicting views about the hostile bid for the Co-op. The Labour Party argued that it was a matter for the company itself. The Trade Union Congress was concerned to protect its members' jobs. Many felt that the Co-op needed reform. The Co-op Bank and Insurance Society were well run but many shops were poorly stocked and maintained. The CWS argued that the Co-op was not an outdated organisation, but had lost its way because it was so diverse, with no overall strategy. It suggested that serving local communities and providing convenience for shoppers may be its role in future. However, it may still face rationalisation and the need for price competition.

Source: adapted from *The Guardian*, 26.4.1997.

Table 5.1 *Co-operative retail societies*

	1994	1997
Number of societies	57	49
Number of shops	4,637	4,600
Trading surplus	£179.3m	£138m

Source: adapted from The Co-operative Union Ltd.

(a) Explain two problems facing the Co-op in 1997.
(b) Explain the phrases:
   (i) 'This perhaps means that it (the Co-op) is not as economically efficient as it could be';
   (ii) 'if a proper value is placed on the social benefits of the local shop then the cost of the inefficiency is cheap at twice the price'.
(c) A Co-op is aiming to set up in an as yet unidentified area of the country. Suggest three features that it might take into account to help it compete with existing supermarket chains.

the objectives of shareholders and employees will be the same. Worker co-operatives can involve the local community, either by giving donations to local bodies or even having them as members of the co-operative.

Building and friendly societies

Most building societies and friendly societies in the UK are MUTUAL ORGANISATIONS. They are owned by their customers, or members as they are known, rather than shareholders. Profits go straight back to members in the form of better and cheaper products. Friendly societies began in the 18th and 19th centuries to support the working classes. Today, there are around 80 friendly societies. They offer a wide range of 'affordable' financial services. These include savings schemes, insurance plans and protection against the loss of income or death. They also provide benefits such as free legal aid, sheltered housing or educational grants to help young people through university. These extra benefits are distributed free of charge, paid for by trading surpluses. The government gives friendly societies special tax treatment, which reduces the amount of tax that members pay.

Building societies used to specialise in mortgages and savings accounts. Savers and borrowers got better interest rates than those offered by banks. This was possible because building societies were non-profit making. In the 1980s building societies began to diversify and compete with banks. In the late 1990s a number of building societies, such as Halifax, Alliance and Leicester and Northern Rock, became public limited companies. The main reason for this was because mutual organisations are restricted by law from raising large amounts of capital which might be used to invest in new business ventures. This **demutualisation** process involved societies giving members 'windfall' payments, usually in the form of shares, to compensate them for their loss of membership.

Charities

Charities are organisations with very specialised aims. They exist to raise money for 'good' causes and draw attention to the needs of disadvantaged groups in society. For example, Age Concern is a charity which raises money on behalf of senior citizens. They also raise awareness and pass comment on issues, such as cold weather payments, which relate to the elderly. Other examples of national charities include Cancer Research Campaign, British Red Cross, Save the Children Fund and Mencap.

Charities rely on donations for their revenue. They also organise fund raising events such as fetes, jumble sales, sponsored activities and raffles. A number of charities run business ventures. For example, Oxfam has a chain of charity shops which sells second hand goods donated by the public.

Charities are generally run according to business principles. They aim to minimise costs, market themselves and employ staff. Most staff are volunteers, but some of the larger charities employ professionals. In the larger charities a lot of administration is necessary to deal with huge quantities of correspondence and handle charity funds. Provided charities are registered, they are not required to pay tax. In addition, businesses can offset any charitable donations they make against tax. This helps charities when raising funds.

Factors affecting the choice of organisation

Age Many businesses change their legal status as they become older. Most businesses when they start out are relatively small and operate as sole traders. Over time, as needs change, a sole trader may take on a partner and form a partnership. Alternatively, a sole trader may invite new owners to participate in the business, issue shares and form a private limited company. Public limited companies are often formed from established private limited companies that have been trading for many years.

The need for finance A change in legal status may be forced on a business. Often small businesses want to grow but do not have the funds. Additional finance can only be raised if the business changes status. Furthermore, many private limited companies 'go public' because they need to raise large amounts for expansion.

Size The size of a business operation is likely to affect its legal status. A great number of small businesses are usually sole traders or partnerships. Public limited companies tend to be large organisations with thousands of employees and a turnover of millions or billions of pounds. It could be argued that a very large business could only be run if it were a limited company. For example, certain types of business activity, such as oil processing and chemicals manufacture, require large scale production methods and could not be managed effectively as sole traders or partnerships.

Limited liability Owners can protect their own personal financial position if the business is a limited company. Sole traders and partners have unlimited liability. They may, therefore, be placed in a position where they have to use their own money to meet business debts. Some partnerships dealing with customers' money, such as solicitors, have to have unlimited liability in order to retain the confidence of their clients.

Degree of control Owners may consider retaining control of their business to be important. This is why many owners choose to remain as sole traders. Once new partners or shareholders become a part of the business the degree of control starts to diminish because it is shared with the new owners. It is possible to keep some control of a limited company by holding the majority of shares. However, even if one person holds 51 per cent of shares in a limited company, the wishes of the other 49 per cent cannot be ignored.

The nature of the business The type of business activity may influence the choice of legal status. For example, household services such as plumbing, decorating and gardening tend to be provided by sole traders. Professional services such as accountancy, legal advice and surveying are usually offered by partnerships. Relatively small manufacturing and family businesses tend to be private limited companies. Large manufacturers and producers of consumer durables, such as cookers, computers and cars, are usually plcs. The reason that these activities choose a particular type of legal status is because of the benefits they gain as a result. However, there are many exceptions to these general examples.

Summary

1. What is the difference between a corporate body and an unincorporated body?
2. State 3 advantages and 3 disadvantages of being a sole trader.
3. What is the advantage of a deed of partnership?
4. State 3 advantages and 3 disadvantages of partnerships.
5. What is meant by a sleeping partner?
6. What is the role of directors in limited companies?
7. What is the difference between the Memorandum of Association and the Articles of Association?
8. What is a Certificate of Incorporation?
9. Describe the advantages and disadvantages of private limited companies.
10. What are the main legal differences between private and public limited companies?
11. Describe the advantages and disadvantages of plcs.
12. How is a company prospectus used?
13. State an advantage and a disadvantage of a holding company.
14. State 3 features of a co-operative.

Question 6

Gwen Watson is a sole trader. She runs a financial services business in London. She rented an office in Fulham and has enjoyed a great deal of success since setting up in 1991. In 1997 the Inland Revenue introduced self assessment for taxpayers. Gwen believed that a lot of new business could be generated as a result. She initially wanted to attract new clients by offering a competitive self-assessment tax service. She then planned to develop further business with these clients by offering a wider range of financial services, such as personal investment plans and private pensions advice.

To carry out her plans Gwen needed to:
- recruit staff experienced in income tax and self-assessment;
- go on a training course to improve her knowledge of the tax system;
- move into larger premises to accommodate the new staff and to build a reception area for clients. The reception area was a drafty corridor which was not in keeping with the image of a forward looking financial services company;
- invest in advertising and promotion to attract new clients.

After a meeting with her bank manager, Gwen was faced with a problem. She needed to raise £75,000 to carry out her plans. The bank, however, would not lend her any of the money as Gwen was unable to offer any collateral against a loan. The bank also felt that she may have difficulty repaying such a large amount given the current position of the business. It suggested that she invite new owners to contribute some capital to the business.

(a) Describe the possible alternative business organisations that may allow Gwen to raise extra funds.
(b) Suggest one type of business organisation that may be suitable for Gwen's business and explain the advantages and disadvantages of your recommendation.

Key terms

Deed of Partnership - a binding legal document which states the formal rights of partners.

Flotation - the process of a company 'going public'.

Holding company - a public limited company which owns enough shares in a number of other companies to exert control over them.

Limited company - a business organisation which has a separate legal entity from those of its owners.

Limited liability - where a business owner is only liable for the original amount of money invested in the business.

Limited partnership - a partnership where some members contribute capital and enjoy a share of profit, but do not participate in the running of the business. At least one partner must have unlimited liability.

Mutual organisation - businesses owned by members who

are customers, rather than shareholders.

Organisation - a body set up to meet a need.

Partnership - a business organisation which is usually owned by between 2-20 people.

Private sector - businesses that are owned by individuals or groups of individuals.

Retail co-operative - a retail business organisation which is run and owned jointly by the members who have equal voting rights.

Sole trader or sole proprietor - a business organisation which has a single owner.

Unlimited liability - where the owner of a business is personally liable for all business debts.

Worker co-operative - a business organisation owned by employees who contribute to production and share in profit.

Case study

Orange

Orange, the well known mobile telephone company, was floated on the stock market in 1996 when it became a quoted public limited company. The company was owned by two businesses - 68.42 per cent by Hutchison Whampoa and 31.58 per cent by British Aerospace. Hutchison Whampoa is one of Hong Kong's largest conglomerates. The two principle shareholders were expected to sell around 25 per cent of Orange. 325,000,000 ordinary shares were offered for sale at a price expected to be between 175p and 205p per share.

Orange began trading in 1994 and grew very rapidly. The group's main business is the operation of the Orange digital PCN telecommunications network in the UK and the sale and marketing of Orange services. Under the brand name of 'Orange' the group offers a wide range of mobile voice and data communication services. In the late 1990s the group was one of four main operators in the industry. The others were Vodafone, One2One and Cellnet.

The total number of subscribers in the UK grew from 1.23 million in 1991 to 5.41 million before the flotation, which is around 10 per cent of the population. Orange expected to attract a huge number of new subscribers from the remaining 90 per cent of the population by the year 2000. In 1998 the total mobile phone subscribers in the UK had risen to 13 million.

The money raised from the flotation was to be used to reduce Orange's debts. About £562 million was to be repaid to the principal shareholders. A large amount of money had been used to set up the company and fund its development. Between its birth and 1996, Orange made continual losses. The company lost £91.7 million in 1994, £117.8 million in 1995, and £177.5 million in 1996 according to its published accounts. However, in 1996 it had 11.5 per cent of the mobile phone market and had seen the number of subscribers increase from 89,000 in 1994 to 785,000 in 1996.

Shares in Orange began trading on 27.6.1996. The offer was oversubscribed many times and immediately the share price rose sharply from its final issue price of 205p. In June 1996 the share price was 245p. By March 1999 it had soared to 865.5p.

Source: adapted from Orange, *Annual Report and Accounts*, various; *Orange Prospectus*, 1996.

(a) (i) **How were the proceeds from the flotation to be used?**

(ii) **Suggest two other ways in which they might have been used.**

(b) **Why do you think the main shareholders only floated around 25 per cent of Orange?**

(c) **The shares were eventually sold for 205p. Calculate the amount of money raised from the flotation.**

(d) **Explain why the share issue was oversubscribed even though Orange had not made a profit between 1994 and 1996.**

(e) **Why might a company like Orange operate more successfully as a public limited company than a private limited company?**

(f) **What problems may Orange face having gone public?**

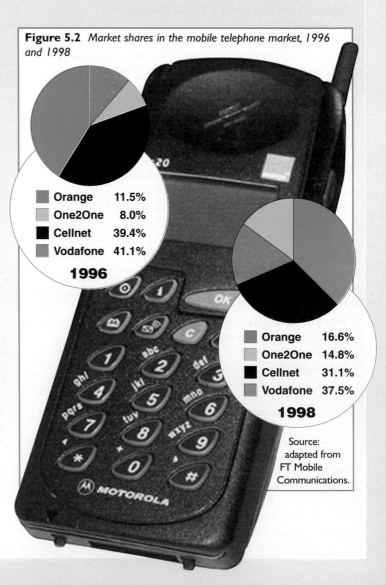

Figure 5.2 *Market shares in the mobile telephone market, 1996 and 1998*

Orange	11.5%
One2One	8.0%
Cellnet	39.4%
Vodafone	41.1%

1996

Orange	16.6%
One2One	14.8%
Cellnet	31.1%
Vodafone	37.5%

1998

Source: adapted from FT Mobile Communications.

Public sector organisations

The PUBLIC SECTOR is made up of organisations which are owned or controlled by central or local government or public corporations. They are funded by the government and in some cases from their own trading 'surplus' or profit. The amount of business activity in the public sector has decreased over the last two decades as a result of government policy. Some public sector businesses have been transferred from the public to the private sector. However, the public sector still has an important role to play in certain areas of business activity.

Which goods and services does the public sector provide?

It has been argued that certain PUBLIC GOODS and MERIT GOODS need to be provided by public sector organisations. Public goods have two features.

- **Non-rivalry** - consumption of the good by one individual does not reduce the amount available for others.
- **Non-excludability** - it is impossible to exclude others from benefiting from their use.

Take the example of street lighting. If one person uses the light to see her way across the street, this does not 'use up' light for someone who wants to look at his watch. Also, it is impossible to stop using the light shining across the street. This means that it would be unlikely that people would pay directly for street lighting. If you paid £1 for light to cross the street, someone else could use it for free! If people will not pay, then businesses cannot make a profit and would not

provide the service. Other examples of public goods may include the judiciary, policing and defence, although in some countries private policing does exist. These public goods are provided free at the point of use. They are paid for from taxation and government borrowing.

Some argue that certain merit goods should be provided by the public sector. Examples include education, health and libraries. These are services which people think should be provided in greater quantities. It is argued that if the individual is left to decide whether or not to pay for these goods, some would choose not to or may not be able to. For example, people may choose not to take out insurance policies to cover for unexpected illness. If they became ill they would not be able to pay for treatment. As a result it is argued that the state should provide this service and pay for it from taxation. The provision of merit goods is said to raise society's standard of living (☞ unit 29).

Public corporations

Like incorporated bodies in the private sector (☞ unit 5), these have a separate legal identity to their owners, the government. They are also organised in a similar way. A government minister will appoint a chairperson and a board to run the corporation. The board will have responsibility for policy and will be accountable to a minister. Public corporations can take a number of forms.

Public utilities These are organisations which supply important services like water and electricity. In England and Wales these have all been transferred to the private sector. However, in 1999 the Scottish Water Authorities were still operating in the public sector, accountable to the Scottish Office.

Nationalised industries NATIONALISED INDUSTRIES played an important role in the economy between 1945-79. They included organisations such as the National Coal Board, British Telecom, British Gas and British Rail. These were private sector companies which were taken into public ownership. Certain motives were put forward for their nationalisation.

- To supply services which were unprofitable, like trains and buses to isolated towns and villages.
- To avoid wasteful duplication where NATURAL MONOPOLIES existed.
- To save jobs when closure was threatened.
- To control and guarantee strategic industries like energy and transport.
- To prevent exploitation from monopolistic operators.
- To allow the profit of business to be shared by the state.

Over the last two decades virtually all the nationalised industries have been transferred back to the private sector. The

Question 1

(a) Is the example in the photograph above a public or a merit good? Explain your answer.

(b) Explain why either the private sector or the public sector may provide such a facility.

Question 2

One reason why many public sector business organisations have been privatised is that they are inefficient and cost the taxpayer money. In 1974 the Post Office, for example, made the biggest ever corporate loss. However, in the 1980s and 1990s the organisation improved its operations. In 1998 it made a pre-tax 'profit' of £651 million. Independent surveys show that the Royal Mail, the biggest part of the Post Office, is the most reliable and cheapest postal service of any major EU country. It is also the most flexible. It is cheaper now in real terms than it was 10 years ago.

One important reason why Royal Mail efficiency has been improved is because of investment . For example, a £600,000 investment in 4 machines tripled the amount of mail passing through part of the sorting procedure. The organisation also more than halved the manpower needed and raised productivity sixfold. In 1997 it invested £200 million in automated sorting offices, where computers read addresses and sort them for

delivery. The £1.5 billion Pathway project will computerise post offices and sub post offices.

The Post Office operates in competitive markets. Government regulations state that no company except the Post Office can deliver parcels or letters for less than £1. This effectively gives the Post Office a monopoly on private mail deliveries as no company can compete on price. However, Parcelforce faces competition for delivery of packages from around 4,000 private companies such as DHL, as parcels cost more than £1. In future, the Post Office is likely to face increasing competition from electronic mail and from foreign delivery services.

Source: adapted from the *Independent on Sunday*, 9.6.1996 and *The Guardian*, September 1998.

Table 6.1 *Comparison of first class EU letter prices, pence*

	Domestic	To the EU
Spain	17	35
Greece	23	35
Netherlands	26	33
Denmark	28	30
Austria	29	34
Luxembourg	29	30
Belgium	30	30
Finland	30	34
France	30	30
Italy	34	34
Ireland	34	34
Germany	34	34
Sweden	35	48
Portugal	41	51
UK	**26**	**26**

(a) Suggest two reasons why the Post Office remained a public sector organisation in the 1990s.
(b) Explain why a loss making public sector business organisation might cost the taxpayer money.
(c) If the Post Office faced competition for the delivery of private letters, suggest how this might affect:
 (i) the Post Office;
 (ii) the public.
(d) What evidence is there to show that there has been an improvement in efficiency at the Post Office?
(e) Suggest three reasons that might account for this improvement.

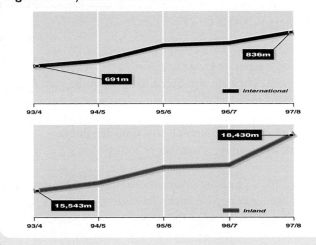

Figure 6.1 *Royal Mail letters delivered*

836m
691m
International
93/4   94/5   95/6   96/7   97/8

18,430m
15,543m
Inland
93/4   94/5   95/6   96/7   97/8

reasons for privatisation are dealt with later in this unit.

Major parts of the Post Office still remained as part of the public sector in the 1990s. Like many organisations still in the public sector, great efforts were made to improve its efficiency. The Post Office has a number of key operating areas - Post Office Counters (running post offices), Parcelforce (handling parcel delivery), the Royal Mail (delivering letters) and Subscription Services (a call centre operation).

The BBC The BBC (British Broadcasting Company) is a unique organisation. The chairperson is accountable to the Home Office and it raises most of its revenue from TV licence money. However, an increasing amount of money is being raised from the sale and production of programmes for other TV broadcasters, particularly overseas.

The Bank of England

The Bank of England is a former privately owned business that was taken into public ownership in 1946. It has a special

role in the monetary system (☞ unit 26). In 1997 it was given powers by the government to decide what the level of interest rates should be in the UK. It is headed by a governor, who is accountable to the Chancellor of the Exchequer.

Local authority services

Some services in the UK are supplied by local authorities. Their structure, composition and responsibilities are laid down mainly in the **Local Government Act 1972**. Local authorities include district, county and unitary councils, metropolitan councils and London boroughs. They provide many services to the local community and local businesses.
● Education and recreation. Local authorities are responsible for distributing most of the money allocated by the government to primary and secondary education. In the 1990s the government allowed some schools to 'opt out' of local government control. This meant that an individual school was accountable to a board of governors rather than the local authority. The governors were accountable to the

Department of Education via a funding council. From 1998 schools granted Foundation Status would obtain funds from local authorities, with some independence of the governing body. Sports halls, libraries, swimming pools and parks are all examples of recreation services provided by local government.

- Housing. This includes the provision of council housing, amenities for the homeless and house renovation. The importance of this provision has diminished greatly since 1979 for many councils because huge numbers of council houses have been sold off to the tenants.
- Environment and conservation. Refuse collection, litter clearance, pest control, street cleaning and beach maintenance are examples of these services. However, an increasing number of councils are employing private sector businesses to carry out these services.
- Communications. The provision of essential services to isolated towns and villages is one responsibility under this heading. Others include road maintenance and traffic control.
- Protection. This involves the provision of fire and police services, local justice, and consumer protection. Local authorities also employ trading standards officers and environmental health officers to investigate business practice and premises.
- Social services. Local government is also responsible for providing services, such as community care, social workers and children's homes.

Most of the funding for the above services comes from central government grants. However, there is some scope for independent funding. For example, local authorities raise some revenue from the council tax. Charges are also made for the supply of services like swimming pools and football pitches.

There are reasons why such services are provided by local rather than central government. First, it is argued that the local community is best served by those who are most sympathetic to its needs. Thus, local authorities should have the knowledge to evaluate those needs and supply the appropriate services. Second, central government is made up of large departments which often have communication problems. The decentralisation of many services should help to improve communication between the providers of services and the public. Finally, local councillors are accountable to the local electorate. If their policies are unpopular in the local community it is unlikely that they will be re-elected.

Central government departments

Central government departments supply some important services. These departments are also used to implement government policy.

- **The Treasury** is responsible for the government's economic strategy. This involves controlling the level of government spending, collecting revenue, monitoring economic performance and making economic forecasts.
- **The Department of Social Services** provides benefits for those in need. Its main task is to assess claims and determine individual benefit entitlements.
- **The Department of Defence** is responsible for the provision and maintenance of the armed forces, both in the UK, and in bases located in other parts of the world.
- **The Department of Trade and Industry's** role is to ensure that company law is enforced. It also aims to protect the public from business and financial fraud. One example of its activities is the work carried out by the Competition Commission (☞ unit 22), investigating the market power which a company might have following a takeover.
- **The Department of Health** is responsible for the running of the National Health Service (NHS) in the UK through the NHS executive and regional offices. From 1999, teams of GPs and community nurses (called Primary Care Groups) will control up to 90 per cent of the NHS budget. They will buy services from hospitals, organised into NHS trusts. The Care Groups are accountable to Health Authorities, which, together with the NHS trusts, are directly accountable to the NHS Executive.
- **The Department for Education and Employment** helps to shape government policy on education and training, and to implement these policies. For example, the department was responsible for introducing the Labour government's New Deal policy in 1998 (☞ unit 79). This was designed to provide young people with training places in business.
- **The Department for the Environment** exists to help protect the environment from threats such as exhaust emissions, illegal dumping and the disposal of sewerage. It has the power to penalise those who break environmental legislation. The Department also monitors levels of pollution in the UK.
- **The Department of Transport** implements the government's transport policy. It is responsible for the construction of new roads and oversees the operation of the London Underground. The 1998 Transport White Paper proposed the first integrated transport policy in the UK since the 1960s. It aimed to encourage the use of public transport, deter over-use of cars and reduce pollution and congestion caused by excess traffic (☞ unit 35).

Much of the work carried out by central and local government departments also benefits businesses in the private sector. For example, the Department of Transport gives contracts to large construction companies like Wimpey and Costain, to build roads and motorways.

QUANGOs

Some activities carried out by the government are said to be politically non-controversial. These are controlled by QUANGOs (quasi autonomous non-governmental organisations). They tend to be specialised bodies providing

The 1997 NHS White Paper promised a change in the structure of the NHS and some populist reforms. Under the old system, individual GPs and Health Authorities were given funds to buy services from competing NHS trust hospitals. It was argued that competition amongst trusts would lead to greater efficiency and that fundholding GPs would be more responsible. However, the system created large numbers of buyers and sellers, which actually led to bureaucracy and inefficiency. The new system would combine GPs and community nurses into teams of Primary Care Groups, with budgets for around 100,000 patients. They would commission health care from the Trusts and develop their own care. Trusts would work with Health Authorities to develop plans and annual contracts would be replaced by 3 year contracts between Trusts and Care Groups. Trusts would also have to publish lists of treatment costs and would have their performance monitored. Other measures to be introduced included an NHS direct 24 hour telephone advice service staffed by nurses and plans to link all hospitals and GPs by computer.

The government announced an extra £300 million for the 1997/8 NHS budget. The extra money was seen as a long term investment designed to improve approaches to health care. It was suggested that between 6-7,000 people were in hospital that did not need to be there if they could be sent home and provided with satisfactory community and social care.

Source: adapted from *The Guardian*, 15.10.1997 and 10.12. 1997.

(a) How might the change in the NHS system improve efficiency?
(b) Using examples from the passage, explain why health care is controlled by a central government department.
(c) Suggest two ways in which the NHS might benefit private sector businesses.
(d) Explain why accountability is important in public sector organisations such as the NHS.

services which central and local government does not have the resources or the expertise to carry out. QUANGOs receive funding from and are accountable to different government departments, depending on their area of specialism. Some examples include research councils, advisory bodies, tribunals and funding councils like the Higher Education Funding Council.

There are around 5,000 QUANGOs in the UK which are responsible for allocating around a third of all public spending. The number of QUANGOs has grown in the last decade and they now have between 50,000 and 70,000 people sitting on them. They have become quite powerful and are involved in a wide range of activities. For example, the Millennium Commission has responsibility for allocating funds to projects designed to celebrate the new millennium. The National Rivers Authority is responsible for the up-keep of the nation's waterways, for example allocating funds to clean-up rivers.

In recent years QUANGOs have attracted an increasing amount of criticism. It is argued that they are not entirely non-political. Members appointed by a government may be biased towards its stance on certain issues. The efficiency of some QUANGOs has also been questioned.

Executive agencies

Executive agencies have become well established since their introduction at the end of the 1980s. They are responsible for the supply of services previously provided by government departments such as:
● the payment of state benefits - the Benefits Office;
● the processing of passport applications - the Passport Office;
● the administering of written driving tests - DVLA.
These have been separated from the policy making bodies which used to deliver them.

Executive agencies are headed by chief executives who are accountable to a government minister. Many of these leaders are recruited from the private sector. They are encouraged to introduce business principles when delivering services. The general policy of the government departments remains the responsibility of the permanent secretaries and senior civil servants.

Since the introduction of executive agencies the efficiency of services has improved considerably. For example, it now takes 7 days on average to process a passport application, compared with as much as 30 days at times in the past. Also, many social security payments are now much cheaper to administer.

Privatisation

PRIVATISATION is the transfer of public sector resources to the private sector. It was an important feature of government policy in the 1980s to the mid-1990s. It is still seen by some as a means of improving efficiency and further privatisation is always a possibility. Privatisation has taken a number of forms.

The sale of nationalised industries The most publicised privatisations were the sales of large, well known nationalised industries. These included British Gas, British Steel, the regional water boards and British Rail.

The sale of parts of nationalised industries Some nationalised industries were broken up by parts being sold off. The Jaguar car company which was part of the then state-owned British Leyland was sold for £297 million. Sealink, a part of British Rail, was sold for £40 million.

Deregulation This involves lifting restrictions that prevent private sector competition. The deregulation of the communications market has allowed Mercury and cable companies to compete with British Telecom. Deregulation has also allowed bus services to be run by private sector businesses.

Contracting out Many government and local authority services have been 'contracted out' to private sector businesses. This is where contractors are given a chance to bid for services previously supplied by the public sector. Examples include the provision of school meals, hospital cleaning and refuse collection. The French company Phoenix won the contract to collect refuse in Liverpool, for example. Wolds Remand Centre, run by the Group 4 security company, was Britain's first privately run prison service. In the early 1990s local authorities were forced into compulsory competitive tendering (CCT). Private businesses **had** to be asked to quote on contracts for services, bidding against council services. The contract was awarded to the most efficient, least cost service. In 1998 the Labour government planned to replace this. Tendering would not be compulsory and contracts would be awarded for 'best value' - based also on effectiveness and quality as well as efficiency.

Table 6.2 *Sale of state owned companies to the private sector since 1979*

Date begun

1979	* British Petroleum	1986	British Gas
	* ICL	1987	British Airways
	* Ferranti		Rolls Royce
	Fairey		Leyland Bus
1981	British Aerospace		Leyland Truck
	* British Sugar		Royal Ordnance
	Cable and Wireless		British Airport
	Amersham International		Authority
1982	National Freight Corporation	1988	British Steel
	Britoil		British Leyland
1983	* Associated British Ports	1989	British Water Authorities
	British Rail Hotels	1990	Electricity Area Boards
1984	British Gas Onshore Oil	1991	Electricity Generation
	Enterprise Oil	1994	British Coal
	Sealink Ferries	1995	British Rail
	Jaguar Cars	1996	British Energy
	British Telecom		Railtrack
	British Technology Group		

* Partly owned by the government at the time of sale.

The sale of land and property Under the 1980 Housing Act, tenants of local authorities and New Town Development Corporations were given the right to buy their own homes. Tenants were given generous discounts, up to 60 per cent of the market value of the house, if they agreed to buy. During the 1980s about 1.5 million houses were sold. Few realise that the sale of land and properties has raised almost as much money as the sale of nationalised industries.

The reasons for privatisation

During the 1980s and 1990s governments transferred a great deal of business activity from the public sector to the private sector. Different reasons have been put forward for this.

● The sale of state assets generates a great deal of income for the government. Table 6.3 shows the revenue raised from privatisation from 1979 to 1997. It also indicates the amounts that could have been raised in 1998 by selling off certain state owned organisations at the time.

● Nationalised industries were inefficient. They lacked the incentive to make a profit, since their main aim was arguably to provide a public service. As a result their costs tended to be high and they often made losses. Also, many believed that they were overstaffed. Supporters of privatisation argued that if they were in the private sector, they would be forced to cut costs, improve their service and return a profit for the shareholders.

● As a result of deregulation, some organisations would be forced to improve their service and charge competitive prices. For example, in many areas, private firms began to compete for passengers on bus and train routes. Electricity and gas prices and telephone charges have also been reduced, arguably as a result of competition. Consumers would benefit from this and should also have greater choice. In addition, it is argued that there would be more incentive to innovate in the private sector.

● Once these organisations had been sold to the private sector there would be little political interference. They would be free to determine their own investment levels, prices and growth rates. In the past government

Table 6.3 *Revenue from privatisation*

UK privatisations: what they raised	£	What the government could have sold, 1998	
1979-80	0.4bn	600m	Air Traffic Control
1980-81	0.2bn	8.0bn	BBC
1981-82	0.5bn	200m	British Waterways
1982-83	0.5bn	20m	Cent. Office of Info.
1983-84	1.1bn	2.0bn	Channel 4
1984-85	2.0bn	50m	Coastguard Agency
1985-86	2.7bn	500m	Commonwealth Dev. Corp
1986-87	4.5bn	5.0bn	Crown Estate
1987-88	5.1bn	500m	Defence Evaluation Off.
1988-89	7.1bn	80m	DVLA
1989-90	4.2bn	30m	Hydrographic Office
1990-91	5.3bn	1.2bn	London Underground
1991-92	7.9bn	100m	Meteorological Office
1992-93	8.1bn	80m	Ordnance Survey
1993-94	5.4bn	10m	Pipelines Agency
1994-95	5.5bn	3.0bn	Post Office
1995-96	1.0bn	20m	QE2 Centre
1996-97	1.0bn	1.0bn	Radio spectrum
		80m	Royal Mint
Source: adapted from the Treasury.		800m	Scottish forests
		400m	The Tote

interference has affected the performance of nationalised industries.

● Privatisation would increase share ownership. It was argued that this would lead to a 'share owning democracy' in which more people would have a 'stake' in the success of the economy. For example, if you bought shares in British Telecom, you would be a part owner of the company and get a dividend each year. Workers were encouraged to buy shares in their companies so that they would be rewarded for their own hard work and success.

● Privatisation should improve accountability. The losses made by many of these nationalised industries were put down to the fact that they were operating a public service. In the private sector these industries would be accountable to shareholders and consumers. Shareholders would expect a return on their investment and consumers would expect a quality service at a fair price. For example, if shareholders were not happy with the dividends paid, they could sell their shares.

Impact of privatisation on business

How have businesses changed after transferring to the private sector?

● Achieving a surplus or profit has become a more important objective. For example, the profits of British Telecom have increased from around £1,000 million in 1984, when the company was first privatised, to around £3,000 million in 1996, to nearly £3,200 million in 1998.

● In some cases prices have changed. This was considerably higher than the rate of inflation over the same time period. In other examples prices are lower. Most analysts would agree that charges made for some telephone services, gas and electricity have fallen since privatisation.

● Some of the newly privatised businesses have cut back on staffing levels. For example, the Rail, Maritime and Transport Union believes that 20,000 to 30,000 job losses are to be expected as a result of rail privatisation. British

Question 4

The Labour government of 1929-31 created a publicly owned authority to run London's transport 'to eliminate wasteful competition'. Nearly 70 years on, the party appeared to have accepted that a degree of private sector involvement would improve services and bring new funds into the London Underground. However, John Prescott, the Deputy Prime Minister, ruled out the 'wholesale privatisation' of London Underground. In March 1998 he announced plans to involve the private sector in the running of the Tube system. He also said the network would receive an extra £365 million of taxpayers' money over the following two years.

Private firms were to be invited to run the track, the signalling and the supply of rolling stock. Trains would still be operated by the public sector, which would pay charges to the private investors. The new spending plans involved an extra injection of cash on top of what was already planned. In total around £1 billion was expected to be generated in the two years before private sector involvement. The moves were in response to the £1.2 billion backlog of investment

over the previous ten years.

Under the plans, ministers would invite bids to break the infrastructure into two or three sections, with private investment being pledged over 15 years. However, the companies would not own the infrastructure. They would have a limited concession of between 25 and 35 years, before being returned to the state. London Underground, which becomes directly accountable to the Greater London Authority in 2000, would still be responsible for operating services, including ticketing, fares and signalling. Private businesses would be responsible for maintenance, refurbishing stations, replacing tracks, upgrading signalling and refurbishing trains. Several businesses, such as GEC Alsthom, Railtrack, Amec and Bechtel, have expressed an interest.

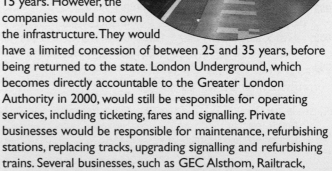

Source: adapted from the *Financial Times*, 21.3.1998

(a) (i) What does Figure 6.2 show?
(ii) How does the trend shown in Figure 6.2 help to explain why the government has promised to increase investment in the tube?
(b) What are the possible motives for involving private sector businesses in the provision of Tube services?
(c) Why do you think that the Labour Party ruled out the 'wholesale' privatisation of London Underground?

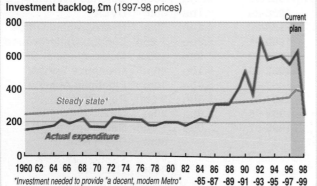

Figure 6.2 *Investment backlog in the Tube*

Investment backlog, £m (1997-98 prices)

Energy shed a quarter of its workforce before privatisation.

● Many companies increased investment following privatisation. For example, British Telecom increased investment between 1994 and 1998 from £2,171 million to £3,030 million. Many of the water companies raised investment levels to fund new sewerage systems and purification plants. Immediately after privatisation investment rose by about £1,000 million in the water industry. However, more recently some figures suggest that investment levels are falling.

● Some of the companies have begun to offer new services and diversify. For example, North West Water offers a Leakline service which promises to repair any leaks on a customer's property provided they are outside the house. Railtrack and Anglia Water want to develop old sewerage works in Cambridge into a regional shopping centre.

● There has been a number of mergers and takeovers involving newly privatised companies. For example, Hanson bought Eastern Electricity and an American railway company bought the British Rail freight service. North West Water and Norweb joined together to form United Utilities and Scottish Power bought Manweb.

Arguments against privatisation

Arguments against privatisation have been put forward on both political and economic grounds. Most of the criticisms below are from the consumer's point of view.

● Privatisation has been expensive. In particular, the amount of money spent advertising each sale has been criticised. The money spent on expensive TV advertising was at the taxpayer's expense.

● It has been argued that privatisation has not led to greater competition. In some cases public monopolies with no competition have become private monopolies. These companies have been able to exploit their position. This has been a criticism levelled at gas and electricity companies.

● Nationalised industries were sold off too cheaply. In nearly all cases the share issue has been over-subscribed. This shows that more people want to buy shares than there are shares available. When dealing begins on the stock market share prices have often risen sharply. This suggests that the government could have set the share prices much higher and raised more revenue. For example, there was an £11 billion rise in the value of electricity companies between privatisation in 1990 and 1996.

● Natural monopolies have been sold off. Some argue that they should remain under government control to prevent a duplication of resources.

● Once part of the private sector, any parts of the business which make a loss will be closed down. This appears to have happened in public transport. Some bus services or trains on non-profitable routes have been cut or stopped completely since deregulation.

● Share ownership arguably has not increased. Many who bought shares sold them very quickly after. In addition, a

Question 5

Supporters of privatisation would claim that one of the major benefits of privatisation is a steady and significant growth in profitability. Figure 6.3 shows the dividend payments made by a selection of newly privatised companies.

(a) Suggest three reasons why profits may have risen since privatisation for certain companies.

(b) State two ways in which these companies may use any rise in profits. In each case explain who might benefit.

(c) (i) Describe the trends in Figure 6.3.

(ii) Do these trends indicate that privatised businesses are making greater profits? Explain your answer.

Figure 6.3 Dividends per share paid by a sample of newly privatised companies, 1994-98 (pence)

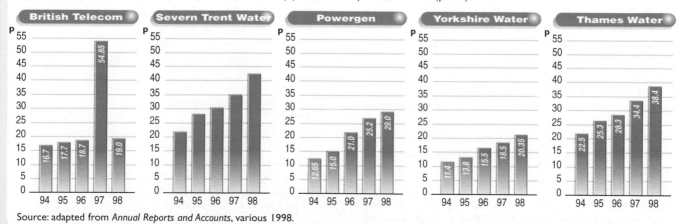

Source: adapted from Annual Reports and Accounts, various 1998.

significant number of new shareowners only own very small shareholdings in just one company.

● Many of the nationalised industries are important for the development of the nation. To put them in private hands might jeopardise their existence. For example, one of the reasons why British Steel was nationalised was to save it from possible closure. If business conditions change for the worse a private company may not guarantee supply. Also, since the shares are widely available, it is possible for overseas buyers to take control of strategic UK firms.

Regulation of privatised industries

One criticism of privatisation was that dominant industries, which were previously state owned, now operated as private sector businesses. They may be able to exploit their position by increasing their prices or reducing services. Because of this they must be controlled. Control of private sector firms is nothing new. The Monopolies and Mergers Commission was set up to monitor firms which might act against the public's interest. They investigate cases where large dominant firms or firms merging might act to exploit their position. Because privatisation created some private monopolies, the government set up specialist 'watchdog' agencies to protect

the public. Examples of these bodies include Oftel (the telecommunications industry), Ofgas (the gas industry) and Ofwat (the water companies). These are discussed in more detail in unit 22.

Key terms

Merit goods - goods which are underprovided by private sector businesses.
Nationalised industries - public corporations previously part of the private sector which were taken into state ownership.
Natural monopoly - a situation where production costs will be lower if one firm is allowed to exist on its own in the industry, due to the existence of huge economies of scale.
Privatisation - the transfer of public sector resources to the private sector.
Public goods - goods where consumption by one person does not reduce the amount available to others and, once provided, all individuals will benefit.
Public sector - business organisations which are owned or controlled by central or local government, or public corporations.
QUANGOs - Quasi Autonomous Non-Governmental Organisations.

Question 6

Yorkshire Water has attracted a great deal of criticism in the last couple of years. At the centre of the criticism is the claim that its customers have had a very raw deal and shareholders have enjoyed significant financial benefits. The trouble really began during the drought of 1995 when Yorkshire Water imposed hose pipe bans and threatened to introduce rota cuts and standpipes. During the summer there was a massive road tanker operation to transport water from other districts into North Yorkshire.

An official inquiry into Yorkshire Water's handling of the water shortage, led by Professor John Uff, accused the company of having no emergency planning and causing public distress. In his report, Professor Uff an engineering expert from the University of London, concluded that:

● Yorkshire Water failed to do enough to modernise its infrastructure and tackle leakage from pipes;
● leakage currently accounts for a similar quantity to the region's entire domestic consumption;
● national and local regulators failed to take enough action to protect customers and the environment;
● the health of local people was put in danger by the company and the needs of businesses were overlooked.
● Yorkshire Water should consider a massive £220 million investment to pipe water from Northumbria to avoid the repeat of the crisis which put industry, education and the health service at risk.

Matters have been worsened by an announcement made in June 1996 that the company's profits increased by 14.2 per cent

during the year of the drought and that the company would be buying back £140 million of shares (this would benefit shareholders). Dividends were also to be increased by 12.2 per cent. By 1997/8 profits before tax were £206 million. Leakages totalled 375 mega litres per day.

(a) What evidence is there in the case to suggest that privatisation has not been in consumers' interests?
(b) In the light of Yorkshire Water's monopoly position in the market, suggest measures that might be taken to improve customer service.

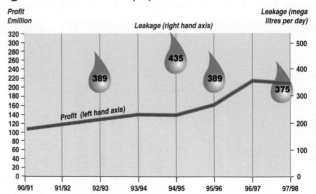

Figure 6.4 *Yorkshire water performance*

Source: adapted from *The Times*, 6.6.1996 and *The Observer*, 25.5.1997 and *Annual Accounts* of Yorkshire Water.

Summary

1. What is meant by a public corporation?
2. What is meant by non-rivalry and non-excludability when describing public goods?
3. Why are certain merit goods provided by the public sector?
4. Why do local authorities provide some public sector services?
5. How are local authority services funded?
6. Describe the responsibilities of 3 government departments.
7. Explain the difference between deregulation and contracting out as methods of privatisation.
8. What are the disadvantages of privatisation?
9. What is the function of Ofgas, Ofwat and Oftel?

Case study

The Rail industry

The privatisation of the rail industry was one of the most complex, widely debated and lengthy privatisations of all. The industry was broken up and sold off in parts. The largest part is Railtrack, which includes the infrastructure of British Rail - the railway lines, stations, bridges, signals and property. Railtrack was floated on the stock exchange in May 1996 and sold for £1.8 billion. In April 1994 Railtrack's assets were valued at £6.5 billion. In addition, a large proportion of Railtrack's debt to the government was written off prior to the sale.

Passenger transport services on the railway system are now provided by private train service operators. These businesses pay Railtrack for using the network. Any company wishing to obtain a franchise to operate a service has to make a bid to the government. In total there were 23 franchises available. One of the first companies to be awarded an operating franchise was Stagecoach, the UK's largest bus company. They operate trains in the South West region. Another franchise was awarded to Great Western Rail, a management buy-out team.

Other Railway businesses, such as the Royal Train, rolling stock companies, maintenance companies, Red Star and depots have also been sold. Most of these were sold (through direct negotiation with potential buyers) to a range of specialist companies and management buy-out teams.

The sale of British Rail was delayed and subject to numerous criticisms. The company suffered from an extremely poor image, a desperate lack of investment and a diminishing subsidy from the government. Only 0.14 per cent of GDP has been given to the railway system in the UK compared with 0.7 per cent of GDP in the rest of Europe. In 1992 British Rail topped the league of public dissatisfaction and the possibility of rail privatisation was described as a 'poll tax on wheels'. Rail privatisation was opposed by the Labour Party at that time, rail enthusiasts, many passenger groups, trade unions and sections of the general public. There is no other country in the world which has a privately run national railway system.

One of the likely effects of rail privatisation was the loss of jobs in the industry. The Rail, Maritime and Transport Union

Figure 6.5 *Railtrack's share price after privatisation*

Share price since flotation relative to the FTSE All-Share index

Source: adapted from Datastream/ICV.

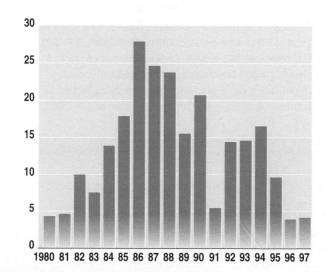

Figure 6.6 *Number of new or reopened stations*

Source: adapted from Railway Development Society.

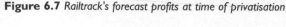

Figure 6.7 *Railtrack's forecast profits at time of privatisation*

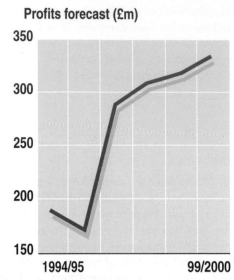

Profits forecast (£m)

Source: adapted from SBC Warburg.

Figure 6.8 *Virgin: subsidies from and payments to UK government*

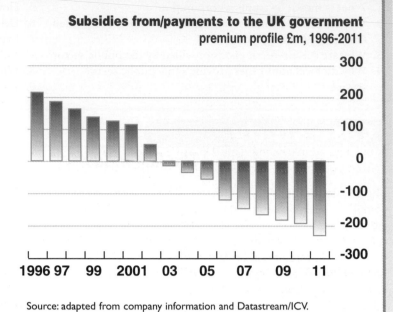

Subsidies from/payments to the UK government
premium profile £m, 1996-2011

Source: adapted from company information and Datastream/ICV.

believed that 20,000 to 30,000 jobs were at risk. In the past, a crude rule of thumb in the City is that the figure for job losses after privatisation will be 30 per cent of the total job cuts in the run up to privatisation. Stagecoach, the South West Trains operator, announced 125 job losses immediately after taking control of the service. South West Trains employed around 4,000 staff. Finally, in a report by a subsidiary of British Rail, Civil Engineering Design Group, it was claimed that around £11 billion needed to be spent by Railtrack on the infrastructure in the 10 years after privatisation. Railtrack had only allowed for £1.4 billion to be spent on repairing bridges and other route structures in the next decade. This suggested that safety standards on the railways might be at risk.

In 1998 Virgin, the private limited company which runs the west coast main line and cross country franchises, announced investment in new trains worth £1.85 billion. It came at a time of growing optimism for the privatised rail industry. Passenger numbers were growing faster than expected. However, subsidies from government will run out in 2002, by which time Virgin will be expected to make payments to run its franchises. In June 1998 Virgin entered into a £158 million deal to sell 49 per cent of shares to Stagecoach, the transport group. This allowed Richard Branson to retain management control of Virgin and avoid the flotation of the company.

Source: adapted from the The *Guardian*, 3.2.1996, The *Independent*, 29.3.1996 and The *Observer*, 28.4.1996, the *Financial Times*, 12.3.1998 and 23.6.1998.

(a) 'Railtrack was floated on the stock exchange.' What is meant by this statement?

(b) Using information from the case study, suggest two reasons why Railtrack might have been attractive for buyers of shares during privatisation.

(c) What factors are likely to determine the success of private rail companies running rail services after the year 2000?

(d) How might the approach of private rail companies running train services be different to that of a state run organisation such as British Rail?

(e) Explain the possible motives that the government may have had in privatising the rail network.

(f) Explain how the privatisation of rail services may have affected:
   (i) a private operator such as South West Trains;
   (ii) an employee working on a line which has been privatised;
   (iii) a passenger on a privatised line.

How are businesses organised?

All businesses need to organise their activities. Running a business involves planning, decision making, co-ordination and communication. In order to simplify these complex tasks it is helpful to organise the business into a number of clearly defined sections. For example, a business selling books to customers by mail order from a warehouse may be organised into a number of departments.

- Buying and marketing. This department purchases books from publishers. It also deals with advertising and handles the production of the mail order catalogue.
- Warehousing/dispatch. This department stores books delivered to the warehouse and deals with requests for books from the orders department. It is then responsible for putting together customers' orders and checking, wrapping, addressing and transporting parcels.

- Orders. This department receives orders from customers and informs the warehouse. It also processes all the paperwork involved in the buying and selling of books.
- Administration and finance. This department deals with payments and receipts of cash. It also handles all the personnel work, including staff wages.

This type of STRUCTURE is simple but effective. Staff in each department will understand their role. They will also know what other departments are doing in relation to their own. Small businesses may feel that they do not need to organise themselves in this way. However, as businesses grow, so does the need for organisation (☞ unit 13). Without this, the efficiency of a business could suffer. Communications may break down, mistakes might be made and staff may become confused about their roles.

The mail order business described here is organised by **function**. This is explained in the next section. There are other methods of organising a business which may be more suitable in certain situations. Large businesses often combine different methods of organisation to gain the benefits of each.

Question 1

Metalmaster Ltd produces housings for air-conditioning units, metal casings and metal signs. The company is organised into departments as shown in Figure 7.1.

(a) What evidence is there to suggest that Metalmaster is organised by function?
(b) The board of directors is concerned that the company is operating too many separate departments. It has discussed merging some departments to improve efficiency.
  (i) Suggest and explain two problems that might arise from having too many departments.
  (ii) Draw a new organisational chart for Metalmaster and give an explanation for your choice of structure.

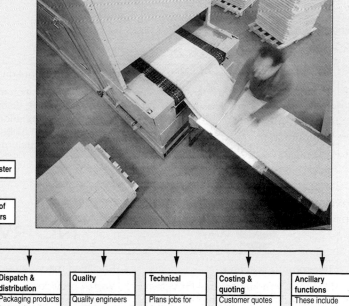

Figure 7.1 *Metalmaster Ltd organisational structure*

Metalmaster
↓
Board of Directors
↓

Sales & marketing	Production	Purchasing	Accounts	Administration	Dispatch & distribution	Quality	Technical	Costing & quoting	Ancillary functions
Dealing with customers, securing new business, and designing promotions and advertising	50 people are employed to manufacture the company's products in a large purpose built factory unit. Punching, cutting, welding, folding, finishing, assembly and painting are examples of production activities.	Buying all the company's material resources including raw materials, office supplies, machinery and other equipment.	Keeping records of all financial transactions. Dealing with invoices, credit control, wages and personnel.	Providing management reports, progress reports, inputting data into computer systems, reception, filing and secretarial work.	Packaging products for transit and transporting finished products to customers.	Quality engineers and inspectors monitor and update the quality system and ensure that work conforms to standards.	Plans jobs for production department, undertakes some research and development and designs prototypes for customers.	Customer quotes for jobs are calculated and individual jobs are costed to check that the costs do not exceed the quote.	These include maintenance, cleaning, storage, tooling and ICT support.

Organisation by function

One of the most common methods of organising a business is by function. This is where a business is divided into different sections or departments according to the operation undertaken. Typical functional departments in many larger businesses include production, marketing, finance and personnel. There is a number of advantages for a business in organising itself in this way.

● Specialisation. It allows each department to focus on just one business area. Specialist staff can be employed in each department. For example, the finance department may employ management and financial accountants and credit controllers. Specialisation should help to improve efficiency (☞ unit 1).

● Accountability. Each department is likely to have a manager who will be responsible for allocating departmental resources, employing staff and achieving departmental goals. The manager will be accountable to a senior executive and will be under pressure to perform. This method of organisation also allows a business to

organise itself into cost or profit centres (☞ unit 53). For example, if a business decides to make one department into a cost centre, it may have to keep its costs within a limit. This will help accountability.

● Clarity. Organisation by function helps staff to understand their role and position in the business structure. For example, staff are likely to be trained in their department, will be familiar with their superiors and will know where to seek help and support.

This method of organisation will also have some drawbacks.

● Communication and co-ordination problems. When businesses are divided by function they often operate as self-contained units. Communication between departments may be limited, resulting in a lack of information sharing and some unnecessary duplication. Senior management may struggle with co-ordination if departments pursue their own objectives rather than those of the whole company. Individual departments may also be reluctant to work with other departments on projects.

● Inertia. Individual departments may become 'set in their ways' over time. They may try to resist change and prefer to continue their current practices.

Question 2

United Utilities is the UK's first multi-utility group. It provides services in water, wastewater, electricity distribution, electricity and gas supply, telecommunications and business operations outsourcing. It operates nationally and internationally. Figure 7.2 shows how the business was organised in 1998.

(a) Using information from Figure 7.2, explain how United Utilities has organised its operations.

(b) Suggest reasons to explain why the business may be organised in this way.

Figure 7.2 *United Utilities, organisational structure*
Source: adapted from United Utilities, *Annual Report and Accounts*, 1998.

Water and wastewater	Electricity distribution	Energy supply
North West Water provides water and wastewater services to 2.8 million domestic, commercial and industrial customers in North West England.	Norweb Distribution maintains a 59,000 kilometre distribution network and 39,501 substations to deliver electricity to 2.2 million domestic and industrial customers in England.	ENERGi from Norweb supplies electricity to 2.2 million customer premises throughout the North West. As the domestic gas market opens to competition 157,000 customers had, at the year end, contracted to buy gas from ENERGi.
Turnover £905.3m Operating profit £394.2m		Turnover £1,120.9m Operating profit £26.2m
North West Water	NORWEB	ENERGi FROM NORWEB
Telecommunications	Facilities management	International operations
Norweb Communications provides voice and data telecommunications services to the business community in North West England.	Vertex provides a wide range of business operations outsourcing services to the United Utilities Group. Business services include customer services, operations systems, information technology, accounting, procurement and training.	United Utilities International develops and operates contracts.
Turnover £23.4m Operating profit £0.2m	Turnover £193.8m Operating profit £28.6m	Turnover £7.7m Operating profit £5.6m
NORWEB communications	vertex	United Utilities

● Bureaucracy. Organisations may become too bureaucratic. For example, there may be a large increase in paperwork if every communication from one department to another has to be made via memo or if transactions between departments have to have written confirmation. E-mail and company **intranets** (☞ unit 82) may solve this problem to some extent. However, time may still be wasted responding to requests.

● Suitability. Very large companies with a diversified product range could find this method of organisation unsuitable. For example, when an organisation grows there will be more departments and more layers of management. In this case senior management may find it increasingly difficult to influence what is happening lower down.

Organisation by product or activity

When a business produces a wide range of different goods or services it could find that organisation by function is not effective. Different products may need different approaches to production and marketing. For example, a multinational group may operate a supermarket chain, a property company and a construction business. It is possible that each of these businesses may have different approaches to marketing which take into account the needs of their markets. It is also possible that different staff with different skills will be needed.

Large diversified companies often organise their business by grouping together different functional staff who are involved in the production of the same product lines or activities. For example, the Burton Group is organised into six divisions - Debenhams, Burton (menswear), Dorothy Perkins, Evans, Topshop (and Topman) and Principles (and Principles for Men). Each division sells clothes to different market segments and is headed by a different managing director. Each division is likely to employ a mixture of specialised functional staff so that it can operate fairly independently.

This method of organisation is often seen as 'a business within a business' and has a number of advantages.

● Each division is able to focus on the needs of a particular market segment. Thus, customers should find that their needs are satisfied more effectively.

● Each division is likely to operate as a profit centre. This will help to measure the performance of each division and allow comparisons in the business. Poor performing sections can be identified and action taken.

● Healthy competition may take place between each division. This could improve the overall performance of the organisation.

● There may be scope for reorganisation. Organisation by product provides some flexibility for the future. Loss making divisions can be closed down. Divisions supplying similar markets can be merged. Businesses that are bought by the company can be absorbed more easily. Divestment (selling) of parts of the business should also be easier.

● Co-operation may improve. Because each division is pursuing the same goal, eg profit, it is possible to share expertise and ancillary services. For example, the Burton Group, in the above illustration, might use the same transport fleet to serve all of its branches.

Disadvantages of organisation by product include the following.

● There may be a duplication of functions in different departments. For example, an accountant may be employed in each division. It may be more cost effective to employ a small team of specialist accountants for the whole organisation.

● Competition between divisions may become counter-productive. This is likely to occur when divisions compete for the organisation's resources. A division which fails to obtain resources may become poorly motivated.

● Senior management might lose control over each individual division. For example, a decision by a junior manager in one division to extend credit to customers for longer than company policy allows might go unnoticed.

Organisation by area

Some businesses prefer to organise their activities on a geographical or regional basis. This is particularly the case if a business has a large number of very similar operations which are widely dispersed either nationally or globally. Many chainstores or multiples (☞ unit 46), for example, have this method of organisation. They tend to have a large number of stores which operate in a very similar or sometimes identical way. For example, they might sell the same products, use the same procedures and look very similar. The stores are then grouped together in regions and will be accountable to a regional or area manager. Multinational businesses operating in many different countries may also organise themselves into regions of the world, such as Europe, North America and the Far East. The advantages of organising a business geographically include the following.

● Local needs. Sometimes the needs of customers, employees and the community vary in different geographical regions. If a business is organised regionally then it should be able to serve the needs of local people more easily. This is particularly the case for multinational companies. For example, the needs of Middle Eastern customers may be different from those of North American customers.

● Improved communications. Operating on a regional basis should improve communications. For example, a regional manager may be able to more easily inform local shops of a decision than all retail outlets. To some extent this benefit is not as important today as information and communication technology allows fast and easy communication around the world.

● Competition. It may be possible to encourage healthy internal competition between different regions in the organisation. For example, prizes or bonuses are sometimes awarded to those regions with the highest sales or profits. In addition, regions are often used as training grounds for senior management.

Some disadvantages of regional organisation include the following.

● Duplication of resources. As with some other methods of organisation, it may not be cost effective for each region to provide certain specialist services, such as accountancy and research and development.

● Conflict. It is possible that local managers may begin to introduce their own policies. They might argue that their local situation requires a different approach from that of the business. This might lead to conflict with senior management as they see their authority being undermined.

Organisation by customer

This method is similar to organising a business by product. It involves grouping together employees who deal with a specific customer or group. This method is particularly useful where the needs of distinct customer groups are different. For example, an advertising agency might organise itself according to customer. Senior staff may be given the accounts of the most important customers. This method of organisation has a number of advantages.

● Customer needs. The needs of different customers will be served more effectively by a department focused on one particular service. Also, customers might prefer to do business with a company that is sensitive to specific customer needs.

● Market segmentation. A business may divide its market into different market segments. The advantages of market segmentation are discussed in unit 38.

However, there may also be some difficulties.

● Customer definition. It is not always possible to clearly define a particular customer group. For example, students at university may be taking a modular course, which involves more than one faculty. This may cause problems for students if different faculties operate in different ways.

● Inefficiency. It is possible that some departments are too small because they do not have enough customers. In this case costs per customer could be high. This may affect the profitability of the whole organisation.

● Control and co-ordination. As with other methods of organisation where the company is split into discrete divisions, there may be problems of control and co-ordination. Communication between departments may be limited, individual departments may pursue their own goals and senior management may find it difficult to control the organisation.

Organisation by process

The production of some products or services requires a series of processes. Departments could be established to take responsibility for each process. For example, a clothing company manufacturing children's clothes may be divided into departments. Each department operates in its own workshop in the factory.

● The first stage in the production process may be design. This department would be responsible for designing new clothes and producing computerised patterns for the cutting department.

Question 3

In its 1998 Annual Report, Arjo Wiggins Appleton p.l.c. states that it is: 'the world's leading manufacturer of premium papers and Europe's leading stock merchant of printing and writing papers'. It manufactures a variety of papers. Thermal papers are used for tickets and labels. Premium and coated papers are used for top of the range books. Speciality papers are used for sterile packaging in the medical industry. Its merchanting division is the third largest paper supplier in the world, supplying paper and writing materials. Soporcel is a joint venture pulp and paper producer.

(a) What two methods of organisation of Arjo Wiggins Appleton p.l.c. are suggested in the data?

(b) Explain the possible advantages of the organisation methods shown in Figure 7.3 and Figure 7.4.

Source: adapted from Arjo Wiggins Appleton p.l.c., *Annual Report and Accounts*, 1998.

Figure 7.3 *Turnover of Arjo Wiggins Appleton p.l.c., 1998*

Carbonless & Thermal 26%
Premium Fine, Speciality & Coated 30%
Merchanting 41%
SOPORCEL 3%
Turnover

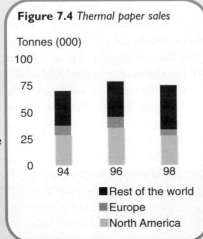

Figure 7.4 *Thermal paper sales*

Tonnes (000)

100
75
50
25
0

94   96   98

■ Rest of the world
■ Europe
■ North America

Unigate is a European food and distribution group. Its businesses include Malton Foods, which manufactures pork, bacon and cooked meats, St.Ivel which makes a range of fresh foods and dairy products and Unigate Dairies, which distributes milk. Another part of the group, Wincanton Logistics, designs, builds and operates automated warehouses and distributes milk, food, chemicals and gases.

Figure 7.5 *Operating profit*

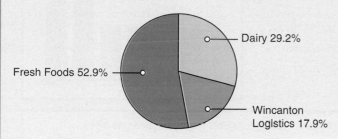

Fresh Foods 52.9%
Dairy 29.2%
Wincanton Logistics 17.9%

Figure 7.6 *Milk sales*

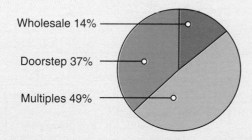

Wholesale 14%
Doorstep 37%
Multiples 49%

Source: adapted from Unigate, *Annual Report and Accounts*, 1998.

(a) What two methods of organisation at Unigate are suggested by Figures 7.5 and 7.6? Explain your answer.
(b) Suggest reasons why Unigate might have organised itself using two or more methods.

● In the cutting department fabrics are cut to size by computer operated machines. The cut fabrics are then taken to the sewing department. Here the separate pieces of fabric are sewn together to form clothes.
● The finishing department is responsible for adding seams, frills, buttons, zips and other accessories.
● The last process in the sequence is dispatch. This department is responsible for packing the clothes and preparing the products for distribution to retailers.

Organisation by process is very similar to organisation by function and has similar benefits. Teams of staff in each department may be more focused. The company may enjoy the advantages of specialisation. There is likely to be regular communication between each stage in the production process. Management will be able to monitor clearly the performance of each department. The main disadvantage of organisation by process is a lack of flexibility. It may be difficult to switch staff from one process to another. This may be because they are not trained to work in other departments or because they do not wish to transfer. In addition, departments will have to operate at the same pace. For example, if the cutting department slows down, resources in the sewing department may lay idle. Communications problems may also arise.

Summary

1. What is meant by organisation by function?
2. Why might a business be organised in more than one way?
3. State 2 advantages and 2 disadvantages of a functional organisational structure.
4. Describe the advantages of a company organising itself by product.
5. When is regional organisation likely to be an appropriate method of organisation for a business?
6. Why might solicitors organise themselves according to customer group?
7. What is meant by organisation by process?
8. Suggest 2 types of business that may organise themselves by process.

Key terms

Structure of a business - the way in which a business is organised.

Case study

East Anglia News Ltd

East Anglia News Ltd is based in Norwich and distributes newspapers to around 280 newsagents in the East Anglia area. The depot receives deliveries of newspapers and magazines from publishers in the early hours of the morning and a team of 30 packers put together the newsagents' orders. These orders are then distributed in a fleet of vans to newsagents and shops in towns and villages by 6.30 am. The company also delivers local and regional newspapers.

In 1997 East Anglia News bought a distributor based in Thetford and merged the activities. The Thetford depot was closed and all operations were transferred to Norwich. The merger resulted in a doubling of turnover, however, profits did not rise in proportion. Figure 7.7 shows the turnover, profits and number of employees for East Anglia News from 1993 to 1998. It was hoped that the merger would result in some economies of scale and a more than proportionate increase in profits. It was the poor financial performance of the company which prompted the owners, George and Albert Rimmer, to employ a consultant to look into the organisation of the business.

The current organisational structure has been established for 24 years, ever since the company was formed. George Rimmer is the managing director and oversees the entire operation. Albert Rimmer, who is a qualified accountant, is responsible for finance, personnel and administration. Dilip Haq is the supervisor on the packing line and is also responsible for the delivery fleet and the van maintenance team. Jane Birkinshaw is in charge of marketing, sales and special promotions.

Quite often newspaper publishers pay East Anglia News to distribute thousands of newspapers at special events which they sponsor. These special promotions are a growing source of income for the company and take up an increasing amount of Jane's time. Figure 7.8 shows the current organisational structure. Since the acquisition of the Thetford company the Rimmers, Jane and Dilip have all received generous wage increases to compensate for the increased workload. However, the extra work has become overbearing and many staff have suggested that the company is now poorly organised. An extract from the consultant's final report on business organisation is shown in Figure 7.9.

(a) Identify the current problems facing East Anglia News Ltd.

(b) Suggest a possible reorganisation of the business and illustrate this using an organisation chart.

(c) Explain how the reorganisation might benefit the business.

(d) Explain any problems that may result from the reorganisation.

(e) Examine how these problems may be solved.

Figure 7.7 *East Anglia News: Turnover, profit and employees*

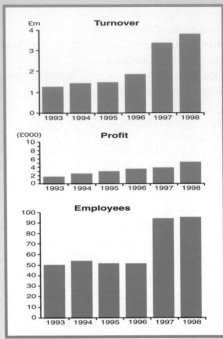

Figure 7.8 *Organisatonal chart for East Anglia News*

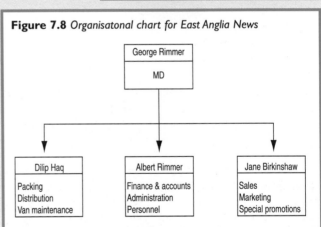

Figure 7.9 *An extract from the consultant's report*

CONCLUSION
A sound and effective organisational structure is vital for the efficient running of a business. A poor or inappropriate structure will result in the following consequences.
- Breakdown in communications.
- Poor staff motivation.
- A lack of guidance and leadership.
- Weak decision making.
- Overwork for certain individuals.
- A lack of promotional opportunities.
- Staff division and a lack of co-operation.
- Inflexibility.
- Duplication of resources.

As outlined in the above report, East Anglia News Ltd has suffered many of these consequences and needs to reorganise its structure immediately.

The basic economic problem

Unit 1 showed that business activity involved satisfying consumers' **needs** and **wants**. Businesses aim to satisfy these wants and needs by producing goods and services. When food is produced or a bus service is provided **resources** (land, labour, capital and enterprise) are used up. These resources are scarce relative to needs and wants. In other words, there are not enough resources to satisfy all consumers' needs and wants. This is known as the BASIC ECONOMIC PROBLEM. This means businesses, individuals and the government must make **choices** when allocating scarce resources between different uses. For example, a printer may have to choose whether to buy a new printing press to improve quality or some new computer software to improve administrative efficiency.

Economics is the study of how resources are allocated in situations where they have different uses. The choices faced by decision makers can be placed in order of preference. For example, a business may be considering three investment options but can only afford one. The decision makers might decide that the order is:

1. a new computer system;
2. a fleet of cars for the sales force;
3. a warehouse extension.

The business will allocate resources to the purchase of the new computer system. The other two options are **foregone** or given up. The benefit lost from the next best alternative is called the OPPORTUNITY COST of the choice. In this example it would be the benefit lost by not having a fleet of new cars.

Question 1

In 1997 Bass, the brewing, leisure and hotel giant, was looking to expand its operations. Previously, it was known to be interested in UK companies, with bookmakers William Hill and disco operator First Leisure being possible targets. Sources close to the company pointed to Europe as its next target. In particular, it was interested in buying an overseas brewing operation and perhaps a foreign hotel chain. In 1998 Bass bought Inter-Continental Hotels, the worldwide hotel chain, for £1.77 billion. Part of the funding for its acquisitions came from the sale of other parts of the business. For example, in 1998 it sold 222 pubs to Avebury Taverns for £40-50 million.

Source: adapted from *The Observer*, 24.8.1997 and *The Times* 22.5.1998.

(a) What choices had to be made by Bass in 1997?
(b) Suggest the possible opportunity costs of the activities of Bass in 1998.

The function of an economy

What is an economy? An ECONOMY is a system which attempts to solve the basic economic problem. In the national economy the resources in a country are changed by business activity into goods and services which are bought by individuals. In a household economy the family budget is spent on a range of goods and services. Local and international economies also act in the same way, but at different levels. The function of an economy is to allocate scarce resources amongst unlimited wants. The basic economic problem is often broken down into three questions.

- **What should be produced?** In developed economies the number of goods and services produced from resources is immense. The economic system must decide which resources will be used to produce which products. For example, what proportion of resources should be used to produce food, housing, cars, cigarettes, cosmetics or computers? Should resources be used for military purposes? Should resources be used to generate wealth for the future? In less developed countries the decision about what to produce may be simpler. This is because the choices available are limited. For example, a very poor African village might be faced with the decision whether to produce wheat or maize. However, this is still a question

Question 2

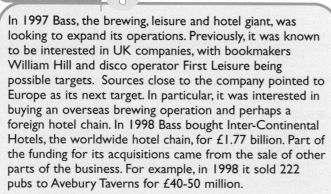

Look at the photographs.
(a) What types of goods are being produced in each case?
(b) Who are the goods being produced for?
(c) Describe the resources used in production in each case.

about resource allocation and what to produce.

● **How should it be produced?** The way in which goods and services are produced can vary. Decisions have to be made about such things as where production will take place, the method of production and the materials and labour that will be used.

● **For whom should it be produced?** An economy has to determine how the final goods and services will be allocated amongst competing groups. For example, how much should go to students, should the unemployed receive a share of output, should Ethiopia receive a proportion of total UK output, should managers get more than workers?

How the above questions are answered will depend on the type of **economic system**. It is usual to explain how resources are allocated in three types of economy - the free market economy, the planned economy and the mixed economy. The way business activity is organised will be different in each of these systems.

The organisation of production in different economic systems is also influenced by the **political system**. For example, in countries where there are free democracies, a significant proportion of goods and services are produced by independent businesses. On the other hand, in those few remaining countries which are dominated by the state, usually **communist** systems, the government plays the most important role in the production of goods and services.

Market economies

In MARKET ECONOMIES (also known as CAPITALIST ECONOMIES or FREE ENTERPRISE ECONOMIES) resources are allocated through markets (☞ unit 1).

The role of government in a free market system is limited. Its main functions are:

● to pass laws which protect the rights of businesses and consumers and punish offenders;

● to issue money and make sure that the monetary system (☞ unit 1) operates so that markets work efficiently;

● to provide certain essential products and services that would not be provided for everyone by firms, such as policing, national defence and the judiciary;

● to prevent firms from dominating the market and to restrict the power of trade unions. These activities would restrict competition and affect the workings of the market.

What to produce This decision is often made by consumers. Businesses will only produce goods if consumers will buy them and so firms must identify consumers' needs and respond to them. Firms which produce unwanted products are likely to fail.

Resources will be used to produce those goods and services which are profitable for businesses. If consumers buy more of a particular product, prices will tend to rise (☞ unit 17). Rising prices will attract firms into that industry as they see

the chance of profit. For example, in recent years, new firms have set up supplying accommodation for the elderly, to exploit rising demand as the population ages in the UK.

As demand for out of date and unwanted products falls their prices will also fall. Firms will leave these industries due to a fall in profit. They will sell unwanted resources like land, buildings and equipment and make labour redundant. These resources will be used by other businesses. For example, many textile mills have closed down due to a lack of demand. Some of the buildings have been bought by other businesses and converted into furniture stores or health centres.

How to produce In market economies businesses decide this. Businesses aim to make a profit. They will choose production methods (☞ unit 91) which reduce their costs. Competition in business forces firms to keep costs and prices low. Consumers will prefer to buy their goods from firms which offer lower prices, although other things such as quality will also influence them.

How are goods and services allocated? Firms produce goods and services which consumers purchase with money. The amount of money consumers have to spend depends on their income and wealth. In market economies individuals own the factors of production. For example, workers earn wages from selling their labour. Owners of capital receive interest, owners of businesses receive profits and the owners of land receive rent. All of these can be spent on goods and services. Those individuals with the most money can buy the most products.

In practice there are no pure market economies in the world. However, some countries such as the USA and Japan have economies which possess many of the characteristics of market economies.

Implications of market economies

The working of a free market economy can affect business and consumers in many ways.

● Resources are allocated automatically by the forces of demand and supply (☞ unit 17). For example, if more people decide to buy a product, the business will expand output, hire more factors of production and earn more revenue.

● Resources are not wasted in the production of unwanted goods.

● There should be a wider choice of goods and services.

● Individuals are free to set up in business and to choose how to spend their income.

● Competition should lead to lower costs and improve quality as firms try to impress consumers. Innovation might also be more widespread as firms try to develop new products to offer more choice and new production techniques to lower costs.

- There is often an unequal DISTRIBUTION OF INCOME. Groups that cannot be involved in economic activity, such as the old or the ill, may have little or no income. Owners of profitable businesses can build up great wealth.
- MARKET IMPERFECTIONS often occur. For example, a large firm may dominate an industry by driving out competition. The large company can then force up prices and exploit consumers.
- Some goods are not provided by private firms. These include defence, but also services where they may not make a profit (☞ unit 6).
- A lot of time and money is wasted when businesses collapse. For example, a failed construction company may own partly completed buildings which can become derelict if buyers cannot be found.
- Resources are often very slow to move from one use to another. For example, some workers may refuse to move from one area to another if a firm closes down resulting in underused resources and unemployment.
- Consumers may lack the information to make choices when buying products. The range of products, their quality and their prices change so frequently that consumers find it difficult to keep up to date. Also, some firms use marketing techniques to influence consumer choice.
- In order to keep costs low, firms may choose to pollute the environment. For example, they might discharge poisonous substances into rivers.

Planned economies

In the decades before 1990 many Eastern European countries such as Romania, Poland and Russia could have been described as PLANNED or COMMAND ECONOMIES. Government has a vital role in a planned economy. It plans, organises and co-ordinates the whole production process. This is unlike a market economy, where planning and organising is carried out by firms. Another difference is that resources in planned economies belong to the state. Individuals are not permitted to own property, land and other non-labour means of production.

What to produce This decision is made by government planners. They decide the type and mix of goods and services to be produced. Planners make assumptions about consumers' needs. For example, they decide how many cars, how much milk, how many shirts and how much meat should be produced. Planners then tell producers, such as farms and factories, exactly what to produce.

How to produce Government also tells producers how to produce. **Input-output analysis** is often used to make plans. For example, with a given level of technology, the state may know the land, labour, tractors and fertiliser (inputs) needed to make 1 million tonnes of wheat (the output). If an area

Question 3

The small Baltic state of Estonia is now reputed to be one of the world's purest free market economies. There are no barriers to trade and politicians frown upon government meddling in the economy. Economy minister, Jaak Leiman, says: 'Our liberal philosophy is due to the fact that we are so small and we just don't like state industry'. Since breaking away from the Soviet Union a number of economic improvements have occurred. It has been calculated that productivity increased by 33 per cent between 1993-98. In 1997 there was an 11 per cent fall in unit labour costs. Improvements are mainly due to revamped, privatised textile, engineering and other foreign owned plants. A combination of better management, access to UK markets and investment in new technology has helped to raise living standards. The open economy has also enjoyed a dramatic expansion of credit, partly financed by foreign borrowing.

Estonian businesses are shifting towards the production of high value-added goods, which is contributing to a growth in exports. Its service economy is also growing rapidly, with developments in transportation, travel and communications. It is able to exploit the country's position as a bridge to Russia and beyond into central Asia. Jaak Leiman says: 'The state is a facilitator not an investor'. The government is ready to support investors in the paper and pulp industry, for example, by guaranteeing long term supply of wood from state forests at market prices.

Source: adapted from the *Financial Times*, 24.2.1998.

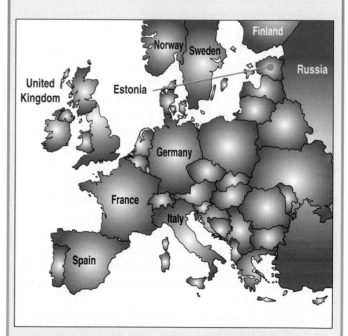

(a) Explain the phrase: 'One feature of Estonia's market economy is its "openness".'
(b) State two possible reasons why a UK business might want to locate part of its operations in Estonia.
(c) Describe the benefits that: (i) businesses; and
   (ii) consumers in Estonia might enjoy as a result of its free market economy.

needs 20 million tonnes, it is possible to work out the inputs needed. A complex table is drawn up which helps planners calculate the resources needed to meet the various output targets. Plans are often for 5, 10 or 15 years.

How are goods and services allocated? Goods and services are distributed to consumers through state outlets. People purchase goods and services with money they earn. Prices are set by the planners and cannot change without state instruction. Sometimes there are restrictions on the amount of particular goods and services which can be bought by any one individual, cars for example. Some goods and services, like education and health care, are provided free by the state.

Implications of planned economies

How does a planned economy affect the businesses and consumers that operate in it?

- There tends to be a more equal distribution of wealth and income. The state provides a minimum level of payment to all individuals. In addition, people are not allowed to own property, so wealth cannot be accumulated through private ownership.
- Resources are not duplicated. There is no competition in the supply of a service like public transport, whereas in a market economy several buses might drive along the same road competing for the same passengers.
- Production is for need rather than profit. Planners decide what is needed and what is produced. Resources are not wasted through businesses producing unwanted goods.
- Long term plans can be made taking into account a range of future needs, such as population changes and the environment.
- Many resources are used up in the planning process. Vast bureaucracies, employing large numbers of people, are needed to supervise, co-ordinate and carry out plans.
- People tend to be poorly motivated. As there is no profit, there is no incentive to motivate entrepreneurs.
- Planners encourage the production of standardised goods with little variety and choice for consumers.
- Planners often get things wrong! This can lead to shortages of some goods and services and surpluses of others. Also, planners' choices are not necessarily those of individuals. For example, many command economies produce large quantities of military goods.
- Shortages of goods often result in long queues outside state shops. This often leads to black markets. Goods and services are sold unofficially by individuals well above the state imposed prices. It is argued that this leads to bribery and corruption.
- The standard of living is often poor compared with countries which use other types of economic system.

Many of the former communist countries, such as Russia, Poland and the Czech Republic, reformed their economic and

In 1999 Cuba still remained a planned economy. However, the collapse of the Communist bloc in 1989 meant that its main trading partner disappeared. The economy, faced with a US trade embargo, collapsed. Its leader, Fidel Castro, had no choice but to introduce reforms. These included limited private ownership, encouragement of foreign investment and the legalising of the use of US dollars to curb the black market.

Most of the Cuban economy remains under state control. However, reforms have resulted in growth of 7.8 per cent in 1996. BAT industries set up a small joint venture in 1995, having left the country 35 years earlier. A partnership between the state and a Canadian company LCI in 1997 planned to build four 5 star hotels in undeveloped parts of Cuba. These hotels would offer inclusive holidays similar to those in the Dominican Republic. The state is willing to work with foreign companies because the poor quality of its own hotels has restricted tourism.

Forty years of Communism have created quirks in the country. Basic food and fuel supplies are a problem, but there is a strong biotechnology industry that is attracting foreign investment. Huge resources have been put into the development of this area. Cuba has an impressive health record, a lower infant mortality rate and a higher life expectancy than the US as a result.

Source: adapted from *The Times*, 12.7.1997, 15.10.1997.

(a) Using examples from the passage, suggest two:
   (i) benefits of a planned economy;
   (ii) problems of a planned economy.
(b) What factors influenced the introduction of some elements of market economies into Cuba?
(c) Suggest two effects that the introduction of elements of market economies might have on businesses in Cuba.

political systems after 1989. They changed from planned economies to mixed economies, with a greater freedom of markets. This led to problems, as described later in this unit. In the late 1990s examples of planned economies might include North Korea, Cuba, Vietnam and China. They have many of the characteristics listed here. However, some have introduced limited private ownership and free markets to help solve some of the problems of state run systems.

Mixed economies

In reality, no country has an economy which is entirely planned or free market. Most economic systems in the world have elements of each system.

They are known as MIXED ECONOMIES. In mixed economies some resources are allocated by the government and the rest by the market system. All Western European countries have mixed economies. The public sector (☞ unit 6) in mixed economies is responsible for the supply

Question 5

The amount of money which a government spends as a proportion of national income could be said to be an indication of the degree of 'mix' in an economy. In the 1980s and 1990s governments in the UK tried to reduce the size of the public sector by transferring many business activities from the public sector to the private sector.
(a) Describe the trends in public sector business activity

suggested by Figure 8.1 and Figure 8.2.
(b) Does your answer in (a) support the view that the amount of business activity in the public sector has declined since 1979?
(c) What might be the effects on businesses in: (i) the construction industry; (ii) the defence industry of falling public expenditure?

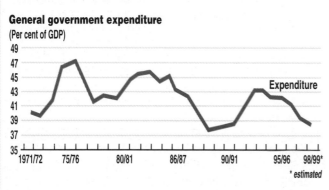

Figure 8.1 *General government spending as a percentage of GDP, UK*

Source: adapted from Red Book.

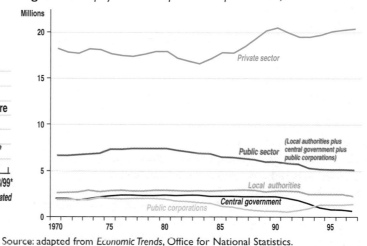

Figure 8.2 *Employment in the private and public sector, UK*

Source: adapted from *Economic Trends*, Office for National Statistics.

of some public goods and merit goods. Decisions regarding resource allocation in the public sector are made by central or local government. In the private sector production decisions are made by firms in response to the demands of consumers.

In the public sector, public goods and merit goods are usually provided free when used and are paid for by taxes. Examples might be roads and street lighting. In mixed economies the state usually provides a minimum standard of living for those unable to work. In the UK the state provides benefits as workers look for work and certain sickness benefits. In the public sector the state will own a significant proportion of production factors and service provision.

In the private sector individuals are allowed to own the means of production. Businesses are set up by individuals to supply a wide variety of goods and services. Competition exists between these firms. As a result, there will tend to be choice and variety. One of the roles of the government is to ensure that there is fair competition in the private sector. All private sector goods and services are allocated as in the market system described earlier.

What should be the 'degree of mixing' in this type of economy? The government will decide how much business activity there will be in the private sector and how much in the public sector. Some countries, like Sweden, allow the government to play a greater role in the supply of goods and services than others, like the UK. For example, in Sweden the government spends around 60 per cent of national income, whilst in the UK the government spends around 40 per cent. In countries where the government plays an important

economic role, social provision will tend to be greater, taxes higher and the distribution of wealth and income more equal. In countries where the private sector plays the most important economic role, social provision will tend to be lower with fewer free goods and services at the point of sale. Also, taxes will be lower and the distribution of wealth and income less equal. For example, in the last two decades, income tax rates have fallen in the UK and fewer services have been supplied by the state. The distribution of income has changed in favour of the 'wealthy' during this time.

Problems of changing systems

In the late 1980s and the 1990s major changes took place in a number of Eastern European countries. The former communist regimes were overthrown and replaced by some form of democracy. In most cases, the new governments wished to introduce market economies to replace the older planned systems which were thought to be inefficient. Although each country has had different experiences, there are some common features which all countries changing to a market system have faced. Many problems have arisen as a result of these changes. Businesses in these countries have had to change how they operate to cope with new demands.

Inflation Most countries have experienced inflation - a rise in the general price level. Under a planned system prices were set by the state and, in theory, inflation did not exist.

However, following liberalisation of their markets former planned economies experienced high inflation rates. In countries such as Armenia, Russia and Georgia inflation rates were more than 1,000 per cent in the early 1990s. By 1999 countries such as Poland and the Czech Republic had inflation rates of less than 10 per cent. Inflation affects the functions of money (☞ unit 23). In some countries businesses have reverted to bartering for resources, exchanging their products for other goods or services. Alternatively, they have exchanged their goods for currencies with stable values, such as the dollar.

Establishing the system A change to a market economy will not take place overnight. The institutions in Western economies which help the market system to work will take time to develop and operate in the former planned

economies. Businesses may have problems raising finance due to a lack of institutions. able to loan money. In many countries there is no stock market where shares in a company can be sold to raise finance. Other problems may result from the previous inefficiencies of planned systems. Transport, communications and markets for buying and selling goods are not yet ready for the level of business activity that will take place under a market system. This can result in late deliveries, a lack of information and a restriction in selling opportunities.

Competition Businesses in former planned economies now face competition from both within the country and from abroad. Some countries have suffered from cheap foreign goods being sold in their economy. Prices of home produced goods and services are likely to be higher than before. Previously the

Question

Poland is one of the Eastern bloc countries which has begun to see some of the benefits of changing from a planned to a more market orientated economic system. The Polish economy entered the 1990s as one of the weakest in central Europe. However, it is expected to begin the new Millennium as one of the strongest. Poland's recovery is largely due to the stabilisation package and market reform policies introduced in 1990 by the first post-communist finance minister. Between 1995 and 1999 economic growth in Poland averaged between 5-7 per cent.

Two businesses which are flourishing in the new environment are Elektrim, an electrical engineering and trading business, and Rolimpex, a leading company in agriculture. Both were large state monopolies operating in the old economic regime. These companies have adapted and helped drive the economic change in Poland. Elektrim, floated on the Warsaw stock exchange in 1992, acquired a number of other companies in the 1990s. Its profits rose from 151.8 million zloty to 170 million zloty in 1996. Rolimpex, floated in 1994, sells over 1,000 products. Its profits rose by 18 per cent in 1996. Both companies are

selling well in domestic markets. However, they are also attempting to increase sales abroad.

One of the problems facing new private sector companies is changing the attitudes of the workforce, management and unions. One pharmaceutical company opposed the creation of a marketing department. Sales fell as a result of foreign competition and the workforce was cut by 40 per cent. Some companies also prefer not to be in debt and so are not prepared to borrow in order to expand.

Source: adapted from the *Financial Times*, 27.3.1996; *The Guardian*, 4.10.1997.

(a) Suggest three possible differences in the ownership and organisation of Elektrim and Rolimpex now that they are not state owned.
(b) What problems associated with changing the economic system are indicated in the article?
(c) What evidence is there in the case to suggest that Polish businesses are benefiting from a more market orientated economy?
(d) Suggest how possible problems of transition to a market system might affect businesses like Elektrim and Rolimpex.

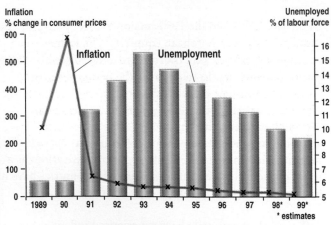

Figure 8.3 *Poland: unemployment and inflation*

Source: adapted from OECD, *World Economic Outlook*.

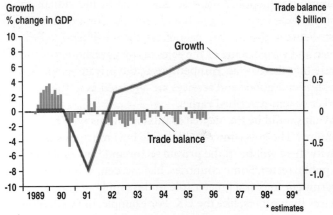

Figure 8.4 *Poland: economic growth and the trade balance*

state had kept the prices of resources low so that the prices of final goods were also low. Removal of these controls would mean having to increase prices to make a profit.

Unemployment In a planned system unemployment should not exist. The state provides work for all individuals and makes sure that they have minimum living standards. In 1999 unemployment in Russia, Bulgaria and the Slovak Republic was forecast to be greater than 10 per cent.

Running the business The new entrepreneurs in former planned economies will be the managers and employees of ex-state run firms. These people have no experience of how to operate in a market system. They face the prospect of making a profit or going out of business, unheard of under a planned system. Also, businesses are not used to operating under a system where profit and earnings motivate people to work. Many would still suffer from the lack of initiative associated with the planned system. Finally, the ability to organise, run and motivate business activity in these countries may not exist, and many people require training, often from Western firms or training agencies.

It has been argued that those countries with the most recent history of a market system have adjusted best to the transition. Before the Second World War, Hungary, Poland, Slovenia and the Czech and Slovak Republics all had market systems. Countries that were part of the former USSR, with communist systems, have not performed as well. In 1996, for example, economic growth in the Slovak Republic was 7 per cent compared to -4.9 per cent in Russia, although by 1999 Russia's growth was forecast to be 4 per cent.

Transfer of ownership One major problem facing all economies changing from a planned to a market system is the transfer of ownership. Previously all resources and businesses were state owned. Farms, factories and shops now have to be passed on to employees and managers. In the former East Germany all state firms were placed in the hands of an agency (the Treuhand) which sold them off. In the former USSR, people were given vouchers which entitled them to a share of a company.

Many Eastern European countries are undertaking a huge privatisation process. In some cases privatisation experts from the UK and other western economies are recruited to advise on the transfer of assets from the public to the private sector.

Key terms

Basic economic problem - how scarce resources with different uses are allocated to satisfy wants.

Distribution of income - the amount of income and wealth different groups have in a particular country.

Economy - a system which attempts to solve the basic economic problem.

Market economy or capitalist economy or free enterprise economy - an economic system which allows the market mechanism to allocate resources.

Market imperfection - any factor which hinders the free operation of markets, such as where one firm dominates resulting in exploitation.

Mixed economy - an economic system which allows both the state and the market mechanism to allocate resources.

Opportunity cost - the benefit of the next best option foregone when making a choice between a number of alternatives.

Planned economy or command economy - an economic system in which the state is responsible for resource allocation.

Summary

1. Why do businesses, individuals and government need to make choices about the resources they use?
2. Give 2 examples of opportunity cost.
3. What is the function of an economy?
4. What are the 3 questions an economy aims to answer?
5. Describe the benefits of market economies for: (a) firms; (b) consumers.
6. Describe the problems of planned economies for: (a) firms; (b) consumers.
7. What determines the degree of 'mix' in a mixed economy?
8. 'A free market system in former planned economies will take time to work.' Give 3 examples which support this statement.

Case study

China

The Chinese economy has experienced more than fifteen years of economic transformation. However, the political system in China remains largely unchanged. China is a communist, one-party state. There are no competitive elections. The government operates a strict regime, but at the same time acknowledges that the standard of living in the country will only improve if it allows free markets to flourish. China has been keen to encourage inward investment (investment in Chinese business from abroad). The country is rich in natural resources and has a huge population (around 2,000 million).

Rupert Murdoch's Hong Kong based Star Satellite television service unveiled a new broadcast network in 1996. It was designed to improve its access to the Chinese market. Star TV hoped to establish three Chinese language channels to broadcast sport, films and popular entertainment as a means of raising its profile in China. Efforts to break into the Chinese market include a $10 million-$15 million investment in a new film studio with Tianjin television in East Beijing and a $4.5 million investment in an on-line computer publishing venture with the People's Daily, the Communist party newspaper. However, resistance to Star TV from the Chinese authorities did exist. Indeed, there was a crackdown on satellite dishes partly in response to Star's own claim about success in viewing figures.

China has been involved in a large scale privatisation programme in the 1990s. However, the performance of the shares following privatisation has not been very impressive. The performance of H-shares, the name given to former Chinese state companies listed in Hong Kong, is shown in Figure 8.5. In 1996, a number of large Chinese companies was being prepared for sale, with the hope of attracting overseas investors. The state has relied heavily on foreign companies buying privatised businesses because of a lack of funds in China.

Figure 8.5 *Performance of H-shares*

Source: adapted from Datastream, Goldman Sachs, Kleinwort Benson.

There appears to be a shortage in China of opportunities for wealthy people to invest their money. HSBC Holdings, the global group that is Hong Kong's biggest bank, sees this as an opportunity to develop its network of banks. Chinese banks have no experience of operating as commercial organisations. In addition, the authorities will not wish to see overseas competitors entering the market until their own banks are capable of competing. Chinese banks are forced to pay out more to depositors than they receive from borrowers. Four Chinese banks have been privatised, but their lack of technology would currently make them vulnerable to competitors with modern technology. All leading banks in Hong Kong have established branches on the mainland.

One of the biggest foreign investors in China is CP Pokphand, a family owned company from Thailand. CP Pokphand has invested around US$2 billion in China. Its main business is the sale of day-old chicks and feed to farmers. It claims to be the first company to establish a genuine business interest in China. It secured the first business registration certificate in 1979. The company now employs 15,000 people in Shenzen where it first set up. Its main business is agriculture, but increasingly, new and unrelated products are being added to its now diverse portfolio. Motorbikes and telecommunications are examples of this. Share prices rose from below 2 Hong Kong dollars in 1994 to over 3.5 HK$ in 1996. One of the reasons for CP Pokphand's success in China might be the number of joint ventures it has established in the country. There are around 80 joint ventures, one in every single Chinese province except Tibet.

In particular this has helped to ease distribution problems. The company has experienced failure though. Its activities in the retail sector fell apart in January 1996. A venture with the US company, WalMart, failed to get going.

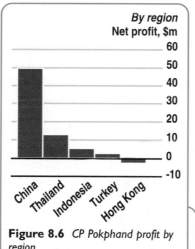

By region
Net profit, $m

China, Thailand, Indonesia, Turkey, Hong Kong

Figure 8.6 *CP Pokphand profit by region*

Figure 8.7 *Share price*

Share price (HK$)

4.5
4.0
3.5
3.0
2.5
2.0
1.5

95   96

In 1997, the French car manufacturer, Peugeot, withdrew from a factory they had set up in Guangzhou, South China. The company lost $100 million as a result of a failed joint venture in the region and was typical of foreign car makers' frustration in China. However, Honda, the Japanese car maker paid $200 million to take over the site. Koji Kadowaki, president of the new Guangzhou Honda Automobile, believed that Honda would succeed where Peugeot failed. Honda already have experience in Asian markets and their management style is different to those of the French. Honda aimed to communicate with local people in Guangzhou and to share responsibility. It also planned to distribute the cars differently. When Peugeot were in control most of their sales were in the local area. Honda planned to set up dealerships around the nation. Only a few foreign car makers have been admitted to the Chinese market. In Shanghai, Volkswagen make Santana saloon cars and General Motors is about to begin making Buicks. No new licenses will be granted for car making until the government drafts its next five year plan for industry in 2000. The Chinese government also imposes certain restrictions on foreign manufacturers. For example, they are not allowed to produce economy cars and there are limits on the numbers of cars which can be produced.

Source: adapted from the *Financial Times*, 15.9.1998.

In September 1997, Zhu Rongji, China's top economic official, set a three year target to revive loss making state owned enterprises. He proposed to introduce incentives for imports of equipment by foreign companies. This he hoped would bring in new technology, which would develop Chinese industry. Between 1994 and 1997 China received more than $100 billion in investment.

Source: adapted from the *Financial Times*, 23.9.1997.

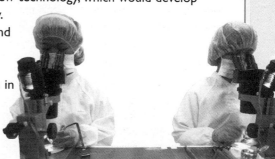

(a) State two possible disadvantages to Chinese businesses of reforms to the Chinese economy.
(b) State two possible advantages to: (i) Chinese people; (ii) foreign companies of markets becoming more open.
(c) Why might CP Pokphand have been successful in China?

(d) Using examples from the articles, suggest two reasons why the Chinese government is keen for overseas businesses to invest in its country.
(e) What changes in the articles show that China is moving towards becoming a market economy?
(f) To what extent do you think Chinese privatisation and market reforms have been a success?

Why do businesses collect data?

Information is a valuable resource in business. Businesses collect large amounts of information or DATA about their own organisations. They may also employ companies such as Dialogue and Reuters, which specialise in the collection and sale of information. Examples of data that a business might collect include:

- costs of production;
- share prices and exchange rates;
- company reports;
- weekly or monthly sales figures;
- business news, for example about a potential takeover;
- market research findings.

Data are collected by businesses for a number of reasons. Most importantly perhaps, data are required in the decision making process (☞ unit 10). Managers, employees and others involved in business activity need up to date and accurate data to help them make effective decisions. For example, a business choosing from a number of investment opportunities would require the latest information on the costs and expected return of each project.

Data are required to monitor the progress of a business. Business performance could be gauged by looking at the growth or decline in turnover or profit. Changes in productivity rates can be calculated if a business has data on its inputs and output.

All businesses keep records which contain a wide range of qualitative (about nature or characteristics) and quantitative (involving measurement) data. These records contain information that is important to the business. Such records might include monthly sales figures, staff files, customer files and market reports. It is important that records are regularly updated so that they are correct when required by the business. Businesses make use of **backdata,** such as sales in previous years, to forecast (☞ unit 51) what might happen in future.

Finally, data are used to aid control in a business. Financial data on payments and receipts are used to control cash flow (☞ unit 59). A financial controller, for example, might delay payment to a supplier until money is received from customers in order to avoid a cash flow problem.

Why do businesses present data?

Once data has been collected it can be stored, retrieved and presented. The volume of data collected by businesses is enormous and it is important to avoid making mistakes. The development of information and communication technology (☞ unit 82) in recent years has made the handling of data far easier and less prone to error. Data can be stored on a computer memory or disc, 'called up' on a computer screen, manipulated and presented in a variety of styles. Businesses may make use of graphs, charts, tables and other pictorial methods of communicating data. Presenting data in this way:

- can be more concise and easier to understand than written information;
- can take less time to interpret;
- can identify trends clearly;
- may be effective in creating an impact or an image;
- can be used to impress a potential client.

The method of presentation a businesses chooses will depend on the type of data collected, who and what it is required for and how it is likely to be used. Data can be presented 'internally' and 'externally'. Examples of data presented to those inside a business might be:

- the sales department presenting a breakdown of regional sales figures to senior management to illustrate the popularity of

Question 1

JD Weatherspoon plc develops, owns and manages pubs throughout the UK. It aims to provide its customers with a clean, safe and attractive environment in which to enjoy good value, high quality food and drink, served by friendly and well trained staff. Figure 9.1 shows data from the company's Annual Report and Accounts about two aspects of the business over the period 1994-98.

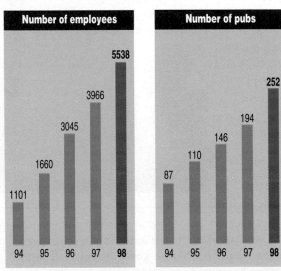

Figure 9.1 *Number of employees and number of pubs owned by JD Weatherspoon plc, 1994-98*

Source: adapted from JD Weatherspoon, *Annual Report and Accounts.*

(a) What data is shown in the diagrams?
(b) Who is the data likely to be presented to?
(c) Suggest reasons why the data is presented in this way.

products in an area or the effectiveness of promotion;
● the production manager presenting the accounts department with weekly time sheets to allow the calculation of wages and costs;
● the research and development department providing an analysis of monthly expenditure to enable budgets to be calculated;
● the personnel manager providing an analysis of staff turnover to illustrate possible problems or improvements in human resource management;
● the market research department providing research data to allow products to be designed to fit consumers' needs.
Examples of data presented to those outside the business could be:
● the accounts department providing Customs and Excise with VAT details to claim back tax on sales which are exempt from VAT;
● the publication of an Annual Report and Accounts to illustrate a company's progress over the last year to stakeholders;
● the presentation of a new market range by the marketing department to a potential customer.

Bar charts

A BAR CHART is one of the simplest and most common means of presenting data. Numerical information is represented by 'bars' or 'blocks' which can be drawn horizontally or vertically. The length of the bars shows the relative importance of the data. Table 9.1 shows data on the profit made by Ragwear PLC, a manufacturer, over the last six years. They are presented as a bar graph in Figure 9.2.

Table 9.1 *Profit for Ragwear PLC over a six year period*

	Yr1	Yr2	Yr3	Yr4	Yr5	Yr6
						£m
Profit	2.1	2.9	3.8	4.1	3.2	4.9

The main advantage of using a bar chart is that it shows results very clearly. At a glance the reader can get a general feel of the information and identify any trends or changes over the time period. Figure 9.2 shows that profit has continued to increase over the period apart from a 'dip' in year 5. This might indicate to the firm that trading conditions in year 5 were unfavourable or that the firm's performance was relatively poor. Bar charts are more attractive than tables and may allow the reader to interpret the data more quickly.

The bars in Figure 9.2 are drawn vertically. They could also, however, be drawn horizontally. They are also 3 dimensional, but they could have been 2 dimensional.

It is possible to produce a bar chart from collected data, such as from market research. This data may be collected in a

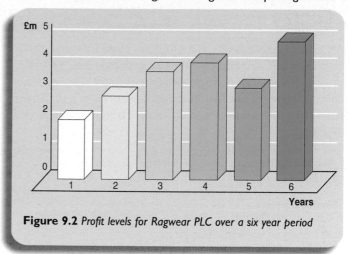

Figure 9.2 *Profit levels for Ragwear PLC over a six year period*

tally chart as in Table 9.2, which shows the results of research into the brands of toothpaste bought by a sample of supermarket customers. The total number of times each item occurs is known as the **frequency** (f). So, for example, the most popular from the survey is Colgate and the least popular is Aquafresh. Figure 9.3 shows the data from Table 9.2 as a bar chart.

Table 9.2 *Survey results into the popularity of toothpaste*

Brand	Tally marks	Frequency
Colgate	ǁǁǁ ǁǁǁ ǁǁǁ etc.	260
Macleans	ǁǁǁ ǁǁǁ ǁǁǁ etc.	190
Sensodyne	ǁǁǁ ǁǁǁ ǁǁǁ etc.	100
Mentadent	ǁǁǁ ǁǁǁ ǁǁǁ etc.	50
Supermarket own brand	ǁǁǁ ǁǁǁ ǁǁǁ etc.	230
Aquafresh	ǁǁǁ ǁǁǁ ǁǁǁ etc.	20
Gibbs SR	ǁǁǁ ǁǁǁ ǁǁǁ etc.	150
Total		1,000

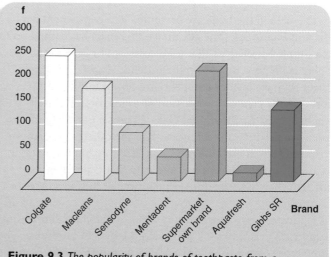

Figure 9.3 *The popularity of brands of toothpaste from a sample of 1,000 customers*

Component bar charts

A COMPONENT BAR CHART allows more information to be presented to the reader. Each bar is divided into a number of components. For example, the data in Table 9.3 shows the cost structures of five furniture manufacturers in a particular year. The total cost is broken down into labour, materials and overheads.

Table 9.3 *Cost structures of five furniture manufacturers and overheads*

£000

	Oakwell	Stretton	Bradford	Jones	Campsfield
Labour	50	36	70	45	90
Materials	18	25	48	23	50
Overheads	10	10	19	9	25

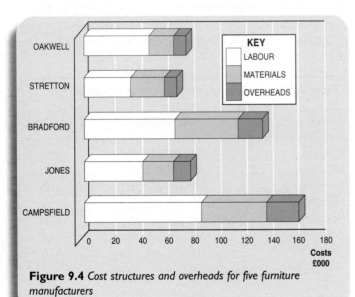

Figure 9.4 *Cost structures and overheads for five furniture manufacturers*

The data in the table are presented as a component bar chart in Figure 9.4. One advantage this chart has compared to the simple bar chart is that total costs can be seen easily. There is no need to add up the individual costs. It is also easier to make instant comparisons. For example, labour costs are the greatest proportion of total cost at Oakwell. This might suggest to a firm that Oakwell uses a more labour intensive production technique than the others. Also, labour costs at Oakwell are higher than at Stretton, but not as high as at Campsfield. This might indicate that Oakwell is less efficient than Stretton and a much smaller business than Campsfield.

Figure 9.5 shows three other styles of bar chart, illustrating data for AVC Holdings. This is a company that produces three types of machine tool, code named BAT 4, BAT 3 and BAT 2.

● The top chart is a **parallel** bar chart. It shows the turnover

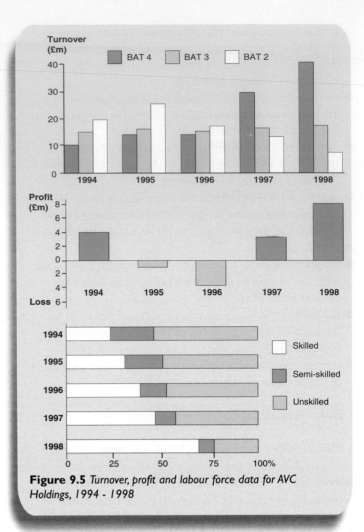

Figure 9.5 *Turnover, profit and labour force data for AVC Holdings, 1994 - 1998*

contributed by each of the company's three products. Over the time period the turnover for BAT 4 has increased from £10 million to £40 million. Sales of BAT 3 have remained fairly steady at around £15 million each year. The turnover from BAT 2 has declined from £20 million to £7 million. This type of graph is similar to a component bar chart. The advantage is that it is easier to compare changes between the components, although it is more difficult to compare totals.

● The middle chart is a **gain and loss** bar chart. It shows the profitability of the company over the time period. The performance of AVC Holdings worsened in the first three years and then improved. The profit in 1998 was £8 million. This type of chart distinguishes very clearly between positive and negative values.

● The bottom chart is a **percentage component** bar chart. It shows the breakdown of the workforce in terms of their skill with each section represented as a percentage of the workforce. In 1994 nearly 25 per cent of the workforce were skilled. In 1998 this had risen to around 70 per cent. The chart also shows that the numbers of semi-skilled workers had fallen as a percentage of the total. This might indicate that the firm had introduced new technology, leading to unskilled staff being replaced with skilled staff.

One disadvantage of this presentation is that changes in the total size of the workforce are not shown.

Question 2

In 1998 Scottish Hydro-Electric and Southern Electric announced that they would join forces to create one of the country's biggest energy businesses. Since the industry was privatised in 1991, many mergers had taken place between energy companies.

Figure 9.6 *Profits of Scottish Hydro-Electric and Southern Electric*

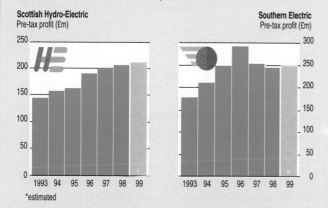

Source: adapted from Datastream/ICV; company information.

(a) Explain briefly what the bar charts are showing.
(b) Discuss whether you think the use of bar charts here is an effective way of presenting the data. Explain your reasons.
(c) Suggest how the bar chart could be adapted into a component bar chart to show profit information.

A pictograph or pictogram

A PICTOGRAPH or PICTOGRAM is another form of chart. It presents data in a similar way to bar charts. The difference is that data are represented by pictorial symbols rather than bars. Figure 9.7 shows an example of the orders which GPA Group has received for its aircraft over a nine year time period. The pictograph shows a general decline in orders. This might indicate that there is a general decline in the market or that customers are delaying future orders. One problem with a pictograph is that it is not always easy to 'divide' the symbols exactly. This makes it difficult to read precise quantities from the graph. For example, in Figure 9.7, in 1996 the number of orders is more than 60, but the last symbol is a fraction of an aircraft which makes it difficult to determine the exact size of orders placed in that year. The main advantage of this method is that the graphs tend to be more eyecatching. Such a method might be used in business presentations to attract clients or in reports to the public.

Pie charts

In a PIE CHART, the total amount of data collected is represented by a circle. This is divided into a number of segments. Each segment represents the size of a particular part relative to the total. To draw a pie chart it is necessary to perform some simple calculations. Table 9.4 shows the details of monthly output at five European plants for a multinational brick producer. The 360 degrees in a circle have to be divided between the various parts which make up the total output of 50,000 tonnes. To calculate the number of degrees each segment will contain, a business would use the following formula:

$$\frac{\text{Value of the part} \times 360°}{\text{Total}}$$

Table 9.4 *Monthly brick output at five European plants*

	Bedford	Brescia	Lyon	Bonn	Gijon	Total
Output (tonnes)	10,000	8,000	5,000	15,000	12,000	50,000

Thus, the size of the segment which represents the monthly brick output in Bedford is:

$$= \frac{10,000}{50,000} \times 360°$$

$$= 0.2 \times 360°$$

$$= 72°$$

Using the same method it can be shown that the size of the other segments representing output at the other plants will be: Brescia 58°; Lyon 36°; Bonn 108°; Gijon 86°.

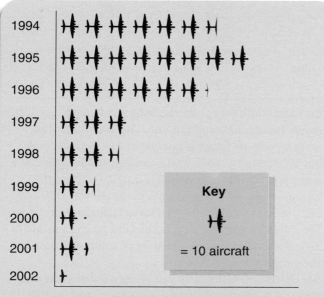

1994	
1995	
1996	
1997	
1998	
1999	
2000	
2001	
2002	

Key

= 10 aircraft

Number of aircraft

Figure 9.7 *A pictograph for GPA Group showing orders for aircraft in March 1994 for each year to 2002*

The number of degrees in each segment added together make 360°. A pie chart can now be drawn using a protractor or a spreadsheet or DTP software pakage on a computer. The pie chart is shown in Figure 9.8. Bonn makes the largest contribution to monthly output with Gijon second. The company might use this information to compare with monthly production targets.

Pie charts are useful because readers get an immediate impression of the relative importance of the various parts. They can also be used to make comparisons over different time periods. There are however, drawbacks with pie charts.

● They do not always allow precise comparisons to be made between the segments.
● If a total consists of a very large number of components, it may be difficult to identify the relative importance of each segment.
● It is difficult to show changes in the size of the total pie. For example, if the total rises over time it is possible to make the 'pie' bigger. However, the exact size of the increase is often difficult to determine because it involves comparing the areas of circles.

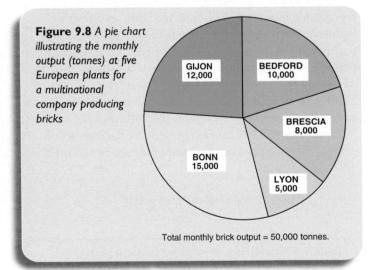

Figure 9.8 *A pie chart illustrating the monthly output (tonnes) at five European plants for a multinational company producing bricks*

GIJON 12,000
BEDFORD 10,000
BRESCIA 8,000
BONN 15,000
LYON 5,000

Total monthly brick output = 50,000 tonnes.

Histograms

Table 9.6 illustrates some data collected by market researchers on behalf of a cinema chain. It concerns the age profile of a sample of cinema goers on a Saturday. The chart shows the number of viewers in the sample that falls into various age ranges (known as **classes**). The total number of times each item occurs in each class is known as the frequency (f). So the total number of viewers in the 10 - 19 age range is 290. This type of data is usually shown as a HISTOGRAM as in Figure 9.9. A histogram looks similar to a bar chart, but there are some differences.

● In a histogram it is the **area** of the bars which represents the frequency. In a bar chart it is the length or height of the bars. For example, in Figure 9.9, all the columns have

In the early 1990s, the television 'listings' market was deregulated. Previously the market had been dominated by the *Radio Times* and the *TV Times*. Competition led to the publication of many new magazines showing television programme schedules. Table 9.5 shows the market shares of the surviving titles after the initial rush of rival launches.

Table 9.5 *TV listings market*

Title	Publisher	Circulation
Sky TV guide	Redwood	3,241,325
What's On TV	IPC	1,692,070
Radio Times	BBC	1,406,417
TV TIMES	IPC	982,007
TV Quick	Bauer	809,000
Cable Guide	Cable Guide	625,019
TV & Satellite Week	IPC	200,061

Sources: adapted from ABC/Bauer/BSkyB.

(a) Using the data in Table 9.5, construct two pie charts: (i) to show the market shares of each title; and (ii) to show the market shares of each publisher.
(b) Describe the advantages of using pie charts rather than the table to illustrate this data.
(c) Discuss the extent to which the market is dominated by a single title or publisher.

Table 9.6 *The age profile of cinema goers on a Saturday*

Age range	Frequency
0-9	180
10-19	290
20-29	500
30-39	400
40-49	350
50-59	280
60-79	200
Total	2,200

the same width except for the last one where the age range covers two decades and not one. This means that the frequency in the figure is not 200 as shown in the table, but 100 (200÷2 = 100). This is because in the table 200 spectators fall into the age range 60 - 79, whereas the histogram shows 100 spectators in the age range 60 - 69 and 100 in the range 70 - 79. However, the area of the last bar coincides with the data in the table, ie it is equal to 200. The total area represented by all columns is equal to the sample size of 2,200.

● Bar charts and histograms can be used for **discrete data** - data which only occur as whole numbers, such as the number of people employed in a store. Histograms are most useful when recording **continuous data** - data which occur over a range of values, such as weight or age.

● Histograms tend to be used for grouped data, for example the number of people between the ages of 0 and 9.

The histogram in Figure 9.9 shows that the most frequently occurring age range of viewers is 20 - 29. The information might be used by the cinema chain to help plan a marketing strategy. It is possible to show the information in Table 9.6 by plotting a curve called a frequency polygon. It is drawn using the histogram and involves joining all the mid-points at the top of the 'bars' with straight lines. The frequency polygon for the data in Table 9.6 is shown in Figure 9.9. Arguably, the visual pattern of the data is shown more clearly by the frequency polygon.

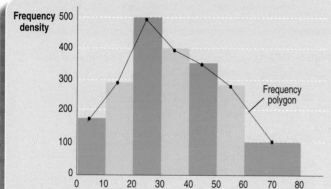

Figure 9.9 *A histogram representing the age profile of a sample of cinema goers on a Saturday - the frequency polygon is also shown*

 Question 4

Orrel Boxes Ltd produces cartons for cereal producers. The marketing manager was asked by the chairperson to supply information regarding the size of customer orders for the last month. After looking through the sales records she was able to draw up Table 9.7.

Table 9.7 *Information regarding the size of orders for Orrel Boxes Ltd*

Order size	Frequency
1,000 - 1,999	34
2,000 - 2,999	52
3,000 - 3,999	86
4,000 - 4,999	100
5,000 - 5,999	189
6,000 - 6,999	60
7,000 - 7,999	48
8,000 - 11,999	40

(a) Why would the marketing manager produce a histogram rather than a bar chart to present the data?
(b) Construct a histogram from the above information.
(c) How might a business make use of data presented in this way?
(d) Construct a frequency polygon. Explain what it shows.

Tables

Tables are used to present many forms of data. They may be used:
● if data are qualitative rather than quantitative;
● where a wide range of variables needs to be expressed at the same time;
● where the numbers themselves are at the centre of attention;
● when it is necessary to perform calculations on the basis of the information.

Some would argue that the use of tables should be avoided if possible. However, a poorly or inaccurately drawn graph would be less effective than a neatly presented table. Table 9.8 shows extracts from a 1998 *Labour Research* earnings survey. It shows the percentage increases or decreases and the wage rates for a sample of 'celebrities' earning over £1 million. Although it may have been possible to present the data using charts, the tables show the 'league positions' clearly.

Table 9.8 *Celebrities' earnings*

Name	Company	Pay (£)	% change
Phil Collins	Philip Collins	11,812,084	+34.5
Sting	Steerpike/ Steerpike O'seas	9,843,000	-4.0
Sir Paul McCartney	Apple/MPL	6,111,798	-16.5
George Harrison	Apple	5,742,530	+41.7
Yoko Ono	Apple	5,742,530	+41.7
Ringo Starr	Apple	5,592,530	+43.3
Mark Knopfler	Chariscourt	1,774,843	+4.8
Peter Gabriel	Peter Gabriel	1,370,000	n.a
Eric Clapton	Marshbrook	1,232,000	-43.1

Source: adapted from *Labour Research,* September 1998.

Line graphs

LINE GRAPHS are probably the most common type of graph used by a business. A line graph shows the relationship between two variables. The values of one variable are shown on the vertical axis and the values of the other variable are placed on the horizontal axis. The two variables must be related in some way. The values of the variables can be joined by straight lines or a smooth curve. If **time** is one of the variables being analysed it should always be plotted on the horizontal axis. Output is usually plotted on the horizontal axis. The main advantage of this type of graph is the way in which a reader can get an immediate picture of the relationship between the two variables. Also, it is possible to take measurements from a line graph when analysing data. It is much more difficult to do this when reading figures from a table. Quite often more than one line is shown on a line graph so that comparisons can be made. **Economic data** is often presented on a line graph. A line graph showing interest rates over the recent period may influence a business's decision to invest, for example.

In the period 1996 to 1998, Somerfield, the supermarket chain, and Booker, the UK's largest cash and carry business, embarked on expansion. Booker suffered as a result of over-ambitious purchases of other businesses. Somerfield bought the Kwik Save chain which made it one of the largest businesses in the supermarket market. In August 1998 Somerfield was interested in taking over Booker.

(a) What information do the line graphs in Figure 9.10 show?

(b) Suggest two other pieces of information that might be illustrated using line graphs.

(c) What are the advantages of illustrating the data in this way?

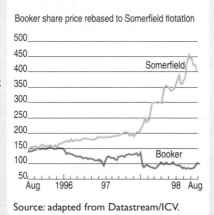

Figure 9.10 *Somerfield and Booker share prices*

Booker share price rebased to Somerfield flotation

Source: adapted from Datastream/ICV.

Cumulative frequency curves

When collecting data and recording it in a table, it is possible to show CUMULATIVE FREQUENCY. This is the total frequency up to a particular item or class boundary. It is calculated by adding the number of entries in a class to the total in the next class - a 'running total'. Table 9.9 shows the weights of cereal packages coming off a production line in a particular time period.

The cumulative frequencies in the table can be plotted on a graph. The graph is called an **ogive** and is shown in Figure 9.11. It can be seen, for example, that 270 packages weigh below 201.5 grams.

Table 9.9 *Cumulative frequency of package weights*

Weights falling within these ranges (grams)	Frequency	Cumulative frequency
198-199	30	30
199-200	50	80 (30 + 50)
200-201	150	230 (30 + 50 + 150)
201-202	70	300 (30 + 50 + 150 + 70)
202-203	40	340 (30 + 50 + 150 + 70 + 40)
203-204	5	345 (30 + 50 + 150 + 70 + 40 + 5)

A Lorenz curve

A LORENZ CURVE is a special type of line graph. It is a cumulative frequency curve which can be used to show the difference between actual distribution and an equal

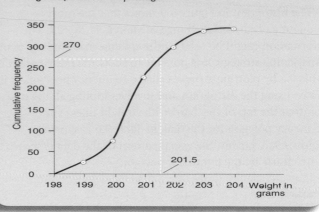

Figure 9.11 *A cumulative frequency distribution (ogive) showing the weights of 345 cereal packages*

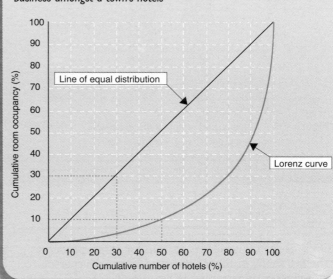

Figure 9.12 *A Lorenz curve illustrating the distribution of hotel business amongst a town's hotels*

distribution. Figure 9.12 is a Lorenz curve which illustrates the way in which business is distributed between different hotels in a town. What does the curve show? If business was shared equally between all hotels then the line would be a straight 45° line. So, for example, 30 per cent of the town's hotels would get 30 per cent of all business, measured here as the number of rooms occupied. The Lorenz curve shows the actual distribution of business amongst the town's hotels. For example, 50 per cent of the town's hotels have only 10 per cent of the total hotel business. This obviously indicates a very unequal distribution of business amongst the town's hotels. The further the Lorenz curve is drawn away from the 45° line the more unequal the actual distribution will be. A business might use this to analyse market share. The Lorenz curve is often used to show the distribution of wealth in a particular country.

Bias in presentation

Just as bias can affect the collection of data it can also affect its presentation. When presenting profit figures to shareholders or sales figures to customers, managers will want to show the business in the best light. There is a danger that figures may be distorted in the way they are presented, in order to make performance look better than it was.

There are two main ways in which bias can occur.

● The method of presentation could exaggerate the actual rate of change shown by the data. This can be done by cutting and expanding one axis of a graph. Darrel Huff, an American statistician, called this a 'Gee-Whiz' graph. Figure 9.13 shows the same data presented in two different ways. In graph (b) the profit axis has been cut and extended. This gives a far better impression of the growth in profit than in graph (a). Similar bias can be introduced into bar charts, pie charts and pictographs.

● A business could leave out figures that do not fit into the 'picture' it wants to portray. For example, in a presentation to customers a firm may show its sales figures have been rising over the past five years, but omit to show that the total market has been increasing at a faster rate. This, in fact, means that the market share of the business has been falling.

Figure 9.13 *The same profit figures for a business presented to show two different pictures*

Question 6

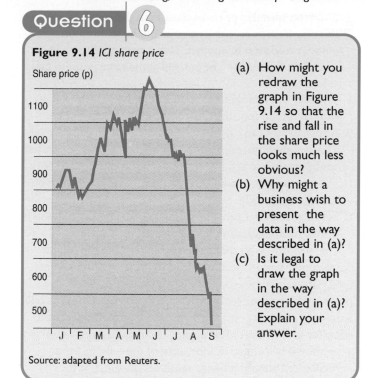

Figure 9.14 *ICI share price*

(a) How might you redraw the graph in Figure 9.14 so that the rise and fall in the share price looks much less obvious?

(b) Why might a business wish to present the data in the way described in (a)?

(c) Is it legal to draw the graph in the way described in (a)? Explain your answer.

Source: adapted from Reuters.

Table 9.10 *An example of a spreadsheet which contains cost data*

	A	B	C	D	E	F	G
1		Jan	Feb	March	April	May	June
2	Labour	200	210	230	210	200	230
3	Materials	100	100	110	130	100	110
4	Fuel	35	35	35	30	30	20
5	Overheads	25	25	30	30	35	35
6	Total costs	360	370	405	400	365	395

The formulae for total costs in row 6 is shown below.

6	Total costs	=SUM(B2..B5)	=SUM(C2..C5)	=SUM(D2..D5)	=SUM(E2..E5)	=SUM(F2..F5)	=SUM(G2..G5)

Spreadsheets

Some types of numerical data can be presented effectively using a SPREADSHEET. A spreadsheet allows the user to enter, store and present data in a grid on a computer screen. Just as a word processor is able to manipulate text, spreadsheets can do the same with numerical data. The grid is made up of a number of 'cells' or blank boxes. These cells are arranged in rows (information across the spreadsheet) and columns (information down the spreadsheet). Each blank cell is able to carry information which will fall into one of three categories.

● Numerical data - these are the numbers entered by the user which will be manipulated by the program.

● Text - this refers to the words used in the spreadsheet, often headings.

● Formulae - these are the instructions given by the user which tell the computer to manipulate the numerical data, for example, add a column of entries to give a total.

An example of a spreadsheet is illustrated in Table 9.10.

It contains data relating to a firm's production costs. Each column (from B to G) shows the costs of various items each month. Each row shows particular costs over the entire period. For example, row 2 shows the labour costs each month. Row 6 shows the total cost each month. The total cost is automatically calculated by the program.

In this case the formula for cell B6 would be B2 + B3 + B4 + B5 or = SUM (B2..B5). If the business changed any of the entries, the totals in row 6 would change automatically.

Some spreadsheets are much larger than the screen itself with up to 250 columns and 8,000 rows. The screen can only show part of the spreadsheet. Scrolling is used to solve this problem. This enables the user to scan over the entire spreadsheet until the section they need is shown on the screen. The advantages of spreadsheets are listed below.

● Numerical data is recorded and shown in a clear and ordered way.

● Editing allows figures, text and formulae to be changed easily to correct mistakes or make changes in the data.

● It is easy to copy an entry or series of entries from one part of the spreadsheet to another. This is particularly useful when one figure has to be entered at the same point in every column.

● The user can add, subtract, multiply and divide the figures entered on the spreadsheet.

● A spreadsheet can calculate the effect of entry changes easily. This is sometimes referred to as the 'what if' facility, eg what would happen to cell X (total costs) if the entry in cell A (labour costs) increased by 10 per cent? The answer can be found very quickly.

● Some spreadsheet programs allow graphs and diagrams to be drawn from figures in the spreadsheet.

One problem with spreadsheets is in printing the results. Some simple spreadsheets will tend to print everything being used. This can be time consuming and wasteful. Other programs allow the user to print specific rows, columns or cells. Some spreadsheets permit the sheet to be printed sideways to allow for a wide sheet to be printed. A further complication is what should be printed out for some of the cells, eg for a particular cell-should it be the result of a formula or the formula itself?

Databases

A DATABASE is really an electronic filing system. It allows a great deal of data to be stored. Every business which uses computers will compile and use databases. The information is set up so that it can be updated and recalled when needed. Table 9.11 shows part of a database of a finance company which gives details about their clients. The collection of common data is called a file. A file consists of a set of related records. In the database pictured in Table 9.11 all the information on Jane Brown, for example, is a record. The information on each record is listed under headings known as fields, eg name, address, age, occupation, income each year. A good database will have the the following facilities.

● 'User-definable' record format, allowing the user to enter any chosen field on the record.

● File searching facility for finding specified information from a file, eg identifying all clients with an income over £24,000 in the above file. It is usually possible to search on more than one criterion, eg all females with an income over £24,000.

● File sorting facility for rearranging data in another order, eg arranging the file in Table 9.11 in ascending order of income.

● Calculations on fields within records for inclusion in reports.

In the world of business and commerce there is actually a market for information held on databases. It is possible to buy banks of information from market researchers who have compiled databases over the years. Names and addresses of potential customers would be information well worth purchasing if it were legally available. The storage of personal data on computer is subject to the Data Protection Act (☞ unit 98). Any company or institution wishing to store personal data on a computer system must register with the Data Protection Office. Individuals have a right under the Act to request details of information held on them.

Key terms

Bar chart - a chart where numerical information is represented by blocks or bars.

Component bar chart - a chart where each bar is divided into a number of sections to illustrate the components of a total.

Cumulative frequency - the total frequency up to a particular item or class boundary.

Data - a collection of information.

Database - an organised collection of data stored electronically with instant access, searching and sorting facilities.

Histogram - a chart which measures continuous data on the horizontal axis and class frequencies on the vertical axis.

Line graph - a line which shows the relationship between two variables.

Lorenz curve - a type of cumulative frequency curve which shows the disparity between equal distribution and actual distribution.

Pictograph or pictogram - a chart where numerical data is represented by pictorial symbols.

Pie chart - a chart which consists of a circle where the data components are represented by the segments.

Spreadsheet - a method of storing data in cells in such a way that a change in one of the entries will automatically change any appropriate totals.

Table 9.11 *An extract from a simple database*

Surname	First name	Address	Town	Age	Occupation	Income p.a
Adams	John	14 Stanley St	Bristol	39	Bricklayer	£15,000
Appaswamy	Krishen	2 Virginia St	Cardiff	23	Welder	£25,000
Atkins	Robert	25 Liverpool Rd	Cardiff	42	Teacher	£21,000
Biddle	Ron	34 Bedford Rd	Bath	58	Civil servant	£40,000
Brown	Jane	111 Bold St	Newport	25	Solicitor	£22,000

Summary

1. Why is it important for a business to present data clearly, accurately and attractively?
2. What are the main advantages of using bar charts?
3. What is the main disadvantage of using pictographs?
4. State 3 types of data that component bar charts can be used to illustrate.
5. What is the difference between a histogram and a bar chart?
6. Why are pie charts a popular method of data presentation?
7. What is the main disadvantage of using tables to present data?
8. State 2 ways in which bias may be shown when presenting data.
9. State the 3 types of information which a cell in a spreadsheet can carry.
10. What are the main advantages of spreadsheets?
11. What are the advantages of databases for firms?

Case study

Zeneca

Zeneca is a large UK pharmaceuticals company. It researches, develops and manufactures medicines for six therapeutic areas - cancer, cardiovascular and metabolism, central nervous system, infection, respiratory, and arthritis and bone diseases. It also has interests in agrochemicals and a range of products such as leather coatings, colours, resins and biocides. Figure 9.16 shows a range of data from Zeneca's 1998 Annual Report and Accounts.

(a) **A company's Annual Report and Accounts often shows sales turnover over the last 5 years. Suggest how this may be presented.**

(b) **(i) Identify the methods that have been chosen to present each type of data in Figure 9.16.**
   (ii) For each piece of data, explain why that method of presentation may have been chosen.

(c) **Write a short introduction to the company's Annual Report and Accounts describing the progress of the business over the period 1995-98.**

(d) **A chemicals company has had a poor trading year. In its presentation at the AGM it hopes to present data showing the company's performance in the best possible light.**
   (i) Suggest how it might do this.
   (ii) Comment on the possible problems it might face as a result of its action in future.

Figure 9.16 *Data for Zeneca*
Source: adapted from Zeneca, *Annual Report and Accounts*, 1998.

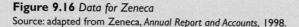

Capital expenditure £m

467
64
379
41 61
283 57
17 140 141
51
91 201
141
124

95 96 97

- Pharmaceuticals
- Agrochemicals (including Seeds)
- Specialties
- Other

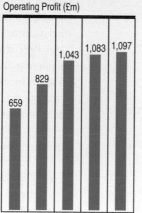

Operating Profit (£m)

659 829 1,043 1,083 1,097

94 95 96 97 98

Operating profit by geographical area including exports

Asia, Africa & Australasia
£54m (5%)

United Kingdom
£417m (38%)

The Americas
£489m (45%)

Continental Europe
£137m (12%)

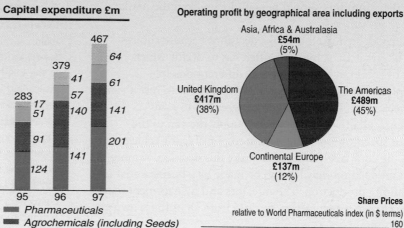

Share Prices
relative to World Pharmaceuticals index (in $ terms)

160
140
120
100
80
60

1993 94 95 96 97 98

Shareholders percenatge analysis at 31 December 1998 of issued share capital.

No. of shares	1998	1997
1 - 250	1.2	1.2
251 - 500	2.0	2.1
501 - 1,000	2.9	3.1
1,001 - 5,000	4.4	4.8
5,001 - 10,000	0.6	0.7
10,001 - 50,000	2.4	2.6
50,001 - 1,000,000	21.2	24.2
over 1,000,000	65.3	61.3
Issued share capital	100.0	100.0

Why do businesses make decisions?

Businesses are DECISION MAKING units. Making the 'right' decisions should allow a business to achieve its objectives (☞ unit 4). Some of the decisions faced by a business might include:

● how much output to produce of different products in a week or a month;
● who should be promoted from the shop floor to a supervisory level;
● whether the price of a product should be raised;
● how the construction of a new warehouse should be financed;
● what should be the design of a new company logo;
● which supplier should be used to provide components;
● whether a product should be withdrawn from the market; and many others.

Businesses are forced to make decisions because choices nearly always exist. A business often has to decide which course of action to take from many different possible alternatives. For example, a company that needs to hire a van for a week might have to choose between 10-15 local companies, all of which are able to supply the van to the required specifications. The person responsible for vehicle hire in the company will need to make this decision. A more important decision may have to be made by a business that is rationalising production. The directors and management may need to choose which factory to close from all of those owned by the business.

Decision making is also necessary to solve problems in a business. For example, if the workforce goes on strike the management may have to decide on an appropriate course of action. A business may also have to take decisions to solve problems such as lengthy queues which develop when consumers are buying goods or possible delays which may take place in the construction of a new factory.

All decisions involve some risk. Decisions where the outcome is unpredictable, where many factors can affect success or which affect a large part of a firm's operations for a long period are most risky. A business may be able to minimise the risk by collecting accurate and comprehensive data and by using decision making models. These are dealt with later in this unit.

Types of decision

It is possible to classify the decisions made by businesses in different ways.

Programmed decisions This idea was put forward by H.A.Simon in his 1965 book *The New Science of Management*

Decisions. These are repetitive decisions. A set routine for making the decisions will have been established. For example, a supermarket branch manager may have to prepare a rota every week. This will involve decisions about which staff should be on duty during various shifts. The decisions are repetitive (carried out weekly). Also, a procedure is likely to have been developed which specifies exactly how decisions should be made. There may be formal rules which control decisions, such as the minimum number of staff stacking shelves at any one time. The rules will have been developed and improved over time. The decisions may even be carried out on a computer. For these reasons the decisions have become programmed.

Competition between the main supermarkets in the UK has intensified in recent years. One aspect of this growing rivalry has been the introduction of loyalty cards. Tesco was one of the first major chains to introduce such a scheme in 1994/5. It launched the Tesco Clubcard, which rewarded customers with 'points' in relation to the value of their expenditure in the stores. Customers receive money off coupons when they accumulate a certain number of points. Safeway also introduced a similar promotion soon after. Sainsbury's initially made the decision not to introduce a version of its own. However, in June 1996 it launched the Sainsbury's Reward Card, offering almost identical benefits to customers as those of its competitors.

In 1997 the major supermarkets expanded their services by offering savings accounts similar to those of banks and other financial institutions. Services provided included instant access via telephone or cash machines. Some supermarkets also provided a visa 'credit' card service.

(a) State 2 possible reasons why:
   (i)   Tesco decided to launch its Clubcard;
   (ii)   Sainsbury's decided not to launch a loyalty card to begin with.
(b) Suggest other possible courses of action that Sainsbury's could have taken in response to Tesco launching a loyalty card.
(c) What risk might Sainsbury's have taken in not launching its own loyalty card at the time of the Tesco launch?

Non-programmed decisions Simon argued that these are novel or unstructured decisions. For example, a business may be forced to move its premises because its current location is subject to a compulsory purchase order by a local authority. This is an unusual problem and it is unlikely that a decision making procedure will have been developed to resolve the problem. A decision like this will also have a long lasting effect on the organisation.

In practice decisions will not fall neatly into the two categories above. Many decisions will be partly programmed and partly non-programmed. For example, managers may develop a decision making structure to apply to unforeseen events. Decisions in a business are also likely to be either strategic, tactical or operational.

Strategic decisions STRATEGIC DECISIONS concern the general direction and overall policy of a business. They are far reaching and can influence the performance of the organisation. They will also be **long term** decisions, which means that they will affect the business for a period of more than one year. Strategic decisions tend to have a high risk because the outcome of the decision is likely to be unknown.

Examples of strategic decisions might include:
- the offering of instant access savings accounts by Tesco in 1997;
- the merger of publishers Reed Elsevier and Wolters Kluwer in 1997 to form the world's largest supplier of technical and professional information;
- the purchase by National Power (the UK electricity generator) of a 48 per cent stake in Elecktarny Opatovic (a Czech Republic electricity company based in Prague) in 1997, making it the largest shareholder;
- the decision of the Nationwide Building Society to remain a mutual in 1998.

These decisions are all likely to have long term effects on the businesses concerned. They often involve moving into new areas which will require new resources, new procedures and retraining. Whether or not the decisions were the 'right' ones may not be known for several years because it will take time to evaluate their effect on the businesses involved.

Tactical decisions TACTICAL DECISIONS tend to be medium term decisions which are less far reaching than strategic decisions. They are tactical because they are calculated and because their outcome is more predictable. In a business, tactical decisions may be used to implement strategic decisions. For example, as a result of Tesco's strategic decision to offer financial services such as savings accounts, some tactical decisions might have been:
- what interest rate should be offered;
- what methods of promotion should be used;
- what staff should be involved in the operation of the new service;

- what should be the size of the maximum and minimum customer deposit.

Operational decisions OPERATIONAL DECISIONS are lower level decisions, sometimes called administrative decisions. They will be short term and carry little risk. Such decisions can normally be taken fairly quickly. They require much less thought and evaluation than strategic and tactical decisions. Every day a business makes a large number of operational decisions.

Question 2

In October 1998, Kingfisher, the owner of B&Q, announced that it would invest £750 million into B&Q Warehouse. B&Q Warehouse is a subsidiary of the market-leading B&Q DIY chain. Kingfisher said that it had decided to increase the number of B&Q Warehouse stores from 30 to 125 by 2003. Around 20,000 new jobs were expected to be created.

Source: adapted from *The Independent*, 28.10.1998.

Table 10.1 *DIY spending, 1992-97*

Current year	£m	Index
1992	8,525	121
1993	9,065	129
1994	9,504	135
1995	9,811	140
1996	10,575	150
1997	11,678	166

Index: 1988 = 100

Source: adapted from ONS, Verdict Analysis.

(a) Suggest two possible examples of operational decisions that a store assistant working in a B&Q Warehouse store might make.
(b) Explain why Kingfisher's decision in the above article might be strategic.
(c) How might the information shown in the table have influenced Kingfisher's decision?
(d) Comment on the likely risk involved in the decision made by Kingfisher.

Examples might include:

● how many checkouts to have open in a retail outlet at a particular time of day;
● how much time should be allocated to a task in a factory;
● how to stagger breaks for sales staff in a department store so that a minimum number are always on the shop floor;
● when to order new invoices for an office and what quantity to order.

Who makes decisions?

Decisions are made by all staff in a business. However, responsibility for the decision will vary according to the employee's position in the hierarchical structure. A senior manager can delegate decision making powers to a junior manager, but will retain ultimate responsibility for decision making. Also, the size of the company will influence who makes decisions. For example, a sole trader with no employees will make all the decisions. As businesses grow and more staff are employed, decision making is likely to be delegated.

Strategic decisions These are likely to be made by the owners of the business. Such decisions are so important and far reaching that only the owners can be responsible for their outcome. However, in some public limited companies these decisions will be made by the board of directors. Directors are appointed to run plcs in the interests of the owners, the shareholders, who can number thousands. Some important strategic decisions may require the shareholders' consent. For example, shareholders at Hanson, the conglomerate business, were consulted before the group was demerged into four smaller companies in 1996.

Tactical decisions Business managers are likely to make tactical decisions. Such decisions are often required to implement the strategic decisions made by the owners or the senior management team. Important tactical decisions, such as the promotion campaign for a new product, tend to be made by those near the top of the business hierarchy. Less important tactical decisions will often be made by middle or junior managers.

Operational decisions Nearly all employees will be involved in operational decisions. Lower level decisions, such as what task should office staff at an NHS trust hospital perform, are constantly taken by all staff in the business. Sometimes managers may be consulted by their subordinates if they need guidance or approval for a decision.

It is argued that delegating decisions to those further down the hierarchy can help motivation. This empowerment (☞ unit 73) of employees can also help to solve problems quickly without the need to consult managers. In the 1990s a number of UK businesses have handed decision making to factory, team or group workers, giving

Question 3

In 1996, Stakis the leisure group, recognised that its casino division was not performing in line with expectations. As a result a number of decisions were made to help overcome trading difficulties. It was decided to:

● sell the Barracuda Casino in London for £1.8 million;
● open new concept casinos which are bigger, much more highly visible and with good parking;
● to focus more on customer service and the quality of their facilities in order to position the casino business firmly in the night time leisure market.

The decisions meant a number of changes in the organisation. For example, around 300 branch managers were put through an intensive training programme placing greater emphasis on staff management, development of team work and customer care. The reception areas in casinos were made to look more friendly and a lot more attention is being paid to the gaming environment. Demonstration tables were introduced in branches to increase members' understanding of the games available.

Source: adapted from Stakis, *Annual Report & Accounts*, 1997.

Figure 10.1 *Members and attendances at Stakis casinos, 1997*

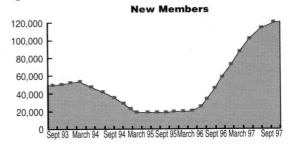

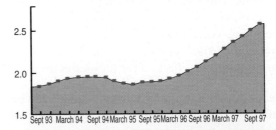

(a) Suggest two examples of decisions that a branch manager may take at a casino.
(b) Who is likely to have made the decisions listed in the article? Explain your answer.
(c) How might the management training programmes have affected the quality of decision making in Stakis casinos?
(d) What evidence is there to suggest that the decisions made may have been the right ones?

them the authority to identify and solve problems before or as they occur. This has led to improvements in both efficiency and quality (☞ unit 96). The removal of layers of management has also improved decision making in some cases by reducing the number of levels in the chain of command, although this can lead to problems if not supported by retraining and changes in organisational culture (☞ unit 14).

The decision making process

A business makes decisions in order to achieve objectives (☞ unit 4). For example, it might decide to launch a new product in order to diversify. Decisions are made at all levels in a business and it is useful to have a flexible and logical process which can be followed by all involved. Figure 10.2 shows the stages in the decision making process.

Identifying objectives The first stage in the process is to identify the objective a business wants to achieve (☞ unit 4). The objective might be a corporate objective, such as growth or survival in a poor trading period. These decisions are likely to be complex and might be taken by the board of directors. For lower level objectives, such as filling a part time vacancy, decisions may be taken by junior managers. A business's objectives might be different at different stages in its growth. Business activities controlled by local government may have different objectives from public limited companies. The business also needs to develop criteria to measure whether it has achieved its objectives. Quite often the objective is to solve a problem. This might be planning for an uncertain future or dealing with a poor level of profitability.

Collecting information and ideas People need information and ideas to make decisions. The amount and nature of the information needed will depend on the decision. For example, the decision whether or not to launch a new product might require some information about possible sales levels and consumer reactions, costs of production and reactions of competitors. It could take several months to collect all this information. Other decisions could perhaps be made from information which the business already has. A decision whether or not to dismiss an employee might be made on the basis of information from the personnel department.

Where does the business get its ideas? It might set up a working party to collect information and ideas from within the firm. The working party would then produce a report or make a presentation to the decision makers. Alternatively, individuals or departments might submit ideas and information. Another way of obtaining information and ideas is to hold discussions amongst staff in the firm.

Analysing information and ideas The next stage in the process is to analyse information to look for alternative courses of action. Possible courses of action may be based on

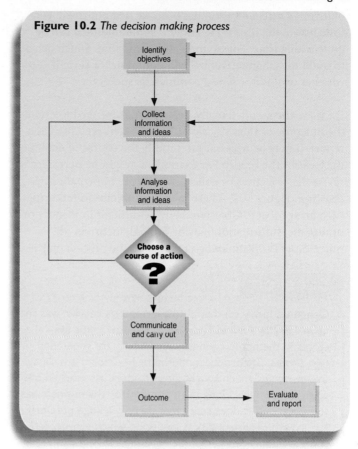

Figure 10.2 *The decision making process*

Identify objectives → Collect information and ideas → Analyse information and ideas → Choose a course of action **?** → Communicate and carry out → Outcome → Evaluate and report

previous ideas or completely new ideas. The aim is to identify which course of action will best achieve the business's objective or solve the problem. It may be possible to test the alternatives before the one that is chosen is carried out.

Making a decision Next the decision has to be made. This is the most important stage in the process. Decision makers have to commit themselves to one course of action. It is difficult to change the decision, so getting it right is vital. For example, once production begins following the decision to launch a new product, it is difficult for the firm to change its mind. If the product does not sell, this can lead to a loss of money. Some decisions can be reversed. For example, if the owner of a shop decides to close on Tuesday afternoons, but then finds that the loss of sales is intolerable, the owner can easily reopen again.

Sometimes the decision makers feel that they cannot reach a decision. They may have to obtain more information and complete the previous two stages in the process again.

Communication Once a decision has been made, personnel are informed and the decision is carried out. Quite often the people making the decisions are not those that carry them out. Instructions may be passed by the decision makers to someone else, probably a manager, explaining what action should be taken. For example, if the directors decide to begin selling their products in a new country, instructions must be sent to the marketing manager. In smaller firms decision makers are more likely to carry out their own decisions.

Outcome Once a decision has been carried out it will take time before the results are known. Sometimes this can be quite a long time. For example, the companies which decided to build the Channel Tunnel will not know for several years whether or not it will be a commercial success.

Evaluate the results Finally, decision makers need to evaluate the outcome of their decisions. This is often presented as a report. It may be necessary to modify the course of action on the basis of the report. For example, it might be necessary to revise the objectives or collect some more information, as shown in Figure 10.2. There may be problems in following such an approach. Objectives may be difficult to identify or unrealistic. Information may be limited, incorrect or misleading. People making decisions in the process may have different views and this may lead to differences of opinion about what is the best course of action, for example.

Decision making models

The decision making process outlined in the previous section is an example of a **normative model**. A normative model describes how decisions should be made, rather than how they are made. It is a subjective proposal of how, ideally, a decision should be made. A normative model provides a structured sequence of activities by which a business can identify and correct problems. The ability of the process to deliver the best decision depends on the activities in the process and the order in which they are carried out.

Positive models, however, deal with objective or value free explanations about how decisions are made. They attempt to show what is, rather than what should be. Positive models attempt to solve some of the problems of normative decision making explained earlier. They are created using a scientific method in the same way that a scientist might. A 'theory' is put forward, evidence is gathered to support or refute (disprove) it and the theory is then accepted, changed or refuted.

The use of 'positive' or 'scientific' MODELS or SIMULATIONS is widespread in business. Models are replicas or copies of problem areas in business. They are theories, laws or equations, stating things about a problem and helping in our understanding of it. There is a number of common features to models.

● They reflect the key characteristics or behaviour of an area of concern.
● They tend to be simplified versions of areas of concern.
● They simulate the actions and processes that operate in the problem area.
● They provide an aid to problem solving or decision making.
● Models often make use of formulae to express concepts. Some models can be carried out using computer software. This allows decisions to be made quickly and many variables affecting decisions to be included.

Management science and operations research are areas which often make use of decision making models. For example, linear programming (☞ unit 103) provides a model which allows decision makers to determine optimal solutions to a wide range of business problems. It has been used to make decisions such as:

● how to minimise waste in production;
● how to allocate resources between two competing tasks;
● how to find the least cost mix of ingredients for a product.
Another example in the area of marketing is the use of Ansoff's Matrix (☞ unit 48). This model is used to help consider the relationship between the strategic direction of the business and its marketing strategy.

A simulation involves trying to mimic what might happen in reality. It allows a business to test ideas and make decisions

Question 4

Opaque, a highly successful soft furnishings retailer, was set up in 1997 by Andrea Thompson. She now owns five stores in the home counties, all of which are generating high profits. The products offered by her stores are classy, expensive and much sought after. Andrea has reached the stage now where a long term strategy for the business has to be clarified. It does seem that there is a huge potential for growth. Andrea's task is to decide which growth path she should take. Three courses of action seem possible:

● borrow £4 million from a bank and retain full control as 10 new shops are opened each year for the next five years;
● float the company on the stock market (this would raise about £16 million) and fund the growth from the proceeds;
● set up a franchising operation which would allow much more rapid growth (around 15 new shops each year).

Figure 10.3 *Franchising turnover*

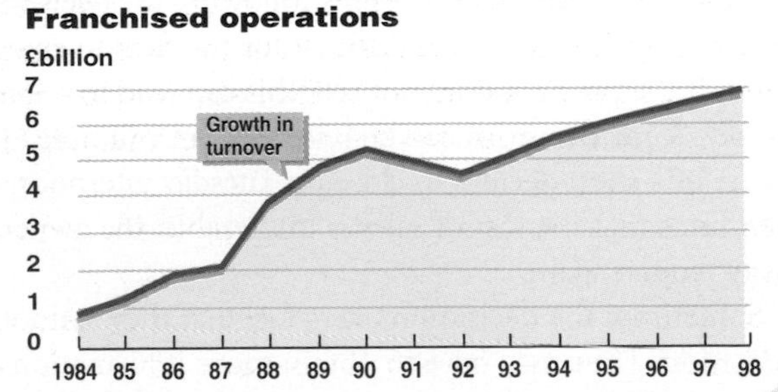

Franchised operations

Source: adapted from British Franchise Association.

(a) What is the objective in the decision faced by Andrea Thompson?
(b) How might the information in Figure 10.3 be helpful in making the decision?
(c) Suggest 3 other pieces of information which might be helpful in making the decision.
(d) What problems may Andrea face when using a decision making process in Figure 10.2 to decide on a suitable course of action?

Question 5

A new approach to corporate portfolio models was developed by W.Chan Kim from the Boston Consulting Group and Renee Mauborgne, President of ITM Research. They divided companies into 3 categories. Settlers are businesses that aim for incremental or small improvements. Migrators are businesses that aim to improve value compared of that of competitors. Pioneers are businesses that innovate. They researched 100 new business launches and found that 86 per cent were settlers, generating 39 per cent of all new business launch profit. The other 14 per cent were pioneers, creating new markets or recreating existing ones. They, however, generated 61 per cent of profits. Examples of Pioneers are the Dyson vacuum cleaner, the Sony Walkman and Swatch watches. The model suggests that businesses should shift the portfolio of products in future from settlers to pioneers as shown in Figure 10.4. This is the path to profitable growth. Procter & Gamble is an example of a company using this approach. It aims to double turnover over the next 10 years by creating and recreating markets.

Source: adapted from the *Financial Times*, 11.8.1998.

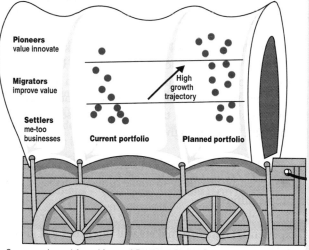

Figure 10.4

The Pioneer-Migrator-Settler map
Where does your portfolio of businesses stand today and where will it stand tomorrow?

Source: adapted from Harvard Business Review.

(a) Using examples, explain why the Pioneer-Migrator-Settler theory might be an example of a positive model.

(b) Suggest how a business like Procter & Gamble could use the model in future.

without bearing the consequences of 'real action' if things go wrong. Imagine a business has a problem. A simulation can be carried out several times, quickly and cheaply, in order to test alternative decisions. There is no risk and resources are not used up. Simulations are often used to deal with problems such as queues in business (☞ unit 104).

Constraints on decision making

Businesses cannot make decisions with complete freedom. In many situations there are factors which hinder, limit or restrict particular courses of action. These CONSTRAINTS may make the decision easier because they eliminate some courses of action. For example, a business may require an agency to carry out market research on its behalf. It may allocate a budget of £5,000 to pay for the research and invite tenders for the work. The tenders received could be:

- Sefton Research Associates - £4,700;
- Aston MR Ltd - £6,100;
- Salford Marketing - £4,900;
- Carlton Marketing - £5,400.

The business can only afford to pay the tenders offered by two of the agencies. Thus its choice is reduced and the decision simplified by its financial constraint. Note, however, that the best quality service may be provided by Aston MR Ltd and so the financial constraint has denied the business using a better quality service.

Internal constraints These may result from the policy of the business itself.

- Availability of finance. Decision makers are often prevented from choosing certain courses of action because the business cannot afford them.
- Existing company policy. For example, to control the wage bill, a firm's policy may be to restrict overtime to a maximum of 10 hours per week. The production manager may want to offer workers more overtime to reach a production target. However, she is not able to do so because of the firm's overtime policy.
- People's behaviour. Decisions may be limited by people's ability. For example, a manual worker is unlikely to be able to run a department if the manager is absent. People are also limited by their attitudes. For example, a company may wish to move three people into one office who work in seperate offices at the moment, but this could meet with resistance.

External constraints These are limits from outside and are usually beyond the control the control of the business.

- Government and EU legislation. Businesses must operate within the law. For example, a manager may require a driver to deliver some goods urgently to a customer 600 miles away, which would require a 17 hour drive. The law restricts the amount of time a person can drive certain commercial vehicles to about 10 hours per day.
- Competitors' behaviour. Say a firm is deciding to introduce a new product. If Mars is enjoying some success with a new product Cadbury's might copy Mars and decide to launch its own version of the product. Because competition has become greater in recent years, this constraint has affected more firms.

Case study

Camellias

Camellias is a UK based, up-market ladies fashion chainstore. It is a large, established business with around 200 high street shops. It has enjoyed a steady growth in sales and profits in recent years. The success of the business has resulted largely from the quality of the after sales service that the stores have to offer to their customers. They offer:

● a low price fitting and adjustment service;
● an exchange facility for mistaken purchases;
● high class dry cleaning.

Many of the customers are regulars and have shopped there for years. The stores also face little competition in the areas in which they operate. Another chainstore, Frock Shop, does offer a similar service in the UK, but operates in different regions to Camellias. As yet there is no high street in which both shops compete.

The board of directors is considering the purchase of 40 high street shops for £4 million from a regional shoe shop that has just ceased trading. Camellias is poorly represented in the region where the shops are situated, but Frock Shop has a number of retail outlets in the area. So far the directors of Camellias have deliberately avoided opening shops in streets where Frock Shop has stores. In addition, Frock Shop has never directly competed in streets where Camellias has operated. The average income per head of the population in the area where the shops are located is relatively high, which is one reason why Frock Shop already has stores in the area.

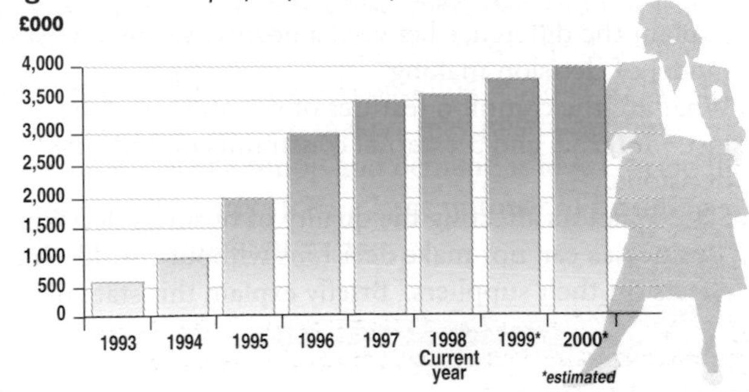

The board realises the importance of the decision to buy the shops. To help it make the 'correct' choice it is using what it considers to be a structured and logical decision making process. It does not, however, make use of decision making models.

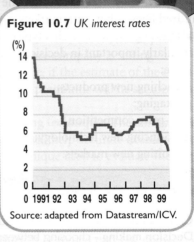

One of the directors involved in the decision is new to the company. She has an excellent record as a marketing director and was recruited with the overwhelming support of the company owners. They were impressed with her ideas on merchandising and also her commitment to rapid growth. This fits in with their view of the company's position over the next few years.

It is likely that Camellias will need to borrow some funds to finance the purchase of the 40 high street shops. However, the bank has told the directors that they must reach a decision by the end of the month otherwise finance will no longer be available.

Figure 10.7 UK interest rates

(%)

Source: adapted from Datastream/ICV.

Figure 10.5 Turnover of Camillias

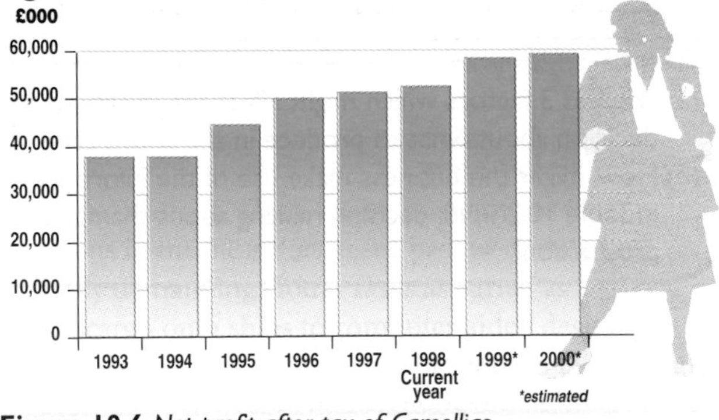

£000

Figure 10.6 Net profit after tax of Camellias

£000

(a) Explain why the decision facing Camellias might be regarded as a strategic decision.
(b) What might be the objectives of Camellias when making its decision?
(c) Identify possible: (i) external; and (ii) internal constraints that there might be on the decision facing Camellias.
(d) (i) What information in the case study might be helpful to the business in making its decision?
(ii) Explain how each piece of information might influence the business's decision.
(e) (i) Discuss the problems that might exist in the decision making process.
(ii) Evaluate the possible effects of these problems on the business's decision.
(f) What decision do you think Camellias might come to? Justify your answer.

11 Decision Trees

Making decisions

Every day, businesses make decisions (☞ unit 10). Most, if not all, involve some risk. This could be because the business has limited information on which to base the decision. Furthermore, the outcome of the decision may be uncertain. Launching a new product in a market abroad can be risky because a firm may not have experience of selling in that market. It may also be unsure about how consumers will react.

When faced with a number of different decisions a business will want to choose the course of action which gives the most return. What if a printing company had to decide whether to invest £750,000 in a new printing press now or wait a few years? If it bought now and a more efficient machine became available next year then it may have been more profitable to wait. Alternatively, if it waits it may find the old machine has problems and costs increase.

When the outcome is uncertain, decision trees can be used to help a business reach a decision which could minimise risk and gain the greatest return.

What are decision trees?

A DECISION TREE is a method of tracing the alternative outcomes of any decision. The likely results can then be compared so that the business can find the most profitable alternative. For example, a business may be faced with two alternatives - to launch a new product in Europe or in the USA. A decision tree may show that launching a new product in Europe would give £5 million profit, whereas launching in the USA would only give a profit of £1 million.

It is argued by some that decision making is more effective if a **quantitative approach** is taken. This is where information on which decisions are based, and the outcomes of decisions, are expressed as numbers. In a decision tree, numerical values are given to such information. The decision tree also provides a pictorial approach to decision making because a diagram is used which resembles the branches of a tree. The diagram maps out different courses of action, possible outcomes of decisions and points where decisions have to be made. Calculations based on the decision tree can be used to determine the 'best' likely outcome for the business and hence the most suitable decision.

Features of decision trees

Decision trees have a number of features. These can be seen in Figure 11.1 which shows the decision tree for a business that has to decide whether to launch a new advertising campaign or retain an old one.

Decision points Points where decisions have to be made in a decision tree are represented by squares and are called decision points. The decision maker has to choose between certain courses of action. In this example, the decision is whether to launch a new campaign or retain the old one.

Outcomes Points where there are different possible outcomes in a decision tree are represented by circles and are called chance nodes. At these **chance nodes** it can be shown that a particular course of action might result in a number of outcomes. In this example, at 'B' there is a chance of failure or success of the new campaign.

Probability or chance The **likelihood** of possible outcomes happening is represented by probabilities in decision trees. The chance of a particular outcome occurring is given a value. If the outcome is certain then the probability is 1. Alternatively, if there is no chance at all of a particular outcome occurring, the probability will be 0. In practice the value will lie between 0 and 1. In Figure 11.1, at 'B' the chance of success for the new campaign is 0.2 and the chance of failure is 0.8.

It is possible to estimate the probability of events occurring provided information about these events can be found. There are two sources of information which can be used to help estimate probabilities. One source is historic **backdata** (☞ unit 51). For example, if a business has opened 10 new stores in recent years, and 9 of them have been successful, it might be reasonable to assume that the chances of another new store being successful is 9/10 or 0.9. Another source is research data. For example, a business might carry out marketing research to find out how customers would react to a new product design. 80 per cent of people surveyed may like the product and 20 per cent may dislike it.

Expected values This is the financial outcome of a decision. It is based on the predicted profit or loss of an outcome and the

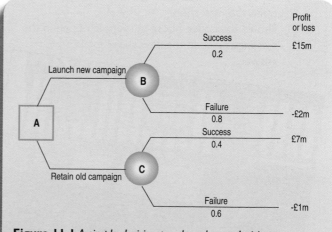

Figure 11.1 *A simple decision tree based on a decision whether to retain an existing advertising campaign or begin a new one*

probability of that outcome occurring. The profit or loss of any decision is shown on the right hand side of Figure 11.1. For example, if the launch of a new campaign is a success, a £15 million profit is expected. If it fails a loss of £2 million is expected.

Question 1

'Coffee houses' are often found in market towns and open during the daytime. Typically they sell coffee, tea, soft drinks. Licensed houses may sell wine. Some offer lunch-type meals such as jacket potatoes, baguettes and speciality meals such as fried brie wedges with salad. It has been suggested that they open later in the evening, develop their existing range of foods and offer restaurant-type meals.

(a) The chances of success and failure and the expected profit or loss of this decision for five coffee houses in different towns are shown below. Calculate the expected values.

	Probability of success	Profit or loss	Probability of failure	Profit or loss
(i) Beverley	0.2	£6,000	0.8	-£1,000
(ii) Norwich	0.5	£8,000	0.5	-£2,000
(iii) Salisbury	0.3	£3,000	0.7	-£1,000
(iv) Chorley	0.6	£2,000	0.4	-£500
(v) Preston	0.7	£3,000	0.3	-£1,500

(b) The coffee house in Norwich has to choose between opening later and opening another shop as a means of expanding. The probability of success and failure and the profit or loss of opening the new shop are:

Probability of success	Profit or loss	Probability of failure	Profit or loss
0.2	£30,000	0.8	-£4,000

(i) Calculate the expected value of the decision to open the new shop.
(ii) Should the coffee house in Norwich open in the evenings or open the new shop? Explain your answer.

Calculating expected values

What should the firm decide? It has to work out the expected values of each decision, taking into account the expected profit or loss and the probabilities. So, for example, the expected value of a new campaign is:

$$\begin{array}{ccc} & \text{Success} & \text{Failure} \\ \text{Expected value} = & 0.2 \times £15m + 0.8 \times (-£2m) \\ & \text{(probability) (expected profit) (probability) (expected loss)} \\ = & £3m - £1.6m \\ = & 1.4m \end{array}$$

The expected value of retaining the current campaign is:

$$\begin{array}{ccc} & \text{Success} & \text{Failure} \\ \text{Expected value} = & 0.4 \times £7m + 0.6 \times (-£1m) \\ = & £2.8m - £0.6m \\ = & 2.2m \end{array}$$

Question 2

Colin Andrews is the owner of Slade farm near Spalding. He specialises in vegetable crops and allocates about 400 acres of land each year to the production of potatoes and swedes. He decides what crops to plant in October each year.

If Colin plants potatoes he estimates that the probability of a good crop is 0.3, which will generate £50,000 profit. The probability of an average crop is 0.3, which would result in £30,000 profit. The probability of a poor crop is 0.4, which would result in only £10,000 profit.

If swedes are planted, either a good crop or a bad crop will result. He estimates that the probability in each case is 0.5. A good crop will generate a profit of £40,000 and a poor crop only £10,000. Figure 11.2 is a decision tree which shows this information.

Figure 11.2 *The alternative courses of action faced by Colin Andrews*

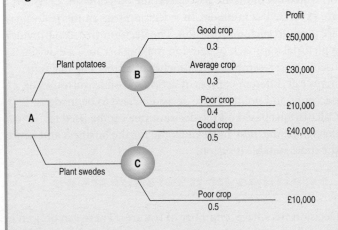

(a) What is happening at points B and C in the decision tree?
(b) Calculate the expected values of each course of action.
(c) On financial grounds, which course of action should Colin take?

From these figures the firm should continue with the existing campaign because the expected value is higher.

Numerous outcomes

It is possible to have more than two outcomes at a chance node. For example, at point 'B' in Figure 11.1 there might have been 3 outcomes:

● the probability of great success may be 0.2 with a profit of £15 million;
● the probability of average success may be 0.4 with a profit of £6 million;
● the probability of failure may be 0.4 with a loss of -£2 million.

The expected value is now:

$$= (0.2 \times £15 \text{ m}) + (0.4 \times £6 \text{ m}) + (0.4 \times -£2 \text{ m})$$
$$= £3 \text{ m} + £2.4 \text{ m} - £0.8 \text{ m}$$
$$= £4.6 \text{ m}$$

Decisions, outcomes and costs

In practice businesses face many alternative decisions and possible outcomes. Take a farmer who has inherited some land, but does not wish to use it with his existing farming business. There are three possible decisions that the farmer could make.

● Sell the land. The market is depressed and this will earn £0.6 million.
● Wait for one year and hope that the market price improves. A land agent has told the farmer that the

chance of an upturn in the market is 0.3, while the probabilities of it staying the same or worsening are 0.5 and 0.2 respectively. The likely proceeds from a sale in each of the circumstances are £1 million, £0.6 million and £0.5 million.

● Seek planning permission to develop the land. The legal and administration fees would be £0.5 million and the probability of being refused permission would be 0.8, which means the likelihood of obtaining permission is 0.2. If refused, the farmer would be left with the same set of circumstances described in the second option.

If planning permission is granted the farmer has to make a decision (at node E). If the farmer decides to sell, the probability of getting a good price, ie £10 million, is estimated to be 0.4, while the probability of getting a low price, ie £6 million, is 0.6. The farmer could also develop the land himself at a cost of £5 million. The probability of selling the developed land at a good price, ie £25 million, is estimated to be 0.3 while the likelihood of getting a low price, ie £10 million, is 0.7.

The information about probability and earnings is shown in Figure 11.3. What decision should the farmer make? The sale of the land immediately will earn £0.6 million.

The expected value of the second option, waiting a year, is:

$$\text{Expected value} = 0.3 \times £1\text{m} + 0.5 \times £0.6\text{m} + 0.2 \times £0.5\text{m}$$
$$= £0.3\text{m} + £0.3\text{m} + £0.1\text{m}$$
$$= £0.7\text{m}$$

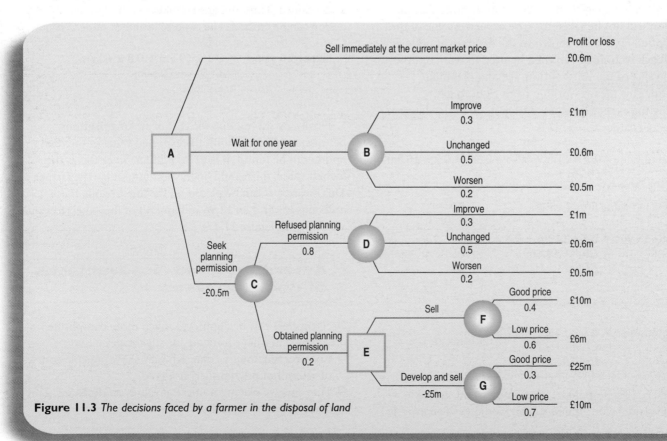

Figure 11.3 *The decisions faced by a farmer in the disposal of land*

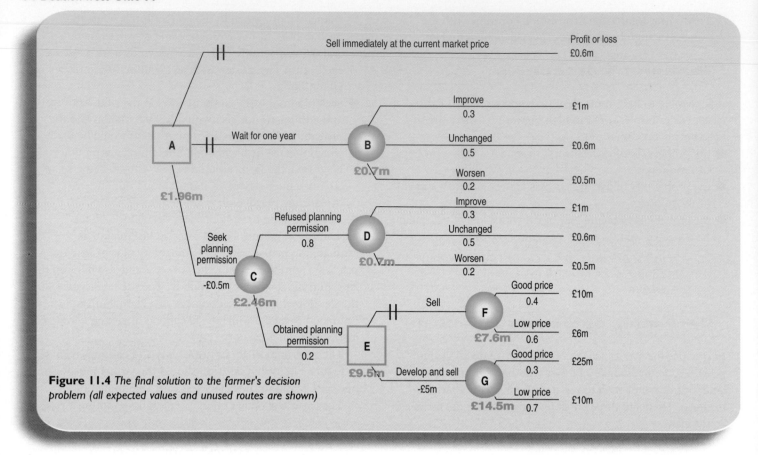

Figure 11.4 *The final solution to the farmer's decision problem (all expected values and unused routes are shown)*

Since this earns more than the first option, it would be a better choice. We could show this in Figure 11.4 by crossing the 'selling immediately' path with a //, indicating that the first option will not be taken up. The expected value of the second option (£0.7m) is shown in the diagram at node B.

A **rollback technique** can then be used to work out the expected value of the third option, seeking planning permission. This means working from right to left, calculating the expected values at each node in the diagram. The expected value at node D is:

Expected value = 0.3 × £1m + 0.5 × £0.6m + 0.2 × £0.5m
= £0.7m

The expected value at node F is:

Expected value = 0.4 × £10m + 0.6 × £6m
= £4m + £3.6m
= £7.6m

The expected value at node G is:

Expected value = 0.3 × £25m + 0.7 × £10m
= £7.5m + £7m
= £14.5m

At node E, a decision node, the farmer would choose to develop the land before selling it. This would yield an expected

return of £9.5 million (£14.5 - £5 million) which is higher than £7.6m, ie the expected return from selling the land undeveloped. Thus, in Figure 11.4 the path representing this option can be crossed. The expected value at node C is now:

Expected value = 0.2 × £9.5m + 0.8 × £0.7m
= £1.9m + £0.56m
= £2.46m

Finally, by subtracting the cost of seeking planning permission (£0.5 million), the expected value of the final option can be found. It is £1.96 million. Since this is the highest value, this would be the best option for the farmer. This means a // can be placed on the line to node B as £0.7 million is lower than £1.96 million. All of the expected values are shown in Figure 11.4.

Advantages and disadvantages of decision trees

Decision trees can be applied to much more complicated problems. They have some major advantages.
● Constructing the tree diagram may show possible courses of action not previously considered.
● They involve placing numerical values on decisions. This tends to improve results.

Question 3

The owner of a popular Torquay restaurant, The Sea Gull's Table, has been advised by a doctor to take a month's holiday for health reasons. As a result the owner is faced with a dilemma regarding the running of his business in his absence. There are three possible courses of action open to him.
- Shut the restaurant for one month and suffer the financial loss which is estimated to be £1,000.
- Place the business in the hands of an inexperienced relative who would receive a payment of £1,000. The probability of the relative securing a good profit, ie £4,000, in the owner's absence is 0.2. The probability of modest profit, ie £2,000, is 0.8.
- Hire a professional manager experienced in the restaurant trade at a cost of £4,000. The probability of the manager making a good profit, ie £5,000, is 0.9, while the probability of a more modest profit, ie £3,000, is 0.1.

This information is shown in a decision tree in Figure 11.5.

(a) Calculate the expected values of the three courses of action.
(b) Which course of action is the most desirable on financial grounds?
(c) What non-financial information might need to be considered in making this decision?
(d) How would your decision in (b) be affected if the amount of good profit made from hiring a professional manager were to rise from £5,000 to £8,000?

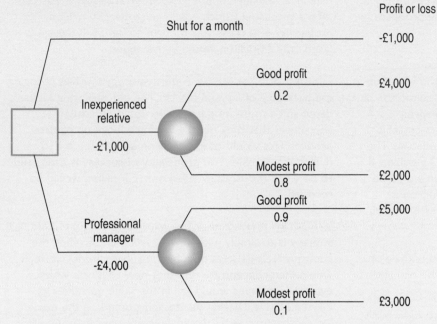

Profit or loss

Shut for a month — -£1,000

Inexperienced relative -£1,000

Good profit 0.2 — £4,000

Modest profit 0.8 — £2,000

Professional manager -£4,000

Good profit 0.9 — £5,000

Modest profit 0.1 — £3,000

11.5 *The alternative courses of action faced by the owner of The Sea Gull's Table*

- They force management to take account of the risks involved in decisions and help to separate important from unimportant risks.

The technique also has some limitations.
- The information which the technique 'throws out' is not exact. Much of it is based on probabilities which are often estimated.
- Decisions are not always concerned with quantities and probabilities. They often involve people and are influenced by legal constraints or people's opinions, for example. These factors cannot always be shown by numerical values.
- Time lags often occur in decision making. By the time a decision is finally made, some of the numerical information may be out of date.

- The process can be quite time consuming, using up valuable business resources.

Summary

1. Why are decision trees useful when a business has to make important decisions?
2. What is meant by a quantitative approach to decision making?
3. What is meant by probability in a decision tree?
4. What is the difference between chance nodes and decision nodes?
5. How is the expected value of a course of action calculated?
6. What are the advantages and disadvantages of using decision trees?
7. State 3 possible situations where a business might make use of a decision tree.

Key terms

Decision trees - a technique which shows all possible outcomes of a decision. The name comes from the similarity of the diagrams to the branches of trees.

Case study

Crystal Holdings plc

Crystal Holdings plc is a large national manufacturer of toiletries. It supplies a range of products such as soaps, shampoos, hair conditioners, shower gels and deodorants to large retailers and wholesalers.

One of its main brands of bathroom soap, Crystal Marble, which has sold well for a number of years, has seen annual sales start to fall recently. The marketing department has investigated how to deal with this. Four proposals have been put forward to deal with the problem. Three of the proposals are aimed at extending the 'life' of the product using extension strategies.

Export to the USA Crystal Holdings has often considered exporting some of its products to the USA, but was concerned that certain products were not suited to consumers' tastes. However, recently other European competitors have been breaking into US markets and this has opened up the possibility of exporting its toiletries. The launch of Crystal Marble is expected to cost £3.5 million. If the launch is successful an estimated £20 million would be generated. If the launch failed, only around £2 million is likely to be recouped. The probability of a successful launch is 0.5.

Modify the product The colour, fragrance and texture of Crystal Marble can be changed in many ways. The company

has identified two possible changes to the design of the product. An initial outlay of £2 million is needed for research and development. Design A would cost a further £5 million to develop. Design B would cost a further £12 million.

If Design A was eventually launched and was successful it would generate £50 million in revenue. The probability of success is estimated at 0.4. If it failed, a gain of only £10 million in revenue could be expected. If Design B was used then a successful launch would generate £90 million. The probability of success was thought to be 0.2. If Design B failed only £4 million would be recouped.

Change the packaging A third strategy involves changing the packaging of Crystal Marble. The old packaging looks dated and a more modern design could persuade consumers that they may be getting a more up to date product. This would cost £2 million and generate £10 million if successful. The probability of success is estimated to be 0.6. If the strategy failed only £3 million would be received.

Withdraw the brand after another two years One final strategy is to simply withdraw Crystal Marble when the company feels its sales no longer justify its manufacture. It would then concentrate on other new products which eventually it hopes would sell in the same quantities as Crystal Marble. Leaving the declining brand on the market for another two years would generate revenue of 6 million.

Figure 11.6 shows a decision tree containing all the information about possible alternative strategies.

Figure 11.6 *A decision tree to help Crystal Holdings plc decide which strategy to use for one of its key brands, Crystal Marble*

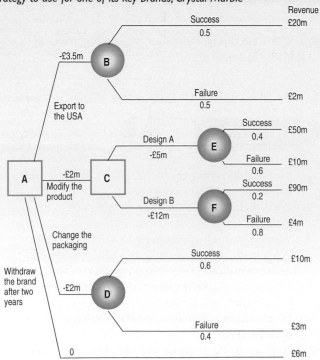

(a) **Suggest two advantages to Crystal Holdings of making decisions using decision trees.**

(b) **How might the probabilities used in this decision tree be estimated?**

(c) **Explain the significance of:**
  (i) **point C;**
  (ii) **node B.**

(d) **Calculate the expected values of the four strategies.**

(e) **On the basis of your answers to (d) evaluate which strategy Crystal Holdings should choose.**

(f) **Assuming the decision tree in Figure 11.6, if the probability of success of export to the USA was 0.9 instead of 0.5, how might the decision in (e) be affected?**

(g) **Assuming the decision tree in Figure 11.6, if the probability of success of modifying Design A was 0.1 instead of 0.4, how might the decision in (e) be affected?**

Why analyse data?

A business can make great use of the data which it has collected about such things as costs, sales, markets and profits. Unit 9 showed that presenting the data will allow a firm to find out important information, such as the proportion of total costs accounted for by employees' wages. However, when looking at more complex problems, the data may need to be analysed in more detail. This can involve:

- finding out the most likely outcome, such as the most likely purchaser of a new product;
- forecasting what may happen in future, such as the need for extra employees;
- finding out variations, such as by how much output changes at different times of the week, day or year;
- finding out whether the quality of a product is being maintained.

Sometimes businesses can use data which has been analysed for them. Government departments produce information on factors which might influence businesses, such as the rate of inflation. Industry bodies may provide data. For example, ABTA give information on the market for tourism.

There is a variety of techniques which can be used to analyse data. This unit looks at measures of central tendency and dispersion, and the next looks at forecasting and predicting from data. While these methods can help a business to make better decisions, they must also take into account the nature of the data they are using. A certain amount of data is unreliable. It may be out of date, collected in less than a thorough way, or incomplete. Analysing this data, and making decisions based on incorrect figures, may cause problems. A firm that decides to increase its stocks because data show they are running low each week may have large quantities of unwanted goods if the data prove to be incorrect.

Central tendency

Much of the information that a business collects will be too detailed to be useful. It is necessary for this raw data to be organised into a form that decision makers can use more effectively. One method allows the business to discover the most **likely** or **common** outcome from the data. This involves calculating the CENTRAL TENDENCY from the data - usually known as the **average**.

Knowing the most likely outcome will be useful in a number of situations. A firm may be interested in:

- the level of stock ordered most often;
- the production level a department achieves most often;
- the average sales each month;
- the average number of days lost through injury.

Table 12.1 shows the amount of stock ordered by a small business over a period of time. How can the business find the average quantity of stock ordered each week? There are three ways of doing this - finding the **mean**, **median** or **mode**.

Table 12.1 *Amount of stock ordered by a business over a 40 week period*

6	8	10	12	8	10	8	10	14	10
10	8	10	12	10	12	12	14	12	12
8	14	10	12	12	12	10	10	12	12
6	10	14	12	8	12	8	12	10	8

Arithmetic mean The arithmetic MEAN is the figure that most think of as an average. Simply, it can be calculated by adding the value of all items and dividing by the number of items. The formula for calculating the arithmetic mean ($\bar{x}$) is:

$$\bar{x} = \frac{\text{sum of items}}{\text{number of items}}$$

The mean for the first four orders in Table 12.1 would be:

$$\bar{x} = \frac{6 + 8 + 10 + 12}{4} = \frac{36}{4} = 9$$

Working out the mean in this way for all figures is time consuming. Imagine a multinational adding up the stock needed by every department for a year!

One method used to save time and improve accuracy is to work out the frequency (f) from the figures. The frequency is the number of times an item occurs. The **frequency distribution** (☞ unit 9) for the figures in Table 12.1 is shown in Table 12.2.

Table 12.2 *Frequency distribution for stock ordered by a business over a 40 week period*

Quantity of stock ordered (x)	Frequency (f)	Quantity (x) x frequency (f)
6	2	12
8	8	64
10	12	120
12	14	168
14	4	56
	$\Sigma f = 40$	$\Sigma f(x) = 420$

where Σ = the sum of (adding up all the values).

The mean can be calculated by:
- multiplying the quantity of stocks ordered (x) by the frequency (f);
- adding up all these values and dividing by the total frequency.

The formula for calculating the mean of a frequency

distribution is:

$$\bar{x} = \frac{\Sigma\ fx}{\Sigma\ f} = \frac{420}{40} = 10.5$$

Therefore, when the business orders stock, on average it orders 10.5 units. The company might use 10.5 as its average order quantity for stock control (☞ unit 94).

The advantage of using the mean as a measure of average value is that it takes into account all data. It is also a figure which is generally accepted as representing the average. However, it can be distorted by extreme values, resulting in a figure which is untypical and which may be misleading. For example, if the stock ordered had been 6 + 8 + 10 + 12 + 69 in Table 12.2, the $\Sigma f(x)$ would have been 640 and the mean would have been 640 ÷ 40 = 16.

The median The MEDIAN is the **middle** number in a set of data. When figures are placed in order, the median would be half way. For example, the median of the figures 3, 6, 8, 10 and 12 would be 8. The median for 1, 2, 3, 4, 5, 6 would be 3.5, the half way point. If a firm had production figures of 200, 220, 240 and 260 units, the median would be half way between 220 and 240. In this case the median is found by an average of 220 and 240:

$$\frac{240 + 220}{2} = \frac{460}{2} = 230$$

Again, these are simple figures. Businesses, however, have large amounts of data and finding the median may require the use of the formula:

$$\frac{n + 1}{2} \text{ (for odd numbers) or } \frac{n}{2} \text{ (for even numbers)}$$

where n is the number of values or total frequency. In practice, with large numbers of figures, the latter formula is used.

In Table 12.2 there are 40 values. The median value would be 40 ÷ 2 = the 20th item if they were placed in order from smallest to largest, ie 6, 6, 8, 8, 8 etc. This is orders of 10 units. You can see this from the cumulative frequency in Table 12.3. The 20th item in the cumulative frequency column must have been for an order of 10 units.

Table 12.3 *Cumulative frequency of stock ordered by a business over a 40 week period*

Quantity of stock ordered (x)	Frequency (f)	Cumulative frequency
6	2	2
8	8	10
10	12	22
12	14	36
14	4	40

The median is a useful measure of the average because, unlike the mean, it is not distorted by extreme values. However, the problem with the median is that it ignores all data other than the middle value.

The mode This is the value that occurs most frequently. From the figures in Table 12.1, the MODE would be 12 units, as this is the order quantity which occurs most often (14 times). As with the median, the mode is unaffected by extreme values and has the added attraction of being easy to calculate. The main problem with the mode value is that it does not take account of all values and might, therefore, prove misleading when taken as a measure of the average. There might also be several modes within a set of data, which will make the measure less useful.

Question

Ashwear is a company that manufactures a variety of clothing. Table 12.4 shows information about the cost of its various products.

Table 12.4

Cost of production	Number of products
£1	4
£2	12
£3	22
£4	15
£5	7
	60

(a) Calculate:
   (i)   the arithmetic mean;
   (ii) the median;
   (iii) the modal;
   cost of production.
(b) The firm is considering launching 2 new products and has estimated that they will both have a production cost of £8. Calculate the likely effect that this will have on your answers to question (a).

Grouped data

Data is often put into convenient groups, called **classes** (☞ unit 9). Table 12.5 shows the results of marketing research into the ages of people buying a particular firm's products. The quantity purchased by each age group (the frequency) is shown in the second column.

How does a business find the average? It is not possible to find the mode, but it is possible to find the **modal group**. This is the group with the highest frequency, in this case consumers between the ages of 30-39 (25).

To find the mean, take points at the centre of each age group, such as 24.5, which is the central point between the ages of 20 and 29. This is shown in column 3. Multiplying the frequency (f) by the central point (x) allows column 4 to be calculated. The **mean** can be found using the formula:

$$\bar{x} = \frac{\Sigma fx}{\Sigma f} = \frac{3,600}{100} = 36$$

where Σ is the sum of all values.

Table 12.5 *Marketing research results showing the ages of people buying a firm's products*

Ages of consumers	Quantity purchased (f)	Centre of of interval (x)	f x
0 - 9	3	4.5	13.5
10 - 19	10	14.5	145.0
20 - 29	21	24.5	514.5
30 - 39	25	34.5	862.5
40 - 49	22	44.5	979.0
50 - 59	14	54.5	763.0
60 - 69	5	64.5	322.5
	$\Sigma f = 100$		$\Sigma fx = 3,600.0$

The figure of 36 is an estimate because it has been assumed that the average age of the 10 people in the age group 10 - 19 is 14.5. In fact, it could have been more or less. This is true of all groups.

The **median** can also only be estimated. To find the median a business would need to calculate a cumulative frequency table. The information in Table 12.5 has been used to do this in Table 12.6 Part (a) shows the original table. Part (b) shows how a cumulative frequency table can be calculated. 3 goods were bought by consumers under the age of 9. 10 goods were bought by consumers aged 10-19, so 13 goods in all were bought by consumers under the age of 19. The last point is 100, showing the 100 goods bought altogether by all consumers. It is possible to draw this as a cumulative frequency polygon or **ogive** (☞ unit 9) as in Figure 12.1.

What is the median age of consumers buying the products? If there are 100 goods, the median value can be found by drawing a line at 50 to the cumulative frequency curve. This gives a median of 35.

Table 12.6 *Frequency and cumulative frequency tables*

(a)		(b)	
Ages of consumers	Quantity purchased	Ages of consumers	Cumulative frequency
0 - 9	3	10 or less	3
10 - 19	10	20 or less	13
20 - 29	21	30 or less	34
30 - 39	25	40 or less	59
40 - 49	22	50 or less	81
50 - 59	14	60 or less	95
60 - 69	5	70 or less	100
	= 100		

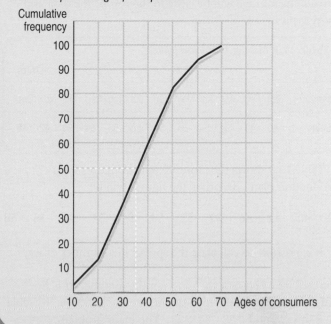

Figure 12.1 *A cumulative frequency polygon showing the ages of consumers purchasing a firm's product*

Question 2

Table 12.7 shows the salary ranges of employees in a business.

Table 12.7

Salary range (£)	Number of employees
8,001 - 9,000	6
9,001 - 10,000	15
10,001 - 11,000	40
11,001 - 12,000	25
12,001 - 13,000	10
13,001 - 14,000	4
	100

(a) What is the modal salary group?
(b) Estimate the mean salary. Use approximate mid class values of 8,500, 9,500 etc.
(c) Estimate the median by drawing a cumulative frequency graph on graph paper.
(d) Why would it be important for the employee representatives at this company to calculate such average figures?

Dispersion

The previous section explained how a firm can calculate an average. The firm may also be interested in how wide the data are spread - the DISPERSION. It may be that information is widely spread or there is a narrow dispersion.

If the data are widely spread, the average is likely to be distant from the rest of the data. If, however, there is a narrow spread, the average will be close to the rest of the data and more typical.

Table 12.8 *Monthly production figures*

												Units
Month	Jan	Feb	Mar	Apr	May	Jun	Jul	Aug	Sep	Oct	Nov	Dec
Sales	40	46	52	54	54	52	58	56	54	56	42	36

Table 12.8 shows the monthly output figures for a production plant. In order, the figures will be:

36 40 42 46 52 52 54 54 54 56 56 58

It is possible to calculate the spread in a number of ways.

Range The RANGE is the most simple method. It is the difference between the highest and the lowest value. In Table 12.8 this would be 58 - 36 = 22. The main problem with the range is that it can be distorted by extreme values. Just one rogue figure can vastly increase the value of the range out of all proportion to its size.

Interquartile range The INTERQUARTILE RANGE considers the range within the central 50 per cent of a set of data. It therefore ignores the bottom and top 25 per cent (quarter). This gives it the advantage of being far less prone to distortion by extreme values than the range.

In order to calculate the interquartile range it is necessary to arrange data with the lowest item first and the highest item last. The first quartile, which is a quarter of the way along, must then be found, followed by the third quartile, which is three-quarters of the way along. The difference between the first and the third quartiles provides the interquartile range.

Using the data in Table 12.8 it is possible to calculate the first quartile using the formula:

$$\text{First quartile (Q1)} = \frac{n}{4}$$

where n equals the number of values. The first quartile shows the value below which 25 per cent of all figures fall. So:

$$Q1 = \frac{12}{4} = 3$$

The third quartile can be calculated using the formula:

$$\text{Third quartile (Q3)} = \frac{3(n)}{4} = \frac{3 \times 12}{4} = \frac{36}{4} = 9$$

In the data the third item is 42 and the ninth is 54. So the

interquartile range is 54 - 42=12. The interquartile range for these production figures is therefore narrower than the range. When dealing with large amounts of data **deciles** or **percentiles** may have to be used as they give more exact figures. Deciles are the 10, 20 etc. per cent values, whereas percentiles are the 1, 2, 3 etc. per cent values. In the production figures, the 50th per cent of the values will be 50 per cent of 12 (6), or the sixth value of 52 units of production.

Mean deviation The range and interquartile range only take into account the spread between two figures in a set of data. However, there are many figures and each will **deviate** from the mean. In business this could be for reasons such as:
● the results from market surveys varying between regions;
● sales varying on a monthly or weekly basis;
● the output from a machine varying in quality as parts begin to wear out;
● the quality of products received from different suppliers varying according to the specifications they have used.
In Table 12.8 the arithmetic mean of the production figures is:

$$\frac{600}{12} = \frac{\text{(total production over the period)}}{\text{(the number of months)}} = 50 \text{ units}$$

The deviation of each production total from the mean is shown in Table 12.9.

Table 12.9

		units
Month	Production (x)	Deviation (x-x̄)
Jan	40	-10
Feb	46	- 4
Mar	52	+ 2
Apr	54	+ 4
May	54	+ 4
Jun	52	+ 2
Jul	58	+ 8
Aug	56	+ 6
Sep	54	+ 4
Oct	56	+ 6
Nov	42	- 8
Dec	36	-14
	Σ (x) = 600	Σ (x-x̄) = 72 (ignoring signs)

The MEAN DEVIATION provides one figure, by averaging the differences of all values from the mean. It is usual to ignore the plus and minus signs and use the formula:

$$\text{Mean deviation} = \frac{\Sigma (x-\bar{x})}{n}$$

where Σ = the total of all values
$(x- \bar{x})$ = the difference between the mean and the value ignoring the sign
n = the number of values.

The mean deviation for the monthly production figures in Table 12.9 would be:

$$\frac{72}{12} = 6$$

This is the average deviation of all values from the mean. The larger the mean deviation, the wider the spread or dispersion. As a method of calculating dispersion, mean deviation has problems, notably the removal of the plus and minus signs. The next section shows two other measures of dispersion, the **variance** and the **standard deviation**, which attempt to deal with this.

Question

Table 12.10 shows the petrol consumption per annum for area sales representatives working for Quantex plc, a producer of office equipment.

Table 12.10 *Monthly production figures*

								Gallons per annum
Region	North West	North East	South West	South East	West Midlands	East Midlands	Wales	Scotland
Number of gallons used	1,200	1,360	1,140	1,000	1,150	1,300	1,250	2,000

(a) Calculate the mean deviation from the figures.
(b) Calculate the:
   (i) range;
   (ii) interquartile range;
   from the figures.
(c) Which of your answers to (b) do you think is of more use to the business?

The variance and the standard deviation

Both the range and the interquartile range are basic measures of dispersion. They only take into account the spread between two figures in a set of data. The mean deviation is also of limited use because of the cancelling out of positive and negative deviations. A more sophisticated measure of dispersion is needed if businesses are going to be able to gain accurate and useful conclusions from a set of raw data.

By using the VARIANCE a business can look at the average of the spread of all data from the mean. Table 12.11 shows the figures for production from Table 12.9. To remove the

plus and minus figures the deviations have to be squared, rather than ignoring the signs as in the mean deviation calculation. This is shown in the fourth column of Table 12.11.

Table 12.11

Month	Production figures	Deviations from mean, $(x-\bar{x})$	Deviations squared, $(x-\bar{x})^2$
Jan	40	-10	100
Feb	46	- 4	16
Mar	52	+ 2	4
Apr	54	+ 4	16
May	54	+ 4	16
Jun	52	+ 2	4
Jul	58	+ 8	64
Aug	56	+ 6	36
Sep	54	+ 4	16
Oct	56	+ 6	36
Nov	42	- 8	64
Dec	36	-14	196
		$\Sigma(x-\bar{x})^2 =$	568

The variance can be calculated by:

$$\frac{\Sigma (x- \bar{x})^2}{n} = \frac{568}{12} = 47.333$$

The original figures were expressed in units of production, but the variance figures are expressed in units 'squared'. To return to the original units it is necessary to find the **square root** of the variance. This is known as the STANDARD DEVIATION, ie:

$$\sqrt{\frac{\Sigma (x- \bar{x})^2}{n}} = \sqrt{47.333} = 6.88$$

Using the variance and the standard deviation

It is possible to use the variance and standard deviation with far more detailed data. Say that a local council is interested in the age profile of its employees because it is considering the introduction of an early retirement policy, and it wants to calculate the likely costs of such a policy over the next few years. Table 12.12 shows how it might use the mean and the standard deviation.

● As group data is shown in the table, the total frequency is found by multiplying the mid-point of each age class (column 2) by the frequency (column 4) and then adding these values (bottom of column 4). The mean age is then found by:

$$\frac{\Sigma f(x)}{\Sigma f} = \frac{8,365}{230} = 36.4 \text{ years}$$

The variance is found first by calculating how much each mid-point deviates from the mean (column 5). Next each of these values must be squared to cancel out the plus and minus signs (column 6). Finally, the frequency of these squared values can be found by multiplying column 6 by column 3 to give column 7.

The variance is the sum of column 7 divided by the total frequency so:

$$\frac{\sum f(x-\bar{x})^2}{\sum f} = \frac{37,673}{230} = 164$$

The standard deviation is:

$$\sqrt{\frac{\sum f(x-\bar{x})^2}{\sum f}} = \sqrt{164} = 12.8$$

The standard deviation is a measure of the average deviation from the arithmetic mean of a set of values. It is calculated by using the formula:

$$1 \text{ standard deviation equals} \quad \sqrt{\frac{\sum f(x-\bar{x})^2}{\sum f}}$$

Table 12.12

1 Age class	2 Age class mid-point (x)	3 Frequency (f)	4 Mid-point x frequency (fx)	5 Deviation from mean $(x-\bar{x})$ mean = 36.4	6 Deviations squared $(x-\bar{x})^2$	7 Frequency of deviations squared $f(x-\bar{x})^2$
16-20	18	25	450	-18.4	338.6	8,465
21-25	23	29	667	-13.4	179.6	5,208
26-30	28	32	896	- 8.4	70.6	2,259
31-35	33	36	1,188	- 3.4	11.6	418
36-40	38	27	1,026	1.6	2.6	70
41-45	43	23	989	6.6	43.6	1,003
46-50	48	18	864	11.6	134.6	2,423
51-55	53	17	901	16.6	275.6	4,685
56-60	58	13	754	21.6	466.6	6,066
61-65	63	10	630	26.6	707.6	7,076
		$\sum f = 230$	$\sum fx = 8,365$			$\sum f(x-\bar{x})^2 = 37,673$

Unlike the interquartile range it takes into account all items in a set of data. It is thus much less likely to be distorted by a 'rogue' piece of data within a range. In the example above of the local council, the data had a mean of 36.4 years with a standard deviation of 12.8 years. This would tell the organisation information about both the average age of its employees and the spread of ages.

The standard deviation can be used in a number of ways by a business.

● To establish whether the results of a market research survey are significant and show variations from what was expected (☞ unit 50).

● To find out the quality of batches of products being bought (eg grain being bought by a flour mill) where it would be impossible to check all the batches.

● To check on the standards of output of a production line.

● To identify the likely range of productivity in a workforce where it would be impossible to carry out a work study of all those employed.

Question **4**

In a market research survey carried out amongst 1,000 consumers across the Midlands, Enigma Research was able to collect the information in Table 12.13 about the amount of milk that households are likely to buy in one week.

Table 12.13

Quantity of milk purchased (pints)	Frequency of response
0 - 2	5
3 - 5	18
6 - 8	55
9 - 11	137
12 - 14	269
15 - 17	271
18 - 20	149
21 - 24	62
25 - 27	22
28 - 30	12
	1,000

(a) From the figures calculate:
  (i) the mean rate of consumption per household;
  (ii) the variance in this sample;
  (iii) the standard deviation.
(b) In what ways might the Milk Marketing Board make use of these figures?

Index numbers

When faced with large amounts of data, it may be difficult for firms to see exactly what is happening. Also figures are often for very large amounts and are measured in different values. This makes interpretation and comparison a problem.

One method to help a business analyse and interpret data is the use of INDEX NUMBERS. Table 12.14 shows the production figures and unit costs for a company manufacturing small components. It is not easy to immediately see the changes in production or costs from the data. Changing these figures into index numbers will make them easier to interpret.

The first stage in working out an index is to decide on a BASE YEAR. This is given a value of 100 and acts as the base from which all other figures in the index can be compared. In the example, 1996 is taken as the base year and has a value of 100 in the index. Next, all other figures must be changed into index figures based upon the base year.

Table 12.14 Production levels and unit costs of a small component manufacturer

Year	1995	1996	1997	1998	1999	2000
Production levels (units)	25,000	24,350	25,500	26,300	26,950	25,950
Unit costs (£)	1.23	1.25	1.24	1.27	1.30	1.31

For production levels in 1996, this is:

$$\frac{\text{Number produced in 1996}}{\text{Number produced in 1995}} \times 100 = \frac{24,350}{25,000} \times 100 = 97.4$$

In 1997, it would be:

$$\frac{\text{Number produced in 1997}}{\text{Number produced in 1995}} \times 100 = \frac{25,500}{25,000} \times 100 = 102$$

A similar process would be carried out for the material costs. The results are shown in Table 12.15 and Figure 12.2.

Table 12.15 Index numbers for production levels and unit costs of a small component manufacturer

Year	1995	1996	1997	1998	1999	2000
Production levels	100	97.4	102	105.2	107.8	103.8
Unit costs	100	101.6	100.8	103.3	105.7	106.5

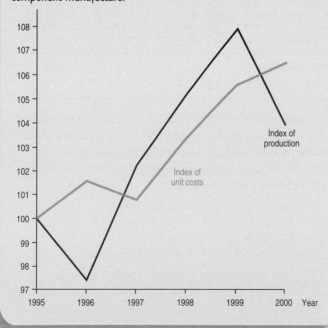

Figure 12.2 Index of production and index of unit costs of a small component manufacturer

It is now easier for the business to analyse this data. It could use the results in a number of ways.
● To identify trends and forecasts.
● The percentage increase in production or costs can be calculated. For example, between 1995 and 2000, the index of unit costs rose from 100 to 106.5 or 6.5 per cent.
● To compare figures that are measured in different values. The production levels of the business are measured in units and costs are expressed in money values. It is possible to compare the trends in both on the same graph. This is particularly useful for the business. Between 1999 and 2000, for example, production had started to fall whereas material costs were continuing to rise, although not at as great a rate.
● Presenting the data in a clear and easy way for shareholders or managers.

Question 5

A manufacturing company in the South East employs 100 workers. It has become concerned at the level of pay increases over recent years. Table 12.16 shows the average level of wages for some groups in the business.

Table 12.16

				£
	1997	1998	1999	2000
Managers	25,000	30,000	32,000	35,000
Administration	10,000	10,500	11,000	12,000
Production	12,000	15,000	16,800	18,000

(a) Using 1997 as a base year, calculate the index for each category.
(b) If 15 per cent of workers are employed as managers, 25 per cent in administration, 55 per cent in production (the other 5 per cent being cleaners etc.), calculate the total cost in 2000 of each category.
(c) How could the business use the index in future pay bargaining?

Problems of index numbers

A business will need to take care when producing its index.
● Updating the base year. From time to time a business will need to change its base year which will affect index figures in the years that follow. After a number of years the firm will no longer be interested in comparing this year's figures with those of, say, 10 years ago (the base year). It will want to compare this year's figures with a more recent base year. So for example, in Table 12.14 if the base year was 1998 instead of 1995, the index of production in 1999 and 2000 would be:

1999 $\dfrac{26,950}{26,300} \times 100 = 102.5$

and 2000 $\dfrac{25,950}{26,300} \times 100 = 98.7$

● Choice of base year. A firm must be careful to choose a base year which is representative. If a year is chosen where costs, prices or output are high, then index figures in later years will be lower than if a more appropriate year was picked. A base year where figures were low will inflate index numbers in following years.

● Nothing has been said so far about the importance of different items that make up an index. A firm's unit costs would be made up of many different items. This is dealt with in the next section.

A weighted index

A more accurate index would take into account that changes in some items are more important than others. The costs of a firm may be made up of labour, capital, electricity, etc. The firm might be able to construct an index showing how costs change over a period. However, if it spends more on, say, machinery than labour, then the figures for spending on capital must be WEIGHTED.

Table 12.17 shows a firm which spends different amounts on various costs of production over a period. Using year X as the base year, the index of total costs is calculated by:

$$\frac{\text{Year Y index}}{n \text{ items}} = \frac{424}{4} = 106 \text{ or } 6 \text{ per cent}$$

where n = total amount.

Table 12.17

				£ per annum
	Year X	Year Y	Year X index	Year Y index ([Costs in Year X÷ costs in Year Y] x100)
Wage costs	100,000	103,000	100	103
Rent/rates	50,000	55,000	100	110
Materials	250,000	260,000	100	104
Production costs	100,000	107,000	100	107
			400 ÷ 4 = 100	424 ÷ 4 =106
Total costs	500,000	525,000		

This says nothing, however, about the weightings of the different costs. Looking at Table 12.17, it is possible to work out the proportion of spending on each item in year X.

Total wage cost   = 20 per cent   (100,000 ÷ 500,000) x 100
Rent/rates   = 10 per cent
Materials   = 50 per cent
Production costs = 20 per cent

A firm can now calculate a weighted index using these figures. This is shown in Table 12.18. The index in year Y is multiplied by the weighting, so the weighted index of, say, total wage costs is 103 x 20 per cent = 20.6.

Table 12.18

	Weighting	Year Y index	Weighted Year Y index (weighting x Year Y index)
Total wage costs	20%	103	20.6
Rates/rent	10%	110	11.0
Materials	50%	104	52.0
Production costs	20%	107	21.4
			105.0

The weighted index is now 105. When the percentage spent on each item is taken into account the increase in prices is 5 per cent rather than 6 per cent, as shown in Table 12.17.

A weighted index over time

The example so far has only dealt with an index over two years. Table 12.19 shows calculations for another 2 years based on changes in the index numbers. The proportion spent on each item is assumed to remain the same. This is known as the **base year** or **Laspeyre** method of calculation.

Table 12.19

	Year X Index	Year Y Index	Year Z Index	Year A Index
Total wage costs	100	103 x 20% = 20.6	105 x 20% = 21	106 x 20% = 21.2
Rent/rates	100	110 x 10% = 11	110 x 10% = 11	108 x 10% = 10.8
Materials	100	104 x 50% = 52	106 x 50% = 53	110 x 50% = 55
Production costs	100	107 x 20% = 21.4	110 x 20% = 22	115 x 20% = 23
Weighted index	100	105.0	107	110.0

It is also possible to recalculate the index each year based on the weightings in the current year. This is known as the **Paasche** method and can be useful if weightings change frequently. In Table 12.19 the weighting in year A (the most recent year) may have been:

Total wage costs   = 15 per cent
Rent/rates   = 10 per cent
Materials   = 45 per cent
Production costs   = 30 per cent

The index numbers for each year would have been multiplied by the current percentages and not the weightings for the base year. So in year A the weighted index using the

Paasche method would be:

Total wage costs	106 × 15% =	15.9
Rent/rates	108 × 10% =	10.8
Materials	110 × 45% =	49.5
Production costs	115 × 30% =	34.5
		110.7

Firms can use weighted indexes in a number of ways, especially where there are a number of items which they wish to include in an index. For example, a firm which sells five products and wishes to construct a single index to show its changes in sales over the last ten years may consider using one. Products with high sales levels could be given a higher weighting than those with low sales levels. In this way, a weighted index would more accurately reflect overall changes in sales.

Probably the best known index in the UK is the Retail Price Index (RPI). This measures the rate of inflation by finding out how the average household spends its money and monitoring any falls or rises in the prices of those goods and services. The RPI is an example of a **weighted index** as it gives greater importance to some items than to others. For example, a rise in the price of petrol is given a higher weighting than a rise in the price of soap. A change in the price of a product with a high weighting will consequently have a relatively greater impact upon the index than a similar change in the price of a product with a low weighting.

Question 6

Table 12.20 shows the expenditure by a bicycle manufacturer over a 3 year period.
(a) Calculate the weightings for each cost item based upon the Year 1 expenditure figures.

(b) Using the base year method, calculate a weighted index for each of the following years shown.
(c) What are the advantages of presenting the data to the business as a weighted index?

Table 12.20

			£000
	Year 1	Year 2	Year 3
Wages	150	180	195
Rent	90	90	99
Materials	90	91.8	93.6
Admin	50	60	70
Production costs	120	120	126
	500		

Key terms

Base year - a period, such as a year, a month or a quarter, which other figures are compared to. It is given a value of 100 in the index.

Central tendency - a measure of the most likely or common result from a set of data (the average).

Dispersion - a measure of the spread of data.

Index number - an indicator of a change in a series of figures where one figure is given a value of 100 and others are adjusted in proportion to it. It is often used as an average of a number of figures.

Interquartile range - the range between the central 50 per cent of a set of data.

Mean - the value in a set of data around which all other values cluster; commonly used in business as the average of a set of data.

Mean deviation - the average deviation of all figures from the mean, which ignores plus and minus signs in its calculation.

Median - the value which occurs in the middle of a set of data when the data is placed in rank order.

Mode - the most commonly occurring item in a set of data.

Range - the difference between the highest and lowest values in a set of data.

Standard deviation - the average deviation from the arithmetic mean of a set of data (accounting for plus and minus signs in the calculation) found by the square root of the variance.

Variance - the average deviation of all figures from the mean, which removes plus and minus signs by 'squaring' the deviation figures.

Weighting - a process which adjusts an index number to take into account the relative importance of a variable.

Summary

1. Why might businesses need to analyse data?
2. What are the differences between the mean, median and mode as measures of central tendency?
3. How is the mean of grouped data calculated?
4. List 5 measures of dispersion that might be used in analysing data.
5. Explain 2 possible uses in business of the standard deviation.
6. Why might a business use index numbers rather than actual figures?
7. State 3 uses that a business might have for index numbers.
8. Why might weighted index numbers be more useful than a simple index?
9. Explain the difference between the Laspeyre and Paasche methods of calculating a weighted index.
10. What does the Retail Price Index show?

Case study

Sarne Co

The management of Sarne Co, a manufacturer of machinery for the textile industry, has set an objective of improving productivity on the assembly line.

A group of work study consultants were employed to analyse existing work methods on the production line and devise new ways of organising the production line. As well as carrying out discussions with the workforce and the production controllers, the consultants also studied the output of a random sample of 100 workers in order to establish their productivity before any changes. The results were as shown in Table 12.21(column a).

Two months later, following a substantial reorganisation both of the layout of machinery and the way the workforce carried out their jobs, the consultants returned to measure the output of another random sample of 100 workers. The results after the reorganisation were as shown in Table 12.21 (column b).

(a) Explain how the work study consultants might have chosen their random sample of workers.

(b) Explain the use of: (i) the mean and (ii) the standard deviation for the business.

(c) Calculate the mean and the standard deviation of output for this sample of workers before and after the reorganisation.

(d) Based on the calculations in (c), evaluate whether the reorganisation was a success.

Table 12.21

Products produced per hour	Number of workers producing these products (a)	(b)
21 - 30	3	0
31 - 40	18	12
41 - 50	36	30
51 - 60	25	30
61 - 70	10	12
71 - 80	8	10
81 - 90	0	6

(e) Discuss whether management might consider the reorganisation a success using only the calculation of the mean and the standard deviation.

13 Business Expansion

Expanding the business

Between 300,000 and 400,000 businesses start up each year in the UK. Five years later less than 70 per cent will still be operating. Those that do survive, however, will hope to grow, expand production, and increase sales and profits.

Growth can take place by producing and selling larger numbers of existing products or services, launching new products or services or by finding new markets. For example, a taxi firm setting up in a town area may gain more customers and increase sales as a result of its prompt timekeeping and helpful drivers. It may then decide to offer a limousine service to drive people to theatre shows or functions, which charges a higher price and raises more revenue.

Growth can also take place when firms join together. A business may decide to buy another. The turnover of the combined businesses will be higher. For example, in 1999 Kingfisher, the retail group that owns Woolworth's, was interested in buying Asda, the supermarket chain. Kingfisher's turnover at the time was reported as £6,407 million. Asda's was £7,619 million.

Some businesses grow by franchising their operations or licensing. For example, a large car manufacturer might give businesses the franchise to sell its products or a multinational manufacturer of drinks may give a foreign business a licence to use the company name abroad for a fee.

As a business grows it is likely to face issues and challenges that may not exist in a smaller organisation. Even if they do, they are likely to be less complex and relatively less important.

Raising finance

Unit 2 explained the different methods of finance that were available for a business that is starting up. Some of these methods will also be suited for a business seeking to expand. The method that a business chooses is likely to depend on how much is required, the position of the business and the use of the funds.

Private funds A small business entrepreneur may be willing to put her savings into a business to expand. Unless she has built up a large amount of savings, has had a windfall gain or has been given a large sum of money, this is only likely to provide limited funds. There are examples, of multi-millionaires ploughing large amounts of their own money into football clubs in order to finance transfers which they hope will bring success and benefit the club in future.

Partners'/shareholders' funds The owner of a small business may decide to bring in a partner to finance expansion. However, the partner is likely to want some control of the business and some reward for the investment. Private limited

companies can raise funds by selling shares to existing or new shareholders. They also have the option of 'going public' and becoming a plc. The shares of plcs may be traded on stock exchanges. The Alternative Investment Market (☞ unit 59) was set up in the mid-1990s to give small, young growing companies the opportunity to raise capital. These methods reduce the control and ownership of existing shareholders. Plcs can fund further expansion by issuing new shares or giving share options to existing shareholders.

Bank loans A business can apply to a bank for a loan, for example to buy more equipment or new technology. The bank may want some **collateral** against the loan in case of failure to pay. It would also consider the current position of the business, perhaps by examining its accounts. The business may also need to write a business plan (☞ unit 2) to explain its strategy to the bank.

(☞ unit 59)
(☞ unit 2)

Question 1

Increasingly companies are mixing and matching lenders to meet funding requirements. Andrew Sumner set up his television editing company in 1992. He has one of only three virtual reality editing studios in the UK. In 1998 he expected to turn over £2 million. The company was going through rapid growth. It was making films for HSBC and editing television shows, such as *The Travel Show.* Expansion from 12 to 20 editing suites required £1.75 million cash. He said: 'We are financed on leasing finance and cash flow, but we knew that the leasing company could not go as high as we needed.' So the company raised £750,000 from 3i the venture capitalist, which took a 25 per cent equity stake, arranged £800,000 worth of hire purchase and took out an overdraft from NatWest. The company leased the machines for 4-5 years, with an option to buy later.

Tangerine Holdings is a family owned company involved in natural animal food supplements. It needed money to buy another company. Initially it approached venture capitalists. However, it rejected them after the chosen funder asked for 35 per cent of the business. David Haythornwaite, who formed the business with his father, said that a lot of people who venture capitalists deal with are: 'managers who are happy to accept 15 per cent of the firm if they start with nothing. I had 100 per cent, so wouldn't give up so much.' The company set up a deal with NatWest to fund half of the £1.6 million purchase price and the rest was provided by equity providers within the family.

Source: adapted from *en*, October, 1998.

(a) Examine the factors that may have influenced the choice of funding methods in each of the companies in the article.
(b) Discuss whether a business would benefit from a mixture of funding methods.

Asset leasing and hire purchase These provide useful sources of finance for funding of new investment when a business lacks sufficient funds, for example to purchase new technology.

Venture capital/business angels These are organisations or individuals that are prepared to invest in growing businesses, hoping to see rewards in future. They often provide funds for businesses that are considered too risky by other investors. The problem is that they often take a certain share in the business as reward for their investment.

Government and EU funds Examples of funds available for expansion include Regional Selective Assistance for projects that would create jobs or loans from the European Investment Bank for capital projects (☞ unit 100).

Merger capital A merger or joint venture with another business may provide capital for growth. For example, one company may have a potentially profitable area into which it can expand, but not have the liquid funds to do so. Another business may have stockpiled money over a period. A merger or joint venture would give the combined business the funds to take advantage of the opportunity for growth.

Retained profit As a business grows, it would hope eventually to make profit. It will be able to use retained profit (☞ unit 55) to fund further expansion. The amount of money available for expansion will depend on the amount of profit from previous years. Large plcs often have huge retained profits in any year.

Accounting

Keeping records As a business expands, the records it keeps become larger and more complicated. A supplier of pine furniture may increase its sales from 20 to 100 retailers over a period of time. The amount of materials it buys from suppliers will also increase. Records of these transactions must be kept. Invoices must be sent out with the products sold. The business may decide that it needs to buy or improve its computers or computer software in order to keep efficient records of these transactions.

Keeping accounts The accounts of a small business, may be fairly straightforward. Sole traders can produce their own accounts and provide information to the Inland Revenue on a self assessment form. As a business grows it may employ an accounting firm to produce its accounts to comply with legal requirements. The annual accounts of sole traders and limited companies have slightly different categories, although all transactions are recorded (☞ units 55 and 56). Very large companies employ their own accountants, not only to produce the accounts but to provide help and guidance to the company when making decisions.

Payments As the number of customers increases, so do problems in getting payments from them. Credit control (☞ unit 60) becomes more complex the larger a business becomes. Computer software may be used to maintain lists of age debtors, people who have been owing money for certain periods. Credit controllers may be employed by the business. Alternatively, a factor (☞ unit 57) may be employed to chase outstanding debt.

Changing legal status

As a business grows it is possible that it will change its legal organisation. A sole trader wishing to expand by bringing in others who will invest and help to run the business may be forced to change to a partnership (☞ unit 5). Partners may want some say in the business. Partnership legislation or a partnership deed of agreement will set out the responsibilities and the rewards to each partner. Some people willing to put money into a business would not be prepared to accept unlimited liability of a partnership. This is because they would be personally responsible for the debts of the business. Changing to a limited company would give them the security of limited liability. Many very large businesses have become public limited companies in order to sell shares on the open market and raise large amounts of finance.

Question

To float or not to float? Transform Medical Group saw its turnover leap 150 per cent and profits 125 per cent in three years between 1995-98. If profit figures were good enough in 1999, John Ryan, the chairperson, hoped to float the company. The company has transformed its operations, setting up a new marketing department, a new accounting system, starting a major computerisation of patient records and changing its management structure. The business has also a three year rolling business plan which is seen as a key document when it goes to the market. Newer faces were brought in with the flotation in mind.

Flotation is mainly to fuel expansion. The business is taking over a hospital in the London area, but wants to build another three and add several more clinics around the country. So far the company's growth has been funded through organic growth, without bank borrowing. But it has to raise some capital before the flotation and would prefer investors rather than loans. It was suggested that the decision whether or not to float would depend on the 1999 results, but it saw no problem in achieving its targets.

Source: adapted from *en*, December 1998, January 1999.

(a) Examine the effects on the business of changes brought about with flotation in mind.
(b) Discuss whether flotation is necessary for business expansion.

Planning and forecasting

Planning and forecasting are vital to all businesses, no matter what size. Even a small retailer must plan what to buy, what to sell, how large the business will be in the next few years and when to employ more staff. The larger a business, however, the more complicated planning becomes. Larger business have more resources. They have more sales, more stocks, more employees etc. This makes accurate marketing, human resource and production plans essential.

● Without careful and coordinated planning, individual departments may make decisions which conflict with each other. Poor communication can raise the costs of the business. This is an example of a **diseconomy of scale** (☞ unit 93).

● Inaccurate forecasts and predictions will lead to greater problems in larger businesses and could increase costs.

● Without planning, the most efficient method of working may not be used. For example, too many workers may be working on a project or workers without suitable skills may be doing a job.

Some companies make use of theories or models to help understand the markets in which they operate (☞ unit 47). Business may even try to develop a corporate culture (☞ unit 14) so that the organisation all works towards the same business goals.

Marketing

An expanding market, increasing output and an increase in sales can have a number of implications for the marketing of a business.

Marketing research A small business such as a window cleaner is likely to know his market. The revenue of the business may be determined by the buildings in the area, how often people want their windows cleaning and the competition faced. A UK retailer selling imported American Comics may know most of his customers personally. As businesses get larger it becomes more difficult to keep and find out information about the consumers of the product.

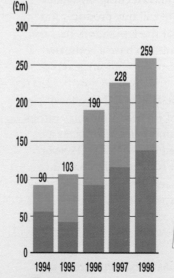

Question 3

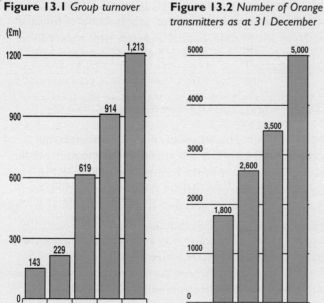

Figure 13.1 *Group turnover*

Figure 13.2 *Number of Orange transmitters as at 31 December*

Source: adapted from Orange plc, *Annual Summary*, 1998 and *Annual Report Form*, 1998.

(a) Explain the trends taking place in Figures 13.1 and 13.2.
(b) Using the information in Figures 13.1-13.4, discuss how the growth of Orange might affect its marketing mix.

Figure 13.3 *Distribution and administration expenses*

Figure 13.4

Unprecedented growth in our customer base put our customer service representatives (CSRs) and their systems to the test. The investments we made last year, primarily in a state of the art call centre and in our customer service systems, helped us to cope with this growth. Over the year, we also increased the number of CSRs by 47% to 1,635 from 1,115.

■ Distribution
■ Administration

The importer of a new comic may know that 100 people will buy it each month. Estimating the sales of a new car is more difficult. This is why large businesses spend great sums on researching the market. They also look for new ways to find out about customers, such as finding out the products bought by holders of loyalty cards in supermarkets. Larger businesses also make use of databases and external research agencies to collect information about the buying patterns of customers (☞ unit 37).

Distribution As a business and its markets grow, the difficulties of getting the product to consumers increase. The producer of a local newspaper perhaps needs to send its current issue to an area such as Yorkshire or an even smaller local region such as Stafford. A multinational company, such as Coca-Cola, has to get its products to customers in many countries around the world. As a business grows the total costs of distribution will increase. The total costs of distributing newspapers nationally will be larger than the costs of circulating a local newspaper. However, the cost for a textile manufacturer transporting 1,000 products to a retailer in a large van instead of a fleet of smaller vans is likely, on average, to be less. This is an example of an economy of scale (☞ unit 93). Some businesses continue to own and distribute their own products as they grow. Others employ specialist businesses to deliver their products.

Marketing methods A small business may be able to advertise its products by a leaflet or an advert in the local paper. As a business grows it may have to consider other methods of advertising and promotion (☞ units 44 and 45). Large businesses make use of relatively expensive television and cinema advertisements. They also make use of other forms of promotion such as free products, display material and exhibitions. As a business grows its name itself may become a marketing tactic. Well known company names become a corporate brand. People will buy products and services of the business because of the reputation. In some cases, certain specialist small firms also have a company brand.

Target markets Businesses that start may sell into local markets or niche markets. One of Richard Branson's earliest business ventures was selling second hand records. As a business expands it may either sell into wider markets or produce other products to sell. It is then said to have a product portfolio (☞ unit 41). Large businesses have many different products selling into a variety of markets.

Production

Changing production methods As a company grows so might its production methods. A small company making hand made furniture may employ a worker to produce the goods from start to finish. This is likely to be time consuming

and costly for a business expecting to produce 1,000 kitchen units a day. It may therefore be necessary to buy new machinery, retrain employees and change methods of production as a business grows. Many large companies use large scale machinery and assembly lines to mass produce products (☞ unit 91). This large scale production of similar products reduces the average costs of each product. Some large businesses are recognising the benefits of combining the advantages of large scale output with producing a product from start to finish. They are organising production into teamwork, known as cell production (☞ unit 92).

Relocation and land As a business grows it may become 'too big' for its premises. It then has a decision to make. Should it expand in its current location or should it relocate? This decision is likely to be based on a number of factors, including available land and employees, the need for related businesses, the market and government and EU aid (☞ unit 100).

Reorganisation As output increases and production methods change, it may be necessary to reorganise production. For example, some businesses have found that time can be saved and efficiency improved if related operations are carried out in a cell, with machines near to each other.

Purchasing A larger business will tend to order more supplies than a smaller business. This will increase total costs, although buying in bulk may be able to reduce the average costs (☞ unit 52). It is vital for all orders to be on time, but perhaps even more so for a larger business. Large amounts of supply will require storage space, as will stocks of finished goods for distribution. Some businesses have reduced this cost by asking for supplies just before production begins (☞ unit 94).

Human resources

Reorganisation The organisation of the business may need to change as it grows. A sole trader making candle holders may be the manager of the business, might make the products and may even deliver them to the retailer. As a business grows the owners may delegate some work to other employees and give them responsibilities. The larger the business grows, the greater may be the need to delegate. A limited company will have a hierarchy (☞ unit 70). The overall responsibility for company-wide policy will be made by the directors. Departmental managers may be responsible for employees in their area. Some large businesses have recognised the problems caused by too many layers in the hierarchy, such as poor communication or task duplication. This has led to delayering (☞ unit 102), for example removing one layer of managers. Businesses that grow by means of a merger sometimes find that jobs are duplicated. This may lead to a reduction in the workforce or redundancies in certain types of jobs and expansion in other areas.

Recruitment As a business grows it will need to recruit more workers. It must make sure that the workers it recruits have the appropriate skills required. It may employ staff from outside the business or from within (☞ unit 102).

Industrial relations A larger business will tend to find that more conflicts of interest develop between different stakeholders. Workers in smaller businesses may feel that they and the owners all have the same interests. In large organisations disagreements can take place over many things. Workers may push for higher wages just at the time that the company needs to control costs. Workers may fell aggrieved

at large dividends paid to shareholders. Individual workers may disagree with the decisions of managers.

Motivation It has been suggested that one problem with larger businesses is the motivation of workers. Some workers feel isolated in large operations. They may feel that they are just a 'cog in the machine' and their work is not valued. Workers on assembly lines have often complained of monotonous and boring operations. Businesses use a variety of motivational techniques to deal with this problem (☞ unit 71). These range from:
● financial incentives such as bonuses;
● reorganising work so that the employee does not carry out the same task all the time;
● other non-financial incentives, such as company health schemes or company cars;
● ideas to develop company loyalty, such as group activities.

Growth and costs

One argument put forward for the growth of businesses is that they can reduce average costs (☞ unit 52). A small business may buy a computer for £1,200. If it is used by a part time worker for 15 hours a week, the average cost per hour each week is £80. If a larger business makes use of the computer for a full working week of 40 hours, the average cost falls to £40. There are other benefits of large size. A large business is more likely to obtain sizable finance than a small firm. A large business may also have a stronger marketing image than a smaller business and be able to buy in bulk.

However, if a business continues to grow it may experience rising average costs. For example, a large factory might find that it has to spend large amounts on pollution control. A number of smaller factories may not generate as much pollution, and may not have to spend as much.

 Question 4

When a small order for commemorative rose bowls turned into a larger proposition, Caithness Glass had to innovate. The Bank of Scotland asked gift manufacturers for ideas for a present costing £100 to mark its 300th anniversary. The design from Caithness Glass appeared in a brochure sent by the bank to its employees along with other products. But a third of employees chose the bowl. Caithness had to make 3,500 by July and the clock was ticking.

The only solution was an accelerated production system. There was no-one in the factory skilled enough to make the bowls. So the designer was brought to the factory and videoed making the product. The skilled craftspeople learned how to make the product and then trained the junior members of the team. Time was tight so yields would have to be very high. 90 plus out of every 100 had to be flawless. Normally the target was around 70-75. Workers took no holidays and worked longer hours.

In order to meet the deadline corners needed to be cut. For example, instead of adding the base to the bowl, which was very complicated work, it was decided to do the whole thing at once. It was also decided to divide the job into seven stages and form two teams of six or seven people with different skill levels. This allowed far greater output.

The business was able to complete the job on time and turned an estimated £350,000 loss into a £40,000 profit. One of the reasons why it was so successful was because of the adaptability of the workforce. Another factor was the training in new skills, although the workforce did not see it as training. As skilled craftspeople they simply saw it as adapting skills they had developed over the years.

Source: adapted from *People Management*, 19.2.1998.

(a) Explain the effects that growth in sales had on: (i) production; and (ii) human resources; at Caithness Glass.
(b) Discuss to what extent these changes might benefit the business in future.

Summary

1. How might a business be able to grow?
2. State 5 ways in which a business might obtain funds for expansion.
3. Why might obtaining funds from partners or shareholders be a problem?
4. Why might a investor in a business wish a partnership to become a limited company?
5. Suggest 2 reasons why planning in a larger company is important.
6. Explain 3 effects that the expansion of a business might have on its marketing.
7. Explain 3 effects that the expansion of a business might have on its production.
8. Explain 3 effects that the expansion of a business might have on its human resource planning.

Case study

Kidstuff

Kidstuff is a business run by Judith and Kim Yip in the North West, Merseyside and the Wirral. The business provides specialised, originally designed and unusual children's clothing. Fabrics are bought in bulk from wholesalers, the clothes are made up and then they are sold in local markets in the area. The average price of a stall per day was £15. The business operated 4 out of 7 days a week. Kim and Judith charged between £7 and £18 for the clothes although the average price was around £12. They felt that they could charge a slightly higher price than other clothing stalls because of the uniqueness of their service. Sometimes customers will suggest their own designs and these can be made up at an extra cost.

The business was set up as a partnership. It was started with the £11,000 that Kim and Judith received when they were made redundant. They were keen not to borrow from a bank. Judith's mother also put in £5,000 of her own savings. Part time machine operators were employed to make the clothes in their own homes. When they were finished, they would be stored at Judith's and Kim's house, ready to be taken to markets in the area.

Figure 13.5 shows the change in revenue, profit and costs of the business in the first three years. Costs include the materials, the wages of the operators, the hiring of stalls and some leaflets to advertise the business. The market for their product was likely to be limited in the areas in which the business operated and they decided that they had to expand. They have had a meeting with an independent adviser. A number of alternatives were suggested.

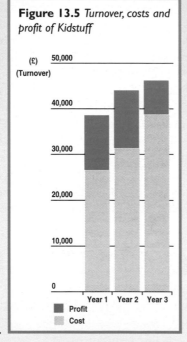

Figure 13.5 *Turnover, costs and profit of Kidstuff*

Markets further afield Markets in Salford and North Wales had not been considered initially because of the distance and greater costs. This might involve leaving earlier in the morning and arriving home later. Costs might include vehicle maintenance, petrol, other costs such as staying overnight at a hotel if they worked late. One problem was that the markets would have to take place on days that they did not work already. It would also mean an increase in the number of days a week they worked. Kim and Judith had considered employing someone from another area to sell their products in these markets.

Other markets Craft fairs, village fairs and other related sales opportunities could be one way of expanding. Again this would mean working extra days, with increased costs, but not further afield. The size of these markets was likely to be fairly limited and people were not likely to spend a great deal. It was suggested that they would only provide a small increase in turnover.

Changing production The success of the business so far had been based on the uniqueness of the product and the chance to charge a relatively high price. Now that it was successful, the business could perhaps offer more standardised clothing at a slightly cheaper price. It may also offer related products, such as hand made table mats or chair backs. They could be sold at existing markets on the same days they were operating. Kim and Judith were concerned that the new products would appear the same as those of others and the price reduction would not make them as profitable.

Opening a shop The business had considered opening its own shop. Premises in Formby, an area of relatively high income earners, had recently become available to rent at £6,000 a year. The shop would give them an established base from which to build up regular clients. They could also use the shop to store stock. The shop could be opened 6 days a week, or even 7 perhaps by employing a part time sales assistant.

If the method chosen was a success and resulted in expansion, this would have a number of implications for the business.

(a) Explain three effects that a growth in sales may have on Judith and Kim's business.
(b) Comment on the situation of the business over the three years shown in Figure 13.5.
(c) Evaluate the methods of business growth available to Judith and Kim's business by:
   (i) discussing the implications of each method on the business;
   (ii) selecting an appropriate method given your analysis.

What is corporate culture?

CORPORATE CULTURE is a set of values and beliefs that are shared by people and groups in an organisation. A simple way of explaining corporate culture might be to say that it is the 'way that things are done in a business', eg the McDonald's way. For example, at Microsoft, the computer company staff work long hours, dress casually and communicate by e-mail. These are the **norms** of behaviour.

The corporate culture of a business can influence decision making. For example, General Electric in the USA stresses that employees should feel ownership for the company. It also encourages low level managers to behave like entrepreneurs. This means that managers tend to make their own decisions and often take risks. Insurance companies may encourage caution and conservative attitudes in employees as they do not want risky decisions to be made.

Business leaders are able to create a corporate culture to achieve the **corporate objectives** and **strategy** of the company (☞ unit 15 and 16). Computer companies often encourage employees to perform tasks in a creative way. This is because they believe that it will lead to innovation, which is the source of their **competitive advantage** (☞ unit 16).

It is important that the corporate culture of a business is understood by all the people that work in the organisation. It is usually transmitted to new members and reinforced informally, by stories, symbols and socialisation, and more formally through training.

The growth of corporate culture

The idea of corporate culture became popular in the 1980s. Tom Peters and Robert Waterman (1982), in their book *In Search of Excellence*, highlighted the potential impact that company values could have on the success of a business. Terrence Deal and Allan Kennedy's (1982) book, *Corporate Cultures*, suggested that the culture of any organisation could be managed to improve the effectiveness of the business. There was a certain amount of evidence to support these ideas.

● The success of Japanese organisations. Japanese businesses appeared able to establish and maintain cooperative, team-based organisational cultures (☞ unit 92).

● A growing awareness that successful leadership was not only concerned with profits, costs and sales, but also with the ability to motivate and to gain the commitment of employees.

● The belief that there was a relationship between a strong corporate culture and improved business performance. It was suggested that a company's corporate culture could be made stronger by the actions of managers.

Management theorists have therefore stressed the importance of developing a strong corporate culture. To help with this, the idea of a '**culture gap**' has been used. This is the difference between the culture that a company possesses and the kind that senior management would like to have. Businesses can fill this gap by techniques that change the corporate culture.

Developing a strong corporate culture?

All organisations have cultures to some extent. However, only a minority have a 'strong' culture that is highly visible and which affects the behaviour of employees and other stakeholders. It has been suggested that firms with a strong culture and little or no 'culture gap' are the ones that are likely to perform effectively. How might a business develop a strong corporate culture? Buchanan and Huczyenski (1991) argued that four areas can be examined.

Core elements of corporate culture The corporate culture of a business is its shared values, beliefs and norms. For a corporate culture to form, a stable collection of people needs to have shared a significant history, involving dealing with problems. This allows a social learning process to take place. Top managers are often viewed as 'culture carriers'. They are the people that set the firm's standards and its values and beliefs. The way that a culture develops is often influenced by the founders of the business. For example, Anita Roddick, the founder of The Body Shop, created a strong corporate culture of fair trade, fair employment practices and ethical standards for products.

Packaging corporate culture The values, beliefs and norms must be effectively 'packaged'. The corporate culture must be embedded into the everyday 'fabric' of the business. It must inform individuals how things are done. Packaging can come in different forms. Each helps to strengthen the company values, beliefs and norms.

● Stories. They are based on original events, but can include a mix of truth and fiction. Stories help to explain current practices. For example, an employee at Procter & Gamble noticed that the labels on a product at his local supermarket were mounted off centre. He bought the whole stock, assuming that P&G would reimburse him, which it did. This story helps to communicate the importance of quality in the business.

● Heroes. These may be living or dead people. Through their deeds and words they represent the culture of the organisation and can be role models for others to follow. They might be company founders, leaders or successful employees. For example, the thoughts of Ray Kroc, who bought the hamburger restaurants from the McDonald brothers, are played to staff who attend the company's training courses.

● Sagas and Legends. These are historical accounts of actual events, which may have become embellished over time. An example is the 3M worker who tried to find a use for rejected sandpaper minerals. He was fired for spending time on this. However, he kept coming back and eventually succeeded. He went on to become vice-president of the company's Roofing Granules Division, which he helped to create.

● Symbols, slogans and mottoes. Examples of symbols include the Coca Cola and IBM logos. Slogans such as Caterpillar's 'Forty-eight hours part service anywhere in the world' are well known. The Hard Rock Café's staff motto is: 'Love All, Serve All'. Mission statements (☞ unit 4) often contain information about companies' cultures.

Communicating corporate culture The corporate culture of the business must be communicated to employees and other stakeholders. Formal and informal methods can be used to do this. Formal methods are highly visible, consciously designed, regular events and activities. They provide opportunities for employees to acquire the company values and beliefs. Examples include:

● rites and occasions - planned, often dramatic, activities that show different aspects of culture. An example may be the unveiling of a product, the honouring of employees' work and a lecture from an inspirational leader about future company prospects;

● rituals - a sequence of activities which reinforce the ideas, values, beliefs and norms of the company. Many American companies arrange regular Friday afternoon 'beer busts' at which employees can get together and relax.

● courses - induction, orientation and training courses which have the values, beliefs and norms of the organisation communicated within them.

Informal cultural transmission refers to the informal way in which culture is passed on. For example, the ways in which employees communicate and express themselves may represent their company's culture.

Cultural networks The strength of a business's corporate culture depends on the homogeneity (similar beliefs and ideas) of group members. It also depends on the length and intensity of shared experiences by members of cultural networks. Cultural networks are groups of individuals that are socialised into the values, norms and beliefs of the business through working together over time.

Types of corporate culture

Studies have shown that there are different ways of categorising corporate cultures. John Kotter and James Heskett (1992) suggested that there are two types of culture.

Question 1

How effective is an image? It was reported that British Airways spent £60 million on its change in identity in the mid-1990s. Priding itself as 'the world's favourite airline', BA introduced colourful multicultural images on the tail fins of its planes instead of the Union Jack. These included Chinese calligraphy and Aboriginal art. In June 1999 the company announced that it would be bringing back the Union Jack on at least 160 out of 340 planes. A spokesperson said: '60 per cent of our passengers who come from abroad tell us they love the world images, but the people of Britain believe their community is not as well represented as it should be.' The announcement came a day before Virgin was due to launch its own Union Jack livery and claim to be the UK's national carrier.

British Steel conceded that after its merger with Dutch company Hoogovens, its new identity would be unlikely to include the national name. This is also true of other businesses such as BP Amoco and BT which have played down their Britishness. This is more a reflection of the changing nature of business. Nationalised industries often stress their nationalness to workers and consumers. But the global nature of business has meant a change in identity.

BA argued that this was one of the reasons for its international livery. A survey of 200 companies in other countries suggested that few found the 'made in the UK label' had a positive impact. Only 39 per cent of US companies and 11 per cent of French companies associated 'made in the UK' with positive attributes.

Source: adapted from The *Guardian*, 7.6.1999 and 8.6.1999

(a) Identify the methods which the businesses in the article have used to create a corporate culture.
(b) Explain why the businesses in the article may have needed to make changes in these methods from the point of view of :
    (i) an employee;
    (ii) other stakeholders.

Adaptive cultures In such businesses managers are able to introduce a culture that allows a business to adapt to changes in its external environment (☞ unit 17). Such businesses are more likely to survive in a changing environment. Features of business with an adaptive culture include:

● a bias for action - employees are encouraged to be entrepreneurial and take risks. Managers have a 'hands on' approach;

● the company sticks to 'what it knows best'. It also emphasises close relations with customers;

● the organisation should be lean (☞ unit 102) and decision making should be decentralised.

Inert cultures These are businesses where managers all accept the values and norms of the business, which never change. Such cultures promote inertia. Decision making is often centralised. The problems with such structures is that managers can not see problems if the environment changes.

Another way of describing cultures is to look at the solidarity and sociability in businesses. This was proposed by Gareth Jones and Rob Goffee (1998) in *The Character of a Corporation*. **Sociability** is the relations between individuals who see each other as friends. **Solidarity** describes cooperation between individuals which takes place when the need arises or when there is a shared interest.

Networked organisations These have high sociability and low solidarity. Examples might be Heineken and Phillips. Such a culture encourages teamwork, creativity and openness. Workers enjoy working. However, discipline may be difficult because of friendships and productivity may suffer. There may also be an over-concerned with compromise, rather than the best solution.

Mercenary organisations These have low sociability and high solidarity. Examples may be PepsiCo and Mars. The culture is about getting things done, now. Targets are set. Roles are clearly defined. People consider: 'What's in it for me' when working. The advantages of this are that a business have a focus. It can respond to threats and does not tolerate poor performance. However, workers only work together if they have to. Also, because roles are clearly defined, there may be conflict over 'grey' areas of work.

Fragmented organisation These have low sociability and low solidarity. Examples might be law firms, consultancies or newspapers. This form of culture is best suited to businesses where individuals do not need to work with each other.

Communal organisations These have high solidarity and high sociability. Examples might be Hewlett Packard and Johnson & Johnson. They are like networked businesses, but more cohesive and goal orientated, and less mercenary than mercenary organisations. They are concerned with shared values and seek to find ways to support and maintain such values. They are careful to recruit, induct and train employees that have similar values to the business. Leaders are important as they guide the business. One problem despite the advantages of shared goals is that they may stifle individual creativity. There is also a need to recruit those who fit in with the culture of the business.

Resistance to change

At times senior management may decide that the corporate culture of a business is not appropriate for the new corporate strategies (☞ unit 15 and 16) that it is trying to introduce. One indication of this might be a CULTURE GAP - a difference in the current culture and the culture that managers want.

To what extent can a business change its culture? Some

Unilever started as an Anglo-Dutch joint venture. Its success was based on its ability to customise its products and marketing for individual markets, such as those in Brazil and Italy, for instance. People worked around the formal system, getting things done through informal networks. Its strength was in sharing information, networks cultivated over many years and fitting in with existing norms and values.

This structure originated in a world where there was time for decision making and people stayed in one company all their careers. But Unilever changed towards a more unified, systematic approach. It was the first organisation to link its global business via e-mail. Richard Greenhalgh, national manager for Unilever UK, said: 'We are adapting to face a world where tough choices have to be taken quickly which calls for common processes and information bases.' But Unilever still aims to recruit workers who share a set of values, to reward people fairly and to offer development in exchange for performance. Part of this is the company's international training centre, where executives discuss work but also socialise and improve contacts.

Source: adapted from *People Management*, 29.10.1998.

(a) What type of organisation (networked, communal, fragmented, mercenary) was Unilever in the past? Explain your answer.
(b) Suggest why this was suited to the business at that time.
(c) Explain the type of business culture that Unilever has moved towards, giving reasons for the change.

argue that if the culture of a business can be sustained by the strength of management, company stories and socialisation, it should be possible for these to be changed. A new culture can then be introduced. On the other hand, the longer a culture is allowed to develop, the stronger it will become. Beliefs and practices become more widely shared and deeply held. This makes them harder to change. A corporate culture learned over many years can not be altered overnight.

There might be certain **constraints** on a business's ability to change corporate culture.

● Structural and technological issues. A company's culture is affected by factors such as businesses procedures, the way buildings and plant are organised, the type of technology used, and the responsibilities of employees in the organisational hierarchy (☞ unit 70). It may be possible to change these over time. In the short term, changing technology, for example, may be difficult and costly.
● Cultural change brought about by managers is often resisted by employees. There is often a limit to the amount of change to values and norms that they will accept. Mergers are a particularly difficult time for staff. Familiar symbols, beliefs, values and shared meanings are often disrupted.

- Managers may be an obstacle to change. They may have an interest in keeping things the same. A change in corporate culture may threaten these interests.
- The effects of external factors. The operation of pressure groups or competitors may constrain how a business can change its culture. For example, it might be difficult for the police force to develop a culture which promotes norms of casual dress, rewards risk takers and encourages radical ideas, such as the legalisation of soft drugs.
- Corporate culture and national cultures. Attempts to establish a corporate culture in a multinational firm can be undermined by the strength of national cultures. Geert Hofstede (1984) examined the attitudes of 116,000 employees in the same multinational company located in 40 different countries. He found, for example, that in countries such as Argentina and Spain, inequality was accepted. Managers were expected to make decisions. There was a lack of trust between superiors and subordinates. Workers wanted to be directed by the boss. In Australia and Canada, however, the relationships between individuals at different levels in the organisation were close and there was mutual trust. Employees expected to be involved in decision making.

Advantages of a strong corporate culture

It is argued that there are certain advantages to a business of

Question 3

In the mid-1990s Bill Cockburn, chief executive, said the corporate culture of WH Smith must be changed if it was to compete effectively in a tough trading environment. He said: 'There is a culture of excuses, complacency and explaining on the night why we haven't done what we said we would do. There is not enough accountability and an attitude that seems to accept mediocrity in areas such as product.' The comments came as he reported a fall in profits, hit by extra costs of £19.8 million over a 31 week period, including increased advertising of £9.1 million.

Mr Cockburn said he was to carry out a strategic review of the entire group, including the WH Smith shops, the Do-it-All joint venture with Boots and a newspaper and magazine distribution business. 'Everything is being reviewed, Nothing is being ruled out.' He would focus mainly on costs. Jeremy Hardie, WH Smith chairman said that sales were encouraging, but profit was unsatisfactory mainly due to increased competition and higher labour costs. It was suggested that offers for parts of the business would not be turned away if a buyer came forward.

Source: adapted from *The Times*, 25.1.1996.

(a) What evidence of a culture gap could be found at WH Smith at the time of the article?
(b) Suggest problems that the business may have faced in trying to change the culture of the organisation.

establishing a strong corporate culture.
- It provides a sense of identity for employees. They feel part of the business. This may allow workers to be flexible when the company needs to change or is having difficulties.
- Workers identify with other employees. This may help with aspects of the business such as team work.
- It increases the commitment of employees to the company. This may prevent problems such as high labour turnover (☞ unit 75) or industrial relations problems (☞ unit 87).
- It motivates workers in their jobs. This may lead to increased productivity.
- It allows employees to understand what is going on around them. This can prevent misunderstanding in operations or instructions passed to them.
- It helps to reinforce the values of the organisation and senior management.
- It acts as a control device for management. This can help when setting company strategy.

Criticisms of corporate culture

It is has been suggested that a business will benefit if management ensures that:
- there is a strong corporate culture:
- the 'culture gap' is kept to a minimum and there is a single corporate culture that all people in the business work towards.
  Certain criticisms of this view have been put forward.

Corporate culture and economic performance John Kotter and James Heskett (1992) researched the relationship between corporate culture and economic performance. They tested the idea that a strong culture improves performance by measuring the strength of the culture of 207 large firms from a variety of industries. A questionnaire was used to calculate a 'culture index' for each firm. They then looked for any correlation between a strong culture and the firm's economic performance over an eleven year period. The research did show a positive correlation, but weaker than most management theorists would have expected. Strong culture firms seemed almost as likely to perform poorly as their weak-culture rivals.

Different perspectives on corporate culture There are other views on the nature of corporate culture.
- A business is made up of sub-cultures which coexist. Sometimes these are in harmony. Sometimes, however, they are in conflict. There may be differences of interests and opinions among different groups. As a result, cultural practices in companies are interpreted in different ways by employees. These may not always be those intended by management. For example, a profit-sharing scheme may be seen as a sign of equality by one group. Everyone gets a share in the profits, not just management and shareholders.

Question 4

Starbucks Coffee Corporation is based in Washington, USA. It roasts and sells whole bean coffees and coffee drinks through its chain of retail outlets. The company believes that happy employees are the key to growth. Whilst enforcing strict standards about the quality of its coffee and service, the culture towards employees is laid back and supportive. Employees are empowered and allowed to make decisions. This is reinforced through generous compensation and benefits packages for full time and part time employees. It includes medical and dental insurance, as well as paid holidays, health benefits and a share option plan. Only 25 per cent of employers offer medical packages to part time workers. It was difficult at first to get insurers to sign Starbucks up as they did not understand why they wanted to include part timers.

Starbucks health care package is relatively inexpensive, at around $150 per employee a month. This is because it has a young workforce, including managers. As workers get older costs were bound to rise. The company hoped this would be offset by lower training costs as a result of the low labour turnover at the company. Starbucks is the only private company in the US to offer stock options to all employees. The larger number of shareholders dilutes the power of existing shareholders and venture capitalists in the business. However, they were won over by a study that showed a positive relationship between employee ownership and productivity. Culture also contributed to profitability. Grants paid to employees were tied to overachieving. It was more

attractive to 'beat the numbers'.

Employees are trained in the culture of the organisation. This includes classes ranging from the history of coffee, to brewing the perfect cup of coffee. Classes teach employees to make decisions. They are given power to replace beans that customers are not satisfied with. They are also trained to hone skills in coffee shops as this protects Starbucks' quality image.

Employees outside the organisation are also taken into consideration. In 1995 Starbucks reacted to leaflets complaining that Guatamalan coffee pickers received less than $3 a day. It implemented a code of practice for foreign sub-contractors which made them pay a satisfactory wage and reduce child labour. Other importers of agricultural products followed this lead and the company earned praise from human rights groups.

Source: adapted from 'Starbuck Corporation: still perking'? by M.A.Shilling in *Strategic Management: An Integrated Approach*, Fourth edition,1998, C.W.L Hill and G.R.Jones, Houghton Mifflin Company, Boston, New York.

(a) Explain the reasons why the corporate culture at Starbucks is so successful.
(b) Examine the possible benefits of the corporate culture at Starbucks for the business.

Another group, however, may see it as a bribe for employees to conform with the company.

● The main feature of business life is ambiguity. Companies lack clear centres due to decentralisation, delegation and the employment of temporary and part-time workers (☞ unit 78). Also, new working practices often leave employees physically separated and socially distant. As a result, employees share some viewpoints, disagree on others and are indifferent to yet others.

These approaches are seen as necessary, to meet the requirements of the complexity of business life. The way businesses do things can be interpreted in a variety of ways. Values, beliefs, and norms may not be shared between individual employees or between employees and management.

The reason why someone does something in the way they do may not be just because management has created a culture that everyone follows. It may be because of other factors, such as outside influences, internal politics, self- interest, the sub-culture of a group, or different individual personalities.

Key terms

Corporate culture - the values, beliefs and norms that are shared by people and groups in an organisation.
Culture gap - a difference between the culture that a business has and what it would like it to be.

Summary

1. How can corporate culture affect decision making?
2. Suggest 3 reasons for the growth in corporate culture.
3. State 4 ways in which a business might develop a strong culture.
4. Suggest 4 different types of culture.
5. How might corporate culture be packaged?
6. How might corporate culture be communicated?

7. What are the constraints on the ability of a business to change culture?
8. How might national culture affect the introduction of a corporate culture?
9. State 5 advantages of a strong corporate culture.
10. Explain 2 criticisms of the idea of a corporate culture.

Case study

Kerry Foods

The direct sales division of the Kerry Group delivers chilled foods to the unsung heroes of retailing - the corner shop, the mini-mart, the petrol station and the cash and carry. The division was created when the group bought up Mattessons, Wall's, Millers and Robirch and merged them into their own delivery business. But this created a problem for Sue Camm, the personnel and development manager. After cutting a quarter of all jobs, she had to harmonise terms and conditions, and change the roles of workers from delivery drivers to sales people.

By January 1999, Sue Camm had to forge a new team ethos. In the past the organisation had often been divided and even unprofessional. There was distrust of head office, absence levels and staff turnover were high and so were customer complaints. A new culture was needed. The difference in performance between depots could not be explained by operational differences. They had the same products and the same vans. It was the atmosphere that was different.

A 'culture health check' was carried out. Staff were asked to assess their employer on factors using a questionnaire, such as fairness, respect, team spirit and trust. It was argued that the skills and motivation of the workforce were essential for developing a competitive edge. Roy Davis, head of SHL which produces such questionnaires, said: 'One key thing that senior managers must understand is the culture of the organisation, but often they don't. Anything that can be done to bring together the values of the organisation and the individual into harmony has to be good'.

The company scored 3.4 overall on this assessment. This was said to be a 'good middle of the road score'. But other surveys found employees disliked initiatives such as expanding the delivery role into sales and the use of hand held computers for stock control. Loaders disliked working at night, often alone and gave the company only 3.1. The main gripe was a lack of identification with the company. The business issued uniforms and Christmas hampers to all workers. This may sound trivial, but previously only delivery workers received hampers. A second survey raised the loaders' rating to 3.8.

Supervisors and managers that adopted an informal management style were ineffective ambassadors for head office. They would often agree with employees complaints. This caused tension. Also individuals still identified with their old companies rather than the new operation. Sue Camm decided not to use team building outdoor exercises as a quick fix solution as it was not a good indicator of behaviour back in the office. Instead managers were involved in improvement programmes involving one-to-one meetings, training courses and incentives. With 27 depots, some in remote areas, building a common team spirit and loyalty was not easy. But take the Rainham depot. It gave 3.0 in its orginal survey. It raised this to 4.2 after Chris Snowsill changed his management style. He had often told them when he disagreed with head office policy and so workers did not 'work for the company'. Now he acted more like a manager. Sue Camm also introduced a number of measures to promote team spirit and encourage friendly rivalry such as:
- weekly and annual performance incentives;
- longer induction training and a three month coaching period with an experienced sales representative;
- staff working in teams of three;
- supervisors regularly working with staff to improve their work, not just when it was poor.

Sue Camm said: 'Staff now trust us. And now the business is successful we can sometimes admit we make operational decisions without thinking about individuals.' She also recognises that a culture needs to be flexible because it is a depot based business. 'Trying to impose exactly the same culture on Aberdeen as at Andover may not be sensible.

Source: adapted from *People Management*, 6.5.1999.

(a) **Explain the problems facing the business as a result of its lack of corporate culture.**
(b) **Discuss whether: 'Anything that can be done to bring together the values of the organisation and the individual into harmony has to be good'.**
(c) **Evaluate the methods used by Kerry Foods to introduce a strong corporate culture.**

What is strategy?

In 1998 Cadbury Schweppes bought the leading chocolate brand in Poland, Wedel. The company argued that acquisitions were an important method of achieving its aim of profitable growth. In the same year Airtours, the travel services group, introduced the first loyalty card for package holiday customers as part of its commitment to customer service.

These are all examples of strategies used by businesses. A business's STRATEGY is the pattern of decisions and actions that are taken by the business to achieve its goals. A business is likely to have a variety of goals and objectives (☞ unit 4). For many businesses, the major goal is to improve performance so that profits increase. For example, over the period 1994-98 the Royal Bank of Scotland's profit after taxation increased every year. It rose from £386 million in 1994 to £715 million in 1998. In its Annual Report, the company argued that its growth was a result of its diverse range of business and flexibility in responding to new business opportunities. In 1997, for instance, it entered into a joint venture with Virgin Direct to launch a bank account, Virgin One.

Changes in the external environment of the business (☞ unit 17) have led many businesses to rethink their strategy. The success of businesses from Japan and other Asian countries in global markets has led Western companies to rethink their approach to quality, delivery, price and satisfying employees' and consumers' needs. Changes such as the opening up of markets in eastern Europe, the introduction of the Euro in 1999 and growing EU regulations are all likely to affect the strategy of UK businesses.

Planning and strategy

It is likely that the strategy of a business will, to some extent, be a planned strategy. Business PLANNING involves deciding what is to be done, setting objectives and developing policies to achieve them. The planning process that a business might carry out is shown in Figure 15.1. It could be argued that businesses go through a number of stages when planning their strategies.

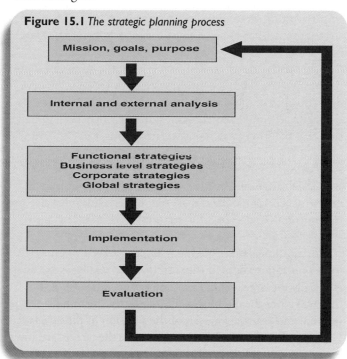

Figure 15.1 *The strategic planning process*

- Mission, goals, purpose
- Internal and external analysis
- Functional strategies / Business level strategies / Corporate strategies / Global strategies
- Implementation
- Evaluation

Identifying missions and goals Unit 4 showed that businesses have many objectives and goals, the things it wants to achieve. A company may want to increase its market share over a period of time or have more specific goals such as achieving a 10 per cent market share over the next 5 years. Companies also have missions. These are the reasons why the company exists and what it is trying to do. They are often found in **mission or corporate statements** (☞ unit 4). For example, in its 1998 Annual Report and Accounts it is stated that: 'Stagecoach is a leading integrated transport business, an international operator of buses, coaches, rolling stock, trains and aviation services in the UK and overseas'.

Analysis of the position of the business A business will analyse the aspects within and outside the organisation. External factors might be the opportunities that exist, such as new markets, and threats, such as increased competition.

Question 1

MEPC is the UK's fourth largest quoted property company. After years of underperformance, it began selling off unprofitable foreign and UK assets, refinancing its debts and improving its low returns to shareholders. Analysts and shareholders, however, questioned whether MEPC had a growth strategy. They argued that investors in property companies were no longer investing capital in companies with a diverse range of assets. Increasingly they were demanding property companies focus on a single narrow geographical area or product type. The new chief executive, Jamie Dundas, hinted that he intended to move MEPC away from the 'asset collector model' that was the norm for most of its biggest competitors. He said that: 'The quoted property sector has to do more than just be best-in-class in driving value out of trading property assets'.

Source: adapted from the *Financial Times*, 7.5.1999.

(a) Outline the old and new strategy at MEPC.
(b) Explain the factors that may have affected this change of strategy.
(c) Examine one possible objective of this change in strategy.

Internal analysis might examine the strengths of the business which give it a **competitive advantage** (☞ unit 16) over rivals, such as the skills of its workforce. It would also consider the company's weaknesses, such as a poor supplier network.

Developing strategies A business may have a number of different strategies and plans that it might use. These might be operational strategies designed to improve the efficiency of marketing, production or human resources. Examples might be building up brand loyalty, introducing Total Quality Management techniques (☞ unit 95) or training the workforce. Business strategies might be differentiating products from those of others. Corporate strategies might involve merging with others. Global strategies may involve setting up production in another country.

Implementing strategies Once a business has identified the strategies it wishes to use it must then carry them out. The business needs to put into place the organisational and management systems needed to carry out the strategies. This might involve adapting existing systems or redesigning new ones. Businesses must also be able to control the way new strategies are implemented. For example, it may need to make sure that the strategy remains within a budget.

Evaluation A business must have some way to decide if its strategies have been effective. To do this it must measure its performance against the targets that it has set. It must also use the outcomes to decide if the strategy needs to be changed.

Not all strategies are planned. Some emerge from the day to day operation of the business. However, strategies are vital, especially for large, complex organisations. The rest of this unit will cover the establishment of effective planning and the internal and external analysis of the position of the business. Unit 16 will deal with different strategies, the factors affecting how they are implemented and their evaluation.

The elements of effective planning and strategy

Purpose A business must be clear about its purpose. This may be defined in terms of the type of products or services it wants to produce or whether it is profit or a non-profit making organisation. If the purpose of the business is unclear, its plans, operations and practices that are devised in the strategy will lack focus and direction.

Vision Without a strategic vision, a business might struggle to succeed. The vision is the creative idea, image or imagination about the business. It is often the idea of the founder of the business or those responsible for particular projects or initiatives. A vision that is communicated effectively to others is likely to be shared by all and to be successful. The visions of businesses such as Virgin are well

Question 2

In 1998 MFI was attempting to change its retail strategy. Sales of core products - kitchens and bedrooms - had performed well. Other product groups were not producing satisfactory returns and costs were rising too quickly. The business stated that it intended to improve its long term profitability and the retail net margin by concentrating on higher margin products and reducing its fixed costs. There were certain elements to its strategy.

FOCUS ON CORE PRODUCTS
'We have identified substantial opportunities in certain segments of our core markets of kitchens and bedrooms particularly at higher price points. We have already made progress in these areas and we now intend to gain further market share.
This will be achieved through targeted advertising, additional brand support, new product development, with improved focus on service in both sales and distribution.
In future our stores will focus on kitchens and bedrooms. Upholstery, textiles, housewares and other small products which cannot be home delivered economically will no longer be sold. The cost of stock to be written off as a result in the current year will be approximately £5m. This rationalisation of the product range will result in a loss of turnover of £90m in a full year.'

HOME DELIVERY AND STORE FORMAT
'The Homeworks stores have much smaller warehouses and were designed to operate with remote warehousing which could handle the bulk of deliveries to the customer's home.
Over the last 18 months we have seen demand from customers for home delivery continue to increase with the result that the level of orders being handled by remote warehouses has risen substantially and the value of the product distributed through branch warehouses has fallen. The running costs of the branch warehouses are essentially fixed at this lower volume of activity, and it now makes commercial sense to distribute all products through Home Delivery Centres. This will enable us to reduce the fixed cost base of the business.'

It was suggested that the changes would result in one-off costs of redundancy payments and written off assets of around £20 million. Redundancies of 1,500 staff would save £25 million in a year. The reorganisation would 'provide a strong platform for profitable growth in future.'

Source: adapted from MFI, *Annual Report and Accounts*, 1998.

(a) Explain the objectives of the business in changing strategy.
(b) Analyse the planning process at MFI using the Annual Report and Accounts information.

publicised. Virgin Atlantic, for example, was created by Richard Branson in the 1980s as a top quality niche airline to fly between London, the USA and the Far East. To promote this Branson created a distinctive image based on quality and the ability to identity with the passenger. He reinforced the image by keeping himself and the company in the public eye. The result has been the creation of a profitable business with strong image and identity.

Commitment Effective strategies have a 'commitment to achieve'. This can be done in a variety of ways, including financial gains and profits, effectiveness and quality of service. Commitment is also reflected in the volume, quality and nature of resources used, the ways of working, management styles and the ethical stance of the company. Table 15.1 shows the corporate purpose of Unilever, reproduced in its Annual Report and Accounts.

Table 15.1 *Unilever's Corporate Purpose*

Our purpose in Unilever is to meet the everyday needs of people everywhere - to anticipate the aspirations of our consumers and customers and to respond creatively and competitively with branded products and services which raise the quality of life.

Our deep roots in local cultures and markets around the world are our unparalleled inheritance and the foundation for our future growth. We will bring our wealth of knowledge and international expertise to the service of local consumers - a truly multi-local multinational.

Our long-term success requires a total commitment to exceptional standards of performance and productivity, to working together effectively and to a willingness to embrace new ideas and learn continuously.

We believe that to succeed requires the highest standards of corporate behaviour towards our employees, consumers and the societies and world in which we live.

This is Unilever's road to sustainable, profitable growth for our business and long-term value creation for our shareholders and employees.

Source: Unilever, *Annual Report and Accounts*.

Customers and clients Effective strategies are geared towards customers and clients. They must take into account:
- the nature, locations, and numbers of customers;
- their needs and wants in relation to the products offered by the business;
- the importance of these products to customers;
- the advantages of products in relation to those of competitors;
- the confidence in and loyalty to the firm by its customers;
- financial viability.

Strategies must be designed to satisfy the needs of customers over the long term. If not, they will go elsewhere.

Timescale A business must make sure that its objectives are achievable in the time it has set for its plans. It is likely that there will be different timescales for different plans and strategies. For example, a business may have a short term objective to train the accounting department to use a software programme. This sort of **operational planning** is likely to be achieved in a relatively short space of time, perhaps a few weeks or months. However, a **corporate**

strategy to enter into a joint venture with an Eastern European country to set up a printing works make take years to research and set up.

Flexibility and dynamism Strategy is a continuous and dynamic process, not a single event. A business needs to allow its staff to seek out commercial opportunities. However, they must not be deflected from the standards and direction set out in the plan. Tom Peters, the management 'guru', calls this the 'simultaneous loose-tight properties'. A business must be 'loose' enough to give employees some responsibility for finding opportunities. But it must be 'tight' enough not to allow employees to take the business into areas not outlined in plans.

Suitability The plans and strategies of the business must be suitable for the goals it is trying to achieve. Businesses often have a variety of plans for different situations. For example, as well as the overall strategic plan of the business, there will be functional plans, such as **marketing plans** (☞ unit 47) and **human resource plans** (☞ unit 88). There may also be plans for unexpected situations. A company may plan to launch a new product in six months, but have a **contingency plan** that it could be introduced the following year if there are production problems. This is explained in the next section.

Crisis planning

At times businesses may face CRISES. These are situations where unstable conditions exist. As a result problems can occur for businesses. Crises are usually unexpected. Effective planning should reduce the impact of the crisis on a business. Firms often have contingency plans to cope with unforeseen or changing conditions. Why might a crisis arise?

Financial crises An example of a financial crisis might be a lack of working capital to pay immediate bills (☞ unit 60). The business could be said to have a liquidity problem. This might arise because the business has too many assets that are not easily converted into cash. Another reason might be because it has built up a large number of long term debts or is unable to recover money owed. Smaller firms may go out of business because they have been unable to collect large amounts of money owed to them.

Production crises An example might be the breakdown of a crucial piece of machinery. This would lead to a loss of production for the manufacturer and perhaps a failure to deliver products on time. Delays in the deliveries of components can cause major problems for businesses that use just-in-time production (☞ unit 92). Other possible crises might include fire or water damage to machinery, premises and stock. Natural disasters such as crop failures may affect the supply of agricultural products. The provision of services may also be affected. For example, a problem with the computer system at an airport may lead to delayed flights or customers might miss flights because they have been given incorrect information.

Human resources problems At times of industrial action businesses may face problems. Production may be halted. Sales may suffer because of a lack of supply or because the image of the business is affected. Unofficial strikes (☞ unit 87), called suddenly, can cause damage and may lead to conflict. Other human resources problems might be very high levels of staff turnover (☞ unit 75) or poor motivation amongst the workforce (☞ unit 71) which lead to a loss of productivity. This may develop over time without the knowledge of management.

Environmental problems A business may find that its operations are leading to environmental damage. This might result in opposition from pressure groups and perhaps the halting of the activity. For example, a road may be re-routed around an area of natural beauty, or a business may be prevented from building a waste incinerator in an area because of opposition from local residents.

Corporate problems Certain crises may affect the whole organisation. An example might be an attempted hostile takeover by a larger company. Another might be a loss of confidence in a public limited company. This might lead to its share price falling greatly on the stock exchange as shareholders sell their shares.

Product and legal problems At times crises take place when faulty or dangerous products are produced which break the law (☞ unit 22). A child's toy that was found to be causing harm could be banned. Products that have been found to cause health problems have led to difficulties for food manufacturers.

Image problems Many of the problems above will affect the image of the business. Consumers may lose faith in its products or change their opinions about a firm being a 'good employer' for example. This is likely to affect the sales and profitability of the business.

Contingency planning

Effective planning will allow a business to cope with the crises mentioned above. The contingency plans of the business should be designed to cope with the problems that arise from crises. How might a business do this?

Finance Large firms may have contingency funds set aside to deal with liquidity problems. Other solutions include finding alternative funds to deal with a short term lack of finance (☞ unit 57). The possible solutions to liquidly problems are dealt with in unit 60.

Production One solution to interruptions in production is to find alternative sources. A business may be able to **outsource** some of the work to other producers. It may also be able to switch production from one machine or one factory to another. It might even rearrange the time of production. If production stops in the day, the product may be manufactured overnight. This is easier if production systems and the workforce are flexible (☞ units 88 and 92). Having a pool of suppliers may prevent problems if components are not delivered on time by one firm. The same method may be used for crises that result in the supply of services. Services may be sub-contracted or an alternative may be offered.

Human resources management Effective consultation and grievance procedures will help to minimise difficulties and may speed up the solution to industrial relations problems. Motivational rewards (☞ units 72 and 73) may be used to deal with poor staff motivation. Establishing a corporate culture (☞ unit 14) may prevent some of these problems occurring in the first place. A business might make use of the flexible workforce (☞ unit 88) to deal with a lack of employees as a result of high labour turnover.

Image Faulty products or damage to the environment can have an enormous effect on the image of a business. A business must act quickly and effectively when faced with an image problem. Faulty products must be withdrawn immediately. The business should attempt to alleviate any public concern for its products. For example, it might promote the fact that it has found the problem and how it has solved it in the media. Other forms of promotion may be used to support the company's image (☞ unit 45). Businesses with operations that affect the environment often spend money on recycling and improving their environmental performance and promote this in their Annual Reports.

Management and communication Management has a vital part to play at times of crisis. There must be strong leadership from the top of the company hierarchy. Others in the business must be clear about their roles and responsibilities. A business also needs clear communication channels (☞ unit 82) to ensure that messages are being passed on effectively. Use should be made of information and communication technology.

While contingency plans are important, a business must not give them too much emphasis. They must not affect the corporate plans of the firm. Keeping a large amount in a contingency fund, for example, may reduce the funds that the business has available for expansion or investment.

Business analysis

Business analysis is the examination of the 'how, what, why' of business activity. It may involve analysing the possible internal problems and advantages that a business has. It might determine the factors external to the business that could affect its strategy. The outcome of analysis should be to find the organisation's strengths and capabilities, its commercial and operational advantages and the wider general pressures and constraints on the business. Businesses have a number of methods to carry out analysis. These are dealt with in the following sections.

SWOT analysis

The purpose of SWOT ANALYSIS (☞ unit 4) is to conduct a general and quick examination of a business's current position so that it can identify preferred and likely directions in future. SWOT analysis involves looking at the internal strengths and weaknesses of a business and the external opportunities and threats.

Strengths These are things that a business and its staff do which:
● they are effective at;
● they are well known for;
● make money;
● generate business and reputation;
● lead to confidence in the market;
● causes customers to come back for repeat business;
● cause other businesses to try to learn from them.

Weaknesses These are the things that the businesses does badly, that it is ineffective at or that it has a poor reputation for. It also includes the factors that cause losses, hardships, disputes, grievances and complaints for a business.

Opportunities These are the directions that the business could profitably take in future because of its strengths or because of the elimination of its weaknesses. This involves a consideration of the business environment from the widest and most creative possible standpoints.

Threats Threats to a business arise from the activities of competitors and from failing to take opportunities or to build on successes. Threats also come from complacency, a lack of rigour, and from falling profits, perhaps due to rising costs.

The analysis is often carried out as a brainstorming discussion. It is an effective way of gathering and categorising information, illustrating particular matters and generating interest in the business and its activities quickly. The result of such an exercise may provide a basis on which a more detailed analysis can be conducted. SWOT analysis is often used as a method by which marketing departments can plan its marketing strategy (☞ units 47 and 48).

PEST analysis

PEST ANALYSIS examines the external environment and the

Question 3

ICL was said to be making a comeback in 1998. A global alliance and a joint marketing agreement with Microsoft, together with 1,000 new jobs over three years appeared to bode well. Part of the deal involved ICL developing all future software for Microsoft's Windows. Keith Todd, ICL's chief executive, reinvented the company as a systems and services company, shedding its manufacturing arm and its PC business.

Computers are now in the hands of high volume specialists. Most of the action is in services, in the heady growth and large margins of the UK's IT sector. Today sales of ICL's computer hardware account for less than 6 per cent of its £2.5 billion turnover. The company sees its future in developing large scale systems and offering consultancy and maintenance services. It is trying to shed its UK tag, but it still earns 57 per cent of revenue from UK sales. To compete worldwide it must fight fierce competition and win contracts against services companies such as Logica and Sema. ICL is strong in the public sector and retail markets and is well placed in new markets such as electronic commerce and education.

But there is still room for improvement according to some. ICL has to show it can make 7-8 per cent profit margins which is the industry average. In 1998 they were estimated at 1.2 per cent. For this reason it was not planning to float on the stock exchange until perhaps 2000 when it would have had three years of improved profits to show and the company might be worth around 2 billion. Another reason to hold off was the automation of Britain's 19,000 Post Offices, when people could claim pensions and benefits with plastic cards. ICL would be paid a tiny payment for every transaction that took place as reward for its enormous investment in creating the system

Source: adapted from *The Observer*, 31.5.1998.

(a) Carry out a SWOT analysis for ICL using information from the article.

global factors that may affect a business (☞ unit 17). It can provide a quick and visual representation of the external pressures facing a business, and their possible constraints on strategy. It is usually divided into four external influences on a business - political, economic, social and technological.

Political This is concerned with how political developments, regionally, nationally and internationally might affect a business's strategy. It might include a consideration of legislation, such as consumer laws, regulation, such as control of water companies, political pressures and the government's view of certain activities. In the late 1990s the following were all political issues facing businesses.
● Regional. Will the government increase financial support for business start-ups in Northern Ireland?
● National. Will the UK government provide increased subsidies to BMW to support investment in the Rover plant at Longbridge?
● International. Given the number of Sino-Western joint ventures in Southern China, would a change in leader in China affect this policy initiative?

Economic This might involve the analysis of a variety of economic factors and their effects on business. They might include:

● consumer activity - confidence, spending patterns, willingness to spend;
● economic variables - inflation, unemployment, trade, growth;
● government policy - fiscal, monetary, supply side, exchange rate;
● fixed and variable costs of the business;
● the effect of changes in product and labour markets.

For example, in a recession (☞ unit 21) demand for many products and services tends to fall. Businesses may also need to analyse the possible effects on its plans of government policy designed to lift the economy out of the recession.

Social What competitive advantage (☞ unit 16) might a business gain by social changes taking place outside of the business? For example, in the year 2000 the UK had a falling birth rate, an increase in life expectancy and an ageing population. This has led to the development of products, particularly private pensions, private medical schemes, sheltered housing developments and 'third age' holidays, aimed at the older age group. Pressure groups can also affect businesses (☞ unit 27). The anti-smoking lobby, for example, has led to smoke free areas in restaurants, in hotels, and on aircraft.

Technological Businesses operate in a world of rapid technological change (☞ unit 98). Organisations need to review the impact of new technologies upon their activities. Products can become obsolescent quickly and production methods can become out of date. Communication may be inefficient as IT develops. New markets may open. For example, some music companies have considered sales via a internet. The strategy towards R&D (☞ unit 99) is vital in industries where technological change is rapid.

The five forces model

Michael Porter developed a model that allows business to analyse competitive forces in an industry in order to identify opportunities and threats (☞ unit 18). These include:

● the risk of entry of new competitors;
● the degree of rivalry amongst established firms;
● the bargaining power of buyers;
● the bargaining power of suppliers;
● the threat of substitute products.

Porter argued that the stronger each of these forces is, the less able a business is to raise prices and profits. For example, when cheap airlines such as Ryannair entered the market in the 1990s, established companies, such as BA when setting up the airline company Go, offered their own service of lower priced flights.

Industry structure analysis

A similar method of business analysis may involve an

Question 4

In 1999, in response to the strength of the yen and price competition, Sony announced that it intended to refocus its activities. It aimed to reduce its manufacturing activities and provide internet-based computer technology services. In a competitive, fast moving market it would invest aggressively in its electronics group, which accounted for 60 per cent of its total revenue. Within the electronics group, the existing operations would be reorganised into three segments - the home network company, the personal IT network company and the core technology and network company. As part of the move Sony was also taking three of its subsidiaries, Sony Music Entertainment (Japan), Sony Chemicals and Sony Precisions Technology back into its ownership.

It argued that in the fast moving age of the internet it was important to act with speed. Sony argued that Japan was way behind in the internet and the gap was widening. The reorganisation was designed to make Sony more in tune with an age in which software and its distribution via the internet can add significantly to profits, which are critical to the success of hardware manufactured by the business. Mr Nobuyuki Idei, its president, said that companies operating on the internet, such as AOL and Yahoo, made Sony look like part of the establishment. Whilst changes in the market place were affecting Sony's decisions, it also needed to be careful to raise shareholder value. 40 per cent of Sony shares were owned by foreigners. The share price could not be allowed to fall or the company may be a target of a takeover.

Source: adapted from the *Financial Times*, 31.5.1999.

(a) Using appropriate PEST factors, analyse the position of Sony in 1999.

examination of the structure of the industry in which a business operates. There are four components to this.

Competitors This examines the nature and extent of the rivalry among organisations operating in a market and the implications of this for the future. A business may consider the extent of product differentiation, the prospects of price wars and profit margins. It may also include questions about the current and future productive capacity of the industry.

Suppliers This focuses on the bargaining power of suppliers, including their ability to withdraw or flood the market. Either will affect a business buying supplies. Scarcity of components, for example, may lead to delays in production, increased costs or loss of business. Flooding the market may lead to falls in supply prices and possible new entrants to the market.

Substitution This looks at the ability of customers to change to the products of a competitor. It is dealt with under 'competitor analysis' below.

Potential entrants This examines the nature of potential entrants and any advantages they would have.

Competitor analysis

This involves assessing rivals. It may examine initiatives that they may take to promote their own strategic advantage. It could also evaluate the likely response to such initiatives by other businesses and consumers. The purpose of competitor analysis is to highlight the strengths and opportunities present in the 'rest of the field' and to learn from other businesses in the industry. Competitor analysis looks at a number of areas.

- The strategy of the competitor.
- The driving forces and constraints upon it.
- Its current business operations, capacities and strengths.
- Its current marketing operations and activities.
- Assumptions about the competitor.

Question 5

Peterson Spring, a West Midlands spring manufacturer, found that one of its competitors in Spain was buying its raw materials cheaper than it was. Ten years before its only competitors were the 30 spring makers in Redditch. By 1998 Edward Roberts, who runs Peterson, considered two companies in Spain and Germany to be its main competition. Peterson was under intense pressure to improve its margins. Its customers, such as Lucas and Ford, were demanding a minimum 3 per cent year on year cost reduction. Peterson was having to push its own suppliers to cut costs. The company spent £1.25 million on materials in 1998.

Faced with a global market, this small manufacturer reorganised its purchasing function. A specialist purchasing manager was employed and given the task of cutting costs by £150,000 in the first 12 months. Employing a specialist for purchasing is unusual for a small business. The number of suppliers was reduced and existing suppliers given larger volumes. This meant more regular deliveries and so suppliers could plan more efficiently. Electronic data exchange systems were also set up with suppliers. Prices paid to sub-contractors were re-examined. When Peterson checked its prices against the market it found that they were ' just awful'. Renegotiating with suppliers proved to be a delicate affair. Some suppliers were no longer used. The company set up long term contracts with suppliers in the same way that Lucas did for its products. For one supplier, Peterson Spring is its second largest customer.' But Mr Roberts says; 'but he has a large number of customers and we represent only 4 per cent of his business'. Still in mid-negotiation with the supplier, he argued: 'we need this supplier, but not at any price.'

Source: adapted from the *Financial Times*.

(a) How might: (i) five forces analysis; (ii) industry structure analysis; be useful to Peterson Spring?
(b) Using one of these models, explain how factors mentioned in the article may have influenced the business.

- Assumptions about the industry itself.
- Detailed profiles of each competitor. This might include an assessment of satisfaction with their current position, likely responses to competitors' strategies, their positions in the market and the extent to which they are operating at under or over capacity.

Product life cycle and product portfolio analysis

The **product life cycle** shows how the sales and profits from a product change over a period of its 'life', from its launch to its withdrawal (☞ unit 41). **Product portfolio analysis** looks at the relationships between the performance of different products sold by a business, each of which is likely to be at different stages in its cycle. These are essential components of a business's analysis. They provide a detailed understanding of what stage of the life cycle each product of a business is at, what is the present mix of products and how that portfolio might be developed in future. It is difficult for a business to develop a strategy for the future if it does not know the performance and mix of its current products.

Cost and value analysis

Cost analysis is essential to business strategy. A detailed knowledge of the costs of machinery, workers and materials will be needed before a strategy can be chosen. It provides the exact costs incurred in manufacturing product or providing a service. It helps a business to calculate margins of profit for each product or service and what each product or service might contribute to fixed costs. A variety of costing methods can be used to do this (☞ unit 53). Value analysis (☞ unit 99) is used to identify activities and areas of a business that add value, and to find out where value is lost. A business can concentrate on solving problems in areas where value is lost and attempt to reproduce or improve activities that add value. Value analysis is a likely indicator of the points in operation where profits and losses are likely to be made.

Key terms

Crises - unstable situations which arise, often in unforseen circumstances.
PEST analysis - an anaysis of the political, economic, social and technological factors affecting a business.
Planning - planning is the process of deciding, in advance, what is to be done and how it is to be done.
Strategy - the pattern of decisions and actions that are taken by the business to achieve its goals and objectives.
SWOT analysis - an analysis of the internal strengths and weaknesses and the external threats and opportunities facing a business.

Summary

1. 'Strategy is designed to achieve business goals.' Explain this statement.
2. Outline the stages of planning strategies, placing them in order.
3. Identify 5 important elements of planning and strategy.
4. Identify the 4 areas of SWOT analysis, stating which are external and which are internal.
5. Identify the 4 areas of PEST analysis, giving an example of each.
6. What are the 5 forces that affect a business's ability to compete?
7. How might a supplier's actions to flood the market with materials affect businesses?
8. State 6 factors about a competitor that a business may be interested in.
9. What does:
   (a) the product mix;
   (b) value analysis;
   tell a business about its operations?

Case study

BSkyB

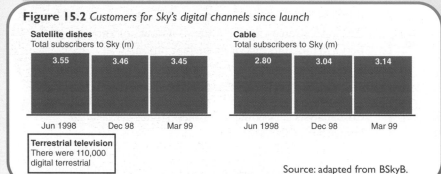

Figure 15.2 *Customers for Sky's digital channels since launch*

Satellite dishes
Total subscribers to Sky (m)

| 3.55 | 3.46 | 3.45 |
| Jun 1998 | Dec 98 | Mar 99 |

Cable
Total subscribers to Sky (m)

| 2.80 | 3.04 | 3.14 |
| Jun 1998 | Dec 98 | Mar 99 |

Terrestrial television
There were 110,000 digital terrestrial

Source: adapted from BSkyB.

In 1998 BSkyB, the satellite broadcasting company, launched 140 digital channels. On May 5, 1999, the company announced that from June onwards it would give away free to subscribers the £200 set top boxes needed to decode digital signals. This was not likely to please the 551,000 existing customers that had already paid for the decoders. Sky also offered free internet access and discounted telephone charges. It was seen as a landmark in television viewing. Previously digital TV had been seen as a luxury good, but this strategy made it available at lower cost to a mass market.

Retailers were drawing parallels with the rapid growth in mobile phone purchasing as prices came down. Some are less than £10 and there are 12 million subscribers. Digital television companies looked set to embark on a price war. On Digital, a rival delivering 30 channels through rooftop aerials, aimed to give away a free decoder to anyone buying a television worth more than £200 in May 1999. However, this offer was likely to continue in response to Sky's actions. Steve Grabiner, chief executive of On Digital said: 'We'll never be in a position where we don't have a competitive offer.'

On Digital was not, perhaps, seen as the main competitor to BSkyB. Mark Booth, chief executive of BSkyB said: 'On digital will be a successful niche player, but it will always be in a niche'. Rupert Murdoch, Sky's owner, said that he thought cable television, which had yet to launch its digital service was the biggest threat to BSkyB. Cable customers would not have to pay for set top boxes when digital was launched in late 1999 as they were included in the monthly subscription. They also received cheap telephone calls. This was why Sky digital subscribers would get a 40 per cent discount on all BT calls. Cable & Wireless Communications, the UK's biggest cable operator, said its 200 channel digital service would be launched in July 1999. It expected to sign up 200,000 customers during the first year. Greg Clarke, CWC's chief executive said it would always be able to charge less for its digital service than BSkyB.

BSkyB's strategy would not come cheap. Its analogue system would be switched off in the year 2002 and it would cost £315 million to change its 3 million analogue subscribers to digital. Giving each customer a set top box would cost £1,555 on average. Dividends were being suspended in favour of investing in digital. It was also suggested that the government would stop all terrestrial digital signals, which provided BBC, ITV and Channel 5, through aerials at some date in the future, perhaps in 2010.

There were also risks. The offer was announced in May but did not begin until June. Some retailers were said to be taking the set top boxes off the shelves as they did not expect to sell any. Despite the competition BSkyB suggested: 'We intend to take Sky into every home in the country'.

Source: adapted from the *Financial Times*, 6.5.1999.

Using information from the article, analyse the position of BSkyB and the possible reasons for its strategy. In your analysis:
● **explain the strategy being used;**
● **suggest possible reasons for the use of this strategy;**
● **carry out an analysis of the current position of the business using a suitable method.**

16 Strategy and Planning 2

Developing, implementing and evaluating strategy

Unit 15 explained that there are steps a business can take when planning its strategies. The first two stages of the process involve identifying the goals to be achieved, and analysing the business's position and the effects on it of internal and external factors. This unit looks at the next stages - developing and implementing strategies, and their evaluation.

A business has to decide on the types of strategy it will use. Some of these are strategies at the functional level, to improve the efficiency of business operations. Generic strategies are designed to improve the ways that a business can compete against its rivals in an industry. A business may also consider strategies designed to compete in global markets (☞ unit 32) and corporate strategy aimed at the long term development of the organisation. Once a business has implemented a strategy it must have some way of assessing how successful the strategy has been.

Functional/operational strategies

These are strategies designed to improve the efficiency of a business's operations. They often focus on one area, such as production methods, marketing, human resources or research and development. However, to be effective they involve cooperation between departments. The different methods of improving efficiency are dealt with in detail in other units in this book. Examples include:

- achieving economies of scale (☞ unit 93). For example, a business will reduce its costs if it delivers products in one large van, making one journey, than in three small vans making three trips;
- lean production methods (☞ unit 92). For example, just in time manufacturing means that a business does not receive materials until they are needed, to save on storage costs and speed up the production process;
- total quality management (TQM ☞ unit 95). For example, giving work groups responsibility for solving quality problems during the process reduces the quantity of wasted finished products;
- matching consumers' needs better, through marketing research for example (☞ unit 37);
- improving customers' response, through better distribution (☞ unit 46);
- improving staff motivation with rewards (☞ units 72 and 73);
- accurately forecasting the need for staff and the loss of staff (☞ units 75 and 88);
- improving staff skills by training (☞ unit 79);
- encouraging research, development, and innovation (☞ units 98 and 99);
- improving waste management (☞ unit 97).

Business level strategies

Business level strategies are plans a company uses to gain a COMPETITIVE ADVANTAGE over rivals in a market. They are sometimes called GENERIC STRATEGIES because all firms can use them, whether manufacturing or service businesses. It is unlikely that a business can serve an entire market all of the time. Competition exists. Consumers have a

Question 1

Robbins Ltd is a bottling plant in Glasgow. It has decided to introduce TQM in order to achieve the ISO 9000 quality standard. A problem facing management is the need to inform all workers that they are now responsible for the quality of their own work. Before a foreman had always checked work that was proceeding to the next stage of the operation.

It was likely that staff would need to be retrained to deal with their new responsibilities. In the short term management expected some staff loss and morale may fall with teething problems. It was considering some way of motivating employees in the change over stage. Part of the new process involved a requirement of suppliers to provide materials just in time. It was likely that some suppliers would not be able to fulfil this and so there would be a rationalising of business suppliers.

The new system would be geared towards quality assurance. Focus groups of consumers would be asked for their views before changes were made. They would also be allowed to inspect production as it took place. Some changes were also likely to be needed in the product itself, to make it more suitable to the new working methods.

(a) How might changes in the strategy of Robbins Ltd affect the following functions?
  (i) Management.
  (ii) Human resources.
  (iii) Marketing.
  (iv) Materials control.
  (v) Production.
  (vi) Research and development.
(b) Explain two reasons why coordination between different areas would be needed.

choice whether to buy a rival's products or not to buy at all. Firms, therefore, have to decide which parts of the market to aim at and how to be distinctive from competitors. Michael Porter in his book *Competitive Strategy* (1980) suggested that there are three generic strategies that could be used to gain competitive advantage - cost leadership, differentiation and focus.

Cost leadership This is where a business attempts to produce goods or services at a lower cost than its competitors. It will do this to charge lower prices than rivals and to compete in price wars that may take place. Organisation, production, marketing and distribution will all be geared at reducing

Question 2

SMH is the producer of Swatch watches. These are cheap and yet stylish Swiss watches. Swatch has established a basis upon which the business can compete and achieve superior performance. It developed a group of products that appeal to various segments of the mass market for watches, on the basis of style. The products are differentiated from those produced by competitors. They project 'a Swatch lifestyle' which is youthful and stylish. The watches appeal to both a basic market and increasingly, through variations in style, to a range of market segments. These include the children's market, young persons' and sporting markets.

American Express cards are only offered to those with a relatively high income. Promotions have been geared at stressing the exclusiveness of the card. Consumers were prepared to pay for this. In the 1990s many companies started to offer credit cards for a variety of uses. Banks and airline companies have offered cards that give air miles to users. The increasing number of financial institutions that are now operating as banks in the UK all offer credit card services, many with lower charges. American Express fought back by offering its own airline mileage programme. It also attempted to make the card available to more people and used in more areas.

Source: adapted from *Decision Making - An Integrated Approach*, D. Jennings and S. Wattam, 1994, Pitman Publishing.

(a) Identify the two types of generic business strategy mentioned in the articles.
(b) Explain the possible benefits that each approach has had for the businesses involved.
(c) Discuss, using information from the article, whether the three approaches to business strategy are mutually exclusive.

costs. These firms are likely to offer standard, adequate, medium quality products. For example, supermarkets Netto and Aldi's strategy may be classified as cost leadership. Their approach to retailing is low cost and price, 'no frills', and cheap packaging and distribution.

Differentiation This is where a business tries to make a product that is seen as unique by customers. A business may carry out promotion to give the goods or services a distinctive identity. A business can charge a PREMIUM price, higher than other prices, and so gain a competitive advantage. Examples of such products might be BMW cars or Rolex watches.

Focus This is where a business concentrates on a particular segment or consumer group. It tries to identify, anticipate and meet the needs of this group. The segment could be a geographical area or a certain income group (☞ unit 38). Once it has chosen a segment, it might then try to take either a low cost or a differentiation approach.

According to Johnson and Scholes (1993), organisations have a variety of strategies. All of these can be cost based, differentiated or focused.

Consolidation This is where a business tries to preserve its position in the market, niche or sector, range of activities and operations, and customer base. This could be achieved by increasing marketing and promotional activities, improvements in productivity, quality or delivery and reductions in costs. Consolidation may take place in declining markets. As a product starts to decline, a firm will try to gain every possible benefit from the product before sales make it unprofitable. Strategies might be the sale of the brand, licences, franchises, technology or distribution rights for a product.

Withdrawal, retrenchment and contraction These strategies are used when a business decides to move out of a particular market or reduce its portfolio of products or services (☞ unit 41). This may not be a negative thing. SWOT or PEST analysis may suggest that certain products are not performing as well as others. For example, in the 1990s, insurance companies and building societies sold their estate agency chains which they had bought in the more profitable mid-1980s, because of the slump in the housing market.

Market entry and penetration This is where a business can see an opening in a market. It will use strategies to gain entry to these markets. Market entry is more likely to occur when certain conditions exist.
● Where the market is growing, can be made to grow or has growth potential. There is likely to be sales potential that existing businesses are unable or unwilling to fill.

- Where organisations leave the market, leaving unfilled demand for products.
- Where the new entrant has a real or perceived advantage. These are likely to be cost, price, value or quality advantages over the existing operators. For example, in the soft drinks market, the perceived or real advantage of Pepsi and Coca-Cola is 'image and lifestyle'. New entrants must be able to compete with this.
- Where existing operators are complacent or where there has been a fall in the level of quality or service.
- Where a business is able to bring its reputation from one area to another, to gain a foothold. Stagecoach, for example, has taken its reputation a a successful bus operator into other transport services, such as railways.

Market development and domination Businesses may try to develop their share of the market, in order to dominate it. Domination of a market can lead to economies of scale (☞ unit 93). These include the ability to negotiate discounts with suppliers, attract the best staff and find the best sites for the business.

New product development Marketing research may indicate the need for a product that has not yet been developed. For example, Saga holidays recognised that there was a growing market for foreign holidays for over 50s which had not been fully exploited by other holiday companies. Technological advances may also result in new products being developed that create a new market. 'New' products may also be created based on existing products (☞ unit 36).

Diversification Diversification strategies occur where a business seeks to extend its current range of products or services. This may be by integration with other business or through new product or market development. Related diversification is where a business develops products which are similar to those that it is currently offering. Similarities may be in:

- existing provision, for example, an industrial building company seeking to diversify in the house building sector;
- existing technology or expertise, for example, an electrical goods company adapting its technology in order to produce digital wrist watches;
- related markets, for example, a confectionery company producing dog and cat biscuits because of the advantages of having the same product outlets;
- complementarity of products or services, for example, moves by dairy companies into the sale of bread (to complement butter);
- extensions of production, for example the output of components for one industry may easily be changed into production of components for others;
- 'New' products may also be created by adapting existing products slightly.

Unrelated diversification is where the organisation moves into completely new areas. For example, the Virgin Group expanded from music retailing into airlines, soft drinks and financial services. This was arguably a complete change in direction.

Question 3

In 1999 Coca-Cola, the world's biggest soft drinks company, announced that it was to launch a range of fashion and sports clothing. This was the first significant extension of the Coke brand. The company was signing up partners and franchisees worldwide to manufacture the products. The range, including jeans, sports clothes and other casual items, would be sold through concessions in department stores and fashion outlets. Clothes were expected to vary to take into account national tastes.

The company said that the clothes would reflect on the brand and 'will reflect Coca-Cola's values of authenticity, genuineness and part of people's lives'. Coca-Cola already licenced its drinks and logo to 10,000 products in 40 countries. This, however, was the first time that the company would use its brand name to give credibility to products not primarily designed to display its logo. Coca-Cola had recently announced its first fall in global sales in recent memory as a result of upheavals in Russia, Asia and Latin America.

Source: adapted from the *Financial Times*, May, 1999.

(a) Identify the strategy being used by Coca-Cola.
(b) Suggest reasons for this strategy.
(c) Explain the implications for the business of this strategy.

Corporate strategy

Corporate strategy is aimed at the long term position of the business. A company, for example, may consider where it will be in 10 years time and how it will get there. Should it expand? If so, how and in what direction? These are all likely to be long term decisions that will affect the entire organisation. There is a variety of methods by which corporate strategic development can be achieved.

Internal development This is where the business grows by increasing sales, output and profit over a period of time. In some ways the internal development can be seen as the least risky corporate strategy that an organisation may pursue. Corporate culture and structure will evolve 'organically' to meet the new requirements of the business. However, one of the disadvantages is that the business may not have all the necessary technology or personnel to implement the new strategy quickly. It may also take time for business to grow internally. This may not fit in with the overall objectives of the organisation.

Takeovers, mergers and acquisitions This involves

companies joining together to form one single organisation (☞ unit 101). A merger is often when two companies of relatively equal size join to become one company. Takeovers or acquisitions usually, though not always, involve a larger company 'buying' a smaller organisation.

This corporate strategy has a number of benefits. An organisation may be able to introduce new products and services quickly by buying a business that is already set up to deliver such a product. Business expansion can lead to reduced costs and other economies of scale. A business may get access to new customers and product portfolios, new markets, specialised technology and expertise, high profile brands and prime retail or manufacturing sites.

Takeovers and mergers are not without problems. They may be resisted. Employees of companies that are taken over may be hostile to the new organisation. This could result in a demotivated and unproductive new workforce. There are also likely to be organisational difficulties, such as duplication of roles and assets and the need for retraining.

Some larger companies have attempted to demerge or divest themselves of unprofitable arms of the business. This allows them to focus on their core products. It may be that two separate companies may operate more efficiently than one large one.

Collaborative strategies and alliances Collaborative strategies and alliances are when organisations work together to the mutual benefit of both. They may remain as separate legal businesses. Sometimes they may have an arrangement where a new separate business is formed. They can come in a number of forms.

● Joint ventures and consortia. Joint ventures and consortia are when two or more organisations pool their resources for projects, research, offensive strategies or initiatives. The principle behind joint ventures is SYNERGY. This explains how the coming together of organisations ends in a greater result than would have been the case if the businesses had done things separately. So, for example, certain car manufacturers may share similar components. Working together, cost reductions can be achieved in the production of each of their new cars.

● Hook-ups, associations and networks. This occurs where, for example, one organisation agrees to give prominence to or provide an exclusive outlet for the products of another. For example, at McDonald's the only soft drinks on sale are products of the Coca-Cola company. Each of the other major fast food chains, Wimpy, Burger King and Kentucky Fried Chicken, has similar hook-ups. Supermarkets and department stores give prominence to major branded suppliers in their sectors. Examples have included Boots plc and Rayban sunglasses, and the John Lewis Partnership and Panasonic microwaves. The aim of the relationship is the mutual benefit of the two organisations.

Global Strategy

Businesses often expand to operate outside their national markets. It is argued that expanding outside national markets can benefit businesses for a number of reasons.

● A business that is successful in one country may have a unique strength or 'distinctive competence'. This may also be the case in other countries. So, for example, McDonald's has been successful in taking its unique skills and products from the USA to countries that did not have fast food chains, such as China and Brazil. This has allowed it to make even greater profit.

● It can reduce its costs. For example, it may be that production is more suited to a location abroad. Manufacturing in a country with lower wage costs may also reduce the production costs of a business. Selling a standard product in a variety of countries is also likely to gain economies of scale for a business.

What strategies might a business use to enter and compete in international markets?

International strategy This is where a business transfers skills or products to a foreign country because competitors in those countries lack these. An example might be a business setting up a computer software business in an eastern European country. This approach is useful if products are not available from competitors in foreign countries.

Multidomestic strategy This approach involves **customising** the product to suit the needs of different foreign markets. It may also mean setting up factories in each particular country. The advantage of this is that products can be targeted to the

 Question 4

In the mid-1990s executives of the multinational British American Tobacco (BAT) were gathering in Hong Kong to plan Project Battalion. This was the new strategy targeted at China and emerging markets. Third world smokers were of growing importance, particularly the 450 million in China. BAT had a state of the art plant in Southampton geared exclusively to the Chinese market. Sales to China contributed £200-£300 million to BAT's profits the previous year. Many cigarettes were allegedly smuggled to China, however, by independent operators. The meeting was designed to find ways to boost sales in China and other emerging markets. These markets had so far been unaffected by health concerns over smoking which dented profits in the west.

Source: adapted from *The Guardian*, 3.1.1996.

(a) Suggest reasons why BAT may be attempting to enter the Chinese market.
(b) Discuss the most suitable strategic approach that the business might take.

needs of particular markets. A problem may be the costs of duplicating production facilities in different countries.

Global strategy This approach means that production is concentrated in a few, favourable locations. Organisations are pursuing a low cost strategy. Companies tend to produce a standard product to reduce production costs. They do this to charge low prices for products in markets where there is pressure for prices to be kept low.

Transnational strategy It has been suggested that markets today are so competitive that a business must gain economies of scale, transfer competences and also pay attention to the needs of different markets. It is also argued that companies can benefit from a flow of skills and products from foreign subsidiaries back to home countries. This is likely to be a very difficult strategy for a business to follow.

Implementing strategy

Once a business has decided and planned its strategy it has to implement it. This may involve a number of features of the business.

Organisational structure A business must organise itself into the structure that best suits its strategies. It may have to decide:
- on the type of hierarchy or organisational hierarchy of the company (☞ unit 70). For example, some businesses prefer to delayer, so that there are fewer layers of management in the hierarchy. They give employees lower down the organisation the power to make decisions;
- whether to organise by function, region, product, process or customer, or some combination of these (☞ unit 7). For example, some businesses prefer to organise by area and have different marketing departments, each with knowledge of the markets in particular parts of the world.

Control systems A business must have some way of controlling its activities. This involves setting targets, measuring and feedback. Controls may be in the form of:
- financial controls, such as the return on investment to be achieved by the new strategy (☞ unit 64);
- output controls, where managers forecasts targets to be met. An example might be management by objectives, which is a way of evaluating the performance of managers (☞ unit 74);
- organisational culture (☞ unit 14) which determines the norms of behaviour in the business;
- the leadership and management style adopted by the business (☞ unit 74);
- reward systems, both financial and non-financial (☞ units 72 and 73).

The implementation of change A business must decide how change is to take place. Strategic change involves a move away from the present method of operation to another method. There is a variety of methods a business might use. Some of these include:
- reengineering, which involves redesigning processes of operation (☞ unit 102);
- Kaizen, or continuous improvement (☞ unit 92);
- restructuring, possibly involving delayering or downsizing (☞ unit 102);
- total quality management (☞ unit 95).

Evaluating strategy

A business must have some way of telling if its strategies have been successful. This will provide important **feedback** which may influence future decisions taken by the business. First a business needs to set strategic performance targets and indicators. No real understanding of the success, failure, viability or otherwise of any strategy can be achieved unless accurate, measurable and achievable performance targets are drawn up. Targets and indicators need to be specific, measurable, achievable, realistic and time based, known as SMART targets. They must be easily understood by all concerned. These may be drawn up in the following ways.

Earnings A number of different measures of earnings could be used to evaluate strategy.
- Earnings per employee, include all the employees of the business, not just the sales force or production line workers.
- Earnings per customer. The total income over a period is measured against the number of customers.
- Earnings per outlet. The outlet could be an office, a sales person, a department store, an airliner or a restaurant.
- Earnings per square foot, for example of individual premises or total premises.

Profit Each of the items above may be represented as profit (per employee, per customer, per outlet, per square foot). Again, this would be calculated over given periods of time.

Returns on capital These are explained in unit 68. Examples might be:
- earnings per share in organisations where share capital has been issued or per partner where this form of organisation exists;
- returns on total capital employed.

Volume The volumes of business conducted and the quantities of products and goods moved may be measured. These may include:
- sales, production or throughput per employee, either overall or by occupation, department or function;
- volume of goods sold per customer or per outlet;
- rate of volume turnover per outlet.

Costs Cost targets may be appropriate in relation to earnings, profits and volumes. They may also be used where a business is seeking constant improvement. A business may take into account premises and equipment costs, capital charges, administrative and bureaucratic charges, and purchasing, lease and rental costs. Target costs per employee, per department, per square metre and per premises may be calculated.

Comparisons It is useful for many businesses to analyse their operations in relation to other companies, particularly competitors in their industry. This benchmarking (☞ unit 95) may help to find out whether there is any scope for improvement overall or in certain activities similar to those of competitors. On the other hand, a business may find that competitive advantage can only be gained by adopting strategies that are different from those of competitors. Comparisons are vital in the area of pricing and customer satisfaction. In certain markets, for instance, a business may find that customers will only buy a quality product and are prepared to pay a premium price, rather than receive a poorer product or service at a lower price.

Comparisons of output, volume, profit margins and turnover are also useful. However, care must be taken to compare like with like. For example, one year Honda UK declared a profit of £300 per car produced. This could be compared to the figure given by the exclusive Morgan company that year of £2,500 per car. However, they are not comparable operators. They do not serve the same market. Honda does not enjoy the price premium advantage that Morgan commands. Morgan does not enjoy or seek the global volumes of Honda.

Percentages and annual comparisons Organisations may set themselves targets of 'increasing sales or output by a particular percentage'. Usually the performance is based on performance in previous years. Care needs to be taken when making this type of comparison. A business may make a 2 per cent increase in sales in one year and not regard that as successful. However, in a year when it is facing a difficult market a sales increase of 2 per cent may be very good.

Qualitative aspects Achieving qualitative targets can be as important as meeting quantitative targets such as sales targets. Being seen as 'the top quality operator in the field' by customers is likely to be a route to success.

Question 5

Caring For You is a chain of 10 salons in the Newcastle area which specialises in all aspects of hair, nail and beauty care. The business was originally set up as a fast and cheap service aimed largely at younger people. It had been relatively successful, but sales had started to decline in recent years. The owner of the business consulted staff and customers about what they wanted and found that the market had moved on.

Customers wanted a slower, more stylish experience and were prepared to pay for it. So the salons were redesigned at great expense. A London consultant was brought in to retrain staff. A customer care training programme was introduced and salaries were increased. These were all aspects of what is known as an 'inclusive' approach to business. Successful companies, it was suggested, focused on all those who contributed to the business including staff, shareholders, customers, suppliers and the community rather than just profit per share.

The redesigned salons were taking 10 per cent more than the old ones, turnover was expected to rise from £1 million to £2.5 million within 5 years and pre-tax profits increased from £80,000 to £500,000.

(a) Explain the aspects of implementing change at Caring For You.
(b) Using information in the article, evaluate the new strategy of the business and discuss how such a business might use other methods of evaluation.

Key terms

Competitive advantage - the advantage that a business has over rivals who are competitiors. It can be gained in a variety of ways.
Generic strategies - strategies that can be used by any type of business organisation.
Premium price - a price above the average charged by businesses in the market.
Synergy - where the activities of two or more businesses when brought together create more value than they do separately.
SMART targets - targets that are specific, measurable, achievable, realistic and time based.

Summary

1. What is meant by functional level strategies of a business?
2. State 5 functional level strategies a business might use.
3. State 3 generic strategies a business might use.
4. In what type of market situation might a consolidation strategy be used?
5. Suggest 3 conditions under which market entry might be a suitable strategy.
6. State 4 circumstances where diversification might be a suitable business strategy.
7. Explain when internal growth may not be a suitable strategy.
8. State 4 approaches to operating in global markets.
9. Why might feedback on the effectiveness of strategy be important to a business?
10. Suggest 5 ways in which a business might evaluate strategy.

Case study

ICI

ICI is now classed as 'a leader in sensory perception products'. This shows how much it had changed in the year to July 1998. Once one of the world's leading producers of industrial chemicals, it had become a major manufacturer of products such as toothpaste, flavourings, fragrances and glue for disposable nappies. A decade ago the industrial chemicals division accounted for two thirds of the company's business. By the end of 1998 it was gone. ICI was left as a collection of consumer related businesses, such as Dulux paint, Cuprinol and the businesses mentioned above. In June 1998 it bought Acheson Industries, a US company which makes electronic materials for switches in computer keyboards and films for medical devices. This followed the purchase of Unilever's specialist chemicals division in 1997 for $4.8 billion.

The strategy is simple. It is to make the business less cyclical and its performance more predictable by reducing reliance on chemicals where competition is fierce, prices are volatile and profits cut to the bone. In the 1980s the then chairman had predicted that ICI would have to transform itself from a business that relied on capital to one that relied on skills. Despite years of restructuring the slimmed down ICI chemicals business continued to make losses. One problem was that no sooner had the company identified an area of competitive advantage, than competitors dived in and stole a march. ICI was an innovative company, but to be successful it needed to sell chemical products on a large scale. To be really competitive in chemicals ICI would have had to have merged, for example by joining with a large petrol chemicals group. But it didn't.

Will the restructuring work? Competition for ICI will be inevitable. But the markets it has chosen to operate in are those where setting up overnight is not easy. Charles Miller Smith, ICI's chief executive, said: 'If you build a £100 million ingredients plant you will not get a sale for 5 years. You have to have the skills to develop and offer a range of 200 flavours to a range of customers across the globe'.

The change had been rapid. ICI's total acquisitions and sales were £9 billion in less than a year, although it was suggested that it may have stretched itself, as year end borrowings were £3.8 billion. The business set demanding targets. Miller Smith insists that the business will make an average 20 per cent return on investment. In 1997 the return was 13.4 per cent. Profit margins which were 6.3 per cent in 1997 were estimated to be in double figures a year later, and within 5 years sales were expected to increase from £8 billion to £12 billion.

The new strategy also dispensed with rationalisation, that promises ever increasing costs savings, but results in ever lower staff numbers. The focus was on creating value through sales growth, improving the supply chain and improving the company's skills.

Source; adapted from *The Observer*, July, 1998.

(a) Examine the reasons for the change in strategy by ICI.

(b) Explain the types of strategy that ICI used and the effects on the business.

(c) Evaluate whether the change in strategy would benefit the business.

Figure 16.1 *ICI share price*

ICI
Indexed against FT All-Share
Apr 1978=100

Source: adapted from Datastream, Nikko Europe.

Figure 16.2 *The restructuring of ICI*

The changing shape of ICI
Breakdown of sales:
1987

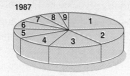

1 Petrochemicals and plastics **23%**
2 Effect products **17%**
3 General chemicals **16%**
4 Paint **11%**
5 Pharmaceuticals **9%**
6 Agrochemicals **8%**
7 Oil **7%**
8 Fibres **6%**
9 Explosives **3%**

1999 (estimates)

1 Speciality chemicals **49%**
2 Paints **29%**
3 Materials **22%**

Source: adapted from Datastream, Nikko Europe.

Markets and the external environment

A market is any situation where buyers come into contact with sellers to exchange goods and services (☞ unit 1). The markets in which a business sells its products are part of the EXTERNAL ENVIRONMENT in which the business operates. Businesses do not operate in a vacuum. There are factors outside the business that may affect its decisions.

● The state of competition. A new competitor entering a market could lead to a reduction in the sales of existing firms.
● The labour market. The availability of low priced labour may influence the location of a business.
● Economic factors and the state of the economy. If people have more money to spend, this may encourage businesses to produce new products. If exchange rates are stable, a business may be more willing to trade on foreign markets.
● Government objectives and government policy. If the government offers training funds, a business may be willing to employ young workers for a period. The reduction of interest rates means that businesses may borrow as they have less to pay back.
● Legislation. There might be laws that affect the product, eg controls on the ingredients that can be used in food.
● Population. The size, age and sex distribution of the population can affect demand for a product, eg an increase in

the birth rate would affect firms marketing baby products.
● Social factors, eg an increase in the amount of crime directed against businesses will affect firms differently. A few, such as security firms, may benefit. Others may find that their costs increase due to, for example, higher insurance premiums.
● Political factors. A shop may change its opening hours because of the influence of a local pressure group.
● Environmental factors. Increased consumer awareness has led many firms to re-evaluate their impact upon the environment. An environmentally friendly business may spend more on waste disposal.
● Technology. The rate of change of technology may influence the type of good produced, eg the development of the microchip has made possible a whole new range of products.

One of the most important influences of markets on businesses is the way in which they help to determine prices. In all markets, buyers (often referred to as consumers) demand goods and services from sellers who supply them. It is the interaction of demand and supply within markets that determines the prices of goods or services.

Demand

DEMAND is the amount of a product that consumers are willing and able to purchase at any given price. Demand is concerned with what consumers are actually able to buy (what they can afford to and would buy), rather than what they would like to buy. So, for example, we could say that the demand for cars in the UK market at an average price of £9,000 might be 130,000 a year.

Table 17.1 shows a **demand schedule** for mushrooms. These figures can be used to draw a **demand curve** as in Figure 17.1. In practice, demand curves are not a straight line, but are usually drawn in this way for simplicity.

The curve shows the quantity of a good or service that will be demanded at any given price. As with nearly all such curves, it slopes downwards from left to right. This is because the quantity demanded is likely to be higher at lower prices and lower at higher prices - **ceteris paribus** (assuming no other things change). In Table 17.1 more mushrooms are bought at

Question 1

Saskia Patel owns a small business that manufactures carpet slippers. She has seen a strong local demand for her products, even though the market demand for slippers has been relatively stable. She wants to expand the business and her bank manager has suggested that now may be a good time to borrow as interest rates are fairly low. One problem she faces is the need to recruit new workers. If she employs skilled workers, they are likely to demand higher wages, increasing her costs. If she employs young workers, she faces training costs, although she will receive some government help for a period. After she employs these workers she may find costs rise after all because of the requirement to pay the minimum wage.

(a) Using an example from the passage, identify the external factors affecting Saskia's business.
(b) In the following year the market demand for slippers increases. How might this solve some of Saskia's problems?

Table 17.1 *The demand schedule for mushrooms*

Price per kilo (£)	Quantity demanded (000 kilos)
0.50	100
1.00	80
1.50	60
2.00	40
2.50	20

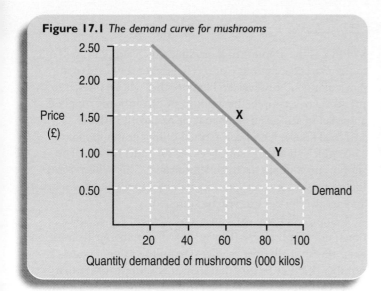

Figure 17.1 The demand curve for mushrooms

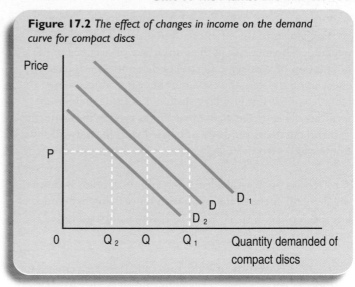

Figure 17.2 The effect of changes in income on the demand curve for compact discs

a price of £0.50 than at a price of £2.50.

A change in the price of a good or service will lead to a change in the quantity demanded. This is shown on the demand curve as a movement along (up or down) the curve. In Figure 17.1, a fall in price from £1.50 to £1, for example, will result in a movement along the curve from point X to point Y.

This will result in a rise in the quantity demanded from 60,000 to 80,000 kilos. The demand curve itself has not moved from its original position. Price changes only lead to an **extension** (rise) or **contraction** (fall) in the quantity demanded.

Changes in demand

As well as price, there is a number of other factors which might affect the demand for a product. Unlike price, a change in any of these factors might cause the whole demand curve to **shift**. This might result in an increase in the demand for a good. The result is that more of a product will be demanded at any given price. Alternatively, it may result in a fall in demand, so less is demanded at any given price.

Income It is reasonable to assume that the higher the incomes of consumers, the more they will be able to buy. When incomes in the country as a whole increase, the demand for products will increase. However, the rise in income is unlikely to be the same for everyone. Some consumers will have large increases in income. Others will find that their incomes do not increase at all. Thus, demand for a product will only increase if the incomes of those consumers buying the product increase.

Assume that consumers of compact discs have had a rise in their income. The demand for compact discs increases as a result. This is shown in Figure 17.2 as a shift to the right of the demand curve from D to D_1. The demand for compact discs has increased at any given price level. In Figure 17.2, demand has risen from OQ to OQ_1. On the other hand, if consumers' incomes were to fall, this would cause the demand

for compact discs to fall at any given price. The result of this would be a shift of the demand curve to the left from D to D_2 in Figure 17.2. Demand will have fallen from OQ to OQ_2.

The price of other goods The demand for one product often depends on the price of another. For example, the demand for one brand of tea bags can be influenced by the price of other brands. A rise in the price of one brand is likely to cause an increase in the demand for others. This is often true of products which have close **substitutes**, such as canned drinks. An increase in the price of cassette tapes may result in a shift in demand from D to D_1, in Figure 17.2. Fewer tapes would be bought if prices rose, leading perhaps to increased demand for compact discs.

Complementary goods are those which are used together. Examples include cars and petrol, and video players and video cassettes. An increase in the price of one will affect the demand for the other. A fall in the price of compact disc players may lead to a shift in demand from D to D_1 in Figure 17.2. More players would be bought and so the quantity demanded of discs would also rise.

Changes in tastes and fashions Some products are subject to changes in tastes and fashions. Skateboards, for example, were bought in huge quantities in the early 1970s. They then went out of fashion for a number of years only to come back into favour again in the late 1980s. It is more usual for a company to stop producing products which have gone out of fashion altogether. Other products have shown more gradual changes in demand. In recent years, the demand for red meat has gradually declined as tastes have changed, often in response to health concerns. This has caused the demand curve for red meat to shift to the left. This means that at any given price, less red meat is now demanded than in previous years. The growth in CD sales over the last decade has shifted the demand curve to the right. Some have suggested that the demand curve for compact discs may shift to the left in the future as internet access to music becomes more popular.

Changes in population As well as changes in population levels, changes in the structure of population can affect demand. The increase in the proportion of over 65s in the population of Western industrialised countries will have an effect upon the demand for a number of products. They include winter-sun holidays, sheltered housing and leisure facilities. This means that, other things staying the same, the demand curve for products associated with the old will shift to the right, with more being demanded at any given price.

Advertising Successful advertising and promotion will shift the demand curve to the right, with more being demanded at any given price. A successful advertising campaign for CDs would have this effect.

Legislation Government legislation can affect the demand for a product. For example, a law requiring all cyclists to wear helmets would lead to an increase in the demand for cycling helmets at any given price.

This section has examined the market demand for goods and services. This is a summing or totalling of the demand curves for individual business's products. So, for example, the market demand curve for CDs, which has been much discussed in this section, is a totalling of the individual demand curves of all the businesses, such as Warner Brothers, Creation and Island, which produce CDs. Unit 42 examines the demand curve for individual businesses.

Question 2

Table 17.2 The demand schedule for ice cream at a local theme park

Price (£)	Quantity demanded
0.80	2,000
0.90	1,600
1.00	1,200
1.10	800
1.20	400

Table 17.2 shows the monthly demand schedule based on the average price of ice creams at a local theme park. It has been predicted that the following changes to the market will occur:
● incomes will rise so that there will be 500 more bought at each level;
● the prices of substitute goods (ice lollies etc.) are likely to rise so that there would be another 500 bought at each price level.
(a) Draw the original demand curve from the figures in the table.
(b) Show the combined effect on the demand curve of the changes in the market.

Supply

SUPPLY is the amount of a product which suppliers will offer to the market at a given price. The higher the price of a particular good or service, the more that will be offered to the market. For example, the amount of mushrooms supplied to a market in any given week may be as shown in Table 17.3.

These figures have been plotted onto a graph in Figure 17.3, which shows the supply curve for mushrooms. The supply curve slopes up from left to right. This is because at higher prices a greater quantity will be supplied to the market and at lower prices less will be supplied.

A change in price will cause a movement either up or down the supply curve. The curve will not change its position assuming that all other factors remain the same. There is a number of other factors that may affect supply other than price. Changes in these factors will cause the whole supply curve to shift.

Table 17.3 The supply schedule for mushrooms

Price per kilo (£)	Quantity supplied (000 kilos)
0.50	20
1.00	40
1.50	60
2.00	80
2.50	100

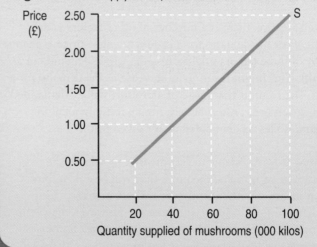

Figure 17.3 The supply curve for mushrooms

Costs of production A fall in the costs of production due, for example, to new technology will mean that more can be offered at the same price. This will cause the supply curve to shift to the right as shown in Figure 17.4, from S to S_1. A rise in the costs of production would cause the supply curve to shift to the left, from S to S_2. A rise in raw material costs or wage costs could lead to such a shift.

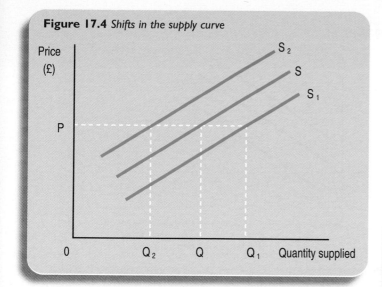

Figure 17.4 *Shifts in the supply curve*

Changes in production Where it is possible to shift production from one area to another, the price of other products can influence the quantity supplied. For example, many farmers are able to produce a wide range of crops on their land. A rise in the price of broccoli, might encourage farmers not only to produce more broccoli, but less of other crops such as turnips. The broccoli price change has affected the quantity of turnips supplied to the market. So a rise in the price of broccoli would shift the supply curve for turnips to the left, in Figure 17.4 from S to S_2.

Legislation A new anti-pollution law might increase production costs causing the supply curve to shift to the left. Similarly, a tax on a product would shift the supply curve to the left.

The objectives of firms Firms might seek to increase their profit levels and their market share. This might reduce the overall level of supply as other firms are forced out of business. The result of this would be a shift of the supply curve in Figure 17.4 from S to S_2.

Expectations If businesses expect future prices to rise they may restrict current supplies. This would be shown as a shift to the left of the supply curve in Figure 17.4, from S to S_2. Similarly, if businesses expect worsening trading conditions they might reduce current supply levels in anticipation of this.

The weather The weather can influence the supply of agricultural products. For example, in the UK a late spring frost can reduce the supply of strawberries, from say S to S_2 in Figure 17.4.

It was shown earlier in this unit that the market demand curve is a summing of individual firms' demand curves. Similarly, the market supply curve is an adding up of the supply curves of individual firms.

Price and output determination

How does the interaction of demand and supply determine the market price and output? Market prices are set where the plans of consumers are matched with those of suppliers. The point at which the demand and supply curves intersect is known as the EQUILIBRIUM PRICE. This is shown in Figure 17.5. The equilibrium price of mushrooms is £1.50. The figure is drawn from Tables 17.1 and 17.3. At this price 60,000 mushrooms will be produced.

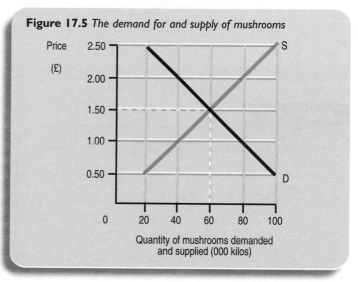

Figure 17.5 *The demand for and supply of mushrooms*

Changes in demand and supply

Shifts in the demand or supply curves will cause a change in the market price.

Changes in demand Assume that there has been a rise in income which has resulted in an increase in demand. The effect of this, as shown in Figure 17.6a, is a shift in the demand curve to the right, all things remaining the same, from D to D_1. This leads to an increase in quantity demanded from OQ to OQ_1. This increase in demand raises the equilibrium price from OP to OP_1. As a result, the quantity supplied extends as well, as producers will supply more at the higher price.

If demand falls, due to lower incomes, from D to D_2, this leads to a fall in quantity demanded from OQ to OQ_2. The equilibrium price falls from OP to OP_2 and at this lower price suppliers will supply less.

Changes in supply Figure 17.6b shows the effect on the equilibrium price of changes in supply. An increase in supply may have been as a result of lower labour costs. This shifts the supply curve from S to S_1. The equilibrium price falls from OP to OP_1 as the supply curve shifts from S to S_1. Consumers are more willing and able to buy goods at the

Figure 17.6 *The effect on equilibrium price of an increase in demand and supply*

(a)

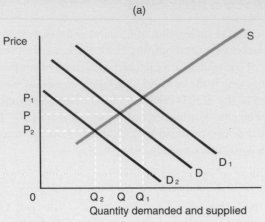

(b)

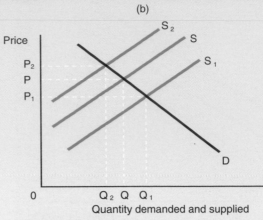

Figure 17.7 *The demand for and supply of organically grown broccoli*

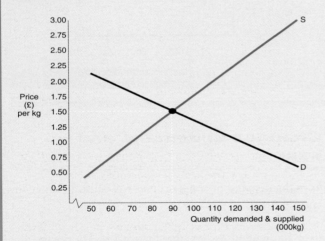

(a) What is the equilibrium price of organic broccoli?
(b) Explain the effect that the following factors will have on: (i) the equilibrium price of organic broccoli; (ii) the demand for broccoli or the supply of broccoli by businesses in the market.
● A reduction in the average incomes of consumers purchasing organic vegetables.
● Improved organic farming methods leading to a reduction in the cost of producing organic broccoli.
● All types of organic vegetables becoming increasingly popular with greater health consciousness amongst food consumers.
● A fall in the price of non-organic broccoli.

Excess demand and excess supply

EXCESS DEMAND occurs when the demand for a product is greater than its supply. This can be illustrated using the demand for and supply of mushrooms shown in Figure 17.8. At a price of £0.50 per kilo, 100,000 kilos of mushrooms are demanded, but only 20,000 kilos are supplied by businesses. This means that there is an excess demand of 80,000 kilos (100,000 - 20,000). This excess demand will result in a shortage of mushrooms, with many consumers being left disappointed.

EXCESS SUPPLY occurs when the supply of a product is greater than the demand for it. In Figure 17.8, at a price of £2.50, 100,000 kilos of mushrooms are supplied by businesses, but only 20,000 are demanded. This means that there is an excess supply of 80,000 kilos of mushrooms. This excess supply will result in a surplus (sometimes referred to as a glut) of mushrooms. This will mean a huge quantity of unsold mushrooms for businesses, with no immediate buyers.

It can be seen in Figure 17.8 that it is only at the equilibrium price, £1.50, that there is no excess demand or supply. At this price all products supplied to the market are purchased and all buyers able to afford the price of £1.50 per kilo will be able to purchase their intended quantity.

Figure 17.8 *The excess demand for and supply of mushrooms*

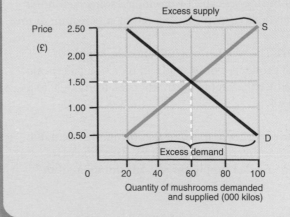

lower price and so the quantity demanded rises as well from OQ to OQ₁.

If supply is cut , the supply curve moves to the left from S to S₂. The equilibrium price rises from OP to OP₂. Consumers are less willing to buy products at this higher price and so the quantity demanded falls from OQ to OQ₂.

Question 4

Table 17.4 *The demand for and supply of sunflower oil*

Price per litre (£)	Quantity demanded (Million litres)	Quantity supplied (Million litres)
0.50	800	500
0.75	700	600
1.00	600	700
1.25	500	800

(a) Draw the demand and supply diagram for sunflower oil using the figures in Table 17.4.
(b) What is the equilibrium price for sunflower oil?
(c) What will be the excess demand or excess supply of sunflower oil at the following prices?
  (i) £0.60;
  (ii) £0.90;
  (iii) £0.70;
  (iv) £1.15.
(d) In each of the examples for (c)(i) to (c)(iv) above, explain the effect on businesses in the sunflower oil market.

Key terms

Excess demand - a situation where the quantity demanded of a product is greater than the quantity supplied at a given price.
Excess supply - a situation where the quantity supplied of a product is greater than the quantity demanded at a given price.
External environment - the factors outside a business that may influence its decisions.
Demand - the quantity of a product purchased at any price.
Supply - the quantity of products which suppliers make available to the market at any given price.
Equilibrium price - the price at which the quantity demanded is equal to the quantity supplied.

Summary

1. State 6 external factors that may affect a business's decisions.
2. What happens to the amount consumers are willing and able to buy as the price of a product falls?
3. State 4 factors that cause the market demand to move to the right.
4. What happens to the amount that businesses are willing to offer to the market as price increases?
5. State 4 factors that cause the market supply curve to shift to the left.
6. What effect will a shift in demand to the left have on equilibrium price and the supply by businesses in a market?
7. What effect will a shift in supply to the right have on equilibrium price and the demand by consumers in a market?
8. What problems will excess supply cause for some businesses in a market?

Case study

Oil

In early 1999 Saudi Arabia, Venezuela and Mexico agreed a deal to shore up oil prices during secret talks. The deal was intended to withdraw around 2 million barrels of oil on a daily basis from world markets. Crude oil prices and oil company shares were expected to react sharply to news of the agreement, which came just after the price of crude oil dropped to a nine year low. Oil prices had fallen by more than a third over the previous five months in reaction to a growing global surplus. The deal between the major oil producing nations took place amid forecasts of a collapse in the oil price unless the main producers took immediate action to curb supply.

Joe Stanislaw, a director of Cambridge Energy Research Associates, predicted that prices could rise by $3-$5 a barrel from their early 1999 level of just over $13. Precise calculations of this nature are, however, hampered by a lack of information about how much oil is at sea being transported in tankers.

Under the terms of the deal Saudi Arabia would match a combined 300,000 barrel a day cut offered by Mexico and Venezuela. Kuwait announced that they would cut production by 125,000 barrels a day, while Algeria said it would reduce supply by 50,000 barrels.

Source: adapted from the *Financial Times*, 23.3. 1998.

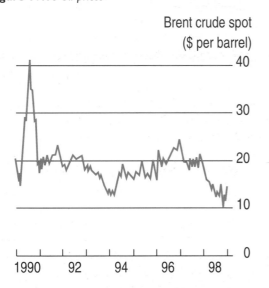

Figure 17.10 *Oil prices*

Brent crude spot
($ per barrel)

Source: adapted from BP, Datastream/ICV.

(a) **Describe the action taken by oil producing countries.**

(b) (i) **Who are likely to be the consumers of oil?**
   (ii) **Suggest two factors which you might expect to determine the demand for oil in the UK.**

(c) **Using a demand and supply diagram and a written explanation, explain how the action taken by oil producing countries will affect:**
   (i) **the equilibrium price of oil;**
   (ii) **production of oil companies;**
   (iii) **consumers of oil.**

(d) **For what reasons do you think that the action taken by Saudi Arabia, Venezuela and Mexico might not work?**

(e) **Using a demand and supply diagram explain why you think that oil companies might be concerned about a global surplus of oil.**

Markets and competition

Unit 17 showed how the prices of products and services can be determined by demand and supply. In market economies, the forces of demand and supply will influence prices in a wide range of different markets. These could be markets divided by geographical boundaries including:

- local markets, such as the market for houses in South London;
- regional markets, such as the market for out of town entertainment in the North West of England;
- national markets, such as the market for personal computers in the UK;
- international markets, such as foreign exchange markets.

On the other hand they could be markets differentiated by use including:

- highly specialised markets, such as the market for water polo playing equipment;
- non-specialist markets, such as the market for potatoes.

The degree of competition in a market will affect how prices are determined. Assessing the level of competition in a market is not as easy as it sounds. Two businesses operating a local bus route, for example, may seem to have little competition except each other. In fact they face competition from other forms of transport such as trains, mini buses and taxis. A new chocolate bar will face **direct** competition from other chocolate bars. But it will also face **indirect** competition from other forms of confectionery, such as crisps or sweets.

Degrees of competition

The amount of competition that exists in a market is known as the MARKET STRUCTURE. There is a number of widely recognised MODELS OF COMPETITION with different market structures. They vary according to:

- the amount of knowledge consumers have about different products;
- the ease with which firms can set up and compete within the market;
- the number of firms operating within the market;
- the extent to which rival products are different.
- The amount of control which businesses exert within their markets.
- The extent to which individual businesses can determine the price of their goods and services.

Perfect competition

The model of PERFECT COMPETITION assumes businesses produce products which are exactly the same. Consumers have 'perfect knowledge' of the market. They are aware of what is being offered by all businesses. There are no barriers to prevent firms from setting up and there is a large number of firms in competition with one another.

Businesses in such markets are known as PRICE TAKERS. Each individual firm has no influence over the price which it charges for its products. If a firm were to charge a higher price than others then no consumers would buy its products, since every product is exactly the same and they would know exactly where to go to buy an alternative. A firm that charged a price below that of others would be forced out of business.

In reality, it is not easy to identify markets which conform to the model of perfect competition. However, there are some which have many of the characteristics of a perfectly competitive market. One example in the UK could be agriculture. There are large numbers of farmers providing farm produce for the market. Farming businesses tend, generally, to be small scale and are unable to influence market price. Furthermore, it is likely that one vegetable will be much the same as another on a different farm. Information about this market is also available in trade journals.

One advantage for businesses of operating in conditions of perfect competition is that they have a strong incentive to operate efficiently. Inefficient businesses are forced out of perfectly competitive markets.

However, there are certain problems.

Question 1

(a) Do you think the businesses producing the above products or services are competing in local, regional, national or international markets? Explain your answer.

(b) What other businesses might: (i) British Telecom; (ii) Nationwide; (iii) Microsoft compete against?

- Businesses only make what are known as 'normal profits'. Normal profits are relatively modest. They are only just enough to prevent new businesses being attracted to the market and existing businesses from leaving the market. Businesses operating under normal competition making larger than normal profits would quickly see these profits eroded by the entrance of new businesses into the market forcing prices, and therefore profits, down.
- Businesses operating under perfect competition are not able to control their prices. This is because of the competitiveness of the markets in which they operate. Such businesses have little control over their own destinies. They are completely governed by market conditions.

It is for the above reasons that businesses prefer to operate in conditions that are less competitive than perfect competition. Wherever possible, the majority of businesses attempt to exert some control over the markets in which they operate.

Monopoly

MONOPOLY occurs when one business has total control over a market and is the only seller of the product. This **pure monopoly** should not be confused with a **legal monopoly**, which occurs in the UK when a firm controls 25 per cent or more of a market.

Monopolists are likely to erect barriers to prevent others from entering their market. They will also exert a strong influence on the price which they charge for their product. However, because monopolists are the only supplier of a product, it does not mean that they can charge whatever they want. If they raise price a great deal demand will fall to some extent. Because of the influence monopolists have on their price, they are often called **price makers**.

Although there are many businesses in the UK which exert a great deal of power in the markets in which they operate, few, if any, could be described as being a pure monopoly. In the past, however, certain businesses have come close to exerting pure monopoly power. Before competitors such as Transco were able to supply gas to consumers, British Gas enjoyed a monopoly position in the gas market. It was the sole supplier of piped gas in the UK. On the other hand, it could be argued that British Gas was operating in the energy market and therefore faced competition from electricity and oil companies. One of the main reasons why British Gas no longer exerts such control over the market for gas is that the government introduced **legislation** to increase competition in markets where monopolies previously existed (☞ unit 22).

From a business's point of view monopoly has certain advantages and problems. To some extent these are the inverse of the benefits and problems of perfect competition. For example, monopolies tend to make 'abnormal' profits compared to competitive businesses. However, there may be little or no incentive to innovate for a large business if it faces a lack of competition. It may therefore be less efficient and

profitable than it is capable. This could lead to bureaucracy, inefficient management and a lower dividend for shareholders.

Monopoly, perfect competition and consumers

Business often attempt to restrict competition in the markets in which they operate. This allows them to have a greater control of prices and to become more profitable. In addition, governments seek to regulate markets in order to control monopolies and protect consumers. This might suggest that competition is better for consumers than monopoly. However, under certain circumstances, consumers may benefit from monopolies.

Prices It might be expected that prices for consumers would be higher under monopolies than under perfect competition. However, monopolies can sometimes provide consumers with lower prices than businesses operating under competitive conditions. This is because the large size of many monopoly businesses allows them to gain economies of scale (☞ unit 93). Costs savings gained by operating on a large scale may allow monopolies to earn large profits. They might then set prices either lower than or the same as low profit making businesses operating under perfect competition.

Choice It could be argued that a large number of businesses competing against each other will lead to greater choice of products for customers. However, there are conditions where competition does not lead to wider choice for consumers. For example, many believe that a wider choice of channels operated by an increasing range of television companies is not improving choice. This is because competing businesses tend to replicate the products of their competitors. In the US, consumers are faced with vast numbers of channels offering what many regard as low quality programmes.

Innovation Businesses in competitive markets have the incentive to innovate as they try to differentiate their products from those of competitors. However, the relatively large profits made by monopolies allow them to invest heavily in research and development which could lead to innovations. Smaller businesses facing intense competition may not be able to finance this research.

Monopolistic competition

This is a market model where there is **imperfect** competition. This means that there is some restriction on competition.

MONOPOLISTIC COMPETITION exists where a large number of relatively small firms compete in an industry. There are few BARRIERS TO ENTRY, so that it is fairly easy for firms to set up and to leave these markets. Firms will also have perfect knowledge of the market.

Each firm has a product that is **differentiated** from the

Question 2

The US based computer giant Intel manufactures microprocessor chips primarily for use in personal computers. In 1996 its profits topped $5.2 billion and it had a turnover of $20.8 billion. At the time it commanded 85 per cent of the world's market for general purpose microprocessor chips and appeared to have an unassailable position. The company is often referred to as Silicon Valley's 'money machine'. The joke is that Intel should give up making chips and simply print dollar bills. To drive its technology forward, Intel planned to spend $4 billion on new plant and equipment in 1997 and $2.5 billion on research and development. No other company could get close to this rate of spending.

Intel does have competitors, albeit distant ones. The company claims to have avoided predatory action against other 'chipmakers' and rather has concentrated on a strategy of growing the market as a whole. The company also has its critics. Internet newsgroups talk of its 'obscene profits'. It also faces discontent from its customers. With its dominant market share, Intel is able to influence industry-wide pricing. It may also allocate scarce chips to individual customers, which gives it enormous power.

Source: adapted from the *Financial Times*, 1997.

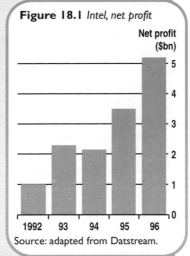

Figure 18.1 *Intel, net profit*

Net profit ($bn)

1992 93 94 95 96

Source: adapted from Datstream.

(a) Which model of competition best describes the market for general purpose microprocessor chips? Explain your answer.
(b) Examine the possible effects of this type of competition on: (i) businesses in the market; (ii) customers, using examples from the article.

others. This is achieved through **branding**, when a product is given an identity of its own (☞ unit 45). A business will face competition from a wide range of other firms competing in the same market with similar, but differentiated, products.

Firms operating under these conditions are not price takers, but they will only have a limited degree of control over the prices they charge. There are few markets of this kind in the UK. Two examples include legal services and the manufacture of certain types of clothing.

Oligopoly

When there are many firms, but only a few dominate the market, OLIGOPOLY is said to exist. Examples include the markets for petrol, beer, detergents, paint and sweets. The majority of businesses in the UK operate under this type of competition.

Under oligopoly, each firm will have a differentiated product, often with a strong brand identity. Several brands may be competing in the same market. Brand loyalty amongst customers is encouraged by advertising and promotion. Firms in such markets are often said to compete in the form of non-price competition. Prices are often stable for long periods, disturbed only by short price wars.

Although brand loyalty does allow some price control, businesses often 'follow' the price of a leader. This means that they tend to be interdependent. In extreme cases firms might even **collude** to 'fix' a price. Sometimes this is illegal and may be called a **restrictive trade practice** (☞ unit 22).

Barriers to entry exist. If it was easy for new firms to enter the industry, they would set up and take the market share of the few large producers. Examples of barriers to entry might be:
● legal restrictions, such as patents which prevent other businesses copying products for a period of time;
● high start up costs, such as the cost of steel manufacturing;
● the promotion or advertising required, for example, in the tobacco or soap powder industries;
● arrangements between businesses, for example in the 1990s newsagents could not stock ice creams by other producers in certain manufacturers' freezers (known as freezer exclusivity);
● collusion between businesses in cartels, which act together to prevent new entrants.

Question 3

Figure 18.2 *Car manufacturer information*

US and Canada
Chrysler
Ford
General Motors (GM)

South Korea
Daewoo
Hyundai
Kia

Japan
Daihatsu
Fuji (Subaru)
Honda
Mazda
Mitsubishi
Nissan
Suzuki
Toyota

Europe
BMW (incl Rover)
Fiat
Ford (incl Jaguar)
General Motors (incl Saab)
Mercedes-Benz
PSA (Peugeot)
Renault
Volkswagen Group
Volvo

Estimated world ranking in year 2005 (millions sold barring mergers)

General Motors	5.2
Toyota	4.4
Ford/Mazda	4.4
Volkswagen	4.0
Fiat	2.4
Nissan	2.3
Honda	2.2
PSA	2.2
Renault	1.9
Mitsubishi	1.4

Market share, Western Europe
Market shares by manufacturer for new registrations, 1997, %

Ford 11, Renault 10, Others 8, BMW 6, Mercedes-Benz 4, Nissan 3, Toyota 3, Volvo 2, Honda 2, Volkswagen 17, GM 12, Fiat 12, Peugeot 11

Total 13.40m

Source: adapted from *Economist Intelligence Unit*.

(a) Which of the models of competition do you think best describes the car market? Explain your answer.
(b) What degree of influence might any one of the top six car manufacturers have on the price of cars in the Western European market?

Table 18.1 *A summary of the characteristics of models of competition*

	Perfect competition	Monopolistic competition	Oligopoly	Monopoly
Barriers to entry	None	Few	Many	Almost impossible for new firms to enter the market
Number of of firms	Many	Many	A few	One
Influence over price	None	Some	Strong	Very strong
Differentiated product	No	Yes	Strong brands	No competition; not necessary

Porter's five forces analysis

The models of competition outlined above provide a useful means of describing markets. It can be argued, however, that they project businesses as being largely passive, simply accepting the constraints of their market structures. Michael Porter (1980) in his book *Competitive Strategy*, suggested that in certain circumstances businesses can influence the markets in which they operate. He outlined five forces that determine the extent to which businesses are able to manage competition within their markets.

Rivalry among competitors Porter argues that competitive rivalry is the main force that affects the ability of businesses to influence markets. This includes:
● the number of competitors - the more competitors the less likely it is that a business will be to have influence;
● their ability to differentiate products - a promotional campaign by a business to differentiate its product will increase its influence;
● the rate of growth of the market - in a fast growing market competition may be less intense and individual firms will have more scope to influence the market;
● the existence of barriers to exit - competition may be intense in markets where businesses are deterred from leaving the market. Exit barriers may include the costs of high redundancy payments or losses as a result of having to sell machinery at reduced prices.

The threat of new entrants The number of businesses in a market may not always be a useful guide to competition in that market. This may also depend on the ability of businesses to enter the market. If it is easy for businesses to enter markets then competition is likely to be greater. This will restrict the ability of a business to influence the market. It is possible that businesses may be prevented or deterred from entering markets due to barriers to entry. For example, the need to invest heavily

in new plant and machinery or to match high levels of promotional spending could deter new businesses from entering a market.

The threat of substitute products This depends upon the extent to which businesses can differentiate their products from those of competitors. A business which struggles to differentiate its products is likely to face intense competition. This is why businesses spend large sums of money attempting to make their products different or seem different from those of competitors. For example, the success of a chain of pizza restaurants may depend on its ability to appear to offer a style of pizza that others do not.

The bargaining power of customers Where customers are strong, there is likely to be more competition between producers and their influence will tend to be weaker. The factors affecting the power of consumers may be:
● the number of customers;
● whether they act together;
● their importance, for example, large supermarket chains have had great influence over food manufacturers;
● their ability to switch products;
● regularity of purchases, for example, consumers on holiday are often 'one-off' purchasers prepared to pay a higher price.

The bargaining power of suppliers Powerful suppliers can increase the costs of a business and decrease the extent to which it can control its operations. The power of suppliers is likely to depend upon the number of suppliers able to supply a business and the importance in the production process of the product being supplied. For example, if a JIT manufacturer can easily switch supplier, the producer will have greater control of the production process.

Question

British Airways turned itself into a world beater on the back of its global network and a protected position at Heathrow airport, the world's busiest airport. However, as markets opened up, due to a huge expansion in the amount of air travel and attempts by governments to increase competition between airlines, heavyweight competitors emerged. International alliances led by United Airlines of the US and Germany's Lufthansa started to take their toll on BA. Nifty niche challengers such as Virgin and British Midland and even the new low-cost European carriers, such as Ryanair and EasyJet, also drew blood. BA's share price fell by more than a half as fears of economic recession and the Asian economic crisis combined with a loss of business travellers on BA to undermine investor confidence in the world's 'most popular airline'.

Source: adapted from *The Observer*, 16.5.1999.

(a) Using Porter's five forces analysis, examine BA's ability to manage competition in the market for international air travel.

Key terms

Barriers to entry - factors that might deter or prevent businesses from entering a market.

Market structure - the characteristics of a market which determine the behaviour of firms operating within it.

Model (of competition) - a simplified theory to explain the types of competition between businesses.

Monopolistic competition - a market structure with freedom of entry and exit, differentiated products and a large number of small firms competing.

Monopoly - a market structure in which only one firm supplies the entire output, there is no competition and barriers to entry exist.

Oligopoly - a market structure with a small number of dominant firms, producing heavily branded products with some barriers to entry.

Perfect competition - a market structure with perfect knowledge, many buyers and sellers, freedom of entry and exit and a homogeneous product.

Price taker - a firm that is unable to influence the price at which it sells its products.

Summary

1. Explain the difference between a local and an international market.
2. What determines the amount of discretion firms have in making their pricing decisions?
3. What is the difference between a price taker and a price maker?
4. What are the 4 models of market competition?
5. Under what conditions might a firm be unable to influence the price it sets for its product?

Case study

Travel trade set for the long haul

More than £30 billion will be spent on overseas travel in 1999 by UK consumers. This was equal to the annual National Health Service budget. £6 billion of that figure would be spent on package tours, of which three quarters would find itself going to just four mega-companies.

The travel trade in 1998 was dominated by takeovers. In just twelve months the big four companies - Thomson, Airtours, First Choice and Thomas Cook - swallowed up more than 10 well known UK tour operators and increased their market share from just over 60 per cent to 80 per cent. The activity was not confined to takeovers of other travel companies. Charter airline companies and travel agents were also included in the merger mania. Despite all the merger activity, increasing numbers of consumers were turning their backs on organised holidays preferring to 'do their own thing'. Ten years before 11 million people took inclusive tours, while 6.5 million tailor-made their own foreign trips. But the number of holidaymakers preferring to do their own thing grew by 77 per cent between 1988-98, compared to growth of 36 per cent in the organised sector.

(a) Are the four travel companies mentioned in the article operating in local, regional, national or international markets? Explain your answer.

(b) Describe the structure of the market in which the holiday companies are operating.

(c) Suggest, using examples, the factors that are likely to influence businesses in the market for holidays.

(d) Why might travel companies wish to take over charter airline companies and travel agencies?

(e) Discuss the extent to which you think that travel companies are able to influence prices in their markets.

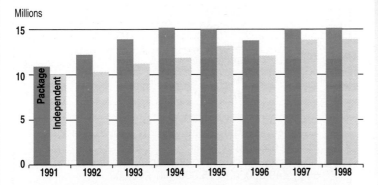

Figure 18.3 *Holidays abroad, by type, 1991-98*

Millions

Source: adapted from *The Guardian*, 23.10.1998 and *The Observer*, 3.1.1999.

The market for labour

Unit 17 looked at the operation of markets for goods and services. It showed how the forces of demand and supply determine prices and the effects of changes in demand and supply on consumers and businesses. It could be argued that the market for labour operates in a similar way. This is because it is concerned with the demand for labour and the supply of labour. Unit 75 explained how an individual business might plan its workforce. It would look at its current and future worker requirements (demand) and the availability of workers (supply).

The demand for labour

In order to produce goods and services businesses need labour (☞ unit 1). Therefore, the demand for labour comes from businesses. The demand curve for labour is determined by the combined behaviour of individual businesses and their approach to employing workers.

To examine the demand for labour it is necessary to consider how businesses reach decisions about taking on extra staff. Most businesses need to make sure that the costs of taking on extra staff are lower than the extra revenue generated by those staff. Take the example of a design business employing another designer at a cost of £2,200 per month. If the additional monthly revenue generated by this designer was more than £2,200 the design business may be satisfied. However, if the extra monthly revenue generated by the new designer was less than £2,200, the design business is unlikely to be satisfied with the decision to take on the new employee.

Table 19.1 illustrates this. It shows that, at a monthly cost of £2,200, Link Design might be prepared to employ five designers. This is because the first to the fifth designers are all adding more to revenue than they are costing Link Design to employ. However, the sixth designer is adding less to revenue than she is costing the business. Therefore, at a monthly cost per designer of £2,200 Link Design would employ five designers. At a monthly cost of £1,300 per designer it would employ six

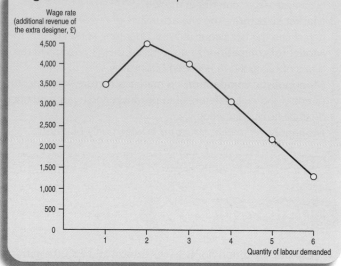

Figure 19.1 *The demand curve for labour*

Wage rate (additional revenue of the extra designer, £)

Quantity of labour demanded

designers. If the cost per month of employing designers were to rise to £3,100, only four designers would be employed.

In general, therefore, it could be argued that the higher the wages of employees, the fewer will be employed by businesses. Similarly, the lower the wages paid to employees the more likely businesses are to employ more workers. This is shown in Figure 19.1, which illustrates the demand curve for labour.

Table 19.1 *Employing extra designers at Link Design Ltd*

Number of designers employed	Total revenue monthly (£)	Additional revenue from each extra designer (£)
1	3,500	3,500
2	8,000	4,500
3	12,000	4,000
4	15,100	3,100
5	17,300	2,200
6	18,600	1,300

Question 1

Stark Ltd is a fish supplying business. Table 19.2 shows information about employees at the business.

Table 19.2

Number employed	Total revenue annually (£)	Additional revenue from each employee (£)
20	350,000	-
21	390,000	-
22	425,000	-
23	450,000	-
24	470,000	-
25	480,000	-

(a) Complete the third column in the above table for the 21st to the 25th worker.
(b) How many workers would Stark Ltd employ at an cost of: (i) £40,000; (ii) £25,000; (iii) £10,000.
(c) What is the most likely employment level in this business? Explain your answer.

Increasing or decreasing demand for labour

Certain factors may increase or decrease the demand for labour.

Changes in labour productivity It is suggested that if workers are able to improve their productivity, the business might be more willing to hire extra workers. For example, Link Design employees may increase productivity so that the additional revenue generated by each employee doubled. This would mean that the sixth worker would now add £2,600 extra revenue (£1,300 x 2). If the wage rate was still £2,200 a month, it would be worth the business employing this worker. If workers in the design industry become more productive, then design businesses may be willing to employ more workers.

Demand for the product The demand for labour is said to be a DERIVED DEMAND for the products or services that businesses produce. For example, Link Design may receive a contract to design a national monthly magazine. It may employ more workers as a result. The design industry may need to employ more workers as a result of demand for promotions for the millennium celebrations in December 1999 and early 2000.

The effect of these changes can be shown by a shift to the right in the demand curve for workers from D to D_1, as shown in Figure 19.2. Businesses will increase the number of workers employed from Q to Q_1. Falls in productivity and reduced sales of products will move the curve to the left, reducing the demand for workers.

The supply of labour

The supply curve for labour shows the amount of labour which will be supplied to the market at a particular wage rate.

Figure 19.2 *Changes in the demand for labour*

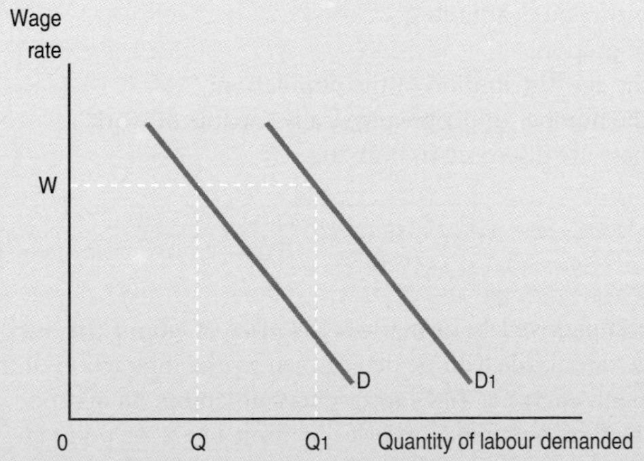

It is possible to show how individual workers, workers in an industry and the total supply of workers will react to a particular wage rate.

Individual workers For an individual worker, the supply of

Question 2

In April 1999 Ford's assembly lines at Dagenham celebrated the first capacity increases at the plant for 20 years. Output increased from 272,000 to 450,000 vehicles a year. Changes in working practices narrowed the productivity gap with European competitors. It was estimated in 1999 that Dagenham was Ford's most productive plant. The start of this improvement came 10 years previously. The company had threatened to close the poorly performing plant unless the workforce could improve quality and productivity to match Ford's other European plants. It was estimated at that time that Dagenham was 30 per cent less efficient than Ford's Cologne factory.

Source: adapted from the *Financial Times*, 22.4.1999.

Figure 19.3 *The best plants in Europe*

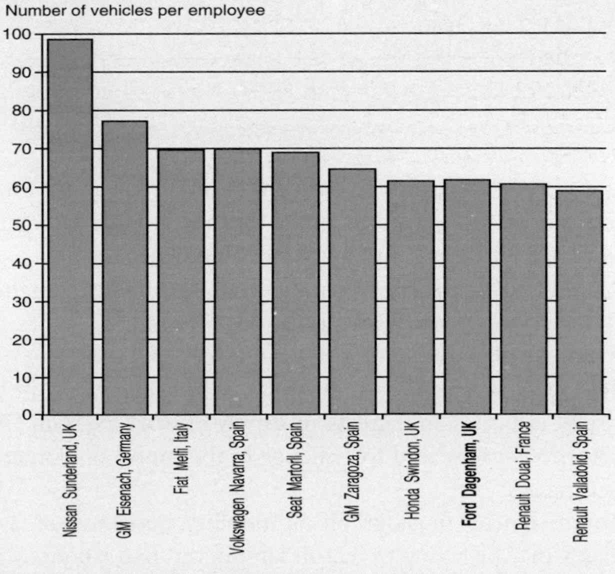

Source: adapted from Economic Intelligence Unit.

(a) Describe the problems faced by the Ford Dagenham plant.
(b) Explain how changes made at the plant are likely to have affected the demand for labour.

labour is the number of hours that he or she is prepared to work. As the REAL WAGE RATE rises, a worker is likely to want to work longer hours. The real wage shows what the wage of the worker can actually buy because it takes into account changes in the prices of goods. This is shown in Figure 19.4. At a real wage rate of OW, OQ hours are worked. Above OW it has been suggested that an increase in the price of labour may lead to less labour being offered to the market. This is because a higher wage may allow individuals to earn the same amount as on a lower wage, but by working for less time. So, for example, someone working for 40 hours per week at £25 per hour would earn £25 x 40 = £1,000 per week. If the wage were to increase to £30 per week, the same person could work for 35 hours per week (£30 x 35 = £1,050) and earn the same quantity. The effect of this tendency for individuals to work less creates the backward sloping individual supply curve for labour, shown in Figure 19.4.

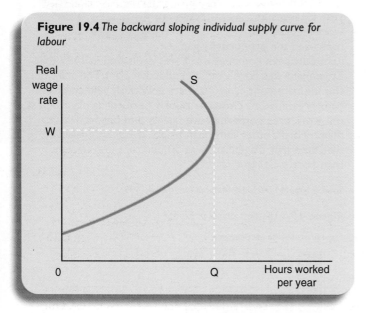

Figure 19.4 *The backward sloping individual supply curve for labour*

may be influenced by people's attitudes to certain areas of the country, family ties to certain areas and government help to change location (☞ unit 100).
● OCCUPATIONAL MOBILITY is the extent to which labour is able to move from one occupation to another. Occupational mobility is linked to the qualifications and skills of labour. Highly qualified and skilled employees tend to be able to change occupations more easily. The level of skills and qualifications required for some occupations are very high. This means that it is not straightforward for those trained in other occupations to move into these jobs. For example, a shortage of forensic scientists could not be quickly solved by recruiting labour from other areas.
● The availability of training schemes (☞ unit 79) may improve the supply of labour. These may be business or industry schemes or government funded schemes. They may retrain existing workers or train unemployed people (☞ unit 24).

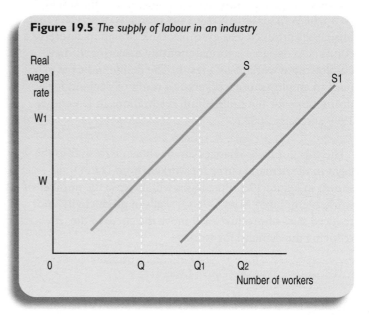

Figure 19.5 *The supply of labour in an industry*

Supply to an industry It is argued that the supply curve for workers in an industry is generally upward sloping, from left to right. This is shown in Figure 19.5. More workers are prepared to offer their services to the labour market at higher real wage rates. As real wages rise from OW to OW_1, more workers are prepared to offer their services, OQ to OQ_1.

Figure 19.5 also shows shifts in the supply curve. A shift to the right indicates an increase in supply of workers, from OQ to OQ_2. What may lead to a change in the supply of workers to businesses?
● Improvements in geographical mobility. Businesses in Essex may be trying to recruit labour, but find labour shortages in the area. The success in recruiting new labour may depend upon the ability to attract employees from other parts of the country. If labour is GEOGRAPHICALLY MOBILE, willing and able to move from one part of the country to another, businesses may be more able to recruit new labour. Geographical mobility

Total supply The total supply curve for labour is also said to be upward sloping. The total supply of labour for the whole population will depend upon a variety of factors, such as:
● birth and death rates;
● migration;
● the age distribution of the population;
● the number of people physically capable of work.
These are discussed in unit 20.

Wage and employment determination

In competitive labour markets the price of labour (the real wage rate) is likely to be determined by the interaction of the demand curve for and supply curve of labour. As in other markets, the equilibrium price (☞ unit 17) is the point at which the demand and supply curves intersect. In

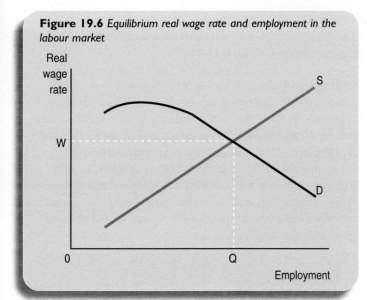

Figure 19.6 *Equilibrium real wage rate and employment in the labour market*

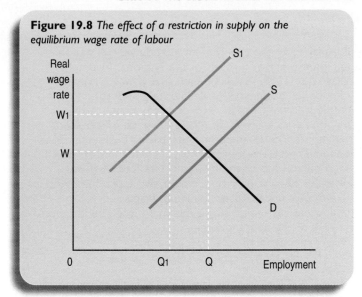

Figure 19.8 *The effect of a restriction in supply on the equilibrium wage rate of labour*

competitive labour markets this will determine the rate that wage earners are paid by businesses. This is shown in Figure 19.6. The diagram also shows the number of workers employed at this equilibrium real wage rate.

Labour market conditions and business

Different conditions in the labour market influence the demand for and supply of labour by businesses. These conditions are influenced by factors that are often outside the control of businesses. They may lead to situations were there are changes in the demand for or supply of labour. They may also create situations of excess demand or excess supply.

Government intervention in the labour market
Governments usually intervene in labour markets in order to

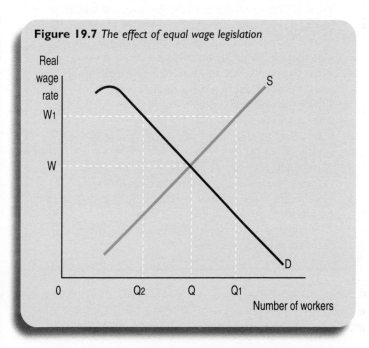

Figure 19.7 *The effect of equal wage legislation*

pursue 'social' aims, such as ensuring that all employees are paid at least a minimum amount or to prevent discrimination. For example, the **Equal Pay Act of 1970** (☞ unit 80) aimed to prevent businesses paying women less than men for the same or similar work. Some businesses which had previously been paying women less than men, faced increased wage costs as a result. In certain circumstances, this led to a reduction in employment. This can be seen in Figure 19.7, which shows the demand and supply curves for labour in an industry. The equilibrium wage rate is OW and employment is OQ. The effect of equal pay legislation is to raise the wage rate to OW_1. As a result of the higher wages, workers are prepared to supply OQ_1 labour, but employers only want OQ_2 workers. Unemployment is therefore OQ_1-OQ_2. The OQ_2 workers still employed have higher wages, but OQ_1-OQ_2 workers have lost their jobs.

Trade unions and professional groups These organisations seek to further the aims of their members (☞ unit 85). One of the ways in which they do this is by attempting to increase or maintain the pay levels of their members. The main way in which they attempt to do this is through collective bargaining (☞ unit 86). Trade unions and professional organisations which are successful may be able to push wage levels above the equilibrium level. The effect of this is similar to that shown in Figure 19.7. This is also the case if the union can negotiate some form of minimum wage.

Unions and professional organisations may also seek to restrict the supply of labour to a particular market. The solicitor's organisation known as the Law Society, for example, has severe examinations which all aspiring solicitors must pass. Many believe that one of the functions which these examinations serve is to restrict the supply of new solicitors. The effect of this is shown in Figure 19.8. It can be seen that a restriction in the supply of solicitors causes a shift to the left of the supply curve from S to S_1. The result in the fall in the supply of labour is a rise in the equilibrium wage

Question 3

In April, 1999 the government introduced the national minimum wage as a result of the National Minimum Wage Act, 1998. The Act meant that it was a criminal offence for businesses to deliberately underpay employees, fail to keep records of payments made to employees or prevent an Inland Revenue officer from seeing records. In addition, underpaying businesses could be fined twice the minimum pay for each day on which each person has been underpaid. The following wage rates for full and part time employees applied in 1999:

● workers under 18: no minimum wage;
● apprentices under 26: no minimum wage for the first year of the apprenticeship;
● workers aged 18 to 21: £3 per hour;
● workers aged over 21: £3.60 per hour.

Figure 19.9 *Number of employees affected by the minimum wage by age and industry (thousands)*

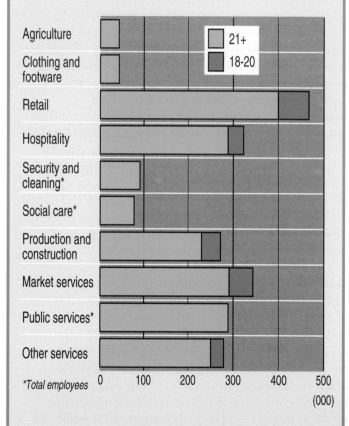

(a) How might the minimum wage affect the supply of labour to businesses forced to increase their pay rates?
(b) Using a demand and supply diagram, illustrate how the minimum wage might affect businesses in: (i) the clothing and footware industry; (ii) the retail sector.

rate from W to W_1. This is because labour is more scarce. The demand for labour by businesses will also fall because of the higher wage rate, from OQ to OQ_1.

The amount of unemployment At higher levels of unemployment businesses are able to recruit from a larger pool of labour. This means that suitable labour may be more readily available and the increased supply of labour may force down the equilibrium wage. Labour shortages at times of high employment, either in the economy as a whole or in particular sectors of the economy, are likely to have the opposite effect. This will mean that businesses have a smaller pool of available labour from which to recruit and upward pressure on the equilibrium wage.

Key terms

Derived demand for labour - when the demand for workers by businesses is the result of demand for the product or service produced by businesses.
Geographical mobility - the ease with which workers can move from one occupation to another in a different location.
Occupational mobility - the ease with which workers can switch from one type of job, with particular skills, to another requiring different skills.
Real wage rate - the value of the wage rate taking into account the effect of prices. It shows how much the value of the money wage rate can purchase.

Summary

1. What is meant by the demand for labour?
2. What is likely to happen to the demand for labour by businesses if wage rates rise?
3. State 2 factors that can lead to an increase in the demand for labour by businesses.
4. What happens to the amount of hours individual workers may want to work at higher wages?
5. What happens to the supply of labour by workers as wage rates rise?
6. State 2 factors that may lead to an increase in the supply of labour by workers.
7. How might a fall in the supply of workers affect: (a) wage rates; (b) demand by businesses?
8. How might wage legislation affect a business's demand for labour?
9. If unemployment is high, how might this affect recruitment by a business?

Case study

Changes in the labour market

Modern apprenticeships (MAs) provide high quality work based training for young people to NVQ level 3. Training is carried out against a series of industry designed frameworks. Orange, the mobile phone company, required highly skilled employees. It decided that the best way to ensure a good supply of technicians was through modern apprenticeships. Nine successful candidates became

Orange's first technician apprentices in 1997. Around 70 per cent of employers agree that MA's provide more benefit to their industry than previous training programmes. They agree that there has been an improvement in alleviating skills shortages, raising skill levels, providing extra funding for training and providing better quality staff.

Source: adapted from *Labour Market Trends*, February, 1999.

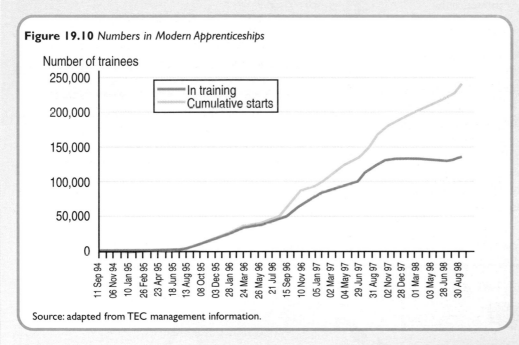

Figure 19.10 *Numbers in Modern Apprenticeships*

Source: adapted from TEC management information.

In 1999 the chairman of the National Skills Task Force, Chris Humphries, suggested that a compulsory levy could be placed on employers to pay for training. It was suggested that the UK was falling behind competitors by not providing workforce training. A 'major skills deficiency' was identified in the UK which could damage productivity among UK craftsmen, technicians and foremen.

(a) **What problems in the UK labour market are suggested in the data?**
(b) **Describe the possible changes that are taking place to deal with these problems in the UK.**
(c) **Explain how 'a major skills deficiency among UK craftsmen, technicians and foremen' might affect: (i) productivity; (ii) the demand for these workers by businesses.**
(d) **Using demand and supply diagrams and explanations, examine how the changes taking place in the labour market might affect: (i) the supply of labour; (ii) the wage rate; (iii) the demand for labour by businesses.**

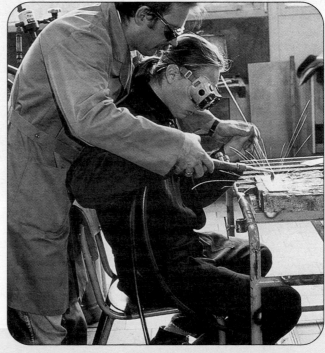

20 Population and Business

The influence of population on business

People are vital to the operation of businesses. They provide organisations with labour (☞ unit 1). People also demand the goods and services that businesses produce. Changes in total population can affect businesses. A growing population is likely to place greater demand on a country's resources. Businesses are also affected by the structure of the population of the markets within which they operate. A higher proportion of people who are elderly means greater need for support. This unit considers the main trends in these DEMOGRAPHIC factors and how they influence the operation of businesses.

Population size and business

In 2000 the world's population was estimated to be around 6 billion people. It was predicted to grow by 90 million a year. This would mean that total world population would double by the year 2050 if this continued.

Different countries have different population sizes. Their populations also grow at different rates. Figure 20.1 shows how the UK population has grown from around 52 million in 1961 and how it is projected to increase to more than 60

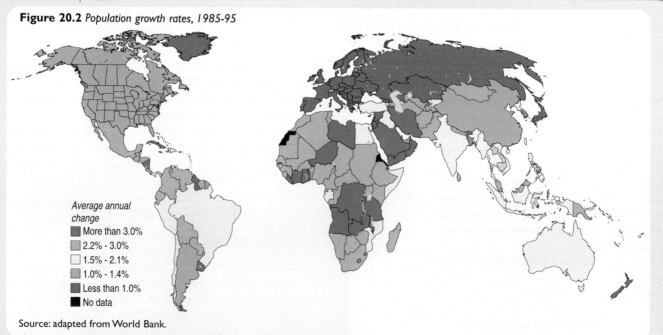

Figure 20.1 *The population of the United Kingdom, 1961-2021*

Source: adapted from *Social Trends*, Office for National Statistics

million by 2021. In 1997 the UK had an estimated population of 59 million. Between 1990 and 1997 the UK had average population growth rate per year of 0.3 per cent. Compare this to Cameroon. In 1997 it had a smaller population of 14 million. Over the period 1990-97, the average population growth rate per year was greater, at 2.9 per cent.

What effect might a growing population have on businesses?

● There is likely to be greater demand for goods and services.

Question

Figure 20.2 *Population growth rates, 1985-95*

Average annual change
- ■ More than 3.0%
- ■ 2.2% - 3.0%
- □ 1.5% - 2.1%
- ■ 1.0% - 1.4%
- ■ Less than 1.0%
- ■ No data

Source: adapted from World Bank.

(a) Describe the trends taking place in Figure 20.2.
(b) Using this information, explain the possible benefits and problems for businesses based in Africa.

● There is likely to be a larger pool of labour.
● There may be growing pressure on resources, if population growth is greater than the growth in output.

The factors affecting population growth and business

What factors might determine the growth of a country's population and how might this affect businesses? It is suggested that there are three main factors which affect population growth - births, deaths, and migration. Table 20.1 shows the effect of changes in these three factors on the population of the UK between 1951 and the projected population in 2021.

Table 20.1 *Population changes*

United Kingdom						Thousands
	Average Annual change					
	Population at start of period	Live births	Deaths	Net natural change	Net migration and other	Overall change
Mid-year estimates						
1951-1961	50,287	839	593	246	6	252
1961-1971	52,807	963	639	324	-12	312
1971-1981	55,928	736	666	69	-27	42
1981-1991	56,352	757	655	103	43	146
1991-1997	57,808	754	640	113	87	200
Mid-year projections						
1997-2001	59,009	719	634	85	69	154
2001-2011	59,618	690	624	66	65	131
2011-2021	60,929	694	628	66	65	131

Source: adapted from *Social Trends*, Office for National Statistics

The number of births If nothing else changes, a greater number of births will increase the population of a country. A larger number of births may affect businesses in a number of ways. This is discussed in the next section.

The number of deaths If nothing else changes, a smaller number of deaths should increase the population. Furthermore, changes in the number of years people are expected to live can affect businesses. This is also discussed in the next section.

Migration NET MIGRATION is the difference between the number of people entering a country (immigration) and the number leaving (emigration). **Positive** net migration occurs when more people enter the country than leave it. **Negative** net migration occurs when more people leave the country than enter it.

Changes in immigration and emigration might affect businesses in a country in a number of ways.
● **Immigration.** The effect of immigration on the demand for a business's products may depend upon the age and income levels of immigrants and where they settle. For example, parts of North London reflect immigration from Arab countries. A range of businesses, such as restaurants and supermarkets, have emerged to meet the needs of those settling in that area. The effects of immigration upon labour supply may depend upon the need for businesses to recruit the skills that immigrants possess. Where there are labour shortages, immigration can be a way of filling vacancies. The National Health Service, for example, has often relied upon immigrants to fill posts. Immigrants may also possess entrepreneurial skills which will help them to set up their own businesses.
● **Emigration.** This occurs when people leave a country. Large scale emigration from certain areas or by certain age groups can affect demand for businesses serving particular parts of the country or age groups. Emigration can also affect the pool of qualified workers that businesses can choose from. There are two reasons for this. First, emigrants tend to be mainly young people between the ages of 20 -40. They are more likely to possess the energy and up-to-date skills and knowledge most in demand by businesses. Second, many emigrants from the UK are amongst the most highly skilled and able employees. They are likely to be tempted away by offers of better salaries and conditions elsewhere.

Between 1985/87 and 1995/97 the average number of people both leaving and entering the UK who were professionals and managers increased. The increase, however, was greater among immigrants.

Age distribution of the population and business

POPULATION STRUCTURE is concerned with the breakdown or distribution of the population according to a variety of categories. This age distribution of the UK population looks at the numbers of people in the total population that fall into different age groups.

The birth rate, death rate and net migration from a country can all affect the age distribution of the population. Changes in these factors can affect businesses in a number of ways.

Birth rate The BIRTH RATE is measured by the number of live births per thousand of the population. The birth rate varies according to many factors. For example, in the UK in the 1970s there was a decline in the birth rate, perhaps due to better contraception and a growing number of women choosing to go out to work. The growing number of births in the 1980s may have been due to the larger number of women of child bearing age. In the late 1990s women in their twenties were having 1.3 children on average, compared to 1.9 thirty years earlier.

How might a fall in the birth rate affect businesses?
● It could be argued that the fall in the birth rate in the 1970s should have led to a decline in the demand for baby

products. However, increases in real incomes may have offset this, so that businesses selling baby products have continued to be successful.

● A decline in the birth rate does have consequences for the future supply of labour. Falls in the birth rate can lead to a 'demographic timebomb', with shortages of young workers available to businesses. The low number of births in the 1970s led to a smaller proportion of teenagers and people in their 20s in the 1990s. It was suggested that there could be labour shortages in the 1990s as a result. The recession in the early 1990s and falls in demand prevented this to some extent.

● Falls in the birth rate can lead to lower school numbers. This may be reflected in a fall in demand for teachers and for school materials.

An increase in the birth rate may also affect businesses. After the Second World War (1945) there was a large increase in the birth rate. These 'baby boomers' were approaching middle age in the late 1990s. Many businesses attempted to target these groups. For example, record companies reissued music on CD that these people may have listened to when they were younger, hoping for them to buy again.

The death rate The DEATH RATE is the number of deaths per thousand of the population. The death rate in the UK and other EU nations has been declining steadily since the end of the Second World War (1945). Combined with increases in the population as a whole in the UK, the decline in the death rate has meant steadily increasing numbers of people in older age categories. It is suggested that the number of people aged 60 and above will continue to increase in the future. The UK is said to have an **ageing population**. This means that there is a growing number of older people as a proportion of the population. What will be the effects of this ageing population?

● Changing patterns of demand. Some elderly people enjoy relatively high retirement incomes. This means that the demand for goods and services associated with the elderly is likely to increase. There could be increasing demand for leisure activities for the elderly, medical products, sheltered housing and specialist household goods. An example of a business which has benefited from this change is Saga holidays. It began by specialising in vacations for over 50s, Now it has expanded its activities into financial services.

● Effects on the labour market. Advances in medicine, better sanitation and housing and increasing affluence have all led to people living longer and healthier lives. One of the side effects of this has been an increasing pool of labour amongst those in their 50s, 60s and even 70s.

● Effects on government. An ageing population is likely to mean more demand for state provided services like hospitals and provisions such as bus passes and state pensions. There is also likely to be a need to raise more money from those in work, for example by taxation, to pay for those who are retired. There will be a rise in the DEPENDENCY RATIO. This is the proportion of

dependants or non-workers to workers.

Migration If large numbers of younger or older people are emigrating from or immigrating to a country, this can affect its age distribution. For example, the emigration of large numbers of younger people from a country will tend to leave it with an older population, as discussed in the previous section.

Question

Peter Cook was 62 when he applied for a job as a DIY adviser at a B&Q centre in Wandsworth, South London. 'I was retired and frankly bored', said Mr Cook. 'I had worked for a construction company for 50 years, so I knew I could do the job. And they wanted someone with experience who could be trusted by the customers.' Although Mr Cook is paid more than some of the younger DIY advisers, he believes the company benefits in the long run. 'A lot of our customers are in the over-50s age group, and I think they prefer talking to someone like me.'

In 1989 and 1990 B&Q opened stores in Macclesfield and Exmouth which were completely staffed by the over 50s. 'More mature employees are likely to have a different perspective of what constitutes good customer service', said Martin Toogood, B&Q's UK managing director.

Source: adapted from *The Guardian*, 17.1.1998.

(a) Explain the possible advantages to B&Q of employing increasing numbers of older employees.
(b) Examine the problems for B&Q of the employment policy it has adopted for its stores in Macclesfield and Exmouth.

Gender distribution of the population and business

There is a higher proportion of women in the UK population than men. In the late 1990s these ratios were 50.8 per cent and 49.2 per cent. This is despite the fact that more boys than girls are born in the UK. The main reason for this is that the death rate is higher for men than for women. On average, women live longer than men. This means that there are higher proportions of women in older age groupings.

Figure 20.3 shows that over the age of 80, there are far more women than men. The gender imbalance amongst younger age groupings is far less marked. Providing services for older, often single women may represent an increasingly important market for businesses. A change in the ratio of men to women may also affect the birth rate. Fewer women may mean fewer children are born.

Although not directly related to the gender distribution, arguably the single biggest change for businesses in this area has been the increasing number of women entering the labour market. Businesses are increasingly targeting women in their marketing of products such as cars and electrical goods. Women are also obtaining senior posts in

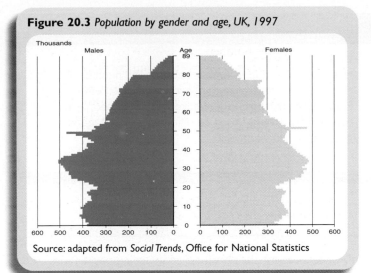

Figure 20.3 *Population by gender and age, UK, 1997*

Thousands

Males / Age 89 / Females

Source: adapted from *Social Trends*, Office for National Statistics

management and becoming a relatively larger part of the workforce. Business have to respond to this in their recruitment and provision of facilities for women (☞ unit 80).

Geographical distribution of population and business

The movement of people between countries is called migration. The location and movement of people within a country may also affect businesses. In the 1990s there were a number of trends in UK population that could have affected businesses.

● Urban and rural location. In Great Britain, almost 90 per cent of people lived in urban areas in the 1990s. In recent years this trend has been reversed in certain parts of the country. For example, there have been noticeable declines in the populations of Inner London, Manchester and Liverpool. In 1997, for example, London experienced a fall in population of 55,000 people. The South West experienced the largest net gain in population.

● Age and location. In general, younger people are more likely to live in urban areas than older people. In the 1990s 41 per cent of the population under 30 lived in urban areas, compared to 36 per cent in rural areas.

● Age and migration. Young people tend to have higher mobility than older people.

How might businesses have been affected? It is possible that businesses may react to demand by younger people in cities. For example, in Inner London and Manchester house builders have responded to these changes by building houses and flats suited to the needs of younger people. Their marketing of these developments has been geared to the needs of younger buyers. The movement out from cities may encourage support businesses to locate in semi-rural or urban fringe areas. Examples may be multiplex cinemas, shopping malls and family orientated pubs.

Figure 20.4 *Economic activity rates of women aged 16-59 by age of youngest dependent child, UK, 1988, 1993, 1998*

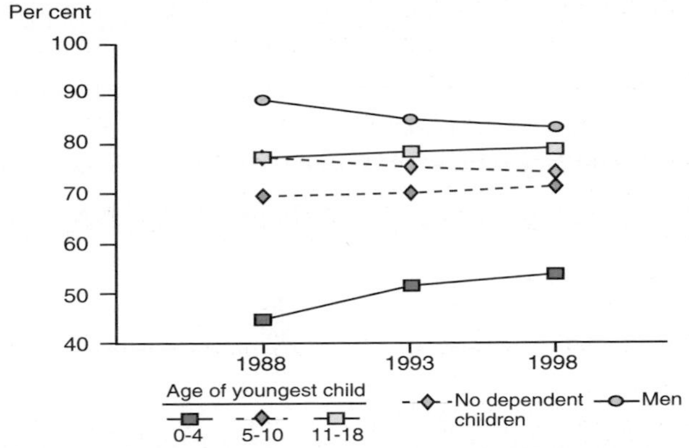

Per cent

Age of youngest child: 0-4, 5-10, 11-18 — No dependent children — Men

Source: adapted from *Labour Market Trends*, Office for National Statistics, March 1999.

Stay beautiful.

Drive the safest car in its class.

The New Mégane

RENAULT

(a) Describe the trends taking place in Figure 20.4.
(b) Comment on the advertisement in the light of your answer to (a).

Other changes in the structure of the population

Households One of the most significant changes in the structure of the population has been changes in the households within which people live. Increasingly people are living in smaller units, especially one person households, and less in extended and nuclear family groups. This has been the result of increases in the number of divorces and older people living longer after their partners have died. Businesses may be able to cater for the needs of people in these groups by developing fast, microwavable food, single accommodation or singles holidays, for example.

Ethnic minority groups The age structure of ethnic minority groups may vary. For example, people from black groups other than Black African and Black Caribbean are more likely than people from the Chinese group to have been born in the UK. Certain ethnic groups have a younger age structure. 45 per cent of Bangladeshis in the UK are under the age of 16, for instance.

Key terms

Birth rate - the number of live births per thousand of the population.

Death rate - the number of deaths per thousand of the population.

Demographic factors - features of the size, location and distribution of the population.

Dependency ratio - the proportion of dependants or non-workers to workers.

Net migration - the difference between the number of people entering a country (or region) and the number leaving it.

Population structure - the breakdown of the people in a country into groups based on differences in age, gender, geographical location etc.

Summary

1. What does the population growth rate show?
2. Suggest 3 effects of a growing population on businesses.
3. State 3 factors that affect population size and growth.
4. What happens to population if net migration is negative?
5. How might immigration affect businesses?
6. State 2 factors that might cause a fall in the birth rate.
7. How might a fall in the birth rate affect a business?
8. State 2 benefits to a business of an ageing population.
9. How might a larger proportion of women than men affect population?
10. State 2 other features of the structure of population that might affect a business.

Case study

The singles club?

Is the UK becoming a singles club? Are more people living on their own? How old are single people in the UK and what do they do in their spare time?

(a) Identify the main trends taking place in the data.

(b) Suggest possible reasons to explain the trends you have identified.

(c) Explain the effects of each of these trends on:
   (i) possible business opportunities;
   (ii) the likely supply of workers to businesses.

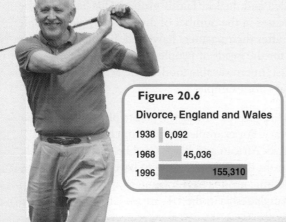

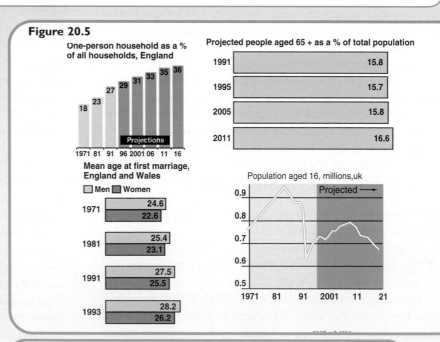

Figure 20.5

One-person household as a % of all households, England

18, 23, 27, 29, 31, 33, 35, 36
Projections
1971 81 91 96 2001 06 11 16

Projected people aged 65 + as a % of total population

1991 — 15.8
1995 — 15.7
2005 — 15.8
2011 — 16.6

Mean age at first marriage, England and Wales
☐ Men ■ Women

1971 — 24.6 / 22.6
1981 — 25.4 / 23.1
1991 — 27.5 / 25.5
1993 — 28.2 / 26.2

Population aged 16, millions, uk
Projected →
0.9, 0.8, 0.7, 0.6, 0.5
1971 81 91 2001 11 21

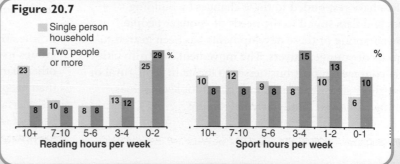

Figure 20.6

Divorce, England and Wales

1938 — 6,092
1968 — 45,036
1996 — 155,310

Figure 20.7

☐ Single person household
■ Two people or more

23, 8, 10, 8, 8, 8, 13, 12, 25, 29 %
10+ 7-10 5-6 3-4 0-2
Reading hours per week

10, 8, 12, 8, 9, 8, 8, 15, 10, 13, 6, 10 %
10+ 7-10 5-6 3-4 1-2 0-1
Sport hours per week

Governments and the economy

Unit 17 explained that a number of external factors can affect businesses. One of these factors is the operation of the economy in which the business operates. Changes in the economy can affect how businesses make decisions. For example, a growing economy, with increased spending by consumers, may encourage a business to expand production. Governments often attempt to influence the economy in order to achieve their objectives. The activities of government can also influence businesses.

How a simple economy operates

A useful tool for analysing how an economy works is the CIRCULAR FLOW OF INCOME. It is often used in **macroeconomics** - the study of the whole economy. The circular flow shows how money flows around the economy. In Figure 21.1, businesses (or producers) buy land, labour and capital from households - the users of goods and services (point 1). Households receive rent, wages, interest and profit (income) in return. This is shown as point 2. The money they earn is spent (point 3) on goods and services produced by businesses (point 4). So, money (or **income**) flows from businesses to households and back again - a circular flow of income around the economy.

How much money is flowing around the economy? The money earned by households, their income (Y), is spent on goods and services (E), which are produced by businesses - their output (O). In the national accounts of economies these are all defined so that they are equal. We can say that the value of:

$$Y \equiv E \equiv O$$
(where $\equiv$ represents **must equal**)

In practice, the way that economies work is more complex, as explained in the next section.

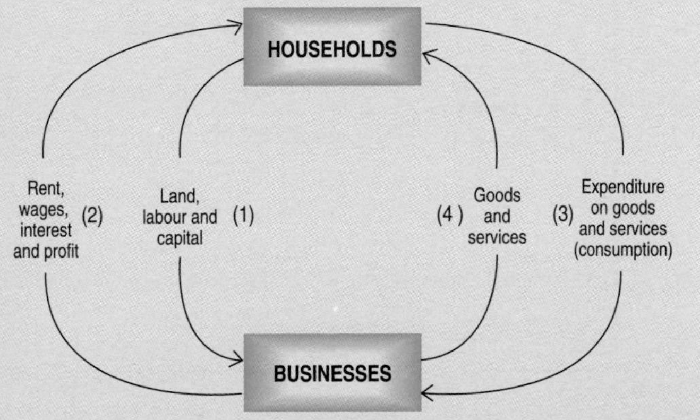

A more complex economy

In Figure 21.1 households spend all of their money on goods and services. Is this likely? In practice they will spend some money (known as consumption) and save some as well. Saving takes money out of the circular flow - a WITHDRAWAL.

What about businesses? They are not likely to spend all their revenue on rent and wages. They will also invest some in machinery and equipment. These are used to produce goods and services which increase money in the economy - an INJECTION.

There is a number of injections and withdrawals in a more complex economy. Injections into the UK economy include:
- investment (I) - spending on fixed capital, such as machinery and factories, and circulating capital, such as stocks and work-in-progress (☞ unit 94) which enter the circular flow;
- government spending (G) - spending by government on new schools and motorways, for example, or subsidies to firms;
- exports (X) - goods and services sold abroad, earning money for the UK which enters the circular flow of income.

Withdrawals can be:
- savings (S) - money saved by households, for example in bank accounts, which is not then available to spend;
- taxation (T) - money taken out of the economy from businesses and households by government through taxation, such as income tax;
- imports (M) - goods and services coming into the country paid for by money leaving the circular flow to be paid to overseas producers.

Injections and withdrawals are shown in Figure 21.2.

How can we measure how much money is flowing around the circular flow? The value of a country's **economic activity** is known as its GROSS NATIONAL PRODUCT (GNP). Figures 21.1 and 21.2 can be used to show how GNP can be measured.
- Income method - adding up all the income earned by households (rent, wages, interest and profit).

Figure 21.1 *The circular flow of income*

HOUSEHOLDS

Rent, wages, interest and profit (2) — Land, labour and capital (1) — Goods and services (4) — Expenditure on goods and services (consumption) (3)

BUSINESSES

Figure 21.2 *The circular flow of income showing injections and withdrawals*

HOUSEHOLDS

Savings ← — → Investment
Taxes ← Income — Expenditure ← Government spending
Imports ← — → Exports

BUSINESSES

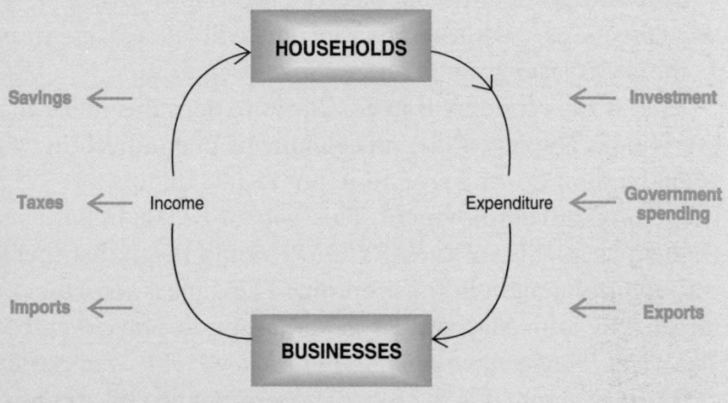

- Output method - adding up the value of all goods and services produced by businesses.
- Expenditure method - adding up the spending of consumers (C), the investment of business (I), the expenditure of government (G) and the spending of people overseas on exports minus the spending of a country on imports from abroad (X - M). These are often known as items which make up AGGREGATE DEMAND. The relationship is often expressed as:

$$Y = C + I + G + (X - M)$$

where Y equals GNP.

Whichever method is used, it will give the same figure for GNP because by definition income = output = expenditure. This is true of all circular flows of income. Another measure of economic activity is GROSS DOMESTIC PRODUCT (GDP). This is GNP less net earnings from property overseas.

Question 1

Using Figure 21.2, describe the possible impact on the UK leisure and entertainment industry of the following events. Explain your answers and, for each event, state whether it will be an injection into or a withdrawal from the circular flow of income.
(a) Greater availability of grants for setting up new businesses.
(b) An increase in the number of British groups in the US album charts.
(c) A developing trend for consumers to devote more of their income to savings.
(d) An increase in the number of British tourists taking holidays in Europe and the US.
(e) A 2 per cent reduction in income tax in the UK.

Equilibrium

Look at Figure 21.2. If injections in any year are the same as withdrawals, the money flowing around the circular flow would remain the **same**. This is known as EQUILIBRIUM. If injections and withdrawals are not the same, the money flowing around the circular flow will change. We can say that:
- if injections = withdrawals - income remains the same;
- if injections > withdrawals - income will rise because more money is entering the economy than is leaving it;
- if injections < withdrawals - income will fall because more money is leaving the economy than is entering it.

Even if the economy is in equilibrium, does this mean that everyone is employed? Say an economy is in equilibrium, with £6,000 billion flowing around it, but £8,000 billion was needed for **full employment**. This 'gap' of £2,000 billion (known as a DEFLATIONARY GAP) would mean that there was unemployment in the economy. These ideas were first put forward by John Maynard Keynes in his book *The General Theory of Employment, Interest and Money* (1936). Supporters of this view argue it is the role of government to fill any gap

that exists by spending more than it receives in taxes. This is known as a **budget deficit**.

Other economists suggest that the economy will be in equilibrium at full employment only if markets are allowed to operate freely. They argue that government spending will only lead to inflation and government policy should be aimed at making markets more efficient. This debate is dealt with in unit 28.

The business cycle

As well as gaining an understanding of how economies work, governments need to be aware of the fluctuations that economies go through over a period of time. These 'ups and downs' indicate how much money is flowing around an economy. A rise in the amount of money flowing around an economy may lead to increased earnings, spending and production. This is known as **economic growth** (☞ unit 29). It is measured by changes in GNP. A fall in the amount of money flowing around an economy may be an indication of a RECESSION.

The BUSINESS CYCLE is a useful way of showing a country's growth record. At the bottom of the cycle, economic growth will be low or perhaps even negative. At the top, economic growth will be relatively high. It is argued that all economies go through these cycles, which illustrate fluctuations in economic activity.

Figure 21.3 shows a typical business cycle. There are four parts to the business cycle.
- Peak or boom. A BOOM occurs when an economy is at a peak. Consumer spending and investment will be high. Many firms will be experiencing high levels of demand from people with increasing disposable income. Profits should be high for most firms, but wages are likely to be rising.
- Recession. A recession occurs when incomes and output begin to fall. Businesses will face a fall in demand for their products. Some may begin to lay off workers.
- Trough or slump. A SLUMP occurs when the economy is at the bottom of the business cycle. Many firms will be going

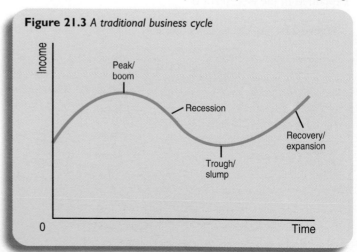

Figure 21.3 *A traditional business cycle*

out of business and unemployment levels will be very high.

● Recovery or expansion. During this stage of the business cycle, income will rise and business output will begin to increase. Firms will invest more and consumers will start to increase spending. Many businesses will be taking on more employees.

Question 2

Table 21.1 shows the government's statistics on the number of new businesses registering and deregistering for VAT. This data can be used as a guide to the number of new businesses starting up and the number of existing businesses closing down.

Table 21.1 *VAT registrations and deregistrations; United Kingdom; 1986-96*

	Numbers registering	Numbers deregistering	Net change
1986	193,754	169,068	
1987	211,793	172,581	
1988	245,802	179,651	
1989	258,838	181,005	
1990	239,107	191,838	
1991	204,564	209,844	
1992	187,000	226,000	
1993	191,000	213,000	
1994	168,240	188,140	
1995	163,960	173,230	
1996	168,200	156,965	

Source: adapted from *Labour Market Trends*, Office for National Statistics.

(a) Complete the net change column in the table above.
(b) Using the data, identify:
   (i) a boom year;
   (ii) a slump year.
(c) What evidence is there that the economy was moving out of recession in 1996? Explain your answer.
(d) Why might the number of business start-ups and closures be a good guide to the state of the economy?

Government objectives

Businesses and consumers have an expectation that governments will try to solve economic problems. The success, or otherwise, of government policies will affect a business's external environment. For example, if a business is thinking of expanding, its decision will be affected by future inflation, which may raise the price of components needed to produce goods. Government policy which controls inflation will result in a more stable climate and will allow the firm to expand with confidence. So if the government is able to meet its objectives, it is likely to create an environment where businesses are also successful. It is argued that governments have some common economic objectives.

Control of inflation Inflation is a rise in the general level of prices. Some are rising and some may be falling, but overall prices are increasing. Governments usually set **target rates** at which they want to keep inflation. In practice, the targets which governments set themselves often depend upon the inflation rate from previous years. The inflation rates of below 5 per cent in the UK in the 1990s meant that the government set a target of 2.5 per cent in the late 1990s. Countries such as Russia, Poland and Bulgaria which experienced inflation rates of over 300 per cent in the 1990s may have been satisfied with inflation rates of less than 20 per cent in the year 2000.

Governments aim to achieve an inflation rate at or below the level of their competitors. An inflation rate which is higher than those of competitors can mean higher prices for exports and a loss of sales by UK businesses to those of other countries. Inflation can also restrict a government's ability to achieve its other economic objectives. The problems that inflation can cause for business are dealt with in unit 23.

Employment Full employment occurs when all who want a job have one at a given wage rate. It is argued that the UK came closest to achieving this in the 1960s. For example, between 1950 and 1970 the rate of unemployment never reached above 4 per cent (about one million unemployed). Since then unemployment levels have risen considerably. Levels of over 3 million were recorded in the 1990s. UK governments over this period arguably abandoned the objective of full employment. Their aim was to reduce unemployment to an acceptable level.

The level of unemployment in an economy can be seen as an indicator of its success. A falling rate may show an economy doing well. Firms employ extra workers to produce more goods and services and new businesses set up in order to take advantage of opportunities which may occur. A rising unemployment rate, on the other hand, could indicate an economy which is in recession. Firms will be making some of their employees redundant. Others may be closing down and new ventures will be put their ideas on ice until conditions improve. Unemployed people will have less to spend and this will affect firms' revenue and profits. The effects of unemployment on business are dealt with in unit 24.

Economic growth Economic growth (☞ unit 29) is said to exist if there is a rise in economic activity. This is often measured by increases in gross national product (GNP). Most governments judge the overall performance of an economy by the figures for growth. Economic growth is good for most businesses. A growing economy should mean that trading conditions are favourable and that there are new business opportunities. However, there is another view that growth harms the environment and that sustaining growth in the long term may be impossible as the world's resources begin to run out.

A growth rate of 3-4 per cent per year may be considered good in Western economies. But some countries such as

Malaysia, China, Vietnam and Uganda experienced average annual growth rates of between 5-10 per cent between 1990 and 1997.

The balance of payments Governments usually attempt to achieve equilibrium or a surplus on the current account of the balance of payments (☞ unit 25). This would mean that the value of exports going out of a country is either the same as or greater than the value of imports coming into a country. At worst they would aim to prevent a long term deficit on the current account of the balance of payments. This occurs when the value of imports exceeds the value of exports. The problem with a current account deficit is that it must be financed either by borrowing from abroad or by running down savings. For one or two years this may not be a problem, but if the deficit persists then the country's debts will increase.

Government policy to prevent a balance of payments deficit can have a major effect on business and is dealt with in unit 26.

It is unlikely that a government will achieve all of its objectives at the same time. For example, say that the government was concerned about the level of inflation. It may try to reduce spending in the economy to keep prices down. However, reduced spending may lead to fewer sales of products and some businesses may have to make workers unemployed (☞ unit 24). The government may then have to find other ways of encouraging businesses to create jobs. In practice, achieving all objectives at the same time has proved difficult for governments.

Governments and business

In order to achieve their objectives and create a climate in which businesses can prosper, governments are involved in a number of activities. These activities often influence business behaviour.

Taxation In order to finance their spending on health, welfare and education governments tax individuals and businesses. In the UK, sole traders such as window cleaners pay **income tax**, a tax on their earnings. Companies also pay tax. **Corporation tax** is a tax on profits made by businesses. **Value added tax** is a tax which is a percentage of the price of the product. Taxes on businesses, along with government spending are an important aspect of FISCAL POLICY (☞ unit 26). This is the means by which governments attempt to control the level of total spending in the economy. Businesses are also affected by the amount of taxes which individual consumers pay. The levels of these taxes can be an important factor in determining how much consumers have to spend on the goods and services provided by businesses.

Government spending Along with taxation, government spending is part of fiscal policy. The levels and direction of government spending can affect businesses in a number of ways. For example, an increase in welfare spending in the form of grants for 16-19 year olds in full time education would increase the incomes of consumers in this age range. Businesses serving the needs of this age group would be likely to benefit. Governments may also spend directly. Expenditure on road building might lead to an increase in revenue for contractors and employment for skilled labour. Incentives for businesses to employ and train workers, such as the New Deal in the UK (☞ unit 79), might encourage businesses to employ young workers.

Money Governments are concerned with the amount of money circulating in the economy. The government in the UK has given responsibility for control of the money supply,

Question 3

Figure 21.4 *UK economic growth and inflation*

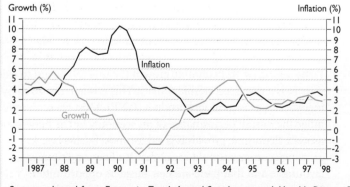

Figure 21.5 *UK unemployment and the current balance*

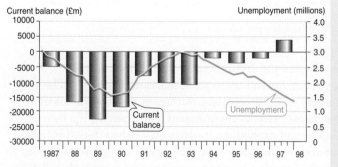

Source: adapted from *Economics Trends Annual Supplement* and *Monthly Digest of Statistics*, Office for National Statistics.

(a) Describe the likely trading conditions for UK businesses in (i) 1989/90 and (ii) 1997.

(b) What does the data tell you about the chances of the government achieving all of its economic objectives at the same time? How might this affect UK businesses?

part of MONETARY POLICY (☞ unit 26), to the Bank of England. The decisions made by the Bank of England on matters such as the level of interest rates can have a great impact upon businesses. A fall in interest rates might encourage businesses to borrow as they have less to pay back in interest.

Trading relations with other countries Countries trade goods and services with each other. One of the most important trading relationship for the UK is that with other countries who are a part of the European Union (EU) (☞ unit 30). Government decisions about the UK participation in the EU can have a major impact upon businesses in the UK, the rest of the EU and non-members. For example, in 1997 the UK signed the Social Chapter of the EU which committed it to a minimum wage (☞ unit 81).

The operation of markets In the 1990s, UK governments attempted to carry out actions to allow markets to operate efficiently. They used a range of policies designed to make markets more competitive. Such policies have included the opening up of services previously only carried out by local authorities to all businesses. This, for example, has led to school meals being provided by private businesses. Other examples include economic policies designed to improve the labour market (☞ unit 26).

Legal framework Businesses are affected by the law in three main ways. First, as employers they are affected by employment laws (☞ units 80 and 81). For example, the UK joining the Social Chapter of the EU has meant that employees are protected against employers who make unreasonable demands upon them in terms of the number of hours worked per week. Second, as producers businesses are affected by laws relating to the way in which they work with other businesses including competitors and suppliers. For example contract laws seek to prevent businesses reneging on their payments to suppliers. Third, a range of laws constrain the way in which businesses behave in relation to consumers and citizens. For example, a number of consumer laws (☞ unit 22) protect consumers against unscrupulous business practices.

The environment Governments are involved in a range of activities which affect the environment. With increasing public concern about its protection, governments have tried to regulate business activity to make sure it does not lead to a deterioration in the quality of the environment (☞ units 27 and 35). There is a number of government policies designed to achieve this.
- Transport policy. In the late 1990s governments taxed petrol and diesel and cancelled new road schemes to control the rate of growth of road transport. Public transport on buses and trains also continued to be

Question 4

In the late 1990s the government was considering the use of 'congestion charges' for cars entering cities. In city areas, heavy traffic leads to traffic jams and pollution from car emissions. It was predicted that road traffic would grow by 24 to 51 per cent by 2020. The charges could be collected by local authorities and ploughed back into public transport in their areas. Suggested charges for motorists were between £2 and £10 per day. Drivers using electronic smart cards fitted to windscreens would be charged for using certain routes into city centres. Charges would vary, depending on the time of day and the level of pollution. Other schemes under consideration to persuade motorists to use their cars less included:
- employers being charged for workplace parking spaces and higher taxes on company cars;
- customers at out of town supermarkets being charged for parking;
- toll charges on motorways;
- even higher taxes on petrol and diesel.

Source: adapted from the *Financial Times*, 21.7.1998 and *The Observer*, 9.11.1997.

How might the following businesses be affected by government policies to control car usage in the UK?
(a) A clothing chain store with branches mainly in city and town centres.
(b) A supermarket chain with branches in various locations throughout the country.
(c) A Derbyshire sheep farm.
(d) A direct insurance business with telephone call centres in Birmingham, Central London and Sheffield.

subsidised at a regional and local level partly to encourage less use of cars.
- Urban policy. During the 1980s and 1990s government spending attempted to regenerate urban areas, particularly in inner cities. One of the biggest urban schemes was the redevelopment of the London docklands with the creation of complexes such as Canary Wharf.
- Housing policy. The term 'green belt' (☞ unit 100) describes areas of land, mostly in the South-East, where the building of new houses is forbidden. The maintenance of green belt land is viewed by many as essential for the preservation of the environment.

Regional aid Regional policy aims to provide aid to businesses in different parts of the country. It has been used to support regions that have suffered from a decline in important industries and high levels of unemployment (☞ unit 100). It has included a range of measures to attract business to these areas, from UK government and EU grants to the offering of 'tax breaks' for a limited period of time. Corporations have also been set up in a number of towns and cities to encourage private sector investment in previously run down sites.

Summary

1. Give examples of 3 injections into and 3 withdrawals from the circular flow of income.
2. Explain the terms:
   (a) income; (b) output; (c) expenditure; in an economy.
3. 'Income must equal output, which must equal expenditure.' Explain this statement in relation to the circular flow of income.
4. What will be the effect on the circular flow if injections are greater than withdrawals?
5. Why might an economy be in equilibrium but not have full employment?
6. What are the 4 main parts of the business cycle?
7. State 4 government objectives.
8. Give an example of:
   (a) taxation on the price of a product;
   (b) taxation on income;
   (c) taxation on profits.
9. How might an increase in government spending affect a business producing hospital beds?
10. What effect would cutting interest rates have on business borrowing?

Key terms

Aggregate demand - a measure of the level of demand in the economy as a whole.
Boom - the stage when an economy is at the peak of its activity.
Business or trade cycle - a measure of the regular fluctuations in the level of economic activity.
Circular flow of income - the flow of money around the economy.
Deflationary gap - when planned expenditure is less than the level of income needed for full employment.
Equilibrium - a balanced state, for example, when withdrawals equal injections in an economy.
Fiscal policy - a policy designed to manage the level of aggregate demand in the economy by changing government spending or taxation.
Gross Domestic Product (GDP) - like GNP, a measure of economic activity, but it does not include net property income from abroad.
Gross National Product (GNP) - a measure of the amount of income generated as a result of a country's economic activity.
Injection - any factor causing income to enter the circular flow.
Monetary policy - a policy designed to control the supply of money in the economy.
Recession - when income and output begins to fall in an economy.
Slump - the lowest point of the trade cycle.
Withdrawal - any factor causing income to leave the circular flow.

Case study

Retail chains tell tales of woe

In 1998 retailers were facing the most dismal Christmas in over a decade. The British Retail Consortium confirmed that spending was lower in November 1998 than in the same month the previous year. This was the first time November sales had fallen since the early 1990s. High street retailers are often a barometer of customers' spending. Many stated that spending in early December was also down. Ranjiv Mann, senior economist at the Confederation of British Industry, said: 'There's enough pessimism among consumers with all the news of job losses for Christmas not to be as strong as last year'.

Shops claimed that the problem was not a lack of money but a lack of confidence amongst customers. More people were in work than last year. Interest rate cuts over the year had left them with more money in their pockets. But they lacked confidence to spend the money, fearing what might happen in future. Even the pharmacist, Boots, normally recession proof, was thought to be finding conditions difficult. Some stores, such as Marks & Spencer, had tried to lure customers by extending Autumn sales into pre-Christmas sales.

Storehouse, parent group of Mothercare *'We will not be able to recover fully from the sharp and sudden downturn in the market during the period from late September to the end of October ... sales volumes have fallen and continue to be volatile.'*

Marks & Spencer *Announced a 23 per cent profits decline.*
John Lewis *Department store sales in the last week in November were down 3.4 per cent. The sales fall per store was around 6 per cent.*
Alders *'Consumer confidence, once eroded, is not easily rebuilt.'*
New Look *Recent like-for-like sales down 1 per cent. 'There is an increasing amount of discounting on the high street. That is what we have always been about. Our performance is better than the market as a whole.*

Source: adapted from *The Observer*, December, 1998.

(a) **Identify the features of a recession that are mentioned in the article.**
(b) **Explain what is meant by the phrase: 'Even the pharmacist, Boots, normally recession proof, was thought to be finding conditions difficult'.**
(c) **Examine how the situation at Christmas might affect government objectives such as: (i) creating employment; (ii) controlling inflation; (iii) achieving economic growth.**
(d) **Explain how government might create more favourable trading conditions for retailers at Christmas.**
(e) **What evidence is there to suggest that consumers are influenced by the state of the economy?**

22 Business and Consumer Protection

The growth of protection

At the beginning of the century consumers and producers were seen as having equal responsibility. Indeed, consumers were expected to ensure that their purchases were satisfactory. This approach can be summarised by the expression caveat emptor, which mean - 'let the buyer beware'.

Today, the relationship between consumers and businesses is viewed differently. Many see consumers as being at the mercy of powerful and well organised producers. This has led to a rise in interest about consumer affairs and increasing pressure on governments to pass legislation to protect consumers. Consumer magazines, such as *Which?*, and consumer television programmes, such as 'Watchdog', have lent pressure to this movement seeking to protect the rights of consumers. There is a number of reasons why consumers may need protecting more than they did in the past.

● The increasing complexity of many goods and services. Technological advances, in particular, have increased the gap between the knowledge of consumers and producers about products. Few consumers have the ability to properly assess the quality of the technology which goes into everyday items such as televisions, washing machines or refrigerators. Such ignorance can leave consumers at the mercy of unscrupulous producers.

● The environment within which firms operate is becoming increasingly competitive. Some believe that this degree of competition encourages firms to take advantage of consumers. This may be in the form of reductions in the level of service or the quality of goods offered, for example.

● The disposable income of many consumers has increased greatly over the last four to five decades. This means that the average consumer purchases far greater quantities of goods and services than would have been the case in the past. It is argued that more protection needs to be offered to consumers as a result.

● The increase in the number of goods and services from abroad. Now that consumers are purchasing increasing numbers of goods and services imported from abroad, they may need protection against the different standards which may operate in other countries. Safety standards on children's toys, for example, have in the past been lower in goods produced in Asia.

● Scientific advances have created a variety of materials that were not previously available. For example, genetically modified products have developed as a consequence of scientific advances in the production of foods. Consumers may need to be protected against any possible harmful effects of such scientific discoveries.

Consumer protection legislation

It could be argued that, in a number of areas, businesses cannot be relied upon to regulate themselves. These include their dealings with employees (☞ unit 81) and other firms, as well as consumers. Governments in the past have found it necessary to regulate businesses, by passing laws which protect consumers from their activities. Some examples are shown below.

Weights and Measures Act, 1951 This act makes it possible for inspectors to test the weighing and measuring equipment used by businesses. Use of false or unfair weighing equipment is an offence. It is also an offence to give short weights or short measures. The Act states that all prepacked goods must have information about the net quantity of their contents.

Trade Descriptions Act, 1968 This prohibits false or misleading descriptions of goods or services. For example, a pair of shoes which are described as made of leather cannot be made of plastic.

Unsolicited Goods Act, 1971 This law seeks to prevent the practice of sending goods to consumers which they had not ordered, and then demanding payment. It states that unsolicited goods need not be paid for and that consumers can keep such goods after six months if the seller does not collect them.

Consumer Credit Act, 1974 This aims to protect the rights of consumers when they purchase goods on credit, such as hire purchase or credit sale agreements. For example, it states that consumers must be given a copy of any credit agreements into which they enter. It also ensures that only licensed credit brokers can provide credit. There are many other offences listed which constitute a breaking of the law. These include credit firms sending representatives to people's homes to persuade them to take credit and credit agreements which have high interest rates.

Consumer Safety Act, 1978 This law was passed in order to prevent the sale of goods which might be harmful to consumers. It concentrates, in particular, upon safety matters relating to children's toys and electrical goods.

Sale of Goods Act, 1979 This law states that goods sold to consumers should meet three main conditions. First, that they are of merchantable quality which means that goods should not have any serious flaws or problems with them. Second, that they are fit for the purpose for which they were purchased. For example, paint which is sold to be used outdoors should not begin to peel or flake with the first outbreak of poor weather conditions. Third, that they are as described. Thus, an anorak described as waterproof should not leak in the rain.

Supply of Goods and Services Act, 1982 This seeks to protect users of services, ensuring services are of 'merchantable quality' and at 'reasonable rates'. For example, a holiday firm which booked clients into a four star hotel that turned out to be of lower quality would be in breach of the conditions. Breaches of this and the 1979 Act are subject to civil law. An injured person can sue for breach of the Act.

Consumer Protection Act, 1987 This law was introduced to bring Britain in line with other European Union nations. It ensures that firms are liable for any damage which their defective goods might cause to consumers. For example, a firm supplying defective electrical equipment would be liable for any injuries caused to consumers using that equipment. It also seeks to outlaw misleading pricing, such as exaggerated claims relating to price reductions on sale items. An example might be a statement that a good is '£2 less than the manufacturer's recommended price' when it isn't.

Food Safety Act, 1990 This law ensures that food is safe and does not mislead the consumer in the way it is presented. It is an offence to:

● sell food that does not comply with regulations, ie is unfit to eat or is contaminated;
● change food so that it becomes harmful;
● sell food that is not of the quality stated;
● describe food in a way that misleads.

Breaches of the Act are a criminal offence, punished by a fine and/or a prison sentence.

Sale and Supply of Goods Act, 1994 This Act amends the Sale of Goods Act, 1979 and the Supply of Goods and Services Act, 1982 in favour of the buyer. For example, consumers now had a right to partial rejection. A buyer of a case of wine, may accept ten bottles, but reject the two which do not match the description ordered.

Food Safety (General Food Hygiene) Regulations, 1995 These list a whole series of regulations about the preparation and storage of food and equipment.

Food labelling regulations, 1996 These specify exactly what information should be included on food labels.

Consumer protection and the European Union

Increasingly the European Union (☞ unit 30) is affecting legislation in member countries. The EU's aim is to harmonise (make the same) consumer laws. It is responsible for a series of directives which all EU nations implement as

Which of the consumer protection Acts might the following contravene? Explain your answer.
● Winston Stanley buys a cotton tee shirt from a shop in Bath. When he takes it home, he discovers that it is made of polyester and cotton and has a small hole in its collar.
● Lena Hardman buys a 400 gramme box of chocolates, but later discovers there are only 250 grammes of chocolates in the box.
● A car dealer advertises that all of his cars have been approved by the AA. Irfan Patel, who has just bought a car from this dealer, rings up the AA and discovers that the car dealer has had no dealings with them.
● Bill Dean urgently requires £1,000 to pay a long overdue loan back to a friend. He goes to a credit agency and arranges a loan of £1,000 to be paid back over 12 months. His repayments on this loan will be £250 a month.
● Aaron Peters bought a can of lemonade. Before he drank it, the smell made him wary of the contents. It was found that the lemonade contained caustic soda.

law and regulations. Examples include:

● EU directive, Unfair Terms in Consumer Contracts, in April 1993, which led to the **Unfair Terms in Consumer Contracts Regulations, 1994** in the UK. This directive sought to prevent consumers being locked into unfair contracts which undermined their rights;
● The EU directive which led to **The General Product Safety Regulations, 1994** in the UK. These state that all products supplied to customers must be safe.
● EU directives 88/314 and 88/315 leading to the **Price Marking Order, 1991** which states that the selling price of goods must be indicated in writing.

Effects of protection on business

The increase in the number of consumer laws and the concern about protecting consumers has a number of possible implications for firms.

● Increases in costs. Improving the safety of a good or ensuring that measuring equipment is more accurate can increase the costs of a firm. For example, an electrical firm producing table lamps may find that its product contravened legislation. The firm would have to change or improve the components used to make the lamps or re-design the lamp itself. Such changes would be likely to raise the firm's costs.
● Quality control. Many firms have needed to improve their quality control procedures as a result of legislation. For example, firms involved in bagging or packaging goods must ensure that the correct quantities are weighed out. Failure to do so could result in prosecution. In addition,

businesses must be careful not to sell substandard or damaged products.

● Dealing with customer complaints. Many businesses now have a customer service or customer complaints department to deal with customers. These allow firms to deal with problems quickly and efficiently and to 'nip problems in the bud' - dealing with any problems before the customer turns to the legal system.

● Changes in business practice. Attempts to ensure that customers are treated fairly by a firm may place pressure on it to become more market orientated (☞ unit 36). The firm would attempt to ensure that it is actually meeting the needs of those people it is attempting to serve. Such a change, for example, may lead to greater use of market research.

Monopolies and mergers

It is argued, by some, that competition between businesses benefits consumers. Such arguments have been one influence upon government's attempts to control monopolies and mergers.

A LEGAL MONOPOLY in the UK is defined as any business which has over 25 per cent market share. Examples may include Microsoft, in its production of operating systems for computers. A merger is the joining together of two or more firms (☞ unit 101). In the 1990s there has been a growth in mergers and takeovers. Examples of mergers between well known companies include:

● the merger between Commercial Union and General Accident insurance companies in the UK in 1998;

● the creation of the world's largest mobile telephone company when Vodaphone merged with US cellular company AirTouch in 1999;

● Ford's £3.9 billion buyout of Swedish car manufacturer Volvo in 1999.

In some cases just one firm or a small group of firms control the market for a particular good or service. Such market strength puts these firms in a position where they have the potential to exploit their consumers. They can also prevent other firms from competing against them. Some criticisms of monopolies and mergers for consumers and businesses include the following.

● They raise prices in order to make excess profits.

● They fix prices. When a small group of firms control the market for a product, it is believed that they may act in unison to fix prices at an artificially high level.

● They force competition out. It has been suggested that monopolists sometimes pursue pricing or promotional strategies designed to force competitors out of the market. For example, some have suggested that the launch of the low cost airline Go, by British Airways, will force other low cost airlines like Ryanair and EasyJet out of the market. It is suggested that BA will be able to subsidise Go, driving down airline prices and gaining market share from its rivals until they are forced out of business.

● They prevent new firms from entering markets.

● They carry out a range of restrictive practices. Examples include putting pressure on retailers not to stock the goods of rival firms and attempting to prevent suppliers from doing business with new entrants to the market.

Question 2

The European market for toilets and other bathroom accessories is becoming dominated by large businesses. Small manufacturers are finding it difficult to compete with multinationals that can supply these products from low cost plants in emerging markets. The production of WCs is notoriously labour intensive. European businesses face increasing pressure to merge or form alliances. The catalyst for this was the takeover of the UK's Armitage Shanks by American Standard. The merged company had 18 per cent share of the European market, twice as big as the second and third largest manufacturers. Size gives it not only considerable pricing and buying power, but the ability to switch to low cost countries if necessary.

Source: adapted from the *Financial Times*, 11.3.1999.

Table 22.1 *Leading sanitary manufacturers*

	Country	Capacity*	Overseas operations**
American Standard	US	24.0	21
(of which Europe)		9.0	
(Armitage Shanks)	UK	4.2	
Keramic Laufen	Switzerland	14.6	9
Sanitec-Laufen	Finland	8.0	10
Roca	Spain	6.5	4
Villeroy & Boch	Germany	4.0	3
Sphinx-Gustavsberg	Netherlands	4.0	5

Source: adapted from *Ceramic World Review*.
*Million pieces
**Number of countries with production plants

(a) Explain two reasons why mergers have taken place in the market for toilet and bathroom accessories.

(b) How might Keramic Laufen react to the merger between American Standard and Armitage Shanks? Explain your answer.

There are, however, a number of arguments which support the continued existence of monopolies.

● Because monopolies often operate on a large scale, they are able to benefit from economies of scale (☞ unit 93). The cost advantages from this can allow monopolies to set prices lower than would be the case if there were a number of firms competing, and still make profits.

● Monopolies can use their large profits to undertake research and development projects. Many of these projects, which result in technological and scientific breakthroughs, could not be afforded by smaller firms.

● Monopolies are much better placed to survive in international markets. It is argued that this is only possible if a firm operates on a large scale.

Anti-competitive practices

Anti-competitive practices restrict competition between businesses. In the UK, the Office of Fair Trading, under the leadership of the Director General of Fair Trading, is responsible for preventing anti-competitive practices. RESTRICTIVE TRADE PRACTICES prevent competition between businesses. Examples of restrictive practices include the following.

● A firm which is a dominant supplier in a particular market may set a minimum price for the re-sale of its products. Such firms may also seek to ensure that retailers stock their products alone. In return, retailers are often given exclusive rights to sell this product within a particular area.

● Firms forming agreements to fix prices and/or limit the supply of a product. Such agreements between firms are often referred to as COLLUSION.

● A dominant supplier requiring retailers to stock the full range of their product lines.

It is usually argued that consumers suffer as a result of these practices. For example, if two businesses join together to fix prices so that another business is forced to close, this will restrict consumers' choice. Such practices may benefit those businesses taking part, but will be against the interest of those that are faced with the restrictive practices.

Legislation in the UK

In the UK there has been legislation over many years to protect consumers from the problems created by monopolies, mergers and anti-competitive practices.

Monopolies and Restrictive Practices (Inquiry and Control) Act, 1948 and Monopolies and Mergers Act, 1965 The 1948 Act established a Monopolies Commission with powers to investigate unfair dealings referred to it by the then Board of Trade. If it believed that a monopoly was 'against the public interest', it could pass on the matter to the government for action. The 1965 act created the **Monopolies and Mergers Commission** (MMC). It extended the powers of the Commission to investigate proposed mergers and the supply of services.

Restrictive Trade Practices Act, 1956 This Act regulated restrictive trade practices. It established a Restrictive Practices Court. All firms engaged in restrictive practices have to register them with this Court, which then decides whether or not they are acceptable. Firms have to prove that their practices are in the public interest. Judgements made by the Court are backed by law. The 1956 Act laid down 8 gateways through which a restriction could be approved. If a business could prove a restrictive practice would prevent the public from injury, for example, it may be allowed to continue. The **1976 Restrictive Practices Act** extended the powers of the Court to cover services as well as goods.

Fair Trading Act, 1973 This act defined exactly what constitutes a monopoly or merger. Monopolies were said to exist if a business had a 25 per cent share of the market or greater. Mergers were said to exist if the combined total assets of firms that join together were greater than £5 million. (In the late 1990s the value of net assets taken over for a merger was £70 million.) It also established the role of the **Office of Fair Trading**. This was able to refer cases to the MMC for investigation. Under the Director General of Fair Trading (DGFT), the Office was given responsibility for overseeing all policy relating to competition and consumer protection. The MMC's scope was extended. It was able to examine local as well as national monopolies and public sector monopolies. The Secretary of State for Trade and Industry could also refer monopolies in the area of labour practices to the MMC.

Competition Act, 1980 This act allowed the Secretary of State for Trade and Industry to ask the MMC to investigate the efficiency and possible abuse of power by nationalised industries and other public bodies. It also extended its work into the examination of anti-competitive practices, to see if they were against the public interest.

Telecommunications Act, 1984 This act marked the start of the role of the MMC as an independent arbiter between newly privatised industries and their regulators (see later in this unit). It increased the number of cases investigated by the MMC. Its role was also extended by the Broadcasting Act, 1990, which gave the MMC powers to investigate competition activities between holders of regional licences for Channel Three.

Competition Act, 1998 This act:
● prohibits agreements, cartels or practices which prevent, restrict or distort competition;
● prohibits conduct which amounts to abuse of a dominant position.

The new legislation is designed to reflect EU law, dealt with in the next section. The DGFT, utility regulators and

Secretary of State will be able to grant exemptions. This act also replaced the MMC with the **Competition Commission** and extended its role to hearing appeals against decisions under the 1998 Act.

The work of the Monopolies and Mergers Commission/ Competition Commission

The role of the MMC had been to investigate and report on matters such as whether or not a particular monopoly, proposed merger or anti-competitive practice is in the public interest. On its own the MMC has had no power to act. It would investigate and report on matters referred to it by the Director-General of Fair Trading, the Secretary of State for Trade and Industry and the regulators of privatised industries. The MMC's approach has been on a case by case basis, refusing to condemn outright certain types of business. Examples of MMC activities have included the following.

● The tool producer Black & Decker withdrew distribution from B&Q stores in response to B&Q's discount campaign. The MMC forced Black & Decker to supply goods again.

● In an investigation into the brewing industry, the MMC reported that the practice by big brewers of producing, distributing and selling their own beer in 'tied' public houses restricted competition. It recommended that no brewer should own more than 5,000 public houses, and that guest beers should be provided in those pubs owned by breweries. As a consequence of this, around 11,000 pubs were sold off by the big brewing companies.

● An investigation into new housing warranty schemes by the MMC looked at the rule of the National House Building Council, which required builders to present every new house for inspection to obtain a warranty from the NHBC. The Commission found that this deterred builders from using other schemes, such as those provided by insurance companies.

● The MMC report on the UK supply of fine fragrances included perfumes, eaux de toilette and aftershave. The MMC received complaints that fragrance houses were discriminating against certain retailers. Suppliers would only distribute to those retailers with the right 'ambience'. The MMC found that a complex monopoly existed, but it was not against the public interest.

The MMC has been criticised for a number of reasons.

● It has had no real power to initiate an investigation.

● Investigations have been lengthy and the limited number of staff (less than 100) has restricted the number of investigations.

● Many findings in the 1990s were argued to favour business rather than consumers. For example, the finding that the monopoly on the sale of fragrances was not against the public interest prevented retailers such as Tesco and Superdrug selling perfume at lower prices.

On April 1, 1999, the MMC was replaced by the **Competition Commission**. The Commission has two sides to its work. The reporting side took on the former MMC role. The appeals side would hear appeals against decisions made

Question 3

The government held out the prospect of lower car prices after the launch of a Monopolies and Mergers Commission inquiry into the new car market in 1999. The inquiry was ordered after John Bridgeman, the Director General of Fair Trading, found evidence that practices employed by manufacturers and dealers were distorting competition. The inquiry followed mounting criticism of the industry for the relatively high prices UK private car buyers face compared with other European countries. Mr Bridgeman said this was partly due to suppliers' (the car manufacturing businesses) refusal to give volume discounts to dealers. One possible reason for the relatively high prices was the treatment of fleet buyers, the purchasers of 'company cars' for business users. Car dealers had long complained that they were not offered the same volume discounts as fleet purchasers by the car manufacturers. Alan Pulham of the National Franchised Dealerships Association said: 'The car market is split half fleet and half retail, but fleet buyers pay 20 per cent less than a retail customer'. The MMC inquiry would also consider whether to lift the car industry's current exemption from EU competition rules. This allows car manufacturers to sell only through exclusively franchised dealers.

Source: adapted from the *Financial Times*, 18.3.1999.

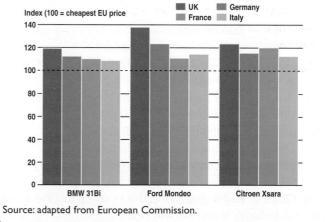

Figure 22.1 *Relative price of cars in European countries*

Source: adapted from European Commission.

(a) What evidence is there in the article that car manufacturers were engaging in anti-competitive practices in the UK car market?

(b) Explain how: (i) customers; (ii) other businesses might be affected by the behaviour of car manufacturers.

(c) Examine how car manufacturers might be affected by a ruling against their practices by the Monopolies and Mergers Commission (now the Competition Commission).

under the prohibition provisions of the new Competition Act 1998.

The European Union

The EU takes a prohibition-based approach to monopolies, mergers and anti-competitive practices.

● Article 85 of the Treaty of Rome prohibits all agreements and concerted practices which may affect trade between member states which aim to prevent, restrict or distort competition within the common market. Exemptions can be granted by the European Commission.

● Article 86 prohibits any undertaking from abusing a dominant position which it enjoys.

In 1989 the EU adopted a regulation on the control of mergers. Mergers of businesses with a combined turnover of £4.2 billion with certain provisions, are subject to control by the European Commission. Some mergers may be reviewed by national bodies. In 1996 the proposed takeover of Lloyds Chemist by GEHE AG was referred to the UK.

The regulation of business

Regulating privatised utilities During the 1980s and early 1990s, former state monopolies were sold off as part of the government's privatisation (☞ unit 6) programme. The aim was to increase efficiency in these firms by removing them from the public sector. However, the creation of private monopolies led to concern that these newly privatised firms would take advantage of their market position and exploit consumers. Agencies were set up to regulate them as a result.

● The Office of Telecommunications (OFTEL) - set up in 1984 when British Telecom was privatised.

● The Office of Gas Supplies (OFGAS) - set up in 1986 when British Gas was privatised.

● The Office of Water Services (OFWAT) - set up in 1989 when the water boards were transferred to the private sector. It joined with OFFER in 1999 to become OFGEM (the Office of Gas and Electricity Markets).

● The Office of Electricity Regulation (OFFER) - set up in 1989 during the privatisation of the electricity industry.

● The Office of Rail Regulation (ORR) - set up in 1993 when the rail industry was privatised.

Each of the regulators has different powers, but all of them are required to carry out two main functions.

● To operate a system of price controls. The regulatory authorities for gas, water, electricity and telecommunications operate according to a Retail Price Index (☞ unit 23) plus or minus formula. Where a firm's costs are falling due, for example, to improvements in technology, it will probably be set an RPI minus figure. As an example, British Telecom was given a figure of RPI minus 7.5 per cent for 1993. In 1996 Transco, the newly formed gas company which owned the gas pipeline network, was given a target to cut gas prices by 20 per cent by 1997, and RPI minus 2.5 per cent each year to 2002.

● To help bring about the introduction of competition wherever this might be possible. In some respects, this is more difficult than implementing price controls. This is because telephone lines, gas pipelines, water pipes and the National Grid are examples of **natural monopolies**. If every house, factory and office were connected with a number of different water pipes or telephone lines from which to choose, the costs within these industries would rise significantly. It therefore makes sense for the regulated firm to operate such services.

However, there is no reason why other firms should not be allowed to transmit their power, gas, telephone calls or water down the existing National Grid, gas pipeline network, telephone lines and water pipes. Indeed, this is the way in which competition has been introduced into these industries. A range of rail passenger businesses such as Virgin and Great Western Railways are, for example, able to operate services on railways lines controlled by Railtrack.

Regulating other businesses Other business are also regulated by government sponsored regulatory bodies. The Financial Services Authority (FSA) is responsible for regulating the performance and behaviour of businesses operating in the financial services industry, such as insurance and pensions companies. Unlike many of the former state utilities, financial service operators do not tend to have monopoly powers. However, this is an industry which has aroused suspicion in the past due to scandals regarding the mis-selling of pensions to consumers, for example. Consequently the government established and funded the FSA in order to regulate the activities of businesses working in this industry.

It is the threat of government regulation which causes many other industries to 'keep their own house in order' by establishing their own regulatory bodies. The Advertising Standards Authority is an example of a self-regulatory body for the advertising industry. The European Petroleum Industry Association (EUROPIA) regulates conduct by businesses operating in the European petroleum producing industry.

Question 4

Losses through leakages by water companies were enough to fill almost 2,000 Olympic size swimming pools on a daily basis. This is according to the water industry regulator OFWAT. Despite such losses water companies had performed better than the targets set for them by OFWAT. According to OFWAT, leakages from water and sewerage operations in England and Wales fell by 12 per cent during the year 1997 to 1998. The water companies have had targets of 9 per cent reduction imposed on them for 1998-99. Ian Byatt, the Director-General of OFWAT, said: 'Looking at these figures, some companies have still got a lot of work to do to ensure they reach next year's targets.'

Source: adapted from the *Financial Times*, 15.7.1998.

(a) Describe the role of OFWAT.
(b) How, other than controlling leakages, might OFWAT influence the operations of water companies?
(c) Why do you think OFWAT has set targets for leakages for the water companies?

Summary

1. What is meant by the term caveat emptor?
2. For what reasons might consumers need more protection today?
3. List 5 main consumer protection acts.
4. In what ways might firms be affected by consumer protection legislation?
5. What are the possible advantages and disadvantages of monopolies?
6. How is a monopoly defined by UK law?
7. What is the role of the Competition Commission?
8. How does EU legislation affect monopolies and mergers?
9. What are the 4 main bodies set up to regulate the former state monopolies?
10. State 2 other industries that are regulated.

Key terms

Collusion - agreements between businesses designed to restrict competition.
Legal monopoly - in the UK, any business with over 25 per cent of the market.
Restrictive trade practices - any attempt by businesses to prevent competition.

Case study

Freezer exclusivity

The ice cream market in Europe is dominated by Birds Eye Wall's, the frozen foods subsidiary of Unilever and Nestlé. In six European countries it enjoys between 42 per cent and 58 per cent of the market. In 1993 the, then, Monopolies and Mergers Commission (MMC) was asked to investigate and report on whether a monopoly situation existed in relation to the supply of ice cream in the UK. The investigation focused upon the restriction of competition through freezer cabinets. Shops could obtain a freezer cabinet free of charge from a company so long as they agreed to stock its products exclusively in the cabinet. Not surprisingly this proved very attractive to small businesses, which accounted for a significant proportion of ice cream sales, many of which had room to stock only one cabinet. The extent of freezer exclusivity is shown in Figure 22.3.

The MMC inquiry arose from complaints by Mars concerning its difficulties in entering the UK ice cream market with its Ice Cream Mars. Although Mars was able to supply all the major grocery multiples with multi-packs, it claimed that the two main market players had a stronghold on distribution in what was termed the 'impulse market'. Mars complained that this stronghold was achieved through freezer exclusivity.

The subsequent MMC report found that freezer

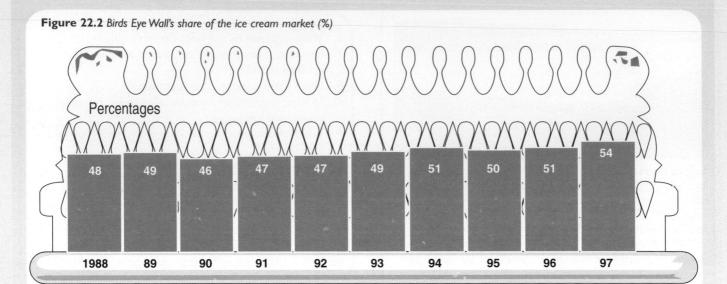

Figure 22.2 *Birds Eye Wall's share of the ice cream market (%)*

Percentages

1988	89	90	91	92	93	94	95	96	97
48	49	46	47	47	49	51	50	51	54

Source: adapted from MMC, BEW.

exclusivity did not operate against the public interest and was not convinced that consumer choice would be significantly improved were exclusivity to be ended. The MMC reported that retailers had several options open to them.

● They could install an exclusive freezer on an agreement terminable by short notice.
● They could buy their own freezer and purchase ice cream at lower prices from any ice cream supplier.
● They could add a second freezer where space permitted. Such space, they found, was available in 80 per cent of outlets.

In 1998, however, the European Commission decided that freezer exclusivity was illegal throughout the EU. Unilever appealed against this judgment and was awaiting the outcome of its appeal in the new millennium. In 1999 Bird's Eye Wall's attempted to head off a threat by the MMC, now named the Competition Commission, to investigate it again. It stated that interference in its business would result in job cuts. It argued that its position in the market had been achieved through investment and strong brands and that allowing competition into distribution would encourage foreign businesses to enter the market.

Source: adapted from 'The Monopolies and Mergers Commission', Peter Maunder, in *Developments in Economics*, vol. 11, GBJ Atkinson, ed, Causeway Press, and the *Financial Times*, 10.6.1999.

(a) **Using evidence from above describe the role of the Monopolies and Mergers Commission (renamed the Competition Commission) in the ice cream market.**

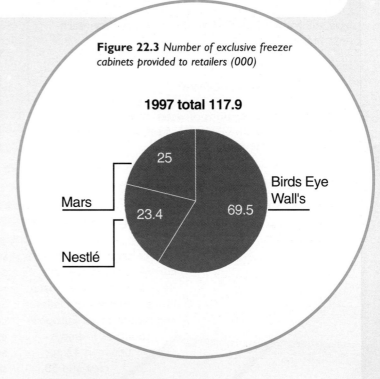

Figure 22.3 *Number of exclusive freezer cabinets provided to retailers (000)*

1997 total 117.9

Mars — 25

Nestlé — 23.4

Birds Eye Wall's — 69.5

(b) **Explain how the removal of cabinet exclusivity might affect Birds Eye Wall's.**
(c) **Explain the effects of freezer exclusivity deals on:**
   (i) Birds Eye Wall's and Nestlé, (ii) Mars;
   (iii) consumers.
(d) **Examine how the ice cream businesses might be regulated other than through the MMC.**
(e) **Why do you think the MMC and the EU arrived at different conclusions regarding cabinet exclusivity?**

What is inflation?

INFLATION can be defined as a persistent tendency for prices to rise. It occurs when there is a general increase in the price level, not just if one business raises its prices. In the UK, inflation is measured by changes in the RETAIL PRICE INDEX, as explained later in this unit. If the index rises from, say, 100 to 105 over a year, then there is an inflation rate of 5 per cent. This means that on average over the year, prices have risen by 5 per cent.

To what extent is this a problem? Low levels of inflation, below 5 per cent, are likely to be considered acceptable in many countries. Governments, consumers and businesses do not suffer the difficulties of high inflation, such as rising costs, and gain benefits from some inflation, such as a fall in the value of repayments on borrowing. Rates of around 10 per cent or more, as experienced by the UK in the early 1990s, may lead to greater problems. HYPER-INFLATION, such as the inflation rate of 1,150 per cent in Croatia in 1993 or 1,500 in Tajikistan in 1995, can cause serious difficulties. Figure 22.1 shows the inflation rate in the UK between 1987 and 1999.

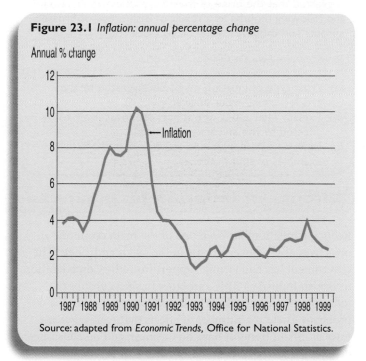

Figure 23.1 *Inflation: annual percentage change*

Annual % change

Source: adapted from *Economic Trends*, Office for National Statistics.

Governments may try to reduce the rate of inflation from 10 per cent to 5 per cent for example. This does not mean that prices are falling, just that the rate of inflation is slowing down. DEFLATION is a situation where average prices actually fall over a period. Governments also set target rates for inflation. They aim for rates that are lower or the same as those of their main international competitors. The UK government in the late 1990s set target rates mainly between 2 and 3 per cent per annum.

The causes of inflation

What causes inflation? Certain arguments may be put forward.

The money supply Some believe that inflation is caused by increases in the MONEY SUPPLY. This is the total amount of money circulating in the economy. This view is often associated with the group of economists known as **monetarists** (☞ unit 28).

Supporters of ths idea believe that any increase in the money supply which is not in line with growth in the output of the economy will lead to inflation. Take, for example, an increase in the money supply of 10 per cent. In the short term, consumer spending would increase, but the output of producers would not be able to expand as quickly. Instead, there would be an increase in prices. Supporters of this view argue strongly that it is important for governments to ensure that the rate of growth of the money supply is kept in line with the rate of growth of output or there will be inflation.

It has been suggested that the excessive inflation levels in Eastern European and some South American countries has been inflamed by governments simply printing money to cope with price rises. This has simply led to further price rises as the money supply has increased over and above any output rise. In the UK the independence of the Bank of England is said to be a factor which may have influenced the low levels of inflation in the late 1990s. Governments could no longer make the Bank increase the money supply before an election in order to gain public support.

Demand Too much spending or **demand** can lead to inflation. This is known as DEMAND-PULL INFLATION. The result is similar to that described under changes in the money supply, but the cause is different. Demand-pull inflation comes about when there is excessive spending in the economy. This expenditure leads to an increase in demand which cannot be matched by the level of supply. Because demand is greater than supply, prices rise. The increase in demand can be due to:
● a rise in consumer spending;
● firms investing in more machinery;
● government expenditure increasing;
● more exports being bought abroad.

Some economists argue that inflation in the UK at the end of the 1980s and early 1990s was caused by earlier tax cuts, leading to increases in consumer expenditure.

Increasing costs Another argument is that rising costs lead to inflation. This is known as COST-PUSH INFLATION, as rising costs force firms to push up their prices. What causes costs to increase?
● Rises in wages and salaries. There may be an increase in

Question 1

Official figures suggested that competitive pricing by retailers, fighting a fall in consumer spending at the start of the year, boosted activity in the shops. 'The 1990s customer is increasingly demanding and looking for real value,' said Sir Geoffrey Mulcahy of Kingfisher. 'I think we can look forward to low growth in consumer spending. It would not be easy to persuade customers to spend. You have to offer real value, real choice and real service. With the latest official inflation figures, the government will be able to take comfort from the fact that traders are having to curb prices in order to maintain demand.' Simon Briscoe, UK economist at Nikko Bank, said: 'The data suggests that retailers, in order to sell goods, have to be price competitive'.

Source: adapted from *The Guardian*, 20.3. 1997.

(a) Describe the consumer demand conditions facing businesses at the time of article.
(b) Explain how the demand conditions might affect demand pull inflation.

labour costs as workers and unions push for and receive an increase in their wages.

● Tax increases. Increases in indirect taxes, such as VAT (☞unit 26), can raise the price of products. They can also increase the costs of production, which causes firms to raise their prices.

● Profits. A push by firms to raise profit levels, due to pressure from shareholders, can increase production costs.

● Imports. An increase in costs can be 'imported' from abroad. The prices of imported raw materials or semi-finished products, such as components, may rise. This could increase the price of home produced goods which use these in production. A rise in the price of imported finished goods can more directly lead to inflation, as it adds to the general level of prices. For example, a sudden fall in reserves of raw materials such as oil will force up the price (☞unit 17). Businesses importing oil or using oil in their production process will have to pay higher costs.

Rises in wages or the price of imports are said to be examples of **supply shocks** because they affect the firms' costs and the supply of their products. Many argued that the high levels of inflation experienced by the UK in the 1970s and early 1980s was due to huge oil price rises. In the 1990s the UK had relatively low inflation rates. Some argued that one of the factors affecting this was the reduced power of trade unions in collective bargaining and their inability to negotiate high wage rises (☞unit 85).

Expectations Many economists believe that employees expecting inflation to occur can actually be a cause of inflation. This is because workers pressing for a pay rise tend to build in an **anticipated** amount of inflation into

their claim. For example, if they expect inflation to be four per cent, and want a two per cent pay rise, they will demand a six per cent pay increase. If awarded, this would give them a two per cent **real** increase in wages and a six per cent **money** increase (☞unit 19). If this was the average for all businesses in the economy, they would be faced with a six per cent increase in their wage costs. This increase in costs may lead businesses to increase their prices, and inflation can occur. If expectations of inflation are reduced, wage costs may be kept down. It is also argued that increases in wages in line with increases in productivity do not lead to higher costs, and higher prices as a result.

Question 2

In November, 1997 torrential rain in Spain and French lorry drivers' strikes combined to send lettuce prices soaring. Supplies of lettuces from Spain were cut by a combination of the downpours and warm temperatures which led to infestation by hungry caterpillars which destroyed the crop. The French lorry drivers' dispute also restricted deliveries to the UK. British supermarkets were hardest hit. The prices in British supermarkets were 55 per cent higher in November than the month before. It was suggested that the price of fresh vegetables would rise in the following months as a result of Irish crops of Brussels sprouts and cabbages being hit by black rot.

Source: adapted from *The Guardian*, 10.12.1997.

(a) What type of inflation might be suggested by the article? Explain your answer.
(b) Explain what types of business are most likely to be affected by the factors in the article.
(c) Examine whether or not the factors in the article are examples of supply shocks.

Effects of inflation on business

Reducing inflation has been one of the main economic objectives of UK governments in the 1980s and 1990s. The government has had strong support from the Confederation of British Industry (CBI) and other business groups in following this approach. Why is inflation seen as such a problem? There is a number of effects that relatively high rates of inflation might have on business, and on consumer demand and confidence.

Increasing costs Inflation leads to an increase in business costs. Examples might be:
● increases in the cost of components or raw materials;
● increase in wages and salaries of employees to keep pace with inflation;
● increasing energy costs;
● rising 'service' costs, such as the cost of calling out technicians.
If a business cannot pass on these costs to consumers as

higher prices or 'absorb' the costs in greater productivity, profits can fall. Higher prices are likely to mean fewer sales. Whether this results in a fall in turnover depends on the response of consumers to a rise in price (☞ unit 42). Businesses may be able to raise the prices of essential products a great deal with little fall-off in sales.

Shoe leather costs During periods of price stability firms are likely to have good knowledge of the price that they will pay for various goods and services. Such purchases might include delivery vehicles, premises insurance, computer equipment and stationery. However, during periods of rising prices firms may be less able to recognise a 'reasonable' price. They may need to spend more time shopping around for the best price (hence the term shoe leather costs). The extra time spent on this can be extremely expensive for some small firms.

Menu costs This refers to the time and money which firms have to spend on changing their price lists. It is a problem for firms displaying their price either on the actual product or on its packaging. Some firms, such as those distributing their goods via vending machines, are particularly affected.

Wage negotiating When inflation is high, firms will be under strong pressure to upgrade wages and salaries in line with expected levels of inflation. As well as the increased wage costs there will be some administrative costs in these changes. Conflict between employees and employers can result from disagreements about the extent to which wages need to be raised to compensate for inflation.

Reduced purchasing power When prices are rising the REAL VALUE of money will fall. This is the value taking into account inflation. A consumer with £200 to spend will be able to buy less if prices are increasing. So will a business aiming to purchase £20,000 worth of raw materials. There is said to be a fall in their **purchasing power**.

In periods of inflation, sales of certain goods are particularly affected. Businesses that produce 'luxury' goods, such as designer footwear, are likely to suffer as consumers switch to more essential products. Producers of goods and services sold to groups that are badly hit by inflation may also lose sales. It is argued that fixed income groups, such as pensioners, are affected most because their earnings do not always keep pace with inflation.

Businesses unable to increase their turnover in line with their costs will suffer similar effects. This may be the case, for example, with a local retailer with a geographically 'fixed' market, who is unable to raise prices for fear of losing customers to a local superstore. Profits will decline as costs, which are not covered by increased turnover, rise.

Borrowing and lending Inflation redistributes money from lenders to borrowers. A business that has borrowed £20,000 is likely to pay back far less in real terms over a ten year period if inflation is high. Those business that owe a large amount of money stand to gain in periods of high inflation as the value of their debts may be 'wiped out'. Businesses that have saved will lose out. Interest rates may fail to keep up with inflation, especially when inflation reaches levels of 10 per cent or more. So, if interest rates are 10 per cent and inflation is 20 per cent, the saver will lose 10 per cent of the real value of savings, but the borrower will find the value to be paid back falls 10 per cent a year.

Investment Views are divided as to the effects of inflation upon investment decisions. Some argue that, in the short term at least, it might increase the amount of investment undertaken by firms. This is because the real rate of interest (taking into account the rate of inflation) is often low during inflationary periods as inflation figures get close to, or exceed, the rate of interest. This makes investment using borrowed money relatively cheap.

Others believe that businesses are less likely to go ahead with investment projects. This is because inflation makes entrepreneurs less certain about the future and less willing to take risks.

Uncertainty Uncertainty may affect decisions other than investment that a business makes. Firms are often unwilling to enter into long term transactions in inflationary periods. Take, for example, a business ordering stocks of sheet metal in March to be delivered in June and paid for in August. Inflation of 24 per cent a year may mean that the price of the good increases by 12 per cent during this period. The firm supplying the sheet metal will receive the amount quoted in March when the payment is made in August. However, by August the value of this money will have declined as a result of the inflation.

Unemployment, growth and trade It is sometimes argued that inflation can actually lead to unemployment and lower economic growth. The uncertainty that inflation creates in the minds of business people means they are less willing to take risks, invest in new ventures, expand production or hire workers. Also, if UK inflation rates are higher than those of our competitors, UK products would be relatively more expensive in markets abroad, whilst foreign products would be relatively cheaper in the UK. An inability to compete on price in both domestic and foreign markets could mean the loss of many jobs. It could also result in a deterioration in the balance of payments (☞ unit 25) as the number of exports sold abroad falls and the number of imports coming into the country increases.

The value of assets The monetary value of assets increases in inflationary periods. Consumers who own antiques or scarce items may find their values soar. The money value of houses, factories, offices and machinery also rises. A business owning an office can sell it for a higher price. Of course, it will have to pay a higher price for any other office it wants to buy.

A footloose business in an area of high demand may be able to sell a factory or a set of offices for a high price and move to an area where property is cheaper. This is true at any time, but in periods of inflation the gains to be made are larger because the difference between prices will be greater.

Question 3

Table 23.1 *Inflation in selected countries*

Percentage changes on previous 12 months

Country	To Dec 1995	To Dec 1996	To Dec 1997	To Oct 1998
United Kingdom	3.4	2.4	3.1	3.1
USA	2.8	2.9	2.3	1.5
Japan	-0.1	0.1	1.7	0.2
Germany	1.8	1.5	1.8	0.7
Czech Republic	9.0	8.8	8.5	8.2
Hungary	28.5	29.5	18.3	12.3
Turkey	89.1	80.4	85.7	76.6

Source: adapted from OECD website,
http://www.oecd.org/news_and_events/new-numbers/cp/cplist.htm

(a) Describe the UK's inflation rate relative to that of its international competitors during the period.
(b) Explain how inflation in 1998 may have affected:
   (i) a small firm that considered investing in a new machine which had to borrow £20,000;
   (ii) a manufacturer of drinks machines for sports centres etc. which had to buy parts from a variety of sources overseas;
   (iii) an exporter of men's suits to the USA.

Measuring inflation

Inflation in the UK is measured by the Retail Price Index. This is an **index** (☞ unit 12) which is constructed to provide an accurate figure on the changes in the prices of goods and services each month. It is based upon a 'basket' of goods and services which is meant to represent the typical purchases of consumers throughout the UK. This basket of goods and services includes a range of items, such as foodstuffs, electrical items and petrol.

Index numbers can be used as indicators of changes and allow comparisons to be made. The Retail Price Index chooses a base year from which changes in prices can be calculated. Average prices are given a value of 100 in the base year. If the index in the following year is 102, then on average prices may be said to have risen by 2 per cent. Table 23.2 shows the changes in the Retail Price Index in the 1990s.

The Retail Price Index is a **weighted index** (☞ unit 12). This means that the importance attached to some goods and services included in the index is higher than for others. For example, petrol will tend to have a higher weighting in the index than soap. This is because petrol represents a higher proportion of the monthly expenditure of consumers than soap. The effect of this on the index is that a two per cent change in the price of petrol will have more impact upon the Retail Price Index than a two per cent rise in the price of soap.

Question 4

Table 23.3 *Percentage changes in retail prices on year earlier, 1998*

All items	3.3	Clothing and footwear	-0.9
Food	0.6		
Catering	3.7	Personal goods and services	3.3
Alcoholic drink	3.2		
Tobacco	9.4	Motoring expenditure	3.5
Housing	8.8		
Fuel and light	-5.8	Fares and other travel costs	3.1
Household goods	1.0		
Household services	2.7	Leisure goods	-0.8
		Leisure services	5.1

Source: adapted from *Labour Market Trends*, Office for National Statistics.

(a) Identify the product with the: (i) largest percentage increase; (ii) smallest percentage increase; (iii) largest percentage decrease in prices in 1998.
(b) Suggest the possible effects on:
   (i) customers buying these products;
   (ii) businesses producing these products;
   (iii) other businesses.

Table 23.2 *The Retail Price Index, Jan 1987 = 100*

	1988	1989	1990	1991	1992	1993	1994	1995	1996	1997	1998
	106.2	115.0	126.2	133.8	138.5	140.7	144.1	149.1	152.7	157.5	163.5

Source: adapted from *Economic Trends*, Office for National Statistics.

Summary

1. How is inflation measured in the UK?
2. Describe the 3 main causes of inflation.
3. What is imported inflation?
4. List 3 ways in which: (a) a business; and
   (b) consumers; might each be affected by inflation.
5. How might inflation lead to unemployment?
6. Explain how the Retail Price Index is compiled in the UK.

Key terms

Cost-push inflation - inflation which occurs as a result of businesses facing increased costs, which are then passed on to consumers in the form of higher prices.
Demand-pull inflation - inflation which occurs as a result of excessive spending in the economy.
Deflation - a situation where prices are falling.
Hyper-inflation - a situation where inflation levels are very high.
Inflation - a continuing or persistent tendency for prices to rise.
Money supply - the total amount of money circulating in the economy.
Real value - any value which takes into account the rate of inflation.
Retail Price Index - an indicator of the changes in average prices of a range of goods typically bought by consumers in the UK.

Case study

Inflation in Brazil

Between 1984 and 1994 Brazil had an annual average inflation rate of 900.3 per cent. Investment decisions were particularly hard to make. Planning for long term investment was impossible because it was difficult to forecast what would happen even 6 months later. Businesses aimed for long lead times in paying suppliers, but fast collection of debts. If a business could sell within 15 days, but have 30 days to pay, it could invest the money for 15 days on money markets. This was profitable because of the high interest rates at the time.

Pricing was also greatly affected by inflation. Prices of goods and services needed to be constantly kept in line with inflation rates. Too low a selling price may attract customers, but the costs of materials may rise more, leading to losses. Too high a price may allow the firm to keep pace with rising costs, but may lead to a loss of customers. Firms tended to ignore production costs and priced at the value customers would pay.

Inflationary expectations dominated negotiations. Renegotiations with suppliers about stocks and unions about wages, which took place each year in many countries, were carried out each month. For retailers with 80,000 items this could mean discussions with up to 6,000 suppliers each month.

By the late 1990s it was suggested that inflation in Brazil had been defeated. The 'Plan Real' in 1994 was designed to stabilise the economy and had created a new currency, the real. The price increases of over 2,000 per cent in 1994 had been reduced to 3.4 per cent by 1997. In 1998 foreign investment in Brazil was expected to reach $22.5 billion. With high inflation, retailers were able to make losses on goods and services, yet make money by delaying payments to suppliers and investing in money markets. With the curbing of inflation, this was no longer possible. Retailers

were forced to make their sales operations more efficient. This meant the introduction of technology, such as bar coding and scanning at checkouts. However, despite the success in controlling inflation there was still concern about the level of government spending in 1998.

Source: adapted from the *Financial Times* and updated, 25.9.1998; *The World Development Report*.

(a) How would you describe the inflation experienced in Brazil between 1984 and 1994?
(b) Explain why Brazilian businesses might have wanted long lead times in paying suppliers during periods of high inflation.
(c) Explain three problems faced by Brazilian businesses during periods of high inflation.
(d) Explain two changes that have taken place in the operation of Brazilian businesses since inflation fell.
(e) Why might Brazilian businesses be concerned about levels of government spending in 1998?
(f) To what extent might expectations have played a part in leading to inflation in Brazil?

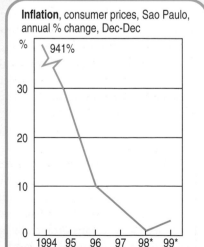

Inflation, consumer prices, Sao Paulo, annual % change, Dec-Dec

What is unemployment?

Unemployment is concerned with people being out of work. Measures of unemployment try to calculate or estimate the number of people out of work at a given point in time. Figure 24.1 shows unemployment rates in the UK in the 1990s. The different measures of unemployment that have been used in the UK are explained later in this unit.

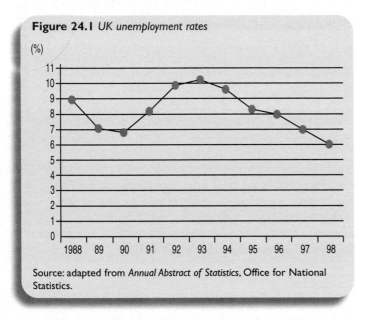

Figure 24.1 *UK unemployment rates*

Source: adapted from *Annual Abstract of Statistics*, Office for National Statistics.

Types of unemployment

There is a number of different types of unemployment.

Seasonal unemployment Some workers are employed on a seasonal basis. In the UK construction, holiday and agricultural industries, workers are less in demand in winter because of the climate. Seasonal unemployment can therefore be high. In summer it may fall, as these workers are hired. It is difficult in practice for governments to 'solve' this type of unemployment, which may always occur. In producing unemployment statistics, governments often adjust the figures to allow for seasonal factors.

Search and frictional unemployment These two types of unemployment are very similar. FRICTIONAL unemployment occurs when people are moving between jobs. Usually it only lasts for a short amount of time. For example, an electrician who had been working in the North East may have a few weeks 'off' before starting a new job in London. It is not seen as a serious problem by government. SEARCH unemployment, however, can last longer. This type of unemployment occurs when people are searching for a new job. The greater the information on job opportunities, the

lower search unemployment is likely to be.

Structural unemployment STRUCTURAL unemployment is caused by changes in the structure of a country's economy which affect particular industries and occupations. Examples include the decline of the coal and steel industries in the second half of the twentieth century. Between 1963 and the mid-1990s almost half a million jobs were lost in the coal mining industry. This indicates the size of the problem in the UK. Because certain industries have traditionally been located in particular parts of the country, their decline can have a dramatic effect upon those regions. As a result, structural unemployment is closely linked with regional unemployment. It may also result from changes in demand for the goods and services produced by particular sectors of the economy. For example, there has been a decline in demand for natural fibres such as jute as a result of the development of synthetic products.

Technological unemployment This occurs when new technology replaces workers with machines. For example, new technology introduced to the newspaper industry has meant the loss of many print workers' jobs.

Cyclical or demand-deficient unemployment CYCLICAL unemployment results from the cycles which occur in most economies. These ups and downs in economic activity over a number of years are known as the business cycle (☞ unit 26). In a recession, at the 'bottom' of a business cycle, unemployment results from a lack of demand. It is argued that demand is not high enough to employ all labour, machines, land, offices etc. in the economy.

Real wage unemployment Unit 19 explained how the demand for workers by business and the supply of workers is influenced by the **real wage rate.** Relatively high real wages mean that workers will want to supply more labour than businesses want to employ. This results in unemployment. In other words, it is argued that workers 'price themselves' out of jobs. There are vacancies, but businesses will only be willing to pay wages which are lower than workers are prepared to accept.

Voluntary and involuntary unemployment Some suggest that unemployment can be voluntary or involuntary. Voluntary unemployment occurs when workers refuse to accept jobs at existing wage rates. Involuntary unemployment occurs when there are not enough jobs in the economy at existing wage rates. Economists sometimes talk about the **natural rate of unemployment.** This is the percentage of workers which are voluntarily unemployed. This is also referred to as the **non-accelerating inflation rate of**

unemployment (NAIRU). This is because it is the rate of unemployment that can be sustained without an increase in inflation. Any attempt to reduce unemployment below this level will simply result in an increase in prices.

Question 1

In 1999 manufacturing employment was expected to fall to its lowest level since the nineteenth century. Job losses were expected to be around 1,000 a day, leading to predicted net job losses of 390,000 over the year. The fall could be even worse, however, as figures were based on an average fall in output and economic growth of 1.5 per cent over the period 1998-2000. In the recession of 1990 output actually fell 5 per cent and this led to 927,000 job losses in manufacturing.

It was also estimated that output in the farming industry would fall and that agricultural employment would be at a record low.

Source: adapted from *The Observer*, 11.10.1998.

(a) Explain three types of unemployment that may occur in the agricultural industry.
(b) What type of unemployment in manufacturing is suggested in the article? Explain your answer.

Effects of unemployment on business

High levels of unemployment have a number of effects on businesses. The majority of the effects of unemployment are harmful for businesses. However, there are some businesses which may be unaffected by unemployment. A small minority may even benefit.

Demand The obvious effect of unemployment is that people are not earning income and are likely to have less to spend. Businesses will suffer a loss of demand for their products and reduced profits as a result. Producers of goods, such as clothing and household furniture, and providers of services, such as insurance and holidays, are all likely to suffer.

Organisation Unemployment can have a number of effects on the internal organisation of a business. It may mean that a firm can no longer afford to recruit new members of staff because of low demand for its products. New, often young, recruits to a firm will no longer be coming through. In addition, new posts which arise may be filled through retraining of existing staff rather than recruitment. This can lead to significant changes in the age profile of an organisation's employees.

Redundancies are also a common feature of a period of high unemployment. Whilst the work of some who are made redundant will not be replaced, the responsibilities and roles of others may be added to the job descriptions of those who remain with the firm. This can lead to increasing demands on existing employees.

During periods of high unemployment, some firms reorganise their internal structure. This may mean the loss of a whole tier in the hierarchy or the changing of individual job descriptions. In recent years, many businesses, such as IBM, have removed large numbers of middle managers.

Payments Businesses may be faced with making redundancy payments to workers. These tend to vary between firms depending upon the average length of service of the employee.

The cost of any reorganisation caused by redundancies will also have to be borne by firms. Such costs may include lost productivity after a reorganisation as employees struggle to cope with new responsibilities.

It may be easier for firms to recruit new employees during a period of high unemployment. This is because there is a larger pool of people to choose from, with more applicants for each available post. In addition, because of the increased competition for new jobs, people may be prepared to work for less money. In this way firms can lower their labour costs.

Output During periods of unemployment, many firms reduce their level of output to compensate for falling demand. This can lead to excess capacity and under-utilisation of capital equipment. In addition, falling levels of demand can interrupt the flow of production, causing production and stock control problems (☞ unit 94).

Government spending High levels of unemployment mean that government spending on social security will be high. Also, the government will lose revenue from tax and National Insurance contributions which people would have paid had they been in employment. To make up for this the government may borrow, increase taxation or reduce other items of spending.

Increased trade and reduced costs The services offered by some firms depend upon other firms going out of business. Firms specialising in receiverships and pawnbrokers may see an increase in the demand for their services. Firms also benefit from 'trading down', ie buying cheaper alternatives. Retailers and manufacturers selling goods aimed at lower income segments of the market tend to do well during periods of unemployment. Supermarkets, in particular, have benefited. It has been argued that this is because consumers spend more on home entertainment and less on going out during periods of high unemployment.

Social issues Research into unemployment has shown that it has a number of possible 'side effects'. These can have consequences for businesses. The suggested side effects include poverty and stress for those individuals, families and communities that have high levels of unemployment. They also include higher levels of vandalism and crime. This can lead to higher insurance premiums for businesses, disruption to businesses caused by crime and, in some cases, loss of custom and the need to relocate premises.

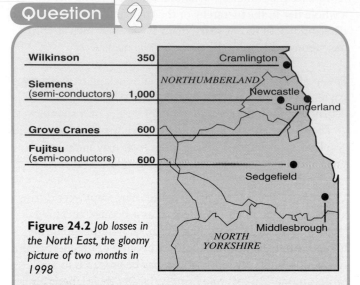

Figure 24.2 *Job losses in the North East, the gloomy picture of two months in 1998*

Wilkinson	350	Cramlington
Siemens (semi-conductors)	1,000	Newcastle
Grove Cranes	600	Sunderland
Fujitsu (semi-conductors)	600	Sedgefield

The North-east of England was dealt another blow in 1998 when Wilkinson Sword announced the closure of its long established factory. This closure brought the number of job losses in the North-east to 4,500 in an eight week period. The job losses were blamed on a global surplus of razor blades, with supply exceeding demand. The closure of the 35 year old plant in Cramlington New Town occurred as the company had been forced to review operations across Europe.

Dick Gibbons, Wilkinson Sword's Director of manufacturing operations, said: 'We realise it is going to be very difficult, given the recent spate of job losses across the North-east'. 'This is a colossal blow to the workers and the local community,' said Davey Hall, regional secretary of the Amalgamated Engineering and Electrical Union. 'It will have a massive knock-on effect on suppliers and is a massive body blow to Northumberland.'

Source: adapted from *The Guardian*, 1998.

(a) What types of unemployment might the loss of these jobs create?
(b) What might be the 'knock-on effects' of the job losses referred to on:
   (i) suppliers;
   (ii) the local community;
   (iii) government revenue?

Measuring unemployment

How many people are unemployed? It is possible to measure unemployment in various ways. In the UK, unemployment has been measured by the number of people claiming unemployment-related benefits. To claim benefits such as Jobseeker's Allowance and National Insurance credits, people must declare that they are out of work and be capable of,

available for and actively seeking work during the week in which the claim is made. This is known as the **claimant count** measure. One problem with this measure is that it does not include people who are unemployed but who do not register.

In the late 1990s the UK government indicated that it wanted the main measure to be the **International Labour Force** (ILO) measure of unemployment. This is based on a survey of people. To be unemployed a person has to be out of work, have looked for work in the last four weeks and be able to start work in the next two weeks.

Figure 24.3 *Unemployment: claimant count and ILO measures, UK, seasonally adjusted*

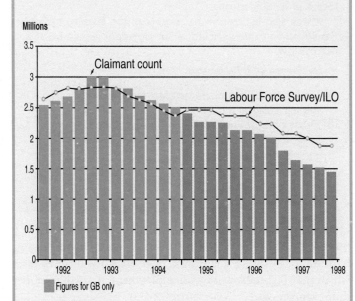

Source: adapted from *Economic Trends, Social Trends,* Office for National Statistics.

(a) Describe the trends taking place in unemployment in Figure 24.3.
(b) What might account for the difference between the two sets of figures?
(c) Explain why the ILO figures might be of greater interest to a business looking to employ workers.

Key terms

Cyclical unemployment - unemployment resulting from the ups and downs (cycles) which occur in most economies.
Frictional/search unemployment - unemployment caused by people moving from one job to another.
Structural unemployment - unemployment caused by changes in the structure of the economy.

Summary

1. What are the different types of unemployment?
2. Why is frictional unemployment not regarded as a problem by government?
3. What are the possible negative effects of unemployment on firms?
4. What are the possible positive effects of unemployment on firms?
5. State 2 methods of measuring unemployment.

Case study

Unemployment in the City, or not?

In 1998 Merrill Lynch, the leading US investment bank, announced 3,400 job losses, with 400 jobs lost in its City of London operations. Merrill Lynch is widely used by many analysts as a benchmark of cutbacks. The removal of 5 per cent of its workforce led to estimates at the time that as many as 80,000 jobs could be lost in the City. Even the most conservative estimates put the cull at 30,000 job cuts or 10 per cent of the City's total workforce.

The jobs losses came in the wake of what was considered to be disastrous investments in high risk markets, with changeable demand conditions. The job losses came as the investment bank announced its first net loss in nine years of $164 million for the third quarter of the year. Defending the job losses, the company said that it was looking ahead to a more challenging trading environment and, as a consequence, was implementing an energetic programme to reduce expenses and selectively resize certain business operations. It was also suggested at the time that in 1999 the world economy would only grow by 1.75 per cent, its lowest rate in six years. There was even a chance of further shocks to financial markets which could trigger a recession in the US and a substantial reduction in growth in Europe.

Experts believed that City firms may have been disguising their job losses by keeping secret the number of temporary or part time workers they were sacking. Under European rules, companies were forced to announce cut-backs if they involved 100 people or more. Banks and other financial institutions hate to admit job losses. It was suggested that most of the big City firms had been laying off their temporary employees, whose departure did not have to be made public. Others were letting high paid dealers and fund managers leave in 'dribs and drabs' to avoid being caught by EU disclosure rules. In some City firms, more than half the staff were temporary and employment agencies announced an upturn in demand for short term workers. The trend was particularly apparent over a two month period which coincided with financial market turbulence.

Source: adapted from *The Guardian*, 1998.

(a) Describe the two types of unemployment suggested in the article.

(b) Suggest types of unemployment that temporary workers in financial firms may face in future having been made redundant.

(c) What might be the possible effects of job losses at Merrill Lynch on the business?

(d) Explain the possible effects of increasing unemployment in the financial services industry in the City of London on:
  (i) a sandwich making business;
  (ii) a financial services employment agency;
  (iii) an estate agency;
  based in the City.

(e) (i) Explain how actions by financial institutions may affect unemployment figures.
  (ii) Why might financial institutions want to hide their redundancies?

The balance of payments

Business transactions often take place across country borders. A UK manufacturer may buy components from the USA. Japanese businesses may use British insurance companies. A UK business may invest in a land reclamation project in a developing country.

All these transactions would be shown in a country's BALANCE OF PAYMENTS. It is a record of transactions between one country and the rest of the world. The balance of payments is usually divided into sections.

The current account The current account of the balance of payments is also divided into a number of sections.

● **Trade in goods.** Examples of traded goods might be computers, machine tools and chemicals. Goods which are manufactured in a country and sold abroad are called EXPORTS. Goods which are brought into a country from abroad are known as IMPORTS. An export from the UK, where goods are sold abroad, earns money for UK businesses. Money flows into the UK, so UK exports are recorded as **credits**. An import to the UK, where UK consumers or businesses buy goods from abroad, leads to an outflow of money from the UK. UK imports are recorded as **debits**. The difference between the value of exports and imports of goods is shown as TRADE IN GOODS on the balance of payments.

● **Trade in services.** Examples of traded services might be banking, shipping, travel and tourism, and insurance. Services which are sold abroad are exports and services bought from abroad are imports. Passenger tickets sold abroad for travel on a UK airline is an export of a service for the UK. The UK business earns money which flows into the UK. It appears as a credit. A UK business which insures with a foreign company is an example of an import of a service to the UK. The UK business spends abroad and money flows out of the UK. It appears as a debit. The difference between the value of exports and imports of goods is shown as TRADE IN SERVICES.

● **Income.** Income may be compensation paid to employees working abroad. Income sent home to the UK by a British computer programmer working in Saudi Arabia would appear as a credit under income on the UK accounts as money is entering the UK. Income may also be investment income. This is the interest, profit and dividends earned by companies abroad or foreign firms in a country. Profits sent to Japan made by a Japanese car firm in the UK would appear as a debit on the UK accounts.

● **Current transfers.** These include central government transfers. They also include gifts from individuals abroad to a country or gifts to foreign countries. For example, a payment to the EU by the UK government would be

shown as a debit under current transfers on the UK current account, as money is leaving the UK.

The difference between the value of money entering a country (credits) and the value of money leaving a country (debits) for:
● trade in goods and services;
● income to/from abroad;
● transfers;
is called the CURRENT BALANCE. We can say that:

Current balance = sales of exports and services, income earned from abroad and transfers to a country *minus* purchases of imports and services, income going abroad and transfers from a country

Capital account This involves the transfer of ownership of assets, transfers of funds associated with the purchase and sale of assets and the cancellation of liabilities. Examples include transfers from the EU regional fund (☞ unit 100) and the forgiveness of debt. This is a small part of the balance of payments account compared to the current and financial accounts.

Question

Jobson plc is a UK based multinational business. It has plants in Singapore, the USA, the UK and Australia. It specialises in the manufacture and distribution of a wide variety of food and drink products. Below are some of its transactions over the past 12 months.
● Profits from plants in Singapore, Malaysia and Ireland taken back to the UK.
● Buying shares in a French drinks producing firm.
● Exporting £30 million of soft drinks to EU nations from its UK plant.
● Holding a conference for senior managers from all of its plants in Bermuda.
● Paying for a team of Japanese management consultants to help with the restructuring of its London headquarters.
● Buying new production machinery from Germany for its UK plant.
● Investing £50 million on upgrading production facilities in its USA, Singapore and Australian factories.

Explain which of the above would be shown as:
(a) exports of services;
(b) imports of services;
(c) exports of goods;
(d) imports of goods;
(e) transactions in liabilities;
(f) the purchase or sale of assets;
in the UK's balance of payments account.

The financial account This covers the flow of money for transactions in **financial assets and liabilities**. For example, a foreign business may buy shares (an asset) in a UK company. Money would flow into the UK and would be shown as a credit on the financial account. Note that any dividend earned by the foreign business on the shares would be shown as a debit under investment income on the UK's current account as money is leaving the country. A transaction in liabilities on the UK accounts would be a UK business borrowing from a foreign bank. This would appear as a credit on the financial account, as money is flowing into the UK.

Balance of payments problems and business

The balance of payments must always 'balance'. Take a situation where a country has a **current account deficit**. This also means that outflows of money are greater than inflows to that country from trade in goods and services, income and transfers.

Where does the money come from to finance this deficit? The UK may, for example, borrow from foreign banks or sell its assets abroad to bring money back in. The Bank of England (☞ unit 26) could sell some of the country's gold or foreign currency reserves. Whatever happens, the deficit on the current account would be made up by a surplus on the capital account and financial account. In practice, if the values do not actually balance a **balancing item** is added. This is a figure for errors and omissions. It is large or small enough so that the accounts always balance.

Although the accounts always balance, individual parts of the balance of payments may not. What if the current account deficit carried on for a long period? This could lead to a number of problems for the UK government and for UK business.

● The country as a whole will get more and more into debt. Other countries may refuse to lend more money, and may insist upon repayment of any debt. Third World and Eastern European countries have faced such problems over the past few decades.

● Loss of jobs. If consumers buy imports, they will not buy home produced goods or services. Thus opportunities for job creation are lost. Similarly, low levels of exports mean the demand by businesses for employees will be lower.

● UK businesses may become dependent on imports of components and raw materials. This may mean that costs are dependent upon the exchange rate value of the pound sterling. This is dealt with later in this unit. It may also make the UK economy more vulnerable to imported inflation (☞ unit 26).

Figure 25.1 shows the current account of the UK over the period 1987-98. For most of the period the current balance was in deficit. This was because the UK tends to be a **net importer** of goods. In other words, it imports more goods than it exports. Although the UK exports a large amount of services (it is a **net exporter**), this is not enough to offset the deficit on the trade in goods (known as the **balance of trade**).

Figure 25.1 *The current account of the UK, 1987-98*

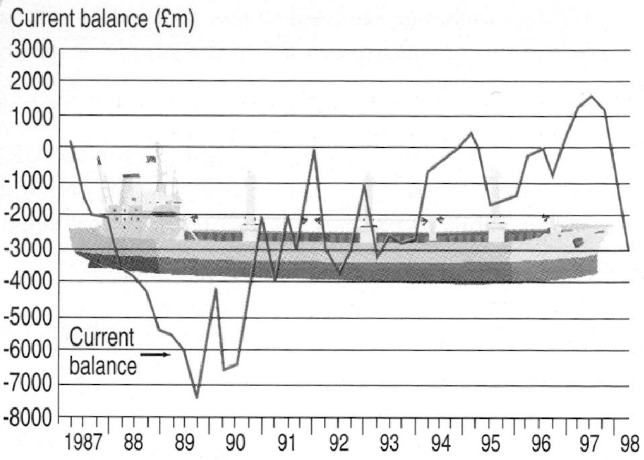

Current balance (£m)

Current balance →

Source: adapted from *Monthly Digest of Statistics*, Office for National Statistics.

Exchange rates

An EXCHANGE RATE is the price of one country's currency in relation to that of another. So, for example, an exchange rate £1 = $2 means that one pound is worth two dollars. Alternatively, one dollar is worth 50 pence.

Exchange rates are determined on foreign exchange markets throughout the world. If an exchange rate is **freely floating,** then changes in the demand for or supply of a currency will result in a change in that country's exchange rate. For example, a fall in the demand for sterling will cause its value to fall. This is the same type of analysis that was used to show the effect of changes in the demand for and supply of goods on prices in unit 17. A **fixed** exchange rate system is where countries do not allow the values of their currencies to change against each other's.

If the value of a currency falls in relation to the value of another currency then the exchange rate is said to have DEPRECIATED. Under a system of fixed exchange rates the currency will be DEVALUED by the government or controlling organisation. If the value of the currency rises against that of another currency then it is said to have **appreciated** (or to have been revalued).

There is a number of factors that can affect the exchange rate of a currency.

The volume of exports An increase in exports by UK firms will mean that more pounds are required to buy these exports. This will result in an increase in the demand for sterling and cause the value of sterling to rise. A decrease in UK exports will have the opposite effect, resulting in a fall in the demand for sterling and a fall in its value.

The volume of imports An increase in imports coming into the UK will mean that more sterling has to be sold in order to purchase the foreign currencies needed to buy imports. This will cause an increase in the supply of sterling, leading to a fall in sterling's exchange rate. A decrease in imports will have the opposite effect, resulting in a fall in the supply of sterling and a rise in its value.

The level of interest rates A rise in interest rates in the UK will attract savings from abroad. This will raise the demand for sterling and thus its price. A fall in interest rates will have the opposite effect.

Speculation The short term price of a country's currency is mainly influenced by speculation. If dealers on foreign exchange markets expect the value of a currency to fall in the future, they may sell their reserves of that currency. This will cause the supply of that currency to increase and its price to fall. It has been argued that speculation led to the collapse in the price of the pound on the so-called 'Black Wednesday' in 1992 and to the collapse of the Russian rouble in 1998. If, however, speculators expect the value of a currency to rise in the future, then they will begin purchasing that currency leading to an increase in its value.

Government intervention Governments may intervene on foreign exchange markets. They may try to influence the price of either their own currency or that of another country. For example, the UK government may attempt to raise the value of the pound by purchasing it on foreign exchange markets. Governments may also raise interest rates in order to increase the value of the pound.

Investment and capital flows An inflow of funds for long-term investment in the UK will cause the demand, and therefore the price, of sterling to rise. Similarly an outflow of investment funds will cause the supply of sterling to rise and its price to fall, other factors remaining the same. Thus, French investment in a UK water bottling plant would cause a rise in the exchange rate.

Capital flows are largely determined by the rate of interest. Thus an increase in UK interest rates would lead to an inflow of funds into the UK and a rise in the value of sterling. Such inflows of funds following interest rate changes tend to be short term money moving from one of the world's financial centres to another in search of the highest rate of return.

Question 2

Discuss the likely effects on the value of the pound against the Japanese yen of the following:
(a) increases in UK residents visiting Japan;
(b) the yen coming under speculative selling pressure as an election comes nearer;
(c) an increase in UK aircraft sales to Japan;
(d) UK interest rates increased to 6 per cent whilst Japanese interest rates remain at 4 per cent.

Exchange rates and business

The main reason why exchange rates are so important to businesses is because of their influence on the price of imports and exports. All but a very few small firms use at least some goods and services imported from abroad. Increasingly, large numbers of businesses are finding that they have to export their products in order to grow or survive. Thus the majority of firms are affected in some way by exchange rates.

The effect of falling exchange rates A fall in the exchange rate (a **depreciation** or **devaluation**) will affect the price of a business's exports and the price it pays for imports. Look at Table 25.1 which shows the effects of a fall in the value of the pound.

Table 25.1 *The effects of a fall in the value of the pound on the price of exports and imports*

	Exchange rate	UK price	USA price
Exported goods	£1 = $2	£10	$20
	£1 = $1.60	£10	$16
Imported goods	£1 = $2	£10	$20
	£1 = $1.60	£12.50	$20

At an exchange rate of £1 = $2, a book priced at £10 that is exported to the USA would cost Americans $20. If the value of the pound fell to £1 = $1.60, Americans would now be able to buy the same book for $16. So a fall in the exchange rate can make UK exports cheaper. What about imports to the UK? A picture frame priced at $20 imported to the UK would cost £10 before the depreciation of the exchange rate. If the exchange rate fell to £1 = $1.60, the picture frame would now cost £12.50 ([$2÷$1.60] x£10) or ($20÷1.60). So a fall in the exchange rate can cause the price of imports to rise.

The overall effect should be beneficial for UK businesses. The price paid for UK exports should fall, allowing businesses to sell more in export markets. The price paid by UK businesses and consumers for imports should rise. This might encourage them to switch their purchases from foreign goods to UK products.

There are problems, however, for firms if exchange rates are falling.
● Rising import prices mean that the amount paid for any inputs, such as raw materials or components bought in from abroad, will rise.
● Rising import prices can lead to IMPORTED INFLATION and the associated problems of this for businesses.
● Uncertainty over future prices of raw materials and components can result.

● Constant price changes may affect foreign demand for products as they are unsettling for customers.

The effect of rising exchange rates This has the opposite effect to devaluation. A rise in the exchange rate can cause the price of exports to rise and the price of imports to fall. For example, in Table 25.1 an increase in the exchange rate from £1=$1.60 to £1=$2 will cause the price of a £10 export to rise from $16 to $20 and the price of a $20 import to fall from £12.50 to £10.

The overall effect is likely to be negative. Not only will it become more difficult for UK firms to compete on price in export markets, but it will put pressure on them in UK markets, as they struggle to compete with lower priced imported goods. However, a rise in the exchange rate could allow UK businesses to buy cheaper imports from abroad.

The stability of exchange rates Unstable exchange rates can make it very difficult for firms to plan for the future. A rise in the exchange rate, for example, could turn a previously profitable export order into a loss maker. A devaluation, on the other hand, could mean that exports which looked unprofitable could now earn a profit for the firm.

Question

Calypso is an importer of ceramics and pottery from around the world. It sells its imported goods in specialist retailers and kitchenware outlets. It has recently imported some ornately decorated serving plates from Mexico at a price of 90 new pesos each. The current exchange rate is £1=15 new pesos. It will sell these in the UK at £6.

(a) Show how the business is likely to have arrived at the UK price of £6 for each plate.
(b) How might a fall in the exchange rate to £1=12 new pesos affect:
    (i) the price of the product sold in Mexico;
    (ii) the price to Calypso of the imported product?
(c) Suggest how Calypso might react to a fall in the exchange rate.

How much are businesses affected?

Not all businesses are affected to the same extent by changes in exchange rates.

The response of consumers Some products have a strong brand identity. Even if their prices increase, consumers do not reduce the amount purchased by a great deal. Unit 42 refers to these products as having an **inelastic** demand. What effect will a fall in the value of the pound from £1=$2 to £1=$1.60 have on UK businesses exporting such goods?

A firm selling 1,000 books to the USA each month for $20

each at an exchange rate of £1 = $2, would receive $20,000 (£10,000) in revenue. If the exchange rate fell to £1 = $1.60, and the demand for books was price inelastic, then the business may be able to keep the price at $20. At this new exchange rate the $20,000 would be worth £12,500 (20,000÷ 1.60). Thus, revenue would increase by £2,500.

Firms with products which are sensitive to price changes are likely to feel the impact of even minor exchange rate changes. If export prices rise the volume of sales will fall by a greater degree, and the overall revenue for exports will fall. If export prices fall, revenue should be greater because the increase in quantity sold is relatively greater than the fall in price.

The degree of control over prices Not all businesses have the same degree of control over the price at which their products are sold. Those with a high degree of control over their prices can adopt market based methods of pricing, such as customer value pricing (☞ unit 43). They might decide not to allow exchange rate changes to alter the price of their exports, although their sales revenue may change. For example, a business selling sportswear with a strong degree of brand loyalty amongst its customers might be unwilling to alter its price as a result of relatively small exchange rate fluctuations. This is because prices will have been carefully chosen to suit particular markets. In this case, only a large rise in the exchange rate, which threatened profits, would cause a pricing re-think.

Importing components and raw materials The effect of a change in the exchange rate on firms that imported components or raw materials would depend on a number of factors. First, whether or not the firms from which they are importing decide to alter their prices. Second, whether or not any long term agreements on prices had been reached. Third, whether the firm had already bought foreign currency to pay

Question

The Reconstruction Company rebuilds cars such as Land Rovers and exports them to countries such as South Africa and Australia. It has exported 5 reconditioned vehicles for use on game reserves, selling each one for 120,000 rand. The exchange rate at the time was £1=10 rand.

(a) Calculate the earnings in rand and in pounds for the business.
(b) The exchange rate fell over the next year to £1=9.6 rand. The South African companies still needed vehicles and were not likely to find a supplier at this price and at short notice. The Reconstruction Company decided to keep its price the same in rand. It sells another 5 vehicles. Calculate the effect of this on the revenue of the business.
(c) Suggest why the company was able to follow this approach.

for future imported components etc. A firm importing fabric from Hong Kong might want to buy a year's supply of Hong Kong dollars to make sure it was unaffected by changes in the exchange rate.

The single European market and the single European currency

In 1992 the single European market was created. This removed restrictions on trade between members of the European Union (☞ unit 30). The next step in European integration took place on January 1 1999 when 11 European countries joined the European Monetary Union (EMU). They included France, Germany, Ireland and Spain, but not the UK. At that time the participating countries fixed their exchange rates so that they could not move at all against each other. They were also to be fixed against a new reference currency, the **euro**. On 1 January 2002, euro notes and coins will become legal tender in these countries. The member countries would then have a **single currency**. At some point later it would replace the national currencies.

Some have suggested that this type of fixed exchange rate could have a number of effects on businesses and consumers in countries within the 'euro zone'.

● Consumers and businesses will be able to see price differences if the prices of products in different countries are all shown in euros.
● There will be less costs in changing from one currency to another to buy foreign goods and services for businesses and consumers, eg commission and time.
● There will be reduced exchange rate uncertainty. If exchange rates are fixed, businesses will not experience a sudden change in exchange rates which might, for example, increase the price of their imported components.
● It is argued that the need to prevent fluctuations in exchange rates by control of interest rates, for example, will keep inflation low. This is especially the case in countries such as Italy which are prone to inflation. The benefits of low inflation for businesses are discussed in unit 26.
● There will be costs of retraining staff in the use of the new currency and in repricing products.

Some people and groups within the UK are opposed to the the single currency. They do not want control of economic policy to be from Europe. They argue that European policies that may suit Europe, such as high interest rates, may not be applicable to the UK at a particular time. UK businesses, they argue, may suffer as a result. The impact of monetary union on business is discussed in detail in unit 30.

Question 5

Table 25.2 *Variations in prices of cars*

Model	Minimum price		Maximum price		% increase on minimum price
Ford Fiesta		Portugal		UK	43.5
VW Golf		Netherlands		UK	40.1
Honda Accord		Netherlands		UK	29.0
BMW 520i		Netherlands		UK	29.5

Source: adapted from Eurostat.

Prices of cars vary from one European country to another. Table 25.2 shows the difference between the minimum price and maximum price of different cars in Europe. When the euro is introduced, cars will be priced in euros and in national currencies in all countries. It is argued that businesses often price products around a fixed amount. For example, a car may be priced at £11,000. A price of £11,365 would look 'odd' to a customer. When euros are introduced, there may be a temptation to round up prices to the nearest full euro by businesses.

Source: adapted from the *Financial Times*, 1998.

(a) What problem for UK consumers might the introduction of the euro help to solve?
(b) Explain how the introduction of the euro might affect:
  (i) consumers;
  (ii) car manufacturers;
  using the information in the article.

Key terms

Balance of payments - a record of the transactions between one country and the rest of the world over a given period of time.
Current balance - the difference between the value of money entering and leaving a country for trade in goods and services income from abroad and transfers.
Devaluation/depreciation - a decline in the value of an exchange rate.
Exchange rate - the price of one currency in relation to another.
Exports - goods and services which leave the country and are sold to foreigners.

Imports - goods and services which enter the country and are bought from foreigners.
Imported inflation - a rise in prices, as a result of exchange rate changes, which raise the price of materials or components brought into a country.
Trade in goods - the difference between imports and exports of physical products.
Trade in services - the difference between the import and export of services.

Summary

1. Give 3 examples of trade in services.
2. Give 3 examples of investment income.
3. What does the financial account of the balance of payments show?
4. What is meant by a deficit on the account balance?
5. Why must the balance of payments always balance?
6. Briefly explain 2 policies used to tackle a balance of

payments deficit and how they can affect business.
7. State 5 factors that determine exchange rates.
8. What is the difference between a fixed and a floating exchange rate system?
9. State 3 ways fluctuating exchange rates can affect firms.
10. State 3 benefits to a business of a single currency.

Case study

Black Wednesday

In 1990 the UK joined an exchange rate agreement with other EU countries which was intended to improve trading conditions within Europe by providing exchange rate stability. Under this agreement, the UK government at the time agreed that the minimum value below which the pound sterling was not allowed to fall was £1 = 2.78 deutschmarks (DM). If there were signs that the pound was in danger of falling below this level, then the Bank of England would intervene on foreign exchange markets. This was done by increasing the demand for, and therefore the value of, sterling by buying appropriate quantities of it. Similarly if the pound sterling was in danger of rising above its agreed limit, then it would sell sterling on the foreign exchange, therefore increasing its supply and lowering its price.

However, there were signs that this approach was going wrong in the week beginning 14 September 1992. On the Tuesday, the moment London foreign exchange dealers began work they started selling sterling. Its value slid. The Bank of England dug into its reserves to buy pounds. Sterling survived the day - bolstered by the Bank of England's support.

Overnight, foreign exchange dealers in New York and Tokyo were frantically selling sterling. London dealers joined in on the Wednesday morning. At 11 am, the Government increased interest rates from 10 per cent to 12 per cent. The government's message was clear: we mean business. Norman Lamont the Chancellor of the

Exchequer at the time, repeated that he would 'do whatever was necessary' to maintain the value of sterling. However, pressure on sterling continued. At 2.15 pm a further interest rate rise, to 15 per cent, was announced by the government. Again it made no difference. This time, the government threw in the towel and announced that it was unable to maintain the value of the pound at the agreed rate of £1 = 2.78 DM.

It has been estimated that the government spent over £10 billion on intervention to support the pound. Despite this, in just one day the value of the pound sterling fell from £1 = 2.78 DM to £1 = 2.70 DM.

(a) Describe the factors that were affecting the exchange rate at the time.

(b) The aim of the ERM, like the single currency, was to keep exchange rates stable. Suggest three benefits of this for businesses.

(c) Explain how a fall in the value of the pound after Black Wednesday might have affected:
(i) UK exports; (ii) UK imports; (iii) the UK's balance of payments.

(d) Using calculations, show the possible effects of the fall in the value of the pound from £1 = 2.78 DM to £1 = 2.70 DM on a UK firm selling ten £5,000 computer systems to Germany each week.

Government policy

Unit 21 considered how and why governments seek to influence the economy. Governments use a variety of methods of intervention, including legislation, spending and taxation. Part of the government's involvement in the economy is the use of policies to control economic variables such as inflation, unemployment and trade. The use of these different policies can affect businesses.

Fiscal policy

Fiscal policy aims to manage the level of total spending or aggregate demand (☞ unit 21) in the economy. The government can use fiscal policy in a number of ways to achieve its objectives.
● It can boost total spending in the economy when there is unemployment (☞ unit 24).
● If there is inflation in the economy, linked to the level of demand (☞ unit 23), fiscal policy can be used to reduce demand in the economy as a whole.
● If there is a current balance deficit the government could raise taxes or cut spending on imports.
● It may try to redistribute income. It may spend money or reduce tax on low income groups to give them more disposable income.
    Fiscal policy may involve governments making the following changes.

Changes in government spending If the economy needs a boost, government expenditure can be raised. For example, spending on building new hospitals can create jobs, income and increased spending by the people in those jobs. On the other hand, if the economy needs to be slowed down, government expenditure can be lowered. This may also be used to control inflation.

Changes in direct taxation **Direct taxes** are those which are levied directly on individuals or businesses. Income tax rates, as part of a fiscal policy, can be lowered in order to encourage consumers to buy more goods and services. This should raise the level of aggregate demand. Corporation tax, a tax on company profits, may be cut to encourage businesses to invest and increase output. Raising income tax is likely to have the opposite effect, ie to lower the level of aggregate demand. This could be used to cut disposable income and control inflation.

Changes in indirect taxation **Indirect taxes** are taxes on goods or services. The main indirect tax in the UK is VAT. Governments raise indirect taxes as part of fiscal policy in order to raise the price of goods and services and discourage spending. Indirect taxes are also used by governments as a

means of raising revenue in order to finance spending plans. There is much debate as to whether it is individual businesses or consumers who have to pay for indirect taxes. Take the example of a 2 per cent increase in VAT. If this was passed on to consumers in the form of a 2 per cent price rise, then consumers would be paying for it. However, firms might be reluctant to pass on the price rise to consumers because of fears of falling demand for their product. In this case, they might only raise the price by 1 per cent and pay the other 1 per cent VAT increase themselves. This would lead to a 1 per cent increase in their costs.

Question 1

Japanese toy makers and video game makers were rubbing their hands with glee as the government decided to give children cash handouts in the latest attempt to get the nation spending. As part of a record £118 billion economic stimulus package, Tokyo plans to hand out about £100 in shopping vouchers to 35 million people - including everyone under the age of 16 and over the age of 64. Unemployment in Japan is at a record high and Japan's gross domestic product is expected to decline by 1.8 per cent during the financial year 1998-99. Underlining the problems, the government announced that bankruptcies had risen for the 22nd consecutive month, while steel production declined by 11 per cent compared with the previous year.

Source: adapted from *The Guardian*, 17.11.1998 and 1.2.1999.

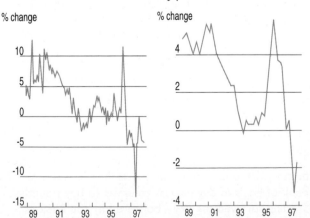

Figure 26.1 *Retail sales in Japan*

Figure 26.2 % *change in GDP in Japan*

Source: adapted from Datastream/ICV.

(a) Describe the way that the Japanese government is using fiscal policy to boost the economy.
(b) Suggest reasons, using information from the article, why the government is using fiscal policy.
(c) Explain the effect that the policy might have on the budget of the country.

If a government spends more than it receives in revenue from taxation and other sources, then it is said to have a **budget deficit**. This will mean it has to raise money from a variety of sources, such as individual members of the public or banks. This is will increase the PUBLIC SECTOR NET CASH REQUIREMENT (PSNCR), formerly the public sector borrowing requirement. In the late 1990s the government has attempted to reduce its PSNCR, by cutting spending and increasing taxes. By the year 2003 it is estimated to reach 0 per cent. In the past years governments have had budget surpluses, ie higher revenue than spending. In such years governments were able to pay off past debts.

Monetary policy

Monetary policy (☞ unit 21) is also used to manage the level of aggregate demand in the economy, with a particular emphasis upon controlling the money supply. Monetary policy can be used to:
- expand the economy by allowing more money to circulate and increase spending;
- control spending and restrict increases in money flowing around the economy which may lead to price rises;
- control spending on imports if there is a current balance deficit.

The government has a variety of methods to control the money supply.

Changing interest rates An increase in interest rates can reduce the money supply. If interest rates increase, the cost of borrowing rises. This could reduce the amount that businesses and consumers borrow from banks and building societies. Raising interest rates may possibly add to inflation. This is because higher interest rates increase firms' costs and these may be passed on to consumers in the form of higher prices.

Restricting bank loans By restricting the ability of banks to give out loans, the size of the money supply can be regulated. The BANK OF ENGLAND could instruct banks to keep a higher proportion of their assets in reserve. This means that they are able to lend less. The government may also sell financial securities. This will reduce the size of the bank's assets and leave banks with less to lend out.

Credit or hire purchase restrictions The government can place controls on the amount of credit and hire purchase agreements which banks and other financial institutions are allowed to give to businesses and consumers. In the 1980s and 1990s the UK government encouraged competition in financial markets. This led to an explosion in the amount of credit available and made restricting credit more difficult.

Independent central banks In certain countries, such as Germany, the central bank has responsibility for control of inflation and the money supply. Governments in the UK traditionally controlled interest rates directly. In 1997, control

of interest rates passed to the Monetary Policy Committee of the Bank of England. It is argued that an independent bank is in a better position to control monetary policy. For example, it will not allow a government to increase the money supply before an election to finance spending in order to win votes.

An increase in interest rates and restrictions of loans and credit are aimed at controlling the money supply and inflation. However, this will also affect spending and may reduce output, employment and imports.

Question ②

The Bank of England yesterday delighted business with a half point cut in interest rates. The unexpectedly large cut suggested that the Bank is worried about the threat of recession. The cut in interest rates was said to be appropriate for maintaining a path for inflation consistent with the government's 2.5 per cent target. Adair Turner, Director-General of the Confederation of British Industry, said: 'we believe half a point is just the right amount'. He added that it would make recession less likely by reducing the chances of rises in sterling and by reviving consumer confidence.

Source: adapted from the *Financial Times*, 6.1.1998.

(a) Why should worries about recession cause the Bank of England to cut interest rates?
(b) Explain how a cut in interest rates might affect:
  (i) the money supply;
  (ii) spending on products;
  (iii) the exchange rate.

Exchange rate policy

The exchange rate is the price of one currency in relation to another (☞ unit 25). The value of the pound, for instance, can be shown against a variety of other currencies, such as the dollar, the yen or the euro. Some governments take the view that the exchange rate should be left to find its own market value. Such governments do not try to intervene in foreign currency markets to influence the exchange rate.

Other governments seek directly to influence exchange rates. This involves the buying and selling of the currency on foreign exchange markets to influence its price. A government may want to:
- support the currency to prevent its value from falling. This might involve buying up currency to restrict its supply. A fall in the exchange rate may raise the price of imported products, possibly leading to **imported inflation** (☞ unit 25);
- allow the value of the currency to fall to improve the competitiveness of businesses in export markets. A fall in the value of a currency should make exports relatively cheaper;
- 'shadow' or follow another currency. For example, the British government has tried to shadow the value of the euro

(☞ units 25 and 30). This is so that UK businesses operating within the single European market do not experience variations in prices compared to those of European competitors.

There is a link between monetary policy, explained in the previous section, and exchange rate policy. Changes in interest rates have an effect on the value of a country's currency. An increase in US interest rates, for example, will tend to raise the value of the dollar. Higher interest rates attract short term investors who buy the currency. This increases the demand for the dollar. As a result its price rises. Lower US interest rates cause short term investors to move assets elsewhere. They will sell the dollar and buy other currencies with which to invest. This increases the supply of the dollar and lowers its price.

Protectionism

This involves the use of controls to restrict the amount of imports coming into a country. TARIFFS are a tax on imports. They raise the price of imports and, hopefully, discourage consumers from buying them. For example, there is a Common External Tariff (☞ unit 30) on goods entering the EU. QUOTAS are a limit on the number of goods that are allowed to enter a country. For example, a government may specify that only 1,000 Japanese television sets are allowed to enter the country each month.

A more subtle approach is to impose technical restrictions or 'waiting' periods on goods entering a country. For example, Japan has been known in the past to reject imports because they do not meet standards they have set for products being sold in domestic markets.

Why might a government impose tariffs?

● To protect INFANT INDUSTRIES or newly emerging industries which have yet to find their feet. This is often used by developing countries to protect their manufacturing industries.

● To protect strategic or declining industries which governments feel are important to the future of the country. Also industries whose decline may lead to a loss of jobs are sometimes protected. Many believe that the UK coal industry should have been protected for this reason.

● Anti-dumping. Dumping occurs when goods are sold in foreign markets at prices below their cost of production. This may occur because of excess capacity in an industry or as a deliberate attempt to quickly gain market share at the expense of domestic businesses. Because dumping is seen as unfair, many governments act to protect their own businesses from its effects.

There are some difficulties with protectionist policies.

● They may lead to retaliation by the exporting country. This may 'cancel out' the effect of protection. It will also harm the imposing country's exports to other countries.

● They can lead to inflation in the country imposing the tariff. This may be the case if, despite the tariff, the country still has to buy the goods. They might be essential raw materials, for example.

● International agreements, such as those controlled by the World Trade Organisation (☞ unit 31), prevent the use of tariffs by those countries that have signed the agreement.

Question 3

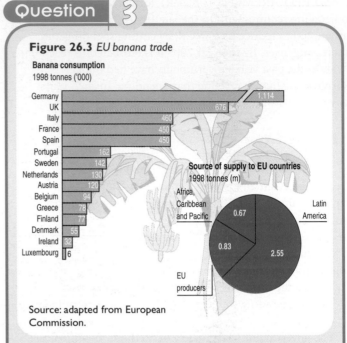

Figure 26.3 *EU banana trade*

Banana consumption
1998 tonnes ('000)

Germany	1,114
UK	676
Italy	460
France	450
Spain	450
Portugal	162
Sweden	142
Netherlands	130
Austria	120
Belgium	94
Greece	78
Finland	77
Denmark	55
Ireland	32
Luxembourg	6

Source of supply to EU countries
1998 tonnes (m)

Africa, Caribbean and Pacific 0.67
Latin America 2.55
EU producers 0.83

Source: adapted from European Commission.

Europe loves bananas, particularly Germany. The single European market, set up in 1992, resulted in a single tariff on all products imported from outside Europe. It also created a licensing agreement which the EU said was geared towards helping the poorer former colonies of France, Spain and the UK, mainly in the Caribbean. In 1999 the EU lost a World Trade Organisation (WTO) ruling for the fifth time in six years.

The EU practices were accused of being against the rules of world trade, which are designed to promote free trade between countries. The major critic of the EU policy had been the USA. It claimed that protecting the poorer former colonies was simply a smokescreen for protecting deals with suppliers in the Caribbean. It even argued that importers in France, Spain and the UK could benefit from the restrictions, as they could sell off licences that they were not using. When the US threatened sanctions against the EU as a result of its actions, before the WTO authorised them, the EU claimed America was the outlaw to the trade system. But the US said that the WTO ruling had proven that it was correct in its interpretation of WTO rules.

Source: adapted from the *Financial Times*, 1999.

(a) What reasons were put forward for protection by the EU?
(b) How might: (i) exporters of bananas from Caribbean countries; (ii) exporters of bananas from Latin America; (iii) importers of bananas in the EU; be affected by the actions of the EU?
(c) Examine the problems of the action by the EU.

If there is a large and persistent current account surplus a country may restrict the amount of exporting its businesses undertake. Due to its large current account surplus, there has been international pressure on Japan to exercise export restraint in recent years.

Supply side policies

SUPPLY SIDE POLICIES are policies that:
● encourage the workings of the free market;
● encourage competition;
● attempt to change the aggregate demand or AGGREGATE SUPPLY in the economy;
● give incentives to businesses and individuals.
Supply side policies can be viewed in two main ways.

Policies which allow the labour market to function efficiently Unit 24 outlined how unemployment can result from real wages being too high. Supply side policies seek to reduce the impact of those factors which are believed to distort the free workings of the labour market. Such policies include the following.
● Reducing the power of trade unions and professional organisations. This would result in them being less able to force wage levels up.
● Cuts in taxation to give lower paid workers a greater incentive to take jobs. This is because such workers will be left with more income.
● Improving the mobility of labour (☞ unit 19). Workers may be encouraged to move to parts of the country where work is available. Such policies might include making the buying and selling of houses more straightforward.
● Greater availability of information about jobs
● 'Job clubs' where people seeking work can find advice and facilities, such as telephones and word processors, to help them apply for jobs.
● Encouraging young workers to find paid work and to provide occupational advice.

Policies to improve the efficiency of businesses and industries Such policies focus upon the competitiveness of business and the markets within which they operate. They also involve the education, skills and training of employees. Policies in this area are based upon the view that competition forces individual businesses and the economy as a whole to operate more efficiently. Such policies include the following.
● Privatisation (☞ unit 6) of industries and the removal of the government from directly controlling businesses.
● Deregulation of industries which results in industries being opened up to competition. This allows businesses the opportunity to enter markets from which they were previously excluded.
● Reducing income and corporation tax to encourage businesses and employees to be more efficient by allowing them to keep more of their income or company profits.

● Supporting businesses that provide training in order to create a more efficient and productive labour force.
● Reduction of the amount of 'red tape', such as form filling and returns required of business
● Removal of restrictions to employment such as the minimum wage or maximum number of working hours in a week.
● Reduction of employers' National Insurance contributions to reduce the cost of employing workers.
Supply side policies are seen by their supporters as anti-inflationary for two reasons.
● They try to remove the ability of trade unions and professional associations to increase wage levels above market rates. This removes one of the main pressures on business costs.
● Policies such as privatisation and deregulation create competition. This should force businesses to lower their prices to compete with rivals.

Incomes policy

This is a means of controlling inflation by imposing limits upon pay or price increases. During the 1970s it was widely used in the battle against inflation. Although not an official incomes policy, there were attempts in the 1990s to restrict pay rises. An example was the pay freeze for public sector workers in 1993.

The effects of government policies on business

The policies outlined above are used to help governments achieve their objectives (☞ unit 21). The effects of these policies upon businesses depends mainly upon the objectives the government is trying to achieve.

Anti-inflationary monetary policy There are two main effects depending upon the type of monetary policy used. First, if interest rates are raised by the Bank of England this will make borrowing by businesses more expensive and might lead to the cancellation of investment projects. Higher interest rates will also hit the pockets of many consumers. They will find it more expensive to borrow money on credit and their mortgage repayments will increase. This is likely to lead to fewer sales, particularly for those firms manufacturing and selling consumer goods.

Second, if bank lending or credit is restricted, loan capital will be harder to come by, particularly for small firms. Again this may result in less investment and a lower level of demand from consumers as they find money harder to come by.

Anti-inflationary fiscal policy This can be in the form of tax (usually direct) increases or public expenditure cuts. Tax increases will mean that consumers have less money in their pockets and they are therefore likely to spend less. This will affect the sales of many firms. Public expenditure cuts will mean less money spent on, for example, schools, colleges, hospitals, road building, and local leisure services. This will hit a wide range of firms, especially those who work for local authorities and central government. The construction industry, for example, is always adversely affected by cutbacks in public expenditure.

Anti-inflationary exchange rate policy Such a policy will try to ensure that the exchange rate does not fall too greatly, as explained earlier in this unit. However, a high exchange rate causes the price of UK products in export markets to be relatively high. This makes it difficult to sell products in foreign markets. It also causes the price of imported goods to be relatively cheap, making it difficult for UK firms to compete 'at home'. Maintaining exchange rates at a particular level often requires a high interest rate. This will also lead to problems for businesses.

Anti-inflationary supply side policies The effects of anti inflationary supply side policies on businesses will depend upon the circumstances of those businesses. Businesses in monopoly (☞ unit 18) positions in their markets may be forced, by deregulation for example, to compete with other businesses. This is likely to have the effect of lowering their profits, at least in the short term. For other businesses, these policies have the potential to create opportunities for entering markets which never previously existed. The bus company Stagecoach, for example, has grown as a result of the deregulation of the coach and bus industries.

Policies to increase demand, output and employment Firms can both benefit and suffer from government policy to increase demand in the economy. Fiscal policy involving increases in the amount of government spending on new capital projects, such as hospitals and colleges, can lead to an increase in the demand for many firms' products. Cuts in income tax may also increase demand. Similarly, monetary policy that reduces interest rates can make the cost of borrowing cheaper for firms, allowing them to invest in new plant and machinery. Lower interest rates also make it cheaper for consumers to borrow. This can increase the demand for a variety of goods, particularly those, such as consumer durables bought on credit.

However, the government may have to finance its spending by borrowing or taxation. The former may involve a rise in interest rates, which makes loans to firms more expensive.

Increased corporation tax or income tax will take away a firm's profits or income. Increasing the money supply or government spending may lead to inflation, which can also be harmful to businesses.

Supply side policies, output and employment Supply side policies can affect the output and employment of businesses in a number of ways.
- Policies which aim to cut wages reduce the cost of employing labour for firms.
- A more mobile and flexible workforce could make recruitment easier for businesses. It may also improve the efficiency of businesses (☞ unit 96 and 102).
- A better trained workforce could improve labour productivity and output (☞ unit 96).
- Greater competition may force businesses to be more efficient.
- Incentives aimed at improving training may lead to increased employment (☞ unit 79).

A criticism of supply side policies is that they can lead to the creation of significant numbers of low paid jobs. Not only may this reduce the morale and motivation of low paid workers, but it may also lead to a lower level of demand in the economy.

There is also concern that supply side policies, giving greater freedom to businesses, could result in damage to the environment. This is because businesses, left to themselves, often fail to take account of the true social costs (☞ unit 27) of their activities.

Trade and exchange rate policy Trade policy by the UK government may affect businesses in a number of ways.
- Quotas can help domestic businesses by restricting competition from imports. However, they may also restrict the supply of components or raw materials available to a business and could result in retaliation from another country which may affect the exports of UK businesses.
- Tariffs tend to raise the price of imports, making them more expensive to UK customers. UK businesses may sell more products as they are relatively cheaper. Tariffs, however, may raise the price of imported materials and may lead to retaliation.
- Allowing the value of the currency to fall should make exports relatively cheaper and businesses should sell more products abroad. The price of imported materials for business may rise, however.

Question 4

In summer 1999 the Japanese government said that it would continue to intervene in markets to stop the value of the yen rising. It was also determined to keep interest rates low. The vice minister for finance said that: 'Too strong a yen is not desirable.' Following intervention by the government the yen was valued at Y120 to the dollar, Y3 down on the previous Friday. Figures published showed that the Japanese economy had grown by 1.9 per cent between the fourth quarter of 1998 and the first quarter of 1999. It was suggested that these figures may have been distorted because retail store sales had been depressed. They were also flattered perhaps by the wave of public spending at the start of 1999 which was due to run out in Autumn.

Source: adapted from the *Financial Times*, 15.6.1999.

(a) Identify the government policies being used in the article.
(b) Explain the effects of these policies on Japanese businesses.
(c) Why might the Japanese government argue that 'Too strong a yen is not desirable'?

Key terms

Aggregate supply - the level of output in the economy as a whole.

Bank of England - the central bank of the UK which controls the supply of money.

Infant industries - newly set up industries that are unable to compete with established foreign competition.

Public sector net cash requirement - the amount of money the government has to raise when spending is greater than receipts.

Quota - a limit placed upon the number of particular categories of goods allowed to enter the country.

Supply side policies - policies designed to make markets operate more efficiently.

Tariff - a tax upon imports.

Summary

1. Give 3 examples of:
   (a) fiscal policy;
   (b) monetary policy.
2. Explain the difference between direct and indirect taxation.
3. What are the methods of controlling the money supply?
4. Briefly explain 2 policies used to tackle a balance of payments deficit.
5. State 6 examples of supply side policies.
6. How might supply side policies control inflation?
7. What is an incomes policy?
8. In what ways might businesses be affected by anti-inflationary policies?

9. What effect would cutting income tax have on:
   (a) businesses;
   (b) consumers?
10. State 3 policies to:
    (a) increase demand;
    (b) increase supply.
11. How might government policy to solve unemployment benefit a firm?
12. Give 2 reasons why government spending to solve unemployment may be a problem.
13. Briefly explain the benefits of supply side policies to firms.

Case study

The ceramics industry

A strong pound, high interest rates, recession in key markets. These all led to a gloomy feeling in the UK ceramics and pottery industry, traditionally one of the country's strong export performers. The strength of the pound accounted for 1,000 job losses in the first four months of 1998. Half of the industry's £1.2 billion annual sales, including tiles and toilets, goes overseas. Japan is the most important market outside the US. The industry sees itself as a victim of the governments strict emphasis on meeting inflation targets. It was hoping to avoid a repeat of the job losses caused by strict monetary control in the 1980s.

There were nearly 900 job cuts at Royal Doulton and Waterford Wedgewood. Hundreds of other workers were working part time and smaller firms had gone broke. 'We haven't seen the full impact yet', said Stephen Roper, chief executive of Churchill China. Some employers feared that up to 10,000 jobs would go, nearly half the workforce, if the pound stayed where it was and the UK went into recession. 'The higher the interest rate, the stronger the pound', commented the Ceramic & Allied Trades Union.

The industry still employs one in ten wage earners in Stoke and Newcastle-under-Lyme. The leader of Newcastle Borough Council hoped that the trend was a short term thing. But he suggested that the government should pull out all the stops to save 'this important industry from declining'. Sales and exports were just about holding up, but the result had been lower profit margins. The industry warned that it was only a matter of time before exports and the contribution to the balance of payments tailed off.

An important European market for Wedgewood is The Netherlands. The pound appreciated 35 per cent against the guilder in a year and the firm's price rose 20 per cent as a result. Villeroy and Boch, one of Wedgewood's German competitors, had taken advantage of the weakness of the deutschmark to cut prices by 10 per cent. Wedgewood chief executive Brian Patterson said: 'Consumers are less likely to buy and retailers on lower margins are less likely to order, stock and sell our products'. As for the UK, where cheap Chinese and Japanese goods have flooded the mid-price section of the market, it was vulnerable to imports.

The pottery industry has often weathered the storm better than competitors. For example, in the eighties German industry was 50 per cent bigger than the UK's. In 1998 it was around four fifths the size.

Source: adapted from *The Observer*, 12.4.1998.

(a) What difficulties were government policies causing for businesses in the ceramics and pottery industry in 1998?

(b) (i) Explain why interest rates were being kept high at the time.

(ii) Explain three possible effects of high interest rates on the ceramics and pottery industry.

(c) Why might businesses in the ceramics industry be vulnerable to changes in the exchange rate?

(d) Analyse how changes in the value of the pound and the deutschmark have affected:
(i) Wedgewood in Holland; (ii) Villeroy and Boch.

(e) Examine and explain three ways in which government policy might solve some of the problems of the businesses mentioned in the article.

Business and social constraints

Businesses affect the societies in which they operate. A sole trader running a small grocery store may benefit local residents by opening for a few hours on a Sunday. On the other hand such a business may have negative effects. Canned drinks bought from the shop may be left in the street. Opening on a Sunday may lead to more traffic in the area. Decisions made by a multinational company (☞ unit 32) can have a huge impact in many different countries. For example, it may decide to relocate its factory from one country to another. This is likely to lead to a fall in income and employment in the country that the company has left. The new location may gain from more jobs, the building of infrastructure, such as roads, and perhaps spending on health care and community projects.

These examples show that businesses do not operate in isolation. The decisions they make can affect a range of other groups and individuals. The businesses can be seen as part of the societies in which they operate. As a result, governments often pass laws and set regulations to control the conduct of businesses. Consumer laws (☞ unit 22) try to ensure that businesses do not deliberately mislead consumers. Employment laws (☞ units 81 and 82) attempt to provide safe working conditions and set standards for working hours and payments.

Such laws tend to set the legal minimum in terms of the way in which businesses behave. However, do businesses have any further responsibilities to society? Should businesses consider the implications of their decisions upon society and not just take into account whether these decisions help the business to achieve its objectives? For example, a cement factory may have emissions within legal limits. The local community might argue that the emissions cause health problems amongst children and the elderly in the area. Should the business try to reduce the emissions?

Some would argue that businesses are self-regulating. They do not need to be controlled by government. If they ignore the views of society, consumers will not buy their products. They will lose trade and perhaps go out of business. Others argue that, without external regulation, businesses may have negative effects upon society. People who are adversely affected by business activity may not be in a position to influence the business. The children and elderly people living near the cement factory may not buy cement. The young and old may not be able to exert any outside pressure by complaining to the management of the business.

is to view all of the groups affected by the behaviour of a business as **stakeholders** (☞ unit 3). The stakeholders in a business are likely to include customers, employees, shareholders, suppliers, government, local communities and businesses, financial institutions and other creditors.

Businesses have tended to be influenced mainly by customers, employees and shareholders. Increasingly, however, other groups are affecting business behaviour. For example, some businesses will only supply their products to other businesses that have an ethical or environmental policy. Some pension companies will not invest in businesses that sell arms. This suggests that businesses need to have a greater SOCIAL RESPONSIBILITY to groups beyond those immediately involved in the business.

Question 1

The human rights of workers who produce goods sold in the developed world are becoming more important to retailers and manufacturers. Campaigners have highlighted the risks of buying goods from suppliers that have unacceptable employment practices. The question is, how do businesses check that their suppliers are not employing child labour, paying their workers starvation wages or putting their health and safety in danger? Such dangers are far from restricted to producing goods in developing countries.

One ambitious initiative designed to address this problem is the SA8000. The SA stands for Social Accountability. It aims to provide a framework which allows businesses to check the employment practices of suppliers of goods made by companies of every size, anywhere in the world. SA8000 has the backing of companies such as Avon, Toys 'R' Us, Sainsbury's and The Body Shop. It stipulates that :
- children under 15 must not be employed;
- forced labour must never be used;
- workers must have the right to join a trade union
Avon became the first business to receive the SA8000 for one of its US factories. The firm now wants to have all its 19 factories certified and is urging its suppliers to do likewise.

Source: adapted from *The Observer*, 1998.

(a) Why might the employees of an African based business supplying Sainsbury's be regarded as stakeholders of Sainsbury's?
(b) What might be the effects on Sainsbury's if it regards the employees of all suppliers as stakeholders?
(c) Why might businesses such as Sainsbury's and Toy 'R' Us be concerned about the rights of workers employed by their suppliers?

Business and stakeholders

One way of considering the impact of businesses upon society

Business ethics

The way in which businesses respond to issues such as the sale of arms or health risks from pollution may depend on their ETHICS. Ethics are the **values** and **beliefs** which influence how individuals, groups and societies behave. For example, an electricity generating business may be operating within legal emissions limits. However, it may feel that it has to change its production methods to reduce emissions even further because it believes businesses should work towards a cleaner environment.

In part the ethics of a business will depend upon the values of its employees. However, the ethical stance of the business is likely to be determined by the values of senior managers, directors and other important stakeholders. It will also be influenced by codes of conduct which may operate in the industry. The term ETHICAL is used to refer to businesses which explicitly recognise the importance of social responsibility and the need to consider the effects of its actions upon stakeholders. Business ethics are examined in detail in unit 33. It is possible that a business following an ethical policy may:

● attract customers and employees who agree with its policy;
● have to change its operations to fit in with this policy, for example approving certain suppliers;
● have to set a policy for all the business in areas such as recruitment and marketing.

Question 2

(a) Using the information in the advertisement, would you describe the Co-operative Bank as ethical? Explain your answer.
(b) Suggest how this policy might affect:
  (i) sales;
  (ii) costs;
  of the business.

The CO-OPERATIVE BANK

The more people join The Co-operative Bank, the less animal testing there'll be.

We promise never to invest our customers' money in companies involved in animal experiments for cosmetic purposes.

Apply now.
☎ Freefone
0800 73 11 299

Business and the environment

It is possible that the activities of business can have certain beneficial effects on the environment. For example, a new factory may be built in a derelict area. The new premises may be landscaped, improving the view. A grass area built might have a bench which could be used by pedestrians.

Businesses are becoming more and more aware of the need to consider the environment in their operations. Many critics of certain business activities suggest that they have a negative effect on the environment in the surrounding area. Some of the negative effects of business activity include:

● air pollution caused by the discharge of emissions into the atmosphere and traffic visiting retail outlets;
● water pollution as a result of the dumping of waste;
● congestion from employees going to work or consumers visiting retail outlets;
● noise from factories and traffic;
● destruction of natural habitats from the building of premises.

How might these effects be controlled? There are laws, such as the **Clean Air Act**, which try to restrict the environmental impact of business activity. The government and the EU have planning regulations and legislation affecting the location of businesses (☞ unit 100). Taxes on petrol and diesel are often raised in an attempt to reduce the use of transport.

In many areas, businesses are becoming responsible for regulating their own behaviour. The ethics of a business can affect the extent to which it controls its impact on the environment. Some businesses have adopted their own stringent codes of practice and policies to control their activities. Unit 35 considers businesses and the environment in greater detail. It is likely that attempts to control the effect on the environment by businesses will lead to:

Question 3

GUINNESS BREWING GB
INFORMATION

ENVIRONMENTAL STATEMENT

Without some of the world's most basic natural resources, there would be no Scotch whisky or Guinness Stout or indeed any of the other alcoholic beverages which have made Guinness PLC the great international company it is today.

Guinness is dependent upon a healthy environment - pure water, clean air and fertile soils - to provide the natural ingredients essential to the creation of the finest spirits and beers, and to sustain the quality that has made our brand names famous around the world.

Consideration for the environment is therefore a major and continuing priority throughout the Guinness group.

Environmental responsibility is inherent in the jobs of all our managers. Environmental assessment is incorporated in all projects for investments, in the acquisition of companies, new plant and equipment, new technologies, and in researching and developing packaging for our product.

Our working practices and procedures will be regularly reviewed to minimise the risk of environmental damage, particularly in our process and production operations. We aim to meet all the relevant government and legislative requirements, and where none exists we will set ourselves high standards.

All new products and processes will be evaluated to assess their environmental impact and we will seek to conserve natural resources by ensuring the responsible use of energy and materials. We will promote recycling and re-use wherever appropriate.

We will assess the environmental procedures followed by our suppliers and ensure that these are consistent with the standard which we set ourselves.

Guinness has established a joint steering group on the environment which monitors all environmental matters and which is responsible for ensuring the company's environmental policies are updated.

PUBLIC RELATIONS PRESS OFFICE
PARK ROYAL BREWERY, LONDON NW10 7RR
TELEPHONE: 0181 965 7700. FACSIMILE: 0181 963 5120

Source: Guinness Brewing, GB.

(a) What evidence is there in the statement that Guinness's policy towards the environment extends across a range of stakeholders?
(b) Explain the aspect of the environment that may benefit from the policy of Guinness.
(c) What might be the: (i) costs; and (ii) benefits; for Guinness of committing itself to the above statement?

● increased costs in the short term;
● the attraction of customers who agree with the policy of the business;
● a change in production methods.

Pressure groups

PRESSURE GROUPS are groups without the direct political power to achieve their aims, but whose aims lie within the sphere of politics. They usually attempt to influence local government, central government, businesses and the media. They aim to have their views taken into account when any decisions are made. Such influence can occur directly, through contact with politicians, local representatives and business people, or indirectly by influencing public opinion.

The use of pressure groups is one way in which stakeholders can exert influence over those making decisions within a business. Pressure groups can represent stakeholders directly involved with the business, such as employees or shareholders. They can also represent those not directly involved in the business, such as local communities or consumer groups.

There are many different types of pressure group and many ways of classifying them. One way is to divide groups into those which have a single cause and those which have a number of different causes.

● Single cause groups include the Campaign for Nuclear Disarmament, Survival International and the NSPCC. Such groups mainly try to promote one cause.
● Multi-cause groups include trade unions, Greenpeace and the Confederation of British Industry. Pressure groups falling into this category tend to campaign on a number of issues. Trade unions, for example, have campaigned on a variety of issues, including the rights of the unemployed and improving the pay and conditions of their members.

Over the last few decades there has been a huge increase in the number of pressure groups and in the scale of their activities. Inevitably this has brought them into much closer contact with businesses. As a result there are now a number of groups which focus their activities upon businesses in general or particular businesses and industries.

● Environmental groups such as Friends of the Earth campaign to prevent businesses from polluting the environment.
● Consumer groups, such as the Consumers' Association seek to protect the rights of consumers in general. Others' include The Football Supporters' Association and rail users' groups.
● Local community groups may, for example, seek to prevent particular business developments or influence the policies of individual firms which operate in their local area.
● Employee groups, such as trade unions and professional associations, try to influence firms on issues such as conditions of work and pay levels.

Pressure groups vary in size. Some, like a local group aiming to divert a by-pass, may be made up of a few local people. Others are national organisations such as Greenpeace or the Royal Society for the Protection of Birds, or international groups such as Amnesty International.

Factors influencing the success of pressure groups

The success of any group, no matter how large or small, will depend on a number of factors.

● Finance and organisational ability. A pressure group with large funds will be able to spend on well organised campaigns. This has been a tactic employed by trade unions and professional groups. A well financed pressure group may also be able to employ full time professional campaigners. Such people are likely to organise more effective campaigns than enthusiasts devoting some of their spare time to such an activity.
● Public sympathy. Capturing the imagination of the public will play an important role in the ability of a pressure group to succeed. The Campaign for Real Ale has been effective in this respect. Almost single handedly they caused a change in the types of beer available in public houses and in the brewing methods of the big brewing companies. As with many successful campaigns, CAMRA's ability to present a clear and simple message to the public was vital.
● Access to politicians. Pressure groups which have access to politicians are able to apply pressure for changes in the law. For example, the International League for the Protection of Horses persuaded the government to ban the export of live horses for human consumption within the EU. Their contacts with politicians were vital in this campaign. The process of applying pressure on politicians is known as lobbying. It has become dominated by skilled professional lobbyists, the fees of whom are out of the range of all but the wealthiest of groups.
● Reputation. Gaining a favourable reputation amongst politicians can be important. The British Medical Association, for example, has a good reputation amongst a variety of politicians and is therefore often consulted on a variety of health matters by the government.

The effects of pressure groups on business

There is a number of ways in which pressure groups can affect firms.

● Pressure groups often seek to influence the behaviour of members of the public about a particular product, business or industry. Friends of the Earth attempt to persuade the public to use cars less and public transport or bicycles more in order to reduce emissions into the atmosphere. This campaign, if successful, would have important implications for a wide range of firms involved in the transport industry.

- Political parties, through their representatives in Parliament, are able to pass laws which regulate the activities of businesses. Therefore it is not surprising that many pressure groups devote resources to lobbying politicians. An example of this is the attempt by the anti-smoking group, ASH, to change the law so that all advertising of tobacco is made illegal.
- The actions of pressure groups can reduce the sales of firms. This is often most successfully achieved when efforts are targeted at particular firms. Consumers are then called upon to boycott these firms.
- Firms can face increased costs as a result of the activities of pressure groups. This may involve new production processes or waste disposal methods. Firms may have to counteract any negative publicity from a pressure group. For example, many believe that the campaign to attract visitors to the Sellafield nuclear site was a result of the negative publicity from environmental groups.
- Businesses with a tarnished reputation as a result of pressure group activity may find it more difficult to recruit employees.

How might businesses react to pressure groups?

- By positively responding to the issues raised by pressure groups. It was argued that pressure from Greenpeace contributed to Shell's decision not to dump the Brent Spar oil platform in the North Sea in 1995. Instead it was

dismantled and used to build a ferry quay in Norway. Similarly, local pressure groups have been successful in persuading some firms to change building plans and landscape nearby areas.

- Through promotions and public relations. Firms can attempt to counteract negative publicity through their own promotional and public relations work. For example, a number of oil companies which have been criticised for their impact upon the environment have sought to deal with this by promoting the 'greener' aspects of their industry, such as the availability of lead free petrol.
- A number of leading firms either lobby politicians themselves or pay for the services of professional lobbyists to represent their interests.
- Legal action. Where pressure groups make false allegations about a business, this can be dealt with by the legal system. For example, allegations by pressure groups that McDonald's were contributing to the destruction of the Amazonian rainforest were dealt with through legal action in the courts.

Key terms

Ethics - the values and beliefs of individuals or groups.
Ethical - behaviour which is viewed as correct.
Pressure groups - groups of people without direct political power who seek to influence decision makers in politics, business and society.
Social responsibility - the responsibility that a business has towards those directly or indirectly affected by its activities.

Question 4

In 1998 150 poster sites across the UK displayed the image of a heavy overcoat composed of pictures of a live fox, along with the words: 'For sale. Fur coat. 20 previous owners.' It was the sort of advert that anti-fur groups used to great effect in the 1990s as they tried to rouse public opposition to the use of fur in clothes. Leading department stores removed fur from their shelves as demand dropped. In 1998, however, the Fur Education Council, which represents manufacturers of fur products, claimed that fur clothes were making a comeback.

Mark Glover, campaign director for Respect for Animals, the pressure group which placed the advert, said: 'We were worried that the fur trade was attempting something of a comeback so we were keen to stem that. The fur industry is putting a great deal of effort into trying to make fur respectable again in Britain. But I have no reason to believe they are succeeding.'

Source: adapted from the *Financial Times*, 13.1.1998.

(a) In what ways are Respect for Animals attempting to influence the behaviour of businesses operating in the fur industry?
(b) How might the fur industry respond to the poster campaign described above?
(c) What factors are likely to influence the success of the campaign by Respect for Animals?

Summary

1. State 2 ways that a large business may affect the society in which it operates.
2. State 3 legal restrictions on the behaviour of businesses.
3. Why might the effect on society of a business's activities be self-regulating?
4. State 3 effects of ethical behaviour on a business.
5. How might a business be of benefit to the environment surrounding it?
6. State 5 problems caused by business activity to the environment.
7. State 3 ways in which the effect on the environment of business may be controlled.
8. What are the main types of pressure groups?
9. Give 3 reasons why a pressure group campaign may fail.
10. How can pressure groups affect the sales of a firm's product?

Case study

Tate & Lyle

TATE & LYLE IN THE COMMUNITY

Tate & Lyle fully acknowledges the contribution it should make to the well-being of the communities in which it operates throughout the world.

We have continued to support a wide range of community projects both at home and overseas, allocating around 0.7% of profit before tax worldwide and 1% of the UK pre-tax profits based on the previous year's results (excluding exceptional items). This year our target percentage for education and youth was increased from 35% to 50% of total donations. Our total charitable donations and support amounted to £1.6 million worldwide of which £0.9 million was donated in the UK.

Below are a few examples of the range of activities.

In the UK, the major emphasis has been on education with continuing support for Reading is Fundamental® and the Newham Reading Project. As one of the main employers in the London Borough of Newham, Tate & Lyle Sugars ('TLS') works in partnership with many local bodies to benefit urban regeneration and improve educational and training opportunities for local youngsters. TLS is a partner in the Newham Consortium for 'New Deal' for the unemployed and the Newham 'Education Action Zone', a Government initiative to raise standards in local schools. We have also worked with the Royal Botanic Gardens, Kew, by sponsoring an educational pack for primary schools linked to a major environmental project to create the world's largest seed bank.

Elsewhere in Europe local sports teams, educational projects and arts-related activities are supported, including Alcantara's scholarships for promising young musicians from low-income families in Portugal.

In Australia, Tate & Lyle Bundaberg supports a number of social, environmental and cultural programmes in the rural communities where it has a presence. The Company is a major donor to a new library complex for the Central Queensland University and is continuing its support for the Queensland Youth Orchestra.

Health and welfare feature strongly in the community activities of Group companies in the developing world. At Zambia Sugar, the company runs comprehensive hygiene, health and education programmes for employees, their families and the local community. This includes mother and baby clinics, immunisation, Aids awareness and skills training programmes. UM HGroup companies based in developing countries also support health and education issues such as the Tom Mboya Unit for celebral palsy in

Kenya and a children's education scheme in Guyana.

More important than any single initiative, the Group has a business culture that recognises the need to support the local community if business development is to be sustained in the long term.

ENVIRONMENT

The Group is committed to a continuing programme of monitoring the environmental impact of its operations. Investment programmes are in place at a number of manufacturing sites to improve the quality of atmospheric emissions, liquid effluent discharges and solid waste and resource utilisation and all sites to improve their environmental performance.

Some examples of environmental improvements from around the Group:

● At Kaba in Hungary, process control integration at the boilers has led to further air purity protection improvements.

● At the Thames refinery in London a 10% production enhancement was achieved with no increase in emission levels.

● At Zambia Sugar the discharge of each type of liquid effluent - suspended solids, nitrates and phosphates - has shown improvement on the previous year.

Source: adapted from Tate & Lyle, *Annual Report and Accounts*, 1998.

(a) **Using information from the extracts, identify and give examples of the stakeholders of Tate & Lyle.**

(b) **Identify the factors that may have influenced the activities of Tate & Lyle mentioned in the extracts?**

(c) **Explain how the factors you identified in (b) may have influenced the business.**

(d) **Examine how the activities of Tate & Lyle may affect the environment.**

(e) **Discuss whether you think that Tate & Lyle is acting in a socially responsible and ethical way.**

Government economic policy and business

A government has a range of **economic policies** at its disposal in order to achieve its **objectives** of low inflation, high economic growth, high employment levels and control of the balance of payments situation (☞ unit 21). These policies include fiscal policy, monetary policy, exchange rate policy and supply side policies. Policies can affect businesses in many ways, as explained in unit 26. It is therefore important for businesses:

● to understand why a government is using a particular policy;
● to be able to respond to policy changes and their effects with appropriate strategies when they occur.

Policy changes and disagreements

There is often disagreement about the **extent** to which changes in economic policies may affect variables, such as inflation and unemployment, and also businesses. At the root of policy disagreements are the different approaches which economists have to solving economic problems.

One approach favours the free operation of markets. Supporters of this believe that the role of government should be limited to providing the right environment for businesses to flourish. Another approach to policy favours using government intervention in the economy.

The operation of markets The free market approach suggests that markets will achieve equilibrium providing they are free to operate. Take the market for labour. Say that in a depressed area there are more workers wanting jobs than are available. This would put pressure on wages to fall. Employers would offer lower wages to workers and some workers would, as a result, not offer their labour to employers at this wage rate. This would occur until the labour market returned to equilibrium, ie to the point where the demand for labour was equal to the supply of labour at a given wage. This approach would argue for the removal of all restrictions to markets and the free movement of wages and prices.

Interventionists argue that the operation of a market economy results in a variety of problems, such as:
● high levels of unemployment;
● inadequate merit goods, such as housing, health care and education (☞ unit 6);
● a lack of provision of some public goods, such as defence;
● inequalities in income.

Wages and unemployment Market supporters suggest that if real wage rates (that take into account inflation) are free to move up and down, the economy would always achieve full

employment. Workers must be flexible in their demands and prepared to react to changes in the market. If there is any unemployment, it is likely to be voluntary. Some people may not want to work by choice at a given wage rate. This is known as the **natural rate of unemployment** (☞ unit 24).

Interventionists believe that in the 1930s depression (and arguably in the 1980s and 1990s recessions) wage rates fell, or were held down, but unemployment was still high. They dispute whether real wage rates will actually operate to allow markets to achieve equilibrium at full employment. In modern economics this is because:
● labour may be reluctant to move from one area to another;
● trade unions protect the real wage rates of their members;
● businesses may not reduce wages because of the dissatisfaction it may lead to.

Instead they argue that unemployment is caused by a lack of aggregate demand in the economy. It is the government's role in such circumstances to use policies which will lead to an increase in consumption, investment, government spending and exports.

Inflation Providing markets operate freely, the economy will achieve full employment, according to market economists. At this point an increase in output would only be possible if the state of technology changed. Increases in aggregate demand by government would simply lead to inflation. Businesses could not take on more workers or produce more output even if they wished. Price increases would be the only result of government spending. Some economists, sometimes called monetarists, argue that increases in the money supply over and above increases in output lead to inflation.

Interventionists argue that money supply increases merely reflect the state of the economy and do not cause inflation. Instead, they believe that inflation is caused by an excess of consumer demand in the economy as a whole or a rise in firms' costs.

Government policy Market economists argue that obstacles to the operation of markets should be removed by government. These occur on the **supply side** of the economy. For example, workers may not be able to move to other jobs because they do not have the skills needed. This will prevent the labour market from working. Incentives to businesses to retrain workers may help solve this. The aim of supply side policies is to increase the level of output in the economy as a whole. This is known as **aggregate supply** (☞ unit 26). Supply side economists believe that this can be increased by using the supply side policies mentioned in the last section.

Interventionists argue that government should attempt to solve problems of the market. They argue that government policy should include:

● fiscal and regional policy to increase employment, generate economic growth, help ailing industry and encourage firms to invest in new plant and machinery;
● protection for UK firms against foreign competition;
● the use of prices and incomes policy to prevent wage costs rising as a result of increases in aggregate demand;
● government ownership or close involvement in particular sectors of the economy.

One of the more significant shifts in policy comes about through the election of a new government. A new government is likely to introduce new economic policies. In the past, in the UK, Labour governments had been associated with interventionist policies and Conservative governments with a more free market approach. Increasingly, political parties in the UK and other countries have placed the operation of markets at the centre of their economic policy approach.

However, different governments do have different approaches to the solving of economic problems. For example, the Labour government elected in 1997 introduced policy initiatives such as New Deal, which was aimed at reducing unemployment, and increased expenditure on education to enhance the UK's future growth prospects. Both of these policies would have a direct effect upon a range of businesses, such as educational supply companies and private training organisations.

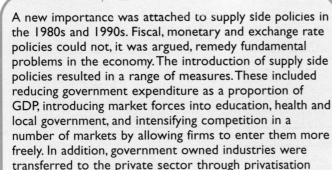

Question 1

A new importance was attached to supply side policies in the 1980s and 1990s. Fiscal, monetary and exchange rate policies could not, it was argued, remedy fundamental problems in the economy. The introduction of supply side policies resulted in a range of measures. These included reducing government expenditure as a proportion of GDP, introducing market forces into education, health and local government, and intensifying competition in a number of markets by allowing firms to enter them more freely. In addition, government owned industries were transferred to the private sector through privatisation and more stress was placed on the individual rather than the collective. For example, managers were encouraged to bargain with individual workers rather than unions.

Source: adapted from the *Economic Review*.

(a) What is meant by the phrase 'Fiscal, monetary and exchange rate policies could not ... remedy fundamental problems in the economy'?
(b) What evidence is there in the above passage to suggest that supply side policies stress the operation of a free market?
(c) Explain briefly how one of the supply side policies in the article might affect a business.

Policy conflicts and business strategy

In practice governments find it difficult to achieve all of their objectives at the same time. This is because of the way in which individual economic policies have varied effects upon employment, growth, inflation and the balance of payments. Businesses need to plan for and respond to policies as they change over time to meet different economic conditions.

Inflation and employment conflicts In order to achieve a targeted level of inflation the Bank of England may make the decision that it is important to maintain interest rates at a high level. High interest rates tend to control inflation. Businesses and people tend to borrow less and spend less. High interest rates may also cause the value of sterling to be high relative to other currencies, which should help to keep the price of imported goods low (☞ unit 26).

However, there can be problems with higher interest rates. They discourage consumer spending, leading to lower levels of output by businesses and possibly job losses. They may discourage investment by businesses in projects such as new factories and offices. Again, this may have the effect of reducing employment or preventing the creation of new jobs.

They can also lead to a higher exchange rates and thus cause higher prices in export markets for UK businesses. This may reduce the competitiveness of UK businesses in export markets and lead to a loss of jobs.

A business may react to higher interest rates by:
● finding alternative methods of borrowing to raise funds;
● finding cheaper suppliers of finance;
● lengthening its periods of repayment;
● passing on its charges to suppliers or consumers.

It may react to a high value of the pound by:
● attempting to improve its competitiveness in foreign markets in other ways, such as improving the quality of its products (☞ unit 95) or changing its marketing mix (☞ unit 40);
● not raising the price of its products in foreign markets and accepting a reduction in profits;
● buying low cost imports as a result of the higher value of the pound;
● concentrating on sales in the home market.

Some economists would argue that conflicts between inflation and unemployment are only likely to be short term. This is because the competitiveness of UK businesses in both domestic and export markets is likely to depend upon low inflation rates.

Economic growth and inflation / balance of payments deficit conflicts British governments have traditionally found it difficult to achieve high rates of economic growth of 3 per cent or more and control inflation at the same time. One of the reasons for this is because economic growth is associated with high levels of aggregate demand, which can lead to inflation. At times of high economic growth many consumers may find their incomes rising and use this income to spend more on goods and services. This leads to increased inflationary pressures in the economy. This increased consumer spending, as a consequence of high economic growth, can also contribute to a deficit on the balance of payments. If the increased spending of consumers is on domestic products, there would be no problem in terms of the balance of payments. However, UK consumers have tended to buy imported goods in growth periods. This high economic growth has tended to be associated with a increased balance of payments deficit in the UK.

In periods of high inflation a business may:

● attempt to reduce its costs by cutting wages, rationalising its organisation (☞ unit 102) or finding cheaper suppliers of materials or components;

● pass on some of the increase in cost to consumers;

● hedge against possible future price rises by agreeing to pay before prices increase;

● sign long term, fixed payment contracts.

Economic growth and the environment Governments are becoming increasingly aware of the need to consider the impact of their policies on the environment. Many commentators are concerned that the high levels of business activity associated with economic growth can have a negative effect upon the environment. For example, the amount of traffic on the roads generally increases in line with increases in business activity. This can lead to air pollution and congestion. Increased business activity also leads to increased usage of non-renewable resources, such as oil and gas, and to the pollution associated with their use.

Growth and business strategy

Unit 21 explained that economies move through booms and slumps in the business cycle. In a boom there are likely to be increased earnings, spending, production and employment. These conditions are associated with growth periods.

What strategies might a business adopt during periods of growth or when high growth is anticipated in future?

● Analyse the extent to which the incomes of existing customers will be affected by economic growth. Although economic growth leads to increased average incomes across the country, not all groups of consumers will experience an increase in their incomes.

● Assess the income elasticity of demand (☞ unit 42) of the business's products. The demand for some products, such as basic foodstuffs, is largely unaffected by increases in consumer incomes. For other products, such as new cars and restaurant services, demand is strongly linked to consumer incomes.

Question 2

Realworks is a manufacturer of children's wooden toys. Towards the end of 1998 it was considering expanding abroad for the first time. It realised that this may involve borrowing to finance the expansion and also charging a competitive price abroad. One of the directors of the business had suggested that expansion would be better in the UK, although it was concerned about whether the costs of materials might rise.

Figure 28.1 *UK economic data*

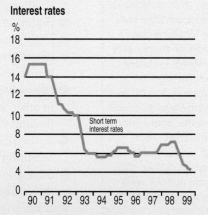

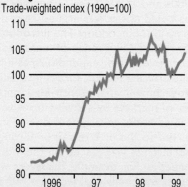

Source: adapted from Primark Datastream.

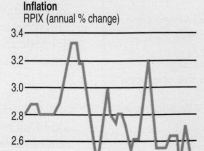

(a) Comment on the relationship between the value of the pound and the rate of interest in Figure 28.1.

(b) Comment on the strategy of Realworks given the data in Figure 28.1.

- Consider market opportunities which may arise in either existing markets where people have more money or new markets that have developed. For example, in a period of growth people may be more prepared to spend on leisure activities or holidays. It may be safer to expand into foreign markets in growth periods.
- Take the opportunity to diversify into new areas which are potentially risky. There might be less of a risk in a period of growth if spending is higher.
- Analyse the likely impact of economic growth on competitor products. For example, in a growth period small producers or service providers may develop which would not survive in a slower growth period.
- Consider the ability of the business's organisational structure (☞ unit 70) to cope with and positively respond to a growing business environment. This might mean employing more specialists or taking the opportunity to use more updated technology.
- Evaluate capacity to provide goods and services in sufficient quantities to meet demand. There may be a need to purchase new equipment to cope with larger quantities being produced.
- Assess the ability of the business to raise finance from either internal or external sources (☞ unit 57) to fund expansion where this is required.

Recession and business strategy

Periods of recession are usually accompanied by falling incomes and spending, and business failure.

It is useful for businesses to find strategies which they can use to weather a recession or increase their chances of doing so. Possible strategies may include some of the following.

- Focusing upon parts of the market where a business has an advantage. A business, for example, may produce a number of product lines. It may close down certain plants or lines and concentrate only on those that are profitable.
- Accurate and up to date financial information. Businesses need to identify quickly where losses are being made and act decisively with the use of this information.
- Credit control. Small firms, in particular, are often forced to close down due to the failure of a major customer to pay their bills. A tight credit control policy which involves promptly chasing up slow payers and taking out credit insurance can be useful.
- Realistic planning. Too many firms set their plans (☞ unit 15) on the assumption that nothing will go wrong. In a recession it is vital that firms build room into their plans for setbacks.
- Identify niche markets. A business may try to find markets which are largely unaffected by recession.
- A business may concentrate on safer home markets or those in countries which are less prone to recession.
- Analyse the extent to which the incomes of existing customers will be affected by recession. Although recession can lead to reduced average incomes across the country not all groups of consumers will experience a reduction in their incomes. Many groups of high earners have, in the past, been largely untouched by recession in terms of their earnings.
- Assess the income elasticity of demand (☞ unit 42) of the business's products. The demand for some products, such as basic foodstuffs, is largely unaffected by decreases in consumer incomes. For other products demand is linked to consumer incomes.

Question 3

Within a few hours of the liquidator arriving at Ms Jennifer Bond's Leicestershire leather-processing business a £65,000 order arrived. The order, for the tanning and dyeing of about 50,000 feet of leather, would have kept the factory busy for more than a month. But underfunding had already brought about the demise of the five year old business, and a meeting of creditors expected to put it into voluntary liquidation. Ms Bond said, 'The recession has passed but we can't finance the orders we are getting.'

Ironically the Leicestershire company's fate was sealed by its efforts to expand the business. It increased turnover by switching from the cheaper leathers and varied colours used in women's shoes to better quality leather for men's shoes, most of which are dyed black. The improvement in business increased the company's need for working capital and put further pressure on its already overstretched finances. 'We were very successful in opening up new markets but we didn't have the money to go on', said Ms Bond. 'We couldn't afford to buy in the chemicals or the other raw materials.'

The problem of how to finance growth is one which faces many businesses in a recession. Ms Bond's company had barely established itself when the recession began to bite and it lost money. The company was unable to return to profit and finally Ms Bond decided to call in the liquidator.

If the creditors approve, the liquidator will sell off the plant and equipment, the remains of the lease on the factory and any other assets he can find. Ms Bond, in spite of her disappointment at the loss of the business and concern at the personal liability she may still face when the business is liquidated, is relieved that it is all over. 'I feel better', she said, after her first meeting with the liquidator. 'It has been two years of ifs and buts.'

Source: adapted from the *Financial Times*.

(a) What factors contributed to the collapse of Ms Bond's business?
(b) Why are small firms likely to suffer from a recession more than larger firms?
(c) Discuss possible strategies that Ms Bond might have used to survive the recession.

Business failure

A number of terms are used to explain business failure. Businesses ultimately fail because they are **insolvent.** This means that they are unable to pay their debts. The **Insolvency Act, 1986** set out certain regulations for terminating businesses that become insolvent.

Sole traders and **partnerships** can be declared BANKRUPT. The process of a person being declared bankrupt begins when one or more creditors of a business present a petition to a court. Petitions can only be presented by creditors who are owed a certain amount by a business. If this is successful, then a receiving order will be made out against the debtor. An OFFICIAL RECEIVER is then appointed who has legal rights over all of the owner's property. Nothing can happen to this property without the permission of the Official

Receiver. If the Official Receiver believes that the business is still a going concern, a manager will be appointed to run the business on the Receiver's behalf. Within a period of time from the bankruptcy being declared, a meeting of creditors will be called. At this meeting the debtor has the opportunity to present proposals to meet debts. If this is unsuccessful, the debtor will return to court and, if the court is satisfied, the debtor will be declared bankrupt.

Private or **public limited companies** face LIQUIDATION. Liquidation can be either compulsory or voluntary, depending upon the circumstances. It involves the appointment of an Official Receiver as a **Liquidator.** This person is responsible for the winding-up of a company, taking control of a company's affairs and gathering assets with a view to finding a buyer. The liquidator is also responsible for paying off any debts the company may have. The law states the order of priority in the payment of debts. For example, payment of taxes comes before payments to firms. Some creditors may receive nothing if the company was heavily in debt.

Question 4

Figure 28.2 *Insolvencies in England and Wales*

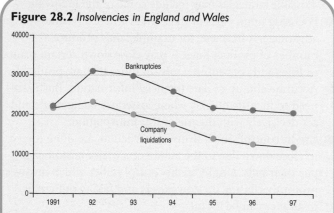

Source: adapted from *Annual Abstract of Statistics,* Office for National Statistics.

Figure 28.3 *Company insolvencies in England and Wales in agriculture*

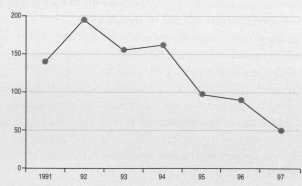

Source: adapted from *Annual Abstract of Statistics,* Office for National Statistics.

(a) Identify the trends taking place in the Figure 28.2.
(b) Comment on the likely changes in conditions over the period.
(c) Discuss possible strategies that a business in agriculture might have considered in 1995.

Key terms

Bankruptcy - declared by a court when a sole trader or partnership cannot meet its debts.
Liquidation - declared by a court when a company is unable to meet its debts.
Official Receiver - the person called in to handle the affairs of a business facing bankruptcy or liquidation.

Summary

1. Briefly explain the free market approach to:
   (a) the operation of markets;
   (b) reducing unemployment .
2. Briefly explain the interventionist approach to:
   (a) the operation of markets;
   (b) reducing unemployment.
3. Identify 3 examples of government policy conflicts.
4. State 3 strategies a business might use when interest rates are high.
5. State 3 strategies a business may use when exchange rates are high.
6. State 3 strategies a business might use in periods of high inflation.
7. State 5 ways in which a business might react during a growth period.
8. Why are small firms especially vulnerable to recession?
9. What is the difference between bankruptcy and liquidation?
10. What strategies might a business pursue in order to survive a recession?

Case study

Is recession around the corner?

A combination of the strong pound, the Asian economic crisis and foreign competition was thought to be putting people in British manufacturing out of work. BOC, the industrial gases group, said it would shed 500 jobs in Britain and 3,200 elsewhere in an efficiency drive to cut costs and boost productivity because of tougher competition from overseas. Molins, the cigarette machinery maker, confirmed it was closing its Peterborough plant because of the strength of sterling.

The latest redundancies raised fears among union leaders that Britain's manufacturing was enduring a repeat of the recession during the eighties which destroyed much of the country's industrial base. Fred Higgs, a senior TGWU official, said the BOC job cuts were taking place despite a 30 per cent cut in costs and a big rise in productivity over the past two years. The company said sterling's strength had cost it £100 million in profit during the same period. 'We have co-operated fully with the company to an extent where we have changed working practices and reduced unit labour costs by 30 per cent. In spite of that, due to the turmoil in Asia, compounded by the high value pound in the UK, and high interest rates, they are having to look at further cost cutting.'

BOC, the world's second largest industrial gas producer, said most of its British job losses would be in Surrey and Sussex where unemployment was the lowest in the country. 'We're instituting changes on a massive scale to accelerate sales growth and productivity,' said Danny Rosenkranz, the chief executive, as he announced that pre-tax profits for the nine months to June 30 were down to £272.4 million after falling sharply in the third quarter. 'We'll be reviewing all of our European assets,' Mr Rosenkranz said. 'It doesn't make enough money for us, and we'll have to find out if we want to stay with them or sell them.' BOC's problems have been compounded by the fact that 35 per cent of its business is in the Far East. The company's restructuring would cost £267 million, partly financed by selling most of its temperature-controlled operations.

BAe said the strong pound was only partly to blame for the latest round of job losses at its Royal Ordnance plant (RO). Since it acquired RO in 1987, BAe has reduced the workforce from 19,000 to below 5,000 and cut overhead and labour costs by 25 per cent. But it said it was being forced to shave costs further because of a 50 per cent reduction in defence spending over the past ten years, overseas competition, and the Asian crisis. The RO has increased export sales from 30 per cent to 60 per cent of turnover, but is fighting rivals like Denel, of South Africa, for diminishing defence orders.

Source: adapted from *The Guardian*, 12.8.1998.

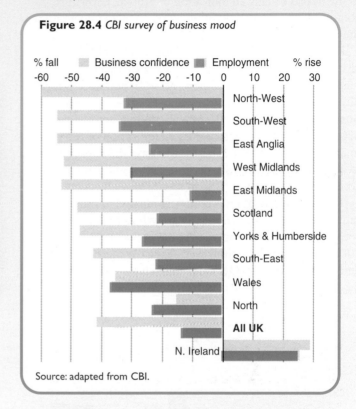

Figure 28.4 *CBI survey of business mood*

Source: adapted from CBI.

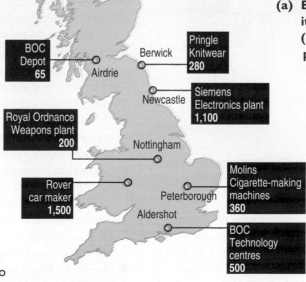

Figure 28.5 *Job losses*

(a) Explain how **BOC** has changed its strategy to account for:
(i) the exchange rate for the pound; and (ii) recession-like conditions.

(b) Discuss how the levels of business confidence shown in Figure 28.4 might affect the strategies adopted by businesses in: (i) the **North West**; (ii) **Northern Ireland**.

(c) To what extent are there likely to be policy disagreements in the methods of dealing with the rising levels of unemployment described in the article?

What is economic growth?

ECONOMIC GROWTH is an indication of the change in the goods and services produced by an economy. One way an economy can tell if growth is taking place is to examine its GDP or GNP figures (☞ unit 21). These show how much money is flowing around the economy. A rise from one year to the next is usually an indication of growth. Growth is measured in **real** terms, in other words, it takes into account the rate of inflation (☞ unit 23).

If economic growth is taking place, there are likely to be favourable trading conditions for business. Many new businesses set up and continue to grow. In periods of growth, businesses may find a healthy demand for their products. Businesses will tend to suffer when growth is zero or even negative. Negative growth may be an indication of recession in an economy (☞ unit 21). This will have the opposite effect to a period of growth, with declining sales and many firms going out of business.

The growth rate of one country compared to others is also important. Figure 29.1 shows the growth rates in the UK compared to other countries over the period 1990-96. The UK has performed relatively well against Western competitors and far better than former communist economies. However, it has lagged behind some countries in Asia.

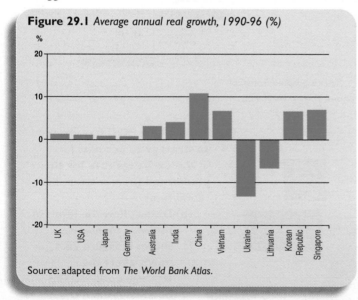

Figure 29.1 *Average annual real growth, 1990-96 (%)*

Source: adapted from *The World Bank Atlas.*

The business cycle

Unit 21 explained how economies move through periods of 'up and downs' over time. This can be shown by the use of the **business cycle** or **trade cycle**. At the top of the cycle, in a boom, growth will be high. As output and income fall, the economy moves into recession. At the bottom of the cycle, in a trough, firms fail and unemployment is high. As the economy recovers, output and income start to rise again.

Figure 29.2 shows the change in GDP at constant prices over a period of 45 years. The trends in the figures show that the performance of the UK economy has, over this period, been similar to that explained by the traditional business cycle. In the 1990s the UK saw periods of recession and growth. In 1990, according to some measures, growth was nearly minus 3 per cent. In 1997 growth was nearly 4 per cent. However, the long term growth rate of the UK, like that of many countries is declining. In the 1960s the average annual growth rate for the decade was over 3 per cent. Between 1990-97 it was 1.6 per cent.

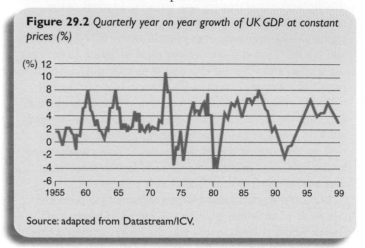

Figure 29.2 *Quarterly year on year growth of UK GDP at constant prices (%)*

Source: adapted from Datastream/ICV.

Factors affecting growth

There is a number of factors that can lead to economic growth.

Land Land includes all natural resources such as forests, lakes and oil and coal deposits, as well as land itself. It is possible for countries to experience economic growth through more effective exploitation of their natural resources. Saudi Arabia, for example, has generated the vast majority of its wealth from its oil reserves and the UK has benefited from North Sea oil.

Labour force/population Increasing the quantity of the labour force can contribute to economic growth.
- One relatively easy way of increasing the labour force is to encourage immigration. The success of the US economy has been partly attributed to the effects of immigration.
- Changes in the demography (☞ unit 20) of a country can be important. More young people will swell the size of the workforce, but an increase in the birth rate will create more dependents for a number of years. The UK is at present experiencing an ageing of its population, resulting in a relative decline in the number of people of working age.
- One of the biggest increases in the UK's workforce over the last thirty years has come about through the increasing participation of women in work. At any given time, there are usually large numbers of women willing to enter the

Table 29.1 *Individual bankruptcies and company liquidations, 1987-97*

	1987	1988	1989	1990	1991	1992	1993	1994	1995	1996	1997
Bankruptcies	6,994	7,717	8,138	12,058	22,632	32,106	31,016	25,634	21,933	21,803	19,892
Total company liquidations	11,439	9,427	10,456	15,051	21,827	24,425	20,708	16,728	14,536	13,461	12,610

Source: adapted from *Annual Abstract of Statistics*, Office for National Statistics

(a) Describe the main trends taking place in the table.
(b) To what extent does the information suggest that there is a business cycle?
(c) What might a business expect to happen in the period 1997-2002 from the figures in the table? Explain your answer.

workforce should suitable employment become available.

Whilst the quantity of labour in a country can be important, the quality of it tends to be especially significant in influencing growth rates. A well trained, well educated workforce, which is flexible and able to respond to change can help to provide favourable trading conditions for businesses, leading to growth.

Investment and technology Economic growth requires an increase in the capital stock of the economy. This means the development of and investment in new technology (☞ unit 98) and the updating of capital equipment. Technological development also allows new products to be created. It is not just the quantity of investment in an economy which is important. Investment needs to be directed into growth industries whose products are likely to be in high demand in the future.

Government policy Governments can use a combination of fiscal, monetary, exchange rate and supply side policies to stimulate growth. The policies a government chooses will reflect its views about the operation of the economy (☞ unit 28). The choice of policy is important. Even if an economy has great natural resources, a well trained workforce and high levels of investment it may be held back by inappropriate government policy.

Competitive advantage Michael Porter has suggested that countries must have strategies that attempt to create a competitive advantage (☞ unit 16) in international trade. This, he suggests, can be done by building up the competitive advantage of particular sectors of the economy, rather than attempting to compete in all sectors. For example, Japan has been successful in achieving growth as a result of its trading policy despite a relatively weak retail and agricultural sector.

The effects of economic growth on business

The majority of firms benefit from a growing economy. There are some, such as pawnbrokers and scrap-metal dealers who

perhaps do better in recessions, but these tend to be exceptions. If a business is operating in a growing economy, experiencing economic growth rates of 3 per cent per annum or more, this is likely to have a number of effects upon it. Not all of them, however, are positive.

Sales revenue Consumer spending should be high during a period of economic growth. This will increase the demand for many firms' products and should lead to an increase in sales revenue. If a firm is able to keep its costs under control, this should also mean an increase in profits.

Expansion An increase in the demand for a firm's products generated by a sustained period of economic growth may lead to expansion. Some businesses are forced into expanding where they find that they cannot meet demand. Others plan their expansion well in advance. Expansion may involve some or all of the following:
● recruiting new staff;
● raising finance;
● increasing the size of premises;
● moving to new premises;
● purchasing more assets, for example, production facilities, machinery or office equipment;
● taking over competitors.

Security In a healthy business climate, a business is likely to feel more secure in its decisions. It will be able to order from suppliers with greater confidence. This may lead to a better and more effective relationship. Businesses should also be able to hire employees without concern about being forced to lay them off within a short period of time. This may result in a firm committing itself more to the workforce, for example, by investing in training programmes.

Planning for the future Economic growth should provide businesses with more confidence in planning for the future. Higher profit levels, for example, should help to provide investment funds for new projects. Year to year or even day to day survival is likely to become less of an issue as a firm seeks

There is, however, a number of potential problems with the single currency for businesses in member countries.

Costs The initial conversion which all businesses will need to make will be costly. It may affect a business in a number of ways. Accounting systems may need to be changed to take into account the new currency. Dual pricing may lead to redesigned packaging, advertising and display material. Staff would need to be trained to use the new currency. There will also be costs in being a member country. For example, competition is likely to increase, which may force down profits. Businesses must constantly review prices due to price transparency.

The impact of the ECB The European Central Bank's central role in setting interest rates and controlling monetary policy (☞ unit 26) for all nations within the euro zone could have a damaging effect upon businesses. This is because the interest rates and monetary policy pursued by the ECB will reflect the needs of the member countries as a whole. If there are inflationary pressures in the euro zone the ECB is likely to pursue tight monetary polices, such as the raising of interest rates. However, there may be particular countries within the euro zone which do not have inflationary pressures, but which are seeking to avoid recession. Such countries would also be subject to tight monetary policies, but for them it would be inappropriate. These policies could help drive these countries into recession with damaging effects for business.

Effects of the euro on non-member countries

Businesses remaining outside the euro zone, such as the UK in the late 1990s, were far less likely to enjoy the benefits or incur the costs of operating within the zone. Many commentators anticipated that the UK would join the euro in the 21st century, although there was still a great deal of debate about whether this would take place.

For businesses outside the euro zone, the introduction of the euro may have a number of effects.

● Businesses trading with the member states would have to quote their prices in euros and be able to make transactions in this currency.
● The uncertainties of dealing with a number of different EU nations, all with their own separate currencies, would be reduced.
● There would be some reduction in transactions costs, although not as great as for members' businesses.
● UK businesses selling into the euro zone may be at a competitive disadvantage against competitors that share the same currency.
● The competitiveness of businesses may depend on the value of their country's currency against the euro. For example, if the value of the Swedish krone against the euro fell, this may make Swedish exports to countries in the

euro zone more attractive.
● Increasing competition within the euro zone may make cross-border mergers more likely. Businesses outside the euro zone therefore have to decide how to compete against these merged firms.

It was suggested that the UK businesses most affected by the euro zone were:
● exporters and importers who would need to quote in euros;
● multinationals (☞ unit 32) such as BP and Rover who adopted the euro as their trading currency. This had an effect upon businesses supplying them. It meant that even businesses trading entirely in the UK were asked to price, invoice and accept payment in euros;
● banks who may be asked to provide euros, make payments

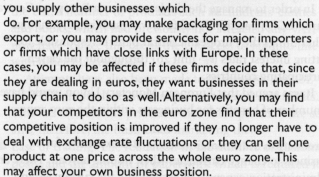

Figure 30.3 *EU members and countries applying to join in 1999*

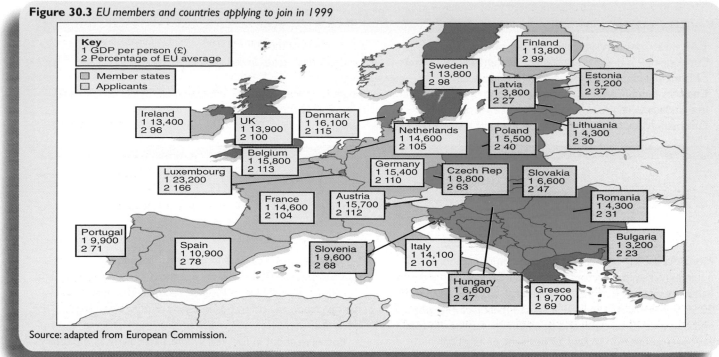

Key
1 GDP per person (£)
2 Percentage of EU average

☐ Member states
☐ Applicants

Finland
1 13,800
2 99

Sweden
1 13,800
2 98

Latvia
1 3,800
2 27

Estonia
1 5,200
2 37

Ireland
1 13,400
2 96

UK
1 13,900
2 100

Denmark
1 16,100
2 115

Netherlands
1 14,600
2 105

Poland
1 5,500
2 40

Lithuania
1 4,300
2 30

Belgium
1 15,800
2 113

Luxembourg
1 23,200
2 166

Germany
1 15,400
2 110

Czech Rep
1 8,800
2 63

Slovakia
1 6,600
2 47

France
1 14,600
2 104

Austria
1 15,700
2 112

Romania
1 4,300
2 31

Portugal
1 9,900
2 71

Spain
1 10,900
2 78

Slovenia
1 9,600
2 68

Italy
1 14,100
2 101

Bulgaria
1 3,200
2 23

Hungary
1 6,600
2 47

Greece
1 9,700
2 69

Source: adapted from European Commission.

in euros and open euro accounts;
● some retailers, perhaps in tourist areas, who may need to quote prices in euros;
● subsidiaries of multinationals in the euro zone who may be asked to deal in euros.

The expansion of the EU

One of the major issues facing the EU in the year 2000 was whether or not to expand, and if so, how rapidly. Figure 30.3 shows the existing members at that time and the countries that were applying to join. It was argued that including countries such as Poland, Romania and Bulgaria would require major changes in the EU.

There is a number of implications of EU expansion into eastern Europe.
● Many of the nations seeking membership of the EU were significantly poorer than existing members. This would inevitably place a strain on the EU's budget. The poorer countries may not be in a position to contribute greatly to EU funds, whilst requiring large amounts in payments to help their development. This could affect businesses operating in existing EU countries.
● By including countries such as Poland, Romania and Bulgaria in the EU there may need to be significant changes to policies. For example, the CAP may need to change to prevent large sums being paid to economies that were largely agriculture based.
● Enlargement to include the countries shown in Figure 30.3 would consolidate the EU's position as the world's largest single market, increasing the number of consumers from 370 million to 500 million. This would provide a huge

increase in the potential number of customers for many EU businesses and offer further opportunities for them to enjoy economies of scale.
● Including many of the former communist eastern European countries within the EU would be likely to generate greater economic and political stability within them. This would provide improved investment opportunities within these countries for existing EU businesses.
● The eventual adoption of the euro by all of these countries could lead to major benefits. The area would also operate as a strong trading bloc (☞ unit 31) with the rest of the world.

Summary

1. Why is the EU said to be a customs union?
2. What is the Common Agricultural Policy?
3. What changes have occurred as a result of the Single Market?
4. State 5 implications of the Single Market for British businesses.
5. State 3 benefits of a single currency for businesses in member countries.
6. State 2 problems of a single currency for businesses in member countries.
7. Explain 3 effects that the single European currency might have on businesses in non-member countries.
8. What effects might EU enlargement in East Europe have on businesses in existing member countries?

Key terms

CAP - the Common Agricultural Policy of the European Community. It is designed to stabilise EC agricultural markets by fixing minimum prices for agricultural products.
Customs union/Common market - a group of countries with free trade between them and a common external tariff.
European Monetary Union - the adoption of a single currency

by members of the EU.
Excise duties - taxes levied on fuel, alcohol, tobacco and betting.
Single European Market - an agreement by EU countries to remove all barriers to trade.

Case study

Motorola

Motorola, the big US manufacturer of communications equipment, semiconductors and automotive components, has had a presence in Europe for 30 years. It employs around 22,500 people across Europe. It has 14 manufacturing plants and operates 18 research and development facilities. In total, Europe accounts for around 23 per cent of its global turnover.

But the Chicago-based group says that its investment approach is still driven mainly by market considerations, rather than production cost factors. Arnold Brenner, Executive Vice-President, says: 'Getting close to the customer has always been a successful way for us to develop products, so we make investments based principally on how large an opportunity we see in the market, and our ability to penetrate that market by knowing a lot about it. 'It's very rare these days to make an investment just because [a place] is the lowest-cost manufacturing base. Cost is important, but it's lower down on the decision-making tree in terms of whether to put investment into a country.'

Mr Brenner admits that, for this reason, a good deal of recent manufacturing-type investment has tended to go into the large continental European markets - for example, the new DM500 million cellular phone plant in Flensburg, Germany, which opened recently.

In other cases, familiarity with a site, and knowledge of the available labour pool, has encouraged reinvestment. Mr Brenner cites the opening last month of a new £82 million GSM worldwide headquarters in Swindon in the UK.

'We've been in the Swindon area for eight years now. We found ourselves needing more capacity and space. It's a very favourable employment atmosphere. So we decided to stay and build the factory.'

Mr Brenner thinks that monetary union itself will have little impact on investment decisions. 'First of all, we support it, and think it will do nothing but help. Having a single currency in Europe is going to simplify matters - marketing, pricing structures across all the countries that participate, and eventually accounting as well - things like payroll, invoicing. We think it'll eventually be reasonably simple.

'We will be euro-capable in January 1999, and we've told our customers that we will invoice them - or receive payment - in either their choice of local currency or the euro. But it has not made any difference in terms of our investment decisions.'

But what about in five years' time, particularly as monetary union fosters greater harmonisation across European nations? Here he acknowledges that this could stimulate the market, and possibly encourage investment inflows.

'I do think harmonisation will probably do things to enlarge the market', he says. He makes a comparison between EMU and the cellular telecommunications business. He recalls the stage when many big countries had different networks, and customers were unable to take a telephone across borders and use it successfully. 'When GSM became standardised, the market grew phenomenally because people could roam freely. Whether emu has that kind of impact or effect, I don't think I can predict. I can't see it would hurt. But I think just having the ability to trade in common denominators is going to make for a successful bringing together of the business community in terms of enlarging the market.'

Source: adapted from the *Financial Times*, 2.11.1998.

(a) Explain, using evidence from the article: **(i)** why Motorola is keen to invest in EU nations; **(ii)** why Motorola may be more likely to invest in a higher cost EU nation such as Germany or the UK than a lower cost eastern European country such as Russia.

(b) How might the expansion of the EU to include a range of eastern European countries within the EU affect Motorola's European investment decisions?

(c) Explain the statement :'I do think harmonisation will probably do things to enlarge the market'.

(d) Using evidence from the article evaluate the likely impact on Motorola of EMU.

Business competitiveness in international markets

Unit 30 explained how the European Union might affect businesses in member and non-member countries. This unit examines the effects of international trading in other areas around the world and the effects of trading conditions on businesses. There is a number of factors that might influence the competitiveness of businesses trading in international markets.

The existence of trade barriers Some countries and groups of countries, known as TRADING BLOCS, such as the EU (☞ unit 30), erect trade barriers. These are designed to prevent businesses based outside the trading areas from competing with those who are members of the trading area.

Tariffs (☞ unit 26), a tax on imports, are one form of restriction. The effect of a tariff on products exported to countries which impose them is to increase the price charged by businesses or to lower their profit margins.

Quotas may also be used, which restrict the amount of a product that can be exported to a particular country or trading bloc. For individual businesses, quotas can mean that they can only export small quantities of their products, or indeed none at all, to countries which impose them. It is easier for businesses exporting abroad to compete with local businesses when they do not have to pay a tariff or have quotas imposed upon them.

The costs of production For some businesses their ability to compete in international markets depends upon their ability to have the same or lower costs of production than their international competitors. Lower costs of production allow businesses to have lower prices and therefore undercut their competitors. Because of the importance of labour costs these have traditionally been taken to indicate the competitiveness of a country and the businesses operating within it.

The behaviour of businesses Keeping production costs low and matching or beating competitors' prices are important in many markets. However, it is increasingly the view of business commentators such as Michael Porter that competitiveness in international markets depends upon how businesses behave. Competitiveness may depend on the extent to which businesses innovate and produce new products desired by consumers. Those businesses which produce quality goods and services, which meet the needs of consumers and stand out from those offered by competitors, are likely to be successful in international markets. The ability of businesses to produce innovative products and make good use of new technology will depend on their ability to recruit and train suitable employees.

Trading agreements In certain international markets, trade agreements regulate competition. For example, countries may belong to The World Trade Organisation, which is committed to increasing free trade. This is discussed in the next section. Another example is Mercosur, a free trade area agreed between Brazil, Paraguay, Argentina and Uruguay.

Question

Crocodile clips became an aspiring global business the moment it doubled its staff to two. The small software company produces multimedia packages for teaching electronics in schools. The company identified a market niche for children between the ages of 11 and 16. It had the advantage that the subject was common to secondary schools all over the world.

About half of the company's turnover was exported and that proportion was expected to grow. The first big step was to translate the package into French and win approval from France's centralised education authorities. This was secured in a matter of weeks once the appropriate official had been located. A similar exercise was carried out in Germany and a Spanish version was under development. However, translation costs were high, so the company had to choose carefully how to expand.

Chris Cytera, the incoming partner at Crocodile Clips, believed that the company had no choice but to trade throughout the world: 'Our four nearest competitors are in Canada, California, Hungary and Israel. We had to be a global company from the word go. If you don't operate in a range of international markets in this sort of business you're sunk.'

This policy has clearly paid off. The company had sales approaching £1 million and received an excellence award for its export successes.

Source: adapted from the *Financial Times*, 20.1.1998.

(a) What trade barriers might have existed for Crocodile Clips?
(b) Analyse the factors which have enabled Crocodile Clips to achieve success in international markets.

Developed economies

Western Europe and, in particular, the EU (☞ unit 30) is now the single most important market for British firms. However, there are many other parts of the world which are significant trading partners for the UK. Particularly important are the US, Japan and Canada. They provide large export markets and have rival firms operating in the UK market. The way these countries trade with the UK and the EU is largely determined by two organisations - the G7/G8 countries and the World Trade Organisation.

The Group of Seven (G7) or G8 countries The G7 nations are the seven leading industrial countries - Germany, Japan, US, UK, France, Italy and Canada. Between them they are responsible for over two-thirds of the world's total output, and a similar proportion of its expenditure. The main aim of G7 is to promote growth in the world economy. Note that it is sometimes referred to as G8, and includes Russia.

The success of G7 nations in reaching agreements has implications for firms trading in all parts of the world. For example, the break-up of G7 nations into rival trading groups centred around Europe, North America and the Pacific Rim could lead to a reduction in the quantity of goods and services traded. This may result in a reduction in business opportunities for firms. The failure of G7 nations to reach agreement on promoting economic growth could have similar effects.

Trading agreements between non-EU G7 nations can also affect EU-based firms. For example, the US and Canada along with Mexico formed the North American Free Trade Area (NAFTA). This is a regional trading bloc similar to the EU. Such regional trade blocs place barriers in the way of external firms seeking to export into them. Trade barriers of this kind can be damaging to firms wishing to enter such markets.

The World Trade Organisation (WTO) The WORLD TRADE ORGANISATION (WTO), formerly the General Agreement on Tariffs and Trade (GATT), came into being in 1995. The aim of GATT was to promote free trade and to prevent protectionist measures by member countries. The WTO is made up of 123 countries that account for around 90 per cent of world trade. It has a number of roles, including being responsible for policing the world trade system. For example, it has annual reviews and also oversees individual members' trade policies. All countries that join the WTO must agree to abide by its decisions.

Decisions taken by the WTO occur in 'Rounds' which last for years. The latest, the Uruguay Round, was completed in 1994 and the final Act was signed in 1995. The main agreements were:

Table 31.1 *Tariff reductions in the Uruguay Round*

Product categories	Value of imports million US$	% reduction in tariffs
All agricultural products	84,240	37
Coffee, tea, sugar etc.	13,610	34
Fruit and vegetables	1,334	36
Oilseed, fats and oils	14,575	40
Other agricultural products	12,584	48
Animals and their products	15,585	32
Beverages and spirits	9,596	39
Flowers, plants, veg mats	6,608	48
Tobacco	1,945	36
Grains	3,086	39
Dairy products	5,317	26

Source: adapted from GATT.

● a phasing out of the Multi Fibre Agreement, which had protected countries' textiles and clothing industries from foreign competition;
● the liberalisation of trade amongst agricultural products;
● rules to cover businesses' intellectual property rights, such as copyright and patents, to prevent them being copied and used by other businesses;
● an aim for a gradual liberalisation of trade in services, for example opening up of competition in nationally provided services such as telecommunications;
● phasing out of voluntary export restraints which had been used particularly by the US and EU to prevent too many cars and electrical goods entering their areas.

Table 31.1 shows the extent to which some tariffs were reduced as a result of the Uruguay Round.

The reason the WTO is important is because of its potential for increasing the amount of trade in the world. Such an increase in trade, many believe, can lead to greater prosperity. Indeed, the increase in the wealth of many nations since the Second World War has, perhaps, been due to the success of the WTO in lowering trade barriers. There are concerns that, without the WTO, the world could divide up into trading blocs resulting in a reduction in trade and possibly a worldwide depression. For individual firms, the WTO makes it more likely that they can operate in export markets on equal terms with locally based companies.

Japan and North America Many of the world's largest and most famous businesses, such as Exxon, Toyota and Microsoft, are based in Japan and North America. In addition to these famous large businesses there is a host of small and medium sized businesses producing innovative and highly sought after products. Despite a severe economic downturn in the late 1990s, the growth of the Japanese economy in the post war years was arguably the most dramatic economic miracle of the 20th century. The US has the largest economy in the world and enjoyed high rates of economic growth throughout much of the 1990s. For UK businesses this means that non-EU developed economies represent both opportunities and threats.
● Opportunities. These arise because the income levels in these countries and the size of their markets provide numerous openings for UK businesses.
● Threats. These arise because many businesses based in non-EU developed nations are renowned for their innovation, use of new technology and general ability to gain a competitive advantage over rivals. Consequently, businesses originating in these countries are able to challenge UK businesses both in domestic and international markets.

Eastern Europe

The fall of the communist governments of Eastern Europe and the countries' attempts to move to market economies in the early 1990s presented many opportunities for UK and EU businesses.

Japanese cars have tended to be more reliable than many cars made by US or European owned manufacturers. Yet US manufacturers have resisted the Japanese challenge and retained the major market share in the US. One reason for this was that customers began to prefer safety at low cost. US manufacturers quickly gave them what they wanted, offering features such as strong bodies, air bags and anti-lock brakes.

Japanese car makers were slow to respond. Their entire system was built to improve reliability and fuel efficiency. Safety was less of a consideration. Even Volvo, the previous leader in the safety niche, was caught off guard. It offered safe cars but at much higher prices. Neither the Japanese manufacturers nor Volvo responded effectively to the shift towards 'safety for the masses'.

Source: adapted from the *Financial Times*, 'Mastering Global Business', Part Two, 1998.

(a) Using evidence from the article, explain why US and Japanese car manufacturers may act as a threat to European car manufacturers.
(b) Analyse the likely impact of changes made in the Uruguay Round on international competition between US, Japanese and European car manufacturers.

Countries such as the Czech Republic, Russia, Poland and Hungary are, with varying degrees of success, introducing the operation of markets into their economies (☞ unit 8). In 1992, East Germany united with West Germany to form one country. This meant that businesses in the former East Germany were faced with the prospect of competing in a market economy with domestic and foreign businesses.

Prior to the dramatic economic changes of the early 1990s, most products in this part of the world were provided by state-owned monopolies. These were protected from overseas competition by trade barriers. Today, most of these state-owned monopolies have been privatised and investment from foreign firms is positively encouraged.

For British firms, the changes in Eastern Europe have presented a number of opportunities. Many UK firms see these economies as largely untapped export markets for their products.

● The opening up of these markets has provided Western-based firms with access to a huge number of consumers. They can be used as a manufacturing base for Western firms, taking advantage of workforces and land prices which are relatively cheaper than those in Western Europe.

● There are opportunities for joint ventures (☞ unit 101) with former state-owned firms. This allows British and other Western firms to combine their international business skills with local knowledge of markets and trading conditions.

● Businesses and individual entrepreneurs have the opportunity to sell their expertise and skills to Eastern

European businesses.

Although there are many opportunities for UK businesses in Eastern Europe, some businesses based in these countries also represent an increasing threat. Countries such as the Czech Republic and Hungary have adapted more effectively to the demands of a market economy than other countries such as Russia. Consequently, the businesses based in more successful former communist countries are beginning to rival their western counterparts. This is a trend which is likely to continue in future years.

There is also a number of problems with trading in Eastern Europe and the former Soviet Union states.

Bureaucracy Many of the institutions and regulations under the old planned system are still in existence. These can present a number of obstacles. For example, there are huge delays in receiving permits and licences for Western businesses wishing to set up and trade in some of these countries.

Political instability Since their transition to market economies, there has been political instability in a number of these countries. This ranges from full scale war, as in Bosnia and Kosovo, to weak and fragile governments. Such instability may be off-putting for potential business investors. They may argue that their businesses are unlikely to flourish in the 'turmoil' which results from such instability.

Low incomes Although Eastern Europe and the former Soviet Union represents a huge potential market for Western-based businesses, opportunities are likely to be limited whilst average incomes remain low. The bulk of the population of these countries is unlikely to be able to afford many of the products manufactured by Western-based firms. This could, however, be less of a problem over time if businesses in these countries develop and earnings increase.

Infrastructure The INFRASTRUCTURE of a country includes roads, railways, schools, airports, hospitals and office accommodation. In many ways the infrastructure of the Eastern European nations is of a high standard. For example, the hospitals and public transport in some of these countries are better than those found in some Western countries. However, there are also problems. Poor telecommunication systems, banking services and law enforcement are all problems which may affect the prospects of Western firms.

Economic conditions After the change to market economies some countries experienced hyper inflation of over 1,000 per cent per year. Economic conditions in some countries are still liable to change quickly. For example, in the late 1990s many of the new shopping malls built as the economy slowly grew in the mid-1990s were finding they had no customers as a result of a currency crisis and high inflation.

The revolution which swept communism out of eastern Europe helped make Jan Kulczyk rich. This 42-year-old Polish millionaire, clad soberly in grey slacks and a blue blazer, has moved with apparent ease from the old world of communist rule to the new one where capitalism holds sway - and where the whole of Europe now appears a place to make money.

Controlling 36 companies with sales approaching 3,000 billion zloty (£124 million), Mr Kulczyk's interests include banking, Volkswagen vehicle distribution in Poland and, above all, agribusiness. Mr Kulczyk made his fortune selling fruit, vegetables and meat to the EU. Now, in addition, he buys western food processing machinery to sell in the east. Prospects for increased EU commerce depend crucially on improving transport links. Mr Kulczyk and other businessmen want to build a 270km toll motorway linking Berlin to his native Poznan and beyond.

In another example of his activities, Mr Kulczyk has teamed up with Krupp to help build, near Poznan, a $100 million 150,000 tonnes per year processing plant, a venture which will increase Poland's rape seed processing capacity by a quarter. 'Workers in the European Community shouldn't feel that low wage employees in Poland are a threat to their jobs', he declares. 'Rather, this offers a chance to expand their companies' business.'

Mr Kulczyk's European horizons stretch east as well as west. Last year he helped set up Euro Agro Centrum, a company which aims to sell food processing equipment from western Europe to countries like Ukraine.

Source: adapted from the *Financial Times*.

(a) What evidence is there in the article of EU firms taking advantage of opportunities in Poland?
(b) What problems related to doing business in Poland are suggested by the article?

Developing economies

These economies are almost always found in the southern hemisphere. They are often known as 'the South', Third World Countries, developing countries or low and middle income countries.

Their main features are that they have poorly developed infrastructures and low average incomes per head of population. However, it is difficult to place countries in the South into one single group. This is because some have developed a wide range of industries which can compete with those in the West. Such countries are sometimes known as the Newly Industrialised Countries (NICs). Others are hardly developing at all. They continue to struggle with a range of economic and social problems on a scale almost unimaginable in the west.

The Newly Industrialised Countries (NICs) Many of these countries are found in South East Asia and include the so called 'tiger economies' of Taiwan, Singapore, South Korea, Malaysia and Hong Kong. Others are in South and Central America, including Mexico and Brazil. Such countries have been developing home-grown businesses with products which are increasingly able to compete in the domestic markets in the West. Examples include Proton cars from Malaysia, Daewoo from South Korea and Creative Technology from Singapore. In addition, multinational companies (☞ unit 32) that locate their production facilities in NICs can take advantage of their relatively cheap wage costs. Businesses in NICs, therefore, present competition to Western companies on two fronts.
● Undercutting the costs of Western producers.
● Companies based in SE Asia are expanding via takeovers or via inward investment into Western countries where their imports have reduced the strength of the competition.

These countries have also experienced a rise in overall income levels. As a result, they now provide significant export markets for Western produced consumer goods.

Low income countries Most of these countries are to be

Figure 31.1 *Where the world's poor are concentrated*

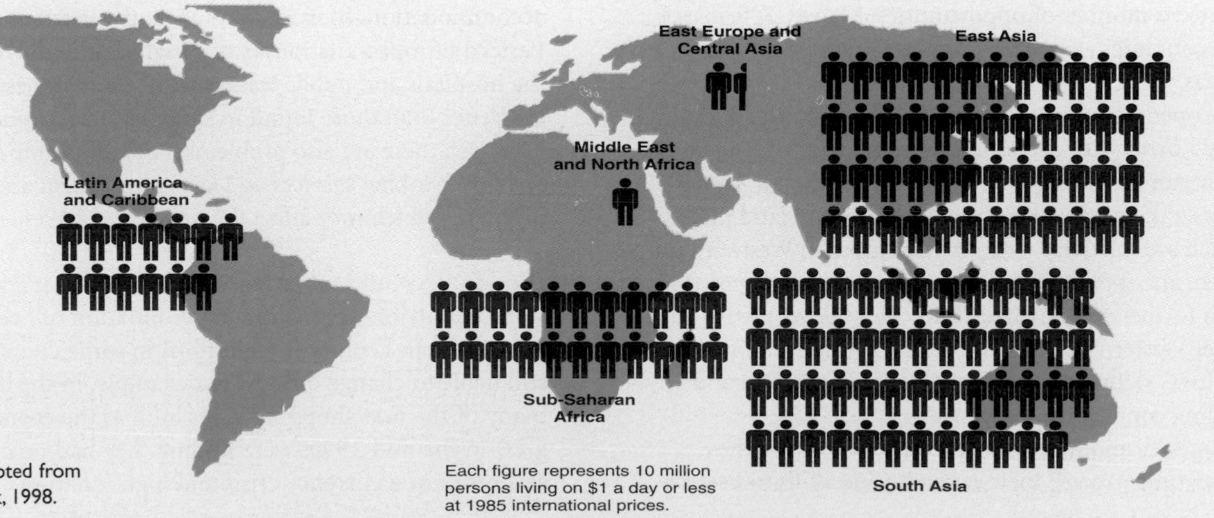

Source: adapted from World Bank, 1998.

Each figure represents 10 million persons living on $1 a day or less at 1985 international prices.

Question 4

A significant development in the final twenty years of the twentieth century has been the rising ambitions of companies that have their roots outside of the traditional homes of North America, northern Europe and Japan. Daewoo of South Korea, for example, comes 52nd, ahead of giants such as Electrolux and Xerox, in rankings based on the value of foreign assets. Third World businesses are catching up in another way too by making strides towards more modern structures. Companies such as Taiwan's Acer do not confine their research and product design to their home countries. They draw heavily upon the skills of the developed world as well. Even where they have strong local skills on which to draw the new entrants establish alliances with

Western companies to gain wider exposure to technological trends.

Source: adapted from the *Financial Times*, 1997.

(a) Examine the significance for European businesses of the emergence of large and successful businesses in NICs.
(b) Explain why some developing countries continue to be unable to nurture large and internationally successful businesses.

Table 31.2 *Multinationals based in less developed countries*

Ranked by intenational exposure

Ranking by index*	Corporation	Industry	Total assets ($)	Of which foreign ($)
1	**Panamerican Beverages** *Mexico*	Beverages	1,372.1	1,003.6
2	**First Pacific** *Hong Kong*	Electronics parts	6,821.2	3,779.2
3	Gruma *Mexico*	Food	1,095.5	992.5
4	**Creative Technology** *Singapore*	Electronics	661.2	405.0
5	Guangdong Investment *Hong Kong*	Miscellaneous	1,519.7	839.6
6	**Fraser & Neave** *Singapore*	Beverages	3,199.0	957.0
7	Jardine Matheson Holdings *Bermuda*	Diversified	11,582.7	3,092.6
8	**Cemex** *Mexico*	Construction	8,407.9	4,226.7
9	Daewoo *S.Korea*	Diversified/trading	28,898.0	11,946.0
10	**Dairy Farm Int'l Holdings** *Hong Kong*	Retailing	2,934.8	965.8

* Index calculated as the average of ratios of foreign assets to total assets, foreign sales to total sales and foreign employment to total employment

Source: adapted from World Investment Report.

found in Africa, Asia and Central/South America as shown in Figure 31.1. For Western businesses, such countries can either provide a base for manufacturing products or act as potential export markets. The infrastructure of such countries however, is often poor. It can be very difficult for multinational companies to establish manufacturing facilities. For example, in Sudan, the largest African country, there is only one purpose-built road of any great distance. Income levels are also very low. Export opportunities for most Western firms are limited to providing goods to very small sections of the population who enjoy Western incomes and lifestyles.

Many of these poorer countries are crippled by debt arising from balance of payment deficits and loans which they had been given by Western banks and governments. This means that they are required to make large, regular payments to Western banks. As a result, despite the aid which is given by those in the richer North, there is a net outflow of money.

Despite these problems, many Western-based businesses continue to operate in these countries. They represent an enormous market. The majority of the world's population lives in these countries and they can provide low cost facilities. Unfortunately, such business activities have often attracted bad publicity.

● Some Western businesses have provided aid for military goods or inappropriate projects, such as enormous hydro-electric schemes, which are unlikely to meet the needs of the majority of the population.
● Some companies have been accused of acting unethically by persuading poor consumers to purchase goods which can be harmful, such as drugs banned in the West.
● Large multinationals (☞ unit 32) are said to exploit cheap labour and raw materials and provide little in return.

Key terms

Infrastructure - those aspects of a country which support its economy. These include schools, roads, airports, telecommunication systems, hospitals etc .
NICs - Newly Industrialised Countries. These are countries such as Singapore, Malaysia and Mexico which have recently gone through the process of industrialisation.
Trading blocs - countries that join together to restrict trade.
World Trade Organisation - an organisation which seeks to promote free trade between nations and monitors world trade.

Summary

1. Why is the EU said to be a trading bloc?
2. Explain 4 facts that may affect the competitiveness of business in international markets.
3. What is the aim of the G7/G8 group of countries?
4. How might the work of the WTO affect trade between businesses?

5. What opportunities have the changes in Eastern Europe presented for British firms?
6. What problems exist in poorer countries which can make it difficult for Western firms to operate within them?

Case study

The Asian Financial Crisis

The Asian financial crisis began with the devaluing of the Thai currency, the baht, in July 1997. It led to a wave of currency crises and financial instability in Indonesia and Malaysia and further afield in Taiwan, Hong Kong and Korea. Suddenly after more than a decade of double digit growth rates people began to wonder whether the events really represented the end of the Asian economic miracle. For the previous two decades the Asian Tigers' economic performance had been stunning. Between 1980 and 1996, annual GDP growth averaged 7 per cent in Malaysia, 7.4 per cent in Taiwan and 7.8 per cent in Thailand.

The effects of the crisis were severe in the countries directly affected. In Korea, for example, it was estimated that 45 companies were going bankrupt each day and that 30,000 small and medium sized businesses would fail in 1998.

Concern also centred upon the wider effects of this crisis. The economies of East and South-East Asia are highly integrated into the international economy. Asia as a whole, for example, accounts for over a quarter of the world's exports and is particularly important in areas such as textiles and clothing and machinery and transport equipment. Asia also accounts for approximately 25 per cent of world imports and the combined economies of the ASEAN countries (Brunei, Indonesia, Malaysia, the Phillipines, Singapore, Thailand and Vietnam) are ranked as the third largest group of importers after the European Union and the US.

Source: adapted from the *Observer*, 31.7.1997, the *Financial Times*, 9.9.1998.

As an economic adviser, you have been asked to write a report on the problems for businesses of the crisis in South-East Asia . In your report:
● **identify the features of the crisis;**
● **discuss the factors which a British business wishing to trade in South-East Asia might have to take into account;**
● **analyse how the crisis might have affected the international competitiveness of businesses based**

in South-East Asia and businesses based in the EU;
● **recommend possible courses of action for UK businesses given this situation.**

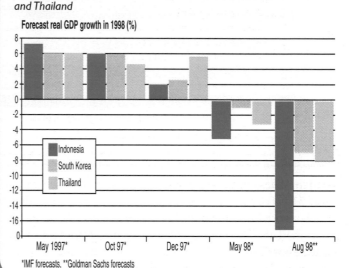

Figure 31.2 *Forecast real GDP growth in Indonesia, South Korea and Thailand*

Forecast real GDP growth in 1998 (%)

Indonesia
South Korea
Thailand

May 1997*   Oct 97*   Dec 97*   May 98*   Aug 98**

*IMF forecasts, **Goldman Sachs forecasts

Table 31.3 *Major economic indicators of the impact of the Asian crisis: affected and non-affected economies, 1991-1997 (per cent)*

Item	Affected economies			Non-affected economies		
	1991-95	1996	1997	1991-95	1996	1997
GDP growth	7.3	7.0	4.4	6.5	5.7	6.5
Inflation rate	6.1	5.8	5.1	4.9	3.7	2.5
Gross domestic saving/GDP	33.9	33.3	32.8	31.8	31.5	31.3
Current account balance/GDP	-3.0	-5.0	-3.0	4.1	4.9	4.2
Fiscal baalnce/GDP	0.3	0.4	-0.2	-0.7	2.0	1.4
Money supply (M2) growth	19.5	18.6	18.5	14.5	9.8	8.1

Note: affected economies include Indonesia, Korea, Malaysia, Philippines and Thailand. Non-affected economies include Hong Kong, China, Singapore and Taipei, China.
Source: Asian Development Bank, 1998.

What is globalisation?

GLOBALISATION is the term used to describe the growing **integration** of the world's economy. It is suggested that as globalisation takes place, national economies are becoming integrated into a single 'global economy' with similar characteristics. There are interrelationships throughout the world between related businesses, between competitors and between businesses and consumers. Decisions taken in one part of the world affect other parts. Businesses base decisions on what is happening in the 'world market' rather than national markets.

Evidence of the integration of the world's economy can perhaps be seen in businesses that design and market their products to a world market, such as Coca-Cola. This product is sold in many countries throughout the world. Consumers in different countries recognise the product easily and have similar tastes for the product. Coca-Cola is able to market its products worldwide. It has close relationships with businesses in other countries, some of which manufacture Coca-Cola products.

Three important aspects of globalisation might be identified.

The growing importance of international trade Between 1980 and 1990 the volume of international trade almost doubled. In part this can be accounted for by increases in production during the same period. However, since 1945, increases in production have been far outstripped by increases in the volume of international trade.

The rise of the multinational business The operation of multinational companies can be seen in many countries around the world. Familiar products and brand names appear worldwide. This is a trend which accelerated in the latter part of the twentieth century. For example, by 1995 the production of foreign branches of multinational companies generated $7,000 billion. This exceeded global exports of goods and services by 20 per cent. The operation and effects of multinationals are discussed later in this unit.

The emergence of businesses which think globally about their strategy Such businesses base their strategic decisions (☞ unit 16) on the global market rather than national markets. For example, a business may make parts for a product in several different countries and assemble them in another because this is the most cost effective and efficient method to get the product to its consumers. They will tend to make use of their business's **competitive advantage** by locating production wherever it is most efficient. This means businesses with widely spread networks of research, component production, assembly and distribution. Asea

Brown Boveri (ABB), the world's leading supplier of power and railway equipment, is an example of a global business. It comprises 1,300 different companies located throughout the world in 140 different countries. Its eight main directors are from five different companies and it has adopted English as its official language for major transactions.

Factors affecting globalisation

It could be argued that certain factors have contributed to the growth of globalisation.

- Technological change has played an important role in globalising the world's economy. More powerful computers and communications technology (☞ unit 82) have allowed the easy transfer of data. The internet is beginning to revolutionise the way in which consumers purchase products.
- The cost of transportation has fallen. Between 1930 and 1990 average revenue per mile in air transport fell from 68 US cents to 11 US cents at 1990 dollar prices. The cost of a three minute telephone call between New York and London fell from $244 to $3.
- The deregulation of business. Throughout the 1980s and 1990s many businesses were privatised in countries throughout the world. In the UK the privatisation of former state owned monopolies (☞ unit 6) allowed competition. The removal of restrictions on foreign businesses operating in former communist countries (☞ unit 8) also increased the ability of businesses to operate globally. New markets such as power generation were opened up to foreign competition.
- The liberalisation of trade. Trade protection has been reduced due to the operation of organisations such as the WTO (☞ unit 31). For example, the agreement to reduce restrictions on trade in textiles set out in the Multi-Fibre Agreement is likely to open up markets in Asia and the West.
- Consumer tastes and their responses have changed. Consumers in many countries are more willing to buy foreign products. Examples might include cars from Korea and Malaysia which are now purchased in Europe. It could also be argued that consumers around the world increasingly have similar tastes. Some food products are sold in many countries with little difference to their ingredients.
- The growth of emerging markets and competition. New markets have opened up in countries that have seen a growth in their national income. Examples might include countries in South East Asia and the more successful former communist countries in Eastern Europe. As businesses in these countries have become more successful, they have been able to compete in Western economies. Figure 32.1 shows the results of a survey from PwC, the

consultants, into the factors thought to be affecting the growth of globalisation.

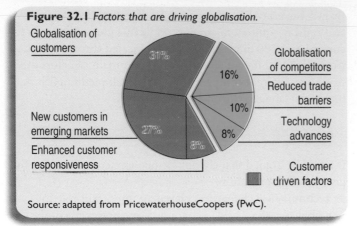

Figure 32.1 *Factors that are driving globalisation.*

Globalisation of customers

31%

Globalisation of competitors 16%

Reduced trade barriers 10%

New customers in emerging markets 27%

Technology advances 8%

Enhanced customer responsiveness

8%

Customer driven factors

Source: adapted from PricewaterhouseCoopers (PwC).

Question 1

Welcome to the global village. While nations may pride themselves on their diversity and sense of identity, the global leisure business is doing its best to ensure that everyone, whether in Europe, Asia, Africa or Australasia is watching and listening to the same product. In short, the world market is dancing to the same pop tune. The first global album chart, compiled for CNN International has, at its top with 20 million units worldwide, James Horner's original soundtrack for Titanic. The global chart - a chart of charts - is compiled using the album charts from 37 countries, weighing the position according to market share. The pan-European chart compiled by Billboard magazine, echoes the global chart with eight of the entries appearing in the top ten of both lists.

Source: adapted from *The Guardian*, 6.6.1998.

(a) Examine the factors that may have led to the globalisation of this market.
(b) Discuss whether the market for CDs is a globalised market.

The effects of globalisation on business

Globalisation has had many effects upon businesses throughout the world. The impact of globalisation has not been evenly spread. Some business, for example those in telecommunications, have witnessed dramatic changes. Others, such as small businesses serving niche markets in localised areas, may have been little affected by globalisation.

There is a number of effects of globalisation upon businesses. Some provide opportunities whilst others present threats.

Competition The impact of globalisation on many larger businesses has been to dramatically increase the level of competition which they face. There is a number of reasons for this.
● Foreign competition has increasingly entered markets

previously served mainly or exclusively by domestic businesses.
● Deregulation has meant that many businesses which previously had little or no competition are now opened up to the forces of global competition. For example, in 1980 British consumers were able to purchase telecommunications services from only one company, BT.
● Globalisation has provided opportunities for new, innovative businesses to enter markets and compete with all comers including well established industry leaders. For example, Microsoft, Intel, Compaq and Dell, all relative newcomers to the computer industry, were able to compete effectively against the market leader IBM. HYPERCOMPETITION has been used to describe competition in the new global economy. This term refers to the disruption of existing markets by flexible, fast moving businesses.

Meeting consumer expectations and tastes Competition by businesses seeking to meet customer needs in increasingly effective ways has raised customer expectations in many markets. Businesses must now meet ever greater consumer demands about quality, service and price. They must also provide the greater choice of products expected by purchasers. The global market has made predicting consumer preferences more difficult. For example, few businesses predicted the huge rise in the popularity of mobile phones or the speed with which consumers would accept the internet.

Economies of scale Businesses able to build a global presence are likely to enjoy a larger scale of operations. This will enable them to spread their fixed costs over a larger volume of output (☞ unit 93) and reduce unit output costs. A larger scale of operations also allows businesses to exercise power over suppliers and benefit from reduced costs. For example, global hotel chains such as Holiday Inn and Marriott are in a position to benefit from volume discounts from catering supply companies.

Choice of location Businesses with a global presence can choose the most advantageous location for each of its operations. When locating its operations, a business may consider:
● reduction of costs. For example, Nike's decision to locate its shoe manufacturing operations in countries such as China and Vietnam was perhaps based on cost reduction factors;
● enhancement of the business's performance. Production and service facilities are located in parts of the world which are likely to improve factors such as product or service quality. For example, Microsoft may have taken this into account when deciding to locate its research laboratories in Cambridge.

Mergers and joint ventures Business are increasingly merging

Question 2

DHL was set up in 1969 to fly shipping documents from San Francisco to Hawaii. The documents arrived ahead of the goods being shipped, reducing customs delays. Today DHL is the world's largest international courier. It is run from a 'global coordination centre' in Brussels and delivers packages to every country there is except North Korea, Iraq and Tunisia. To achieve the $5 billion it forecasts for 1997 DHL employs 53,000 people of many different nationalities spread all around the globe.

One of the challenges faced by DHL is the increasing trend for electronic communication to allow businesses a 'global reach without the need for physical presence'. Documents can now be sent via computer, fax or e-mail without the need to physically transport them. To offset any threat to this area of its business, DHL was seeking to expand into high value 'parts' shipments for the auto, pharmaceutical and medical equipment markets. It was also aiming to develop its own 'logistics' computer system, although it was likely to face competition from post offices, freight forward companies and contract distributors.

Source: adapted from the *Financial Times*, 1.10.1997 and 17.6.1999.

(a) What evidence is there that DHL is a global businesses?
(b) How might changes to the global business environment highlighted in the article be seen as: (i) a threat to DHL; and (ii) an opportunity for DHL?

or joining with others (☞ unit 101), often in other countries, in order to better provide its goods or services to a global market. Both manufactures and retailers are operating on a global basis. A manufacturer, for example, may merge with another in order to make products in the country in which they will be sold. A DIY retailer may merge with a supplier of toilet seats in another country in order to distribute its products more easily to customers in that country.

Multinationals

A MULTINATIONAL company is an organisation which owns or controls production or service facilities outside the country in which it is based. This means that they do not just export their products abroad, but actually own production facilities in other countries.

These companies usually have interests in at least four countries, but there are many which operate in a huge range of countries throughout the world. Examples of multinationals include Ford, British American Tobacco, Volkswagen, Matsui (producers of electrical goods), Unilever, Mobil, Sony and Ciba-Geigy (producers of chemicals). The very largest of the multinationals such as Exxon (which trades as Esso in the UK), General Motors and Royal Dutch Shell are enormous organisations. They have turnovers that are in excess of the GNPs of all but the wealthiest countries.

Question 3

Unilever is an Anglo-Dutch business formed in 1930. It is one of the world's largest producers of consumer goods and is known for its branded food and drinks, detergents and personal products. Such brands include Birds Eye Wall's, Surf, Vaseline, Mentadent, Magnum, Flora and Brooke Bond. Unilever employs around 265,000 people worldwide.

Business Overview

We sell our products and services in 150 countries. Our portfolio includes some of the world's most famous brands: some are sold around the world, such as Dove, Organics and Magnum, others are tailored to meet the needs of different regions or countries.

Our largest markets are Europe and North America. We also invest heavily in promising emerging and developing markets and have identified five priority regions. These are Central and Eastern Europe, China, India, South East Asia and Latin America.

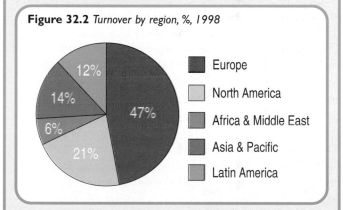

Figure 32.2 *Turnover by region, %, 1998*

- Europe 47%
- North America 21%
- Africa & Middle East 6%
- Asia & Pacific 14%
- Latin America 12%

Operating profits improved in most European markets. France advanced in oil and dairy based foods and personal care. Italy achieved good results in ice cream and personal care, and the United Kingdom did well in culinary, beverages and frozen foods. The results in Germany and Sweden fell because of lower ice cream sales.

Given the difficult circumstances caused by Russia's economic crisis, we delivered creditable results in this priority region. Sales rose 4% and underlying volumes by 5%. Profits overall were slightly ahead of 1997 and we were able to maintain operating margins.

Source: adapted from Unilever, *Annual Report and Accounts*, 1998.

(a) Using examples from the data, explain why Unilever might be described as a multinational.
(b) Expalin why the company may have become a multinational.

There is a number of reasons why firms become multinationals.

- To avoid protectionist policies. By actually producing within a particular country, a firm can usually avoid any tariffs or quotas which that country may impose. This is why Japanese car firms, such as Nissan, Toyota and Honda, have established themselves within EU countries in recent years.
- The globalisation of markets. National boundaries, many believe, are becoming irrelevant for firms as instant communications and high speed travel make the world seem smaller. This is sometimes referred to as the 'global village'. Multinationals, which are global or international in outlook, are the ideal type of business organisation to take advantage of this situation.

The influence of multinationals

There is great debate as to the actual effects of multinationals. Whilst there are clear benefits of multinationals operating in a particular country, there are also a number of problems associated with them.

The balance of payments and employment One benefit of multinationals is their ability to create jobs. This, along with the manufacturing capacity which they create, can increase the GNP of countries and add to the standard of living. As well as this, multinationals benefit the balance of payments of a country if their products are sold abroad. The setting-up of a car manufacturing plant by Toyota in Derby helps to illustrate this. Not only has this plant created jobs, but it has raised the GNP of the UK. The balance of payments has also been helped as a large proportion of the Derby plant's cars are shipped out to other EU nations.

However, whilst multinationals can create jobs, they are also capable of causing unemployment for two reasons. First, they create competition for domestic firms. This may be beneficial, causing local firms to improve their efficiency, but it can also be a problem if it results in these firms cutting their labour force or closing down plants. Second, multinationals often shift production facilities from one country to another in order to further their own ends. The effect of this is that jobs are lost and production is either reduced or completely stopped.

In addition, multinationals can have a negative impact upon the balance of payments. This is because many of them receive huge amounts of components from their branches abroad, thus adding to the total quantity of imports.

Technology and expertise Multinationals may introduce new

technology, production processes and management styles and techniques. This has been one of the benefits to Western countries of Japanese multinationals. Techniques such as just-in-time stock control (☞ unit 94) and management methods such as quality control circles (☞ unit 91) have been successfully used by Japanese firms in foreign countries. Such techniques have also been adopted by home based firms. These raise the standards of local firms who become aware of these new developments. The process by which multinationals benefit countries in this respect is known as **technology transfer.**

Technology transfer can be especially important to developing countries, which may lack technical expertise and know-how. However, this is not always the case. Managers and supervisors are often brought in from the multinationals' home country, with little training being given to locally recruited staff. As a consequence locals may be employed in low skilled jobs.

Social responsibility Multinationals have often been criticised, especially in their dealings with low income economies. The Union Carbide disaster in Bhopal, India, when hundreds were killed by the release of poisonous gases into the atmosphere, raised serious doubts about the safety measures used by multinationals in low income economies.

They have also been accused of marketing harmful products. One example was the aggressive selling of milk powder to mothers with new born babies when medical research indicated that breast feeding is far more likely to benefit infant health. In addition, environmentalists are concerned about the impact of multinationals on tropical rainforests and other natural resources. On the other hand, large multinationals are in a better position to finance projects that protect the environment from their activities. They also tend to offer better pay than local firms in developing economies.

Government control Because of the size and financial power of many multinationals, there are concerns about the ability of governments to control them. For example, they may be able to avoid paying corporation tax in particular countries.

Taxation can be avoided by the use of TRANSFER PRICING. This involves declaring higher profits in those countries with lower taxation levels, thus reducing the overall tax bill. A company may charge subsidiary branches in low taxation countries low prices for components bought in from overseas branches of the same firm. This means that costs in the low tax country are kept low and high profits can be declared. Similarly, subsidiary branches in high tax countries are charged high prices for components bought in from overseas branches. This means little or no profit is recorded.

Question 4

Figure 32.3 *Capital flows to developing countries*

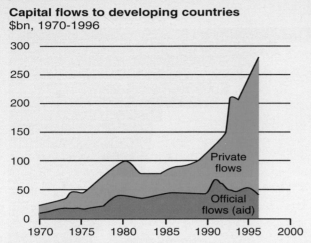

Capital flows to developing countries
$bn, 1970-1996

Private flows

Official flows (aid)

Source: adapted from World Bank.

Are multinationals the big, bad, exploitative businesses they are made out to be or not? It has been argued that given the crises in Mexico and Asia in the late 1990s, too much foreign investment is not a bad thing. *The State of the World 1998* publication by the WorldWatch Institute in Washington said that if a Multilateral Agreement on Investment (MAI) negotiated by the OECD in 1999 went through, it would: 'constrain the ability of countries to put in place policies that would minimise the environmental damage and social disruption of foreign investment projects'. The agreement was designed to set in place common legally binding rules that applied to national and multinational businesses equally, which would reduce government regulation and control of foreign investors. An OECD spokesperson said that the agreement was not: 'a carte blanche for multinationals to pollute the planet', but an agreement to make foreign investment easier.

Source: adapted from *The Independent*, 22.1.1998.

(a) Using evidence from the article, evaluate the impact of multinationals on developing economies.

Summary

1. What is meant by a global market?
2. State 3 important aspects of globalisation.
3. Suggest 5 factors which have contributed to the growth of globalisation.
4. How might globalisation affect the location of a business?
5. Why might globalisation increase competition for businesses?
6. For what reasons do firms become multinationals?
7. What are the potential benefits of multinationals?
8. What problems might be created by multinationals?

Case study

Coca-Cola

In English-speaking countries, the C on the kitchen tap stands for cold water and the H for hot. But Coca-Cola boss Roberto Goizueta used to say he would never rest until the C stood for Coke. It was estimated in the late 1990s that Coca-Cola had around 50 per cent of the world's soft drinks market.

Douglas Ivester was appointed as Mr Goizueta's successor, in 1997. But few industry observers expected other than evolutionary changes to a marketing strategy that has proved as successful as Coca-Cola's. That strategy rests on the unshakeable belief that there is no such thing as a mature market or, to put it another way, that the world offers a virtually infinite opportunity for growth.

The average person requires an intake of 64 ounces of liquid per day, but around the world Coca-Cola supplies less than 2 ounces per person per day. 'We remain resolutely focussed on going after the other 62', Mr Goizueta said.

For Mr Goizueta, it was irrelevant that Coca-Cola already had nearly half the world's soft drink market. Instead, he said, Coca-Cola was focussed on expanding its share of every human beings liquid intake. 'In some cases, that means taking on other international soft drink companies. In other cases, indigenous beverages are our biggest contenders. When it comes to availability, however, only one beverage is our true rival: tap water.'

In pursuing Mr Goizueta's ambition of replacing water with Coca-Cola, Mr Ivester starts with the advantage that the company's biggest-selling product seems to have almost universal appeal. In spite of worries that Coke would not be accepted in societies with strongly entrenched preferences for other drinks, it out-sells the leading tea in Britain, the leading bottled water in France, and the leading coffee in Brazil.

After 111 years of advertising, it also boasts the advantages of being the world's best-known brand name and the world's best known expression after 'okay'.

Name recognition, Coca-Cola says, gives the company the opportunity to make its case, but it is down to the company itself to make that case relevant and compelling. Years ago, advertising might have been seen as the best way to achieve that objective. Indeed, in 1971, Coca-Cola came up with one of the most memorable commercials ever made when it put a multi-ethnic crowd of 200 youngsters on a hilltop in Italy and conducted them in a rendition of 'I'd like to teach the world to sing.'

The advertisement succeeded in emphasising the global appeal of Coca-Cola, and gave a lot of people a sentimental glow. But Mr Goizueta grumbled that it never sold much Coke. When he became Chairman and Chief Executive in 1961 he put more emphasis on distribution. He wanted Coke to be put at 'arm's reach of desire'.

Coca-Cola's distribution machine is probably the most powerful and pervasive on the planet. Its bottling partners - the companies that buy soft drink concentrate from Coca-Cola and mix it with water before bottling or canning it for local markets - deploy a fleet of more than 180,000 delivery vehicles and service more than 6.6m vending machines, coolers and dispensers.

Coca-Cola further strengthened distribution by buying its smaller bottlers and invested in them to get them into better shape. It then sold them to bigger and more powerful 'anchor' bottlers set up on a regional basis. These anchor bottlers have the management and financial resources to match Coca-Cola's growth targets.

A sign of Coca-Cola's aggressiveness has been its attempts to shove other companies aside. It tried to push Cadbury Schweppes' drinks out of thousands of McDonald's fast-food outlets in the US by offering McDonald's franchisees gifts of up to 600 gallons of free soft-drink syrup if they would only serve Coca-Cola products in their restaurants.

The advertising has changed, too. The problem with single-theme advertising, the company decided, was that by talking to everyone at once, it reached nobody very effectively. So

Figure 32.4 *Coca-Cola per capita consumption, servings of company beverages per person, per year*

Coca-Cola per capita consumption*

363	US
332	Mexico
308	Australia
291	Chile
266	Norway
253	Israel
201	Germany
187	Argentina
184	Canada
181	Spain
177	Benelux/Denmark
153	Hungary
149	South Africa
144	Japan
131	Brazil
117	Philippines
115	Colombia
114	UK
82	Italy
74	France

*Servings of company beverages per person per year, excludes products distribution by The Minute Maid Company

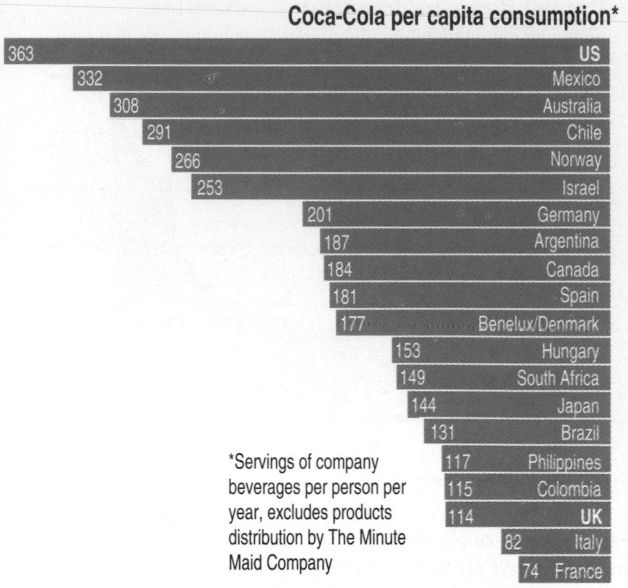

Source: adapted from Coca-Cola, *Annual Report and Accounts*.

four years ago Coca-Cola replaced single-theme advertising with the 'Always Coca-Cola' campaign, the most notable feature of which is its sheer diversity. It comprises a portfolio of commercials aimed at different audiences, from teenagers to pensioners.

There has also been a bigger emphasis on other aspects of marketing. Coca-Cola has been differentiating Coke from other colas by trading on its famous 'contour' bottle trademark, achieving surprisingly large increases in sales by using the shape for its plastic Coca-Cola bottles. It is now looking for new ways to exploit its powerful association with the colour red and its famous logo.

Source: adapted from the *Financial Times*, 1997.

(a) **Why might Coca-Cola be described as a multinational business?**

(b) **Explain why Coca-Cola might benefit from operating globally.**

(c) **Examine the possible threats that globalisation might pose for Coca-Cola.**

(d) **Examine the reasons why Coca-Cola might operate on a global basis.**

(e) **Discuss the implications for a new entrant to the cola market, such as Virgin Cola, attempting to compete with Coca-Cola on a global scale.**

33 Business Ethics

What are business ethics?

Ethics are a set of values and beliefs which influence how individuals, groups and society behave (☞ unit 27). BUSINESS ETHICS are concerned with how such values and beliefs operate in business. They help firms to decide what actions are right or wrong in certain circumstances. Ethics might influence the following business decisions.

● Should products which might damage the health of consumers be withdrawn from the market?
● What efforts, if any, should be made to ensure that business activities do not damage the environment?
● Should money be spent on wheelchair access to workplaces and retail outlets?
● Should a firm reject a bribe given to secure an overseas contract?
● Should part time staff be offered the same employment rights as full time staff?
● Should a workplace creche be provided for working mothers?
● Should a contribution be made to a local charity?

A business that says 'yes' to some or all of these questions might be described as ethical. A firm which is ethical with regard to society as a whole and the community within which it is based might also be described as 'socially responsible'. **Corporate responsibility** (☞ unit 34) is the term used to describe attempts by individual businesses to behave in an ethical manner.

Different individuals and groups have different viewpoints. It is these which can determine what they see as ethical business behaviour. For example, a firm polluting a river might only be able to take action against further pollution through savings made by job losses. What is ethical behaviour in this case - preventing the pollution or saving jobs?

To some extent the law attempts to ensure that businesses act ethically. However, obeying the 'letter' of the law does not necessarily mean that a firm is behaving in an ethical way. For example, some would regard water companies which pump untreated sewerage into the sea as unethical, even if the activity is legal. This is due to the possible pollution and health problems associated with such an activity.

There have been a number of businesses that could be described as acting unethically in the past. Examples which some believe fall into this category include British Airways for the 'dirty tricks' which it allegedly used against its competitor Virgin Airlines and Exxon for the safety standards on its oil tanker Exxon Valdez which sank in Alaskan waters. Other examples may include the large salary increases given to the chief executives of privatised companies, insider share dealing in the City of London, the trade of some businesses with countries that have oppressive regimes, or the trade in arms. Individuals within businesses also act 'unethically'. A well

Question 1

Figure 33.1

YOU GET EXCELLENT COFFEE. YOU DON'T GET COCAINE.

The coffee growers of Latin America face a problem. Either they get paid a fair price for their coffee, or they face bankruptcy and may have to turn their land over to the illegal production of the coca plant for cocaine.

Cafédirect helps avoid this problem, because more of the money you pay for Cafédirect roast and ground coffee goes directly to the growers.

The result? They continue to produce high quality Arabica coffee for Cafédirect.

Cafédirect. Fair trade. Excellent coffee.

(a) Would you describe the above as ethical behaviour? Explain your answer.
(b) Why might the: (i) owners and (ii) customers of Cafédirect be concerned about Latin American coffee workers?

publicised example is the behaviour of Robert Maxwell, former owner of Maxwell Communications

Corporation. After his death, it was found that he had been supporting his business empire with money 'borrowed' from his employees' pension fund.

The ethical behaviour of businesses is, to some extent, controlled by laws and regulation. Increasingly, however, businesses and industries are placing greater emphasis on developing their own codes of conduct and practice. For example, the Chemical Industries Association has a Responsible Care programme which includes the requirement that individual chemical businesses must be open about giving relevant information to interested parties. They must also work closely with local communities in achieving required levels of performance. In the late 1990s PepsiCo stopped selling Pepsi in Burma, a country with a history of human rights abuse. Previously, Apple and Kodak had stopped selling products to the country.

The benefits of ethical behaviour

There are certain advantages for businesses in behaving in an ethical or socially responsible way.

Consumers' views Increasing numbers of consumers are taking into account a firm's 'behaviour' when buying products. As a result, ethical behaviour can be good for sales. Body Shop is a good example of this. A feature of Body Shop's marketing is that its products are not tested on animals. The company has also lent support to groups helping firms in the world's poorest countries. This stance has perhaps helped Body Shop become a successful business. There is a number of other firms which have responded in a similar way. The Co-operative Bank, for example, has conducted a wide ranging campaign. It refuses to invest money in or finance a variety of concerns. These range from countries with poor human rights records to companies using exploitative factory farming methods. This policy was introduced as a result of a survey carried out amongst the bank's customers, which found that they regarded a clear ethical policy as important for the bank.

Improvements in the recruitment and retention of staff Firms with an ethical approach believe that they will be more able to recruit well qualified and motivated staff. In addition, ethical firms argue that they are able to retain their staff better if they adopt a more caring approach to employees. Polaroid

Question 2

Industry exposure

Investments considered appropriate will typically have interests in one or more of the following areas:

Air quality/emissions control	Pollution analysis
Drinking water purification	Recycling
Energy conservation	Site remediation
Environmental assessment	Waste reduction/disposal
Geothermal energy	Wastewater treatment
Natural gas	Wind power

Share Selection Criteria

The fund manager will seek to avoid companies which are involved in:
1 The production, sale or distribution of fur products.
2 The production, sale or distribution of cosmetics where animal testing may be involved.
3 The manufacture of ozone depleting chemicals (CFCs and halons).

4 The manufacture or distribution of harmful pesticides.
5 The supply of tropical hardwood.
6 The production, processing or sale of meat products.
Other types of company, which would normally be ineligible for an ethical portfolio, will also be avoided as they are inconsistent with Evergreen's objectives. These are companies which are involved in:
7 The manufacture or provision of armaments.
8 Companies involved in repressive regimes to a total extent of no more than 10% of group turnover. For this purpose 'repressive regimes' are those listed by the Ethical Investment Research Service (EIRIS).
9 The provision of gambling services.
10 The production of tobacco products.
11 The production or distribution of pornography.

Source: Clerical Medical, Evergreen Trust Investment information.

In 1998 The Body Shop planned a new marketing campaign to make women feel more comfortable with themselves, irrespective of size or age. It refused to portray the images of perfection used by competitors, but went for the anti-sell of realism. From July posters appeared in Body Shop windows saying: 'There are 3 billion women who don't look like super-models and only 8 who do'. Anita Roddick, founder of the company said: 'We do not lie to women. We try to expose the stereotypes that make so many women feel they'd be better off shutting up, going on a diet and having a facelift'. The company magazine also advertised: 'The Body Shop products

won't change your life. They won't make you more popular. Does this help to sell our moisturisers? Probably not. We want to change how you feel about the way you look. If we can help you feel good, then we have given you something you can't buy - a sample of self-esteem'. The company was trying to get women to break out of the stereotypes. Whether the campaign would change women's views or not, Alexander Shulman, editor of *Vogue* and Wendie Stone, from advertising agency TBWA GGT Simons Palmer, said it was good publicity.

Source: adapted from The *Times*, 10.7.1998.

(a) Why might these companies be said to be acting in an ethical manner?

(b) Using information above discuss the benefits to these businesses of an ethical stance.

in the US, for example has, subsidised child-care expenses for their lower paid workers. Marks and Spencer provide their staff with a range of benefits, over and above those usually provided in the retail sector. They have benefited by achieving one of the lowest rates of staff turnover in the UK. This has cut their recruitment and retraining costs.

Improvements in employee motivation Firms which behave in an ethical manner believe that their employees are more committed to their success as a result. They may be prepared to work harder to allow the business to achieve its aims.

Effects of ethical behaviour

What effect will acting in an ethical way have on a business?

Increasing costs Ethical behaviour can result in an increase in costs for a firm. An ethical firm may, for example, be forced to turn down cheaper supplies from a firm which tests its products on animals. Similarly, costs may be raised by pollution-reducing filters put on coal-fired power stations.

Loss of profit Firms may be forced to turn down profitable business due to their ethical stance. A business, for example, may reject a profitable investment opportunity in a company which produces animal fur, as this is against its ethical policy. However, the ethical firm would hope that the gains it makes from its policy, by attracting increased numbers of customers, would outweigh these costs.

Conflict When a firm's overall profitability comes into conflict with its ethical policy, problems may result. In such cases the shareholders of a firm may object to the ethical policy as the return on their investment is harmed.

Business practice A firm seeking to act more ethically may need to alter the way in which it approaches a huge range of business matters. Such a firm might, for example, need to consider the impact of its activities on the environment (☞ unit 35), whether or not its recruitment policy was providing equal opportunities for all applicants regardless of age, sex, ethnic background or disability (☞ unit 80), the extent to which its advertisements are offensive or in poor taste, and the protection given to consumers buying their products (☞ unit 22).

Relations with suppliers Some suppliers will only supply products to businesses that meet ethical criteria. This might include agreeing not to trade with certain countries or businesses that deal in arms, that exploit workers or that abuse human rights.

Question 3

In the late 1990s Littlewoods, the retail group, was embarking on a programme to impose ethical practices on all its international suppliers. The aim of the policy was to make ethical standards as important an element in awarding new contracts as the traditional requirements of technical standards, quantities and production.

Equal opportunities measures are now a requirement for all new contracts awarded by Littlewoods in the UK. Contractors must ensure that sub-contractors fulfil the same criteria. As Surinder Sharma, Littlewood's corporate equal opportunities manager, said: 'We ask contractors, "Do you have an equal opportunities policy and do you have any industrial tribunal cases against you?" and ask them to explain if they do. It's part of our values, just like health and safety'.

Littlewoods concedes that the situation with overseas suppliers is more complicated. However, it plans to train hundreds of buyers to carry out inspections of overseas suppliers.

James Ross, Littlewood's chairperson, won a silver award in the Campaign for Racial Equality leadership section. The business has also established a reputation for a comprehensive package of good practice measures. These include generous maternity leave, bereavement leave, mosque facilities, prayer rooms and company publications in a range of languages.

Source: adapted from *People Management*, 26.11.1998.

(a) Identify the elements of Littlewood's ethical behaviour using examples from the article.
(b) Why might the company have extended its ethical code to sub-contractors?
(c) Explain the effects of Littlewood's ethical stance on:
(i) the company itself;
(ii) suppliers.

Should businesses be expected to act ethically?

There is considerable debate about how businesses should actually behave.

Some argue that businesses have a responsibility to act ethically. Those who hold this view stress the fact that firms do not operate in isolation. They are a part of society and have an impact upon the lives of those communities in which they operate. As such they should act in a responsible manner and consider the possible effects of any decisions they make. This means that profit making should not be the only criterion used when making decisions. Other factors which firms might consider include the effect of their decisions upon the environment, jobs, the local community, consumers, competitors, suppliers and employees.

Others argue that businesses should not be expected to act ethically. There are two main views in support of this argument. The first is from supporters of free market economics (☞ unit 28). They argue that the primary responsibility of businesses is to produce goods and services in the most efficient way, and make profit for shareholders. Firms should attempt to do this in any way they can, providing it is legal. Only by doing this will the general good of everyone be served. If firms are expected to act 'ethically', then consumers may suffer because the ethical behaviour could lead to inefficiency, higher costs and higher prices.

A second argument is that in most cases it is naive to expect businesses to act ethically. Whenever there is a conflict between acting ethically and making greater profits, the vast majority of firms will choose the latter. Those firms which do act in an ethical manner only do so because it is profitable. This view is often held by those who favour government intervention to regulate business. They argue that it is necessary for the government to force firms to behave responsibly through a variety of laws which it must enforce.

Are businesses becoming more ethical?

It could be said that the late 1980s and 1990s have seen a move towards a more 'caring' attitude by businesses. The growth of companies producing health care products which are not animal tested, the use of recyclable carrier bags and the sale of organically grown vegetables by many retailers could all be an indication of this. Some pension funds and a number of investment schemes are now termed 'green'. They will only invest savers' money in companies which promote the environment.

Others argue that ethical attitudes have failed to penetrate the boardrooms of the UK and that firms continue to act unethically in a variety of ways. An extensive survey undertaken by the University of Westminster found that junior executives and women took the moral 'high ground', with more concern about green issues, staff relations and trade with countries that had records of abusing human rights. This was in contrast to the greed driven motives of company directors, the majority of whom were old and male. One respondent summed up the climate. 'In general, business ethics does not come very high in the scale of human behaviour. Professional standards and levels of caring sometimes leave a lot to be desired.'

One explanation for the findings of the survey is that

business culture (☞ unit 14) continues to be driven by short term profit. This suggests that the stakeholders, such as shareholders and directors, hold most influence in setting the objectives of the business. These groups tend to be most interested in the profit of the business.

Question 4

Mr Richard Branson and his Virgin Atlantic airline won near record libel damages of £610,000 at the end of a two year 'dirty tricks' legal battle against British Airways. In charging BA with going 'beyond the limits of commercially acceptable practice', Mr Branson listed details of its rival's campaign to discredit Virgin. These included:
- the illegal use of Virgin Atlantic computer information;
- the poaching of Virgin passengers by bogus Virgin representatives;
- the shredding of documents relating to Virgin activities;
- the spreading of hostile and discreditable stories to destabilise Virgin.

BA, which also had to meet several million pounds in legal costs, apologised 'unreservedly' to Mr Branson in court for alleging that Virgin Atlantic, in claiming BA was conducting a 'dirty tricks' campaign, was only seeking publicity.

Sir Colin Marshall, BA's chief executive and deputy chairman, said his airline was taking steps to ensure 'regrettable incidents' undertaken by BA employees did nor occur again.

In a special message to BA staff intended to bolster morale, Sir Colin said the 'overwhelming majority' of the airline's workforce had no involvement whatsoever in the campaign against Virgin. He urged them not to be distracted by the publicity surrounding the affair.

Mr Branson also demanded BA directors give a full explanation of a separate covert activity targeted at Virgin which, he alleged, was carried out by private investigators.

Source: adapted from the *Financial Times*.

(a) What elements of BA's behaviour could be termed
  (i) illegal;
  (ii) unethical?
(b) What evidence is there to suggest that this was the action of individuals rather than a corporate policy?
(c) Which view about the behaviour of the firms would BA's actions lend support to? Explain your answer.

Key terms

Business ethics - the influence of values and beliefs upon the conduct and operation of businesses.

Summary

1. Give 5 examples which might indicate a business is behaving ethically.
2. Give 5 examples which might indicate a business is behaving unethically.
3. Why might firms draw up a code of ethics?

4. Briefly explain 5 effects that ethical behaviour may have on businesses.
5. 'Businesses should not be expected to act ethically.' Explain the 2 sides to this argument.

Case study

Are businesses becoming more ethical?

A 1996 Nestlé advertisement made claims about its responsible involvement in the developing world. But in 1999 the Advertising Standards Authority claimed Nestlé had disregarded a World Health Organisation (WHO) code of practice which restricted the use of manufactured formula baby milk and its marketing because of fears over diarrhoea in babies as a result of unhygienic bottle feeding. Nestlé had supported the code since 1984. It argued that the advertisement was an isolated incident and that it was determined to comply with the code.

Many companies are striving to show corporate responsibility. Greenpeace, the environmental and ethical pressure group, is prepared to work with Tesco on sourcing products that do not contain genetically modified ingredients, for example. In 1999 it also launched a range of environmentally friendly fridges with Iceland. Peter Melchett, Director of Greenpeace, praised the food manufacturers and retailers that had come out against genetically modified foods. He argued that the about turn

from some companies was because of the harm to their reputation, staff morale and customers' perceptions. He said: 'it's not quite as simple as: "sales fall, so change policy". It is reputation as much as sales that people start to worry about.'

Mr Melchett argued that many of the big companies were making progress, but some were still in the firing line. The World Development Movement (WDM) in 1999, for example, attacked multinationals on a range of issues, including targeting children with cigarettes. The common thread was the need to protect the poor in developing countries and the belief that this should be the job of governments. Barry Coates, WDM director, said: 'Some leading companies are doing good things. But the fear is that they are undercut by less scrupulous ones unless there is regulation'.

Source: adapted from *The Guardian*, 12.5.1999.

(a) Give examples of what might be described as: (i) unethical; and (ii) ethical behaviour; mentioned in the article.
(b) Explain what is meant by the phrase: 'sales fall, so change policy'.
(c) Using information from the article, explain the possible effects of following ethical practices on businesses.
(d) Why might the WDM be particularly concerned about the ethical behaviour of businesses in developing countries?
(e) Evaluate the extent to which businesses are becoming more ethical, using information in the article.

Business responsibility

Unit 27 explained that the influence of stakeholders has led many businesses to take into account the effect of their activities on others. A business that accepts CORPORATE RESPONSIBILITY will be prepared to be responsible for and to justify its actions. It will also consider the impact of its actions on a variety of individuals and groups, both inside and outside the organisation.

For example, a mobile phone business will aim to provide as wide a coverage as possible for its customers. However, in order to do so it is likely to have to erect masts in the places that give the best reception. Masts tend to be fairly ugly and may disrupt the environment in which they are placed. If the business accepts this and is prepared to pay for innovative designs that blend in with the environment then it could be said to be accepting corporate responsibility. In 1997 Orange, the mobile phone company, for example, introduced tree shaped transmitters which blended in with the surrounding area and were also comfortable enough for squirrels to live in.

Methods of encouraging corporate responsibility

There is a number of ways in which businesses can be encouraged to accept corporate responsibility.

Government intervention Governments can intervene directly to ensure that a business accepts the consequences of its behaviour. One of the most common methods of achieving this is through the creation of legislation which businesses must adhere to. For example, in Germany all retailers and manufacturers are required to recycle 80 per cent of their packaging. Although legislation can control the behaviour of businesses and the creation of negative externalities (☞ unit 35), there are some problems with this method of control. First, businesses can obey the 'letter of the law' rather than the 'spirit of the law'. This might mean, for example, a business adopting practices which are legal, but which do not greatly reduce negative externalities. Second, legislation which only applies within national boundaries may not affect businesses in other countries. For example, legislation governing the behaviour of the UK or EU nuclear industry would have had no impact on the Chernobyl disaster in the former Soviet Union. This led to radioactive materials being deposited in the UK and other Western European countries.

Self-regulation Governments can work with particular industries and business sectors to encourage the creation of regulatory bodies which help to control the activities of business. These tend to be voluntary organisations which aim to monitor the behaviour of relevant firms. The Press Complaints Authority and The Advertising Standards Authority are examples of such organisations. The Press Complaints Authority aims to encourage newspapers and other media organisations to act in a responsible way. Governments can help such organisations to control businesses by threatening legislation if the self-regulatory bodies are not seen to be working.

Market pressures Some commentators believe that there is no need for governments to exert direct pressures on businesses to act responsibly. This is because the free market will act effectively to police less responsible businesses. The argument is that such businesses will be unpopular with consumers, who will be less likely to purchase their products. Thus consumer behaviour will force irresponsible businesses to act with greater accountability. Businesses which refuse to act responsibly will fail. This is only likely to be the case, however, if consumers have information about the behaviour of businesses. Without sufficient information, consumers will be unable to make judgments about the levels of corporate responsibility of companies. For this reason, some firms have

Question 1

In 1997 Marks & Spencer announced that it had negotiated supplies of free range eggs for all its British stores. Does this show that the consumer is king? Perhaps, but only if power is focussed and widespread. Few shoppers are concerned enough about issues to go out of their way or are prepared to pay more, for ethical products. Furthermore, supermarkets have only slowly responded to concerns about animal welfare, food purity and healthy eating because they see the prospect of selling profitable products, often at premium prices.

It has been argued that Marks & Spencer in the past has resisted external pressure from campaigners. However, it aimed to introduce a scheme to end the use of tethering for pigs and caging of animals. A spokesperson said that the changes were nothing to do with pressure group influence but: 'Our goal is to supply the safest quality goods on the high street. We aim to ensure that all animals and animal products operate to the highest standards of welfare'. However, the company suggested that pressure groups did have some role to play, by making businesses aware of situations that need to be addressed.

Source: adapted from *The Guardian*, 1.10.1997.

(a) Identify the factors that may have influenced the decision of Marks & Spencer to change its policy on supplier conditions.
(b) Evaluate the extent to which these factors are likely to have influenced its decision.

tried to make more information about their activities available to the public. The EU has introduced an Eco-Label system which identifies products which have had the least negative impact upon the environment.

Pressure groups Pressure groups can sometimes affect businesses. Unit 27 explained the ways that pressure groups are able to exert influence over firms. In recent years, certain groups have had notable successes. For example, animal welfare pressure groups have encouraged cosmetics businesses not to test their products on animals. The campaign of some pressure groups for a complete ban on animal testing continues, however. Some pressure groups, frustrated in their attempts to change corporate behaviour, have called for greater democracy in the corporate decision making process. This would involve stakeholders (☞ unit 27) being involved as a matter of routine in decisions that have a direct effect upon them.

Barriers to corporate responsibility

There is a number of incentives for businesses to behave in a responsible manner. They might attract more customers as a result of their stance or avoid penalties from legislation. However, there are certain reasons why businesses may fail to act in a responsible manner.

Costs and profit Responsible behaviour can raise the costs of businesses. Some businesses may consider that the costs of accepting corporate responsibility are too great. For example, a business which uses the cheapest overseas contractors, regardless of how it treated its workforce, may find that it is able to achieve lower production costs. This could enable the business to price its product more competitively than rival products and possibly make higher profits. Similarly, a local garage may find it cheaper to dispose of engine oil in a local stream than to pay for it to be disposed of in an environmentally friendly manner.

Values and beliefs The values and beliefs of the senior managers and employees of a business may not correspond with what the majority of others in a society regard as responsible. For example, a public house or bar which continued to serve alcoholic drinks to a drunken customer may be regarded as irresponsible. However, the manager or employee of the business may regard this as the concern of the customer and a matter in which he should not become involved. This view may lead him to continue serving alcoholic drinks to the customer. In this case the business is not accepting the responsibility of possible problems that the customer may have, nor the potential danger to others as a result.

Information available to consumers, governments and pressure groups In the absence of useful information about the behaviour of a business it is difficult for interested parties to monitor its activities. For example, the nuclear industry has been accused by pressure groups of being secretive about its activities. Nuclear industry representatives have argued that this is due to defence and national security reasons. However, this secrecy has made it difficult for consumers and pressure groups to make judgments about its behaviour. For other businesses it is the complexity and scope of their activities that makes it difficult to evaluate their actions. Multinationals, in particular, because of their global activities, can be very difficult to monitor. Other businesses are involved in such technically complex work that it can be difficult for consumers, governments and pressure groups to understand issues relevant to their behaviour. Businesses involved in genetic modification may fall into this category.

Question 2

Nike, in the past, had faced criticism for its policy of sub-contracting the manufacture of sports shoes to overseas contractors in low income countries. Complaints of worker mistreatment centred on factories in Indonesia some of whom:
● provided unacceptable working conditions for local employees;
● demanded excessive working hours of employees;
● failed to pay the local minimum wage.
  Nike initially dismissed criticism of its record. One company representative remarked: 'I don't know that we need to know'. However, after further investigation the Chairman and Chief Executive of Nike announced that the company would sever ties with three Indonesian contractors that manufactured its shoes.

Source: adapted from the *Financial Times*, 'Mastering Global Business', Part 9, 1997.

(a) Analyse why Nike may not have initially severed its ties with its contractors.

Social auditing

A business that produces its final accounts must have them **audited** by law (☞ unit 62). An audit is a check to make sure the financial performance of the business, shown in its accounts, are accurate.

SOCIAL AUDITING is the process by which a business organisation attempts to assess the impact of the entire range of its activities on stakeholders. It might try to produce a set of 'social accounts' to evaluate its performance against a set of non-financial criteria. This might include its effect on the environment and its attempts to meet social obligations to employees. Social auditing may involve:

- identifying the social objectives and ethical values of the organisation;
- defining the stakeholders of the business;
- establishing social performance indicators;
- measuring performance, keeping records and preparing social accounts;
- submitting the accounts to an independent audit and publishing the results.

The social audit might include details such as:
- the salary difference between the highest and lowest paid employee;
- health and safety information;
- the extent to which employees feel valued;
- the views of consumers about whether the business is living up to its ideals.

The benefits of social auditing

Increasingly businesses are carrying out their own social audit. Some publish the results in their Annual Report and Accounts. Businesses as wide ranging as The Co-operative Bank, Ben & Jerry's, the US ice cream manufacturer, and St Lukes, the ethical advertising agency, have carried out social audits. Why might they be seen as useful?
- They provide valuable information to pressure groups and consumers about the corporate responsibility of a business. Consumers can take account of this information, often issued through press reports, when making purchasing decisions. Pressure groups can use them as the basis for further enquiries.
- They allow the managers of a business to gain a complete picture of the impact of the business's activities. Especially in large businesses, managers may be unaware of some practices which they would regard as undesirable. This can allow the business to make better informed decisions about the impact of its activities upon stakeholders.
- A business can use a social audit as a means of preventing future criticism of its activities. By opening up its activities to scrutiny a business can deflect suspicions which some stakeholders may have about less than responsible behaviour. The use of an independent social audit is especially valuable. There can be a lack of credibility associated with social audits which are generated from within the business itself. It is also important that a business commits itself to full publication of an independent social audit. Edited versions are unlikely to persuade more critical stakeholders.
- A business will be able to identify the extent to which it is meeting some of its non-financial objectives. For example, a social audit may indicate a growing agreement with the corporate culture of the business (☞ unit 14).
- Shareholders can use social audits to raise questions about a business's activities at annual shareholder meetings.
- Governments can use social audits of a range of businesses in a particular industry as one means of assessing the need

for legislation or regulation of businesses in the industry.

As businesses are subjected to increasing levels of scrutiny and as consumers and pressure groups have access to more information about business behaviour, it is likely that an increasing number of businesses will use social audits.

Question 3

The Body Shop introduced a 'values report' in 1996. This provided what the company believed to be an independently verified audit of its activities in the areas of the environment, human relations and animal protection. The report was put together using a number of attitude surveys among customers, suppliers, employees, franchisees and shareholders. 'At a time when lots of people are talking about the stakeholder economy, this is a way of identifying how a company acts upon its own stakeholders and using the information to improve the company,' said D. Wheeler, manager of the Body Shop ethical audit department.

Source: adapted from *The Business Environment*, I. Worthington and C. Britton, Pitman.

(a) Why might the Body Shop's 'values report' be an example of a social audit?
(b) How might the Body Shop benefit from its 'values report'?
(c) Comment on the extent of the usefulness of the report.

Summary

1. Give an example of a business acting with corporate responsibility.
2. State 4 ways in which corporate responsibility may be encouraged.
3. Why might legislation to control companies be a problem?
4. State 3 possible barriers to corporate responsibility.
5. What might be involved in social auditing for a business?
6. What details might be included in a social audit?
7. How might a business benefit from a social audit?
8. How might other stakeholders benefit from a social audit?

Key terms

Corporate responsibility - the willingness of a business to accept responsibility for its actions and their impact on a range of stakeholders.
Social auditing - the process by which a business evaluates the effect of its activities on all of its stakeholders.

Case study

The Co-operative Bank

In 1997 the Co-operative Bank, famed for its ethical stance, issued a new challenge, stating its customers were sick of increasing profits of UK businesses. Highlighting industrial problems at other businesses, it said that its research showed that companies should recognise the crucial importance of their workforce. The chief executive at the time, Terry Thomas, said that: 'Aggressive treatment of staff sends out a negative message to consumers. It says this company is more concerned about profits and keeping its shareholders happy than its staff and customers who actually create profit potential in the first place'. The information came from research by the bank, which was the first stage in its attempt to publish a social audit which would assess the performance of the bank against a number of criteria. The information below shows the results of the research. Percentage figures indicate the support for each area from customers.

Our Ethical Policy

It's our customers' money, so we asked for their views on how it should and shouldn't be invested. To make it easy for you to see how opinions have been taken into account, we've indicated the changes to our Ethical Policy and shown how much support each received from our customers.

Human Rights

We will not invest in or provide financial services to:

- 96% any regime or organisation which oppresses the human spirit or takes away the rights of the individual
- 96% manufacturers of torture equipment or other equipment that is used in the violation of human rights

Armaments

We will not invest in or provide financial services to any business involved in the:

- 94% manufacture
- 94% sale
- 95% licensed production
- 95% brokerage of armaments to any country which has oppressive regime

Trade and Social Involvement

We will seek to support and encourage:

- 95% the business of organisations which promote the concept of fair trade
- 93% business customers and suppliers to take a pro-active stance on ethical sourcing with any Third World suppliers they may use
- 91% organisations participating in the UK social economy e.g. co-operatives, credit unions and charities
- 95% suppliers whose activities are compatible with our Ethical Policy

In addition, our customers' money will not be used to finance any of the following activities:

- 95% we will ensure that our financial services are not exploited for the purpose of money laundering

relating to the proceeds of drug trafficking, terrorism and other serious crime

- 90% we will avoid investment and currency trading in developing countries which does not support productive purposes
- 84% we will not participate in currency speculation which consciously damages the economies of sovereign states
- 75% we will not invest in or provide financial services to tobacco product manufacturers.

Environmental Impact

- 94% We will encourage business customers to take a pro-active stance on the environmental impact of their own activities and will invest in companies that avoid repeated damage to the environment.

In line with the principles of our Ecological Mission Statement we will not invest in any business or organisation that, as core activity, relies on:

- 92% the extraction or production of fossil fuels, which contribute to problems such as global climate change and acid rain
- the manufacture of unnatural chemicals which may contr ibute to problems such as ozone depletion, or which may accumulate in nature
- the unsustainable harvest of natural resources such as timber clearance, which leads to deforestation.

Animal Welfare

We will not invest in, or provide financial services to, organisations involved in the following activities:

- 88% animal testing
- 88% exploitative factory farming methods
- 86% blood sports, which involve the use of animals or birds to catch, fight or kill each other
- 83% fur farming and the trade in animal fur.

Customer Consultation

We will regularly re-appraise customers' views on these and other issues and develop our ethical stance accordingly.

- 92% From time to time we seek to represent our customers' views on the issues contained within the Ethical Policy and other ethical issues.
- 89% On occasion we will make decisions on specific business ethical issues not included in our Ethical Policy.

(a) **Explain reasons why the Co-operative Bank might have accepted corporate responsibility and taken an ethical stance.**

(b) **Analyse the possible information that could be included in the social audit of the company.**

(c) **Evaluate the stance taken by the company using information in the data.**

(d) **Discuss the value of the questionnaire data for the Co-operative Bank in making future decisions about its ethical stance.**

The costs and benefits of business activity

When businesses produce and sell a product or a service it is relatively easy for them to see the costs involved and the benefits they will gain. These costs are known as PRIVATE COSTS. They might include such things as the wages paid to employees, the cost of an advertising campaign or the purchase of raw materials. The PRIVATE BENEFITS to the business and its owners include the total revenue earned from sales, any resulting profit and the dividends paid to shareholders.

A business may find, however, that it creates other costs. Take a factory producing cement which is located in a small 'scenic' town. The firm may dispose of some of its waste in a local river or discharge dust into the atmosphere. Lorries making deliveries to the factory may disturb the local residents. The factory may be sited close to a local beauty spot, ruining the view. These are all examples of spillover effects or EXTERNALITIES. So the costs to the whole of society, the SOCIAL COSTS, are made up of the private costs of the business plus **negative externalities** (the costs to the rest of society). Social audits (☞ unit 34) seek to take into account the social costs of business activity.

There may also be **positive externalities** which result from the business. It may create other jobs in the area for companies producing components or design a factory that complements the landscape. The firm may create skills which can be used for other jobs in the area. We can say that SOCIAL BENEFITS to society are the private benefits to business plus positive externalities (the benefits to the rest of society).

There are obvious problems that result from negative externalities. Many externalities affect the environment. Furthermore, when firms set their prices these usually only reflect the private costs of production. Prices will not, therefore, reflect the cost of pollution, noise etc. As a result of this firms may not be concerned about negative externalities as they do not have to pay for them. For example, a chemical company may produce toxic waste from its production process. It might be faced with two choices - disposing of this waste in a nearby river without treating it, or treating it and removing any toxins. The first measure would cost next to nothing, but the second measure could be relatively expensive. The rational choice for the firm, assuming this is legal, is to dispose of the waste untreated in the river. However, for other users of the river, such as anglers and water sports enthusiasts, this decision would have serious effects.

In order to assess the impact of business activity, cost - benefit analysis is sometimes used, particularly for large projects (☞ unit 104).

Question 1

In 1991 Shell, the owner of the Brent Spar oil platform, was looking for ways to dispose of the structure. With the approval of the UK government, it decided to sink it in a deep part of the Atlantic. Sinking it in its place of operation in the North Sea would have caused a hazard to shipping and would have caused further environmental damage to an already polluted area. In 1995 the platform was towed to the Atlantic for sinking. Pressure from groups such as Greenpeace led to Shell abandoning the plan to dump the platform. In 1998 Shell decided to dismantle the platform and use the parts to construct a ferry quay in Norway. Shell had already spent £20 million preparing the platform for sinking. It would cost £26 million for the recycling of the structure.

Using examples from the article, outline the possible:
(a) private costs;
(b) negative externalities;
(c) positive externalities;
of the proposed methods of disposal of the Brent Spar oil platform.

Environmental costs

There are many different types of negative externality that may result from business activity. Some are dealt with in other units, eg consumer exploitation (☞ unit 22) and employee exploitation (☞ units 80 and 81). This section will focus on environmental costs.

Air pollution This is pollution from factories, machines or vehicles emitting poisonous gases into the atmosphere. We need only look into the sky above some factories to see evidence of this. Other forms of air pollution may be catastrophes such as at the Chernobyl nuclear plant in 1986, when massive quantities of radioactive materials were released into the atmosphere and surrounding countryside. The results have been seen in many countries in Europe. Even now the area around the Chernobyl nuclear plant is uninhabitable.
 What are the main causes of air pollution?
● Acid rain. Thousands of acres of forests have been destroyed by acid rain, as a result of sulphur dioxide emissions into the atmosphere.
● Chlorofluorocarbons (CFCs). The use by some firms of CFCs in aerosols and refrigerators has contributed to the breakdown of the earth's ozone layer. The ozone layer acts as a filter for the sun's rays. Without it, exposure to sunlight can increase the risk of skin cancer.

● Carbon dioxide (CO2) and other gases. There has been a growing awareness that the release of CO2, and other gases such as methane and nitrous oxide, into the atmosphere is causing a 'greenhouse effect'. The build-up of these gases is associated with the rise in the use of cars and with the generation of electricity using fossil fuels such as coal.

Scientists argue that the 'greenhouse effect' could result in the earth's atmosphere warming up (**global warming**) to such an extent that the polar ice caps melt. This could lead to significant areas of land being submerged by rising sea levels. The 'greenhouse effect', many scientists believe, has also been responsible to some extent for the climatic extremes experienced in parts of the world in the 1990s.

Figure 35.1 shows the emissions of air pollutants in the UK over twenty five years. It suggests that concern over their effect on the environment has led to an effort to cut emissions.

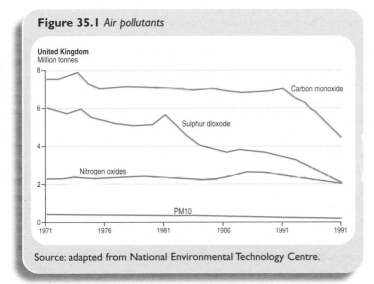

Figure 35.1 *Air pollutants*

United Kingdom
Million tonnes

Source: adapted from National Environmental Technology Centre.

Water pollution Water pollution can occur in a number of ways. Many industries, such as brewing and chemical manufacturing, use water in production. Their plants are usually located by rivers and it is fairly easy, therefore, for them to dispose of waste into nearby water. It is also possible for our drinking water from reservoirs to be polluted by chemicals used in agricultural production. People are starting to drink bottled water or have water filters fitted to their water supply in the home as a result.

The sea has also been polluted over many years. Industries sited near to the coast have used the sea as a dump for their waste. The effluence and cargo of ships are also sometimes dropped into the sea. The North Sea, for example, is one of the most polluted seas in the world as a result of years of discharges from a variety of industries. These have included sewage and the by-products of chemical production. A number of beaches in the UK are unsafe for bathing, according to the European Union, which grades the quality of beaches.

Congestion and noise Business activity has resulted in more roads becoming congested with traffic. For example, many

firms now transport their goods by rail rather than road. Estimates have put the cost of this congestion on British roads as high as £15 billion. Studies of traffic in Central London suggest that it now moves more slowly than it did in the last century, before the days of motorised transport.

Some business activity can also result in noise pollution. For example, a decision by an airport to open a new runway would affect noise levels experienced by local residents.

Destruction of the environment One example of this is logging and associated industries, which have been responsible for the destruction of sections of the Amazonian rainforests. Another example might be the effects of new buildings in a rural area. A new housing estate in a village, for example, may deprive villagers and visitors of previously unspoilt countryside. It may also increase noise and congestion levels in the village.

Waste disposal Many business operations result in waste products (☞ unit 97). This may be in the form of waste chemicals resulting from the manufacture of plastics or waste materials from the manufacture of wooden products. The packaging used in products can also be waste and needs to be disposed of.

It has been suggested that some water operators in the UK impose external costs. If a company does not maintain its pipes and leaks occur, this can result in hosepipe bans. It also means that it has to take more water from reservoirs and rivers because of the waste water it has created by leakages.

The impact on the environment of business is not always

Question

ICI's Runcorn factory has been criticised by local residents, environmental activists, the national media and the Environmental Agency, the pollution watchdog. ICI was fined £300,000 after it admitted it had polluted water near the factory with chloroform, a suspected carcinogen (a cancer causing substance).

ICI's Runcorn plant is one of the biggest chemicals employers in Cheshire. At first sight the factory appears to exist in harmony with its environment - set next to marshland which teems with waterfowl and rabbits. But ICI's opponents say the image is misleading. They point to the plant's 444 breaches of Environment Agency regulations during 1995 and 1996.

The Managing Director of halochemicals for ICI, believed the factory has been unfairly portrayed. He points out that ICI tests itself 30,000 times a year and 29,850 tests prove to be negative.

Source: adapted from the *Financial Times*, 17.3.1998.

(a) Explain why chloroform might be regarded as a negative externality.
(b) What externalities, other than chloroform, might be produced by the ICI Runcorn factory?

negative. In derelict urban areas, for example, businesses have converted rundown buildings into office space and have landscaped waste land around the site. Also, some of the buildings may be thought to have architectural merit.

Controlling environmental costs

Because of concern about the impact of business on the environment, attention has been focused on how pollution, congestion and other environmental costs can be controlled. There is a number of ways this can be done.

Government regulation Laws can be passed which make it illegal for firms to pollute the environment. The **Clean Air Act** and the **Environmental Protection Act** seek to achieve this in the UK. They set limits on the maximum amount of pollution. For example, there are controls on the quantities of certain gases which firms are allowed to release into the atmosphere.

In the US a highly powerful body, the Environmental Protection Agency, attempts to ensure that US firms do not contravene legislation.

Taxation The aim of taxation in this context is to ensure that the social cost of any pollution caused by a firm is paid for. This means that the government must estimate the actual cost to society of different types of pollution. As a result prices would more accurately reflect the true cost of using environmental resources. So, for example, a firm which produced a £5 product with 'environmentally unfriendly' packaging might be taxed 50p for this packaging, raising the price to £5.50. There are two advantages to this. First, the tax revenue might be used to minimise the impact of this packaging on the environment. Second, it might act as an incentive for the firm to produce more environmentally sensitive packaging, so that the tax is either reduced or removed.

In this example the consumer pays for the environmentally unfriendly packaging in the form of a price rise. Some would argue that the firm itself should pay for such costs. In this way, the price would remain at £5.00, but the firm would be taxed 50 pence for externalities created by its packaging. The consumer would not directly suffer as a result of the taxation.

Increases in fuel prices in the UK have been justified by governments on the grounds that consumers should pay prices which accurately reflect the impact of car use on the environment. In the late 1990s the UK government introduced a **landfill tax**. This taxed businesses £10 per tonne in 1999 for dumping waste on a landfill site.

Compensation Firms could be forced by law to compensate those affected by externalities. For example, it is common for airports to provide grants to nearby residents. This allows them to purchase double glazing and other types of insulation, which provides protection from aircraft noise.

Businesses may also be forced by court action to pay compensation to people affected by their actions.

Government subsidisation This involves governments offering grants, tax allowances and other types of subsidy to business in order to encourage them to reduce externalities. Such subsidies can allow environmentally desirable projects, which otherwise might not be profitable, to go ahead. For example, a business may be given a grant so that it could build a recycling plant for plastics. This should encourage domestic and industrial users to recycle rather than dump plastic products.

Government subsidies could also be used to encourage more environmentally friendly habits amongst consumers. For example, many councils in the UK are attempting to encourage the use of bicycles through schemes such as setting up cycle lanes and giving grants to employees wishing to use bicycles for travelling to and from work.

Road pricing and charges Charging road users could be used to reduce pollution and congestion. There is a long history of charging for motorways in European countries such as France, Spain and Italy and the first toll motorway will soon be built in Britain in the West Midlands. Similarly, vehicle users could be charged for entering cities at certain times of the day, as happened in a scheme in Cambridge.

Park and ride schemes These are also designed to encourage a reduction in car use in city areas. They are often run by local authorities. Car users, for a fee, can park their cars outside the city areas and are taken by bus into and out of the city. A single bus reduces traffic in the city area and also reduces the need for inner city car parking spaces.

Pollution permits In the USA pollution permits have been introduced. These allow businesses a certain amount of emissions. If the business reduces its pollution below a certain level, it can save the allowance for later or even sell it. Some have argued that Western economies should adopt the same approach to developing countries as they pollute the atmosphere across the world.

Working together It may be possible for business and/or government to work together to control the effect of business activity on the environment. Examples might be:
● the sharing of best practice on environmental controls;
● producing environmental codes of practice;
● developing waste strategies.

Education Governments and other agencies, such as charities, could try to influence consumers and producers through educational and promotional campaigns.

Consumer pressure Consumers have forced a number of firms to consider the impact of their activities on the environment. There is evidence that a new breed of consumer is emerging, who considers factors other than price and quality when buying products. Such consumers take into account the effect on the environment and society of those products which they purchase. So, for example, such a consumer may not buy aerosols containing CFCs, furniture made from trees which have been chopped down in the Amazon rainforest or cosmetics which have been tested on animals.

Although this approach has influenced a wide range of firms, it does have one major problem. Consumers often do not have sufficient information with which to evaluate the impact of business activity upon the environment. Such information is often not disclosed to members of the public. Also, many firms have not been slow to realise that presenting themselves as being environmentally conscious can be very good for sales. However, the actual record of such firms with regard to the environment may well fall short of the claims which they make for themselves. For example, a battery producing company placed an environmentally friendly label on its products. However, this had to be removed when it was revealed that batteries use up more energy in their construction than they create in their use.

Environmental audits An environmental audit is one method by which consumers have a fairer chance of assessing the environmental impact of a firm. This could be much like the financial audits which all companies are at present required to have by law. An environmental audit can be one part of a wider social audit (☞ unit 34). This perhaps indicates the growing pressure put on firms to be concerned about their impact on the environment.

Business and environmental policies

With public concern increasing about the dangers of damaging the environment, pressure is building on many firms to become more environmentally friendly. Adopting such environmental policies can affect businesses in a number of ways.

● They may need to change production techniques or the materials which they use. Such changes may range from the simple, such as the use of recycled paper in offices, to the complex, such as the installation of new recycling plants.

● Businesses may have to change their operations. For example, they may have to seek different methods of waste disposal. They may have to reduce or alter the packaging used in products. They may consider reducing the size of company cars or encouraging transport on trains by representatives.

● Firms may find that their costs increase. For example, a firm previously dumping waste products into the sea

would find it more expensive to process this waste. Similarly, a firm which encouraged its employees to use bicycles rather than cars on company business might find that this takes employees longer and is, therefore, more expensive. Such increases in costs may well be passed on to customers in the form of higher prices.

● Some activities which improve a firm's environmental practices may lead to lower rather than higher costs. For example, a firm which sought to improve its energy efficiency might insulate the workplace, turn down heating appliances and turn off unused lights. Such actions are likely to reduce fuel bills and thus reduce costs. Encouraging employees to re-use items, such as paper clips, envelopes and elastic bands, is likely to have a similar effect.

Question 3

In 1999 Geoff Gilbert, managing director of Geoff Gilbert International, a road haulage business, planned to move his operations from Boston, Lincolnshire to the Netherlands. The company employed 55 staff and ran 40 trucks. Many other UK companies were considering following suit by moving their operations to Europe to benefit from lower fuel and vehicle duties. It is suggested that the business could save more than £200,000 a year by moving 90 per cent of its business from the UK to Europe. Moving is not without problems. Unless the business can move all of its operation it may have to run from two centres. This can lead to higher costs. Dick Denby, from haulage firm Denby Transport, argued: 'It is the British manufacturing industry in general that will pay the price.'

Source: adapted from the *Financial Times*, 17.3.1999.

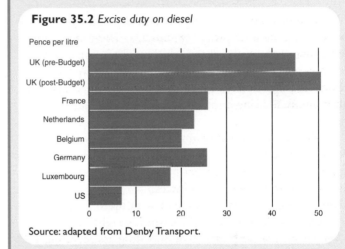

Figure 35.2 *Excise duty on diesel*

Source: adapted from Denby Transport.

(a) Explain the: (i) methods used to control the road haulage industry in the UK; and (ii) reasons why the road haulage industry may have faced control by the government.
(b) Explain the effects that these regulations might have on UK road haulage businesses.
(c) Suggest two other methods that might be used to regulate this industry.

- There may need to be a change in its ethical stance (☞ unit 33). This may have a knock-on effect on other aspects of a firm's activities and lead to a re-examination of a number of its business practices.
- There is growing evidence that consumers are attracted to firms with environmentally friendly policies. Adopting such policies may lead to an increase in sales and possibly in profit levels.
- Research and development expenditure may need to increase as a firm seeks to find new, more environmentally friendly, products and production processes. Such an increase in expenditure may go on testing and creating new packaging materials or materials to be used in production.

Conservation

All businesses depend, to a greater or lesser degree, on the use of non-renewable resources (☞ unit 97). These are resources which cannot be replaced and which might in some cases, with current usage, run out within the next 100 years. Such resources range from raw materials, like oil, iron, copper and aluminium, to living creatures like whales, elephants and dolphins.

Conservation ranges from banning the use of such resources altogether, to encouraging businesses to use them sparingly. There is a number of measures which seek to conserve non-renewable resources.

- Recycling schemes. Bottle banks set up to help the recycling of glass are now a common sight in supermarket car parks. Not only do glass recycling schemes help to conserve natural resources, but they can be profitable for those companies involved. Recycling schemes also exist in the paper, plastics and aluminium industries.
- Multilateral agreements. These are agreements between a number of countries which seek to limit the use of natural resources. Agreements now exist which place limits on the amount of fishing and whaling which countries are allowed to carry out. In addition, some countries now have import bans on commodities, such as ivory, which come from endangered species.
- Government subsidies. These have been used to encourage farmers to conserve the countryside through retaining features such as dry stone walls and hedgerows, for example.

Business opportunities

The growth in the importance of conservation and the management of waste (☞ unit 97) in recent years has led to

Question 4

In the late 1990s UK detergent manufacturers were launching an unusual marketing drive urging consumers to use less soap. This was part of a campaign to reduce the impact of domestic laundry products on the environment across the EU. The aim was to cut energy consumption, solid waste production and water pollution. The opportunities to make these cuts in production and distribution are limited as shown in Figure 35.3. Most energy is used in home washing machines. Powder used in the home also produces most solid waste. Washing machines produce most effluence. Most of the remaining waste is packaging.

The campaign, masterminded by the Soap and Detergent Industry Association called Wash Right, urged users to do fewer washes at lower temperatures. Some environmental issues about washing powder are already covered by legislation such as the EU's packaging directive and regulations on the biodegradability of products. Detergent packaging is being redesigned to include Wash Right advice. This will be followed up by mailings to more than half the households in the UK from the databases of Unilever and Proctor & Gamble. In the past, producers have said they could only control what goes on in factories and distribution to reduce the effects on the environment.

Source: adapted from the *Financial Times*, 1999.

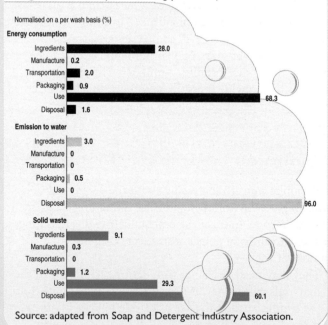

Figure 35.3 *European washing powder information*

Normalised on a per wash basis (%)

Energy consumption
Ingredients	28.0
Manufacture	0.2
Transportation	2.0
Packaging	0.9
Use	68.3
Disposal	1.6

Emission to water
Ingredients	3.0
Manufacture	0
Transportation	0
Packaging	0.5
Use	0
Disposal	96.0

Solid waste
Ingredients	9.1
Manufacture	0.3
Transportation	0
Packaging	1.2
Use	29.3
Disposal	60.1

Source: adapted from Soap and Detergent Industry Association.

(a) Suggest the methods that could be used by detergent manufacturers to be more environmentally friendly.
(b) Evaluate the possible effects of these methods on the manufacturers of detergents.

a huge expansion in commercial opportunities in the provision of waste management services. Examples of businesses that have grown as a result of these trends include:

- chemical treatments such as metal precipitation, pH adjustment and acid/alkali neutralisation, cyanide treatment and ammonia stripping and recovery;
- special waste transfer stations where a wide range of waste material can be dealt with;
- domestic refuse collection on behalf of local authorities;
- clearing contaminated land;
- waste transportation from business sites to disposal or treatment points;
- clinical waste disposal on behalf of hospitals, dentists and veterinary surgeons;
- laboratory chemicals' packing and disposal;
- dry waste disposal services;

- on-site treatment technologies;
- water jetting and air conveyancing;
- backtrack services to help businesses recycle and recover difficult and special wastes;
- drainage systems and support services;
- integrated waste management services;
- sewer surveying services.

Key terms

Externalities - occur when private costs are different to social costs and private benefits are different to social benefits.
Private benefits - the benefit of an activity to an individual or a business.
Private costs - the cost of an activity to an individual or a business.
Social benefits - the benefit of an activity to society as well as to a business.
Social costs - the cost of an activity to society as well as to a business.

Question 5

Skyscrapers are often criticised as wasteful energy guzzlers. They need huge air conditioning and heating systems, and banks of lifts. Computers gulp electricity. A new building under construction in Times Square, New York, was set to create a new standard however. The Durst Organisation, developer of the project, described it as the first environmentally responsible high rise.

The 48 storey building has a strict ecological code. Large windows give maximum light. Fuel cells on the roof and solar panels of the sides reduce the dependency on electricity. Recycled materials are used for construction where possible. Occupiers have different chutes for different types of waste. A powerful ventilation system regularly moves fresh air around the offices to prevent 'sick building syndrome'. The builders estimated that the building's greenness had increased construction costs by between 5-10 per cent. It anticipated that it would recoup this within 5 years through lower energy use.

Source: adapted from the *Financial Times*, 1998.

(a) Explain how the initiatives used in the building might conserve resources.
(b) Explain the possible advantages for:
  (i) The Durst Organisation;
  (ii) the tenants; of conserving energy in the building.

Summary

1. Give an example of:
  (a) a private cost;
  (b) a positive externality;
  (c) a private benefit.
2. State 5 examples of negative externalities that may be created by a business.
3. Briefly explain the effect that:
  (a) a tax on a business;
  (b) a subsidy from government to a business;
  might have on the creation of negative externalities.
4. Why might a business be concerned about the views consumers have about how it affects the environment?
5. Briefly explain 3 consequences of following an environmentally friendly policy for a business.
6. 'Conservation can be profitable for a business.' Explain this statement with an example.
7. State 5 examples of businesses that may develop as a result of the growth of concern over the effect of businesses on the environment.

Case study

Savco plc

Traditionally beer has been sold in glass bottles. However, there is growing interest in beer in plastic bottles. Initially the plastic bottles may cost around 9p a bottle, compared to 6p for a glass bottle. Costs will come down with larger scale production. Transport will also be easier and more cost effective as plastic is around half the weight of glass. This could be particularly useful for exporters.

One problem is that PET (polyethylene tetraphthalate), the plastic used for soft drinks bottles, does not keep beer for as long as glass. Oxygen, which gives beer its taste and carbon dioxide, which gives it fizz, seeps out. In 1997, a new plastic PEN (polyethylene napthalate), often in multi layers, was used which acted as a barrier. PEN is 10 times the cost of PET. There were initially concerns over these new methods. They had recycling problems, because it is difficult to separate the layers. Using a 'spray on' coating on a bottle made from PET solves this problem.

One concern was the beer drinkers would be put off by beer in plastic bottle. Tests showed that consumers, after drinking the beer, did not find the plastic bottle a problem. Young people who had been brought up with plastic bottles instead of glass bottles may well be a group attracted by the product.

Source: adapted from the *Financial Times*, 17.3.1999.

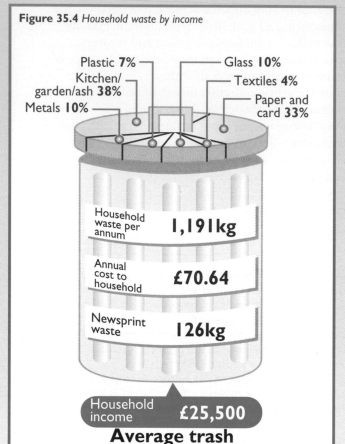

Figure 35.4 *Household waste by income*

Plastic **7%** — Glass **10%**
Kitchen/garden/ash **38%** — Textiles **4%**
Metals **10%** — Paper and card **33%**

Household waste per annum	**1,191kg**
Annual cost to household	**£70.64**
Newsprint waste	**126kg**

Household income **£25,500**

Average trash

Plastic container manufacture: cost savings in production and distribution

Distribution It has been estimated that as each inefficient vehicle is replaced, an annual saving of over 15,000 litres of fuel is made.

Material savings Savings can be made in the areas of reduced weight of plastics, use of recycled plastics, collection of plastic bottles and scrap management. Savings account for 1,000 tonnes less plastic for the same production output as a result.

In the late 1990s the UK government was considering a charge on the amount of rubbish that individual households dispose of per week. In many cases there is no real limit to the amount of household waste that is left out for refuse collectors. The government argued that imposing a charge would give individuals incentives to reduce the amount of waste. One problem with such a tax is that people may try to dispose of the waste elsewhere to avoid paying the tax.

Source: adapted from *The Guardian*, 21.7.1998

Increasingly businesses are asking suppliers to provide evidence that they are environmentally friendly organisations. They may refuse to stock the products of businesses that are not following environmentally friendly practices. Suppliers may have to show that they are following policies that reduce waste, that they are using energy and material conserving processes, and that they are following environmentally friendly transport policies.

The 1998 Transport White Paper made a number of proposals to reduce traffic congestion.
● Local authorities may be given powers to charge motorists for driving into town centres. In Liverpool it was suggested that a charge of £6 could be made for entering the town centre in a car.
● Parking provided by employers in city centre areas may be taxed.
● Drivers on motorways could be made to pay a toll.
Most car users drive the car for under one mile. This is shown in Figure 35.5.

Source: adapted from *The Guardian*, 21.7.1998.

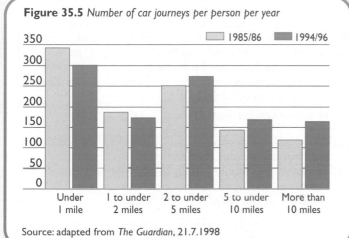

Figure 35.5 *Number of car journeys per person per year*

Legend: 1985/86, 1994/96

| | Under 1 mile | 1 to under 2 miles | 2 to under 5 miles | 5 to under 10 miles | More than 10 miles |

Source: adapted from *The Guardian*, 21.7.1998

Table 35.1 *Average daily flow of motor vehicles: by class of road*

Great Britain				Thousands
	1981	**1991**	**1996**	**1997**
Motorways	30.4	53.8	62.4	65.3
Built-up major roads				
Trunk	14.0	18.6	19.6	19.6
Principal	12.2	15.2	15.1	14.8
Non built-up major roads				
Trunk	9.0	15.0	15.6	16.2
Principal	4.5	6.8	7.5	7.6
All major roads	9.1	13.8	14.9	15.3
All minor roads	1.0	1.4	11.4	1.4
All roads	2.2	3.1	3.3	3.3

Source: Department of the Environment, *Transport and the Regions*.

Savco plc is a manufacturer of plastic containers. They are used to hold a variety of liquid materials. The company has a head office in Liverpool and a factory in Blackburn. It delivers supplies to manufacturers of liquid products in both the UK and abroad. After extensive market research the company has decided to aim at the potentially enormous market for beer in plastic bottles. This will involve marketing representatives visiting the head offices of customers in order to vigorously promote the product. The company has decided that all aspects of its operations will be as environmentally friendly as possible.

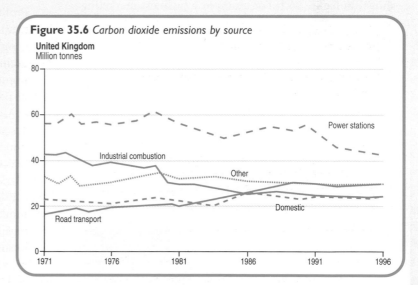

Figure 35.6 *Carbon dioxide emissions by source*

United Kingdom
Million tonnes

Labels: Power stations, Industrial combustion, Other, Domestic, Road transport

Write a report as the project controller of a team set up by the company to design an environmentally friendly policy. The team will consist of members of various departments, including production, marketing, finance and human resources and will report to the directors of the business. In your report:
● **suggest suitable strategies that could be used by the business and justify the use of these strategies;**
● **evaluate possible implications for the business of the strategies suggested.**

36 What is Marketing?

Marketing - a possible definition

A market is any set of arrangements that allows buyers and sellers to exchange goods and services (☞ unit 1). It can be anything from a street market in a small town to a large market involving internationally traded goods. But what is meant by the term MARKETING? Some definitions which suggest that marketing is the same as advertising or selling are incorrect. Selling is, in fact, just one of many marketing functions. One definition, from the Institute of Marketing, which has gained wide acceptance is that:

'Marketing is the management process involved in identifying, anticipating and satisfying consumer requirements profitably.'

There are some features of business marketing behaviour that may have led to this definition.

● Consumers are of vital importance. A product has a far greater chance of being a success if it satisfies consumers' needs. Marketing must be aimed at finding out what these needs are and making sure that products meet them. Marketing research (☞ unit 37) is often used by businesses for this purpose. Managers, however, also place stress on having a 'feel' for the market. This could be very important in a market with changing trends, such as fashion clothing or home decoration products.

● Marketing is a process. It does not have a start and an end, but is ongoing all the time. Businesses must be prepared to respond to changes that take place. This is shown in Figure 36.1. For example, a business marketing its own range of office furniture would be unwise to decide on a strategy and then not take into account consumers' reactions. If the firm sold modern designs, but sales were poor, it might consider designs for offices that wanted a traditional look.

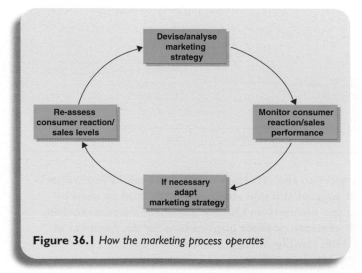

Figure 36.1 *How the marketing process operates*

(Diagram cycle: Devise/analyse marketing strategy → Monitor consumer reaction/sales performance → If necessary adapt marketing strategy → Re-assess consumer reaction/sales levels → back to Devise/analyse marketing strategy)

When researching the market for jeans in the US, Levi Strauss discovered that many potential purchasers of jeans could not find a pair to fit them. Such customers, the vast majority of whom were women, found a variety and combination of problems with 'off the peg' jeans. The solution developed by the company to deal with this problem was to individualise the manufacture of its jeans for the US market. They achieved this by arranging for sales assistants in Levi Strauss retail outlets to take the measurements of customers dissatisfied with the fit of 'off the peg' jeans. These measurements were then entered into a computer. Three weeks later the customer received the personalised jeans for an extra ten dollars.

Source: adapted from the *Financial Times*, 20.1.1997.

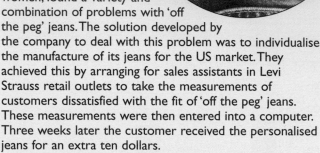

(a) Why might the actions of Levi-Strauss have helped to build good customer relations?
(b) To what extent would you say that Levi-Strauss 'identified, anticipated and satisfied consumer requirements profitably' at that time?

● Marketing involves building relationships with customers. Profitable businesses are often built upon good customer relations. This might involve dealing with customer complaints in a careful and considered manner, for example. Customers, as a result, are likely to develop a favourable view of the business. They also continue to buy its products over a long period of time. RELATIONSHIP MARKETING is now used by some businesses, such as Tesco. This is an approach to marketing which stresses the importance of developing relationships with customers which last longer than the short term.

● Marketing is a business philosophy. It is not just a series of activities, such as advertising or selling, but more a 'way of thinking' about how to satisfy consumers' needs. A business selling good quality products, cheaply, may be unsuccessful in its marketing if it has dirty, badly organised or poorly lit facilities. Retailers such as IKEA, Safeway, Asda and Carpetworld have large 'superstores' with restaurants and play areas for children. They could be said to cater for all their consumers' shopping needs.

● Marketing affects all aspects of a business. A production department would not continue making a product that does not satisfy the needs of the consumers at whom it is aimed. In the same way, pricing decisions cannot be made without knowing how much consumers are prepared to pay.

● Marketing is not just about selling. Selling is only one part of the marketing process. Before selling their products, many businesses carry out a range of activities which take into account consumer preferences. These include market research, the testing of products on consumers and the design of products.

● Marketing and advertising are not the same. Advertising is just one of a number of tactics used by marketing departments. Other marketing methods include promotions, such as free gifts and competitions.

● Many businesses regard profit making as their main objective (☞ unit 4). Firms in competitive markets must make a profit in the long run to survive. Marketing must therefore satisfy consumers' wants **profitably**. Even when profit is not the main objective, marketing has a vital role to play. Charities, such as Oxfam and many public sector organisations such as colleges and hospitals, adapt and change the marketing of their services to satisfy their consumers' needs.

The rise in the importance of marketing

It is only in the last fifty years in the UK that marketing has begun to assume such an important role in business. What factors may have led to this?

Economic growth Economic growth (☞ unit 29) in the UK since the Second World War has led to an increase in the REAL DISPOSABLE INCOME of many consumers. This has resulted in a growth in demand for products and services and for a far wider range of choice. In response, businesses have developed an array of products and services which are available to the consumer. We need only think of goods that were not available twenty years ago, such as compact discs and personal computers. Services, such as credit cards and mail order, have also been developed in response to consumers' needs.

Fashion There have been considerable changes in fashion and in the tastes and lifestyles of many consumers. For example, large numbers of people today buy products for sports which were new or were mostly ignored just a few years ago. These include mountain biking, snowboarding and hang gliding.

Technology Rapid technological change has taken place in recent years and continues to do so. Firms constantly invent, design and launch new and advanced products onto the market. One example is the electronics industry. During the 1980s and 1990s, Sony was able to launch a range of products that were not previously feasible in technical terms. These included the compact disc player, the camcorder and digital audio tape players.

Competition The number of products competing for the consumer's attention is constantly increasing. There has been increased competition from foreign products in UK markets and a greater availability of foreign services. Competition is nothing new, but the scale of it is. Japanese and US businesses, with efficient production methods and sophisticated marketing, have been successful in UK markets. More open trade in European Union countries (☞ unit 30) has also created more competition for UK firms.

Effects on business

How have the factors in the last section affected the marketing of UK businesses?

Economic growth Businesses are now aware of the growth in demand and the wide variety of tastes of consumers. Successful marketing is essential if businesses are going to gain their share of a growing market and increase their turnover and profit. Larger markets can pose a problem. The investment needed to launch a product onto a large market is enormous. Marketing must make sure that such products will succeed or the business can face large losses.

Fashion Tastes and fashions in today's markets are changing faster than ever before. Marketing must anticipate and respond to these changes. Toy manufacturers, for example, try to be aware of the next 'craze'. Marketing has become more important as firms have realised that consumers' tastes may be influenced. There is a variety of techniques that can be used to achieve this (☞ units 43-45).

Technology Businesses must respond to changes in technology. A firm's products can become obsolete very quickly unless it is able to respond to such changes. Marketing and production departments now work closely together to anticipate new opportunities that arise. Marketing must also provide consumers with technical details about products. It is unlikely that consumers will know all the uses of new products which have previously been unavailable. Technology has influenced the marketing methods that businesses use. Examples of technical marketing media now used by firms include electronic billboards and satellite TV.

Competition Competition, both at home and from abroad, has meant that successful marketing is vital to maintain a firm's market share. UK businesses have also had to respond to the sophisticated marketing techniques of foreign companies. This has meant that the expenditure on marketing by many UK firms has risen as a share of total spending in the last few decades.

The British motorcycle industry serves as a warning to those firms which fail to respond. British companies such as Triumph and BSA had dominated the market for motor

Nintendo's launch of a new 3-D video game featuring the old favourite 'Super Mario' was part of a determined effort to win back old customers and gain new customers using the very latest in technology. The moustachioed plumber featured strongly in the elaborate 3-D games on the Nintendo 64 console. The console took four years to develop and leapfrogged competing systems in terms of computing power. It could handle information more quickly. Graphics moved more smoothly with a high degree of detail, landscapes were interactive and objects had shadows. The console had an innovative control pad and was the first to use a thumb sized joystick as well as buttons. Industry experts predicted that the N64 would trigger a revival in home entertainment systems. Video games had been losing market share in recent years, with consumers choosing to buy personal computers rather than consoles.

Source: adapted from *The Times*, 1.3.1997

(a) What factors might have influenced Nintendo's decision to market its new console?

cycles in the UK ever since the 1930s. When the Japanese company Honda launched its 50 cc moped in the UK, British companies did not see this as a threat. Their lack of response allowed Honda and other firms, such as Yamaha and Kawasaki, to almost completely take over the market for motorcycles in the UK. By the 1980s, the British motorcycle industry had effectively collapsed.

Product orientation

Many businesses in the past, and some today, could be described as PRODUCT ORIENTATED. This means that the business focuses on the production process and the product itself.

In the past, many businesses producing consumer goods were product orientated. When radios and televisions were first produced in the UK, it was their novelty and the technical 'wonder' of the product that sold them. There were few companies to compete against each other, and there was a growing domestic market. There were also few overseas competitors. The product sold itself.

Some industries today are still said to be product orientated. The machine-tool industry has to produce a final product which exactly matches a technical specification. However, because of increased competition such firms are being forced to take consumers' needs into account. The technical specification to which a machine-tool business produces might be influenced by what customers want, for example.

The Concorde aircraft project has often been described as being product orientated. The main question was whether the aircraft was technically possible. Whether or

not it could be produced at a price which would attract companies was less important. The developers assumed that a supersonic aircraft would 'sell itself'. In fact the only airlines which did buy it were British Airways and Air France, largely because of the involvement of the British and French governments in its development. For other airlines the price was too high and the number of passengers Concorde could carry was too low. Several airports, most especially New York, had indicated that they might ban supersonic aircraft because of noise. Although the project was thought to be a technological success, its failure to take into account the needs of the market meant that it was not a commercial success.

Every business wants something special to market - a unique proposition, something which marks out a product from its competitors. In textiles this is difficult to achieve. Cotton is cotton, polyester is polyester, and it is difficult to establish a product which stands out from the rest. Tencel, however, is just that product for Courtaulds the chemical business. It is a fibre which can be used to create clothes which are remarkably soft and comfortable to wear. It is machine washable and has qualities which mean that it can be used to manufacture high quality, smart and casual clothing. In a clothing market which is increasingly orientated towards casual rather than formal clothing, Tencel has the right qualities - the strength and convenience of polyester, the comfort of cotton and the drape of silk. These factors have meant that Tencel is now being used to manufacture clothes by big names such as Calvin Klein and Armani and newer companies such as Democracy. Tencel emerged, however, almost by accident from attempts to improve on methods of producing viscose. Ironically the process used to create Tencel is simple when compared to the complex methods needed to produce arguably inferior fabrics such as viscose. Despite the early success of Tencel, Courtaulds still has the problem of establishing a place for Tencel in the competitive textiles market. Lycra, for example, took over 30 years to establish itself.

Source: adapted from *The Guardian*, 28.6.1997.

(a) Would you say that Courtaulds was product orientated or market orientated in the development of Tencel?
(b) Suggest reasons why Tencel might ultimately become successful.

Tencel Products

Product orientated businesses thus place their emphasis on developing a technically sound product, producing that product and then selling it. Contact with the consumer comes largely at this final stage.

There will always be a place for product orientation. A great deal of pure research, with no regard to consumers' needs, still takes place in industry.

Market orientation

A MARKET ORIENTATED business is one which continually identifies, reviews and analyses consumers' needs. It is led by the market.

Henry Ford was one of the first industrialists to adopt a market orientated approach. When producing the Model T, he did not just design a car, produce it as cheaply as possible, and then try to sell it to the public. Instead, in advance of production, he identified the price at which he believed he could sell large numbers of Model T's. His starting point was the market and the Model T became one of the first 'mass-market' products. This illustrates the market orientated approach - consumers are central to a firm's decision making.

Sony is one of many modern businesses that has taken a market orientated approach. The Sony Walkman is an example of a product developed in response to the wishes of consumers.

A market orientated business will have several advantages over one which is product orientated.
● It can respond more quickly to changes in the market because of its use of market information.
● It will be in a stronger position to meet the challenge of new competition entering the market.
● It will be more able to anticipate market changes.
● It will be more confident that the launch of a new product will be a success.

What effect will taking a market orientated approach have on a business? It must:
● consult the consumer continuously (marketing research);
● design the product according to the wishes of the consumer;
● produce the product in the quantities that consumers want to buy;
● distribute the product according to the buying habits and delivery requirements of the consumer;
● set the price of the product at a level that the consumer is prepared to pay.

The business must produce the right product at the right price and in the right place, and it must let the consumer know that it is available. This is known as the **marketing mix** (☞ unit 40). We will consider each aspect of the mix in more detail in subsequent units. Here it is enough to say that it involves the product, price, promotion and place.

It would be wrong to assume that the adoption of a market orientated approach will always be successful. Many well-researched products have been failures. Coloroll was a business which started in the wallpaper market and, expanded into home textiles and soft furnishings. Its attempt to enter the DIY burglar alarm market, however, was a failure. The company's reputation and design skills had little value in that section of the DIY market compared with other companies, whose reputations were based on home security or electronics.

Influences on product and market orientation

Whether a business places emphasis on the product or on the market will depend on a number of factors.

The nature of the product Where a firm operates in an industry at the edge of new innovation, such as bio-technology, pharmaceuticals or electronics, it must innovate to survive. Although a firm may try to anticipate consumer demand, research is often 'pure' research, ie the researcher does not have a specific end product in mind.

Policy decisions A business will have certain objectives. Where these are set in terms of technical quality or safety, the emphasis is likely to be on production. Where objectives are in terms of market share or turnover, the emphasis is likely to be on marketing.

The views of those in control An accountant as a managing director may place emphasis on cash flow, profit forecasts etc., a production engineer may give technical quality control and research a high priority and a marketing person may be particularly concerned with market research and consumer relations.

The nature and size of the market If production costs are very high, then a company is likely to be market orientated. Only by being so can a company ensure it meets consumers' needs and avoids unsold goods and possible losses.

The degree of competition A company faced with a lack of competition may devote resources to research, with little concern about a loss of market share. Businesses in competitive markets are likely to spend more on marketing for fear of losing their share of the market.

Asset-based marketing

It has been suggested that in recent years companies have been taking an asset-led approach to marketing. ASSET-BASED or ASSET-LED MARKETING (☞ unit 48) is where a business develops those goods or services that make the best use of its **major strengths** or assets. This means concentrating on what the business is 'good at', although this approach would still take into account the needs of the market. For instance, many businesses have attempted to produce 'new' products that are related to successful existing products. An example might be the development of ice cream versions of best selling chocolate bars, such as the Mars Bar and Bounty. The use of this approach has certain implications for a business. It must:

- identify the main competences and strengths of the business;
- aim to produce those products that make the best use of its resources.

Key terms

Asset-based (asset-led) marketing - where a business develops and markets products based on its main strengths.

Marketing - the management process involved in identifying, anticipating and satisfying consumer requirements profitably.

Market orientation - an approach to business which places the requirements of consumers at the centre of the decision making process.

Product orientation - an approach to business which places the main focus of attention upon the production process and the product itself.

Real disposable income - the income with which consumers are left after taxes (other than VAT) have been deducted and any state benefits added on. Any changes in the rate of inflation are also taken into account.

Relationship marketing - an approach to marketing which seeks to strengthen a business's relationships with its customers.

Question 4

Changing lifestyles, changing work patterns and shifts in expectations among customers are three reasons why telephone banking continues to increase in popularity since the pioneer development by First Direct in the early 1990s. Prior to telephone banking the only way in which customers could undertake banking transactions was by visiting their local branch. Such branches were difficult for many customers to use because of their town centre locations and opening hours which coincided with normal working hours.

The introduction and development by the former TSB (now Lloyds TSB) of a state of the art telephone banking system reflected the demand from banks' customers for a 24 hour a day, 365 days a year banking service. The business invested heavily in technology which allowed it to provide customers with a wider range of services, but with shorter and simpler calls. In less than two seconds the bank's computer system retrieves the customer's details from it's main customer database. All transactions, such as the payment of bills, are applied immediately and loans and overdrafts can often be agreed on the spot.

To operate this system the bank employed 750 phone banking staff, taking 25,000 - 50,000 calls a day from 600,000 customers. The call centre ensures that at least 90 per cent of calls are answered within 15 seconds. Fewer than 3 per cent of customers ring off before being answered. 'We had to build in a two-ring delay so the customer is ready for us when we answer', said Graham Duke, the head of telephone banking operations. The bank calculated that through its improvements to the computer system it had halved the average length of calls.

Source: adapted from *The Sunday Times*, 20.4.1997.

(a) What evidence is there that the bank has become more market orientated?
(b) How has technology enabled the bank to become more market orientated?
(c) Advise the bank on the implications for their local branches of the shift to a more market orientated approach.

Summary

1. What is meant by the term marketing?
2. Distinguish between marketing and advertising.
3. Why is marketing described as a process?
4. How can marketing techniques be employed by non-profit making organisations?
5. What factors have made marketing so important in today's business environment?
6. Why might product orientation still be important today?
7. What are the main advantages of a market orientated approach?
8. Why might a market orientated approach be unsuccessful?

Case study

3M and Daewoo

3M What's yellow, tacky and very successful? The answer can be found easily in stationery shops and newsagents throughout the country. The 'Post-it-note' has become as indispensable as paper clips in many offices. It is a best seller for its producer The Minnesota Mining and Manufacturing Company, known as 3M, in 50 countries around the world.

The 'Post-it-note' was the brainchild of Art Fry, a chemical engineer who was a researcher in product development at 3M. He was looking for a method of preventing his notes from falling out of a hymn book - a sort of 'book mark that stuck'. He remembered that a colleague had previously developed a rather strange low tack adhesive and wondered if there was a way in which he could use it. At the time the company had no idea what to do with the adhesive. Fry found it was perfect for his ideas. The adhesive was not so sticky as to cause the paper to rip if it was removed. However, it was sticky enough to keep things in place. That was in 1975. "The processing equipment and the marketing of the product then had to be invented', he said. In 1979, after an initial failure with 'Press and feel pads', 'Post-it-notes' were trialled. They were given away free to a sample of people, with detailed notes on how they could be used. The company found that 90 per cent of those receiving free copies wanted to buy more.

By the mid-1990s 3M had developed a 'Post-it-note' for use with computers. A software package enabled the 'Post-it-note' to appear on the computer desktop, and then to be dragged onto documents and stuck on. It could be enlarged and reduced as necessary and messages typed onto the note. The note goes wherever the document goes. When it is no longer needed it can be thrown away.

Source: adapted from *The Observer* and *The Times*, 30.10.1996.

Daewoo is a manufacturer of motor vehicles based in Korea. Technically its products have been said by some to compare unfavourably with other manufacturers, such as Ford, Vauxhall and Rover. In Spring 1995 it entered an already crowded UK market. There were around 40 manufacturers selling in the UK car market, but less than half had market shares of over one per cent. In fact, since 1971, no new car manufacturer entering the car market had gained a market share of 1 per cent or over. Many independent car dealers

had exclusive relationships with manufacturers, which restricted them to selling only one manufacturer's vehicles.

After one year of selling Daewoo had broken through the 1 per cent market share barrier. It identified as its target market those drivers who were mainly interested in the reliability of the car and the ability to get from one place to another cheaply, rather than other factors. Its surveys also showed that customers found salespeople pushy, showrooms intimidating and after sales service poor. 84 per cent of those surveyed said that treatment from the salesperson was at least as important as their own opinions about the car.

Using the results of the surveys, Daewoo developed a number of aspects to its marketing.
- It dealt directly with customers through its own dealers.
- Its dealer retail outlets had free cafes, creches and computer terminals with product information.
- Sales people were on a fixed salary with no commission. Prices were fixed - there was no haggling.
- A variety of guarantees was provided, such as a three year warranty, three years' free servicing and three years' free AA cover.
- Other free customer services were available, such as a courtesy car during servicing and free delivery.

Source: adapted from the *Financial Times*, September 1998.

(a) **Are these businesses product or market orientated? Explain your answer.**
(b) **What factors may have influenced their approach to marketing?**
(c) **Explain the possible: (i) advantages; and (ii) disadvantages; to each business of its approach to marketing.**
(d) **Advise each business on how it may take an asset-based approach.**

What is marketing research?

Unit 1 explained that business activity will only be successful if the output produced can satisfy people's wants and needs. Information about the things people want will help businesses to decide what to produce. This information is often found by MARKETING RESEARCH.

Marketing research can be defined as the collection, collation and analysis of data relating to the marketing and consumption of goods and services. For example, a business might gather information about the likely consumers of a new product and use the data to help in its decision making process. The data gathered by this research might include:

● whether or not consumers would want such a product;
● what type of promotion will be effective;
● the functions or facilities it should have;
● what style, shape, colour or form it should take;
● the price people would be prepared to pay for it;
● where people would wish to purchase it;
● information about consumers themselves - their age, their likes, attitudes, interests and lifestyles;
● what consumers buy at present.

Some, mainly smaller or local, businesses have just a few customers who are well known to them. For these businesses, information about their markets can be relatively easy to find. This may be through personal and social contact with their customers. Such businesses, however, must be careful that they do not misread their customers' views and actions.

Other businesses have a more distant relationship with their customers. This may be because they have a large number of customers, operate in a range of different markets or market their products in international as well as national markets. For these businesses market information may be less easy to come by. Such businesses often find that in order to gather marketing information they need to use complex and sophisticated marketing research methods.

The terms **market research** and **marketing research** are usually used interchangeably in business books and in the media. This is the approach taken in this book. Some have suggested a distinction between the two terms. Market research, they argue, is about researching consumers' preferences and tastes. Marketing research is a wider term, which also includes the analysis of marketing strategies, for example the effect of promotions such as advertising.

The uses of marketing research

A market is anywhere that buyers and sellers come together to exchange goods and services (☞ unit 1). Markets are in a constant state of change. As a result a business is likely to use marketing research on a regular basis for a number of reasons.

 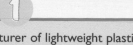
Plysu is a manufacturer of lightweight plastic containers for the British dairy industry. Containers, known as polybottles, manufactured by the company are used to hold liquids as diverse as lubricating oil, milk, fruit juice and detergents. Figure 37.1 shows information that may be useful to manufacturers of plastic containers.

(a) Explain what the marketing research information tells a business like Plysu.
(b) Suggest how the business might use this information.
(c) Why might Plysu find it difficult to rely upon personal contacts when researching the market for plastic containers?

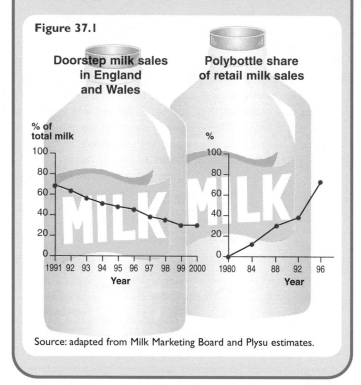

Figure 37.1

Doorstep milk sales in England and Wales

Polybottle share of retail milk sales

Source: adapted from Milk Marketing Board and Plysu estimates.

● Descriptive reasons. A business may wish to identify what is happening in its market. For example, a brewery may want to find trends in its sales of various types of beer over a certain period, or to find out the types of customers who are buying a particular beer.
● Predictive reasons. A business may wish to predict what is likely to happen in the future. For example, a travel company will want to discover possible changes in the types of holiday that people might want to take over the next 2-5 years. This will place it in a better position to design new holiday packages that will sell.
● Explanatory reasons. A business may want to explain a variety of matters related to its marketing. This may include sales in a particular part of the country. A bus company, for example, might wish to research why there

has been a fall in the number of passengers on a specific route.

● Exploratory reasons. This is concerned with a business investigating new possibilities in a market. For example, a soft drinks manufacturer could trial a new canned drink in a small geographical area to test customer reaction before committing itself to marketing the product nationally.

Once a business has decided how it wishes to use marketing research data, the next stage is to identify the **aspects** or **areas** that it wants to concentrate on. Table 37.1 shows the different areas that could be researched and some possible elements that might be considered in each.

Table 37.1 *The scope of marketing research*

Area of research	Possible elements to be considered
The market	Identifying market trends Discovering the potential size of the market Identifying market segments Building up a profile of potential/actual consumers Forecasting sales levels
Competition	Analysing the strengths and weaknesses of competitors Identifying relative market shares Identifying trends in competitors' sales Finding information on competitors' prices

Promotion	Analysing the effectiveness of promotional
	    materials
	 Deciding upon choice of media for
	    promotions

The product	Testing different product alternatives Identifying consumer wants Developing new product ideas Assessing consumer reaction to a newly launched product
Distributing the product	Identifying suitable retail outlets Exploring attitudes of distributors towards products

Pricing the product	Discovering the value consumers place on
	    the product
	 Identifying the sensitivity of the demand for
	    the product to changes in its price

Desk research

Desk research involves the use of SECONDARY DATA. This is information which **already exists** in some form. It may be existing business documents or other publications. Some secondary data may be available from within a business. This may include the following.

● Existing market research reports.

● Sales figures. The more sophisticated these are the better. For example, sales figures which have been broken down according to **market segments** (☞ unit 38) can be particularly useful.

● Reports from members of the sales force resulting from direct contact with customers.

● Annual Report and Accounts published by businesses.

● Internet data. Businesses are increasingly planning websites on the internet giving up to date information (☞ unit 82).

● Stock movements. These can often provide the most up-to-date information on patterns of demand in the market. This is because they are often recorded instantly, as opposed to sales figures, which tend to be collected at a later date.

Secondary data will also be available from sources outside the business. Individuals or other organisations will have collected data for their own reasons. A business might be able to use this for its own market research.

● Information from competitors. This may be, for example, in the form of promotional materials, product specifications or price lists.

● Government publications. There are many government publications which businesses can use. These range from general statistical publications such as *Social Trends*, the *Census of Population* and the *Annual Abstract of Statistics* through to specialist publications, such as country profiles produced by the Department of Trade and Industry and *Business Monitor*.

● Data from customer services on complaints which have been received about a product.

● The European Commission. The EU now provides a wide range of secondary data which can be highly valuable to businesses operating within EU countries. Such publications include *European Economy* and *Panorama of EU Industry* which are published by Eurostat (the Statistical Office of the European Union).

● International publications. There is a huge amount of information about overseas marketing published each year by organisations such as the World Bank and the International Monetary Fund.

● Commercial publications. A number of organisations exist to gather data about particular markets. This information is often highly detailed and specialised. Mintel, Dun and Bradstreet and Verdict are examples.

● Retail audits. The widespread use of Epos (electronic point of sale) has meant that it is now much easier to collect detailed and up to the minute data on sales in retail outlets such as supermarkets and other retail chains. Retail audits provide manageable data by monitoring and recording sales in a sample of retail outlets. Businesses find these audits especially helpful because of the way in which they provide a continuous monitoring of their performance in the market. A well known example is data on the best selling records or CDs which make up weekly music charts. This information is collected from retail outlets in the UK.

● General publications. A business may use a range of publications widely available to members of the public for their market research. These include newspaper and magazine articles and publications such as the *Yellow Pages*.

The main advantage of secondary information collected externally is that it has already been collected and is often available at little or no cost. However, it is not always in a form the firm would want. This is because it has been collected for another purpose. Consequently, secondary

Question 2

Stephanie and Tahira are considering setting up a bridal shop selling gowns and other wedding accessories in their home town of Bolton (population 260,000). Before doing so they have decided to research the market. The latest edition of Social Trends tells them that each year there are 252,000 first marriages. They calculate, with the UK's present population of 58 million, that this means one first marriage for every 230 people.

(a) Why is the information which Stephanie and Tahira are using known as secondary data?

(b) Explain how Stephanie and Tahira might use the information to predict likely sales. Suggest possible problems with using the data to predict demand.

(c) What other sources of secondary data would you suggest that they use when examining the potential market?

information needs to be adapted before it can be used in particular marketing research projects.

Field research

Field research involves collecting PRIMARY DATA. This is information which does not already exist. In other words, it has to be collected by the researcher. Field research can either be carried out by a firm itself or by a market research agency.

The main advantage of primary data is that the firm which

Question 3

In 1997 the Co-operative Bank undertook a £1 million exercise to research its customers' views on the bank's ethical stance. It sent 2 million customers a brochure containing a questionnaire. The questions included asked for comments on a range of issues, such as its ethical position, its service and its responsibility to stakeholders. By June 1997 over 50,000 replies had been received.

Source: adapted from *The Observer*, 1,6,1997.

(a) Explain why this type of research is an example of field research.

(b) Suggest the advantages to the Co-operative bank of carrying out field research to find the information it required.

(c) To what extent do you think the field research was effective by June 1997?

initially collects it will be the only organisation with access to it. Primary information can therefore be used to gain marketing advantages over rival firms. For example, a package holiday firm might discover through its field research that the use of a particular airline is a major attraction for its customers. This information can then be used to win a share of the market from rival firms by using it as a feature in promotional materials. The main disadvantage of primary information is that it can be very expensive to collect. This is because field research, if it is to generate accurate and useful findings, requires specialist researchers and is time consuming.

Most primary information is gathered by asking consumers questions or by observing their behaviour. The most accurate way to do this would be to question or observe all consumers of a particular product (known as the **population**). However, in all but a few instances this would be either impractical to carry out or expensive. It is usual to carry out a survey of a **sample** of people who are thought to be representative of the total market. Methods of choosing samples are dealt with later in this unit.

Methods of field research

There is a number of different field research methods a business can use.

Questionnaires Personal interviews, telephone interviews and postal surveys (see below) all involve the use of questionnaires.

There are certain features that a business must consider when designing a questionnaire. If it is poorly designed it may not obtain the results the business is looking for.

- The balance between closed and open questions. **Closed** questions, such as 'How many products have you bought in the last month', only allow the interviewee a limited range of responses. **Open** questions, however, allow interviewees considerable scope in the responses which they are able to offer. Open questions allow certain issues to be investigated in great detail, but they do require a high degree of expertise in the interviewer. For example, an open question might be 'Suggest how the product could be improved'.

- The clarity of questions. The questions used must be clear and unambiguous so that they do not confuse or mislead the interviewee. 'Technical' language should be avoided if possible.

- The use of leading questions. Leading questions are those which encourage a particular answer. For example, a market research agency investigating the soft drinks market should avoid the question: 'Do you think that Diet Pepsi is better than Diet Coke?' A better question would be: 'Which brand diet cola do you prefer - Pepsi or Coke?'

Personal interviews This involves an interviewer obtaining information from one person face-to-face. The interviewer rather than the interviewee fills out the responses to questions on a questionnaire, which contains mainly 'open' questions.

The main advantage of interviews is that they allow the chance for interviewees to give detailed responses to questions which concern them. Long or difficult questions can also be explained by the interviewer and the percentage of responses that can be used is likely to be high. If needed, there is time and scope for answers to be followed up in more detail. Interviews, however, can be time consuming and rely on the skill of the interviewer. For example, a poorly trained interviewer asking questions on a product she did not like may influence the responses of the interviewees by appearing negative.

Telephone interviews This method allows the interview to be held over the telephone. It has the advantage of being cheaper than personal interviewing and allows a wide geographical area to be covered. However, it is often distrusted by the public and it is only possible to ask short questions.

Postal surveys This involves the use of questionnaires sent to consumers through the post. It is a relatively cheap method of conducting field research. It also has the advantage that there is no interviewer bias and a wide geographical area can easily be covered. Unfortunately, the response rate to postal questionnaires is poor, often falling to 20 per cent, and responses can take as long as six weeks. In addition, questions must be short, so detailed questioning may not be possible. Questionnaires must also be well designed and easy to understand if they are to work.

Observation Observation is often used by retail firms 'watching' consumers in their stores. Observers look out for the amount of time consumers spend making decisions and how readily they notice a particular display. Its advantage is that a tremendous number of consumers can be surveyed in a relatively short space of time. However, observation alone can leave many questions unanswered. For example, it may reveal that a particular display at a supermarket is unpopular, but provide no clues as to why this is the case.

Use of technology Technology is constantly developing new ways in which businesses can carry out marketing research.
- Many businesses use information gathered from electronic point of sale (Epos) systems which give details of items bought and the time and date.
- In the UK over 90 shopping centres in 1998 had videos installed which recorded where customers shop. Certain videos have been developed which 'count' the number of customers entering a shop and some even differentiate between adults, children and pushchairs. The technology

provides information which allows shops to see which areas of the centre attract most shoppers. It can also be used to compare shopping centres.
- Interactive methods can also be used to gather information. Consumers may be able to express their views via internet websites or digital television. Information can be collected when orders are placed directly via the internet or digital tv link.
- Spending patterns may be analysed from the use of credit cards and store loyalty cards. Loyalty cards allow customers to obtain a certain amount of benefits and discounts with each purchase they make within a shop or supermarket.

Focus groups This involves a group of customers being brought together on one or a number of occasions. They are asked to answer and discuss questions prepared by market researchers. The groups contain a range of individuals who are thought to be representative of the customers of the business or a particular segment of customers. Because they only involve a small number of customers, focus groups are a relatively cheap and easy way of gathering marketing research information. A problem is that the views of a fairly small number of customers may not reflect the views of the market or the market segment in which the business is interested.

Consumer panels This involves a group of consumers being consulted on their reactions to a product over a period of time. Consumer panels are widely used by TV companies to judge the reaction of viewers to new and existing

Question 4

Vegran is a company that has developed a healthy lunch bar made from carob and oats. Initially, it has decided to sell the bar in the South West for a trial period, before launching the product throughout the country. Before this, however, it wants to collect views of consumers on the taste and appearance of the bar. It is particularly interested to find out whether consumers would notice a difference in taste between chocolate and carob and their views on the bar's size and packaging.

Vegran is only a small company with a limited budget for its marketing projects.

(a) What potential advantages might test marketing have for Vegran?
(b) Comment on the usefulness of:
   (i) postal surveys;
   (ii) consumer panels;
   (iii) personal interviews;
   for this company in gathering information.
(c) Suggest how Vegran might make use of the internet when collecting marketing research information.

programmes. Their main advantage is that they can be used to consider how consumer reaction changes over time. Firms can then build up a picture of consumer trends. Their disadvantage is that it is both difficult and expensive to choose and keep a panel available for research over a long period.

Test marketing Test marketing involves selling a product in a restricted section of the market in order to assess consumer reaction to it. Test marketing usually takes place by making a product available within a particular geographical area. For example, before the Wispa chocolate bar was marketed nationally, it was test marketed in the North East of England.

Sampling methods

Carrying out a survey of every single potential consumer (known as the POPULATION) of a firm's product would be impractical, time-consuming and costly. Businesses still, however, need to collect enough primary data to have a clear idea of the views of consumers. This can be done by taking a SAMPLE of the population. This sample group should be made up of consumers that are representative of all potential buyers of the product.

There is a number of ways in which a sample can be chosen.

Random sampling This method gives each member of a group an equal chance of being chosen. In other words, the sample is selected at random, rather like picking numbers out of a hat. Today computers can be used to produce a random list of numbers which are then used as the basis for selecting a sample. Its main advantage is that bias cannot be introduced when choosing the sample. However, it assumes that all members of the group are the same (homogeneous), which is not always the case. A small sample chosen in this way may not have the characteristics of the population, so a very large sample would have to be taken to make sure it was representative. It would be very costly and time consuming for firms to draw up a list of the whole population and then contact and interview them.

One method sometimes used to reduce the time taken to locate a random sample is to choose every tenth or twentieth name on a list. This is known as systematic sampling. It is, however, less random.

Stratified random sampling This method of random sampling is often preferred by researchers as it makes the sample more representative of the whole group. The sample is divided into segments or strata based on previous knowledge about how the population is divided up. For example, a business may be interested in how employment status affected the demand for a food product. It might divide the population up into different income groups, such as higher managerial and professional occupations, small employers and 'own account' workers etc. A random sample

Late one Friday afternoon, the Senior Management Team of Northminster College, a large college, had gathered to have a brief discussion on undertaking market research into the provision of a number of new courses in the next academic year. Due to financial constraints, it had already been agreed that the college would need to undertake its own research.

Sheila Whittle, the Principal, opened the discussion. 'This would have been a lot easier 20 years ago when I first started in this game. All of our students lived within five miles of the college and were aged between 16 and 19. Nowadays, we get a range of students and office workers some of whom live forty miles away. We also get adults returning for retraining and retired people wanting to study.'

Roy Erkule, the marketing manager, offered the first suggestion: 'Why don't we just draw up a list of our potential students and then take a random sample from the list? That way, everyone will have an equal chance of being selected and our results will be totally reliable.'

Kerry Chan, the finance officer, disagreed. 'I think that'll be far too complicated. We need to identify the different groups of students who might attend the college and then interview a specified number from each of these groups.'

Ian Jackson, the curriculum manager, was already tiring of the discussion: 'Look, I've got better things than this to do on a Friday afternoon. Can't we just select a group of students, give each one a set of ten questions and get them to pass them around their friends?'

(a) Is it necessary for Northminster College to use sampling when carrying out this research? Explain your answer.
(b) What might be the problems of using random sampling in this case?
(c) Identify the sampling methods mentioned by Kerry Chan and Ian Jackson.
(d) Which sampling method would you recommend to the college? Explain your answer.

could then be chosen from each of these groups making sure that there were the same proportions of the sample in each category as in the population as a whole. So if the population had 10 per cent upper class males, so would the sample.

Quota sampling This sampling method involves the population being segmented into a number of groups which share specific characteristics. These may be based on the age and sex of the population. Interviewers are then given targets for the number of people out of each segment who they must interview. For example, an interviewer may be asked to interview 10 males between the ages of 18 and 25, or 15 females between the ages of 45 and 60. Once the target is reached, no more people are interviewed from that group. The advantage of this sampling method is that it can be cheaper to operate than many of the others. It is also useful where the proportions of different groups within the population are known. However, results from quota sampling are not statistically representative of the population and are not randomly chosen. They must therefore be treated with caution.

Cluster sampling This involves separating the population into 'clusters', usually in different geographical areas. A random sample is then taken from the clusters, which are assumed to be representative of the population. This method is often used when survey results need to be found quickly, such as opinion polls.

Multi-stage sampling This involves selecting one sample from another sample. So, for example, a market researcher might choose a county at random and then a district of that county may be selected. Similarly, a street within a city may be chosen and then a particular household within a street.

Snowballing This is a highly specialised method of sampling. It involves starting the process of sampling with one individual or group and then using these contacts to develop more, hence the 'snowball' effect. This is only used when other sampling methods are not possible, due to the fact that samples built up by snowballing cannot be representative. Businesses operating in highly secretive businesses such as the arms trade may use this method of sampling. Similarly, firms engaged in producing highly specialised and expensive one off products for a very limited range of customers may need to rely upon snowballing when engaged in market research. Examples might include firms engaged in the nuclear and power generating industries.

Sample results

A business will be interested in the **range** of results it gets from the surveys it carries out. In particular, it will want to know the **significance** of any sample result. It can use **standard deviations** (☞ unit 50) to find out how confident it can be about a particular sample. For example, a business might look at marketing research information about the possible sales of a new product. It might expect that the average sales per week will be 1,000 and the standard deviation from the average will be 100. The business can use CONFIDENCE LEVELS to analyse the data.

● It will be 68 per cent confident that sales will be plus or minus one standard deviation from the average. So it is 68 per cent confident that sales will be between 900 (1,000 - 100) and 1,100 (1,000 + 100) a week.

● It will be 96 per cent confident that sales will be plus or minus 2 standard deviations from the average - between 800 (1,000 - [2 x 100]) and 1,200 (1,000 + [2 x 100]) a week.

● It will be nearly 100 per cent confident, ie certain, that sales will be plus or minus 3 standard deviations from the

average - between 700 (1,000 - [3 x 100]) and 1,300 (1,000 + [3 x 100]) a week.

These figures assume that the survey is carried out without bias and that the results resemble a normal distribution. Standard deviations can then be used to tell a business what the expected range of outcomes from a particular population will be.

The benefits of marketing research

An aid to decision making Perhaps the main benefit of marketing research is that it allows a business to make more informed decisions. This is especially important in fast changing markets. Businesses operating in such markets constantly need to adjust their marketing activities.

Reducing risk Whilst the reliability of marketing research information cannot be guaranteed (see later in this unit), it does reduce risk for a business. Without marketing research, a business might spend large sums developing and launching a new product which could prove to be unsuccessful. Businesses are less likely to waste resources on failed activities if careful marketing research is carried out.

Providing a link with the outside world Without marketing research businesses may operate in a vacuum. They would have little or no way of finding out the views of their actual and potential customers. They would also find it difficult to identify future trends in their existing markets and the markets in which they plan to operate in future.

The size of markets As markets become ever larger and as new markets open up, marketing research becomes ever more important. In international and global markets it is impossible for businesses to operate without precise information about the needs of their customers. This is because of the huge number of customers and the large differences in their tastes.

Public relations Carrying out market research may be good for the image of a business. Consumers may feel that their views are being considered. They may also think that the business is concerned that its customers are happy. This may lead to 'corporate' brand loyalty.

The problems of marketing research

If marketing research was totally dependable, businesses could use marketing research when introducing or changing products and then be completely confident as to how consumers would respond to them. This would mean that all new products launched onto the market, which had been researched in advance, would be a success. Similarly, no products would flop because businesses would receive advance warning from their research and take any necessary measures.

In reality, things may be different. It has been estimated that 90 per cent of all products fail after they have been initially launched. Some of this, no doubt, can be put down to a lack of, or inadequate, market research. However, a number of businesses that have conducted extensive research amongst consumers before committing a product to the market place have launched products which have failed. Given estimates which suggest that the minimum cost of launching a new product nationally is £1 million, this is a risky business.

Famous examples of thoroughly researched products which have turned out to be flops include the Sinclair C5, a cheap vehicle with more stability than a moped and lower costs than a car. In research, consumers enthused over this vehicle. In reality, it was almost impossible to sell. Similarly, when Coca-Cola launched 'New Coke' with a new formula flavour onto the market, research suggested it would be a huge success. In practice, 'New Coke' was quickly withdrawn from the shops.

The problem is often the **reliability** of data. This can be a problem for both primary and secondary data.

Primary data There is a number of reasons why 'field' research does not always provide reliable information to businesses.

● Human behaviour. Much marketing research depends upon the responses of consumers who participate in the collection of primary data. Whilst the responses of consumers may be honest and truthful at the time, it does not mean that they will necessarily respond in the same manner in future. This is because all human behaviour, including the act of consuming and purchasing goods, is to some extent unpredictable.

● Sampling and bias. As noted earlier in this unit, when undertaking marketing research it is usual to base the research upon a sample of the total population. This is because it would be impossible and costly to include every person when dealing with a large population. It is possible, however, that results from the sample may be different from those that would have been obtained if the whole population had been questioned. This is known as a **sampling discrepancy**. The greater the sampling discrepancy, the less reliable will be the data obtained.

   Sampling discrepancies are caused by **statistical bias**. One reason why a sample may be not representative of the whole population is because it is not large enough. A very small sample may be different from the whole population. Another problem is that some methods of sampling are likely to introduce a higher degree of statistical bias than others. Random sampling introduces little or no bias into the sample because each member of the population has an

equal chance of being selected. On the other hand, there is likely to be a high degree of bias with snowballing as the sample selected is unlikely to be representative of the population as a whole.

● Other forms of bias. It is not only the process of sampling which can introduce bias into market research. As mentioned earlier in the unit, questionnaires need to be carefully constructed to avoid the problem of encouraging particular responses from consumers through the use of leading questions. Similarly, the behaviour of interviewers can affect the outcome of interviews.

Secondary data Businesses must also be careful when using secondary data. Secondary data has often been collected for a purpose other than that for which it is being used. For example, many businesses use the government (DTI) publication *Business Monitor* to estimate the size of markets in which they might wish to operate. However, these market sizes do not always accurately match the product market being researched.

Another problem is that much secondary data, including government publications and internal business publications, is out of date almost as soon as it goes into print. In fast changing markets in particular this can reduce the reliability of such data.

Summary

1. Why is marketing research important to businesses?
2. Explain the difference between:
   (a) descriptive research;
   (b) predictive research:
   (c) explanatory research.
3. State 5 areas that marketing research could concentrate on.
4. What is meant by desk research?
5. What is meant by field research?
6. Why might field research be of benefit to a business?
7. In what circumstances might:
   (a) postal surveys;
   (b) questionnaires;
   (c) observation;
   be useful?
8. What is meant by sampling?
9. Why might a stratified random sample be preferred to a random sample?
10. Briefly explain how a business might obtain a quota sample.
11. Suggest 3 benefits of marketing research to a business.
12. Why might sampling result in statistical bias?

Key terms

Confidence level - a statistical calculation which allows a business to gauge the extent of its confidence in the results of research.

Marketing research - the collection, collation and analysis of data relating to the marketing and consumption of goods and services.

Population - the total number of consumers in a given group.

Primary data - information which does not already exist and is collected through the use of field research.

Sample - a group of consumers selected from the population.

Secondary data - data which is already in existence. It is normally used for a purpose other than that for which it was collected.

Case study

Bemrose Corporation plc

In the mid-1990s Bemrose Corporation PLC, a firm of printers, was in the process of making a decision about buying a new item of machinery. It wanted to be certain about the most suitable machinery to purchase and did not want to waste money buying technology which was unsuitable for its needs. It was also keen to keep pace with developments and did not want to lose vital orders from customers because of an inability to carry out work that was required. All concerned at the company agreed that information was needed before a decision could be taken.

Mr Roger Norton, the Southern area sales manager, was given the task of designing research into actual and potential customers.

Customers were mainly businesses wanting books, magazines and manuals printed. Mr Norton drew up a questionnaire designed to discover information about the printing requirements of publishing companies. Part of the questionnaire concentrated on the colours required in each publication, the number of copies required, the types of publications they produced etc., as shown in Figure 37.2.

The questionnaire was sent by post to 1,653 book publishers based in the UK. Names of publishers were found from a list produced by J. Whitaker & Sons Ltd, which includes nearly all book publishers in the UK. Some small publishers, magazine publishers and large publishers (such as *Yellow Pages*) were excluded from the research, although these accounted for a very small proportion of the total number of publishers. A free pen was offered to all firms responding to the postal survey. 336 responses were received representing a rate of response of 20 per cent.

Source: Mr Roger Norton, *Bemrose Publishing Survey.*

(a) **Would you describe the data gathered by Bemrose as primary or secondary data? Explain your answer.**

(b) **What reasons might Bemrose have had for carrying out the research?**

(c) **Did Bemrose use sampling techniques? Explain your answer.**

(d) **Comment on Bemrose's decision to use a questionnaire to gather data, using the results of the survey to illustrate your answer.**

(e) **Using the survey results, what advice would you give Bemrose on the type of machinery it may require?**

(f) **Why might Bemrose need to be cautious about the results of the survey?**

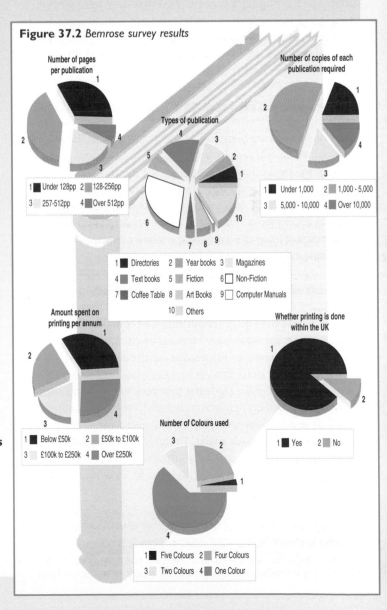

Figure 37.2 *Bemrose survey results*

Number of pages per publication
1 Under 128pp 2 128-256pp
3 257-512pp 4 Over 512pp

Number of copies of each publication required
1 Under 1,000 2 1,000 - 5,000
3 5,000 - 10,000 4 Over 10,000

Types of publication
1 Directories 2 Year books 3 Magazines
4 Text books 5 Fiction 6 Non-Fiction
7 Coffee Table 8 Art Books 9 Computer Manuals
10 Others

Amount spent on printing per annum
1 Below £50k 2 £50k to £100k
3 £100k to £250k 4 Over £250k

Whether printing is done within the UK
1 Yes 2 No

Number of Colours used
1 Five Colours 2 Four Colours
3 Two Colours 4 One Colour

38 Market Segmentation

Market segments

Unit 37 showed the different marketing research methods that a business might use. Marketing research provides a wide variety of information about the people who may be interested in buying a business's products. For example, it might tell a business that a new chocolate bar will mainly be bought by people aged 16-25. It might indicate that older people have bought more of a magazine than younger people in the last year.

Producers may use this information to identify people with similar needs. Breaking down a market into sub-groups with similar characteristics is known as MARKET SEGMENTATION. A business can then target these groups and develop products and services for each of them.

Threshers, the off-licence chain, has in the past made use of such information. Each branch stocked goods which were suitable to the population of the area that they were serving. Branches in towns such as Eastbourne or Cheltenham, for example, had products geared towards the 'older' customer. They were, therefore, more likely to promote whisky and sherry than lager and vodka.

Segmentation by age

Many businesses are beginning to pay attention to the age of their customers. Of particular interest is the segment that includes the over 60s as this segment is growing as a proportion of the total population. The marketing of financial services for older people has become popular in recent years. So has a number of other products and service areas, ranging from the growth of mobility shops to the development of retirement housing.

Segmentation by gender

Manufacturers may target either males or females. Some car producers, for example, have targeted women in their promotional campaigns for smaller hatchbacks. Manufacturers of perfumes and related products have realised the growing market for personal care products amongst men. Major brand names such as Armani and Yves Saint Laurent, as well as sports companies, have produced a range of products geared towards males. In the late 1990s, mobile phone manufacturers targeted a growing number of females buying the latest 'technological gadgets', by designing phones to suit their requirements.

Segmentation by level of education or occupation

Sometimes a business can segment its market based on how

Question 1

A report published in 1997 by Datamonitor showed that sales of Kellogg's products were suffering faced with competition from other producers. For the first time, Kellogg's share of the cereal market in the previous year fell below half to 48 per cent of the market. It was suggested that shoppers may have been drawn increasingly to supermarket own brand products, as well as to other cereals. Own label brands accounted for a fifth of the cereal market at the time. Kellogg's Corn Flakes was believed to be immune from the own-labels assault. However, it had seen its share of the cereal market fall from 12 per cent two years before to just below 10 per cent. Kellogg's responded by launching Nutri-Grain bars. They were advertised as cereal bars suited to the needs of those such as young professionals, who tend to skip breakfast.

Source: adapted from *The Guardian*, 9.9.1997.

(a) Identify and explain three pieces of marketing research information that appeared in the Datamonitor report.
(b) What evidence is there in the article that Kellogg's had been breaking down the market into segments?

far the consumer has progressed through the education system. The market is usually divided into those who have or have not studied at higher education level. An example might be a magazine aimed at those with certain qualifications. Magazines are also sometimes geared towards particular occupations such as farming. Others are geared towards a type of employee, such as a manager or outworker (☞ unit 78).

Segmentation by social class

Markets are often divided by social class. Table 38.1 shows two measures of social class used in the UK. For the 2001 population census, the Registrar General will divide social class into eight areas. Classes are based on employment status and conditions. This division is usually used in government reports and surveys. The Institute of Practitioners in Advertising (IPA) divides social class into six categories. These are used to decide which group to target for promoting a product. Because of regular changes in the pay and status of different occupations, these categories are revised from time to time. For example, the Registrar General's classification previously had only five classes.

Research often breaks these categories down even further. For example, AB, C1, C2 and DE are sometimes used to highlight the difference between levels of management, and skilled and unskilled manual workers. The media often refers to ABC1s. It is suggested that some businesses are particularly interested in people who might fall into this category as they tend to have higher incomes and levels of spending. Figure

38.1 shows the leisure activities of consumers broken down according to the IPA social classification. Restaurants may promote to AB class. 87 per cent of this group ate meals in a restaurant in the three months before they were interviewed. Bingo operators may promote to groups D and E.

Segmentation by income

Although linked to some extent to 'social classes' described above, income groups can be different. For example, a self-

---

Table 38.1 *Segmentation by social class*

Registrar General's classification
Class 1 Higher managerial and professional occupations
  1.1 Employers in large organisations
    (eg corporate managers)
  1.2 Higher professionals (eg doctors or barristers)
Class 2 Lower managerial and professional occupations (eg journalists, actors, nurses).
Class 3 Intermediate occupations (eg secretary, driving instructor).
Class 4 Small employers and own account workers (eg publican, taxi driver).
Class 5 Lower supervisory, craft and related occupations (eg plumber, butcher, train driver).
Class 6 Semi-routine occupations (eg shop assistant, traffic warden).
Class 7 Routine occupations (eg waiter, road sweeper).
Class 8 Never worked/long-term unemployed.

IPA classification
A - Higher managerial, administrative or professional.
B - Middle management, administrative or professional.
C1 - Supervisory or clerical, junior management.
C2 - Skilled manual workers.
D - Semi and unskilled manual workers.
E - State pensioners, casual or lowest paid workers, unemployed.

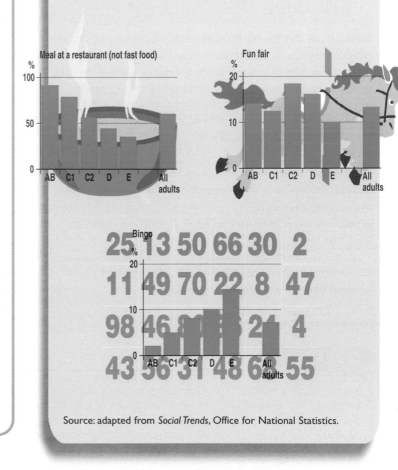

Figure 38.1 *Participation in leisure activities away from home by social grade (GB): percentage aged 16 or over participating in each activity in the three months before interview*

Source: adapted from *Social Trends*, Office for National Statistics.

Question 2

In 1998 ITV considered moving its popular News at Ten to a new 6.30pm slot. It hoped to launch a new schedule of evening programmes running to 11pm. This would be made up of entertainment, drama and popular factual programmes, followed by a new late night news bulletin. It believed that the new schedule would arrest a declining audience share.

Independent research by the consultant Paradigm for ITV, however, suggested that the television company ran the risk of losing for good the highly desirable up-market viewers who watched News at Ten. It argued that they were unlikely to be home from work by 6.30 to watch its replacement. News at Ten's audience was skewed towards ABC1s, especially ABC1 men. 42.7 per cent of its News at Ten

audience was in the ABC1 category. This compared with a national average of 33.2 per cent. This made it the most upmarket of all prime time television news. Despite this, the decision went ahead.

Source: adapted from *The Times*, 15.5.1998.

(a) Identify and explain the methods of segmenting the market that are mentioned in the article.
(b) Why might News at Ten's audience have been skewed towards ABC1 men?
(c) Suggest why a television company might be concerned about losing a male ABC1 audience.

employed skilled manual worker, such as an electrician, may receive the same income as a middle manager. However, because of his or her occupations the two people will be in different social classes.

Segmentation by religion

Businesses may divide markets by religious groups. Food producers, for example, may specialise in producing Kosher food for Jewish people. Digital television may see the growth of American style Christian television channels in the UK.

Segmentation by ethnic grouping

Markets can sometimes be segmented by country of origin or ethnic grouping. Radio stations have been geared towards African-Caribbean groups. Some products, such as clothing or hair accessories, are also geared towards this grouping.

Segmentation by family characteristics

The features of entire families may be used to segment the market. Examples of these segments include 'young singles, married with no children' (if both partners have jobs they are sometimes referred to as 'DINKIES' - double income, no kids) and 'older singles'.

Segmentation by political voting preference

Newspapers are an example of a product that is geared towards people who are likely to vote for a particular political party. *The Guardian*, for example, is arguably aimed at Labour or Liberal Democrat voters, whereas the *Daily Telegraph* is perhaps geared towards Conservative voters. The Labour Party has a credit card which is available for those who support the Party.

Segmentation by geographical region

This might include considering the region of a country that consumers live in and the nature of the region, eg rural, urban, semi-rural or suburban. It may also consider the type of house, road or area of a city that people live in. This method can be especially useful in large or highly culturally diverse markets, where buying patterns are influenced by region. Businesses selling into the European Union are likely to break this area down into more manageable segments. Many large businesses selling into global markets have different products for different countries or areas. For example, Nestlé sells refrigerated profiteroles in France and a fortified drink called Milo with a malted taste in Japan. The Maggi and Cross & Blackwell soups are adapted to suit different tastes, by varying the ingredients from one country to another.

Segmentation by personality and lifestyle

Consumers are sometimes classified according to their psychological characteristics. So, for example, sports products may be aimed at those who are interested in 'extreme' sports such as skiboarding. Chocolate

Question **3**

Is your house a suburban mock Tudor effort or a terraced lookalike? The style of your house is very much of interest to market researchers. Linking people's housing preferences to database information about car ownership, drinking habits and working hours allows a photo-fit picture of the way we live to be compiled. 'Mosaic' is one of several systems of social classification based on house type. It cross references postcodes with Census and other information to classify people into 52 types based on 12 lifestyle groupings, each with a short description. The grouping 'stylish singles' includes:
- bedsits and shop flats (may enjoy commercial advertising as an art form);
- studio singles (time may be at more of a premium than money, consumer products purchased on the basis of convenience);
- college and communal (limited sales opportunities);
- chattering classes (predominate in high density suburbs of Edwardian terraces; avid readers of newspapers).
  Most people who buy this information are trying to sell a product. Mail order companies use it to avoid selling lawnmowers to people living in high rise flats. Holiday companies avoid selling youth orientated holidays to over 65s. It prevents a great waste of resources for businesses.
  Once a business has decided which Mosaic group resembles its target market, a printout can be given of all the names and addresses of everyone in that category. A business might be interested in:
- M7 - pebble dash subtopia - people living in 1930s semis, with a residual ageing population, misses out on new fashions;
- M45 - gentrified village - high landscape value, excellent commuting distance, estate versions of upmarket cars sell well, good prospects for suppliers of garden products;
- M12 (Smokestack shiftwork) and M30 (Bijou homeowners).

Source: adapted from *The Observer*, 4.5.1997.

(a) Explain how the market is being segmented in the article.
(b) Why might businesses be interested in segmenting the market in this way?
(c) Suggest businesses that might be interested in groupings:
(i) M45; (ii) studio singles;
giving reasons for your answers.

manufacturers have identified two categories of chocolate eaters. 'Depressive' chocolate lovers eat chocolate to unwind predominantly during the evening. 'Energetic' chocolate eaters eat chocolate as a fast food and live life at a fast pace. People's attitude to life may also be used to segment the market. Some pension funds are geared towards those who only want investments in 'ethical' businesses. Clothes may be geared at those who are interested in 'retro' fashions from earlier decades.

Segmentation by purchases

This segments consumers according to their behaviour when purchasing a product. So, for example, consumers may be categorised according to the quantity and frequency of their purchases. One example of this is British Airways who have established an 'Executive Club' to encourage and develop the custom of regular business travellers.

Uses of market segmentation

Why might a business attempt to identify different market segments?
● The main reason is that it would hope that the information would allow it to sell more products overall and perhaps increase its profit.
● It would hope to be able to gain greater knowledge about its customers so that it could vary its products to suit their needs better.
● It might be able to target particular groups (☞ unit 48) with particular products.
● It would hope to prevent products being promoted to the wrong people which would waste resources and possibly lead to losses.
● It might hope to market a wider range of differentiated products.
In many cases a business might employ a variety of the segmentation methods explained above. So, for example, a manufacturer of luxury apartments may be interested in

Question

Table 38.2 *Participation[1] in sports, games and activities by gender*

Great Britain *Percentages*

	Males			Females		
	1987	1990-91	1996-97	1987	1990-91	1996-97
Walking	41	44	49	35	38	41
Snooker/pool/billiards	27	24	20	5	5	4
Cycling	10	12	15	7	7	8
Swimming	–	14	13	–	15	17
Darts	14	11	–	4	4	–
Soccer	10	10	10	–	–	–
Golf	7	9	8	1	2	2
Weightlifting/training	7	8	–	2	2	–
Running	8	8	7	3	2	2
Keep fit/yoga	5	6	7	12	16	17
Tenpin bowls/skittles	2	5	4	1	3	3
Badminton	4	4	3	3	3	2
At least one activity[2]	70	73	71	52	57	58

1 Percentages aged 16 and over participating in each activity in the four weeks before interview.
2 Includes activities not separately listed.

Source: *General Household Survey*, Office for National Statistics.

Source: adapted from *Social Trends*, Office for National Statistics.

Your company, Sportswear Ltd, is developing new ranges of leisurewear. Using the information in Table 38.2, write a letter to the marketing director.
(a) Suggest market segments the company should aim at and the type of clothing it might produce.
(b) Justify your decisions.

Table 38.3 *Buyers' profile of the Mini*

- Predominantly women accounting for 70% of buyers.
- Married - 56%.
- 13% of Mini sales are to people in the 17-24 age bracket 16% are 65+.
- Majority of buyers come from clerical occupations - 39%.
- The car is bought primarily as the second car in the household and driven mainly around town.
- 76% of Mini owners had a Rover product previously (this is the second highest manufacturers loyalty rating, the first being the Metro).

Source: adapted from *Small Wonder, The History of the Mini*, Rover Group Product Communications.

Summary

1 What is meant by a market segment?
2 Explain the difference between segmenting by age and by gender.
3 What are meant by social classes when discussing market segments?
4 Explain how markets can be segmented by types of purchase.
5 What might be the advantages to a business of segmenting the market?

segments that included single men or women with no children, in the 30-40 age range, with high incomes that fall into social class AB. Table 38.3 shows the buyers' profile of the Mini motor car in the 1990s.

Research into why businesses are successful has shown why market segmentation is so important. One survey, for example, revealed that Japanese businesses paid far more attention to market segmentation than British businesses. A number of the UK businesses surveyed did not see their markets as made up of segments. They felt that anyone in the market could be a customer and that there was little real purpose in 'breaking down the market'. As a result, such businesses were pushed into low quality, low price segments. The Japanese businesses, however, had been able to successfully target more up-market segments.

Question 5

March 26th 1998 is a day the shareholders and directors of Next would probably rather forget. Share prices fell. Certain factors were argued to have caused the fall. There was concern that falls in sales would leave profits below the previous years' levels. The City also suspected that Next, which was regarded as one of the high street's best operators, had lost the plot.

The cause of Next's problems was widely believed to have been its failure to target the right segments of the clothing market. Instead of aiming for 'thirty somethings' and their young children, an established and successful target group for the company, it attempted to capture younger, more volatile customers. In short, the fickle finger of fashion, which has been the downfall of so many clothing retailers and manufacturers, was placed upon Next.

The effect of this miscalculation was that Next was left with too many lingerie dresses and micro minis on its shelves and far too few daily wear jumpers and tailored business suits for office workers.

Source: adapted from *The Guardian*, 27.3.1998.

(a) How has the market for clothing been segmented in the above extract?
(b) In what other ways might the clothing market be segmented?
(c) How might market segmentation assist Next in its efforts to reverse declining sales?

Key terms

Market segmentation - breaking down a market into sub-groups which share similar characteristics.

Case study

Time called at the local pub

Ten years ago it was almost unthinkable that the good old British pub would play host to one of the biggest business revolutions ever. In less than a decade Britain's pubs have undergone unprecedented change. Many traditional 'locals' have died and, in their place, institutions aimed at different types of drinker have sprung up.

There are now, for example, bars for young professionals, family pubs, student pubs, cafe bars, real ale pubs, sports bars and gay pubs. Bob Cartwright of Bass Taverns explained this as follows: 'We had faced the decline of the pub traditionalist - largely male, blue collar workers. We had two options: to preside over a gently declining industry; or to seek new ways of attracting people in white collar occupations who eat out and drink out on a regular basis.' All the big pub owning groups have analysed market opportunities in a fast changing market and have tended to focus upon four main groups:

● women who want to go for a drink without entering an all male environment;

● young professionals who are single or childless;

● families with children;

● seniors and empty nesters - senior citizens and older people who no longer have any family responsibilities and often have a large disposable income.

In order to attract young professionals and women pubs have been created which look more like wine bars or continental cafes than the traditional British pub. Bass's All Bar One chain, for example, has bright decor, stripped wood furniture, floor to ceiling glass fronts and an emphasis upon sitting down rather than thronging around the bar. For families Whitbread's Brewer's Fayre chain, for example, has Charlie Chalk Fun Factory, while Allied Domecq has more than 115 Wacky Warehouses. Other pubs are concentrating on the student market.

One potential disadvantage in aiming at only one segment of the market is that it could leave a pub under-used during part of the day, particularly town centre pubs which can pull in youthful drinkers only at night. Many of the operators are developing 'Chameleon' brands which change their atmosphere throughout the day to appeal to different groups. One is the Rat and Parrot chain, created by Scottish and Newcastle, the UK's largest brewer. Jeremy Blood, Brand Marketing Director, says: 'The daytime customers wouldn't recognise it by late evening'.

An alternative approach, adopted by Scottish and Newcastle and Allied Domecq's with their Mr Q's chains, is for a pub to attract a variety of segments of the market much like the traditional pub. Mr Q's has one area for 18-25 year olds with games and music, another for their parents to prop up the bar and a third for their grandparents to sit and chat.

Sources: adapted from *The Guardian*, 22.9.1997 and the *Financial Times*, 13.3.1998.

(a) Identify the different methods of market segmentation referred to in the article.

(b) What characteristics might pubs need to have which are aimed at:
  (i)   families with children;
  (ii) students?

(c) Identify and explain the potential dangers of designing and running pubs to suit the needs of particular market segments.

(d) How might market segmentation have enabled pub owners to reverse the decline in their sales?

(e) Explain how a pub might be changed to suit different market segments at different times of the day.

(f) Suggest and explain two other methods which a pub can use to segment its market.

(g) Leisure Inc is a private limited company that is trying to break into the market for themed pubs and bars. Suggest a possible theme for the new bar and the market segments that it might be aimed towards.

Table 38.4 *The changing face of the traditional British pub.*

Pub chain	No. of managed outlets	Women	Young professionals	Families	Students/ real ale	Seniors/ empty nesters
Bass	2,562	All Bar One	All Bar One	Harvester	It's A Scream	Toby Restaurants
Allied Domecq	2,165	Carpe Diem	Mr Q's	Big Steak Pub	Firkin	Nicholson's
Scottish & Newcastle	1,900	Bar 38	Rat & Parrot	Homespreads	T&J Bernard	Chef & Brewer
Whitbread	1,700	Peppers	Tut 'n' Shive	Brewer's Fayre	Hogshead Alehouses	Wayside Inns
Greenalls Group	790	Henry's Café Bars	Squares	Miller's Kitchen	-	Red Rose Inns
Wolverhampton & Dudley	650	-	Taphouse	Poacher's Pocket	Varsity	Milestone

39 Marketing Objectives

The objectives of marketing

MARKETING OBJECTIVES are the **goals** that a business is trying to achieve through its marketing. A company's marketing objectives will be influenced by its objectives (☞ unit 4). For example, if the objective of the business is to maximise profit, marketing will be geared at achieving this. Firms' marketing objectives are likely to include some of the following.

● To target a new market or market segment. A business must decide which markets it will aim to sell its products into. It might decide that a product will sell better in a market abroad than one at home. It may also decide to target a section or **segment** (☞ unit 38) of the market. So, for example, the product could be sold to a certain 'class' of customer or a certain age group.

● To achieve or maintain market share. A business may attempt to gain a certain MARKET SHARE or percentage of a market. It may set goals, such as 'gaining 10 per cent of all market sales within three years of launching a new product'. Once a business has achieved a particular market share, it must decide how to maintain it or increase it in the face of competition.

● To develop a range of products. A business might aim to develop products which market research has indicated would be successful. Goals may also be set on how existing products could be improved or how products can be differentiated from rivals' products.

● To increase profitability and revenue. A business might set profit or revenue targets. It may also set goals for making products more profitable and assessing which products give the greatest profit.

● To prevent losses or declining sales. Marketing may be used to prevent losses. For example, a new product may initially be expected to have low sales until it takes off. Marketing may be aimed at increasing these sales. A 'mature' but popular product may face declining sales. The objective of marketing may be to prevent this decline, perhaps using marketing extension strategies (☞ unit 41).

● To favourably position a product. MARKET POSITIONING is concerned with the way in which consumers view a product relative to those of its competitors. Businesses often plan 'positions' that will maximise the sales of their products. They use promotions such as advertising (☞ units 44 and 45) in an attempt to influence the position of their products. An example might be a business trying to change the image of its product to appeal to a younger market.

● To create a competitive advantage. Competitive advantage (☞ unit 16) is the advantage that one business has over other businesses against which it is competing for customers' spending. Marketing may be used to develop a brand loyalty for a particular product. This may give a business an advantage, particularly over new competitors entering the market.

There is a relationship between these objectives. For example, in the early 1990s Adidas found that its market share in the European sports shoe market was under threat. This was partly as a result of a successful promotional campaign by its competitor, Nike, using the slogan 'Just Do It'. In order to regain its market share, it attempted to REPOSITION its trainers as less dull and with more 'street credibility'. Similarly, a business aiming to develop a new product is likely to be trying to increase its revenue and profit.

The marketing objectives chosen must also take account of the constraints under which a business operates. For example, products such as Lada cars have traditionally been sold to lower income groups. Huge sales increases are unlikely amongst higher income groups in a short period of time. Also, a business cannot expect to launch a major new product onto the market unless it has the finance. Other constraints may include legal requirements, competition that a business faces and economic changes that may take place.

Market share

MARKET SHARE is the term used to describe the proportion of a particular market that is held by a product or business. Figure 39.1 shows the share of the European market in 1999

Question 1

Table 39.1 Chocolate: European market share (per cent)

	UK	Germany	France	Italy	Spain	Netherlands	Total Europe
Nestlé Switz	28	13	27	22	36	15	20
Mars US	26	17	11	10	1	23	16
Suchard Switz/US	2	19	14	3	14	9	12
Cadbury Schweppes UK	30	-	8	-	1	-	10
FERRERO ROCHER Italy	2	16	6	28	-	-	9
All others	12	37	33	37	46	53	33

Source: adapted from BZW estimates.

(a) What marketing objectives might:
  (i) Mars set in the UK;
  (ii) Ferrero Rocher set in the UK;
  (iii) Cadbury/Schweppes set in Italy?
Explain your answers.

held by telephone companies operating fixed lines, ie not including mobile phone services. The figure shows that British Telecom, for example, had a smaller share of the market than its French and German rivals.

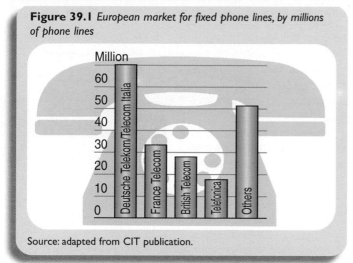

Figure 39.1 *European market for fixed phone lines, by millions of phone lines*

Source: adapted from CIT publication.

Why might the measurement of market share be important? It might indicate a business that is a **market leader**. This could influence other companies to follow the leader or influence the leader to maintain its position. It might influence the strategy (☞ unit 16) or objectives (☞ unit 4) of a business. A business that has a small market share may set a target of increasing its share by 5 per cent over a period of time. It may also be an indication of the success or failure of a business or its strategy.

Illustrating the market share held by different businesses is not as straightforward as it may seem. There are problems that must be taken into consideration when calculating and interpreting the data.

● The share of the market may be measured in different ways. These might include sales revenue, profit, or the quantity of goods produced or services sold or provided. For example, the share of BT in Figure 39.1 may have been different if sales revenue from calls or the number of calls had been used as a measure of market share.

● The type of product on which the market share is based can affect the results. For example, the market shares of the companies in Figure 39.1 may have been different if mobile phone companies had been included, such as Orange or One2One.

● The data in Figure 39.1 related to the European market. However, the market share figures are likely to have been different if national markets or global markets were taken into account. BT, for example, would have the largest share of national fixed phone lines.

● The type of business to be included can often influence market share. For example, in 1998 it was reported that Tesco, Sainsbury's, Asda and Safeway sold 45 per cent of British groceries. This measure, however, excluded small shops and petrol stations which also sell groceries. If they were included, the percentage would be lower.

Targeting the market

Sometimes businesses attempt to market products to all consumers. At other times they may **target** particular groups to concentrate on. What strategies might a business use in each case?

Undifferentiated marketing This is aimed at most sections of

Question 2

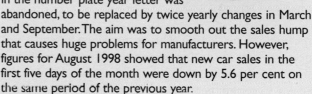

August had traditionally been a boom time for car manufacturers. It was the month of the year when the first letter on registration numbers changed. In August 1998 car manufacturers had been anticipating a bumper year. This was because it was the last before the annual change in the number plate year letter was abandoned, to be replaced by twice yearly changes in March and September. The aim was to smooth out the sales hump that causes huge problems for manufacturers. However, figures for August 1998 showed that new car sales in the first five days of the month were down by 5.6 per cent on the same period of the previous year.

Table 39.2 *Car sales*

	Units sold	Market share (%)		
	August 1-5	Jan-Aug 97	Jan-Aug 98	1-5 Aug 98
Ford	43,369	17.85	17.95	16.39
Vauxhall	33,796	13.74	12.49	12.77
Peugeot	21,391	7.64	8.04	8.08
Rover	20,829	9.84	9.07	7.87
Renault	20,123	7.30	8.08	7.60
Volkswagen	17,734	5.78	5.39	6.70
Toyota	11,730	3.44	3.80	4.43
Nissan	10,913	4.29	4.27	4.12
BMW	10,045	3.32	3.11	3.80
Honda	8,982	2.59	2.75	3.39
Citroen	8,527	3.91	3.51	3.22
Fiat	6,640	3.95	3.95	2.51
Audi	6,566	1.68	1.94	2.48
Volvo	5,320	1.86	1.63	2.01

Source: adapted from *The Observer*, 16.8.1998.

(a) Compare the percentage market shares of Peugeot and Rover over the period January to August 1998.
(b) Which car manufacturers are:
    (i) most likely to be satisfied with their sales during the period 1-5 August 1998;
    (ii) least likely to be satisfied with their sales during the period 1-5 August 1998?
    Give reasons for your answers.
(c) Suggest two ways in which figures for car manufacturers' market shares could be misleading.

the market, or possibly the whole market. It is likely to be expensive because of the need to sell to the whole market. A business will probably face competition from those firms aiming at certain segments within the market. This strategy is likely to suit those products which cannot easily be differentiated to suit the needs of particular groups of people.

Some businesses are moving away from undifferentiated marketing strategies as they attempt to target customer needs. Milk, for example, was in previous years largely marketed in an undifferentiated way. There was little choice for customers other than sterilised or pasteurised. Today milk is differentiated according to a variety of factors such as its fat levels, ie skimmed, semi-skimmed, full fat and the sources it comes from, ie cows, goats and soya.

Differentiated marketing This can involve marketing different products or services to different groups of people or promoting the same product by different means. An example of the former is the way in which banks have different types of bank accounts. There are now bank accounts specifically designed for teenagers and students, and others geared up to the needs of retired couples.

Concentrated marketing This occurs when a firm concentrates its marketing upon a specific section of the market. An example might be a product that is only available to certain people, such as the under-26s European rail pass, or because the business only expects a certain **market segment** (☞ unit 38) to buy the product. This strategy is often used by small firms as well as those in specialist markets, as it is not as expensive as other methods.

Niche marketing

NICHE MARKETING involves a business aiming a product at a particular, often tiny, segment of a market. It is the opposite of mass marketing, which involves products being aimed at whole markets rather than particular parts of them. Tie Rack, Knickerbox and Classic FM are all examples of attempts to exploit niche markets.

Why do firms attempt this type of marketing?
● Small firms are often able to sell to niche markets which have been either overlooked or ignored by other firms. In this way, they are able to avoid competition in the short run at least.
● By targeting specific market segments, firms can focus on the needs of consumers in these segments. This can allow them to gain an advantage over firms targeting a wider market.

There is, however, a number of problems with niche marketing. These include the following.
● Firms which manage successfully to exploit a niche market often attract competition. Niche markets, by their very nature, are small and are often unable to sustain two or

Nestlé is a major manufacturer of food products, with sales of over £25 billion. It has a wide product range including beverages, milk products, prepared dishes, chocolate and confectionery and pharmaceutical products. Figure 39.2 shows extracts from its *Management Report*.

Figure 39.2
The Nestlé range of chocolate bars, specialities and boxed chocolates includes not only such strategic international brands as *Nestlé, Crunch, KitKat, Smarties, Lion, After Eight, Quality Street* and *Baci*, but also brands specific to a single geographic region or country, like *Butterfinger, Baby Ruth, Charge, Femina* and *Especialidades*.

A diversified range of soups, bouillons, sauces and culinary preparations is sold under the *Maggi* and *Crosse & Blackwell* labels. The range is adapted to suit the taste, recipes and local ingredients of each individual country. In the area of Italian cuisine, Nestlé offers long-life and refrigerated sauces under the *Buitoni* brand (*Contadina dalla Casa Buitoni* in the United States). The *Buitoni* product range also includes a complete line of pizzas and frozen dishes. Chief among Nestlé's miscellaneous activities is pet food. Nestlé is well known for its cat and dog foods sold under the *Friskies* and *Alpo* brands, along with pet accessories.

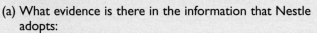

Source: adapted from Nestlé, *Management Report*.

(a) What evidence is there in the information that Nestle adopts:
   (i) undifferentiated;
   (ii) differentiated;
   (iii) concentrated;
   marketing strategies?
(b) Which of these strategies might be used by:
   (i) a multinational pharmaceutical company;
   (ii) a multinational publisher of paperback books?
   Explain your answer.

more competing firms. Large businesses joining the market may benefit from economies of scale which small firms are unable to achieve.
● Many small firms involved in niche marketing have just one product aimed at one small market. This does not allow a business to spread its risks in the way that a business producing many goods might be able to.
● Because niche markets contain small numbers of consumers, they tend to be faced by bigger and more

frequent swings in consumer spending than larger markets. This may mean a rapid decline in sales following an equally rapid growth in sales.

Market positioning

Market positioning is concerned with the perceptions which consumers have about products. To simplify the choice from a vast array of products, consumers categorise products according to a range of factors. Such factors tend to include the quality, status and value for money of products. It is the categories into which consumers place products that define their 'position'.

Businesses know that consumers will position their products in relation to those of competitors. This is often in the form of a 'pecking order' or product ladder. Firms will, therefore, attempt to plan marketing activities to achieve a desired position. Some of the ways in which businesses position products include the following.

● The benefits offered by the product. For example, Ready Break is 'positioned' as providing warmth and energy predominantly for children going to school. In contrast Special K promises low calories and a contribution to slimming.

● The UNIQUE SELLING PROPOSITION (USP) of the product. This is the key aspects of the product or service which sets it apart from those of its competitors. For example, the USP of Polo Mints is that they are a mint with a hole in the middle.

● The attributes of the product. This can be especially important for technical products. Orange, the mobile phone company, for example, ran a campaign emphasising the percentage of the country covered by its network. The manufacturers of mobile phones themselves, such as Nokia and Ericsson, tend to emphasise the weight and number of features on their phones.

● The origin of the product. In the beer market Castlemaine emphasises its Australian origin, whilst Boddingtons has stressed its connections with Manchester.

● The classification of the product. 'I can't believe its not butter' is clearly an attempt to position margarine against butter, despite the fact that it is not butter.

As markets change in response to shifting consumer demand, many businesses find they need to **reposition** their products. This usually involves changing the target market, the features of the product or the image of the product which enables consumers to distinguish it from others. An example may include Lucozade being changed from a drink taken by people who are ill to one which is used by sportspeople. Another might be Rugby League being changed from a winter to summer sport in the UK.

Question 4

'We are quite content to be the mouse under the elephants' table', says Stephen Falder of paint manufacturers H.Marcel Guest (HMG). He is referring to the position of his company in relation to the West European paint market which has major players such as ICI, Akzo Nobel and Courtaulds competing with much smaller operators such as HMG.

HMG has only 200 employees and £12 million per annum turnover. It survives by specialising in niche markets, supplying paints to the industrial market. 'It is about knowing your market and your place in it', Stephen Calder comments. Its paint can be found on the new safety railings outside Buckingham Palace and many of Britain's cast-iron lampposts, bollards and park benches. Other niche markets include painting spectacle frames and model trains. One research project is on behalf of a motorcycle crash helmet manufacturer that wants a shinier gloss on its products.

In contrast to the market for domestic paints sold in outlets dominated by large retailers such as B&Q, most industrial paints are not made in large quantities even by the larger manufacturers. As Mr Calder comments: 'We can compete very effectively. All industrial coatings are supplied in small quantities to a lot of relatively small markets.'

Source: adapted from the *Financial Times*, 16.10.1997.

(a) Explain why HMG is engaged in niche marketing.
(b) How effectively do you think HMG would be able to compete in:
  (i) the domestic paint market;
  (ii) industrial paint markets?

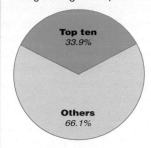

Figure 39.3 *Western Europe leading coatings manufacturers*

Top ten 33.9%

Others 66.1%

Source: adapted from *The Coatings Agenda*, James Consulting.

Key terms

Marketing objectives - marketing goals that businesses try to achieve.
Market positioning - the view consumers have about the quality, value for money and image of a product relative to those of its competitors.
Market share - the proportion of total sales in a particular market for which one or more firms are responsible. It is usually expressed as a percentage.
Repositioning - an attempt to change the views of consumers about a product relative to its competitors.
Unique selling proposition (USP) - the aspects of a product that makes it different from other products.

Question 5

In the late 1990s the manufacturers of Bunty, the girls' comic, were attempting to reverse years of declining popularity. The comic had seen its circulation slump from over 200,000 in the late 1970s to 65,000. 'We are trying our best to be optimistic', said Jim Davie, Bunty's editor. 'But fewer and fewer girls are interested in this type of magazine. I suppose they are too busy going to the cinema or watching television.' He believed that girls are growing up much faster. Whereas they used to read Bunty until the age of 12 or 13, they now graduated to the burgeoning 'teen-mag' market by the age of 10. As a result the publishers were seeking to introduce a more grown up feel to the magazine. They were including new photo stories and concentrating on boys and relationships. One thing did not change. The price of joining the Bunty club remained at 25p.

Source: adapted from *The Guardian*, 12.1.1998.

(a) Why were the publishers of Bunty seeking to reposition this product?
(b) What strategies were they using to reposition Bunty?
(c) What other strategies would you suggest to improve the circulation of Bunty?

Summary

1. Identify 5 marketing objectives.
2. What constraints might be placed on a firm's choice of marketing objective?
3. Give 3 examples of problems of measuring market share.
4. Explain the difference between differentiated and undifferentiated marketing.
5. Give 2 examples of a niche market.
6. Why might a business concentrate on niche marketing?
7. Give 4 examples of how a business might reposition its product.

Case study

Levis shrinks to reflect new blue reality

Wearing Levi-Strauss jeans has long existed in US mythology. Old western movies, James Dean, 60s flower power children and Bruce Springsteen all conjure up images of the American in blue denim. In 1997, however, the company closed 11 of its 37 factories. Competition from large retailers' own brand jeans and the high cost of US workers relative to those in other countries had all taken their toll.

After 10 years of growth, turnover had risen to $7.1 billion in 1996. However, Levis' market share for men's jeans slipped from 48 per cent in 1990 to around 26 per cent in 1997. Levis had about one-fifth of the market. To some extent it was having to cope with the same problems that faced the whole industry. Growth in demand for jeans had slowed to 3 per cent after a decade of running at 10 per cent.

But what happened to Levis itself? It faced increasing competition at both ends of the market. Mass market retailers such as Gap and low cost brands cut into its markets. Cheaper brands had around 19 per cent of the mens' and 30 per cent of the womens' market in 1997, compared to only 3 per cent each in 1990. At the top end of the market designer labels such as Donna Karan had 5 per cent of the mens' market. Traditional competitors such as Wrangler had also taken around £1 billion of annual sales.

Another problem was that Levis failed to see shifts in fashion. Large jeans with 40 inch legs were 'in'. Levis' largest was only 23 inches wide. Also young people were buying trousers made of non-denim fabrics. They disliked the idea that they would be wearing the same trousers as their older but 'young at heart' parents. Rivals to Levis branched out into non-traditional fabrics such as velveteen and moleskin. But Levis did not really innovate. Its own brand of loose fitting khaki chinos, Dockers, aimed at baby boomers with growing waistlines, also faced growing competition from cheaper brands.

Levis changed its strategy. It aimed to be a smaller operation, geared towards profitable market niches, such as custom made jeans. It also intended to attract more young consumers. However, there were concerns that repositioning the brand, perhaps by dropping the 501 label, may alienate existing customers. In 1997 Wal-Mart, the low cost US retail chain, offered to buy a million pairs of jeans from Levis. A Levis' company spokesperson said: 'it is not a discount brand' and intended to refuse the offer.

Source: adapted from *The Observer*, 9.11.1997.

(a) Using evidence from the article, describe three possible marketing objectives of Levis.
(b) Why might Levis be reluctant for the discount retailer Wal-Mart to stock its product?
(c) (i) Explain how Levis attempted to reposition its brand.
   (ii) What might be the problems with this?
(d) Why might the market for custom made jeans be an example of a niche market?
(e) What evidence is there to suggest that Levis has used differentiated strategies?
(f) Discuss the factors that may have affected the repositioning of the product.

The Marketing Mix

In order to achieve its marketing objectives (☞ unit 39), as well as the overall objectives of the company, a business must consider its MARKETING MIX. The marketing mix refers to those elements of a firm's marketing strategy which are designed to meet the needs of its customers. There are four parts to the marketing mix - product, price, promotion and place. These are often known as the four 'Ps', as illustrated in Figure 40.1. To meet consumers' needs, businesses must produce the right product, at the right price, make it available at the right place, and let consumers know about it through promotion.

Product Businesses must make sure their product is meeting the needs of their customers. This means paying close attention to a number of the features of the product.
- How consumers will use the product. A furniture manufacturer, for example, would market different products for home use than it would for office use. Products created for the office would need to be sturdy, able to withstand regular use and long lasting. Products created for the home would need to stress features such as the quality of the fabric, design and the level of comfort.
- The appearance of the product. This is likely to involve a consideration of such things as colour. Food manufacturers, for example, go to great lengths to ensure that their products have an appealing colour. In some cases this means adding artificial colourings to alter the appearance. There are many other factors to be taken into account during the product's design (☞ unit 99). These include shape, taste and size. Deodorant manufacturers and toilet cleaning fluid producers amongst others might also consider aroma.
- Financial factors. There is little point in a firm producing a product which meets the needs of consumers if it cannot be produced at the right cost. All things being equal, a good produced at high cost is likely to be sold for a high price. Unless consumers are convinced that a product is value for money, they are unlikely to purchase it. They

Figure 40.1 Elements of the marketing mix

```
                    MARKETING
                       MIX
     ┌─────────────┬──────┴──────┬─────────────┐
  PRODUCT        PRICE         PLACE       PROMOTION
 Appearance    Cost based     Retailers    Advertising
 Function    Competitor based Wholesalers Sales promotion
   Cost      Consumer based  Distribution Personal selling
```

Question 1

One of the great products of a civilisation marching into the third millennium was launched at the Candy and Cards shop in Bolton, Greater Manchester in the late 1990s. All that was needed was 55 pence paid to the owner, Varsha Halai. Pull off the ring pull and you would drink 190 ml of PG Tips brewed in Manchester, canned in Belgium and heated for three hours in Bolton at between 55-75°C. Brooke Bond, which had produced tea granules and the pyramid-shaped tea bag, had invested £6 million in the canned drinks. Consumers had a choice of tea with milk, with or without sugar, Red mountain coffee or hot chocolate. Jill Winter, Brooke Bond's marketing controller, said that the biggest challenge was getting the tea right. 'We spent three years trying to get that fresh brewed taste.'

Source: adapted from *The Guardian*.

(a) Identify elements of the marketing mix mentioned in the article.
(b) Explain how these elements might help Brooke Bond to gain a competitive advantage over its rivals.

might take into consideration factors such as the quality of the product or **after sales service**.
- The product's life cycle (☞ unit 41). After a period of time the sales of all products rise and then later start to fall. A business must decide whether to allow the product to decline and cease its production or to try to revive it in some way.
- A product's unique selling proposition (☞ unit 39). This is the aspect or feature of the product that may differentiate it from its rivals. It may help a business to gain a **competitive advantage** (☞ unit 16) over competitors.
- Market position (☞ unit 39). This is the view that consumers have of a product compared to that of its competitors. For example, a product might be seen as 'up market' or alternatively 'low cost' by buyers.

Price The pricing policy that a business chooses is often a reflection of the market at which it is aiming. Prices will not always be set at the level which will maximise sales or short run profits. For example, a business may charge a high price because it is aiming to sell to consumers who regard the product as exclusive rather than because production costs are high. The way in which the customers influence the pricing policy of a business is dealt with in unit 42. However, factors such as production costs do also influence pricing (☞ unit 43).

Promotion There is a number of promotional methods a business can use including above the line promotions, such as TV advertising, and below the line promotions such as personal selling (☞ units 44 and 45). A business will choose a promotion method it feels is likely to be most effective in the market in which it operates. For example, methods such as '10 per cent off your next purchase' are used with 'fast moving consumer goods', such as canned food and packets of biscuits. National television advertising will only be used for products with a high sales turnover and a wide appeal.

Place This refers to the means by which the product will be distributed to the consumer (☞ unit 46). The product must get to the right place, at the right time. This means making decisions about the way in which the product will be physically distributed, ie by air, sea, rail or road. It also means taking into account how the product is sold. This may be by direct mail from the manufacturer or through retail outlets such as supermarkets.

Choice of marketing mix

Each business must decide upon its own marketing mix. It is important that the right **balance** between price, product, promotion and place is achieved. It could be argued that as businesses become more market orientated all elements are important. However, at times businesses may stress one or more elements of the mix. The mix a business chooses will depend upon certain factors.

● The type of product it is selling. For example, a business marketing highly technical products is likely to emphasise its products' qualities rather than giving a free good as a promotion. However, a business marketing a product very similar to that of its competitors may wish to emphasise a lower price or use some method of promotion.

● The market they are selling to. Businesses selling consumer goods aimed at the mass market are likely to emphasise the promotional and price aspects of their marketing mix. Firms selling machinery or industrial goods are likely to stress the product itself.

● The degree of competition it faces. A business operating in a competitive market, with many close rivals, is likely to stress the importance of price in its marketing mix. In less competitive markets price might not be seen as being so important.

● The marketing mix of competitors. Businesses cannot afford to ignore the mix chosen by competitors. For example, confectionery manufacturers lay particular emphasis upon the availability of their products in a wide

Question 2

Steinway, the traditional supplier, and Yamaha, its Japanese rival, have long been competing for the attention of pianists and composers. Yamaha is the world's largest manufacturer of musical instruments. It has attempted to gain a greater market share in one of the most prestigious areas of the business - grand pianos. The market leader is Steinway, set up in 1853. It claims its pianos are played by 90 per cent of concert pianists.

But Yamaha hit back in the late 1990s. Its pianos were to be found in the London Royal College of Music. As part of its promotion campaign it negotiated to provide the official pianos for the Metropolitan Opera House in New York. It loaned 40 pianos free of charge and also made a $40,000 'contribution' in exchange for the Met's endorsement. Some Steinway artists were also courted by the company, and their flattering reviews of Yamaha products were used in advertisements. Quality was also improved and Yamaha unveiled what it claimed to be the 'finest piano ever'. The price of a Yamaha concert grand piano retailed at £51,490, £20,000 less than the cheapest Steinway. This price differential gives Yamaha an advantage at the commercial end of the market, such as pop concerts and television work.

Source: adapted from the *Financial Times*, 9.8.1997.

(a) Suggest three factors mentioned in the article which might influence the marketing mix of Yamaha pianos.
(b) From the information provided, advise Yamaha on the aspects of its marketing mix that it could emphasise for its pianos.

range of retail outlets. These include petrol stations, newsagents, off-licences and DIY stores. The emphasis here is on place. Any business wishing to compete in this market would, therefore, be unable to overlook the importance of place in this marketing mix.

● The position of a business within an industry. Businesses that are leaders within their industries tend to have a greater degree of freedom over the particular marketing mix which they choose. Such businesses include McDonald's, Kodak and Coca-Cola. Other businesses are in less strong positions, but may operate in industries with strong market leaders. Where this occurs the relatively weaker businesses often choose to 'mimic' the marketing mix of the dominant business.

The marketing mix and the scope of business activity

A wide range of organisations is engaged in marketing activities. Marketing is not confined to well known businesses, such as BMW and PepsiCo, operating in a national and international environment. It is also used by smaller firms operating in local markets. However, the size of a business and the extent to which it operates in the private or public sector can affect its marketing mix.

Non-profit making organisations There has been a huge increase in the marketing activities in which non-profit organisations (☞ unit 5) such as schools and colleges, charities and hospitals engage. One of the reasons for this is that non-profit organisations in the public sector (☞ unit 6) increasingly need to compete with other similar businesses for their customers (who are still usually called patients, students, clients or other appropriate terms by these organisations). The funding of such organisations is now usually linked to their ability to attract 'customers'. For example, if a college student chooses to attend College A to study for a course, rather than College B, College A will receive funding for this student and College B will not. This provides an incentive for public sector organisations to attract students. Not surprisingly they have employed marketing strategies and techniques to help them meet consumer needs and gain an advantage over rival organisations.

For many non-profit organisations, particularly those in the public sector, price may be less important as a component of the marketing mix than for other businesses. There are two reasons for this. First, such organisations often do not receive any money directly from their customers. For example, colleges and hospitals receive their money through funding organisations set up by the government. Second, the price which their customers are charged is often set by the government and is, therefore, out of the control of individual organisations.

For charities, pricing is also likely to be a less important element of the marketing mix. This is because they do not have a priced product in the sense that many other businesses do. Instead they rely on donations from individuals and groups.

Small businesses For many small businesses, particularly sole proprietors, sophisticated marketing strategies are beyond their means. They often have so much work keeping their businesses ticking over on a day to day basis, they do not get the chance to think strategically about their marketing. Certain elements of the marketing mix may be out of the control of small business owners. For example, a survey by Barclays Bank found that 60 per cent of small businesses depend upon word of mouth to promote themselves. In addition, many small businesses do not have the opportunity to alter the way in which their goods or services are distributed. Thus, the importance of place in the marketing mix may be less.

Businesses operating in industrial markets Such firms have other businesses as their consumers. For example, the manufacturers of fork lift trucks do not market their products for use in consumers' homes. Instead, they are aimed at businesses who are interested in buying these products, such as warehouses. The differences between consumer and industrial markets mean that the marketing mix for businesses operating in these two areas may vary a great deal. Whereas the marketing mix for many mass market consumer goods often places emphasis upon advertising campaigns in the media, industrial marketing tends to rely upon personal contacts and the role of personal selling (☞ unit 45). International shows or fairs are important events, where producers can make contact with industrial customers.

Consumer markets Many marketing theories and concepts have been developed to explain the behaviour of consumer markets, especially those for high sales, mass market goods. Most businesses operating within such markets tend to focus upon all aspects of the marketing mix, paying a great deal of attention to every element.

International marketing Businesses engaged in international marketing (☞ unit 49) will often vary their marketing mix from one country or region of the world to another. Product names, product specifications, prices, distribution networks and promotional campaigns may all be different. For example, car and paper prices are often lower in Europe than in the UK.

Key terms

Marketing mix - the elements of a business's marketing that are designed to meet the needs of its customers. The four elements are often called the 4 'Ps' - price, product, promotion and place.

Summary

1. Identify the 4 elements of the marketing mix.
2. What features of a business's product are important in the marketing mix?
3. Explain the difference between price and place in the marketing mix.
4. State 4 factors that influence a business's choice of marketing mix.
5. 'The size of a business is likely to affect its marketing mix.' Explain this statement.
6. Why might advertising be less important to a supplier of industrial equipment than personal contact with possible customers?

Question 3

British universities are becoming increasingly dependent on income generated from overseas students. They have been competing for such students both with themselves and with higher education providers in other countries, especially the USA and Australia. Economic crises in Asian countries, such as Malaysia and South Korea, had hit UK universities hard. These students accounted for 53,988 places in 1997.

Universities responded to changes in their recruitment patterns by exploring potential student markets in countries such as China, India, South Africa and South America. A British Education Exhibition in Beijing, the Chinese capital, attracted 30,000 visitors. Universities also set up schemes for emergency financial support and relaxed deadlines for paying tuition fees. Another solution was to allow colleges and universities overseas to deliver UK degree courses with UK university supervision. This however, has raised concerns about quality control.

Source: adapted from the *Financial Times*.

(a) Using examples from the article, explain why it is important for non-profit making bodies such as

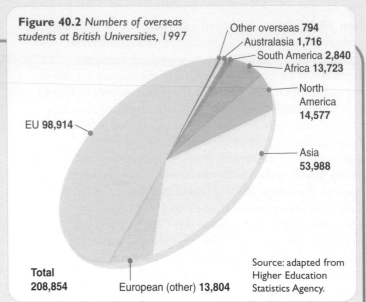

Figure 40.2 *Numbers of overseas students at British Universities, 1997*

Other overseas **794**
Australasia **1,716**
South America **2,840**
Africa **13,723**
North America **14,577**
Asia **53,988**
EU **98,914**
European (other) **13,804**
Total **208,854**

Source: adapted from Higher Education Statistics Agency.

universities to engage in marketing activities.

(b) Explain the elements of the marketing mix that British universities wishing to attract overseas students might need to consider.

Case study

Waxing lyrical

Price's Candles has seen the light after two decades of problems. Founded in the nineteenth century, this global manufacturer provided illuminations to royalty and air fresheners to the masses. Richard Simpson bought Price's for £250,000 from Shell in the early 1990s. Using an old factory at the side of the Thames, he streamlined production, brightened up the product and raised turnover to £15 million. In 1996 it made the first operating profit of the 1990s of £600,000.

Christmas is always a busy time for Price's. It sells three times as many candles then as in the rest of the year. The company also benefited from increased demand after the death of Diana, Princess of Wales. It supplied candles at the official funeral. However, it declined the offer of supplying newspapers with tea 'lights' to be given away as a free promotion.

The success of Price's has coincided with the reemergence of candles as a 'must buy' product. For people brought up on electricity, the candle at a barbecue, a romantic dinner or a student get together has become an important accessory. There is still a market for the traditional product. Retailers such as Past Times sell traditional historical candles. Churches still need traditional candles, although candles for different religions are given different names.

But designs are changing. Christmas candles are not just Santa candles. People's needs are becoming more sophisticated. The company produces church candles with gold scripts from carols. Retailers are demanding candles and lights for fresheners and for aroma therapy, smelling of

lemons and spices. The perfume is added into the wax candle. Producing a whole candle from perfumed wax would cost around £40. This is a price most consumers would not pay. Supermarket chains are big buyers of Price's candles. People seem to want candles lit all the time, even in the bath! However, to retain exclusivity some ranges are limited to gift shops or the packaging is made differently. The key to future success appears to lie in capturing the mass market. Price's has outlets in factory villages, as well as displays in department stores.

In 1997 the business operation was to be moved to a new factory in Bicester. Some of the land surrounding the old building had been sold. The old factory was to be done up and used as a visitors' centre. Some candles would still be made there, but mainly for show.

Source: adapted from the *Observer*, 21.12.1997.

(a) How might Price's Candles be operating in:
   (i) consumer markets;
   (ii) industrial markets?
(b) Explain the factors that may have influenced Price's marketing mix.
(c) Using the information in the article, analyse the four elements of the marketing mix of Price's candles.

The product life cycle

A business aiming to achieve its marketing objectives (☞ unit 39) must be aware of the PRODUCT LIFE CYCLE. The product life cycle shows the different stages that a product passes through and the sales that can be expected at each stage. Most products pass through six stages - development, introduction, growth, maturity, saturation and decline. These are illustrated in Figure 41.1.

Development During the development stage the product is being designed. Suitable ideas must be investigated, developed and tested. If an idea is considered worth pursuing then a **prototype** or model of the product might be produced. A decision will then be made whether or not to launch the product. A large number of new products never progress beyond this stage. This is because management is often reluctant to take risks associated with new products.

During the development stage it is likely that the business will spend to develop the product. As there will be no sales at this stage the business will initially be making a 'loss' on the product.

Introduction This stage is when the product is new on the market and sales are often slow. Costs are incurred when the product is launched. It may be necessary to build a new production line or plant, and the firm will have to meet promotion and distribution costs. Therefore, it is likely that the product will still not be profitable.

The length of this stage will vary according to the product. With brand new technical products, eg washing machines, compact disc players and personal computers, the introduction stage can be quite long. It takes time for consumers to become confident that such products 'work'. At first the price of such products may be quite high. On the other hand, a product can be an instant hit resulting in very rapid sales growth. Fashion products and some FAST MOVING CONSUMER GOODS may enjoy this type of start to their life.

Growth Once the product is established and consumers are aware of it, sales begin to grow rapidly. The product then becomes profitable. If it is a new product and there is a rapid growth in sales, competitors may launch their own version. This can lead to a slowdown of the rise in sales.

Maturity At some stage the growth in sales will level off. The product has become established with a stable market share at this point. Sales will have peaked and competitors will have entered the market to take advantage of profits.

Saturation As more firms enter the market it will become saturated. Some businesses will be forced out of the market, as there are too many firms competing for consumers. During the maturity and saturation stages of the product life cycle many businesses use extension strategies to extend the life of their products. These are discussed below.

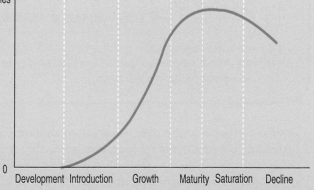

Figure 41.1 *The various stages of the product life cycle*

Sales

0 | Development | Introduction | Growth | Maturity | Saturation | Decline

Question 1

James Dyson is the ingenious creator of a household suction cleaner that was awarded a leading European prize for its design. He began his career as an artist, invented a new kind of boat called the Sea Truck and then developed the ballbarrow, which is easier to steer than a conventional wheelbarrow and does not leave tracks on the grass.

In 1979 Dyson was cleaning his house and became frustrated with how poorly his vacuum cleaner was working because it kept on getting clogged up. He came up with the idea of using centrifugal force in a cyclone tower to allow the cleaner to operate more effectively. This would mean the creation of the first bagless vacuum cleaner. He spent five years perfecting the machine, made a staggering 5,000 prototypes, and the whole process nearly bankrupted him. He was given a lot of advice at this time which he worked hard to disprove. He was told that he could not sell a cleaner for twice the price of his rivals - he now outsells the nearest competitor by more than two to one.

After a struggle to raise enough finance to fund the setting up of a factory to produce the new suction cleaner, Dyson was reduced to selling the rights to the machine in Japan for £1,000,000. The product was launched in 1993 and has since experienced a rapid growth in sales. By 1997 Dyson had 560 employees and a sales turnover per annum of over £100 million.

Source: adapted from *The Times*, 8.2.1997.

(a) Draw a product life cycle. Indicate the stages that the Dyson household suction cleaner was at during the period 1979 to 1997 using the information in the article.
(b) Using the product life cycle, explain what is likely to happen to sales of the Dyson household suction cleaner in future.

Decline For the majority of products, sales will eventually decline. This is usually due to changing consumer tastes, new technology or the introduction of new products.

Different product life cycles

Many products have a limited life span. Their product life cycles will look similar to that shown in Figure 41.1. For some products there is a very short period between introduction and decline. They are sometimes called 'fads'. The slope of the product life cycle in the introduction and growth period will be very steep and the decline very sharp. Examples of such products might be Rubik cubes in the 1980s and children's toys, such as the 'Tamagochi' virtual pet, in the 1990s. Once consumers lose interest in a product and sales fall, a business may withdraw it from the market. It may be replaced with another new product. Sometimes poor selling products are withdrawn in case they damage the image of the company.

However, businesses must take care not to withdraw a product too early. Over time certain products have become popular again. For example skateboards which were popular in the 1980s regained popularity in the mid-1990s. 1998 saw sales of the yo-yo boom, a toy not fashionable since the 1960s.

Some businesses still enjoy profits from products which were launched many years ago. The Oxo cube was launched in 1910, Kellogg's Cornflakes were launched in 1906 and Theakston's Old Peculiar, a strong ale, was launched in the eighteenth century. These products still sell well today in a form fairly similar to their original.

Because of the high cost of investment, car producers often set product life cycles of 10 years for their models. For many products life cycles are getting shorter, especially in areas like electronics. In the computer industry, some models and software have become obsolete within a very short period as new versions appear which are more technically advanced. For example, in 1995 Microsoft launched its operating software Windows 95. It was later replaced by Windows 98 and Windows 2000.

Extension strategies

It is clear from the product life cycle that the sales of products decline, although at different rates. Firms can attempt to extend the life of a product by using EXTENSION STRATEGIES. They may decide to use one or more of the following techniques.
- Finding new uses for the product. Video tape which had previously been used for video recorders attached to televisions was adapted to be used with portable camcorders.
- Finding new markets for existing products. During the 1990s there was a boom in the sales of sports clothing. This was largely due to a significant increase in the use of sports clothing as fashionwear.
- Developing a wider product range. Lucozade was originally

Question 2

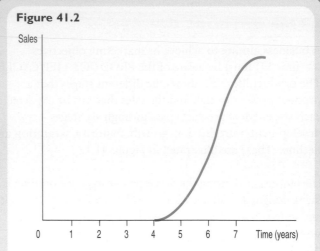

Figure 41.2

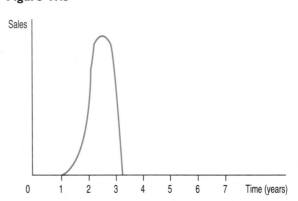

Figure 41.3

(a) Examine Figures 41.2 and 41.3. For each of these, name a product which you think might have a similar product life cycle.
(b) Why do some products have a very long life cycle (greater than 50 years)?
(c) Sketch the current product life cycle of three of the following products:
　(i)　A compact disc by a leading performance artist/group (you will need to specify the name of the CD);
　(ii)　ice cream Mars Bars;
　(iii)　Coca-cola;
　(iv)　Hovis bread;
　(v)　Rice Krispy bars;
　(vi)　Buzz Lightyear dolls associated with the film 'Toy Story';
　(vii)　the Volkswagen Golf;
　(viii)　a football strip of a Premier League team (you will need to specify the team).

sold as a product to those recovering from an illness. By extending the product range to include a 'Sports' version, a huge increase in sales has been achieved. Lego constantly develops new versions of a product that started out as a plastic set of building blocks.

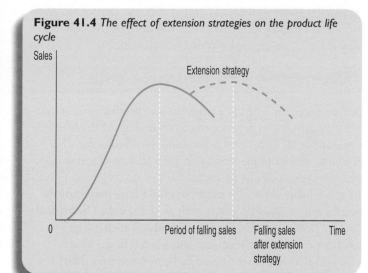

Figure 41.4 *The effect of extension strategies on the product life cycle*

Sales

Extension strategy

0   Period of falling sales   Falling sales   Time
                                    after extension
                                    strategy

- Gearing the product towards specific target markets. In 1998 mobile phone companies were introducing mobile phone packages geared to the needs of 18-21 year olds. Banks have accounts for teenagers under 17 which provide cheques books and cash dispenser cards but not cheque guarantee cards.
- Changing the appearance, format or packaging. Coca-cola is available in traditional sized cans, in glass or plastic bottles, or in mini sized cans. Swatch constantly redesigns its entire range of watches as a means of stimulating consumer interest.
- Encouraging people to use the product more frequently. Manufacturers of what were previously known as 'breakfast cereals' have used promotional campaigns to encourage the use of their products at different times throughout the day.
- Changing the ingredients or components. Many microwave food products are available as 'weight watchers' or 'low fat' meals, as well as more traditional meals. In 1998 Ford Mondeos were equipped with CD players and air conditioning as standard.

The effect that an extension strategy can have on the product life cycle is shown in Figure 41.4. As the market becomes saturated and sales begin to fall, the decline in sales is delayed by the use of an extension strategy.

It would be sensible for a business to try to extend the life of a mature product **before** sales start to decline. Firms that can predict falling sales from **market forecasts** (☞ unit 51) may attempt to use extension strategies before the decline takes place.

Uses of the product life cycle

Why might a business be interested in analysing the product life cycle of its existing products or anticipating the life cycle of new products?
- It will illustrate the broad trends in revenue that a product might earn for the business.
- It will identify points at which businesses may need to

Question 3

The long-running soap wars saga took another twist in 1998 with Lever Brothers, the Unilever subsidiary, claiming to have gained the initiative. The battle had been raging for many years. The Persil name was first registered in 1909. In 1968 Lever introduced Persil automatic. It was followed closely in 1969 by Ariel, produced by Lever's rival Procter & Gamble. Lever Brothers' new Persil Tablets had stormed the market, taking Persil back to the number one detergent brand in the UK. Lever launched the white, peppermint style, individually wrapped soap tablets in June 1998. This was enough, Lever argued, to take Persil's market share above that of Ariel, for the first time in four years.

Procter & Gamble reacted by test marketing its own tablets, Ariel Discs. It expected to launch the tablets in autumn 1998. However, it was suggested that Lever would gain by being first in the market, although the success of the tablets would depend on whether they would wash better than liquid or powder versions. Euromonitor, a research agency in a study of the detergents market, argued: '... the constantly shifting sand amongst different formats ... disguises the fact that this is a mature market in which the two main protagonists are fighting hard just to stand still'.

Source: adapted from *The Observer*, 6.9.1998.

(a) What evidence is there in the article to suggest the use of extension strategies in the market for soap powder?
(b) Explain why: (i) Unilever may have made use of extension strategies for Persil; (ii) Procter & Gamble made use of extension strategies for Ariel.
(c) Advise soap powder manufacturers on another extension that could be used in future.

consider launching new products, as older ones are in decline.
- It will identify points at which extension strategies may need to be introduced.
- It may help a business to identify when and where spending is required, eg on research and development at the start, on marketing at the introduction and when extension strategies are required.
- It may help to identify points at which a business should no longer sell a product.
- It will help a business to manage its product portfolio - its mix of products. This is discussed in the next section.
- It will identify points at which revenue from products should be growing and points where it may be declining. This may help a business when managing cash flow (☞ unit 59).

- It will give an indication of the profitability of products at each stage in its cycle.
- It will allow a business to plan different styles of marketing that a product might need over its life cycle.

The product mix

Product life cycle analysis shows businesses that sales of products eventually decline. It is possible to delay this decline using extension strategies.

A well organised business will attempt to phase out old products and introduce new ones. This is known as managing the PRODUCT MIX (or PRODUCT PORTFOLIO). With a constant launch of new products, a business can make sure a 'vacuum' is not created as products reach the end of their life.

Figure 41.5 shows how a business can manage its product mix. Say that a business over a particular time period aims to launch three products. By organising their launch at regular intervals, there is never a gap in the market. As one product is declining, another is growing and further launches are planned. At point (i), as sales of product X are growing, product Y has just been launched. This means that at point (ii), when sales of product X have started to decline, sales of product Y are growing and product Z has just been launched.

This simple example shows a 'snapshot' of three products only. In practice, a business may have many products. It would hope that existing products remain in 'maturity' for a long period. The profit from these mature products would be used to 'subsidise' the launch of new products. New products would be costly at first, and would make no profit for the business.

Examples of businesses that have successfully managed their product mix are sweet manufacturers. Companies such as Nestle produce a wide range of products, including KitKat, Milky Bar and Yorkie, and constantly look to launch new products.

The product mix includes **product lines**. These are groups of products which are closely related to each other. One example is the launch of a range of products associated with a new film. Product lines in this area include anything from T-shirts and mugs to books and CDs for films such as

Jurassic Park, the Full Monty and Star Wars. One of the most successful product lines of all time has been the Mickey Mouse merchandise of the Walt Disney Company.

Managing the product mix

One problem for firms in planning their product mix is that it is very difficult in practice to tell what stage of the life cycle a product is at. Also, there is no standard lifetime for products. For example, young people's fashion clothing has life cycles which can be predicted with some certainty. Others are less reliable. Who, for example, could have predicted the lengthy life cycles of products such as Heinz baked beans and the VW Beetle, or the short life of products such as the Sinclair C5 - a sort of 'mini-car' introduced in the 1980s.

A useful technique for allowing firms to analyse their product mix is the **Product Portfolio Matrix** developed by the Boston Consulting Group. It is sometimes called the **Boston Matrix**. This matrix places products into four categories.

- 'Star' products are those with a large share of a high growth market.
- 'Problem children' might have future potential as they are in growth markets, but their sales are not particularly good.
- 'Cash cows' are those which are able to generate funds, possibly to support other products. They are mature products with a stable market share.
- 'Dogs' are products that may be in decline.

These are shown in Table 41.1.

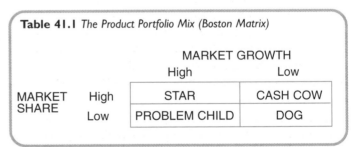

Table 41.1 *The Product Portfolio Mix (Boston Matrix)*

		MARKET GROWTH	
		High	Low
MARKET SHARE	High	STAR	CASH COW
	Low	PROBLEM CHILD	DOG

Businesses must ensure that their product mix does not contain too many items within each category. Naturally, firms do not want lots of 'Dogs', but they should also avoid having too many 'Stars' and 'Problem children'. Products on the left hand side of the table are in the early stages of the product life cycle and are in growing markets, but the cost of developing and promoting them will not yet have been recovered. This will drain the firm's resources. Balancing these with 'Cash cows' will mean the revenue from the 'Cash cows' can be used to support products in a growing market. The development cost of 'Cash cows' is likely to have already been recovered and promotional costs should be low relative to sales.

This does not mean though that firms would want lots of 'Cash cows' and few 'Problem children' and 'Stars'. This is because many of the 'Stars' and perhaps some 'Problem children' might become the 'Cash cows' of the future.

The Boston Matrix has not been without its critics. They

Figure 41.5 *Launching products successively (as older products decline, new products are launched onto the market)*

Sales

PRODUCT X   PRODUCT Y   PRODUCT Z

(i)   (ii)   (iii)   Time

Question 4

Lokotronics is a company producing a range of electrical goods. Table 41.2 shows the sales from just four of its products over the period 1990-1998.

Table 41.2

Sales (000)

Year	Product A	Product B	Product C	Product D	All products
1990	2	8	-	-	
1991	4	10	-	-	
1992	8	6	9	-	
1993	12	3	15	-	
1994	18	1	18	2	
1995	20	-	16	6	
1996	22	-	11	15	
1997	22	-	10	20	
1998	21	-	8	25	

(a) From the sales figures, describe the product life cycles of:
 (i) Product A;
 (ii) Product B.
(b) Calculate the total sales of all products in each year.
(c) Comment on the management of the product mix over the period.

argue that the matrix can cause businesses to focus too much upon pursuing increases in market share as opposed to, for example, attempting to consolidate market share or improve other aspects of the performance of a product. It is also suggested that the model fails to take account of the way in which products within a business can support one another.

New product development

Planning the product mix requires the continual development and launch of new products. New products are needed to replace products coming to the end of their life cycle and to keep up with changes in the market. This is called **new product development**.

In some industries the need to plan ahead is very important. In the chemical industry, development work is done on products which might not reach the market for over ten years. In the motor industry many cars take over five years to develop.

New products normally pass through five stages when they are being developed.

Generating ideas The first stage is when firms generate ideas. Ideas for new products come from a variety of sources.
● Identifying gaps in the market, perhaps through market research. An example of this has been the development of vegetarian microwave dishes by food producers.

● Scientific research. Firms such as ICI devote huge amounts to research and development expenditure. As a result they have developed products ranging from 'non-drip paint' to bio-degradable plastics.
● Creative ideas or 'brainstorming'. Products such as the jet engine have come about as a result of this.
● Analysing other products. When developing new products many businesses will analyse products manufactured by competitors. They aim to include, adapt or improve upon the best features of these products in their own designs. Some businesses adapt their own successful products to make new products.

Analysis The second stage is the analysis of those ideas generated in the first stage. There are a number of questions a firm might ask. Most importantly, it must find out if the product is marketable - if enough consumers wish to buy it to allow the firm to make a profit. Businesses must also decide if the product fits in with the company's objectives, if it is legal and if the technology is available to produce it.

Development The third stage is the actual development of the product. This may involve technical development in the laboratory or the production of a prototype. Such work will be carried out by the **research and development** department. An important part of this process is the actual design of the product (☞ unit 99). Some preliminary testing may be carried out to find out whether or not the product actually meets consumers' needs.

Test marketing Stage four involves the test marketing (☞ unit 37) of a product. TEST MARKETING occurs when a new product is tested on a small, representative section of the total market. The test market area should share characteristics which are similar to those found in the market as a whole. The benefit of test marketing is the high degree of reliability of results gained. It is carried out because of the high cost and risk of launching a product in a large, usually national, market. Test marketing can itself be costly, but not as expensive as a national launch which fails. One problem is that it allows competitors to see the new product and gives them the chance to take counter action before a national launch.

Commercialisation and launch The final stage is the launch and commercialisation. Here any problems found during test marketing must be solved. The firm will then decide on the 'marketing package' it will use to give the product launch the

Table 41.3

Stage	Number of ideas	Pass rate
Generation of ideas	40	1 in 5
Business analysis	8	1 in 2
Development	4	1 in 2
Test marketing	2	1 in 2
Commercialisation and launch	1	1 in 1

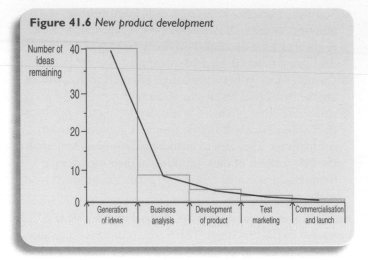

Figure 41.6 *New product development*

greatest chance of success.

At each of the five stages, many ideas are rejected. This means that very few ideas generated in the first stage will actually end up as a product launched onto the market. In Figure 41.6 and Table 41.3, an example is shown where 40 ideas were put forward for a new product. In this company the majority of ideas do not get beyond the first stage. The pass rate at this stage is only 1 in 5, with 4 out of 5 ideas being rejected. After that, the number of ideas which survive from one stage to the next increases as the pass rate falls from 1 in 5 ideas to 1 in 2. At the end of the process, only 1 out of a total of 40 ideas has survived to be launched onto the market.

Constraints on new product development

There is a wide range of **constraints** on businesses. These will restrict the number of new products developed.

Availability of finance and resources In highly competitive markets businesses find that their profit margins are squeezed. This means that financial and human resources are often not available to develop new products. An example of this is in the market for budget fashion clothing. Businesses in this market tend to copy products developed for designer labels.

Cost Even when businesses have resources, the cost of developing new products may be prohibitive. The development of products in the electronics market can cost millions of pounds. As technological boundaries have been pushed forward, the cost of even modest new product development has risen sharply. Also, in many markets products have increasingly shorter life spans. This means that less time is available to recover development costs.

Market constraints There is little point in a business developing a new product unless consumers are prepared to purchase it at a price which can cover development and production costs. Many so-called 'tremendous ideas' for new products have been abandoned. This is because firms believe

they cannot find a profitable market for the product. In addition, consumers can be resistant to change. This is often because of the time and effort consumers need to spend in getting to know how new products 'work'. There is also evidence that consumers are resistant to new products which represent a radical departure from existing products. New versions of existing products are sometimes more popular with consumers than totally new ideas for this reason.

Legal constraints Firms cannot develop whatever new products they wish. Legislation must be taken into account. For example, a pharmaceutical company wishing to develop a new product must be sure that it adheres to health legislation.

Technology The development of technology can affect the type of product or service provided. 100 years age computers did not exist. Today they are sold in a variety of ways to different businesses. Internet cafes have also been set up which allow consumers to pay for time on the internet. Technology may also affect manufacturing processes. Developing a new material for use in clothing which it is not possible to produce in the quantities required is unlikely to be successful.

Question

Sir Clive Sinclair, famous for being the inventor of calculators and digital watches, believed that he had spotted a gap in the market for people who like to cycle without breaking a sweat. He produced a kit for converting a conventional bicycle into one equipped with a motorised boost for the tougher parts of a ride. Called the Zeta II, it was an updated version of the original model, and could be fitted to just about any model of bicycle with the aid of a cycle spanner and screwdriver in about 20 minutes. The motor limited the rider to a speed of about 15 miles per hour, because that is the level below which anybody aged over 14 could use a powered machine without a licence, tax, insurance or helmet. One of the main reasons behind the original idea for this product was the belief that people do not like cycling to work because they arrive hot and sweaty and in need of a shower.

The original Zeta was well received, particularly among the middle aged and over. However, Sir Clive and his team were confident that they could appeal to young people as well. 'It is about putting the fun back into cycling and providing a viable, convenient alternative for the many thousands of short car journeys carried out each day,' he said.

Source: adapted from the *Independent on Sunday*, 20.7.1997.

(a) From where might the ideas for such a product have come?
(b) Identify the constraints which may have restricted the development of the Zeta II.
(c) Suggest factors that you think might determine the success or failure of this product.

Key terms

Extension strategies - methods used to extend the life of a product.

Fast moving consumer goods - products with high levels of sales which are sold within a short period of time, such as soap powder or tinned foods.

Product life cycle - this shows the different stages in the life of a product and the sales that can be expected at each stage.

Product mix (product portfolio) - the particular mix of products which a firm is marketing.

Test marketing - testing a product out on a small section of a market prior to its full launch

Summary

1. Briefly describe the various stages in the product life cycle.
2. Why might a product have a 'steep' life cycle?
3. How can a firm extend the life of its products?
4. Explain how a business can prevent a 'vacuum' in its product mix.
5. What is meant by a product line?
6. What is meant by the Product Portfolio Matrix?
7. How can the Product Portfolio Matrix help a business to manage its product mix?
8. What is meant by new product development?
9. State 2 ways in which a business can generate new product ideas.
10. What is meant by the 'pass rate' of new products?

Case study

Murphy Drinks Ltd

Murphy Drinks Ltd had been producing powdered chocolate drinks for just over thirty years. The company was set up as the market for vending machines producing hot drinks had just begun to mushroom in the 1960s. Its first product, 'Murphy's Vending Chocolate', came onto the market in 1963. Its success in gaining a 35 per cent share of the market for vended chocolate drinks in under five years acted as the foundation stone for the future actions of the company. Ever since 1968, the percentage market share held by Murphy's vending chocolate had never fallen below this 35 per cent mark and, at times, had risen as high as 42 per cent. Sales generated by this product were in excess of £160,000 in the financial year ending in 1998.

The success of the vending chocolate gave Murphys the confidence to develop a new product in 1969 called 'Catering Chocolate'. This was aimed at the hotel, canteen and restaurant market. Although 'Catering Chocolate' was successful in gaining a 20 per cent share of its market, the cost of developing it made Murphys cautious about attempting to launch any further products. In total, almost £15,000 was spent over a two year period in the process leading up to the product being marketed to hotels, restaurants and canteens throughout the country.

It wasn't for another eighteen years that Murphys attempted to launch a new product. This time, in response to changing tastes in the hot drinks market, it developed a low calorie chocolate drink called 'Lifestyle'. This low calorie drink was sold in sachets and distributed mainly through the larger supermarket chains. Despite its past successes, Murphys initially found it difficult to establish a firm footing for this product. However, the last two years, 1997 and 1998, had witnessed a substantial growth in the sales of 'Lifestyle' as consumer and retailer resistance to it was broken down by a series of promotional campaigns. Sales revenue in 1998 amounted to over £100,000.

Encouraged by the success of 'Lifestyle' in the retail sector, Murphys had made the decision in 1998 to launch a product line which they had been developing for a number of years. This was a range of flavoured chocolate drinks called 'Hi-lifes'. There was a high degree of initial interest from consumers in this product range, but it was too early - only six months after the launch - to evaluate its likely success.

Murphys also wanted to develop a new chocolate drink (called Bliss) and had a number of ideas which needed to be considered. However, members of the board of directors were split on this issue. Some were keen to go ahead with the new product development programme for two main reasons: first, out of concern about the falling sales of

'Catering Chocolate' and second, because they felt that now was the time to capitalise upon their recent success with 'Lifestyle'. Other members of the Board were much more cautious. Not only were they concerned about upsetting their present product mix, but there were worries about the cost of developing this product.

Table 41.4 shows the different stages involved in the development of this new product and the cost at each stage.

Table 41.4 *Cost of developing a new chocolate drink (Bliss)*

	Cost per idea	No. of ideas	Pass rate
Generation of ideas	£50	40	1 in 5
Analysis of ideas	£500	8	1 in 2
Development	£8,000	4	1 in 2
Test marketing	£13,000	2	1 in 2
Launch and commercialisation	£35,000	1	1 in 1

(a) **At what stage of the life cycle were each of Murphy's products in 1998?**
(b) **From the figures given in the table, calculate the total cost to Murphys of developing the new chocolate drink, Bliss.**
(c) **Other than cost, what might prevent Murphys from developing a new product?**
(d) (i) **Suggest possible extension strategies that Murphys might use for Catering Chocolate.**
   (ii) **In each case explain why the technique might be suitable for this product.**
(e) (i) **Describe Murphy's existing product mix.**
   (ii) **Evaluate the extent to which the product mix is well managed.**

Price and demand

Unit 17 explained how the interaction of market demand and supply can determine the price of a good or service. The operation of markets is considered to be an 'external' influence on a business's decisions. This unit considers the factors affecting the demand for an individual business's products and the way in which these factors can influence the price that the business might charge.

The demand curve of a business

Businesses need to understand how the demand for a product can affect the price that they can charge for it. This relationship can be shown by a demand schedule and a demand curve. For most products the relationship between demand and price is inverse. As the price goes up, the quantity demanded goes down. As the price goes down, the quantity demanded goes up. So, for product A shown in Figure 42.1, a rise in price from OP to OP_1 (£20 to £40) will lead to a fall in the quantity demanded from OQ to OQ_1 (£5,000 to £3,000).

Some products have a demand curve which looks different to that shown in Figure 42.1. 'Prestige' perfumes are designed to appeal to wealthy consumers. A low price might put off

Table 42.1 *The demand schedule for Product A*

Price (£)	Quantity demanded
10	6,000
20	5,000
30	4,000
40	3,000
50	2,000

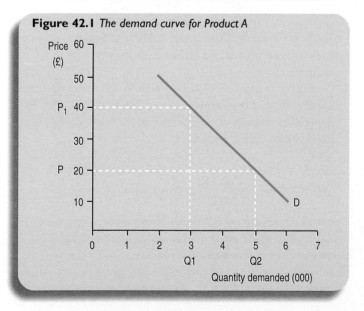

Figure 42.1 *The demand curve for Product A*

Table 42.2 shows the demand schedules for three products manufactured by different businesses.

Table 42.2 *The demand schedule for products A, B and C*

Price (£)	Quantity demanded(A)	Quantity demanded(B)	Quantity demanded(C)
5	50,000	10,000	40,000
10	30,000	15,000	30,000
15	20,000	25,000	25,000
30	10,000	16,000	20,000

(a) Draw the demand curve for each product.
(b) For each product, describe the relationship between price and quantity demanded, giving examples.
(c) Which demand schedule might show demand for commemorative coins from mail order collectors? Explain your answer.

consumers of such a product, given the association made between a higher price and high quality. This means that the quantity demanded over lower price ranges may increase as price rises for such a product. This would create an entirely different demand curve. Figure 42.2 shows the demand curve for such a product. An increase in price from OP to OP_1 causes the quantity demanded for this perfume to increase from OQ to OQ_2. However, an increase in price from OP_1 to OP_2 causes the quantity demanded to fall from OQ_2 to OQ_1. In this part of the curve a more normal relationship between demand and price exists. An increase in price leads to a fall in the quantity demanded. Speculative goods are also said to have upward sloping demand curves. As prices rise people buy more of them, hoping to sell them for a profit at a later date.

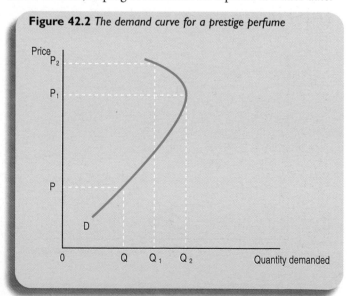

Figure 42.2 *The demand curve for a prestige perfume*

Other factors influencing the demand for a business's products

Other than price there is a range of factors affecting the demand for an individual business's products. A change in any of these factors can cause a shift in the whole demand curve (as opposed to a change in price which causes a movement along the demand curve). Figure 42.3 shows an increase in the demand for a product by the demand curve moving outwards from D to D_1. A decrease in the demand for the product is shown by the demand curve shifting inwards, from D to D_2. What factors might lead to a change in demand and how will this affect a particular business?

● The consumers at which the product is aimed may experience an increase in income. The business may be able to sell more of the product at a given price (OQ - OQ_1) or charge a higher price (OP - OP_1). If incomes fall, the demand curve shifts inwards and the quantity demanded may fall (OQ - OQ_2) or the price may fall (OP - OP_2). An example may be increased demand for Zanussi freezers as incomes increase.

● The price of a rivals' goods may change. If a rival's price goes up, customers may be more willing to buy more of this product. If rival's prices fall customers may reduce demand for this product. An example may be a fall in demand for one newspaper as another cuts its price.

● The price of a complementary product may fall. For example, the price of portable radios, CD players or other similar products may fall. People may buy more of these products and as a result the demand for Duracell batteries could increase. A rise in the price of a complementary product may lead to a fall in demand for the related product.

● Changes in tastes and fashion. The Body Shop, for example, has seen a rapid rise in demand over the last 20 years as its products appeal to environmentally

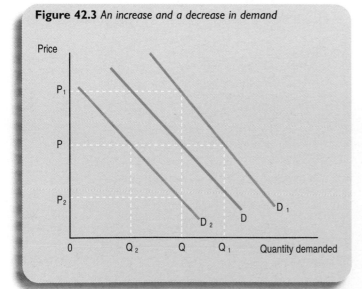

Figure 42.3 *An increase and a decrease in demand*

Question 2

Table 42.3 shows the demand for Robinson's petrol lawn mowers in the UK market. Market analysis by experts employed by Robinson's indicated the following changes for the year 2000.

● A series of newspaper advertisements for Robinson's lawn mowers leading to 4,000 more V28s being demanded over the entire price range shown in Table 42.3.

● A rise in the level of income of males in social class A and B between the ages of 35 and 55 (the target market for V28 lawn mowers). Market analysis indicates that this will lead to 2,000 more V28s being demanded over the price range shown in Table 42.3.

Table 42.3 *The demand schedule for Robinson's V28 petrol lawn mower, 2000*

Price (£)	Quantity demanded
130	30,000
140	26,000
150	22,000
160	18,000
170	14,000
180	10,000

(a) Draw the original demand schedule for the V28 from the figures in Table 42.3.
(b) Show the effect on the demand curve of the changes as predicted by the market analysts. Explain your answers.

conscious customers.

● Promotional campaigns. Examples of well known advertisements which may have led to increased demand include the controversial Benetton posters in the 1990s or the use of the slogan 'The United Colours of Benetton'.

● Changes in population. A large shopping mall such as the Trafford Centre in Manchester is likely to find an increase in demand if offices and housing are drawn close to its location.

● Government legislation and regulation can affect demand. Local pubs and breweries, for example, may find a fall in demand as a result of a reduction in the legal alcohol limit for drinking and driving.

How businesses use demand curves

Demand curves are useful tools to businesses in terms of analysing and planning their marketing activities. In particular they enable businesses to:
● calculate revenue to be earned for any given price change;
● predict the likely reaction of consumers to price changes;

- predict the likely impact upon revenue of price changes.

Calculating revenue

One of the reasons why businesses are interested in their demand curve is because it enables them to calculate revenue that may be earned for a particular price that is charged. Revenue can be calculated using using a simple formula:

Price x quantity demanded = total revenue

Table 42. 4 reproduces Table 42.1 showing the revenue that a business will earn for product A at different prices, given its demand schedule.

Table 42.4 *The demand schedule for Product A*

Price (£)	Quantity demanded (Q)	Total revenue (P x Q)
10	6,000	60,000
20	5,000	100,000
30	4,000	120,000
40	3,000	120,000
50	2,000	100,000

So, for example, the revenue of the business at a price of £30 would be £30 x 4,000 = £120,000. If the price were to change to £20 the revenue would be £20 x 5,000 = £100,000. Thus we can see that a change in price from £30 to £20 has led to a fall in revenue from £120,000 to £100,000, a fall of £20,000.

This process can help a business to identify the point on the demand curve and the price at which revenue is maximised. This can be seen from Table 42.4. At prices below £30 the business actually increases the revenue by raising its price. At prices above £40 revenue falls as prices are increased. The business earns most revenue between £30 and £40.

It is also possible to show the effect of changes in demand on revenue. Table 42.5 shows the effect on Product A's revenue of an increase in demand of 2,000 at each price level.

Table 42.5 *The demand schedule for Product A*

Price (£)	Quantity demanded (Q)	Total revenue (P x Q)	Quantity demanded (+2,000) (Q)	Total revenue (P x Q)
10	6,000	60,000	8,000	80,000
20	5,000	100,000	7,000	140,000
30	4,000	120,000	6,000	180,000
40	3,000	120,000	5,000	200,000
50	2,000	100,000	4,000	200,000

Question 3

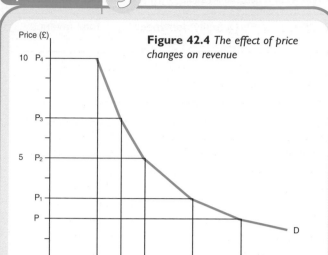

Figure 42.4 *The effect of price changes on revenue*

Using Figure 42.4 calculate the change in the revenue of the business of the following.
(a) An increase in price from P to P_1.
(b) An increase in price from P_3 to P_4.
(c) A decrease in price from P_2 to P_1.
(d) An increase in demand of 200 units at price P_2 assuming price remains the same.

Price sensitivity

All businesses are likely to be concerned about the sensitivity of the demand for their products to price changes. In other words, they will want to predict what will happen to the quantity demanded of their product if there is a change in price. The sensitivity of quantity demanded to changes in price is known as the PRICE ELASTICITY OF DEMAND (PED). It can be calculated using the following formula:

$$PED = \frac{\text{Percentage change in quantity demanded}}{\text{Percentage change in price}}$$

or

$$\frac{\text{Change in quantity demanded}}{\text{Original quantity demanded}} \div \frac{\text{change in price}}{\text{original price}}$$

Inelastic demand A business selling its product in a particular market may face the demand schedule and demand curve in Table 42.6 and Figure 42.5. If the price is raised from £5 to £6 (a 20 per cent change), the quantity demanded falls from 10,000 to 9,000 units (a 10 per cent change). This is shown in Figure 42.5. The price elasticity of demand is:

$$PED = \frac{-10\%}{20\%} = (-)0.5$$

$$\text{or} \quad PED = \frac{-1,000}{10,000} \div \frac{1}{5} = \frac{-1}{10} \times \frac{5}{1} = \frac{-1}{2} \text{ or } (-)0.5$$

Table 42.6 A demand schedule

Price £	Quantity demanded (units)	Total revenue £
4	11,000	44,000
5	10,000	50,000
6	9,000	54,000

Figure 42.5 The effect of a change in price on quantity demanded

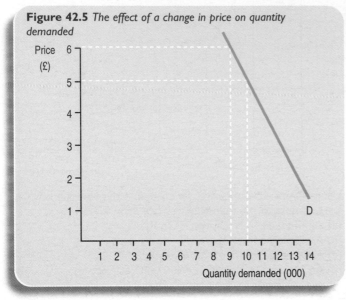

It is usual to ignore the minus sign, so that a figure that is less than 1 but greater than 0 tells the business that demand for the product is **price inelastic**. This means that the percentage change in quantity demanded is less than the percentage change in price. In other words, consumers do not change the quantity of a good they demand proportionally more than any change in price.

What effect will a change in price have on a business's total revenue? Table 42.6 and Figure 42.5 show that a rise in price from £5 to £6 will increase revenue from £50,000 to £54,000. This is because the rise in price is proportionally greater than the fall in the quantity demanded. A business which raises its price will hope that demand for the product is price inelastic.

A reduction in price from £5 to £4 will result in a fall in revenue from £50,000 to £44,000, even though the quantity demanded has increased from 10,000 to 11,000 units.

Elastic demand A business operating in a different market may face the demand schedule in Table 42.7. An increase in price from £20 to £24 (a 20 per cent change) results in a fall in quantity demanded from 10,000 units to 6,000 units (a 40 per cent change). Price elasticity of demand is therefore:

$$PED = \frac{-40\%}{20\%} = (-)2$$

$$\text{or} \quad PED = \frac{-4,000}{10,000} \div \frac{4}{20} = \frac{-1}{10} \times \frac{5}{4} = \frac{-1}{10} \text{ or } (-)2$$

As this figure is greater than 1, the business can conclude that demand for its product is relatively **price elastic**. This means that the percentage change in quantity demanded is greater than the percentage change in price. When demand is price elastic, consumers react to changes in price by changing the quantity they demand by a greater proportion.

Table 42.7 and Figure 42.6 show that if the business reduces its price from £20 to £16, quantity demanded will increase from 10,000 to 14,000 and total revenue will increase from £200,000 to £224,000. This is because the

Table 42.7 A demand schedule

Price £	Quantity demanded (units)	Total revenue £
16	14,000	224,000
20	10,000	200,000
24	6,000	144,000

Figure 42.6 The effect of a change in price on quantity demanded

Question 4

Ratcliffe and Sons, manufacturers of top of the range turntables for hi-fi systems, were analysing the effects of recent price changes. They had increased the price of their turntables from £200 to £240. Sales fell from 800 per month to 600 per month as a result. Questions were now being asked about the effectiveness of these price changes.

(a) Calculate the price elasticity of demand for Ratcliffe turntables.

(b) Is the price elasticity of demand relatively elastic or inelastic?
Explain why you think this is so.

(c) In terms of sales revenue, was the decision to raise prices wise?
Explain your answer showing all calculations.

increase in quantity demanded is proportionally greater than the fall in price. If a business is aiming to cut its price, it will hope demand for the product will be price elastic. An increase in price from £20 to £24 will lead to a fall in revenue from £200,000 to £144,000.

Factors affecting price elasticity of demand

There are two main factors which are thought to affect the price elasticity of demand.

● The number of substitutes for a product. A product with a wide range of substitutes is likely to be highly sensitive to price changes and relatively price elastic. This is because the more substitutes there are for a particular product, the more easy it is for consumers to purchase another product when price changes occur. For example, most types of fish are likely to be relatively price elastic. This is because if the price of one type of fish goes up, consumers can easily swap to another type of fish.

● Time. The longer the period of time, the more price elastic the demand for a product is likely to be. The more time consumers are given, the more able and willing they are to adjust their buying habits. Take, for example, a rise in the price of gas. Over a short period of time, it would be difficult for consumers to buy less gas. Ownership of a gas cooker and gas central heating systems means in the short term that it is difficult to use other types of power. However, over a longer period of time it may be possible for consumers to switch to oil or electricity.

Income elasticity of demand

INCOME ELASTICITY OF DEMAND is a measure of the sensitivity of demand to changes in income. It can be calculated using the formula:

$$\frac{\text{Percentage change in quantity demanded}}{\text{Percentage change in income}}$$

Businesses will want to know the income elasticity of demand for their products. This will help them to judge the effect of a change in their consumers' income on the demand for their products.

● If a rise in income leads to a relatively greater rise in quantity demanded then income elasticity of demand is positive and greater than one.

● If a rise in income leads to a relatively smaller rise in quantity demanded then income elasticity is positive but less than one.

● If a rise in income leads to no change in quantity demanded then income elasticity of demand is zero.

● If a rise in income leads to a fall in quantity demanded then income elasticity of demand is negative.

Advertising elasticity of demand

ADVERTISING ELASTICITY OF DEMAND is a measure of the responsiveness of demand to changes in advertising expenditure. It is measured by the following formula:

$$\frac{\text{Percentage change in quantity demanded}}{\text{Percentage change in advertising expenditure}}$$

Businesses need to be able to measure the effectiveness of their advertising campaigns. One way of doing this is to consider the impact on consumer demand of spending on advertising. This can provide businesses with valuable data which can enable them to judge how far consumers are influenced by advertising campaigns. It also allows businesses to evaluate the relative success of advertising campaigns. If the percentage increase in quantity demanded is a great deal larger than the percentage increase in advertising spending, then advertising elasticity of demand is strong and positive. This may tell a business that advertising is effective in influencing consumers.

Cross elasticity of demand

The CROSS ELASTICITY OF DEMAND shows the response of quantity demanded of one good to a change in the price of another. It allows a business to gauge how demand for its products will react if the price of either rival's products or complementary goods change. It can be calculated using the formula:

$$\frac{\text{Percentage change in quantity demanded of good X}}{\text{Percentage change in price of good Y}}$$

● Goods which are substitutes and compete with each other have a positive cross elasticity. An increase in the price of one newspaper (good Y) should lead to a fall in demand for this product and an increase in demand for another newspaper (good X). Both changes are positive. A fall in the price of good Y will lead to a fall in the demand for good X. Two negatives cancel out to make a positive.

● Goods which are complements to each other have a negative cross elasticity. An increase in the price of an electrical product (good Y) should lead to a fall in demand for this product and a fall in demand for batteries (good X). One change is positive, the other is negative.

Limitations of demand curves

It is often very difficult for an individual business to develop its own demand curve. This is because many businesses do not have sufficient information to construct their individual demand curves. They do not have the market research data to enable them to assess the likely demand for their products over a given range of prices. Often this is because of the high cost of collecting such market information. Such businesses tend to develop a PERCEIVED DEMAND curve. This is a demand curve based upon the 'feel' which managers and owners have for their market. It will involve rough estimations of the likely impact upon demand of upwards or downwards changes in prices.

Some larger businesses with access to detailed market information are in a much better position to develop demand curves which can assist them in making more informed decisions about their prices. However, even for such businesses the demand curve may be of limited value. This is because the demand curve can only provide information about the likely response of consumers to a change in the price of a particular product at a given point in time. In fast changing markets such information may quickly go out of date and will be of limited value unless it is regularly updated.

Summary

1. What does the demand curve of a business show?
2. What might the demand curve for a product judged on quality rather than price look like?
3. What are the factors affecting the demand for a product?
4. How is price elasticity of demand calculated?
5. What is the difference between inelastic and elastic demand?
6. What effect will a change in price have on the revenue of a firm facing inelastic demand for its product?
7. State 2 factors affecting the price elasticity of demand for a product.
8. Why might a business be interested in its advertising elasticity of demand?
9. Suggest a limitation when using a demand curve for a business.

Key terms

Advertising elasticity of demand - the responsiveness of demand to a change in advertising expenditure.
Cross elasticity of demand - the responsiveness of the demand of one product to a change in the price of another.
Income elasticity of demand - the responsiveness of demand to a change in income.
Price elasticity of demand - the responsiveness of demand to a change in price.
Perceived demand - the demand which the managers and owners of a business believe exists for their products in a particular market.

IceStyle is a manufacturer of skiing products, including skis, snowboards and skiboards, outdoor clothing and skiing accessories. Recently it has found that the price of skiing holidays for its customers has risen by 4 per cent due to the level of the exchange rate. This resulted in a 6 per cent fall in sales last year. In an attempt to battle against the fall in demand, the business launched a high profile marketing campaign designed to promote skiwear as leisure clothing. It particularly targeted the 'youth' market, attempting to stress a link between extreme sports and fashion. So far a 10 per cent increase in advertising expenditure has resulted in a 2 per cent increase in sales.

(a) Why might IceStyle be interested in:
   (i) cross elasticity of demand;
   (ii) advertising elasticity of demand?
(b) Using the figures above calculate the:
   (i) cross elasticity of demand;
   (ii) advertising elasticity of demand;
   and in each case comment on the results from the point of view of IceStyle.

Case study

Bodyline

Bodyline is a small firm based in the West Midlands which manufactures womens' swimwear. Their products are distributed through four main types of outlet - mail-order catalogues, department stores, womens' clothing chains and independent retailers.

The business was set up in early 1998. The two women, Elaine and Penny, who started up the firm had originally been friends at University. One had studied for a degree in Art and Design, the other in Business Studies.

Their main product was to be a swimsuit, the Californian, which had been designed in a wide range of dazzling colours. Their marketing strategy had been to aim for the bottom end of the market, offering a cheap, but fashionable garment which would be within the reach of a wide number of consumers' pockets. Marketing research into the demand for the Californian showed that sales at different prices were likely to be as in Table 42.8.

Elaine and Penny found that they were able to sell all of their production at a price of £9. They sold Californians at this price for 6 months and made a fair profit. The market was fairly stable at this time and few sudden changes were expected in the near future. Penny felt that by reducing the price a little they would be able to capture more of the market. Elaine was not so sure and the two debated the decision over the next six months without taking any action.

By early 1999 a number of rival businesses developed similar product lines using bright colours, having seen the initial success of Bodyline in the market.

As Elaine had commented, one of the worst things about the new products was that 'the Californian designs no longer stood out in the shops and are the same as other products now available'. In what had seemed like a short period of time to these two entrepreneurs, their niche in the market had all but disappeared.

After their initial success in the market, many of the new businesses had attempted to undercut Bodyline's prices. The effect on the demand curve for the Californian is shown in Table 42.9.

One business in particular, Johnson Peters, which produced a swimsuit called Ebony, claimed that its novel fabric would cut down on resistance in the water and was also designed to reduce chaffing. It had increased its advertising budget by 5 per cent and had seen a 25 per cent increase in sales as a result.

(a) Draw the demand curve for Californians from the figures in Table 42.8.

(b) Calculate the elasticity of demand for Californians for a reduction in price from:
  (i)   £10 to £9;
  (ii) £9 to £8;
  (iii) £8 to £7.

(c) (i)   Calculate the advertising elasticity of demand for Johnson Peters.
  (ii) Explain how this might be of use to the business.

(d) Using Table 42.9 explain the idea of cross elasticity of demand for Californians.

(e) Given your answer to question (b) do you think Penny was right to suggest cutting the price of Californians at the time she did? Explain your answer using figures or a diagram.

Table 42.8 *Demand curve for Californians*

Price	Quantity of Californians
£7	18,000
£8	14,000
£9	10,000
£10	6,000

Table 42.9 *Effect of a change in competitors' prices on the demand for Californians*

Price of other products	Quantity of Californians
£7	16,200
£6	12,600
£5	9,000
£4	5,400

Pricing strategies

Unit 18 showed that the extent to which a business can influence its price will depend on the degree of competition it faces. When a business does have scope to set its price there is a number of PRICING STRATEGIES or policies it might choose.

- Penetrating the market. A business may set its price in order to gain a footing in a market. This could be a new product being launched or an existing product being launched into a new market.
- Destroying competition/capturing the market. Some firms may seek to 'capture' a market by trying to force other firms out of business.
- Being competitive. Businesses may be concerned about their ability to compete with others. This may mean following another firm's price increase or cut. An example may be the pricing of petrol companies.
- Skimming or creaming. A business may be in a position to skim or cream a market as a result of having a unique product. This usually involves charging a high price for a limited period of time in order to take advantage of the unique nature of the product. For example, video cameras were highly priced when first launched.
- Discriminating between different groups of consumers. A business may be in a position to charge different prices to different groups of consumers for the same product. For example, BT charges higher rates for telephone calls at certain times of the day.

Factors affecting pricing decisions

What factors influence the price a business sets for its product?

Objectives The pricing strategy chosen by a business is likely to reflect the extent to which it wants to maximise profits or sales. A business seeking to maximise short term profits may use more aggressive and perhaps risky pricing strategies.

The marketing mix The price chosen by a business must complement the other aspects of the marketing mix (☞ unit 40). This means that the price must fit in with the nature of the product itself and the way in which it is being promoted and distributed to consumers. For example, a low quality product being sold in retail outlets at the bottom end of the market is likely to be sold at a fairly low price.

Costs A business which cannot generate enough revenue over time to cover its costs will not survive. In the long run, a business must charge a price which earns enough revenue to cover its total cost of production (fixed and variable) at any level of output. This means that businesses must take account

all of their costs when setting price. In the short run, however, it is unlikely that a business would expect to cover the fixed costs of its factory or machinery (☞ unit 52). Providing its price is high enough to generate revenue that covers its variable costs, the firm will stay in business. Revenue below this will cause the firm to cease production. As a result businesses may have greater flexibility in the short term when making pricing decisions.

Competition Unit 18 explained how competition can affect pricing decisions. For a market trader, the price of her goods is largely determined by prices on nearby stalls selling similar goods. Such a trader will have little room for manoeuvre compared to a business which faces less competition.

Consumer perceptions and expectations Businesses must pay attention to what consumers think a product is worth. A product priced above what consumers consider its value to be may generate low sales because of doubts about its **value for money**. A product priced too low may also generate low sales. This is because consumers often suspect that such products have something wrong with them or that they are of inferior quality. For example, a business marketing high fashion clothing would be careful to ensure that its products were priced higher than those offered to the mass market.

Businesses have the opportunity to influence consumer perceptions through aspects of the marketing mix, such as advertising. By improving the view consumers have of the product, businesses can give themselves more scope when setting prices. In some cases firms actually encourage consumers to think of their products as expensive. For example, After Eight Mints have been marketed as a high quality item.

Market segment Businesses that produce a range of products are likely to have some aimed at particular market segments (☞ unit 38). This is true, for example, of all major car manufacturers. They are, therefore, likely to charge different prices for each segment. However, the price which they charge to one segment of the market will affect the prices charged to other segments. A product competing in the top end of the market will need to have a different price from one aimed at the middle or bottom end of the market.

Legal constraints The price of a number of products is affected by **taxation**. This raises the price above the level that might have been set by manufacturers. Products affected greatly by taxation include cigarettes, alcoholic drinks and petrol. There is also a number of products which are offered to consumers below the price that producers would normally charge. Such products are **subsidised** by the government. An example might be low priced travel on public transport for young people and pensioners. The prices of products such as

The price of each product in a market will be influenced by a variety of factors. For some products, the ability of a business to set its price is limited. For others, there will be more scope for a business to set the price it wants to charge.

(a) What factors do you think have influenced the price of the products in the photographs?

gas and water are determined by regulatory bodies such as OFGAS and OFWAT (☞ unit 22).

Cost based pricing

COST BASED PRICING is an example of a **marketing strategy** that a business might use (☞ unit 48). All businesses are influenced by their costs when setting prices to some extent. For this reason many businesses use their costs as the floor or 'bottom line' when choosing a price. Businesses using cost based pricing methods are mainly influenced by cost, more than other factors such as market conditions or competitors' prices, when setting their price.

There is a number of methods that businesses use to set their prices which are based upon particular costs.

Cost plus pricing This involves setting a price by calculating the average cost (☞ unit 52) of producing goods and adding a MARK-UP for profit. If a business produces 10,000 goods costing £50,000, the average cost would be £5.00. A mark up of 20 per cent would mean goods would cost an extra £1.00

and the price would be £6.00 per product. Retailers often use this method of pricing. Say that a department store buys a colour TV from wholesalers for £200 and their mark-up to allow for a profit is 100 per cent. The retail price to consumers will be £400.

The attractiveness of cost plus pricing is that it is a quick and simple way of setting a selling price. It also ensures that sales revenue will cover total costs and generate profit. A criticism, however, is that a fixed mark-up does not allow a business to take market needs into account when setting prices. In addition, no attempt is made to allocate indirect costs to particular products. This means they do not reflect the resources being allocated by the business to that particular product or product range.

Contribution pricing This method takes into account that different products within a company might need to be priced using different criteria. For each product, a price is set in relation to the **direct costs** of producing that product and any **contribution** (☞ unit 53) that the business wants that product to make towards covering its **indirect cost** and towards profit. Thus for a manufacturer of electrical goods, some prices might be as set out as in Figure 43.1.

No one product will be **expected** to account for all the indirect costs of the business. Each product's selling price would make some contribution to meeting indirect costs. If the producer expected to sell 100 items of each product and had to cover indirect costs of £6,500 and generate profit of £2,000 (£8,500) then:

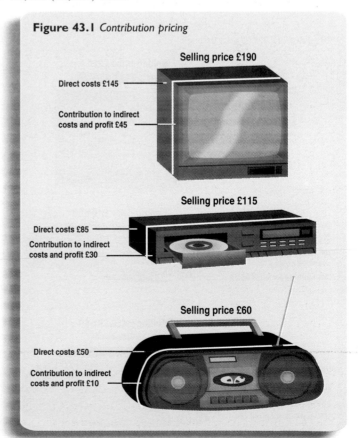

Figure 43.1 *Contribution pricing*

Selling price £190
Direct costs £145
Contribution to indirect costs and profit £45

Selling price £115
Direct costs £85
Contribution to indirect costs and profit £30

Selling price £60
Direct costs £50
Contribution to indirect costs and profit £10

Product A   £45×100 = £4,500   contribution
Product B   £30×100 = £3,000   contribution
Product C   £10×100 = £1,000   contribution
<u>   </u>
£8,500

This allows businesses more flexibility than the cost plus approach. Successful products can be priced to make a large contribution. Less successful products or new products can be priced more competitively, as they need only to make a lower contribution to overheads and profits. Indeed, new products might even be making a negative contribution, ie their price does not even cover the **marginal cost** of production. Demand factors as well as cost factors are now being taken into account.

Absorption cost/full cost pricing A business may attempt to take into account the indirect costs that can be attributable to a particular product in deciding on a price. In its simplest form (known as **full cost pricing** ☞ unit 53) a 'blanket' formula is used to allocate indirect cost to each product, for example, a percentage of total sales of each product. The electrical goods manufacturer might charge the prices in Figure 43.2. A mark-up is then added for profit.

A more sophisticated method of allocation can also be used. This is known as **absorption cost pricing** (☞ unit 53). Instead of a 'blanket' formula being used to allocate indirect costs, each element of the cost will be treated separately. This means the selling price of a product will absorb elements of

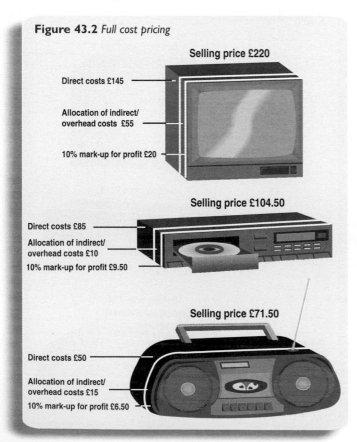

Figure 43.2 *Full cost pricing*

Selling price £220

Direct costs £145

Allocation of indirect/ overhead costs £55

10% mark-up for profit £20

Selling price £104.50

Direct costs £85

Allocation of indirect/ overhead costs £10

10% mark-up for profit £9.50

Selling price £71.50

Direct costs £50

Allocation of indirect/ overhead costs £15

10% mark-up for profit £6.50

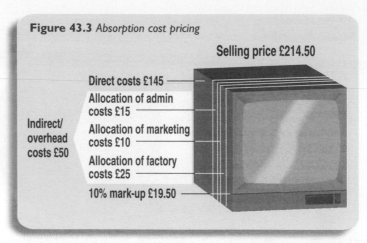

Figure 43.3 *Absorption cost pricing*

Selling price £214.50

Direct costs £145

Allocation of admin costs £15

Indirect/ overhead costs £50

Allocation of marketing costs £10

Allocation of factory costs £25

10% mark-up £19.50

each overhead cost.

As we can see from Figures 43.2 and 43.3 the price of the TV is different according to the method used. A different costing formula will lead to a different final price. Under the full cost method a larger allocation of indirect/overhead costs was made to the television's final price than in the absorption cost approach.

Target pricing This is sometimes known as **target profit pricing**. It involves businesses setting prices that will earn them a particular level of profit, which has been clearly targeted. When setting a target price (or profit) businesses make use of break-even analysis (☞ unit 54). Figure 43.4 shows the break-even chart for a small business producing leather briefcases. It is based upon a selling price of £90, fixed costs of £30,000 and variable costs of £30 per briefcase. In order to break-even the business must produce and sell 500 briefcases. If, however, it wishes to target a profit of £30,000 then it must produce and sell 1,000 briefcases. Using break-even analysis in this way businesses can target a particular level of profit for their product.

We know from unit 42 that the price which is charged for a product affects the demand for a product. The precise relationship between demand and price is measured by price **elasticity** of demand. Thus the briefcase manufacturer may

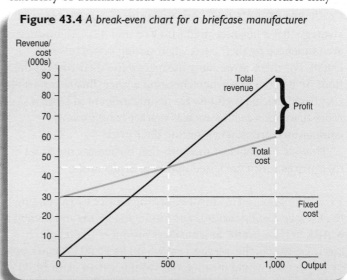

Figure 43.4 *A break-even chart for a briefcase manufacturer*

Revenue/ cost (000s)

Total revenue

Profit

Total cost

Fixed cost

Output

wish to estimate the demand for its briefcases at various price levels. It can then choose a price and associated sales which will enable it to make the profit that it wants. This is shown in Table 43.1.

Table 43.1 *Profits and break even at different price levels for a briefcase manufacturer*

Price	Estimated demand at given price	Total revenue	Total costs (Fixed costs = £30,000 variable costs = £30)	Break-even point	Profit
(£)		(£)	(£)		(£)
80	1,100	88,000	63,000	600	25,000
90	1,000	90,000	60,000	500	30,000
100	800	80,000	54,000	429	26,000

Problems of cost based pricing

Cost based pricing does have a number of problems. It is a product and cost orientated approach with little reference to consumers' wishes or flexibility.

Contribution pricing does, however, allow more flexibility than cost plus pricing for a particular marketing strategy. Full or absorption cost pricing will result in prices being set too high or too low in relation to consumers' wishes or competitors' prices. They are also inflexible in response to market changes, as these would not necessarily be reflected in the costs of a company. The more sophisticated the costing method used when pricing, the more accurate is the allocation of costs to a product, but the further the price might be from what the market will bear.

Market orientated pricing

MARKET ORIENTATED PRICING methods are those which are based upon an analysis of the conditions in the market at which a product is aimed. As such, they are much better suited to market orientated businesses.

Penetration pricing This is used by businesses seeking to gain a foothold in a market, either with new products or with established products being placed in new markets. It involves pricing a product at a low level so that retailers and consumers are encouraged to purchase the product in large quantities.

There are two main reasons why businesses use penetration pricing.
- Consumers are encouraged to develop the habit of buying the product, so that when prices eventually begin to rise they will continue to purchase it.
- Retailers and wholesalers are likely to purchase large quantities of the product. This should mean that they will

Question 2

Patel and Co has been manufacturing aluminium ladders since the business was set up in 1988. Its sales up to now have been based upon two products, a 10 metre and a 15 metre folding ladder. The business has adopted a cost plus method of pricing for each ladder, as illustrated in Table 43.2.

Table 43.2

10 metre ladder	Average cost per unit £92	20% mark-up to cover profit £18.40	Selling price to trade £110.40
15 metre ladder	Average cost per unit £125	20% mark-up to cover profit £25.00	Selling price to trade £150.00

Because of the success of these two products and pressure from competition, the company has developed a new product, a ladder which would allow people to gain constant access to their lofts, but which will be permanently attached to the loft entrance. With a third product, the company's accountant felt that a contribution pricing approach should now be used to price each of their products. He set out some initial calculations of their likely prices, as in Table 43.3.

Table 43.3

	Direct costs per unit	Contribution to indirect cost and profit	Price
10 metre ladder	£80	£35	£115
15 metre ladder	£105	£40	£145
Loft ladder	£185	£5	£190

The pricing for the loft ladder was set at a level which was in line with the price of competitors, which was £190.00.
(a) Identify the benefits to the company of using a contribution pricing approach compared to a cost plus approach for their ladders.
(b) Is the loft ladder a viable product for the company to produce given the figures produced by the accountant? Explain your answer.

not buy from other suppliers until they have sold most of their stock. Businesses can thus gain a significant slice of the market.

Penetration pricing, because of its high cost, is often used by large firms operating in mass markets, such as those selling biscuits, sweets, washing powder and canned drinks. It is also a policy used by new businesses or established businesses in other areas to break into a new market. It is not a policy that is suitable for products with short life cycles. There is usually not enough time to recover the cost of lost revenue from the initially low price. One exception to this is new CD singles. They are often launched at £1.99 in the first few weeks of release before being raised to their full price.

Market skimming Market skimming involves charging a high price for a new product for a limited period. The aim is to gain as much profit as possible for a new product while it remains unique in the market. It usually means selling a product to the most profitable segment of the market before it is sold to a wider market at a lower price.

There are two reasons why businesses adopt market skimming. They may try to maximise revenue before competitors come into the market with a similar product. Often new techniques or designs mean that entirely new products, or new versions of a product can be offered. Examples include new fashions in clothes, new childrens' toys and new inventions. When first launched, a basic digital watch could cost as much as £50 or £60. Now they often sell for as little as a few pounds. Market skimming can also be used to generate revenue in a short period of time so that further investment in the product can be made. Companies in the electronics and pharmaceutical industries often use skimming for this reason.

Customer value pricing This involves charging the price that consumers are prepared to pay. Products which have prestige names attached to them, such as Rolex, may be able to command a higher price because of the status of these names. Products for one-off events, such as music festivals or sports finals, may be given a high price because they are unique.

Loss leaders LOSS LEADERS are products priced at very low levels in order to attract customers. The price of a loss leader is set lower than the average total cost of producing the product. The company selling the product makes a 'loss' on each product sold. Businesses use this pricing technique because they expect the losses made on the loss leader to be more than compensated for by extra profits on other products. It is often used by larger supermarkets. Safeway, for example, has sold its baked beans at prices as low as 5p per can. Its aim is to attract more customers into stores, drawn in by the low prices. The 'captive' customers will then buy more highly priced and profitable items.

Psychological pricing Many businesses seek to take account of the psychological effect of their prices upon consumers. This is known as psychological pricing. A common example is the use of prices just a little lower than a round figure, such as £199.99 rather than £200, or £29.99 rather than £30. Businesses using these slightly lower prices believe that they will influence the consumers' decision as to whether or not to purchase. Such slightly lower prices also suggest that consumers will be looking for value for money. For this reason, the producers of high status products such as prestige cars or designer clothing tend to avoid such prices. Instead, they often choose prices which psychologically match their consumers expectations of higher quality. So, for example, a price of £110 may be charged for a designer shirt rather than £99.99.

Price discrimination Price discrimination occurs when a

Question 3

The phenomenon of geographical pricing, charging different prices for the same product in different geographical areas has always been a feature between countries. New cars in the UK, for example, have for a number of years been priced more highly than the same models in other European countries. However, the use of geographical pricing is becoming increasingly widespread within countries. Sainsbury's was criticised for charging up to 60 pence more for a range of products including coffee and sherry in one of its Hampshire stores. One Vauxhall dealer in Hull might charge about £106.50 for a new exhaust for a Vauxhall Cavalier. In another part of the country, such as Bristol, a Vauxhall dealer might charge about £173 for the same product. Virgin Direct charges a 36 year old non-smoking man living in Hull £15.64 for a 15 year £100,000 life insurance policy. The same man living in Bristol would pay £15.05 for the same policy.

Source: adapted from the *Sunday Times*, 23.3.1997 and *The Guardian*, 10.5.1997.

(a) How would you account for the price differences between products mentioned in the article in different parts of the country?
(b) Do you think geographical pricing is mainly a cost or a market based pricing method? Explain your answer.
(c) How might businesses benefit from using geographical pricing?

firm offers the same product at different prices when consumers can be kept separate. An example is British Telecom's (BT's) policy of charging different prices to business and residential users at different times of the day and the weekend. This allows BT to take into account the differences in cost which exists at peak and off peak times. So, for example, local calls may be charged around four times more on Monday to Friday, 8am-6pm, than at weekends. BT's price discrimination is **time based**. The price you pay for a phone call is based upon the time of day or the day of the week when you use the service. Other businesses which use this policy are rail companies (cheaper off peak travel), and holiday firms which charge higher prices for their product during school holidays.

Price discrimination can also be **market based**. This involves offering different market segments the same product at different prices. An example of this is students being given discounts on coach and bus travel.

Discounts and sales These tend to support the pricing strategies used by businesses. They often mean a reduction in the standard price for particular groups of consumers. A very common form of discount is the seasonal 'sales' of retailers. The aim is to encourage purchasers at times when sales might otherwise be low and to clear out of date and out of fashion stock. Discounts may also be given to those customers who buy in bulk or in large quantities.

Competition based pricing

With COMPETITION BASED PRICING it is the prices charged by competitors which are the major influence on a producer's price. It is used mostly by businesses which face fierce and direct competition. As a rule, the more competitive the market and the more homogeneous the products competing in that market, the greater the pressure for competition based pricing. Markets similar to the model of oligopoly (☞ unit 18) will often use this form of pricing. For example, soap powder producers tend to be influenced by the price of competitors' products.

Going rate pricing This occurs in markets where businesses are reluctant to set off a price war by lowering their prices and are concerned about a fall off in revenue if prices are raised. They examine competitors' prices and choose a price broadly in line with them. It also occurs when one dominant business establishes a position of **price leadership** within a market. Other firms will follow suit when the price leader changes its prices. This type of policy can be seen when a petrol company changes the price of a gallon of petrol or when banks and building societies change interest rates.

Companies which operate in markets where going rate pricing occurs will often be frustrated by their inability to control their prices more closely. A strategy often used in such circumstances is to establish a strong **brand** identity for your product and to differentiate it from others on the market (☞ unit 45). This would be through unique design features or quality of service. BP's Amoco's decision to upgrade all of its service stations is an example of an attempt to achieve this. A strong brand identity and unique product features allow firms much greater scope for choosing their own price levels.

Destroyer pricing The aim of destroyer pricing is to eliminate opposition. It involves cutting prices, sometimes greatly, for a period of time, long enough for your rivals to go out of business. It could be argued that the reduction in the price of *The Times* in the early 1990s was an attempt to force other newspapers out of the business. Others then responded by following the 'going rate price'.

Close bid pricing This method of pricing occurs when firms have to TENDER a bid for work which they are going to carry out. This is common practice for firms dealing with the government or local authorities. For example, if a new road is to be built firms will be invited to put in a bid to win a contract for the work. Firms will clearly need to pay very close attention to the price at which they expect their competitors to bid. Sometimes, when a number of firms bid for a contract, those with the highest prices are likely to be rejected. Another example of this type of pricing was the bids to operate Independent Television stations. A round of bids saw TV-AM replaced by GMTV for the breakfast news slot in the mid-1990s.

Question 4

Price wars in the late 1990s were said by some to be healthy for business, with the consumers being the ultimate winner. Ryanair, the budget airline operator, had taken a growing share of the market for UK and European flights by offering cheap, no-frills deals. British Airways and other airline 'giants' had been forced to rethink their ticket prices as a result of the success of such airlines. BA responded by launching its own low cost airline, Go, in 1997. In 1998, for example, it offered one million cheap seats. Ryanair criticised the offer because of the restricted availability. In September 1998 Ryanair promised one-way tickets to Italy, Sweden and France for prices undercutting those of BA, Virgin Express and other low cost airlines, such as EasyJet. Michael O'Leary, the chief executive of Ryanair, warned that fierce competition would drive some airlines out of business.

Figure 43.5 *Ryanair prices*

Route	One-way	Return
Luton-Dublin	£16.99	£33.98
Liverpool-Dublin	£16.99	£33.98
Stansted-Prestwick	£16.99	£33.98
Stansted-Pisa (Italy)	£29.99	£59.98*
Stansted-Oslo (Norway)	£29.99	£59.98*
Stansted-Carcassonne (France)	£29.99	£59.98*
Stansted-Stockholm (Sweden)	£29.99	£59.98*

*Tax to be added.

Source: adapted from the *Daily Mail*, 4.9.1998.

(a) What might have been the pricing policies of: (i) BA in 1997; (ii) Ryanair in 1998? Explain your answer.
(b) Explain the possible effects on: (i) the businesses involved in the airline market; and (ii) customers; of these types of pricing policy.
(c) What do you think are the risks to Ryanair of pursuing its pricing policy?

Key terms

Competition based pricing - methods of pricing based upon the prices charged by competitors.
Cost based pricing - methods of pricing products which are based upon costs.
Lost leaders - products with prices set deliberately below average total cost to attract customers who will then buy other, more profitable, products.
Market orientated pricing - methods of pricing based upon the pricing conditions in the market at which a product is aimed.
Mark-up - that part of a price which seeks to provide a business with profit as opposed to covering its costs. It is used in cost plus pricing.
Pricing strategy - the pricing policy or method of pricing adopted by a business.
Tender - a bid to secure a contract for work.

Summary

1. State 5 pricing strategies a business might use.
2. What are the main factors affecting a firm's pricing decisions?
3. Explain the difference between cost plus pricing and contribution pricing.
4. State one advantage and one disadvantage of cost plus and contribution pricing for a firm.
5. What is meant by absorption cost pricing?
6. Why might a firm use penetration pricing?
7. What is market skimming?
8. What types of firm might use market skimming as a pricing strategy?
9. Why might a business sell a product as a loss leader?
10. What is meant by psychological pricing?
11. What is meant by price discrimination?
12. Under what circumstances might a firm use competition based pricing?
13. Explain the terms:
    (a) going rate pricing;
    (b) destroyer pricing;
    (c) close bid pricing.
14. Give 2 examples of tendering.

Case study

Make or break?

In 1992 Compaq turned itself into a major player in the computer industry by designing a line of affordable computer products. It decided that consumers were paying too much for designing their own computers. Compaq argued that people would sacrifice this flexibility for an effective computer at a low price. It was proven right. Lee Iaccocca came up with the idea for one of Ford's most successful cars, the Ford Mustang. He asked designers to build a more affordable sports car rather than a better car. Buyers did not want the engine of a sports car, he reasoned. They wanted the look. The Mustang sold more in its first year than any other car that Ford built.

Setting a lower price is not always the answer. Luxury products, such as Godiva chocolates and Rolex watches, may possibly see sales revenue decline if the price was cut for the mass market. Porsche, for example, made an error according to Tom Nagle, a pricing guru, when it offered a new cheaper model, the Boxster, for $30,000. 'Porsche undermined its image and underestimated the demand for the Boxster'. As a result of shortages, dealers started charging customers higher prices. They were able to take the profits, rather than Porshe.

When setting the price of a product, it is important to consider not what customers are willing to pay, but what the company can convince them to pay. The sound equipment group Bose used such a strategy with its wave radio. The radio retailed at $300 (around £190). Many analysts thought no-one would pay such an amount for a radio alarm clock. Using a smart advertising campaign, the company convinced customers that the superior sound quality of the radio was worth the extra money.

But how much are people prepared to pay? Suppliers' figures have suggested that British supermarkets are charging shoppers up to 60 per cent more for products than they pay suppliers for them. Figure 43.6 shows the mark-ups on various products. Supermarkets often place 'value products' or 'own brands' next to higher priced well known brands, so that they look cheaper. In fact, because value products are cheaper to

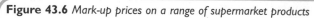

Figure 43.6 *Mark-up prices on a range of supermarket products*

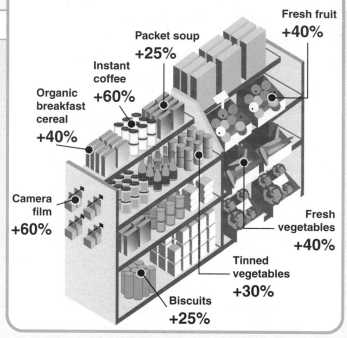

Fresh fruit **+40%**
Packet soup **+25%**
Instant coffee **+60%**
Organic breakfast cereal **+40%**
Camera film **+60%**
Fresh vegetables **+40%**
Tinned vegetables **+30%**
Biscuits **+25%**

manufacture they have a much higher mark-up. UK supermarkets argued that net margins were actually only 5.9 per cent.

Source: adapted from the *Financial Times*, 12.10.1998 and *The Sunday Times*, 8.11.1998.

(a) **Using an example from the article, explain what is meant by cost-plus pricing.**
(b) **Explain two market orientated pricing strategies that may be used by supermarkets.**
(c) **Explain the factors that may have influenced Bose when setting a price of $300 for its radio alarm clock.**
(d) **How would you describe the pricing strategy used by Compaq when becoming a 'major player in the computer industry'? Explain your answer.**
(e) **Discuss the extent to which pricing a product cheaply may be a successful strategy, using evidence from the article.**

What is promotion?

PROMOTION is the attempt to draw attention to a product or business in order to gain new customers or to retain existing ones. Different methods of promotion are shown in Figure 44.1.

Businesses often refer to promotion **above the line** and **below the line**. Above the line promotion is through independent media, such as television or newspapers. These allow a business to reach a wide audience easily. Most advertising is carried out 'above the line'. Some advertising, however, is carried out by methods over which a firm has direct control, such as direct mailing. These and other direct methods of promotion (known as below the line promotion) are dealt with in unit 45. This unit looks at how businesses advertise their products through different media.

The objectives of promotion

A business must be clear about exactly what it is trying to achieve through its promotion. The main aim of any promotion is to obtain and retain customers. However, there is a number of other objectives, some or all of which any successful campaign must fulfil.

- To make consumers aware or increase awareness of a product.
- To reach a target audience which might be geographically dispersed.
- To remind consumers about the product. This can encourage existing consumers to re-purchase the product and may attract new consumers.
- To show a product is better than that of a competitor. This may encourage consumers to switch purchases from another product.
- To develop or improve the image of a business rather than a product. Much **corporate advertising** is carried out with

this in mind, and is dealt with later in this unit.
- To reassure consumers after the product has been purchased. This builds up confidence in the product and may encourage more to be bought at a later date.
- To support an existing product. Such promotions may be used to remind consumers that a reliable and well thought of product is still available.

Businesses sometimes consider their promotion using **models**. For example, AIDA is a method used to consider advertising. It suggests that effective advertising will raise awareness (A) and encourage interest (I), desire (D), and action (A), so that consumers buy the products. The DAGMAR (defining advertising goals for measured advertising results) model is also used to measure the effect of advertising. A business can measure how far the group that is targeted has progressed along a scale of unawareness, awareness, comprehension, conviction and action, as a result of advertising.

Question 1

(a) Identify the objectives that the businesses involved might have had when using these promotions.

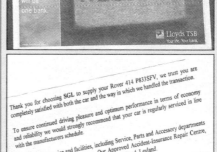

The growth of advertising

Faced with competition, firms have come to realise the importance of advertising. The extent of advertising in the UK can be seen in numerous poster, TV and newspaper campaigns of companies as diverse as pet food manufacturers and merchant bankers. It has been estimated that the drinks industry spends over £200 million on advertising and that between 1 and 2 per cent of national income is spent on advertising in the United Kingdom.

Advertising is often placed into different categories. INFORMATIVE ADVERTISING is designed to increase consumer awareness of a product. Examples include the

Figure 44.1 *Methods of promotion*

- Advertising
- Sales promotions
- Exhibitions and trade fairs
- Personal selling
- **PROMOTION**
- Direct mail
- Merchandising
- Public relations

classified advertisements in local newspapers, new share offers, grants available to small firms and entries in the Yellow Pages. New products may be launched with informative advertising campaigns to make consumers aware of their presence. It is usually argued that this type of advertising helps consumers to make a rational choice as to what to buy.

PERSUASIVE ADVERTISING tries to convince consumers to purchase a product, often by stressing that it is more desirable than others. It is argued that this type of advertising distorts consumer buying, pushing them to buy products which they would otherwise not have bought. In reality, almost all advertising is persuasive to some extent. Very few major campaigns aim to be entirely informative.

Types of advertising media

There is a wide range of ADVERTISING MEDIA that firms can choose from in order to make consumers aware of their products.

Television Because of its many advantages, television advertising is often used by businesses marketing consumer goods to a mass market. The fast changing trends in television are likely to provide opportunities for television advertising after the year 2000. 99 per cent of males and females watch television in the UK. The growth of cable, satellite and digital television may attract companies to advertise on television. In 1998 over a quarter of UK households owned a satellite dish. Businesses may be particularly attracted to advertise on satellite television. As shown in Figure 44.2, households headed by skilled manual workers or professionals are most likely to subscribe. They tend to be higher income groups.

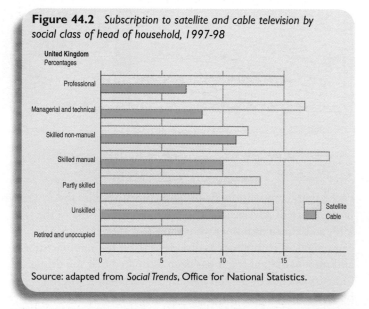

Figure 44.2 *Subscription to satellite and cable television by social class of head of household, 1997-98*

Source: adapted from *Social Trends*, Office for National Statistics.

Newspapers and magazines Newspapers are a very important medium for the advertising of mass market consumer goods, because of the numbers of readers. In 1998, for example, 56 per cent of all adults regularly read a daily newspaper.

A quarter of all males read *The Sun*.

Newspapers can be important in reaching a target audience. Newspapers and magazines are often read by people sharing similar characteristics. The readership of the *Financial Times* and the *Independent* is mainly from social classes A and B. Newspaper advertising is important to small firms. The only promotion they can afford may be in a local paper.

Cinema Cinema attendances fell from a high of around 1.4 billion in 1951 to reach a low of 53 million in 1984. The 1990s, however, saw a revival in attendances, partly as a result of the better facilities offered by large multiplex cinemas. By 1997 attendances had improved to 124 million. As a result, advertisers began to pay greater attention to this medium. Firms such as Wrangler have even produced advertisements principally designed for use on large cinema screens. Of all the advertising media available to a business, the cinema has the greatest potential for having a strong impact on its audience.

Radio In recent years there has been a growth in the number of independent radio stations in the UK. These include local stations, such as Capital in London and Piccadilly in Manchester, to national stations such as Virgin and Kiss FM and specialist stations such as Jazz FM and Classic FM. For advertisers this has meant an increase in both the number and type of radio stations on which they can advertise.

There has also been an increase in the amount of radio listening in recent years. The growth in the number of local commercial radio stations has been of particular benefit to small and medium sized firms.

Posters Posters appear in a variety of locations and tend to carry short messages. This is because motorists and pedestrians usually only have a few seconds to consider them. An effective poster is likely to be large, attention grabbing and placed in a site where it is highly visible to large numbers of people.

The internet Of growing interest to businesses in the 1990s was advertising on the internet. The 'worldwide web' offers the opportunity for businesses to advertise their products to countries throughout the world. Any computer linked to the internet can call up 'home pages' of companies or search for these using search indexes. Many well known companies such as The Body Shop, Boots the Chemist and Sainsbury's have their own web sites.

The advantages and disadvantages of different advertising media are shown in Table 44.1.

Choice of advertising media

How do firms decide which medium will be most suitable for their product? There are a number of factors that advertisers may take into account.

Table 44.1 *Advertising media*

Medium	Advantages	Disadvantages
Television	• Creative advertisements can attract attention and have a great impact. • Advertisements can demonstrate the product in use. • Can reach a vast audience. • Increased scope for targeting the audience, eg digital television. • The message can be reinforced by continuous advertisements.	• Relatively expensive initial cost. • The message is short lived. • Consumers may not watch commercials. • Technical information is difficult to explain. • There may be a delay between seeing the advert and visiting the shops.
National newspaper	• National coverage. • Reader can refer back. • Relatively cheap. • Detail of the product can be provided.	• No movement or sound. • Usually limited to black and white. • Individual adverts may be lost amongst large quantities of other advertisements.
Regional newspaper	• Good for regional campaigns and test marketing. • Can be linked to local conditions.	• Cost per reader higher than national newspapers. • Reproduction, layout etc. may be poor.
Magazines	• Colour advertisements possible. • Targeting possible with specialist magazines. • Advertising can be linked to features. • Magazines may be referred to at a later date.	• A long time exists between advertisements being placed and magazine being printed. • Competitors' products are also being advertised. • No movement or sound.
Cinema	• Colour, sound and movement can be used. • Advertisements can be highly localised. • A 'captive' audience for advertisements. • Great impact on the consumer. • Age groups can be targeted.	• Limited audience. • Message is short lived. • Message may only be seen once.
Radio	• Enables use of sound. • Most consumer groups covered. • Minority programmes can target audiences. • Produced cheaply. • Younger audience targeted.	• Not visual. • No copy of material. • Interruptions to music may prove irritating. • May not capture the audience's attention.
Posters	• National campaigns possible. • Most groups covered. • May encourage impulse buying through location close to shops. • Seen repeatedly. • Excellent for short, sharp messages, eg, election 'promises'.	• Limited amount of information. • Difficult to measure effectiveness. • Weather and graffiti can ruin the poster.
Internet	• Relatively cheap and easy to set up. • Number of 'hits' can be monitored. • Can be targeted. • Can be easily changed.	• Limited audience. • Possible technical problems of connection, viewing, ordering, maintaining.

Cost Small firms will be mainly concerned with what media they can afford. Larger firms will need to consider the cost effectiveness of each of the different media. For example, although television is the most expensive medium, it reaches huge numbers of consumers. This means the cost per sale from a television advertisement may be relatively low. The internet is a relatively low cost method of advertising.

The audience reached Given that many products are aimed at certain segments, it makes sense for firms to place their advertisement in a medium which the target audience is likely to see or hear. Firms must aim to reduce **wastage** in their advertising. 'Wastage' means advertising to those other than the target audience. Clearly a certain amount of wastage

will occur with most TV advertising, whilst very little will occur when advertising in, say, specialist magazines. Advertising on the internet can be targeted, but the audience may be limited.

The advertising of competitors A major TV advertising campaign by one firm may, for example, be followed by a counter campaign from its competitors.

The impact Firms will aim to make the greatest impact when advertising. Different products will require different media to do this. For example, some products such as sports equipment will benefit from being shown in action to have the most impact on an audience. Television and cinema are the obvious choice of media in such cases.

The law There are legal restrictions in the UK which mean that some products cannot be advertised in particular media. This is discussed in detail later in this unit. One example of this is the ban on advertising tobacco on TV in the UK.

The marketing mix The advertising campaign should be integrated with other types of below the line promotion (☞ unit 45). For example, sponsorship of a sports event and an advertisement for the product on the sports pages of a newspaper may be effective.

The presentation and recording of information If an advertisement is designed to be visual, with little written information, then posters on billboards or magazine articles can be effective. Magazine advertisements can also include a lot of text, usually in small print. Advertising on television will also be useful for visual images and has the advantage that words can be spoken at the same time. A short radio advert can provide a certain amount of spoken information, although it will be difficult for the listener to remember everything. Advertising on the internet allows large amounts of information to be downloaded free of charge.

Question 2

The Body Shop, founded by Anita Roddick in 1976, has spurned traditional advertising channels. Its tactical use of posters sets its advertising apart from competitors. The shop windows of its 1,500 plus outlets in 47 countries around the world are seen as prime advertising sites. Designers in London work specifically on producing posters which fit in with the identity of the company.

All the posters everywhere in the world are changed every two weeks to highlight a particular issue or a new product. Roddick is pushing for posters to have even more attitude and strong primary colours. She says 'You need to set yourself apart from the rest'. Care must be taken over the posters' design. Nudity can not be used in certain countries.

Source: adapted from *Design*, The Journal of the Design Council, Summer 1996.

(a) Suggest the benefits to The Body Shop of using posters as an advertising medium.
(b) What factors may have influenced The Body Shop in choosing posters as an advertising medium?

Controls on advertising

Consumers sometimes complain that advertisements either mislead or exploit. For this reason, there are legislation and codes of practice to protect the consumer.

Legislation The **Trades Descriptions Act, 1968** is the most important piece of legislation in the control of advertising. The law states that products must correspond to the claims made for them in advertisements. It is, therefore, illegal to include ingredients on a label which are not present or make unproven claims about the effects of, say, weight loss products. Descriptions of services provided by firms must also be accurate. The Act prevents businesses from misleading the consumer about 'sales'.

Under the **Monopolies and Restrictive Practices Act, 1948**, the **Office of Fair Trading** and the **Competition Commission** have been given powers to investigate anti-competitive behaviour by firms (☞ unit 22). Such anti-competitive behaviour may be in the form of high levels of spending on advertising. This raises costs within an industry and acts as a barrier to prevent other firms from entering the market.

Independent bodies The **Advertising Standards Authority (ASA)** is a body set up to monitor advertising in the UK. It is responsible for making sure that advertisers conform to the **British Code of Advertising and Sales Promotion Practice**. This code stresses that advertisements must be legal, decent, honest and truthful and must not cause grave or widespread offence. Around 10,000 advertisements are referred to the ASA each year by consumers and businesses. Around one-third of these are investigated. If the ASA finds that an advertisement infringes the codes of practice it may ask the business involved to withdraw the advertisement. Although it has no legal power to force a business to withdraw an advertisement, it can put pressure on it to do so. It may threaten to refer a business to the Office of Fair Trading (OFT). The OFT has the power to take out an injunction preventing certain advertisements appearing at a later date. It may also put pressure on the media to refuse to handle the advertisement and may ask to see future advertisements before they are used.

An example in the 1990s of an advertisement criticised by the ASA and then withdrawn was a Barclays Bank advertisement aimed at teenagers. The advertisement had the headline '10 things you should have done before you're 18' included advice to 'stay out all night without ringing home.' The ASA upheld a complaint, deeming the advertisement likely to encourage irresponsible or anti-social behaviour.

The Independent Television Commission (ITC) controls advertising on television and radio. There is a variety of rules which are used to judge such advertising. Examples are that current newsreaders cannot appear in adverts to endorse products and actors cannot be used in commercial breaks during programmes in which they appear.

Pressure groups Certain pressure groups (☞ unit 27) seek to influence advertising. FOREST, for example, is a pressure group which aims to defend the rights of tobacco firms to advertise. The British Medical Association (BMA) and Action on Smoking and Health (ASH) take the opposite view. Women's groups have sought to influence firms to produce advertisements which are not sexist. Pressure groups campaigning for better safety on roads have sought to persuade car and tyre manufacturers to produce advertisements showing less aggressive driving.

 Question 3

In an increasingly competitive market place, colleges and universities have taken up advertising as a means of assisting their campaigns to recruit students. However, this shift towards a more market driven approach has been accompanied by complaints to the ASA that some colleges and universities are misleading potential students. An ASA report criticised the advertising of certain colleges and universities. One, for example, claimed that it had been educating people since 1878. In fact the former polytechnic only became a university in 1992. The 1878 date referred to a college which had once stood on the site of one of the present campus buildings. Another university was criticised for claiming to offer 'the UK's leading Public Relations Master's Degree'. In fact, there were only two such courses at the time of this claim and the university could not substantiate that it was the best.

Source: adapted from *The Guardian*, 11.2.1998.

(a) Explain the possible constraints on advertising by universities and colleges.
(b) How might these constraints influence the approach to advertising by universities and colleges in future?

Advertising and society

Advertising has the potential to affect the lives of many people. This is because, for most, regular exposure to advertising is almost unavoidable. How might advertising affect individuals?

● It adds to the cost of marketing products. This money could have been spent on improving products or price reductions. It is likely that consumers will pay more of any advertising costs than firms.

● It is argued that advertising encourages people to buy products which they might not otherwise have purchased. This may, perhaps, lead to a society where people are judged according to how much they consume rather than their value as human beings.

● Environmentalists are concerned about high levels of consumption and the role of advertising in encouraging this. They doubt whether the earth's resources can sustain current levels. There is a growing trend amongst

consumers to look at the type of goods they buy and also how much they consume, as they become more aware of long term problems.

● Advertising can encourage people to buy products which are regarded as being damaging to society.

● Advertisements often encourage behaviour which might be to the detriment of society as a whole. An example is the fast 'macho' driving often seen in advertisements for cars and related products.

In its defence, the advertising industry would point to a number of arguments to justify its role.

● Advertisements offer a choice to consumers which allows them to make more informed consumption decisions.

● Advertisements give valuable information to consumers which might otherwise be difficult to come by.

● Advertisers respond to and reflect the needs, wishes and attitudes of consumers; they do not 'create' them.

● Advertising earns revenue for television and radio and allows newspapers and magazines to be sold at lower prices.

● The advertising industry employs large numbers of people. They are employed directly, through advertising agencies, and indirectly through jobs that may result from a successfully advertised product.

 Question 4

Sony pulled the plug on a multi million pound advertising campaign after complaints that it used explicit drugs language to sell a computer game to children and teenagers. The advertisements, for a £34.99 snowboarding game for the best selling games console, PlayStation, referred to a body 'aching for powder' and 'needing a rush'. The game was called Coolboarders 2.

After 10 complaints from members of the public to the Advertising Standards Authority and condemnation by drugs help agencies, Sony withdrew the advertisement from poster sites all over the country. A TV and magazine campaign was also abandoned. 'There is something rather unpleasant about a large corporation exploiting the drug scene to make ever greater profits', said Greg Porter of the drugs charity Release.

Source: adapted from *The Guardian*, 18.2.1998.

How might the events described above affect:
(a) the business's target audience;
(b) the business itself?

Corporate advertising

CORPORATE ADVERTISING is concerned with promoting a company as a whole, rather than individual products. An example of corporate advertising can be seen in the detergent market. Companies such as Unilever, a subsidiary of Lever Bros, now have their name on all branded packets.

The amount spent on corporate advertising has doubled in recent years and this trend is expected to continue.

Companies ranging from ICI to Benetton to BP Amoco have jumped on this bandwagon.

There are two reasons why companies need to sell themselves now more than ever. First, companies must now be seen to be responsible good 'citizens' (☞ unit 27). This means communicating. Second, there is growing pressure for the company to become a **brand** (☞ unit 46). Companies need to ensure that their corporate image is positive.

Corporate advertising often makes use of **slogans** or **catchlines**. Nestlé, for example, has started to identify its name on products. So, for example, all Kit Kats now have the name Nestlé clearly marked on their covers. Even more dramatically, the Chambourcy brand of yoghurt has been renamed Nestlé. Shell tried to build up its reputation as a much trusted institution with the slogan 'You can be sure of Shell' and BA has advertised itself as the 'World's Airline'.

Corporate advertising allows a company to advertise its whole philosophy. Corporate messages are aimed at a variety of different, yet connected, audiences. These include employees, local groups, the trade, government, the media, financial institutions and the 'general public', as well as consumers themselves. There are problems, however. The corporate values of one company may not be different to those of another, so that target audiences may not be able to distinguish between the messages of different firms. Also, less may be spent on advertising individual brands, as a business uses resources to promote the whole company.

Key terms

Advertising media - the various means by which advertisements can be communicated to the public.

Corporate advertising - advertising which is meant to promote a whole company rather than a particular product or product line.

Informative advertising - advertising which primarily seeks to provide consumers with information about a product.

Persuasive advertising - advertising which seeks to influence and persuade consumers to buy a product.

Promotion - an attempt to retain and obtain customers by drawing attention to a firm or its products.

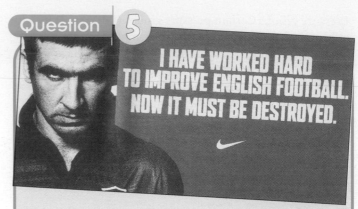

Question 5

The market for sportswear and training shoes is highly competitive. In the 1980s and 1990s sportswear crossed the threshold into leisurewear. Ever since, marketing experts have fought to stay one step ahead. At the forefront of this have been attempts to cultivate an image. Nike, arguably the market leader, has gone to great lengths to associate itself with sport's controversial characters - McEnroe, Cantona, Agassi. Its image is about the streetwise. 'We like to ruffle a few feathers', says Peter Bracegirdle, from Nike's UK advertising agency. Nike advertisements have aggressive images and words. On all advertisements can be found the famous Nike 'Swoosh' logo.

Reebok tends to promote a caring, sharing image. The company motto is 'making a difference' and it has the 'Planet Reebok' slogan. Its advertisements have included Greg Norman, Ryan Giggs and ice skater Nancy Kerrigan. Jeremy Bowles at Reebok's UK advertising agency says, 'Our approach is more about taking part, that our shoes will enhance your performance at whatever level of sport you participate in.'

Adidas suffered during the 1980s. However, it gained credibility again in the 1990s as music artists went for 'retro' styles. Adidas was able to draw on its heritage, reissuing its 'classic' shoes for a new young audience. After all Adi Dasler, its founder, was supposed to have invented the first training shoe in 1920. Its slogan is, 'We knew then, we know now'.

Source: adapted from *Design*, The Journal of the Design Council, Summer 1996.

(a) What examples of corporate advertising are suggested in the article?

(b) Contrast the corporate philosophies of the sportswear manufacturers and explain how they have influenced corporate advertising.

(c) Suggest possible advantages of corporate advertising for these businesses.

Summary

1. What is above the line promotion?
2. Why might advertising be both above and below the line promotion?
3. What are the objectives of promotion?
4. What choices of advertising media do firms have?
5. What criteria might firms use in order to decide upon their choice of advertising media?
6. What is the role of an advertising agency?
7. What is the role of the ASA?
8. Why might an advertisement be banned under the Trade Description Act 1968?
9. State 3 arguments for and 3 arguments against advertising.
10. What is the objective of corporate advertising?

Case study

Conrack and Eco-Store

Conrack

Conrack Ltd is a private limited company which specialises in manufacturing products from 'managed' wood. Managed wood is wood which when cut down for timber is replaced by planting a new tree. Its policy is only to purchase wood from suppliers that guarantee to conform with these requirements.

The business has been successful in selling to customers who are interested in preserving the environment. They are attracted by the idea that the products they buy do not use up the earth's resources, which are preserved for future generations. Conrack's slogan is 'What we use, we replace'. Products include kitchen and dining tables. It also manufactures housing 'parts', such as window ledges and doors, from managed wood, as well as conservatories and garden outhouses.

In 1999 the business had a manufacturing factory just outside Manchester and two retail outlets in the area North of Manchester. Its turnover was £800,000 and it had a promotion budget of around £15,000 per annum. It had concentrated mainly on local advertising in the region. The managing director, Kim Barnett, argued that small scale but thought provoking advertisements might be particularly influential in attracting interest in the company's products.

Conrack and The Eco-Store are considering what promotion media they will use.

(a) **What might be the objectives of the promotion for each company?**

(b) **For each company, identify the factors that are likely to affect their choice of advertising medium.**

(c) **Select the most suitable media to be used by each business. Explain why the media you have chosen are suitable. Note that the business may choose more than one medium.**

Eco-Store

The Eco-Store is a company with a national chain of stores in the UK. The shops are based on 'old style' American stores. Food is sold loose from barrels and sacks to remove the need for packaging and waste. Liquids and drinks are filled into bottles or containers rather than being sold in plastic or glass bottles. Environmentally friendly goods are also sold. These include products made from recycled plastic and wood and recycled paper. The company has seen rapid growth in the 1990s. By 1999 it had a turnover of £200 million. It had decided to review its marketing strategy. It particularly wished to develop a caring image for the company. It hoped in its advertisements to stress the 'homely nature' of the stores and products. It felt that this would attract families to shop at its stores.

Table 44.2

Advertisement in local newspaper per week -
£51 per issue (based on a business card sized advertisement of 5 cm x 2 cm)

Advertisement on local radio
Fixed costs - £500-£1,000
Cost per minute - £100-£200

Leaflets
Single colour
Fixed costs - £125
Cost per thousand - £50
Full colour
Fixed costs - £200
Cost per thousand - £200

Internet website
£1,000 per year

Poster on a fleet of buses for a month - £300

Insert into *Yellow Pages* per annum
1.5 cm box - £154
3 cm box - £272
4.5 cm box - £367

Advertising in a specialist magazine (per issue)
1/4 page black and white £400
Full page 2 colour £1,300
Full page full colour £1,700

Advertising in a national newspaper -
£20,000 per quarter page advert

Television advertising - £50,000 per 30 seconds, plus fixed costs.

45 Promotion Below the Line

Promoting below the line

Promotion below the line refers to those promotional methods which do not depend upon media such as newspapers and TV. Instead, it takes place by methods over which firms have some degree of control. These include direct mail advertising, exhibitions and trade fairs, sales promotions, merchandising, packaging, personal selling and public relations. A business, such as Forte, might promote its hotels by using a combination of promotions, for example public relations and sales promotions.

Below the line promotion allows a business to aim its marketing at consumers it knows are interested in the product. Above the line advertising in newspapers means that the promotion is seen by most of the readers, even though some will not be interested. With below the line promotions, firms are usually aiming their message at consumers who are either known to them or who have been chosen in advance. For example, direct mail advertisers will pick exactly which consumers they wish to send their mail to, rather than going for blanket coverage. Businesses promoting through exhibitions, such as the Boat Show, can be certain that the majority of those attending will be interested in the products on show.

There may be problems that result from below the line promotions.
- As with advertising, they are expensive and their outcome is difficult to predict.
- They are often 'one off' events, which have an impact for a limited period.
- Some types of promotion, such as direct mail and personal selling, are disliked by consumers.

Direct mailing

Direct mailing involves sending information about a product or product range through the post. The consumer can usually buy the product by placing an order by post or telephone. Although sometimes unpopular with the public, direct mail is a fast growing area of promotion. It has proved very effective for firms trying to reach a target audience.

Direct mail is one means of **direct marketing** (☞ unit 46), which is often seen as part of a firm's distribution network.

Exhibitions and trade fairs

Exhibitions and trade fairs are used by firms to promote their products. They are visited by both industrial and ordinary consumers. Examples of better known fairs and exhibitions include the Motor Show, the Boat Show and the Ideal Homes Exhibition. Why do businesses find them useful?
- They give the chance to show how a product actually

works. This is important in the case of bulky or complex technical products. The marketing of industrial and agricultural machinery is often done through trade fairs.
- Consumer reaction to a product can be tested before it is released onto the market.
- Some trade fairs and exhibitions are held overseas. They can form a part of a firm's international marketing strategy (☞ unit 49).
- A fair or exhibition may attract press coverage. New products may be launched to take advantage of this. The Motor Show is widely used for this purpose.
- They allow customers to discuss a product with members of the management team. It is not unusual for the managing directors of a business to attend a trade fair. For industrial consumers, in particular, this can be a valuable point of contact.
- Technical and sales staff are available to answer questions and discuss the product.

 Question 1

One of the USA's major trade exhibitions is the PC Expo which is held at New York's Javitz Centre, the city's main exhibition venue. It draws in over 50,000 people during its three day existence, and receives a tremendous amount of press and TV coverage. The principal players in the personal computer market, such as Apple, IBM and Compaq, all have stands there and it is used as a platform to make major new business announcements.

(a) Why is it important for a business such as IBM to use a trade exhibition as part of its promotional mix?
(b) Why might trade fairs be more effective in promoting personal computers than direct mail advertising?

Sales promotions

Sales promotions are the incentives offered to consumers to encourage them to buy goods and services. They are used to give a short term 'boost' to the sales of a product. This is different to building up brand recognition and loyalty, which may be a longer term aim. There is a variety of sales promotions that a business can use.
- Coupons, refunds and loyalty or reward cards. These involve either refunding money to the customers or allowing savings to be made on repeat purchases. Many supermarkets and high street retail chains have loyalty cards. The Boots loyalty card, launched in 1997, had 8.7 million holders by mid-1998.
- Competitions. Prizes are sometimes offered for competitions. To enter, consumers must first buy the product. Tabloid newspapers often use this type of promotion. They try to attract customers through large

cash prizes in their 'bingo' competitions.

● Product endorsements. These are widely used by sports goods manufacturers. Sports personalities and teams are paid to wear or use particular products. A crucial element of the competition between Nike and Adidas, the two leading sportswear manufacturers, is their signing of sports personalities. In 1998 Nike were lining up Ronaldo, Michael Jordan and Ian Wright against Tim Henman, David Beckham and Naseem Hamed for Adidas.

● Product placing. This is a recent innovation. It involves a firm paying for product brands to be placed on the sets of films and TV programmes. Car manufacturers are often eager to see their vehicles driven by Hollywood stars in popular movies.

● Free offers. A free 'gift' may be given with the product. An example of this is the music magazine, Q, which regularly offers its readers free CDs of featured artists.

● Special credit terms. This has been increasingly used by firms. It includes offers such as interest free credit and 'buy now pay later' schemes.

Why have these methods become popular?

● Sales promotions can be used as a method to break into a new market or introduce a new product into an existing market. They can also be used as a means of extending the **product life cycle** of an existing product (☞ unit 41).

● They are a means of encouraging consumers to sample a good or service which they might not have bought otherwise. Once the initial good has been purchased it is likely that further goods will be bought. Many magazines offer free gifts ranging from CD Roms to make-up in their first issues hoping that their consumers will continue to buy.

● Customers feel 'rewarded' for their custom. They may, as a result, develop a loyalty to a particular product or business.

● Customers identify products or businesses with things that they like or are attracted to. A customer is therefore more likely to purchase a product.

● Sales promotions provide businesses with feedback on the impact of their marketing expenditure, for example, through the number of coupons returned or the amount spent on loyalty cards.

Sales promotions are not without problems. The free flight offer of Hoover in 1992 is one example. It offered two free flights to the US with the purchase of products worth over £200. The company misjudged the number of people taking advantage of the offer. This meant extreme pressure on the company to produce the goods consumers were demanding. Also many consumers did not receive the holidays on dates or at times they wished. By 1993 there were so many complaints that Maytag, Hoover's US parent company, had to intervene to make sure flights or compensation were provided. It was estimated that the cost of dealing with these problems was £21.1 million.

Question 2

Are customers selling themselves for points? Many retail outlets now offer loyalty cards to customers. Those who sign up receive a number of points per £100 spent. The points can be redeemed against future purchases in participating outlets. They are designed to encourage repeat purchases by customers, who know that they will gain more points the more they spend. Table 45.1 shows examples of the different amounts that can be redeemed per £100 spent on certain cards. Some cards have been extremely successful, with millions of carriers.

However, there is a growing number of criticisms. *Which?* magazine calculated that a family spends £2,900 a year on average on food. If this was all spent in one supermarket, the reward could be as little as £29. Some retailers, such as Do-It-All, have scrapped their schemes and it is predicted that 'umbrella cards' gaining points in a number of stores will soon take their place. Somerfield, for example, has linked with BP Amoco, Mobil and Southern Electric to offer points redeemable at Argos stores.

Source: adapted from *The Observer*, 18.10.1998.

Table 45.1 *Loyalty cards*

	Where it can be used in UK	Points per £100 spent	Actual monetary value for £100 spent	Real rate of return on money spent %
Boots (1997)	Boots stores 1,300 outlets	400 points	£4	4
Co-op Wholesale Society (1998)	CWS stores 650 outlets	n/a	£2 average	2
WHSmith Clubcard (1997)	WHSmith stores 500 outlets	1000 points	£2	2
Texaco Global (1994)	Texaco petrol stations 1,000 outlets	16.66 Global stars	£1-£1.10	1-1.1
Sainsbury Reward (1996)	Sainsbury stores & petrol stations, Savacentres 400 outlets	100 Reward points	£1	1
Tesco Clubcard (1997)	Tesco stores, petrol stations & B&Q 640 outlets	100 points	£1	1

Source: adapted from table provided by Professor Steve Worthington, Staffordshire University.

(a) Identify the sales promotion method illustrated in the above passage.

(b) For what reasons might this particular sales promotion be: (i) successful; or (ii) unsuccessful?

(c) What other types of sales promotion might be used by a supermarket?

Branding

A BRAND is a name given by a producer to one or more of its products. The main aims of this are to differentiate the product from others and to make it distinctive to consumers. Choosing a brand name is an important part of a firm's **marketing strategy** (☞ unit 48). An effective brand name is likely to be short and easy to identify and remember. It must also project the required image and, if possible, the positive characteristics of the product. Examples of strong brands include Coca-Cola, Kodak, Porsche, Jaguar, Persil, Mars and Fairy Liquid. Figure 45.1 shows the world's most popular brands in 1997.

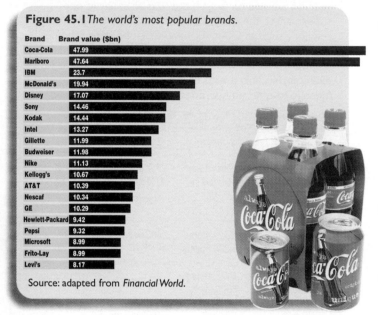

Figure 45.1 *The world's most popular brands.*

Brand	Brand value ($bn)
Coca-Cola	47.99
Marlboro	47.64
IBM	23.7
McDonald's	19.94
Disney	17.07
Sony	14.46
Kodak	14.44
Intel	13.27
Gillette	11.99
Budweiser	11.98
Nike	11.13
Kellogg's	10.67
AT&T	10.39
Nescaf	10.34
GE	10.29
Hewlett-Packard	9.42
Pepsi	9.32
Microsoft	8.99
Frito-Lay	8.99
Levi's	8.17

Source: adapted from *Financial World*.

Popular brands have often been supported and developed by CATCHLINES. These are phrases which seek to strengthen the identity of a brand. Famous examples include 'A Mars a day helps you work, rest and play' and 'The future's bright, the future's Orange'.

For a business with only one product, deciding upon a brand strategy is relatively straightforward. For those companies with a range of products it is more complex. The majority of businesses fit into one of the categories below.

● Multiple branding. This involves a business using a range of brand names for its products. An example is Unilever which produces Radion, Surf, Persil and other detergents. The main advantage of this strategy is that different brands with separate identities can be developed to meet the needs of different segments of the market. Another advantage is that failure by one brand will not have an adverse effect on another.

● Corporate branding. This is where a business uses its corporate name as the principal brand identity. Heinz, BMW and Sony are examples of businesses which adopt this approach. This form of branding allows new products to be more readily accepted by consumers if they already

trust the existing corporate brand. It also enables marketing campaigns to be spread across a range of products. This can enable a business to benefit from marketing economies of scale (☞ unit 93).

● Corporate and individual branding. This is a middle way between the two previous branding strategies. It involves an emphasis being placed upon both the corporate and the individual brand name. This is a strategy which has been used to good effect by Cadbury Schweppes. It has a range of products such as Wispa, Milk Tray, Flake and Dairy Milk. All of these brands have a strong identity. However, the limelight is always shared with the name Cadbury's, so that for consumers the two brand names appear to naturally go together.

● Retailers' own brands. These are products which are branded with the name of the retailer selling them rather than the manufacturer. Examples include Sainsbury's, Tesco, Boots and Marks & Spencer own brand products. Manufacturers of own brands can supply products to be sold under the name of another business, such as a retailer. This allows the responsibility for the marketing of the product to be passed on to the retailer. Own brands help retailers to gain customer loyalty. They also increase their bargaining power when dealing with manufacturers.

There is a number of reasons why businesses use branding.

● To create brand loyalty. Consumers often have a high degree of loyalty to popular, well established, brands. In many markets it can be very difficult for firms to compete unless they have a strong brand identity.

● To differentiate the product. Especially in markets where products are fairly similar, it is important for a firm that its own products can be clearly distinguished from others. A clear brand identity can help to achieve this.

● To gain flexibility when making pricing decisions. The greater the loyalty of consumers to a particular brand, the more room for manoeuvre a firm will have in its pricing decisions. A survey by Business Marketing Services found that consumers were reluctant to switch from well known brands in the hotel, car hire, computer and transatlantic flights markets. For example, in the car hire market pricing discounts of over 20 per cent were required to persuade consumers to switch from Hertz or Avis to one of the lesser known companies.

● To help recognition. A product with a strong brand identity is likely to be instantly recognised by most consumers. This may mean consumers trust the product and are therefore more willing to buy it. Some brand names are used to describe whole classes of products, such as Sellotape and Hoover.

● To develop a brand image. It is argued that customers respond to brand images with which they identify. Some consumers respond to brands that allow them to pursue multiple goals. Volvo, for example, stress that its cars not only protect but allow the user to escape to remote places.

Question 3

The distinctive slanted lettering is almost exactly as it was 40 years ago and the slogan remains: 'Have a break, have a Kit Kat'. In all that time the only noticeable break with tradition has been the replacement of the discreetly lettered 'made by Rowntree' with the prominently displayed 'Nestlé' (Nestlé took over Rowntree in the 1980s) now found on the cover of this chocolate bar.

Peter Brabeck, Nestlé's chief executive, explains the strategy as follows: 'Nestlé is a brand in its own right. If we want to be perceived as the world's leading food company, we have to offer consumers an increasing amount of products that they can identify as Nestlé's. The approach is a shift away from what was once regarded as traditional marketing wisdom. The argument used to be that an organisation that owned a number of diverse product brands should remain firmly in the background, rather than get in the way of the individual brand's communication with consumers.

Source: adapted from the *Financial Times*, 5.6.1998.

(a) Identify the branding strategy used for the Kit Kat:
 (i) 40 years ago; (ii) at the time the above article was written.
(b) What are the likely advantages and disadvantages of this change in branding strategy for Nestle?

Consumers also react to brands that offer 'extreme consumption experiences' such as Haagen-Dazs ice cream or Starbucks coffee.

Merchandising

Merchandising is an attempt to influence consumers at the POINT OF SALE. The point of sale is anywhere that a consumer buys a product. It may be, for example, a supermarket, a department store, a bank or a petrol station. Consumers are intended to buy based on 'what they see' rather than from a sales assistant. The aim of merchandising is to encourage sales of a product and therefore to speed up the rate at which stocks are turned over (☞ unit 94).

There is a number of different features of merchandising.
● Display material. A good display should attract attention, enhance certain aspects of a product and encourage the 'right frame of mind' to make a purchase. Department

stores lay great stress on window displays. Banks make sure that the services which they offer, such as insurance and loan facilities, are well displayed in their branches.
● The layout of products at the point of sale. Many retail outlets, such as supermarkets, design the layout of their stores very carefully. Their aim is to encourage consumers to follow particular routes around a store. Retail outlets often place popular items at the back or sides of a store. Consumers, on their way to these, are encouraged to walk past other items which they might buy. Another tactic is to place related products next to each other, so consumers buy both.
● Stocks. A firm must make sure that stock levels are maintained and shelves are quickly restocked. Shelf space is usually allocated according to the amount of a product which a business expects to sell. For example, a supermarket will give more space to products on special offer.
● Appropriate lighting and the creation of desirable 'smells'. Generally lighting is kept soft where browsing is encouraged and bright where there is a need to suggest cleanliness as, for example, at a cosmetics counter. Smells are used to encourage the right atmosphere. Bread smells are often wafted into supermarkets and food retailers.

Packaging

A product's packaging is important in its overall marketing. This is because consumers often link the quality and design of a product's packaging with the quality of the product itself. Unsuitable packaging may affect sales.

What factors should firms consider when deciding upon how to package their product?
● Weight and shape. These can affect the cost of distributing a product. For example, bulky packaging may mean high distribution costs.
● Protection. Products must not be damaged in transit or in storage. They must also be protected against light, dust and heat.
● Convenience. The packaging must be easy to handle by the consumer and distributors.
● Design. The design of the packaging should be eye catching and help the consumer to distinguish it from others. It should also fit in with the overall marketing of the product and project the brand image. Colour is likely to be important here.
● Information. It is likely that the package will contain information required by the consumer. For technical products, the packaging will need to include information about how the product should be used. For food products, there are legal requirements about the information that must be on the package, such as details of the ingredients contained.
● Environmental factors. Manufacturers are facing increasing

pressure to cut down on the amount and type of packaging placed around products. Consumers and pressure groups (☞ unit 27) stress the wastefulness of this and its impact upon the environment. The response of some manufacturers to this pressure has been to use recyclable materials.

☞ unit 27

Question 4

Caribbean Ltd is a manufacturer of soft drinks. It has recently produced a new additive-free kiwi fruit drink, which it initially aims to target at business people who are looking for something a little different for a lunchtime drink. It has arranged for retailers to stock the new drink and keep a display on view for an initial trial period.

(a) Advise the marketing department of Caribbean Ltd on the:
  (i) features of its merchandising;
  (ii) packaging;
  that it should use in attempting a successful launch for its product.
(b) What are the likely constraints on the packaging of this product and how are they likely to affect its success?

Personal selling

Personal selling occurs when a company's sales team promotes a product through personal contact. This can be done over the telephone, by setting up meetings, in retail outlets, or by 'knocking on doors'. In general, the more highly priced, technically complex or individual the product, the greater the need for personal selling. Most firms supplying industrial markets rely upon personal selling in the form of **sales representatives**.

The main advantage of personal selling over other methods is that individuals can be given personal attention. Most forms of promotion tend to deliver a 'standard message' to a 'typical' consumer. With personal selling the individual consumer's needs can be dealt with and the product shaped to meet these needs.

There are certain purposes which personal selling can serve.
● Creating awareness of and interest in a product.
● Explaining the functions and technical aspects of a product.
● Obtaining orders and, in some cases, making deliveries.
● Encouraging product trials and test marketing.
● Providing rapid and detailed feedback from the consumer to the producer via the sales representative.

One disadvantage with personal selling is that it can be expensive. The cost of maintaining a team of sales representatives can be very high. Another problem is the dislike of 'callers' by consumers. There are also legal and ethical issues about the way products are sold that need to be considered.

Question 5

In recent years the banks, such as Lloyds TSB, NatWest and HSBC, have been placing increasing emphasis upon the marketing of financial services, such as household insurance, holiday insurance and life assurance. In the past they were largely seen as sidelines to the main business of banking. Merchandising, personal selling and packaging have all played key roles in a promotional mix with a high emphasis placed upon below the line promotions.

(a) What would be the likely point of sale for these services?
(b) Which aspects of their merchandising would you advise the banks to pay particular attention to?
(c) What might be the particular benefits of personal selling in marketing these 'products'?

Public relations

PUBLIC RELATIONS is an organisation's attempt to communicate with groups that form its 'public'. Such groups may include the government, shareholders, employees and customers. The aim of such communications is to increase sales by improving the image of the firm and its products. This can be done directly by the business itself through a public relations activity. On the other hand a television programme or a newspaper could be used.

Consumers appear to attach great importance to messages conveyed through public relations. Take the example of a new restaurant which has just opened. It would expect to promote a positive image of itself through its own promotional materials. Such communications may, therefore, be taken 'with a pinch of salt' by consumers. However, a good write-up in a newspaper or restaurant guide is likely to be taken much more seriously by consumers.

Businesses often use **press conferences** to attract publicity. These might involve inviting journalists to a company presentation, where they are given information. The business may take the opportunity to launch a new or updated product. Sometimes, businesses provide free products for conference members to try out. Conferences may also be used for presentations to trade customers.

Businesses also make use of **press releases**. These are written accounts of events or activities which may be considered newsworthy. For example, new multi-million pound contracts gained by firms such as British Aerospace are announced on TV news bulletins. Such news stories usually originate from press releases issued by businesses themselves.

Because of the importance of maintaining good relations with the media, a business may appoint a **publicity manager**. As well as promoting favourable press stories, publicity managers must respond to criticisms and try to ensure that there are no unfavourable press notices.

Other than conferences what other public relations activities may firms use?

● Donations to charities etc. These can range from a small contribution to a college mini bus appeal to a large donation to Comic Relief's 'Red Nose Day' or the 'Children in Need' appeal . Whilst some make payments anonymously, others take advantage of the opportunity for a good public relations event. The approach of a firm to such an event is likely to be determined by its particular ethical stance (☞ unit 33).

● Sponsorship. This is popular in the sporting world. Examples have included the links between Coca-Cola and the Olympic Games, McDonald's and the World Cup, Sharp electronics and Manchester United, and Nike and Michael Jordan. Other types of sponsorship take place in the arts world with ballet, opera and theatre being

sponsored by businesses. Firms such as ICI and BP Amoco choose to sponsor educational programmes.

● Company visits. Jaguar Cars and Warburtons Bakeries have allowed members of the public to visit their manufacturing and research plants as part of their public relations activities.

Key terms

Brand - a name given by a business to one or more of its products, as a means of identification by the customer.
Catchline - a memorable phrase which seeks to strengthen a product's brand identity.
Point of sale promotion- a promotion at any point where a consumer buys a product.
Public relations - an organisation's attempts to communicate with interested parties.

Summary

1. What is below the line promotion?
2. What is direct mailing?
3. Why do businesses promote their products at trade fairs and exhibitions?
4. Identify 4 different types of sales promotions.
5. What is branding?
6. What are the main methods of branding?
7. Where is merchandising likely to take place?
8. Which aspects of their merchandising should businesses pay attention to?
9. What factors do businesses need to consider when packaging their products?
10. What is the main advantage of personal selling?
11. What is public relations?
12. Under what circumstances might public relations activities be most effective?

Case study

Wine producers hope to create brands with mass appeal

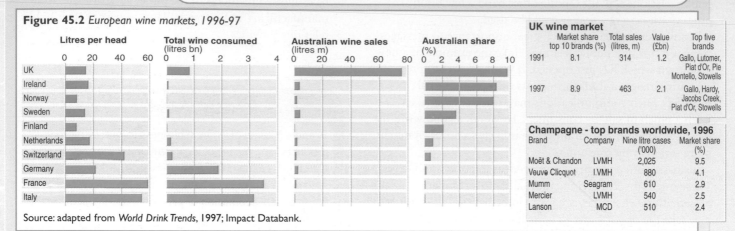

Figure 45.2 *European wine markets, 1996-97*

Source: adapted from *World Drink Trends*, 1997; Impact Databank.

Leading wine producers remain convinced that they can create retail brands with mass appeal to emulate the likes of Johnnie Walker whisky, Buitoni pasta or L'Oreal cosmetics. Yet most of the wine brands over the years - including Hirondelle, Ernesto and Julio Gallo, Mateus Rose, Jacob's Creek, Blue Nun and Piat D'Or - have succeeded in winning no more than a few per cent of the market in one or two countries. Even Gallo, the world's biggest wine brand, has less than one per cent of global sales.

The wine trade should be ripe for branding. Most consumers are baffled by the complexities of choosing between countries, regions, types and grapes. That is where brands should help, says branding expert Jonathan Knowles: 'They help the customer choose between the enormous number of bottles on the shelf, offering a guarantee of value'.

Retailers provide some of that reassurance with their own label products which have taken more than half the market in countries such as the UK and Belgium. But stores are also keen to have branded wines priced just above their own label products. Jacob's Creek is one such brand in the UK. 'Recognisable brands provide a reference point on price and quality that encourages them to make a purchase', says Jonathan Knowles. 'Our research shows that 63 per cent of consumers enter the store without knowing which wine they intend to buy. The appeal for producers is also clear. It would be too expensive to advertise a single wine, but branding across several varieties allows the marketing costs to be spread.'

In spite of these arguments the wine trade has proved impervious to branding. In the UK, the top 10 brands have less than 9 per cent of the market and the picture is little different elsewhere in Europe. Jean-Louis Dumeu, head of the Paris offices of a leading firm of wine distributors, believes that the product itself does not lend itself to branding. 'The promise of a brand is that it will be the same quality every time' he says. 'A brand is a contract with the consumer which says: "I will not be a bad surprise when you buy me again".' As Monsieur Dumeu points out, however, each variety of wine is unique, and yet the same wine can taste quite different from one year to the next.

Wine consumers might also be a problem. As Jonathan Knowles acknowledges, 'wine lovers look for something they haven't heard of'. Even if consumers start off drinking branded wine, they quickly become educated about the product and feel less need for the reassurance of a brand.

Source: adapted from the *Financial Times*, 23.2.1998.

(a) Explain how wine producers might use:
   (i) sales promotions;
   (ii) trade fairs;
   (iii) public relations;
   to promote their products.
(b) (i) Explain the difference between personal selling and direct mail as a means of promotion for a wine manufacturer.
   (ii) Suggest problems of using personal selling and direct mail for wine businesses in their attempts to improve their share of the wine market.
(c) What are the possible benefits of branding wine for:
   (i) consumers;
   (ii) producers;
   highlighted in the article?
(d) Using information from the article and Figure 45.2, evaluate the success of branding as a means of promotion for wine manufacturers.
(e) Traditionally English wine has not had the reputation of European or New World (Australia, Chile, South Africa, California) wines. In the 1990s a small number of English wines were getting rave reviews in wine circles. A wine producer in Kent is considering the use of below the line promotion in the local area to take advantage of the growing reputation of English wines. Advise the wine producer on the most effective methods that could be used.

Channels of distribution

Distribution is about one of the 4 'Ps' of the marketing mix (☞ unit 40) - place. A business must get the product to the right place, at the right time. A product which is effectively priced and promoted may not be a success unless the consumer is able to purchase it easily.

A CHANNEL OF DISTRIBUTION is the route taken by a product as it passes from the producer to the consumer. Figure 46.1 shows some of the most popular channels of distribution that are open to a business. A producer can sell its products:
● directly to the consumer (channel 1);
● through a retail outlet (channels 2, 4, 6, 7);
● through a wholesaler (channels 3, 4, 7);
● using an agent (channels 5, 6, 7).

Sometimes the channel of distribution can be straightforward. Take the example of a village bakery. The bread and cakes are baked in the same place as they are sold. Consumers buy direct from the producer (channel 1 in Figure 46.1). Other examples include the sale of 'home' produced local computer software, hand made guitars or the sale of farm products 'on site'.

Many firms manufacture their goods and provide their services from large, central units in order to benefit from **economies of scale** (☞ unit 93). Their consumers, however, may be located over a wide geographical area. Having a distribution channel similar to that of the village baker could spell disaster. It is likely, in this case, that more complex methods of distributing the product are needed. This usually involves the use of INTERMEDIARIES - wholesalers, retailers or agents.

Intermediaries

What intermediaries are involved in the distribution of products?

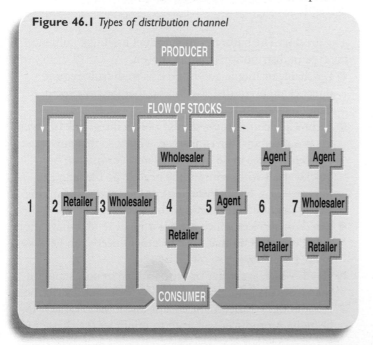

Figure 46.1 *Types of distribution channel*

Wholesalers These often act as links between producers and retailers. Their main task is to buy in bulk from manufacturers and to break this down into smaller quantities which can then be handled by retailers. Examples in the UK include Makro and Costco. Channel 4 in Figure 46.1 has traditionally been the most common method of distribution because of the benefits for the businesses involved. Wholesalers can benefit **manufacturers** in a number of ways.
● They have well established distribution networks and are likely to have strong links with retailers.
● By breaking the manufacturers' products down into smaller batches and taking care of distribution problems, they free the manufacturer to concentrate upon production.
● For multi-product firms, they can help to solve distribution problems, especially when wide geographical areas are involved. Figure 46.2 shows how wholesalers are able to help a firm producing six products distributed over a wide area. By using a wholesaler, the manufacturer is able to deliver all six products to one site. Imagine the difficulties if the manufacturer had to deliver every one of the products to each of the retailers.
● They can bear the cost of storage or warehousing.
● They provide a source of market research information, for example, by asking retailers how their stock is selling in different areas.

Wholesalers also help **retailers**. They offer a choice of products from a variety of manufacturers and provide a 'local' service, often delivering products. Wholesalers sometimes sell direct to the public (channel 3). An example might be a kitchenware wholesaler holding a one week sale for members of the public in order to clear out old stock.

Despite the benefits wholesalers offer, they are not without their problems. Some wholesalers may not promote the products as a business might want, which might harm the firm's marketing efforts. By using a wholesaler the business is passing on the responsibility for marketing - possibly a risky venture. The wholesaler is also likely to take some of the profit.

Retailers Because of the problems of wholesalers, a number of manufacturers now prefer to deal with retailers directly, by setting up their own distribution networks. Many of the larger retail outlets, such as Sainsbury's and Marks and Spencer, deal directly with the manufacturer. This is shown as channel 2 in Figure 46.1. Retailers are an important part of distribution, particularly to manufacturers selling to consumer markets. Retailing is dealt with in more detail later in this unit.

Agents and brokers The usual role of agents is to negotiate sales on behalf of a seller. A ticket agency, for example, will sell tickets to consumers for a range of events, such as concerts and plays. The ticket agency does not usually take

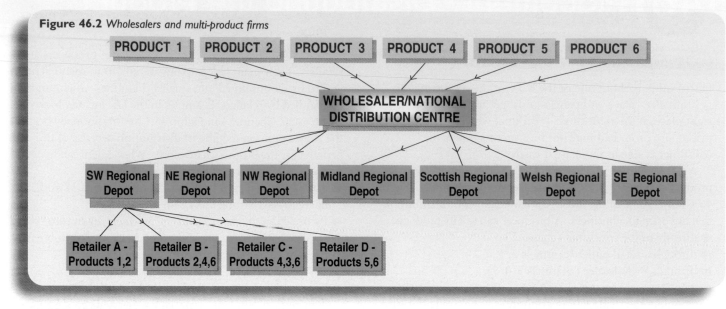

Figure 46.2 *Wholesalers and multi-product firms*

ownership of the tickets it offers. Instead it takes a
commission (☞ unit 72) on those which it does sell and
returns the rest.

Most travel agencies operate in this way. They earn
commission on those holidays which they sell, but never
actually buy 'blocks' of holidays. The agents are the link
between those providing a good or service and those wishing
to buy them (channel 5 in Figure 46.1).

Agents are often used by firms wishing to break into a
foreign market (☞ unit 49). They are helpful to businesses
which are unsure about the trading practices and legal
requirements in foreign countries. They help to take the risk

out of trading abroad. People and organisations which are
involved in the buying and selling of commodities, such as
copper, tin, coffee or sugar, in international markets are
known as brokers. After being bought these commodities are
broken down and sold on to firms for processing or to be
used in manufacturing.

The choice of distribution channel

How does a producer decide which channel of distribution will
get the product to the right place at the right time? An efficient
channel of distribution will allow a business to make products
available to consumers quickly, when required, and at a
minimum distribution cost to the firm itself. Large firms often
choose different channels for different products.

There are many factors that can influence a business'
decision.

The product The nature of the product itself will influence
the type of distribution channel chosen.

● Perishable or fragile goods, such as fresh fruit, require
direct channels of distribution, so that the time spent
handling the product is reduced.

● Technically complex goods also need a direct link between
the producer and the consumer. This is so that any
problems which arise from installation or use can be
quickly dealt with, without the need to go through an
intermediary. Firms installing computers operate in this
way to maintain close links with consumers.

● Goods or services which are tailor made tend to have more
direct channels, so that the consumer's needs can be passed
to the producer.

● Goods which are heavy or are packaged in non-standard
shapes are likely to require a direct channel of distribution.
If handling is difficult, the cost of distribution is likely to
be high. A producer will want to minimise the charges for

 Question 1

In 1998, Campbell Soup, the US food manufacturer, was
considering the idea of selling soup in free standing kiosks
set up in shopping malls, railway stations and at airports. It
was responding to a growing trend of people eating 'on
the hoof' and eating take away meals, rather than cooking
at home.

Its new division 'Campbell Away from Home' would
concentrate on non-traditional distribution channels. The
company's product was already sold to many restaurants,
hospitals and schools, but consumers did not know that
they were eating Campbell's soup. This was a way of
getting the company name on the product at the point of
sale, hoping that people would buy the soup because they
knew it was produced by Campbell Soup.

Source: adapted from the *Financial Times*, 1998.

(a) What is likely to be meant by the phrase 'traditional
distribution methods' when referring to the sale of
soup?
(b) What channel of distribution was Campbell thinking of
using in 1998?
(c) Suggest possible benefits to Campbell of using this
channel of distribution.

the handling of such products.

- Convenience goods, such as canned drinks and food, need to be widely available through retailers. Firms that are unwilling to sell to a wide range of retailers are likely to find rival brands on shop shelves.
- Producers wishing to sell large quantities of low valued goods are likely to use a wholesaler. They will not want to keep stocks of low valued goods if they are receiving orders for more highly priced goods. Selling through wholesalers will mean they can sell low valued products in bulk, as quickly as possible.

The market

- Large and dispersed markets usually require intermediaries. Smaller, local markets can often use a system where consumers buy directly. This is also true of the size of an order, where smaller orders can be sent by a more direct channel of distribution.
- The market segment (☞ unit 38) at which the product is aimed may influence the retail outlet at which the product is made available. For example, products aimed at travelling business people may be sold near to railway stations. Consumer goods are often sold via a retailer or directly to the consumer, whereas industrial products may pass through an agent or

wholesaler. International sales may also need to be made through an agent.

- The time period within which consumers expect a response to orders is sometimes an influence. A business may be forced to find the most direct means of distribution, or lose an urgent order to a rival.

Legal restrictions Legislation may influence the channel that can be used for particular products. Certain drugs, for example, can only be sold by pharmacists through a prescription. Alcohol cannot be sold at petrol stations and only those with special gaming licences are able to operate casinos.

The company Larger companies are often able to set up their own distribution networks. They have the resources to set up warehouses, build and operate distribution sites and purchase transport. They are also often able to take advantage of **economies of scale** (☞ unit 93). For example, a large firm may be able to purchase a fleet of lorries. Manufacturers may open up their own retail outlets, but this will only be effective if the value of the product is high, a wide range of goods or services are sold or large quantities are sold. An alternative is for a producer to develop links with retailers. Raleigh bicycles, for example, provides financial and managerial help to small retailers.

Smaller firms are far less likely to be able to set up their own distribution system. They would tend to use intermediaries, such as wholesalers.

Physical distribution

Physical distribution is the movement of products from one place to another. It is an important part of the marketing process for two main reasons.

- Failure to deliver a product in the right quantities, at the right place and at the right time can damage an effective marketing effort.
- The cost of physical distribution can be high - in some cases higher than the cost of actually producing the product.

Two aspects of physical distribution are important to a business-holding stocks and transporting products.

Holding stocks Ideally a business would be able to guarantee every customer the product they wanted, whenever they wanted it. To do this a firm would have to hold huge amounts of stock. Holding excessive amounts of stock is very costly. Holding very low stock levels, however, could mean turning down orders.

The solution is for a business to assess the level of stocks needed to maintain an agreed level of customer service. This often means holding enough stock to satisfy regular orders, but not enough to deal with sudden changes in demand. This will depend on the market in which the product is selling.

Transporting products This is concerned with how goods

Question 2

Oakham Dairies, a small Leicestershire based firm, specialises in the production of cheeses. Traditionally, the business had serviced mainly the Leicestershire and South Lincolnshire markets. But a series of prizes in cheese fairs and a few flattering write-ups in national newspapers meant that its demand had spread. Requests were being received from customers in London and areas surrounding the capital. Since its cheeses had been mentioned on a television food programme, it had been besieged with requests for its product from restaurants, hotels, market stallholders, cheese shops and individual consumers, not to mention some world famous retailers. Oakham Dairies had a significant amount of excess capacity and was sure that it could go a long way to meeting this surge in demand. However, it was less sure about its ability to distribute the cheeses. It had always relied upon its 'fleet' of two vans, but one of them had broken down.

(a) Advise Oakham Dairies on which channel of distribution would best suit its purpose.
(b) Identify the main factors that influenced your choice in (a). Explain how each of these factors affected your decision.

can be physically delivered to markets. Firms need to consider the relative costs and speed of transporting their goods by road, rail, sea or air. For example, aeroplanes are faster than ships when transporting exports from the UK. However, firms must decide whether this advantage outweighs the costs which result from using this mode of transport. There are times when the nature of a product dictates the transport. For example, an Orkney Islands based firm which sells freshly caught lobsters to Paris restaurants has little choice but to fly this product to France.

When transporting goods, firms must also consider possible damage to or deterioration of goods. Packaging may help to reduce damage and deterioration, for example, if vacuum packs are used.

Retailing

Retailers are responsible for the sale of products to the final consumer. It is unlikely that products bought by a consumer from a retailer will be sold again, in the way that wholesalers distribute to many different retailers. Second hand exchanges are perhaps the only exception to this.

Retailers have a major role to play in the distribution of most products. This is because they have the ability to reach huge numbers of consumers, in different markets, over a wide area. Retailers, therefore, can influence manufacturers, insisting on high standards of product quality and delivery times.

Marks and Spencer, for example, is particularly concerned about the quality of products supplied to it. It has an advantage over some retailers because the products which it stocks are OWN BRANDS and because of its size and influence in the retail sector. Smaller retailers may have little influence over manufacturers. This is because the success of such retailers in attracting customers is often dependent upon whether or not they stock brands which are currently in demand.

Retailers can be grouped according to their characteristics.

Multiple shop organisations These are businesses with perhaps ten or more establishments, or a group of specialist shops dealing in a particular group of products. Examples include Oddbins, the wine merchants, and B&Q, the DIY specialists. For consumers, multiple shops have two benefits. They usually offer a wide choice of products in their specialist area. Also, they have often developed an established image, so consumers will be familiar with the level of service, value for money and quality which they can expect.

Supermarkets These sell mainly foodstuffs in premises with a minimum of 400 square metres of floor space. Many buy direct from manufacturers rather than through wholesalers and sell products which are fast moving, ie with a short SHELF LIFE, in large volumes. The majority of supermarkets are part of chains, such as Sainsbury's, Tesco, Safeway, Waitrose and Asda. There is an growing trend for supermarkets to provide 'own-brand' goods. There has also been a growth of supermarkets stressing lower prices and selling less well known brands. Examples include Aldi and Netto.

Superstores or hypermarkets These are huge stores which divide their stock nearly equally between food and other goods, such as electricals. They occupy 2,500 square metres of selling space or more and tend to be found on the outskirts of towns and cities. Their advantage is the ability to offer a wide range of goods and services under one roof. Examples include the French supermarket chain Mammouth and some Sainsbury's stores in the UK. Many of the multiple organisations mentioned above now have superstores in out of town locations. Examples include PC World, Comet and Marks & Spencer.

Department stores These sell five or more different lines of products and occupy at least 2,500 square metres of selling space. They tend to sell more highly priced goods and increasingly parts of these stores are run as franchises (☞ unit 2). Examples include Selfridges, Debenhams and the John Lewis Partnership.

Retail co-operatives Retail co-operatives (☞ unit 5) differ from other types of retail organisation in terms of their ownership and the way in which profits are distributed. They are owned by 'members' rather than shareholders and profits are distributed to customers in the form of a dividend rather than being given to shareholders. Retail co-operatives have faced extreme competition from large superstores and hypermarkets in the 1990s. They attempted to compete by setting up their own superstores. However, this strategy did not prove successful and by the late 1990s they were concentrating on convenience stores with late night opening hours, geared to the needs of the local community. Parts of the Co-operative organisation, such as the travel business and

---

Question 3

Toys R Us is the world's largest retailer of toys. Most of its stores are in out of town locations and carry 30,000 or more different products. In the UK market, in which it has been the leading operator since 1992, it faces competition from specialist retailers such as the Early Learning Centre, catalogue companies such as Argos, department stores such as the John Lewis Partnership and mail order companies such as Littlewood's. By stocking such a large range of product lines, it offers largely unrivalled choice to customers. This saves time shopping around. Toys R Us also seeks to match or better the prices of competitors.

(a) What type of retail organisation is Toys R Us? Explain your answer.
(b) Compare the benefits and problems of this type of retailer to those of an independent retailer from a consumer's point of view.

the funeral service operation, continue to thrive.

Independent retailers The smaller local shop, often owned by a sole trader, is still important for selling many types of products, eg newspapers and tobacco. These rely heavily on the supply of nationally known or branded goods through a wholesaler or a manufacturer's agent. Groups of independent retailers might also join together in order to benefit from the bulk purchasing of stock or joint advertising. These are sometimes known as **voluntary chains**, eg Spar. They are an attempt by independent retailers to match the strengths of large chains.

Direct marketing

DIRECT MARKETING is sometimes thought to be the same as direct mailing (☞ unit 45). In fact, it is just one type of direct marketing. Direct marketing occurs when sales are made without intermediaries being involved. For consumers, this means being able to make purchases from their own homes.

Direct marketing is perhaps the fastest growing means of distribution and is expected to continue into the future. There is a number of reasons for this. Changing work patterns mean that many now find it easier to shop from home. The increased range of products available, and their specialised nature, mean that certain products cannot be purchased from 'usual' outlets such as shops. Also, the increased use of credit cards makes buying in this way easy and direct.

Direct marketing also has advantages for firms. There are no intermediaries to take part of the profits. The producer is able to control its own marketing and also has a chance to reach consumers, who might not otherwise have bought from shops.

Direct marketing can be achieved through a variety of methods.

Direct mail This involves posting promotional materials to homes and workplaces. Consumers then place an order and products are sent to the buyer's address. At present, the average British adult receives five items of direct mail each month. This is just half the average in Europe, and one-tenth of what floods through the average US letterbox.

There is a number of benefits of direct mail for businesses and consumers.
● Personalised communications with the potential purchaser's name on a letter can improve sales.
● Groups of consumers or **market segments** can be targeted.
● Detailed information can be provided.
● Groups of consumers who are widely dispersed can easily be reached.

Despite its benefits, it is unpopular in some quarters and also suffers from a number of disadvantages.
● Consumers do not like the personalised nature of direct

mail and the amount sent to their home address.
● The databases with potential consumers' names and addresses on them quickly go out of date, so that a large amount of mail goes to the wrong people.
● It is felt to be a 'waste of paper' which uses up a valuable resource - wood.

For many businesses, such as Readers Digest, direct mailing has been very successful. In addition, many charities such as Oxfam and Greenpeace are able to raise large sums in this way.

Question 4

Figure 46.3 *Mail order sales and shares of sales*

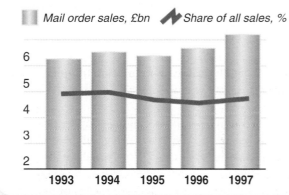

After struggling in the early 1990s, sales from mail order recovered in the period 1995 to 1997. This was as a result of a number of successful launches of mail order operations by companies such as Marks & Spencer and Arcadia (formerly Burton). Traditional catalogues offered commission to agents who sold the products to customers on credit terms. The new direct catalogue selling involves sending catalogues to homes where products can be ordered and viewed, and then paid for or returned. This follows the style of the successful Next Directory as an alternative to buying clothes from a retail outlet.

Retailers are also experimenting with internet shopping and a new television shopping channel, a venture between Granada and Littlewoods, was to be launched in future. The research agency Verdict said at the time that it was not sure whether this type of shopping would replace catalogues totally or whether both would exist together, helping to expand the market.

Source: adapted from *The Guardian*, 1998.

(a) What examples of direct marketing are suggested in the article?
(b) Contrast the advantages of these types of direct marketing with sales of clothing through a retail outlet.
(c) A theatre company has a new play which begins later in the year. It hopes to advertise the play so that it has advanced bookings before the show begins. Suggest two types of direct marketing that could be used. Explain which of the methods of direct marketing chosen would be most suitable.

Direct response advertisements These are advertisements placed in newspapers and magazines, and on the TV and radio. Consumers are encouraged to fill in a coupon or make a telephone call in order to purchase a product. There should be enough information in the advertisement to allow people to make a decision.

Direct response broadcasting is relatively new. It is the selling of products through TV commercials, often in late night slots. Records, CDs and car telephones have been sold in this way. There are now TV channels devoted entirely to direct response advertising, such as QVC on Sky Television. The introduction of digital television in 1998 increased this type of marketing. Consumers with digital television are linked to a telephone line which allows interactive television and the direct ordering of products. It is also possible to order products from advertisements on the **internet** (☞ unit 82)and to pay by credit card.

Personal selling This can be a useful form of direct marketing. It is dealt with in unit 45.

Telephone selling This involves ringing people up at their home or workplace and trying to sell a good or service. The advantage is that the seller can deal personally with a consumer. However, it is felt to be intrusive by many consumers. It has often been used as a means of marketing financial services, such as insurance, and advertising space on products such as calendars.

Catalogues This involves a range of products being included in a catalogue which people can read through at home. Orders can usually be placed by telephone or in writing. It has been seen recently as an outdated means of marketing, but innovations such as the Next Directory with 24 hour delivery have breathed new life into it. Market leaders in this area are Littlewoods and Great Universal Stores.

Trends in retailing and direct marketing

Retailing is a fast changing sector of the UK economy. Today's retail scene is very different from that which existed 30 years ago. Changes in direct marketing have also greatly affected the way in which goods and services are purchased by customers. What are the changes that have taken place?

Shopping centres A number of American-type shopping 'malls' were built in the UK in the 1980s and 1990s. These include the MetroCentre in Gateshead, The Mall near Bristol and the Trafford Centre in Manchester. They contain a wide range of retail outlets, cafes and restaurants and other services, such as theatre booking. They are designed to provide all the shopping facilities that customers need in one place. They promote shopping as a leisure activity and a 'day out for the family'. They are often found away from city areas because of their size.

Retail parks There has been a growth of out-of-town retail 'parks', such as Kinnaird Park near Edinburgh and Fosse Park South near Leicester. They are usually sited on the edges of urban developments as a result of a lack of building land and relatively high rents in city and town areas. Retail parks often contain superstores of high street chains, supermarkets or hypermarkets and restaurant chains. The extent to which they will benefit customers depends on a variety of factors. Those able to travel may benefit from a wider choice of products in a particular superstore. Another benefit is the ease of parking. However, if there is a limited number of retailers, customers may be unable to compare prices as they might in the 'high street' or city centre. Those without transport may face increased prices at local shops as retailers attempt to cover their costs. Retail parks are sometimes criticised for leading to traffic congestion and also for a decline in city centre retailing.

Call centres These are usually large offices with staff sitting at telephones who deal with customers. They are mainly used to sell insurance, airline tickets and hotel rooms. They also act as information centres for providers of rail or telephone services. In 1998 there were 3,500 call centres in the UK employing 400,000 people.

Changes in technology Many developments in retailing have resulted from new technology. For example, bar codes on products (read by laser beams) are a common feature in most retail outlets. They recognise the cost of products, allowing them to be quickly totalled. Some supermarkets have facilities for customers to 'read' prices as they shop around the supermarket, which saves time at checkouts. Increasingly electronic point of sale (Epos) data is used to gauge consumer tastes, so that trends can be identified and particular groups targeted. Tesco, for example, has used the information from loyalty cards to select wine buyers for 'cheese and wine tasting evenings'. Bar codes can also be used to update stock levels. Many retailers use in-store cameras to record when and where consumers are tempted to pause and consider whether to buy a product. Cameras are also used for in-store security.

The growth of 'online shopping' Shopping via the internet is increasing in popularity. amazon.co, for example, is the world largest bookseller. Customers with a computer can search the internet for businesses selling products. They are able to browse through the range of products and make purchases, with the use of credit cards. Goods are then delivered to the home of the purchaser. Many commentators predict a huge growth in online shopping as more homes have their own computer and as more companies make their products available using this form of distribution. The development of digital television makes the continued growth of this trend even more likely.

Variable opening hours There has been a growing trend for longer opening hours to fit in with patterns of work and leisure. Some 'convenience stores' attract customers by staying open until 11pm at night. Flexible opening hours were previously an advantage of small businesses. However, some supermarkets, remain open until late on certain days. Some have all night shopping. Increasingly, city centre retailers are opening on Sunday. A survey in 1998 found that 5 million people shop after 10.00 pm. This suggests a change in consumer attitudes towards nighttime and daytime shopping.

Diversifying Increasingly retailers are offering a wider variety of products and services. The traditional products for sale at one type of retailer are changing as they are faced with growing competition. Many garages, for example, now sell food and magazines as shown in Figure 46.4. Some even offer microwave cooking facilities. Financial services are also becoming available in places where they were unlikely to be sold previously. Pensions are available from Marks & Spencer and some supermarkets offer banking facilities and pharmacies.

The relative decline of independents In the last 40 years the number of independent grocers in the UK has been cut by over two-thirds. This has largely been due to the increasing growth of supermarket and hypermarket chains selling food.

Reductions in costs Businesses have increasingly been looking for ways to reduce distribution costs. This has led to businesses wishing to supply in larger quantities to retailers in order to achieve economies of scale (☞ unit 93). Retailers can also benefit from lower costs by buying in bulk. The larger retail chains are in a stronger position to do this. This has, to

some extent, accounted for the decline in the independent retailer. Remaining open for longer hours may also reduce a business's average total costs (☞ unit 52). This is because the fixed costs of the business, such as the retail outlet, are being spread over a greater output. Even though variable costs may increase, average total costs may fall.

Second hand shops In the mid-1990s there were over 6,000 retail outlets in the UK selling second hand goods. They accounted for 2.2 per cent of all retail outlets (compared to 1.9 per cent in the early 1990s) and just under 1 per cent of all retail turnover. There have been second hand shops in the UK for many years, including second hand car dealerships. The 1990s saw a number of charity shop chains, such as Age Concern and Scope gaining a higher profile in town centres in certain parts of the UK. It is likely, however, that this will always be a small part of the total retail market.

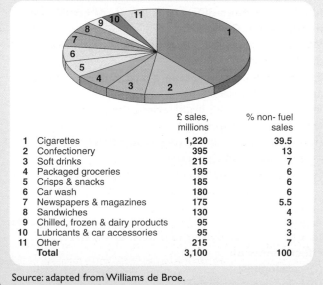

Figure 46.4 *Goods and services sold at petrol stations other than fuel in 1997*

		£ sales, millions	% non-fuel sales
1	Cigarettes	1,220	39.5
2	Confectionery	395	13
3	Soft drinks	215	7
4	Packaged groceries	195	6
5	Crisps & snacks	185	6
6	Car wash	180	6
7	Newspapers & magazines	175	5.5
8	Sandwiches	130	4
9	Chilled, frozen & dairy products	95	3
10	Lubricants & car accessories	95	3
11	Other	215	7
	Total	**3,100**	**100**

Source: adapted from Williams de Broe.

Question 5

In 1998 the £600 million Trafford Centre opened on the South-Western edge of Manchester. It was amongst the last to gain government approval before a tightening of planning rules in 1996. By the end of 1999 the UK would have eight centres. With no new proposals at the time this seemed like an end to their development. Those who argue that such centres only lead to pollution, take trade away from town centres and favour car users could breath a sigh of relief.

Older centres wanted to grow to compete with the newer centres being developed. Lakeside in Thurrock, for example, was faced with competition from Bluewater, an even bigger centre in nearby Dartford. It promised 300 shops and over 13,000 car parking spaces. Over 5,000 houses were planned for the area around Bluewater, with more than 20,000 in the surrounding area. Bluewater's developers suggested: 'it looks like out-of-town now, but in 10 years time it will be something quite different'. Some suggested that the decline in town centres was not directly the result of the new shopping centres. Newcastle, Sunderland and Durham seemed to be successful despite the Gateshead MetroCentre. On the other hand, two other towns in the area, Morpeth and Hexham, had problems. However, they were losing trade to a variety of retail outlets, not just the centres.

Critics of the new centres forecast that trade would be taken away from surrounding areas. The North-West feared the impact of the Trafford Centre on nearby towns. Altrincham and Stockport were predicted to lose 27 per cent of trade in the first three years of opening. Even Manchester city centre initially faced a 5 per cent slump in trade.

Source: adapted from *The Guardian*, 5.11.1997 and the *Financial Times*, 10.9.1998.

(a) What trends in distribution are suggested in the article?
(b) Why might businesses welcome the trends identified in the answer to (a)?

Summary

1. Why is distribution so important to a firm's marketing mix?
2. What is a channel of distribution?
3. List the 5 types of organisation which can be involved in a channel of distribution.
4. What is the main role of an intermediary?
5. Explain the difference between a wholesaler and a retailer.
6. Why do manufacturers use wholesalers?
7. What is the difference between an agent and a broker?
8. What factors might influence the choice of distribution channel?
9. What is the difference between direct mailing and direct marketing?
10. Why might a business be reluctant to use direct mailing?
11. Explain 4 trends in retailing and their effect on business.

Key terms

Channel of distribution - the route taken by a product as it passes from producer to consumer.
Direct marketing - a method of distributing products directly to consumers, without the use of intermediaries such as wholesalers and retailers.
Intermediaries - firms which act as a link between producers and consumers in a channel of distribution.
Own brands - products which have the brand name of their retailer on them.
Shelf life - the average length of time it takes for a product to be sold, once it has been displayed by a retailer.

Case study

When is a bookshop not a bookshop? When it's a cafe

In September 1997 the largest bookshop to open for 50 years was unveiled in Glasgow. Waterstone's new branch boasted 350,000 books, 28,000 square feet of sales area and computer search facility. However, it also had two sofas, two cafes, a coffee cart and CD listening posts. It was an attempt to encourage browsing in the store. Browsers could then be turned into customers. Once over the threshold, 'it's up to us to use our retailing skills to get them to buy something', said Waterstone's MD, Alan Giles. A similar store in London was promised by Dillons, with sofas, coffee and cafes.

Bookshops have traditionally been a convenient way for publishers to distribute their products to the customer. Customers can view a wide range of books in one place. Publishers may sometimes sell to an intermediary, such as a wholesaler, or have facilities to take single orders from customers over the phone. The new 'lifestyle' stores are modelled on the Barnes & Noble bookstores in America. They transformed bookselling in the US by encouraging people to sit and read at leisure rather than hurrying them into buying. The company's sales nearly tripled between 1992 and 1995.

This trend was perhaps a response to the growth of aggressive discounting. Until 1995 the net book agreement allowed publishers to set minimum prices below which retailers could not sell. Its end meant that many bookshops sold bestselling paperbacks and hardbacks at reduced prices. Booksellers also faced competition from other retail groups which began selling popular books. Asda, in particular, successfully moved into this market. Another attack has come from the growth of direct selling. Publishers selling via the internet could remove some of the custom of bookshops.

Bookshops were likely to have to set up their own internet sites in future if they wished to compete.

The new style of shop was an attempt to deal with some of these problems. It tried to appeal to the need of customers to physically buy objects and flick through books, rather than impersonal buying via computer. Bookshops also hoped that visiting a bookshop would be more like visiting a library or gallery. Potential customers would perhaps spend up to four hours simply browsing. The main problem with this approach was that it required increases in costs. Barnes & Noble, for example, saw little increase in profit despite the rise in turnover. It was also likely that smaller bookshops would be unable to offer such a service, due to lack of space or finance.

Source: adapted from The *Guardian*, 22.9.1997.

(a) Identify the three different channels of distribution mentioned in the article.

(b) What factors might influence these channels of distribution?

(c) Explain why certain retailers have changed their approach to bookselling.

(d) What might be the implications for book retailers of this change of approach?

(e) (i) What type of direct response advertising is mentioned in the article?

(ii) What might be the implications for publishers of the growth in this method of direct response advertising?

(f) A publisher wishes to promote a new range of books to a bookshop. Advise the publisher on the effectiveness of:
(i) catalogues;
(ii) sales representatives;
as methods of marketing books.

Marketing Planning and Budgeting

Marketing planning

To help make marketing decisions a business must plan effectively. MARKETING PLANNING is the process by which future marketing activities are systematically planned. Not all businesses have a marketing plan. Some smaller businesses, for example, may make marketing decisions on a short term basis or in response to changing conditions. However, we will see later that planning has a number of benefits for all businesses.

A business's MARKETING PLAN is influenced by the **strategic plans** of the business (☞ units 15 and 16) and the overall corporate objectives (☞ unit 4). A large public limited company such as Unilever, Nestlé, Unigate or the Rank Group will have an overall plan for the business and objectives that it wishes to achieve. Companies within the business will then develop marketing plans for their businesses and for individual products which fit in with the overall strategic plan. For example, the Rank Group plc will have an overall corporate strategy. This will influence the plans of its leisure division. Detailed marketing plans may be drawn up for Top Rank Bingo outlets, for Odeon Cinemas and for Tom Cobleigh pub-restaurants. A manufacturer such as Unigate will have corporate objectives, but detailed marketing plans will be drawn up by St.Ivel, which is part of Unigate, and even for individual products such as St.Ivel Shape yogurt and St. Ivel Golden sunflower spread.

The marketing plan

The marketing plan is concerned with a number of questions.

Where is the business at present? A business can only plan where it is going if it knows where it is starting from. Finding out where a business is at the moment involves a MARKETING AUDIT. This analyses the **internal** and **external** factors which affect a business's performance. Most businesses analyse their current position by using SWOT analysis (☞ units 4 and 15), which identifies the business's strengths, weaknesses, opportunities and threats. Table 47.1 shows a possible SWOT analysis for a manufacturer of soft drinks. The business will have some control over internal factors. External factors are out of the control of a business. These include political, economic, social and technological (PEST) factors outlined later in this unit.

Where does the business wish to be in future? This involves the business setting **objectives** to be achieved (☞ unit 4). The objectives provide goals and targets for the business to aim at. They may include such goals as a growth in sales or gaining a certain market share in future.

Table 47.1 *SWOT analysis of a soft drinks manufacturer*

STRENGTHS (the strong points of the business)

- Current products are market leaders in some countries in terms of sales and market share.
- Brand loyalty to products and to the corporate identity.
- Effective promotion.
- Flexibility in production methods.
- Excellent distribution network.
- Constant R&D leading to new ideas.

WEAKNESSES (the problems it has at present)

- Age of the life cycle of certain products.
- Restricted product range could cause problems if sales suddenly fall.

OPPORTUNITIES (that may arise in future)

- Expansion into newer markets such as sports drinks, low calorie drinks and drinks with new flavours.
- Expansion into new geographical areas such as Eastern Europe.
- Development of a global brand and possible global marketing.
- Possible growing demand for soft beverages.
- Legislation on drink driving may encourage growth of soft drink sales.

THREATS (that may arise and should be avoided/prevented if possible)

- Growing competition from supermarket own brands.
- Increasing competition from competitors bringing out new products.
- Competition from alcoholic beverages and non-alcoholic beers and lagers.
- Legislation on ingredients could force changes in production.

How will a business achieve its objectives? A business must decide how to get where it wants to go. It will have **marketing strategies** (☞ unit 48) which it will use to achieve its objectives. For example, if it wishes to increase its market share at the expense of a market leader then it may use market challenger strategies. Marketing strategies can be expressed in terms of the 4P's (☞ unit 40). So a company wishing to gain a 10 per cent increase in market share must make sure that it has the the right product, at the right price, with an effective promotion and distribution policy.

Chairman Dennis Henderson believed that in the past marketing had not had enough attention in ICI. ICI had not, in his judgement, concentrated sufficiently on looking ahead at customers' needs, at how markets are changing and how to present products in the optimum way to solve customers' problems.

He recognised that in some of its businesses there was a lot of market expertise. These businesses tended to be of more recent origin, international and nearer to the ultimate consumer. On the other hand some areas of ICI had been less market orientated.

He had an answer to this problem. 'Improve the flow of information about marketing across business boundaries and urge people in the various businesses that there is much valuable information within the group', Mr Henderson said. 'We have a collection of very independent businesses, each convinced that its problems and markets are unique so they can appear unwilling to learn from each other's experiences.'

'Another barrier can be the technical/commercial interface. For as long as I can remember it has been a running joke that the production people think marketing people can't move the product and the marketing people think that production can't produce in the right quantities when it is needed. A company like ICI will continue to succeed if it produces first class technology and incorporates it into the best products. There is still a bit of an attitude which says,

"This commercial hype is not quite nice - why can't we stick to inventing new molecules, making the resultant products and distributing them to our customers?" One difficulty is that the market often requires fairly minimal change in the product to excite consumers, whereas the scientists, not unnaturally, want a major breakthrough.'

'One example of minimal change was the natural whites campaign in paints. Brilliant white paint had, for a long time, been a loss leader which was heavily discounted in all supermarkets. Somebody said, "How can we add value?", "How can we differentiate?" and the answer was special shades, such as apple white and rose white.'

In the future Mr Henderson stated that he would like to see marketing given a higher priority and suggested that ICI should be more proactive in looking at customers' needs and problems and in using science expertise to solve them.

(a) From the information in the article, identify the:
   (i) strengths;
   (ii) weaknesses;
   of ICI in the past.
(b) Suggest two possible objectives that ICI may have wanted to achieve in future.

Factors influencing the market plan

A marketing audit should identify the internal and external factors which affect a business. There is a number of possible factors that may fall into each category.

Internal factors
- The marketing mix. Of great importance to the internal audit will be an examination of the effectiveness of the marketing mix (☞ unit 40). This will include an analysis of each element of the marketing mix. For example, projections regarding the life span and future profitability of each of the firm's products may be carried out. It should also include an analysis of how well the elements of the marketing mix fit together, for example, the extent to which distribution channels are compatible with the promotions may be considered.
- People. A huge range of people will be involved in devising and implementing marketing plans. The objectives of these people will determine the targets set in the plan. Also the skills and abilities of those people working for a firm will determine whether targets can be met.
- Finance. Firms can set themselves ambitious marketing goals. However, unless finance is available to fund plans, such goals are unlikely to be achieved. This is discussed later in this unit under the heading 'Marketing Budgeting'.
- Production processes. Any marketing plan must take into account whether the firm can produce the product. There is little point in planning to increase market share unless enough of the product can be produced to achieve this. Similarly, a firm cannot plan to launch a new product if it cannot manufacture it.

External factors An analysis of the external influences on a business usually involves a consideration of PEST factors. These are the political, economic, social and technological factors which affect a business's performance.
- Political. There is an increasing amount of legislation and regulation that may affect the marketing plans of a business. It can vary from controls on the ingredients of products to restrictions on price changes of the privatised utilities, such as water and gas. Much of the new legislation affecting the UK is from the European Union.
- Economic. A wide range of economic factors may affect a business's marketing plans. A buoyant economy, for example, may lead to increased demand for products, higher incomes and the possibility of price increases. Growing unemployment may lead to a fall in future levels of demand. Marketing plans should also take into account the pricing, promotion, distribution and product policies of rival businesses (☞ unit 18).
- Social. Changes in society can have consequences for marketing planning. The decline of the so-called nuclear

family and the changing role of women may influence how a business promotes its products. The ageing of the population may influence the types of products which are developed and the channels of distribution used to deliver products to customers.
- Technological. Changes in technology can affect marketing plans in a variety of ways. It may make it possible for businesses to manufacture products that were previously thought to be too costly. It may also lead to greater obsolescence and shorter product life cycles. New technological developments such as interactive television and the internet may change the promotional methods that a business uses.

Businesses should be careful to consider how each of the above factors affects consumers and their buying behaviour. Changes in external factors can cause changes in the wants and needs of consumers. An effective plan should anticipate these changes as well as any other issues affecting consumers' needs.

Question 2

Figures in 1997, showing that England and Wales had the worst crime figures in the industrialised world, led to quiet anticipation in the security industry. The 1990s saw a relentless growth in the use of steel fencing, closed circuit television cameras (CCTV) and uniformed security guards. Although familiar in factories and offices, they were increasingly appearing in hospitals, schools and residential areas.

Security companies' services range from providing guards, carrying cash and making and installing safes and alarms to access control and closed circuit television monitoring. The industry is highly fragmented. There were around 1,500-2,000 companies providing security guards and safe installation and hundreds more providing high-tech security equipment.

Growth in manned security has been characterised by cutthroat competition. Small, unscrupulous operators have given the industry a bad name. Larger businesses feel that regulation is the answer. This would limit the ability of 'cowboy' operators to undercut the prices of the big boys. Providing guards, however, was regarded as a saturated market and many of the larger operators were moving into CCTV and electronic detection equipment. Jim Harrower, chief executive of Group 4, believed that there were still growth opportunities in the market. For example, some security companies were moving into facilities management, taking responsibility for catering and cleaning as well as security. Clients such as the Prison Service and the Ministry of Defence were early takers of this facility.

Source: adapted from *The Observer*, 8.6.1997.

(a) Identify the: (i) internal; and (ii) external factors; in the article that might affect the marketing planning of a security business.
(b) Discuss the possible effects that these factors may have on the marketing planning of the business.

The benefits of marketing planning

- The main benefit of marketing planning is that it ensures a business takes time to reflect upon its marketing activities. In today's competitive environment it is not enough for businesses to carry on doing what they have done successfully in the past. They must constantly evaluate and develop their marketing policies. The marketing plan allows them to do this and can be seen as a means of ensuring the survival of the business.
- The marketing plan co-ordinates the various aspects of marketing. It takes a holistic view of a business's marketing activities. This should lead to better co-ordination and integration of the different elements of marketing. It should also allow all employees and all areas of the business to be aware of marketing objectives, helping to ensure that they 'pull in the same direction'.
- The marketing plan makes sure that human and financial resources are used where they are most needed. It will also make sure resources will not be wasted on unprofitable activities.
- Businesses will set marketing objectives and targets in their marketing plan. Management, as a result, will have a clear set of criteria against which they can evaluate the success of products.
- Marketing plans may encourage greater employee motivation. Employees are likely to be more prepared for changes in company policy and in the climate of trading. They should therefore be able to act in a more confident and informed manner. They are also likely to feel more secure in the knowledge that the business has planned for the future.
- A marketing plan should make banks feel more confident about offering loans to a firm. Shareholders may also be more confident about buying shares in a business.

Problems with marketing planning

For many businesses the main problem with marketing plans lies in their confusion as to what marketing actually is. Marketing plans often concentrate upon issues such as product development or increasing sales, but ignore customers' needs. Satisfying consumers' needs should be at the forefront of any marketing plan. A plan which centres around the expected success of a new advertising campaign, for example, is unlikely to be successful unless consumers' needs are satisfied. British Airways, Dunlop, and Woolworths are all companies which have won awards for advertising campaigns in the past. It is arguable whether these campaigns directly led to any improvement in sales.

Many businesses in the UK are organised into personnel, finance, production, and marketing departments. The success of the marketing plan will depend upon each of these areas being prepared to put aside their own goals to satisfy consumers' needs. This can be difficult, especially in a large business, where loyalty to the department can override more important goals. One suggested way of solving this problem is for businesses to be organised around customer groups rather than 'functions' (☞ unit 7).

Marketing plans often include too much information for them to be useful to managers. In order to overcome this problem, plans should be brief and concentrate upon key factors.

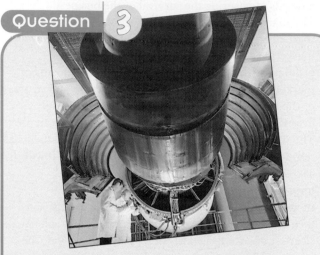

Paul Rossington had just been appointed Marketing Manager of SBC plc, a firm which had forty years experience of supplying a range of instrumentation and components to the aircraft industry.

Paul had decided that his first act would be to involve a range of managers in drawing up a marketing plan. To this end, he called a meeting requesting the presence of all senior managers within the firm.

At the meeting, he began with a short presentation outlining the advantages to SBC plc of marketing planning. He then invited comments from all those assembled. The sales manager chipped in with the first comment; 'It's about time we started advertising more heavily in trade journals and stopped turning out products with the wrong specifications'. The production manager came next; 'I don't know why you dragged me up here to this meeting. You concentrate on the marketing and I'll get on with the production side. So long as you keep me informed of developments we'll be happy down in production.'

Paul was beginning to feel uncomfortable, but it wasn't until the senior accountant's remark that he really felt worried about having accepted this new post. 'I suggest you go away and write this plan and then call another meeting when you're in a position to discuss it with us', she had said.

(a) What advantages of marketing planning would you have advised Paul to mention in his brief presentation?
(b) From the comments made at the meeting, explain any problems which you think SBC plc will have with marketing planning.

There is a danger that a business may embrace the planning ethos too eagerly. This may lead to the establishment of planning departments which become isolated from those responsible for carrying the plans out. This can have the effect of further divorcing marketing plans from the needs of customers.

Marketing plans often fail to **prioritise** objectives. Plans may include as many as 100 objectives. This means that it becomes difficult to decide whether objectives are being met.

Overall, it is important that a business's marketing plan is geared up to the particular set of circumstances in which it operates. This means a marketing plan which is sensitive to prevailing market conditions, the nature of the markets in which the business is operating and the customers at which the business's products are aimed.

Evaluating marketing plans

It is essential that businesses evaluate the success of their marketing plans. This will provide them with information on which to base future plans. Businesses also need to know whether or not planned activities were carried out in the manner which was planned.

The evaluation of marketing plans can take place both during the period of time in which the plan is being carried out and at the end of the time period (often one year) that the plan covers. Evaluation which takes place during the period of implementation may allow managers and directors to better control marketing activities.

It is important that marketing plans are evaluated against clear, measurable criteria. To do this, clear performance targets must be agreed and set during the process of marketing planning. Such performance targets are often time specific. This means that they are expected to be achieved by a certain date during the implementation of the plan. For example, a plan may require a 5 per cent growth in market share by the end of the first six months. A business may use a number of methods to evaluate a marketing plan.

Sales analysis This is an analysis of either the volume or the value of sales. If a business achieves a sales target then it may consider its marketing plan to be successful. This method is the most commonly used to evaluate marketing plans. Sales analysis is especially valuable to a business as it can be linked to a whole range of variables such as:
● sales by region;
● sales by product;
● sales by customer types;
● sales via different distribution channels.

The problem with using sales analysis in isolation is that it may not be related to what is taking place in the wider market. For example, a business may be experiencing high sales growth and so consider its marketing plan successful. However, it may be operating in a growing market in which competitors are experiencing even higher sales growth.

Question 4

Figure 47.1 show the results of research by Tim Ambler and Flora Kokkinaki of the London Business School. They carried out a survey of 531 finance officers and marketers who were asked: 'What measures does your company use to track marketing ... performance?' From the results 5 main categories, shown in Figure 47.1, were identified. The figure indicates how frequently senior management used these measures according to marketers and finance officers.

Figure 47.1 *Importance of measures of marketing effectiveness for senior management (average)*

Financial	6.51
Direct trade customer	5.53
Customer awareness, attitudes & satisfaction	5.42
Competitor	5.42
Consumer purchases, market share & prices paid	5.38
Innovation	5.04

531 senior marketers and finance officers were asked to rate the importance that senior management attaches to different measures of market effectiveness in a 7 point scale.

Source: adapted from LBS.

(a) Explain what is likely to be included in 'Financial' measures of marketing effectiveness.
(b) Why are senior managers likely to regard this as the most important measure of marketing effectiveness?
(c) Suggest reasons why other measures of marketing effectiveness may be more important in certain instances.

Market share analysis This method examines a business's sales in terms of market share. It enables performance in relation to competitors to be more accurately gauged. For example, if a business meets its target of an increase in market share of 5 per cent over a year then it may consider its marketing planning to be successful. Together, sales analysis and market share analysis are a powerful tool for evaluating marketing planning.

Marketing profitability analysis Profitability is concerned with the relationship between profits and costs (☞ unit 52). In the context of marketing planning, profitability analysis is calculated by subtracting the marketing costs of a product from the revenue gained from the product:

Marketing profit = sales revenue of a product
(quantity sold x price) - marketing costs (marketing research, advertising, distribution, promotion etc.)

Thus a product with high revenue and relatively low marketing costs will be highly profitable. In contrast a product with low sales revenue and relatively high marketing costs will be less profitable.

The main benefit of calculating marketing profitability is that it can highlight some of the most and least profitable markets. Take the example of a business seeking to increase sales of a particular product by moving into two new markets A and B. In market A, an increase in sales of 10 per cent can be achieved with additional marketing costs of 5 per cent. In market B an increase in sales of 45 per cent can be achieved with additional marketing costs of 5 per cent. This business may wish to focus upon the more profitable market B.

The problem with calculating marketing profitability is that it is often difficult to calculate the marketing costs of particular products. For example, many promotional activities, such as trade fairs (☞ unit 45) and corporate advertising (☞ unit 44), cannot be easily apportioned to individual products in businesses with a range of products.

Satisfaction surveys Many businesses undertake analysis of their customer satisfaction surveys. These are detailed surveys designed to identify the reactions of customers to their products. They use this data to assess the extent to which marketing plans are leading to increases or decreases in customer satisfaction.

Number of enquiries generated Many businesses pay very careful attention to the numbers of enquiries generated in particular aspects of their business. For example, financial service businesses monitor and evaluate the enquiries generated by direct mailshots (☞ unit 7) as a means of evaluating the success of such promotions.

The marketing budget

The MARKETING BUDGET specifies and sets out clearly the financial elements of the marketing plan. Like budgets for other aspects of business activity (☞ unit 61), the marketing budget is a plan of what the business hopes to achieve in the forthcoming period. Marketing budgets focus mainly upon sales revenue, marketing expenditure and profit.

When setting marketing budgets a balance must be maintained. On the one hand businesses must set precise financial plans associated with marketing activities. It is important that plans are precise if managers are to use the budget to control spending and to set targets for sales. However, changes in the internal and external marketing environment mean that some flexibility must be built into the budget.

There is a number of ways in which a business might construct a marketing budget.

The affordable budget This is where the budget for marketing expenditure is based upon what is expected to be left over after more important expenses have been met. So a business might decide, for example, that once it has paid for its raw materials, labour costs and overheads, it has £10,000 left over to spend on marketing. The problem with this method is that it takes no account of market requirements and conditions. It could be that the business actually needs to spend £30,000 for its marketing to be effective.

Historical budgeting This is where the budget for marketing expenditure is based upon what has been spent on marketing activities in previous years. Sometimes an extra amount is added to allow for the effects of inflation. As with affordable budgets, it takes no account of market factors. It is also based upon the sometimes mistaken assumption that previous years' expenditures have been appropriate.

As a percentage of past sales This is where the budget for marketing expenditure is based upon previous sales of a product. Products are allocated a marketing budget in line with their sales records. So, for example, a product that has sold particularly well in the past may have a higher amount spent on its advertising than a product with poor sales.

The benefit of this method is that successful products are rewarded with high promotional budgets. This should help their future success. Businesses using this method sometimes refer to their ADVERTISING:SALES RATIO. This is the means by which businesses decide on the proportion of sales revenue to allocate to future advertising. Businesses in the cosmetics industry, for example, generally have a ratio of 20 per cent or more. Businesses operating in industrial markets may have ratios as low as one per cent or even less. For example, scrap metal dealers may have advertising expenses per annum of less than 0.1 per cent of their sales revenue.

The problem with this budgeting method is that it can lead to particular products being sent on a downward spiral. Falling sales lead to lower marketing expenditure, which leads to lower sales and so on. Sometimes, however, it may be in the strategic interest of a business to increase marketing expenditure on a product with falling sales.

Competitor based budgeting This involves setting marketing budgets in relation to competitors' spending. It may mean spending amounts similar to that of competitors, matching competitors' spending exactly, or exceeding competitors' spending. The problem with this method is that marketing expenditure may not be set in relation to the marketing objectives of a business itself. Instead such expenditure may be set in relation to the marketing objectives of the competitor.

Objective and task budgeting This method involves setting marketing expenditure in relation to marketing objectives and the tasks or actions which must be completed to achieve these objectives. To do this a business must cost all of the

marketing activities in which it expects to be engaged over a particular period of time. Many regard this as the most desirable method of marketing budgeting. This is because it is based upon the needs of particular businesses and products operating in particular market conditions.

Question 5

The total amount spent on marketing in the UK in 1997 was £20 billion. Or it could have been £25 billion or £30 billion. No-one really knows. This uncertainty is evidence of a paradox. On the one hand marketing accounts for large sums of money and yet much of it is poorly defined and unaccountable. There is little agreement on how to measure the effectiveness of marketing. There is also little agreement on what spending on marketing actually is. It probably includes spending on advertising and promotion, but what about price maintenance?

Few businesses admit it, but setting a marketing budget amounts to little more than guesswork. The problem, according to Keith Holloway, former commercial director of Grand Metropolitan, is that the number of variables is so great. Setting budgets must take into account what competitors are doing, the economic climate and media costs. One way to set a budget is to take last year's spending and add a bit more. It sounds crude, but at least it is based on experience, not guesswork.

Visa is a company that is careful in setting its marketing budget. Aidan New, head of brand management at VisaEurope, says: 'We look at our business requirement, work out what marketing activity we need to meet and then cost that activity. We know that we have to hit x per cent of the population y times with a message successfully to achieve marketing objective z, so we can work out how much money we need'.

Others take a different approach. David Payne, of Pepe Jeans, says: 'We just spend what we can afford. We have recently increased our budgets by 50 per cent. There was no rationale, we just felt we needed to meet our business objectives of building a strong long term brand.

Source: adapted from the *Financial Times*, 19.5.1997.

(a) Identify the approach to marketing taken by:
(i) Keith Holloway;
(ii) VisaEurope;
(iii) Pepe Jeans.
  Explain your answer.
(b) Critically examine the approaches to setting a marketing budget taken by the three businesses.

Summary

1. How is a marketing plan affected by a business's strategic plan?
2. State 3 aspects of the marketing plan.
3. What does SWOT analysis show?
4. State 3 internal and 3 external factors that may be taken into account when carrying out a SWOT analysis.
5. State 3 benefits of marketing planning.
6. State 3 problems of marketing planning.
7. Suggest 4 ways in which a business might evaluate its marketing plan.
8. Explain the difference between historical budgeting and task based bugeting.

Key terms

Advertising: sales ratio - advertising expenditure expressed as a proportion of sales revenue.

Marketing audit - an analysis of the internal and external factors which may affect a business's performance.

Marketing budget - a plan agreed in advance of the funds to be used for marketing and how they will be used.

Marketing planning - the process by which marketing activities are identified and decided upon.

Marketing plan - a detailed account of the company's marketing at present, what it wants it to be in future and how it intends to change it.

Case study

Are you being served?

There was no business in late 20th Century Britain, perhaps, that struck a stronger chord with the public than Marks & Spencer (M & S). However, a drop in profits of 23 per cent in 1998, the first such drop for ten years, suggested that all may not be well. A range of different factors may explain the situation that faced this high street giant in the late 1990s.

Food division

M & S was widely recognised as a market leader in terms of providing quality food to well heeled customers. However, some believed that its leadership had passed to Tesco and other supermarkets that were pushing high-quality lines. Tesco sold two Barbary ducks with orange and lemon sauce for £6.99 - just the sort of price and product that M&S used to sell exclusively. Food sales were on the slide. In part, it was argued, this could be explained by increasing sophistication among other high street food retailers. Products such as extra virgin olive oil and balsamic vinegar had become commonplace. Competitors such as Tesco, Sainsbury's and Waitrose were able to challenge M & S's marketing of ready prepared meals in terms of price, packaging and product sophistication.

Strategy abroad

The decision by the Chief Executive of M & S, Sir Richard Greenbury, to go slow on the company's international growth strategy was questioned. He had planned to have in place a network of 60 stores encompassing much of continental Europe, including Germany, by the year 2000. The decision to halt this process, including the new German stores, was a sharp break with M & S's long-term approach to developing businesses.

The company had 600 branches in 32 countries in 1998. In countries outside the UK it was promoted as a premium brand store. In parts of Asia, prices could be as high as 70 per cent more than in the UK. This strategy was deliberate. It was argued that Asian customers are label-mad, and M & S offers an 'aspirational brand'. In 1998 it was considering reviewing its marketing policy abroad, perhaps moving back to the middle market position it knows best and takes in its UK stores. The problems in Eastern economies in 1997/98 led to low sales, which particularly hit retailers trying to sell upmarket brands. However, it was unlikely the business would pull out, preferring to wait until things improved.

Clothing

The rest of the high street was sharpening up its act. M & S, for example, was the first high street giant to secure designer input, but other big names were starting to do the same. Unlike modest M & S, they were screaming it from the rooftops. Dorothy Perkins had a Clements Ribiero range and at Debenhams Philip Treacy designed hats were clearly signposted. Other commentators challenged this view, arguing that nothing had changed in terms of M & S's clothing. Shoppers, they believed, were still able to count on M & S as a source of discreetly fashionable, reasonably priced, good quality clothes that wouldn't fall apart when they were put in the washing machine.

Figure 47.2 *Non-food production, (M & S)*

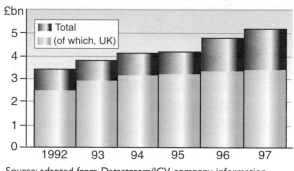

Source: adapted from Datastream/ICV, company information.

Management

Some were concerned about M & S's hierarchical top down management structure. They questioned the suitability of such a structure in an age when the more open structures of the kind pioneered by Archie Brown at Asda were winning out. Was the top management of M & S, much of it home bred with mainly domestic experience, good enough since the company had become an international retailer with interests from Hong Kong to Germany?

Profits and Investment

A deeper analysis of the company suggested that pessimism surrounding M & S in 1998 may have been overdone. Although profits had fallen dramatically, people were still shopping in M & S in ever-increasing numbers. In fact British consumers spent over £3 billion in M & S in the first six months of 1998. This was around £375 per head for every man, woman and child in the country. St Michael may not have been as trendy as Next, Wallis, Gap or the designer names that spread out across the modern high street, but it was never meant to be.

The fall in profits could largely be attributed to a massive investment programme paid for mainly out of current profits. Much of the money had gone on integrating into the M & S network some 440,000 square feet of stores acquired from Littlewoods. This was the biggest rebranding operation ever undertaken on the high street. As a continental retailer M & S was also anxious to be euro-ready from January 1st 1999. It had spent up to £3,200 million putting in new tilling and stock systems that were ready for the euro's introduction in 1999. It was the only retailer to have done so. Finally, M & S had moved into upmarket home shopping for the first time, producing glossy brochures, selling top-of-the-range products from Italian suits to Christmas hampers.

Figure 47.3 *Yearly increase in selling space '000 sq.ft, M&S*

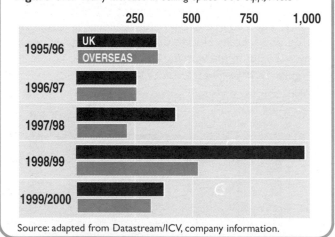

Source: adapted from Datastream/ICV, company information.

Figure 47.4 *Share price relative to FTSE All-Share, M&S*

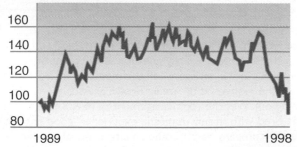

Source: adapted from Datastream/ICV, company information.

Table 47.2 *A decade's perspective, M & S*

Year ending March

	Sales	Pre-tax profit	Net profit after tax	Net margin*
	£bn	**£m**	**£m**	**%**
1989	**5.1**	**529**	-	**11.0**
1990	**5.6**	**604**	-	**11.2**
1991	**5.8**	**615**	-	**11.0**
1992	**5.8**	**589**	368	**11.7**
1993	**5.9**	**736**	495	**12.3**
1994	**6.5**	**851**	578	**13.1**
1995	**6.8**	**924**	623	**13.2**
1996	**7.2**	**965**	652	**13.1**
1997	**7.8**	**1,102**	756	**13.2**
1998	**8.2**	**1,168**	829	**13.3**

*operating profit as percentage of sales

Figures for the six months to September 1998 (£m)

	Sales	Profits
UK:	**3,075**	**271.6**
Europe:	241	**(69.3*)**
The Americas:	291	1.2
Far East	43	(1.2)
Financial Services:	156	44.9

*after exceptional provision of £64m

Source: adapted from Datastream/ICV, company information.

In the late 1990s chain stores such as Marks & Spencer and Next were at the forefront of a revival in mail order sales. Sales increased from £4.2 billion in 1994 to £8.2 billion in 1997. Glossy catalogues and the ease of shopping had encouraged customers to increasingly use a method of shopping believed to be on the wane in the early 1990s.

Source: articles adapted from *The Guardian*, 5.11.1998, *The Observer*, 8.11.1998, *The Mirror*, 12.11.1998, the *Financial Times*, 4.11.1998.

(a) **What might be the benefits for Marks & Spencer of engaging in marketing planning?**

(b) **Using information from the data, outline any constraints which may have been operating upon Marks & Spencer's marketing plan.**

(c) **What effect might the decision to go slow on the company's strategy of opening new shops in Europe have had on M&S's marketing budget? Explain your answer.**

(d) **Using the information in the article, carry out a SWOT analysis for Marks & Spencer.**

(e) (i) **Using information from the article, examine how Marks & Spencer might evaluate its marketing planning.**

   (ii) **Using a suitable method, evaluate the effectiveness of Marks & Spencer's marketing in recent years.**

Marketing analysis and strategy

Units 36 and 37 explained how important it is for a business to understand the needs of its customers. An understanding of customers' needs helps a business to determine how to price, promote and place a product. For example, information gained from marketing research by a company may indicate that the most likely buyers of a new product will be females, over the age of 25, who are professionals. Finding out about the needs of this group should allow the company to decide how to target the market and the best marketing mix for those consumers being targeted. The business may decide to promote the product in colour supplements of quality newspapers, to use high quality paper in the product and to charge a relatively high price.

Such strategies tend to be operational (☞ unit 10). However, many businesses have to make marketing decisions which include wider and longer term marketing issues. These include matters such as how a business can gain a competitive advantage (☞ unit 16), in which markets a business should operate and where a business wishes to be in future years. These MARKETING STRATEGIES can affect the entire business.

Marketing strategies will vary in different circumstances. Sometimes marketing decisions will be based on the 'hunches' of decision makers. This may be the case in smaller businesses where one person or a few people make decisions. For example, the partners in a typesetting business may decide to increasingly promote its design services at the expense of its production of film or printing because they 'feel' that they will gain more customers and increase turnover. Larger businesses often make use of **decision making models** (☞ unit 10) to analyse marketing behaviour and the possible effects of changes in marketing strategy. These are discussed later in this unit.

Factors influencing a business's marketing strategy

There is a number of factors that may influence a business's marketing strategy.

The objectives of the business The marketing strategy that a business uses must reflect the objectives of the business as a whole. Marketing strategies must therefore be consistent with the wider corporate objectives of the organisation (☞ units 4 and 15). For example, a business which is aiming to reduce the number of countries into which it operates should not develop international marketing strategies which go against this wider, corporate strategy (☞ unit 16). However, marketing strategies are not always secondary to corporate objectives. In some businesses, marketing

Question 1

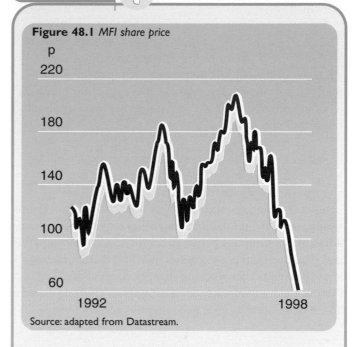

Figure 48.1 *MFI share price*

Source: adapted from Datastream.

MFI, the furniture retailer turned its back on tradition in 1998. Floated in 1992 on the stock exchange, the company was famous for cheap and cheerful flatpack furniture which could be loaded into the car and assembled at home. Faced with a number of problems in the latter part of the 1990s the company decided on a change of strategy. This change involved:
● cutting 60 per cent of its product range, around 7,000 products;
● concentration mainly on kitchen and bedroom furniture, with a small amount of office furniture;
● ordering of products which will be delivered to homes within 2 weeks.

The company had a target operating profit of 11-12 per cent. John Randall, MFI's chief executive argued that this was not 'pie in the sky' but is achievable. It was suggested that results were due to poor performance of the economy, although many other stores such as Boots and Dixons had strategies that kept customers spending profitably during this period. Costs had been a problem for MFI. Randall argued that: 'We know the cost structure necessary (for 11-12 per cent growth) and the steps we are taking will get us there'.

Source: adapted from *The Observer*, 5.7.1998.

(a) Examine the objectives that MFI may have had when changing its marketing strategy, using examples from the information above.
(b) What other factors may have influenced the marketing strategy of the business?

information and strategies often have a strong influence upon corporate objectives and strategy. A growing market amongst ethical customers, for example, may persuade the business to deal only with those businesses that conform to certain ethical principles.

The strategies of competitor businesses As shall be seen later in this unit, many businesses take account of the strategies of their competitors when setting their own marketing strategies. For example, if a competitor promotes all of its company products on the internet successfully, other businesses may follow.

The structure of the market Marketing strategies will be influenced by the level of competition and the degree of change within different markets (☞ unit 18). In less competitive markets, with relatively little change, for example, businesses may find that their strategies require only minor adjustments from one period to another. In more competitive and dynamic markets businesses may find that marketing strategies require far reaching changes on an annual basis. For example, a manufacturer of active wear clothing aimed at 16-24 year olds may need to constantly monitor changes in tastes.

The attitudes of key decision makers within businesses Marketing strategies are likely to be influenced by the attitudes of decision makers towards matters such as the desirability of risk and change. Such attitudes are influenced by the environment within which a business operates, but also by the views of managers and directors and the culture of the business itself (☞ unit 14). For example, new managers aiming to alter the 'direction' of a business may decide to change the entire distribution network to mail order and sell off its retail outlets because this has worked successfully in other businesses.

The size of the business Larger businesses are likely to be strongly influenced by one or more of the above factors when making decisions about their marketing strategies. Smaller and medium sized businesses, however, often find strategic decision making more challenging. This is because the owners and managers of such businesses are often so immersed in the operational side of their work that they take few opportunities to adopt a strategic outlook. As a result, marketing strategy may be influenced by 'intuition' and responses to daily pressures.

The strengths of the business Unit 36 explained that **asset-based or asset-led marketing** is where a business develops those products that make the best use of its 'core competences'. These are the major strengths of the firm. It produces goods or services that make the best use of its resources. Many businesses see brand loyalty (☞ unit 45) or goodwill as a major **intangible asset** (☞ unit 56).

The marketing strategy adopted by such businesses will therefore attempt to develop products that can be associated with the brand names of its successful products. Many food manufacturers have followed this marketing strategy in recent years. Examples have included Milky Way crispy rolls and ice cream Mars Bars. One of the most successful companies in the world, the Walt Disney Company, has perhaps followed this strategy into a number of areas. The launch by IKEA of a new range of furniture or a construction company moving into house renovation might be other examples. Examples in the service industry might include travel companies buying cottages to let for holidays or buying ships to sell cruise holidays.

 Question 2

'Have a break, have a ***'. If you are not able to fill in the gap then you are one of only two people in a hundred who can't. The slogan has been used in television advertisements since 1957. Kit Kat was originally launched in 1937. The new advertisements in 1999 included a baby trying to blow out trick candles and a group of Loch Ness Monster spotters. The idea was to keep the customers guessing about the product. This could only work with such a well known brand.

There have been numerous developments over the years. A two finger version was launched in 1951 and it was sold in multipacks in 1963. In 1996 Kit Kat Orange was launched followed by a mint version. These were mainly special promotions designed to stir up interest in the brand name. In 1999 Nestlé, the owners, launched Kit Kat Chunky. It was a single chunky bar aimed at teenagers, competing directly with chocolate brands such as Wispa.

Source: adapted from *The Guardian*, 12.6.1999.

(a) Identify the factors that may have affected the launch of Kit Kat related products.
(b) To what extent would you say that Nestlé was taking an asset-based marketing approach when launching Kit Kat Chunky?

Competitive marketing strategies

Many businesses are finding that the markets in which they operate are increasingly competitive. Two factors might explain this. First, the increasing internationalisation of trade means that many markets that were dominated by domestic business are now open to foreign competition. Businesses operating within the EU have experienced such increases in competition since the creation of the single European market (☞ unit 30). Second, government attempts throughout the world to release market forces have led to many markets being privatised and liberalised (☞ unit 6). This has often led to greater competition.

These changes have led businesses to pay careful attention to their competitors when creating marketing strategies.

Question 3

Disney is in a dominant position in terms of its share of the theme park market. In 1996 it ran the six most popular sites throughout the world, attracting nearly a quarter of the 320 million admissions in that year. The most popular theme park in the world was Tokyo's Disneyland, where attendance topped 15.5 million. Figure 48.2 shows that Disney's operations accounted for two-thirds of all trips by Britons to foreign parks, with Disney parks occupying all top five slots. Only Alton Towers in Staffordshire, with 2.7 million customers, and Chessington World of Adventures attracted more Britons than Disneyland Paris.

The biggest rivals to Disney's 24 per cent share of the world market for theme parks were all American. These included Six Flags, with ten parks across America (8 per cent), Anheuser Busch with six attractions including Sea World at Orlando, Florida and San Diego, California (6 per cent), and Universal and Paramount both attracting 4 per cent.

Source: adapted from *The Guardian*, 11.9.1997.

(a) Using the three methods of identifying competitors on page 328, examine the possible businesses that may compete against Disney.

(b) Discuss the possible objectives of:
   (i) Disney in relation to its share of world tourists;
   (ii) Alton Towers in relation to its share of UK tourists;
   (iii) Legoland in Windsor.

Figure 48.2 *UK tourists to foreign theme parks*

	UK visitors as a % of total	Visits by UK tourists, 1996, 000s
Disneyland, Paris	10	1,180
Disney Magic Kingdom, Florida	3.0	414
Disney EPCOT, Florida	3.0	337
Disney-MGM Studios, Florida	3.0	299
Disneyland, California	1.6	225
Universal Studios, Florida	2.0	170
Port Aventura, Spain	5.4	162
Parc Asterix, France	6.8	115
Sea World, Florida	2.0	102
Busch Gardens, Tampa, Florida	2.0	83

Source: adapted from Mintel.

Table 48.1 *Visits to most popular tourist attractions that charge admission, GB*

Attractions charging admission	Millions
Alton Towers	2.7
Madame Tussaud's	2.7
Tower of London	1.7
Chessington World of Adventures	1.7
Canterbury Cathedral	1.7
Natural History Museum	1.6
Science Museum	1.5
Legoland	1.4
Windsor Castle	1.2
Blackpool Tower	1.2

Source: adapted from British Tourist Authority.

Table 48.2 *Participation in leisure activities away from home, GB*

Great Britain	Percentages
	All adults
Visit a public house	65
Meal in a restaurant (not fast food)	62
Drive for pleasure	47
Meal in a fast food restaurant	42
Library	39
Cinema	36
Short break holiday	29
Disco or night club	27
Historic building	24
Spectators sports event	22
Theatre	20
Museum or art gallery	20
Fun fair	15
Exhibition (other than museum/gallery)	14
Theme park	12
Visit a betting shop	9
Camping or caravanning	9
Bingo	7

Source: adapted from *Leisure Tracking Survey*, The Henley Centre.

Businesses often carry out COMPETITOR ANALYSIS. This provides businesses with a variety of information about their rivals. Businesses can then use this information to develop suitable COMPETITIVE STRATEGIES. Competitive strategies allow businesses to compete most effectively with their rivals and to maximise their competitive advantage.

Competitor analysis

Competitor analysis allows a business to develop a knowledge and understanding of its competitors' behaviour before deciding on a suitable strategy. There is a number of aspects to competitor analysis.

Identifying competitors This would appear to be a straightforward task for a business. For example, a cinema complex in Bristol may consider that its competitors are other cinemas in the same city. However, this would be based upon the assumption that the Bristol cinema defines its competitors as other businesses offering the same or similar products. Further analysis of a cinema's competitors might reveal that cinema complexes are competing not only with other such complexes, but also with a range of other leisure based businesses, such as bowling alleys, football clubs and sports centres. Businesses can define their competitors in three main ways.

● Other businesses providing the same or a similar product. For example, P & O, the business which operates cross Channel ferries, might identify Stena Sealink, Brittany Ferries and Sally Line as its competitors. This is because all these competitor companies also offer cross Channel ferries. Some businesses may wish to take this aspect of competitor analysis further by identifying those businesses providing the same or a similar product to the same market segment (☞ unit 38). Here P&0 would analyse the market segments using Stena Sealink, Brittany Ferries and Sally Line.

● Other businesses with products which provide the same service. In this case P & O might regard its competitors as Hoverspeed, who operates Seacats and hovercrafts across the Channel and Le Shuttle which, like cross Channel ferries transports passengers and vehicles between Folkestone and Calais. A wider interpretation of this category would include Eurostar, the train service which uses the Channel Tunnel to transport passengers from Britain to continental Europe and airline companies offering flights from London to cities such as Paris and Brussels.

● Other businesses seeking to satisfy the same or a similar customer need. Here P & O may see themselves as competing with other travel businesses competing for holiday spending money.

Michael Porter developed a model which identified five 'forces' of competition which affect a business (☞ unit 16

and 18). These include new market entrants competing with established businesses, competition from substitute products, competition from the rivalry of established firms, the bargaining power of consumers and the bargaining power of suppliers. Porter supports the view suggested above, that an analysis of competition should not be restricted to businesses producing the same or a similar product. He extends his view of competition not only to businesses competing for the same customers, but also to businesses competing for suppliers and to future competitors entering markets.

Examining competitors' strengths and weaknesses Here a business will wish to examine a whole range of elements of competitors' businesses, from the specifications and technical aspects of competitors' products, through to relationships with suppliers and customers. Especially important in this type of competitor analysis is the identification of **critical success factors**. These are the factors which may give a competitor an edge in the market and allow it stand out from others. For example, the critical success of a business could be identified as the quality of its product or the after sales service provided to customers.

The main problem associated with examining customers' strengths and weaknesses is the difficulty of obtaining data. In general there is a need to rely upon secondary data (☞ unit 37) and the experiences of customers, suppliers and others associated with the competitor business.

Identifying competitors' objectives and strategies It is important that not too much emphasis is placed upon the assumption that competitors will be attempting to maximise their profits. Some businesses attempt to satisfice (☞ unit 4) rather than to maximise profits. Other businesses have objectives which do not directly relate to increased profits even if, in the longer term, the aim is to create additional profits. Such objectives include entering new markets, improving cash flow and leading a market technologically. Again, businesses will need to rely heavily upon secondary data when undertaking competitor analysis in this area.

Competitive strategies - cost leadership, differentiation and focus

It is suggested that there are three main competitive marketing strategies.

Cost leadership The aim of following a cost leadership strategy is to gain a cost advantage over competitors. This cost advantage can then be passed on to consumers in the form of lower prices. Businesses can gain a cost advantage by having higher levels of productivity (☞ unit 96) and more efficient supplier and distribution networks. Amstrad is an example of a business which has pursued this strategy. It provides electrical goods cheaper than those of competitors. The main problem with cost leadership is that it focuses upon costs of production and lower prices rather than the needs of customers. This may create certain problems. For example, consumers might not always wish to purchase the lowest price product as it may have been perceived as being of lower quality.

Differentiation This strategy is where a business offers consumers something different from that which is offered by its competitors, in order to gain an 'edge' over them. The difference can be in terms of something real, such as a technical difference in the product itself, or perceived, such as a strong brand identity developed through a promotional campaign. In the latter case, consumers must actually believe the perceived difference. Guinness, for example, has been differentiated both in terms of its smooth consistency and taste, and through a campaign which promotes it as an 'intelligent' drink.

Focus Businesses adopting focus strategies concentrate upon particular market segments (☞ unit 38) rather than the market as a whole. They attempt to meet effectively the needs of a clearly defined group of consumers. By following this strategy, a business seeks to gain a competitive advantage over other businesses which spread their efforts over a wider range of consumers. For example, there is a small but thriving market for hand made, made to measure suits.

Competitive strategies - market positioning

Another set of alternative competitive marketing strategies is based upon the 'position' which a business wishes to occupy in relation to other businesses operating in the same market.

Market leader strategies In many markets there is one business which is generally recognised as the leader. Market leaders tend to have the largest share (☞ unit 39) of a particular market. Market leaders may also be businesses which lead the market in terms of price changes and promotional spending. Examples of market leaders might be Microsoft in the software market and Kodak in the camera film market. There is a number of strategies which market leaders can adopt to improve or maintain their market leadership.

● Expanding the total market. As holders of the largest market share, market leaders stand most to gain by expanding the market. Expanding the market can be achieved by attracting new product users, promoting new uses for the product or encouraging greater product usage. For example, breakfast cereal manufacturers have tried to get consumers to eat cereal at different times of the day.

● Expanding market share. Market leaders may use the range

of elements in the marketing mix (☞ unit 40) to expand their current market share at the expense of competitors'. For example, Microsoft increased its share of the computer software market by establishing its product as the standard PC operating system.

● Defending current market share. The aim here is to prevent competitors from increasing their market share at the expense of the market leader. Most market leaders take the view that defending market share can best be achieved by continually improving the way in which they meet consumer needs. Often this is achieved with the use of complex and sophisticated marketing strategies. For example, some commentators have seen the development by Nestlé of a range of brands in the instant coffee market not only as an example of meeting new needs, but also as a sophisticated form of defence. The development of the Alta Rica, Cap Colombie and Blend 37 brands can be seen as a defence of Nescafé and Gold Blend from competitors seeking to damage Nestlé's share of this market by gaining a foothold in smaller segments.

Question 4

In the late 1990s Boeing, the Seattle based leading aircraft manufacturer, was struggling to take its 238,000 employees into a new era. The company faced stiff competition from a much younger rival, Airbus Industrie, a tie up of European manufacturers including British Aerospace. Airbus Industrie was threatening to steal Boeing's crown by claiming a greater share of new orders and, further ahead, of the overall market.

Airbus won a deal worth potentially £5.5 billion from British Airways (BA) for up to 188 shorthaul jets. Although BA ordered some long haul Boeing 777s, the US firm was bitterly disappointed at losing a mainstay client. To add to its troubles the company was rocked by its own inability to manage its production processes and keep its costs down. Blinded by the need to win orders against Airbus, it made the mistake of committing itself to making huge numbers of aircraft then found that it could not deliver. Despite buoyant demand, Boeing's profit margins plunged as it paid through the nose for overtime, rush delivery of parts and compensation to airlines for late delivery. The effect was Boeing's first loss in fifty years. Airbus was aiming to raise the stakes with the development of the A3XX, a new longer range jumbo jet with an increased seating capacity of 555.

Source: adapted from *The Guardian*, 31.10.1998.

(a) How would you describe: (i) Boeing's; and (ii) Airbus Industrie's; position within the aircraft industry?
(b) Identify the marketing strategy being adopted by Airbus Industrie. Explain your answer.
(c) Using the evidence in the above article, comment on the possible marketing strategies that Boeing might use in order to maintain its current position in the aircraft industry.

Market challenger strategies Market challengers are those businesses with a substantial share of the market. However, they hold second, third or lower positions in the market in relation to the market leader. Not all businesses with lower market shares than the leader are market challengers. To be defined as market challengers businesses must be in a strong enough position to challenge the leader and be willing to adopt strategies to win more market share. There are three main types of strategies which market challengers can adopt.

● Direct attacks on the market leader. Here the market challenger must be prepared to directly compete in terms of the market leaders' strengths and also to match its marketing mix. To do this the market challenger must be able to match the resources of the market leader and to respond to retaliatory actions by the market leader. Such retaliatory action often takes the form of price cutting and aggressive promotion and distribution campaigns.

● Indirect attacks on the market leader. Because of the problems involved in mounting a direct attack upon a market leader, many market followers choose to adopt less confrontational strategies. One of the most common is to identify areas in which the market leader is less strong and to develop products designed to address these weaknesses. For example, businesses have attempted to compete with crisp manufacturers Walkers by offering exotic snack foods such as popadums and Chinese rice crackers.

● Attacking firms other than the market leader. This allows a business to increase its market share by attacking relatively weaker businesses. For example, many of the larger brewing businesses have increased their market share in this way in the UK by taking over smaller breweries.

Market follower strategies Many businesses occupying lower positions in a market do not wish to challenge the market leader. Challenges on a market leader often lead to retaliatory action and cause expensive battles which often hurt challengers more than they do leaders. For this reason many businesses choose to follow the strategy of market leaders. There are three main types of market followers.

● Those who imitate market leaders. Own brand products in supermarkets fall into this category, as do canned drinks such as Virgin Cola. In more extreme cases imitation may lead to cloning. This occurs when one business seeks to copy the market leaders' products without originating anything itself.

● Innovative businesses. Such businesses lack the resources to challenge market leaders. They tend to willingly follow moves made by market leaders so that they do not change the structure of the market.

● Businesses not capable of challenging market leaders which are content to satisfice. It is not unusual to find such businesses in the take away food market. These businesses have little competitive advantage. They tend to be vulnerable to changes in the market and may fail as a consequence.

Market niche strategies As explained in unit 38, market niches are very small segments of the market. They are sometimes described as segments within segments. The majority of businesses which operate in niche markets tend to be small and medium sized. However, some larger businesses have divisions specialising in market niches. Niches can be based upon geographical location, specific product differentiation, customer group or product type. Examples of businesses adopting market niche strategies include Tie Rack, Reuters and TVR, the sports car manufacturers.

Marketing strategies for growth

Many businesses operate in or intend to move into markets where business growth is both desirable and possible. Businesses operating in such markets will tend to emphasise growth in their corporate (☞ unit 4) and marketing objectives. Growth may be in the form of increased sales revenue or turnover, greater profits, increased capital or more land and employees. There is a range of marketing strategies that growth orientated businesses can adopt. Growth orientated marketing strategies are not suited to all businesses, however. In shrinking markets, for example, a business may wish to maintain previous sales levels or just survive rather than aim for growth.

The ANSOFF MATRIX is a useful tool for businesses aiming for growth. The Ansoff Matrix shown in Figure 48.3 illustrates both existing and new products within existing and new markets. Four possible marketing strategies to achieve growth are revealed by the Matrix.

Figure 48.3 *The Ansoff Matrix*

		PRODUCT	
		Existing	**New**
MARKET	**Existing**	Market penetration	Product development
	New	Market development	Diversification

Market penetration As suggested by the Ansoff Matrix, the purpose of market penetration is to achieve growth in existing markets with existing products. There is a number of ways in which businesses can achieve this.

● Increasing the brand loyalty (☞ unit 45) of customers so that they use substitute brands less frequently. Well known brands such as Kellogg's Corn Flakes and Lurpak butter make use of this strategy.

● Encouraging consumers to use the product more regularly. An example might be encouraging people to drink canned drinks at breakfast.

● Encouraging consumers to use more of the product. An example might be a crisp manufacturer producing maxi sized crisp packets rather than standard sized crisp packets.

Product development This is concerned with marketing new or modified products in existing markets. The development of the Ford Focus, launched in 1998 and intended to act as a replacement for the Ford Escort, is an example of product development. Confectionery manufacturers such as Cadbury and Nestlé regularly use this strategy in order to stimulate sales growth.

Market development This involves the marketing of existing products in new markets. For example, the Halifax has extended its banking activities to the Spanish market and Harvey Nichols, a retail outlet previously limited to London, has opened a branch in Leeds.

Diversification This occurs when new products are developed for new markets. Diversification allows a business to move away from reliance upon existing markets and products. This allows a business to spread risk and increase safety. If one product faces difficulties or fails, a successful product in another market may prevent the business overall facing problems. However, diversification will take a business outside its area of expertise. This might mean that its performance in new markets is relatively poor compared to more experienced operators. The move by Mercedes Benz into the market for small, high volume cars and the move by Virgin into financial services and the air passenger business are perhaps examples of this marketing strategy.

Question 5

Reckitt & Colman is a multinational producer of household and pharmaceutical products, selling in over 120 countries. One of its most well known brands is Dettol. The original Dettol product was an antiseptic disinfectant. The brand was first established in 1933. This is still available to consumers, but in a range of different bottle sizes. The company now offers other products in the Dettol range. These include soap, shower foam, antiseptic cream, antiseptic spray, mouthwash and antiseptic wipes. In 1997 Sporox was sold for the first time in North America. The US Food and Drugs Administration approved the sale of Sporox, a sterilising disinfectant for use in hospitals and clinics. Sales of Disprin were particularly strong in Africa and South Asia. In India, for example, sales increased by 24.7 per cent after it was relaunched with a new claim about the speed with which it kills pain. The company stated in its 1997 *Annual Report and Accounts* under the heading brand leadership that: 'The first priority is to continue to refine the focus of our business on household and over the counter pharmaceutical brands. In December we announced our intention to spend £96 million on the acquisition of important US household brands ... which are a natural fit with our core categories. We disposed of minor businesses outside our strategic focus.'

Source: adapted from Reckitt & Colman, *Annual Report and Accounts.*

(a) Using Ansoff's Matrix, analyse the strategies used by Reckitt & Colman for its products.
(b) Discuss how the view of the company in 1997 may have affected its marketing strategy.

Key terms

The Ansoff Matrix - a model which identifies growth strategies for businesses based on an analysis of their products and their markets.
Marketing strategies - approaches to marketing taken by a business which enable it to achieve its objectives.
Competitor analysis - identifying the strengths and weaknesses of competitors and their products.
Competitive marketing strategies - marketing strategies directly based upon particular approaches to dealing with competitors.

Summary

1. What is meant by a strategic marketing decision?
2. What factors will affect a business's marketing strategy?
3. State the 3 aspects of competitor analysis.
4. How might a business define its competitors?
5. What are the 5 forces of competition according to Porter?
6. What is meant by a critical success factor?
7. Explain the difference between a cost leadership and a differentiation strategy.
8. Suggest 3 ways in which a market leader might protect its market position.
9. Suggest 3 ways in which a market challenger might improve its market position.
10. What is meant by a market follower?
11. What 4 methods of growth strategy are suggested by the Ansoff Matrix?
12. How might a business gain greater penetration in an existing market with an existing product?

Case study

Burger King vs McDonalds

Pepsi-Cola has been left trailing by Coca-Cola. Microsoft has trounced all opposition. But sometimes the number two in the market can get the upper hand - as in the US burger wars between McDonald's and Burger King.

Burger King seems to have gone from strength to strength, opening more restaurants in the US than ever before. It scored a publicity coup by declaring a Free FryDay and gave away a bag of French fries to anyone who walked into, or drove up to, one of its 7,000 restaurants. In total 15 million bags were handed out. This event was staged to mark the launch of its new weapon in the war with its bigger rival, McDonald's, a hotter, crispier potato chip that is cheekily promoted with the slogan, 'The taste that beat McDonald's fries'.

The launch of the new fries came only four months after the introduction of another new Burger King product aimed squarely at McDonald's customers. The Big King burger was a shameless imitation of the Big Mac, but with 75 per cent more meat. Burger King launched it with the slogan: 'Get ready for the taste that beats Big Mac'.

McDonald's has many more restaurants than Burger King. At September 30 1997, it had 12,249 restaurants in the US, compared with Burger King's 7,414, and 9,997 in the rest of the world, compared with Burger King's 1,986. But recent experience has shown that biggest is not necessarily best

With its 'size is everything strategy', McDonald's has sought to increase sales by opening more restaurants. Marketing research has shown that some 70 per cent of visits to a fast food restaurant are made on impulse. So, theoretically, more restaurants should mean more spur-of-the-moment trade. But in the US, McDonald's now has so many outlets that it appears to be close to saturation point. In 1996, sales growth failed to keep up with the pace of restaurant openings, so sales per store fell, hitting profits. Consequently, McDonald's sharply cut back the pace of expansion in 1997.

The store opening programme might not have hurt profits if McDonald's had been able to attract more customers with

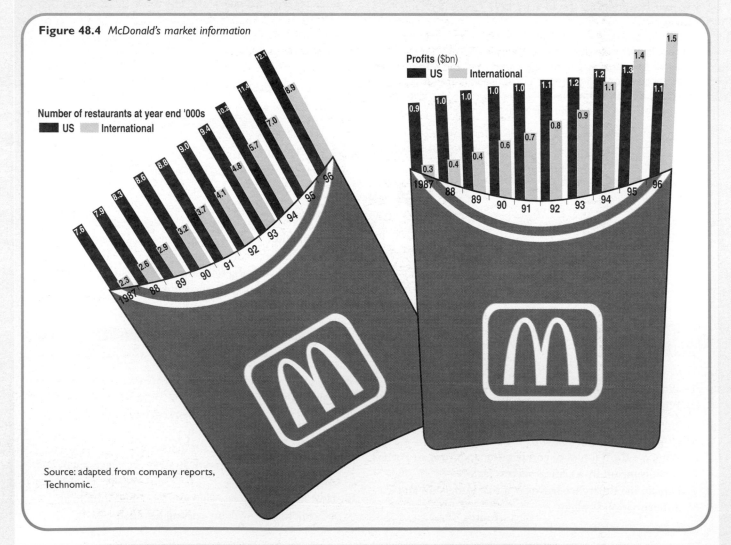

Figure 48.4 *McDonald's market information*

Number of restaurants at year end '000s
■ US ■ International

US: 1987 7.6, 88 7.9, 89 8.3, 90 8.6, 91 8.8, 92 9.0, 93 9.4, 94 10.2, 95 11.4, 96 12.1
International: 1987 2.3, 88 2.6, 89 2.9, 90 3.2, 91 3.7, 92 4.1, 93 4.8, 94 5.7, 95 7.0, 96 8.9

Profits ($bn)
■ US ■ International

US: 1987 0.9, 88 1.0, 89 1.0, 90 1.0, 91 1.0, 92 1.1, 93 1.2, 94 1.2, 95 1.3, 96 1.1
International: 1987 0.3, 88 0.4, 89 0.4, 90 0.6, 91 0.7, 92 0.8, 93 0.9, 94 1.1, 95 1.4, 96 1.5

Source: adapted from company reports, Technomic.

Figure 48.5 *McDonald's and Burger King: market comparison*

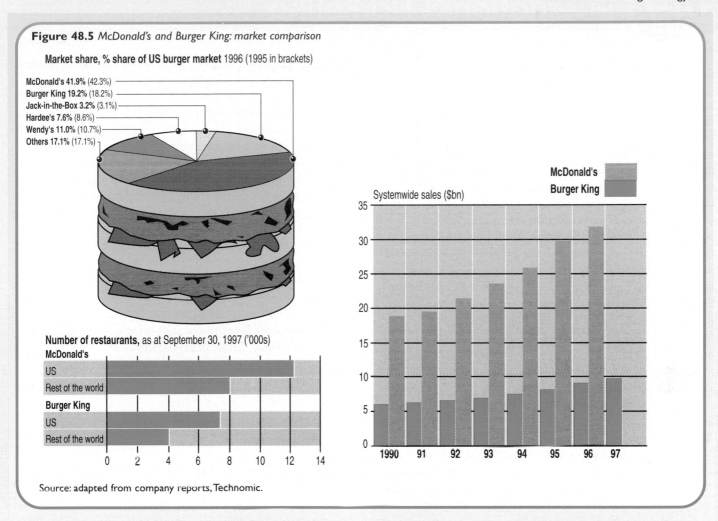

Market share, % share of US burger market 1996 (1995 in brackets)

McDonald's 41.9% (42.3%)
Burger King 19.2% (18.2%)
Jack-in-the-Box 3.2% (3.1%)
Hardee's 7.6% (8.6%)
Wendy's 11.0% (10.7%)
Others 17.1% (17.1%)

Number of restaurants, as at September 30, 1997 ('000s)

McDonald's — US, Rest of the world
Burger King — US, Rest of the world

Systemwide sales ($bn)

McDonald's
Burger King

1990 91 92 93 94 95 96 97

Source: adapted from company reports, Technomic.

exciting products. But McDonald's has a poor record for innovation. It has failed to come up with a successful new product since the introduction of Chicken McNuggets in 1983, and the Big Mac is now 30 years old.

In most markets outside the US, however, Burger King's advantage is not so clear. Saturated markets are not an issue for either company, but McDonald's has already succeeded in building a global brand, while Burger King is still at the starting post. According to the Interbrand consultancy, McDonald's was the world's best known brand in 1996, while Burger King ranked nowhere in the top 100.

The Chief Executive of Burger King, Dennis Malamatinas, says Burger King is building a global brand in a disciplined way, country by country and that his company has no ambitions to oust McDonald's from its number one spot. 'If there is one critical element to our strategy, it is revenues per store as opposed to number of restaurants. Offering the best food to consumers and driving revenues per store: that is the way to make money', he commented.

Source: adapted from the *Financial Times*, 16.7.1997 and 5.1.1998.

(a) **Describe Burger King's and McDonald's position in the US and world burger market.**

(b) **Outline the main marketing strategies used by the two companies.**

(c) **Examine the factors that may have influenced the different strategies of the two businesses.**

(d) **Evaluate the success of these strategies in America and outside the US.**

(e) **Discuss possible future scenarios in burger markets if the businesses continue with their current strategies.**

The importance of international marketing

At one time businesses may have thought that marketing products overseas was an adventurous act. It was generally undertaken by large businesses which had grown too big for domestic markets. Today, however, the world has 'shrunk' due to, amongst other things, rapid changes in international transport and telecommunications. One effect of this is that a business now needs to consider the threat from foreign competition and the opportunities which might be gained from marketing internationally. For many firms international marketing is no longer an option. It is necessary if a business is to survive in a competitive business environment. For British firms this was very much the case after trade barriers between European Union nations were lifted on the last day of 1992 (☞ unit 30). The increase in the size and number of multinationals has contributed to the increase in international trading. The globalisation of business activity (☞ unit 32) has also affected business marketing strategy.

Why might businesses market their products internationally?

● Profits. By selling in overseas markets, a business might have the potential to increase its profits through an increase in sales. Overseas markets may be more lucrative than domestic ones. Manufacturing and distribution costs may be lower abroad. The product might also sell at a higher price on foreign markets than in the home market.

● Spreading the risk. If a business only produces in one country then it may face problems caused by downturns in demand due to recession (☞ unit 21). The more countries a firm operates in, the less vulnerable it is to changes in the business climate of any single country.

● Unfavourable trading conditions in the domestic market. Businesses often find that the market for a product is saturated or in decline. One option for a firm is to try and breathe new life into the product by introducing it into an overseas market. This is an example of an **extension strategy** (☞ unit 41). British American Tobacco industries, for example, have started to sell in developing countries as domestic market sales have declined.

● Legal differences. Legal restrictions on the sale of products vary from one country to another. For example, developing countries have fewer restrictions on which drugs can be offered for sale. Some pharmaceutical companies (in what many regard as unethical practice) have sold drugs banned on health grounds in the UK to these nations.

Why the overseas market is different

There can be many rewards for a business entering an overseas market.

One problem that it will face, however, is that market conditions will be different to those in the domestic market.

Question 1

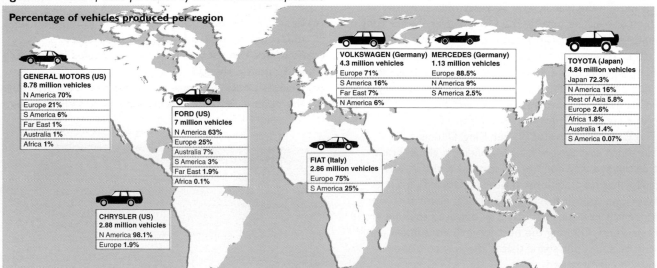

Figure 49.1 *Sites of world production by motor vehicle manufacturers*

Percentage of vehicles produced per region

GENERAL MOTORS (US)
8.78 million vehicles

N America	70%
Europe	21%
S America	6%
Far East	1%
Australia	1%
Africa	1%

FORD (US)
7 million vehicles

N America	63%
Europe	25%
Australia	7%
S America	3%
Far East	1.9%
Africa	0.1%

CHRYSLER (US)
2.88 million vehicles

N America	98.1%
Europe	1.9%

FIAT (Italy)
2.86 million vehicles

Europe	75%
S America	25%

VOLKSWAGEN (Germany)
4.3 million vehicles

Europe	71%
S America	16%
Far East	7%
N America	6%

MERCEDES (Germany)
1.13 million vehicles

Europe	88.5%
N America	9%
S America	2.5%

TOYOTA (Japan)
4.84 million vehicles

Japan	72.3%
N America	16%
Rest of Asia	5.8%
Europe	2.6%
Africa	1.8%
Australia	1.4%
S America	0.07%

Source: adapted from *The Observer*, 10.5.1998.

(a) Using information from Figure 49.1, comment on the extent to which motor vehicle manufacturers operate in overseas markets.

(b) Examine reasons why the vehicle manufacturers in Figure 49.1 are so keen to operate in overseas markets.

This makes selling abroad very risky. What are the differences that are likely to affect the success of foreign sales?

Political differences A firm must take into account the political stability of the country in which it plans to sell. Political instability, such as existed in Lebanon over a number of years, can make trading almost impossible. Also, a change of government can bring about a change in attitude towards foreign companies. A firm thinking of investing a large sum in its operations abroad will need to weigh up the political situation carefully. A number of businesses, for example, were affected by the change in government in Hong Kong in 1997 as ownership was transferred from the UK to China.

Cultural differences One difference which often causes problems for British businesses is that English is not the main or even the second language in many countries. In Eastern Europe for example, German and Russian are more widely spoken than English.

Other cultural differences may influence the way a product is marketed. For example, a product name suitable in one country may have a totally different meaning in another - the French lemonade Pssschit would require a new name were it to be sold in the UK! Colours have different meanings throughout the world. In the Far East, white rather than black is associated with mourning. In India fashion models of the sort used to promote products in the West are considered too thin. In some countries, what may be regarded as a 'bribe' in the UK is common business practice. Payments to government or industry officials may be required to get things done, from electricity connection to securing contracts.

Differences in legislation Such differences can affect the way in which a business produces and markets its products.
● Product labelling. US laws are far more stringent than UK laws about the amount of information which should be included on food labels.
● Product safety. Some countries have very strict legislation governing safety standards on childrens' toys. Others are less strict.
● Environmental impact. All cars sold in California must be fitted with a catalytic convertor. This is not the case in Europe, but may be in future.
● Advertising. Cigarette advertising on television is outlawed within EU countries.

Economic and social differences Some of the economic factors which businesses must consider include levels of income, levels of sales and corporation tax, how income is distributed, the use of tariffs or other import barriers and the level and growth of population. For example, after 1998 businesses were waiting to see how the severe downturn in the growth of 'tiger economies', such as Malaysia and Indonesia, would affect trading conditions before they invested in these countries.

Social factors which firms may need to consider include literacy levels, the role of women, religious attitudes, readiness to accept new ideas, and the habits and attitudes of social groups.

Differences in business practice The usual amount of time it take to receive payment may vary in different countries. Other differences include accounting techniques, company ownership (most British companies are relatively independent whereas those in other EU nations are often controlled by families or banks) and distribution (in many EU countries greater use is made of rail transport than in the UK).

Adapting products to fit in with local, national and regional needs can be costly. It is cheaper to have one product with one brand name and a promotional package which fits all markets. Businesses must attempt to cater for national consumer tastes, whilst trying to gain economies of scale from operating in international markets.

Methods of entering overseas markets

Once a business has made the decision to enter an overseas market, it must decide the best way to do this.

Exporting This is often the first step for a business wishing to enter an overseas market. It involves manufacturing products at home but selling them abroad. The great advantage of exporting is that it minimises the risk of operating abroad. It

Question 2

Whirlpool, a US based company, is one of the world's biggest manufacturers of 'white goods', household appliances such as fridges, dishwashers and cookers. In 1997 Whirlpool gained one third of its $8.5 billion sales outside of the US. As a company it therefore had plenty of experience of developing and producing products to suit the needs of different markets.

In the case of dishwashers, the products for the main markets in North America and Europe are quite different. Because in many US homes the machines double as garbage disposers, US-style dishwashers have mechanisms for chopping up bits of food. They also use more energy and water and tend to be noisier.

Consumers' tastes for fridges vary even more. US consumers prefer 'larder-size' cabinets which nearly all contain air-blowing systems to make them frost-free. The Germans want lots of space for meat, while the Italians are keen on special vegetable compartments. To cater for the large number of vegetarians in India, often within families that contain meat eaters, the fridges often require internal sealing systems to stop smells of different foods intermingling.

Source: adapted from the *Financial Times*, 26.3.1998.

(a) In what ways does Whirlpool's product differentiation between different countries reflect differences in the various overseas markets in which it operates?
(b) How might the need to develop different products for different markets affect Whirlpool?

can also be used as a means of testing out the ground.

Sometimes, the business may have little or no control over how the product is actually marketed in the countries to which it is sent. For this reason many firms exporting abroad make use of overseas agents (☞ unit 46). These agents are able to play an active role in the marketing of the product.

Franchising (☞ unit 2) This involves one business selling a licence to others. The licence allows one firm to use another's name, product or service in return for an initial payment and further commission or royalties.

This is a quick and relatively easy way into foreign markets and it allows the franchiser a high degree of control over the marketing of its product. However, a share of the profit does go to the franchisee. Firms such as PizzaExpress, Budget Rent-a-Car and Kentucky Fried Chicken have used this as a way of entering overseas markets.

Licensing This is similar to franchising. Franchising is used in service industries, such as fast foods and car hire. Licensing, however, involves one firm producing another's product and using its brand name, designs, patents and expertise under licence. This means that goods do not have to be physically moved abroad. Instead they are produced abroad by the foreign licensee. Also, it means that firms can avoid operating overseas. The main disadvantage is that the success or failure of the venture is largely in the hands of the licensee.

Joint ventures (☞ unit 101) This involves two companies from separate countries combining their resources. One new enlarged company is formed to launch a product onto one market. An example of this is the Royal Bank of Scotland's alliance with Banco Santander of Spain to provide banking and financial services throughout Europe. Joint ventures are increasingly being used by businesses wishing to enter Eastern European markets.

One advantage of this form of venture is that the risks are shared between two firms. Also, each business can draw on the strengths of the other. One business may have research and development strength, for example, while others may have strengths in manufacturing. However, many joint ventures have broken down due to conflicts which occur.

Direct investment Direct investment requires the setting up of production and distribution facilities abroad. They can be obtained by merger or takeover, or they may be built for this specific purpose. It is an increasingly common way for firms to reach overseas markets. For example, many Japanese manufacturers such as Nissan and Toyota set up plants in the UK in the 1990s. It was argued that there were a number of advantages to these businesses of direct investment.

- They could avoid paying import duties (☞ unit 26) that were placed on foreign products entering the EU.
- They could take advantage of the relatively low costs and availability of relatively cheap labour in the UK.

- They could take advantage of government and EU incentives to invest in the area (☞ unit 100).
- There would be lower distribution costs.
- They could take advantage of local knowledge.

Mergers or takeovers Buying a business in another country may allow a company to produce and sell its products more easily. This method of entering foreign markets has similar advantages to direct investment and is most often used by **multinationals** (☞ unit 32).

Question 3

The New Covent Garden Soup Company, which makes premium priced chilled soups and has built up a turnover of £20 million a year in the last 10 years, started selling direct to the US in 1995.

The customers are middle to up-market delicatessens. Only one large supermarket chain buys the product. 'Many large UK food retailers have made it easy for small suppliers of specialised products to get on the shelves, but US retailing is structured very differently', said William Kendall, the Managing Director. 'Part of our UK success has come through positioning ourselves as David versus Goliath. It does not work in the US. They think that because we are exporting from the UK, we must be big'.

US prices have been pushed as high as the market will bear, but that has not covered the cost of flying chilled soup on Virgin Atlantic and distributing direct to retailers. Nevertheless, the US has generated £1 million in revenue and the brand has gradually established itself with target customers in key cities. New Covent Garden is currently backing a Scot based company in San Francisco to build a factory there. The UK company will provide the manufacturing know how.

Source: adapted from *The FT Exporter*, March 1998.

(a) Identify New Covent Garden's method of entering the US market.
(b) Examine the possible problems that the method identified in (a) might have caused for the company.
(c) (i) In what other ways do you think that New Covent Garden might attempt to develop its position in the US market?
    (ii) Discuss the possible advantages of the methods you have chosen.

Summary

1. Give 5 reasons why international marketing can be so important to firms.
2. How does entering an overseas market allow a firm to spread its risks?
3. State 3 differences between overseas and domestic markets.
4. How can an agent help a business to export its products?
5. In what ways can a business enter an overseas market?
6. What is meant by licensing?
7. What is the difference between direct investment and joint ventures?

Case study

Coca-Cola

Coca-Cola is the world's largest soft drinks manufacturer. In the 1990s it has increasingly expanded its sales into foreign markets. Smaller beverage companies have found it difficult to grow in the face of competition from Coca-Cola and the second largest drinks manufacturer, Pepsi-Cola. Only companies that were able to invest in marketing and distribution were likely to succeed. Coca-Cola has aimed to have Coke within 'arms reach of desire'. This has meant having bottling plants and distribution systems in foreign markets. Coke has a network of independent bottling companies abroad. They handle the distribution and marketing of the product. Coca-Cola takes a large stake in the companies to protect its interests. In central and eastern Europe, for instance, Coke invested more than £500 million in bottling plants and a fleet of trucks.

Hefty marketing has also been required, including special offers to supermarkets for good shelf positions and generous supply terms to persuade fast food dealers to stock only Coke in drinks dispensers. Coca-Cola also has a number of other marketing strategies when selling abroad. For example, it changes the flavour of the soft drink to take into account local tastes. Coke in the US tastes different from Coke in the UK and Coke in India.

In 1999 Coca-Cola had plans to acquire interests in Cadbury Schweppes. However, it faced the prospect of fines from the European Union for failing to seek EU approval for its $1.85 billion acquisition of the Cadbury drinks business, Schweppes, in 120 countries. Coca-Cola's plans to buy Orangina from Pernod Ricard of France for around £500 million were blocked by the French authorities.

Source: adapted from the *Financial Times*, 30.4.1999 and *Mastering Marketing*, part ten, the *Financial Times*.

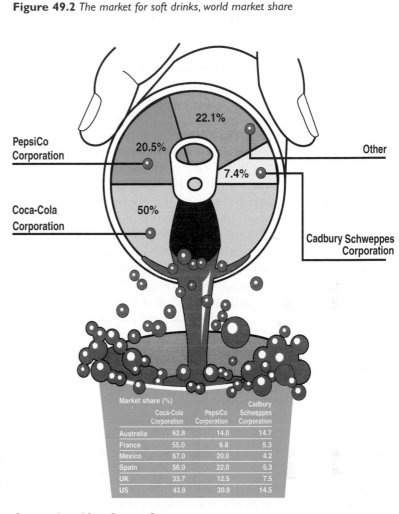

Figure 49.2 *The market for soft drinks, world market share*

PepsiCo Corporation 20.5%

22.1%

Coca-Cola Corporation 50%

7.4%

Other

Cadbury Schweppes Corporation

Market share (%)	Coca-Cola Corporation	PepsiCo Corporation	Cadbury Schweppes Corporation
Australia	62.8	14.0	14.7
France	55.0	6.8	5.3
Mexico	67.0	20.0	4.2
Spain	56.0	22.0	5.3
UK	33.7	12.5	7.5
US	43.9	30.9	14.5

Source: adapted from *Beverage Digest*.

(a) **Identify possible differences in overseas markets mentioned in the article.**

(b) **Explain how Coca-Cola has entered overseas markets.**

(c) **Examine the factors that might influence the future success of Coca-Cola in expanding into foreign markets.**

(d) **To what extent do you think that:**
   (i) **Coca-Cola has been successful in entering foreign markets;**
   (ii) **small US businesses might be successful in entering overseas markets for soft drinks in future?**

Sample results

Unit 37 showed that businesses carry out marketing research to find out what their customers want. It is highly unlikely that a business will be able to carry out marketing research on everyone in the population. So businesses tend to choose a **sample** of people to survey. There is a variety of sampling techniques that can be used. These vary from completely random samples, where everyone has an equal chance of being chosen, to quota sampling, where the population is segmented into groups with similar characteristics and a certain number of people are selected out of each segment.

Marketing research will provide a wide variety of information about the people in the sample. Businesses then analyse this data to find out the significance of the sample results. For example, a business may be interested to know the likely proportion of the population that would pay between £10 and £20 for its product or whether a new promotional campaign has increased the sales of its product.

To analyse sample marketing research data, businesses make use of probability, average and standard deviation calculations (☞ unit 12) and the normal distribution.

Probability and sampling

The reason why businesses carry out surveys and take samples is to try to reduce the risk and uncertainty that exists in every business decision. PROBABILITY is a technique that helps a business to quantify risk and it forms a basis for the analysis of sampling data.

A probability is a simple ratio between the event the business is interested in and the total number of events that could occur, ie:

$$\text{Probability (P)} = \frac{\text{Required event}}{\text{Total events}}$$

Take an example of a card drawn from a pack of 52 playing cards. The probability of drawing a 'Heart' would be:

$$\text{P(a Heart)} = \frac{13}{52} = \frac{1}{4} = 0.25$$

Similarly, for drawing a card that is from one of the other suits:

$$\text{P(a Club)} = \frac{13}{52} = \frac{1}{4} = 0.25$$

$$\text{P(a Diamond)} = \frac{13}{52} = \frac{1}{4} = 0.25$$

$$\text{P(a Spade)} = \frac{13}{52} = \frac{1}{4} = 0.25$$

There are three important laws of probability:

● The sum of the probabilities of all the possible events will equal 1. Thus the probability of drawing a Heart, a Club, a Diamond or a Spade will equal 1 (0.25 + 0.25 + 0.25 + 0.25 = 1).

● To obtain the probability of one event or another event occurring, **add** the probabilities (the addition rule). Thus the probability of drawing a Diamond or a Spade = 0.25 + 0.25 = 0.5.

● To obtain the probability of one event and another occurring, **multiply** the probabilities (the multiplication rule). Thus the probability of drawing a Diamond and a Spade on two successive draws = 0.25 x 0.25 = 0.0625.

Two examples can be used to illustrate how probability might affect a business. The first example considers its use in marketing. However, it is possible to use probability in other areas of the business, such as production or stock control. The second example shows how the business might evaluate problems arising in its administration department.

To quantify the risk associated with making a decision Say that a business has the following information about the launch of a new product.

● Probability of gaining a high demand = 0.6, expected return £6 million.

● Probability of gaining a medium demand = 0.2, expected return £3m

● Probability of gaining a low demand = 0.2, expected return £1 million.

This information about the likelihood of high, medium or low demand would have been derived from market research. The likely outcome from the decision to launch the new product will be:

● 0.6 probability of a return of £6m = 0.6 x £6m = £3.6m;

● 0.2 probability of a return of £3m = 0.2 x £3m = £0.6m;

● 0.2 probability of a return of £1m = 0.2 x £1m = £0.2m.

Given that these are the only three outcomes possible (the sum of the three probabilities = 1), then the average return the company can expect from the launch of such a product = £3.6m + £0.6m + £0.2m = £4.4m. If, for example, the cost to the business of launching such a product is £3m, then by the laws of probability, such a launch would be worth the risk. This use of probability is found in decision trees (☞ unit 00).

To establish the possible range of events that might occur in business situations Say an estate agency has three photocopiers in operation. The photocopiers are known to break down one day in every ten. What is the chance that all three are out of operation at once? There is a number of alternative combinations to consider.

● All 3 copiers are working.

● 2 copiers are working and 1 is faulty.

● 1 copier is working and 2 are faulty.
● All 3 copiers are faulty.

If a working copier is (w) and a faulty copier is (f), the possible combinations amongst the three machines are:

Machine	1	2	3	
	w	w	w	All 3 machines are working
	w	w	f	
	w	f	w	} 2 are working and 1 is faulty
	f	w	w	
	w	f	f	
	f	w	f	} 1 is working and 2 are faulty
	f	f	w	
	f	f	f	All 3 machines are faulty

If the probability of a working machine (p) is 0.9 then the probability of a faulty machine (q) is 0.1. It is possible to work out the probability of all these combinations.

● All 3 machines working = 1 x 0.9 x 0.9 x 0.9 = 0.73 (or 73%).
● 2 machines working and 1 faulty = 3 x 0.9 x 0.9 x 0.1 = 0.24 (or 24%).
● 1 machine working and 2 faulty = 3 x 0.9 x 0.1 x 0.1 = 0.027 (or 2.7%).
● All 3 machines are faulty = 1 x 0.1 x 0.1 x 0.1 = 0.001 (or 0.1%).

In algebraic terms the probabilities are worked out using the binomial expansion:

$$p^3 + 3p^2q + 3pq^2 + q^3 = 1$$

Thus for this business there is only a 0.001 chance (0.1 per cent) of all three machines being out of action at once. But there is a 0.24 (24 per cent) chance of at least one machine being out of action, which might be a problem for the company. Although 3 machines have been used in this example, a business might need to look at combinations involving 2, 4 or more machines. Probabilities would then be worked out using, for example:

$$p^2 + 2pq + q^2 = 1 \text{ (for 2 machines)}$$

$$p^4 + 4p^3q + 6p^2q^2 + 4pq^3 + q^4 = 1 \text{ (for 4 machines)}$$

The normal distribution

The NORMAL DISTRIBUTION is a statistical model that will tell a business what the expected range of outcomes from a particular population will be. It is used where businesses have been carrying out large scale sampling (☞ unit 37), for example in marketing research or in quality control, where they want to find out what range of results to expect.

The normal distribution occurs in many different contexts. For example, if a large group of sixth form students, representing the full ability range, took a Business Studies examination, then the frequency distribution of their marks may resemble a normal distribution, as shown in Figure 50.1.

Question 1

Littlehurst is a manufacturer of electronic sensor equipment. Its most popular product is a sensor device that is used to test corrosion in metal on equipment. It has tested two new hand held sensor devices with a sample of its customers and has found the following information.

Test product A Probability of success - 0.3 Expected revenue - £200,000
Probability of failure - 0.7 Expected revenue - £50,000
Cost of launch - £90,000

Test product B Probability of success - 0.5 Expected revenue - £120,000
Probability of failure - 0.5 Expected revenue - £30,000
Cost of launch - £80,000

(a) Calculate:
(i) the returns that the company can expect from each product;
(ii) the profit or loss that the company can expect from each product.
(b) Suggest which product the company should launch based on the above information alone.
(c) If the cost of the launch of product B fell to £65,000, how might this affect your answer to (a)?

Some students will do very well, some students will do very badly, but the majority of students will fall close to and either side of the average (mean) score.

The resulting CURVE shows all the possible outcomes (range of marks) and the frequency at which they occurred (number of students at each mark). It is 'bell-shaped' and symmetrical about the mean value.

Normal distributions will differ in their shallowness or steepness. The weights of people in a population are likely to be quite evenly spread as in Figure 50.2(a), whilst IQ scores in a population are likely to be more closely bunched around the average, with few high or low scores as in Figure 50.2(b). It is the spread of the data that determines the curves' steepness or shallowness. This spread can be measured by the use of **standard deviations** (☞ unit 12).

Whatever the spread of the normal distribution curves,

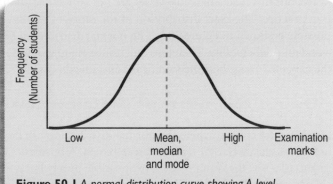

Figure 50.1 *A normal distribution curve showing A level examination scores*

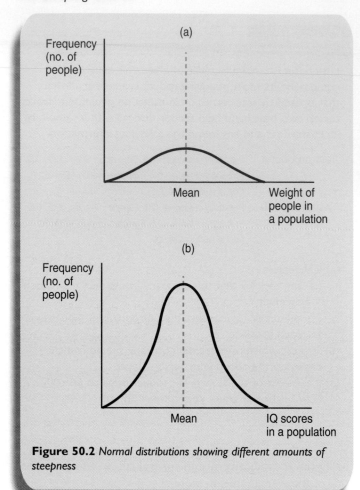

Figure 50.2 *Normal distributions showing different amounts of steepness*

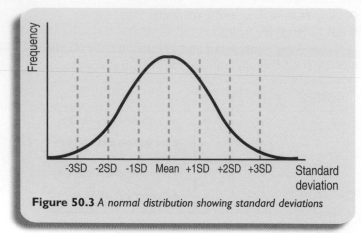

Figure 50.3 *A normal distribution showing standard deviations*

they have particular features in common.
● The curve is symmetrical about the mean.
● The mean, mode and median of the distribution is equal.
● 50 per cent of all values lie either side of the mean value.
● The curve can be divided into 3 standard deviations (SDs) either side of the mean.
   68 per cent of the population will lie between + or - 1 SD.
   96 per cent of the population will lie between + or - 2 SDs.
   99.8 per cent of the population will lie between + or - 3 SDs.
   Thus nearly all results will lie within + or - 3 SDs of the mean. A small proportion (0.2 per cent) will lie outside this range, but this is so small businesses are not concerned about it in practice. The exact distribution of the range of results possible is shown in Figure 50.3. The normal distribution has a certain predictability. Therefore any results that lie outside the expected range become significant and unexpected.

Using the normal distribution

One business context where the normal distribution can be used is in the analysis of market research data. A business might ask, 'was the result of a survey possible purely by chance or was there a significant difference between the actual result and the expected one?'

Say that a company which manufactures potato crisps has used a market research company to discover whether their new 'Sweet and Sour' flavour, which has been heavily promoted since its launch, is well known by the public. On average, the company would expect 50 per cent of those asked to recognise a flavour, but following the promotion they would expect a higher recognition. If the market research company asks 900 consumers, what results might the company expect to get to measure whether the promotion was successful?

The first stage in the use of normal distribution to answer this question involves the calculation of the expected RANGE OF RESULTS from such surveys. To do this it is necessary to calculate the mean and the standard deviation for this particular distribution.

The mean for a normal distribution can be calculated using the formula:

$$mean = n \times p$$

where n = the sample size
and p   = the probability of an event occurring.

The standard deviation for a normal distribution can be calculated using the formula:

$$1 \text{ standard deviation (1SD)} = \sqrt{npq}$$

where n =   the sample size;
      p =   the probability of an event occurring;
and   q =   the probability of an event not occurring.
For the market research on the 'Sweet and Sour' crisps:
   n = 900
   p = 0.5
   q = 0.5

Therefore, for such surveys as this:

$$mean = 900 \times 0.5 = 450$$

$$1SD = \sqrt{900 \times 0.5 \times 0.5} = \sqrt{225} = 15$$

The full range of results can be + or - 3SD from the mean where:

2SD = 30
3SD = 45

Therefore, the range for this normal curve will be:

450 + or - 45 = 405 to 495.

The normal curve can now be drawn based on this information as in Figure 50.4. For the company, this normal curve provides a tool to help it analyse any market research results.
● 68 per cent of all results will show that between 435 and 465 people recognise the flavour (given a mean of 450).
● 96 per cent of all results will show that between 420 and 480 people recognise the flavour.
● 99.8 per cent of all results will show that between 405 and 495 people recognise the flavour.
These percentages are usually referred to as confidence levels (☞ unit 37).

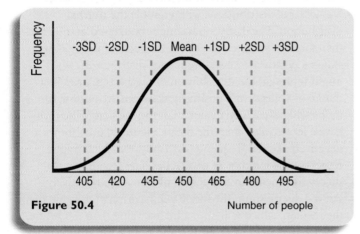

Figure 50.4   Number of people

Question 2

A manufacturer of dental products is particular interested in the hygiene habits of its customers. The business expects that the average length of time people take before changing their toothbrush is 90 days and the standard deviation is 20 days.

(a) Draw a normal distribution. Assuming that the information is normally distributed, calculate and plot onto the graph:
  (i) the expected average length of time people take to change their toothbrush;
  (ii) the range of results between minus 3 and plus 3 standard deviations (in days);
(b) What percentage of its customers might the business expect to change their toothbrush:
  (i) after 70 days;
  (ii) after 130 days?

Confidence levels

Look again at the previous example about sweet and sour flavoured crisps. Only if marketing research results showed more than 495 people recognised the flavour could the company be totally confident that its promotion had been effective in increasing recognition above the 50 per cent level. Suppose the actual result was 486 people recognising the product? How significant would this be? We can find this in terms of standard deviations (z) by using the formula:

$$z = \frac{x - m}{s}$$

where x = the value
m = the mean
s = the standard deviation

so:

$$z = \frac{486 - 450}{15} = \frac{36}{15} = 2.4 \text{ SDs from the mean}$$

To find out what percentage of the population lies between the mean and +2.4SDs, a normal distribution table, as in Table 50.1, can be used. This shows the areas under the standard normal distribution from the mean. Because this is a frequency distribution, the area represents the number in the population between each value.

Reading from the left hand column of the table, 49.18 per cent (or 0.4918) of the population will lie between the mean and +2.4SDs. To include all values up to and including 486 it is necessary to add this to the 0.5 or 50 per cent on the other side of the mean. This gives a total of:

0.5 + 0.4918 = 0.9918 or 99 per cent

This is shown as a shaded area on Figure 50.5. The company can therefore be 99 per cent certain or confident that a result of 486 represents an improvement over the 50 per cent average. If it wanted to be even more certain, it would need to take 3 standard deviations (rather than 2.4) into account.

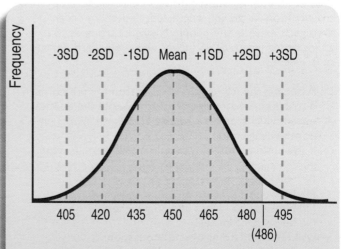

Figure 50.5 *A normal distribution showing standard deviations*

Table 50.1 *Table of standard normal curve areas*

(z)	.00	.01	.02	.03	.04	.05	.06	.07	.08	.09
0.0	.0000	.0040	.0080	.0120	.0160	.0199	.0239	.0279	.0319	.0359
0.1	.0398	.0438	.0478	.0517	.0557	.0596	.0636	.0675	.0714	.0753
0.2	.0793	.0832	.0871	.0910	.0948	.0987	.1026	.1064	.1103	.1141
0.3	.1179	.1217	.1255	.1293	.1331	.1368	.1406	.1443	.1480	.1517
0.4	.1554	.1591	.1628	.1664	.1700	.1736	.1772	.1808	.1844	.1879
0.5	.1915	.1950	.1985	.2019	.2054	.2088	.2123	.2157	.2190	.2224
0.6	.2257	.2291	.2324	.2357	.2389	.2422	.2454	.2486	.2517	.2549
0.7	.2580	.2611	.2642	.2673	.2704	.2734	.2764	.2794	.2823	.2852
0.8	.2881	.2910	.2939	.2967	.2995	.3023	.3051	.3078	.3106	.3133
0.9	.3159	.3186	.3212	.3238	.3264	.3289	.3315	.3340	.3365	.3389
1.0	.3413	.3438	.3461	.3485	.3508	.3531	.3554	.3577	.3599	.3621
1.1	.3643	.3665	.3686	.3708	.3729	.3749	.3770	.3790	.3810	.3830
1.2	.3849	.3869	.3888	.3907	.3925	.3944	.3962	.3980	.3997	.4015
1.3	.4032	.4049	.4066	.4082	.4099	.4115	.4131	.4147	.4162	.4177
1.4	.4192	.4207	.4222	.4236	.4251	.4265	.4279	.4292	.4306	.4319
1.5	.4332	.4345	.4357	.4370	.4382	.4394	.4406	.4418	.4429	.4441
1.6	.4452	.4463	.4474	.4484	.4495	.4505	.4515	.4525	.4535	.4545
1.7	.4554	.4564	.4573	.4582	.4591	.4599	.4608	.4616	.4625	.4633
1.8	.4641	.4649	.4656	.4664	.4671	.4678	.4686	.4693	.4699	.4706
1.9	.4713	.4719	.4726	.4732	.4738	.4744	.4750	.4756	.4761	.4767
2.0	.4772	.4778	.4783	.4788	.4793	.4798	.4803	.4808	.4812	.4817
2.1	.4821	.4826	.4830	.4834	.4838	.4842	.4846	.4850	.4854	.4857
2.2	.4861	.4864	.4868	.4871	.4875	.4878	.4881	.4884	.4887	.4890
2.3	.4893	.4896	.4898	.4901	.4904	.4906	.4909	.4911	.4913	.4916
2.4	.4918	.4920	.4922	.4925	.4927	.4929	.4931	.4932	.4934	.4936
2.5	.4938	.4940	.4941	.4943	.4945	.4946	.4948	.4949	.4951	.4952
2.6	.4953	.4955	.4956	.4957	.4959	.4960	.4961	.4962	.4963	.4964
2.7	.4965	.4966	.4967	.4968	.4969	.4970	.4971	.4972	.4973	.4974
2.8	.4974	.4975	.4976	.4977	.4977	.4978	.4979	.4979	.4980	.4981
2.9	.4981	.4982	.4982	.4983	.4984	.4984	.4985	.4985	.4986	.4986
3.0	.4987	.4987	.4987	.4988	.4988	.4989	.4989	.4989	.4990	.4990

Limitations of the normal distribution

As with all models used in business decision making, there are possible problems with its use.

- The sample size has to be large otherwise it is unlikely that the distribution will be normally distributed. A large sample size helps to smooth out the peaks and troughs in smaller frequency distributions.
- The calculation of the mean and the standard deviation are based on probability figures that themselves might be based upon estimates rather than exact figures. In the example of market research, the 0.5 probability used to calculate the likely response to the market research on crisps was an estimate based upon previous experience.
- Especially in the area of quality control, a 'one-off' reading which is a long way from the expected mean may not be sufficient to reject a batch or shut down a machine. Further sampling would be important to confirm the evidence of the first sample before costs are incurred by the business.
- Not all large distributions will resemble the normal distribution. The distribution might be skewed and therefore not symmetrical about the mean. Figure 50.6(a) shows a positively skewed frequency distribution, which might represent the distribution of teachers' salaries in a school or college. In a positively skewed distribution, the mode will have a lower value than the median, which will have a lower value than the mean. Figure 50.6(b) shows a negatively skewed frequency distribution, which might represent the number of people per day attending a successful cinema over a period of time. In a negatively skewed distribution, the mode will have a higher value than the median, which will have a higher value than the mean. Normal distribution analysis could not be used with such skewed distributions.

Question 3

High Style is a manufacturer of clothing for tall people. It provides a bespoke leg length service. It will turn up trousers to suit the leg length specified on an order. On average, it expects the people buying its trousers to have an inside leg length of 35 inches with a standard deviation of 0.5 inches.

(a) Assuming the leg lengths of its customers are normally distributed, what range of lengths would the business expect its customers to have? Plot these figures onto a normal distribution.

(b) If the business tested a sample of 100 people, what percentage would it expect to be:
   (i)   above 36.5 inches;
   (ii) between 35 inches and 36 inches;
   (iii) between 35 inches and 35.8 inches;
   (iv) below 34.2 inches?
   Use Table 50.1 to answer this question.

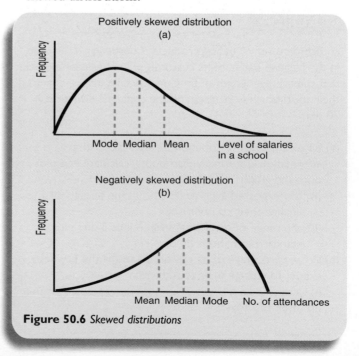

Figure 50.6 *Skewed distributions*

Key terms

Normal distribution curve - a graphical representation of the normal distribution.
Normal distribution - a naturally occurring frequency distribution where many of the values cluster around the mean, but where there are a few high and low values away from the mean.
Probability - a quantification of the likelihood of an event occurring.
Range of survey results - the highest and lowest results from market research surveys.

Summary

1. What statistical concepts are used to analyse market research data?
2. What does probability measure?
3. Why is the normal distribution a useful tool for businesses to use in analysing data?
4. What are the distinguishing features of a normal curve?
5. What is the difference between a normal distribution and a skewed distribution?

Case study

Heritage Cottages Ltd

Heritage Cottages Ltd is a company which hires out cottages in various areas of England. Most customers book directly with the business via the telephone and use the company brochure which shows the cottages that are available. The brochure is produced each November and Heritage has traditionally advertised the availability of the brochure in a range of weekly magazines between December and April. The management was always careful to analyse the number of responses that resulted from these advertisements each week. Over a five year period it calculated that the mean number of responses was 1,500

each week with a standard deviation of 125.

For the 1998-99 season Heritage decided to shift its advertising over the December to April period to the Sunday papers, such as the *Sunday Times* and *The Observer*. It wanted to see if this resulted in a significant increase in the number of customer enquiries. Again it kept a careful record of the number of responses over the twenty week period that It ran the advertisements. Heritage found that the mean level of response had risen to 1,800 for the 1989-99 season. The company was pleased with the outcome and decided, on the basis of these figures, to continue advertising in the Sunday papers for the following season.

(a) **Why might it be expected that the results from the 5 year analysis by Heritage of responses to a magazine advertisement would be normally distributed?**

(b) (i) **Draw a normal distribution curve which shows the full range of responses that the company achieved.**
　　(ii) **How many standard deviations from the mean did the 1,800 responses from the Sunday newspaper advertisements represent?**

(c) **Was the business right to be pleased with the outcome from the switch to newspaper advertisements? Explain your answer with reference to the normal distribution diagram in your answer to (b).**

(d) **If the company continued with newspaper advertising over the next 5 years and achieved a mean of 2,000 responses, what would that tell the business?**

(e) **Discuss the other factors that Heritage might need to take into account in evaluating the move from magazine to newspaper advertising.**

51 Forecasting

Forecasting

Businesses are keen to know about what might happen in the future. Anything they can predict accurately will reduce their uncertainty and will allow them to plan. Predictions may be based on a variety of data. They could be based on current information provided by managers. Most forecasts are based on **backdata** gathered from a variety of marketing research techniques (☞ unit 37). The accuracy of forecasts will depend on the reliability of the data.

What might a business like to predict with accuracy? Some examples might include:
- future sales of products;
- the effect of promotion on sales;
- possible changes in the size of the market in future;
- the way sales fluctuate at different times of the year.

A variety of techniques can be used to predict future trends. One of the most popular is **time series analysis**, which is discussed in the next section.

Time series analysis

TIMES SERIES ANALYSIS involves predicting future levels from past data. The data used is known as **time series data** - a set of figures arranged in order, based on the time they occurred. So, for example, a business may predict future sales by analysing sales data over the last 10 years. The firm, of course, is assuming that past figures are a useful indicator of what will happen in the future. This is likely to be the case if trading conditions are **stable** or if the business needs to forecast trends in the short term. Time series analysis does not try to explain data, only to describe what is happening to it or predict what will happen to it.

There are likely to be four components that a business wants to identify in time series data.
- **The trend**. 'Raw' data can have many different figures. It may not be easy to see exactly what is happening from these figures and so a business often tries to identify a trend. For example, there may be a trend for sales of a new product to rise sharply in a short period as it becomes very popular.
- **Cyclical fluctuations**. For many businesses there may be a cycle of 'highs and lows' in their sales figures, which rise over a number of years and then fall again. It is argued that these are a result of the recession-boom-recession of the trade cycle in the economy (☞ unit 21). In a recession, for example, people have less money to spend and so the turnover of a business may fall in that period.
- **Seasonal fluctuations**. Over a year a business is unlikely to have a constant level of sales. The seasonal variations are very important to a business such as a travel agent or a 'greetings card' producer, where there may be large sales at

some times but not at others.
- **Random fluctuations**. At times there will be 'freak' figures which stand out from any trend that is taking place. An example may be the sudden boost in sales of umbrellas in unusually wet summer months or the impact on consumers' spending of a one-off event such as a summer music festival.

Question 1

Unigate plc is a manufacturer and distributor of food products including milk, fruit juices and low fat spreads. Table 51.1 shows its annual sales turnover over the period 1991 to 1998.

Table 51.1 *Unigate plc, turnover (£ million)*

1991	1992	1993	1994	1995	1996	1997	1998
2,142	2,021	1,925	1,980	1,893	2,134	2,414	2,311

Source: adapted from Unigate Website and *Annual Report and Accounts*.

(a) What trend is likely to be taking place over the period shown?
(b) To what extent do the figures show cyclical fluctuations?
(c) How might a long hot summer in a future year affect the trend?

Identifying the trend

An analysis of figures will tell a business whether there is an upward, downward or constant trend. Identifying the trend allows the business to predict what is likely to happen in future. The first step is to smooth out the raw data. Take an example of a toy manufacturer, whose yearly sales over the past 10 years are shown in Table 51.2.

Table 51.2 *Yearly sales of a toy manufacturer (£000)*

1991	1992	1993	1994	1995	1996	1997	1998	1999	2000
300	500	600	550	600	750	850	1,100	800	1,100

It is possible to calculate a trend by using a MOVING AVERAGE. The average can be taken for any period the business wants, such as a year, a month or a quarter. For now we will assume the toy manufacturer uses a 3 year average. The average of sales in the first 3 years was:

$$\frac{300 + 500 + 600}{3} = \frac{1,400}{3} = 466.7$$

The first year's sales 'drop out' and the next year's sales are added to give a moving average. The average for the next three years was:

$$\frac{500 + 600 + 550}{3} = \frac{1,650}{3} = 550$$

If the business continues to do this, the results will be as shown in Table 51.3. Notice that the moving average is placed at the centre of the 3 years (ie the average for 1991-1993 is plotted next to 1992).

Table 51.3 *3 year moving average for sales of a toy manufacturer (£000)*

1991	1992	1993	1994	1995	1996	1997	1998	1999	2000
300	500	600	550	600	750	850	1,100	800	1,100
	466.7	550	583.3	633.3	733.3	900	916.7	1,000	

What if the firm had used a 4 year period instead of 3 years? No one year is the centre point and simply placing the figure in between two years may result in misleading predictions in future. The solution is to use CENTRING. This uses a 4 and 8 year moving **total** to find a mid point. So, for example, in Table 51.2:

Year	1991	1992	1993	1994	1995
(£000)	300	500	600	550	600

1,950 + 2,250 = 4,200
(4 year moving totals) (8 year moving total)

This can then be used to find the mid-point, which is 1993. The trend or moving average can be found by dividing the 8 year moving total by 8, the number of years, as shown in Table 51.4.

Table 51.4 *Calculating a 4 year moving average for a toy manufacturer*

£000

Year	Sales	4 year moving total	8 year moving total	Trend (4 year moving average = 8 year moving total ÷ 8)
1991	300			
1992	500	1,950		
1993	600	2,250	4,200	525
1994	550	2,500	4,750	593.75
1995	600	2,750	5,250	656.25
1996	750	3,300	6,050	756.25
1997	850	3,500	6,800	850
1998	1,100	3,850	7,350	918.75
1999	800			
2000	1,100			

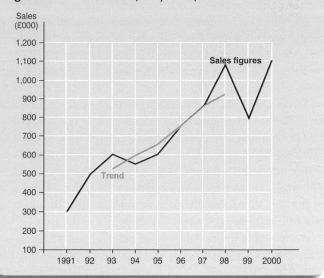

Figure 51.1 *Annual sales of a toy manufacturer*

Question 2

A business has recently gathered data on its sales revenue as shown in Table 51.5, and wants to calculate a 3 and 4 period moving average.

Table 51.5 *Sales revenue*

(£000)

Period	1	2	3	4	5	6	7	8	9	10
Sales revenue	100	130	160	175	180	190	190	180	220	250
3 period moving average		130	155							
4 period moving average			151.3							

(a) Calculate the 3 and 4 period moving averages for as many years as you can to complete the table.
(b) Plot the sales figures and both trend lines onto a graph on graph paper.
(c) Comment on the relationship between the trend and the actual sales revenue figures.

Plotting the moving average figures onto a graph (as shown in Figure 51.1) shows the trends in the figures. It is clear to see that sales appear to be rising over the period. The trend line is 'smoother' than the line showing the actual sales figures. It eliminates any fluctuations in sales each year and gives a more obvious picture of the trend that has been taking place.

Predicting from the trend

Having identified a trend that is taking place the business can now predict what may happen in future. Figure 51.2 shows the trend data from Figure 51.1, but with a line drawn to predict the likely sales in 2001. The graph shows that sales of the toy manufacturer's goods may reach about £1,160,000.

The business has made certain assumptions when predicting this figure. First, no other factors were likely to have changed to affect the trend. If other factors changed, resulting in different sales figures, then the prediction is likely to be inaccurate.

Second, the sales figures are predicted by drawing a line through the trend figures and extending it to the year 2001. The broken line through the trend in Figure 51.2 is called the LINE OF BEST FIT. It is the best line that can be drawn which matches the general slope of all points in the trend. The line is an average, where points in the trend on one side of the line are balanced with those on the other. In other words, it is a line which best fits **all** points in the trend.

It is possible to draw the line of best fit by plotting the trend figures on graph paper accurately and then adding the line of best fit 'by eye', so that points fit equally either side of the line. Extending the line carefully should give a reasonable prediction. To help draw the line, it should pass through the coordinates $(\bar{X}, \bar{Y})$ where $\bar{X}$ is the average of the years and $\bar{Y}$ is the average sales. These coordinates can be calculated using the figures in Table 51.4.

$$\bar{X} = \frac{\Sigma X \text{ (the total years)}}{N \text{ (the number of years)}} = \frac{1993+1994+1995+1996+1997+1998}{6} = \frac{11,973}{6} = 1995.5$$

$$\bar{Y} = \frac{\Sigma Y \text{ (the total sales in the trend)}}{N \text{ (the number of years)}}$$

$$= \frac{£525,000 + £593,750 + £656,250 + £756,250 + £850,000 + £918,750}{6} = \frac{£4,300,000}{6}$$

$$= £716,667$$

This point is shown on Figure 51.2. The actual predicted figure for the year 2001 is £1,162,550. This can be found by a method known as 'the sum of least squares'. Computer software can be used by businesses to calculate the line of best fit and to predict from the trend.

Variations from the trend

How accurate is the prediction of **around** £1,160,000 sales of toys by the year 2001? Even allowing for the assumptions above, the prediction may not be accurate because it is taken from the trend, and the trend 'smoothed out' variations in sales figures. To make an accurate prediction, the business will have to find the average variation over the period and take this into account.

We can find how much **variation** there is from the trend by calculating:

Actual sales - trend.

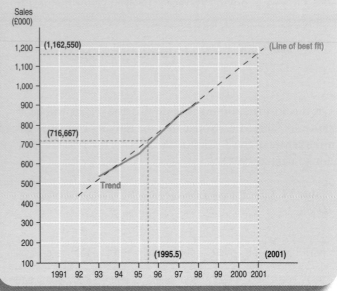

Figure 51.2 *Annual sales of a toy manufacturer*

Table 51.6

(£000)

Year	Sales	Trend (4 year moving average)	Variation in each year
1991	300		
1992	500		
1993	600	525	+75
1994	550	593.75	-43.75
1995	600	656.25	-56.25
1996	750	756.25	- 6.25
1997	850	850	-
1998	1,100	918.75	+181.25
1999	800		
2000	1,100		

So, for example, the **cyclical** variation in Table 51.4 would be as shown in Table 51.6. The average of the variations over the period 1991-2000 is (in £000):

$$\frac{+75 - 43.75 - 56.25 - 6.25 +/-0 +181.25}{6} = \frac{+150}{6} \text{ +25 (or +£25,000)}$$

If the predicted value based on the trend was £1,160,000, then adding £25,000 may give a more accurate predicted figure of £1,185,000.

Seasonal variations

Earlier it was stated that a business may be interested in variations in any one year. It is possible to predict from a trend and use **seasonal** variations to make a more accurate prediction. Table 51.8 shows sales of a business over a 3 year

Table 51.7 shows the yearly sales figures of a furniture manufacturer over a period of 10 years.

Table 51.7

units

Period	1	2	3	4	5	6	7	8	9	10
Sales	5,000	5,200	5,800	6,000	5,800	7,000	8,200	7,400	7,600	8,400

(a) Calculate a four yearly moving average from the figures to show the trend taking place.
(b) Plot the trend onto a graph on graph paper and predict the likely output in year 11, stating your assumptions.
(c) Calculate:
  (i) the cyclical variation for each year;
  (ii) the average cyclical variation over the period.
(d) Explain how the average variation will give a more accurate figure, using your answers to (a)-(c).

period, including sales in each quarter. A 4 quarter moving average has been calculated and also the variation in each quarter.

Carrying on the trend to predict the sales for the fourth quarter of the year 2000 might give a figure of £470,000. (It would be possible to find this by drawing and extending a line of best fit through the trend.) As we know, this is a 'smoothed out' figure. A more accurate prediction might be to calculate the **average seasonal variation** in the fourth quarter, for example (in £000):

$$\frac{-97.125 - 117.5}{2} = \frac{-214.625}{2} = -107.313$$

By subtracting it from the total of £470,000, this gives a more accurate prediction of £362,687.

Table 51.8

(£000)

Year	Quarter	Sales	4 quarter moving average	Variation
1997	3	460		
	4	218		
1998	1	205	328.5	-123.5
	2	388	346	+42
	3	546	358.25	+187.75
	4	272	369.125	- 97.125
1999	1	249	383.625	-134.625
	2	431	396.625	+34.375
	3	619	404	+215
	4	303	420.5	-117.5
2000	1	277		
	2	535		

Causal modelling

Time series analysis only describes what is happening to

information. Causal modelling tries to explain data, usually by finding a link between one set of data and another. For example, a business may want to find whether there is a link between the amount that it spends on advertising and its sales.

Table 51.9 shows data that has been collected about advertising and sales by a business at different times. The data in the table is plotted onto a SCATTER GRAPH in Figure 51.3. Advertising (the **independent** variable) is shown on the horizontal (X) axis. Sales (the **dependent** variable) are shown on the vertical (Y) axis. The figure shows, for example, that in one period (E) the business had advertising spending of £1,500 and sales of 1,800 units. In another period (G) the business had advertising spending of £3,500 and sales of 5,800 units.

Looking at the graph, there appears to be a positive CORRELATION between the two variables. The more that is spent on advertising, the higher the level of sales. The line of

Table 51.9

Period	Advertising expenditure (£000)	Sales (000)	(£million)	(million)	(£million)
	X	Y	X²	Y²	XY
A	1.0	3.2	1.0	10.24	3.2
B	2.0	4.5	4.0	20.25	9.0
C	3.0	1.8	9.0	3.24	5.4
D	4.0	3.0	1.6	9.0	12.0
E	1.5	1.8	2.25	3.24	2.7
F	2.5	1.6	6.25	2.56	4.0
G	3.5	5.8	12.25	33.64	20.3
H	1.2	4.7	1.44	22.09	5.64
I	2.7	5.9	7.29	34.81	15.93
J	3.0	3.5	9.0	12.25	10.5
K	3.6	3.1	12.96	9.61	11.16
L	7.0	3.5	0.49	12.25	2.45

$\Sigma X^2 = 81.93 \quad \Sigma Y^2 = 173.18 \quad \Sigma XY = 102.28$

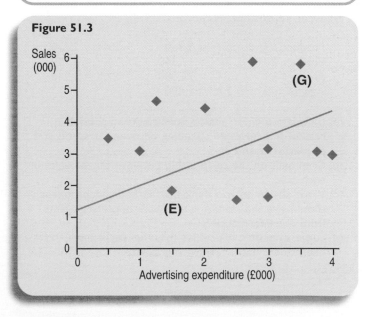

Figure 51.3

best fit is drawn through the data to show this relationship better. It is also possible to calculate the extent of the relationship by means of a CORRELATION COEFFICIENT, using the formula:

$$r = \frac{\Sigma XY}{\sqrt{(\Sigma X^2)\ (\Sigma Y^2)}}$$

Using the data in Table 51.9, the correlation coefficient for advertising and sales can be calculated as follows.

$$r = \frac{£102.28m}{\sqrt{£81.93m \times 173.18m}}$$

$$r = \frac{£102.28m}{£119.117m}$$

$$r = \quad +0.86$$

● A correlation coefficient of +1 means that there is an absolute positive relationship between the two variables. All points in the scatter graph fall on the line of best fit and the line slopes upwards from left to right. As the values of the independent variable increase, so do the dependent variable values.

● A correlation coefficient of 0 means that there is no relationship between the variables.
● A correlation coefficient of -1 means that there is an absolute negative relationship between the two variables. All points in the scatter graph fall on the line of best fit and the line slopes downwards from left to right. As the values of the independent variable increase, the values of the dependent variable fall.

The formula itself does not show **positive** and **negative** values. However, it is easy to see whether the relationship is positive or negative from the graph. A positive coefficient of 0.85 suggests a strong correlation between the spending on advertising and the level of sales. As advertising increases, so do sales. This information could help a business in future when making decisions about its marketing. It is suggested that if the figure falls below 0.7 it becomes difficult to see any correlation from the scatter graph. An example of a negative correlation might be the relationship between prices and customers' demand. As prices rise, demand falls (☞ unit 17).

Businesses must be careful when basing decisions on such calculations.

● A large quantity of sales in any period may be due to factors other than advertising, such as other forms of promotion.
● There are sometimes examples of 'nonsense correlations'. These are correlation coefficients that appear to show a strong relationship between two variables, when in fact the relationship between the figures is pure coincidence.

Qualitative forecasting

Qualitative forecasting uses people's opinions or judgements rather than numerical data. A business could base its predictions on the views of so-called experts, or on the opinions of experienced managers in the marketing or production department. Such methods are usually used by firms:

● where there is insufficient numerical data;
● where figures date quickly because the market is changing rapidly.

Question 4

Denten Limited is a manufacturer of bins and other storage equipment. It exports a large amount of its products abroad. It makes use of direct sales to customers and also employs some overseas agents. The managing director has asked the marketing department to examine the relationship between the number of agents it employs and sales of three of its most popular products and make recommendations. The research found the following information.

Product 1	$\Sigma Y^2 = 5,360$	$\Sigma XY = 2,720$
Product 2	$\Sigma Y^2 = 17,360$	$\Sigma XY = 3,200$
Product 3	$\Sigma Y^2 = 25,080$	$\Sigma XY = 3,240$
Agents	$\Sigma X^2 = 1,400$	

(a) Calculate the correlation coefficients to show the relationship between spending on overseas agents and products 1, 2 and 3.
(b) Comment on the relationship between the variables in each case.
(c) What advice do you think the marketing department should give the managing director concerning agents from this information?
(d) Suggest possible difficulties that the marketing department may have in giving advice.

Summary

1. Why might a business want to predict the future?
2. What are the four components of time series data that a business might be interested in?
3. What does a trend show?
4. How might a business use the calculation of a trend?
5. What is meant by causal modelling?

Key terms

Centring - a method used in the calculation of a moving average where the average is plotted or calculated in relation to the central figure.
Correlation - the relationship between two sets of variables.
Correlation coefficient - a measure of the extent of the relationship between two sets of variables.
Line of best fit - a line plotted through a series of points which balances those on one side with those on the other, and best represents the slope of the points.
Moving average - a method used to find trends in data by smoothing out fluctuations. It involves calculating an average for a number of periods, then dropping the first figure and adding the next to calculate the average that follows.
Scatter graph - a graph showing the performance of one variable against another independent variable on a variety of occasions. It is used to show whther a correlation exists between the variables.
Time series analysis - a method which allows a business to predict future levels from past figures.

Case study

Box Wrap Ltd

Box Wrap Ltd is a UK based company that manufactures cardboard packaging and boxes. In the late 1990s the business experienced a rapid increase in sales and turnover as more companies found a use for the materials. In particular, orders came from food producers and confectioners. The company expanded as a result. Table 51.10 shows the sales of the business over the period 1997-2000.

Table 51.10 *Box Wrap Ltd, (£000)*

Year	Quarter	Sales revenue (£000)
1997	3	115
	4	101
1998	1	112
	2	80
	3	105
	4	130
1999	1	115
	2	90
	3	105
	4	140
2000	1	125
	2	105

(a) **Using a 4 quarter moving average, calculate the trend from the figures in Table 15.10 that the business might have found.**
(b) **Explain why centring might be used by the business when calculating the trend in (a).**
(c) **Calculate:**
   (i) **the seasonal variation for as many quarters as you can;**
   (ii) **the average seasonal variation for the fourth quarter.**
(d) **Plot the trend onto a graph and, using your answer to (c ii), predict the likely sales in the fourth quarter of 2000, stating any assumptions you have made.**

The costs of production

A business needs accurate and reliable cost information to make decisions. A firm that is aiming to expand production to meet rising demand must know how much that extra production will cost. Without this information it will have no way of knowing whether or not it will make a profit. You will be familiar with your own costs. These are the expenses you have, such as travel costs to school or college. Similarly, businesses have expenses. These might include wages, raw materials, insurance and rent.

Economists usually think of costs as **opportunity costs** (☞ unit 8). The opportunity cost is the value that could have been earned if a resource was employed in its next best use. For example, if a business spends £40,000 on an advertising campaign, the opportunity cost might be the interest earned from depositing the money in a bank account. A business is concerned, however, with ACCOUNTING COSTS. An accounting cost is the value of a resource used up in production. This is shown in the business accounts as an asset or an expense. For example, if a firm buys some fuel costing £5,500, this is shown as an expense in the accounts.

It is also important to understand how a firm's costs change in the SHORT RUN and the LONG RUN.

● The short run is the period of time when at least one factor of production (☞ unit 1) is **fixed**. For example, in the short run, a firm might want to expand production in its factory. It can acquire more labour and buy more raw materials, but it has a fixed amount of space in the factory and a limited number of machines.
● In the long run, all factors can vary. The firm can buy another factory and add to the number of machines. This will increase **capacity** (the maximum amount that can be produced) and begin another short run period.

Fixed costs

Costs which stay the same at all levels of output in the short run are called FIXED COSTS. Examples might be rent, insurance, heating bills, depreciation (☞ unit 63) and business rates, as well as **capital costs** such as factories and machinery. These costs remain the same whether a business produces nothing or is working at full capacity. For example, rent must still be paid even if a factory is shut for a two week holiday period when nothing is produced. It is worth noting that 'fixed' here means costs do not change as a result of a change in **output** in the short run. But they may increase due to, say, inflation. Figure 52.1 shows what happens to fixed costs as a firm increases production. The line on the graph is horizontal which shows that fixed costs are £400,000 no matter how much is produced.

What happens over a longer period? Figure 52.2 illustrates

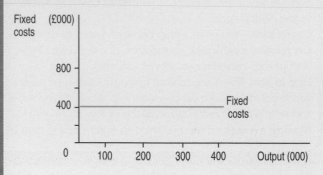

Figure 52.1 *Fixed costs*

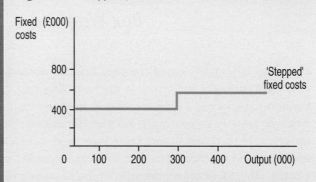

Figure 52.2 *'Stepped' fixed costs*

Question 1

Paul Helder runs a mail order company. He places a small advert costing £200 in a newspaper every week for his products. A full time employee deals with all the orders, which are entered into a computer as soon as they arrive. Paul also employs 6 part time staff to pack and dispatch the products. Orders are sent out within 2 days from the warehouse, which is rented for £250 per week. The weekly wage bill ranges from £900 to £1,400 per week depending on how many orders are received. When Paul's business is busy, part time staff have to work more hours. The computer system is leased at a cost of £2,600 per year.

(a) Explain why the weekly advert is a fixed cost.
(b) Suggest why the weekly rent might rise in the long run.
(c) Using the information above, calculate the weekly fixed cost of Paul's mail order business.

'stepped' fixed costs. If a firm is at full capacity, but needs to raise production, it might decide to invest in more equipment. The new machines raise overall fixed costs as well as capacity. The rise in fixed costs is shown by a 'step' in the graph. This illustrates how fixed costs can change in the long run.

Variable and semi variable costs

Costs of production which increase directly as output rises are called VARIABLE COSTS. For example, a baker will require more flour if more loaves are to be produced. Raw materials are just one example of variable costs. Others might include fuel, packaging and wages. If the firm does not produce anything then variable costs will be zero.

Figure 52.3 shows a firm's variable costs. Assume that the firm buying new machinery in Figure 52.1 produces dolls and that variable costs are £2 per doll. If the firm produces 100,000 dolls it will have variable costs of £200,000 (£2 x 100,000). Producing 500,000 dolls it will incur variable costs of £1,000,000 (£2 x 500,000). Joining these points together shows the firm's variable costs at any level of output. As output increases, so do variable costs. Notice that the graph is **linear**. This means that it is a straight line.

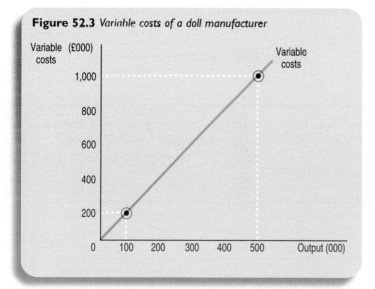

Figure 52.3 *Variable costs of a doll manufacturer*

Some production costs do not fit neatly into our definitions of fixed and variable costs. This is because they are not entirely fixed or variable costs. Labour is a good example. If a firm employs a member of staff on a permanent basis, no matter what level of output, then this is a fixed cost. If this member of staff is asked to work overtime at nights and weekends to cope with extra production levels, then the extra cost is variable. Such labour costs are said to be SEMI-VARIABLE COSTS. Another example could be the cost of telephone charges. This often consists of a fixed or 'standing charge' plus an extra rate which varies according to the number of calls made.

Question 2

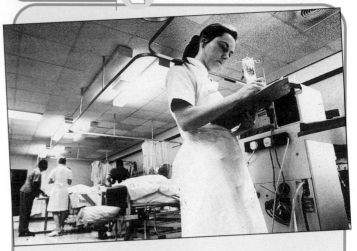

(a) Look at the photograph. State 2 examples each of:
   (i) fixed costs; and (ii) variable costs; which the hospital ward might incur.
(b) Explain which of the above costs would rise if more patients were admitted to the ward.
(c) Explain why some nursing costs on the ward might be semi-variable costs.

Total costs

If fixed and variable costs are added together they show the TOTAL COST of a business. The total cost of production is the cost of producing any given level of output. As output increases total costs will rise. This is shown in Figure 52.4, which again shows the production of dolls. We can say:

Total cost (TC) = fixed cost (FC) + variable cost (VC)

The business has fixed costs of £400,000 and variable costs of £2 per doll. When output is 0 total costs are £400,000. When output has risen to 300,000 dolls, total costs are £1,000,000, made up of fixed costs of £400,000 and variable costs of £600,000 (£2 x 300,000). This information is summarised in Table 52.1. Figure 52.4 shows the way that total costs increase as output increases. Notice that as output increases fixed costs become a smaller proportion of total costs.

Table 52.1 *Summary of cost information for the doll manufacturer*

			£000
Output (units)	Fixed cost	Variable cost	Total cost
0	400	0	400
300	400	600	1,000

Direct and indirect costs

Costs can also be divided into direct and indirect costs. DIRECT COSTS or PRIME COSTS are costs which can be identified with a particular product or process. Examples of direct costs are raw materials, packaging, and direct labour.

Figure 52.4 *Total costs of a doll manufacturer*

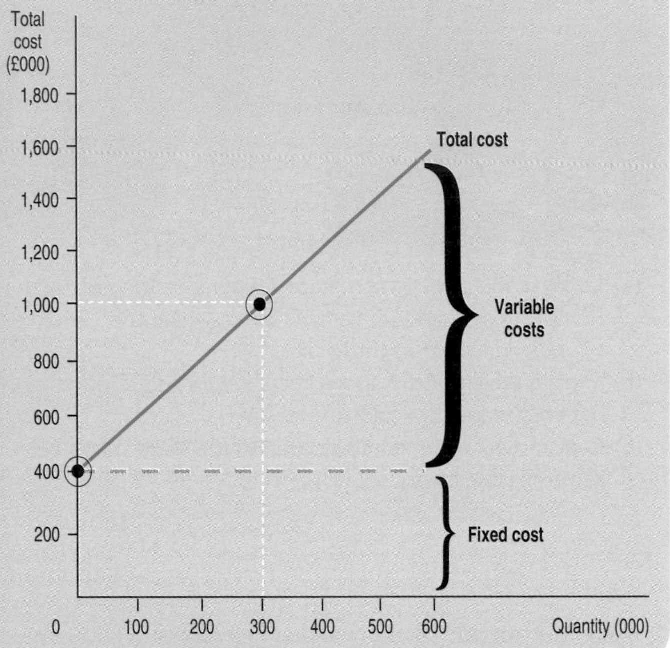

INDIRECT COSTS or OVERHEADS result from the whole business. It is not possible to associate these costs directly with particular products or processes. Examples are rent, insurance, the salaries of office staff and audit fees. Indirect costs are usually fixed costs and direct costs variable costs, although in theory both direct and indirect costs can be fixed or variable. The methods used to apportion indirect costs to individual products are discussed in unit 53.

Average and marginal costs

The AVERAGE COST is the cost per unit of production, also known as the UNIT COST. To calculate average cost the total cost of production should be divided by the number of units produced.

$$\text{Average cost} = \frac{\text{Total cost}}{\text{output}} \quad \text{or} \quad \frac{\text{Fixed cost} + \text{variable cost}}{\text{output}}$$

It is also possible to calculate **average fixed costs**:

$$\text{Average fixed cost} = \frac{\text{Total fixed cost}}{\text{output}}$$

and **average variable costs**:

$$\text{Average variable cost} = \frac{\text{Total variable cost}}{\text{output}}$$

Question 3

Robinson Wire Ltd produces wheels for bicycle manufacturers. Originally it produced a wide range, but this proved to be uneconomical. Since securing a large contract with a number of Belgian bicycle manufacturers it has reduced its range considerably. The wheels are produced in batches of 1,000 and the main variable costs are materials (£4 per wheel), labour (£5 per wheel) and packaging (£1 per wheel). An incomplete cost schedule for the wheels is shown in Table 52.2.

Table 52.2 *Cost schedule*

£

Number of wheels	1,000	2,000	3,000	4,000	5,000	6,000	7,000	8,000	9,000	10,000
Fixed costs	20,000	20,000	20,000	20,000	20,000	20,000	20,000	20,000	20,000	20,000
Materials										
Labour										
Packaging										
Total variable costs										
Total costs										

(a) State two examples of: (i) direct costs; (ii) indirect costs; which Robinson Wire Ltd might incur.
(b) Complete the cost schedule shown in Table 52.2.
(c) Using a range of output from 0 to 10,000 wheels, plot the fixed costs, variable costs and total costs onto a graph.
(d) Show the effect on your graph of an increase in fixed costs to £30,000.

Take the earlier example of the doll manufacturer with fixed costs of £400,000 and variable costs of £2 per unit. If output was 100,000 units:

$$\text{Average fixed cost} = \frac{£400,000}{100,000} = £4$$

$$\text{Average variable cost} = \frac{£2 \times 100,000}{100,000} = £2$$

$$\text{Average total cost} = \frac{£400,000 + (£2 \times 100,000)}{100,000}$$

$$= \frac{£600,000}{100,000} = £6$$

MARGINAL COST is the cost of increasing total output by one more unit. It can be calculated by:

$$\text{Marginal cost} = \frac{\text{change in total cost}}{\text{change in output}}$$

For example, if the total cost of manufacturing 100,000 dolls is £600,000 and the total cost of producing 100,001 dolls is £600,002, then the marginal cost of producing the last unit is:

$$\text{Marginal cost} = \frac{£600,002 - £600,000}{100,001 - 100,000} = \frac{£2}{1} = £2$$

The relationship between average and marginal cost and their uses for the business are discussed in unit 53.

Standard costs

Some businesses use the term STANDARD COST in their operations. A standard cost is a predetermined cost. It is the cost normally associated with a specific activity or what the activity ought to cost. A business, for example, may know that the cost of transporting a regular 30 tonne load from its premises in Rochdale to Liverpool docks is £80. This £80 is a standard cost - the **usual** cost of that activity.

If the actual cost of an activity is different from the standard cost a business might investigate why the difference occurred. The information collected might help the business to improve efficiency. In the above example, if the journey from Rochdale to Liverpool actually costs £100 because of motorway congestion, the business might consider another route in the future.

The problems of classifying costs

There is a number of possible ways in which costs can be classified.
● By type. This involves analysing business costs and deciding whether they are **direct or indirect**.
● By behaviour. Economists favour this method. They classify costs according to the effect that a change in the level of output has on a particular cost. **Fixed, variable, semi-variable, average and marginal costs** all fall into this category.
● By function. It is possible to classify costs according to the business function they are associated with. For example, costs could be listed as **production, selling, administrative or personnel**.
● By nature of resource. This involves classifying costs according to the resources which were acquired by a business, for example, **materials, labour or expenses**.
● By **product, job, customer or contract** A multi-product manufacturer, such as Heinz for example, might classify costs according to the product line (beans, soups, puddings) they are associated with. Solicitors might classify costs by identifying them with particular clients.

The classification of costs is not always straightforward. In some cases the same business cost can be classified in several ways. For example, the earnings of a full time administrative assistant may be classified as a fixed cost, if they do not vary with output, and an indirect cost, if they are not associated with a particular product. The costs of a worker earning piece rates might be a direct cost if they can be associated with a particular product and a variable cost if they rise as the output of the worker increases.

Another problem relating to costs concerns the allocation of indirect costs. When calculating the cost of producing particular products it is necessary to allocate indirect costs to each of the different products a business manufactures. In practice this may be difficult. The methods of allocation are discussed in unit 53.

The way in which costs are classified will depend on the purposes for which the classification is being undertaken and the views of the management team.

Long run costs

Most of the costs discussed so far in this unit have been short run costs, ie the time period where at least one factor of production is fixed. In the long run, all production factors are variable, and the behaviour of costs are subject to new economic 'laws'. This is dealt with in detail in unit 65.

Total revenue

The amount of money which a firm receives from selling its product can be referred to as TOTAL REVENUE. Total revenue is calculated by multiplying the number of units sold by the price of each unit:

Total revenue = quantity sold x price

For example, if the doll producer mentioned earlier sells

300,000 dolls at a price of £5 each:

Total revenue = 300,000 x £5 = £1,500,000

Figure 52.5 shows what happens to total revenue as output rises. Notice that the graph is **linear**.

Profit and loss

One of the main reasons why firms calculate their costs and revenue is to enable them to work out their **profit** or **loss.** Profit is the difference between revenue and costs.

Profit = total revenue - total costs

For example, if the doll manufacturer in the earlier example produces and sells 300,000 dolls, they sell for £5, fixed costs are £400,000 and variable costs are £2 per unit, then:

Profit = £5 x 300,000 - (£400,000 + [£2 x 300,000])

= £1,500,000 - (£400,000 + [£600,000])

= £1,500,000 - £1,000,000

= £500,000

It is possible to calculate the profit for a business at any level of output using this method.

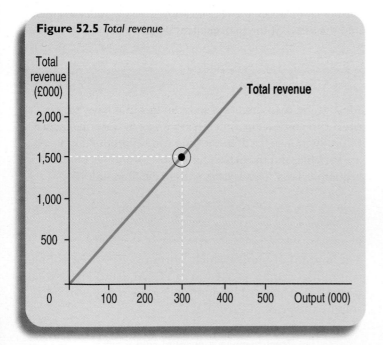

Figure 52.5 *Total revenue*

Question 4

Jushna Begum grows tomato plants which she sells to a local garden centre. She rents a large greenhouse from a local farmer and grows the plants from seeds. The seeds are grown in trays to begin with and then replanted into pots which are sold a month later for 40p per pot. Each pot has one plant. When Jushna is busy she employs two students from a local horticultural college to help out at weekends and in the evenings. Her costs are:

fixed cost = £5,000 each year
variable cost = £0.20 per pot

(a) This year Jushna supplied 120,000 tomato plants to the local garden centre. Calculate: (i) total revenue; (ii) total cost; (iii) average cost; (iv) profit.
(b) At the end of this year's growing season Jushna was approached by a garden centre in another town 24 miles away with a new order. It wanted to buy 40,000 tomato plants next year, but in a more advanced stage of growth (1 extra month). It also wanted her to deliver the plants at regular intervals. Jushna calculated that variable costs for this new order would be £0.30 per pot and that there would be additional fixed costs of £2,000.
  (i) State two non-financial considerations which Jushna might have to take into account before accepting the order.
  (ii) Calculate the profit for this extra order.
  (iii) Calculate and explain the effect that this extra order would have on Jushna's total profit if accepted.

Summary

1. What is the difference between opportunity costs and accounting costs?
2. How do you account for a 'stepped' fixed cost function?
3. Why are some costs said to be semi-variable?
4. What happens to variable costs as a proportion of total costs when output rises?
5. Explain the difference between direct and indirect costs.
6. How is:
   (a) average fixed cost;
   (b) average variable cost;
   calculated?
7. How is total revenue calculated?
8. What information is required to calculate a firm's profit?
9. What problems might there be when clarifying costs?

Key terms

Accounting cost - the value of an economic resource used up in production.

Average cost or unit cost - the cost of producing one unit, calculated by dividing the total cost by output.

Direct cost or prime cost - a cost which can be clearly identified with a particular unit of output.

Fixed cost - a cost which does not change as a result of a change in output in the short run.

Indirect cost or overhead - a cost which cannot be identified with a particular unit of output. They are incurred by the whole organisation or department.

Long run - the time period where all factors of production are variable.

Marginal cost - the cost of increasing output by one more unit.

Semi-variable cost - a cost which consists of both fixed and variable elements.

Short run - the time period where at least one factor of production is fixed.

Standard cost - the usual cost of a specific activity.

Total cost - the entire cost of producing a given level of output.

Total revenue - the amount of money the business receives from selling output.

Variable cost - a cost which rises as output rises.

Case study

Banbury Paper Supplies Ltd

Table 52.3

	£
Rent p.a.	30,000
Business rates p.a.	10,000
Raw materials (per batch)	200
Fuel (per batch)	100
Directors' salary p.a.	20,000
Labour (per batch)	1,700
Equipment leasing charge p.a.	16,000
General overheads p.a.	4,000

Banbury Paper Supplies Ltd is a small paper manufacturer which produces rolls of newspaper for the Oxford Chronicle, a local newspaper. At the end of the year its current contract with the newspaper expires. It is rumoured that the Oxford Chronicle, which has always been supplied by the Banbury producer, is looking for a cheaper source of material in an effort to cut its costs. Gillian Cowbridge, the managing director and controlling shareholder of Banbury Paper Supplies Ltd, is obviously concerned. She is aware that the costs of her own company's operations have been escalating recently and profit margins have been squeezed. One of the problems is the location of the factory. Although it is small, it is located in the most expensive part of Banbury. The premises are owned by a property company who refuse to sell the freehold. Gillian
has tried to get planning permission for alternative sites but applications have been repeatedly turned down by the local council.

Banbury Paper Supplies Ltd does not have any debt, but leases all of its equipment. Rolls of newspaper are produced in batches of 100. Raw materials are very cheap since recycled paper is used. Details of all business costs are shown in Table 52.3.

(a) **Which of the above costs are fixed or variable (assume that there are no semi-variable costs)?**

(b) **Draw up a table of costs over a range of output from 0 to 20 batches. (Use only even numbers of output.) Include fixed cost, variable cost, and total cost.**

(c) **Plot the fixed, variable and total cost on a graph.**

(d) **Examine the cost breakdown of Banbury Paper Supplies Ltd. What is its main problem? What might Gillian do to overcome the problem?**

(e) **The Oxford Chronicle currently purchases 20 batches of newspaper per annum at an agreed price of £7,000 per batch. What is the level of profit made?**

(f) **After a meeting with the purchasing officer for the Oxford Chronicle, Gillian is told that the Oxford Chronicle is now only prepared to buy 20 batches at £6,500 or 10 batches at £8,500. On purely financial grounds which is the best deal for Banbury Paper Supplies?**

Collecting cost data

A business incurs costs at all stages of production. It will have to pay for resources bought from outside the business, such as raw materials. There are also costs when a service is bought from another department within the business. Business managers must record all these costs as they occur. One method used to do this is to find a point where the costs occur and can easily be recorded (a cost collection point). These are known as COST CENTRES. A cost centre may be:

- a geographical location, eg a factory, sales region or department;
- a person, eg, a director, salesperson or maintenance worker;
- an item of equipment, eg a photocopier, telephone line or vehicle.

Charging **direct costs** to a cost centre is simple. For example, a vehicle will be charged with the expenses it incurs,

Table 53.1 *Direct costs for two components*

			£000
Component	ZX 1	ZX 2	Total
Direct cost	200	300	500

eg petrol, oil, repairs, servicing and road tax. Charging indirect costs is more involved, and is dealt with later in this unit.

Cost centres have two benefits for managers. First, they provide a very sound foundation for a costing system. Second, they enable managers to make comparisons between the cost of operating a cost centre and the benefit it provides. For example, if a salesperson costs a company £30,000 per year and only generates £25,000 worth of sales, it may be more profitable to find another method of selling.

Costing methods

The process of measuring the likely consequences of a business activity is called COSTING. Costing systems benefit a business in a number of ways. They provide managers with financial information on which to base decisions. They help to identify the profitable activities, avoid waste and provide information for cost cutting strategies. Costing can also assist the marketing department in setting the price of products. Examples of costing exercises include:

- measuring the cost of manufacturing individual products;
- calculating whether or not it would be more economical to contract out a particular business operation, eg security;
- determining the cost of moving to a new business location;
- estimating the cost of decorating the office.

What costing methods might be used by firms? Methods include full, absorption, standard and marginal costing.

Full costing

When a business produces several products in the same factory and is trying to calculate the cost of producing one individual product, it faces a problem. How should it allocate indirect costs? In other words how can it decide how much each product is contributing to total indirect costs? FULL COSTING solves the problem by allocating indirect costs in an arbitrary way, such as a percentage of direct costs. For example, a manufacturer which makes two metal components code named ZX 1 and ZX 2 may have the direct costs of producing 100,000 of each component shown in Table 53.1.

Assume that total indirect costs are £300,000. We need to calculate the percentage each component contributes to total direct cost.

Question 1

Maria and Patricia Evans own a small chain of shoe shops in the South East. They have six shops in Croydon, Brighton, Dover, Bexley, Redhill and Crawley, all with similar turnover. Maria and Patricia employ managers in each shop. Maria is responsible for the day to day coordination of the business, whilst Patricia is responsible for buying and marketing. One reason for their success has been due to their effective cost control. Each shop is a cost centre. Annual total cost information for each centre, over a three year period, is shown in Figure 53.1.

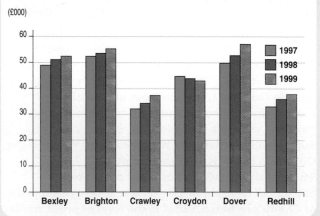

Figure 53.1 *Total costs for Maria's and Patricia's shoe shop business*

(a) Explain the advantages to Maria and Patricia of recording costs using the cost centres described above.

(b) Given that all the shops have roughly the same annual turnover, what conclusions might you draw from the above information?

$$\text{For ZX 1} = \frac{200}{500} \times 100 = 40\%$$

$$\text{For ZX 2} = \frac{300}{500} \times 100 = 60\%$$

The £300,000 indirect costs can now be allocated to each component.

For ZX 1 indirect costs = 40% x £300,000 = £120,000
For ZX 2 indirect costs = 60% x £300,000 = £180,000

The total cost or **full cost** of producing 100,000 of each component can now be calculated. This is done by adding the allocated indirect costs to the direct costs.

For ZX 1 full cost = £120,000 + £200,000 = £320,000
For ZX 2 full cost = £180,000 + £300,000 = £480,000

Full costing is often criticised for the arbitrary way it allocates indirect costs. It could result in misleading costings because the allocation of indirect costs is not based on any actual indirect costs incurred.

Question 2

Bantom Ltd manufactures motorbikes in its Bristol factory. It makes three models:
● the Fury - a racing bike with a 1000 cc engine;
● the Trialmaster - a popular trials bike;
● the XL10 - a standard 500 cc road bike.
Details of the direct production costs are shown in Table 53.2. Bantom also incurs indirect costs of £600,000 per month. The company manufactures 100 of each bike per month.

Table 53.2 Direct costs for Bantom Ltd

			(£ per bike)
	Fury	Trialmaster	XL10
Direct labour	250	150	200
Raw materials	150	120	100
Components	400	300	340
Other direct costs	200	130	160

(a) Calculate the direct costs of producing 100 of each motorcycle.
(b) Allocate the indirect costs of production to each product as a percentage of direct costs.
(c) Calculate the full cost of producing 100 of each bike.
(d) Bantom sets the price of its bikes by adding on 25 per cent of the full cost. Calculate how much profit it would hope to make during one month if all the bikes it produced were sold.

Absorption costing

ABSORPTION COSTING is a traditional method of cost determination. It involves charging or 'absorbing' all the costs associated with business operations individually to a particular cost centre. This includes all direct and indirect costs. Absorption costing differs from full costing in the way indirect costs are allocated. Full costing uses a 'blanket' method, whereas absorption costing apportions indirect costs more accurately. How costs are **apportioned** can vary according to the nature of the indirect cost. For example:
● costs like rent, rates, heating and lighting can be apportioned according to the area or volume in a building that a particular operation occupies;
● personnel expenses could be apportioned according to the number of people employed in a particular operation;
● depreciation and insurance costs could be apportioned according to the book value (☞ unit 63) of the assets used.
To illustrate absorption costing take the example of Dudley Car Exhausts which manufactures three types of exhaust systems, the E1, E2, and E3. Factory time and direct cost details (per system) are shown in Table 53.3. Annual indirect costs include rent, selling costs, overheads and administration. These are £12,000, £18,000, £24,000 and £4,000 respectively. Rent is apportioned according to the factory time used by each system. Selling costs and overheads are apportioned equally between all systems. Administration is apportioned according to the labour input of each system (most administration costs in this case are labour related, eg wages). Dudley Car Exhausts produces 1,000 of each system every year.

Table 53.3 Factory time and direct costs for Dudley Car Exhausts

System	Labour (£)	Materials (£)	Fuel (£)	Factory time(hrs)
E1	2	3	1	1
E2	2	4	2	3
E3	4	4	2	2
Total	8	11	5	6

Using the absorption costing method it is necessary to allocate every single business cost to the production of the three systems. For E1 the total direct cost is calculated by adding labour, materials and fuel, ie (2 + 3 + 1 = £6). To apportion rent to the production of one E1 system it is necessary to take into account the amount of factory time one E1 system uses, ie 1/6 of the total time and also the number of E1 systems produced, ie 1,000 during the year. The following calculation must now be performed:

Rent apportioned to one E1 system $= £12,000 \times \dfrac{1}{6} \times \dfrac{1}{1,000}$

$$= \frac{£12,000}{6,000}$$

$$= £2$$

Selling costs and overheads are split equally between each system, so that selling costs are £6 and overheads £8 for each system. Administration costs are apportioned according to the amount of labour used to make each system. For the E1 system the allocation can be calculated as follows.

Administration costs
apportioned to one E1 system

$$= £4,000 \times \frac{£2}{£8} \times \frac{1}{1,000}$$

$$= £4,000 \times \frac{1}{4} \times \frac{1}{1,000}$$

$$= \frac{£4,000}{4,000}$$

$$= £1$$

The complete cost schedule for all three systems is shown in Table 53.4.

Table 53.4 *The cost of producing the three exhaust systems using the absorption method of costing*

(£)

System	Direct	Rent	Selling	Overheads	Admin.	Total
E1	6	2	6	8	1	23
E2	8	6	6	8	1	29
E3	10	4	6	8	2	30
Total	24	12	18	24	4	82

Some businesses use the absorption method to set the price of their products. Once the cost of each unit has been calculated a profit percentage is added to determine the selling price (☞ unit 43).

The absorption costing method is popular in practice, although there are some criticisms of its use. It is difficult to apportion indirect costs accurately to each unit when a firm produces a very wide range of products. Although less so than full costing, any method of apportionment will still be arbitrary to some extent. It is, therefore, important for a business to be consistent in the way it apportions indirect costs to different cost centres.

Standard costing

Standard costs (☞ unit 52) are those costs which a business expects to incur for particular activities when they are carried

Question 3

Using the information in the above text about Dudley Car Exhausts, answer the following questions.
(a) Show why the rent, per exhaust, is £6 for the E2 system.
(b) Calculate the selling price of each system if a 25 per cent mark-up is used.
(c) Using the absorption method, calculate the cost of producing each system if (i) rent and selling costs double; (ii) rent falls by 20 per cent.

out efficiently. They are known in advance. STANDARD COSTING involves calculating the expected costs of an activity and then comparing these with the actual costs incurred. The difference between the standard cost and the actual cost is called a **variance** (☞ unit 61). Standard costing helps businesses to monitor and control costs. For example, the standard cost and actual cost of making a circuit board for an electronics company is shown in Table 53.5. In this example the actual cost is 50p more than the standard cost.

Table 53.5 *The standard cost and actual cost of producing a circuit board*

Description	Standard cost	Actual cost
Materials	90p	90p
Components	120p	120p
Labour	350p	400p
Indirect costs	140p	140p
Total	700p	750p

This means that there is a variance of 50p. Such a variance is likely to result in the business carrying out an investigation to determine why the actual cost of manufacturing the circuit board was higher than expected, ie higher than the standard cost. In this case the actual cost is higher because the labour cost was £4 compared with an expected labour cost of £3.50. This may have been caused by, say, a new recruit working a little more slowly than a fully experienced operative. By comparing standard costs with actual costs a business can quickly identify poor performance or inconsistencies which might be indicated by large variances.

Marginal costing

Marginal cost is the cost of increasing output by one more unit. The MARGINAL COSTING approach used in business is based on this idea. It allocates direct costs (likely to be variable costs), but not indirect costs (likely to be fixed). In marginal costing, decisions are based upon the value of the CONTRIBUTION that a product or process makes to the indirect costs (fixed costs) and profit. The contribution is the

value of fixed assets is reduced each year by the amount shown as depreciation in the profit and loss account.

Public limited company accounts

Public limited companies have similar accounts to those of private limited companies, such as Virginian Carpets. They must also publish their accounts by law. This allows the public to see the financial position and performance of the company and decide if buying its shares is worthwhile. Existing shareholders can also gauge the company's performance.

It is likely that the published profit and loss account of a large public limited company will be slightly different from that of a private company. Accounts often show the **earnings per share** (☞ unit 68) in the appropriation account. This is calculated by dividing the profit after tax by the total number of issued shares. For example, if a company's net profit after tax is £1.6 million and 5 million shares have been issued:

$$\text{Earnings per share} = \frac{\text{Net profit after tax}}{\text{No. of shares issued}}$$

$$= \frac{£1.6m}{5m}$$

$$= 32p$$

The earnings per share gives an indication of a company's performance.
- Plcs usually pay dividends twice a year. About half way through the financial year a company might pay an **interim dividend**, usually less than half the total dividend. At the end of the financial year the **final dividend** is paid.
- From time to time business may make a 'one-off' transaction. An example of an **exceptional item** might be a very large bad debt which is deducted as normal in the profit and loss account, but disclosed separately in the notes. In recent years some of the commercial banks have had to make such entries after incurring bad debts from Third World countries. An example of an **extraordinary item** might be the cost of management restructuring. Generally they arise from events outside the normal business activities and are not expected to occur again. The expenditure would normally be listed in the profit and loss account, below the line showing profit after tax.
- Finally, in the profit and loss appropriation account of a public limited company, the retained profit figure is sometimes called **transfer to reserves**.

Sole trader accounts

Table 55.6 shows the trading and profit and loss account for Joanna Cullen, a retailer selling PCs. The differences and similarities between the profit and loss account of a sole trader and a limited company can be illustrated from Table 55.6. The profit and loss account of a sole trader normally shows how the year's purchases are adjusted for stock by including opening and closing stocks. In addition, a more detailed list of expenses is included. This allows a comparison with the previous year. A profit and loss appropriation account is not included since there is only one owner and all profit is transferred to the capital account in the balance sheet.

The uses of profit and loss accounts

- Business owners are keen to see how much profit they have made at the end of the trading year. The size of the profit may be a guide to the performance of the business. A comparison is also possible because a profit and loss account will show the previous year's figures. It is possible to calculate the gross profit and net profit from the profit and loss account. The ratio of gross profit to sales turnover is known as the GROSS PROFIT MARGIN. It can be calculated by:

$$\frac{\text{Gross profit}}{\text{Turnover}} \times 100$$

The gross profit margin of Virginian Carpets in 1999 would have been:

$$\frac{£400,000}{£900,000} \times 100 = 44.44\%$$

A rise in the gross profit margin may be because turnover has increased relative to costs of sales. A fall may be because costs of sales have risen relative to turnover. Gross profit does not take into account the general overheads of the business. So a business may be more interested in the ratio of net profit to turnover or the NET PROFIT MARGIN. This can be calculated by:

$$\frac{\text{Net profit}}{\text{Turnover}} \times 100$$

Question 5

Compare the two accounts in Table 55.1 and Table 55.6.
(a) Why do you think that more detail is shown in a sole trader's profit and loss account compared with a limited company's?
(b) Explain why a £20,000 increase in turnover for Joanna Cullen between 1998 and 1999 in Table 55.6 only led to a £11,500 increase in net profit.

Table 55.6 *The profit and loss account of Joanna Cullen, a sole trader*

JOANNA CULLEN
Trading and profit and loss account for the year ended 31.5.99

1998 £		1999 £	£
130,000	Turnover		150,000
25,000	Opening stock	30,000	
65,000	Purchases	70,000	
90,000		100,000	
30,000	*less* Closing stock at selling price	35,000	
60,000			65,000
70,000	Gross profit		85,000
	less:		
1,000	Casual labour	2,000	
2,500	Motor expenses	3,000	
800	Telephone	1,000	
2,500	Printing, stationery and advertising	3,000	
1,300	Electricity	1,500	
8,000	Rent and rates	9,000	
400	Insurance	500	
2,500	Bank interest and charges	2,500	
2,000	Depreciation - car	2,000	
900	Depreciation - fixtures and fittings	900	
21,900			
			25,400
48,100	Net profit		59,600

The net profit margin of Virginian Carpets in 1999 would have been:

$$\frac{£110,000}{£900,000} \times 100 = 12.22\%$$

- A profit and loss account can be used to see how well a business has controlled its overheads. If the gross profit is far larger than the net profit, this would suggest that the company's overheads are quite high. However, if there is little difference between the two this could suggest that a business has controlled its overheads.
- A business can use the profit and loss account to help measure its growth. A guide to a business's growth may be the value of turnover compared with the previous year's. If the turnover is significantly larger than the previous year's, this could suggest that the business has grown.
- The earnings per share is also shown on the profit and loss account for limited companies. This shows shareholders in a limited company how much each share has earned over the year. However, this is not necessarily the amount of money which they will receive from the company. This is

the dividends per share.

Limitations of profit and loss accounts

- Business accounts cannot be used to show what is going to happen in the future. The profit and loss account uses historical information. The account shows what has happened in the past. However, it may be possible to identify future trends by looking at the accounts for a longer time period, say, four or five years. The cash flow forecast statement and other budgets may be helpful in predicting future business performance. These are discussed in units 59 and 61.
- Stakeholders who are interested in the accounts must be aware that it is possible to disguise or manipulate financial information in the accounts (☞ unit 69). For example, a business may attempt to hide its profits to reduce tax or to deter a potential takeover. Alternatively, a business may try to show a greater profit to satisfy shareholders.

Question 6

Table 55.7 *Financial information for Precoat International plc*

	1998	(£000) 1997
Turnover	57,190	49,325
Cost of sales	49,980	42,897
Gross profit	7,210	6,428
Administrative expenses	3,074	2,888
Operating profit	4,136	3,540
Interest receivable and similar income	14	4
Interest payable and similar charges	(422)	(258)
Profit on ordinary activities before taxation (net profit)	3,728	3,286

Source: adapted from Precoat International plc, *Annual Report and Accounts*, 1998.

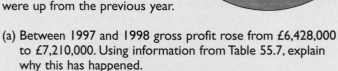

Precoat International plc operates the leading precoated steel service in the UK and Canada. Precoated steel is manufactured by coating wide strip steel with paint or polymer film on a continually operating coating line. In 1998 the business had record sales and earnings. Both gross profit and pre-tax profit were up from the previous year.

(a) Between 1997 and 1998 gross profit rose from £6,428,000 to £7,210,000. Using information from Table 55.7, explain why this has happened.
(b) (i) Calculate the gross profit margin and the net profit margin for 1997 and 1998.
   (ii) Suggest reasons why this has happened.
(c) Explain two uses of the information in Table 55.7 for the business.

Key terms

Gross profit - turnover less cost of sales.
Gross profit margin - expresses operating profit before tax and interest (gross profit) as a percentage of turnover.
Net profit - profit on ordinary activities before taxation.
Net profit margin - shows the ability of a business to control overheads and expresses net profit before tax as a percentage of turnover.
Overheads - indirect business expenses which are not chargeable to a particular part of work or production, eg

heating, lighting or wages.
Profit and loss account - shows net profit after tax by subtracting business expenses and taxation from operating profit.
Profit and loss appropriation account - shows how the profit after tax is distributed between shareholders and the business.
Trading account - shows operating profit by subtracting the cost of sales from turnover.

Summary

1. What is meant by profit from an accountant's point of view?
2. What is likely to happen to a business if normal profit is not made?
3. Distinguish between gross and operating profit.
4. What adjustments might need to be made to turnover during the year?
5. Why is it necessary to adjust purchases for changes in stock levels?
6. What is meant by non-operating income?
7. How might a limited company appropriate its profits?
8. How are earnings per share calculated?
9. What is the difference between the interim and the final dividend?
10. What is the difference between an extraordinary item and an exceptional item?
11. How might the profit and loss account of a sole trader be different from that of a limited company?
12. How might the profit and loss account be used by a business?
13. How might a business calculate its: (a) gross profit ratio; (b) net profit ratio?
14. 'A business may disguise its accounts.' Why might this be a problem for a business attempting a takeover?

Case study

Carpetright plc

Carpetright plc is a specialist carpet retailer. In the financial year to May 1998 the company traded from 307 outlets in Britain. These included:

● Carpetright - a value for money outlet aimed at the middle and lower end of the market, where the majority of sales are from large roll-stock carpets available to take away immediately;

● Carpet Depot - which offers mid-range and more expensive carpets.

The policy of working closely with suppliers led to the launch of the Crossley brand in Summer 1997. This was a collection of mid-priced carpets with a five year stain resistant guarantee, exclusive to Carpetright plc. It was successful in improving sales margins and value for the customer.

Over the year the number of Carpetright and Carpet Depot stores increased by 23 and 11 respectively and the business expanded store space from 2.6 million square feet to 2.94 million square feet. Carpetright plc faced a large rise in property costs over the period. There was only a modest rise in rents, but the cost of new stores, particularly on better sites, had increased substantially.

Table 55.8 *Profit and loss account for Carpetright plc, 1998*

	53 weeks to 2 May 1998 £000	52 weeks to 26 April 1997 £000
Turnover	269,340	233,860
Cost of sales	(131,726)	(119,221)
Gross profit	137,614	114,639
Distribution costs	(1,629)	(1,538)
Administrative expenses	(109,213)	(83,294)
Other operating income	2,021	1,178
Operating profit	28,793	30,985
Profit on disposal of fixed assets	203	492
Net interest receivable and similar income	158	688
Profit on ordinary activities before taxation	29,154	32,165
Tax on profit on ordinary activities	(8,453)	(9,649)
Profit for the financial period	20,701	22,516
Dividends	(17,522)	(15,366)
Profit retained	3,179	7,150
	pence	pence
Earnings per share	26.0	28.5

Source: adapted from Carpetright plc, *Annual Report and Accounts*, 1998.

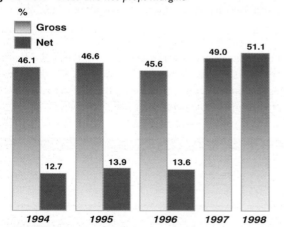

Figure 55.3 *Gross and net profit margins*

%

■ Gross
■ Net

1994: Gross 46.1, Net 12.7
1995: Gross 46.6, Net 13.9
1996: Gross 45.6, Net 13.6
1997: Gross 49.0
1998: Gross 51.1

(a) Give examples of:
(i) cost of sales;
(ii) administrative expenses;
(iii) distribution costs;
using examples from Carpetright plc.
(b) Calculate the number of shares that the company has issued using the 1998 figures.
(c) Explain what has happened to net interest over the period 1997-98 and the effect this will have on net profit.
(d) (i) What has happened to: (i) turnover; (ii) gross profit and (iii) the gross profit margin over the period 1997-98?
(ii) Suggest reasons why these changes may have taken place.

(e) (i) Explain how the distribution of profit has changed over the period 1997-98.
(ii) How might this affect the business in future?
(f) (i) Calculate the net profit ratio for 1997 and 1998.
(ii) What has happened to net profit and the net profit margin over the period 1997-98?
(iii) Explain why these changes may have taken place.
(iv) Discuss how the business might attempt to deal with any problems raised by these changes.

Introduction to the balance sheet

What does a BALANCE SHEET show? It is like a photograph of the financial position of a business at a particular point in time. The balance sheet contains information about the **assets** of a business, its **liabilities** and its **capital**.

● ASSETS are the valuable resources that a business **owns**. They are resources that can be **used** in production. Assets are usually divided into current assets and fixed assets. Current assets are used up in production, such as stocks of raw materials. Fixed assets, such as machinery, are used again and again over a period of time.

● LIABILITIES are the debts of the business, ie what it **owes** to other businesses, individuals and institutions. Liabilities are a **source** of funds for a business. They might be short term, such as an overdraft, or long term, such as a mortgage.

● CAPITAL is the money introduced by the owners of the business, for example when they buy shares. It is another source of funds and can be used to purchase assets.

In all balance sheets the value of assets (what a business owns) will equal the value of liabilities and capital (what the business owes). Why? Any increase in total assets must be funded by an equal increase in capital or liabilities. A business wanting to buy extra machinery (an asset) may need to obtain a bank loan (a liability), for example. Alternatively, a reduction in credit from suppliers (a liability) may mean a reduction in stocks that can be bought (an asset). So:

$$\text{Assets} = \text{capital} + \text{liabilities}$$

This is shown in Figure 56.1. The diagram shows the types of asset and liability that might appear on the balance sheet of a private limited company. There are differences in the assets and liabilities shown in the balance sheets of sole traders and limited companies. This is explained later in this unit.

Question 1

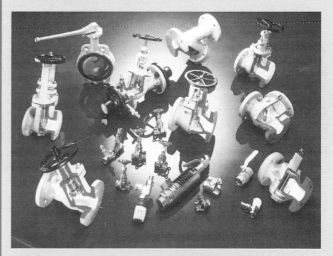

(a) AJ Crisp is a manufacturer of valves used in radiators, for example. The value of AJ Crisp's assets is £6 million. The value of the company's capital and liabilities is also £6 million. Next year the value of its assets increases to £8 million. What will happen to the value of liabilities and capital? Explain your answer.

(b) The photographs above show:
(i) production of valves at the manufacturing plant;
(ii) finished products.
Where might the items shown in the photographs be included in Figure 56.1? Explain your answer.

Figure 56.1 *The assets, liabilities and capital of a private limited company*

Sources of funds		Uses of funds	
Liabilities	£000	**Assets**	£000
Current liabilities		**Fixed assets**	
Trade creditors	120	Premises	200
Taxation	70	Plant and equipment	100
Dividend	80	Financial investments	120
Long term liabilities			
Mortgage	150	**Current assets**	
Capital and reserves		Stocks of goods	180
Shareholders' capital	400	Debtors	200
Retained profit	170	Cash at bank	190
	990		990

Table 56.1

BREAKOUT LTD
Balance sheet as at 31 August 1999

	£000	£000
Fixed assets		
Premises	1,200	
Fixtures and fittings	1,100	
Equipment	700	
		3,000
Current assets		
Stocks	800	
Debtors	500	
Cash at bank	400	
	1,700	
Current liabilities		
Trade creditors	200	
Taxation	300	
Dividends	200	
	700	
Net current assets		
(working capital)		1,000
Total assets less		
current liabilities		
		4,000
Creditors: amounts		
falling due after one year		
Mortgage	1,100	
Bank loan	200	
		1,300
Net assets		**2,700**
Capital and reserves		
Ordinary share capital		
(2,000,000 shares at £1)	2,000	
Retained profit	700	
		2,700

FIXED ASSETS are assets with a life span of more than one year. They might include the buildings, musical and lighting equipment, drinks equipment behind the bar, tables and seats.

CURRENT ASSETS are assets that are likely to be changed into cash within one year. They might include cash deposited at the bank and stocks of goods, such as cigarettes and drinks. They might also include customers or businesses that owe money to Breakout Ltd - the debtors of the business.

CURRENT LIABILITIES are debts that have to be repaid within 12 months. They might include money owed to suppliers of drinks or food, telephone and electricity bills - the creditors of Breakout Ltd. They may also include corporation tax payable to the Inland Revenue for profit earned in the past or dividends owing to shareholders. Bank overdrafts are also a current liability.

*The value of NET CURRENT ASSETS or **working capital** can be found by:*
Current assets - current liabilities
Calculating working capital is important for a business. The working capital a firm has indicates whether or not it can afford to pay its day to day bills.

*The value of **total assets less current liabilities** can be found by:*
(Fixed assets + current assets) - current liabilities

The debts that a business owes which are payable to creditors after 12 months are LONG TERM LIABILITIES. They might include a mortgage which has been taken out to purchase buildings. They could also include any long term loans used to buy equipment, for example.

The value of NET ASSETS can be found by:
(Total assets less current liabilities) - long term liabilities

*The **capital and reserves** figure is equal to the value of net assets. The total of capital and reserves is sometimes called **capital employed** or **shareholders' funds**. Capital and reserves are a liability for the business - money that it owes. Shareholders' funds include the money that is put into the business by people purchasing shares. It is the value of shares when first sold rather than the current market value. Retained profit is profit that the business has made in previous years. It is money which is owed to the owners. However, it has been retained in the business to buy equipment or to help cash flow rather than distributing it as a dividend.*

Question 2

Barden Ltd manufactures components for forklift trucks. It is located in Bristol and serves a major manufacturer of forklift trucks in Cardiff. Table 56.2 shows information that may be contained in the balance sheet for Barden Ltd as at 30.4.99.

(a) Suggest two examples of:
  (i) other current liabilities;
  (ii) creditors falling due after more than one year;
  that the business might have.

(b) Explain why:
  (i) the value of debtors is shown as an asset;
  (ii) the value of creditors is shown as a liability.

(c) From the information in Table 56.2, calculate the value of:
  (i) net current assets;
  (ii) total assets less current liabilities;
  (iii) net assets;
  (iv) capital and reserves.

Table 56.2 *Information from a balance sheet for Barden Ltd as at 30.4.99*

	£000	£000
Fixed assets		
Factory	11,000	
Plant and machinery	5,000	
Equipment	2,500	
Financial assets	1,000	
		19,500
Current assets		
Stocks	3,000	
Work-in-progress	2,500	
Debtors	3,500	
	9,000	
Current liabilities		
Trade creditors	3,500	
Other liabilities	2,500	
	6,000	
Net current assets		****
Total assets less current liabilities		****
Creditors falling due after more than one year	6,000	
Net assets		****
Capital and reserves		
Share capital	9,000	
Other reserves	2,000	
Retained profit	5,500	
		****

Presenting the balance sheet

Table 56.1 shows the balance sheet of Breakout Ltd. It is a business that owns a small chain of nightclubs. It is presented here in a vertical format. Businesses now use this method when presenting their accounts, although in the past they were shown in a horizontal format similar to Figure 56.1. The balance sheet is a record of the company's assets, liabilities and capital.

One advantage of presenting the balance sheet in this format is that it is easy to see the amount of **working capital** (current assets - current liabilities) that a business has. This is important because the working capital shows whether a business is able to pay its day to day bills (☞ unit 60). The net assets (total assets - current liabilities - long term liabilities) of a business are also clearly shown.

The balance sheets of public limited companies

Table 56.3 shows the balance sheet of a public limited

company, Crestfell plc. It is a major manufacturer of food products. A number of new balance sheet items are included compared to those of a private limited company. They reflect the type of transactions of a public limited company.

- **Investments** might be shares held by Crestfell in another company. Investments can be fixed or current assets.
- **Tangible fixed assets** could be factories and equipment.
- **Intangible assets** might be the value of the company's good name with customers (goodwill, ☞ unit 58).
- The value of **provision for liabilities and charges** would include a variety of charges such as reorganisation costs, post retirement benefit payments and deferred taxation.
- **Called up share capital** might include different types of shareholders' funds, including ordinary and preference share capital.
- **Revaluation** sometimes appears under capital and reserves to balance an increase in the value of fixed assets. A business may buy a building for £100,000. Later it may be worth £160,000. This £160,000 would be included in the tangible assets figure. However only £100,000 would appear under capital and reserves as this was the original amount spent. Capital and reserves have to be revalued by

Table 56.3 *The balance sheet of Crestfell plc, 31 August 1999*

Crestfell plc
Balance sheet as at 31 August 1999

	1999 (£m)	1998 (£m)
Fixed assets		
Tangible assets	920	780
Intangible assets	150	140
Investments	20	10
	1,090	930
Current assets		
Stocks	220	210
Debtors	410	390
Cash at bank	70	40
	700	640
Creditors		
(amounts falling due in one year)	(550)	(500)
Net current assets		
(working capital)	150	140
Total assets less current liabilities	1,240	1,070
Creditors		
(amounts falling due after more than one year)	(350)	(240)
Provision for liabilities and charges	(70)	(70)
Net assets	**820**	**760**
Capital and reserves		
Called up share capital	110	100
Revaluation	130	130
Retained profit	580	530
	820	**760**

Figures in brackets show values to be subtracted.

£60,000 so that assets still equal liabilities plus capital and reserves.

Company law requires both **private and public** limited companies to show both this year's and last year's figures in published accounts. This allows comparisons to be made. When the balance sheets for Crestfell plc as at 31 August 1998 and 1999 are compared, most of the figures have changed.

Depreciation and the balance sheet

The value of assets falls over time. A machine bought one year is worth less the next. Vehicles lose a large amount of value after one year. This is DEPRECIATION. Accountants must make an allowance for this when

Table 56.4 *Notes to the accounts of Crestfell plc showing depreciation of tangible fixed assets*

Tangible assets

	Land & buildings £m	Plant, machinery & vehicles £m	Fixtures & fittings £m	Total £m
Cost	380	950	70	1,400
Depreciation & amortisation	50	400	30	480
Net book value	330	550	40	920

showing the value of assets. They estimate the amount by which asset values depreciate. They then deduct depreciation from the value of assets before placing the value on the balance sheet. The term AMORTISATION is used for the changing value of fixed assets with a limited life. For example, a business may pay to lease a building. The lease has a value. When the lease runs out after, say, 10 years, it has no value.

Details about depreciation are shown in the **notes to the accounts**. An example of these notes is shown in Table 56.4. Unit 63 shows how depreciation can be calculated.

Sole trader balance sheets

Earlier it was mentioned that sole trader balance sheets will be different to those of limited companies.

Take the example of Joanna Cullen, a sole trader running a retail outlet that sells computers. Her balance sheet is shown in Table 56.5. There is a number of differences between a sole trader and a limited company balance sheet.

- The sole trader has a capital account rather than a 'capital and reserves' section. Sole traders are set up with the personal capital introduced into the business by the owner. Joanna Cullen introduced a further £4,500 into the business during 1999, according to the balance sheet in Table 56.5.
- It is likely that a sole trader will need to withdraw money from the business for personal reasons during the year. This is subtracted from the capital account and is shown as DRAWINGS in the balance sheet. The balance on the capital account is the amount owed to the owner. This is equal to the assets of the company.
- A limited company has many sources of capital and reserves. However, all companies will show shareholders' funds (often listed as capital and reserves), which will not be in a sole trader's balance sheet.
- The shareholders of a limited company are paid a dividend. This appears in the figure for current liabilities. As sole traders do not have shareholders no such figure will be included in their accounts.

Table 56.5 *Balance sheet for Joanna Cullen as at 31 May 1999*

JOANNA CULLEN
Balance sheet as at 31 May 1999

1998 £		1999 £	£
	Fixed assets		
10,000	Car		8,000
7,900	Fixtures and fittings		7,000
17,900			15,000
	Current assets		
30,000	Stocks	35,000	
4,000	Debtors and prepayments	5,000	
3,000	Bank account	4,000	
1,000	Cash in hand	1,000	
38,000		45,000	
	(less) Current liabilities		
20,000	Creditors and accrued charges	25,000	
18,000	Working capital		20,000
35,900	**NET ASSETS**		35,000
	(FINANCED BY)		
30,000	**Opening capital**		35,900
-	Capital introduced		4,500
48,100	*(add)* Net profit		59,600
78,100			100,000
42,200	*(less)* Drawings		65,000
35,900			35,000

The use of balance sheets

The balance sheet has a number of uses for a business.
● In general, it provides a summary and valuation of all business assets, capital and liabilities.
● The balance sheet can be used to analyse the **asset structure** of a business. It can show how the money raised by the business has been spent on different types of asset. The balance sheet for Crestfell plc in Table 56.3 shows that £1,090 million was spent on fixed assets in 1999. Current assets, however, accounted for only £700 million.
● The balance sheet can also be used to analyse the **capital structure** of a business. A business can raise funds from many different sources, such as shareholders' capital,

Question 3

Look at Table 56.5.
(a) What is the value of total assets for Joanna's business?
(b) What will be the value of opening capital in 2000?
(c) (i) Calculate the percentage increase in drawings over the two years.
    (ii) Explain one possible reason why the increase is so large.
(d) According to the capital account Joanna introduced £4,500 into the business during 1998.
    (i) Where might this money have come from?
    (ii) What do you think it was used for?

retained profit and long term and short term sources.
● Looking at the value of working capital can indicate whether a firm is able to pay its everyday expenses or is likely to have problems. The value of working capital is the difference between current assets and current liabilities. In the 1999 balance sheet for Crestfell plc the value of working capital was £150 million.
● A balance sheet may provide a guide to a firm's value. Generally, the value of the business is represented by the value of all assets less any money owed to outside agents such as banks or suppliers. The value of Crestfell plc in 1998 was £820 million.

Limitations of balance sheets

● The value of many assets listed in the balance sheet may not reflect the amount of money the business would receive if it were sold. For example, fixed assets are listed at cost less an allowance for depreciation (☞ unit 63). However, the depreciation allowance is estimated by accountants. If estimates are inaccurate, the value of assets will also be inaccurate.
● Many balance sheets do not include intangible assets (☞ unit 58). Assets such as goodwill, brand names and the skills of the workforce may be excluded because they are difficult to value or could change suddenly. If such assets are excluded, the value of the business may be understated.
● A balance sheet is a static statement. Many of the values for assets, capital and liabilities listed in the statement are only valid for the day the balance sheet was published. After another day's trading, many of the figures will have changed. This can restrict its usefulness.
● It could be argued that a balance sheet lacks detail. Many of the figures are totals and are not broken down. For example, the value of tangible assets for Crestfell plc in 1999 was £920 million. This figure gives no information about the nature of these assets.

Question 4

Most football clubs do not include the value of their players on the balance sheet. In 1998, some players featuring in the World Cup were transferred to English clubs for large fees. These included Marcel Desailly from World Cup winners, France, who was transferred to Chelsea, a public limited company. Others already playing for English clubs included Holland's Bergkamp and Overmars, both of Arsenal.

(a) In what way does the above example highlight the limitations of business balance sheets?

(b) Recently, some football clubs have considered the inclusion of player's values on their balance sheets. Why do you think this is?

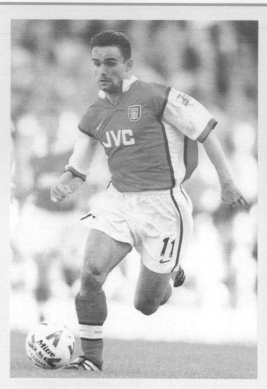

Key terms

Amortisation - the gradual reduction in value of an asset with a fixed life.

Assets - resources owned by the business used in production.

Balance sheet - a summary at a point in time of business assets, liabilities and capital.

Capital - a source of funds provided by the owners of the business used to buy assets.

Current assets - assets likely to be changed into cash within a year.

Current liabilities - debts that have to be repaid within a year.

Depreciation - the fall in value of an asset.

Drawings - money withdrawn by a sole trader from the business for personal use.

Fixed assets - assets with a life span of more than one year.

Liabilities - the debts of the business which provide a source of funds.

Long term liabilities - debts that are payable after 12 months.

Net assets - the value of total assets minus current liabilities minus long term liabilities. The value is equal to capital and reserves on the balance sheet.

Net current assets - current assets minus current liabilities. Also known as working capital.

Summary

1. What is a balance sheet?
2. Why is a balance sheet a static business document?
3. Why must the value of assets on a balance sheet be equal to the value of liabilities plus capital?
4. What is the difference between fixed and current assets?
5. State 3 examples of the fixed assets that a business might have.
6. State 3 examples of the current assets that a business might have.
7. Why is the balance sheet shown in a vertical format?
8. What is the difference between tangible and intangible fixed assets?
9. What is the difference between current and long term liabilities?
10. State 3 current liabilities that a business might have.
11. Why is revaluation of assets sometimes included under capital and reserves?
12. How does depreciation affect the balance sheet?
13. State 3 items that might appear on the balance sheet of a public limited company but not a sole trader.
14. Suggest 3 uses of balance sheets for a business.
15. Suggest 3 limitations of balance sheets.

Case study

Cadbury Schweppes

Cadbury Schweppes is a major global manufacturer of beverages and confectionery. Its products are sold in over 190 countries worldwide.

(a) Give an example of:
   (i)   stocks;
   (ii) intangible assets;
   (iii) revaluation reserve;
   (iv) creditors: amounts falling due within one year;
   that Cadbury Schweppes may have.
(b) Calculate the value of Cadbury Schweppes':
   (i)   current assets;
   (ii) net assets;
   (iii) capital and reserves;
   in 1997 and 1998.
(c) Explain the effect that depreciation has had on the balance sheet.
(d) (i)   Who are likely to be the debtors of Cadbury Schweppes?
   (ii) Calculate the percentage increase or decrease in debtors over the period shown.
   (iii) Suggest possible reasons for any increase or decrease in debtors.
   (iv) How is any change in the value of debtors likely to affect the business?
(e) (i)   Compare the value of current assets in relation to current liabilities in 1998 and 1997.
   (ii) Explain how any change in the relationship might affect the business.
(f) Examine how the capital and reserves part of the balance sheet may be of use to the business and its stakeholders.

Table 56.6 *Balance sheet at 2 January 1999*

	1998	1997
	(£m)	(£m)
Fixed assets		
Intangible assets and goodwill	1,607	1,575
Tangible assets	1,126	1,221
Investments	171	73
	2,904	2,869
Current assets		
Stocks	409	419
Debtors	760	711
Investments	416	682
Cash at bank and in hand	104	86
	****	****
Current liabilities		
Creditors		
(amounts falling due within 1 year)	(1,744)	(1,828)
Net current assets	(55)	70
Total assets less current liabilities	2,849	2,939
Non-current liabilities		
Creditors (amounts falling due after 1 year)	(551)	(716)
Provisions for liabilities and charges	(158)	(248)
	(709)	(964)
Net assets	****	****
Capital and reserves		
Called up share capital	254	252
Revaluation reserve	63	67
Profit & loss account	523	385
Other*	1,300	1,271
	****	****

* Includes the value of:
- shares issued to shareholders as part of the share options scheme ;
- share issues of subsidiary and acquired companies.
- shares issued by a subsidiary

Source: adapted from Cadbury Schweppes, *Annual Report and Accounts*, 1998.

The need for funds

Firms need money to get started, ie to buy equipment, raw materials and obtain premises. Once this initial expenditure has been met, the business can get under way. If successful, it will earn money from sales. However, business is a continuous activity and money flowing in will be used to buy more raw materials and settle other trading debts.

If the owner wants to expand, extra money will be needed over and above that from sales. Expansion may mean larger premises, more equipment and extra workers. Throughout the life of a business there will almost certainly be times when money has to be raised from outside.

The items of expenditure above fall into two categories - REVENUE EXPENDITURE or CAPITAL EXPENDITURE. Capital expenditure is spending on items which may be used over and over again. A company vehicle, a cutting machine and a new factory all fall into this category. Capital expenditure will be shown in a firm's balance sheet because it includes the purchase of fixed assets (☞ unit 56). Revenue expenditure refers to payments for goods and services which have either already been consumed or will be very soon. Wages, raw materials and fuel are all examples. Revenue expenditure will be shown in a firm's profit and loss account (☞ unit 55) because it represents business costs or expenses.

Internal sources of funds

Figure 57.1 is a summary of all sources of funds, both internal and external. This unit is concerned mainly with external sources, but there are three internal sources for a company.

- Profit. A firm's profit, after tax, is an important and inexpensive source of finance. A large proportion of finance is funded from profit.
- Depreciation. This is a financial provision for the replacement of worn out machinery and equipment. All businesses use depreciation as a source of funds (☞ unit 63).
- Sale of assets. Sometimes businesses sell off assets to raise money. Occasionally a company may be forced to sell assets because it is not able to raise finance from other sources. The sale of business assets such as an associated company or a subsidiary of a business is called **divestment**.

External long term sources of funds

External long term capital can be in the form of share capital or loan capital.

Share capital For a limited company this is likely to be the most important source of funds. The sale of shares can raise very large amounts of money. Share capital is often referred to

Question 1

(a) Look at the photographs. State which transactions to buy these items are revenue expenditure and which are capital expenditure.
(b) Why might expenditure on equipment need to be repeated?
(c) Explain why it might be easier to cut capital expenditure rather than revenue expenditure.

Equipment

Building materials

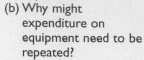

Petrol

as PERMANENT CAPITAL. This is because it is not normally **redeemed**, ie it is not repaid by the business. Once the share has been sold, the buyer is entitled to a share in the profit of the company, ie a **dividend** (☞ unit 3). Dividends are not always declared. Sometimes a business makes a loss or needs to retain profit to help fund future business activities. A shareholder can make a CAPITAL GAIN by selling the share at a higher price than it was originally bought for. Shares are not normally sold back to the business. The shares of public limited companies are sold in a special share market called the STOCK MARKET or STOCK EXCHANGE, dealt with later in this unit. Shares in private limited companies are transferred privately (☞ unit 5). Shareholders, because they are part owners of the business, are entitled to a vote. One vote is allowed for each share owned. Voting takes place annually and shareholders vote either to re-elect the existing board of directors or replace them. Different types of shares can be issued:

- **Ordinary shares**. These are also called EQUITIES and are the most common type of share issued. They are also the riskiest type of share since there is no guaranteed dividend. The size of the dividend depends on how much profit is made and how much the directors decide to retain in the

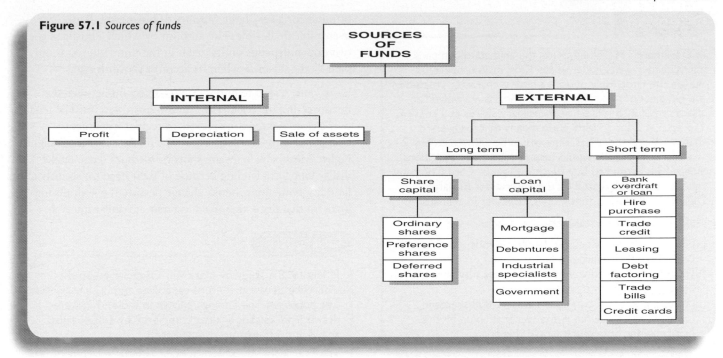

Figure 57.1 *Sources of funds*

Table 57.1 *Summary and explanation of the ways in which new shares can be made available to investors on the stock exchange*

BY PROSPECTUS

Public issue	Potential investors might apply to an ISSUING HOUSE, such as a merchant bank, after reading the company prospectus. This is an expensive method, but suits big issues.
Offer for sale	Shares are issued to an issuing house, which then sells them at a fixed price. This is also expensive but suits small issues.
Sale by tender	The company states a minimum price which it will accept from investors and then allocates shares to the highest bidders.

PLACING

Private placing	Unquoted companies (who do not sell on the Stock Exchange) or those with small share sales approach issuing houses to place the shares privately with investors.
Stock exchange placing	Less popular issues can be placed by the stock exchange with institutional investors, for example. This is relatively inexpensive.

AN INTRODUCTION	Existing shareholders get permission from the Stock Exchange to sell shares by attracting new shareholders to the firm. No new capital is raised.
RIGHTS ISSUE	Existing shareholders are given the 'right' to buy new shares at a discounted price. This is cheap and simple, and creates free publicity. Issues can be based on current holdings. A 1 for 5 issue means that 1 new share is issued for every 5 currently held.
BONUS ISSUE	New shares are issued to existing shareholders to capitalise on reserves which have built up over the years. No new capital is raised and shareholders end up with more shares, but at lower prices.

business. All ordinary shareholders have voting rights. When a share is first sold it has a nominal value shown on it - its original value. Share prices will change as they are bought and sold again and again.

● **Preference shares**. The owners of these shares receive a fixed rate of return when a dividend is declared. They carry less risk because shareholders are entitled to their dividend before the holders of ordinary shares. Preference shareholders are not strictly owners of the company. If the company is sold, their rights to dividends and capital repayments are limited to fixed amounts. Some preference shares are **cumulative**, entitling the holder to dividend arrears from years when dividends were not declared.

● **Deferred shares**. These are not used often. They are usually held by the founders of the company. Deferred shareholders only receive a dividend after the ordinary shareholders have been paid a minimum amount.

When a company issues shares there is a variety of ways in which they can be made available to potential investors as shown in Table 57.1.

Loan capital Any money which is borrowed for a lengthy period of time by the business is called loan capital. Loan capital comes from four sources.

● Debentures. The holder of a debenture is a creditor of the company, not an owner. This means that holders are entitled to an agreed fixed rate of return, but have no voting rights. The amount borrowed must be repaid by the expiry date.

● Mortgage. Only limited companies can raise money from the sale of shares and debentures (☞ unit 5). Smaller enterprises often need long term funding, to buy premises for example. They may choose to take out a mortgage. A mortgage is a long term loan, from, say, a bank or other financial institution. The lender must use land or property as security on the loan.

● Industrial loan specialists. A number of organisations provide funds especially for business and commercial uses. These specialists tend to cater for businesses which have difficulty in raising funds from conventional sources. In recent years there has been a significant growth in the

Question 2

In December 1998 Sleepy Kids, the animation company, announced a rights issue. Sleepy Kids' main property is Budgie the Little Helicopter, a cartoon character created by the Duchess of York. The 2-for-3 rights issue involved an allocation of 20.3 million new ordinary shares at a cost of 15p each. A 2-for-3 rights issue means that for every 3 shares a shareholder has, they would be allowed to buy 2 shares. The proceeds would help to fund two acquisitions. Sleepy Kids agreed to buy Richard Digance Card Company, the media group created by the entertainer Richard Digance, and Musical Tunes, the Cardiff-based animator.

Source: adapted from the *Financial Times*, 4.12.1998.

(a) Explain why a rights issue by Sleepy Kids is an example of an external source of funds.
(b) Suggest two reasons why the business may have chosen to raise money in this way.
(c) One shareholder currently owns 12,000 shares in Sleepy Kids. If the full rights were taken up by this shareholder, how much would this cost?

number of VENTURE CAPITALISTS. These provide funds for small and medium sized companies that appear to have some potential, but are considered too risky by other investors. Venture capitalists often use their own funds, but also attract money from financial institutions and '**Business Angels**'.

Business Angels are individuals who invest between £10,000 and £100,000, often in exchange for an equity stake. A typical Angel might make one or two investments in a three year period, either individually or together with a small group of friends, relatives or business associates. Most investments are in start-ups or early stage expansions. There are several reasons why people become Business Angels. Many like the excitement of the gamble involved, or being part of a new or developing business. Others are attracted by the tax relief offered by the government. Some are looking for investment opportunities for their unused income, such as retired business people and lottery winners.

● Government assistance. Both central and local government have been involved in providing finance for business. The scale of the involvement has varied. Nationalisation of large industries took place between 1945-79. In the 1990s Business start up schemes (☞ unit 2) have provided a small amount of income for those starting new businesses for a limited period of time, providing they meet certain criteria. Financial help is usually selective. Smaller businesses tend to benefit, as do those setting up in regions which suffer from heavy unemployment (☞ unit 100).

External short term sources of funds

Bank overdraft This is probably the most important source

of funds for a very large number of businesses. Bank overdrafts are flexible. The amount by which a business goes overdrawn depends on its needs at the time. Interest is only paid by the business when its account is overdrawn.

Bank loan A loan requires a rigid agreement between the borrower and the bank. The amount borrowed must be repaid over a clearly stated time period, in regular instalments. Compared with a bank overdraft the interest charged is slightly higher. Most bank loans are short or medium term. Banks dislike long term lending because of their need for security and liquidity. Sometimes, banks change persistent overdrafts into loans, so that firms are forced to repay at regular intervals.

Question 3

In July 1998 a study by Mark Van Osnabrugge on the difference between venture capitalists and business angels was published. The findings, shown in Table 57.2, were drawn from questionnaires completed by 143 business angels and 119 venture capitalists.

Table 57.2

● Business angels tend to be wealthy individuals, usually with an entrepreneurial background, who invest their own money, often in small businesses.
● Angels tend to have practical experience. Venture capitalists are more academically qualified.
● 92 per cent of angels had worked in small companies compared with just over 50 per cent of venture capitalists.
● Angels are more likely to invest in unfamiliar business sectors, but are less happy with high technology companies than venture capitalists. 59 per cent of angels have minimal experience in the sector of their most recent involvement.
● Venture capitalists invest on average £945,000 into businesses valued at £3.3 million, giving them a 32 per cent stake. This compares with the average angel investment of £55,000 into firms valued at £289,000 for a 24 per cent stake.
● Angels were concerned with the 'enthusiasm' and 'trustworthiness' of the entrepreneur. Venture capitalists were more interested in the business concept, growth prospects and the product's market.
● Venture capitalists are more diligent when investigating prospective businesses for investment. More than half of the angels admitted to undertaking minimal or no research. Instead they rely on the entrepreneur's own projections.
● Contracts between angels and firms tend to be basic. Venture capitalists often insist on meaningful covenants and will charge substantial arrangement fees.
● Angels hope for an average 29 per cent return on their investment. Venture capitalists expect about 39 per cent.
● Venture capitalists want to exit from investments more quickly than angels. Angels want more involvement and tend to stick around for a lot longer.

Source: adapted from the *Financial Times*, 23.7.1998.

(a) Using details from the report, describe the type of business a venture capitalist might be looking to invest in.
(b) What evidence is there in the study to suggest that venture capitalists are more cautious than business angels when investing?
(c) Why might business angels and venture capitalists prefer to take a stake in businesses when they make an investment?

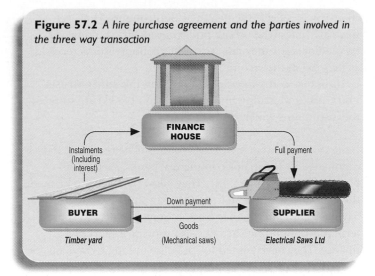

Figure 57.2 *A hire purchase agreement and the parties involved in the three way transaction*

FINANCE HOUSE

Instalments (Including interest)

Full payment

Down payment

BUYER

Timber yard

Goods

(Mechanical saws)

SUPPLIER

Electrical Saws Ltd

Hire purchase This is often used by small businesses to buy plant and machinery. Sometimes, a hire purchase agreement requires a down payment by the borrower, who agrees to repay the remainder in instalments over a period of time. FINANCE HOUSES specialise in providing funds for such agreements. Figure 57.2 illustrates the working of an agreement and the parties involved. The buyer places a down payment on a machine with the supplier and receives delivery. The finance house pays the supplier the amount outstanding and collects instalments (including interest) from the buyer. The goods bought do not legally belong to the buyer until the very last instalment has been paid to the finance house.

If the buyer falls behind with the repayments the finance house can legally repossess the item. Finance houses are less selective than banks when granting loans. Hence their interest rates are higher. They add a servicing charge for paying in instalments which also leads to higher rates.

Trade credit It is common for businesses to buy raw materials, components and fuel and pay for them at a later date, usually between 30 - 90 days. Paying for goods and services using trade credit seems to be an interest free way of raising finance. It is particularly profitable during periods of inflation. However, many companies encourage early payment by offering discounts. The cost of goods is often higher if the firm does not pay early. Delaying the payment of bills can also result in poor business relations with suppliers.

Leasing Leasing is becoming increasingly popular. It allows businesses to buy plant, machinery and equipment without having to pay out large amounts of money. When equipment is leased the transaction is recorded as revenue expenditure rather than capital expenditure. An **operating lease** means that the leasing company simply hires out equipment for an agreed period of time. The user never owns the equipment, but it is given the option to purchase the equipment outright if it is leased with a **finance lease**. There are some advantages of leasing.

● No large sums of money are needed to buy the use of equipment.
● Maintenance and repair costs are not the responsibility of the user.
● Hire companies can offer the most up to date equipment.
● Leasing is useful when equipment is only required occasionally.
● Leasing payments can be offset against tax.
However:
● over a long period of time leasing is more expensive than the outright purchase of plant and machinery;
● loans cannot be secured on assets which are leased.

Debt factoring When companies sell their products they send invoices stating the amount due. The invoice provides evidence of the sale and the money owed to the company. Debt factoring involves a specialist company (the factor) providing finance against these unpaid invoices. A common arrangement is for a factor to pay 80 per cent of the value of invoices when they are issued. The balance of 20 per cent is paid by the factor when the customer settles the bill. An administrative and service fee will be charged.

Trade bills This is not a common source of funds, but can

Question 4

Winters, a small building contractor, has just won a contract to build an extension to a local factory. The contract is worth £78,000 and is expected to take two months. Nick Winter, the owner, employs two other staff and operates from a small builder's yard in Leamington Spa. The contract, Winters' second big job this year, requires the use of an excavator. The business does not own an excavator, but has found that it is having to lease one from a Warwick-based plant hire company more and more often. The hire charges for a JCB are £19 per hour, including the driver. Nick expects to need the excavator for six full working days. Not for the first time Nick felt frustrated at the high cost of acquiring specialised equipment. Before going ahead with the lease he enquired about the cost of a brand new JCB. A local dealer quoted a price of £39,000. At the moment, he could not raise the finance to buy a JCB outright.

(a) Explain the advantages to the business of using a lease to fund the acquisition of the excavator.
(b) Calculate the cost of leasing the excavator. State any assumptions you feel are necessary.
(c) Suggest how Nick might fund the purchase of a new excavator.
(d) What factors might encourage the business to buy an excavator outright?

play an important role, particularly in overseas trade and commodity markets. The purchaser of traded goods may sign a **bill of exchange** agreeing to pay for the goods at a specified later date. Ninety days is a common period. The seller of the goods will hold the bill until payment is due. However, the holder can sell it at a discount before the maturity date to a specialist financial institution. There is a well developed market for these bills and all holders will receive payment at the end of the period from the debtor.

Credit cards Businesses of all sizes have uses for cards. They can be used by executives to meet expenses such as hotel bills, petrol and meals when travelling on company business. They might also be used to purchase materials from suppliers who accept credit cards. Credit cards are popular because they are convenient, flexible, secure and avoid interest charges if monthly accounts are settled within the credit period. However, they tend to have a credit limit, This may make them unsuitable for certain purchases.

Capital and money markets

Businesses have to look to external sources for their funds. **Financial intermediaries** are the institutions responsible for matching the needs of **savers**, who want to loan funds, with those of **investors**, who need funds. These groups do not naturally communicate with each other. Intermediaries provide the link between them.

A number of financial institutions hold funds for savers, paying them interest. In addition, they make funds available to investors who, in turn, are charged interest. Some deal in capital, ie permanent and long term finance, while others deal in money, ie short term loans and bills of exchange. They offer a variety of commercial and financially related services.

The stock market The capital market is dominated by the London Stock Exchange, which deals in second hand shares. The main function of a stock exchange is to provide a market where the owners of shares can sell them. If this market did not exist, selling shares would be difficult because buyers and sellers could not easily communicate with each other. Savers would be less inclined to buy shares and so companies would find it more difficult to raise finance by the issue of shares.

A stock exchange enables mergers and takeovers to take place smoothly (☞ unit 101). If the price of a company's shares begins to fall due to poor profitability, a predator may enter the market and begin to build up a stake in that company. Once the stake is large enough a predator can exert control over the company.

A stock exchange also provides a means of protection for shareholders. Companies which have a stock exchange listing have to obey a number of Stock Exchange rules and regulations, which are designed to safeguard shareholders from fraud.

Finally, it is also argued that the general movement in

share prices reflects the health of the economy. However, there are times when share price movements could be very misleading, eg if they rise when the economy is in a recession as they did in the second half of 1992.

Insurance companies, pension funds, investment trusts, unit trusts and issuing houses (merchant banks) are some of the institutions which trade in shares.

Banks and other financial institutions The money market is dominated by the major commercial banks, such as the NatWest Bank or the HSBC. They allow payments to be made through the cheque system and deal in short term loans. Savings banks and finance corporations also deal in short term funds. Building societies also provide a source of finance. They have tended to specialise in long term loans for the purchase of land and property.

At the heart of this highly complex market system is the **Bank of England**. This is the government's bank and tends to play a role in controlling the amount of money loaned and interest rates (☞ unit 26).

In recent years many of the above institutions have changed in nature. Due to competition, changes in legislation and mergers there has been a great deal of diversification. In particular, there is now little real difference between the role of a building society and that of a bank.

The Alternative Investment Market and OFEX In June 1995 the Alternative Investment Market was established. Its purpose was to give small, young and growing companies the chance to raise capital and trade their shares more widely, without the cost of a full stock market listing. In order to join the market, a nominated adviser must be appointed, such as a stockbroker, banker or lawyer. The adviser must supervise the admission procedure and be responsible for ensuring that the company complies with AIM regulations. The admission procedure takes three months. The cost of a listing is about £100,000. Another market called OFEX was set up by J.P. Jenkins, the specialist market-maker in small company shares. It is not regulated by the stock exchange, but only stock exchange member firms can deal directly on OFEX. OFEX offers a market place in the shares of unlisted companies that have no interest in joining AIM. Two of Britain's biggest private companies, Weetabix and National Parking Corporation, both feature on OFEX. Also, OFEX acts as a 'feeder' to AIM because flotation and other costs are less at the initial stages.

The choice of the source of funds

A number of factors are important when choosing between alternative sources of funds.

Cost Businesses obviously prefer sources which are less expensive, both in terms of interest payments and administration costs. For example, share issues can carry high

Saeed Mustaq is a timber merchant. He operates as a sole trader from a yard in Birmingham. Most of his sales are credit sales to builders in the area. Other customers pay cash. In March 1999 one of his larger customers went out of business, leaving Saeed with a bad debt of £2,200. As a result he was likely to have problems paying day to day expenses. For example, he needed £4,000 immediately or he would run low on timber stocks. Saeed identified three possible sources of finance.

● His bank agreed to extend his overdraft to £3,500 at a rate of 13 per cent per annum.
● The bank offered a debt collection service. They would pay 90 per cent of any invoice issued to a regular customer. Because of the bad debt charges for the service were high - 20 per cent per annum. However, it allowed Saeed access to larger amounts of cash.
● A new timber supplier has offered Saeed favourable credit terms. But he insisted the first three months' purchases must be made in cash.

(a) Using examples from the case, explain the factors that may have influenced Saeed's choice of finance.

administration costs while the interest payments on bank overdrafts tend to be relatively low.

Use of funds When a company undertakes heavy capital expenditure, it is usually funded by a long term source of finance. For example, the building of a new plant may be financed by a share issue or a mortgage. Revenue expenditure tends to be financed by short term sources. For example, the purchase of a large amount of raw materials may be funded by trade credit or a bank overdraft.

Status and size Sole traders, which tend to be small, are limited in their choices of finance. For example, long term sources may be mortgages and perhaps the introduction of some personal capital. Public and private limited companies can usually obtain finance from many different sources. In addition, due to their size and added security, they can often demand lower interest rates from lenders. There are significant economies of scale (☞ unit 93) in raising finance.

Financial situation The financial situation of businesses is constantly changing. When a business is in a poor financial situation, it finds that lenders are more reluctant to offer finance. At the same time, the cost of borrowing rises. Financial institutions are more willing to lend to secure businesses which have **collateral** (assets which provide security for loans). Third World Countries which are desperate to borrow money to fund development, are forced to pay very high rates indeed.

Gearing GEARING (☞ unit 68) is the relationship between the loan capital and share capital of a business. A company is said to be **high geared** if it has a large proportion of loan

capital to share capital. A **low geared** company has a relatively small amount of loan capital. For example, two companies may each have total capital of £45 million. If the first has loan capital of £40 million and share capital of only £5 million it is high geared. The other company may have share capital of £30 million and loan capital of £15 million. It is relatively low geared.

The gearing of a company might influence its funding. If a business is high geared, it may be reluctant to raise even more finance by borrowing. It may choose to issue more shares instead, rather than increasing the interest to be paid on loans.

Table 57.3 *Advantages and disadvantages of being high geared and low geared*

	Advantages	**Disadvantages**
Low geared	The burden of loan repayments is reduced. The need for regular interest payments is reduced. Volatile interest rates are less of a threat.	Dividend payments have to be met indefinitely. Ownership of the company will be diluted. Dividends are paid after tax.
High geared	The interest on loans can be offset against tax. Ownership is not diluted. Once loans have been repaid the company's debt is much reduced.	Interest payments must be met. Interest rates can change, which causes uncertainty. Loans must be repaid and may be a burden, increasing the risk of insolvency.

Capital structure

The CAPITAL STRUCTURE of a business refers to the different sources of funds a business has used. Capital structures can vary considerably depending on the type of business. For example:

● sole traders will not have any share capital in their capital structure;
● firm's such as JCB, which have funded expansion by reinvesting profits, may not show any long term loan capital in their capital structure;
● debt laden companies, such as Queens Moat Houses, have large amounts of loan capital in their capital structure.

Source of funds and the balance sheet

Unit 56 showed how a balance sheet is produced. The liabilities 'side' shows the debts of the company, ie the money owed to others. It is made up of:

● capital - money introduced by the owners of the company;
● other liabilities - money owed to people and institutions other than the owners, such as a bank.

It was also stated that these are the **sources** of funds used by the business, for example to buy assets. The liabilities side is divided into three sections - capital and reserves, long term liabilities and current liabilities.

Capital and reserves Capital is the amount of money owed by the business to the owners. If all the company's assets were sold and the liabilities paid off, any money remaining would belong to the owners. Initially, capital represents the amount of money used to start a business.

During the life of a business the amount of capital changes. It will increase if the owners introduce money or if profits are retained. If the owners withdraw money from the firm or a loss is made then the capital of the business will fall. Because of this, capital is known as an **accumulated fund**. Capital is not physical in nature, and the term is used differently by business personnel and economists. To the accountant, capital is the difference between assets and liabilities.

Capital = total assets - total liabilities

If there is negative capital, where liabilities are greater than assets, then the firm is said to be INSOLVENT. In this situation it is illegal for the firm to continue trading. **Working capital** or circulating capital, is the amount of money a business needs to fund day to day trading. This could be payment of wages and energy costs or the purchase of components. Unit 60 shows how a business calculates its working capital. Here we can say:

Working capital = current assets - current liabilities

In the case of a sole trader or a partnership, capital might be introduced from personal savings or a loan. For a public limited company, the main source of capital is from the sale of **ordinary shares**, ie SHARE CAPITAL. The total value of ISSUED SHARE CAPITAL is shown in the **shareholders' funds**. This is the money raised from the sale of shares. It is calculated by multiplying the number of shares sold by the price at which they were originally sold, ie the nominal value. In the notes to the accounts the AUTHORISED SHARE CAPITAL will be stated. This is the maximum amount of share capital that shareholders want the company to raise. The authorised share capital is often larger than the issued share capital, but never smaller, as companies keep their options open to issue more shares later. For tax reasons preference shares are much less popular in today's business.

Reserves are shareholders' funds which have been built up over the life of the company. Three kinds are shown in the balance sheet.
- Share premiums. If a company issues shares, and the price they charge is higher than the nominal value, the share premium will be the difference. For example, if a 25p share is issued at 40p, the share premium is 15p. Dividends cannot be declared by the business as a result of such premiums.
- Revaluations. At times, particularly during periods of high inflation, some of the company's assets increase in value. If the values are updated on the asset side of the balance sheet then it is necessary to make an equal adjustment on the liabilities side. The entry is recorded under the heading of revaluation. It is a reserve because the benefit of any increase in asset values will be enjoyed by the owners of the company.
- Retained profits. The directors always retain a part of the

company's profits as a precaution or to finance new business activities. When profits are not paid as dividends they are retained in reserve.

Long term liabilities Long term loans over a year must be repaid by the company and are called **long term liabilities** (☞ unit 56). The most common listed in company balance sheets are debentures and mortgages.

Current liabilities **Current liabilities** (☞ unit 56) are those short term financial debts which must be repaid within one year.
- Trade creditors. This is when goods are purchased from suppliers and paid for at a later date. Another current liability which is very similar is an accrued charge. Certain expenses occur from day to day, but are only invoiced periodically. For example, most firms use electricity every day but are billed only four times a year. If at the end of a trading year a bill has not been received, accountants will estimate the charge for the electricity used and record it in the balance sheet as an accrued charge.
- Bank loans and overdrafts. Loans which are repayable within twelve months are classed as current liabilities. In addition, even if bank overdrafts last for more than a year, because they are repayable 'on demand' they are shown as current liabilities.
- Taxation. Most firms pay tax at the latest possible date. When a company has been notified by the Inland Revenue, the amount owed to them is shown in the balance sheet as a current liability.
- Dividends payable. Once a dividend has been declared it has to be approved at the Annual General Meeting by the shareholders. It is assumed that the proposed dividend will be approved and because it will be paid shortly after it is listed as a current liability

Summary

1. Why do businesses need to raise funds?
2. State the internal sources of funds.
3. What is the difference between ordinary, preference and deferred shares?
4. State the advantages to a business of a bank overdraft compared with a bank loan.
5. What is the difference between a finance lease and an operating lease?
6. What is the function of financial intermediaries?
7. Describe the functions of a stock exchange.
8. What factors affect the choice of source of finance?
9. 'Capital structures can vary depending on the type of business.' Explain this statement with an example.
10. Why is share capital described as permanent capital?

Table 59.4 Railtrack, cash flow statement

	1998 £m	1997 £m
Net cash inflow from operating activities	**362**	**608**
Returns on investments and **servicing of finance**		
Interest received	**13**	10
Interest paid	**(40)**	(39)
Net cash outflow from returns on **investments and servicing of finance**	**(27)**	**(29)**
Taxation paid	**(109)**	**(17)**
Capital expenditure		
Purchase of tangible fixed assets	**(620)**	(462)
Sale of tangible fixed assets	**47**	39
Net cash outflow from capital expenditure	**(573)**	**(423)**
Equity dividends paid	**(80)**	**(106)**
Management of liquid resources		
Purchase of short term investments	**(8)**	(15)
Financing		
New loans	**565**	283
Payment of discount and fees on new loans	**(5)**	-
Repayment of loans	**(218)**	(350)
Capital element of finance lease rental payments	**-**	(6)
Capital element of finance lease receipts	**15**	12
Capital grants received	**73**	63
Net cash inflow from financing	**430**	**2**
(Decrease)/Increase in cash	**(5)**	**20**

Table 59.5 Railtrack, net cash inflow from operating activities

	1998 £m	1997 £m
Operating profit	**380**	339
Depreciation and amortisation (net of capital grants amortised)	**137**	119
(Increase)/decrease in stocks	**(6)**	1
(Increase)/decrease in debtors	**(35)**	20
(Decrease)/increase in Asset Maintenance Plan accrual	**(145)**	10
Increase in other creditors	**23**	64
Increase in provisions	**8**	55
Net cash inflow from operating activities	**362**	**608**

Source: adapted from Railtrack, *Annual Report and Accounts*.

companies to publish a CASH FLOW STATEMENT in the annual accounts. Note that this is **not** the same as a cash flow forecast statement. Cash flow statements may include receipts and payments from the previous two years. These may not be disclosed elsewhere in published financial statements. Another advantage is that a cash flow statement must be shown in a standardised presentation. This allows a comparison between different companies.

FRS 1 requires cash flows to be disclosed under standard headings. These are:

- operating activities;
- returns on investments and servicing of finance;
- taxation;
- investing activities;
- financing;

in that order.

Table 59.4 shows a cash flow statement for Railtrack, the provider of railway line infrastructure in the UK. In 1998 the net cash inflow from operating activities was £362 million. The ways in which the business earned this are shown in Table 59.5. Added to this was £13 million interest received. Subtracted was £40 million interest paid. During the year tax paid by the company was £109 million. In addition, the company bought a net £573 million (£620 million-£47 million) worth of new tangible assets. Dividends of £80 million were paid to shareholders, and £8 million worth of short term investments were bought. Railtrack took out £565 million of new loans during the year, and together with other financing adjustments, resulted in a net cash inflow from financing of £430 million. Thus the total net cash outflow for the year was £5 million.

The inclusion of cash flow statements helps to clarify the cash position of a business. However, there are some criticisms of cash flow statements.

- In practice, little new information is shown in the statements. The law encourages disclosure but does not enforce it.
- Small limited companies are not bound to publish a cash flow statement because they are owner managed. However, medium sized firms are. This seems to lack a little logic since most medium sized firms are also owner managed.
- Cash flow statements, like funds flow statements, are based on historical information. It is argued that cash flow statements based on future predictions are more useful.

Question 4

Look at Table 59.4 and Table 59.5.

(a) (i) What has happened to net cash inflow between 1997 and 1998?
   (ii) How has this affected the cash flow statement of Railtrack in 1998?
(b) Look at the cash flow statement for Railtrack in Table 59.4. Describe the main changes that have taken place in the flows of cash into and out of the business over the two years.
(c) How might the cash flow statement be useful to Railtrack?

The difference between cash and profit

It is important for businesses to recognise the difference between cash and profit. At the end of a trading year it is unlikely that the value of profit will be the same as the cash balance. Differences between cash and profit can arise for a number of reasons.

● During the trading year a business might sell £200,000 worth of goods with total costs of £160,000. Its profit would be £40,000. However, if some goods had been sold on credit, payment by certain customers may not yet have been received. If £12,000 was still owing, the amount of cash the business had would be £28,000 (£40,000-£12,000). Thus, profit is greater than cash.

● A business may receive cash at the beginning of the trading year from sales made in the previous year. This would increase the cash balance, but not affect profit. In addition, the business may buy resources from suppliers and not pay for them until the next trading year. As a result its trading costs will not be the same as cash paid out.

● Sometimes the owners might introduce more cash into the business. This will increase the cash balance, but have no effect on the profit made. This is because the introduction of capital is not treated as business revenue in the profit and loss account. The effect will be the same if a business borrows money from a bank.

● Purchases of fixed assets will reduce cash balances, but have no effect on the profit a company makes. This is because the purchase of assets is not treated as a business cost in the profit and loss account.

● Sales of fixed assets will increase cash balances but have no effect on profit. This is because the cash from the sale of a fixed asset is not included in business turnover.

● The amount of cash at the end of the year will be different from profit because at the beginning of the year the cash balance is unlikely to be zero. If, at the beginning of the year, the cash balance for a business is £23,000, then the amount of cash a business has at the end of the year will exceed profit by £23,000.

It is possible for a business to trade for many years without making a profit. For example, British Biotech, a pharmaceuticals company, traded between 1985-98 without ever making a profit. The company survived because it was able to generate cash. Extra cash was introduced by shareholders on several occasions since 1985. In 1998 the company lost £44.8 million. However, the cash in the bank was £132.8 million. Shareholders may be happy to contribute more capital if they think that a company has a lot of potential. However, it is possible for a profitable business to collapse if it runs out of cash. This is likely to happen if a business has to meet some substantial unexpected expenditure or if a bad debt occurs.

Question 5

Woolwear Ltd produces sweaters and jumpers for the mail order market. It advertises products in weekend newspaper supplements. It has enjoyed some success in recent years. However, the directors believe that profits could be raised if it could cut costs. At the beginning of 1999 it was decided that a new computer system would be installed. This was expected to reduce administrative overheads and the monthly wage bill. Table 59.6 shows a cash flow forecast statement and profits for the six month trading period starting in July 1999. It was anticipated that the computer system will be bought and installed in December. Part of the cost would be met by a bank loan.

Table 59.6 *Cash flow forecast statement for Woolwear Ltd, July to December*

£

	Jul	Aug	Sep	Oct	Nov	Dec
Receipts						
Cash sales	40,000	50,000	50,000	70,000	90,000	90,000
Bank loan						30,000
Total cash receipts	40,000	50,000	50,000	70,000	90,000	120,000
Payments						
Cost of sales	18,000	30,000	30,000	40,000	60,000	60,000
Wages	8,000	8,000	8,000	10,000	10,000	8,000
Overheads	10,000	18,000	10,000	15,000	20,000	15,000
Computer system						50,000
Total payments	36,000	56,000	48,000	65,000	90,000	133,000
Net cash flow	4,000	(6,000)	2,000	5,000	-	(13,000)
Opening balance	12,000	16,000	10,000	12,000	17,000	17,000
Closing balance	16,000	10,000	12,000	17,000	17,000	4,000

Table 59.7 *Profit per month Woolwear Ltd*

	Jul	Aug	Sep	Oct	Nov	Dec
Profit*	4,000	(6,000)	2,000	5,000	0	7,000

* Cash sales - operating costs (cost of sales + wages + overheads)

(a) What is the difference between the profit made by the business over the period and the closing cash balance?

(b) Suggest two reasons why there may have been this difference.

(c) Explain the effects on the: (i) cash flow; (ii) profit of the business; if the computer system had not been bought.

Summary

1. Explain the operation of the cash flow cycle.
2. Why is it important that a business:
   (i) does not hold too much cash;
   (ii) holds sufficient cash?
3. Briefly explain what a cash flow forecast statement includes.
4. How does a cash flow forecast statement indicate whether a business faces cash flow problems in future?
5. Explain why a business prepares a cash flow forecast statement.
6. What are the advantages of businesses preparing cash flow statements?
7. How is it possible for a profitable business to collapse?

Key terms

Cash flow cycle - the continuous movement of cash in and out of a business.
Cash flow forecast statement - a prediction of all expected receipts and expenses of a business over a future time period which shows the expected cash balance at the end of each month.

Cash flow statement - a financial statement which shows sources and uses of cash in a trading period.
Liquid asset - an asset which is easily changed into cash.
Receivership - the liquidation (selling) of a firm's assets by an independent body following its collapse.

Case study

Superfix

Superfix operates a 24 hour repair and maintenance service for photocopying machines. The company, which was set up 3 years ago, employs four people and is based in Ealing, West London. It relies mainly on emergency calls from customers who obtain Superfix's number from *Yellow Pages* when their machines malfunction. At the moment the company faces two main problems. First, it can struggle to receive payment from customers after work has been carried out. Indeed, bad debts are common for Superfix. Second, it faces quite high labour costs because its staff are highly skilled. In addition, sometimes the staff are not gainfully employed because there are no calls. The managing director of Superfix is about to draw up the cash flow forecast statement for the next trading year. The monthly sales revenue figures are shown in Table 59.8.
- Wages are expected to be £4,000 per month.
- Motor expenses are expected to be £650 per month.
- Telephone charges are expected to be £150, £150, £170 and £170 in March, June, September and December respectively.
- Insurance is £450 and paid in July.
- Accountancy fees are expected to be £700 and will be paid in December.
- Advertising is paid twice a year in February and August, approximately £300 each time.
- An allowance of £200 per month is made for miscellaneous expenditure.
- Drawings of £1,000 per month will be made by the managing director.
- Annual ground rent of £4,000 is payable in June.
- The opening cash balance for Superfix is £850.

(a) Why do you think Superfix incurs regular bad debts?
(b) Produce a cash flow forecast statement for Superfix.
(c) How will this cash flow forecast statement help the company?
(d) Using examples from the tables, illustrate how a profitable business can still have cash flow problems.

After analysing the statement, the managing director decides that something positive must be done to improve the company's position. It is decided that Superfix will launch an insurance scheme which will be sold by a specialist salesperson directly to users. For an annual fee the insurance scheme will provide annual maintenance and free callout and labour charges for emergency calls. As a result of this scheme a number of additional cash inflows and outflows are to be expected.
- A new salesperson will be recruited at the start of April at a cost of £1,500 per month, for the rest of the year.
- Extra revenue will be generated resulting from the sale of insurance policies (May £1,000, June £1,500 July £2,000 August £2,500 September £3,000, October £3,100, November £3,200 and December £3,300).
- Motor expenses will rise by £150 per month from 1st April onwards.

(e) Produce an amended cash flow forecast statement.
(f) What effect does the new venture have on:
  (i) the cash flow;
  (ii) the profit;
  of the business?
(g) The managing director plans to introduce some new capital into the business. How much do you think it should be and when should it be introduced?

Table 59.8 *Sales revenue for Superfix, January - December (£)*

Jan	Feb	Mar	Apr	May	Jun	Jul	Aug	Sep	Oct	Nov	Dec
6,000	5,800	5,500	6,500	6,600	6,000	6,800	6,700	6,800	7,000	6,900	7,200

What is working capital?

WORKING CAPITAL (sometimes called circulating capital) is the amount of money needed to pay for the day to day trading of a business. A business needs working capital to pay expenses such as wages, electricity and gas charges, and to buy components to make products. The working capital of a business is the amount left over after all current debts have been paid. It is:

● the relatively liquid assets of a business that can easily be turned into cash (cash itself, stocks, the money owing from debtors who have bought goods or services);

minus

● the money owed by a business which needs to be paid in the short term (to the bank, to creditors who have supplied goods or services, to government in the form of tax or shareholders' dividends payable within the year).

In the balance sheet of a company (☞ unit 56) working capital is calculated by subtracting current liabilities from current assets:

Working capital = current assets - current liabilities

Working capital problems

Provided that current assets are twice the size of current liabilities, working capital is usually large enough for most businesses to avoid problems. However, if the value of current assets is less than one and a half times the size of current liabilities, a business may be short of working capital. It might then have problems meeting its immediate debts. Some businesses, such as supermarkets and retailers, can operate if their working capital is smaller than this. These businesses have a very quick turnover of goods and sales are usually for cash which prevents possible problems developing.

Cash is only part of working capital. It is possible for a business to have adequate working capital because its current assets are three times the size of its current liabilities. However, over a very short period of time it may have insufficient cash to pay its bills. It will therefore have a cash flow problem (☞ unit 59).

The working capital cycle

Managing working capital in a business is crucial. In many types of business, particularly manufacturing, delays or **time lags** exist between different stages of business activity. For example, there is a lag between buying materials and components and changing them into finished goods ready for sale. Similarly, there may be a delay between finishing the goods and the goods being sold to a customer. The

Question 1

National Power is the UK's largest generator of electricity. The company also has significant business interests overseas. Table 60.1 contains information about National Power's current assets and current liabilities.

Table 60.1 *National Power's current assets and current liabilities, 1997 and 1998*

	(£ million)	
	1998	1997
Current assets		
Stocks	167	181
Debtors: recoverable within one year	500	711
Debtors: recoverable after one year	165	170
Investments	788	330
Cash and short term deposits	281	109
	1,901	1,501
Current liabilities		
Bank loans and overdrafts	327	413
Trade creditors	76	141
Other creditors	21	13
Other taxation and social security	43	32
Corporation tax	183	169
Windfall tax	133	-
Accruals and deferred income	307	368
Dividends payable and proposed	222	234
Finance leases	23	-
	1,335	1,370

Source: adapted from National Power, *Annual Report and Accounts*, 1998.

(a) Calculate the size of National Power's working capital in 1997 and 1998.

(b) Explain whether National Power's working capital position has improved or worsened over the two years.

(c) Would the level of working capital be considered adequate in 1998? Explain your answer.

WORKING CAPITAL CYCLE, shown in Figure 60.1, helps to illustrate the intervals between payments made by a business and the receipt of cash. The cycle shows the movement of cash and other liquid resources into and out of a business.

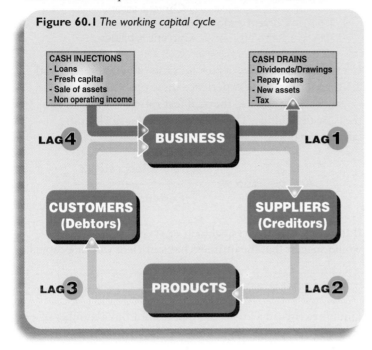

Figure 60.1 *The working capital cycle*

Time lags can occur at a number of stages in the working capital cycle.

Lag 1 Businesses usually purchase resources such as raw materials, components, fuel and other services from suppliers on credit. This means that a business can obtain resources without having to pay for them immediately. There might be a lag of up to 90 days before payment to suppliers has to be made. The length of the lag depends on suppliers' conditions. When a business is first set up, trade credit may not be granted until that business has proved to be creditworthy.

Lag 2 The next lag may occur as resources are turned into products using fixed assets, such as equipment. Work-in-progress (partially finished goods) is created and other costs are incurred, such as wages. The production process can take a long time depending on the nature of business activity. For example, for a cereal farmer this time lag could be about nine months. This would be the time it takes for corn seeds to be planted, grow into plants and eventually ripen so that the corn can be harvested. Alternatively, a furniture manufacturer might take about four to six weeks to make two armchairs and a settee for a customer.

Lag 3 Even when production is complete, a time lag can exist. Businesses may store their finished goods before they are sold to customers. This can be expensive. There may be warehousing costs and opportunity costs. However, storage enables a business to cope with unexpected increases in demand and allows continuous production. In recent years many businesses have adopted just-in-time (☞ unit 92)

manufacturing methods. Goods are only produced to order. This minimises stock holdings and reduces this time lag. When goods are distributed to customers further costs result, such as transport and handling costs.

Lag 4 A fourth time lag occurs when goods have finally been sold to customers. It is common business practice to allow customers to pay their bills over 30-90 days. However, depending on the nature of the business activity, this time lag can vary. For example, in many areas of retailing, goods are sold for cash only and this time lag is eliminated. Once cash has been collected from customers much of it is used to keep the process going, for example buying more materials and paying wages.

Figure 60.1 also shows that a business can enjoy injections of cash from sources other than the sale of products. Loans, the sale of assets and new capital are common examples. However, at the same time there will be cash drains from the business. Cash will leak from the cycle to pay dividends or drawings, to pay tax, to repay loans and to purchase new fixed assets.

Question 2

(a) (i) Arrange in order, according to the length of their working capital cycle, the activities to produce the goods or services in the photographs. Start with the longest working capital cycle and end with the shortest.
   (ii) Give reasons for the order you have chosen.
(b) Select one activity and explain the time lags that could occur in the working capital cycle.

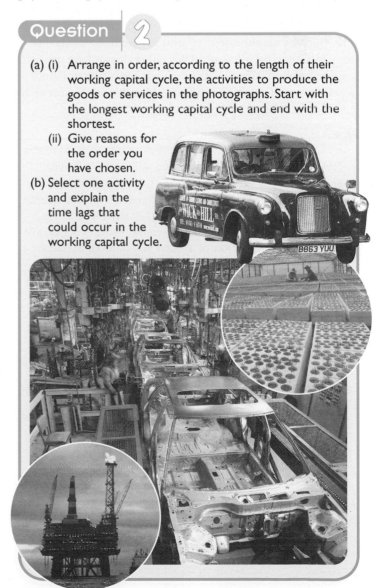

Managing working capital

The length of time lags can be crucial when managing the working capital cycle. Business managers must attempt to prolong the first time lag by delaying payments to suppliers. However, this requires careful judgment because a business would not want to damage relations with valuable suppliers. Also, if payments are delayed for too long this could cause hardship for suppliers and eventually contribute to their downfall. Managers would ideally want to reduce:

- production time;
- the storage time of finished goods before they are dispatched to customers, by reducing stock holdings or encouraging just-in-time manufacturing, for example;
- the time it takes for customers to settle their bills, by monitoring and checking late payments or offering discount for early settlement, for example.

Liquidity and profitability

Businesses that have difficulty controlling their cash flow and working capital are often said to have LIQUIDITY PROBLEMS. Liquid assets (☞ unit 59) are those assets that are easily changed into cash. They either do not have enough cash to pay immediate debts or cannot convert their liquid assets into cash quickly enough. It is possible for businesses to calculate whether they have sufficient working capital using a ratio such as the **current ratio** (☞ unit 68). This is calculated by:

$$\text{Current ratio} = \frac{\text{Current assets}}{\text{Current liabilities}}$$

If a typical business has a current ratio of between 1.5:1 and 2:1 then it should not experience these problems.

A business could use the **acid test ratio** (☞ unit 68) as a measure of liquidity. This method excludes stock from current assets as stock is not a very liquid asset.

$$\text{Acid test ratio} = \frac{\text{Current assets - stocks}}{\text{Current liabilities}}$$

If the acid test ratio is equal to 1, or very close to 1, this would suggest that the business has sufficient working capital.

Sources of liquidity problems

Liquidity crises in a business often result from a number of errors in the control of working capital.

Overtrading Young and rapidly growing businesses are particularly prone to OVERTRADING. Overtrading occurs when a business is attempting to fund a large volume of production with inadequate working capital. Established companies trying to expand can also face this problem. This was arguably one of the factors leading to the demise of Sock Shop in 1990, after expansion plans in the USA failed.

Investing too much in fixed assets In the initial stages of a business, funds are limited. Spending large amounts quickly on equipment vehicles and other capital items drains resources. It may be better to lease some of these fixed assets, leaving sufficient cash funds.

Stockpiling Holding stocks of raw materials and finished goods is expensive. Money tied up in stocks is unproductive. Stocks may become obsolete. In addition, stocks of raw materials in particular cannot be easily changed into cash without making a loss. Stock control is an important feature of managing working capital. Firms should not buy in bulk if discounts are not enough to compensate for the extra cost of holding stocks.

Allowing too much credit A great deal of business is done on credit. One of the dangers is that firms allow their customers too long for payment. This means that the firm is waiting for money and may actually be forced to borrow during this period. Failure to control debtors may also lead to bad debts. Taking early action is the key to the effective control of debtors. At the same time businesses must

Question 3

Oldbury Metal Fittings Ltd makes a wide range of metal brackets, hinges, handles and other small metal products for manufacturers in the West Midlands area. All of its products are made to order and are sold on 120 day credit terms. Most of its suppliers offer 60 day credit terms. Products are manufactured in batches of around 500 - 1,000. An order takes no more than two days to complete. On the 12.6.1999 the managing director of the company received a memo from the company accountant.

OLDBURY METAL FITTINGS LTD
MEMO

To: MD   **From:** Patricia   **Date:** 12.6.1999.

I think we should meet urgently to discuss the company's working capital. Once again the timing of payments and receipts is causing problems.

(a) Describe the nature and length of the four time lags in the working capital cycle for Oldbury Metal Fittings.
(b) Suggest why the problem in the memo has probably arisen.
(c) Explain two possible measures which might help to overcome the problem.

maintain good relations with customers. Small firms are particularly vulnerable if they are owed money by much larger companies. Powerful businesses are often accused of endangering smaller companies by delaying payments to them.

Taking too much credit Taking more credit might appear to help a firm's cash position since payments are delayed. However there are some drawbacks. Taking too much credit might result in higher prices, lost discounts, difficulties in obtaining future supplies and a bad name in the trade. At worst, credit might be withdrawn.

Overborrowing Businesses may borrow to finance growth. As more loans are taken out interest costs rise. Overborrowing not only threatens a firm's cash position, but also the overall control of the business. It is important to fund growth in a balanced way, by raising some capital from share issues. A well publicised example was the overborrowing by Robert Maxwell from the employees' pension fund of Maxwell Communications.

Underestimating inflation Businesses often fail to take inflation into account. Inflation raises costs, which can cause cash shortages. This is often the case if higher costs, such as wages or raw materials, cannot be passed on in higher prices. Inflationary periods are often accompanied by higher interest rates which place further pressure on liquid resources. Inflation is also a problem because it is difficult to predict future rates. Although it can be built into plans, firms often underestimate it.

Unforeseen expenditure Businesses are subject to unpredictable external forces. They must make a financial provision for any unforeseen expenditure. Equipment breakdowns, tax demands, strikes and bad debts are common examples of this type of emergency expense.

Unexpected changes in demand Although most businesses try to sustain demand for their products, there may be times when it falls unexpectedly. Unpredicted changes in fashion could lead to a fall in demand. This could lead to a lack of sales and cash flowing into a company. Travel companies in the UK arguably faced this problem in the early 1990s. Companies have to 'buy' holidays before they are sold. External factors, including the recession, led to many of these holidays remaining unsold as consumers changed their holiday buying patterns. Firms also lost revenue as holidays were discounted in an attempt to sell them.

Seasonal factors Sometimes trade fluctuates for seasonal reasons. In the agriculture industry, cereal farmers have a large cash inflow when their harvest is sold. For much of the year, though, they have to pay expenses without any cash flowing in. This situation requires careful management

Question 4

Airwave Gliders was established about 18 years ago and markets hang gliders and para gliders. The company is slowly returning to profit after surviving a difficult two years. It is now leaner, better-stocked and better able to cope with overseas competitors.

Problems began in the early 1990s after 12 years of stability and profit. Airwave was established as a world leader in hang gliders. It sold units for around £5,000, each largely tailor made for customers. Then para gliders arrived on the scene. They were lighter and cheaper. Airwave responded to the market change by opening a second factory and employing 30 more staff. This enabled the company to produce greater volumes. Unfortunately its profit margins fell to 30 per cent. Margins of key competitors were 45 per cent. One problem was that Airwave lacked the necessary working capital to buy sufficient materials and build up stock. This sometimes meant that customers were let down. In addition, dealers were not prepared to hold stock. Gliders came in a very wide variety of shapes, sizes, designs and colours. Customers insisted that manufacturers held large stocks.

In 1995 Airwave made a £110,000 loss on a £2.2 million turnover. Toby Parker was appointed as the new managing director and some changes followed. In 1996 Airwave began to purchase components from the Far East like its competitors. It produced about 300 hang gliders, but only 200 of the 2,000 para gliders it sold were made in-house. In 1997 it closed its second factory and reduced the total workforce to 20. In the last financial year Airwave made a £113,000 profit on a £1.8 million turnover. It took out a £200,000 loan, guaranteed by the Small Firms Loan Guarantee scheme, which provided the working capital it required to build up stock. However, it would still welcome a further £250,000 to wipe out the bank overdraft. In addition, it received two grants totalling £75,000 to help fund research and development into new materials and designs for gliders.

Source: adapted from the *Financial Times*, 14.3.1998.

(a) Suggest reasons why Airwave encountered liquidity problems.
(b) Explain how Airwave overcame its problems in the short term.
(c) Suggest how Airwave may solve its liquidity problems in the long term.

indeed, although it is possible to predict these changes.
Poor financial management Inexperience in managing cash
or a poor understanding of the working capital cycle may
lead to liquidity problems for a business.

Resolving a liquidity crisis

Liquidity problems can be prevented by keeping a tight
control on working capital. Inevitably though, there will be
occasions when firms run short of liquid resources. When
this does happen the firm's main aim will be survival rather
than profit. The following measures might be used to obtain
liquid resources.

● Stimulate sales for cash, offering large discounts if
necessary.
● Sell off stocks of raw materials - below cost if necessary.
● Sell off any fixed assets which may not be vital for
operations.
● Sell off fixed assets and lease them back.
● Mount a rigorous drive on overdue accounts.
● Sell debts to a factoring company.
● Only make essential purchases.
● Extend credit with selected suppliers.
● Reduce personal drawings from the business.
● Negotiate additional short term loans.
   In all cases, action must be taken quickly. If the firm

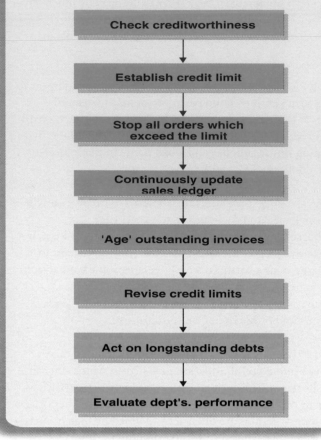

Figure 60.2 *A summary of a typical credit control procedure*

Check creditworthiness

Establish credit limit

Stop all orders which exceed the limit

Continuously update sales ledger

'Age' outstanding invoices

Revise credit limits

Act on longstanding debts

Evaluate dept's. performance

Question 5

Late payment can place a huge burden on businesses,
particularly small firms. A variety of measures have been
suggested to ease the burden. Two of these include the:
● Forum of Private Business's recommendation that there
should be a statutory right to interest on overdue
payments;
● CBI Prompt Payers Code which sets out best practice and
identifies companies which adhere to it.
   However, Richard McCrochan, Managing Director of Equifax
(UK) Ltd, believes that businesses can help themselves to a
large extent. Much of the information and tools needed to
keep customer payments up to date already exists. For
example, Equifax have launched a Windows-based credit
information access system - Prophet 1.1. This enables user-
friendly access to a wide range of Equifax information
solutions. A number of steps can be taken to improve the
working capital and cash flow position of the business. Initially
it is important to ensure that customers are creditworthy.
Extensive information is available on all limited companies and
many sole traders and partnerships. It might also be useful to
check the creditworthiness of individuals behind businesses.
Subscribers to Prophet 1.1. can cross refer to Equifax Europe's
data base which covers some 45 million individuals. Credit
ratings on businesses based on sophisticated scoring
techniques are also available. These enable small businesses to
make judgments on whether to extend credit immediately.

Subscribers to the system will also be alerted if there are
any changes to a customer's financial circumstances. This could
act as a signal for a business to speed up the collection of
outstanding payments if some negative information is received
about a customer. It has been suggested that more than half of
late payments are unintentional. Thus, an effective credit
control system could cut late payments by half. One way of
doing this is to pass all overdue invoices to a debt recovery
service run by a credit information organisation. Often no
charge is made until the outstanding debt has been recovered.
This means that the service is a no-lose arrangement. Also, the
credit information organisation's reputation will add weight to
its role as a recovery agent, while the small business is able to
maintain good relations with its customers. If more serious
action needs to be taken a debt recovery agent can carry out
a pre-check to evaluate whether court action to recover a
debt would be worthwhile.

Source: adapted from the *Manchester Evening News*, 10.7.1996.

(a) State three advantages of using the debt recovery service
described in the case.
(b) Explain what is meant by a credit rating and why it is
important to a business giving credit to a customer.
(c) Explain how the services offered by Equifax might be
helpful to a business.

survives the liquidity crisis, it is important to identify the causes and make sure it does not happen again.

Credit control

Most businesses have some sort of CREDIT CONTROL system, so that money owing can be collected quickly and easily. A 'tight' or 'easy' credit policy may be adopted. Tight credit terms may be used to improve liquidity, reduce the risk of bad debts, exploit a sellers market, or maintain slender profit margins. Easy credit terms may be designed to clear old stocks, enter a new market or perhaps help a regular customer with financial difficulties.

The company accountant and the sales manager often work closely with the credit controller, since credit policy will affect the financial position of the firm and sales. Between them they set targets for the credit control department such as the value of bad debts or the length of time it takes to collect debts.

Firms have procedures to help credit control. Figure 60.2 shows an example. Many firms will not do business with a new customer until their creditworthiness has been checked. This can be done by asking for references from a supplier, a banker's reference, or a credit rating agency's report. From this information the credit controller can set a credit limit based on the risk involved.

When an order exceeds the credit limit, the credit controller should investigate. The result may be a stop being placed on the order, a request to the customer to pay any outstanding debt, or simply allowing the order to go ahead.

Credit control records, which show customer orders and payments, must be up to date. Every month outstanding invoices must be 'aged', to identify customers who owe money over 30, 60 and 90 days.

If there are persistent debts, the credit controller must take action. A statement of the account should be sent, followed by a second one with a letter. Next a telephone call to the debtor should be followed by a personal visit. Finally, as a last resort, it may be necessary to take legal action to recover the debt.

Some firms use an independent **debt factor** (☞ unit 57) to assist in credit control. There has been quite a growth in this type of business in recent years. A factor is a business that will provide finance to a business against its debts for a fee. It often pays a certain amount to the business 'up front' and the remainder as debts are collected.

Key terms

Credit control - the process of monitoring and collecting the money owed to a business.
Liquidity - the ease with which an asset can be changed into cash.
Liquidity problems - difficulties that arise because of the lack of assets that can easily be converted into cash to make immediate payments.
Overtrading - a situation where a business attempts to raise production without increasing the size of its working capital.
Working capital - the funds left over to meet day to day expenses after current debts have been paid. It is calculated by current assets minus current liabilities.
Working capital cycle - the flow of liquid resources into and out of a business.

Summary

1. How is the value of working capital calculated?
2. At what point does a business have sufficient working capital to avoid a problem?
3. State 4 time lags that exist in the working capital cycle.
4. State 2 ways in which time lags can be reduced.
5. What is meant by a liquidity problem?
6. What does the current ratio show?
7. State 5 causes of a liquidity crisis.
8. What could a business do with its stocks of raw materials to help in a liquidity crisis?
9. What steps should a credit controller take to deal with persistent debts?
10. How might a business prevent a debt problem before it gives credit to a customer?

Case study

Torbay Cleaning Services

Torbay Cleaning Services was established in the early 1980s when two smaller businesses merged. Following the merger, the company won a number of contracts from smaller hotels to provide cleaning services. These contracts have been renewed several times since and the company has enjoyed a growing reputation for providing a quality service. In the early 1990s Torbay Cleaning Services developed new markets by extending its services to some business offices and guest houses in the region. The company is based in Torquay and employs 30 staff. The business has enjoyed modest but consistent profits since it was established. It has survived one or two difficult trading periods when new competitors threatened to take away its business.

In the last few years Torbay Cleaning Services has encountered a new problem. Nearly all of its customers are granted 60 days trade credit. However, some important customers are taking considerably longer to settle their accounts. The company does not have a credit control system and the member of staff responsible for accounts is often absent sick. As a result some of the records regarding paid and unpaid bills are incomplete. It is now becoming apparent that some customers owe money from as far back as 1997.

The managing director of the company has been asked to attend an urgent meeting with the bank manager to discuss the worsening cash position. She is aware of the problem regarding the non-payment of accounts by some customers but has very little detailed information about who owes what.

Unfortunately the accounts clerk is absent again and no one else really knows where or what to look for.

Table 60.2 *Current assets and current liabilities for Torbay Cleaning Services, 1996-1999*

				(£)
	1996	1997	1998	1999
Current assets				
Stocks and work-in-progress	3,000	3,400	4,200	3,600
Debtors	4,500	5,100	7,200	8,900
Cash at bank	1,900	200	-	-
Current liabilities				
Trade creditors	2,700	3,500	3,800	5,100
Taxation	1,700	2,200	2,300	2,400
Bank overdraft	-	-	4,200	5,800

(a) How would the business know if it had liquidity problems from the figures?

(b) How might an aged debtors schedule be helpful to the company?

(c) (i) Calculate the value of Torbay Cleaning Services' working capital for each year between 1996 and 1999.

(ii) Calculate the current ratio for each year.

(iii) Using these calculations, comment on the company's working capital position over the time period.

(d) Explain what might happen to Torbay Cleaning Services if the trend shown in Table 60.2 continues.

(e) (i) Outline the problems faced by Torbay Cleaning Services.

(ii) Suggest measures which the company might introduce to resolve the problems.

(iii) Explain how the measures you have suggested would resolve the problems.

What is budgeting?

As businesses expand the need for control grows and becomes more difficult. A small business can be run informally. The owner is the manager, who will know everyone, be aware of what is going on and will make all decisions. In larger firms work and responsibility are delegated, which makes informal control impractical. To improve control, budgeting has been developed. This forces managers to be accountable for their decisions.

A BUDGET is a plan which is agreed in advance. It must be a plan and not a forecast - a forecast is a prediction of what might happen in the future, whereas a budget is a planned outcome which the firm hopes to achieve. A budget will show the money needed for spending and how this might be financed. Budgets are based on the objectives of businesses. They force managers to think ahead and improve co-ordination. Most budgets are set for twelve months to coincide with the accounting period, but there are exceptions. Research and Development budgets, for example, may cover several years.

Information contained in a budget may include revenue, sales, expenses, profit, personnel, cash and capital expenditure. In fact, budgets can include any business variable (known as a budget factor) which can be given a value.

One very well known budget is 'The Budget'. The Chancellor of the Exchequer prepares a budget for a particular period. It will take into account the government's spending plans and how these plans will be financed by taxes and other sources of funds.

Approaches to budgeting

Budgets can be divided into different categories. Objectives budgets and flexible budgets take different approaches to planning.

- **Objectives budgets** are based on finding the best way of achieving particular objectives (☞ unit 4). They contain information on how a business will achieve these objectives. For example, a sales budget might show how a sales target will be met.
- **Flexible budgets** are designed to change as business changes. Changes in business conditions may result in very different outcomes than those budgeted for. A flexible budget takes these into account. For example, the sales budget may be altered if there is sudden increase in demand resulting in much higher sales levels.

A business will also set budgets over the long term and short term.

- **Capital budgets** plan the capital structure and the liquidity of a business over a long period of time. They are concerned with equity, liabilities, fixed and current assets and year-end cash balances.

- **Operating budgets** plan the day to day use of resources. They are concerned with materials, labour, overheads, sales and cash. There are three important operating budgets. The **profit budget** estimates the annual business costs, the year's turnover and the expected profit for the year. The **cash budget** simply plans the receipts and payments. It shows a firm its cash balance at specified times in the budget period. The **budgeted balance sheet** incorporates the budgeted profit and loss account and the closing balance in the cash budget. It also takes into account planned changes in assets and liabilities.

The preparation of budgets

The way in which a budget might be prepared is shown in Figure 61.1. It is a step by step process. The first step is to decide upon a budget period and state the objectives which are to be achieved. The budget period may vary according to the type of budget, but one month or one year is usual. Often the objectives will be set at board level. Targets for performance, market share, quality (provided it can be quantified) and productivity are all examples.

The next stage involves obtaining information upon which the budget can be based. Some information can be obtained from previous results. Historic information can be useful, although some budgetary techniques ignore the past and make a fresh start. Forecasts are another source of information. These are estimates of likely future outcomes.

Question 1

Michael Herriot is a student who works part time for a local hotel. He hopes to tour Europe in the summer holidays and is wondering whether or not he can afford the £500 cost. He draws up a budget showing his planned income and expenditure for the next ten months before the date of the proposed holiday in August.

Table 61.1 *A budget showing Michael Herriot's planned income and expenditure for a ten month period*

(£)

	Oct	Nov	Dec	Jan	Feb	Mar	Apr	May	Jun	Jul
Income	80	80	120	80	80	80	120	80	80	200
Expenditure	40	40	100	40	40	40	40	100	40	100

(a) Given the information in Table 61.1 calculate whether or not Michael can afford the proposed holiday based on his current plans.
(b) Explain how the preparation of this budget can help Michael.

Some business variables are easier to forecast than others. It is fairly easy to predict future costs, but difficult to estimate future sales. This is because sales levels are subject to so many external factors.

It is then possible to prepare two important budgets - the sales budget and the production budget. These budgets are related and affect all other budgets. For example, sales targets can only be met if there is productive capacity. Also, a firm would be unlikely to continue production if it could not sell its products. The sales budget will contain monthly sales estimates, expressed in terms of quantities per product, perhaps, and the price charged. From the sales budget, and with knowledge of stock levels, the production budget can be determined. This will show the required raw materials, labour hours and machine hours. At this stage the business should know whether or not it has the capacity to meet the sales targets. If it is not possible, then it may be necessary to adjust the sales budget.

Subsidiary operating budgets can be drawn up next. These will be detailed budgets prepared by various departments. Budgets are often broken down, so that each person in the hierarchy (☞ unit 70) can be given some responsibility for a section of the budget.

The master budget is a summary statement. It shows the estimated income, anticipated expenditure, and, thus, the budgeted profit for the period. The cash budget can also be prepared when all other budgets are complete. This budget is particularly useful since it shows the monthly flows of cash into and out of the business. It will help to show whether future cash flow problems might occur.

The final step is to prepare the projected balance sheet. This shows the financial position that will result from the firm's budgets.

Problems of preparing budgets

Business may sometimes find that there are problems when preparing budgets.

Using planned figures Problems tend to arise because figures in budgets are not actual figures. The figures are plans, which could be based on historical data, forecasts or human judgment. A business might simply take historic data and add an arbitrary percentage to arrive at the budgeted value. The most important data in the preparation of nearly all budgets is sales data. If sales data is inaccurate, many of the firm's budgets will be inexact. The accuracy of sales data might be improved if marketing research is used (☞ unit 37). However, it may be difficult to estimate sales of new products for a future period.

Collecting information The preparation of budgets is a managerial process. It requires a great deal of co-ordination. This is because different parts of the organisation provide information for budgets. Some businesses appoint a budget officer. This person is responsible for collecting data and opinions, keeping managers to the budget timetable and carrying out budgetary administration.

Time Preparing budgets can be time consuming and use up resources. The whole process can also be held up. This is because many of the major budgets, such as the master budget, cannot be prepared until other smaller budgets have been produced. A delay in approving budgets is also likely to cause problems. If budgets are prepared after the start of the time period in which they will be used, their value is reduced. To avoid delay, a business must prepare a careful timetable for their approval and stick to it.

Conflict The preparation of budgets may lead to conflict between departments or members of staff. For example, a business may only have limited funds. The marketing department may want to promote a product but new machinery may be needed in the R&D department.

Preparing a sales revenue budget

A sales revenue budget will show the planned revenue for a period of time. Emerald Artwork produces four products,

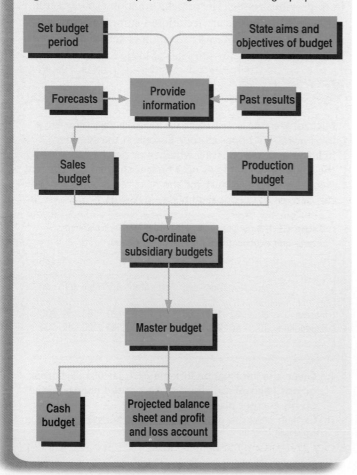

Figure 61.1 *A summary of the stages involved in budget preparation*

AD23, AD24, AE12 and AE13. They sell for £12, £20, £25 and £30 respectively. The planned sales levels for a four month period are shown in Table 61.2.

Table 61.2 *Planned sales figures for Emerald Artwork*

	FEB	MAR	APR	MAY
AD23	100	100	100	100
AD24	50	80	80	100
AE12	40	50	40	50
AE13	30	30	50	50

The sales revenue budget is prepared by showing the planned revenue in each month. This is calculated by multiplying the predicted sales levels by the prices. The sales revenue budget is shown in Table 61.3

Table 61.3 *A sales revenue budget for Emerald Artwork*

	FEB	MAR	APR	MAY
AD23	£1,200 (£12x100)	£1,200 (£12x100)	£1,200 (£12x100)	£1,200 (£12x100)
AD24	£1,000 (£20x50)	£1,600 (£20x80)	£1,600 (£20x80)	£2,000 (£20x100)
AD12	£1,000 (£25x40)	£1,250 (£25x50)	£1,000 (£25x40)	£1,250 (£25x50)
AD13	£900 (£30x30)	£900 (£30x30)	£1,500 (£30x50)	£1,500 (£30x50)
Total	£4,100	£4,950	£5,300	£5,950

A production budget

Once Emerald Artwork has produced a sales budget, it is possible to calculate its production budget. The example in Table 61.4 assumes stock levels stay the same throughout the

Table 61.4 *A production budget for Emerald Artwork covering production of all 4 products*

	FEB	MAR	APR	MAY
Cost of materials (£3 per unit)	£660 (£3x220)	£780 (£3x260)	£810 (£3x270)	£900 (£3x300)
Direct labour costs (£4 per unit)	£880 (£4x220)	£1,040 (£4x260)	£1,080 (£4x270)	£1,200 (£4x300)
Indirect labour costs (£2 per unit)	£440 (£2x220)	£520 (£2x260)	£540 (£2x270)	£600 (£2x300)
Overheads (10% of direct & indirect costs)	£1,320x10% = £132	£1,560x10% = £156	£1,620x10% = £162	£1,800x10% = £180
Total	£2,112	£2,496	£2,592	£2,880

Question 2

Williams & Son Ltd produces Christmas crackers and decorations for large retailers and other chainstores. Its small factory is based in Tamworth, Staffordshire and the production manager has produced a labour, materials and machinery budget for the next twelve months. The figures are based on the sales budget. The cost of direct and indirect labour is £5 and £4 per hour respectively. The cost of the cutting and packing machines are £10 and £20 per hour respectively.

Table 61.5 *The labour, materials and machinery budgets for Williams & Son*

Labour budget

(hours 000)

	JAN	FEB	MAR	APR	MAY	JUN	JUL	AUG	SEP	OCT	NOV	DEC
Direct labour	10	10	10	10	10	30	30	30	40	40	80	60
Indirect labour	4	4	4	4	4	6	6	6	6	6	6	6

Materials budget

(£000)

	JAN	FEB	MAR	APR	MAY	JUN	JUL	AUG	SEP	OCT	NOV	DEC
Paper & card	22	24	23	24	24	70	75	80	80	90	150	100
Other materials	10	10	10	12	12	36	38	45	45	50	80	60

Machinery budget

(hours 000)

	JAN	FEB	MAR	APR	MAY	JUN	JUL	AUG	SEP	OCT	NOV	DEC
Cutting	8	8	8	8	8	25	25	25	30	30	50	30
Packing	2	2	2	2	2	6	6	6	8	8	10	8

(a) What might be the danger of basing production budgets on sales budgets?
(b) Calculate a twelve month production cost budget for Williams & Son.
(c) Account for the pattern of monthly costs shown in your budget.

4 month period. The figures are based on expected sales in Table 61.2.

The benefits of budgets

- Budgets provide a means of controlling income and expenditure. They regulate the spending of money and draw attention to losses, waste and inefficiency.
- They act as a 'review' for a business, allowing time for corrective action.
- Budgets can emphasise and clarify the responsibilities of executives.

- They enable management to delegate responsibility without losing control, because subordinates are expected to meet budget targets which are known in advance by senior management.
- Budgets help ensure that capital is usefully employed by checking that the capital employed is consistent with the planned level of activity.
- They help the co-ordination of the business and improve communication between departments.
- Budgets provide clear targets which can be understood by personnel lower down in the organisational structure (☞ unit 70). They should also help to focus on costs.

The drawbacks of budgets

- Budgets might lead to resentment from some of the firm's personnel, particularly if they are not involved in the preparation. This could result in poor motivation and targets being missed.
- If budgets are too inflexible then it is possible that the business could suffer. For example, a member of the sales team may be prevented from finalising an overseas contract because the overseas travel budget is spent.
- If the actual business results are very different from the budgeted ones then the budget can lose its importance.

Variances

A VARIANCE is the difference between the figure that the business has budgeted for and the actual figure. Variances are usually calculated at the end of the budget period, as that is when the actual figure will be known. They can be **favourable** (F) or **adverse** (A).

Favourable variances occur when the actual figures are 'better' than the budgeted figures.
- If the sales revenue for a month was budgeted at £25,000, but turned out to be £29,000, there would be a £4,000 favourable variance (£29,000-£25,000).
- If cost were planned to be £20,000 and turned out to be £18,000, this would also be a favourable variance of £2,000, as actual costs are lower than planned.

Adverse variances are when the actual figures are worse than the budgeted figures. Actual sales revenues may be lower than planned, or actual costs may be higher than planned.

Managers will examine variances and try to identify reasons why they have occurred. By doing this they might be able to improve the performance of the business in the future. The determination and use of variances is discussed in more detail in unit 66.

Question 3

Andy Van Neuman runs AVN Ltd, a publishing business in Sandbach, Cheshire. His company publishes six specialist magazines. One magazine, *Linedancing Monthly*, was due to be published in February 1999. Andy's 1999 sales budget for the six magazines is shown in Table 61.6. Actual sales levels and the sales variances are also shown.

Table 61.6 *Sales variances for AVN Ltd, 1999*

Magazine	Budget	Actual	Variance
BigPop	120,000	97,280	22,720 A
Linedancing Monthly	60,000	140,001	80,001 F
Wine Weekly	100,000	102,900	2,900 F
Netware	50,000	56,000	6,000 F
The Speculator	76,000	76,120	120 F
Fun City	45,000	43,300	1,700 A

(a) Using the information in Table 61.6, explain what is meant by: (i) a favourable and (ii) an adverse variance.
(b) Using examples from Table 61.6, explain how this information might help Andy in future.

Key terms

Budget - a quantitative economic plan prepared and agreed in advance.
Variances - the difference between the actual value and the planned value in a budget.

Summary

1. How might a budget improve managerial accountability?
2. What is the difference between objectives budgets and flexible budgets?
3. State examples of 3 types of budget.
4. Suggest 3 problems when preparing a budget.
5. Describe the benefits of budgets.
6. Describe the drawbacks of budgets.
7. What does an adverse variance tell a business?
8. What might cause a sales variance?

Case study

Whittaker & King

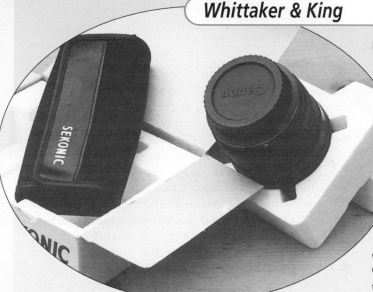

because of its commitment to research and development. The department was well ahead of the field in packaging technology. In 1999, it won a Queens Award for Industry for the development of a new packaging material. Colin Drake is the budget holder for the R&D department. In February there had been a row between Melissa and Colin. When preparing the 1999 budget, Colin had requested £83,000 for 'other R&D expenses'. Melissa asked him to justify this expenditure, since it was double that of the previous year. An allocation of £83,000 would have taken the R&D budget over half a million for the first time ever. Colin couldn't identify specific items of spending. He simply argued that: 'such expenses will be necessary if we want to win another Queens Award'. Melissa cut the item to £43,000. This kept the total below her target of half a million pounds. Table 61.7 shows the final R & D Budget for 1999. Table 61.8 shows the factory overheads budget for 1999.

Whittaker & King is a manufacturer of synthetic packaging. It supplies a range of industries with specialist plastic and polystyrene packaging. For example, it makes the protective blocks which protect electrical goods, such as computers and hi-fi systems, in transit. Its factory is based in Slough, in the M4 corridor. It employs 68 staff. The company prides itself on careful planning and strict financial control.

Profits have risen consistently in the last 4 years since Melissa Todd, a graduate of the Harvard Business School, was appointed financial director. She introduced a simple, but effective, budget system. This created 8 budget holders in the company. Each was responsible for spending in his or her own department. Melissa negotiated the budget with each budget holder in February, two months before the next financial year. Every budget holder had to justify their expenditure plans. Rarely did budget holders get the full amount they requested.

Another reason why Whittaker & King was successful was

Table 61.8 *Factory overheads budget for 1999*

	(£000)											
	JAN	FEB	MAR	APR	MAY	JUN	JUL	AUG	SEP	OCT	NOV	DEC
Rent & rates	12	12	12	12	12	12	12	12	12	12	12	12
Insurance	2	2	2	2	2	2	2	2	2	2	2	2
Cleaning	21	11	11	22	11	11	25	11	11	14	11	11
Electricity	32	30	25	20	20	20	25	30	30	20	41	38
Maintenance	1	1	1	23	1	1	1	1	1	28	1	1
Other O'heads	9	8	11	21	11	8	8	9	9	5	9	8
Total	77	64	62	100	57	54	73	65	65	81	76	72

Table 61.7 *R & D budget for 1999*

Description	£
Wages	120,000
Administration	24,000
Consumables	65,000
Equipment	230,000
Insurance	12,000
Other R & D expenses	43,000
Total	494,000

(a) Where might the information contained in the overheads budget have come from?

(b) The information in both of the above budgets could be used in other budgets. Give an example and explain why.

(c) Explain, using evidence from the case, the problems of preparing an R&D budget.

(d) Explain the: (i) benefits; and (ii) drawbacks to Whittaker & King of using budgets, using examples from the case study.

(e) In April the actual value of factory overheads was £61,000. Examine what this would mean for the business.

Recording business transactions

All businesses, whatever their size and nature, must keep records and accounts of their FINANCIAL TRANSACTIONS. At the very least, they must provide financial information for the Inland Revenue. A sole trader might use a self-assessment declaration to declare income for tax purposes. Larger companies need to provide financial information for their shareholders and for internal use, eg to show their performance.

A wide range of financial information needs to be collected if records are to be accurate. Figure 62.1 illustrates how financial information can be used and who might need it. The information may be useful to all of the stakeholders discussed in unit 4.

A self assessment tax return is a document used by sole traders, such as window cleaners, to declare their income and profit to the Inland Revenue.

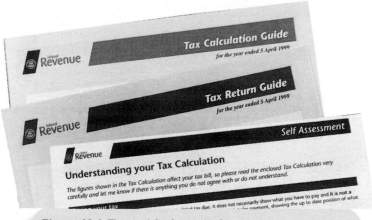

Figure 62.1 *The need for financial information*

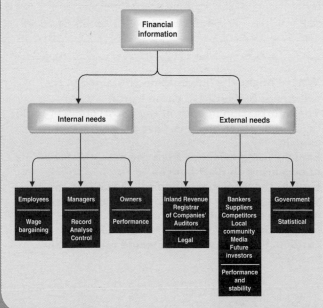

Who uses the records? - internal needs

The main users of financial information are likely to be **management**. Up to date and accurate financial data will help to improve the running of the business. It can also be used for a number of other activities.

- Recording. The values of all of a company's resources and lists of its transactions can be recorded by hand or on computer. The records can then be used to show company assets, **liabilities** and **capital**, for example. Here it is enough to say that assets are the resources of the business, such as equipment, liabilities are amounts of money owed by the business, such as a bank loan, and capital is the money introduced into the business by the owners.
- Analysis and evaluation. It is possible to evaluate the performance of the company, make comparisons with competitors and keep a record of the firm's progress over a period of time.
- Control. Financial information helps the control of money flowing in and out of the business. This becomes more important as the firm grows and the amounts of money used increase.

Employees are another group of people who might need financial information. During wage bargaining, information about the profitability, liquidity and financial prospects of the business could be used to decide if management can meet a particular wage demand.

The **owners** (internal or external, or both) will have a vested interest in the company's financial position. They will naturally assess its performance. For example, shareholders will decide whether any dividend is satisfactory or not. On the other hand, a sole trader might look at the annual profit and decide whether or not they could earn more from another activity.

Who uses the records? - external needs

Certain external parties, from time to time, need financial information about the company.

There are **legal needs** which businesses must satisfy. Every year the accounts of limited companies have to be checked by independent auditors. In addition, companies must send a copy of their final accounts to the Registrar of Companies. All businesses must declare their annual income to the Inland Revenue at the end of a trading year, so that their tax position can be assessed.

Some groups might be interested in the **performance** and **stability** of the business.

- Bankers. If a firm is trying to obtain a loan, or has already received a loan, bank managers will insist on access to records. This will allow them to assess whether the

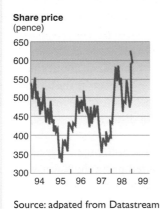

WH Smith, the high street retailer, announced its annual results in January 1999. Figure 62.2 shows a range of financial information about the business. During the year WH Smith changed its business structure, selling Virgin, Our Price, Waterstones and The Wall and acquiring Menzies, IBS and Helicon.

Source: adapted from *The Independent*, 8.1.1999.

Figure 62.2 *Financial information for WH Smith*

Market value: £1.49bn, share price 597.5p (+7.5p)

Trading record	1994	1995	1996	1997	1998
Turnover (£bn)	2.4	2.7	2.8	2.7	3.4
Profit for the year (£m)	83.4	101.0	-194.0	51.0	257.0
Earnings per share (p)	19.9	23.9	-71.4	8.6	77.0
Dividends per share (p)	15.4	10.7	15.65	15.65	20.75

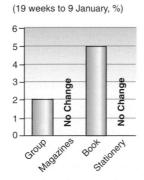

Share price (pence)

WH Smith core Chain
Sales growth by product
(19 weeks to 9 January, %)

Source: adpated from Datastream

(a) State: (i) three internal; (ii) three external potential users of the information shown in Figure 62.2.
(b) Suggest reasons why these potential users might wish to see the information.
(c) A newspaper is writing a short report on the performance of WH Smith for its financial page. Evaluate the performance of WH Smith in the form of a short newspaper article.

company can repay the loan.
● Suppliers. If a business intends to order large quantities of materials or components on credit, the supplier might wish to assess its creditworthiness.
● Competitors. It is usual for businesses to make comparisons with their rivals using financial information. Also, if a company is thinking about an aggressive takeover it can use the information to help make a decision.
● Local community. From time to time the local community might show an interest in the stability of a company, to assess employment prospects perhaps.
● Media. Newspapers and television companies, for example, often make use of financial information when reporting.
● Future investors. Companies, financial institutions and private investors may require information when deciding where to invest their funds. Venture capitalists provide sources of funds (☞ unit 57) for a business. They invest in up-and-coming businesses which they feel will do well in future.

Finally, the **government** may have an interest in a company's financial information. It employs personnel to compile statistics on output, income and employment in the economy. Much of this data is published in journals and is available to the public in libraries.

Who produces the accounts?

Accountants are responsible for supplying and using financial information. They are employed by businesses specialising in accountancy, or by large firms which have their own financial departments. Accountancy specialists sell their services to small and medium sized firms as well as self-employed individuals. They use the transactions recorded by these groups to produce final accounts. They may also advise clients on various financial matters such as taxation and investment.

Another function of these specialists is AUDITING. Businesses which produce their own final accounts must by law have them checked for authenticity by an independent firm of accountants. This audit is performed annually. Accountants also carry out internal audits of businesses. These are audits which check that internal procedures are being carried out correctly. For example, a business may audit its pension fund arrangements to prevent misuse of funds.

There are two branches of accounting - FINANCIAL ACCOUNTING and MANAGEMENT ACCOUNTING. The role of financial accountants is to make sure that a company's accounts are a 'true and fair' record of its transactions. They supervise the book-keeping process, which involves recording the value of every single business transaction. From time to time they summarise these records and convert them into statements which may be used by those parties described earlier in the unit.

Financial accountants are concerned with the past. They

Question 2

Accountants have made an increasing contribution to the running of businesses in recent years. There has been a huge growth in the number of employment opportunities in the field and the amounts of money earned by accountants have risen significantly. Figure 62.3 shows a job advertisement for an accountant placed by an agency attempting to recruit a suitable candidate for a client.

GROUP ACCOUNTING

to £50,000 + car + n/c pension

Central London

Our client is a £3 billion+ Anglo-French Group with operations throughout Europe and in the USA, manufacturing and distributing a range of premium products. The Group's decentralised structure demands strong financial controls exercised through a small high-calibre headquarters team. The Consolidation Manager now to be appointed will make a key contribution to the production of the Group's plan, budget, forecast, management and statutory consolidated financial statements. The experience and high-level exposure associated with this position will provide a valuable platform for career development within the Group.

Applicants must have a recognised UK accounting qualification and have had exposure to the organisational complexity and demanding technical standards of a large group. This could have been gained directly or through their experience in the profession. Age is not critical but future opportunities would be most appropriate for those who have qualified within the last 3-5 years.

Please write with full CV, including current salary and daytime telephone number, quoting reference 1796/FT, to Dick Phillips ACIS, Phillips & Carpenter, 2-5 Old Bond Street, London W1X 3TB. Tel: 0171-493 0156 (24 hours).

Phillips & Carpenter

Search and Selection

Figure 62.3 *Employment advert for an accountant*

(a) What type of accountant is the client seeking to employ?
(b) Suggest two possible:
   (i) characteristics for a successful applicant; and
   (ii) tasks that this type of accountant may be expected to perform.
(c) What might be the advantages and disadvantages of the business employing this type of accountant?

need to know about accounting techniques, company law, auditing requirements and taxation law. The ability to work under quite severe time pressure with a variety of personnel, at all levels in the business, is also important.

Management accountants are more concerned with the future. They do need knowledge of accounting concepts and methods, but they also require training in economics and management science. Such accountants are involved in decision making and problem solving in the business. They are responsible for producing cost and financial data, interpreting financial statements and preparing forecasts and budgets. They act as 'information servants' to the management team, but also help in planning and control.

A subsidiary of management accounting is cost accounting. Cost accountants carry out detailed costing projects. This involves working out the cost of particular business activities, such as calculating the cost of opening a new store, launching a new product or changing working practices.

Accounting concepts and conventions

The accounting process must produce accurate business statements which reflect a 'true and fair' view of a business's financial position. To achieve this, accountants use a series of accounting **concepts** and **conventions**. They allow accountants to communicate in a common language. By using agreed concepts and conventions accountants are being **objective** in their work. If every accountant attempted to use his or her own **subjective** choice of method, this would lead to confusion and misunderstanding. What are the main concepts used in accounting calculations?

Going concern Accountants assume that the business will continue for an indefinite period of time. Assets are valued as if they will continue in their present use, rather than at NET REALISABLE VALUE - the value the asset would raise if it were sold. Assets are therefore valued at the cost when they are bought, known as HISTORICAL COST. This holds even if the asset is bought at a bargain, eg half the manufacturer's recommended price. If things change, and it is necessary for the business to cease trading, assets may be valued according to what they 'might realise'. In some cases this might be less than their cost. Special accounting techniques will then be used to deal with the situation.

Accruals or matching This means that costs and revenue should be matched with the period in which they occur. For example, at the end of the trading year a company may have an outstanding electricity bill for power used in that trading period. According to this principle, the cost should be included even though the bill is unpaid. Related to this is the **realisation** concept. This states that profit occurs when goods or services change hands and not when payment is made.

Consistency Once a decision has been made about the allocation of costs or the valuation of assets it should not be changed. This will make comparisons more meaningful and reduce the chance of figures being distorted.

Prudence and caution If an asset is bought at a bargain price, rather than the recommended price, the lower value is always recorded. This conforms with the concept of **prudence** and **caution**. Accountants undervalue future revenue or profit until it is realised. In contrast, they make provision for costs or losses immediately they occur, even if they are only forecast.

Materiality Accountants should avoid wasting time trying to accurately record items of expenditure which are trivial. For example, a business might purchase a waste paper bin for the office for £1.50. This bin might last for 15 years or more. However, the bin is not a 'material' item. Even though it is expected to be used for many years the purchase should be recorded once and treated as an expense in the year it was bought. No attempt should be made to 'write off' the expenditure over the period of time the bin is in use. There is no law which governs materiality. Different firms may use a variety of arbitrary methods to determine which items of expenditure are material and which are not. For example, a business may decide that all items of expenditure under £50 should be treated as expenses in the period for which they were bought, even if some items are actually used for many years. The method of assessing materiality will be selected by accountants using their judgment.

There is also a number of common conventions which are accepted by all accountants.

Separate entity A business is a 'legal' person in its own right and has a separate identity from that of the owners. Where a sole trader, for example, uses a van for personal reasons and business, it is important to divide the running costs between the owner and the business.

Double entry Double entry accounting is a system of recording transactions. It uses the fact that there are always two sides to a transaction, ie a 'source' of funds and a 'use' of funds. This will be explored later in this unit.

Money terms When recording business transactions, it has long been common practice to record them in money terms. Money acts as a unit of account (☞ unit 1). This allows the values of goods and services to be expressed accurately and makes comparison easier. Financial statements only include those matters which can be easily expressed in money terms. For example, the skills of the workforce would not be included.

Historical cost All assets are valued according to their original cost rather than what they are currently worth. Accountants prefer to deal with values which have, in the past, been confirmed with evidence. They do not like to rely on estimates, even if the historical entries are dated. This convention has been subject to change, particularly when, due to inflation, the historical cost values become inaccurate and do not provide a true and fair view of the company's financial position.

Although the accounting process uses agreed concepts and conventions, the interpretation of business statements relies on the judgment of accountants. Therefore, it is always possible that different individuals may draw different conclusions from the same information.

Question 3

Christine Thompson runs an employment agency for nursing staff in Ealing, London. She has made an appointment with her accountant and is in the process of updating her business records in preparation for the visit. Five transactions are giving her some concern.

● One month before the end of the trading year Christine paid her annual office rent of £12,000. However, Christine decided not to include the payment in her records because nearly all of the amount related to next year.

● During the year Christine purchased the following items:
  Calculator £12; Office Kettle £9; Wall painting £8.50. These items are expected to be used by the business for many years to come and Christine wonders whether the expenditure should be 'written off' over their life, just like the office computer.

● Christine uses her car for business purposes throughout the week. However, at weekends she uses the car for personal travel. Total motor expenses for the whole year are £6,700. She is not sure how to divide the motor expenses between business and personal use.

● During the year Christine purchased a new printer for her computer which cost £400. However, she noticed that the supplier had reduced the price of the printer three months later to £199. She is not sure which value to record.

● Christine has been supplying relief nursing staff to a small private hospital in West London for 3 months, but has not yet received payment for their wages from the hospital, a total of £24,000.

(a) Explain how Christine should treat each of the above transactions according to the appropriate accounting concepts and conventions.

Recording business transactions in practice

Book-keepers are responsible for recording transactions. Many sole traders keep their own records because they cannot afford to employ book-keepers. As a firm grows, it becomes cost effective to take on a book-keeper, part time perhaps. In large businesses, with their own finance departments, book-keepers will work under the supervision of accountants.

Figure 62.4 illustrates the stages in book-keeping. When a transaction takes place, it should be verified by a **document** - an invoice, receipt or cheque stub perhaps. From these documents entries are made in the company's books. The first entries are likely to be made in the **subsidiary** books, where details of all transactions may be recorded almost as they happen. The **day books** will contain records of purchases and sales, while the **cash book** lists the flows of money into and out of the business. At the end of the month, entries in these books will be totalled and recorded in ledgers. The main purpose of these subsidiary books is to avoid overloading the ledgers.

Ledgers form the basis of any book-keeping system. A ledger contains details of individual business accounts. The **sales ledger** records transactions with customers and the **purchase ledger** records those with suppliers. The accounts of customers and suppliers are called personal accounts. All others are impersonal and are recorded in the nominal ledger. The headings in the nominal ledger might include:

- the wages account, which records the wages paid to employees;
- the purchase account, which records all business purchases from suppliers;
- the sales account, which records all business sales.

From time to time a company may wish to check that all previous entries were made correctly. This can be done by producing a TRIAL BALANCE. Finally, various accounts can be produced using the information gathered from book-keeping. The trial balance and the different accounts are discussed in the next sections.

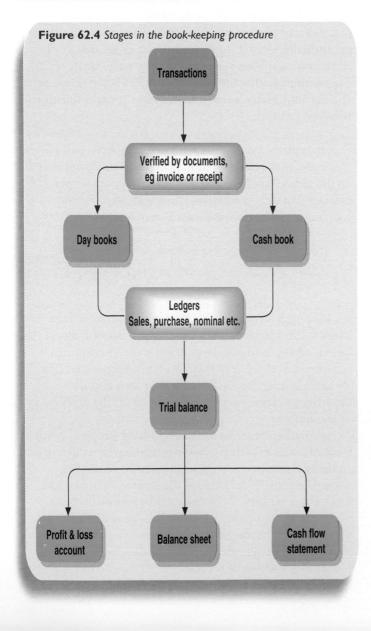

Figure 62.4 *Stages in the book-keeping procedure*

Double Entry

All businesses keep a record of their transactions. During the trading year, this could involve hundreds, thousands, or even millions of entries being made in the records. The system used today was probably developed by Luca Pacioli in the fifteenth century. It was called the 'Italian method' and forms the basis of the present DOUBLE ENTRY SYSTEM.

The term double entry comes from the principle that every transaction has two parts. For example, if you sell something you give away that item, but gain cash. In order to explain how the system works it is necessary to define two terms - **debit** and **credit**.

A debit involves an entry on the left hand side of an account, indicating a **receipt of value**. A credit is entered on the right hand side, indicating that **value has been given out**. For example, a second hand car dealer might put £20,000 of his own money into the business. Two entries are made in the records (which contain many different accounts). The cash account is debited because cash is received and the capital account is credited because capital is owed to the owner. Here we will show the effects on debits and credits simply in one table (Table 62.1).

Table 62.1 *The effect of the introduction of new capital*

Receipt/debit		Payment/credit	
Cash received from owner	£20,000	Capital owed to owner	£20,000

Similarly, what if a car was sold for £10,000? The cash account would be debited because cash was received. The sales account would be credited because the car was 'given out'. Again, we can show this more simply using one table (Table 62.2).

Table 62.2 *The effect of a car sale on the business accounts*

Receipt/debit		Payment/credit	
Cash received from owner	£20,000	Capital owed to owner	£20,000
Cash received from sale of car	£10,000	Capital sold	£10,000

We can see that every transaction has two equivalent entries in the records. Debits and credits affect a business' assets, liabilities and capital.

We can write:
Debits	- increase assets
	- decrease capital and liabilities
Credits	- decrease assets
	- increase capital and liabilities

In the above example the debit entry for the car sale increased the firm's cash balance. The credit entry has reduced the company's stock of cars. In other words, the debit entry has increased one of the assets and the credit entry has reduced another.

You will notice that the debit and credit side of the accounts are both equal (£30,000). This must be the case if equal and opposite entries are made. The advantage of this process is that it provides a self-checking facility. This is the **trial balance** mentioned in the last section. Since every transaction appears twice, when all different account balances are added (such as from the sales account, cash account, purchase account etc.), the debit total must equal the credit total. If it doesn't there must have been a mistake when recording took place.

Bank accounts treat the terms debit and credit differently. If you are overdrawn at the bank then you are said to be in debit. If there is money to withdraw, then you are in credit.

Question 4

In a four day trading period T W Norman, a second hand car dealer, recorded the following transactions:

3.7.99 Introduced £1,000 capital to fund the business venture.
3.7.99 Bought a car for resale for £600 and paid cash.
3.7.99 Bought some spare parts for £50 cash.
5.7.99 Sold the car for £850 cash.
6.7.99 Paid £100 wages to a mechanic in cash.
7.7.99 Bought a car on credit from Fast Motors Ltd for £500

(a) Produce a simple receipts and payments table to illustrate these transactions.
(b) Why must the totals on both sides be equal?
(c) Explain the effect that each transaction would have on:
  (i) assets;
  (ii) liabilities.

The Accounting Standards Board

In the past a number of concerns were raised about the lack of uniformity in accounting. The main problem was that businesses used a wide range of different methods to calculate their profit. This was confusing and made inter-firm comparisons particularly difficult. As a result the Accounting Standards Committee was formed and over a period of two decades 25 Statements of Standard Accounting Practice (SSAPs) were established. Although accountants and auditors were expected to comply with these SSAPs, some variety in presentation and interpretation was still permitted.

One example of a SSAP is SSAP 18: Accounting for Contingencies. Contingency is defined as 'a condition which exists at the balance sheet date, where the outcome will be confirmed only on the occurrence or non-occurrence of one or more uncertain events'. An example might be the outcome of legal action where the case is yet to be decided. In such a

case the treatment of a contingency profit and a contingency loss is different. If a loss can be reasonably estimated it should be included in the accounts. However, a profit should not be incorporated into the accounts. This ruling conforms with the concept of prudence and caution. In 1990 the Accounting Standards Board was set up and took over SSAPs. In addition, any new standards developed by the board are now called Financial Reporting Standards (FRSs).

The use of IT in accounts

Many businesses now use IT in their accounts department. A number of companies, such as Sage, provide fully integrated software packages which handle the whole accounting function. Such packages are very sophisticated and provided details of all transactions are entered into the system they are capable of numerous tasks. These might include:

● keeping records of transactions with all customers showing up to date balances on all accounts;
● keeping records of transactions with all suppliers showing up to date balances on all accounts;
● producing daily, weekly, monthly or annual sales figures;
● producing an aged debtors list (☞ unit 68);
● producing an aged creditors list (☞ unit 68);
● producing trial balances;
● producing profit and loss accounts;
● producing balance sheets;

Question 5

Sports UK publishes a small number of magazines aimed at the sporting industry. It has built up a solid base of customers. Many are businesses that manufacture sporting equipment. One of its most popular magazines, World Sports Technology, provides articles on developments in technology in the sporting world. Four issues are provided each year to subscribers, who renew their subscription annually. So far the accounts information has been written in files. Invoices were typed when required. It has been difficult to find out if a client had received all four issues in a year. Lapsed subscriptions and late payment have not been checked effectively.

In March 1999 the two shareholders decided to invest in a software package to handle the accounts. Keeping records of customers had become time consuming and inefficient. Four staff were employed in the accounts department. They often had to be paid overtime as a result of errors and the process used to record and check accounts. Introducing IT to handle the accounts was expected to result in a reduction in labour costs and improve the monitoring of accounts. The initial costs of the package and the training required by the staff, however, were worrying the partners.

(a) Suggest two effects that the introduction of IT might have on the staff at Sports UK.
(b) Explain the possible; (i) benefits; and (ii) problems to Sports UK of introducing IT.

● calculating staff wages and producing wages slips;
● producing stock details.

The main advantage of using IT in accounts is the speed at which tasks can be undertaken. For example, at the end of a day's trading a business can produce financial documents almost instantaneously. It is also possible to 'call up' financial information on screen if required. The checking of numerical information is also easier and more accurate. In addition, access to up to date financial information can help a business to make more effective decisions.

However, it does not eliminate operator error. Inputting of incorrect data can lead to problems. Extreme care must be taken that work carried out every day is 'backed up' or saved onto disk, or it could be lost if there was a computer or power failure. Computers can also suffer from viruses that destroy information. Virus correction software can be used to solve this problem. One problem facing businesses in the year 2000 is the 'Millennium bug'. Computer systems are usually run on two digits, so that 1999 is represented as 99 for example. If 00 is inputted instead of 2000, however, the machine will interpret this as 1900 and not 2000.

Business statements

At the end of a trading year all businesses produce final accounts. These are the result of the process shown in Figure 62.4. A balance sheet and a profit and loss account generally form the basis of these accounts, although public limited companies publish a full annual report which contains a wider range of financial statements and reports.

Balance sheet A balance sheet provides information about the company's funds and how they are used in the business (☞ unit 56). It lists the assets, liabilities and capital of the business and, to some extent, shows the wealth of the company. A balance sheet describes the financial position of a business at a particular point in time.

Profit and loss account The profit and loss account provides a summary of the year's trading activities, stating the revenue from sales (the turnover), business costs, profit/loss and how the profit is used (☞ unit 55).

Cash flow statement From 1992 onwards companies were required to produce cash flow statements in their accounts. A cash flow statement shows the flows of cash into and out of a business in a trading year (☞ unit 59).

Notes to the accounts The balance sheet and profit and loss account show summarised information. 'Notes to the accounts' are a more detailed analysis of some entries in these statements.

Directors' report This statement, written by the directors, is required by law. It contains information which might not be shown in other financial statements, such as the number of employees, changes of personnel on the board of directors and any special circumstances arising.

Chairperson's statement One of the chairperson's roles is to communicate with the shareholders. She can do this by making a statement in the annual report. The chairperson discusses the company's general performance and comments on events during the trading year which might be of interest to the shareholders. Future prospects are also discussed and shareholders are encouraged to remain loyal to the company.

Auditor's report Auditors must make a brief report to confirm that the accounts give a 'true and fair view' of the firm's financial position, assuming, of course, that they do!

Statistics Companies often include tables and graphs in their annual report. They can be used to illustrate trends and comparisons. They might show turnover, profit, dividends or earnings per share, for example.

Summary

1. Why is it so important for management to have access to financial information?
2. List all potential users of accounts and state whether they are internal or external.
3. What might be the role of a management accountant in a business?
4. What are the fundamental concepts and conventions which aim to make the accounts a 'true and fair view' of the firm's financial position?
5. Why are concepts and conventions needed in accounting?
6. Explain how a double entry system of book-keeping 'balances'.
7. Define the terms 'debit' and 'credit' in double entry accounting.
8. What is the difference between day books and ledgers?
9. What is the function of the trial balance?
10. What is the function of the Accounting Standards Board?
11. Suggest two advantages and two disadvantages of using IT in the accounting process.
12. List the financial statements which might appear in the annual report of a public limited company.

Key terms

Auditing - an accounting procedure which checks thoroughly the authenticity of a company's accounts.

Double entry system - a recording system which enters every business transaction twice in the books, once as a debit and once as a credit.

Financial transactions - payments made when buying goods and services and money received from selling them.

Financial accounting - the preparation of company accounts from business records.

Historical cost - the value of an asset when purchased, ie the amount paid.

Management accounting - the preparation of financial statements, reports and data for use by managers.

Net realisable value - the value of an asset when sold, ie the amount received.

Trial balance - a statement which lists all the balances on all the accounts in the double entry system.

Case study

PizzaExpress PLC

PizzaExpress PLC provides 'high quality food served with style in an attractive environment'. In 1999 it aimed to have over 200 company-owned PizzaExpress restaurants in the UK. It also operates franchises abroad in Egypt, France and India, and in June 1998 acquired Cafe Pasta Limited and the Cafe Pasta restaurants.

Source: adapted from PizzaExpress PLC, *Annual Report and Accounts*, 1998.

Chairman's Statement

PizzaExpress continues to move steadily from strength to strength and we are now in our 33rd year of growth. The company continues to operate on guidelines established by our founder Peter Boizot MBE in 1965. Excellent pizze, good value pricing, friendly and efficient service in clean attractive restaurants. These operating principles are enhanced by a strong management team and staff with many years experience and ability in depth. The 32 previously franchised restaurants we acquired in November 1996 have now been fully integrated.

New sites have been acquired which will ensure organic growth from the present 179 UK company owned pizza restaurants to over 200 by June 1999.

Our ongoing strategy is to maintain and improve every facet of our business. We aim to serve the best pizza and provide the best service possible in our interesting and individually designed restaurants.

These qualities lead to high customer loyalty and satisfaction. In a January 1998 survey 71% of our customers ate at PizzaExpress at least once a month and 92% thought our pizze were superior to those of any other pizza restaurant, whether owned by a chain or an independent operator. Our progress is built upon this solid, reliable, repeat customer business. In tandem with these operating attributes and steady volume increases we aim to provide a superior investment by achieving a high return on capital and stable margins. We now have a five year record of expansion since flotation and our objective is to sustain all our growth characteristics in

the coming years.

In May we started trading from three locations as Pasta di Milano, which is a new restaurant operation with a single menu serving freshly prepared pasta dishes.

In June we acquired Café Pasta Limited, a business with a similar culture and customer base to PizzaExpress. We trade alongside each other in several existing locations and our restaurants are complimentary rather than competitive. This concept has the potential to markedly increase its number of outlets throughout the UK.

In June we also purchased two of our previously franchised PizzaExpress restaurants in West Didsbury in Manchester and Blackheath in London.

Early indications of trade in these new and acquired businesses give us cause for cautious optimism and we expect them to be earnings enhancing in the financial year ending June 1999.

There has been recent speculation about what impact a slowdown in the economy could have on restaurant businesses. There have been three recessions in the UK since 1965 and our previous experience was that like for like sales growth slowed but remained positive. During an economic slowdown there are also more opportunities for new sites at lower rents and reduced building costs.

Nigel Colne CBE was recently appointed as a non-executive director. We now have three non-executives and are looking for one more individual to complete the balance of the board.

David Page
Chairman   21 September 1998

Report of the Auditors to the Members of PizzaExpress PLC

We have audited the financial statements on pages 14 to 29 which have been prepared under the historical cost convention and accounting policies set out on page 18.

Respective responsibilities of directors and auditors

As described on page 12 the Company's directors are responsible for the preparation of financial statements. It is our responsibility to form an independent opinion, based on our audit, on those statements and to report our opinion to you.

Basis of opinion

We conducted our audit in accordance with Auditing Standards issued by the Auditing Practices Board. An audit includes examination, on a test basis, of evidence relevant to the amounts and disclosures in the financial statements. It also includes an assessment of the significant estimates and judgements made by the directors in the preparation of the financial statements, and of whether the accounting policies are appropriate to the Company's circumstances, consistently applied and adequately disclosed.

We planned and performed our audit so as to obtain all the information and explanations which we considered necessary in order to provide us with sufficient evidence to give reasonable assurance that the financial statements are free from material misstatement, whether caused by fraud or other irregularity or error. In forming our opinion we also evaluated the overall adequacy of the presentation of information in the financial statements.

Opinion

In our opinion, the financial statements give a true and fair view of the state of affairs of the Company and the Group as at 30 June 1998 and of the profit and cash flows of the Group for the year then ended and have been properly prepared in accordance with the Companies Act 1985.

PricewaterhouseCoopers
Chartered Accountants and Registered Auditors
1 Embankment Place
London WC2N 6NN

21 September 1998

Notes to the Financial Statements

Dividends and earnings per share	1998	1997
	£'000	£'000
Ordinary - interim paid 6 April 1998 - 1.05p per share (1997: 0.85p)	696	558
Ordinary - final proposed - 3.2p per share (1997: 2.5p)	2,137	1,656
	2,833	2,214

Contingent right to the allotment of shares

Details of outstanding executive share options for employees to subscribe for ordinary shares of 10p each are:

Subscription price per share £	Date granted	Period within which options are exercisable	Number of shares for which rights are exercisable	
			1998	1997
0.42	Mar 1993	Mar 1996 - Mar 2000	200,000	200,000
1.28	Mar 1994	Mar 1997 - Mar 2001	20,000	60,000
2.17	Jan 1996	Jan 1999 - Mar 2003	520,000	530,000
3.50	May 1996	May 1999 - Mar 2003	175,000	185,000
4.99	Dec 1996	Dec 1999 - Mar 2003	530,000	530,000
6.775	May 1997	May 2000 - May 2004	455,000	485,000
7.456	Nov 1997	Nov 2000 - Nov 2004	100,000	-

Group Balance Sheet

as at 30 June 1998

	1998	1997
	£'000	£'000
Fixed assets		
Tangible assets	65,429	42,739
Investments:		
In subsidiary undertakings	-	-
In joint ventures	55	-
Other	267	533
	65,751	43,272
Current assets		
Stocks	4,086	3,362
Debtors	6,497	4,994
Cash at bank and in hand	5,382	6,812
	15,965	15,168
Creditors: amounts falling due after more than one year	(40,400)	(28,348)
Net current (liabilities) assets	(24,435)	(13,180)
Total assets less current liabilities	41,316	30,092
Creditors: amounts falling due after more than one year	(3,076)	(112)
Provisions for liabilities and charges	(378)	(470)
	37,862	29,510
Capital and reserves		
Called up share capital	6,919	6,783
Share premium reserve	35,911	35,789
Profit and loss account	39,470	24,267
Goodwill reserve	(44,438)	(37,329)
Shareholders' funds (including non-equity interests)	37,862	29,510

(a) (i) What is the function of the chairperson's statement?

(ii) Describe the performance and outlook which the chairman of PizzaExpress PLC is trying to convey.

(b) (i) Suggest three stakeholders who might be interested in the information presented in the accounts and the type of information that may be of interest to them.

(ii) Explain why the information might be of interest to these groups.

(c) (i) Why do you think that the Report of the Auditors is a legal requirement?

(ii) Identify the factors that may have influenced the accountants when preparing the accounts of Pizza Express PLC.

(ii) Explain how these factors might have been important when producing the accounts in 1998.

How are assets valued?

One of the problems in financial accounting is how to place a value on assets. Unit 62 stated that accountants value assets at **historical cost**, ie the cost of the asset when it is first purchased.

There are reasons why assets should be valued in this way. Business transactions are entered into records as they occur. For example, if a firm buys a vehicle for £15,000 and pays cash, two entries will be made in the records. Also, accountants would argue that historical cost can be checked. It is based on actual costs and is better than methods which involve estimates. Other methods of valuation, such as those which take into account inflation, are also used. As yet, though, a suitable replacement has not been found.

One problem with historical cost accounting is how to put a value on fixed assets like property. In recent years there have been times when the values of land and buildings have risen sharply - as much as 30 or 40 per cent in one year. Unless the accounts are amended, they will not reflect the true value of the business. It is common now to revalue assets such as property every few years. Inflation distorts the value of assets and any other value which is measured in money terms.

This unit considers the valuation of two sets of assets - fixed assets, such as machinery, and current assets, such as stock. The valuation of these assets causes particular problems for accountants.

Valuing fixed assets - the use of depreciation

Fixed assets are used again and again over a long period of time. During this time the value of many assets falls. This is called **depreciation** (☞ unit 56). Figure 63.1 shows the reasons why the value of assets might fall.

Question 1

Seton Healthcare Group PLC manufactures and supplies over-the-counter therapy products. Some of its most well known brands include Resolve, Diocalm, Gripewater, Earex and Paramol.

Table 63.1 *An analysis of Seton's tangible assets*

	Land and buildings £'000	Plant and equipment £'000	Motor vehicles £'000	Total £'000
Cost At end of year	19,177	33,361	1,324	53,862
Depreciation At end of year	2,643	14,937	554	18,134
Net book value At 28th Feb. 1998	16,534	18,424	770	35,728

Source: adapted from Seton Healthcare Group plc, *Annual Report and Accounts*, 1998.

(a) What is the total depreciation provision for 1998?
(b) Using the information in Table 63.1, explain what is meant by the term 'net book value'.
(c) Suggest possible reasons why Seton's assets have depreciated.
(d) Which of Seton's assets have depreciated the most? Explain your answer.

● Some assets fall in value because they wear out. Vehicles, machinery, tools and most equipment all deteriorate when used, and have to be replaced. Figure 63.2 shows the value of different cars depreciate at different rates. Some cars lose their values faster than others. Note that over seven

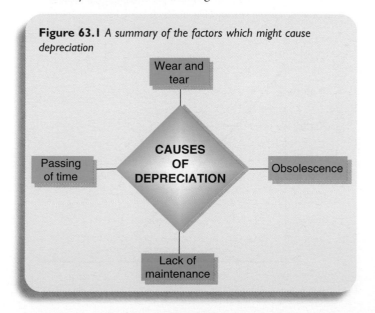

Figure 63.1 *A summary of the factors which might cause depreciation*

Wear and tear

Passing of time

CAUSES OF DEPRECIATION

Obsolescence

Lack of maintenance

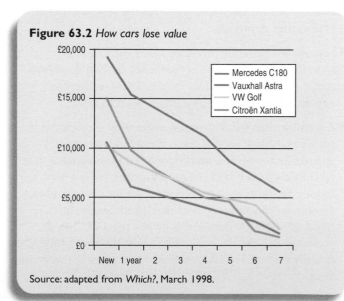

Figure 63.2 *How cars lose value*

Mercedes C180
Vauxhall Astra
VW Golf
Citroën Xantia

New 1 year 2 3 4 5 6 7

Source: adapted from *Which?*, March 1998.

years the value of the Mercedes C180 falls by around 68 per cent. The value of the lower priced Citroën Xantia falls by around 87 per cent.

● Changing technology can often make assets OBSOLETE. Although a machine may still work, it may not be used because a new machine is more efficient.
● Capital goods which are hardly used or poorly maintained may loose value quickly. The life of machinery can be prolonged if it is 'looked after'.
● The passing of time can also reduce the value of assets. For example, if an asset is leased, the 'buyer' can use the asset for a period of time. As the expiry date gets close, the lease becomes worth less and less.

Depreciation and the accounts

Each year accountants must work out how much depreciation to allow for each fixed asset. This can then be used in the balance sheet and the profit and loss account.

The balance sheet (☞ unit 56) will show the BOOK VALUE of assets. This is their original value minus depreciation. So if a piece of machinery is bought for £10,000 and depreciates by £3,000 in the first year, its book value would be £7,000. The book value falls each year as more depreciation is deducted.

Depreciation is shown in the profit and loss account under expenses (☞ unit 55). This indicates that part of the original value is 'used up' each year (known as revenue expenditure (☞ unit 57). Eventually the entire value of the asset will appear as expenses, when the asset depreciates fully. This process of reducing the original value by the amount of depreciation is known as WRITING OFF.

There are good reasons why a firm should allow for depreciation each year in its accounts.

● If it does not, the accounts will be inaccurate. If the original value of assets was placed on the balance sheet this would overstate the value. The value of assets falls each year as they depreciate.

● Fixed assets generate profit for many years. It seems logical to write off the value of the asset over this whole period, rather than when it is first bought. This matches the benefit from the asset more closely with its cost.

● A sensible firm will know that assets must be replaced in future and allow for this. Even though depreciation appears as an expense on the profit and loss account, it is actually a PROVISION. Expenses involve paying out money. In the case of depreciation, no money is paid out. A business simply recognises that assets have to be replaced and provides for this by placing a value in the accounts. In practice, it is unlikely that the firm would actually put money aside each year to replace the worn out asset.

Calculating depreciation - the straight line method

The STRAIGHT LINE METHOD is the most common method used by business to work out depreciation. It assumes that the net cost of an asset should be written off in equal amounts over its life. The accountant needs to know the cost of the asset, its estimated residual value, ie its 'scrap' value after the business has finished with it, and its expected life in years. The formula used is:

$$\text{Depreciation allowance (each time period)} = \frac{\text{Original cost - residual value}}{\text{Expected life (years)}}$$

Assume a delivery van costs £28,000 to buy and has an expected life of 4 years. The residual value is estimated at £4,000.

$$\text{Depreciation allowance} = \frac{£28,000 - £4,000}{4 \text{ years}}$$

$$= \frac{£24,000}{4}$$

$$= £6,000$$

Table 63.2 *A summary of the annual depreciation allowance and book value of the van using the straight line method*

Year	Depreciation allowance (each year) £	Net book value £
1	6,000	22,000
2	6,000	16,000
3	6,000	10,000
4	6,000	4,000

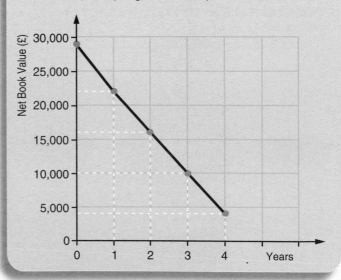

Figure 63.3 *A graph illustrating the book value of the delivery van over its lifetime (straight line method)*

When calculating depreciation it is helpful to draw up a table to show how an asset is written off over its lifetime. Table 63.2 shows the depreciation allowance charged to the profit and loss account each year, and the net book value which is listed in the balance sheet. We can illustrate this on a graph as shown in Figure 63.3. These are some advantages to using this method.

● It is simple. Little calculation is needed and the same amount is subtracted from the book value each year.
● It is useful for assets like a lease, where the life of the asset and the residual value is known precisely.

Question 2

Karren Jennings runs a haulage company in Stafford. She operates from a depot one mile from Junction 15 on the M6. She owns 12 articulated lorries and employs 19 staff. At the beginning of the financial year in 1999 she bought a new lorry for £90,000. Karren expects to use the lorry for 6 years, when it will have a residual value of £12,000.
(a) Calculate the annual depreciation allowance using the straight line method.
(b) Draw up a table to show how the lorry is written off over its life.
(c) What is the book value of the lorry at the end of year 4?
(d) (i) Draw a line graph to show the annual book value over the life of the lorry.
(ii) What is the book value of the lorry after 2.75 years? Read the answer from your graph.

Calculating depreciation - the reducing balance method

The REDUCING BALANCE METHOD assumes that the depreciation charge in the early years of an asset's life should be higher than in the later years. To do this, the asset must be written off by the same percentage rate each year. This means the annual charge falls.

Assume a vehicle is bought for £28,000 and has a life of four years. Table 63.3 shows how the vehicle can be written off using the reducing balance method. A 40 per cent charge will be made each year and the firm expects a **residual value** of £3,629.

Table 63.3 shows the depreciation allowance in the profit

Table 63.3 *A summary of the annual depreciation allowance and book value of the van using the reducing balance method*

Year	Depreciation allowance (each year) £	Book value £
1	11,200 (28,000 x 40%)	16,800
2	6,720 (16,800 x 40%)	10,080
3	4,032 (10,080 x 40%)	6,048
4	2,419 (6,048 x 40%)	3,629

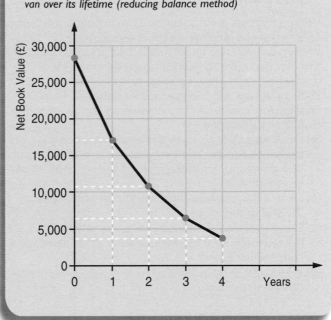

Figure 63.4 *A graph illustrating the book value of the delivery van over its lifetime (reducing balance method)*

and loss account in each of the four years. It also shows the book value which would be listed in the balance sheet. Notice that the depreciation allowance falls every year. This is shown in Figure 63.4. What if the business expected the residual value to be £4,000? The depreciation charge for this can be calculated using the formula:

$$\text{Depreciation rate} = \left[1 - \sqrt[n]{\frac{\text{Residual value}}{\text{Cost}}} \right] \times 100$$

Where n = estimated life of the asset, ie 4 years, so:

$$\text{Depreciation rate} = \left[1 - \sqrt[4]{\frac{4,000}{28,000}} \right] \times 100 = 38.52\%$$

There are some advantages to using the reducing balance method.

● It takes into account that some assets, machinery for example, lose far more value in the first year than they do in the fifth year, say. So the book value reflects more accurately the real value of the asset in the balance sheet.
● For many assets, maintenance and repair costs grow as the asset ages. Using the declining balance method results in a more equal total expense each year for fixed assets related costs. For example, at the end of year 1 the depreciation charge for a machine might be £4,500 with only a £500 maintenance charge. In year 5 the depreciation charge might have been £1,500 and repairs and maintenance may have been £3,000. Although the two totals are not the same (£5,000 and £4,500), as the depreciation charges fall the maintenance and repair costs rise.

William Marshall owns an arable farm in Suffolk. He farms 6,000 acres and employs 4 staff. In the summer of 1999 William decided that he was no longer prepared to lease a combine harvester to harvest his cereal crops. He purchased a brand new combine harvester for £75,000. With good care and maintenance he hoped to keep the machine for 5 years. (After five years a residual value of £5,832 was estimated.)

(a) Draw up a table to show the annual depreciation allowance and the book value at the end of each year. Use the reducing balance method and write off 40 per cent each year.

(b) Draw a line graph to show the annual book value at the end of each year.

(c) Explain why the reducing balance method of depreciation might be more suitable for an asset like a combine harvester.

(d) Why might William Marshall have chosen a discount rate of 40 per cent?

Other methods of calculating depreciation

The **sum-of-the-years' digits method** assumes that fixed assets depreciate quicker in the early years. The calculation is based on the sum-of-the-years' digits, given the expected life of an asset, less the residual value. For an asset which has an expected life of 4 years the sum-of-the-years' is 10, ie 4+3+2+1 = 10. The depreciation charge for the first year will be $4/10$ of the original cost, the second year it will be $3/10$ of the original cost and so on.

Assuming a cost of £28,000, a life span of 4 years and a residual value of £4,000, the **net value** of the asset is £24,000 (£28,000 - £4,000). We can draw up a table to show the annual depreciation charge and the book value each year (Table 63.4).

Table 63.4 *A summary of the annual depreciation allowance and book value of the asset above, using the sum-of-the-years' digits method*

Year	Depreciation allowance (each year)	Book value
	£	£
1	9,600 (24,000 x 4/10)	18,400
2	7,200 (24,000 x 3/10)	11,200
3	4,800 (24,000 x 2/10)	6,400
4	2,400 (24,000 x 1/10)	4,000

From Table 63.4 we can see that the depreciation allowance falls in a similar way to the reducing balance method.

Another method called the **usage method** (or **machine hour method**) takes into account that some assets wear out more rapidly the more they are used. Thus, depreciation is based on the number of hours a machine, for example, is used

during the accounting period. It is not a method that is often used by firms.

The disposal of assets

The book value of assets very rarely reflects their true value. So if an asset is sold, a business usually makes a profit or a loss. This is likely if the asset is sold before the end of its expected life. For example, if a machine is bought for £100,000 with an expected life of 10 years and residual value of £15,000, the depreciation allowance each year will be £8,500 (using the straight line method). If the firm decides to sell the machine at the end of year 7 and receives £44,000, it earns a profit of £3,500 because the book value at the end of year 7 is £40,500. A firm must show this in the accounts. It is common practice to deal with profit or loss on disposal by adjusting that year's depreciation charge. If a profit is made, the depreciation charge will be reduced by the amount of the profit. If a loss is made, the depreciation charge will be increased by the amount of the loss. If the profit or loss is very large then it will be treated as an exceptional item in the accounts (☞ unit 55).

Venetta Gains runs a design business in Cheltenham. Due to the rapid growth in her business in areas such as fabric design, she has decided to buy a new computer. She spent £5,000 on a system which would include a software design package. Venetta planned to use the computer for 8 years, by which time it would have a scrap value of £200.

(a) Calculate the annual depreciation allowance using the straight line method and draw up a table to show the book value at the end of each year.

(b) At the end of the third year Venetta was forced to upgrade her system because it had become outdated. Venetta sold her old system for £1,000. Calculate the profit or loss on disposal.

(c) Comment on the size of the profit/loss.

Valuing current assets - stock valuation

When accounts are produced, a firm must calculate the quantity and value of the stocks which it is holding. The value of **stocks** at the beginning and the end of the trading year, ie the **opening stock** and the **closing stock**, will affect the gross profit for the year. This is because the cost of sales in the trading account is adjusted for changes in stock. If, for example, the closing stock is overvalued, then the cost of sales will be lower and the gross profit higher. This is shown in Tables 63.5 and 63.6. In Table 63.5 the closing stock is

Table 63.5

	£	£
Turnover		97,900
Opening stock	12,300	
Cost of sales	56,400	
	68,700	
Less closing stock	11,300	
		57,400
Gross profit		40,500

Table 63.6

	£	£
Turnover		97,900
Opening stock	12,300	
Cost of sales	56 400	
	68,700	
Less closing stock	14,100	
		54,600
Gross profit		43,300

£11,300, the cost of sales (adjusted for stock) is £57,400 and gross profit is £40,500.

In Table 63.6 the closing stock is now valued at £14,100 instead of £11,300, so the cost of sales (adjusted for stock) is lower at £54,600 and the gross profit higher at £43,300.

A **stock take** can be used to find out how much stock is held. This involves making a list of all raw materials, finished goods and work-in-progress. Stock valuation is more difficult. The 'prudence' concept in accounting (☞ unit 62) does not allow selling prices to be used because profit is only recognised when a sale has been made. So stocks are valued at historic cost or net realisable value, whichever is the lowest. Normally stocks would be valued at cost. But there are circumstances when net realisable value is lower. If goods are damaged in stock, they may sell for a lot less than they cost to produce. Also, some products face severe changes in market conditions. Clothes tend to fall in value when fashions change, and may need discounts to sell them.

What happens to stock valuation when the cost of stock changes over time? Say a business buys some goods at the start of the year, but finds that half way through their cost of replacement has gone up. How are they valued? Three methods can be used.

● FIFO (first in first out).
● LIFO (last in first out).
● Average cost.

First in first out

The FIRST IN FIRST OUT method assumes that stock for production is issued in the order in which it was delivered. Thus, stocks that are bought first are used up first. Any unused stocks at the end of the trading year will be those most recently bought. This ensures that stocks issued for production are priced at the cost of earlier stocks, while any remaining stock is valued much closer to the replacement cost. Assuming that the opening stock is zero, consider the following stock transactions in Table 63.7.

On 1.6.98 a business receives 100 units of stock at £5, which means it has £500 of goods in stock. On 4.6.98, an extra 200 units at £6 (£1,200) are added, making a total of £1,700. On 25.6.98, 100 units are issued from stock for production. As it is first in first out, the goods are taken from the 1.6.98 stock, priced at £5 - the first stock to be received. This means £500 is removed from stock leaving 200 units valued at £6 (£1,200) left in stock.

By using the FIFO method, the value of stocks after all the transactions is £650.

Table 63.7 *A record of stock transactions showing how a closing stock figure is calculated using the FIFO method of stock valuation*

Date	Stock received and price	Stock issued and price	Stock valuation Goods in stock	Total £
01.6.98	100 @ £5		(100 @ £5 = £500)	500
04.6.98	200 @ £6		(100 @ £5 = £500) (200 @ £6 = £1,200)	1,700
25.6.98		100 @ £5	(200 @ £6 = £1,200)	1,200
02.7.98		100 @ £6	(100 @ £6 = £600)	600
12.7.98	200 @ £6.50		(100 @ £6 = £600) (200 @ £6.50 = £1,300)	1,900
23.7.98		100 @ £6	(200 @ £6.50 = £1,300)	1,300
24.7.98		100 @ £6.50	(100 @ £6.50 = £650)	650

Table 63.8 *A record of stock transactions showing how the closing stock figure is calculated using the LIFO method of stock valuation*

Date	Stock received and price	Stock issued and price	Stock valuation	
			Goods in stock	Total
				£
01.6.98	100 @ £5		(100 @ £5 = £500)	500
04.6.98	200 @ £6		(100 @ £5 = £500) (200 @ £6 = £1,200)	1,700
25.6.98		100 @ £6	(100 @ £5 = £500) (100 @ £6 = £600)	1,100
02.7.98		100 @ £6	(100 @ £5 = £500)	500
12.7.98	200 @ £6.50		(100 @ £5 = £500) (200 @ £6.50 = £1,300)	1,800
23.7.98		100 @ £6.50	(100 @ £5 = £500) (100 @ £6.50 = £650)	1,150
24.7.98		100 @ £6.50	(100 @ £5 = £500)	500

Last in first out

The LAST IN FIRST OUT method assumes that the most recent deliveries are issued before existing stock. In this case, any unused stocks are valued at the older and probably lower purchase price. Table 63.8 shows how the previous transactions are adjusted for a LIFO stock valuation. On 1.6.98, 100 units of stock are received at £5, meaning £500 of goods are in stock. On 4.6.98 an extra 200 units of stock valued at £6 are added (£1,200) - a total of £1,700. When 100 units of stock are issued on 25.6.98 they are taken from the most recent (last) stock received, priced at £6. So £600 of stock is removed. This leaves 100 units at £5 and 100 units at £6 in stock - a total of £1,100.

This time the value of stocks remaining after the transactions is £500. If the value of stocks is rising, the LIFO method gives a lower finishing stock than the FIFO method.

Average cost

This method involves recalculating the average cost (AVCO) of stock every time a new delivery arrives. Each unit is assumed to have been purchased at the **average price** of all components. In practice the average cost of each unit is a weighted average and is calculated using the following formula:

$$\frac{\text{Existing stock value + value of latest purchase}}{\text{Number of units then in stock}}$$

Using the same stock transactions as before we can find the closing stock by drawing up Table 63.9. This time the weighted average cost method is used.

When the AVCO method is used the value of stock following the transactions is £622. This stock figure lies closer to the FIFO method of stock valuation. It is often used when

Table 63.9 *A record of stock transactions showing how the closing stock is calculated using the weighted average cost method of stock valuation*

Date	Receipts	Issues	Weighted average cost £	Stock valuation	Total £
01.6.98	100 @ £5		5.00	(100 @ £5 = £500)	500
04.6.98	200 @ £6		5.67	(300 @ £5.67 = £1,701)	1,701
25.6.98		100	5.67	(200 @ £5.67 = £1,134)	1,134
02.7.98		100	5.67	(100 @ £5.67 = £567)	567
12.7.98	200 @ £6.50		6.22	(300 @ £6.22 = £1,866)	1,866
23.7.98		100	6.22	(200 @ £6.22 = £1,244)	1,244
24.7.98		100	6.22	(100 @ £6.22 = £622)	622

stock prices do not change a great deal. In practice it is the FIFO and average cost methods which are most commonly used by firms. Once a method has been chosen it should conform with the 'consistency' convention and not change. This is also true for calculating depreciation.

Inflation accounting

Inflation could cause quite serious problems when valuing assets. Inflation causes the value of assets to rise, whilst a balance sheet would show them at historical cost. During periods of very high inflation the effects can be quite serious. Profit may be overstated. This may lead to dividend payments and wage settlements which are too high, and inadequate funds to replace worn out assets. Any value which is measured in money terms will be distorted. During the 1970s, when inflation was over 20 per cent for a time, the problem was given a great deal of thought by accountants. Two possible solutions were suggested - constant purchasing power accounting and current cost accounting.

Constant purchasing power accounting (CPP) During periods of high inflation, measuring values in terms of money becomes unreliable. CONSTANT PURCHASING POWER ACCOUNTING replaces money values with an index of general purchasing power, ie the Retail Price Index (☞ unit 23). All transactions measured in money terms are translated into 'units of constant purchasing power', depending on the date when they took place. There are two main advantages of this method.
● It reflects the general increase in the price of goods and services.
● Since shareholders spend dividends from profit, the amount that they can buy depends on inflation and hence the Retail Price Index.
There are two main disadvantages.

Question 5

During a trading period the following stock transactions were recorded for a company:
01.7.98 50 units were bought @ £2 per unit.
03.8.98 100 units were bought @ £2.20 per unit.
19.8.98 100 units were issued.
23.9.98 200 units were bought @ £2.30 per unit.
25.9.98 150 units were issued.
(a) Assuming that the opening stock was zero, calculate the value of closing stock using the:
(i) FIFO method; (ii) LIFO method; (iii) AVCO method. Present your answers in tables using a spreadsheet.
(b) If the stock listed in the transactions above was perishable, which of the three methods is most suitable for the physical issuing of stock? Explain why.
(c) Why do you think that the LIFO method is the least favoured by firms?

● The Retail Price Index is a measure of the general price level. Some items in the Index may be moving far more quickly or slowly than others. Thus a general index can be misleading.
● The Retail Price Index is based on consumer goods and may not reflect business assets and expenditure.

Current cost accounting CURRENT COST ACCOUNTING involves changing all historic cost entries in the profit and loss account and the balance sheet into current values. A variety of indices are used to value stocks and fixed assets. Any adjustments made to fixed asset values are shown on the liabilities side of the balance sheet under revaluation (☞ unit 56). In the profit and loss account, adjustments are made for depreciation and cost of sales (similar to the LIFO method). Concern about accounting for inflation declined in the 1990s as inflation rates remained relatively low. Accountants have returned to traditional conventions of 'money terms' and 'historical cost' as a result.

Key terms

Book value - the historical cost of an asset less depreciation accumulated each year.
Constant purchasing power accounting - a complete accounting system which replaces money with an index of general purchasing power.
Current cost accounting - a method of accounting which replaces all historic cost values with current valuations.
First in first out (FIFO) - a method of stock valuation which involves issuing stock in the order in which it is delivered, so that the remaining stock is valued closer to its replacement cost.
Last in first out (LIFO) - a method of stock valuation which involves issuing more recent deliveries first, so that closing stock is valued at the older and possibly lower

purchase price.
Obsolete - an asset that is no longer any use to a company.
Provision - an allowance made in the accounts for depreciation.
Reducing balance method - a method used to calculate the annual depreciation allowance which involves writing off the same percentage rate each year.
Straight line method - a method used to calculate the annual depreciation allowance by subtracting the estimated scrap value from the cost and dividing the result by the expected life of the asset.
Writing off - the process of reducing the value of an asset by the amount of depreciation.

Summary

1. Why are assets valued at historical cost in the accounts?
2. Explain why assets fall in value.
3. Why is it necessary to provide for depreciation?
4. What are the main differences between the straight line and reducing balance methods of calculating depreciation?
5. What is meant by opening stock and closing stock?
6. Explain the difference between the LIFO and FIFO methods of stock valuation.
7. Why is stock not valued at its selling price?
8. What effects might inflation have on the valuation of assets?
9. Distinguish between current cost accounting and constant purchasing power accounting.

Case study

West End Service Station

Ross Wilson runs a small service station in Colchester. His core business is the sale of petrol. Petrol is delivered to his service station fairly regularly because the station's storage tanks are relatively small. Movements of petrol stocks for the first month of 1998 are shown in Table 63.10.

Ross has also set up a car hire operation from the same premises which he calls West End Car Hire. He has four small saloon cars which were purchased for £15,000 each. He plans to keep them for four years, by which time he estimates their residual value will be £3,000 each.

Table 63.10

Date	Purchases (litres)	Stocks used (litres)
04.01.98	400,000 @ 55p	
07.01.98		350,000
07.01.98	400,000 @ 55p	
12.01.98		410,000
14.01.98	400,000 @ 55p	
18.01.98		360,000
19.01.98	400,000 @ 58p	
23.01.98		460,000
24.01.98	400,000 @ 58p	
28.01.98		410,000

(a) **Calculate the value of closing stock at the end of the first month, January, using the FIFO method.**
(b) **Assuming that petrol sales for January 1998 were £1.2 million, calculate the gross profit for the month. (Gross profit is turnover minus costs of sales. Cost of sales can be calculated using opening stock, closing stock and purchases. Assume opening stock for the month is zero.)**
(c) (i) **Calculate the closing stock using the LIFO method.**
    (ii) **Show the effect on gross profit at the end of January.**
(d) **Using the straight line method of depreciation calculate:**
    (i) **the annual depreciation provision for each car;**
    (ii) **the book value of each car at the end of each year.**
(e) **If Ross sold the four cars for £8,000 each at the end of their second year, what would be the profit/loss on disposal?**

The nature of investment

Investment refers to the purchase of capital goods (☞ unit 1). Capital goods are used in the production of other goods, directly or indirectly. For example, a building contractor who buys a cement mixer, some scaffolding, a lorry and five shovels has invested. These goods will be used directly in production. If the contractor buys a typewriter, a filing cabinet and a photocopier for the firm's office, this is indirect investment. Although these items will not be used in production the business would not run as efficiently without them.

Investment might also refer to expenditure by a business which is likely to yield a return in the future. For example, a business might spend £20 million on research and development into a new product or invest £10 million in a promotion campaign. In each case, money is being spent on projects now in the hope that a greater amount of money will be generated in the future as a result of that expenditure.

Investment can be **autonomous** or **induced**. Autonomous investment is when a firm buys capital goods to replace ones which have worn out. Any new investment by the firm resulting from rising sales or expansion is induced investment.

Types of investment

Investment can be placed into various categories.

● Capital goods. This includes the purchase of a whole variety of mechanical and technical equipment. Vans, lathes, computers, robots, tools, vehicles and information technology are examples.

● Construction. This includes spending on new buildings that are bought or constructed by the firm. Factories, shops, warehouses, workshops and offices are examples.

● Stocks. This is a less obvious item of investment, since it does not fit neatly into the earlier definition. However, because stocks of finished goods and work-in-progress (☞ unit 94) will earn income in the future when they are sold, they are classed as investment.

● Public sector investment. Central and local government fund about twenty five per cent of all investment in the economy. Examples of public sector investment include the building of schools, motorways, hospitals and expenditure on goods like buses, dustcarts and equipment for the civil service. The factors which influence the level of public sector investment are often very different from those which affect private sector investment. This is dealt with later in this unit.

Risk in investment

The decision to invest by business is the most difficult it has

---

Since the privatisation of the water industry, OFWAT (the government water industry regulator) has put pressure on water companies to invest in new infrastructure, to replace old and worn out pipes and to prevent leakages. The amount of investment undertaken by Thames Water in the last 5 years is shown in Figure 64.1. Thames Water is the largest water and wastewater services company in the UK. The company serves 11.9 million domestic and commercial customers in London and the Thames Valley.

During the last financial year the business invested heavily in improving, expanding and replacing water and wastewater assets. The company spent £165 million on sludge incineration facilities at Beckton and Crossness wastewater treatment works in east London. Thames Water also received a Heritage Award for their new sewerage pumping station at Abbey Mills. These projects contributed to the investment total of £485 million for the year. Since privatisation, Thames Water has invested around £3 billion.

Figure 64.1 *Thames Water capital investment, 1994-98, £m*

Year	£m
94	377
95	314
96	349
97	410
98	485

Source: adapted from Thames Water, *Annual Reports and Accounts*, 1998.

Source: adapted from Thames Water, *Annual Reports and Accounts*, 1998.

(a) What type of investment is Thames Water likely to spend most money on? Explain your answer.

(b) Explain why the activity shown in the photograph may be described as autonomous investment.

(c) Suggest two possible reasons for the pattern of investment by Thames Water over the last 5 years.

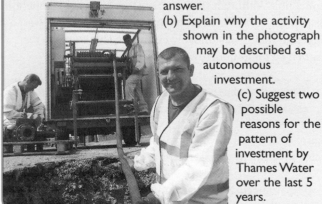

---

to make because of the risk involved. There is often a number of alternative choices. A firm buying a new fleet of cars for its sales staff has to decide which model of car will suit the company best of all. There may also be a considerable choice of projects. For example, a firm may need to choose whether investment in a new packaging machine which increases efficiency would be more profitable than a new computer system.

If all cost and revenue data upon which a decision would be based was accurate, there would not be a problem. However, revenue information in particular comes from predictions. It may be based on forecasts of future demand and conditions in the economy. Even costs, which are perhaps easier to predict, can vary. For example, few would have predicted the oil price increases in 1990.

Most investment decisions are uncertain because they are long term decisions, where resources are committed for a period of time. Investment projects have failed both in the private sector and the public sector. An example in the private sector might be the Nationwide Telephone, a Bury-based telephone maintenance business which went into receivership in 1997 due to problems resulting from the purchase of a rival company, Microcare. In the public sector, the government spent a lot of money on equipment which was used in the development of the Concorde aircraft. This also proved to be commercially unsuccessful.

Even joint arrangements can have problems. In 1994 Lancaster City Council licensed Noel Edmunds' Unique Group to create a 'Crinkley Bottom' theme park at Morecambe, agreeing to pay the company a fee. The park was only open for 13 weeks. Visitor numbers were poor and losses were estimated to massively exceed first year projections.

Investment is also said to be risky because it is often funded with borrowed money. This means that the return on any investment project must also cover the cost of borrowing. Also, if the investment project fails the company may be left with a heavy debt burden and possibly without the means to repay it. The Channel Tunnel project experienced such problems in the late 1990s. Around £5 billion was owed to several hundred banks following the construction of the tunnel link. Although the company was covering its operating costs, it has ceased interest payments to the banks. It was suggested that it was unlikely ever to be able to repay the original £5 billion borrowed.

The factors affecting private sector investment

Figure 64.2 shows the factors which might affect private sector investment decisions.

Motives To begin with, firms must have a reason to invest.
● All firms have to replace worn out equipment.
● To be competitive on costs, price and quality, firms may have to invest or risk losing customers to their rivals. For example, most building societies invested in the refurbishment of their branches in the early 1990s. Once

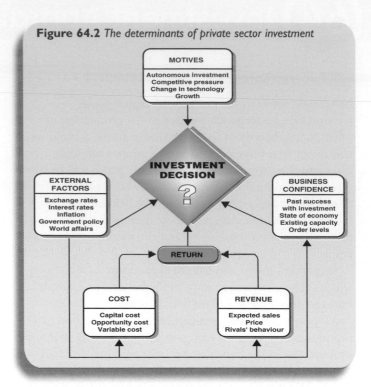

Figure 64.2 The determinants of private sector investment

one society improved its branch most others copied.
● The availability of new technology (☞ unit 98) may persuade firms to invest. When technology becomes available, firms are often keen to use it if they can afford to.
● Firms may wish to grow, to be more profitable or to increase their market influence. Growth involves investment in more plant, equipment and other productive assets.

Return If firms have a reason to invest, they must then decide whether it is worthwhile. One influence on this is the return on the investment. The return on an investment project can be found by subtracting the cost of the project from the expected revenue. There are three major costs. Capital costs might be the cost of a new factory. Opportunity costs (☞ unit 8) are the foregone alternatives the investment funds might have been used for, eg higher dividends to shareholders. Direct variable costs include the running costs of the project, eg labour or fuel costs.

Calculating the expected revenue is not easy. Expected sales are hard to predict with accuracy because many factors affect them. Marketing research (☞ unit 37) can only predict sales to some extent. Sales can also be influenced by the price set by the business in the future and by rivals' behaviour. Both of these factors are unpredictable.

Confidence Entrepreneurs and managers will be either optimistic or pessimistic about the future. Confidence may be influenced by a range of factors. These include whether or not previous investment has been a success, the state of the economy, the existing level of capacity and future order levels. A pessimistic business person may be less likely to invest than an optimistic one.

External factors External influences can be direct or indirect. For example, high interest rates may directly affect the cost of investment. If money is borrowed the business will pay back more. This can indirectly affect confidence. Inflation could affect costs, revenue and confidence. World affairs, such as problems in far Eastern economies in 1998, or rising exchange rates (☞ unit 25), may make investment abroad seem less attractive.

The factors affecting public sector investment

What factors influence investment by central government and local authorities?
- Investment in new schools, roads, and hospitals, for example, will be influenced by national and local needs. As the demands of the population grow, more of these facilities will be needed.
- Political factors may also influence the quantity and type of investment. In the recent past, the government has

aimed to reduce public investment in order to reduce the size of the public sector in general. It has also reduced it in specific areas, such as on defence.
- The availability of government funds and the opportunity cost of investment spending. If revenue from taxes is falling, there may be fewer investment funds. If the opportunity costs of investment projects are high, then they may be cancelled. The state of the economy will be important. For example, falling unemployment in the late 1990s has reduced government spending on unemployment benefit. This has perhaps meant that extra funds were available for spending on health or education.

Investment appraisal - payback method

INVESTMENT APPRAISAL describes how a private sector firm might objectively evaluate an investment project, to determine whether or not it is likely to be profitable. It also allows firms to compare projects.

Question

In 1995 Sony, the global electronics and entertainment group, launched a $30 million gamble on one of its most valuable corporate assets. The asset was the 'pop superstar', Michael Jackson. The gamble was an investment in the marketing campaign to launch his new album HIStory Jackson had sold 100 million albums for Sony. He was so valuable that the company was prepared to pay him 22 per cent royalties on album sales. Most other artists are paid 10 per cent. Michael Jackson helped Sony to establish its music division as one of the top five in the world.

Jackson is regarded as eccentric by many. He was reported to have had extensive plastic surgery. He goes on spending sprees in toyshops and developed a friendship with a chimpanzee called Bubbles. However, this did not have a negative impact on sales of his records. Indeed, the eccentric behaviour, which prompted the UK tabloids to dub him 'Wacko Jacko', may have helped to further his success. But allegations about his private life threatened to affect his appeal to children. Children are an important target in the entertainment market. Their spending power tends to be higher than that of students who follow fashionable bands such as Oasis. Similarly, child-orientated stars are likely to clinch more lucrative tour sponsorship and product endorsement deals.

Sony, however, was willing to gamble on Jackson's popularity and invest heavily in the promotion of HIStory, a double album. The promotion included giant floating Michael Jackson statues on eight European rivers and heavy investment in publicising singles taken from the album. This included a $7 million contribution towards the cost of making a video to promote 'Scream', the first single. Sony also subsidised sales of a cassette version of the second single, 'You Are Not Alone'. It was sold in the US for 49 cents compared with a normal market price of $3.49. Although the second single sold about 2.4 million copies, the

large discounting meant that Sony was unlikely to make a profit. The company was content to suffer losses on the singles provided the album sold well. However, the 11 million sales of HIStory by 1996 were well below Sony's expectations.

Source: adapted from the *Financial Times*, 25.6.1996.

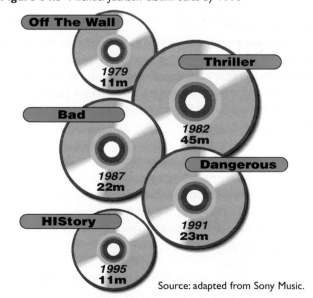

Figure 64.3 *Michael Jackson album sales by 1996*

Off The Wall — 1979 11m
Thriller — 1982 45m
Bad — 1987 22m
Dangerous — 1991 23m
HIStory — 1995 11m

Source: adapted from Sony Music.

(a) Explain, using the above case as an example, why investment is risky.
(b) Explain the factors which might have influenced Sony in their decision to invest $30 million in the promotion of Michael Jackson's new album.
(c) How might Sony be affected by this relative failure?

PAYBACK PERIOD refers to the amount of time it takes for a project to recover or pay back the initial outlay. For example, an engineer may invest £500,000 in new cutting machinery and estimate that it will lead to income over the next five years, as in Table 64.1.

Table 64.1 *Expected income from some new cutting machinery*

Year 1	Year 2	Year 3	Year 4	Year 5
£100,000	£125,000	£125,000	£150,000	£180,000

Here the payback period is four years. If we add together the income from the project in the first four years it amounts to £500,000.

When using this method to choose between projects, the project with the shortest payback will be chosen. Assume a business is appraising three investment projects, all of which cost £70,000. The flow of income expected from each project is shown in Table 64.2.

Table 64.2 *Expected income from three investment projects*

(£000)

	Year 1	Year 2	Year 3	Year 4	Year 5	Year 6	Total
A	10	10	20	20	30	40	130
B	20	20	20	20	20	20	120
C	30	30	20	10	10	10	110

In this example project C would be chosen because it has the shortest payback time, ie $2\frac{1}{2}$ years. Project A's payback stretches into the fifth year and project B's into the fourth. Note that total income is not taken into account in this method. In fact project C has the lowest total return over the six years!

Advantages
- This method is useful when technology changes rapidly, such as in the agriculture industry. New farm machinery is designed and introduced into the market regularly. It is important to recover the cost of investment before a new machine is designed.
- It is simple to use.
- Firms might adopt this method if they have cash flow problems. This is because the project chosen will 'payback' the investment more quickly than others.

Disadvantages
- Cash earned after the 'payback' is not taken into account in the decision to invest.
- The method ignores the profitability of the project, since the criterion used is the speed of repayment.

Question 3

Natalie and Liam Mead run a 4,600 acre arable farm in Steeple Aston, Oxfordshire. They grow barley and wheat and have enjoyed rising profitability in the last 5 years despite EU instructions to set aside some of their land each season. Natalie believes that a lot of their success is down to their investment strategy. They invest regularly in up-to-date agricultural technology and use the payback method when evaluating alternative projects. In 1999 they were considering four purchases:
- new state-of-the-art bailer at a cost of £20,000;
- replacing one of the tractors at a cost of £60,000;
- five new corn trailers at a cost of £3,000 each;
- four new storage silos at a total cost of £40,000.

The expected income stream from each of the above investments is shown in Table 64.3.

Table 64.3 *Expected income from investments made by Natalie and Liam Mead*

(£000s)

Year	1	2	3	4	5	6	7	8	9	10	Total
Bailer	4	4	4	4	4	4	4	4	4	4	40
Tractor	10	10	10	10	10	10	10	8	8	8	94
Trailers	2	2	2	2	2	2	2	2	2	2	20
Silos	10	10	10	6	6	6	4	4	2	2	60

(a) What particular external factors might influence Natalie and Liam's investment decisions in future years?
(b) Calculate, to the nearest month, the payback period for each purchase.
(c) If Natalie and Liam decide to make just one purchase, which should be undertaken according to this method of appraisal?

Investment appraisal - average rate of return

The AVERAGE RATE OF RETURN (ARR) method measures the net return each year as a percentage of the initial cost of the investment.

$$\text{Average rate of return (\%)} = \frac{\text{Net return (profit) per annum}}{\text{Capital outlay (cost)}} \times 100$$

For example, the costs and expected income from three investment projects are shown in Table 64.4.

A business would first calculate the total net profit from each project by subtracting the total return of the project from its cost, ie £70,000 - £50,000 = £20,000 for project X. The next step is to calculate the net profit per annum by dividing the total net profit by the number of years the project runs for, ie £20,000 ÷ 5 = £4,000 for X. Finally, the ARR is calculated by using the above formula, ie

$$\text{ARR (Project X)} \quad = \quad \frac{£4,000}{£50,000} \quad \times 100$$

$$= \quad 8\%$$

The results for all three projects are shown in Table 64.5. Project Y would be chosen because it gives a higher ARR (10 per cent) than the other two.

Table 64.4 *The costs and expected income from three investment projects*

	Project X	Project Y	Project Z
Cost	£50,000	£40,000	£90,000
Return Yr 1	£10,000	£10,000	£20,000
Yr 2	£10,000	£10,000	£20,000
Yr 3	£15,000	£10,000	£30,000
Yr 4	£15,000	£15,000	£30,000
Yr 5	£20,000	£15,000	£30,000
Total	£70,000	£60,000	£130,000

Table 64.5 *The average rate of return calculated for three investment projects*

	Project X	Project Y	Project Z
Cost	£50,000	£40,000	£90,000
Total net profit (return - cost)	£20,000	£20,000	£40,000
Net profit p.a. (profit ÷ 5)	£4,000	£4,000	£8,000
ARR	8%	10%	8.9%

The advantage of this method is that it shows clearly the profitability of an investment project. Not only does it allow a range of projects to be compared, the overall rate of return can be compared to other uses for investment funds. In the example in Table 64.5, if a company can gain 12 per cent by placing its funds in a bank account, it might choose to postpone the investment project until interest rates fall. It is also easier to identify the **opportunity cost** of investment.

However, the method does not take into account the effects of time on the value of money. The above example assumes that, for project X, £10,000 of income for the firm in two years time is the same as £10,000 in one years time. Some allowance must be made for the time span over which the income from an investment project is received for it to be most useful.

Investment appraisal - discounted cash flow

This method of appraisal has certain advantages. It deals with the problems of **interest rates** and **time**. The return on an

Question 4

Scotmart is a small supermarket chain based in the north of Scotland. It has stores in Sutherland, Caithness, Inverness, Moray, Nairn, Cromarty and Perth. Its success in the past few years has resulted in the company building up a large reserve of cash. Scotmart is now considering a substantial investment programme to consolidate its position in the Scottish grocery market. The following investment projects are under consideration:
● acquiring Aberdeen Provisions, a small regional supermarket chain, for £30 million;
● building some brand new stores in Ullapool, Wick, Helmsdale and Elgin at a cost of £40 million;
● diversifying into DIY supplies in its current stores at a cost of £25 million.
The expected revenue from the three investment projects is shown in Table 64.6.

Table 64.6 *Expected income from investment projects of Scotmart*

(£ million)

Year	1	2	3	4	5	6	7	8	9	10	Total
Acquisition	0	0	5	5	5	8	8	8	12	12	63
New stores	4	5	6	6	8	8	9	9	12	12	79
Diversify	5	5	5	5	5	5	5	5	5	5	50

(a) Suggest reasons why Scotmart may be keen to use its large reserve of cash.
(b) Calculate the average rate of return for each project.
(c) Which project should Scotmart invest in according to this method of investment appraisal?
(d) What might be the opportunity cost of the investment chosen in your answer to (c)?

investment project is always in the future, usually over a period of several years. Money earned or paid in the future is worth less today. Why?

What if £100 is placed in a bank account when the rate of interest is 10 per cent? At the end of the year it will be worth £110 (£100 + £100 x 10 per cent) or (£100 x 1.1). At the end of two years it will be worth £121 (£110 + £110 x 10 per cent) or (£110 x 1.1). This shows that money grows over time if it is deposited or lent with interest. Table 64.7 shows how the value of £100 grows over a 10 year period if left in a bank account when the rate of compound interest is 10 per cent.

Table 64.7 *The value of £100 over a 10 year period if left in a bank account when the compound rate of interest is 10 per cent (rounded to the nearest pound).*

Year	Value of £100 at compound rate of interest of 10 per cent
0	£100
1	£110
2	£121
3	£133
4	£146
5	£161
6	£177
7	£195
8	£214
9	£236
10	£259

Put another way, a fixed sum paid in the future is worth less than a fixed sum paid today. Why? The £100 could have been placed in a bank account for 3 years and could have grown to £133. So a fixed sum of £100 received in 3 years time will be far less than £100 today. The value today of a sum of money available in future is called the PRESENT VALUE. What is the present value of £100 in 3 years? This can be found by the formula:

$$\text{Present value} = \frac{A}{\frac{(1 + r)^n}{100}}$$

where A = amount of money, r = rate of interest and n = number of years. The present value of £100 received in three years time is (assuming a 10 per cent interest rate):

$$\text{Present value} = \frac{£100}{\frac{(1 + 10)^3}{100}} = \frac{£100}{(1.1)^3} = \frac{£100}{1.331} = £75.13$$

This shows the £100 received in 3 years time is worth less than £100 today. How much less depends on two things.

● Interest rates. If interest rates rise to 20 per cent then present value would be:

$$\frac{£100}{\frac{(1 + 20)^3}{100}} = £57.78$$

● The length of time. If £100 was received in 25 years time the present value would be:

$$\frac{£100}{\frac{(1 + 10)^{25}}{100}} = £9.23$$

DISCOUNTED CASH FLOW takes into account that interest rates affect the present value of future income. It shows that the future cash flow is discounted by the rate of interest.

How can this be used to decide whether investment should take place? Assume an investment project costs £100,000 and yields an expected stream of income over a 3 year period - year 1, £30,000; year 2, £40,000; year 3, £50,000. The rate of interest remains at 10 per cent over the time period. The present value of the future income stream using the technique described above will be:

$$\text{Present value} = \frac{£30,000}{(1 + 0.1)^1} + \frac{£40,000}{(1 + 0.1)^2} + \frac{£50,000}{(1 + 0.1)^3}$$

$$\text{Present value} = \frac{£30,000}{(1.1)^1} + \frac{£40,000}{(1.1)^2} + \frac{£50,000}{(1.1)^3}$$

$$\text{Present value} = \frac{£30,000}{1.1} + \frac{£40,000}{1.21} + \frac{£50,000}{1.331}$$

Present value = £27,272 + £33,057 + £37,565 = £97,894

The above investment project is not viable since the present value of the return (£97,894) is less than the cost (£100,000). The NET PRESENT VALUE (NPV) of the project which shows the return on the investment less the cost is:

NPV = Present value of return - cost

= £97,894 - £100,000 = - £2,106

Before the DCF procedure was applied, the total income would have been £120,000 (£30,000 + £40,000 + £50,000). A decision maker may have thought the project profitable without the use of DCF. It is sometimes mistakenly thought that DCF is used to take the effects of inflation into account. In fact it is used to take into account the effect of **interest rates**.

Alternative calculations

Sometimes it may not be necessary to use the DCF formula. Information is sometimes available which makes the DCF procedure much easier. We may be **given** the present value of £1 at the end of a number of years at a particular rate of interest. For example, Table 64.8 shows the present value of £1 receivable at the end of 6 years if the interest rate is 5 per cent. Note that the values are rounded off to two decimal places.

Table 64.8 *Present value of £1 receivable at the end of 6 years at 5 per cent*

After	1 yr	2 yrs	3 yrs	4 yrs	5 yrs	6 yrs
Present value of £1	£0.95	£0.90	£0.86	£0.82	£0.78	£0.75

Again assume that an investment project costing £100,000 yields an expected income stream over a three year period of £30,000 (year 1), £40,000 (year 2) and £50,000 (year 3). The present value of an income stream can be calculated using information from Table 64.8.

Present value of income in yr 1 = 30,000 x £0.95 = £28,500
Present value of income in yr 2 = 40,000 x £0.90 = £36,000
Present value of income in yr 3 = 50,000 x £0.86 = £43,000
Total present value of all income = £107,500

This investment project is viable because the present value of the return (£107,500) is greater than the cost (£100,000). The NPV is £7,500.

Question 5

The Tyneside Oil Company, located in Newcastle, processes oil in its large and highly automated refinery. It is now considering the development of its own distribution arm. A distribution operation would involve the purchase of several oil tankers, the acquisition of some adjacent land and a purpose built loading unit. In total the investment would cost the company £25 million. The revenue expected from the investment in the next 5 years is shown in Table 64.9. It is anticipated that the rate of interest over the next five years will be 5 per cent.

Table 64.9 *Expected revenue from the oil company's investment*

Year	1	2	3	4	5	Total
	£4m	£4m	£8m	£8m	£8m	£32m

(a) Calculate the present value of the future income from the investment project.
(b) Calculate the net present value and state whether the business should go ahead with the investment.
(c) How might the answer to (b) be different if the interest rate was 10 per cent throughout the 5 year period? Show the calculations of the present value of future income and the net present value in your answer.

Investment appraisal - internal rate of return

This technique also makes use of discounted cash flow. To decide on the INTERNAL RATE OF RETURN (IRR) a firm must find the rate of return (x) where the net present value is zero. This internal rate of return is then compared with the market rate of interest to determine whether the investment should take place. Assume an investment project costs £10,000 and yields a one year return only of £13,000. The market rate of interest is 14 per cent. To calculate the IRR (x):

$$\text{Cost} = \frac{A}{(1+x)^1}$$

$$10,000 = \frac{13,000}{(1+x)^1}$$

$$(1+x) = \frac{13,000}{10,000}$$

$$1+x = 1.3$$

$$x = 1.3 - 1$$

$$= 0.3 \text{ or } 30\%$$

Since the IRR (x) of 30 per cent is greater than the market rate of interest (14 per cent) the firm should invest in the project. When this is applied to projects over a longer period the calculation becomes more complex. However, the method remains the same.

An alternative approach is to use trial and error. This means choosing a discount rate, calculating the net present value (NPV) and seeing whether it equals zero. If it does not then another rate must be chosen. This process is continued until the correct rate is found. For example, assume that an investment project costs £50,000 and earns a five year return.

Table 64.10 *The NPV of an investment project at three different discount rates*

(£)

		Present value of income at:		
Year	Income	10%	7.5%	5%
1	5,000	4,545	4,651	4,762
2	5,000	4,132	4,325	4,555
3	10,000	7,513	8,045	8,643
4	20,000	13,661	14,970	16,447
5	20,000	12,442	13,828	15,661
Total	60,000	42,273	45,919	50,048
NPV		-7,727	-4,081	48

Table 64.10 shows the actual return and the present value of the return over the five year period at different discount rates. If a 10 per cent discount rate is used the NPV is less than zero, ie -£7,727. Also, if a 7.5 per cent discount rate is

used the NPV is less than zero, ie -£4,081. If a 5 per cent rate is used the NPV is as near to zero as is needed, ie just £48. Thus, 5 per cent is the internal rate of return. Figure 64.4 shows the relationship between the discount rate and the NPV. As the discount rate increases the NPV falls. The IRR is shown on the discount rate axis where NPV is zero.

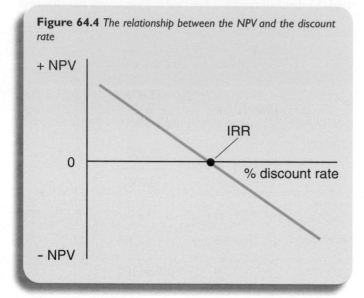

Figure 64.4 *The relationship between the NPV and the discount rate*

Other factors influencing investment decisions

In addition to the factors which might influence investment decisions already outlined in this unit, a number of other factors might be considered.

Human relations Some investment projects can have a huge impact on the staff in an organisation. For example, investment in plant automation might lead to mass redundancies. A business might decide to postpone plans to automate their plant if it thought the damage to human relations in the organisation would be too severe.

Ethical considerations Along with many other business decisions, managers are taking more of an ethical stance when choosing courses of action. For example, a chemicals producer might decide to build a new plant in a location which does not minimise financial costs but does reduce environmental damage. Such a decision might help to enhance the image of a company.

Corporate strategy Many businesses have long term corporate objectives (☞ unit 15) which are laid down in their corporate strategy. Such long term objectives might influence short term investment decisions. For example, a business operating a chain of theme pubs might be considering some repairs to a fire damaged pub. Repairs might be postponed because the pub in question was due for complete refurbishment in the next financial year.

Availability of funding A large number of investment projects fail to get started because businesses are unable to raise the necessary money to fund the project. A significant proportion of these will be small businesses which have difficulty in persuading investors and lenders to provide funding.

Current cash flow A firm's cash flow position (☞ unit 59) may influence investment decisions. Investment projects are a notorious drain on a firm's resources. Businesses often underestimate the cost of investment and struggle to fund their usual activities because money is being directed to the new project. Consequently, if a business has a poor cash flow position it might postpone or cancel investment projects to avoid cash flow problems.

Question 6

In February 1999 residents in Southport's Derby Road expressed horror at proposals to build a new supermarket on the corner of their street. Sefton Council had received an application for a one or two storey retail development on the corner of Kensington Road and Derby Road. One resident said the area would be severely affected by the constant flow of shoppers in cars and delivery lorries. She also complained about the effects of the store staying open till 10 pm in the evening. Another resident feared that vibrations from traffic could damage the 100 year old houses in the area. The Council confirmed that they had received an outline planning application from Boots Properties, the potential builder. The plan included 100,000 square foot of non-food retail area, 75,000 square feet of food retail area and 654 car parking spaces.

Source: adapted from *The Champion*, 10.2.1999.

(a) Describe the problems for residents of a new supermarket in their area.
(b) What strategies might the supermarket owners use to win support of local residents?
(c) (i) Explain the factors that may influence whether the investment would go ahead.
    (ii) Evaluate the extent to which residents' disapproval would be likely to influence the decision.

Key terms

Average rate of return (ARR) - a method of investment appraisal which measures the net return per annum as a percentage of the initial spending.

Discounted cash flow (DCF) - a method of investment appraisal which takes interest rates into account by calculating the present value of future income.

Internal rate of return (IRR) - the rate of return (x) at which the net present value is zero.

Investment appraisal - the evaluation of an investment project to determine whether or not it is likely to be worthwhile.

Net present value - the present value of future income from an investment project, less the cost.

Present value - the value today of a sum of money available in the future.

Payback period - the amount of time it takes to recover the cost of an investment project.

Summary

1. What is meant by the term investment?
2. Explain the difference between autonomous and induced investment.
3. State the 4 types of investment.
4. Why is the investment decision risky?
5. State the factors that might influence: (a) private sector; (b) public investment?
6. What is the function of investment appraisal in business?
7. Explain briefly how a business would appraise investment using the payback period.
8. What are the advantages and disadvantages of the payback method?
9. What does the average rate of return method of investment appraisal aim to measure?
10. Why is the discounted cash flow method of appraisal used in business?
11. Suggest how environmental considerations may affect an investment decision.

Case study

The Hertford Tennis Club

In 1996-98 tennis was growing in popularity in the UK. Greg Rusedski had reached the final of the US Open Championship in 1997. Tim Henman had won a number of world ranking tournaments and had reached a Wimbledon semi-final. Both had a top 20 world ranking in 1998. Seeing a business opportunity, Ruth and Caroline Lee decided to invest in a new tennis school. They were both keen tennis players with coaching qualifications. The sisters were promised a substantial amount of funding from their parents provided they produced a well thought out business plan. However, they indicated that they would only be willing to loan the money for a few years, after which they would want to see it repaid in stages. Ruth and Caroline believed that there would be demand for tennis facilities if only they were easily available and widely publicised.

In their planning and research the sisters found what they thought to be an ideal location for their tennis club. An independent school in St Albans was selling its playing fields to pay for a new roof on the school. The school governors were very keen for a quick sale and preferred a buyer who was going to use the land for sporting purposes. They thought that in future pupils from the school might be able to benefit in some way from a sporting development. Located on the land was a building which Ruth thought could easily be converted into a clubhouse with changing rooms, lounge, bar area, storage space for equipment and reception area.

Caroline had spent some of her time researching into the costs of what was now looking to be quite a substantial investment. The costs of the investment are shown in Table 64.11.

Table 64.11 *Costs of The Hertford Tennis Club*

Description	Cost
Land	£120,000
Refurbishment of building	£100,000
Marketing research	£10,000
Construction of 10 floodlit courts	£80,000
Tennis equipment	£12,000
Legal fees	£4,000
Miscellaneous expenses	£4,000

Table 64.12 *Present value of £1 receivable at the end of 6 years at 5 per cent*

After	1 yr	2 yrs	3 yrs	4 yrs	5 yrs	6 yrs
Present value of £1	£0.95	£0.90	£0.86	£0.82	£0.78	£0.75

The sisters were convinced that there would be enough demand for their facilities. In their catchment area:

● there were no other tennis facilities;

● people were generally employed and had a relatively high income per head;

● the success of British tennis players had everyone in the local nightspots talking about tennis;

● Caroline and Ruth were prepared to invest heavily in marketing.

However, as a precaution they employed a marketing research agency to estimate demand. The marketing research agency used by Caroline and Ruth were able to provide estimated revenue data for the next six years. These are presented in the bar chart shown in Figure 64.5. The revenue includes membership and tuition fees. The pie chart in Figure 64.6 shows the age profile of the market which Caroline and Ruth will be operating in.

Having gathered the information, Caroline and Ruth had to decide whether to go ahead with the investment or not.

Write a report by the marketing agency evaluating the viability of Ruth and Caroline Lee's investment proposal. Consider both financial and non-financial factors in your discussion and show all calculations (assume that the rate of interest remains at 5 per cent for the next six years). Recommend whether or not they should go ahead with the investment.

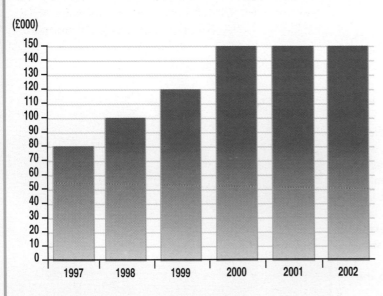

Figure 64.5 *Estimated revenue for The Hertford Tennis club (£000s)*

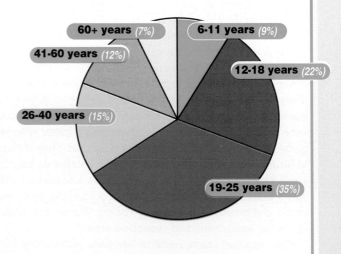

Figure 64.6 *Age profile of expected market for The Hertford Tennis Club*

Constructing break-even charts

Break-even charts (☞ unit 54) provide a visual means of analysing the effect of changes in output on total cost, total revenue, profit and the margin of safety. The effects of changes in fixed costs, variable cost and price on profit and the margin of safety can also be shown. A break-even chart can be constructed by plotting the total cost and total revenue equations on a graph. The graph should measure output on the horizontal axis and costs, revenue and profit on the vertical axis.

Consider Reidle Bros, a small canoe manufacturer. It incurs fixed costs of £20,000 per annum and variable costs of £75 per canoe. The canoes are sold for £125 to agents and wholesalers. The following steps can be used to construct a break-even chart.

Calculating the break-even point It is helpful to calculate the break-even point before constructing the graph. For Reidle Bros the total costs (TC) and total revenue (TR) equations are:

$$TC = £20,000 + £75Q \text{ (fixed costs + variable costs)}$$

$$TR = £125Q \text{ (price x quantity)}$$

Reidle Bros will break-even when total revenue equals total costs. This is where:

$$£20,000 + £75Q = £125Q$$
$$£20,000 = £125Q - £75Q$$
$$£20,000 = £50Q$$
$$\frac{£20,000}{£50} = Q$$
$$400 = Q$$

Therefore, Reidle Bros will break-even when it manufactures 400 canoes.

Calculating points on the total revenue and total cost functions Both the total cost and total revenue functions are **linear** or straight. Therefore the lines can be drawn by joining two points which lie on each function. To plot the total revenue function we need to choose two levels of output and calculate the total revenue at each level. Any two levels of output could be chosen. However, construction will be

simpler if 0 is chosen as one of the points. It is also helpful to choose a second value which is twice that of the break-even point. This would be 800 (2 x 400) in the case of the canoe manufacturers. This will ensure that the break-even point is in the centre of the chart. This improves presentation. The value of total revenue at each of these output levels is shown in Table 65.1.

Plotting the total revenue (TR) function The TR function can now be plotted on the graph. The output axis should run from 0 to 800 canoes and the other axis from 0 to £100,000. Using the information in Table 65.1, the two points, or coordinates, on the TR function are (0, 0) and (800, £100,000). If these are plotted on the graph and joined up the TR function will appear as shown in Figure 65.1.

Plotting the total costs (TC) function To plot the TC function we need to calculate the total cost at two levels of output. It is useful to use the same values as those used for the TR function, ie 0 and 800. The TC function can now be plotted on the graph. From Table 65.1 the two points which lie on the TC function are (0, £20,000) and (800, £80,000). If these are plotted on the graph and joined up the TC function will appear as shown in Figure 65.1. Note that the total cost function does not start at coordinates 0,0. At an output of zero, the business still has fixed costs of £20,000.

Analysis from the diagram The break-even chart is now complete. An analysis of certain points on the diagram can be made.

● The break even point can be identified and plotted. It is usual to draw lines to show the number of canoes Reidle Bros must sell to break-even (400), and the value of TR and TC at this level of output (£50,000). The break-even point should coincide with the calculation made in the first step, ie 400 canoes.

Table 65.1 *Values of TR and TC at two levels of output for Reidle Bros*

Q	TR	TC
0	0	£20,000
800	£100,000 (125 x 800)	£80,000 (20,000 + [75 x 800])

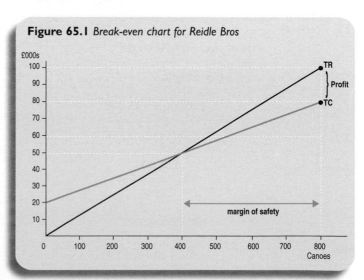

Figure 65.1 *Break-even chart for Reidle Bros*

- The profit at certain levels of output may be indicated. For example, at an output of 800 canoes, the profit is £100,000 - £80,000 = £20,000.
- The margin of safety can be indicated. This is the difference between the output of the business and the break-even point. At an output of 800 canoes it is 800 -400 = 400 canoes.

Question 1

Joanne Williams, a student, believed she could make some money during the summer holidays by operating as a mobile ice-cream vendor. She hired a purpose built van from one of the national ice-cream producers. This cost £200 per week. The variable costs per ice-cream cone were 30p. Joanne was under contract to sell ice-cream cones for 80p each. In order to analyse the profit potential at different sales levels she drew up a break-even chart.

(a) Draw a break-even chart for Joanne Williams.
(b) Using your chart state: (i) the number of cones needed to break-even; (ii) the profit she would make if she sold 700 cones.
(c) On your chart show the margin of safety if 700 cones were sold.
(d) In the last week of the summer holidays Joanne decided to break her contract and charge £1.10 per cone.
  (i)   Construct the new TR function on the break-even chart.
  (ii) Using your chart, state how much profit she makes if 600 are sold.
  (iii) In financial terms, was it worth Joanne breaking the contract?

Target rate of profit

Break-even analysis can be used to calculate the amount of output needed to generate a certain level of profit. For example, if Reidle Bros wanted to make £15,000 profit, the level of output required to do this would be:

$$\frac{\text{Fixed cost + profit target}}{\text{Contribution}}$$

$$= \frac{£20,000 + £15,000}{£50 \ (£125 - £75)}$$

$$= \frac{£35,000}{£50}$$

$$= 700 \ \text{canoes}$$

Thus, when Reidle Bros produces and sell 700 canoes profit is:

$$
\begin{aligned}
\text{Profit} &= \text{total revenue - total costs} \\
&= £125 \times 700 - (£20,000 + [£75 \times 700]) \\
&= £87,500 - (£20,000 + £52,500) \\
&= £87,500 - £72,500 \\
&= £15,000
\end{aligned}
$$

Question 2

Palmer and Minton manufacture lawn tractors in their Hereford factory. They are sold through mail order for £900 each. Their fixed costs are £50,000 p.a. and variable costs £700 per tractor. Palmer and Minton established their partnership in 1998 and for the first two trading years they broke-even. In the next financial year they set a profit target of £150,000.

(a) Calculate how many lawn tractors Palmer and Minton need to produce and sell to reach their profit target.
(b) Calculate the margin of safety if the profit target is reached.
(c) Comment on how realistic the sales target calculated in (a) is, given the previous two years of sales?

Break-even price

Sometimes a business may want to know how much to charge for its product to break-even. In these circumstances a business must know how much it is going to produce and sell. For example, assume Reidle Bros aimed to sell 500 canoes and its objective was to break-even at that level of output. The price it should charge to break even would be :

$$\text{Break-even price} = \frac{\text{Total cost}}{\text{Output}}$$

$$= \frac{£20,000 + (500 \times £75)}{500}$$

$$= \frac{£20,000 + £37,500}{500}$$

$$= \frac{£57,500}{500}$$

$$= £115$$

Thus, if output was 500, Reidle Bros must charge £115 per canoe to break-even.

Julia Robinson owns a large farm and supplies apples to cider producers. Apple production is only part of the farm's output. Most of the profit is generated from milk production. Julia is happy if apple production breaks even each year. The orchard was inherited from her grandfather and Julia does not wish to cease apple production for sentimental reasons, even though it is generally unprofitable. Whether she achieves her aim depends on how many apples she harvests and the going market price. At the end of the 1999 season Julia had picked 60,000 kilos. The fixed costs associated with apple production were £6,000 for the year. Variable costs were 40p per kilo.

(a) Given that Julia is a 'price taker' in the apple market, state two ways she might increase the performance of apple production.
(b) Calculate the price per kilo Julia would need to receive in order for apple production to break-even.
(c) Calculate the profit Julia would make from apple production if the market price was: (i) 48p per kilo; (ii) 51p per kilo.

Aimsley House is a private nursing home located in Bournemouth. It is well established and has served the local council for many years. Aimsley House generally operates at full capacity. It can accommodate up to 25 patients. Up until 1998 Aimsley House and the local council had negotiated financial terms upon which patients would be accepted. However, in 1999 the council informed the management of Aimsley House that, in the future, terms would not be negotiable. The council would state how much they are prepared to pay per patient and local homes would have to tender for the business at the 'going price'. This announcement was a cause of concern for the management of Aimsley House. They wondered whether the business would continue to make a healthy profit. The fixed costs at Aimsley House are £150,000 per annum and variable costs are £5,000 per resident.

(a) Assuming that Aimsley House continues to operate at full capacity, calculate the price that would enable the management to make £50,000 profit per annum.
(b) Assume that the council offers a price of £12,500 per patient every year.
    (i)   Calculate the amount of profit Aimsley House would make.
    (ii) Discuss whether the management of Aimsley house should accept this offer.

Price needed to reach a target rate of profit

A business may want to determine the price it needs to charge in order to reach a target rate of profit. For example, if Reidle Bros wanted to make a profit of £40,000, and its production capacity was 1,000 canoes, the price it would need to charge to reach this target rate of profit would be:

$$\text{Price} = \frac{\text{Profit target} + \text{total cost}}{\text{Output}}$$

$$= \frac{£40,000 + (£20,000 + 1,000 \times £75)}{1,000}$$

$$= \frac{£40,000 + £95,000}{1,000}$$

$$= \frac{£135,000}{1,000}$$

$$= £135$$

Thus, Reidle Bros would have to charge £135 for each canoe in order to make £40,000 profit if it produced and sold 1,000.

Accounting for changes in costs and revenues

One of the weaknesses of break-even analysis discussed in unit 65, is the assumption that the total cost and total revenue functions are **linear.** This indicates that as output increases, total cost and total revenue rise by the same proportion. What actually happens to total costs and total revenue as output increases can affect the decisions a business makes based on its break-even analysis, given a fixed amount of capital.

Total cost Assume a factory is built for 1,000 workers. As more workers are employed they can specialise in different tasks (☞ unit 1). 500 workers are likely to be more productive than one, for example. At some point, however, the opportunity to take advantage of specialisation may be used up and although total output will continue to rise, each extra worker will be less productive. For example, if 2,000 workers were employed in the above factory, there would not be enough machinery available for all workers to be usefully employed.

This is called the law of DIMINISHING RETURNS. It states that as more of a variable factor (labour here) is added to a fixed factor (say capital) the output of the extra workers will rise and then fall. In other words output will rise but at a diminishing rate. In extreme cases output may even fall. This is called negative returns.

Table 65.2 *The effect on output and total cost as a firm employs more workers given a fixed amount of capital*

Capital (machines) costing £100 each	Labour (workers) costing £200 per week	£ Fixed costs (machinery)	£ Variable costs (labour)	Total cost (£)	Output (units)
10	0	1,000	0	1,000	0
10	1	1,000	200	1,200	20
10	2	1,000	400	1,400	54
10	3	1,000	600	1,600	105
10	4	1,000	800	1,800	152
10	5	1,000	1,000	2,000	180
10	6	1,000	1,200	2,200	192

How does this affect the costs of a business? Table 65.2 shows the effect on output and total cost of hiring labour at £200 per week with fixed capital costs of £100 per machine. The output per worker always rises, but eventually at a diminishing rate. For example, when the fourth worker is employed output rises by 47 units, but the fifth worker adds only 28 units. Total costs rise as the firm employs more labour. The effect of diminishing returns on the firm's total cost function is shown in Figure 65.2. Notice that it is non-linear.

Total revenue The total revenue function drawn in unit 10 assumed that each unit would be sold for the same price. In reality, it is unlikely that a firm can continually sell its output for the same price. There reaches a point where additional sales can only be made if the price is lowered, for example a business may offer lower prices to customers who buy larger quantities. Figure 65.3 shows that as the price is lowered to encourage more sales the total revenue earned by the business falls.

The graph also shows a total cost function subject to diminishing returns. Notice that there are now two break-even points, Q_1 and Q_2. When linear functions are used on a

Figure 65.2 *A total cost function subject to the law of diminishing returns*

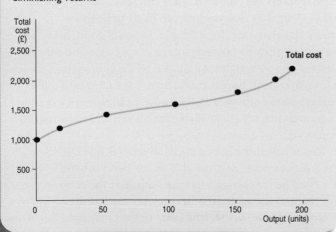

break-even chart, as output is increased beyond the break-even level of output, profit continues to increase indefinitely. When non-linear functions are used profit can only be made over a particular range of output, ie between Q_1 and Q_2. If production is pushed beyond Q_2 losses are made.

Figure 65.3 *A break-even chart with non-linear total cost and total revenue functions*

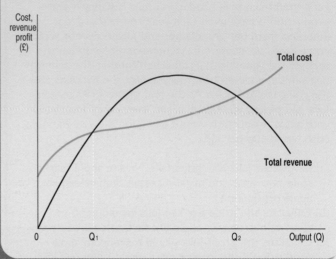

Question 5

JT Edinburgh & Son manufactures standard housebricks. The total revenue and total costs for a range of output between 0 and 100,000 tonnes are shown in Table 65.3.

Table 65.3 *Cost and revenue data for JT Edinburgh & Son*

Tonnes (000s)	0	10	20	30	40	50	60	70	80	90	100
Total costs (£000)	10	22	25	27	28	29	31	35	40	48	56
Total revenue (£000)	0	14	25	33	38	41	42	42	40	34	24

(a) Plot the total cost and total revenue functions for JT Edinburgh. Show the two break-even levels of output.
(b) Reading from your graph, what will be the profit or loss when: (i) 90,000; and (ii) 20,000 tonnes of bricks are produced?
(c) If the total revenue function was linear, how might your answers in (b) be different?

Key terms

Diminishing returns - the eventual decline in output each extra worker adds to total output when the opportunity to specialise is used up.

Summary

1. What might be the first step when constructing a break-even chart?
2. What should be plotted on the horizontal axis when constructing a break-even chart?
3. When constructing a break-even chart which two levels of output might best be chosen to plot the functions?
4. How is the break-even point identified on a break-even chart?
5. How is the margin of safety identified on a break-even chart?
6. What formula is used to calculate the amount of output needed to reach a profit target?
7. What is meant by the break-even price?
8. If total cost = £200,000 and output = 10,000 units, what price must a business charge to make a profit of £40,000?
9. In reality, why is the: (i) total cost function; (ii) total revenue function; likely to be non-linear?

Case study

Dorking Toolmaster Ltd

Dorking Toolmaster Ltd manufactures a range of tool kits, consisting of tools such as hammers, screwdrivers, saws, drills, micrometers and chisels. Until recently it rarely received large standard orders. Indeed, the profitability of the business was beginning to suffer because the company was finding that many of its small orders were not really economical, generating only small amounts of profit. To change direction the company employed a full-time salesperson to find some larger, more profitable orders. Within two months a huge order for a large standard tool kit was received from a French company. The new salesperson also anticipated further European orders.

The board of directors decided that investment would be required to meet the order. It also agreed to focus more sharply on the European market, even though this would mean neglecting some of its more traditional customers. It was clear that a bank loan would be required to fund the investment. Dorking would need new machinery and an upgrade of its premises. After a meeting, the bank had requested a break-even chart on the new European business. The standard tool kits would be sold for £600 each. The costs attributable to the production of tool kits are shown in Table 65.4.

Table 65.4 *Costs attributable to tool kit production at Dorking Toolmaster Ltd*

Overheads per annum	£80,000
Raw materials (per kit)	£190
Labour (per kit)	£140
Administration (per kit)	£50
Exporting cost (per kit)	£20

The French order was for 500 tool kits in the first year. Although there were no formal orders for kits in subsequent years from the French company, it was expected that they would be forthcoming provided delivery dates were met and quality standards were maintained. Dorking had a good record in both these aspects of business.

(a) **Show the equations for the total cost and total revenue functions facing Dorking.**
(b) **Calculate the break even level of output.**
(c) **Construct a break-even chart and show the margin of safety if the French order was for 500 tool kits.**
(d) **Calculate how much profit would be made from the French order in the first year.**

In a further meeting, however, the bank refused the loan. The bank manager raised a number of concerns. She was particularly worried about the low margin of safety on the French order. She suggested that the loan could still be considered if the margin of safety was increased to 200 tool kits. In order to raise the margin of safety Dorking would have to reduce costs, raise price or persuade the French company to buy more kits in the first year.

The only realistic option was to reduce costs. The production manager and accountant were asked to investigate whether this was possible. By rearranging working practices in the factory, contracting out some work and finding cheaper suppliers it was thought that labour costs could be reduced to £90 per kit and material costs to £140 per kit.

(e) **Apart from the low margin of safety, explain three other reasons why the bank may have been reluctant to grant Dorking the loan.**
(f) **Explain how an increase in price might affect the margin of safety.**
(g) **Examine the effect of the reduction in costs on the break-even chart.**
(h) **Discuss to what extent break-even analysis is useful for a bank when deciding whether to grant companies a loan.**
(i) **Evaluate whether the bank would now be in a position to grant the loan after the changes had been made by the company.**

What is budgetary control?

BUDGETARY CONTROL involves a business looking into the future, stating what it wants to happen, and then deciding how to achieve these aims. The control process is shown in Figure 66.1.

● Preparation of plans. All businesses have objectives (☞ unit 4). If the sales department increases sales by ten per cent, how does it know whether or not this is satisfactory? Targets are usually set which allow a business to determine if its objectives have been met. The results it achieves can then be compared with the targets it sets.

● Comparisons of plans with actual results. Control will be effective if information is available as quickly as possible. Managers need budgetary data as soon as it is available. Recent developments in information technology have helped to speed up the supply of data. For budgeting purposes the financial year has been divided up into smaller control periods - usually four weeks or one calendar month. It is common to prepare a budget for each control period. At the end of the period the actual results can then be compared with targets set in the budget.

● Analysis of variances. This is the most important stage in the control process. VARIANCE ANALYSIS involves trying to find reasons for the differences between actual and expected results. An unfavourable variance, when planned sales are 1,000 units and actual sales are 800 units, for example, might be due to inefficiency. It is then up to the management to take some action. A variance might be the result of some external factor influencing the business (☞ unit 17). In this case the business may need to change its business plans and adjust the next budget.

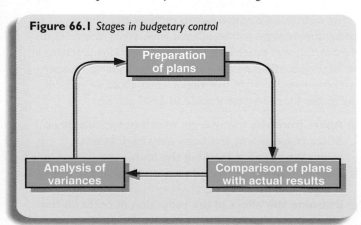

Figure 66.1 *Stages in budgetary control*

Zero-based budgeting

The financial information used in most budgets is based on **historical** data. For example, the cost of materials in this year's production budget may be based on last year's figure, with perhaps an allowance for inflation. Production and manufacturing costs, such as labour, raw materials and overheads, are relatively easy to value and tend to be controlled using methods such as standard costing (☞ unit 53).

However, in some areas of business it is not so easy to quantify costs. Examples might be certain marketing, administration or computer services costs. Where costs are unable to be justified then no money is allocated in the budget for those costs. This is known as ZERO-BASED BUDGETING (ZBB). A manager must show that a particular item of spending generates an adequate amount of benefit in relation to the general objectives of the business for money to be allocated in a budget.

This approach is different to the common practice of extrapolating from past costs. It encourages the regular evaluation of costs and helps to minimise unnecessary purchases. The concept of **opportunity cost** (☞ unit 8) is linked to ZBB. Opportunity cost is the cost of the next best alternative. When choices are made, businesses try to minimise the opportunity cost. ZBB also involves a cautious approach to spending, so that costs are minimised. Both include an element of 'value for money'.

The main advantages of ZBB are that:

● the allocation of resources should be improved;

● a questioning attitude is developed which will help to reduce unnecessary costs and eliminate inefficient practices;

Question

Questcorp plc is a large provider of security systems in the UK. It specialises in systems which protect business premises in rural locations. The financial controller of Questcorp has suggested that expenditure in some departments could be better controlled if the company used zero-based budgeting. The expenditure for four departments is shown in Table 66.1.

Table 66.1 *Expenditure in four key departments for Questcorp plc*
£

	1994	1995	1996	1997	1998
Marketing	120,000	140,000	178,000	219,000	270,000
R&D	250,000	321,000	377,000	679,000	900,000
Production	300,000	400,000	560,000	780,000	980,000
Admin.	45,000	50,000	54,000	79,000	93,000

(a) How might the R&D budget holder justify spending in her department?

(b) Why might zero-based budgeting be a problem for the marketing department launching a new product?

(c) To what extent might Questcorp benefit from zero-based budgeting?

- staff motivation might improve because evaluation skills are practised and a greater knowledge of the firm's operations might develop;
- it encourages managers to look for alternatives.

ZBB also has some disadvantages.

- It is time consuming because the budgeting process involves the collection and analysis of quite detailed information so that spending decisions can be made.
- Skilful decision making is required. Such skills may not be available in the organisation. In addition, decisions may be influenced by subjective opinions.
- It threatens the status quo. This might adversely affect motivation.
- Managers may not be prepared to justify spending on certain costs. Money, therefore, may not be allocated to spending which could benefit the business.

To deal with these possible problems, a business might give each department a 'base' budget of, say, 50 per cent. Departments could then be invited to bid for increased expenditure on a ZBB basis.

Types of variance

Unit 61 explained that a **variance** is the difference between the the actual and the planned figure that the business had budgeted for. It can be calculated by:

Variance = actual value - planned value

A favourable variance is where, for example, actual sales revenues are greater than planned revenues or actual costs are lower than planned. An adverse variance may be where actual sales revenues are less than planned or actual costs are higher than planned.

Figure 66.2 shows examples of variances that a business might decide to calculate and analyse. The profit variance is influenced by all other variances. A change in any one of the variances will affect profit. Most variances are linked to the costs incurred by a business. This suggests that variance analysis

provides a very good way of monitoring business costs. There may be other variances which are not shown in the diagram. The number of possible variances is equal to the number of factors which can influence business costs and revenue.

Profit variances

The most important of all variances is the **profit variance**. Differences between actual profit and planned profit will be of particular interest to business owners, managers and other stakeholders. The performance of most businesses is often measured by profit. All other variances will affect the profit variance, though not by the same magnitude. For example, if planned sales in January are £45,000 and actual sales are £48,500, there is a favourable sales variance of £3,500 (£48,500 - £45,000). This does not necessarily mean that the profit variance will improve by £3,500. This is because the extra sales are likely to generate a cost variance. This will offset some of the benefit.

Question 2

Llantrisant Holdings design and manufacture dials, instruments and sensor equipment for the electronics industry. The company relocated when it won a substantial contract to supply a large South Korean electronics company. The South Korean company set up a factory in Cardiff in 1998 and was keen for its suppliers to be located in close proximity. Llantrisant Holdings delivers just-in-time to its Korean customer. Llantrisant has begun to enjoy substantial efficiency gains in the last 18 months. Representatives from its South Korean customer visited the Llantrisant factory before awarding the contract. During their visit they made helpful recommendations about alternative working practices.

Table 66.2 *Budgeted profit and loss account and actual figures for Llantrisant Holdings (1999)*

			(£)
	Budgeted	**Actual**	**Variances**
Sales revenue	7,435	7,546	
Cost of sales	4,950	4,100	
Gross profit	2,485	3,446	
Overheads	1,250	1,280	
Operating profit	1,235	2,166	

(a) (i) Complete Table 66.2 by calculating the variances.
  (ii) Explain whether the operating profit variance is adverse or favourable.
(b) Analyse the variance which has had the most influence on the operating profit variance.

Direct materials variance

Figure 66.2 shows that the **total cost variance** can be influenced by several cost variances. One of these is the **direct materials**

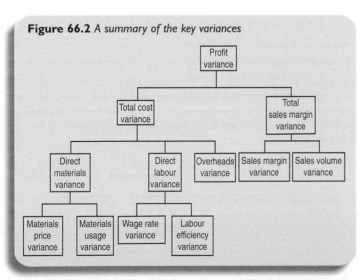

Figure 66.2 *A summary of the key variances*

variance. This is the difference between budgeted direct materials costs and actual direct materials costs. Direct materials include raw materials, components and any other resources used directly in production. For example, a biscuit manufacturer may use flour as one of its raw materials. Table 66.3 shows the budgeted and actual price of flour and the budgeted and actual usage of flour in a particular budget period. According to the table, the budgeted direct materials cost of the flour is £3,000. However, the actual direct materials cost is £2,860. This gives a favourable direct materials variance of £140 in this budget period.

Table 66.3 Cost and usage of flour for a biscuit manufacturer

	Price (per kilo)	Usage (kilos)	Direct materials cost
Budgeted	£1.50	2,000	£3,000
Actual	£1.30	2,200	£2,860
Direct materials variance			£140 (F)

The favourable variance in Table 66.3 is influenced by two other variances.

Materials price variance This will result when the actual price of direct materials is different from the budgeted or standard price. In Table 66.4 this is calculated by:

Materials price variance = (budgeted price - actual price) x actual usage
= (£1.50 - £1.30) x 2,200
= £0.20 x 2,200
= £440 (F)

The materials price variance is favourable because the actual cost is lower than the budgeted cost. This variance may be the responsibility of the purchasing department. Materials price variances could arise for a number of reasons, for example:
● materials may be obtained at a special discount;
● a new supplier might have been found;
● unexpected inflation may raise prices;
● a price war may have broken out in the market.

Materials usage variance A materials usage variance is found by comparing the actual usage of materials and the budgeted usage. The difference is valued at the budgeted price. For the biscuit manufacturer above the variance is:

Materials usage variance = (budgeted usage - actual usage) x budgeted price
= (2,000 - 2,200) x £1.50
= -200 x £1.50
= £300 (A)

The materials usage variance is adverse because the actual usage is greater than the budgeted usage. The effect will lead to lower profit. This variance might be the responsibility of the production manager. Materials usage variances might arise

because materials are:
● wasted in production due to sloppy or careless work;
● wasted because they are inferior;
● used more efficiently because staff take more care in their work;
● wasted due to a machine malfunction.

The direct materials variance for the biscuit manufacturer is £140 (F). It is influenced by both the materials price variance which is favourable, £440, and the materials usage variance which is adverse, £300. Notice that the adverse usage variance is outweighed by the favourable price variance.

Simpson's potato chips are produced by Simpson Ltd. It supplies the retail trade in Yorkshire and a few other outlets in the north. Its factory is located in Dewsbury and it employs 24 staff. The most important raw material is potatoes which it purchases from a large potato farmer in Lincolnshire. Table 66.4 shows the budgeted and actual prices paid for potatoes and the budgeted and actual usage of potatoes in a particular budget period.

Table 66.4 Budgeted and actual prices and usage of potatoes for Simpson Ltd

	Price (per kilo)	Usage (kilos)	Direct material cost
Budgeted	10p	20,000	£2,000
Actual	12p	24,000	£2,880

(a) For the budget period calculate:
(i) the materials price variance;
(ii) the materials usage variance;
(iii) the direct materials variance.
(b) Explain how the results in (a) might affect the business.

Direct labour variances

The direct wage bill is the amount of money paid to workers involved in production. A direct labour variance will occur when the budgeted direct wage bill is different to the actual direct wage bill. In the case of the biscuit manufacturer, the budgeted wage rates and actual wage rates, and the budgeted

Table 66.5 Budgeted and actual wage rates and labour hours for the biscuit manufacturer

	Wage rate	No. of labour hours	Direct wage bill
Budgeted	£5.00	1,500	£7,500
Actual	£5.20	1,600	£8,320
Direct labour variance			£820 (A)

number of labour hours and the actual number of labour hours used in a particular budget period, are shown in Table 66.5. The planned direct wage bill is £7,500. However, the actual wage bill is £8,320. This results in a £820 adverse variance. The direct labour variance is influenced by two other variances.

Wage rate variances A wage rate variance will result if there is difference between the budgeted wage rate paid to workers and the actual wage rate paid. In the case of the biscuit manufacturer the wage rate variance is :

Wage rate variance = (budgeted wage rate - actual wage rate) x actual hours
= (£5.00 - £5.20) x 1,600
= - £0.20 x 1,600
= £320 (A)

The wage rate variance is adverse because the actual wage rate is higher than the budgeted wage rate. The personnel manager may be responsible for this variance. The factors which might influence wage rates could include:
● trade union pressure;
● shortages of skilled labour;
● using a different type of labour;
● government legislation, such as raising the minimum wage.

Labour efficiency variances There will be a labour efficiency variance if there is a difference between the budgeted number of labour hours required in a budget period and the actual number of labour hours used. In the case of the biscuit manufacturer, the labour efficiency variance is:

Labour efficiency variance = (budgeted hours - actual hours) x budgeted wage
= (1,500 - 1,600) x £5.00
= - 100 x £5.00
= £500 (A)

The labour efficiency variance is adverse because the actual

number of hours worked is greater than the budgeted number. The production manager may be responsible for this variance. The factors which might influence the number of labour hours used might include:
● the productivity of workers;
● the reliability of machinery used by workers;
● how well trained workers are.

The direct labour variance for the biscuit manufacturer is £820 (A). It is influenced by the wage rate variance, £320(A), and the labour efficiency variance, £500 (A).

Overheads variances

Overheads variances arise when planned overhead costs are different from the actual overhead costs. Overheads are the general expenses incurred by a business (☞ unit 55). Table 66.7 shows the annual budgeted and actual overheads for the biscuit manufacturer. The overhead variances are also shown. The total overheads variance is adverse (£4,200). The main reason for this is the adverse distribution variance of £7,000. Some of the overheads in Table 66.7 do not have any variances. This is because the budgeted figures are exactly the same as the actual figures. This may happen when a business pays some of its bills in advance. For example, a business will normally know what rent is going to be charged in the next twelve months. This helps businesses to produce more accurate budgets.

Sometimes a business might separate overheads into fixed and variable costs (☞ unit 52). A business could then calculate the fixed overhead variance and the variable overhead variance. Overhead variances might be caused by:
● excessive or under utilisation of a service, such as wasteful or uneconomic use of a service;
● price changes for a service, such as an increase in accountancy fees;
● a change in the nature of a service, such as using oil for heating instead of electricity.

 Question 4

Wallace & Co. makes a range of swimwear which it sells to retailers in the UK. It operates six monthly budget periods. The direct labour budget is shown in Table 66.6. The actual figures for 1999 are also shown. Although swimwear is subject to seasonal demand, Wallace & Co. prefers to keep production fairly constant and build up stocks during the winter. This has helped to maintain good industrial relations in the past.
(a) For the six month budget period calculate:
  (i) the wage rate variance;
  (ii) the labour efficiency variance;
  (iii) the direct labour variance.
(b) Explain what is likely to have caused the direct labour variance.

Table 66.6 Direct labour budget and actual figures for Wallace & Co., 1999

	Jan	Feb	Mar	Apr	May	Jun
	Btd. Act.	Btd. Act.	Btd. Act.	Btd. Act.	Btd. Act.	Btd. Act.
Labour (hrs)	800 810	800 820	800 810	800 200	800 800	800 810
Wage rate	£5 £5	£5 £5	£5 £5	£5 £5	£5 £5	£5 £5
Direct lab. costs (£)	4,000 4,050	4,000 4,100	4,000 4,050	4,000 1,000	4,000 4,000	4,000 4,050

Btd.= budgeted Act.= actual

Table 66.7 *Annual budgeted and actual overheads for the biscuit manufacturer*

Description	Budgeted	Actual	Variance
Rent	£60,000	£60,000	0
Rates	£5,500	£5,500	0
Insurance	£1,200	£1,300	£100 (A)
Maintenance	£16,000	£15,000	£1,000 (F)
Distribution	£78,000	£85,000	£7,000 (A)
Telephone	£1,700	£1,600	£100 (F)
Administration	£64,000	£62,000	£2,000 (F)
Accountancy fees	£4,500	£4,700	£200 (A)
Depreciation	£20,000	£20,000	0
Total	£250,900	£255,100	£4,200 (A)

Sales margin variances

A sales margin variance will arise if there is either a change in the price charged by the business or a change from the budgeted volume of sales. Table 66.8 shows budgeted and actual prices and budgeted and actual sales volumes for cases of biscuits in a particular budget period. The budgeted value of sales is £20,000. However, the actual sales value is £21,320. This generates a favourable sales margin variance of £1,320 in this budget period.

Table 66.8 *Budgeted and actual prices and sales volumes for cases of biscuits*

	Price (per case)	Sales (cases)	Sales value
Budgeted	£2.50	8,000	£20,000
Actual	£2.60	8,200	£21,320
Sales margin variance			£1,320 (F)

The favourable variance shown in Table 66.8 is influenced by two other variances.

Sales margin price variance This will occur if the actual price charged by a business is different from the budgeted price. For the example above this is:

Sales margin price variance = (actual price - budgeted price) x actual sales
$$= (£2.60 - £2.50) \times 8,200$$
$$= £0.10 \times 8,200$$
$$= £820 \text{ (F)}$$

The sales margin price variance is favourable because the actual price charged is higher than the budgeted price. This variance may be the responsibility of the sales or marketing department. Such variances might arise due to:
● the chance to charge premium prices;
● sales in non-planned markets with different prices;

● changes in market conditions, such as a rival leaving the market.

Sales volume variance This will occur if the actual level of sales is different from the budgeted sales. For the biscuit manufacturer this is:

Sales volume variance = (actual sales - budgeted sales) x budgeted price
$$= (8,200 - 8,000) \times £2.50$$
$$= 200 \times £2.50$$
$$= £500 \text{ (F)}$$

The sales volume variance is favourable because the actual number of sales is greater than the budgeted number. This variance is likely to be the responsibility of the marketing department or the sales manager. Sales volume variances may arise due to:
● changes in the state of the economy;
● competitors' actions;
● changes in consumer tastes;
● government action, such as a cut in income tax;
● changes in the quality of the product;
● changes in marketing techniques.
     The sales margin variance for the biscuit manufacturer is £1,320 (F). It is influenced by both the sales price margin variance, £820 (F), and sales volume variance, £500 (F).

Question 5

Bromford Motors is a large car dealership based in Wimbledon, London. It sells cars for a Japanese car manufacturer. The company operates a very strict budget regime. The five sales staff have a fraction of their pay linked to budget performance. Table 66.9 shows the budgeted and actual prices and volume of cars sold for a particular budget period.

Table 66.9 *Budgeted and actual prices and sales of cars for Bromford Motors*

	Average price	Volume	Sales value
Budgeted	£9,500	250	£2,375,000
Actual	£9,325	269	£2,508,425

(a) For the budget period calculate the:
  (i) the sales margin price variance;
  (ii) the sales volume variance;
  (iii) sales margin variance.
(b) If the sales staff receive an equal share of half of any favourable variance generated, calculate how much they will each receive in the above budget period.
(c) Explain the possible causes of the variances in (a).

Cash variances

One variance not shown in Figure 66.2 is the cash variance. This is because cash and profit are not the same (☞ unit 59). Cash budgets are concerned with liquidity, not profitability. A

Table 66.10 Budgeted and actual cash flows for a carpet retailer

(£)

	JANUARY			FEBRUARY			MARCH		
	Budgeted	Actual	Variance	Budgeted	Actual	Variance	Budgeted	Actual	Variance
Cash receipts	25,000	25,600	600F	26,000	27,100	1,100F	30,000	29,800	200A
Cash inflow	25,000	25,600	600F	26,000	27,100	1,100F	30,000	29,800	200A
Purchases	15,000	17,000	2,000A	15,000	16,000	1,000A	20,000	22,000	2,000A
Wages	6,500	6,600	100A	6,500	6,700	200A	8,000	7,600	400F
Overheads	2,000	2,100	100A	2,000	1,800	200F	2,500	2,000	500F
Cash outflow	23,500	25,700	2,200A	23,500	24,500	1,000A	30,500	31,600	1,100A
Net cash flow	1,500	(100)	1,600A	2,500	2,600	100F	(500)	(1,800)	1,300A
Opening balance	4,000	4,000	0	5,500	3,900	1,600A	8,000	6,500	1,500A
Closing balance	5,500	3,900	1,600A	8,000	6,500	1,500A	7,500	4,700	2,800A

cash variance will show the difference between budgeted cash flows and actual cash flows. Table 66.10 shows the budgeted and actual cash flows for a carpet retailer in a three month budget period. The cash variances are also shown. A favourable cash variance arises when more cash flows in than was planned and if cash outflows are lower than planned. An adverse cash variance is caused by more cash flowing out than budgeted or less cash flowing in. In Table 66.10 all the closing balance cash variances are adverse. This means that the amount of cash actually left at the end of each month was lower than budgeted. For example, in January it was planned to have £5,500 at the end of the month. However, the actual closing balance was £3,900 giving an adverse variance of £1,600.

Cash variances can be caused by many factors. Some examples include:

● lower or higher than expected cash sales;
● customers not settling their accounts on time;
● unexpected costs;
● unexpected inflation.

Benefits of variance analysis

● It allows senior managers to monitor the performance of the organisation as a whole, as well as different sections of the organisation. For example, analysing departmental cost variances may allow a business to find out why certain costs are too high. Alternatively, it allows businesses to identify good practice and discover why some costs are lower.
● Prompt variance analysis allows managers to assess whether variances are caused by internal or external factors. Once causes have been traced, they can be corrected.
● By identifying variances and their causes managers may be able to produce more accurate budgets in future. This will aid planning and perhaps improve the performance of the business.
● Budgetary control in general helps to improve

accountability in businesses. It can also be linked to performance related pay. For example, budget holders may receive a bonus payment at the end of the budget period if they can show favourable variances.

Summary

1. Describe the 3 steps in budgetary control.
2. Why is the profit variance probably the most important of all?
3. What is the difference between the materials price variance and the materials usage variance?
4. What might cause a direct materials variance?
5. What is the difference between the wage rate variance and the labour efficiency variance?
6. What might cause a direct labour variance?
7. Why might some overhead variances be 0?
8. Explain the difference between the sales margin price variance and the sales volume variance.
9. What is a cash variance?
10. State 4 benefits of variance analysis.

Key terms

Budgetary control - a business system which involves making future plans, comparing the actual results with the planned objectives and then investigating causes of any differences.
Variance analysis - the process of calculating variances and attempting to identify their causes.
Zero-based budgeting - a system of budgeting where no money is allocated for costs or spending unless they can be justified by the fund holder (the items are given a 'zero' value).

Case study

Windrush Training Services

Windrush Training Services is a small company quoted on AIM. When it was floated in 1990 it offered a range of training services to businesses in London. However, it got into difficulties and its shares were suspended in 1996. A new management team was appointed and the company became more focused by specialising in training courses for the financial services sector. The new managing director identified a market niche. There was a need for employees in the financial services sector to be kept in touch with a

growing body of regulatory guidelines. Windrush used direct marketing to sell its short, update courses to financial analysts, stockbrokers, equity houses and financial advisers

The company raised some fresh capital through a rights issue and trading in its shares began again in January 1998. The new management team recognised a greater need for financial direction. It produced a twelve month cash budget for 1999 and used variance analysis to aid cash control.

Table 66.12 *Cash budget for Windrush Training Services, 1999*

(£000)

	JAN	FEB	MAR	APR	MAY	JUN	JUL	AUG	SEP	OCT	NOV	DEC
Fresh capital	800											
Course fees	200	200	220	220	250	250	300	300	350	350	300	300
Total inflow	1,000	200	220	220	250	250	300	300	350	350	300	300
Wages	100	100	100	100	100	110	110	110	110	110	110	220
Rent	10	10	10	10	10	10	10	10	10	10	10	10
Marketing	20	20	15	15	10	10	10	5	5	5	5	5
Heat & light			5			5			5			5
VAT			92			108			142			142
Other expenses	25	25	25	25	25	25	25	25	25	25	25	25
Total outflow	155	155	247	150	145	268	155	150	297	150	150	407
Net cashflow	845	45	(27)	70	105	(18)	145	150	53	200	150	(107)
Opening balance	(990)	(145)	(100)	(127)	(57)	48	30	175	325	378	578	728
Closing balance	(145)	(100)	(127)	(57)	48	30	175	325	378	578	728	621

Table 66.12 *Actual cash movements for Windrush Training Services, 1999*

(£000)

	JAN	FEB	MAR	APR	MAY	JUN	JUL	AUG	SEP	OCT	NOV	DEC
Fresh capital	800											
Course fees	160	180	170	160	190	240	300	310	390	590	530	200
Total inflow	960	180	170	160	190	240	300	310	390	590	530	200
Wages	100	100	100	100	100	110	110	110	110	110	110	300
Rent	10	10	10	10	10	10	10	10	10	10	10	10
Marketing	20	20	15	15	20	20	25	25	25	30	30	30
Heat & light			5			5			5			5
VAT			76			88			150			196
Other expenses	20	19	21	10	23	19	15	5	21	17	19	32
Total outflow	150	149	227	135	153	252	160	150	321	167	169	573
Net cashflow	810	31	(57)	25	37	(12)	140	160	69	423	361	(373)
Opening balance	(990)	(180)	(149)	(206)	(181)	(144)	(156)	(16)	144	213	636	997
Closing balance	(180)	(149)	(206)	(181)	(144)	(156)	(16)	144	213	636	997	624

(a) **Explain how budgetary control can help a company like Windrush.**

(b) **Evaluate the cash flow budget of Windrush using variance analysis.**

   (i) **Calculate the annual variances for each item of receipts and expenditure and show whether**

the balances are favourable or adverse.

  (ii) **Examine possible reasons for adverse or favourable balances.**

  (iii) **Discuss the possible effects of variances on the business.**

67 The Compilation of Accounts

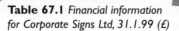

When are accounts compiled?

The compilation of accounts is the final task in the book-keeping process outlined in unit 62. It involves using the information generated by recording business transactions to produce a balance sheet, profit and loss account and cash flow statement. Some businesses use computer software to compile accounts on a regular basis.

Final accounts are compiled at the end of the trading year. Small businesses such as sole traders, partnerships and small limited companies may employ chartered or certified accountants to compile their accounts. Business owners provide records of transactions and supporting documents. Most large companies and many medium-sized companies employ their own accountants who compile accounts for the business. However, companies which produce their own accounts must get them audited by an independent firm of accountants.

Once the accounts have been compiled they can be used by the various stakeholders. Public limited companies distribute their annual reports and accounts to all their shareholders.

Compiling the balance sheet

The structure of a balance sheet was explained in unit 56. Figure 67.1 shows a summary of the balance sheet structure. Accountants produce balance sheets according to accounting convention set out by the Accounting Standards Board (ASB) and the **Companies Act, 1985**.

A balance sheet can be compiled by inserting the appropriate information in the correct positions in the structure. Consider the financial information in Table 67.1 for Corporate Signs Ltd, a business which makes neon signs for

Figure 67.1 Balance sheet summary diagram

	£	
Fixed assets	A	
Current assets	B	
Current liabilities	C	
Net current assets (working capital)	D	B-C
Total assets less current liabilities	E	(A+B)-C or A+D
Creditors: amounts due after one year(Long term liabilities)	F	
Net assets	G	E-F or (A+D)-F
Capital and reserves (Capital employed or shareholders' funds)	H	G=H

Table 67.1 Financial information for Corporate Signs Ltd, 31.1.99 (£)

Mortgage	100,000
Share capital	100,000
Other reserves	71,000
Premises	231,000
Debtors	75,000
Vehicles	87,000
Stocks and work in progress	98,000
Plant and equipment	199,000
Current liabilities	201,000
Retained profit	290,000
Cash at bank	112,000
Unsecured bank loan	60,000
Intangible assets	20,000

companies. All the information relates to the assets, liabilities and capital of the company on 31.1.1999.

To compile the balance sheet for Corporate Signs Ltd, the following step-by-step approach might be used.

- Identify which of the items are assets, which are liabilities and which are capital and reserves.
- Write the title and date at the top of the account.
- List the fixed assets and add them up. Fixed assets are premises (£231,000), plant and equipment (£199,000) and vehicles (£87,000). All these are tangible assets (a total of £517,000). Intangible assets are £20,000. Fixed assets are therefore tangible plus intangible assets, a total of £537,000.
- List the current assets and add them up. Current assets are stocks and work in progress (£98,000), debtors (£75,000) and cash at bank (£112,000) which total £285,000.
- List the current liabilities and add them up. Current liabilities are stated as £201,000. These are the amounts falling due within one year.
- Enter the value for net current assets by subtracting current liabilities from current assets (£285,000 - £201,000 = £84,000).
- Enter the value for total assets less current liabilities by adding fixed assets to net current assets (£537,000 + £84,000 = £621,000).
- List the creditors: amounts falling due after one year and add them up. These are the mortgage (£100,000) and the unsecured bank loan (£60,000) which total £160,000.
- Enter the value for net assets by subtracting creditors: amounts falling due after one year from total assets less current liabilities (£621,000 - £160,000 = £461,000).
- List the capital and reserves and add them up. Capital and reserves are share capital (£100,000), other reserves (£71,000) and retained profit (£290,000) which total £461,000.

● Check that the value of capital and reserves (also shown as shareholders' funds or capital employed on some balance sheets) are the same as net assets. If the balance sheet has been compiled accurately, the value of net assets should be exactly the same as capital employed.

If the above steps are followed the result should be the same as the balance sheet shown in Table 67.2. Remember that normally both the current trading figures, and the previous year's figures, are shown in the accounts.

Table 67.2 *Balance sheet for Corporate Signs Ltd, 31.1.99*

CORPORATE SIGNS LTD - BALANCE SHEET AS AT 31 JANUARY 99

	£
Fixed assets	
Tangible assets	
Premises	231,000
Plant and equipment	199,000
Vehicles	87,000
	517,000
Intangible assets	20,000
	537,000
Current assets	
Stocks and work in progress	98,000
Debtors	75,000
Cash at bank	112,000
	285,000
Current liabilities	201,000
Net current assets	84,000
Total assets less current liabilities	621,000
Creditors: amounts falling due after one year	
Mortgage	(100,000)
Unsecured bank loan	(60,000)
Net assets	461,000
Capital and reserves	
Share capital	100,000
Other reserves	71,000
Retained profit	290,000
Capital employed	461,000

Transactions and the balance sheet

How might a transaction affect the balance sheet? There are two sides to every transaction and transactions can affect both assets and liabilities. For example, when a business makes a sale it will receive cash (an increase in assets) but reduce its stock of finished goods (a decrease in assets). Table 67.4

Question 1

Drew Scientific Group plc designs and manufactures diagnostic instruments, associated software and the consumables needed to carry out clinical tests. The core business of the group is diabetic monitoring. Table 67.3 shows some financial information about the assets, liabilities and capital of Drew Scientific Group plc.

Table 67.3 *Financial information for Drew Scientific Group plc 1998 and 1997*

	(£000)	
	1998	**1997**
Share capital	286	242
Share premium	6,467	3,405
Tangible assets	754	703
Debtors	897	660
Stocks	562	686
Other reserves	(191)	(191)
Intangible assets	266	275
Investments (short term)*	1,000	-
Long term liabilities	45	81
Cash at bank	604	61
Retained profit	(2,961)	(2,487)
Current liabilities	437	1,335

* current assets

Source: adapted from Drew Scientific Group, *Annual Report and Accounts*, 1998.

(a) Compile the balance sheet for Drew Scientific using the information in Table 67.3. Note that the retained profit and other reserves are both negative values.
(b) Comment on any significant differences between the two years.

shows the balance sheet of Gregory Issacs plc, a construction company, as at 31 August 1999. How might four transactions affect the balance sheet?

● **Transaction 1.** The company buys a range of new equipment for one division of the business for £1 million. It arranges to pay by credit. This will increase fixed assets (equipment) by £1 million and current liabilities (trade creditors) by £1 million.

● **Transaction 2.** A consignment of stocks are ordered costing £500,000 on credit. This will increase current assets (stocks) by £500,000 and current liabilities (trade creditors) by £500,000.

● **Transaction 3.** The company makes an interim dividend payment to shareholders of £1.8 million. This will decrease current assets (cash at bank) by £1.8 million and creditors: amounts due within one year (dividend) by £1.8 milion.

● **Transaction 4.** A debtor repays £200,000 to the company.

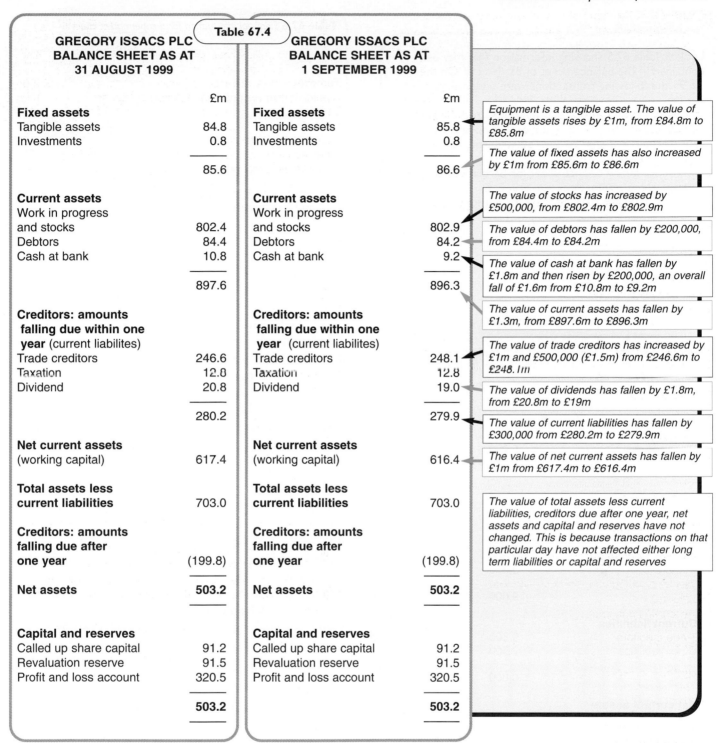

Table 67.4

GREGORY ISSACS PLC BALANCE SHEET AS AT 31 AUGUST 1999

	£m
Fixed assets	
Tangible assets	84.8
Investments	0.8
	85.6
Current assets	
Work in progress and stocks	802.4
Debtors	84.4
Cash at bank	10.8
	897.6
Creditors: amounts falling due within one year (current liabilites)	
Trade creditors	246.6
Taxation	12.8
Dividend	20.8
	280.2
Net current assets (working capital)	617.4
Total assets less current liabilities	703.0
Creditors: amounts falling due after one year	(199.8)
Net assets	**503.2**
Capital and reserves	
Called up share capital	91.2
Revaluation reserve	91.5
Profit and loss account	320.5
	503.2

GREGORY ISSACS PLC BALANCE SHEET AS AT 1 SEPTEMBER 1999

	£m
Fixed assets	
Tangible assets	85.8
Investments	0.8
	86.6
Current assets	
Work in progress and stocks	802.9
Debtors	84.2
Cash at bank	9.2
	896.3
Creditors: amounts falling due within one year (current liabilites)	
Trade creditors	248.1
Taxation	12.8
Dividend	19.0
	279.9
Net current assets (working capital)	616.4
Total assets less current liabilities	703.0
Creditors: amounts falling due after one year	(199.8)
Net assets	**503.2**
Capital and reserves	
Called up share capital	91.2
Revaluation reserve	91.5
Profit and loss account	320.5
	503.2

Equipment is a tangible asset. The value of tangible assets rises by £1m, from £84.8m to £85.8m

The value of fixed assets has also increased by £1m from £85.6m to £86.6m

The value of stocks has increased by £500,000, from £802.4m to £802.9m

The value of debtors has fallen by £200,000, from £84.4m to £84.2m

The value of cash at bank has fallen by £1.8m and then risen by £200,000, an overall fall of £1.6m from £10.8m to £9.2m

The value of current assets has fallen by £1.3m, from £897.6m to £896.3m

The value of trade creditors has increased by £1m and £500,000 (£1.5m) from £246.6m to £248.1m

The value of dividends has fallen by £1.8m, from £20.8m to £19m

The value of current liabilities has fallen by £300,000 from £280.2m to £279.9m

The value of net current assets has fallen by £1m from £617.4m to £616.4m

The value of total assets less current liabilities, creditors due after one year, net assets and capital and reserves have not changed. This is because transactions on that particular day have not affected either long term liabilities or capital and reserves

This will only affect current assets. Debtors will fall by £200,000 and cash at bank will increase by £200,000.

It is assumed here that all these transactions are carried out on 1 September 1999. The effects of these transactions are shown in Table 67.4.

Compiling the profit and loss account

The structure of a profit and loss account was explained in unit 55. Accountants produce profit and loss accounts according to accounting convention set out by the ASB and the Companies Act. There is, however, some variation when looking at the profit and loss accounts of limited companies.

The profit and loss account will contain three key sections.
- The trading account, where gross profit is calculated.
- The profit and loss account, where net profit is calculated.
- The profit and loss appropriation account, which shows how the net profit is distributed.

Consider the financial information in Table 67.6, which shows the revenue and expenses incurred by a supermarket chain. The following steps could be used when compiling a

Look at Table 67.5 showing information that may be contained in the balance sheet of Barden Ltd. On the 1.5.99 the following transactions were undertaken by Barden.

- Debtors repaid £1,000,000, deposited into the bank.
- £2,500,000 of materials were bought on trade credit.
- A machine was sold off for £500,000 and money paid into the bank.

(a) Produce a new balance sheet for Barden Ltd which takes these transactions into account.

(b) A year later the balance sheet for Barden Ltd showed the following values:
- fixed assets of £20,000,000;
- current assets of £12,000,000;
- current liabilities of £8,000,000;
- long term liabilities of £4,000,000.

Calculate the value of:
(i) net current assets;
(ii) total assets less current liabilities;
(iii) capital and reserves.

Table 67.5 *Information from a balance sheet for Barden Ltd, as at 30.4.99*

	£000	£000
Fixed assets		
Factory	11,000	
Plant and machinery	5,000	
Equipment	2,500	
Financial assets	1,000	
		19,500
Current assets		
Stocks	3,000	
Work-in-progress	2,500	
Debtors	3,500	
	9,000	
Current liabilities		
Trade creditors	3,500	
Other liabilities	2,500	
	6,000	
Net current assets		3,000
Total assets less current liabilities		22,500
Creditors falling due after more than one year	6,000	
Net assets		16,500
Capital and reserves		
Share capital	9,000	
Other reserves	2,000	
Retained profit	5,500	
		16,500

Table 67.6 *Financial information for a supermarket chain*

	£m
Turnover	3,000
Administrative expenses and distribution costs	400
Taxation	45
Cost of sales	2,500
Interest paid (net)	5
Dividends	30
Non-operating income	30

profit and loss account from a set of figures:

For the trading account
- Write the title and date at the top of the account.
- Enter the value for turnover (£3,000m).
- Enter the value for cost of sales (remember that the cost of sales must be adjusted for stock (☞ unit 55). The value of cost of sales has already been adjusted in Table 67.6 and is £2,500m).
- Enter the value for gross profit by subtracting cost of sales from turnover (£3,000m - £2,500m = £500m).

For the profit and loss account
- Enter the administrative/operating expenses underneath the gross profit (£400m).
- Enter the value for operating profit by subtracting operating expenses from gross profit (£500m - £400m = £100m).
- Enter the value of other income below operating profit (£30m).
- Enter the value for profit before interest and tax by adding non-operating income to operating profit (£100m + £30m = £130m).
- Enter the value for (net) interest payable underneath the value of profit before interest and tax (£5m).
- Enter the profit on ordinary activities before tax by subtracting (net) interest paid from profit before interest and tax (£130m - £5m). This gives a total of £125m.

For the profit and loss appropriation account
- Enter taxation underneath profit on ordinary activities before tax (£45m).
- Enter the value for profit on ordinary activities after tax by subtracting taxation from profit on ordinary activities before tax (£125m - £45m) which gives £80m.
- Enter dividends underneath profit on ordinary activities after tax (£30m).
- Enter the value for retained profit (or loss) for the financial year by subtracting dividends from profit on ordinary activities after tax (£80m - £30m = £50m).

The retained profit for the financial year figure is the last entry in the accounts (although the earnings per share is usually listed in PLC accounts underneath retained profit). If the above steps are followed then the result should be the same as the profit and loss account shown in Table 67.7.

Table 67.7 *Profit and loss account for a supermarket chain*

PROFIT AND LOSS ACCOUNT
YEAR ENDED 31.1.99

	£m
Turnover	3,000
Cost of sales	2,500
Gross profit	500
Administrative expenses and distribution costs	400
Operating profit	100
Non-operating income	30
Profit before interest and tax	130
Interest (net)	5
Profit on ordinary activities before tax	125
Taxation	45
Profit on ordinary activities after tax	80
Dividends	30
Retained profit	50

Additional entries for inclusion in the profit and loss account

The profit and loss account shown here is fairly simple. Profit and loss accounts for other businesses may appear slightly different. This is because they contain additional information. Whether they do or not depends on the nature of their business and what has happened during the trading year. Some possible differences are described below.

● Exceptional items, if they occur, should be included after operating profit in the account. If the exceptional item is a cost, such as a bad debt, then it should be subtracted from operating profit. If it is revenue, it should be added.
● Sometimes the operating expenses are split into specific expenses. For example, they might be divided between distribution costs and administration expenses. It is quite normal to show these items separately and then subtract them from gross profit.
● The figure for interest paid shown here is a net figure (net interest = interest paid - interest received). The actual breakdown of interest paid and received would be shown in the notes to the accounts. Net interest can be positive or negative. Some businesses receive no interest, so the figure would simply be for interest paid. In other accounts both the figures for interest paid and received will be shown
● Some businesses do not calculate gross profit in the

account. This might be because they provide services rather than make goods. If this is the case all costs and expenses are added together and subtracted from turnover to calculate operating profit.

The list above is not definitive. In reality it is rare to find two companies with identical entries in their profit and loss accounts.

The trial balance

In practice accountants use the **trial balance** (☞ unit 62) to

Question 3

Oasis Stores Plc Annual Report and Accounts stated that: 'The principal activities of the company are the origination and production of exclusive ladies clothing under the "OASIS" name for sale through its own retail outlets in the United Kingdom, Ireland and Germany and to licensees for sale through outlets in Europe, Taiwan and the Middle East'.

Table 67.8 *Financial information for Oasis, 1997 and 1998*

	1998 (£000)	1997
Turnover	92,936	81,651
Cost of sales	46,665	36,828
Distribution costs	30,739	24,900
Administrative expenses	6,828	5,693
Other operating income	43	95
Non-operating income	-	-
Interest receivable and similar income	1,624	1,308
Interest payable and similar charges	8	20
Taxation	3,479	5,376
Dividend	3,934	3,672

Source: adapted from Oasis, *Annual Report and Accounts*, 1998.

(a) Using the information in Table 67.8, compile a profit and loss account for Oasis Stores Plc by calculating: (i) gross profit; (ii) operating profit; (iii) profit before interest and taxation; (iv) profit on ordinary activities before taxation; (v) profit on ordinary activities after tax; (vi) retained profit for the financial period.
(b) Comment on any significant changes over the two years.

compile final accounts. The trial balance is an account which lists all the debit balances and all the credit balances in the entire book-keeping system. In the trial balance:

- **debit entries** represent assets and expenses. They show where money has gone, for example, expenditure on assets such as plant, equipment and vehicles or expenses such as wages, advertising and materials.
- **credit balances** represent liabilities and revenue. They show inflows of money from sales, loans, capital and other sources.

In the trial balance the debit total should equal the credit total. This is because all transactions have been entered twice using the double entry system of recording. This helps to check that transactions have been entered accurately. However, it is still possible for the trial balance to balance even if errors have been made. This is because some errors will not be traced, for example, if a transaction is not recorded at all.

Table 67.9 shows the trial balance for Kingsmead Leisure Park. The debit side shows all balances relating to expenses, such as marketing expenses, and assets such as cash. The credit side shows all balances relating to revenue, such as turnover, and liabilities, such as creditors. Note that the total value of debits £4,901,000 is equal to the total value of credits £4,901,000.

Table 67.9 *Trial balance for Kingsmead Leisure Park as at 31.7.99*

	(£000)	
	Debit	Credit
Turnover		2,413
Purchases	380	
Marketing expenses	920	
Operating expenses	712	
Non-operating income		100
Interest paid	200	
Taxation	80	
Debtors	71	
Stock as at 31.7.98 (opening stock)	34	
Bank account	804	
Tangible assets	1,700	
Creditors		901
Long term loan		1,000
Share capital		200
Profit and loss account		287
	4,901	4,901

Compiling the profit and loss account from the trial balance

By following the steps described earlier it is possible to compile a profit and loss account for the Kingsmead Leisure Park, from the information in the trial balance. However, there are some additional factors which need to be taken into account.

- Only the revenue and expense entries in the trial balance are needed to compile the profit and loss account.
- The cost of sales figure needs to be adjusted for stock. In the case of Kingsmead Leisure Park the opening stock is given in the trial balance (£34,000). If the closing stock is £40,000, cost of sales can be calculated by:

Opening stock	£34,000
Add purchases	£380,000
	£414,000
Less closing stock	£40,000
Cost of sales	£374,000

- In the case of Kingsmead Leisure Park there is no dividend payment for the year. As a result retained profit will be the same as profit after tax.

The completed profit and loss account for Kingsmead is shown in Table 67.10.

Table 67.10 *Profit and loss account for Kingsmead Leisure Park*

KINGSMEAD LEISURE PARK - PROFIT AND LOSS ACCOUNT YEAR ENDED 31.7.99

	(£000)
Turnover	2,413
Cost of sales	374
Gross profit	2,039
Marketing expenses	920
Operating expenses	712
Operating profit	407
Non-operating income	100
	507
Interest paid	200
Profit on ordinary activities before tax	307
Taxation	80
Profit on ordinary activities after tax	227
Dividends	-
Retained profit	227

Compiling the balance sheet from the trial balance

By following the steps listed earlier it is possible to compile a balance sheet from the trial balance. The asset and liability entries in the trial balance are transferred into the normal balance sheet structure. However, when preparing a balance sheet in this way a number of factors must be taken into account.

- The stock figure in the current assets section of the balance sheet will be the closing stock figure (£40,000) not the opening stock figure in the trial balance.

● The retained profit in the profit and loss account (£227,000) is added to the profit and loss account entry in the trial balance (£287,000). This gives a new profit and loss account balance of £514,000.

The completed balance sheet for Kingsmead Leisure Park is shown in Table 67.11.

Table 67.11 *Balance sheet for Kingsmead Leisure Park*

KINGSMEAD LEISURE PARK - BALANCE SHEET AS AT 31.7.99

	(£000)
Fixed assets	
Tangible assets	1,700
Current assets	
Stock	40
Debtors	71
Cash at bank	804
	915
Current liabilities	901
Net current assets	14
Total assets less current liabilities	1,714
Long term liabilities	(1,000)
NET ASSETS	714
Capital and reserves	
Share capital	200
Profit and loss account	514
CAPITAL EMPLOYED	714

Compiling accounts for sole traders

The examples used so far in the unit have involved the accounts of limited companies. When compiling the accounts of sole traders the same principles for account construction still apply. However, there are some important differences to be recognised.

● The bottom of the balance sheet for a limited company shows capital and reserves. For a sole trader the bottom of the balance sheet shows the capital owed to the owner (☞ unit 56). It is made up of the opening balance plus the net profit for the year.

● Drawings (☞ unit 56) will usually appear on the trial balance for a sole trader. Drawings are usually transferred to the capital account in the balance sheet. They are

Paulo Campolucci runs a small shoe manufacturing business in Bath. At the end of each trading year his daughter, Ellen, compiles his business accounts. Ellen handles her father's tax affairs and the first task before completing his self-assessment tax form is to compile the business accounts. The trial balance for the business is shown in Table 67.12.

Table 67.12 *Trial balance for Paulo Campolucci*

PAULO CAMPOLUCCI - TRIAL BALANCE AS AT 31.1.99

	Debit	Credit
Turnover		121,001
Purchases	52,009	
Stock at 31.1.98	5,991	
Operating expenses	36,002	
Non-operating income		567
Interest paid	21,000	
Tools and equipment	13,532	
Vehicle	12,500	
Debtors	4,399	
Cash at bank	10,000	
Current liabilities		16,001
Long term bank loan		14,000
Drawings	12,000	
Capital account		15,864
	167,433	167,433

(a) What is the advantage to Paulo Campolucci of producing a trial balance?

(b) Compile the profit and loss account for Paulo Campolucci from the trial balance and show that net profit is equal to £12,897. Note that the closing stock is £6,331.

(c) Compile the balance sheet for Paulo Campolucci from the trial balance and show that the value of closing capital is £16,761.

subtracted at the end of the capital account to determine the closing capital balance. For example, the closing capital for G.M.Smith, a market trader, is:

Opening capital	£56,811
Add net profit	£21,006
	£77,817
Less drawings	£15,000
Closing capital	£62,817

Summary

1. When do businesses normally compile their accounts?
2. Which assets are listed first in the balance sheet?
3. How is net current assets calculated in the balance sheet?
4. How is the net assets figure calculated in the balance sheet?
5. How is gross profit calculated in the trading account?
6. What entries will appear in the profit and loss appropriation account?
7. How are exceptional items dealt with in the profit and loss account?
8. Under what circumstances might gross profit not appear in a profit and loss account?
9. What do: (a) debit entries; (b) credit entries; represent in the trial balance?
10. Why should the value of debit entries equal the value of credit entries?
11. Does the trial balance include closing stock or opening stock for a business?
12. State 2 differences between a sole trader balance sheet and a limited company balance sheet.

Case study

Cafe Inns

Cafe Inns operates about 15 public houses and a handful of restaurants and cafe bars in the North West region. Some examples include Hartley's at Warrington, The Cricketers at Ormskirk, Harry's Bar at Oldham and Burlington's restaurant at Preston.

During the year the company increased its turnover marginally by 1.9 per cent. However, its profit margin increased to 13.5 per cent from 10.5 per cent in the previous year. Operating profit increased by 32 per cent and the company raised its dividend payment to 3.3p per share, an increase of 10 per cent.

During the year Cafe Inns invested around £1,000,000. This included the refurbishment of the Swan and Royal at Clithero. Finally, as a result of some capital restructuring, the company's debt was reduced and gearing fell from 81 per cent to 49 per cent. Table 67.13 shows some financial information for Cafe Inns relating to assets, liabilities, revenue and expenses.

Table 67.13 *Financial information for Cafe Inns 1997 and 1998*

(£000)

	1998	1997
Turnover	9,085	8,915
Operating expenses	3,716	3,441
Taxation	92	173
Tangible assets	15,129	11,200
Stocks	106	74
Cash	262	395
Current liabilities	1,539	1,668
Share premium	2,355	993
Cost of sales	4,144	4,542
Net interest	(378)	(367)
Dividends paid	260	175
Investments (Short term)	123	123
Debtors	922	843
Long term liabilities	5,270	5,165
Share capital	6,132	4,058
Profit and loss account	1,246	751

Source: adapted from Cafe Inns, *Annual Report and Accounts*, 1998.

(a) **Using the information in Table 67.13, compile the 1998 profit and loss account for Cafe Inns (include also the 1997 figures).**
(b) **Using the information in Table 67.13, compile the 1998 balance sheet for Cafe Inns (include also the 1997 figures).**
(c) **Based on your answers to (a) and (b) comment on the performance of Cafe Inns over the two year period.**

The investigation process

Unit 3 showed stakeholders who may be interested in a company's accounts. Different users are interested for different reasons. For example, shareholders may want information to assess the rewards for holding shares. Managers may try to gauge performance. This unit explains how the information in the final accounts can be interpreted. It is possible to base investigation on some of these figures alone. Also, information can be obtained by combining some of these figures and carrying out a RATIO ANALYSIS. The chairperson's report, the directors' report and the notes to the accounts provide extra material as well.

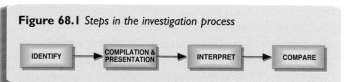

Figure 68.1 *Steps in the investigation process*

IDENTIFY → COMPILATION & PRESENTATION → INTERPRET → COMPARE

The investigation process is shown in Figure 68.1. The first step is to **identify** the figures that are relevant from the final accounts. Suitable data must be used. For example, an accountant might need information on current assets and current liabilities, rather than total assets and liabilities, in order to assess the solvency (☞ unit 57) of the business.

Once the correct figures have been chosen they can be **compiled** and **presented** into a useful form, such as percentages.

To **interpret** ratios an understanding of their significance is needed. Ratios can be used to find out the firm's financial position, assess performance, analyse capital structure and help shareholders when deciding whether to invest.

Finally, ratios may be used to make a variety of **comparisons**. For example, it is common to compare this year's figures with those of last year.

What are ratios?

Financial ratios can be calculated by comparing two figures in the accounts which are related in some way. It may be one number expressed as a percentage of another or simply one number divided by another. For an accounting ratio to be useful the two figures must be connected, eg profit is arguably related to the amount of capital a firm uses.

Ratios on their own are not particularly useful. They need to be compared with other ratios. For example, knowing that a firm has a net profit to sales ratio of 11 per cent may not be helpful. However, if it was 9 per cent the year before, this can be compared with the present figure. There is a number of ways in which ratios can be compared.

Over time The same ratio can be compared in two time periods, eg the current financial year and the previous one. Comparisons over time also show trends. This allows a

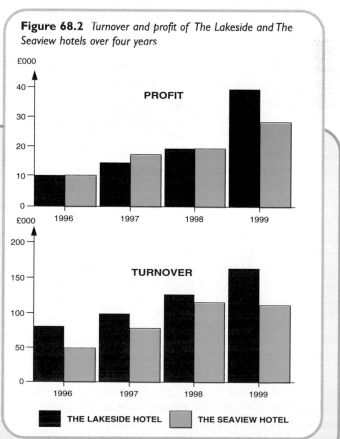

Figure 68.2 *Turnover and profit of The Lakeside and The Seaview hotels over four years*

Question 1

The Lakeside and The Seaview are two hotels of a very similar size situated in Scarborough. Some information regarding their turnover and profit is illustrated in Figure 68.2.

(a) Study the data in Figure 68.2. Make an interfirm comparison of the two businesses over the period 1996-99. (The use of mathematical ratios is not required.)

(b) Explain why it is important to compare 'like with like' when making statistical comparisons.

business to decide whether or not certain aspects are improving.

Interfirm comparisons It is possible for a business to compare its results with others in the same industry. This could highlight particular strengths or weaknesses. For example, a handbag manufacturer with a turnover of £120,000 might think its £30,000 profit satisfactory. Another manufacturer may have a profit of £50,000 on a turnover of £130,000. Assuming that the two firms are very similar, the relative profit of the first business is not as good. It is important that firms compare 'like with like'.

Interfirm comparisons over time Using the two standards above we can make interfirm comparisons over time. This shows trends that may exist. Such comparisons are quite popular and could help analyse the behaviour of a whole industry, over a lengthy time period.

Results and forecasts Management, for example, may want to compare actual results with predicted results. Management prepare budgets and make forecasts about the future. Decision makers will also try to account for differences which exist between the actual results and their estimates. This is called variance analysis (☞ unit 66).

Types of ratios and their users

Ratios fall into one of four general categories.

Performance ratios Performance ratios help to show how well a business is doing. They tend to focus on profit, capital employed and turnover. Stakeholders such as owners, managers, employees and potential investors are all likely to be interested in the profitability and efficiency of a business. However, when measuring performance a business must take into account its objectives. For example, a performance ratio using profit may not be appropriate if the business is pursuing another objective, such as survival. Competitors might also use performance ratios to make comparisons of performance. Activity ratios are likely to be used internally by managers. This is because they focus on how well a business uses its resources. For example, the performance of the credit control department could be assessed by looking at how quickly debts are collected.

Liquidity ratios Liquidity ratios illustrate the solvency of a business - whether it is in a position to repay its debts. They focus on short term assets and liabilities. Creditors are likely to be interested in liquidity ratios to assess whether they will receive money that they are owed. Money lenders and suppliers, for example, will be interested in how easily a business can repay its debts. Potential investors might also have an interest in liquidity ratios for the same reason. In addition,

Question 2

(a) If growth is a company's objective, what type of ratio might be used to evaluate whether it is achieving its objective?
(b) What types of ratios might be of interest to:
   (i) the senior management of a plc;
   (ii) a debenture holder;
   (iii) a pension fund manager?
(c) Suggest reasons why the types of ratio would be important for each answer given to question (b).

managers might use them to aid financial control, ie to ensure that they have enough liquid resources to meet debts.

Gearing ratios Gearing ratios show the long term financial position of the business. They can be used to show the relationship between loans, on which interest is paid, and shareholders' funds, on which dividends might be paid. Creditors are likely to be concerned about a firm's gearing. Loans, for example, have interest charges which must be paid. Dividends do not have to be paid to ordinary shareholders. As a business becomes more highly geared (loans are high relative to share capital) it is considered more risky by creditors. The owners of a business might prefer to raise extra funds by borrowing rather than from shareholders, so they retain control of the business. Gearing ratios can also show the relationship between fixed interest bearing debt and the long term capital of a business. This is discussed later in this unit.

Shareholders' ratios The owners of limited companies will take an interest in ratios which help measure the return on their shareholding. Such ratios focus on factors such as the earnings and dividends from shares in relation to their price. Potential investors will also show an interest in shareholders' ratios.

There may be other bodies or institutions which might use the above ratios. The media produce reports about businesses which they publish. They might use a range of ratios when reporting on particular businesses. In some newspapers the dividend yield and price/earnings ratio are actually published every day for a range of public limited companies. The Inland Revenue might also use ratio analysis when investigating the performance of a business. Some businesses collect business data and sell it to other users. For example, an agency might write a financial report on a business and part of it might consist of comments about particular ratios.

Ratio analysis

Tables 68.1-68.3 show the profit and loss account and balance sheet for Crowmarsh plc and some additional information

Table 68.1 *Profit and loss account of Crowmarsh plc*

CROWMARSH PLC PROFIT AND LOSS ACCOUNT
Year ended 31st July 1999

	1999 £000	1998 £000
Turnover	69,618	63,718
Cost of sales	45,272	39,945
Gross profit	24,346	23,773
Operating expenses	19,476	18,160
Operating profit	4,870	5,613
Income from investments	-	35
Profit on ordinary activities before interest and tax	4,870	5,648
Interest receivable	351	218
	5,221	5,866
Interest payable	1,058	568
Profit on ordinary activities before taxation (net profit)	4,163	5,298
Tax on profit on ordinary activities	1,494	1,987
Profit on ordinary activities after taxation	2,669	3,311
Extraordinary items	1,224	-
Profit for the financial year	1,445	3,311
Dividends	761	712
Retained profit for the period	684	2,599
Earnings per share	41.42p	51.41p

Table 68.2 *Additional information for the accounts of Crowmarsh plc*

	1999	1998
(i) Long term loan capital	£2,454,000	£2,589,000
(ii) Fixed interest preference share capital	£250,000	£250,000
(iii) Preference shareholders' dividend	£9,000	£9,000
(iv) Number of ordinary shares	£6,423,000	£6,423,000
(v) Share price 31st July	1950p	1845p

Table 68.3 *Balance sheet of Crowmarsh plc*

CROWMARSH PLC BALANCE SHEET
31st July 1999

	1999 £000	1998 £000
Fixed assets		
Tangible assets	10,092	9,811
Investments	59	44
	10,151	9,855
Current assets		
Stocks	18,162	16,981
Debtors	11,488	10,674
Cash at bank and in hand	7,219	3,516
	36,869	31,171
Creditors: amounts falling due within one year	20,203	14,148
Net current assets	16,666	17,023
Total assets less current liabilities	26,817	26,878
Creditors: amounts falling due after more than one year	(2,514)	(2,834)
Provisions for liabilities and charges	(997)	(1,010)
Minority interests	-	(75)
Deferred income	(279)	(485)
	(3,790)	(4,404)
Net assets	23,027	22,474
Capital and reserves		
Called up share capital	1,856	1,856
Share premium account	169	169
Revaluation reserve	893	893
Other reserves	147	278
Profit and loss account	19,962	19,278
Shareholders' funds	23,027	22,474

Current liabilities bracket for the first Creditors row. *Long term liabilities* bracket for Creditors due after more than one year through Deferred income.

from the notes to the accounts. Crowmarsh plc is a manufacturer of a wide range of clothing and sportswear. It sells to a worldwide market. The figures shown in the accounts can be used to calculate ratios and analyse the financial position of the company.

Performance ratios

Assuming that a company's main aim is to make a profit, performance ratios will focus on the year's trading profit. The profit figure alone is not a useful performance indicator. In 1999, for example, Crowmarsh made a pre-tax profit (profit on ordinary activities before tax) of £4,163,000, shown in Table 68.1. In 1998 the figure was £5,298,000. Does this mean that Crowmarsh performed worse in 1999 than in 1998? To answer this question it is necessary to see how this profit was generated.

Return on capital employed The return on capital employed (ROCE) measures the return on the capital invested in the business. It expresses profit before tax and interest are taken into account as a percentage of capital employed. The advantage of this ratio is that it relates profit to the size of the business. It can be calculated using the formula:

$$\text{RETURN ON CAPITAL EMPLOYED (ROCE)} = \frac{\text{Profit on ordinary activities before tax and interest}}{\text{Capital employed}} \times 100$$

There are many different ways in which businesses calculate this ratio. The choice of method depends upon what figures are presented and what relationships in the accounts the business wants to investigate. For example, the figure for **profit on ordinary activities before tax and interest** for Crowmarsh in 1999 is £4,870,000 as shown in Table 68.1. Taxes are ignored because they are set by factors outside the control of the business, eg government. Interest is also ignored. Alternatively, a business may want to look at the relationship between all sources of finance and capital employed. Thus it would use the figure for **profit plus interest payments**. This is £5,221,000 for Crowmarsh in 1999 (£4,870,000 + £351,000).

A business may also consider the returns from different types of **capital employed**.

● **Total capital.** Total capital employed can be defined as total capital - share capital, reserves, long term liabilities (such as loans) and current liabilities. The ROCE can be calculated using the formula:

$$\text{Return on capital employed (ROCE)} = \frac{\text{Profit on ordinary activities before tax and interest}}{\text{Total capital employed}} \times 100$$

For Crowmarsh the profit before tax and interest in 1999 was £4,870,000, shown in the profit and loss account (Table 68.1).

A simple method of calculating total capital employed is to add the fixed assets and current assets together. Fixed assets for Crowmarsh in 1999 were £10,151,000 and current assets were £36,869,000, as shown in Table 68.3. The total capital employed was £47,020,000.

Total capital employed can also be calculated by adding: capital and reserves (£23,027,000); plus long term liabilities (£3,790,000); plus current liabilities (£20,203,000); shown in Table 68.3. Total capital again equals £47,020,000.

Calculating a ROCE figure for 1998 allows a comparison over time.

$$\text{For 1999} \quad \text{ROCE} = \frac{£4,870,000}{£47,020,000} \times 100 = 10.4\%$$

$$\text{For 1998} \quad \text{ROCE} = \frac{£5,648,000}{£41,026,000} \times 100 = 13.8\%$$

The return on capital employed will vary between different industries. Generally, the higher it is the better. Over the two years Crowmarsh has seen a worsening in the ratio from 13.8 per cent to 10.4 per cent. Comparing the returns from capital employed with other possible returns will help Crowmarsh to decide if the ratio is satisfactory. For example, around 6 per cent could have been earned from a low risk deposit account in 1998-99. Crowmarsh may decide that a return of 10.4 per cent in 1999 is adequate, given that it is above the returns from such an account. Higher risk accounts, on the other hand, may yield higher returns.

● **Long term capital.** It is also possible to calculate capital employed as long term capital. For Crowmarsh the long term capital is capital and reserves (£23,027,000 in Table 68.3) **plus** long term loans (£2,454,000 in Table 68.2) which gives capital employed of £25,481,000. Profit before tax and interest in 1999 was £4,870,000.

$$\text{For 1999} \quad \text{ROCE} = \frac{£4,870,000}{£25,481,000} \times 100 = 19.1\%$$

$$\text{For 1998} \quad \text{ROCE} = \frac{£5,648,000}{£25,063,000} \times 100 = 22.5\%$$

● **Net assets.** This is a simplified method of calculating ROCE using capital and reserves. These are equal to net assets on the balance sheet. Liabilities are excluded.

$$\text{ROCE/RETURN ON NET ASSETS} = \frac{\text{Profit on ordinary activities before tax and interest}}{\text{Net assets}} \times 100$$

For Crowmarsh the profit before tax and interest in 1999 was £4,870,000 shown in Table 68.1. The net assets figure for 1999, £23,027,000, is shown clearly in the balance sheet in Table 68.3.

$$\text{For 1999} \quad \text{Return on net assets} = \frac{£4,870,000}{£23,027,000} \times 100 = 21.1\%$$

$$\text{For 1998} \quad \text{Return on net assets} = \frac{£5,648,000}{£22,474,000} \times 100 = 25.1\%$$

Over the two years, returns have deteriorated from 25.1 per cent to 21.1 per cent. However, whether Crowmarsh's returns are satisfactory depends on factors such as the current rate of interest, competitors' returns and the state of the economy. The return on net assets will always be higher than other calculations of ROCE because the denominator is lower.

Gross profit margin This shows the gross profit made on sales turnover.

$$\text{GROSS PROFIT MARGIN} = \frac{\text{Gross profit}}{\text{Turnover}} \times 100$$

For Crowmarsh in 1999 gross profit was £24,346,000 and turnover was £69,618,000, shown in Table 68.1.

For 1999
$$\text{Gross profit margin} = \frac{£24,346,000}{£69,618,000} \times 100 = 34.9\%$$

For 1998
$$\text{Gross profit margin} = \frac{£23,773,000}{£63,718,000} \times 100 = 37.3\%$$

An improved gross profit margin may be a result of an increase in turnover relative to costs of sales or a fall in costs of sales as a percentage of turnover. Higher gross profit margins are preferable to lower ones. However, they vary significantly according to industry type. As a rule, the quicker the turnover, the lower the gross profit margin. A car retailer with a slow turnover is likely to have a higher gross profit margin than a supermarket with a higher turnover. Car distributors have high stock values with slow turnover. Higher profits help to compensate for this. Similarly, a specialist retailer of expensive electrical goods with a slow turnover might expect a higher gross profit margin than a large supermarket with a much higher turnover.

The gross profit margin of Crowmarsh is lower in 1999 than in 1998 - 34.9 per cent compared to 37.3 per cent. Interfirm comparisons would help to confirm whether this was a satisfactory performance.

Net profit margin This ratio helps to measure how well a business controls its overheads. If overheads are low then there will be less of a difference between the gross and net profit margins. This is because net profit is gross profit minus overheads. The net profit ratio can be calculated by:

$$\text{NET PROFIT MARGIN} = \frac{\text{Net profit before tax}}{\text{Turnover}} \times 100$$

For Crowmarsh in 1999 net profit before tax was £4,163,000 and turnover was £69,618,000, shown in Table £68.1. Note that the net profit figure here is net profit after interest has been paid - it is the figure for 'Profit on ordinary activities before taxation'.

For 1999
$$\text{Net profit margin} = \frac{£4,163,000}{£69,618,000} \times 100 = 5.98\%$$

For 1998
$$\text{Net profit margin} = \frac{£5,298,000}{£63,718,000} \times 100 = 8.3\%$$

Again, higher profit margins are better than lower ones. The net profit margin of Crowmarsh has fallen over the two years from 8.3 per cent to 5.98 per cent. This might suggest

Question 3

Glassic Ltd manufactures glassware for restaurants and the retail trade. The two main shareholders in the company are Holly Baron and Diana Scott. They are actively involved in running the business and both share the view that to improve performance they must set annual targets. Holly is the financial manager and is responsible for setting such targets. She monitors a number of important ratios. The targets for 1999 are shown in Table 68.4. Table 68.5 shows some financial information for Glassic Ltd for the financial years 1998 and 1999.

Table 68.5 *Financial information for Glassic Ltd*

	1998	1999
Turnover	2,765,000	2,980,000
Gross profit	1,042,000	1,241,000
Profit before interest and tax	850,000	740,000
Net profit	745,000	699,000
Net assets	5,120,000	5,570,000

Table 68.4 *Ratio targets for Glassic Ltd (1999)*

Gross profit margin	40 per cent
Net profit margin	25 per cent
Return on net assets	15 per cent

(a) Calculate: (i) the gross profit margin; (ii) the net profit margin; (iii) the return on net assets for Glassic Ltd for 1998 and 1999.

(b) What might account for the change in the net profit margin between 1998 and 1999?

(c) Evaluate the performance of Glassic Ltd on the basis of your answers in (a).

that the performance of the business according to this measure was not as good in 1999. Note that there is quite a difference between the gross profit and net profit margins - the net profit margin is a lot lower. This might suggest that Crowmarsh incurs quite high overheads. According to the profit and loss account (Table 68.1), operating expenses were £19,476,000 in 1999. This is nearly 80 per cent of the gross profit figure.

The net profit margin is only suitable for comparisons over time. Interfirm comparisons could be misleading because different businesses have different patterns of spending, which affect this ratio.

Activity ratios

Activity ratios or asset usage ratios allow a business to measure how effectively it uses some of its resources. A number of these ratios exist. Three are perhaps used most by businesses.

Asset turnover This ratio measures the productivity of assets. It shows the value of sales generated by every £1 of net assets. Higher ratios show that assets are more productive, ie assets are being used more effectively.

$$\text{ASSET TURNOVER} = \frac{\text{Turnover}}{\text{Net assets}}$$

The turnover for Crowmarsh in 1999 was £69,618,000, shown in Table 68.1. The value of net assets shown in the balance sheet in Table 68.2 was £23,027,000.

For 1999
$$\text{Asset turnover} = \frac{£69,618,000}{£23,027,000} = 3.02$$

For 1998
$$\text{Asset turnover} = \frac{£63,718,000}{£22,474,000} = 2.84$$

According to the calculations above the productivity of assets for Crowmarsh has improved over the two years.

Stock turnover This ratio measures the number of times during the year that a business sells the value of its stocks.

$$\text{STOCK TURNOVER} = \frac{\text{Cost of sales}}{\text{Stocks}}$$

The cost of sales for Crowmarsh in 1999 was £45,272,000 shown in Table 68.1. The value of closing stocks as shown in the balance sheet in Table 68.3 was £18,162,000.

For 1999
$$\text{Stock turnover} = \frac{£45,272,000}{£18,162,000} = 2.49 \text{ times}$$

For 1998
$$\text{Stock turnover} = \frac{£39,945,000}{£16,981,000} = 2.35 \text{ times}$$

Stock turnover can also be expressed in terms of the number of days it takes to sell stocks. This is found by:

$$\text{STOCK TURNOVER} = \frac{\text{Stocks}}{\text{Cost of sales}} \times 365$$

For 1999
$$\text{Stock turnover} = \frac{£18,162,000}{£45,272,000} \times 365 = 146 \text{ days}$$

For 1998
$$\text{Stock turnover} = \frac{£16,981,000}{£39,945,000} \times 365 = 155 \text{ days}$$

High stock turnovers are preferred (or lower figures in days). A higher stock turnover ratio means that profit on the sale of the stock is earned more quickly. Thus, businesses with high stock turnovers can operate on lower margins. A declining stock turnover ratio might indicate higher stock levels, a large amount of slow moving or obsolete stock, a wider range of products being stocked or a lack of control over purchasing.

Over the two years Crowmarsh's stock turnover ratio has improved. In 1999 it has been selling its total stock in 146 days, compared to 155 days in 1998. However, a stock turnover ratio of 2.49 a year means that, on average, money is tied up in stock for 146 days. This may give cause for concern, although again the nature of the business needs to be taken into account.

Debt collection period This measures the number of days it takes to collect debts on average.

$$\text{DEBT COLLECTION PERIOD} = \frac{\text{Debtors}}{\text{Turnover}} \times 365$$

According to the balance sheet in Table 68.3, the value of Crowmarsh's debtors in 1999 was £11,488,000. Turnover was £69,618,000, shown in Table 68.1.

For 1999
$$\text{Debt collection period} = \frac{£11,488,000}{£69,618,000} \times 365 = 60 \text{ days}$$

For 1998
$$\text{Debt collection period} = \frac{£10,674,000}{£63,718,000} \times 365 = 61 \text{ days}$$

Businesses often vary in the amount of time they give customers to pay for goods or services. Credit periods may be 30, 60, 90 or even 120 days. Obviously businesses prefer a short debt collection period. Crowmarsh's performance has only slightly improved between 1998 and 1999. A debt collection period of over 60 days could be a problem for a small business. Even for a larger company it may indicate a need to improve the credit control (☞ unit 59). The point at which the debt collection period becomes a problem may also depend on the industry in which the business operates.

Businesses often draw up a list of the 'ages' of debtors. Some debts will be outstanding over 30 days, some over 60 days, some over 90 days and some even longer. A business with large amounts of longer outstanding debts may have a problem with payment. Again, credit control may need to improve to solve this.

Liquidity ratios

Unit 59 showed that effective cash management, as well as profitability, is essential for business survival. Companies must have access to liquid assets - assets that can be turned easily into cash, to meet day to day payments. Liquidity ratios are concerned with a business's ability to convert its assets into cash. Two of the ratios already considered, stock turnover and the debt collection period, give some indication of a firm's liquidity. If these ratios are poor then it means that money is tied up in stock and debtors. It is, therefore, not immediately available to make payments. Two other ratios can be used to assess liquidity.

Current ratio The current ratio shows the relationship between the current assets and the current liabilities.

$$\text{CURRENT RATIO} = \frac{\text{Current assets}}{\text{Current liabilities}}$$

For Crowmarsh in 1999 current assets were £36,869,000 as shown in Table 68.3. Current liabilities were £20,203,000.

$$\text{For 1999} \quad \text{Current ratio} = \frac{£36,869,000}{£20,203,000} = 1.82$$

$$\text{For 1998} \quad \text{Current ratio} = \frac{£31,171,000}{£14,148,000} = 2.2$$

It is suggested that a business should aim for a current ratio of between 1.5:1 and 2:1. A business operating below 1.5:1 may face working capital problems (☞ unit 60). For example, a business may be **overtrading** or **overborrowing**, which could result in difficulties when paying immediate bills. Operating above 2:1 may suggest that too much money is tied up unproductively. The current ratio of Crowmarsh has changed from 2.2:1 in 1998 to 1.82:1 in 1999. Crowmarsh is in a comfortable position with a ratio of 1.82:1. It might

Question 4

Melvyn Sykes runs a second hand car dealership in Tewkesbury. Most of his sales are for cash and he deals in middle-of-the-range vehicles. Willoughby's Ltd produces a range of boiled sweets in its Rochdale factory. These are sold to supermarkets and marketed under supermarket brand names. Extracts from the accounts of the two companies are shown in Table 68.6.

Table 68.6 *Extracts from the accounts of Melvyn Sykes and Willoughby's Ltd*

| | Melvyn Sykes | | Willoughby's | |
	1998	1999	1998	1999
Turnover	£131,000	£145,000	£5.781m	£6.762m
Cost of sales	£86,000	£89,000	£4.670m	£5.791m
Gross profit	£45,000	£56,000	£1.113m	£0.971m
Current assets				
Stocks	£89,000	£101,000	£0.122m	£0.143m
Debtors	£1,000	£1,500	£1.011m	£0.993m
Cash at bank	£23,000	£27,000	£0.223m	£0.129m

(a) Calculate:
  (i) stock turnover in days;
  (ii) gross profit margins;
  for both businesses for 1998 and 1999.
(b) Compare the ratios in (a) and account for the differences between the two businesses.
(c) (i) Calculate the debt collection period for both businesses.
  (ii) Account for the differences between them.

even be argued that Crowmarsh is in a better position in 1999 because it had assets tied up unproductively in 1998 with a ratio of 2.2:1. Many businesses are able to operate safely outside these limits however, especially if most of their sales are for cash.

Acid test ratio The acid test or **quick ratio** is a more severe test of liquidity. This is because it does not treat stocks as a liquid asset. Stocks are not guaranteed to be sold, they may become obsolete or deteriorate. They are therefore excluded from current assets in the calculation.

$$\text{ACID TEST RATIO} = \frac{\text{Current assets - stocks}}{\text{Current liabilities}}$$

All the figures required for this ratio are listed in the balance sheet in Table 68.3.

$$\text{For 1999} \quad \text{Acid test ratio} = \frac{£36,869,000 - £18,162,000}{£20,203,000} = 0.93$$

For 1998
Acid test ratio $= \dfrac{£31,171,000 - £16,981,000}{£14,148,000} = 1.00$

A quick ratio of 1:1 is desirable. In both years Crowmarsh's ratio is nearly 1:1. This suggests that the company has adequate liquid resources according to this measure.

Gearing ratios

The gearing ratio looks at the balance of funding in the capital structure of a business. In the USA, gearing is called **leverage**. This term is often used in the UK today.

Gearing ratio There are several ways in which gearing ratios can be expressed. One simple method is to look at the relationship between loans and equity. Many company accounts express equity as capital plus reserves. Therefore, gearing can be calculated by:

$$\text{GEARING RATIO} = \dfrac{\text{Loans}}{\text{Equity}} \times 100$$

For Crowmarsh in 1999 the value of long term loans in Table 68.2 was £2,454,000. The value of its capital and reserves was £23,027,000 as shown in Table 68.3.

For 1999
Gearing ratio $= \dfrac{£2,454,000}{£23,027,000} \times 100 = 10.66\%$

For 1998
Gearing ratio $= \dfrac{£2,589,000}{£22,474,000} \times 100 = 11.52\%$

Another method involves looking at the relationship between the long term capital of the business and fixed interest/dividend bearing capital. Long term capital includes shareholders' funds and long term loans. Fixed interest/dividend bearing capital includes long term loans from banks, certain preference shares and debentures. The gearing ratio can be calculated by:

$$\text{Gearing ratio} = \dfrac{\substack{\text{Long term loan capital + other fixed} \\ \text{interest/dividend bearing capital}}}{\substack{\text{Long term loan capital +} \\ \text{Shareholders' funds}}} \times 100$$

For Crowmarsh in 1999 the value of long term loan capital in Table 68.2 was £2,454,000. The other fixed interest bearing debt shown in Table 68.2 is preference shares, with a value of £250,000. The value of shareholders' funds was £23,027,000, shown in Table 68.3.

For 1999
Gearing ratio $= \dfrac{£2,454,000 + £250,000}{£2,454,000 + £23,027,000} \times 100$

$= \dfrac{£2,704,000}{£25,481,000} \times 100 = 10.61\%$

For 1998
Gearing ratio $= \dfrac{£2,589,000 + 250,000}{£2,589,000 + 22,474,000} \times 100$

$= \dfrac{£2,839,000}{£25,063,000} \times 100 = 11.3\%$

If the ratio is less than 50 per cent then the company is said to be low geared. This means that the majority of the capital of a business is likely to be raised from shareholders. Conversely, if the ratio is greater than 50 per cent the company is said to be high geared. This means that most of the capital is borrowed. With a gearing ratio of around 10-11 per cent, Crowmarsh is low geared. Only a small fraction of its capital is borrowed. Over the two years the gearing ratio actually fell slightly.

Why is the gearing ratio important to a business? A business **has** to pay interest on some long term debts, such as loans, debentures and certain preference shares. Raising a large amount in this way is likely to commit the business to fixed interest payments which it has to pay, even in difficult trading periods. However, if it raises money from ordinary shares, it has the option not to pay a dividend to ordinary shareholders if it does not have sufficient profit. High geared businesses, therefore, are likely to be in a weaker position as they are committed to greater interest payments.

Creditors prefer lending to low geared companies as there is less risk. Shareholders may prefer businesses to raise money from methods other than increasing shareholders' funds. Raising extra capital from loans, rather than issuing shares, means that they retain greater control of the business. They would not, however, want the business to be so highly geared that it faced problems. The advantages and disadvantages of being low geared and high geared are discussed in detail in unit 57.

Interest cover The gearing ratio is a balance sheet measure of financial risk. Interest cover is a profit and loss account measure. This ratio assesses the business's ability to pay interest by comparing profit and interest payments.

$$\text{INTEREST COVER} = \dfrac{\text{Profit before tax and interest}}{\text{Interest paid}}$$

In 1999 Crowmarsh's profit before tax and interest was £4,870,000, shown in Table 68.1. Interest paid was £1,058,000.

For 1999

$$\text{Interest cover} = \frac{£4,870,000}{£1,058,000} = 4.6 \text{ times}$$

For 1998

$$\text{Interest cover} = \frac{£5,648,000}{£568,000} = 9.9 \text{ times}$$

A figure of 1 means that a business would need to use all its profit to pay interest. This is obviously not a good position to be in. A figure of 1-2 is also likely to cause problems. An interest cover of about 5 or 6 is said to be adequate. Over the two years Crowmarsh's interest cover has deteriorated from 9.9 to 4.6. However, for a low geared business like Crowmarsh this is likely to be satisfactory.

Shareholders' ratios

Investors are interested in the returns or dividends (☞ unit 3) they may get from holding shares. A number of ratios can be used to measure these returns.

Shareholders' ratios focus on shares where dividends can vary from one year to another. These are mainly ordinary shares (☞ unit 57), although there are other shares with variable returns. Debentures and certain preference shares tend to have fixed returns. This means that the business has to pay a fixed dividend or interest payment.

Earnings per share The earnings per share (EPS) measures how much each share is earning. It does not show how much money is actually paid to shareholders, but how much is available to be paid to shareholders. Shareholders may not be paid all of the money because the business will wish to hold back an amount for other purposes. The EPS is always shown in the accounts at the bottom of the profit and loss account.

For Crowmarsh, which has ordinary shares and fixed interest preference shares:

$$\text{EARNINGS PER SHARE (EPS)} = \frac{\begin{array}{c}\text{Net profit after tax - payment on fixed}\\\text{interest bearing capital}\\\text{(or profit accruing to ordinary shareholders)}\end{array}}{\text{Number of (ordinary) shares}}$$

For Crowmarsh in 1999 the net profit (after tax) was £2,669,000, shown in Table 68.1. The payment of fixed interest bearing capital in Table 68.2 is the value of preference shareholders' dividends, £9,000. So the net profit accruing to ordinary shareholders was £2,669,000 - £9,000 = £2,660,000. There were 6,423,000 shares issued as shown in Table 68.2.

For 1999

$$\text{Earnings per share} = \frac{£2,660,000}{£6,423,000} = 41.42\text{p}$$

For 1998

$$\text{Earnings per share} = \frac{£3,302,000}{£6,423,000} = 51.41\text{p}$$

Over the two years the earnings per share of Crowmarsh has deteriorated. However, whether this is a satisfactory return or not depends on the share price in each year. On its own the EPS is not particularly helpful.

Price/earnings ratio The price/earnings ratio (P/E) is said to reflect the confidence shown in the company. It shows how many years, at current earnings, it will take an investor to recover the cost of the share. The market prices of shares are not shown in the annual reports. However, they are listed in many newspapers every day.

Question 5

In the last few years Greenwich Shields has enjoyed an enormous boost in contracts. The company, based in London, manufactures and supplies high precision shields for use at military bases all over Europe. The shields are partly made up in the Greenwich factory and then completed on site. The shields, made from 3mm steel, are to protect equipment from radio waves which might penetrate normal buildings. Although the company has enjoyed more business, they began to suffer from overtrading. Table 68.7 shows some financial information for Greenwich Shields. The company also had to acquire more equipment to meet increasing orders. This was funded by long term borrowing.

Table 68.7 *Financial information for Greenwich Shields*

	1996	1997	1998	(£000s) 1999
Stocks	581	667	712	912
Debtors	1,221	1,556	1,871	2,011
Cash	1,444	1,001	598	23
Current liabilities	2,401	2,770	2,008	3,390
Long term loans	1,001	1,490	2,900	3,700
Equity	2,000	2,000	2,000	2,000

(a) Calculate the current ratios and acid test ratios for Greenwich Shields for 1996 to 1999.

(b) What evidence is there to suggest that the company is overtrading?

(c) (i) Calculate the gearing ratios for Greenwich Shields between 1996 and 1999.
(ii) Comment on and account for the pattern of gearing shown in (i).

$$\text{PRICE/EARNINGS RATIO (P/E)} = \frac{\text{Market price per share}}{\text{Earnings per share}}$$

For Crowmarsh on 31 July 1999 the share price was 1950p, shown in Table 68.2. The earnings per share were 41.42p, shown in Table 68.1.

For 1999
$$\text{Price/earnings ratio} = \frac{1950p}{41.42p} = 47.08$$

For 1998
$$\text{Price/earnings ratio} = \frac{1845p}{51.41p} = 35.89$$

The higher the ratio the more confidence investors have in the future of the company. Acceptable price/earnings ratios will tend to vary from industry to industry. Generally, price/earnings ratios of between 10 and 15 are said to be acceptable. Investors in Crowmarsh would presumably be happy with a ratio of 35.89 in 1998 and with an improvement to 47.08 in 1999. These ratios may seem quite high. However, price/earnings ratios can be considerably higher than the norm due to:
● the high status of a company;
● the share price being overvalued;
● investors expecting future profits to grow significantly.

Return on equity This ratio measures the 'return on investment'. It shows the profit to the shareholder as a percentage of the shareholders' equity. For Crowmarsh, which only has ordinary shares and fixed interest preference shares:

$$\text{RETURN ON EQUITY} = \frac{\begin{array}{c}\text{Net profit after tax - payment on fixed}\\\text{interest bearing capital}\\\text{(or profit accruing to ordinary shareholders)}\end{array}}{\text{Equity - fixed interest bearing capital}}$$

For Crowmarsh in 1999 the net profit (after tax) was £2,669,000, shown in Table 68.1. The payment of fixed interest bearing capital in Table 68.2 is the value of preference shareholders' dividends, £9,000. So the net profit accruing to ordinary shareholders was £2,669,000 - £9,000 = £2,660,000. Equity, defined as capital and reserves, was £23,027,000 as shown in Table 68.3. Fixed interest bearing capital was £250,000, shown in Table 68.2. So for Crowmarsh:

For 1999
$$\text{Return on equity} = \frac{£2,669,000 - £9,000}{£23,027,000 - £250,000}$$

$$= \frac{£2,660,000}{£22,777,000} = 11.7\%$$

For 1998
$$\text{Return on equity} = \frac{£3,311,000 - £9,000}{£22,474,000 - £250,000}$$

$$= \frac{£3,302,000}{£22,224,000} = 14.85\%$$

The higher the return is, the better. Crowmarsh's ratio has deteriorated from 14.85 per cent to 11.7 per cent from 1998 to 1999. However, whether 11.7 per cent is high enough depends on other interest bearing accounts. For example, around 6 per cent could have been earned from a low risk deposit account in 1998-99. Shareholders may decide that the return on equity was adequate. As with the EPS, this ratio does not illustrate how much money is **actually** paid to shareholders, but how much is **available** to be paid to shareholders.

Dividends per share This ratio does show how much money is actually paid to shareholders. For Crowmarsh, it can be calculated as:

$$\text{DIVIDENDS PER SHARE} = \frac{\text{Dividend (on ordinary shares)}}{\text{Number of (ordinary) shares}}$$

In 1999 Crowmarsh's ordinary shareholders were paid a total of £761,000 in dividends, shown in Table 68.1. Preference shareholders were paid £9,000, shown in Table 68.2. So the dividend paid to ordinary shareholders was £761,000 - £9,000 = £752,000. There were 6,423,000 shares issued as shown in Table 68.2.

For 1999
$$\text{Dividends per share} = \frac{£752,000}{6,423,000} = 11.7p$$

For 1998
$$\text{Dividends per share} = \frac{£703,000}{6,423,000} = 10.9p$$

This ratio is quite important to shareholders. It enables them to calculate their total dividend payment by multiplying dividends per share by the number of shares they hold. They did see a slight improvement from 10.9p to 11.7 p over the two years. Whether or not 11.7p per share is a good return depends on how much was paid for the shares and what could be earned elsewhere.

Dividend yield This ratio helps to measure the value of the return on the share for an investor. It shows the dividend per share as a percentage of the market price.

$$\text{DIVIDEND YIELD} = \frac{\text{Dividends per share}}{\text{Market price}} \times 100$$

For Crowmarsh, the market price of shares in July 1999 was 1950p, shown in Table 68.2. The dividends per share were 11.7p, as calculated earlier.

For 1999
$$\text{Dividend yield} = \frac{11.7p}{1950p} \times 100 = 0.6\%$$

For 1998
$$\text{Dividend yield} = \frac{10.9p}{1845p} \times 100 = 0.59\%$$

A higher dividend yield is preferred. Comparison with other firms could tell whether a dividend yield of 0.6 per cent is satisfactory for shareholders. The level of interest rates at any given time will also influence the value of dividend yield. An unusually high dividend yield might suggest to investors that a company has problems. This is because a falling share price will raise the dividend yield and a falling share price might be the result of a loss of confidence in the company.

Dividend cover This ratio takes into account the chance of capital growth. There are two financial motives for holding shares - to earn dividends and to make a capital gain. If a company's share price rises over time an investor can make a capital gain when the shares are sold. Dividend cover links profit after tax with the dividend payment.

$$\text{DIVIDEND COVER} = \frac{\begin{array}{c}\text{Net profit after tax - payment on}\\\text{fixed interest bearing capital}\\\text{(or profit accruing to ordinary shareholders)}\end{array}}{\text{Dividends (on ordinary shares)}}$$

For Crowmarsh in 1999 the net profit (after tax) was £2,669,000, shown in Table 68.1. The payment of fixed interest bearing capital in Table 68.2 is the value of preference shareholders' dividends, £9,000. So the net profit accruing to ordinary shareholders was £2,669,000 - £9,000 = £2,660,000. Crowmarsh's ordinary shareholders were paid a total of £761,000 in dividends, shown in Table 68.1. Preference shareholders' were paid £9,000. So the dividend paid to ordinary shareholders was £761,000 - £9,000 = £752,000.

For 1999
$$\text{Dividend cover} = \frac{£2,669,000 - £9,000}{£761,000 - £9,000}$$

$$= \frac{£2,660,000}{£752,000} = 3.5 \text{ times}$$

For 1998
$$\text{Dividend cover} = \frac{£3,311,000 - £9,000}{£712,000 - £9,000}$$

$$- \frac{£3,302,000}{£703,000} = 4.7 \text{ times}$$

This ratio shows how many times the dividend could have been paid out of current earnings. For Crowmarsh the cover has deteriorated over the two years from 4.7 to 3.5 times. A figure of 3.5 suggests that the dividend could have been paid 3.5 times over. If the cover is too high shareholders might argue that the company should pay higher dividends. If the cover is too low it may mean that profits are low for the year or that the company is not retaining enough profit for new investment.

Question 6

Amanda Collins is a fund manager for National Union, a pension company based in Manchester. She is looking for investment opportunities in the food processing industry and has received a copy of the financial information shown in Table 68.8.

Table 68.8 *Financial information for three companies*

	Carrows	Wrights	Shepards
Net profit (after tax)	£19.6m	£45.9m	£129.9m
Dividends	£8.0m	£22.9m	£47.0m
Share price	102p	339p	390p
Number of shares	250m	455m	1,289m

None of the businesses have any fixed interest/dividend capital.

(a) Calculate: (i) the earnings per share; (ii) the price/earnings ratio; (iii) the dividends per share; (iv) the dividend yield (v) the dividend cover for all three companies.

(b) If Amanda only wanted to buy shares in one of the above companies which one would you choose? Support your answer using evidence from (a).

(c) What other information might have been helpful in making your decision in (b)?

Limitations to ratio analysis

Ratio analysis does not provide a complete means of assessing a company's financial position. There are also problems when using ratios.

When making comparisons over time, it is necessary to take into account the following:
- inflation;
- any changes in accounting procedures;
- changes in the business activities of a firm;
- changes in general business conditions and the economic environment.

It is also important that firms compare 'like with like' when using ratios, especially when making comparisons between businesses. Even firms in the same industry may be different. Their size, product mix or objectives might differ. Different accounting techniques might be used, eg different stock valuation and depreciation methods. The financial year endings may not be the same. We also need to account for differences in human judgement. Some information is estimated, eg provision for bad debts. Firms may window dress their final accounts (unit 69) to show they are in a better position. One way of doing this is by chasing debts just before the end of the financial year.

Ratio analysis is based on historic information and does not include other useful information, such as the chairperson's and directors' reports. It does not include some of the positive factors within a business such as the quality of the staff or the location, both of which affect performance. Providing these problems are recognised, ratios can be a useful tool for evaluating the accounts.

Summary

1. Briefly describe the steps involved in the investigation process when analysing a set of accounts.
2. Why might interfirm comparisons be useful?
3. What is the difference between performance and activity ratios?
4. What is the difference between liquidity ratios and gearing ratios?
5. How do gross and net profit margins differ?
6. What do stock turnover and debtors turnover measure?
7. Describe the difference between the current ratio and the acid test ratio.
8. What is meant by a high geared company?
9. Why is interest cover a profit and loss account measure of financial risk?
10. Which of the shareholders' ratios measures the actual financial return shareholders receive?
11. Which ratio reflects the prospect of capital growth?
12. Describe the limitations of ratio analysis.

Key terms

Acid test ratio - similar to the current ratio but excludes stocks from current assets. Sometimes called the quick ratio.

Asset turnover - a measure of the productivity of assets.

Current ratio - assesses the firm's liquidity by dividing current liabilities into current assets.

Debt collection period - the number of days it takes to collect the average debt.

Dividend cover - how many times the dividend could have been paid from the year's earnings.

Dividends per share - the amount of money a shareholder will actually receive for each share owned.

Dividend yield - the amount received by the shareholder as a percentage of the share price.

Earnings per share - the amount each ordinary share earns.

Gearing ratios - explore the capital structure of a business by comparing the proportions of capital raised by debt and equity.

Gross profit margin - expresses operating profit before tax and interest, ie gross profit, as a percentage of turnover.

Interest cover - assesses a firm's ability to meet interest payments by comparing profit and interest payable.

Net profit margin - shows the firm's ability to control overheads and expresses net profit before tax as a percentage of turnover.

Price/earnings ratio - relates the earnings per share to its market price and reflects the return from buying shares.

Ratio analysis - a numerical approach to investigating accounts by comparing two related figures.

Return on equity - measures the return on shareholders investment by expressing the profit earned by ordinary shareholders as a percentage of total equity.

Return on net assets - expresses profit as a percentage of long term assets only.

Return on capital employed - the profit of a business as a percentage of the total amount of money used to generate it.

Stock turnover - the number of times in a trading year a firm sells the value of its stocks.

Case study

Glyme Valley Farm and Cold Aston Farm

Patrick and Gillian O'Rourke have always wanted to own a farm. Patrick has worked on farms all his life and has a great deal of experience in mixed farming. Gillian, on the other hand, has been in publishing and recently sold her Gloucester-based publishing business for £350,000. They are now in a position to buy a small farm, although they expect to have to borrow some money to help fund the purchase. After several months of searching they have identified two possible targets. Both farms are private limited companies and both owners are keen for a quick sale.

Glyme Valley Farm - Price £400,000

Table 68.9 *Glyme Valley Farm profit and loss account, 1999*

GLYME VALLEY FARM -
PROFIT AND LOSS ACCOUNT
Y/E 31.1.99

	£
Turnover	1,532,000
Cost of sales	451,000
Gross profit	1,081,000
Overheads	900,000
Operating profit	181,000
Non-operating income	2,000
Profit before interest	183,000
Interest (net)	152,000
Profit on ordinary activities before tax	31,000
Taxation	11,000
Profit for the year after tax	20,000
Dividends	8,000
Retained profit for the period	12,000

Table 68.10 *Glyme Valley Farm Balance sheet, 1999*

GLYME VALLEY FARM - BALANCE SHEET
Y/E 31.1.99

	£
Fixed assets	
Buildings	610,000
Machinery	567,000
	1,177,000
Current assets	
Stocks	13,000
Debtors	15,000
Cash at bank	1,500
	29,500
Creditors: amounts falling due in one year	28,000
Net current assets	1,500
Total assets less current liabilities	1,178,500
Creditors: amounts falling due after one year	(800,000)
Net assets	378,500
Capital and reserves	
Share capital	200,000
Retained profit	178,500
	378,500

Glyme Valley Farm is located in Glympton, Oxfordshire. It consists of 1,200 acres of arable land owned by a local educational establishment, farm buildings, agricultural machinery and a flock of 400 sheep. The current owner, 72 year old Reginald Enser, has recently been taken into care and the farm is up for sale so that the sale proceeds can be used to meet the cost of caring. The profit and loss account and balance sheet are shown in Tables 68.9 and 68.10.

Cold Aston Farm - Price £450,000

Table 68.11 *Cold Aston Farm profit and loss account, 1999*

COLD ASTON FARM - PROFIT AND LOSS ACCOUNT Y/E 31.3.99

	£
Turnover	1,141,000
Cost of sales	322,000
Gross profit	819,000
Overheads	761,000
Operating profit	58,000
Non-operating income	2,000
Profit before interest	60,000
Interest (net)	15,000
Profit on ordinary activities before tax	45,000
Taxation	18,000
Profit for the year after tax	27,000
Dividends	9,000
Retained profit for the period	18,000

Table 68.12 *Cold Aston Farm Balance sheet, 1999*

COLD ASTON FARM - BALANCE SHEET AS AT 31.3.99

	£
Fixed assets	
Buildings	210,000
Machinery	167,000
	377,000
Current assets	
Stocks	36,000
Debtors	27,000
Cash at bank	5,000
	68,000
Creditors: amounts falling due in one year	36,000
Net current assets	32,000
Total assets less current liabilities	409,000
Creditors: amounts falling due after one year	(56,000)
Net assets	353,000
Capital and reserves	
Share capital	100,000
Retained profit	218,000
Other reserves	35,000
	353,000

Cold Aston Farm is situated in Cold Aston, Gloucestershire, near to where Patrick and Gillian currently live. The farm has more land, 1,700 acres, but some of it is prone to flooding. As a result, yields from the land can be quite variable. The land is owned by a wealthy landowner. The farm is also quite run down. For example, the cattle sheds are derelict and the barn roof has been blown off. The agricultural machinery is also old and much of it needs replacing. The farm is owned by Roger and Davina Bartlett who inherited it from their father two years ago. Roger and Davina have lost interest in farming and want to sell up. The profit and loss account and balance sheets are shown in Tables 68.11 and 68.12 .

Patrick and Gillian have approached an independent financial adviser for advice. Evaluate the information in the case and write a report from the adviser recommending which farm they should buy. Use financial ratios in your evaluation and outline the limitations of your analysis in the report.

The valuation of a business

Unit 68 showed that financial ratios can be used to investigate a company's accounts. A relatively high net profit margin might show that one business has performed better than another. It might also show that its own performance has improved over time. A relatively low gearing ratio might indicate that a business has raised most of its finance from its shareholders, rather than through loans.

To some extent, calculating financial ratios can help place a VALUE on a business. For example, businesses which have adequate working capital and high profit margins and returns on capital employed will tend to have more value than those which do not. The value of a business is how much it is worth to a **stakeholder** (☞ unit 3) or any other interested party, such as a potential buyer. In December 1998, Pendragon, the UK's second largest motor dealership, bought Evans Halshaw, the Birmingham-based car dealer. The takeover price was £83.7 million. This was the agreed value of the business at the time of sale.

Different people might place different values on the same business. A seller is likely to place a higher value on a company than a buyer. This is sometimes called the **expectation gap**. Differences in value might also occur because a business might be worth more to one particular buyer. For example, Asda might place a higher value on an independent supermarket located in a town where it was not represented than Tesco might if they already had a store in that town. The difference in value occurs due to strategic considerations.

Reasons for valuation

There may be times when it is necessary to have some idea how much a business is worth.

Planning a sale If the owners are considering the sale of a business, it will be necessary to know its value before putting it 'on the market'. Homeowners will normally ask an estate agent to value their house before putting it up for sale. Similarly, business owners might consult an accountant to help place a value on their business. Such valuations normally provide a starting point for negotiations between buyers and sellers. In many cases the agreed sale price will be different from the original valuation.

A takeover One company may be thinking about taking over another. In this case it will need to know the value of the company it is buying in order to decide whether it has enough funds to go through with the acquisition. Sometimes a takeover can work out more expensive than anticipated. This is often the case in a hostile takeover (☞ unit 101). The

Question 1

In February 1999, Coates Viyella, the textiles and engineering group, announced that it had agreed to sell its Dynacast precision engineering division to Cinven, the venture capitalist, for £322 million cash. Analysts who had expected the business to raise between £200 million and £300 million were upbeat about the sale. The sale proceeds were to be used to help reduce the company's debt. Dynacast made operating profits of £35.4 million from turnover of £319 million in 1997. It manufactures metal and plastic components, including the handle for Gillette's Mach 3 three-bladed razor, in the UK, North America, Mexico and Asia. Cinven was expected to enlarge the business, both organically, and through acquisition.

Source: adapted from the *Financial Times*, 22.2.1099.

(a) What was the value of Dynacast in February 1999?
(b) Why was it necessary to value the company at that time?
(c) Dynacast was worth between £200 million and £300 million according to analysts. How might you explain the sale price of £322 million?

current owners might resist the takeover by refusing to sell their shares. This could drive up the price. Also, another company might want to take over the same firm. This could result in a bidding war. The price may be inflated until the business is eventually sold to the highest bidder.

Merging When two companies merge, they need to know the value of each business. This is because the conditions of the merger have to be determined so that both companies can agree. For example, if one firm is twice the value of the other, it might mean that the new board of directors is made up of six representatives from the highest valued company and three from the other. It is also necessary to know the value of the merging companies so that accountants can merge their financial affairs.

Demerger or management buy-out This is very similar to the sale of a business. In the case of a demerger it is necessary to calculate the value of the company before it is divided into smaller units. This helps to calculate the value of the new, smaller companies when demerger takes place. Valuation of the new companies is required so that the number of new shares being issued, and their price, can be determined. In the case of a management buy-out or buy-in, valuation of the business or part of the business being sold is necessary to help set the sale price.

Flotation If a business, or part of a business, is being floated on the stock exchange (☞ unit 57) it is necessary to know the value. Again, this is required so that the number of shares being issued and their price can be determined. During the privatisation era of the 1980s it was suggested that many companies, such as BT and Powergen, were sold off by the government way below their true value. The government argued that it was necessary to price the share issues attractively in order for the flotation to be a success.

Securing loans When a business wants a loan the bank may require some collateral for security. If this is the case, the business, or part of the business, may be used. The bank may need to know the value of the business in order to clarify the value of the collateral.

Other reasons It may be necessary to calculate the value of the business if:
● the owner is involved in a divorce settlement, where the business is being shared out between husband and wife;
● a business has been inherited and inheritance tax is being calculated by the Inland Revenue;
● business owners or shareholders are curious about how much their business would be worth if sold;
● a business person is considering the sale of the business to retire;
● to make financial comparisons between businesses in an industry, for example, in an industrial survey.

Methods of valuation

There is a number of techniques which could be used to value a business.

Market capitalisation This can be calculated using the formula:

MARKET CAPITALISATION
= the current share price x the number of shares issued

For example, on 27 February 1999, the share price for BT was £10.81 and the number of shares issued in the company was 6,463,922,294. The value of the company could have been £69,875 million using this measure. This method of valuation may be distorted because external factors can cause the share price to change, such as interest rates and the actions of speculators. If the share price falls by 10 per cent due to one of these factors, this does not necessarily mean that the value of the company has fallen by 10 per cent.

Capitalised earnings This method is often used to value the holdings of the majority shareholders in a business. When shareholders buy shares, they buy the right to a future stream of profits that the business will make, known as **maintainable earnings**. Multiplying these maintainable earnings by the price/earnings ratio of a company gives the capitalised earnings. So:

CAPITALISED EARNINGS
= price/earnings ratio (P/E) x maintainable earnings

Unit 68 explained that the price earnings ratio shows the relationship between the amount each share earns for the investor and the current market price of the share. The P/E ratios of plcs are published each day in newspapers such as the *Financial Times*. A discount is often applied to the P/E ratios of private limited companies as their shares are not sold openly.

Maintainable earnings are the sustainable profits, after tax, that a business is capable of generating on a recurring basis. How can a value for maintainable earnings be estimated? It is necessary to consider all factors affecting a company's ability to maintain its current level of profit. This usually means starting with profits after tax for the current financial year. Then the figure is adjusted for one-off items of income or expenditure and directors' payments in excess of the market rate. So the estimate of maintainable earnings requires some human judgment. A subjective decision needs to be made about what non-recurring income and spending to take into account.

Discounted cash flow (DCF) This method may be used to value an entire company. It may also be used as a benchmark to compare the capitalised earnings value. To calculate the DCF a business needs to forecast annual cash flows and a discount factor. The discount factor will be the purchaser's cost of capital, such as the interest rate. Unit 64 explained how it is possible, using the DCF method, to calculate the net present value of a future stream of income. This will tell a business what the value of any future income streams is worth now.

Financial institutions, such as banks and venture capitalists, tend to prefer this method. It focuses on future cash flows rather than historic profit. They argue that valuations based on forecasts of future cash flows provide a better guide to the firm's ability to repay capital than a valuation based on past profits.

Net assets This method is most suitable when assets make up a major part of the value of the business. This might be the case with property or investment companies, for example. It might also be used if the company is a loss maker and the buyer of the business intends to sell the assets and then reinvest the cash. It might be used if a business has had difficulties and is being purchased from a receiver (☞ unit 28) for example. In this case the business may be

$$ROI = \frac{\text{Maintainable operating profit}}{\text{Purchase price}}$$

When using this method to choose between different businesses for acquisition, the business with the highest ROI will be selected. Again, a subjective judgment is required regarding non-recurring income and spending when estimating maintainable operating profits.

The pricing curve Accountants have developed a rule-of-thumb measure to determine the value of a business. The pricing curve shown in Figure 69.1 can be used to give some idea of a company's value. The curve is based on aggregate sales values of private companies from the database of the magazine, *Acquisitions Monthly*. To use the curve it is necessary to determine the operating profits of the company before tax and interest. However, the profit figure must be adjusted to take into account factors specific to the company. For example, if the current owners are paying themselves too much money, the profit figure should be raised accordingly. Once profits have been adjusted the curve can be used to obtain a value. For example, if earnings (profits) before interest and tax were £3 million, reading from the curve, the business would be worth £35 million.

Problems of valuation

The valuation of a business is often difficult. A company's value may not be known until it is placed on the market and sold. Certain problems exist when calculating the value of the business using the methods in the last section.

● When calculating the market capitalisation of a business the current share price is used. Sometimes the share price does not reflect accurately the performance of the business. Share prices can be influenced by external factors, such as interest rates and the actions of speculators. Also, the share price of a particular company may be a lot lower than one would expect because the company is 'out of favour' with the City. If share prices

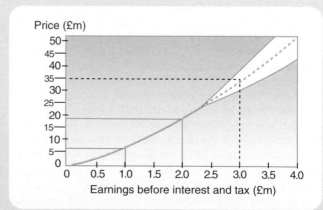

Figure 69.1 *The PCPI Pricing Curve*

Price (£m)

Earnings before interest and tax (£m)

Source: adapted from *en*, August 1998.

Care UK plc is an outsourcing business, which has contracts with the NHS and social services. It has three divisions.
● Care UK Community Partnerships owns and operates nursing and residential homes for the elderly and the mentally ill under long term contracts with the NHS and social services.
● Haven Care and the Care Partnership provides a personal care service to people in their own homes.
● Care Solutions provides residential housing for people with learning difficulties.
  In 1998 the company raised its turnover by 49 per cent from £27.6 million to £41.2 million. Profits before tax rose by 20 per cent from £4,416,000 to £5,457,000.

Table 69.1 *Financial information for Care UK*

	1998	1997
Fixed assets	£48,766,000	£41,438,000
Current assets	£ 8,282,000	£ 5,135,000
Creditors: amounts falling due within one year	£12,934,000	£10,104,000
Long term liabilities	£20,066,000	£14,346,000
Share price: September 30th	176p	119p
No. of shares issued	46,228,004	46,087,553

Source: adapted from *Care UK, Annual Report and Accounts*, 1998,

(a) Calculate the value of Care UK in 1997 and in 1998 using two different valuation methods.
(b) (i) Comment on the difference between the two years for each method.
    (ii) Comment on the differences between the two methods.
(c) A possible purchaser of the businesses is considering the value of the business in 1998. Evaluate which method of valuation is likely to be of most use.

---

bought at a discount to the value of net assets. The net assets of a business are:

Net assets = (fixed assets + current assets) - (current and long term liabilities)

This is quite a simple method of valuation because the value of net assets is shown clearly on all business balance sheets.

Return on investment (ROI) This method might be used, for example, when a choice has to be made about which business to buy from two alternatives. This method uses similar techniques to the calculation of capitalised earnings. However, rather than maintainable earnings after tax it uses **maintainable operating profits** (profit before interest and tax). ROI can be found by:

do not reflect the performance of the business the valuation will be inaccurate.
- The determination of maintainable earnings and maintainable operating profit require some human judgment. They are both concerned with the sustainable profits that a business is capable of generating on a **recurring** basis. The profit figures in the current accounts therefore need to be adjusted for non-recurring income and spending. This decision about what is non-recurring is likely to vary depending on who is making it.
- The DCF method also requires some human judgment. It is necessary to predict future cash inflows. This is difficult because a wide range of external factors, such as competitor's actions and the state of the economy, might influence future cash inflows.
- When using net assets to value a company, the true value of some assets may not appear on the balance sheet. These are intangible assets such as goodwill, brand names and copyrights. Therefore, if excluded, the value of the company would be understated. Many accountants choose

not to include the value of intangible assets because they are difficult to value. Also, the value of intangible assets can change quite sharply and suddenly (☞ unit 58).

To overcome some of the problems, businesses might use more than one method of valuation.

The regulation and manipulation of accounts

The preparation of financial accounts in the UK is subject to regulation. This is necessary to establish some uniformity in accounting. Before the regulatory framework existed it was difficult to make comparisons between company accounts. There were serious differences in the way accountants calculated profits due to the different methods they used. To overcome this problem the Accounting Standards Committee (ASC) was formed. Over a period of about 20 years this committee issued 25 STATEMENTS OF STANDARD ACCOUNTING PRACTICE (SSAPs). The statements provided uniform methods for practice, such as

Question

Football clubs are notoriously difficult to value for a number of reasons.
- Apart from tangible assets, such as the stadium and the training ground, a club's most precious assets are the players. These are virtually impossible to value. They are not like the raw materials, plant and machinery and products of a traditional business.
- The future cash flows of football clubs are unpredictable. Certain income is known in advance, such as season ticket sales and revenue from TV rights. However, a significant proportion is determined by the team's performance in the league, cups and Europe.
- Transactions in the transfer market complicate matters. Pre-tax profits can be hit if a club makes an expensive acquisition in the transfer market. The sale of a star player could move a club from the red into the black.

In September 1998, BSkyB made a takeover bid for Manchester United FC. At the time BSkyB valued the club at £575 million. Before the takeover interest shown by BSkyB, MUFC's share price was 167p. Based on pre-transfer pre-tax profits of £27 million in 1997/98, the P/E ratio for MUFC was 23. This was higher than the average for football stocks, but justified because of the club's status and worldwide popularity. The original BSkyB offer was said to undervalue MUFC and overlooked some of its strengths. These included its relatively low wage-to-turnover ratio, its cash pile, possible earnings from lucrative pay-per-view deals, involvement in European competitions and the club's ability to generate huge amounts of cash. In 1999 the Competition Commission (formerly the Monopolies and Mergers Commission) ruled that the takeover could not go ahead.

Source: adapted from the *Financial Times*, September 1998 and updated.

Figure 69.2 *Share prices*

Figure 69.3 *Manchester United, profit before transfer fees*

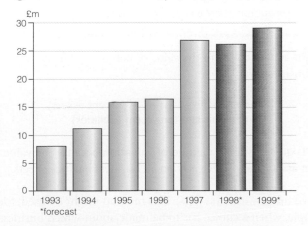

Source: adapted from Datastream/ICV, FTSE International, company.

(a) Using examples from the article, explain why it is difficult to value a football club that is being sold.

dealing with VAT (SSAP 5) and accounting for depreciation (SSAP 12). These SSAPs did help to reduce the variations in profit reporting. However, during the 1980s the ASC was subject to criticism because it had no legal power to enforce its standards, the standards were often too general and they were slow.

The regulatory framework is now the responsibility of the **Accounting Standards Board**. The board took over SSAPs. Any new standards are now called Financial Reporting Standards (FRSs). By 1998 the ASB had issued 8 FRSs. For example, FRS1 deals with the preparation of cash flow statements. In addition, Company Acts have certain requirements regarding accounting procedures. For example, businesses should adopt the accounting conventions discussed in unit 62, such as prudence, caution and going concern. Company accounts should also be presented in certain formats (☞ unit 67). Generally, the law requires that accounts should give a 'true and fair view' of a company's financial position.

Despite the existence of a regulatory framework, it is still possible to disguise the true financial position of a business. Information may be presented so that the financial position appears to be different than it really is. This is called MANIPULATING or WINDOW DRESSING the accounts.

Why might accounts be manipulated?

There is a number of reasons why accounts might be manipulated.

To appease shareholders Stakeholders may not be satisfied with the performance of the business. Shareholders might also be concerned that poor performance might affect the size of the dividend. The accounts might exaggerate the performance of the company to pacify these groups.

To attract investment A business might be trying to raise funds externally. Overstating the financial position of the company might persuade lenders to provide funds. They might be attracted by the potentially large future returns.

To fend off a takeover bid By making a company look stronger than it really is, a predator might decide against a bid for a business. If a company looks as though it is financially sound and performing well, it will appear to be more expensive to buy.

To show a stronger market position A company might want to suggest to outsiders, such as competitors, that it is financially sound. It might hope to show that it is in a stronger position to compete in the market. It might also try to show that it is the market leader and hope that this may influence customers when buying its products.

To affect share sales If the accounts show that the business is performing poorly, this might panic shareholders into selling their shares. They may be prepared to sell shares at lower prices to avoid holding unprofitable assets. Current directors might then be able to buy up shares at these lower prices, knowing that the business is actually in a stronger position than is indicated. On the other hand, this may have the adverse effect of allowing outsiders to buy shares in a plc.

To reduce taxation The accounts may disguise the true financial strength of the business to reduce tax liability. Reducing the profit of a business should reduce the amount of corporation tax paid.

Methods of manipulation

There is a number of ways in which accounts can be manipulated.

Depreciation It is possible for assets to be depreciated at a slower or faster rate. This will affect both the balance sheet and the profit and loss account. A change in the depreciation charge can be achieved by changing the method of calculating depreciation. For example, if a company buys a new machine for £100,000 (with a 6 year estimated life and

Question

Caldy plc is a company which operates a chain of 'themed' restaurants. The company, which is listed on AIM, has seen its market capitalisation fall recently since it published its annual accounts. This is illustrated by movements in the share price shown in Figure 69.4. However, this has not discouraged the three executive directors in the company from purchasing substantial blocks of shares.

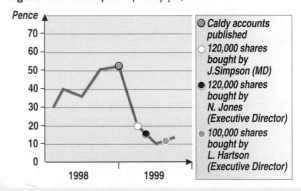

Figure 69.4 *Share price of Caldy plc, 1998-99*

(a) What evidence is there to suggest that the accounts of Caldy plc may have been window dressed?
(b) State two reasons, apart from window dressing, why share prices may not reflect the value of the business.
(c) (i) What stakeholders may be interested in the information in the accounts suggested by Figure 69.4 and the article?
(ii) Evaluate how they may react to this information.

residual value of £10,000), the depreciation allowance in the first year could be £15,000 using the straight line method (SLM) or £40,000 using the reducing balance method (RBM) (☞ unit 63). If the RBM is used rather than the SLM, the higher depreciation charge would reduce the company's profit by £25,000 (£40,000 - £15,000). The choice of method would also mean that the book value of the machine would be lower in the balance sheet. Therefore the value of tangible assets and net assets would be lower.

Creditors and debtors By changing the value of creditors or debtors the solvency of a company can be manipulated. For example, if a business makes a serious effort to collect outstanding debts before the end of the trading year then the value of liquid assets will increase. The company will therefore appear to be in a healthier position. Similarly, if the value of creditors can be reduced on the balance sheet by repaying outstanding debts, the company will appear to be financially stronger.

Balance sheet format It is possible to exaggerate the value of net assets in the balance sheet by changing the position of **creditors: amounts falling due after one year** (long term liabilities). The usual accounting convention is for companies to present their balance sheet with 'creditors: amounts falling due after one year' listed after **total assets less current liabilities**. The value of 'creditors: amounts falling due after one year' is then subtracted from the value of 'total assets less current liabilities'.

However, some plcs include it at the 'bottom' of the balance sheet, in the capital and reserves section. By doing this the value of net assets will rise by the value of 'creditors: amounts falling due after one year'. This is shown in Tables 69.2 and 69.3. In Table 69.2, the value of 'creditors: amounts due after one year' (£900,000) is shown in the position required by accounting convention. This gives a net asset value of £2,300,000. In Table 69.3 the accounts have been manipulated and the value of 'creditors: amounts due after one year' has been moved. The net assets figure is now higher at £3,200,000.

Stock valuation By changing the method of stock valuation (☞ unit 63) the book value of stock might be increased or decreased. This will affect the profit and loss account and the balance sheet. For example, by using the FIFO method of stock valuation, a firm's closing stock might be £2,400,000. By using the LIFO method it might be reduced to £1,900,000 (if stock prices have risen during the year). By switching from FIFO to LIFO the value of cost of sales will be increased by £500,000 and therefore the value of profit will fall by £500,000. In the balance sheet if the value of stocks is £500,000 lower, the value of current assets will also be lower by the same amount. This will also reduce working capital and net assets.

Table 69.2 *Barnes plc - Balance sheet as at 31.12.99*

	(£000)
Fixed assets	2,500
Current assets	1,200
Current liabilities	500
Net current assets	700
Total assets less current liabilities	3,200
Creditors: amounts due after one year	(900)
Net assets	**2,300**
Capital and reserves	2,300
Capital employed	**2,300**

Table 69.3 *Barnes plc - Balance sheet as at 31.12.99*

	(£000)
Fixed assets	2,500
Current assets	1,200
Current liabilities	500
Net current assets	700
Total assets less current liabilities	3,200
Net assets	**3,200**
Capital and reserves	2,300
Creditors: amounts due after one year	900
Capital employed	**3,200**

Writing off A business can reduce its profits by 'writing off' investments or debt. This means, for example, if a debt of £40,000 is 'written off', it is called a bad debt and included as an expense in the profit and loss account. It is subtracted from gross profit and as a result net profit would fall by £40,000. The same would happen if an investment was written off.

Profits By suppressing costs, accountants can show greater profits. For example, a business might decide to pay month 12 salaries to staff in month 1 of the next trading year. This will reduce the salary bill in the current year, which is part of the operating expenses on the profit and loss account. Reducing the value of operating expenses will increase the value of net profit. The amount of retained profit can be manipulated by raising or lowering the dividend payment for the current trading year. If the dividend payment is

At the beginning of 1997 Associated Nursing Services (ANS), the care home operator, had to amend its accounts after an investigation by regulators. The Financial Reporting and Review panel, which took two years over its investigation, hoped that its ruling would put an end to the practice of sale and leaseback schemes designed to flatter a company's financial performance. The schemes aim to improve gearing and earnings per share by removing property assets from the balance sheet. However, not all schemes break the regulations, only those which the risks and burdens of holding property do not properly switch from the owner

Sir Neil Macfarlane, ANS's chairperson, predicted that hundreds of companies could be affected by the ruling. Accountants believe that the sectors vulnerable to challenge are those which seek to manage large property costs. 'People with big property needs want to make the profit out of running it not owning it', said one auditor. Building construction, retailing, hotels and petrol stations are sectors which often sell property and lease it back.

Source: adapted from the *Financial Times*, 19.2.1997.

(a) Explain with an example how ANS may have been said to have manipulated its accounts.
(b) Explain why it is possible that hotel and construction companies might manipulate their accounts in this way.

company's gearing may be:

$$\text{Gearing} = \frac{\text{Loans}}{\text{Equity}} \times 100 = \frac{£12m}{£24m} \times 100 = 50\%$$

If fixed assets of £4 million are sold and then leased back, with the money being used to repay loans, gearing is now:

$$\text{Gearing} = \frac{£8m}{£24m} \times 100 = 33.3\%$$

As a result of this the company has become more low geared. However, it will have to meet the cost of leasing assets in the future. This will reduce profit.

Any manipulation made to the accounts in the current trading year will usually show up in the next trading year. For example, an effort to suppress costs this year by postponing certain payments will mean that profit this year will be higher. However, assuming that the payments are made in the next trading year, the profit for that year will be lower.

Key terms

Capitalised earnings - the value of a company determined by multiplying the P/E ratio by maintainable earnings.
Manipulating or window dressing - where accounts are presented in such a way that the financial position of a business appears to be different than it really is.
Market capitalisation - the value of a company determined by multiplying the share price by the number of shares in an issue.
Statements of Standard Accounting Practice - a list of rules to provide uniformity in specific accounting practices.
Value (of a business) - the amount a business is worth to a stakeholder or any other interested party.

reduced then retained profit for the year will be higher.

Asset manipulation A company can improve its gearing (☞ unit 68) by selling fixed assets and leasing them back. By selling fixed assets the business can use the proceeds to repay debt, such as loans. Reducing the amount of money raised from loans relative to the amount raised from shareholders will improve the gearing of the business. For example, a

Summary

1. What is meant by the expectation gap in relation to the value of a business?
2. Explain 2 reasons why a hostile takeover might lead to a rise in the value of a business.
3. State 5 reasons for valuing a business, other than for a takeover.
4. What information is needed to calculate: (a) market capitalisation; (b) maintainable earnings?
5. How does DCF allow a business to be valued?
6. State 4 problems which might occur when valuing a business.

7. Why is it necessary to regulate the presentation of accounts?
8. State 4 reasons why the accounts might be manipulated.
9. Briefly explain 2 ways in which accounts could be manipulated to exaggerate the value of a company.
10. Briefly explain 2 ways in which accounts could be manipulated to show a company in a poorer light.
11. How can the gearing of a company be affected by window dressing?

Case study

VDR plc

VDR plc, a company based in Sheerness, provides engineering services and equipment to the nuclear power industry. More than 80 per cent of its business is now overseas. The company obtained a full stock market listing in 1992 and has enjoyed mixed trading fortunes since. During 1998 some institutional shareholders began to express concern about the financial position of the company. As a result the share price began to fall and on 31.1.99 VDR shares were trading at 143p. The previous high, in 1997, was 421p.

As a short term solution, to appease shareholders, the senior accountant suggested that the accounts should be window dressed. This was agreed and three manipulations were introduced.

- The balance sheet was presented in such a way that 'creditors: amounts falling due after one year' would be included in the 'capital and reserves' section of the balance sheet.
- The method of calculating depreciation would change this year. The effect of this would be to lower the depreciation charge from £350,000 to £200,000 for the year. This would affect the book value of tangible assets and the value of profit and loss.
- Tangible assets worth £220,000 would be sold off and leased back. The proceeds would be used to repay some long term creditors.

As a result of these manipulations the balance sheet was presented in the way shown in Table 69.4.

(a) Describe two other ways in which VDR may have manipulated its accounts to make it look more favourable.

(b) How might the window dressing affect the performance of the business next year?

(c) Discuss how shareholders may react if they discover that the accounts have been window dressed.

(d) Redraw the balance sheet to show the true financial position of VDR before the manipulations were introduced by:
- **(i)** placing 'creditors: amounts falling due after one year' in the correct accounting convention position;
- **(ii)** calculating the effect on tangible assets and profit of changes in depreciation calculations;
- **(iii)** calculating the effect on tangible assets and long term creditors of selling and leasing back assets.

(e) Calculate the gearing ratio for both balance sheets.

(f) Comment on the differences between the two balance sheets using the results in (d) and (e).

(g) Explain how the value of the company is affected by window dressing if: (i) the net assets; (ii) market capitalisation; methods of valuation are used (the number of shares issued by VDR is 1,500,000).

Table 69.4 *VDR plc - Balance sheet as at 31.12.99*

	(£)
Fixed assets	
Tangible assets	1,490,000
Intangible assets	451,000
Investments	190,000
	2,131,000
Current assets	
Stocks	531,000
Debtors	1,341,000
Cash at bank and in hand	290,000
	2,162,000
Creditors: amounts falling due within one year	(1,844,000)
Net current assets	318,000
Total assets less current liabilities	2,449,000
Net assets	2,449,000
Capital and reserves	
Called up share capital	500,000
Other reserves	564,000
Profit and loss account	780,000
Creditors: amounts falling due after one year	605,000
Capital employed	2,449,000

Human resources

Unit 1 explained that different resources or factors of production are involved in business activity. The HUMAN RESOURCES of the business are the people employed by the business. In a small business, such as a window cleaning service, the owner might be the only human resource. He or she will carry out most, if not all, tasks. In a large multinational company there are likely to be thousands of workers. Some will be manual workers. Some will be skilled workers or administration staff. There will also be managers and directors. The organisation of these human resources is vital if a business is to be successful.

The formal organisation of a business

There are several types of business organisation, including sole traders, partnerships, limited companies and public sector organisations (☞ units 5 and 6). However, each will have its own internal structure - the way in which human resources are organised. This is known as the FORMAL ORGANISATION of the business. It takes into account such things as:
- the relationships between individuals;
- who is in charge;
- who has authority to make decisions;
- who carries out decisions;
- how information is communicated.

Different businesses tend to have different objectives (☞ unit 4). There will also be differences in relationships, how they are managed and how decisions are made. Because these activities can be arranged in various ways, businesses tend to have different STRUCTURES. There are, however, likely to be some similarities. For example, many large companies are controlled by a few directors, are divided into departments with managers, section heads and have many workers in each department.

One method of organising a business is where managers put people together to work effectively based on their skills and abilities. The structure is 'built up' or it 'develops' as a result of the employees of the business. In contrast a structure could be **created** first, with all appropriate job positions outlined, and then people employed to fill them. It has been suggested that the entrepreneur Richard Branson worked out a complete organisation structure for his Virgin Atlantic airline before setting up the company and then recruited the 102 people needed to fill all the positions.

Organisation charts

Many firms produce ORGANISATION CHARTS. These illustrate the structure of the business. Figure 70.1 shows a 'traditional' type of chart. It is a chart for an engineering firm, Able Engineering. Different types of businesses are likely to have different charts. The chart in Figure 70.1 may be simpler than one drawn for a large public limited company, although the style will be similar. It may be more involved, however, than a chart for a partnership.

Why do businesses draw such charts?
- To spot communication problems. An organisation chart indicates how employees are linked to other employees in the business. If information is not received, the business can find where the communication breakdown has occurred by tracing the communication chain along the chart.
- Organisation charts help individuals see their position in a

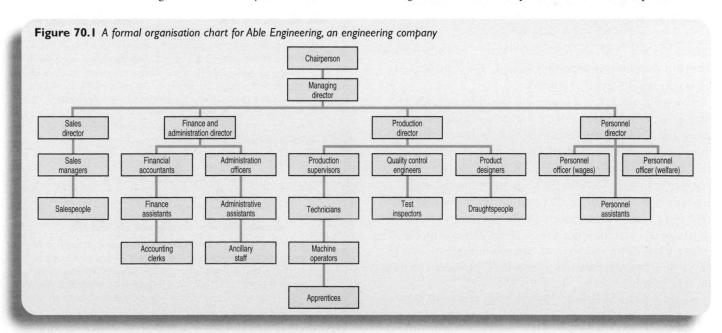

Figure 70.1 *A formal organisation chart for Able Engineering, an engineering company*

business. This can help them appreciate their responsibilities, who has authority over them and who they are accountable to.

● Organisation charts allow firms to pinpoint areas where specialists are needed. For example, in Figure 70.1 Able Engineering recognises it needs designers and draughtspeople as part of the production 'team'.

● Organisation charts show how different sections of the firm relate to each other. For example, the chart for Able Engineering shows the relationship between salespeople and technicians. They are both at the same level in the hierarchy, but work in different departments and are responsible to different managers.

Simply producing an organisation chart is of limited use to a business. The business will only achieve its objectives if it understands the relationships between employees and other parts of the business.

Question 1

Ainscough Engineering Ltd produces ground support equipment for the aviation industry. The company has a traditional organisational structure. The managing director is responsible to the chairperson and has a sales director, finance director, personnel director and production director accountable to her. On the production side of the business, there are a works manager, technicians, test engineers and machine operators. In addition, the company employs a number of personnel assistants, financial and administrative staff, and salespeople.

(a) Draw an organisation chart from the information about Ainscough Engineering Ltd.
(b) Briefly explain two ways in which the business might use the chart.

Chain of command and span of control

When deciding on its organisation structure, a business must take into account two important factors - the management **hierarchy** and the **span of control**.

The HIERARCHY in a business is the order or levels of management in a firm, from the lowest to the highest rank. It shows the CHAIN OF COMMAND within the organisation - the way authority is organised. Orders pass down the levels and information passes up. Businesses must also consider the number of links or levels in the chain of command. R. Townsend, in his book *Up the Organisation* , estimated that each extra level of management in the hierarchy reduced the effectiveness of communication by about 25 per cent. No rules are laid down on the most effective number of links in the chain. However, businesses generally try to keep chains as short as possible.

Another factor to be taken into account is the SPAN OF CONTROL. This refers to the number of subordinates

working under a superior or manager. In other words, if one production manager has ten subordinates his span of control is ten. Henri Fayol (☞ unit 74) argued that the span of control should be between three and six because:

● there should be tight managerial control from the top of the business;
● there are physical and mental limitations to any single manager's ability to control people and activities.

A narrow span of control has the advantage for a firm of tight control and close supervision. It also allows better co-ordination of subordinates' activities. In addition, it gives managers time to think and plan without having to be burdened with too many day to day problems. A narrow span also ensures better communication with subordinates, who are sufficiently small in number to allow this to occur.

A wide span of control, however, offers greater decision making authority for subordinates and may improve job satisfaction (☞ unit 71). In addition, there are likely to be lower costs involved in supervision. Figure 70.2 shows two organisation charts. In the first (a), there is a long chain of command, but a narrow span of control. The second (b) shows a wide span, but a short chain.

Many businesses in the 1990s changed their organisations to make them into 'flatter' structures. This often meant taking out layers of middle management. This process is often called **downsizing** or **de-layering** (☞ unit 102). It is likely to affect

Figure 70.2

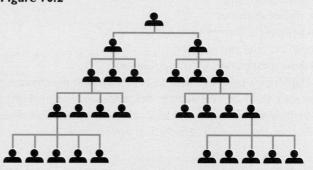

(a) A long chain of command and a narrow span of control. A production department may look like this. One manager is helped by a few assistant managers, each responsible for supervisors. These supervisors are responsible for skilled workers, who are in charge of a group of semi-skilled workers. Close supervision is needed to make sure quality is maintained. This is sometimes referred to as a tall organisational structure.

(b) A short chain of command and a wide span of control. A higher or further education department may look like this, with a 'head' of department, a few senior staff and many lecturing staff. Staff will want a degree of independence. This is sometimes referred to as a flat organisational structure.

the organisation chart, the chain of command and the span of control of a business.

Authority and reponsibility

Employees in the hierarchy will have responsibility and authority. However, these terms do not mean the same thing.

RESPONSIBILITY involves being accountable or being required to justify an action. So, for example, managers who are responsible for a department may be asked to justify poor performance to the board of directors. The personnel department may be responsible for employing workers. If a new worker was unable to do a particular job, they would be asked to explain why.

AUTHORITY, on the other hand, is the ability to carry out the task. For example, it would make no sense asking an office worker to pay company debts if she did not have the authority to sign cheques. Employees at lower levels of the hierarchy have less responsibility and authority than those further up. However, it may be possible for a superior to **delegate** (pass down) authority to a subordinate, eg a

Question 2

Senior and middle managers were hit hard by the wave of downsizing in the UK. This was the conclusion of a study by Cranfield University's School of Management of 90 large UK organisations that were downsizing in the mid-1990s. This is one of the first major surveys of downsizing in the UK, where companies such as BT and BP had shed tens of thousands of jobs. The study found the two most common reasons for downsizing were restructuring and delayering. These had an impact on managerial ranks and their morale. Downsizing was also, however, felt to have had some positive effects on employees. Just under half of those questioned felt the performance of survivors had increased after downsizing. 46 per cent felt that downsizing did not make any difference. 5 per cent felt performance had decreased. Strikingly, 78 per cent reported that survivors had become more task-focused. Downsizing was thought to have helped create clearer lines of accountability, resulting in managers taking personal ownership of results. It also helped break departmental barriers and cleared 'dead wood'.

The drawback was that the workload of survivors had increased in the view of 81 per cent of the managers. According to 75 per cent of respondents, stress levels had gone up. 63 per cent reported a decrease in feelings of job security and 41 per cent said they felt motivational levels had gone down.

Source: adapted from the *Financial Times*, 6.8.1997.

(a) What have been the organisational changes to the businesses studied by the Cranfield Institute?
(b) Explain the possible advantages and disadvantages to the business of changes in the answer to (a).
(c) Examine how the changes are likely to have affected:
(i) the span of control; (ii) chain of command.

manager to an office worker, but retain responsibility. Increasingly, businesses are realising the benefits of delegating both authority and responsibility.

Line, staff and functional authority

Line, staff and functional authority are terms used to describe the type of relationship that managers may have with others in the hierarchy.

Line authority Line authority is usual in a hierarchy. It shows the authority that a manager has over a subordinate. In Figure 70.1, the production director would have line authority over the designers. Communication will flow down from the superior to the subordinate in the chain of command. The advantage of this is that a manager can allocate work and control subordinates, who have a clear understanding of who is giving them instructions. The manager can also delegate authority to others if they feel this will make decision making more effective.

In large organisations, the chain of command can be very long. This means that instructions given by those at the top of the chain of command may take time before they are carried out at a lower level.

Staff authority Many larger organisations now have staff authority. Staff authority might be when a manager or department in a business has a function within another department, for example, giving specialist advice. A marketing manager may give advice to the production department based on market research into a new product. Personnel managers have responsibilities for personnel matters in all departments. Although the specialist can give advice, they have no authority to make decisions in the other department.

Functional authority Functional authority is when a specialist has the authority to make a line manager accept his or her advice. It is different from staff authority, where the specialist can only advise. For example, the finance manager may have overall authority over the budget holder in the marketing department.

Problems may occur in a business if people do not understand where authority and responsibility rest. This means that managers must know whether their authority is line, staff or functional. Unfortunately, this can lead to friction. Line managers are sometimes thought of as 'first class citizens' and staff managers are thought of as costly 'overheads' who are not contributing anything of worth to the organisation. Also, the authority of functional managers is not accepted by line managers at times.

Delegation

Managers are increasingly being asked to carry out strategic activities that affect the whole business (☞ unit 15). This has resulted in the need to DELEGATE authority and responsibility for certain tasks to employees further down the hierarchy. Delegation can provide benefits to a business, as explained in the next section. When is delegation likely to be effective?

● Researchers such as Spetzer (1992) have suggested that employees need to be **empowered** (☞ unit 73) in order to make effective decisions. They need to be given self-confidence and control of what they do.

● If managers only delegate when they are overloaded, subordinates may be resentful.

● Delegation requires planning. Managers must be clear about what needs to be done. Instead of freeing time, poor delegation may take up managers' time as they try to correct problems.

● Managers must take time to explain delegated tasks clearly. Employees may waste time or make mistakes because of lack of information. Telling subordinates why the work is important helps to create shared values.

● Allow participation. It is useful to discuss the task with those to whom it has been delegated. Subordinates will then know from the start what the task will include. It also helps managers to decide if delegation is appropriate. A person may feel they do not have the skills to carry out the task.

● The employee given a delegated task should also be given the authority and responsibility to carry it out. Managers must tell others in the business that the delegated person is acting on his or her behalf. This will avoid difficulties, such as the questioning of authority.

● Managers must avoid interfering with delegated tasks.

● Delegated tasks should be given to suitable employees. It would be inappropriate to delegate a marketing task to an employee in personnel. Employees must also have the training to carry out the task.

● Provide support and resources. If an employee is delegated a task without suitable support and resources this could lead to anxiety, frustration and the task being badly done.

Research has shown that when factors like these are taken into account, delegation was four times as likely to be successful.

Centralisation and decentralisation

Centralisation and decentralisation refer to the extent to which authority is delegated in a business. If there was complete centralisation, then subordinates would have no authority at all. Complete decentralisation would mean subordinates would have all the authority to take decisions. It is unlikely that any business operates in either of these ways. Even if authority is delegated to a subordinate, it is usual for the manager to retain responsibility.

Certain functions within a business will always be centralised, because of their importance. For example, decisions about budget allocation are likely to be centralised

---

Question 3

The Manchester Film Association is an SME in the centre of the city's 'cultural quarter'. Its main activities are video, film and multimedia production. It employs 9 full time staff. Mike joined the company 6 months ago. He recently graduated, but has little work experience. However, he has proven so far in the work that he has done for clients to be innovative. He often has ideas that no-one else has considered. Shoaib has worked for the business for 15 years. He has built up considerable production and post-production skills. Lisa had previously set up her own website design and consultancy operation. She has experience in managing projects, working to deadlines and taking responsibility for clients' requests.

The managing director of the business, Paula, has been approached by a fast growing leisure company to produce an innovative multi-media training programme on CD Rom for newly recruited employees. The company wants the programme to be interactive, but it must be ready within two months. Paula decided to ask Mike to look after the project. However, almost from the start he seemed to have problems. He did not ask for help when it would have been useful. He found it difficult to organise others and often missed deadlines he had set. After four weeks, Paula was concerned that the project would not be completed.

Source: adapted from company information.

(a) Define delegation using an example from the case.
(b) Explain why delegation may not have been effective in this case.
(c) Discuss what action Paula should now take.

---

as they affect the whole company. The decision to distribute profits is also taken only by a few.

Advantages of centralisation Why might a business centralise authority?

● Senior management have more control of the business, eg budgets.

● Procedures, such as ordering and purchasing, can be standardised throughout the organisation, leading to economies of scale and lower costs.

● Senior managers can make decisions from the point of view of the business as a whole. Subordinates would tend to make decisions from the point of view of their department or section. This allows senior managers to maintain a balance between departments or sections. For example, if a company has only a limited amount of funds available to spend over the next few years, centralised management would be able to share the funds out between production, marketing, research and development, and fixed asset purchases in different departments etc.

● Senior managers should be more experienced and skilful in making decisions. In theory, centralised decisions by senior people should be of better quality than decentralised decisions made by others less experienced.

● In times of crisis, a business may need strong leadership by a central group of senior managers.
● Communication may improve if there are fewer decision makers.

Advantages of decentralisation or delegation Some delegation is necessary in all firms because of the limits to the amount of work senior managers can carry out. Tasks that might be delegated include staff selection, quality control, customer relations and purchasing and stock control. A greater degree of decentralisation - over and above the minimum which is essential - has a number of advantages.
● It empowers and motivates workers (☞ unit 73).
● It reduces the stress and burdens of senior management. It also frees time for managers to concentrate on more important tasks.
● It provides subordinates with greater job satisfaction by giving them more say in decision-making, which affects their work (☞ unit 71 on McGregor's Theory Y).
● Subordinates may have a better knowledge of 'local' conditions affecting their area of work. This should allow them to make more informed, well-judged choices. For example, salespeople may have more detailed knowledge of

their customers and be able to advise them on purchases.
● Delegation should allow greater flexibility and a quicker response to changes. If problems do not have to be referred to senior managers, decision-making will be quicker. Since decisions are quicker, they are easier to change in the light of unforeseen circumstances which may arise.
● By allowing delegated authority, management at middle and junior levels are groomed to take over higher positions. They are given the experience of decision making when carrying out delegated tasks. Delegation is therefore important for management development.

Different forms of business structure

Despite the variety of formal business organisation that exists, there are four main types of structure most often found.

The entrepreneurial structure In this type of business structure, all decisions are made centrally. There are few collective decisions and a great reliance on 'key' workers. It is often found in businesses where decisions have to be made quickly, such as newspaper editing.

Most small businesses also have this type of structure, as illustrated in Figure 70.3(a). These businesses rely on the expertise of one or two people to make decisions. Decision making is efficient up to a point because:
● decisions can be made quickly;
● subordinates understand to whom they are accountable;
● little consultation is required.
However, as the business grows, this structure can cause inefficiency as too much of a load is placed on those making decisions.

The bureaucratic or pyramid structure This is the traditional structure for most medium sized and large businesses and perhaps the most well known. It is illustrated in Figure 70.3(b). Decision making is shared throughout the business. Employees are each given a role and procedures are laid down which determine their behaviour at work.

Specialisation of tasks (☞ unit 1) is possible. This means that a departmental structure, with finance, personnel, production and marketing employees, can be set up (☞ unit 7). Specialisation may allow the business to enjoy economies of scale. Recently, this type of structure has been criticised for its inability to change and meet new demands.

The matrix structure This emphasises getting people with particular specialist skills together into project teams, as illustrated in Figure 70.3(c). Individuals within the team have their own responsibility. The matrix structure was developed to overcome some of the problems with the entrepreneurial and bureaucratic structures.

 Question 4

McDonald's, the hamburger chain, decided to make large scale changes to its top management structure in an effort to jump-start its flagging sales and make it more competitive. Jack Greenberg, head of US operations, sent an internal memo to franchisees and employees saying that the company had to make fundamental changes to its business structure. McDonald's was widely regarded as having had a top heavy management since the early 1950s.

The changes included sweeping away the eight zone managers in the US, the company's top executives in America. They were to be replaced by a smaller number of national and more autonomous divisions, similar to the way McDonald's is managed in Britain and other overseas markets. The change overturned the 40-year-old centralised management structure based at the company's corporate headquarters in Illinois. The new structure was designed to make McDonald's more flexible and responsive to the market, where the company faced increasing competition from national rivals such as Burger King, owned by Grand Metropolitan, and from small regional operators. The group's 2,000 US franchisees had often complained that the company's stagnation in sales was partly because centralised management had stifled innovation.

Source: adapted from the *Financial Times*, 10.7.1997.

(a) Explain the possible: (i) benefits; (ii) problems; for the business of the change in its organisation.
(b) To what extent were the changes at McDonald's likely to make it a more centralised or more decentralised organisation?

Figure 70.3 *Alternative forms of organisation structure*

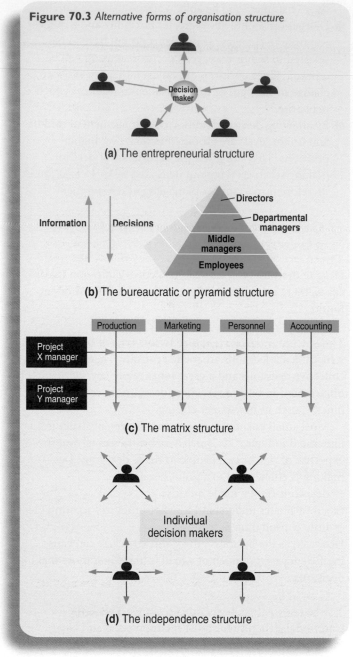

(a) The entrepreneurial structure

(b) The bureaucratic or pyramid structure

(c) The matrix structure

(d) The independence structure

Managers often argue that this is the best way of organising people, because it is based on the expertise and skills of employees and gives scope for people lower down the organisation to use their talents effectively. For example, a project manager looking into the possibility of developing a new product may draw on the expertise of employees with skills in design, research and development, marketing, costing etc. A college running a course for unemployed people may draw on the skills of a number of lecturers in different departments. In this way, a matrix structure can also operate within a business that has a bureaucratic structure. The matrix model fits in with managers who have a Theory Y view of employees (☞ unit 71). It is suggested that this structure improves flexibility and motivation of employees. It has recently lost favour because it often needs expensive support systems, such as extra secretarial and office staff.

There may also be problems with co-odinating a team drawn from different departments and the speed of decision making.

The independence structure This emphasises the individual and is almost a 'non-organisation'. The other three methods put together the contributions of a number of people so that the sum of their efforts is greater than the parts. All efforts are co-ordinated so that the business benefits. The independence structure is a method of providing a support system. Barristers' chambers and doctor's clinics have worked in this way. It is attractive to independent people who are confident of their ability to be successful. This form of organisation tends to be unsuitable for most types of business because of the lack of control and co-ordination.

Informal business structure

Organisation charts show the formal organisation of a business. However many relationships between employees in business are INFORMAL. The informal business structure is the network of relationships that develop between members on the basis of their common interests and friendships. These relationships can affect the way a business operates. Krackhardt and Hanson (1993) in a study of informal networks in the banking industry found three types of relationship.

● Advice networks - who depends on who to solve problems and provide information.
● Trust networks - which employees share potential information and back each other up in times of crisis.
● Communication networks - which employees regularly talk to each other on work related matters.

They recommended that businesses use informal structures to solve problems. For example, a study showed that a bank's task force group was unable to find ways of improving the bank's performance. The leader of the task force held a central position in the 'advice network'. Employees relied on her for technical advice. However, she only had one 'trust link' with a colleague. Management did not want to label the group as a failure or embarrass a valued employee by dismissing her as team leader. Instead, it redesigned the task force in line with the informal organisation of the business by adding a person in the trust network to share responsibility for group leadership.

Factors influencing organisational structures

There is a number of factors which might influence the organisation and the structure of a business.

● Size. As a business grows, it is likely to move away from an entrepreneurial structure towards one where authority is passed to other employees. A large firm will also tend to have a longer chain of command, with more levels in the hierarchy.
● Views of the owners or leadership styles. If owners wish to retain control in the business, they will want a narrow span

of control. Owners or managers who wish to motivate or encourage employees may delegate decision making.

● Business objectives. If the business decides to expand rapidly, perhaps by merger, it is likely to find that its span of control gets wider. An example might be a business setting up an operation in a foreign country or deciding to sell into a foreign market.

● External factors. Changes in external factors can often influence business organisation. In periods of recession or rising costs, a business may be forced to reduce its chain of command to cut costs. Similarly, in a period of growth (☞ unit 21), a firm may employ extra managers as specialists to gain economies of scale.

● Changes in technology. The introduction of new technology can change the structure of a business. For example, a new system of production may remove the need for quality controllers, or an information technology system could reduce the role of administration.

● The informal structure. If the informal structure does not complement and support the formal structure, this may lead to problems.

Key terms

Authority - the right to command a situation, a task or an activity.

Business structure - the way in which a business is organised.

Chain of command - the way authority and power are passed down in a business.

Delegation - authority (and sometimes responsibility) passed down from superior to subordinate.

Formal organisation - the relationships between employees and the organisational structure determined by the business, as shown in an organisation chart.

Hierarchy - the order or levels of management of a business, from the lowest to the highest.

Human resources - the employees of a business.

Informal organisation - the relationships between employees that are based on the common interests of employees.

Organisation chart - a diagram which illustrates the structure of an organisation.

Responsibility - the duty to complete a task.

Span of control - the number of subordinates working under a superior.

 Question 5

Wesley Carrington runs a card design business in Cardiff. He employs four staff - Laura, Mitchell, Kieran and Ella. Laura manages the office in Cardiff dealing with telephone enquiries, visitors, administration and a small amount of marketing. Mitchell, Kieran and Ella are card designers and all work from home in various parts of the country. Mitchell lives and works in a small croft in Glen Cona in North West Scotland. The designers are all linked by computer to the main Cardiff office. This ensures good communications. For example, design briefs are sent direct by Wesley using e-mail and design copy is transmitted direct to Wesley's terminal when designs are completed. Some specialisation takes place amongst the designers. Mitchell designs birthday cards, Kieran designs postcards and Ella works on specialist projects. Wesley is occupied with customers, ensuring that design briefs are satisfied by his designers and looking for new business. He spends three days a week out of the office.

Figure 70.4 *Wesley Carrington's organisational structure*

(a) What type of organisational structure does the business have at present?

(b) Describe the advantages to the business of being organised in this way.

(c) In September, Wesley secured a contract with an American card manufacturer. Wesley had to recruit four more designers as a result. He decided to employ a full-time salesperson to sell designs in the US. He also bought a small printing business in Newport to print and supply cards as well as designing them. Explain why Wesley might decide to change the organisational structure of his business.

Summary

1. What are the features of the internal structure of a business?
2. How might an organisation chart be used in a firm's induction programme?
3. Draw a simple organisation chart showing:
   (a) a partnership with two partners and 6 employees;
   (b) a large company with a board of directors, six departments, and two more levels in the hierarchy.
4. What is meant by a 'wide span of control'?
5. What problems might a 'wide span of control' have for a business?
6. Explain the difference between line, staff and functional authority.
7. Why might businesses have line, staff and functional

authority?
8. Give three situations where centralised decision making may be useful for a business.
9. What factors influence effective delegation?
10. Why is empowerment important when tasks are delegated?
11. State 4 advantages of delegation.
12. What problems might a matrix structure cause for a business?
13. What type of business might be organised with:
    (a) an entrepreneurial structure;
    (b) an independence structure?
14. Why is it important for businesses to understand their informal business structures?

Case study

House proud

In 1996, two years after its stock market flotation, House of Fraser was regarded by some analysts as failing to meet its potential. Slow decision making and inefficient work practices were suggested as the reasons. The survival of the business depended on radical changes to practices and staffing structures. House of Fraser's 51 stores were semi-autonomous. Each operated under its own conditions, job titles and management structure. Careers paths were ambiguous. There was a lack of clarity in what people did, how they did it and where it was done. A job in one store would have different responsibilities to a job in another just 20 miles away.

The first decision was a review of management structure. A half hearted attempt to rationalise a hotchpotch of systems and job descriptions had already been tried. But it had been left to individual store managers. This time change was from the top. The existing management structure was top heavy. Too many managers spent too much time on excessive paperwork. Caroline Mason, the group's communications manager, said: 'It is pointless having loads of great sales staff who never get an opportunity to sell because they spend most of their time chasing pieces of paper.' It was anticipated that management numbers would need to be cut by a third.

The new management structure had no room for assistant managers. They had had a wide, but poorly defined, role. There had been an assistant manager for almost every manager. The scope and responsibilities of the managerial positions that would remain would increase. Each store section - fashion, home, visual and commercial - was to be put under a single manager, supported by sales staff. New

jobs covered areas of expertise. Sales staff would sell. Support staff dealt with the administration.

The rationalisation was not without costs. Everybody had to reapply for their jobs. Certain skills were bound to be lost as a result. The company tried to solve this problem by organising regional offices, each containing a human resources and training manager. However, the new system provided a clear promotion structure. Jobs were graded and everyone could see what skills were needed to progress to the next scale.

Source: adapted from *People Management*, 12.11.1998.

(a) What 'form' of business organisational structure is House of Fraser likely to have had? Explain your answer.
(b) What factors might have influenced the reorganisation at House of Fraser?
(c) Explain how the organisation chart at House of Fraser might have altered as a result of the reorganisation of the business.
(d) Explain the possible advantages and disadvantages of the reorganisation for:
   (i) House of Fraser's management;
   (ii) House of Fraser's employees.

The satisfaction of needs

If asked, most people who work would probably say they do so to earn money to buy goods and services. However, this is not the only **need** that is satisfied by working.

A list of people's needs that may be satisfied from work might be very long indeed. It could include, for example, the need for variety in the workplace, which may be satisfied by an interesting job. Employees may also need to feel appreciated for the work they do, which could be reflected in the prestige attached to their job.

Individuals are not the same. Therefore, it is likely that lists made by any two people of their needs and how they can be satisfied will be very different. There are some reasons for working that could apply to everyone, such as the need to earn money. However, some reasons have more importance for particular individuals than others. One employee may need to work with friendly colleagues, whereas another might be happy working on his own.

Why is it important for a business to find out what satisfies the needs of its employees? It is argued that if an individual's needs are not satisfied, then that worker will not be MOTIVATED to work. Businesses have found that even if employees are satisfied with pay and conditions at work, they also complain that their employer does not do a good job in motivating them. This applies to all levels, from the shopfloor to the boardroom. It appears in many companies that employers are not getting the full potential from their employees because they are not satisfying all of their employees' needs. Figure 71.1 shows one example of how a business might make decisions, having first identified an employee's needs.

It is important for a business to motivate its employees. In the short run a lack of motivation may lead to reduced effort and lack of commitment. If employees are watched closely, fear of wage cuts or redundancy may force them to maintain their effort even though they are not motivated. This is **negative motivation**. In the long term, a lack of motivation may result in high levels of absenteeism, industrial disputes and falling productivity and profit for a business.

Maslow's hierarchy of needs

The first comprehensive attempt to classify needs was by **Abraham Maslow** in 1954. Maslow's theory consisted of two parts. The first concerned classification of needs. The second concerned how these classes are related to each other.

Maslow suggested that 'classes' of needs could be placed into a **hierarchy**. The hierarchy is normally presented as a 'pyramid', with each level consisting of a certain class of needs. This is shown in Figure 71.2.

The classes of needs were:
- physiological needs, eg wages high enough to meet weekly bills, good working conditions;
- safety needs, eg job security, safe working conditions;
- love and belonging, eg working with colleagues that support you at work, teamwork, communicating;
- esteem needs, eg being given recognition for doing a job well;
- self-actualisation, eg being promoted and given more responsibility, scope to develop and introduce new ideas and take on challenging new job assignments.

Figure 71.2 can also be used to show the relationship between the different classes. Maslow argued that needs at the bottom of the pyramid are basic needs. They are concerned with survival. These needs must be satisfied before a person can move to the next level. For example, people are likely to be more concerned with basic needs, such as food, than anything else. At work an employee is unlikely to be concerned about acceptance from colleagues if he has not eaten for six hours.

Once each level is satisfied, the needs at this level become less important. The exception is the top level of SELF-ACTUALISATION. This is the need to fulfil your potential. Maslow argued that although everyone is capable of this, in practice very few reach this level.

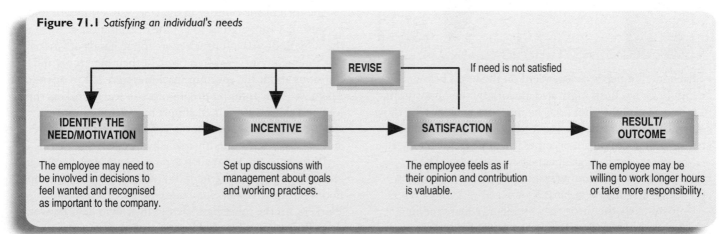

Figure 71.1 *Satisfying an individual's needs*

REVISE — If need is not satisfied

IDENTIFY THE NEED/MOTIVATION → INCENTIVE → SATISFACTION → RESULT/OUTCOME

The employee may need to be involved in decisions to feel wanted and recognised as important to the company.

Set up discussions with management about goals and working practices.

The employee feels as if their opinion and contribution is valuable.

The employee may be willing to work longer hours or take more responsibility.

Question 1

Call centres employ thousands of people in the UK. They are set up by businesses to provide information on everything from train times to technical information on computers, and to sell theatre tickets, pensions and mobile phones. Jobs for operators usually pay better than other similar clerical salaries and offer a great degree of flexibility of work time. However, questions are being asked about the quality of employment. Many organisations have a flat structure. Most staff in junior posts, mostly women, are employed to undertake only basic operations. The Equal Opportunities Commission's research suggests that there are barriers stopping women joining senior management. Other research has shown that job satisfaction is short lived. It rises during the first five months in post and then falls over the next year and a half.

Direct Line Financial Services in Glasgow accepts that many of its jobs are demanding and not to everyone's tastes. However, it argues that it has no difficulty keeping staff and that there are incentives and bonus schemes to keep people interested. There are also opportunities to retrain and work in a different department or on a new product on a regular basis. Research at Newcastle University's Centre for Urban Development suggests that the key to a long life in call centres may well be acquiring new skills rather than promotion.

Source: adapted from *The Sunday Times*, 23.2.1997.

(a) Identify the needs of employees mentioned in the passage.
(b) How has Direct Line Financial Services attempted to satisfy these needs: (i) in the short term; and (ii) in the longer term?
(c) Examine the likely problems of dissatisfaction at call centres for businesses.

Each level of needs is dependent on the levels below. Say an employee has been motivated at work by the opportunity to take responsibility, but finds he may lose his job. The whole system collapses, as the need to feed and provide for himself and his dependents again becomes the most important need.

Maslow's ideas have great appeal for business. The message is clear - find out which level each individual is at and decide on suitable rewards.

Unfortunately the theory has problems when used in practice. Some levels do not appear to exist for certain

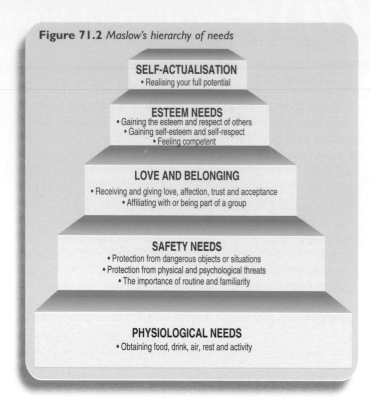

Figure 71.2 *Maslow's hierarchy of needs*

SELF-ACTUALISATION
• Realising your full potential

ESTEEM NEEDS
• Gaining the esteem and respect of others
• Gaining self-esteem and self-respect
• Feeling competent

LOVE AND BELONGING
• Receiving and giving love, affection, trust and acceptance
• Affiliating with or being part of a group

SAFETY NEEDS
• Protection from dangerous objects or situations
• Protection from physical and psychological threats
• The importance of routine and familiarity

PHYSIOLOGICAL NEEDS
• Obtaining food, drink, air, rest and activity

individuals, while some rewards appear to fit into more than one class. Money, for example, needs to be used to purchase 'essentials' such as food, but it can also be seen as a status symbol or an indicator of personal worth.

There is also a problem in deciding when a level has actually been 'satisfied'. There will always be exceptions to the rules Maslow outlined. A well motivated designer may spend many hours on a creative design despite lack of sleep or food.

Taylor's Scientific Management

Research into the factors that motivate individuals had been carried out long before Maslow's 'hierarchy' of needs. **Frederick W. Taylor** set out a theory of SCIENTIFIC MANAGEMENT in his book *The Principles of Scientific Management* in 1911. Many of the ideas of today's 'scientific management school' come from the work of Taylor.

The turn of the century in the USA was a time of rapid expansion. Compared to today, the organisation of work on the shop floor was left much more in the hands of workers and foremen. Workers often brought their own tools and decisions about the speed of machines were left to operators. There were few training programmes to teach workers their jobs and skills were gained simply by watching more experienced colleagues. Decisions about selection, rest periods and layoffs were frequently made by foremen.

Taylor suggested that such arrangements were haphazard and inefficient. Management did not understand the shop floor and allowed wasteful work practices to continue. Workers, on the other hand, left to their own devices, would do as little as possible. 'Soldiering' would also take place

Question 2

Research from the Industrial Society shows managers believe that being ethical in relations with employees is important. However, in practice being ethical does not seem to figure highly in managers' work. The Industrial Society's Jo Gardiner says: 'The gap between what managers know is good practice and what they see happening in their organisations is particularly worrying.'

The research, published in *Managing Ethics*, asked executives to say what they regarded as the essential aspects of being ethical in their management of people. Then they were asked whether those practices were followed in their own businesses. The two sets of answers matched in only one in five organisations. Answers from the 313 respondents provide a useful insight into what managers regard as the crucial aspects of behaving ethically in relation to employees. Nearly 50 per cent of managers thought that employers should not worry too much about the domestic and family concerns of their staff. On the other hand, almost all agreed that people's dignity should be respected. Between these two extremes, there was widespread support for the ideas that:

● people should be consulted before decisions were taken which affected them;
● rewards should be fair;
● open, honest communications with employees were important.

Practice was very different, however. More than half said that their organisations did not consult people. Only 59 per cent said that they communicated with employees openly, honestly and frequently. Two-thirds said staff were not paid fairly. And even though almost everyone agreed that people's dignity should be respected, a quarter of managers said that this did not happen in their organisations.

Source: adapted from the *The Guardian*, 7.9.1996.

(a) What stage in Maslow's hierarchy of needs are:
   (i) family and domestic concerns;
   (ii) the dignity of staff;
   (iii) open and honest communications;
   likely to be? In each case explain your answer.
(b) Using Maslow's hierachy of needs, explain the problem with paying attention to employees' dignity, but not to domestic and family commitments.
(c) Using information in the article, examine reasons why a manager might believe that certain factors in the hierarchy of needs are important, but be unwilling to use these ideas in practice.

Table 71.1 *Taylor's method, designed to find the 'best way' to carry out a task at work*

- Pick a dozen skilled workers.
- Observe them at work and note down the elements and sequences adopted in their tasks.
- Time each element with a stop watch.
- Eliminate any factors which appear to add nothing to the completion of the task.
- Choose the quickest method discovered and fit them in their sequence.
- Teach the worker this sequence; do not allow any change from the set procedure.
- Include time for rest and the result will be the 'quickest and best' method for the task. Because it is the best way, all workers selected to perform the task must adopt it and meet the time allowed.
- Supervise workers to ensure that these methods are carried out during the working day.

---

partnership between manager and worker, based on an understanding of how jobs should be done and how workers are motivated.

Taylor's approach How did Taylor discover what the 'best way' was of carrying out a task? Table 71.1 shows an illustration of Taylor's method.

Taylor had a very simple view of what motivated people at work - money. He felt that workers should receive a 'fair day's pay for a fair day's work', and pay should be linked to output through piece rates (☞ unit 72). A worker who did not produce a 'fair day's work' would face a loss of earnings; exceeding the target would lead to a bonus.

In 1899 Taylor's methods were used at the Bethlehem Steel Works in the USA, where they were responsible for raising pig-iron production by almost 400 per cent per man per day. Taylor found the 'best way to do each job' and designed incentives to motivate workers.

Taylor's message for business is simple - allow workers to work and managers to manage based on scientific principles of work study. Many firms today still attempt to use Taylor's principles. In early 1993 the Bishop of Salford, when shown around a Littlewoods store, was told by the store manager that what he was looking for from potential Littlewoods workers was 'strong backs and nimble fingers'. This may not have been the official approach from Littlewoods, but it was seen locally as the use of Taylor's ideas.

Problems with Taylor's approach There is a number of problems with Taylor's ideas. The notion of a 'quickest and best way' for all workers does not take into account individual differences (☞ unit 83). There is no guarantee that the 'best way' will suit everyone.

Taylor also viewed people at work more as machines, with financial needs, than as humans in a social setting. There is no doubt that money is an important motivator. Taylor overlooked that people also work for reasons other than

---

(working more slowly together so that management did not realise workers' potential) and workers would carry out tasks in ways they were used to rather than the most efficient way. Taylor's scientific principles were designed to reduce inefficiency of workers and managers. This was to be achieved by 'objective laws' that management and workers could agree on, reducing conflict between them. Neither party could argue against a system of work that was based on 'science'. Taylor believed his principles would create a

money. A survey in the early 1980s (Warr, 1982) asked a large sample of British people if they would continue to work if it were not financially necessary to do so. Nearly 70 per cent of men and 65 per cent of women said they would. This suggests there may be other needs that must be met at work, which Taylor ignored, but were recognised in Maslow's ideas which came later.

Human relations

Taylor's scientific management ideas may have seemed appealing at first glance to business. Some tried to introduce his ideas in the 1920s and 1930s, which led to industrial unrest. Others found that financial incentives did motivate workers, and still do today. However, what was becoming clear was that there were other factors which may affect workers' motivation.

The Hawthorne studies Many of the ideas which are today known as the 'human relations school' grew out of experiments between 1927 and 1932 at the Hawthorne Plant of the Western Electric company in Chicago. Initially these were based on 'scientific management' - the belief that workers' productivity was affected by work conditions, the skills of workers and financial incentives. Over the five year period, changes were made in incentive schemes, rest periods, hours of work, lighting and heating and the effect on workers' productivity was measured. One example was a group of six women assembling telephone relays. It was found that whatever changes were made, including a return to the original conditions, output rose. This came to be known as the HAWTHORNE EFFECT.

Question 3

Anmac Ltd is a small expanding high-tech company. It employs approximately 25 workers in two factories, one at Chester and one at Stafford. The employers organise work on a fairly informal basis. Workers work at their own pace, which often results in a variable level of output. Recently orders for their advanced micro-electronic circuit boards have increased rapidly. The firm has decided that, to cope with the orders, increased production is needed. Two suggestions have been put forward.
● Encourage the workers to work overtime at the Chester plant.
● Redeploy some of the workers from Chester to Stafford where there is a shortfall of workers.
The workers at the Chester plant are mainly married women in their twenties, many with young, school aged children and husbands who also work.

(a) Explain how Taylor's scientific management principles might be used to solve the problems faced by Anmac Ltd.
(b) What problems might Anmac Ltd find in using such principles?

The study concluded that changes in conditions and financial rewards had little or no effect on productivity. Increases in output were mainly due to the greater cohesion and communication which workers in groups developed as they interacted and were motivated to work together. Workers were also motivated by the interest shown in their work by the researchers. This result was confirmed by further investigations in the Bank Wiring Observation where fourteen men with different tasks were studied.

The work of **Elton Mayo** (and Roethlisberger and Dickson) in the 1930s, who reported on the Hawthorne Studies, has led to what is known today as the human relations school. A business aiming to maximise productivity must make sure that the 'personal satisfactions' of workers are met for workers to be motivated. Management must also work and communicate with informal work groups, making sure that their goals fit in with the goals of the business. One way to do this is to allow such groups to be part of decision making. Workers are likely to be more committed to tasks that they have had some say in.

There are examples of these ideas being used in business today. The Volvo plant in Uddevalla, opened in 1989, was designed to allow workers to work in teams of 8-10. Each team built a complete car and made decisions about production. Volvo found that absenteeism rates at Uddevalla averaged 8 per cent, compared to 25 per cent in their Gothenburg plant which used a production line system. Other examples might be:
● Honda's plant in Swindon where 'teamwork' is emphasised - there are no workers or directors, only 'associates';
● McDonald's picnics, parties and McBingo for their employees where they are made to feel part of the company;
● Mary Kay's seminars in the USA, which are presented like the American Academy awards for company employees;
● Tupperware sales rallies, where everyone gets a 'badge' and has their achievements recognised.

Problems There is a number of criticisms of the human relations school.
● It assumes workers and management share the same goals. This idea of workplace 'consensus' may not always exist. For example, in the 1980s Austin Rover tried to introduce a programme called 'Working with Pride'. It was an attempt to raise quality by gaining employee commitment. This would be achieved by greater communication with employees. The programme was not accepted throughout the company. As one manager stated: 'We've tried the face-to-face communications approach. It works to a degree, but we are not too good at the supervisory level ... enthusiasm for the Working with Pride programme is proportionate to the level in the hierarchy. For supervisors it's often just seen as a gimmick ...'.
● It is assumed that communication between workers and

management will break down 'barriers'. It could be argued, however, that the knowledge of directors' salaries or redundancies may lead to even more 'barriers' and unrest.

● It is biased towards management. Workers are manipulated into being productive by managers. It may also be seen as a way of reducing trade union power.

Theory X and Theory Y

In 1960 **Douglas McGregor** published *The Human Side of Enterprise*. It was an attempt to apply the implications of Maslow and the work of Taylor and Mayo to business. In it, he gives different reasons why people work. He coined the terms Theory X and Theory Y to describe these differences.

Question 4

Table 71.2 *The effect of introducing a piece rate system into clothes manufacture*

Group	Number in group	Action taken to introduce system	Resignations within 40 days of introduction	Change in output
A	100	Group told the changes will take place next week	17%	-2%
B	150	Management introduces changes with the help of group to suit their needs	0%	+10%
C	200	Group told the changes will take place next week	7%	0%
D	50	Management explains the need for change to group	2%	+2%
E	100	Management explains the need for change and discusses this with the group	0%	+5%

Table 71.2 shows the results of a survey carried out in Bryant and Gillie, a manufacturer of children's clothing. The company introduced a piece rate system of work - a system where employees are paid according to the number or quantity of items they produce. Five groups were involved in the new system. Different actions were taken to introduce the system to each group. The table shows the effect on labour turnover and output of these actions.

(a) To what extent do the results support the human relations explanation of workers' motivation?
(b) Using the results of the survey in Table 71.2, advise the management on the likely action needed to motivate workers when changing work practices.

Table 71.3 *Theory X and Theory Y*

Theory X	Theory Y
• Workers are motivated by money	• Workers have many different needs which motivate them
• Workers are lazy and dislike work	• Workers can enjoy work
• Workers are selfish, ignore the needs of organisations, avoid responsibility and lack ambition	• If motivated, workers can organise themselves and take responsibility
• Workers need to be controlled and directed by management	• Management should create a situation where workers can show creativity and apply their job knowledge

Table 71.3 shows the main ideas of the two theories.

Theory X assumes that people are lazy. If this is accepted, then the only way to get people to work is by using strict control. This control can take one of two forms. One method is to use coercion - the threat of punishment if rules are broken or targets not achieved. This is often known as the 'stick' approach. The problem with threats is that they are only effective if the person being threatened believes that they will be carried out. Modern employment laws and company wide agreements, have made this difficult for managers. For this reason, a 'carrot' approach may be more suitable. People have to be persuaded to carry out tasks by promises or rewards. In many ways this theory is similar to Taylor's view of people at work as shown earlier in this unit.

Theory Y, on the other hand, assumes that most people are motivated by those things at the top of Maslow's hierarchy. In other words, people are responsible, committed and enjoy having control over work. Most people, given the opportunity, will get involved in work, and contribute towards the solution of a problem that may arise. This theory is similar in some ways to the **human relations school**.

Business managers tend to say that their own assumptions are closer to Theory Y than to Theory X. But tests on management training courses tend to show that their attitudes are closer to Theory X than they might like to admit. In addition, many managers suggest that, while they themselves are like Theory Y, workers are closer to Theory X.

In practice, it could be argued that most firms behave according to Theory X, especially where shopfloor workers are concerned. The emphasis is on the use of money and control to encourage workers to behave in the 'correct way'. The same organisations might behave according to the assumptions of Theory Y when dealing with management. A representative of a banker's union wrote in the *Independent on Sunday*, 'The lower down the ladder you are, the less control you have over your work environment. Managers can do as they please, stretch their legs whenever they want. Clerical workers, if they are working in a data-processing centre, for example doing entries for cheques or credit cards, are disciplined if they don't complete a given number of key strokes in an hour or a day. Half the time they don't know what they are doing. They don't see any end product. More and more work has been downgraded.'

Herzberg's two-factor theory

In 1966 **Fredrick Herzberg** attempted to find out what motivated people at work. He asked a group of professional engineers and accountants to describe incidents in their jobs which gave them strong feelings of satisfaction or dissatisfaction. He then asked them to describe the causes in each case.

Results Herzberg divided the causes into two **categories** or **factors**. These are shown in Figure 71.3.

- MOTIVATORS. These are the factors which give workers **job satisfaction**, such as recognition for their effort. Increasing these motivators is needed to give job satisfaction. This, it could be argued, will make workers more productive. A business that rewards its workforce for, say, achieving a target is likely to motivate them to be more productive. However, this is not guaranteed, as other factors can also affect productivity.
- HYGIENE FACTORS. These are factors that can lead to workers being **dissatisfied**, such as pay or conditions. Improving hygiene factors should remove dissatisfaction. For example, better canteen facilities may make workers less dissatisfied about their environment. An improvement in hygiene factors alone is not likely to **motivate** an individual. But if they are not met, there could be a fall in productivity.

There is some similarity between Herzberg's and Maslow's ideas. They both point to needs that have to be satisfied for the employee to be motivated. Herzberg argues that only the higher levels of Maslow's hierarchy motivate workers.

Herzberg's ideas are often linked with **job enrichment** (☞ unit 73). This is where workers have their jobs 'expanded', so that they can experience more of the production process. This allows the workers to be more

involved and motivated, and have a greater sense of achievement. Herzberg used his ideas in the development of

Question 5

Is making a contribution to society more important than money? Some secretaries regard a congenial atmosphere as more important than financial rewards. Best of all is a job which relates to their own interests. These include the arts, the media, the environment, education or helping the sick or underprivileged. Many of the secretaries registering with Permanent Prospects, a recruitment agency for the non-commercial sector (ie charities), have some kind of moral conscience, according to its managing director Maggie Heap. But to what extent do they sacrifice pay for their ethical stance? The Charities Aid Foundation says it is difficult to draw any conclusion. Fundraising has become more and more competitive and salaries have risen accordingly. Charities are paying the going rate for good secretaries. A survey showed that the salary of a director's secretary was £15,500 on average and that of a manager's secretary was £13,500.

The RSPCA in Horsham, West Sussex felt its pay rates were comparable to other local employers. So did Blue Cross. Both allowed pets to be brought to work. Diana Bray who works as a secretary for six managers at Oxfam says: 'Salary is not an issue for me.' She suggests that the ability to make a difference to people's lives and working with dedicated people is more important. The arts is another area where pay may be of secondary importance. A secretary may be expected to earn £13,500 - £14,500 a year on average.

Source: adapted from *The Times*, 10.9.1997.

(a) Identify the factors in: (i) Theory X and; (ii) Theory Y which may influence secretaries in the non-commercial sector.
(b) Suggest three other types of business where employees are likely to take this view. Explain your answer.
(c) To what extent is Theory X or Theory Y more likely to explain the factors which motivate secretaries in the non-commercial sector?

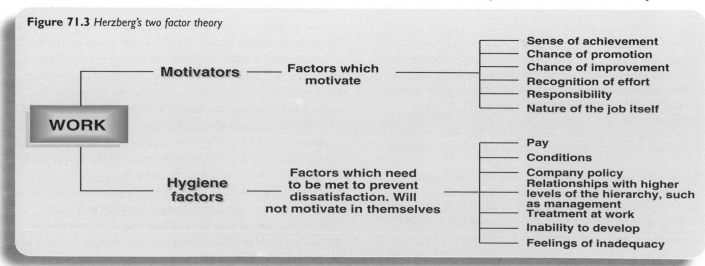

Figure 71.3 *Herzberg's two factor theory*

WORK

Motivators — Factors which motivate
- Sense of achievement
- Chance of promotion
- Chance of improvement
- Recognition of effort
- Responsibility
- Nature of the job itself

Hygiene factors — Factors which need to be met to prevent dissatisfaction. Will not motivate in themselves
- Pay
- Conditions
- Company policy
- Relationships with higher levels of the hierarchy, such as management
- Treatment at work
- Inability to develop
- Feelings of inadequacy

clerical work. He selected a group of workers in a large corporation. Performance and job attitudes were low. Herzberg redesigned these jobs so that they were given more responsibility and recognition.

Problems Herzberg's theory does seem to have some merits. Improving pay or conditions, for example, may remove dissatisfaction at first. Often, however, these things become taken for granted. It is likely that better conditions will be asked for in following years. Evidence of this can be seen in wage claims which aim to be above the rate of inflation in some businesses every year. Job enrichment may also be expensive for many firms. In addition, it is likely that any benefits from job improvements will not be seen for a long time and that businesses will not be able to continue with such a policy in periods of recession.

Surveys that have tried to reproduce Herzberg's results have often failed. This may have been because different groups of workers have been examined and different techniques used. Also, there is a problem in relying too much on what people say they find satisfying or dissatisfying at work as this is subjective. For example, if things go wrong at work individuals have a tendency to blame it on others or factors outside of their control. On the other hand if individuals feel happy and satisfied when they are at work then they tend to see it as their own doing.

McClelland's managerial needs

David McClelland suggested that what motivates people is that they learn in early childhood that certain types of behaviour lead to 'gratification'. They develop needs based on this behaviour. For example, a girl may have a great need to achieve, encouraged by parents who help her to be successful at school. When she becomes employed, she will behave in a similar way. There are, McClelland argues, three basic needs - achievement, affiliation, power.

- The need for achievement. This is one of the keys to a company's success. People who have high achievement needs often become successful entrepreneurs (☞ unit 3). Such people like to take responsibility and risks, and want quick feedback on how they have performed. They like to set their own goals and standards and achieve these on their own. However, it is also likely that people with a need to achieve will not work well in groups.
- The need for affiliation. McClelland found that some successful people in business did not, as he expected, score high on the need to achieve. In large firms, managers' goals can often by achieved by working with others, rather than by their own efforts. Such managers have a need to relate to others and will try to gain the acceptance of their superiors and work colleagues.
- The need for power. Some individuals with high achievement and affiliation needs still had problems in influencing or controlling others, McClelland found. To be

Question 6

Good work practices can have a beneficial effect on employees' attitudes and behaviour. BNL, a small, highly successful plastic-bearing company, has attempted to improve the working environment and change the culture of the business. David Garnett, BNL's managing director, recognised the need to involve the 100-strong workforce in decision making. BNL also improved conditions by putting in natural lighting, painting the walls and ceiling in attractive colours, commissioning artists to design murals and installing ionisers to improve air quality. Improvements in communication have also been a priority. Shop floor workers are encouraged to spend time in the offices and office staff to work in the factory. To help reduce the isolation of its overseas staff, BNL introduced videoconferencing and manufacturing staff are allowed to visit overseas offices as much as possible.

Managing stress may also be important. Zeneca Pharmaceuticals has a strategy for dealing with stress. Its approach teaches stress management to its 5,000 employees. The company argues that: 'some pressure ... leads to job satisfaction, motivation and good performance. Too much on people who are unable to cope is bad for them and the business'. Businesses that fail to take into account employees' needs after a merger can often have difficulties. A merger between two large companies in 1997 led to integration of departments. One company's department became dominant, leading to a bureaucratic structure. Valuable staff began to leave as a result. A report which highlighted poor communication between managers and staff was 'shelved' as managers did not like the criticism. Staff felt let down and cynical.

Source: adapted from *The Sunday Times*, 18.5.1997.

(a) Identify from the passage the hygiene factors that might affect employees' satisfaction.
(b) What 'motivators' at BNL might, according to Herzberg, help to improve their motivation of their employees? Explain your answer.
(c) Why might improvements in employees' satisfaction or motivation not necessarily lead to improvements in the performance of a business?

successful there was often a need to get people to work together. McClelland called this the power motive. He recognised that although the need for power is often seen as undesirable (where one person dominated others) it can also be seen in a positive light. It might reflect the ability of an individual to persuade, influence or lead people. Research suggests that people with a need for power tend to be in higher and more influential positions in business.

According to McClelland, a business needs to know how these three needs affect an individual. For example, a person that has high affiliation needs may not make a good marketing manager. Such a person would, based on the theory, constantly look for acceptance and support for all decisions. It is likely that this job would need someone who was far more self-motivated.

Vroom/Lawler and Porter

The theories of motivation that have been dealt with so far assume that people try to meet goals and so satisfy their needs. Vroom's and Lawler and Porter's theories state that this relationship is not so simple. First, each individual will have different goals. Secondly, people only act to achieve their goals if they feel there is a chance of success. Thirdly, the value of the goal to the individual will also affect that person's motivation.

These theories might affect the way a business designs its pay and benefit systems and also the design of tasks and jobs to enable people to satisfy their needs. They take into account that people have different needs, and that some may want autonomy and responsibility at work, whereas others may not.

Criticisms of motivation theories

At first sight it would appear that a business interested in increasing its employees' motivation at work has a fairly simple task. The theories in this unit are divided into two groups. The scientific management/Theory X group argues that workers are lazy, need controlling and are only interested in monetary rewards. The human relations school/Theory Y/Vroom group argues workers have many needs that might be achieved if they have more control and responsibility. A business, it seems, only needs to identify which view is effective and use the findings to motivate its workforce.

In practice it is difficult to conclude whether either one of these broad perspectives is 'right or wrong'. Any one view may be right or wrong depending on the circumstances. If the business is geared towards hierarchy and authority, and work is routine and monotonous, people may choose to do such work in return for cash. For example, in 1969 Goldthorpe and Lockwood in their famous study, The Affluent Worker, found that workers on a Vauxhall car assembly line saw work as a means to earn high wages. This would allow workers to enjoy life outside work more. Wedderburn and Crompton's study in 1972 of a large chemical plant in North East England found much the same thing. Their results showed that the level of pay, job security and good welfare benefits were far more important to workers than job interest. In such cases, individuals regard monetary rewards as being more important than such factors as responsibility.

However, at other times, job interest and involvement may outweigh financial rewards. This may be true, for instance, in worker buyouts, when employees are prepared to accept lower financial rewards to maintain job security and have a say in the running of the business.

It is also argued that many motivation theories were developed in earlier times, when work conditions were different. Work methods did not need the advanced levels of technological knowledge and problem solving skills that they do today. These skills now require higher levels of education and a change in the relationship between management and the shop floor.

Maccoby (1988) suggested that motivation theories which are too concerned with giving promotion and control to the individual employee may be misdirected. He argued that individuals can be given extra responsibilities in a variety of ways, such as dealing with more customers, teaching other employees, solving problems and making deals. This type of employee does not need as much management, since she is more likely to manage herself or to work as part of a team with shared management. The word **empowerment** (☞ unit 73) is often used to describe this view of motivation. Team empowerment is used to describe teams that are given discretion to make unsupervised decisions.

What conclusion can be drawn from these points?
- Employees are likely to have different priorities at different times and in different circumstances.
- Employees aiming to increase their wage or salary are not likely to show much interest in job satisfaction (at that time).
- When employees are not involved in pay bargaining then they are likely to be interested in the quality of working life and job satisfaction.
- A business cannot generalise about what motivates people. It must try to understand the views workers may have at any one time, before deciding how best to motivate them.
- Employees in modern organisations are likely to be more skilled in team working, problem solving and the use of information technology. Motivation theories have to take this into account to be useful to a business.

Key terms

Hawthorne effect - the idea that workers are motivated by recognition given to them as a group.
Hygiene factors - those things that can lead to workers being dissatisfied.
Motivated - being encouraged to do something.
Motivators - those things that can lead to workers being satisfied.
Self-actualisation - a level on Maslow's hierarchy where an employee realises his or her full potential.
Scientific management - a theory that suggests that there is a 'best' way to perform work tasks.

Summary

1. Why is it important for business to satisfy workers?
2. Name 5 needs in Maslow's hierarchy that an individual might have at work.
3. What are the aims of Taylor's scientific management theory?
4. According to Taylor, how are people motivated?
5. What is meant by the human relations school of thought?
6. What, according to the human relations school, is the main motivator at work?
7. Explain the difference between Theory X and Theory Y.
8. How is Theory X like Taylor's view of scientific management?
9. According to Herzberg's theory, what factors are likely to:
   (a) increase job satisfaction;
   (b) reduce dissatisfaction at work?
10. What general conclusions can a business draw from the criticisms of motivation theory?

Case study

British Telecom

In 1990 British Telecom (BT) employed 250,000 people. In 1998 this had fallen to 110,000. But they achieved higher standards than ever before. Change was tough. The cuts in staff sapped morale. Staff attitude surveys began to highlight motivation and morale problems. As a result, the company launched a new way of working called, '... for a better life'. To survive in a competitive telecommunications market BT needed a motivated, well trained and customer-orientated staff. To allow staff to respond effectively to consumers' needs, the business had to communicate with staff more, to give staff a sense of how the business was doing and to encourage them to stretch themselves.

The new way of working attempted to make clear what was expected of staff and instil in them a sense of excitement and belonging. BT used to be a company that had a manual for everything, including exactly what operators should say to customers. With the new approach staff were expected to be creative and assertive, and approach their jobs more flexibly. Staff were encouraged to develop four attributes:

- to know instinctively how to contribute to BT's success;
- to take accountability for customers' requirements;
- to take decisive action on behalf of the customers
- To take considered risks to 'delight' the customer.

This was known as 'own, decide, do'. It appeared to work. Staff attitude surveys showed the number of people who felt able to take risks increased, as shown in Table 71.4. Staff were also happier with the way they were managed. In 1998 84 per cent reported they were satisfied with their relationship with their line manager. Three years before it was 61 per cent. The new approach meant changes for managers, who had to take more of a coaching role to help people make decisions.

The new approach involved a massive and continuous coaching programme for managers and employees. To embed the new culture at BT a series of competitions were held. For example, the 'Images' video competition was designed to ask employees for illustrations of how they had applied principles of '...for a better life.' One employee, who found that the

Table 71.4 *Employee attitudes in BT's consumer division*

	% of staff agreeing			
	Mar 95	Sep 95	Sep 96	Jan 98
Are you satisfied with your line manager?	61	74	83	84
Do you have a sense of ownership of your job?	73	86	90	94
Are you confident about making decisions?	84	91	95	94
Do you feel able to take a considered risk?	64	83	89	86
Have you received enough coaching to be completely helpful to customers?	-	54	81	82

phone a customer wanted was out of stock, tracked down a phone and delivered it to the customer's house. The best half dozen entries were filmed and an awards ceremony held.

The opportunity to make decisions really appeared to 'turn people on at BT'. The new approach seems to have spilled over into people's everyday lives. Staff were found to be keen to develop their skills. The 'Roots and Wings' campaign was created, which allowed staff to mentor school children in underprivileged areas.

Source: adapted from *People Management*, 29 October, 1998.

(a) **Using an example from the article, explain what is meant by motivational problems.**
(b) **Has BT taken a theory X or theory Y approach to motivation? Explain your answer.**
(c) **Identify and categorise the needs of employees at BT according to Maslow's hierarchy.**
(d) **Explain two ways in which BT's measures have been a success.**
(e) **Using Herzberg's two factor theory, examine how the measures taken by BT are designed to motivate and prevent demotivation.**

Financial and non-financial rewards

Unit 71 outlined theories which have tried to explain the factors that motivate people at work. Some of these theories stress that money is the most important factor. The scientific/Theory X approach, in particular, argues that workers respond to **financial rewards**. It is argued that such rewards are necessary to motivate a reluctant workforce. Employees see work as a means to an end. As a result they are far more likely to be interested in monetary rewards.

In contrast, the human relations/Theory Y view argues that workers are motivated by a variety of factors. An employee working in a car assembly plant, for example, may be highly motivated by working as part of a team. Poor pay may lead to employees being dissatisfied, which can make other **non-financial rewards** less effective in motivating them.

The next two units examine how these theories can be used. This unit looks at how a business might use financial rewards and incentives.

Payment schemes

How are employees rewarded for the work they do? There is a number of methods that may be used.

Time rates TIME RATES are used when workers are rewarded for the amount of time they spend at work. Employees are paid in the form of weekly **wages** or monthly **salaries**. For many workers in the UK, pay is fixed in relation to a standard working week of, say, 37.5 hours. Workers who work longer than this may be paid **overtime**, perhaps at a higher rate. In addition, holidays with pay are included for most British industries. Examples of time rates are the £22,000 (approximately) a year paid to teachers with experience at the top of the standard national scale or the £3.60 per hour paid to a cleaner in, say, Newcastle.

Time rates are a simple way of calculating pay for a business. They are useful when a business wants to employ workers to do specialist or difficult tasks that should not be rushed. Employees can ensure that work is of a high quality without worrying about the time they take.

Time rates are also useful when working out the pay of service sector employees or people working in groups. In these cases it is very difficult for a business to work out the exact value of the employee's output. An example might be doctors, where it is virtually impossible to calculate the value of work. From an employee's point of view, time rates guarantee income.

Annualised hours Many employers have found that payment based on a fixed working week can be inflexible. For example, half the year employees may be idle after 3pm every day, but are still paid for a 'full day's' work. The other half of the year they may work into the evening and be paid overtime. To cater for fluctuations in demand some employers pay staff on the basis of a certain number of hours to be worked in a year. These are known as ANNUALISED HOURS CONTRACTS.

Question **1**

In November 1998 workers at Rover's Longbridge plant were poised to vote on a revolutionary new pay structure. Unions had agreed to radical new work measures including:
● a fall in hourly wages;
● no overtime;
● no annual Christmas bonus;
● working week cut from 37 to 35 hours;
● flexible hours - workers to put in extra hours during busy periods and take prolonged holidays in quiet periods;
● workers to move from one Rover factory to another in response to changes in demand;
● annual salary to replace hourly wages, overtime and bonuses.

The deal meant that 3,000 jobs would be lost but the other 12,000 jobs in the company would be secure. It was suggested that the measures would save the company £150 million a year. Transport Union leader Bill Morris said: 'Both sides recognise the importance of an agreement to protect jobs and defend the interests of the motor industry'. He argued that it would create new principles but admitted that other industries would be affected by the deal.

Source: adapted from *Personnel Management*, 28.1.1999.

(a) Explain how employees were traditionally paid at Rover.
(b) Explain how the payment scheme was to be changed by the business.
(c) How might these changes affect:
   (i) Rover;
   (ii) employees at Rover;
   (ii) employees in other industries?

For annualised hours contracts, the number of hours to be worked each year is fixed. However, the daily, weekly or monthly hours are flexible. So employees may have a longer working day at peak times and work less when demand is slack. Employee's pay is calculated on the basis of, say, an average working week of 36 hours, which is paid regardless of the actual number of hours the employee is required to work.

There are certain advantages. An employee has a guaranteed income each week. Employers often see this as a way of avoiding overtime, reducing costs, increasing flexibility and improving efficiency. One water company found that its service engineers would leave a job part completed in order to get back to their depot by 5pm, even if the job only required a further hour's work. When the company introduced annualised hours contracts the engineers had to complete any job they had started, even if it meant working beyond 5pm. The advantage for the water company was much greater customer satisfaction and efficiency, as service engineers did not have to make two round trips to a job. The engineers were able to negotiate a higher basic pay. They also benefited from a more flexible shift system, which meant they could increase their number of rest days.

Piece rates A system of PIECE RATES is the easiest way for a business to make sure that employees are paid for the amount of work they do. Employees are paid an agreed rate for every item produced. For this reason it is known as a PAYMENT BY RESULTS system. It is often used in the textile industry. Piece rates are arguably an INCENTIVE to workers. The more they produce, the more they earn.

From a business's point of view, this system links pay to output. However, there is a number of problems. Employees have no basic pay to fall back on if machinery fails or if the quality of the goods produced is unacceptable. Trade unions, in particular, have campaigned against this method of payment as it often results in low pay and low living standards. There have also been disputes in the past about what 'rate' should be paid. Some firms may feel that the method encourages workers to sacrifice quality in favour of higher rewards.

Because of the problems of lack of basic pay, most firms use a system where pay is made up of two elements. There is a fixed or basic pay, calculated on the time worked and a variable element, often when a **target** has been reached. It is argued that this extra element motivates workers to increase productivity, while the time element gives security. Incentive schemes are dealt with later in this unit.

Commission In some businesses COMMISSION makes up the total earnings of the workers. This is true of some insurance salespeople and some telesales employees. Commission, like piece rates, is a reward for the quantity (or value) of work. Employees are paid a percentage of the value of each good or service that is sold. It could be argued that it suffers from the same problems and gives the same incentive

as a piece rate system. The benefit to the employer is that it can indicate the level of business 'won' rather than just output achieved. Earnings surveys have shown that the numbers of people receiving commission is falling. The proportion of people's total earnings made up of commission is also declining.

Fees Fees are payments made to people for 'one-off' tasks. Tasks tend to be geared towards the needs of the client, rather than a standard service or product. The amount paid will depend on a variety of factors. These might include the time taken to finish the task or the difficulty of the task. Often fees are paid to people providing services, such as solicitors, performers etc.

Fringe benefits FRINGE BENEFITS are payments other than wages or salaries. They include things like private medical insurance, profit-related bonus schemes, a company car, subsidised meals, transport allowances, loan or mortgage facilities etc. Fringe benefits have grown in importance. This is especially the case in the executive, management and professional area. From an employer's view, providing benefits rather than pay may actually be cheaper as they do not need to pay National Insurance contributions. An employee might also prefer to receive benefits such as private medical insurance, that avoids waiting for treatment, rather than pay. Despite their attraction, fringe benefits can cause status

Table 72.1 *Fringe benefits*		
Company	**Function**	**Fringe benefit**
Dyson Appliances	Vacuum cleaner manufacturer	Dyson cleaner at reduced rate for new employees
Text 100	PR Agency	2 'Duvet days' (unscheduled holidays) a year
Air products	Industrial gas supplier	Free exercise classes and subsidised gym and yoga classes, free annual medical checks
Saatchi & Saatchi	Advertising agency	Company pub - 'The Pregnant Man'
Virgin Group	Travel, entertainment, media, retail and financial services	24 hour parties
Body Shop	Cosmetics manufacturer and retailer	£100 a year to 'buy' a training course in new skill of their choice
Tesco	Food retailer	SAYE tax free share option scheme

Source: adapted from *The Mirror Works*, 9.7.1998.

problems. Also, benefits such as a company car may be liable for tax, although some benefits avoid tax such as certain company pension schemes.

Table 72.1 shows some of the fringe benefits that have been offered by companies in the UK.

Employer objectives for pay

There is a number of objectives employers will have when paying their workforce.

Motivation It has been argued that workers are motivated by money (☞ unit 71). This may be a rather simple view of workers' behaviour. Yet it is clear from the way that employers use money incentives that they believe employees react to the prospect of increasing their earnings. For example, many firms are attempting to link pay with performance because they believe that employees care about pay.

Employers must give consideration to any system they use. For example, if payments are made when targets are achieved, these targets must be realistic. Payment systems are often negotiated between **groups**, such as company representatives and trade unions.

Cost Employers are interested in the profitability or cost-effectiveness of their business. Any system that is used by the business must, therefore, attempt to keep the cost of labour as low as possible in relation to the market wage in that industry. This should enable the firm to increase its profits.

Prestige Managers often argue that it is a 'good thing' to be a

good payer. Whether high pay rates earn an employer the reputation of being a good employer is arguable. What seems much more likely is that the low-paying employer will have the reputation of being a poor one in the eyes of employees.

Recruitment and labour turnover Payment rates must be competitive enough to ensure the right number of qualified and experienced employees stay within the business. This will prevent a high level of **labour turnover** (☞ unit 75). This is also true of vacant posts. A business must pay rates which encourage the right quality and quantity of applicants.

Control Certain methods of payment will reduce costs and make the control of labour easier. These are examined later in this unit.

Employee objectives for pay

Employees will have their own objectives for the payment they receive.

Purchasing power A worker's standard of living is determined by the level of weekly or monthly earnings. The **purchasing power** of those earnings is affected by the rate of inflation (☞ unit 23). Obviously, in periods of high inflation workers are likely to seek higher wages as the purchasing power of their earnings falls. Those whose earnings fall behind the rate of inflation will face a decline in their purchasing power.

Fair pay Employees often have strong feelings about the level of payment that is 'fair' for a job. The employee who feels underpaid may be dissatisfied and might look for another job, be careless, or be absent a great deal. Those who feel overpaid may simply feel dishonest, or may try to justify their pay by looking busy.

Relativities Employees may be concerned about how their earnings compare with those of others. 'How much do I get relative to ... ' is an important factor for a worker. Workers with a high level of skill, or who have trained for a long period, will want to maintain high wages relative to less 'skilled' groups. **Flat rate** pay increases, such as £10 a week for the whole workforce, would erode differences. A 5 per cent increase would maintain the differences.

Recognition Most people like their contribution to be recognised. Their pay gives them reassurance that what they are doing is valued.

Composition Employees often take into account the way their earnings are made up. It is argued that younger employees tend to be more interested in high direct earnings rather than indirect benefits like pensions. Incentive payments are likely to interest employees who want to

Question 2

In the mid-1990s Marks & Spencer was set to stop providing free breakfasts for staff. Staff discounts were also to be changed. The maximum annual discount of £300 for 'full timers' was not changing, but discounts were being linked closely to the number of hours worked. Employees working fewer than five hours a week would have their discount entitlement halved, from £75 to £37.50. Staff would have to negotiate their new positions individually as Marks & Spencer did not recognise a trade union. M&S was concerned about reactions to the loss of the free breakfast. Thousands of employees who open up the stores get this perk. A spokesperson said: 'It was felt that it was no longer appropriate for one group of staff to have the benefit of the breakfast. We have to make sure everyone is fairly treated.' Marks & Spencer also has a number of other staff benefits. For example, it runs a non-contributory pension scheme and provides reduced rates for hairdressing and chiropody.

Source: adapted from *The Observer*, 21.4.1996.

(a) What fringe benefits did M&S provide to its employees?
(b) What might have been the effects of changes in fringe benefits on M&S's employees?

increase their pay. Married women and men are generally less interested in overtime payments, for example, and regard other factors more highly.

Incentive schemes

Paying money can be an incentive to motivate workers to work harder. Businesses may have incentive schemes for manual and non-manual employees, managers and directors.

Incentive schemes for manual and non-manual employees
Incentive payments have been widely used in the management of manual workers in the past. Increasingly, incentives are being paid to workers not directly involved in production. Schemes are now being used for administrative workers and in service industries. For example, a business may set sales targets for its departments. Employees in those departments can then be rewarded with bonuses once targets are reached. Sales representatives in many companies are set targets each month and are paid bonuses if they reach them. Bonus payments come in many forms. One method is a bonus paid per extra output above a target as in the piece rate system. However, one-off payments are often used by businesses to motivate workers. Bonuses can be paid at certain times of the year in a lump sum (often at Christmas). They can also be built into the monthly salary of some workers, such as staff working in certain hospitals.

Although the bonus may be paid for reaching a target, it may also be for other things. Rewards for punctuality or attendance are sometimes used. Some businesses reward their 'best' salesperson with a bonus. One unusual example of this is Richer Sounds, the hi-fi retail outlet, where workers in a retail outlet that performed best over a period were rewarded with the use of a Rolls Royce for a month!

The problem with regular bonuses is that they are often seen as part of the employee's basic pay. As a result, they may no longer act as a motivator.

Productivity agreements are also a form of bonus payment, where rewards are paid providing workers achieve a certain level of 'productivity'. They are usually agreed between employees' groups and management to 'smooth over' the introduction of new machinery or new techniques that workers need to learn.

Incentive schemes fall into three categories.
- Individual schemes. Individual employees may be rewarded for exceeding a target. The benefit of this scheme is that it rewards individual effort and hence employees are more likely to be motivated by this approach.
- Group incentives. In some situations, like assembly lines, the need is to increase group output rather than individual output. Where one worker relies on the output of others, group incentives may also have benefits. They can, however, put great pressure on all group members to be productive. It can also be difficult for a new recruit to become part of the group, as existing members may feel

they will have to compensate for his inexperience.
- Factory-wide schemes. Employees are given a share of a 'pool' bonus provided the plant has reached certain output targets. The benefit to management is that incentives are related to the final output rather than sections of the plant. Furthermore, in theory at least, employees are more likely to identify with the company as a whole.

The difficulty with this type of scheme is that there is no incentive to work harder, as there is no direct link between individual effort and reward. Some employees that work hard may have their rewards reduced by others who do not - the same problem as group incentives.

Incentive schemes for managers and directors In the 1990s there has been a large increase in the use of incentive schemes for managers and directors. These have usually been linked to how well the company has performed, often following restructuring, delayering (☞ unit 102) or the privatisation of companies such as the public utilities (☞ unit 6). Share ownership schemes are often used to motivate managers.

Question 3

In 1997, IBM, the computer company, paid a record $1.2 billion to its employees as part of an incentive scheme. The company's 241,000 employees would receive an average of $4,979, about 10 per cent of the average pay for an employee in America. Payments were linked not only to IBM's overall performance, but to the performance of each business and employee. In 1996 IBM had record sales of $75.9 billion and profits of $5.9 billion. The bonus payout would be about 20 per cent of the group's earnings, making it one of the most generous of any industrial company. The bonus programme began in 1992 when IBM was encountering severe financial problems, with falling sales and a declining reputation. Since then, IBM has recovered much of its market position and is in a far stronger financial position.

'The whole idea is to recognise employees for their hard work. It's linked to how they do, how the business unit does and how the overall corporation does', said a spokesperson. Customer satisfaction is also considered. Large incentive payments are common in the computer industry. Businesses, faced with competition, are increasingly paying attention to employees' performance. Microsoft, for example, pays moderate salaries, but gives shares in the company. The rise in its share price during the last few years has created many millionaires among its staff. Employees at Intel, the computer chip maker, receive about a third of their salary in bonus payments.

Source: adapted from *The Times*, 18.3.1997.

(a) What are the: (i) employee incentives; (ii) management incentives; mentioned in the article?
(b) Identify the possible objectives that computer companies may have had when introducing these incentive schemes.
(c) To what extent are these incentive schemes productivity agreements?

There is evidence to suggest that management perform better if they 'own' part of a business, for example after an internal buyout. However, other research indicates that incentive schemes may not necessarily be the most important motivator at work for many managers. The Ashridge Management Index is a indicator of managers' attitudes based on a survey of 500 middle and senior managers. When asked in 1997 what motivates them, 61 per cent of managers placed challenging work first. Other high-scoring motivators included 'letting people run their own show' and 'seeing the impact of decisions on the business'. These factors, along with high basic salary (35 per cent), topped the motivation league table.

Types of incentive scheme

Piece rate schemes We have already seen that piece rates can be an incentive. Producing more will earn the worker more. Each unit, over and above a target, is rewarded with a BONUS or commission payment. In the past there have often been disputes about the rate that should be paid for each unit produced. Businesses have tried to solve this by using individual time-saving schemes - the incentive is paid for time saved when carrying out a task. Using Taylor's work study methods (☞ unit 71) a work study engineer calculates the **standard time** that an employee should take to complete a task. The employee then receives incentive payments if the task is completed in a shorter time. If it is not possible to work due to shortage of materials or some other reason, the time involved is not counted. Such schemes, however, mean employees still suffer from variable payments. Despite these problems this type of incentive can be used when carrying out short, manual tasks where output can vary.

Measured daywork The idea of measured daywork may provide the answer to the problems of piece rate schemes. Instead of employees receiving a variable extra amount of pay depending on their output, they are paid a fixed sum as long as an agreed level of output is maintained. This should provide stable earnings and a stable output, instead of 'as much as you can, when you can, if you can'.

The first major agreement based on the principles of measured daywork was the National Power Loading Agreement in coal mining in 1966. London Docks and British Leyland both reverted to more traditional 'payment by result' methods in the late 70s. Although productivity gains may not have been great, most surveys found that measured daywork improved industrial relations and that less expenditure was spent on dealing with grievances. Furthermore, measured daywork seemed to give management a greater control over such payment schemes. In practice, the need for flexibility in reward schemes has meant that measured daywork is rarely used as an incentive scheme today.

Profit sharing Profit sharing takes place in business organisations such as partnerships (☞ unit 5). Profits are either shared equally or as agreed in any partnership deed of agreement drawn up by the business. Partners or employees of business have an incentive to be as productive as possible. The more profit the business makes, the more they earn.

Profit related pay Profit related pay involves employees being paid a cash 'bonus' as a proportion of the annual profits of the company. In previous years a certain amount of profit related pay has been exempt from taxation. However, this was no longer to be the case after the year 2000. Profit related pay has a number of problems for employees. It is not linked to individual performance and rewards can fluctuate from year to year depending on the performance of the business.

Share ownership Businesses may offer the possibility of purchasing shares in the company as an incentive. This is sometimes reserved for managers. In large businesses wider share ownership amongst all employees may be encouraged. There is a number of different employee share schemes. **Savings-related** share option schemes, for example, allow an employee to save each month over, say, five years. They can then take up an option to purchase a number of shares at a value stated when the shares are offered - the option price. The advantage of buying shares to employees is that they feel part of the company and are rewarded with **dividends** (☞ unit 3) if the company performs well.

In the 1990s evidence suggested that share ownership was slowly spreading among growing businesses. Out of 63 companies floated on the Stock Exchange in 1996, 39 operated all employee share schemes. However, 52 companies had Inland Revenue approved executive share schemes. Even more had non-approved schemes for top executives.

A UK index of quoted employee-owned companies showed that share prices had outperformed those of conventionally owned rivals over the past few years. The index tracked 30 companies where more than 10 per cent of shares were held by or for employees. The index rose threefold since January 1992, outstripping the FT-SE All Share index by 89 per cent.

Performance related pay PERFORMANCE RELATED pay (PRP) schemes link the annual salary of an employee to their performance in the job. PRP schemes have spread rapidly in recent years and now form an important part of white collar pay in the public and private sector. Nearly all the major banks, building societies and insurance companies now use performance systems. A number of large manufacturers, such as Cadbury's and Nissan, have introduced schemes (at times extending them to the shop floor) as well as public sector industries, such as the civil service, NHS and local government.

The shift towards PRP can be seen as part of a more general movement towards 'pay flexibility' in British industry.
● Organisations have sought to tie pay increases to measures

of business performance, not just through PRP schemes but through other mechanisms, such as profit sharing.

● There has been a move away from national, industry- wide pay agreements to local, plant-wide agreements. This has given managers greater discretion in the way they match rewards to particular business units.

● There is a new focus on the individual employee and rewards which reflect her performance and circumstances, which has meant that collective methods of pay determination have become less important.

PRP schemes come in many forms, but the majority have some common features.

● Individual performance is reviewed, usually over a year. This may take the form of comparing performance against agreed objectives.

● At the end of the review the worker will be placed in a 'performance category'. The 'excellent' performer, for instance, may have exceeded all his agreed targets and produced work of a high standard. The category the worker falls into will determine the size of payment or whether payment is made at all.

● The performance payment can vary. Sometimes there may be a small cash bonus or the award of increments on a pay scale. In others, the entire salary and progression through scales can depend on the results of the performance review. This kind of 'merit only' scheme means a 'poor' performer will be punished, as they will not receive extra pay.

There are problems with PRP. It is based on individual achievement, so the better a person does the more that person is paid. However, there may be disputes about how performance is to be measured and whether a person has achieved enough to be rewarded. Also, the system is not likely to work if people do not react to the possibility of rewards by working harder.

The following example of two sales consultants highlights some practical problems. Jane and Ruth are sales consultants for an insurance company and both had set targets for a six month period. Ruth met her target comfortably and received the agreed bonus of £5,500 for reaching on-target earnings. Jane failed to reach her agreed target because her sales manager left the company and poached three of Jane's best customers just before they signed agreements with Jane. Jane's bonus was therefore reduced to only £2,500 for a lower level of sales. Jane had no control over this, but felt she had worked just as hard as Ruth and therefore deserved a similar bonus.

Research also shows that many organisations may be out of tune with their employees, placing too much emphasis on incentives. The effectiveness of performance related pay, in particular, is called into question. Ashridge researchers describe it as 'the biggest mismatch between what organisations are seen to be relying on to motivate managers and what actually motivates them'. Research by ACAS also suggests that PRP schemes tend to demotivate rather than

Question 4

The bosses of Britain's 30 largest companies saw the value of their share options triple in a year between 1997 and 1998. However, the 'fat cats' of industry might not be the only ones to benefit. Jackie Neale, a part time Sunday night shelf stacker at Tesco's Cheshunt store in Hertfordshire, saved £4,800 as part of the company's savings related share option scheme. These savings were used to buy Tesco shares worth £20,000 at market prices. She said that some of the shares would be cashed in to pay for a family holiday, but the rest were to be kept as an investment.

Many employees in relatively poorly paid jobs have benefited in this way. Rising stock market prices have led to great gains for savers. The schemes also benefit from tax concessions. They are also low risk. Employees do not have to buy shares at the end of the savings period of, say, five years if their price has not risen. Even if shares are not bought, employees receive a bonus payment for five years saving.

Source: adapted from *The Observer*, 12.4.1998.

(a) What type of incentive scheme is suggested in the article?
(b) Describe three advantages to lowly paid employees of this type of incentive scheme.
(c) Explain why some businesses might be introducing this type of incentive scheme for low paid workers as well as managers or directors.

motivate staff.

Problems with incentive schemes

There is a number of problems that financial incentives schemes have.

● Operating problems. For incentives to work, production needs to have a smooth flow of raw materials, equipment and storage space, and consumer demand must also be fairly stable. These conditions cannot be guaranteed for long. If raw materials did not arrive or ran out, for example, the worker may not achieve a target and receive no bonus for reasons beyond his control. If this happens the employee is unlikely to be motivated by the scheme, and may negotiate for a larger proportion of earnings to be paid as guaranteed 'basic' pay.

● Fluctuating earnings. A scheme that is linked to output must result in fluctuating earnings. This might be due to changes in demand, the output of the worker or machinery problems. As in the case above, the worker is likely to press for the guaranteed part of pay to be increased, or store output in the 'good times' to prevent problems in the 'bad'. Alternatively, workers may try to 'slow down' productive workers so that benefits are shared out as equally as possible.

● Quality. The need to increase output to gain rewards can affect quality. There is an incentive for workers to do things as quickly as possible and this can lead to mistakes.

Case study

Empowerment at BP Chemicals

A 1995 survey by the Industrial Society showed that by 1998, employers expect there to be a trend towards greater empowerment in business. Only 20 per cent of managers described their businesses as 'empowering'. But over 50 per cent felt that they would be by 1998. But what is empowerment? For some it is a response to competitors, a way to use their resources better or a method to boost productivity. For others, it's a way to cut the costs of supervision.

Empowerment is supposed to be a departure from the methods of control found in hierarchical businesses. There should be a move towards making things happen, through coaching and providing help to employees. By empowering employees and removing layers of supervision, the role of manager should be changed from one of command to one of support.

Some businesses that consider themselves to be empowering still have many managers who talk in terms of power differentials between themselves and staff. Empowerment is used to describe what the manager will empower (tell) the employee to do. But if employees to feel properly empowered, they need to feel trusted, not to be told what to do. This requires great commitment from senior managers and a change in approach for the whole company. Good managers create an environment in which people believe they are trusted to do their job. There is no need for constant checks to be made. Where trust is lacking, individuals feel isolated and cautious. Teamworking is inefficient because teams treat each other with suspicion. There is often speculation and rumour mongering. Where trust does exist, individuals feel comfortable with colleagues and teams tend to function effectively and to collaborate.

BP Chemicals at Baglan Bay in South Wales was part of the survey. The company employed more than 2,000 in the 1970s. Reorganisation since that time meant that it had only 350 employees by the mid-1990s. In 1991 the business felt that it was overstaffed, that costs were too high and that training was insufficient (2-3 days per year per person, compared to 15-20 days by competitors). To identify changes that were needed, the business set up a number of 'corrective action teams' involving a cross-section of employees. The empowerment process, which the company claims to be one of the first to be introduced in the UK chemical industry, grew out of the recommendations from these teams.

What does empowerment involve at BP Chemicals? Management decisions at plant level are taken by people in the front line of maintenance and production. Conventional foremen were done away with. Round-the-clock shift teams share day-to-day responsibilities and rotate work patterns. This means that they have the ability to tackle most of the maintenance work at the factory. Special training gives employees freedom to use their own initiative. This allows the business to have the best staff possible to operate the plant safely and efficiently.

46-year-old Phil Williams is a member of a four person team which has the power to carry out on-the-spot decisions. Team members use their own initiative. There is no longer a foreman to supervise their work. Williams thinks the changes have been: 'a positive move towards high efficiency and improved staff productivity.' He says: 'Before empowerment, I was basically in charge of a control panel with a foreman giving orders from an office. Any changes in chemical feed rates would be decided by the foreman, but nine times out of 10 an operator would be vastly more experienced. After the introduction of multiskilling and teams, we have taken on the work of the foreman. We pull together as a team and make decisions collectively.' He says each employee is skilled at all the disciplines and capable of tackling a broad range of jobs. 'At first we were wary of the system, but everyone has grasped it. We have realised that industry cannot stand still and must move with the times in a competitive world. Productivity counts, because if another company can produce the goods cheaper than you, they will see you off.'

Gareth James, the BP works' general manager, has no doubt about the beneficial impact of empowerment. 'Productivity has increased significantly and we have seen a reduction in the fixed-cost base of running the factory.' He also believes, however, that further changes are necessary. 'The empowering process is continuous because there is always more that people can do, and making that happen is an essential part of my job.'

Source: adapted from *The Guardian*, 11,5,1996.

(a) Give an example of:
  (i) multiskilling;
  (ii) job enrichment:
  at BP Chemicals.
(b) Explain why team work may have been necessary for 'round-the-clock' shift teams in the factory.
(c) Examine possible problems of team work for:
  (i) employees at BP Chemicals;
  (ii) the business itself.
(d) Using examples from BP Chemicals explain the benefits of empowerment for:
  (i) employees at BP Chemicals;
  (ii) the business itself.
(e) A competitor of BP Chemicals has decided to introduce an empowerment scheme for employees. Discuss the conditions that may need to exist for the scheme to be successful.

What is management?

Unit 3 explained that managers are an important group involved in business activity. It is difficult to define exactly what is meant by 'management'. However, many agree that managers are responsible for 'getting things done' - usually through other people. The term manager may refer to a number of different people within a business. Some job titles include the word manager, such as personnel manager or managing director. Other job holders may also be managers, even though their titles do not say it.

It could be argued that managers:

● act on behalf of the owners - in a company, senior management are accountable to the shareholders;

● set objectives for the organisation, for example, they may decide that a long term objective is to have a greater market share than all of the company's competitors;

● make sure that a business achieves its objectives, by managing others;

● ensure that corporate values (the values of the organisation) are maintained in dealings with other businesses, customers, employees and general public.

The functions of management

Henri Fayol, the French management theorist, listed a number of **functions** or '**elements**' of management.

Planning This involves setting objectives and also the strategies, policies, programmes and procedures for achieving them. Planning might be done by line managers (☞ unit 70) who will be responsible for performance. However, advice on planning may also come from staff management who might have expertise in that area, even if they have no line authority. For example, a production manager may carry out human resource planning (☞ unit 75) in the production department, but use the skills of the personnel manager in planning recruitment for vacancies that may arise.

Organising Managers set tasks which need to be performed if the business is to achieve its objectives. Jobs need to be organised within sections or departments and authority needs to be **delegated** so that jobs are carried out. For example, the goal of a manufacturing company may be to produce quality goods that will be delivered to customers on time. The tasks, such as manufacturing, packaging, administration, etc. that are part of producing and distributing the goods, need to be organised to achieve this goal.

Commanding This involves giving instructions to subordinates to carry out tasks. The manager has the authority to make decisions and the responsibility to see tasks are carried out.

Question 1

Simon Kukes is president of Tyumen Oil Company (TNK), one of the largest oil companies in Russia. He is very different from the typical Soviet manager who was trained to raise production no matter what the cost in the old USSR. He says that the answer to the problems of the Communist era, such as shoddy equipment and dated technology, lies in an incremental, step by step, long term strategy. First, the neglected factories, equipment and roads must be repaired. Only then can costs be reduced, productivity raised and investment take place.

Kukes launched a plan to integrate the company, from the oilfield to the petrol pump. He also began looking for foreign finance for investment projects. The workforce was cut by 20 per cent to 40,000. Productivity was increased and the quality of refined petrol from the company's refinery was improved. Kukes and his team of managers pushed ahead with a petrol station franchising programme which gave the business 400 outlets in and around Moscow by the end of 1998. Kukes also realised that there was a need to modernise the old Ryazan refinery, with potential capacity of 17 million tons a year. TNK employed ABB Lummus, a subsidiary of Swiss-Swedish engineering group ABB, to carry out the work.

TNK also attempted to raise its profile with foreign banks and domestic customers. A low budget, snappy five part commercial was aired on Russian TV. A tank filled up with 'the best and the strongest' TNK petrol and then roared off to destinations throughout the world. Unlike many of his counterparts in Russian industry, Mr Kukes has the full backing of the majority shareholders of the business. They are Alfa Bank and Renova, a small group of US and Russian private investors, who own 51 per cent of shares. In 1998 Kukes negotiated a £65.5 million, 18 month loan from a German bank and credit of $550 million to cover the import of US oil lifting equipment. He aims to turn TNK into a world class oil company, which it already is in terms of reserves.

Source: adapted from the *Financial Times*, 14.12.1998.

(a) What objectives did Simon Kukes set for the business?
(b) Explain the functions of management that Simon Kukes might be carrying out in his attempt to revitalise TNK.

Co-ordinating This is the bringing together of the activities of people within the business. Individuals and groups will have their own goals, which may be different to those of the business and each other. Management must make sure that there is a common approach, so that the company's goals are achieved.

Controlling Managers measure and correct the activities of individuals and groups, to make sure that their performance fits in with plans.

The management process

Peter Drucker worked in the 1940s and 1950s as a business adviser to a number of US firms. He is credited with the idea of MANAGEMENT BY OBJECTIVES, used by some businesses today. Drucker grouped the operations of management into five categories.

- Setting objectives (☞ unit 4) for the organisation. Managers decide what the objectives of the business should be. These objectives are then organised into targets. Managers inform others of these targets.
- Organising the work. The work to be done in the organisation must be divided into manageable activities and jobs. The jobs must be integrated into the formal organisational structure (☞ unit 70) and people must be selected to do the jobs (☞ unit 71).
- Motivating employees (☞ unit 71) and communicating information (☞ unit 82) to enable employees to carry out their tasks.
- Job measurement. It is the task of management to establish objectives or yardsticks of performance for every person in the organisation. They must also analyse actual performance and compare it with the yardstick that has been set. Finally, they should communicate the findings and explain their significance to others in the business.
- Developing people. The manager should bring out the talent in people.

Every manager performs all five functions listed above, no matter how good or bad a manager, Drucker suggests. A bad manager performs these functions badly, whereas a good manager performs them well. He also argued that the manager of a business has a basic function - economic performance. In this respect the business manager is different from the manager of other types of organisation. Business managers can only justify their existence and authority by the economic results they produce.

Being a manager

In contrast with Fayol or Drucker, **Charles Handy** argued that any definition of a manager is likely to be so broad it will have little or no meaning. Instead he outlined what is likely to be involved in 'being a manager'.

The manager as a general practitioner Handy made an analogy between managing and staying 'healthy'. If there are 'health problems' in business, the manager needs to identify the symptoms. These could include low productivity, high labour turnover or industrial relations problems. Once the symptoms have been identified, the manager needs to find the cause of trouble and develop a strategy for 'better health'. Strategies for health might include changing people, through hiring and firing, reassignments, training, pay increases or

Question

Leyland Trucks, the UK's largest commercial vehicle maker, enjoyed great success in the 1990s after its management buyout in 1993. This was to a large extent the result of innovative management. The workplace culture was transformed. The company conducted a survey which found employees thought they were not being given enough responsibility for their work. Management practices were also heavily criticised.

Employees who used to follow instructions exactly were given responsibility to generate their own production improvements. The contributions of workers were also recognised. Certificates of achievement were handed out for good work. Suggestions for improvements received a £1 shopping voucher and a thank you from management. One idea was for litter bins to be suspended on the production line near each lorry cab. Rubbish used to accumulate in the cabs during assembly and contractors were hired to clean them at the end of the line. Now rubbish is binned during production.

At one end of the factory was a new 15,000 square feet space cleared for assembly of Izuzu N series trucks. In the old days a team of engineers would have been put on the reorganisation. Instead, employees were asked to look at the problem and shopfloor teams devised their own plan. One result was a reduction of work in progress by between £180,000 and £200,000. Another production process called 'zig-zagging', where teams move between two parallel production lines, was also devised by shopfloor employees. Allister Butler, manufacturing engineering manager, says: 'I guess that in our minds we didn't trust the people on the shop floor.

The one thing we have learned is that the real experts are those who build the trucks.'

The old system of working involved groups led by a foreman and overseen by an inspector

who checked work. Today work teams have a coordinator, who is paid the same as other members of the team. Clocking on and off was abandoned. There has also been a big improvement in communications, using a variety of methods including regular question-and-answer sessions between the chief executive and groups of employees. The production line is stopped for two hours every month to allow teams to discuss ideas. Improvements can be measured in a variety of ways. The plant's break-even figure for truck production has dropped from 11,500 vehicles in 1989 to between 5,500 and 6,000 in 1997. Defects per vehicle fell from 27-28 in 1986 to 4-5 in 1997. Managers believe the regime can be improved further to achieve the company's stated goal of making 20,000 trucks in 2005, up from an expected 9,200 in 1997.

Source: adapted from the *Financial Times*, 9.7.1997.

(a) Give examples from Leyland Trucks of the five operations of management suggested by Drucker.
(b) Explain how the management at Leyland attempted to:
  (i) give employees more responsibility;
  (ii) improve communication.

counselling. A manager might also restructure work through job redesign, job enrichment (☞ unit 73) and a redefinition of roles. Systems can also be improved. These can include communication systems, reward systems, information and reporting systems budgets and other decision making systems, eg stock control.

Managerial dilemmas Handy argued that managers face dilemmas. One of the reasons sometimes given for why managers are paid more than workers is because of the dilemmas they face.

● The dilemma of cultures. When managers are promoted or move to other parts of the business, they have to behave in ways which are suitable for the new position. For example, at the senior management level, managers may deal more with long term strategy and delegate lower level tasks to middle management more often. If a promoted manager maintains a 'culture' that she is used to, which may mean taking responsibility for all tasks, she may not be effective in her new position.

● The trust-control dilemma. Managers may want to control the work for which they are responsible. However, they may have to delegate work to subordinates, trusting them to do the work properly. The greater the trust a manager has in subordinates, the less control she retains for herself. Retaining control could mean a lack of trust.

● The commando leader's dilemma. In many firms, junior managers often want to work in project teams, with a clear task or objective. This can mean working 'outside' the normal bureaucratic structure of a larger organisation. Unfortunately, there can be too many project groups (or 'commando groups') for the good of the business. The manager must decide how many project groups she should create to satisfy the needs of her subordinates and how much bureaucratic structure to retain.

The manager as a person Management has developed into a profession and managers expect to be rewarded for their professional skills. Managers must, therefore, continue to develop these skills and sell them to the highest bidder.

Managerial roles

Henry Mintzberg suggested that, as well as carrying out certain functions, the manager also fulfils certain roles in a firm. He identified three types of role which a manager must play.

● Interpersonal roles. These arise from the manager's formal authority. Managers have a **figurehead** role. For example, a large part of a chief executive's time is spent representing the company at dinners, conferences etc. They also have a **leader** role. This involves hiring, firing and training staff, motivating employees etc. Thirdly, they have a **liaison** role. Some managers spend up to half their time meeting with other managers. They do this because they need to know what is happening in other departments. Senior managers spend a great deal of time with people outside the business. Mintzberg says that these contacts build up an informal information system, and are a means of extending influence both within and outside the business.

● Information roles. Managers act as channels of information from one department to another. They are in a position to do this because of their contacts.

● Decision making roles. The manager's formal authority and access to information means that no one else is in a better position to take decisions about a department's work.

Through extensive research and observation of what managers actually do, Mintzberg drew certain conclusions about the work of managers.

● The idea that a manager is a 'systematic' planner is a myth. Planning is often carried out on a day-to-day basis, in between more urgent tasks.

● Another myth is that a manager has no regular or routine duties, as these have been delegated to others. Mintzberg found that managers perform a number of routine duties, particularly 'ceremonial' tasks.

● Mintzberg's research showed that managers prefer verbal communication rather than a formal system of communication (☞ unit 82). Information passed by word of mouth in an informal way is likely to be more up to date and easier to grasp.

Leadership

The ability to lead within organisations is of growing interest to businesses. This has resulted from the need to lead companies through change, brought about by an increase in competition and changes in technology and economic conditions.

Earlier in this unit it was shown that a manager might have a leadership **role**. To be a good leader in business it has been suggested that a manager must know what direction needs to be taken by the business and plan how to achieve this. Leaders will also be able to persuade others that the decisions that they have taken are the correct ones.

Leaders are often thought to be charismatic people who have 'something about them' that makes them stand out from others. It has been argued that there are certain personality traits (☞ unit 83) that are common to leaders. However, studies have failed to prove this is the case.

In order to identify 'leadership', studies have shifted to examine what leaders, and in particular managers, do - that is, what behaviour is associated with leadership. This is dealt with in the next sections.

The qualities of leadership

One approach to find out what makes good leaders is to identify the qualities that they should have. A number of **characteristics** have been suggested.

● Effective leaders have a positive self image, backed up with a genuine ability and realistic aspirations. This is shown in the confidence they have. An example in UK industry might be Richard Branson, in his various pioneering business activities. Leaders also appreciate their own strengths and weaknesses. It is argued that many managers fail to lead because they often get bogged down in short term activity.

● Leaders need to be able to get to the 'core' of a problem and have the vision and commitment to suggest radical solutions. Sir John Harvey-Jones took ICI to £1 billion profit by stirring up what had become a 'sleeping giant'. Many awkward questions were raised about the validity of the way things were done, and the changes led to new and more profitable businesses on a worldwide scale for the firm.

● Studies of leaders in business suggest that they are expert in a particular field and well read in everything else. They tend to be 'out of the ordinary', intelligent, and articulate. Examples might be Anita Roddick, the founder of Body Shop or Bill Gates, the founder of Microsoft.

● Leaders are often creative and innovative. They tend to seek new ideas to problems, make sure that important things are done and try to improve standards. One example might have been the restructuring of BHS by David Dworkin. He reorganised the business so that stock did not remain on the shelves until it sold at full price. The price of slow selling stock was cut immediately to get rid of it and new stock brought in.

● Leaders often have the ability to sense change and can respond to it. A leader, for example, may be able to predict a decline of sales in an important product or the likelihood of a new production technique being available in the future.

One of the key leadership issues after the year 2000 is likely to be how to deal with international markets and globalisation (☞ unit 75). Leaders may face challenges such as:

● international recruitment to overcome domestic staff shortages (☞ unit 75);

● cross-border mergers, acquisitions and joint ventures (☞ unit 101);

● the opening of new markets in Eastern Europe, South East Asia and China (☞ unit 31);

● European social policy directives, like the Social Chapter (☞ unit 81);

● developments in information and communications technology (☞ unit 82).

Leadership styles

Another approach is to examine different styles of leadership. There are a number of styles that managers might adopt in the work setting. Table 74.1 shows the different ways in which leaders can involve others in the decision making process.

Autocratic An AUTOCRATIC leadership style is one where the manager sets objectives, allocates tasks, and insists on obedience. Therefore the group become dependent on him or

---

Question 3

In 1989 Rupert Murdoch delivered a speech at the Edinburgh International Television Festival. He warned that regulation was protecting a monopoly and championed a multi-channel environment. At the time top brass at the BBC and ITV laughed.

In August 1993 Murdoch was preparing for the launch of multi-channels, BSkyB's package of new TV channels. His predictions about the future of TV had been accurate. Despite a shaky start, his satellite channel was flourishing. Not only had Murdoch revolutionised British TV, he was making people pay for it. In early 1993 Murdoch had clinched a $525 million deal for a 63 per cent stake in the South-East Asian satellite operator Star TV, a company well placed to carry advertising to Asia's growing middle class audience. This further expanded the possible business opportunities for the Murdoch empire.

In October 1998 Murdoch's Sky Television, as it was then called, was the first digital channel to be launched in the UK. Digital television promised better quality pictures and the possibility of hundreds of channels. Existing Sky subscribers were given financial incentives to switch to digital television. New subscribers were faced with a barrage of promotional publicity. A vast number of channel combinations was available. Subscribers could choose from sports, entertainment and movie packages. They could also receive BBC, Channel 4 and Channel 5 and watch one-off pay per view events, such as boxing matches or concerts. Again, despite reservations about its success, there was great initial consumer demand. There were likely to be major benefits from being first into the market. Customers who signed up were unlikely to be willing to change and goodwill and brand loyalty could be built up before other companies entered the market.

Examine the leadership characteristics shown by Rupert Murdoch which are mentioned in the article.

---

her. The result of this style is that members of the group are often dissatisfied with the leader. This results in little cohesion, the need for high levels of supervision, and poor levels of motivation amongst employees.

Autocratic leadership may be needed in certain circumstances. For example, in the armed forces there may be a need to move troops quickly and for orders to be obeyed instantly.

Democratic A DEMOCRATIC leadership style encourages participation in decision making. Democratic leadership styles can be persuasive or consultative.

● Persuasive. This is where a leader has already made a decision, but takes the time to persuade others that it is a good idea. For example, the owner of a business may decide to employ outside staff for certain jobs and persuade existing staff that this may ease their work load.

● Consultative. This is where a leader consults others about their views before making a decision. The decision will take into account these views. For example, the views of the marketing department about whether to launch a new range of products may be considered.

Democratic leadership styles need good communication skills. The leaders must be able to explain ideas clearly to employees and understand feedback they receive (☞ unit 82). It may mean, however, that decisions take a long time to be reached as lengthy consultation can take place.

It has been suggested that a democratic style of leadership may be more effective in business for a number of reasons.

● There has been increased public participation in social and political life. Democratic management reflects this trend.

● Increasing income and educational standards means that people now expect greater freedom and a better quality of working life.

● Research suggests that this style is generally more effective. Managers are able to 'tap into' the ideas of people with knowledge and experience. This can lead to better decisions being made.

● People involved in the decision making process are likely to be more committed and motivated, to accept decisions reached with their help, to trust managers who make the decisions and to volunteer new and creative ideas.

Laissez-faire A LAISSEZ-FAIRE type of leadership style allows employees to carry out activities freely within broad limits. The result is a relaxed atmosphere, but one where there are few guidelines and directions. This can sometimes result in poor productivity and lack of motivation as employees have little incentive to work hard.

Factors affecting leadership styles

The type of leadership style adopted by managers will depend on various factors.

● The task. A certain task may be the result of an emergency, which might need immediate response from a person in

Table 74.1 *Leadership styles*

Type of leadership	Method
Autocratic	Leader makes decisions alone. Others are informed and carry out decisions.
Persuasive	Leader makes decisions alone. Others are persuaded by the leader that the decision is the right one, ie leader 'sells' the decision to the group.
Consultative	Leader consults with others before decision is made. There will be group influence in the final decision, even though it is made by the leader.
Laissez-faire	There is no formal structure to decision making. The leader does not force his or her views on others.

authority. The speed of decision needed and action taken may require an authoritarian or autocratic style of leadership.

● The tradition of the organisation. A business may develop its own culture which is the result of the interactions of all employees at different levels. This can result in one type of leadership style, because of a pattern of behaviour that has developed in the organisation. For example, in the public sector (☞ unit 6) leadership is often democratic because of the need to consult with politicians etc.

● The type of labour force. A more highly skilled workforce might be most productive when their opinions are sought. Democratic leadership styles may be more appropriate in this case.

 Question 4

An American electronics company asked researchers William Pasmore and Frank Friedlander to study work injuries which were reducing productivity. About a third of the company's 335 employees had complained about pains in their wrists, arms and shoulders. Some had undergone surgery and one woman had permanently lost the use of her right hand. A series of medical and technical investigations carried out by management failed to find the cause of the injuries.

But the company management had never thought of asking the employees themselves about the possible causes of their injuries. So the researchers suggested that a 'Studies and Communication Group' be set up, drawing workers' representatives from each area of the factory. The group members discussed their own experiences and injuries, designed a questionnaire, surveyed over 300 other employees, and produced 60 recommendations for solving the injury problem. Management at first rejected the group's solutions because management practices were identified as the main cause of the problem. The group had found that the injuries were related to inadequate training, rapid and repetitive arm movements, badly adjusted machines, frustration at machine breakdowns, stress from supervisors' behaviour such as favouritism and pressure from management for more output.

The first attempts by management to solve the problem had in fact made it worse. When workers were injured, production fell. So management increased the pressure for more output, which increased workers' stress, which in turn led to more injuries.

The researchers concluded that a change in the relationships between workers and management was necessary to create a climate of effective participation. The managers in this company felt that they had lost over the situation. But as the workers' recommendations were gradually implemented, the number of injuries fell and the overall performance of the factory rose.

Source: adapted from D.Buchanan & A.Huczynski, *Organisational Behaviour*, 3rd edition, 1997, Prentice Hall.

(a) What two types of leadership style are suggested in the article?

(b) How might the new leadership style benefit the business?

- The group size. Democratic leadership styles can lead to confusion the greater the size of the group.
- The leader's personality. The personality of one manager may be different to another manager and certain leadership styles might suit one but not the other. For example, an aggressive, competitive personality may be more suited to an authoritarian leadership style.
- Group personality. Some people prefer to be directed rather than contribute, either because of lack of interest, previous experience, or because they believe that the manager is paid to take decisions and shoulder responsibility. If this is the case, then an autocratic leadership style is more likely to lead to effective decision making.
- Time. The time available to complete a task might influence the leadership style adopted. For example, if a project has to be finished quickly, there may be no time for discussion and an autocratic style may be adopted.

Why do leaders adopt different styles?

A number of theories have been put forward to explain the most appropriate leadership style when dealing with certain situations or groups at work.

Fiedler In 1976, F. Fiedler argued that 'it is easier to change someone's role or power, or to modify the job he has to do, than to change his leadership style'. From his 800 studies he found that it is difficult for people to change leadership styles - an 'autocrat' will always lead in autocratic style whereas a leader that encourages involvement will tend to be 'democratic'. Different leadership styles may also be effective depending on the situation. He concluded that, as leaders are unable to adapt their style to a situation, effectiveness can only be achieved by changing the manager to 'fit' the situation or by altering the situation to fit the manager.

In business it is often difficult to change the situation. Fiedler suggested that a business should attempt what he called **leadership match** - to choose a leader to fit the situation. Leaders can be either **task orientated** or **relationship orientated**. So, for example, a business that faced declining sales might need a very task orientated manager to pull the business around, even if the tradition of the firm might be for a more democratic style of leadership.

Hersey and Blanchard P. Hersey and K.H. Blanchard argued that a leader's strategy should not only take account of the situation, but also the maturity of those who are led. They defined maturity as the ability of people to set targets which can be achieved and yet are demanding.

A leader will have **task behaviour or relationship behaviour**. Task behaviour is the extent to which the leader has to organise what a subordinate should do. Relationship

behaviour describes how much support is needed and how close personal contact is. Together these will decide which of the following leadership styles will be used.

- **Delegating** leadership is where a leader allows subordinates to solve a problem. For this type of leadership style to work, subordinates need to be mature and require little support at work.
- **Participating** leadership is where a leader and subordinates work on a problem together, supporting each other. In this situation subordinates are slightly less mature than when a leader delegates and so need more support.
- **Selling** leadership is where a leader persuades others of the benefits of an idea. Workers are likely to be only moderately mature and require a great deal of support.
- **Telling** leadership is where a leader tells others what to do. Workers are fairly immature. They are told exactly what to do and little contact or support is needed.

Wright and Taylor In 1984, P. Wright and D. Taylor argued that theories which concentrate on the situation or maturity of those led ignore how skillfully leadership is carried out. They produced a checklist designed to help leaders improve the performance of subordinates. It included the following.

- What is the problem? An employee may, for example, be carrying out a task inefficiently.
- Is it serious enough to spend time on? This could depend on the cost to the business.
- What reasons may there be for the problem? How can it be solved? These are shown in Table 74.2.
- Choosing a solution and evaluating if it is the most effective one.
- Evaluation of the leader's performance.

This can be used to identify the most suitable leadership style in a particular situation. For example, if the problem above is caused because the employee has been left to make his own decisions and is not able to, a more autocratic leadership style may be needed. On the other hand, if the employee lacks motivation or does not have the authority to make decisions, greater discussion or delegation may be needed.

Key terms

Autocratic leadership - a leadership style where the leader makes all decisions independently.
Democratic leadership - a leadership style where the leader encourages others to participate in decision making.
Laissez-faire leadership - a leadership style where employees are encouraged to make their own decisions, within limits.
Management by Objectives (MBO) - a management theory which suggests that managers set goals and communicate them to subordinates.

Table 74.2

Possible reasons for performance problem	Possible solutions
Is the person fully aware of the job requirements?	Give guidance concerning expected goals and standards. Set targets.
Does the person have the ability to do the job well?	Provide formal training, on the job coaching, practice, etc.
Does the person find thetask rewarding in itself?	Simplify task, reduce work load, reduce time pressures, etc.
Is good performance rewarded by others?	Reward good performance and penalties for poor performance.
Does the person receive adequate feedback about performance?	Provide or arrange feedback.
Does the person have the resources and authority to do the task?	Provide staff, equipment, raw materials; delegate if necessary.
Do working conditions interfere with performance?	Improve lighting, noise, heat, layout; remove distractions etc.

Summary

1. State 5 functions of management.
2. Briefly explain the process of management by objectives.
3. Give 3 examples of a managerial dilemma.
4. Why might a good manager not always be a good leader?
5. Briefly explain 5 qualities of leadership.
6. State 6 factors which might affect the choice of leadership style.
7. According to Fiedler's theory, why should a business attempt a leadership match?

Case study

Leadership at Semco

When Ricardo Semler joined Semco at the age of 18, his main interest was playing in a rock band. Three years later he was running the Brazilian engineering and consulting group. He is an advocate of the idea that companies perform best when left to themselves. Semler inherited the job from his father, Antonio Curt Semler. Bit by bit he dismantled the company's conservative structure. First to go was searching of employees as they left at the end of each day. Time clocks were next, followed by all controls over working hours. He said: 'I was testing some of the things I'd learnt in the rock group. If the drummer doesn't feel like coming to rehearsals, you can hassle him as much as you want, but the problem remains. At Semco, the question we work on is, how do you get people to want to come to work on a grey Monday morning, which is 100 per cent a motivation issue.'

In the early days his approach caused havoc. Some senior managers left. Since the mid-1980s, however, turnover has risen. By 1996 it was $100 million. Dress and working hours are up to individuals. One-third of employees set their own salaries. The rest are negotiated according to performance. Meetings are open to everyone. There are no receptionists and no secretaries. If there is one rule it's 'keep it sound'. 'Some business units will come back with a budget that says they are going to make 2 per cent and some 18 per cent. I didn't say that 2 per cent was too little. I said whatever you think is sound and you're happy with, we'll accept. My point is that it's financial solidity that gets rid of what I call the boarding school issues. But if financial solidity isn't there, all we have is a kind of Woodstock association of co-operatives for peace, and I don't believe in that.'

Freedom has its responsibilities. Managers are elected by subordinates and evaluated by them every six months. Those who don't come up to scratch may be fired. One manager had this experience soon after finding his wife had a terminal illness. 'He was very depressed,' Semler remembers, 'and the system still expelled him. There's no room for compassion when the bottom line has taken its place.' Semler admits that some of his ideas may look wacky. One example is a board with three pegs by each employee's name for them to hang a coloured flag on each morning. Green means 'good mood', yellow for 'careful' and red for 'not today thank you'. Workers took to it immediately. Semler is most proud of the fact that many successful ideas have come from the factory floor and management. Indeed, he hardly 'runs' the company at all. He has no office and works mostly from home. Management decisions are taken by a 'committee of counsellors'. Another committee takes decisions at shop floor level.

Some of the methods used at Semco have been picked up by organisations around the world, such as manufacturing companies in the US, schools in Finland, an Australian hospital and the Amsterdam police force. 'I'm absolutely convinced that all businesses could be run along these lines,' he says.

Source: adapted from the *Financial Times*, 15,5,1997.

(a) Give an example of: (i) organising; (ii) setting company values.
(b) (i) What type of leadership style does Ricardo Semler demonstrate?
    (ii) What evidence does the article contain which suggests this type of leadership style?
(c) Examine the possible: (i) benefits and; (ii) problems to the business of this leadership style.
(d) Explain the factors that may have influenced this choice of leadership style.
(e) Explain the dilemmas that may have faced Ricardo Semler when changing the business organisation.
(f) Discuss the extent to which the change in management and leadership style was successful.

The work of the personnel department

Many large and medium sized businesses today have a personnel department. Its main role will be to manage the firm's HUMAN RESOURCES. These are the employees or personnel in a business that help it to achieve its objectives. They might include production workers, office staff, members of the marketing team, accountants or cleaners.

The personnel department will deal with many factors associated with employees. These include:

- human resources or workforce planning;
- recruitment and selection;
- induction and training;
- promotion and transfers;
- appraisal and termination of employment;
- discipline;
- rewards and conditions of employment;
- working conditions;
- career development and welfare;
- wage bargaining.

What is human resources planning?

HUMAN RESOURCES PLANNING or WORKFORCE PLANNING is the method by which a business forecasts how many and what type of employees it needs now and in future. It also involves matching up the right type of employees to the needs of the business. A business will work out its labour requirements, its **demand**, and make sure that an appropriate **supply** is planned. For example, a growing business, such as a call centre, might find that it needs an extra 20 telephone operators over the next year. It may, therefore, plan to recruit an extra 20 operators over the period. An engineering business that loses a large order for parts may plan to make 50 workers redundant.

The HUMAN RESOURCES or WORKFORCE PLAN is usually one of the responsibilities of the personnel or human resources department and is one part of **human resources management** (☞ **unit 88**). It is also linked to the plans of the organisation. For example, in 1999 two businesses, Cooper & Lybrand and Price Waterhouse planned to merge. They anticipated a growing demand for accounting skills, particularly in areas such as Eastern Europe, Latin America and China, and felt that the combined firm would be better able to cope. The companies planned to take on an extra 1,000 employees a week worldwide as a result. If staff were not used in one country, they would be deployed elsewhere.

The steps that a business takes when planning its workforce are shown in Figure 75.1. So:

Change in demand for workers = workers from within the business + workers from outside the business

Planning can be **short term** or **long term**. Short term planning is aimed at the immediate needs of the business, such as filling vacancies left, say, as a result of maternity leave. Long term planning will try to plan for the future. For example, if a company was aiming to change its production techniques in the next few years, it would need to plan the number of employees, training needed and perhaps the incentives and motivation that workers would require.

Forecasting employee demand

In the future a business may need more workers, less workers

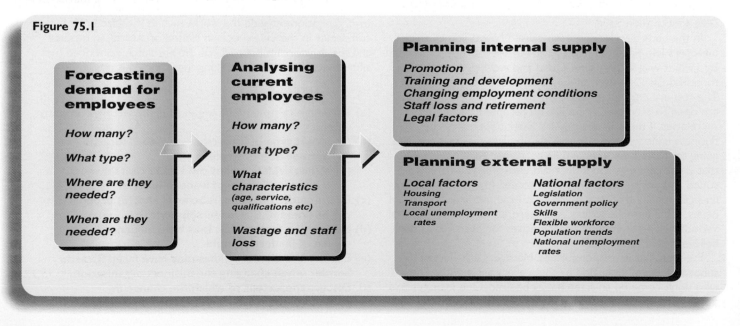

Figure 75.1

Forecasting demand for employees

How many?

What type?

Where are they needed?

When are they needed?

Analysing current employees

How many?

What type?

What characteristics (age, service, qualifications etc)

Wastage and staff loss

Planning internal supply

Promotion
Training and development
Changing employment conditions
Staff loss and retirement
Legal factors

Planning external supply

Local factors
Housing
Transport
Local unemployment rates

National factors
Legislation
Government policy
Skills
Flexible workforce
Population trends
National unemployment rates

Question 1

In 1998 Somerfield, the supermarket chain, was planning to deal with the effects of the 'Millennium bug' on its computer systems. The bug is a problem for many older computers. Because they recognise only two digits in a date, so 1997 would be seen as 97, they will not recognise the date 2000 because it will be seen as 00. The company decided to recruit 15 computer experts to deal with the problem in its Bristol Support Centre. However, recruitment was not as simple as it may have seemed. Somerfield advertised in Australian newspapers and aimed to send six staff 'down under' in March 1999 to conduct interviews. A spokesperson for the company said: 'Travelling to the other side of the world to find new staff may seem to be taking recruitment practices to the extreme, but there is a shortfall of UK citizens with suitable experience that are not tied to their present jobs'. The IT experts would be employed for two years.

Source: adapted from The *Sunday Times*, 27.12.1998.

(a) Using examples from the experience of Somerfield, explain the steps a business takes in planning its workforce.

or workers with different skills. How might a business predict the workers it needs in future?

Using past information Forecasting techniques allow a business to predict what will happen in future from past figures (☞ unit 51). Figures collected from years in the past are referred to as **time series** data or **backdata**. So, for example, if a business has had a steady increase in staff of 2 per cent a year over the last five years, it might expect this to continue. However, this method is not very sophisticated. It does not take into account the development of the business that may be outlined in a business plan. It predicts the number of employees required based on previous growth or reduction figures, without considering future plans. A business, for example, may decide to install new machinery, which might reduce the number of employees it needs.

Workers' productivity A manufacturer may employ a total of 50 staff and produce 550 products a week. This means that it

has an output per worker of 11 products (550 ÷ 50). If it wanted to produce an extra 55 products, it would need to employ an extra 5 staff (55 ÷ 11). If output had to be cut to 495 products, only 45 workers would be needed (495 ÷ 11). This is a rather simple way of predicting demand. It does not take into account **economies** and **diseconomies** of scale (☞ unit 93). As demand for products increases, a business may be able to raise output by using equipment more efficiently rather than hiring more workers. In addition, an increase in output will have a smaller effect on non-production workers. For example, if the amount of work doubled, support services may only need to increase by 30-50 per cent. Although more technical and production staff may be employed, this may not be matched by an increase in management and office staff.

Work study This allows a business to find the numbers of staff needed to carry out a task efficiently (☞ unit 96). For example, a business may decide to change its production methods so that all of a product was manufactured in a 'cell' rather than as parts in batches (☞ unit 91). This would mean that workers would work in teams, take responsibility for decisions and have to be multi-skilled (☞ unit 73). Careful consideration would need to be made of exactly what extra work staff would be doing and whether more or less staff would be needed. Without suitable work studies, a business may over or underestimate the actual number of staff needed to carry out future business plans.

Using business and management knowledge A business may ask experienced managers at all levels for their views on the employees needed in the future. For example, the manager of a large firm of solicitors may know that more part time staff are likely to be needed in the near future as there is a growing number of clients suing others for personal accident compensation. The manager of an advertising agency may predict that staff may be needed for the growing market in internet advertising. The manager of a hotel chain may predict that fewer staff are needed for catering as the demand for conference meals has fallen off.

Calculating staff loss Workers leave their jobs from time to time. They may retire, be promoted, be dismissed, join other businesses, leave to have children or simply resign. If a worker leaves a job then a **vacancy** exists which the business has to fill. One useful indicator of people leaving a business is the **percentage wastage rate** or the **labour turnover index** (☞ unit 88). This shows the number of employees leaving as a percentage of those who could have left. For example, if a business employing 70 staff finds that 18 left the previous year, the wastage rate or LABOUR TURNOVER is:

$$\frac{\text{Number of staff leaving per period}}{\text{Average number of staff in post during the period}} \times 100 = \frac{18}{70} = 25.7\%$$

This could be used to predict the numbers of employees that may leave in future and the need to employ new workers. Similar predictions may be made about the numbers of employees that are likely to be promoted or to retire.

Many factors might influence the demand by a business for workers. If more products are sold, more workers may need to be employed to increase output. New equipment may require workers with different skills. Labour saving equipment might reduce the need for workers. Businesses that have a high labour turnover might need to employ new workers on a regular basis. Promotion or retirement will also create vacancies. A change in the goals of the business may increase or decrease demand for staff. A business aiming to reduce the layers in its hierarchy may demand fewer workers in future. Changes in production techniques, such as a move from assembly line production to team work or cell production, might mean that fewer or different types of workers are demanded by a business. The latest business theories can also affect demand. The move to teamwork in the 1990s in some businesses may have increased demand for 'team leaders'.

Analysing current employee supply

Once a business has decided on the number and type of employees it needs in future, its next step is to ask: 'how do we ensure that we have the right people at the right time to meet the workforce planning requirements?'

A starting point is for a business to analyse the current position of its employees. This is likely to involve calculating the number of employees working in particular jobs and identifying their category and function. It may also mean gathering information on their age, length of service, qualifications and performance results. For example, a business that wants to employ managers may look at the number of graduates on its staff. A business trying to reduce its workforce by retirement may examine the ages of its employees. Data relating to employee 'flows' through the business, staff loss and how the nature of the present staff is changing are also important. For example, a business that wants to introduce flexible work practices may take into account the number of part time staff it has or the percentage of the business that is made up of teleworkers (☞ unit 78).

From the analysis of future demand and the current workforce, a business can decide on the number and type of employees that it may plan to recruit **internally** and **externally** in future to achieve its targets (☞ unit 76). It can also decide how it might reduce its existing workforce if necessary. These are discussed in the next sections.

Planning internal employee supply

A business may plan to meet future changes in demand from workers from inside the organisation. It may also plan to

The number of jobs advertised in magazines for personnel staff fell in the third quarter (August-October) of 1998 compared to the first two quarters. This perhaps indicated that there was a falling demand for workers in personnel departments. However, the demand for certain jobs, such as those with salaries over £50,000 a year and jobs related to human resources management, increased. This may have been because of current fashion or the strategic direction of businesses.

Figure 75.2 *Advertised job titles in the private sector*

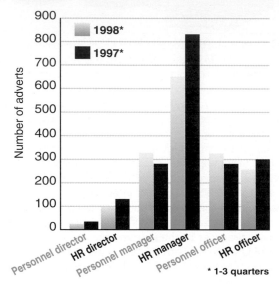

Source: adapted from *People Management*, 29.10.1998.

(a) What type of jobs are in demand in personnel departments?
(b) Explain why demand for these jobs might have increased.
(c) What would you predict might have happened to the demand for jobs in personnel departments in 1999? Explain your answer.

reduce its workforce. Whether a business can meet its future workforce requirements from existing employees may depend on a number of factors.

Promotion A business may decide to promote employees from inside the organisation. Some businesses encourage internal promotion (☞ unit 76). The advantage of promoting existing workers is that they already know about the business's practices and culture. They may also be able to adapt more easily to a new job than an outsider. Some workers may also have been 'filling in' temporarily and have experience of the job. Promoting internally would leave a vacancy further down the hierarchy which would need to be filled. This would add costs and time to filling the vacancy.

Staff development and training A business is more likely to be able to find a suitable employee from inside the organisation if it has training and development programmes (☞ unit 79). Training may provide the skills needed to allow an employee to move to a new position. For example, many larger businesses have graduate training programmes which train employees with degrees for management positions. Businesses that have development programmes which identify how workers can improve, appraise workers' abilities and view the development of employees as important, are more likely to employ an internal candidate. If a business needs to reduce its workforce in a particular department it may consider retraining its employees and **redeploying** them to another part of the organisation.

Staff loss and retirement A workforce supply plan should also take into account staff loss and rates of retirement. High rates of labour turnover, as explained earlier, create vacancies. However, they may also lead to large numbers of skilled workers leaving a business which can affect the number of suitable internal candidates for a job. If large numbers of employees are retiring, this may lead to problems when trying to fill senior management posts which require experienced employees. A business may make use of retirement as a means of reducing the workforce if necessary. People can sometimes be encouraged to take 'early retirement', before 65 for men and 60 for women, if they are given a financial incentive (☞ unit 78).

Flexibility A business may be able to change its workforce practices and conditions in order to meet its labour supply requirements. For example, a business may change the number of hours that people work in a period (☞ unit 78). Employees may be asked to work 1,950 hours in a year rather than 37.5 hours a week. This means that a business can have employees in work for longer than 37.5 hours when they are needed at peak times. If a business wants to add extra responsibility to the role of workers it may encourage team work or the multiskilling of workers (☞ unit 73). It may also decide to make new jobs part time or jobs that can be shared by two people in order to increase the flexibility of the business (☞ unit 88).

Legal factors If a business finds that its demand for workers is likely to fall in future it may decide to make workers redundant. There are legal conditions which affect how and when workers can be made redundant (☞ unit 78). They may also be entitled to redundancy or **severance** payments.

Planning external employee supply

A business may plan to employ workers from outside the organisation. There are local and national factors that have to be taken into account by a business when planning its external employee requirements.

- The availability and price of housing in an area. Some employees may not be able to afford housing in a highly priced area such as London, for example. The availability of new housing on a nearby estate may encourage young families with children to move to a area.
- The ease and availability of public transport. Working at a factory in a remote area may prove difficult for an employee without a car. Areas with efficient rail or bus links may prove popular for some workers. Possible restrictions or charges on cars in city areas may influence external employee supply in future.
- Competition. The closing or opening of other businesses in an area may either help or hinder external supply of labour. If businesses close there may be more skilled labour from which to choose. New businesses may reduce the availability of skilled workers. However, they are also likely to train workers, so that it may be possible to 'headhunt' required employees more easily (☞ unit 76).
- Unemployment. High rates of unemployment in an area lead to a large supply of workers who are available for

Question 3

In 1996 House of Fraser, the clothing and home fashion group, was criticised in the media for its poor performance and working practices. Its 51 stores were run fairly independently, each with its own job conditions, job titles and management structure. Career paths for employees were unclear and systems were buried in paper work.

The business made a number of radical changes to work practices and the workforce. The management structure was changed, with the number of managers cut. In particular, many stores had assistant managers with poorly defined roles. Rationalisation was needed and there were fewer new jobs than old ones. Previously each store had a training and personnel manager. Some of their tasks were given to managers in stores and four regional HR offices were set up as support, each with a training manager, a HR manager and administrative and support staff. This cut the HR staff from 100 to 24. A new system of promotion was set up. Jobs were graded and personal development plans introduced. Each job in the new system covered a precise area and was tied to a set of responsibilities and competences. People could see the abilities they would need for promotion and were given more responsibility for deciding on the training they needed to be promoted. Once the new system was in place, staff were assessed against the new competences. 3,000 lost their jobs. Some were redeployed in the company, or offered advice on redundancy.

Source: adapted from *People Management*, 12.11.1998.

(a) How did the House of Fraser plan to meet its human resource requirements?
(b) Explain the possible advantages to the business of using these methods.

work. This increases choice for a business looking to recruit from outside the organisation. High rates of national unemployment may make workers more willing to travel.

- Availability of skills. Specialist skills may be found in particular areas. For example, the area around Stafford, known as the Potteries, traditionally had skilled pottery workers. Some workers made unemployed in shipyard areas such as Tyneside were able to transfer their skills to other related industries when shipyards closed.
- The availability of flexible workers. Many businesses are taking advantage of the use of teleworkers (☞ unit 78). These are people who are employed to work at home and make use of technology such as the fax and computer to communicate with the business. They work from home which reduces business costs. Some workers are 'employed' by the business, but are not guaranteed work. They are brought in only when required, such as when demand is high. An example might be a delivery firm asking drivers to be 'on call' in case of busy periods. The availability of these workers increases the flexibility of businesses (☞ unit 88).
- Government training and subsidies. Government funded training and employment schemes subsidise businesses for taking on young workers for a period of time (☞ unit 79). This reduces their cost to a business and allows a 'trial run' of a possible employee.
- Population and demographic trends. Changes in the structure of the population can affect external recruitment (☞ unit 20). In the UK there is a growing number of older workers who are available for work. The increase in the number of women joining or returning to the workforce is also likely to affect the supply plans from outside the organisation.
- Government legislation. There are restrictions on the nature and type of advertisements that can be used when recruiting from outside the business. There are also laws which protect the pay and conditions of workers when they are employed (☞ unit 81).

Key terms

Labour turnover - the number of people that leave a business over a period of time as a percentage of the number of people employed.
Human resources plan or the workforce plan - the suggested quantity, quality and type of employees a business will require in future and how this demand is to be met.
Human resources planning/workforce planning - the process of calculating the number of employees a business needs in the short term and the long term and matching employees to the business's requirements.

Summary

1. State 5 tasks that the personnel department may carry out.
2. What are the steps a business takes when planning its workforce?
3. Explain 3 ways that a business might forecast its demand for employees.
4. Suggest 3 reasons why a business may demand more employees.
5. State 3 features of a business's current workforce that it may be interested in analysing.
6. Suggest 5 factors that might affect the possibility of recruiting employees from within the business.
7. Why is labour turnover important to a business?
8. Explain 2 ways in which a business might make itself more flexible.
9. Explain the difference between redeploying workers and retirement as a means of reducing the workforce.
10. Suggest 5 factors that might affect the external supply of workers.

Case study

Stewart and Mathers

Stewart and Mathers is a solicitor, with offices in Lancashire and London. Its head office is situated in Skelmersdale, a 'new town' created to rehouse the overspill of people moving out of Liverpool in the 1960s as inner city housing was knocked down. It is situated next to the M58 and is a half an hour's drive from the cities of Manchester and Liverpool. The planners decided that:

● high private car usage must be catered for, while still encouraging public transport;
● pedestrians and traffic should be separated in the town centre and residential areas;
● industry should be concentrated in separate, but easily accessible areas;
● open spaces should be provided but the housing should be designed to foster a close community atmosphere;
● there must be no urban sprawl, and a clear boundary between town and country;
● the town must try and attract a balanced population structure;
● housing in Skelmersdale was to be high density but without high rise flats;
● residential areas were to be close to the town centre where most facilities were concentrated.

In the mid-1990s the business saw a steady growth in its sales of services. Table 75.1 shows figures relating to the workforce over the period. Stewart and Mathers realised that more cases were being taken out against individuals and companies for accidents which led to personal injury. This mirrored the situation in the USA. Large sums were often paid to employees injured at work, people who had been hurt in 'road rage' attacks and for complaints against the

Table 75.1

	Sales revenue (£m)	Total employees	Employees leaving
1993	1.1	70	3
1994	1.2	72	4
1995	1.4	75	5
1996	1.6	80	5
1999	2.0	100	6

state for injuries as a result of badly maintained roads or pavements. Most of the decisions in the business were taken by the three partners, two of whom had previous experience of working in other countries. There were 10 people in the business who were 'fee earners'.

The organisation decided that it wanted to expand to take advantage of growing business in this area. It encouraged its administrative staff lower in the hierarchy to train in law qualifications or take the Institute of Law examination. This would allow them to progress to become a solicitor's assistant. It advertised widely in the local area to fill vacancies and 'headhunted' graduates of the ILEX (Institute of Legal Secretaries) courses at local colleges who had been trained in basic law skills. It would also be able to take advantage of the government's new deal by employing young workers for a small number of posts.

However, some of its senior management positions needed to be filled quickly and so the business advertised in national magazines and quality newspapers. If necessary it was prepared to subsidise managers for a short time if they were prepared to move to the area immediately. This might mean that they have to leave property unsold in a different part of the country or leave family and work away from home for a period.

(a) What factors could have affected the promotion of internal employees within the business to higher posts?
(b) Explain how the business may have forecasted the increased need for employees in the late 1990s.
(c) (i) Calculate the labour turnover of the business over the period.
    (ii) Examine the possible effects of changes in labour turnover on the business.
(d) To what extent might the business be able to recruit workers from outside the business for:
    (i) jobs at the base of the hierarchy;
    (ii) managerial jobs?

The need for effective recruitment

This unit concentrates on the first stage in the management of human resources - recruitment. The personnel department will aim to attract the the 'best' candidates for the job and then to choose the most suitable. If the wrong person is recruited, this can cause problems for a business. The person appointed may find the job boring or too difficult, which could lead to a lack of motivation and poor productivity. If the person leaves, there will be administration costs for the personnel department. The business will face the extra costs of advertising, interviewing and training. There will also be a settling in period until the new employee has learned the job.

Employing a suitable person should allow the business to get the most out of its human resources. In addition, recruiting the best employees may give a business a competitive edge over rivals (☞ unit 15). To make sure the 'best' person is chosen, businesses must be clear about:
● what the job entails;
● what qualities are required to do the job;
● what rewards are need to retain and motivate employees.

Recruitment is becoming more and more important in business. This is especially the case where employees need to be flexible or work autonomously, or where direct control over workers is difficult.

Job analysis

Before a business recruits new employees, the personnel department usually carries out some form of JOB ANALYSIS. Job analysis is a study of what a job entails. It contains the skills, training and tasks that are needed to carry out the job.

Job analysis can be used by firms in many ways. These include selecting employees, setting pay, disciplinary interviews, promotion and job appraisal (dealt with later in this unit). For example, if a firm was trying to choose an applicant for the post of systems analyst, it may use job analysis to find out exactly what a systems analyst does in that firm.

In order to find out about what is involved in a job, the personnel department must gather data about all the different elements in that job. It is likely that people associated with the job will have different views about what is involved.
● The occupant of the job. She will have the most detailed knowledge of what the job requires. However, she might change the information to exaggerate her own status, or leave parts of the job out because they are taken for granted.
● The job holder's superior. She will have her own view of what the job involves, but is unlikely to be fully aware of all job details.

● Subordinates and others with whom the job holder is in regular contact. They are likely to have observed the behaviour of the job holder over a period of time. Once again, any bias or error which the observer may have must be taken into account.
● Specialist observers, such as job analysts. These can provide an independent view of the work being carried out. The major problem is that the job holder, knowing she is being observed, may adjust her behaviour.

Having collected this information, it must then be analysed. This is often done by using five categories.

Task analysis This involves the study of those tasks an employee carries out when doing their job. Any job will be made up of a variety of tasks. A task is seen as a collection of activities that result in an objective being achieved. For example, an employee may have the task of reporting on stock levels in the company.

Activity analysis This is a study of the activities which make up a task. These will include physical activities and the intellectual demands of the job. So an employee whose task is to do a stock check might need to understand how to use the computerised stock control program and understand the concept of lead time (☞ unit 94).

Skills analysis This involves a study of the skills that are needed to do the job. These could be motor skills, such as the ability to use a computer program, or other skills, such as the ability to work with others.

Role analysis This is the information gathered from the job holder, superiors and colleagues. The duties, responsibilities and behaviour expected from the job holder are discussed to produce a role description which all involved agree upon.

Performance analysis This attempts to set the criteria that will be used when evaluating how well a job holder carries out the job. It involves identifying standards and expectations. For example, an employee may need to ensure that stock wastage is kept to a certain level. This will give a target to aim at while carrying out stock control.

Job description

Once a business has analysed what a job entails, it is important to draw up a description of the job. The JOB DESCRIPTION is a simple 'word picture' of the job. It will often contain some of the elements in Table 76.1.

The job description has a number of uses. It allows the firm to tell candidates for a job what is expected of them. It also helps personnel officers to decide on the qualities that successful candidates must have.

Table 76.1 *Possible job description of a design artist*

General information	Job title, such as 'designer'. Place of job within the business. Job summary, eg main tasks.
Job content information	Tasks involved, eg details of tasks. Purpose of tasks, eg develop designs for products. Methods involved, eg drawing, CAD etc. Other duties, eg part of design team. Responsibility, eg control of other staff.
Working conditions	Physical environment, eg work area. Social environment, eg holidays. Economic conditions, eg length of working day.
Performance information	Criteria for measuring performance, eg quality of designs.

When candidates are appointed, the job description can be used to gauge whether the employee is doing the job 'properly', by comparing their activities with the description. Disputes about the work an employee has to do can also be settled by looking at the job description.

A good example of 'tight' job descriptions are those for

Table 76.2 *A possible person specification of a draughtsperson*

Attainments	Essential to have evidence of application and capacity for detailed work.
	Desirable to have some knowledge of technical drawing and of engineering terms.
	Must have at least technical training and possess 4 GCSEs grade C or above, or NVQ in engineering or manufacturing at equivalent level.
	Previous experience of record keeping in technical office or library is essential.
	Experience of working with engineering drawings is desirable.
General intelligence	Brisk reactions and accurate memory are needed.
Specialised aptitudes	Neat, quick and accurate at clerical work.
Interests	Practical and social.
Disposition	Self-reliant, helpful, friendly.
Circumstances	Likely to stay for at least 3 years.

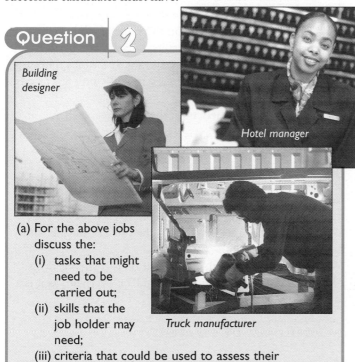

Question 2

Building designer

Hotel manager

Truck manufacturer

(a) For the above jobs discuss the:
 (i) tasks that might need to be carried out;
 (ii) skills that the job holder may need;
 (iii) criteria that could be used to assess their performance.
(b) Suggest problems that a business might have if it did not carry out a job analysis for the jobs in the photographs.

McDonald's employees. They are given because employees are expected to be very flexible and interchangeable in their jobs (☞ unit 88) - so that when a worker comes to a job or task, they know exactly what to do. McDonald's employees have in the past been given a 385 page operations manual. It was full of details on how each task should be performed. It included instructions such as 'Cooks must turn, never flip, hamburgers... once, never two at a time ... Cashiers must make eye contact and smile at every customer'.

The job description is a means of communication (☞ unit 82). It suffers from the usual problems of misunderstanding and distortion. It is also a simplification, as it is rarely possible to include every feature of a particular job.

Person specification

Once the skills and knowledge needed to perform a particular job have been outlined in the job description, they are often reworded into a PERSON SPECIFICATION (sometimes referred to as the human specification or the job specification). This shows a profile of the type of person needed to do the job.

Such a description can then form the basis for the selection of the most suitable person to fill the job. Table 76.2 shows a possible example.

It is important that the person specification fits the 'culture' of a business (☞ unit 14). Goffee (London Business School) and Jones (Henley Management College) suggest that there are two cultures in the workplace - sociability and solidarity. The sociable workplace has a friendly atmosphere, openness and a sharing of ideas. A workplace with solidarity has mutual interests and shared goals. A business must ensure that individuals who are recruited fit the culture of the organisation or they may be an unsuitable appointment.

Job evaluation

A business can use JOB EVALUATION to compare the value of different jobs. Any job can be broken down into a number of factors. These are the skills, effort, responsibility, knowledge and tasks that the job entails. This allows the business to decide on the wages or salary for that job. If another job has greater skill or responsibility, then the business may award it at a higher rate of pay.

Job evaluation has become more popular over the last decade. It has been seen by businesses as a rational way of working out why some jobs are paid more than others. It has also been used in equal pay cases (☞ unit 80). For example, if there is a dispute about equal pay, the job evaluation will help to show if employees are doing work of equal value. When using job evaluation, a business must remember certain points.

● Job evaluation is about the job and not the performance of the employee in the job.

TRAINER/ADMINISTRATOR

Hamptons International is one of the UK's leading Estate Agents employing 800 staff mainly in London and the Home Counties.

THE CHALLENGE
● Working within the Training Team based at Pimlico office.
● Reporting to the Training Director.
● Building relationships internally and working closely at all levels to develop best practice.
● Personally deliver a number of programmes.
● Assist in the administration and creation of a learning organisation.

THE PERSON
● "Hands on" self starter ideally with at least 1 year's stand-up training experience.
● Dynamic presence coupled with sales, coaching and administrative skills.
● Ability to write and design courses a plus.
● The ability to carry out five tasks at the same time and retain a sense of humour.
● Car owner essential.

If you meet the above requirements, please send your CV and current salary details to:

Mrs Sarah Gore
Hamptons International
8 The Quadrant
Richmond
Surrey TW9 1BP

Fax: 0181 940 6887 E-mail: recruitment@hamptons-int.com
All applications will be dealt with in the strictest confidence

Figure 76.1 *A job advertisement*

(a) Use the information in the advertisement above to show the difference between a job description and a person specification.

● Experienced people decide on the value of a job. Whilst this is likely to give useful results, they are not 'perfect'.
● It allows firms to set differential rewards for jobs. This does not rule out collective bargaining (☞ unit 85) to raise these rates.
● Only pay is determined, not other earnings, such as incentives.

The most popular method of job evaluation is a points scheme. A number of factors (skill, problem solving etc.) are found which are common to all jobs. Each factor is given a weighting according to its importance. A job description is then prepared and points are allocated to each factor. The total number of points determines the value of the job, and the wages or salary to be paid.

Whilst it can be useful, job evaluation is costly for firms. Also, some jobs will still be 'underpaid' or 'overpaid', as it is a matter of human judgement.

Methods of recruitment

If vacancies do exist then the personnel department must fill them. Often firms fill vacancies by recruiting new employees - **external** recruitment. An alternative is to appoint **internally** from within the business. In the short term, particularly if funds are not available for extra workers, it may be possible to reorganise the work in order to fill the 'gaps' left by vacant positions. For example, the work could be shared out between the remaining employees.

This option might be used if the workload was felt to be too light in the department before the vacancy existed, or if the section is very 'tightly knit'. A further option is to pay existing workers overtime rates to cover the output lost by the employee who has left. Internal reorganisation is not without its problems. These include how the work should be divided and what rewards employees should receive for 'extra' work.

External recruitment to fill vacancies is likely to become increasingly difficult given the population trends in some Western developed countries. In the UK, skills shortages and demographic changes (☞ unit 20) may make recruitment from outside more difficult. Employers will either need to change their strategies to take into account the falling number of potential recruits in competitive markets, or be faced with vacant positions. This may require the use of innovative forms of recruitment, employing previously inactive workers, flexible working (☞ unit 88) or job sharing. In addition, with many jobs now requiring high levels of skill, some businesses may find a shortage of appropriately qualified and experienced people.

Internal recruitment

It is argued that internal recruitment strengthens employees' commitment to the company. The personnel department of Kellogg's, for example, have stated the following courses of action in their recruitment policy handbook.

'(a) Offer the job to an existing employee, as a promotion or transfer.

(b) Advertise internally, if a suitable candidate is likely to be available internally.

(c) Advertise externally if no suitable candidate is likely to exist internally (and display notice internally to the effect that the advertisement is appearing).

Except in special cases, all vacancies should be advertised internally before external recruitment methods are used.'

There is a number of advantages to advertising jobs 'inside' the business.

● It gives employees within the company a chance to develop their career.

● There may be a shorter induction period as the employee is likely to be familiar with the company.

● Employers will know more about internal candidates' abilities. This should reduce the risk of employing the 'wrong' person.

● Internal recruitment may be quicker and less expensive than recruiting from outside the business.
However, there are also disadvantages.

● Internal advertising limits the number of applicants.

● External candidates might have been of better quality.

● Another vacancy will be created which might have to

be filled.

● If, having investigated ways of filling the vacancy internally the business still does not appoint, then it must find ways to obtain candidates externally.

External recruitment

There are many ways of attracting candidates from outside the company. The choice of method often depends on the type of vacancy and the type of employee a business wants. Each method has its own benefits and problems, although it could be argued that the overall advantages of external advertising are the opposite of the disadvantages of internal advertising, for example, there is a wider number of applicants.

Commercial employment agencies These are companies that specialise in recruiting and selection. They usually provide a shortlist of candidates for a company to interview, but can also provide temporary workers. Examples include Alfred Marks, HMS and Kelly Accountancy Personnel.

The advantage of commercial agencies is that they are experienced in providing certain types of worker, such as secretaries and clerical staff. They also minimise the administration for the employer involved in recruiting staff. Their main drawback is that they tend to produce staff who only stay in a job for a short time. Another problem for the business is the cost of paying fees to the agency.

Job centres and professional recruitment agencies These are government run and private organisations which try to help people obtain work. Their main advantage is that they can find applicants easily and can quickly draw from local or national databases.

Headhunting 'Headhunting' involves executive agencies approaching individuals, who have a reputation in a field of work, with employment offers. The main advantage is that a business can directly approach someone with a known specialism. This is of particular use to employers not experienced in a specialist field. The main disadvantages are the cost, the fact that the recruit may remain on the consultant's list even after they have changed jobs, and that candidates outside the 'network' are excluded.

The Careers Service As well as providing careers guidance to young people and adults, the Careers Service also collects local job vacancies and distributes them to their clients in schools and in the local area. Their main advantage is that they can produce regular enquiries from young people who are likely to be looking no further than the local area for employment and who would be able to take up a post quickly. Their disadvantage is that they work on a local rather than a regional or national basis.

Question 4

Figure 76.2 *Percentages of single and married mothers with dependent children who were working full time or part time*

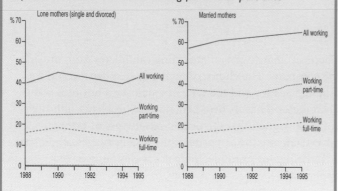

Source: adapted from *Population Trends*, Office for National Statistics.

CRT, the biggest recruitment group for the computer industry, launched a programme in the mid-1990s to relieve the industry's skills shortage. The Career IT Recruitment and Training Programme hoped to attract up to 2,000 new computing staff, at a cost of up to £70 million over four years. The company launched an advertising campaign aimed at recruiting people who may not have considered such a career, such as the over 40s and lone mothers. Advertisements would run in women's magazines and tabloid newspapers. CRT said that there was a growing need for more IT employees. Its chief executive suggested that: 'between 30,000 and 50,000 new people are needed in the IT skills pool by the end of 2000'. The need to upgrade older computer systems to cope with the date change at the turn of the century and the new euro currency increased the need for employees with IT skills.

Source: adapted from the *Financial Times*, 5,11,1997.

(a) What method of recruitment is CRT using? Explain your answer.

(b) Why was there likely to be a need for greater recruitment in the IT industry in the late 1990s and after the year 2000?

(c) Assume that CRT aims to recruit 'people who may not have considered such a career, such as the over 40s and lone mothers'. Comment on the implications of this from the data in Figure 76.2 and Figure 76.3.

Figure 76.3 *Population projections by age, UK, millions*

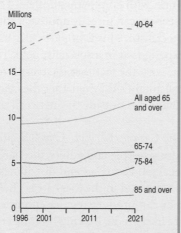

Source: adapted from *Social Trends*, Office for National Statistics.

Government funded training schemes Government funded training schemes (☞ unit 79) provide training for the young, long term unemployed, lone parents and disabled in order to improve their job prospects. They include for, example:

● New deal, which allows people aged 18-24 to have subsidised employment and training with a business or work experience with a voluntary organisation or environmental task force;

● Modern Apprenticeships, run by businesses and training providers, where employees and apprentices sign a 'training agreement' for the period of the apprenticeship. Employees are usually given employed status and train towards an NVQ qualification.

The advantage to a business of offering such a scheme is that the costs of employing workers will be reduced because of the funding from government. The business will also have a 'free trial' of a potential employee.

Visiting universities - 'the milkround' This involves companies visiting universities around the country with the aim of recruiting employees. Its main advantage is that it provides easy access to candidates of graduate standard. It is also fairly inexpensive and convenient through using the free services of the University Appointments Service. The main drawbacks are that often the interviewees are simply enquiring about a job and that interview schedules can be very time consuming and tiring. These problems have become worse as student numbers have increased in recent years.

Advertising agencies Apart from using the above methods, employers will often advertise their jobs to a wider audience. They may deal with advertising agencies to gain help with drafting advertisements and placing them in suitable media. The agency will usually book the space in the chosen media, prepare the layout, read and correct proofs, and check that the right advertisement has appeared in the right publication, at the right time. The agency will usually be aware of the following methods of job advertising.

● Vacancy lists outside premises. This is an economical method, but it will only be seen by a few people and little information can be included.

● Advertising in the national press. This has the advantage of wider coverage. However, it can be costly and may reach people who are not interested.

● Advertising in the local press. This will be read by local people seeking employment. Evidence suggests, however, that the local press is not read by professionals.

● Advertising in the technical press. This reaches the appropriate people, but may be published infrequently.

● Television advertising. This reaches large numbers, but can be expensive.

● Advertising on the internet. Businesses can advertise on their own web site or hire space on other sites. The upkeep of a web site may be relatively expensive compared to a 'one-off' advertisement. However, information can be included which is easily updated. The problem with this method is that not everyone looking for a job has access to the internet. Newspapers advertising jobs now reproduce these jobs on their own website to make searching for a post quicker, such as the *Times Educational Supplement* advertising teaching jobs.

A job advertisement

As important as choosing the most appropriate media through which to advertise a vacancy is the drafting of the advertisement. The decision on what to include in a recruitment advertisement is important because of the high cost of space and the need to attract attention. Both factors will encourage the use of the fewest number of words. Figure 76.4 shows some of the items that could be included.

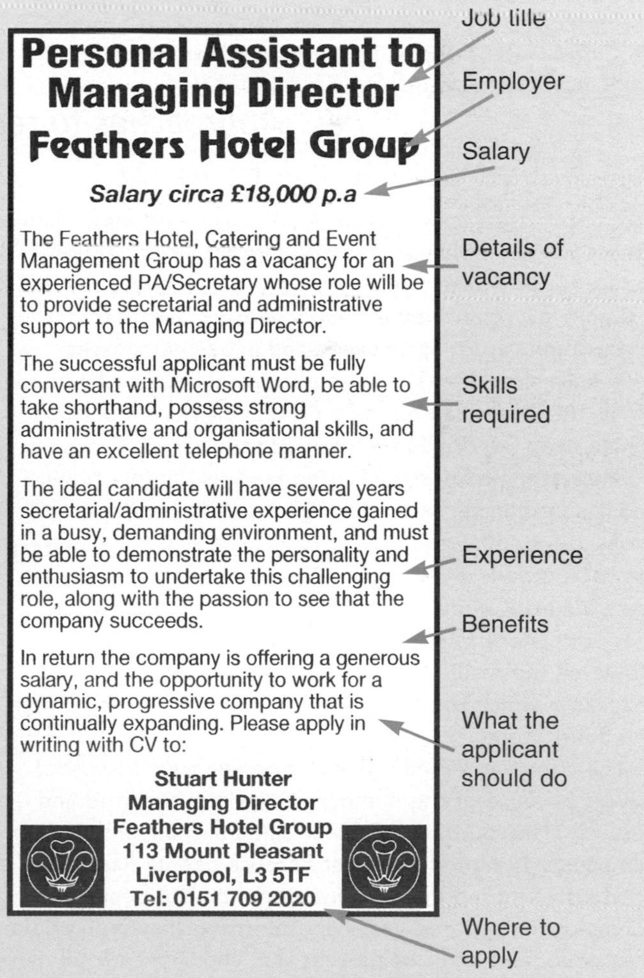

Question 5

Two London-based recruitment businesses have identified ways in which they can benefit businesses looking for new employees. Headfirst, in London's dockland, recognises the potential of headhunting clients. Job advertisements attract only those who are looking to apply. Headhunting, however, is designed to seek out the best candidates whether they are thinking of a move or not. Juliana Edwards, one of the few black search executives in the UK, and co-director Callum Forrest at Headfirst carry out general searches which are aimed at finding the best candidate for the job. They argue, however, that good contacts among ethnic communities enable them to tap into a rich and often undervalued seam of talent. One of their finds was Angela Sarkis, chief executive of the Church Urban Fund, the Anglican charity which supports inner-city projects. Finding such people can be difficult for big headhunting firms, argues Edwards, because few black and Asian people have been able to develop careers in executive search.

Tate Appointments, a London agency supplying temporary staff, such as secretaries and clerical assistants, offers a money-back guarantee to clients if they are dissatisfied with its temporary employees. Julia Robertson, Tate's managing director, argues that such promises will help to improve employment terms for temporary staff. The guarantee, she says, ensures that Tate has to provide well trained and efficient workers. The company has the solution to another problem as well. Temporary staff are often underused by businesses. Tate offers to supply line managers whose job is dedicated to making the best use of temporary staff.

Source: adapted from the *Financial Times*, 9.4.1997.

(a) (i) What are the three external methods of recruitment mentioned in the article?
 (ii) Why are the methods of recruitment in this article likely to be 'external' methods of recruitment?
(b) Contrast the benefits of a job advertisement in a national newspaper by a business to using the services of Headfirst as a means of recruiting staff.
(c) Explain the possible benefits of using temporary staff provided by Tate Appointments as a means of recruiting staff?
(d) Examine the problems of using temporary staff for a business.

Personal Assistant to Managing Director
Feathers Hotel Group

Salary circa £18,000 p.a

The Feathers Hotel, Catering and Event Management Group has a vacancy for an experienced PA/Secretary whose role will be to provide secretarial and administrative support to the Managing Director.

The successful applicant must be fully conversant with Microsoft Word, be able to take shorthand, possess strong administrative and organisational skills, and have an excellent telephone manner.

The ideal candidate will have several years secretarial/administrative experience gained in a busy, demanding environment, and must be able to demonstrate the personality and enthusiasm to undertake this challenging role, along with the passion to see that the company succeeds.

In return the company is offering a generous salary, and the opportunity to work for a dynamic, progressive company that is continually expanding. Please apply in writing with CV to:

Stuart Hunter
Managing Director
Feathers Hotel Group
113 Mount Pleasant
Liverpool, L3 5TF
Tel: 0151 709 2020

Labels: Job title — Employer — Salary — Details of vacancy — Skills required — Experience — Benefits — What the applicant should do — Where to apply

Figure 76.4 *Producing a job advertisement*

Key terms

Job analysis - a study of what the job entails, such as the skills, tasks and performance expected.

Job description - a simple word picture of what the job entails.

Job evaluation - a method used by businesses to compare the value of different jobs and perhaps set wages or salaries.

Person specification - a profile of the type of person needed to do a job.

Summary

1. Why do businesses need to recruit effectively?
2. Give 2 reasons why companies carry out job analysis.
3. How is a job description useful to the personnel department?
4. What is the difference between a job description and a person specification?
5. Give 5 factors that might be on a person specification.
6. How might job evaluation be used by a business?
7. State two ways in which a business could reorganise instead of appointing internally or externally to cover a vacancy.
8. What is meant by:
   (a) internal recruitment;
   (b) external recruitment?
9. Give 3 reasons why a business might recruit internally.
10. State 5 methods of external recruitment.
11. Why might a business recruit using an advertising agency rather than a job centre?
12. What factors are important to show in a job recruitment advertisement?

Case study

Approaches to recruitment

Lend Lease

Talk about large scale recruitment! Imagine having to find almost 7,000 employees in seven months. Imagine having to find these workers mainly from the long term unemployed, school leavers, early retirees, lone parents and women returning to work, and in a labour market with skills shortages. This was the task that faced Lend Lease, the Australian business developing the Bluewater centre near Dartford in Kent in 1998.

Bluewater was designed to be Europe's largest retail and leisure centre, with over 300 retailers, bars, sports shops, cafes and a golf driving range. The signs of achieving the recruitment target had always been promising. People were inquiring about vacancies for their children when they left school as soon as the project was announced. However, the main method to promote vacancies was a roadshow which toured shows and fetes in North London and South Kent.

The company aimed to recruit people such as school leavers because of the number of workers required and because it has a policy of 'minimising poaching' from other companies. It argued that: 'Just because people had previously worked in a cement works or had been unemployed for three years doesn't mean they won't do a great job'. Training of employees was important for all new employees at the centre. There were over 2,000 lone parents in the catchment area. However, with very few child care places available, Bluewater recognised the need to provide a workplace nursery. This would provide work

and training for childminders.

Job applications for Bluewater are handled by the government's employment service, which advertises in local job centres. Bluewater expected up to 35,000 applications for jobs as wide ranging as gardeners, unicyclists and nursery nurses. Once staff were appointed they would be trained not only in the skills of the job but also in personal development skills and the 'customer satisfaction ethos' of the company. This would help employees deal with customers. Bluewater would also offer apprenticeships run jointly with North West Kent college.

Source: adapted from the Financial Times, September, 1998.

The Ceramic Company

The Ceramic Company is a business based just outside Norwich. It is owned by Geoff and Janet Kelsey. It employs 10 staff, some of which are part time. It also makes use of outworkers at times when demand is high. Its main products are clay pots. Small pots are manufactured for earthenware and household goods retailers. Larger pots are manufactured for outside use and are sold to garden centres in the East Anglia area. The business also manufactures hand painted tiles. This is a time consuming and fairly labour intensive process, but has been a growing proportion of total sales over the last year. In particular, orders from independent retailers have been growing. This includes craft shops, small tile shops on industrial estates and retailers selling products with an environmentally friendly tag.

As sales have expanded, particularly to areas outside the locality, Janet is spending more time away from the workshop. Janet feels that she needs to appoint one of the staff to be the manager in her absence. The person would handle the ordering of materials, coordinate work to meet deadlines and deal with full time and part time staff as well as outworkers. Both Geoff and Janet feel that it would be easier to promote someone from within the business as there may not be enough work to justify the appointment of a full time manager.

However, they are both concerned that although two possible candidates have worked for the business for eight years, they do not have the experience of organisation. In particular, when a large order comes in, there is often a need to quickly order materials and perhaps organise part time workers to work extra hours. Of the other two possible candidates, one is part time, but has had experience of managing a garden centre in the area. The other is the youngest worker in the business, although she is keen to develop with the company. She has seen the possibility of moving into other craft areas. Recently she was interviewed for a business that specialised in interior design, but she turned down the job.

Source: adapted from company information.

(a) **Which methods of recruitment are being used by Lend Lease and The Ceramic Company?**
(b) (i) **What information may have been included in a job description for childminders at Bluewater?**
   (ii) **Explain why it might have been important for Lend Lease to carry out job analysis and have a job description for vacancies at Bowater.**
(c) **Explain the advantages and disadvantages of the recruitment methods used by Lend Lease and The Ceramic Company.**
(d) **Examine the factors which may have influenced the choice of recruitment methods by Lend Lease and The Ceramic Company.**
(e) **To what extent do you think that recruitment by Lend Lease and The Ceramic Company will be successful?**

77 Selection

Effective selection - making the right choice

Selection is growing in importance for firms. As explained in unit 76, businesses need to recruit and then select the 'right' person for the job. If the candidate chosen is unsuitable, the business may be faced with the cost of poor performance by the employee. There will also be extra costs in selecting and training a replacement when that employee leaves.

Businesses have also realised the need for a fair and valid choice of candidate. The most suitable applicant will only be chosen if selection is based on ability, skills and knowledge, rather than race or gender, for example. **Equal opportunities** legislation has helped to make impartial selection more likely, although there are still arguments about the 'fairness' involved in selection (☞ unit 80).

Effective selection should lead to the most suitable candidate being employed, in terms of their skills and motivation, as well as reducing the cost of selection. Personnel managers play an important part in this. They help to prepare the job analysis, job description and person specification, and decide exactly how to recruit. They also advise on the nature of application forms, how to SHORT LIST from them, and how to conduct tests and interviews. Finally, they will influence how the information is evaluated and what decisions should be made about candidates.

Application

The first time that a business receives information about candidates for a job it is advertising is when they apply for the job. Applicants may have collected details about the job from the business itself or from a job centre, for example. Some jobs ask for a letter of application from the applicants in which they explain why they want the job. This is often accompanied by a CURRICULUM VITAE (CV). The CV is a list of the applicant's:

● personal details (name, address, nationality etc.);
● educational qualifications;
● hobbies and interests;
● past job experience;
● reasons why the candidate is suitable for the job (strengths);
● references or names and addresses of referees who will provide references. **References** are a confirmation of the abilities, skills and experience of the candidate.

Growing use is being made of application forms by businesses. They have a number of benefits. All applicants give details in a standard way, rather than the different approaches of letters of application. This makes sorting applications and short listing far easier. This task is often called 'pre-selection'. It involves the 'sifting out' of applicants

who least fit the requirements of the person specification and job description. The application form is often used as the basis of the interview and can be a starting point for personnel records.

The application form covers the information contained in a CV, such as personal details, education and job experience. Certain forms leave out some of the above, while others include much more. Whatever the format, the form helps applicants 'present' their case. Also, by gaining biographical information, the personnel department has a simple way of matching the applicant's qualifications, interests, past experience etc. to their person specification (☞ unit 76). This allows the firm to decide quickly which of the applicants is suitable for a job. Table 77.1 shows a checklist of points which

---

Table 77.1

● Handwriting is often larger than type. Do the boxes/areas on the form give enough room for the applicant to complete the information?
● Forms that take too long to complete may be completed haphazardly or not at all. Is the time the form takes to complete appropriate to the information the employer needs?
● Some questions may be illegal, offensive, or not essential. Does the form ask only for information appropriate to the job?
● Word processors make it possible to produce separate application forms for each post advertised and to make them user friendly. One way of doing this is to use introductory paragraphs explaining why the information in each section is being sought.

Question

Frost Frame is a small company producing double glazed windows. It has decided to expand production. In particular, it is looking for someone with skills in working with stained glass. Having placed an advertisement in the local newspaper, the company sent out application forms. The standard application form was used which had been devised for all general workshop employees. It did not ask any questions related to the applicant's specific skills. After four weeks it has received three applications and only one candidate looks worth interviewing. However, it is unclear from his answers whether he will be entirely suitable.

(a) Identify problems that Frost Frame may have had with its application form.
(b) Explain one way in which it could improve the form.
(c) Analyse the possible implications for the company if it decides not to interview the candidate.

can be used to help a business design an application form.

Testing

Businesses appear to be taking a greater interest in testing. There are strong arguments for and against the use of tests in selection. Those in favour argue that interviews (dealt with in the next section) do not really allow a business to predict performance and point to the greater accuracy and objectivity of test data. Those against dispute this objectivity. They also argue that predictions from test results can mislead. For example, does a high test score mean high job performance and a low score mean low job performance?

There is a number of tests that are used in selection. These are often associated with different levels of staff.

- Aptitude tests measure how well a candidate can cope when faced with a business situation or problem.
- Attainment tests measure an individual's ability using skills they have already acquired. For example, a candidate for an administration post may take a word processing test.
- Intelligence tests aim to give an indication of overall 'mental' ability. A variety of questions are asked in such tests covering numeracy and literacy skills, as well as general knowledge. It is assumed that a person who scores highly will be able to retain new knowledge and to succeed at work.
- Personality tests, also known as psychometric tests, examine the **traits** or **characteristics** of employees. For example, they might indicate that a manager does not change her mind once her decision is made or that an employee is willing to experiment and adapt to change. Personality tests may allow a business to predict how hard working or motivated a employee will be or how suited she is to a job. The usefulness of such tests depends on whether the business feels that they are a suitable way of selecting employees. The business must also have qualified personnel to carry out the tests. Such tests do have problems. There is unlikely to be a standard personality profile of the 'ideal employee' to compare test results against. The tests also rely on the individual being honest. Often, however, candidates try to pick the answer that they feel is wanted. In addition, some traits measured in the tests may not be relevant to job performance.

Interviews

Most people have at least one experience of being interviewed prior to employment. Few people enjoy interviews. Often this is because the interviewer appears to be more interested in finding fault than being helpful.

The personnel department is usually involved in interviewing, both in carrying them out and helping managers to adopt good interview practice. By following certain guidelines, the business hopes to employ the 'right' person for the job. It also aims to carry out the interview in a

way that is fair to all candidates. These guidelines might include the following.

- The interview should allow information to be collected from candidates which can be used to predict whether they can perform the job. This can be done by comparing replies with the criteria that successful applicants should have.
- The business should give candidates full details about the job and the organisation. This will help them decide whether the job would suit them.
- The interview should be conducted so that candidates can say that they have had a fair hearing.

The interview has, however, been criticised as not always being an effective 'tool'. Some of the main criticisms are:

- interviewers often decide to accept or reject a candidate within the first three or four minutes of the interview, and then spend the rest of the time finding evidence to confirm their decision;
- interviews seldom change the initial opinion formed by the interviewer seeing the application form and the appearance of the candidate;
- interviewers place more stress on evidence that is

Question

Tol Bedford is chief psychologist at PSL. It is a company which specialises in psychological assessments of candidates for senior posts. He carries out psychometric tests which encourage people to discuss their opinions of others. A candidate will be presented with two people, say Lady Thatcher and Tony Blair. They are asked to say which they regard most highly and why. This approach, argues Mr Bedford, is much more difficult to fake than a traditional personality test. Such tests are often used to identify the traits of senior executives during selection. For example, a person who has the characteristic of making instant decisions may make a good executive because they are decisive.

Certain tests have been criticised because they put women and ethnic minorities at a disadvantage. For example, it is suggested that women do worse than men in traditional attainment tests involving numeracy. Tests that are based on a particular culture may lead to discrimination against candidates from other cultures. Oxford Psychologists' Press (OPP) and Dr S. Blinkhorn have developed a new range of tests, Aptitude for business learning exercises (Able), which they claim get around these problems. People are given fictitious concepts, eg financial ratios, and are tested on how well they apply them. OPP argues that these are fairer than many psychometric tests as they provide candidates with a more 'level playing field'.

Source: adapted from the *Financial Times*, 23.7.1997 and *The Sunday Times*, 9.8.1998.

(a) What type of tests are mentioned in the article?
(b) What reasons might be given for using such tests?
(c) Examine the possible problems of psychometric tests.

unfavourable than on the evidence that is favourable;
● when interviewers have made up their minds very early in the interview, their behaviour betrays their decision to the candidate.

The problem with these criticisms is that they do not solve the problems, only identify them. No matter what other means of selection there may be, the interview is crucial. If it is thought to be unreliable, it should not be discarded. Businesses must simply make sure they carry it out properly.

Conducting an interview

There is a number of factors which could be taken into account when carrying out interviews. The interview should be conducted around a simple plan and be based on a number of questions against which all candidates will be assessed. It is also considered good practice to prepare a suitable place for the interview, such as a warm, quiet, ventilated room. The interviewer should also ensure that the candidates have a friendly reception and are informed of what is expected of them.

The average interview takes around 30 minutes. The interview plan organises the time to cover the important areas in assessing applicants. The plan must be flexible enough to allow the interviewer to explore areas that may come up during the interview. An example is shown in Table 77.2.

Many recruitment handbooks spell out the 'dos and don'ts' of interviewing. Some of the 'dos' that the interviewer may take into account include the following.
● Introduce yourself to the candidate.
● Adopt a suitable manner, show respect and be friendly.
● Make sure the interview is not interrupted.
● Conduct the interview at an unhurried pace.
● Have a list of questions that need to be asked.
● Encourage the candidate to talk by using 'open' questions such as:
> 'Tell me about your present/last job ...'
> 'What is your opinion on ...?'
> 'What do you find interesting in ...?'
● Concentrate on those areas not fully covered by the application form.
● Be alert for clues in the candidate's answer, probe where necessary, and be more specific in the questioning if you are not satisfied.
● When the interview has ended, make sure the candidate has no further questions and let the candidate know when the decision will be made, eg within seven days.

Question 3

How long does it take to employ a secretary? It used to be said that interviewers made up their minds within the first few minutes. But as employing secretaries can now have important implications, as they are often in direct contact with customers, businesses are reviewing their interview procedures.

Some businesses interview secretaries twice. In the first interview candidates may be asked about their abilities and experience. They might also be given the chance to ask their own questions. For example, they might ask about opportunities for training and promotion. Candidates who ask whether training is carried out by the organisation or externally are likely to be more successful than those who ask: 'Do you have a canteen?' In the second interview candidates may be asked to take a psychometric test. The Tussauds Group employs around 100 secretaries in its leisure attractions. The results of the psychometric tests it gives to candidates are analysed by computer, which gives information on their personality, style of work and their ability to work in teams.

The Electronic Boutique in Bracknell uses a five minute personality psychometric test when assessing candidates for a position as a secretary as well as an interview. Julia Birkett, its human resource manager, says that shorthand and IT skills are important, but she really looks for someone who is bright and eager. The company employs eight secretaries who often work as a team. Secretaries are appointed with a view to promotion, especially as the business is expanding into Europe.

Source: adapted from *The Times*, 14.1.1998.

(a) What characteristics might The Tussauds Group and The Electronic Boutique be looking for from a successful candidate ?
(b) Explain the possible advantages for: (i) candidates; (ii) The Tussauds Group of using an interview.
(c) Discuss whether the use of psychometric tests might solve some of the problems of interviews.

Table 77.2 *Organising an interview*

Organisation	Tasks	Time (minutes)
Introduction	Who are they?	2
	Who are you?	3
Body of interview	Begin questioning. Ask questions which probe what they have learnt from their experiences/qualifications /interests and how they would apply this to their new position.	10
	Let the candidate ask questions. Explain about the organisation.	5
	If any questions are left, clear them up.	5
	Tell the candidate what happens next, eg 'We will let you know in 10 days'.	3
Close of interview	Finish tidily.	
After the interview	Assess the candidate.	10/15
	Prepare for next interview.	10/15

● Write up your assessment notes immediately.
● Prepare for the next interview.

The interviewer will have gained a great deal of information from the interview. It will help the interviewer to have a checklist of the criteria used when assessing candidates. Table 77.3 shows two possible lists. The interviewer can make notes about candidates next to each criterion and compare the information with the person specification after the interview, to decide if the person is suitable.

Table 77.3 *Criteria used in assessing candidates*

Rodgers' 7 point plan	Munro-Fraser 5 point plan
Physical make-up	Impact on others
Attainments	Qualifications
General intelligence	Innate abilities
Specialised aptitude	Motivation
Interests	Emotional adjustment
Disposition	
Circumstances	

Interviewing and technology

Falling technology costs mean that some businesses now use videoconferencing as an interviewing tool (☞ unit 82). For example, it can cost less than £1,000 for a recruiter in the UK to interview six candidates in the US by video link. Videoconferencing is not likely to replace the face-to-face interview because people still need the 'human touch'. However, it will help to save time and money. SmithKline Beecham, the pharmaceuticals company, has used video-interviewing in the initial screening of candidates. It has found this to be a way of saving on travel expenses, particularly when an interview would have involved international air travel.

There is a growing trend among companies to select candidates by using the telephone. Phone interviews have a number of advantages. Savings can be made on travel costs and managers need to spend less time away from their desks. However, according to a study by Shell UK, there is evidence that candidates interviewed over the phone are not rated as highly by interviewers as those interviewed face-to-face.

Selection exercises

As well as interviews and tests, more and more companies are using a variety of role play exercises, group presentations and simulations to help them analyse the capabilities of candidates. These exercises allow candidates to demonstrate social skills and problem solving skills which they may need to use in the job. For example, a salesperson may show persuasive communication skills in a role play situation. The

Question 4

Research into graduate recruitment has shown that personnel managers use many different approaches to interviews. Some use a standard approach. Others felt that this means graduates are too well rehearsed for the interview, which leads to a false picture of the candidate. Some comments made during research included the following.

Personnel manager from Scicon - a computer software house
'I don't ask the standard questions about why have you applied to Scicon or what in your degree has prepared you for this job, because all that's testing is one's ability to prepare for interviews. So I ask questions candidates haven't remotely prepared for. I might talk about what's going on in the teachers' dispute with testing, not because I'm interested in the subject itself ... but I'm interested in how people think quickly on a subject they haven't been expecting.'

Personnel manager from Great Universal Stores
'We are obviously anxious to get the right people for the right job. Having said that if we give the game away and say this is the sort of person we want then there are some clever people around who can manipulate their behaviour and do it in a way to show they are best. I want to make sure that they know where they stand with us as well as us finding out about them. It is very difficult to hit a happy medium between not leaving them totally confused in the questions asked but at the same time not giving so much away that some candidates can manipulate their behaviour to put on a good performance. It is very difficult.'

A comment made by a 'typical' candidate
'The interviewer asks about GCSEs, A levels, why are you doing your present degree, why this company - you know, the usual thing. You get to the situation with interviews where you know what they are going to ask and what your answers are going to be.'

Source: independent research by the author.

(a) What might be meant by 'the standard approach to interviewing'?
(b) Why might some personnel managers be unhappy with adopting a 'standard approach'?
(c) Explain the methods that personnel managers might adopt which could avoid the pitfalls of a 'standard approach'.
(d) Based on these comments, do you think that interviewing is a reliable way of selecting individuals for jobs?

use of exercises has a number of benefits for a business.
● They allow more information to be gathered about a candidate than other methods of selection.
● They show how well candidates react to situations such as team working, responding to customers or meeting deadlines.
● They allow large numbers to be assessed and may save on costs.

Evaluating selection

How can a business tell if selection has been effective? It could simply decide that if it has appointed the 'right' candidate, then its aim has been achieved. However, selection will involve costs to a business. There will be expenses in sending out application forms and perhaps travelling expenses for candidates. Staff will also have to give up time to carry out the interviews.

So, for example, if 10 people were interviewed for 3 posts, but only one applicant was suitable, selection may not have been effective. In this case the firm would have to readvertise and interview other candidates as 2 posts would be unfilled. The personnel department's role would be to check all stages of selection to find out where problems had arisen. For example, when short listing, a suitable candidate may have been 'left out'. At an interview a possible candidate may have been rushed, so he was not given the chance to do his best.

Key terms

Curriculum Vitae - a list of the applicant's personal details, experience and qualifications.
Short listing - reducing the original number of candidates to a manageable number to be interviewed.

Summary

1. Why has selection become increasingly important to businesses?
2. State 5 features covered in an application form.
3. What criteria might a personnel department take into account when designing an application form?
4. Name 4 types of tests that a personnel department might carry out when selecting applicants for a job.
5. What are the main problems with personality tests as a method of selection?
6. Explain the main problems with interviews.
7. State 5 'dos' when conducting an interview.
8. How might a business evaluate its selection procedure?
9. How might a business make use of technology when conducting an interview?
10. What is meant by a selection exercise?

Question 5

25 men were busily drawing pictures of pigs, windmills, castles, whales and kites in a conference centre in London. Why? The exercise was designed to relax applicants for jobs with the home delivery service launched by Iceland, the frozen food retailer. The group was inundated with applications. In Scotland more than 8,000 people applied for 84 job vacancies. This forced a rethink of the group's traditional recruitment policies. 'You cannot possibly do one-to-one interviews with 8,500 people,' said Alan Fordham, the home-delivery coordinator.

The result was a two-hour selection session. Applicants were divided into teams, assigned an assessor, and asked to take part in a series of exercises and discussions. These were designed to find candidates with the best social skills. The idea, said Fordham, is to relax people to allow their personalities to shine through. 'We are not just looking for drivers. At the end of the day, they will be ambassadors for the company.' One of the Yorkshire drivers, for example, passed a nunnery every day on his delivery rounds. But he had never seen a nun in his Iceland store and wondered how they eat. So he went to the nunnery and since then they have spent a great deal with the business.

The selection process is not cheap. In London, costs are almost £2,000 a day. The assessors admit that the most likely candidates can often be spotted within minutes. 'It is something in the eye contact when you first meet them,' said Steve Nockels. 'There is something that says, "Hi, I'm friendly". But there is a danger that making a snap judgment could mean that more suitable candidates are passed over. That is why each group session ends with quick individual interviews. Iceland argues that the process has made the selection process far more efficient. 'The labour turnover of our drivers is only half that of our store staff at about 7 per cent,' said Fordham. Some candidates felt the selection process relaxed them. But others thought the jollity grating. 'It is mind games from my point of view,' said one candidate. 'What is wrong with the old-fashioned interview? After all, I cannot see it leading to much else other than driving.'

Source: adapted from the *Financial Times*, 13.8.1997.

(a) What selection exercises were used by Iceland?
(b) Explain the possible advantages of this method of selection for:
   (i) employees;
   (ii) Iceland.
(c) Examine the potential drawbacks of using such exercises for:
   (i) employees;
   (ii) Iceland.

Case study

Recruitment in London Boroughs

Reports in the 1990s highlighted the need for better selection procedures in childrens' homes. The Warner Report in 1992 argued that employers must tighten up selection and appointment procedures, staff training and supervision. A report by Sir William Utting in 1998 said that: 'urgent action is required to raise standards' in personnel procedures for staff working with children. A number of specific criticisms were put forward.

- The Warner Report suggested that homes that had problems tended to prefer mainly internal applicants. It also suggested problems with using agencies for recruitment.
- Some authorities applied equal opportunities policies 'in ways which unreasonably constrained' the interview process according to Warner. For example, some asked set questions without allowing follow up discussion.
- It had been alleged that some interviewers were unwilling to question the backgrounds of gay or ethnic minority candidates. As a result, weak staff were appointed. Recruiters asked standard questions and also allowed preparation time for answers.
- There has been concern over the length of time it takes to check the records and history of applicants.
- Selection procedures have failed to prevent cases of child abuse. People have been appointed who have passed competence tests and interviews, but have been found guilty of abuse. A national register of convicted paedophiles was drawn up by the police as a result.

Examples from Southwark, Lewisham and Islington show how three London Boroughs have responded to the need for improvements in selection procedures.

Southwark

In the early 1990s, Southwark took into account many of the issues raised by the Warner Report. The selection process started with detailed job descriptions and person specifications being produced. Jobs were advertised both internally and externally. All agencies that were used had to carry out detailed checks on staff background.

Before interviews, shortlisted candidates carried out written exercises based on the abilities needed to do a particular job. An applicant for a care plan officer's post might have been asked to estimate a budget. Communication and literacy tests were carried out to test that staff could express themselves clearly to children. Southwark developed personality tests that did not discriminate against candidates, such as those speaking English as a second language. This was important given that members of ethnic minorities made up a large proportion of the borough's population. Interview panels had to reflect a mixture of gender and race. They consisted of three managers, all trained in interviewing techniques. Although interview questions were prepared in advance, interviewers could probe further. Candidates were also asked to make presentations to show their ability to cope with practical problems. These revolved around 'what if' scenarios, such as: 'What would you do as head of a home if you arrived to find all your staff striken with flu?' Southwark also used police checks into the candidates' backgrounds. At the time however, like many London authorities, it only took up references after the successful applicant was appointed. Where concerns were raised, a second interview was carried out.

Lewisham

Lewisham's policy is never to let a new recruit start without checking references. When it opened a new children's home in 1998 the staff went through a stringent selection process. This included psychometric testing, role play exercises, criminal records checks, observed interaction with children and interviews by a panel of young people. The council worked with the 'Making it better group', a collection of young people who represented children in care. Three of the group were used in the selection process.

Islington

Islington has reviewed its policies on selection, interviewing, reference checking and equal opportunities. It has a formal interview and also a personal one. This examines people's motivations, how they deal with stress and their reaction to power.

Source: updated and adapted from *People Management*, 19.2.1998.

(a) **What types of test were used by Southwark before an interview took place?**

(b) **Using examples from the article, explain the:**
   (i) advantages; and (ii) disadvantages of interviews as a means of recruiting staff.

(c) **Explain why registers and background checks might be important for selection of people to work in children's homes.**

(d) **Account for approach to interviews taken by Lewisham Council.**

(e) **Assess the most suitable methods of selection for candidates seeking to work in children's homes.**

The contract of employment

Once a business has selected an employee (☞ unit 77), the successful candidate must be **appointed**. Once appointed, employees are entitled to a CONTRACT OF EMPLOYMENT. This is an agreement between the employer and the employee under which each has certain obligations. It is 'binding' to both parties in the agreement, the employer and the employee. This means that it is unlawful to break the terms and conditions in the contract without the other party agreeing.

As soon as an employee starts work, and therefore demonstrates that she accepts the terms offered by the employer, the contract comes into existence. It is sometimes a written contract, although a verbal agreement or an 'implied' agreement are also contracts of employment. The **Employment Rights Act, 1996** requires employers to give employees taken on for one month or more a **written statement** within two months of appointment. This written statement sets out the terms and conditions in the contract. Some common features shown in the written statement are:

● the names of the employer and the name of the employee;
● the date on which the employment is to begin;
● the job title;
● the terms and conditions of employment.

The duties and rights of employees and employers

Employees that are appointed by a business are covered by certain employment protection rights. Government legislation makes it a duty of employers to safeguard these rights. They fall into a number of areas.

● Discrimination. Employees can not be discriminated against on grounds of gender, race or disability (☞ unit 80). So, for example, a business can not refuse to appoint a candidate for a job only because that person is female.
● Pay. Employees must be paid the same rate as other employees doing the same job, a similar job or a job with equal demands. They also have the right to itemised pay statements and not to have pay deducted for unlawful reasons.
● Absences. Employees have a right to maternity leave, ante-natal leave, time off for union or public duties and time off to look for training or work at times of redundancy. They also have a right to guaranteed payments during a period of lay off or medical suspension. Employees have a right to return to work after maternity leave.
● Dismissal. Employees have the right not to be dismissed or face disciplinary action for trade union activity or on health and safety grounds. They also have a right to notice

of dismissal.

In 1995 differences in the rights of part time workers and full time workers in certain areas were abolished. So, for example, all workers with two years continuous service were entitled to the unfair dismissal and redundancy payment rights above. The **1999 Employment Relations Bill** aimed to increase employee's rights. For example, the qualifying period for protection against unfair dismissal was to be reduced and maternity leave was to be extended.

Employers also have duties to provide a safe environment in which employees can work. In the UK the **Health and Safety at Work Act 1974** ensures that Health and Safety Executive and local inspectors check workplaces (☞ unit 81). It imposed criminal liability on employers failing to meet standards. EU regulations in 1992 set out rules about the safe

Question 1

In 1996 Safeway, the supermarket giant, won its appeal against an Employment Appeal Tribunal (EAT) ruling that its dress code discriminated against males. The company's dress code contained details of the length of a person's hair. Females could have long hair if tied back, but men had to have short hair.

An employee who worked in the delicatessen section was dismissed when he refused to have his hair cut. The EAT had ruled that this was discrimination, but a judge overturned the decision. He said that the Sex Discrimination Act 1975 outlawed discrimination **against** one or other of the sexes and not **between** sexes. He suggested that this was the latter case, discriminating between the appearance of males and females, and so was not discriminatory. Appearance, he argued, might include hair, tattoo and other features as well as dress. The judge also suggested that dress code which attempted to apply a conventional standard of appearance was an 'even handed approach' which did not discriminate.

Source: adapted from *Labour Research*, April 1996.

(a) What duties of: (i) employers; and (ii) employees are mentioned in the article?
(b) Suggest three other duties that employers at Safeway may have to its employees.
(c) Why might employers and employees have these duties?

use of machinery, the use of protective clothing and equipment, the handling of loads and the use of computer screens.

The duties of employees may be set out in the written statement of the contract of employment. For example, employees are expected to conform to standards of behaviour and conduct at work. These may include standards of attendance, punctuality, dealings with colleagues and dress. Standards of quality and accuracy of work, speed of work and safety are also likely to be expected of employees.

In certain circumstances legislation forces businesses to have **vicarious liability**. This is where the business accepts responsibility for the actions of its employees.

Conditions of work and service

The written statement of the contract of employment will contain information about the conditions of work and service agreed by the employer and employee. Conditions may include the following.

The number of hours to be worked The statement will show the hours to be worked per week or over a period such as a year in the case of annualised hours (☞ unit 72). The number of hours must conform to legislation. For example, in 1998 the **European Union Working Time Directive** allowed workers to limit their working hours to a maximum of 48 hours per week, although workers such as junior doctors and senior executives were excluded. Details of the start and finish times may also be included, along with any meal or rest breaks. If an employee is expected to work 'shifts', this should be stated. Shift work is where an employee may work, for example, from 9am-5pm in the day for a week and then from 9pm-5am at night the following week.

The designation of the job Workers may be employed in **full time** jobs or **part time** jobs. They may also be given a **permanent job** or a **temporary job** that only lasts for a period of time. The period of employment would usually be stated in the case of a temporary job. If a worker is expected to be based in a factory or office, this place of employment should also be mentioned. Some employees may be expected to work from home or to travel. If this is the case then arrangements that cover this such as support from the employer or travel expenses should be mentioned. These are discussed in the next section.

Pay The method of payment used to reward the employee is usually included in the written statement (☞ unit 72). She might be paid a wage or a salary. Payment may be by cheque or directly into a bank account. The rate of pay would be specified, such as £5 per hour or an annual salary of £20,000 a year. There may also be an indication of any bonuses, commission or overtime, incentive schemes and deductions from wages. Pay must conform to legislation. For example, employers are bound by the **Equal Pay Act 1970** (☞ unit 80). This states that an employee must be paid the same rate as another employee doing the same job, a similar job or a job with equal demands.

Benefits Benefits that the employer is offering to the employee are usually included. The annual number of days paid holiday is often stated and any restrictions on when they can be taken. Statutory holidays are often stated as being taken. If the business runs its own pension scheme or offers to contribute to individual pensions, this may be stated along with contribution rates. There may also be information on the length of time and the rate at which sick pay is available. Any other benefits, such as paid maternity leave and fringe benefits such as a company car (☞ unit 73) may be included.

Disciplinary procedures The written statement may indicate the immediate superior of the employee, who might be responsible for induction, training, supervision and discipline. In a larger business these are likely to be carried out by the personnel department. The **Contracts of Employment Act, 1972** and the **Employment Protection Act, 1975** state that employers must explain their disciplinary procedures. These are the rules that set standards of conduct at work. Employees must also be clearly informed of the consequences of breaking these rules, how this will be investigated and the rights of appeal against a decision (☞ unit 81). Employees that break rules could be liable for disciplinary action. This may be in the form of a verbal or written warning, suspension or even dismissal in some cases.

Notice Employees may leave a business to change jobs, to stop work totally or to have children. When employees do not intend to return they have to 'hand in their notice'. In other words they have to inform (or notify) the employer before they leave. The length of time that notice must be given by employees before they leave may be indicated in the written statement. This may be 'one weeks' notice' or 'one month's notice' for example. Similarly, the contract may state the length of 'notice' to be given by employers to employees before making them redundant or dismissing them. The length of notice will vary depending on the length of service.

Grievance procedures If an employee has a complaint against other staff or against their treatment at work then a business may have its own internal grievance procedure. Details of these procedures and who to contact in case of complaints may be included in the written statement. Employees should also be aware of how to contact an industrial tribunal (☞ unit 81), ACAS (the arbitration service, ☞ unit 86) or a trade union in the case of a complaint.

Employee rights The rights of employees to union representation, time off and equality of treatment as explained above may be outlined in the written statement of the contract of employment.

Types of employment

A number of different definitions can be used to classify the

The 1998 EU Working Time Directive limited the working week to a maximum of 48 hours for most workers. Other changes that were introduced included compulsory paid holidays for all workers, starting at three weeks a year, and a rest period of 20 minutes for anyone working six hours consecutively. In the UK around 2 million workers previously received no paid holiday at all. It was suggested that the cost to businesses of changes as a result of the Directive could be as high as £2 billion.

There was evidence that some employers were attempting to get around the Directive. Workers at Forte Hotels, part of the Granada Group, were sent letters asking them to accept a new hours of work clause in their contracts. Some employers were persuading employees to sign a waiver agreeing to give up their rights to cap their hours. There was also concern about loopholes in the Directive. Some categories of workers were excluded from the 48 hour a week limit, such as 'senior executives'. There could be disputes about exactly who is a senior executive and therefore about who should have a limit on their hours. Another problem with the 48 hour limit is: 'what actually is work?' Employees' and employers' opinions may differ. For example, if an employee travels on an overnight train to an essential meeting, does this constitute time spent at work ?

Source: adapted from *The Observer*, 27.9.1998 and *Labour Research*, November 1998.

(a) What changes are being made to employees' conditions of service as a result of the EU Working Time Directive?
(b) What problems are likely to arise when implementing these changes?
(c) Explain how the changes might affect:
   (i) employees;
   (ii) businesses?

way in which people are employed.

Employees and self-employment If an employer provides and controls work, supplies equipment and pays tax and National Insurance contributions for the worker, then the worker is an EMPLOYEE. An employee will work under the conditions of the contract of employment agreed with the employer. If the worker makes her own decisions about accepting work and conditions of work, and pays her own tax and National Insurance contributions, the worker is likely to be SELF-EMPLOYED. Working at home does not necessarily mean a worker is self-employed, as discussed in the section on homeworkers later in this unit. To be self-employed, a worker must be in business on her own account. Businesses sometimes 'contract out' work to self-employed people to save on the costs of extra employees. For example, buildings in city centres which are mainly glass may hire window cleaners rather than employing staff, even though regular cleaning may be needed.

Permanent and temporary employment PERMANENT workers are employed by a business for an indefinite period of time. For example, a flour mill may employ a full time quality controller to check wheat as it arrives. He will work for the business until he leaves, either by choice, because he is forced to by the business or when he retires. TEMPORARY workers are employed for a limited period. For example, the mill may employ temporary workers for a period of six months to operate machines that 'mill' the wheat into flour.

In the UK, around 10 per cent of all workers are temporary workers. Businesses needing casual work at busy times employ temporary workers. So do farms, which employ seasonal workers as 'pickers' during the harvesting period. Shops employ retail assistants at Christmas for a fixed period. One advantage of temporary workers is that they no longer have to be employed once demand falls off. They can also be hired when required, for example to cover staff on maternity leave or for 'one-off' tasks. Costs may be lower because temporary workers do not receive the benefits of permanent workers. Some businesses use temporary jobs to try out workers who may later become permanent. One problem with temporary workers, businesses argue, is that they are less reliable than permanent staff.

Full and part time employment Workers may be employed full time or part time by a business. Part time workers are defined in *Labour Market Trends* published by The Office for National Statistics as 'people normally working for not more than 30 hours a week except where otherwise stated'. There has been a large increase in the number of part time workers in the UK in recent years. One advantage of part time workers is the flexibility they provide for a business (☞ unit 88). For example, part time workers may be employed at times of peak trade, such as in public houses at the weekend. They may be employed to allow supermarkets to stay open later in the evening. **Job sharing** is becoming more popular as people seek part time work. This is where the tasks involved in a job description are divided between two people, for example. They often work at different times. Examples could be a legal secretary's job, part of which is carried out by one person from 9am to 12am and another person from 12am to 5pm, or two GPs in a doctors practice working on different days or weeks. Another advantage is reduced costs for the business because they often try to pay lower wages and benefits to part time staff.

Part time work can also benefit employees. It allows workers such as lone parents who have difficulty working full time to be employed. Students or others with low incomes can supplement their wages. The long term unemployed or people who are retraining may find it a way to 'get back to work'.

As Figure 78.1 shows, the majority of men and women in employment in the UK are full time employees. Full time employees tend to work over 30 hours a week. The average number of hours worked by full time workers in 1998 was

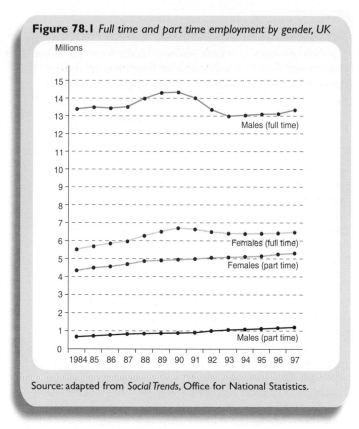

Figure 78.1 *Full time and part time employment by gender, UK*

Millions

Source: adapted from *Social Trends*, Office for National Statistics.

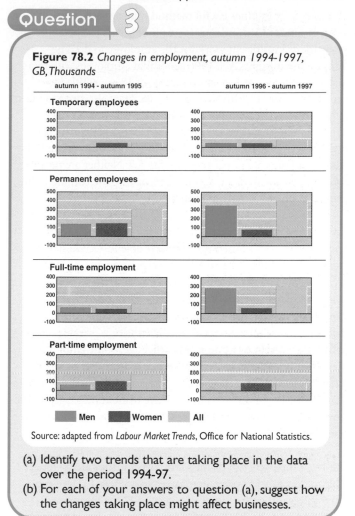

Figure 78.2 *Changes in employment, autumn 1994-1997, GB, Thousands*

autumn 1994 - autumn 1995   autumn 1996 - autumn 1997

Temporary employees

Permanent employees

Full-time employment

Part-time employment

Men   Women   All

Source: adapted from *Labour Market Trends*, Office for National Statistics.

(a) Identify two trends that are taking place in the data over the period 1994-97.
(b) For each of your answers to question (a), suggest how the changes taking place might affect businesses.

38.6 hours. Businesses that employ full time workers expect that they will remain with the firm for a period, will be well motivated by rewards (☞ units 72 and 73) and will benefit from training and promotion. This they hope should ensure that workers are efficient and will justify the higher cost of full time workers.

Homeworkers and teleworkers A wide range of different people working in the UK might be classed as **homeworkers**. It may include for instance farmers, shop owners, representatives, telesales people, hotel owners and some computer operators. They may be employed by a business to work at home or they may be self-employed. They may be full time or part time. **Teleworker homeworkers** are people who work from their own home, or use it as base, and who could not do so without a telephone or computer.

For an employer, the use of homeworkers has a number of advantages. As these workers are not based at the place of employment, the cost of equipment is reduced and less space is needed. There are also fewer problems with absenteeism and transport delays, such as people arriving late to work or who are unable to get to work because of bad weather. People with children are able to work more easily, at times when they want. However, there may be communication problems if staff can not be contacted. Also, it is far more difficult to monitor and control the work of employees.

Termination of contracts

Why might a contract of employment come to end? The contract may be terminated either by the employee or the employer for a number of reasons.

Changing jobs and promotion Employees may leave a business to change jobs. Their existing contract would end and they would be given a contract for their new job. As stated earlier, employees can not usually leave immediately. They often have to work out a period of 'notice', such as one week or one month. Employees who are promoted internally (☞ unit 77) are also likely to be given a new contract of employment as their terms and conditions may have changed. For example, a machine operator who was appointed to be supervisor may have different wages, benefits, deductions and leave entitlements.

Dismissal Employees may be dismissed for a number of reasons (☞ unit 81). These may be for unfair reasons, such as joining a trade union. If an industrial tribunal finds that a person has been dismissed unfairly, it has the power to reinstate the employee. There are lawful reasons, however, for dismissing an employee. These may include misconduct or because an employee is incapable of doing a job. A period of notice is required, but the length will vary depending on how long the employee has worked for the business.

Redundancy Another lawful method of dismissing an employee is on grounds of redundancy (☞ unit 81). This is where there is no work or insufficient work for the employee to do. The **Employment Rights Act, 1996** states that employees with two years' continuous service since the age of 18 are entitled to redundancy or SEVERANCE payments. They also need to meet other criteria. For example, they must have a contract of employment (ie not be self-employed). Some people, such as members of the armed forces, The House of Commons and the House of Lords are not covered by the Act. Neither are people who are retiring over the age of 60/65 or who are coming to the end of a contract or an apprenticeship.

Retirement and early retirement In the UK in the late 1990s men aged 65 and women aged 60 were able to receive state pensions. Between 2010 and 2020 the 'pensionable age' for women is to be raised to 65 to avoid discrimination. Some people decide to leave work when they are entitled to this state pension. However, many take 'early retirement' and finish work before. They will then live on state benefits or a private pension which they can draw upon at an earlier age. Some employers that want to get rid of older workers or reduce staff numbers offer attractive 'early retirement' packages to encourage people to leave work. People do not have to leave work at these ages. Some employees are now seeing the benefit of employing workers over the age of 65 (☞ unit 80).

Illness Employers can dismiss employees if they are no longer able to do a job. However, employees may chose to leave a job themselves if they are too ill to continue. Some businesses provide private health cover for employees who need to finish work. Other employees would need to live on state benefits or private insurance benefits.

End of duration of contract Some temporary employees are only given a contract to work for a limited period of time. For example, contractors may hire construction workers to work on a large project, such as a shopping centre, for a period of two years. After the project finished the employees contract would end.

Breach of contract

If either the employee or employer suffers a financial loss as a result of a BREACH OF CONTRACT by the other party, they may claim damages. For example, an employee on a fixed term contract who is asked to work an extra two weeks to finish the job, but is not paid, may claim as a result. Claims by employees and employers are normally taken to either the the county court or another civil court. An employee can take a claim to an industrial tribunal if an amount is outstanding when the contract is terminated and if it is not related to certain categories, such as patents. Industrial tribunals often settle claims quicker than courts but there is a limit to the amount they can award.

Key terms

Breach of contract - breaking of terms agreed in the contract of employment by the employers and the employees.
Contract of employment - an agreement between an employer and an employee in which each has certain obligations.
Employee - a worker for whom an employer provides and controls work, supplies equipment and pays tax and National Insurance contributions.
Permanent employment - employment for an indefinite period of time.
Self-employed - a worker who makes his or her own decisions about accepting work and conditions of work, and pays his or her own tax and National Insurance contributions
Severance pay - an amount payable to an employee on termination of contract.
Temporary employment - employment for a limited or finite period of time.

Summary

1. 'A contract of employment is an agreement that is binding to both parties.' Explain this statement.
2. What is a written statement of the contract of employment?
3. State 3 rights of employees of a business.
4. State 3 duties of employees of a business.
5. Suggest 5 conditions of work that may appear on the written statement.
6. Explain 3 differences between an employee and a person who is self-employed.
7. Why might a business employ temporary workers?
8. What is meant by job sharing?
9. What are the advantages of job sharing for an employee?
10. What is meant by a homeworker?
11. Suggest 3 advantages of homeworkers for a business.
12. State 5 reasons why a contract of employment may be terminated.

Case study

The growth of teleworkers

Teleworking is becoming popular for both employers and employees. Estimates of the number of teleworkers in the UK vary from a quarter of a million by The Labour Force Survey (LFS) of The Office for National Statistics to 4 million by the Henley Business School. The LFS defines teleworkers as 'people who do some paid or unpaid work in their own home who could not do so without using both a telephone and a computer'. This includes:

- people who work in their own home (teleworker homeworkers);
- teleworkers who work elsewhere but use home as a base;
- occasional teleworkers who spend at least one day a week working in their own home or using home as a base.

Tables 78.1 and 78.2 show data about teleworkers in the UK from the LFS in 1998. But who are the teleworkers, why do they want to work in this way and how does this affect businesses?

Martin and Gaby Allen Soccer Schools

Martin and Gaby Allen conduct business from their home in Winchester. They run soccer schools for children, possibly the largest operation of its type in the UK. The business involves travelling to sites with two lorries full of kits and equipment to set up temporary, soccer schools.

Working from home was not planned and has become a little cumbersome. The garage and rooms in the house are used as office space and storerooms. The former dining room is now full of posters, T-shirts and medals. 'There are good points', says Martin. There is no rent on premises and work is in a pleasant location. In summer planning can be carried out sitting in the garden, not in a stuffy office.

However, there is a constant need to maintain and upgrade equipment. The Apple Mac computer at times needs more memory to handle the size of the database. There are also two telephone lines for phone calls and faxes and a mobile phone. Increasing demand means that more are likely to be needed in future. At times of extra demand the business hires temporary and part time employees to help. One of the problems of working from home, according to the Allens, is that 'you can't escape'.

Campbell Gordon

Campbell Gordon is a Reading-based commercial property agent. One of the company's surveyors, Tara Lee, now works effectively and efficiently outside the office. 50 per cent of her time is spent on development sites in the Thames Valley area. The use of a mobile phone, a laptop computer and an ISDN line allows her to make on-site valuations with a computer link to the office. She can also visit clients to make suggestions. It is argued that this method of working increases productivity, improves the quality of service to customers and reduces costs for the business. Some activities, such as Campbell's, are ideally suited to teleworking. These include management, sales, marketing, administration and secretarial work. However, to carry out teleworking effectively:

- a teleworker must be able to do a job without the need for continuous face to face contact;
- work must be capable of being delivered electronically;
- information must be able to be retrieved and sent electronically.

When setting up workers to work at home businesses must also take into account insurance for equipment and health and safety legislation regarding the use of computers and computer screens. Despite these restrictions, a teleworker trial at Campbell Gordon showed that this method of work 'leads to a significant increase in productivity'.

Source: adapted from *The Times*, 31.5.1997, *The Sunday Times*, 24,5,1998 and *Labour Market Trends*, October 1998.

Table 78.1 *Teleworkers: employees and self-employed, part time and full time*

Per cent

Teleworker homeworkers

	All	Men	Women
Employees	40	30	49
Self-employed	60	70	51
Full-time	51	71	34
Part-time	49	29	66

Teleworkers who work in different places using home as a base

	All	Men	Women
Employees	44	44	47
Self-employed	56	56	53
Full-time	84	90	62
Part-time	16	10	38

Occasional teleworkers

	All	Men	Women
Employees	80	78	83
Self-employed	20	22	17
Full-time	90	96	77
Part-time	10	*	23

Source: adapted from Labour Force Survey.

Table 78.2 *Teleworkers by occupation*

Per cent

Teleworker homeworkers

	All	Men	Women
Managers & administrators	29	32	26
Professional occupations	17	28	*
Associate professional & technical occupations	23	30	18
Clerical, secretarial occupations	24	*	*
Craft and related occupations	*	*	*
Selling	*	*	*
Other	*	*	*

Teleworkers who work in different places using home as a base

	All	Men	Women
Managers & administrators	20	20	21
Professional occupations	20	20	20
Associate professional & technical occupations	17	15	26
Clerical, secretarial occupations	4	2	10
Craft and related occupations	22	27	*
Selling	12	11	16
Other	5	5	*

Occasional teleworkers

	All	Men	Women
Managers & administrators	37	40	29
Professional occupations	35	34	37
Associate professional & technical occupations	15	13	19
Clerical, secretarial occupations	4	*	*
Craft and related occupations	*	*	*
Selling	4	5	*
Other	*	*	*

Source: adapted from Labour Force Survey.

(a) **Explain why the Allens and Tara Lee might be examples of teleworkers.**

(b) **What duties do employers have to teleworkers that are mentioned in the article?**

(c) **Outline three: (i) benefits; (ii) problems; of telework for the businesses mentioned in the article.**

(d) **Why might The Allens employ part time rather than full time workers in periods of high demand?**

(e) (i) **What types of occupations are most suited to telework?**

(ii) **Explain why these occupations are suited to telework.**

(f) (i) **Compare the percentage of full time and part time male and female teleworkers.**

(ii) **Examine reasons to explain these differences.**

Induction

Newly appointed employees are most likely to leave the business in the early weeks of employment. This is called the **induction crisis**. How can employers prevent this? One approach is to help the new employee settle in quickly and feel comfortable in the new job by using an INDUCTION programme. Induction programmes are not usually about a specific job the employee will be doing, but the way in which the business works. They may contain information about some or all of the following.

- The organisation - history, development, management and activity.
- Personnel policies.
- Terms of employment - including disciplinary rules and union arrangements.
- Employee benefits and services.
- Physical facilities.
- General nature of the work to be done.
- The role and work of the supervisor.
- Departmental rules and safety measures.
- The relationship of new jobs to others.

They may also contain:

- a detailed description of the employee's job;
- introduction to fellow workers;
- an explanation of the values that the business feels are important, such as good attendance;
- follow up after several weeks.

Even with these, induction is unlikely to work without careful timing and without making sure that the employee adjusts to the new social and work environment. Experiments have shown that it is possible for the time taken for induction to be halved and costs reduced by two-thirds if it is well planned. To do this, the programme must focus on the anxieties of the new employees, instead of on what it is thought they should be told.

The aims of training

Training involves employees being taught new skills or improving skills they already have. Why might a business train its employees? It is argued that a well trained workforce has certain benefits for the business.

- Well trained workers should be more productive. This will help the business to achieve its overall objectives, such as increasing profit.
- It should help to create a more flexible workforce (☞ unit 88). If a business needs to reorganise production, workers may have to be trained in new tasks.
- It will help the introduction of new technology. New machinery or production processes can be introduced more quickly if workers are trained to use them effectively.

- It should lead to increased job satisfaction for employees. Well motivated workers are more likely to be more productive.
- It should reduce accidents and injuries if employees are trained in health and safety procedures.
- It may improve the image of the company. Customers are more likely to have confidence in personnel who are confident, competent and have knowledge of products or processes. Good applicants are also more likely to be attracted if a training programme is part of the job.
- It can improve employees' chances of promotion. The business, as a result, should have qualified people in important posts.

The need for training

It has been suggested that businesses in the UK need to increase spending on training. A Confederation of British Industry (CBI) report in 1997 found that UK companies were not as competitive as overseas rivals. US firms were 60 per cent and Japanese firms 26 per cent more productive. On a range of measures, including training, many UK companies rated only poor or fair. Research by the Qualifications and Curriculum Authority (QCA) found that a third of all UK workers had no vocational training. 45 per cent of employees from the survey who received training felt it was inadequate.

Another problem in the 1990s was SKILLS SHORTAGES amongst workers. Between 1996 and 1997 the proportion of manufacturing companies reporting skills shortages rose by 70 per cent. The government's skill needs survey found employers were having difficulty filling 60,000 IT posts, 10,000 jobs in engineering and 5,000-10,000 construction posts because of the lack of basic skills. Skills shortages cost small firms one in four of their orders, according to research for Lloyds TSB by the Small Business Research Trust.

This evidence seems to suggest that businesses would benefit from training. Employees are likely to be better educated and have greater skills, and should be more productive. Since the early 1990s, governments have set education, training and learning targets to be met. The targets to be met by 2002 are shown in Table 79.1.

Identifying the need for training

How does a business know if training is required? One method might be to use the job description (☞ unit 76) to find the skills and knowledge needed to do the job. If there is a difference between the knowledge and skills of the employee and those actually required, this may indicate a need for training.

Employees can also be asked about areas where they feel

Question 1

Table 79.1 *Government learning targets for 2002*

- Targets for 16 year olds - 50 per cent of 16 year olds to get 5 GCSEs at grade C or above; 95 per cent to get at least 1 GCSE.
- Targets for young people - by age 19, 85 per cent of young people to achieve GCSE at grade C or above, Intermediate GNVQ or NVQ level 2; by age 21, 60 per cent of young people to achieve two GCE A levels, Advanced GNVQ or NVQ level 3.

- Targets for adults - 50 per cent of adults to be qualified to NVQ level 3, Advanced GNVQ or two A level standard; 28 per cent of adults to have a vocational, professional, management or academic qualification at NVQ level 4 or above.
- Targets for organisations - 70 per cent of organisations employing 200 or more employees and 45 per cent of organisations employing 50 or more to be recognised as Investors in People; 10,000 small organisations to be recognised as Investors in People.

Figure 79.1

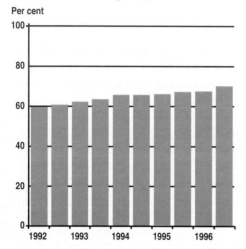

(a) Proportion of 19 year olds qualified to at least NVQ level 2 or equivalent, UK

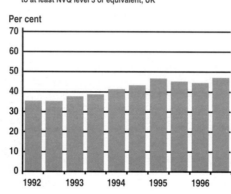

(b) Proportion of 21 year olds qualified to at least NVQ level 3 or equivalent, UK

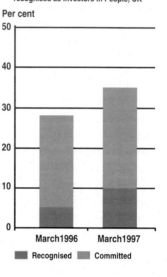

(c) Proportion of organisations with 50 or more employees, committed to or recognised as investors in People, UK

Source: adapted from Labour Force Survey; DfEE; Welsh Office and Scottish Office; Investors in People UK; Advisory Scottish Council for Education and Training Targets.

(a) Describe the trends taking place in Figure 79.1.
(b) Explain two ways in which the trends might affect a business.

(c) Discuss whether the data shows that progress is being made towards achieving government targets.

their performance is inadequate, areas where they have problems, and any 'gaps' in their knowledge and skills. This should make them more committed to training. Training needs are found at different levels within a business.

- The organisational level. A business may need to train workers if there have been changes in a company's goals or objectives, or an introduction of new processes. For example, a move to 'Just-in-time' methods of stock control (☞ unit 94) may mean that workers must be able to constantly monitor stock. Training may also be needed as a result of company surveys or changes in the law. Sometimes workers find that their jobs no longer exist, due to changes in technology or reorganisation of the business for example. As a result, it may be necessary to **retrain** these workers in the knowledge and skills needed for completely new jobs.
- The departmental level. An indication of the need for training may come from personnel statistics, such as

absence levels, turnover levels, production levels and customer complaints. Any differences between departments could show that training is needed.
- The individual level. At this level information from appraisal may be useful. Managers may also request that employees receive extra training. Increasingly, however, workers are identifying their own needs and designing their own personal development plans.

Once a need for training has been identified, a business must decide what skills and approaches should be achieved at the end of the training period. They may be something as simple as 'be able to replace a tyre'. There may also be some criteria to measure how well the trainee has learnt the skill, such as 'type a letter with no more than one mistake', and details on how to perform a task, such as 'always be polite and helpful when taking telephone calls'.

Training needs may be put together as a training or staff development plan. However, the business must take into account whether it has the financial resources to carry out the plan. This will depend on its **training budget**.

The cost of training

Businesses faced with problems may see spending on training as a luxury which has to be cut. This is often the case in times of recession (☞ unit 21). In 1991, for example, the number of people receiving job-related training fell by 177,000 in the UK from the 1990 figure. This was the first fall since figures were first recorded in 1984. Businesses often argue that training leads to increased costs, disruption, wasted time and more effort on their part. Financial costs might include the wage allowance paid to the employee, supervision costs, fees for training at a local college and equipment and travel allowances. To some extent these costs are offset by government payments for training schemes paid to the employer. In 1998 the Institute of Employment Research calculated the costs of training an employee to NVQ level 2. These varied from one industry to another, as shown in Table 79.2.

Table 79.2 *Average annual net costs of training to NVQ level 2*

Industry	Excluding government funding (£)	Including government funding (£)
Electronics	1,010	(345)
Food retailing	1,153	255
Financial services	1,619	1,463
Hotel and catering	3,384	2,384
Construction	8,994	5,354

Figures in brackets show net benefit
Source: adapted from Institute for Employment Research.

On-the-job and off-the-job training

The Spring 1998 Labour Force Survey showed that nearly 3.4 million employees of working age said that they had received job-related training in the four weeks before the survey. The figure for Spring 1995 was 2.8 million. Training is sometimes divided into two types. **On-the-job training** takes place when employees are trained while they are carrying out an activity, often at their place of work. **Off-the-job training** takes place away from the job at a different location. It may, for example, involve release from the job for periods of time to attend a course at a college.

Methods of training

Business may use a variety of training methods. Some might be carried out as the job is being done. Others might take place away from the job. Sometimes training may be a combination of training whilst doing the job and away from

An Institute of Personnel and Development (IPD) report suggested that employees get most of their job knowledge from colleagues, not from courses. Pilkington UK, the glassmaker, developed 220 supervisors and managers as trainers and assessors to maintain standards of production techniques. Over three years the initial 220 passed on their knowledge to 900 employees. The employees benefited by earning higher pay as they learned more skills. Not all on-the-job training is so well-organised. The IPD concluded that too many companies allow on-the-job training to be carried out in a way which does not make the most of its potential, despite the fact that it can be a cost-effective method of training.

Source: adapted from the *Financial Times*, 6.3.1997.

(a) Why was training at Pilkington an example of on-the-job training?
(b) Explain why on-the-job training was a cost effective method of training at Pilkington.

the place of work.

Sitting next to 'Nellie' This is a traditional type of on-the-job training. 'Nellie', the experienced worker, shows the trainee exactly what to do. It can vary from working next to a machine operator to travelling with a salesperson. One-to-one training like this has complications for a business. Where one employee is training another, the quality of the training will depend on the ability, willingness and time available to the tutor. Such training may mean that one employee does not 'produce' themselves, while they are training the other employee. In cases where a specialist is employed to train others, this can be costly for the business.

Coaching This is where a coach will guide the trainee through the use of the equipment or a process in the same way that swimmers are trained. An example might be a technician being trained how to operate a heart monitor whilst working in a hospital.

Mentoring This involves the trainee being 'paired' with a more experienced employee. The trainee carries out the job but uses the 'tutor' to discuss problems that may occur and how best to solve them

Job rotation In some large companies this has been used for the training of 'high fliers'. The employee works in different departments for short periods - picking up skills from each. The aim is that when the person is promoted and reaches the 'top' of the business, she will have a range of experiences which can be used.

In-house courses Businesses may put on courses for their employees and staff them from their own workers. One example is induction courses, which are used to introduce new recruits to a business and help them settle in. A firm might also run a course aimed at achieving a specific goal. For example, if a new computer system was introduced into a department, employees in the section may be trained in its use on a short course. Courses may also be run by the personnel department for marketing and finance managers in the business, to help them improve staff motivation. Some businesses have their own training centres. For example, the former Yorkhill NHS Trust in Glasgow has its own centre where staff can learn skills as varied as word processing and negotiating. Barclays Bank and many insurance companies have similar centres.

Another option is for a business to run its own courses away from the place of work. It could be for one day, a weekend, a week or a longer period. Courses are often for specialist reasons, such as working in teams or Total Quality Management (☞ unit 95). These courses can make use of simulations. One example is in the training of pilots, when trainee pilots can learn to fly a plane without the worry of accidents. Businesses sometimes simulate business activity during courses. Trainees are divided into teams and compete with each other, making business decisions and carrying out tasks. Other forms of simulation might include an 'in-tray exercise', where the trainee might be told they are leaving the country tomorrow and must clear an in-tray of letters and memos. Sometimes these course lead to qualifications.

Self-awareness training This is where trainees complete self-assessment questionnaires, such as a Myers-Briggs. Questions may be asked about personal values, individual learning styles, how the individual interacts with others, personality and interests. The trainee then receives feedback from the person carrying out the questionnaire.

Traditional apprenticeships In the past, businesses took on 'trainee' workers. They served an 'apprenticeship' over a period of time, often in a skilled trade to become a tradesperson, such as a carpenter. When they 'qualified' they were made employees of the business.

Graduate training Some businesses run graduate training programmes. These are designed for graduates with degree qualifications and are often used to train employees for senior or management positions in the business. The Labour Force Survey estimated that employees with a degree or equivalent qualification are five and a half times more likely to receive job-related training than those with no qualifications.

Vocational courses There are may different organisations that provide work related or 'vocational' training. Trainees usually work towards a vocational qualification. These are awarded by organisations such as BTEC (Edexcel), RSA (OCR), City & Guilds (AQA) and professional bodies such as

The Institute of Personnel Management and the Royal College of Nursing. National Vocational qualifications (NVQs) are work based qualifications in areas ranging from hairdressing to engineering. They are offered by businesses, often as a combination of work within the business and release to attend a college. General National Vocational Qualifications (GNVQs) are offered by schools and colleges. They are aimed mainly at 14-19 year olds. Vocational training

Question 3

According to Adrian Furnham, Professor of Psychology at University College London, company training departments should be made redundant. He argues that it is inefficient and counter-productive to employ in-house, full-time trainers. As organisations like Shell and Du Pont have discovered, the attitude to, enthusiasm for, benefit of, and cost of training is improved if it is carried out elsewhere. He suggests that staff need specialist technical and managerial training, refresher courses to practice skills, and training on ever-changing computer systems. They also need to be trained in business skills such as letter writing, understanding financial statements and project management. But this is best done by carefully selected, audited and monitored outside specialists. Why?

● To get cost effective use out of trainers, they need to be 'in the classroom' about 70 per cent of the time. That is a lot of training time, perhaps too much for the organisation and even the trainer.
● Trainers burn out easily. Training is an exhausting task. The working life expectancy of full-time trainers is rather short.
● Trainers are difficult to manage. This is partly due to the sort of people that are trainers. They tend to be performers. They get attracted by new-fangled ideas. They may often talk scientific nonsense because they cannot keep up to date.
● Most in-house trainers are not interested in or do not understand business issues.
● Training must be flexible and dynamic. Yet in-house courses tend to be repeated because this is easier for the trainer.
● Over time trainers tend to know more about their own business and less about outside matters. Outsiders, on the other hand, have a wealth of comparative knowledge.

The solution to these problems is to buy in trainers from outside. Ideally the businesses will have a portfolio of tried and trusted trainers with individual expertise in areas required. 'Hired when required; fired when tired', is his optimal solution.

Source: adapted from the *Financial Times*, 3,3,1997.

(a) Using information from the article, suggest three benefits of a training course.
(b) Discuss why external courses may be better able to provide these benefits than in-house courses.
(c) Examine the possible implications for a business of switching its training from in-house to external sources.

is simulated in areas such as art and design and health and social care. Universities may also provide vocationally related courses.

Self-paced/distance learning There is a number of terms for self-paced learning. These include distance learning, open learning and flexible learning. The main feature of all these approaches is that the trainee controls the pace and the timing of their own learning. Learning is often from materials provided by a tutor. There may be a meeting at the end of a certain period. The main problem with this form of training is the lack of help when the trainee finds the materials difficult.

Training initiatives

In the 1990s, various attempts were made to improve training in the UK.

Modern Apprenticeships (Mod App) These were launched in 1994. By 1998 over 225,000 people had started a Mod App and 133,000 were still training. They aim to increase the number of young people undergoing training who achieve NVQs of at least level 3 for technical, craft and junior management skills. In most firms, Mod Apps have employee status and earn a wage. The scheme is administered through employers, Training and Enterprise Councils (TECs) and industrial training organisations. Government funding covered about £6,000 of the average £25,000 cost of an apprenticeship, which takes up to three years to complete. There are Modern Apprenticeships in more than 72 industries. Many are in traditional areas, such as engineering and manufacturing, but one aim is to improve training standards in services. One of the strongest attractions of apprenticeships is the employment prospects they offer.

New Deal In 1998, 20,000 employers had signed up to The New Deal. This is a scheme which provided subsidised training and employment for 18-24 year olds. 75,000 young people had joined the scheme by 1998 and just over half of all people leaving the scheme found unsubsidised jobs. Those who do not find jobs could either:
- take a job with an employer that would receive a subsidy;
- work on an environmental task force;
- work in the voluntary sector;
- have up to 12 months education and training.
Each would include one day a week training towards a qualification.

National Training Organisations (NTOs) The government has set up National Training Organisations (NTOs) for specific industries, a Training Standards Council to monitor training quality in businesses, schools and colleges, and a Skills Taskforce to develop national skills.

DfEE and TECs The Department for Education and Employment is responsible for training. At a local level, Training and Enterprise Councils (TECs) (unit 2) identify, encourage and deliver training needs in areas in which they operate. They are responsible for managing government funding, making payments to businesses that were training employees. It was proposed in the late 1990s that after the year 2001 some of the work of TECs may be taken over by Learning and Skills Councils.

National Traineeships (NT) These would include occupational and key skills training to NVQ level 2 and include the same features as Modern Apprenticeships. After completion trainees progress onto a Mod App or another form of training. NTOs in industries such as travel agencies and plumbing would design training for their own needs and help in its delivery. By 1998 over 23,000 young people were taking NTs.

Work based training for adults This was aimed at adults who had been employed for a period of time. Between 1997-98, over 116,000 adults had started on WBT. 71 per cent completed the training and 43 per cent gained a job after training.

Question 4

The National Museums and Galleries on Merseyside (NMGM) runs eight museums including the award winning Conservation Centre in Liverpool. It gained Investors in People (IiP) recognition after more than eighty staff took part in the first NVQ in cleaning building interiors. They were learning a range of specialist skills, including machine buffing, carpet cleaning and customer care. NMGM had become an accredited assessment centre for NVQs as a result.

Cleaning services manager Pauline Coughlan, who designed the course, said: 'the museums and galleries represent Merseyside, so it is essential that we provide a quality service, ensuring all venues are sparkling clean. The cleaners are proud of their work and gaining NVQs has boosted their morale and confidence.' It was also suggested that gaining IiP status was a great boost to NMGM. Staff could understand that they had a valuable contribution to make to the organisation and could look to further their careers.

Source: adapted from *Employment News*, DfEE, May 1998.

(a) Identify the features that were designed to improve training at NMGM.
(b) Explain how these training initiatives could benefit the organisation.

Investors in People This is a DfEE initiative, set up in 1991, to encourage the development of skills in the workplace. It provides a training and employee relations quality standard to which employers can commit themselves. To achieve the standard, employers must meet certain criteria. These include a commitment to develop all employees, regular planning to review training, action to develop new recruits and existing staff, and evaluating investment in training. Companies that achieve the standard can display a plaque, which is valid for a certain period.

Evaluation of training

As businesses have demanded greater value for money, it has become important to evaluate training. Evaluation is simple when the result of the training is clear to see, such as when training workers to use new technology. Where training is designed to give a certain result, such as:

● a health and safety course;
● a word processing course;
● a design course;

evaluation can be based on observed results. This may be a reduction in accidents, increased typing speed or designs with greater impact.

It is more difficult to evaluate the success of a management training course or a programme of social skills development. It is usual to use end of course questionnaires, where course members answer a number of questions. The problem is that the course will have been a break for most employees from the normal work routine. This can make the participants' view of training appear of more value than it is. Also questionnaires tend to evaluate the course and not the learning. This often means that the person attending the course is assessing the quality of the tutors and visual aids, instead of what has been learnt.

To overcome these problems a business might:
● ask participants and managers to complete a short questionnaire at the start of the course to focus their minds on what they hope to get from it;
● give out another questionnaire at the end of the course focusing on learning and what could be applied back at the job;
● give further questionnaires to review the effects of the course on performance.

This helps employees to concentrate on what has been learnt. This process may, however, be costly for the business.

Appraisal

After a period of time working in a job (and regularly after), a firm may APPRAISE the employee. This is an attempt by the business to find out the qualities, usefulness or worth of its employees.

Appraisal can be used by a business to:
● improve performance;
● provide feedback;
● increase motivation;
● identify training needs;
● identify potential for promotion;
● award salary increases;
● set out job objectives;
● provide information for human resource planning;
● assess the effectiveness of the selection process.

The problem with having all of these aims is that the person carrying out the appraisal may have conflicting roles. If appraisal is designed to help performance and to act as a basis for salary awards, the appraiser would have to be both judge and helper at the same time. This makes it difficult to be impartial. It is also difficult for the person being appraised. A worker may want to discuss problems, but is likely to be cautious about what they say in case they jeopardise any possible pay rise. One way around this is for the appraisal system to review the performance of the worker only.

Many appraisal schemes have been linked to **performance appraisal**. This involves observing, measuring and developing the performance of employees. Performance can be 'measured' against criteria such as output, quality and speed.

Carrying out appraisal

Appraisal has, in the past, been seen as most suitable for employees in management and supervisory positions. Increasingly, clerical, secretarial and manual staff, with skilled or technical jobs, are also being appraised.

Who carries out the appraisal? There is a number of people that might be involved in appraising an individual. Appraisers may be referred to as **raters**. These are people who 'rate' the performance of an individual.

● Superiors. Most appraisals are carried out by the employee's superior. The advantage of this is that the supervisor usually has intimate knowledge of the tasks that a worker has been carrying out and how well they have been done.
● People 'above' the immediate superior can be involved in appraisal in two different ways. They may 'approve' the superior's appraisal of the employee. A manager further up the hierarchy may also directly carry out the appraisal. This is more likely to happen when individuals decide if a worker has the potential for promotion, for example.
● Self appraisal. This is a relatively new idea and not greatly used. Individuals do carry out self appraisal in traditional appraisal schemes, although the superior's decision officially 'counts'. The ratings that the employer has given may be changed, however, in the light of the employee's comments.
● Peer appraisal. It is sometimes argued that appraisal by peers is reliable and valid as they have a more comprehensive view of the employee's job performance. The main problem, though, is that peers may be unwilling to appraise each other. This can be seen as 'grassing'.
● Subordinates. Appraisal by subordinates is another less

A letter in the *Financial Times* asked whether the effectiveness of managers could be improved by introducing 360 degrees feedback. The person writing the letter said that the idea sounded fraught with danger and asked: 'Don't you think it's asking for trouble to encourage subordinates to criticise their managers?' Part of the response from Professor Hunt said: 'You're right to be concerned: done badly, 360 degrees feedback is potentially lethal. But handled carefully, these surveys can provide a powerful lever for change. For the first time in many organisations, the capability of the manager is assessed by those he or she manages.

You probably already have an annual appraisal system where you as a boss assess the performance of your direct subordinates, help them establish goals and prioritise them, and discuss their training needs. The annual review is one way to ensure the flow of feedback that we need to keep us well adjusted. Companies rarely jump straight from a traditional appraisal scheme to 360 degrees feedback. Usually they experiment with a survey of the direct subordinates of a manager - called in the trade a 180 degrees feedback survey. Most frequently the survey is part of a management development course. If this were you, you would select one of the feedback questionnaires on the market, or design your own, distribute it to your direct subordinates and ask them to complete it. They would then send it anonymously to an outside agent for processing. The aggregated results would be fed back to you as part of the management development course and would provide the structure for the skills training on that course. From

180 degrees the surveys might be extended from your direct subordinates to include bosses and peers. You would also complete the survey as a self-assessment to compare your results with those of the others.

Why do I say feedback like this is potentially lethal? There have been numerous examples where the trust that is essential to the success of this process has been violated. For example, managers who do not like their feedback conduct an inquisition by asking respondents to indicate which were their responses. If this happens, it is essential that the person handling the survey becomes involved immediately, confronts the manager and puts out a potential bush fire. Otherwise, the process of introducing a more open feedback of opinion can be set back for years.

You are clearly worried that your managers might be demotivated by negative comments. It is true that people tend to remember the negative and ignore the positive feedback. But the fact is that in the 15 years that we have been using 360 degrees feedback the vast majority of feedback on managers is positive.'

Source: adapted from the *Financial Times*, 8.12.1997.

(a) What objectives of appraisal are highlighted in the article?
(b) (i) What methods of carrying out the appraisal schemes are explained in the article?
    (ii) Who is involved in each method of appraisal?
(c) Explain the: (i) advantages; and (ii) disadvantages; of the appraisal schemes mentioned in the article.

well used method. It is limited, as subordinates will only know certain aspects of the work of other employees.

- 360 degrees appraisal. This method gathers ratings from a combination of supervisors, peers and subordinates. Self-ratings and customer ratings may also be used. It provides feedback to individuals on how their performance is viewed by business stakeholders (☞ unit 3). It also encourages individuals to self-diagnose their strong and weak areas and identifies where training is needed. The information from 360 degrees appraisal can help a business when making personnel decisions, such as who to choose for promotion.

Many firms have used appraisal systems only to find that they have to change or abandon them after a short time. Others 'battle' on with the system, but recognise that it is inadequate or disliked. What factors influence the success of an appraisal system?

- Purpose of the system. Effectiveness will be greater if all involved are clear about what the system is for.
- Control. It is vital that the system is controlled by senior and line management and isn't something done simply 'for the personnel department'.
- Openness and participation. The more feedback that appraisees are given about their ratings, the more likely they are to accept the process. Similarly, the more the employee is allowed to take part in the system, the greater the chance of gaining their commitment.

- Appraisal criteria. The criteria must be related to the job, be easy to use and appear fair to the worker.
- Training. Training may be needed in how to appraise and how to conduct interviews.
- Administrative efficiency. Appraisal must be carried out so that it causes as few problems as possible for both parties. It also needs to be confidential.
- Action. Appraisal needs to be supported by follow-up action. Plans that are agreed by appraiser and workers must be checked, to make sure they take place.
- Selection of raters. The choice of rater should be carefully controlled to avoid, for example, individuals nominating only 'friendly raters' to provide them with feedback.
- Anonymity of raters. Ratings should be made anonymously to encourage honest appraisal.
- Training of raters. Raters should be trained to complete rating and appraisal forms accurately.

Key terms

Appraisal - evaluating the usefulness of the employee to the business.
Induction - the introduction of a new employee to the business.
Skills shortages - where potential employees do not have the skills demanded by employers.

Summary

1. Briefly explain the purpose of induction.
2. Why is training important to a business?
3. Give 5 aims of training.
4. State 4 methods which could be used to identify training needs.
5. What is the difference between on-the-job and off-the-job training?
6. Briefly explain 3 methods of off-the-job training.
7. How can training be evaluated?
8. What is meant by performance appraisal?
9. How can appraisal help a business?
10. Who might carry out appraisal in a business?

Case study

The North East marine and offshore industry

North-East England's marine and offshore industry is benefiting from a dramatic increase in orders. The last three years have seen a shift from mass redundancies at former shipbuilder Swan Hunter to a position where Liebherr, the Sunderland cranemaker, is importing Austrian workers to meet demand.

The days when Tyneside yards could telephone experienced workers on the dole and have them in work by lunchtime are a memory. 'It's all down to success,' says Mr Alastair Rodgers, director of the Northern Offshore Federation (NOF), which represents 280 North-Eastern and Cumbrian companies. 'Skill shortages are set against a background of a high success rate.' The area's offshore industry skills are currently in great demand.

For the last 25 years the industry, which supplies oil and gas companies, has directly employed about 20,000 workers. It was geared in the 1980s to making sections of North Sea rigs, but has also performed strongly in new undersea and floating installations. But while the declining shipbuilding industry was a major training ground, interest in long-term training has suffered because of its project-based and cyclical nature. With a £885,000 European Regional Development Fund grant, the NOF wants to foster a proactive, long-term approach to skills availability. Its survey of 94 members shows 43 per cent have recruitment problems. Pipefitters and specialised welders are particularly in demand. Employers believe the shortage could be due to high demand for ship repairers, local economic growth and retirement of skilled shipbuilders. The NOF is concerned that the shortages will lead to big companies raising wages to lure employees from small businesses. Quality matters as much as quantity; raising skills levels is crucial to international competitiveness in an industry driven by technological change.

One remedy lies with the new skills-based Modern Apprenticeships. In Tyne-Tees about 115 young people are apprenticed under initiatives involving marine and offshore industry. 'It's probably 115 more than two to three years ago,' says Mr Jim Kinson, NOF's training manager. However, it will be 2002 before these trainees are fully skilled. 'We see Modern Apprenticeships as the future, but we also have to address the present and near future,' says Mr Rodgers.

The NOF also plans a mentor scheme for pre-retirement workers to train new entrants, traineeships for unemployed adults and short skills courses. Through work placements, the NOF hopes graduates will view the industry as a potential long-term career. Keeping pace with technology is another issue. 'We have always had surface coating but it was called painting,' says Mr Rodgers. The NOF is training assessors and creating National Vocational Qualifications, in a bid to upgrade skills and reward employees.

To tackle labour shortages, the NOF says some companies must pool labour, encourage multi-skilling, employ more permanent staff and increase automation.

It believes commitment to training is increasing, and some companies such as Northumberland-based Hedley Purvis clearly take it seriously. Yet Hedley Purvis, a family owned business, illustrates the difficulties of balancing a cyclical order book with skills retention. Sales are up about 20 per cent annually, but its need for mechanical fitters can halve when autumn and winter weather cuts demand. Hedley Purvis has 90 employees working on NVQs, including some temporary staff. 'We try to retain the best ones and take the pain during the winter months,' says marketing manager Mr David Brown. Contracting out by big companies aggravates matters, says Mr Brown. 'The largest companies are expecting the smaller companies to solve their manpower problems.'

Source: adapted from the *Financial Times*, 29.1.1997.

(a) (i) **What is meant by the term 'skills shortages'?**
(ii) **Suggest reasons why these skills shortages exist in the North East.**
(b) (i) **Explain the types of on-the-job and off-the-job training mentioned in the article.**
(ii) **Examine possible advantages and problems of these types of training for businesses in the North East.**
(c) **What are the: (i) aims of training; (ii) problems of training; highlighted in the article?**
(d) **Discuss the problems that a business may have in appraising a welder or a pipefitter.**

What are equal opportunities?

Unit 77 explained the methods used to select candidates. Choosing one candidate rather than another is known as DISCRIMINATION. If a man is chosen rather than a woman, when they are both equally qualified, the business has discriminated in favour of the man and against the woman.

Some discrimination is legal and may be considered reasonable. For example, a business may choose a candidate for the post of quality controller in a meat factory because he has 10 years experience, rather than a school leaver. However, if another person with experience did not get the job because she was a woman, or from an ethnic minority, this is illegal in the UK. It could also be said to be unreasonable. The rest of the unit will use the term discrimination in this way. Discrimination occurs not only in selection, but areas such as training, promotion and wages.

EQUAL OPPORTUNITIES mean that everyone has the same chance. In other words, a candidate or employee is not discriminated against because of their sex or race. UK legislation helps to promote this. So do EU laws.

Why are businesses concerned about equal opportunities? We will see that giving everyone the same chance can affect the productivity, costs and organisation of a business.

Reasons for discrimination

There are certain groups of individuals in society and in business that are arguably discriminated against. Such groups may include:
● women;
● people from ethnic minorities;
● disabled people;
● older people.
Discrimination often occurs because of **unproven** ideas or stereotypes about certain groups, such as the following examples.
● Women should not work because their place is in the home or with children; women don't want to take too much responsibility at work because of home commitments; women who are married are less likely to want to be relocated; women with children will be less reliable than men because their main responsibility is to their children.
● Members of certain ethnic minority groups are difficult to employ because of problems with religious holidays. Also, some overstate their qualifications to obtain jobs.
● A person in a wheelchair will be an embarrassment to other workers or is somehow 'mentally' disadvantaged; someone who has suffered from mental illness will crack up under the pressure.
● Older people are less adaptable, are not interested in

coping with new technology and work much more slowly.
All these and many other unproven ideas can affect the way people view these groups during recruitment and selection, and when they are employed.

Women at work

Women form a large and increasing proportion of the working population. In 1979 women accounted for around 38 per cent of all people of working age in employment. By 1997, this had risen to nearly 42 per cent and was 44 per cent in 1998.

The 1990s saw a growth in women's employment opportunities. The need for a more flexible workforce and demographic changes (☞ unit 20) meant that businesses increasingly looked to women to fill vacancies, especially part time jobs. Some businesses offered creche facilities to encourage women workers with children. More women wanted to return to work after having children. Increasing numbers of women returned to study and gained qualifications.

However, there was still evidence to suggest that women were discriminated against at work.
● There were differences between men's and women's earnings. In 1998 women's average gross weekly earnings were 73 per cent of men's in full time jobs. Differences in earnings varied from one occupation to another. Women's earnings in full time jobs were 90 per cent of men's in transport and storage industries, but 72 per cent in manufacturing. Average gross hourly earnings including overtime were also different. For women in full time jobs it was £8.23 an hour compared to £10.20 for men, as shown in Figure 80.1.
● Certain occupations, such as skilled construction work, are almost exclusively male. This is shown in Figure 80.2.

Figure 80.1 *Average gross hourly earnings, employees on adult rates; GB, April 1986-98, £*

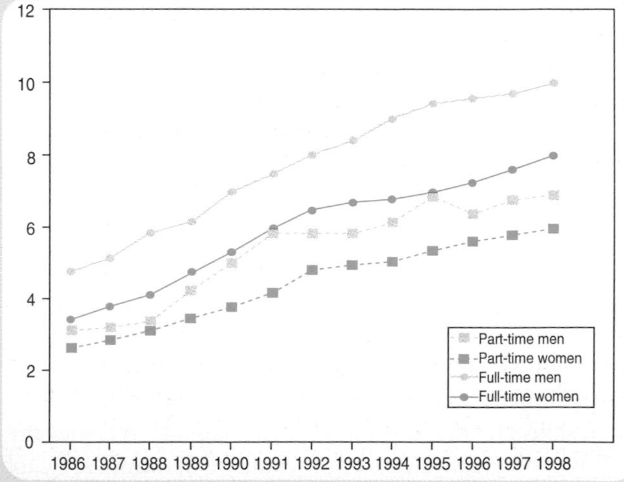

Source: adapted from New Earnings Survey.

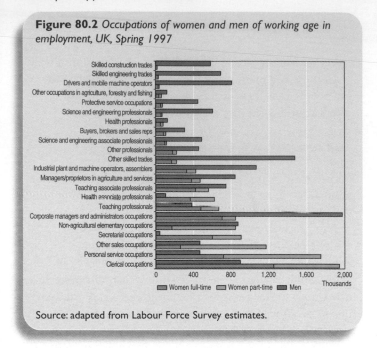

Figure 80.2 *Occupations of women and men of working age in employment, UK, Spring 1997*

Skilled construction trades
Skilled engineering trades
Drivers and mobile machine operators
Other occupations in agriculture, forestry and fishing
Protective service occupations
Science and engineering professionals
Health professionals
Buyers, brokers and sales reps
Science and engineering associate professionals
Other professionals
Other skilled trades
Industrial plant and machine operators, assemblers
Managers/proprietors in agriculture and services
Teaching associate professionals
Health associate professionals
Teaching professionals
Corporate managers and administrators occupations
Non-agricultural elementary occupations
Secretarial occupations
Other sales occupations
Personal service occupations
Clerical occupations

0   400   800   1,200   1,600   2,000
Thousands

Women full-time   Women part-time   Men

Source: adapted from Labour Force Survey estimates.

● Those occupations that employ mainly women tend to involve low pay. Personal services, such as hairdressing, might be an example, as shown in Figure 80.2.

● In the late 1990s nine out of ten male employees worked full time, compared to only six out of ten female employees.

● Women may leave work to have children. When they return, they will not be as far along the pay scale as men and so may have lower wages. They also tend to take part time work. This has meant that employers are unwilling to employ females in demanding, well paid jobs for fear they will leave. It has also meant that they have been overlooked for promotion.

Legislation and guidance

There are two main laws that deal with the promotion of sexual equality at work.

The **Equal Pay Act 1970** stated that an employee doing the same or 'broadly similar' work as a member of staff of the opposite sex is entitled to equal rates of pay and conditions. The Act aimed to eliminate discrimination (mainly against women) in wages and other conditions of work, such as holidays, overtime, hours and duties. The Equal Pay Act was amended in 1983 to allow female employees to claim equal pay for work of 'equal value' to that done by a man. The 1970 Act ruled that women should be paid equal pay for work which is 'like work' or 'work rated as equivalent' to that of a man. But the 1983 amendment made it possible for equal pay to be claimed for work of equal value in 'terms of the demands made on her'. Such demands could include the effort, skills and decisions made by a woman. Whether the work was of equal value or not would be determined by job evaluation (☞ unit 76).

The **Sex Discrimination Act 1975** made it generally unlawful to discriminate either directly or indirectly against someone on grounds of their sex or being married. Direct discrimination is where an employer treats someone less favourably than another person because of their sex. An example would be where a woman was not employed because it was felt she would not fit in because of her sex. It would also include harassment at work. Indirect discrimination is where an employment condition is applied equally to men and women, but women have less chance of complying with it. An example might be if an employer insists on an employee being over, say, six feet tall when it is not necessary for the job. Discrimination is unlawful in areas such as job advertisements, selection, interviews, promotion, training, dismissal and terms of employment. In 1986 the Act was updated, removing restrictions on women's hours of work. This meant that women were more able to take jobs with flexible hours or shift work.

These two Acts have implications for recruitment and selection.

● Advertisements must not discriminate on the basis of sex or marital status. This means that job titles should be sexless, as in 'cashier' or 'salesperson.'

● There is a greater need for job analysis, job descriptions and person specifications (☞ unit 76). In particular, a person specification must not restrict the job to men or women, unless it is essential.

● Interviews carried out in a structured way can help to limit any prejudice that an interviewer may have.

The effects on the whole business are dealt with later in this unit. If employees feel that they have been discriminated against, they can take their cases to an **industrial tribunal**. They can also request help from the **Equal Opportunities Commission (EOC)**, a government body which:

● works toward eliminating discrimination;

● tries to promote equal opportunities;

● helps employees making complaints;

● investigates complaints of discrimination;

● issues notices preventing a business from discriminating;

● reviews the Equal Pay Act.

In 1997 the EOC drew up a statutory code of practice on equal pay. This contained descriptions of how businesses could organise their pay systems to avoid unfair discrimination. By 1998, however, the EOC was arguing for reform of equal pay legislation. In particular it called for a new Sex Equality Bill to deal with the 'pay gap' between men and women, a ban on sexual harassment, tighter rules to deal with clubs that exclude women and a requirement of public bodies to promote equal opportunities.

The European Union (EU) has legislation regarding equal pay. Article 119 of the Treaty of Rome says that men and women should receive equal pay for equal work. The Equal Pay Directive 75/119 states that for the same work or work of equal value sex discrimination must be eliminated in all aspects of pay. It also states that where a job classification is used to determine pay, it

Question 1

A A £75,000 settlement was paid to Patricia Gordon in a discrimination case. She had worked for the London Borough of Hackney between 1987-92 and held senior posts before a job cutting exercise identified that her post was no longer needed. She was offered another post, but that new post was then deleted. Other colleagues in exactly the same position, whose posts had been deleted, were given retraining and help and advice on job opportunities. The UNISON legal officer said that there was still an 'old boy network culture' in the authority.

B Teachers at the City of London School for Girls had traditionally been paid less than those at the City of London School for Boys. In 1995 the pay scales were merged, but teachers were slotted into the new scales at their existing rates of pay. Eileen Halloran, a former PE teacher at the City of London School for Girls, was earning £7,000 a year less than a male PE teacher at the boy's school. A tribunal found that this was a case of discrimination. It rejected the arguments that male teachers were paid more because they were harder to find and women were paid less because parents paid lower fees to educate girls.

C Lasertop, a company setting up as a women only health club, advertised vacancies at the new business. A man who applied was told that posts were only suitable for women. He complained to an industrial tribunal. He argued that this was discrimination because jobs that he could not have performed, such as work in the changing rooms, could have been done by other female employees. The tribunal rejected the claim, as the company had no female employees to carry out these personal duties at the time the advertisement was placed.

Source: adapted from *Labour Research*, November 1997, May 1998.

(a) Explain whether or not discrimination took place in the examples above using sexual equality at work legislation to support your arguments.

(b) A sports centre is advertising for an administrative assistant to take bookings and organise activities. Explain three features of the person specification that it may need to consider to avoid sex discrimination.

---

must be based on the same criteria for men and women. The European Court of Justice (ECJ) hears cases and passes rulings relating to sex discrimination in EU countries.

Ethnic minorities

There is evidence that certain ethnic groups are discriminated against, often in recruitment and selection. Figure 80.3 shows that unemployment rates of ethnic minority groups are higher than those of whites for all social classes.

Figure 80.3 *Unemployment rates by social class and ethnic origin, average, Spring 1996-98*

Professional, managerial and technical
Skilled non-manual
Skilled manual
Partly skilled
Unskilled

□ White
■ Ethnic minority groups

Per cent 0 2 4 6 8 10 12 14 16

Source: adapted from Labour Force Survey.

Legislation and guidance

An awareness of the position of ethnic groups has led to anti-discrimination legislation. The **Race Relations Act 1976** makes it generally unlawful to discriminate directly or indirectly on grounds of race. Racial grounds included colour, race, nationality or ethnic origin. Direct discrimination is where a person is treated less favourably compared to someone else on racial grounds. An example would be a person not being employed because it was felt they belonged to a racial group that might be unreliable. Indirect discrimination is where an employment condition is applied equally but a racial group has less chance of complying with it. An example would be not allowing the wearing of turbans, which would rule out Sikhs from being employed. Under the Act an employer can not discriminate on grounds of race:

● in making arrangements for deciding who should be offered the job;
● in the terms offered;
● in refusing or deliberately omitting to offer employment.

The implications for the employer are similar to those of the Sex Discrimination Act. Advertisements should be worded so that there is no indication that some ethnic groups are preferred to others. Writing a job description and person specification will also be useful. The use of selection tests should be monitored. Many tests discriminate against people from minority backgrounds in the way they are designed. Also, people from some ethnic backgrounds may be at a disadvantage because the method of testing is alien to their culture.

The **Race Relations Code of Practice** helps employers and personnel managers when recruiting. It states that:

- employers should not confine advertisements to those areas or publications which could exclude or reduce the number of applicants of a particular ethnic group;
- employers should avoid stating requirements, such as length of residence or experience, and should make clear that overseas qualifications are acceptable;
- any literature sent to applicants should include a statement that the business is an equal opportunity employer.

Guidance is also given when using employment agencies and about selection testing and applications. A guidance pack for employers was published by the Department for Education and Employment in the 1990s titled *Equal Opportunities, Ten Point Plan for Employers*. The pack shows a business how to develop and implement good equal opportunities policies and practices in ten 'points'. For example, point 2 explains how to set targets for the percentage of employees from an under-represented group that the businesses will employ. Point 5 shows a business how to review its recruitment, selection, promotion and training procedures to ensure that they are not discriminating against ethnic minority groups.

It is argued that POSITIVE ACTION by employers is an important part of a good equal opportunities policy. Positive action describes a range of measures that can be taken under the Race Relations Act to provide equality of opportunity for people from certain ethnic groups. Examples of positive action are training to meet the needs of racial groups and encouragement to apply for particular jobs. Positive action is only lawful if people of the racial group are **under-represented** in work.

Employees who feel that they have been discriminated against on grounds of race can take their case to an **industrial tribunal**. The number of claims taken to tribunals in the UK rose from 1,000 a year to 2,000 a year over the period 1986-96. However, more than six out of ten people withdraw their claim before the hearing. The success rate of cases taken to tribunal is low, at under 15 per cent. Modifications to the Treaty of Rome proposed in 1997 meant that European-wide rules on race discrimination were likely to be introduced by the EU after the year 2000.

Disabled people

There are many different ways of defining disabled people. The Labour Force Survey (adjusted) defines them as 'those with a long-term health problem/disability that limits the kind or amount of paid work they can do'. In 1997 nearly 5.8 million people of working age had a disability. Nearly 2.3 million of these were in employment as shown in Table 80.1

Legislation

The **Disability Discrimination Act, 1995** defines disability as 'a physical or mental impairment which has a substantial and long term (at least 12 months) adverse effect on people's

Question 2

Targets for the recruitment of more black and Asian police officers were to be extended to other public services in the late 1990s. These included the armed forces and the fire, immigration and probation services. The changes in public services policy aimed to employ the same percentage of ethnic minorities as there were in the population, around 6 per cent. Nationally just 2 per cent of police officers are from ethnic minorities. In areas where ethnic minorities made up a higher percentage of the population, recruitment targets might be higher. In some parts of London, for example, ethnic minorities made up nearly 20 per cent of the population.

The Home Secretary stated: 'It is not enough for police forces to pay lip service to equal opportunities. It is vital the police demonstrate minority ethnic officers are needed in the force and that they can progress through the ranks on equal terms with colleagues'. The Metropolitan Police announced schemes to recruit the best black and Asian graduates into the Met. A bursary scheme would pay their way through university if they agreed to serve in the force.

Source: adapted from *The Daily Mail*, 20.10.1998.

(a) What ways in which discrimination take place in public services are mentioned in the article?
(b) Explain the possible benefits to police forces of the new recruitment policies.
(c) To what extent do the changes in the police force policies represent positive action by the employer?

Table 80.1 *Number of disabled people, GB*

000s

	All	In employment	of which full-time
Spring 1992	4,557	1,769	1,282
Summer 1992	4,665	1,816	1,320
Autumn 1992	4,808	1,879	1,332
Winter 1992/3	4,906	1,868	1,322
Summer 1993*	5,112	2,001	1,429
Winter 1993/4*	5,180	1,995	1,434
Summer 1994*	5,059	1,957	1,420
Winter 1994/5*	5,176	1,956	1,395
Summer 1995*	5,280	2,012	1,423
Winter 1995/6*	5,307	2,009	1,425
Spring 1996*	5,510	2,181	1,562
Summer 1996*	5,663	2,250	1,636
Autumn 1996*	5,735	2,311	1,665
Winter 1996/7*	5,778	2,289	1,649

Source: adapted from Labour Force Survey (*adjusted for changes in frequency of disability questions).

ability to carry out normal day-to-day activities'. The Act makes it unlawful for a business (with 20 or more employees in 1996, although this figure may change) to discriminate

against a person in:
- recruitment;
- selection or dismissal;
- the terms of employment offered;
- promotion, transfers, training or other benefits.

A business would discriminate if it treats one person **less favourably** than others for a reason relating to disability, unless the treatment is **justified**.

What is less favourable treatment? An example of discrimination might be if two people applied for a job as a translator, but a disabled person in a wheelchair did not get the job because of his disability, even though he was the better translator. Discrimination would also take place if a business asked the disabled person for a driving licence when no driving was involved in the job of translator. To avoid discrimination, a disabled person must be given the job if he is the best candidate.

When is less favourable treatment justified? There must be relevant and substantial (ie not trivial) reasons to treat people less favourably to avoid discrimination. For example, if the employer had to move to new premises just for one disabled candidate to be employed, this might be a substantial reason not to employ the worker. However, employers must make 'reasonable' adjustments for disabled workers. These are adjustments that involve relatively little cost or disruption. They might include:
- changing fixtures, fittings, furniture and equipment, such as modified telephones for people with hearing difficulties or workstations for people in wheel chairs;
- improving access to a building, such as adding a ramp for a wheelchair user;
- changing building features, such as braille in a lift to help a visually impaired employee;
- changing work conditions, such as allowing absences for treatment;
- providing extra training.

Older people

There is some evidence to suggest that older people are discriminated against.
- Despite their willingness to work, older people find it more difficult to get jobs. The proportion of unemployed people out of work for more than a year is 50 per cent for men and 30 per cent for women aged 20-24. For people aged 50-64 it is 60 per cent for men and 50 per cent for women.
- Employment rates fall as people get older as shown in Table 80.2. The employment rate is the percentage of the population in a given age group in employment.
- The earning power of men falls after age 50 and women age 40 as shown in Table 80.3.
- Training opportunities fall as workers get older. The proportion of employees being trained fell from 14 per cent for workers aged 20-24 to 6 per cent for men and women aged 50-64.

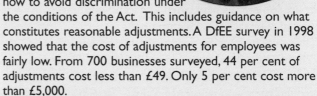

Question 3

The Disability Discrimination Act places a duty on a business to make 'reasonable adjustments' to working conditions for disabled employees. The Department for Education and Employment publishes guidance for employers on how to avoid discrimination under the conditions of the Act. This includes guidance on what constitutes reasonable adjustments. A DfEE survey in 1998 showed that the cost of adjustments for employees was fairly low. From 700 businesses surveyed, 44 per cent of adjustments cost less than £49. Only 5 per cent cost more than £5,000.

Despite this, there is still evidence that discrimination takes place. A visually impaired chemist was awarded £100,000 compensation when a tribunal decided he had been discriminated against by British Sugar. The worker was made redundant in March 1997. The tribunal found that his assessment under redundancy selection criteria was influenced by his disability. He scored 0 out of 10 for performance and competence even though this had never been criticised before. He also had points deducted for absenteeism despite the fact that his absences were related to his disability.

Source: adapted from *Labour Research*, April 1998, May 1998.

(a) Why might there have been discrimination against the disabled worker?
(b) Using information from the article, discuss what is meant by a 'reasonable adjustment' for a business.
(c) Suggest possible 'reasonable' adjustments that could be made for a visually impaired worker and the effects that they might have on a business.

Table 80.2 *Employment rate by age (%)*

	All	Men	Women
25-24	79.4	87.0	71.7
50-54	74.9	81.2	68.6
55-59	59.7	68.6	51.0
60-64	36.7	48.0	-
all workers	73.4	78.6	67.8

Source: adapted from Labour Force Survey.

Legislation

In the 1990s the main protection for older employees was against redundancy (☞ unit 78). Older employees made redundant are often entitled to severance pay. In difficult periods, older people may be the first to be made redundant.

Table 80.3 *Full time workers' average gross weekly earnings*

Age range	Male manual	Male non-manual	Female manual	Female non-manual
under 18	130.00	152.00	143.40	117.80
18-20	188.50	192.60	150.90	174.80
21-24	256.50	296.10	189.20	241.00
25-29	302.30	374.80	208.30	304.90
30-39	329.60	493.80	213.30	355.30
40-49	336.60	551.60	205.10	339.00
50-59	315.40	539.60	199.30	312.70
60-64	283.10	464.10	184.20	285.60
65+	202.80			

Source: adapted from New Earnings Survey, 1997.

They are sometimes persuaded to accept voluntary redundancy by taking early retirement.

There was no specific protection against age discrimination when seeking employment and in training or promotion. However, cases taken to an industrial tribunal have often been won using using sex or race discrimination in relation to age. For example, a case by an employee against the Civil Service bar on people aged over 32 was judged to discriminate against black people, since black employees were older than white employees at the time due to adult immigration. After the year 2000 there is likely to be increasing pressure for laws to prevent age discrimination in the UK.

Some argue that there are actually advantages to a business in employing workers 'over 40'.

● The over 40s have greater experience and better judgement in decision-making.
● The over 40s have already satisfied many of their needs for salary and status and are able to concentrate more on job responsibilities.
● The over 40s have a greater 'social intelligence' and the ability to understand and influence others.

B&Q, the chain of DIY stores, has recognised the benefits of employing older people, and has adopted a policy of hiring over 50s in its stores.

Equal opportunities policies

Certain businesses operate an **equal opportunities policy**. This means that the firm is committed to giving all applicants an equal chance of, say, selection, no matter what their sex, sexuality, race, age, marital status, religion or disability. The aim of such a policy is to remove discrimination in all areas of the business, including promotion, training and financial rewards. Examples of employers that operate such a policy are Ford, Kingfisher (the retail group that comprises Woolworth's) and The Clydesdale Bank.

How will such a policy affect business?

● A business is far more likely to employ the 'best' person for the job if everyone is given an equal opportunity.
The quality of applicants may also improve.
● Equal opportunities for training are likely to lead to a

Question **4**

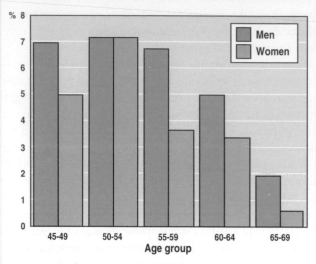

Figure 80.4 *People who think their job application was affected because they were too old, by age and sex, GB*

Source: adapted from Family and Working Lives Survey.

Figure 80.5 *Percentage of older people with health problems, by age and sex, GB*

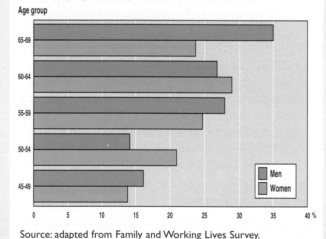

Source: adapted from Family and Working Lives Survey.

(a) Describe the trends taking place in Figures 80.4 and 80.5.
(b) How might these trends explain why age discrimination takes place?
(c) Examine the possible benefits to a business of:
　(i)　training older workers;
　(ii)　employing older workers in a bank;
　(iii)　employing older workers in a job that demands travelling or working away from home.

better qualified workforce in key positions, although the cost of training could increase.

● Workers may become better motivated if, for example, the chances of promotion are more equal.
● Production may need to be reorganised. This might include more flexible hours, job rotation or even job

sharing. For example, an office job could be carried out by a mother in the morning (when children are at school) and by a male in the afternoon. A more flexible workforce may be better able to respond to change (☞ unit 102).

● There may be extra wage costs. Paying women equal wages to men will raise the total wage bill.

● Extra facilities may be needed. This can vary from ramps for wheelchairs to children's creches.

● Recruitment, selection and training procedures may have to change. In some cases there may even be **positive action**. This is where employers discriminate in favour of minority groups or women who may be under-represented in work.

● The image of the business or jobs in it may have to change. This could improve the image to the customer. Rank Xerox, for example, found that jobs in the business were often seen as 'men's' jobs or 'women's' jobs and tried to change this.

Effective equal opportunities policies must also take into account discrimination against which there is no legislation. It is suggested that employers discriminate against candidates with regional accents in interviews. A survey of recruitment specialists found that they felt Liverpool, Manchester and Birmingham accents were negative. 'Upper class accents' led to hostility in Scotland. Discrimination also takes place against people who employers perceive as being 'fat'. One NHS Trust, for example, set a size limit when recruiting which would have ruled out any candidate over 5 feet 10 inches, weighing over 12 stone 12 pounds.

Question 5

The R Stewart Group is a family owned construction business. It is based on Merseyside and employs around 140 people. In 1989 it developed an equal opportunities policy after winning a contract which required it to employ local workers. At the time it had no workers from ethnic minorities, although they made up 8 per cent of the local population. Part of the business's policy involves offering training to ethnic minority school leavers in building skills. Two trainees coming to the end of their three year course were looking forward to applying for jobs as qualified bricklayers. Young people from ethnic minorities in the area are now starting to become more interested in construction work. They see employees on sites from their own racial group.

Source: adapted from *Positive Action*, DfEE.

(a) Why might the R Stewart Group have developed an equal opportunities policy?
(b) Explain the possible benefits for:
 (i) employees;
 (ii) the business;
 of this policy.
(c) Examine how an equal opportunities policy may affect a construction business.

Key terms

Discrimination - to make a selection or choice from alternatives, such as an applicant for a job. The term is often used to mean an illegal or unreasonable selection in the context of equal opportunities.
Equal opportunities - where everyone has the same chance.

In business this can mean the same chance of selection, promotion etc.
Positive action - measures geared towards improving the employment opportunities and training of groups that are under-represented at work.

Summary

1. State 4 groups that are often discriminated against by businesses.
2. Why might there have been an improvement in employment opportunities for women?
3. What are the main points of:
 (a) The Equal Pay Act 1970 and the 1983 amendments;
 (b) The Sex Discrimination Act of 1986;
 (c) The Race Relations Act of 1976;
 (d) The Disability Discrimination Act, 1995?

4. What effect will equal pay legislation be likely to have on wages and opportunities for women in the UK?
5. State 3 ways in which an employer might avoid discriminating against minority groups when recruiting for jobs.
6. What advantages might candidates over 40 have for a business when compared to younger applicants?

Case study

Promoting equal opportunities in health services

Is there discrimination in the medical profession? Half of the medical students in the UK are female. Yet fewer than 20 per cent of consultants are women. Some NHS trusts employ women in as few as 9 per cent of consultancy posts. In surgery the ratio of males to females can be as extreme as 42:1. But what if a women patient attends a hospital with no female obstetrician, as is the case in some NHS trust hospitals? This is perhaps unreasonable since obstetrics deals with patient care before, during and after child birth, and all obstetric patients are women. Many patients might feel uncomfortable being examined by a man.

A study by Leicester University based on a Department of Health survey of 9,000 nurses found that female and Asian nurses moved more slowly up the promotion ladder than male and white colleagues. This was despite their disproportionately larger numbers in the profession. The study found that men were likely to be promoted to higher grades 5-14 years earlier than women. Frank Dobson, the health secretary, at the NHS Equality awards in 1998 spoke about the lack of prospects for large groups of NHS staff. He said: 'Around 8 per cent of the workforce are from ethnic minority backgrounds. Yet they account for fewer than 3 per cent of NHS managers'. Only 21 per cent of black or Asian doctors are consultants, compared to 38 per cent of white doctors.

Janey Huber qualified and then practised as an eye surgeon. After taking time off to have children she went back to work part time as a registrar in the hospital in which she previously worked. However, she felt ignored and simply tolerated. When she refused to take on extra work because of commitments with her children she was said to be non-cooperative. In the end she left.

But do all females in the profession feel this way? Many struggle with the long hours and balance a life at home with a demanding job. Medical organisations are sensitive to the pressures faced by women. The Good Medical Practice Guide of the General Medical Council has an equal opportunities policy in place. In late 1998 a spokesperson said that it had not received any complaints on grounds of sexual discrimination. This is perhaps because such charges are difficult to prove.

Industrial tribunals do hear and rule on cases of discrimination. For example, Ruth Chigwada-Bailey sued the Community Health Services NHS Trust in Camden and Islington, where she worked as a nurse. She claimed discrimination and a racist conspiracy, saying a senior colleague suggested she used black magic to win the lottery for the staff syndicate. The tribunal ruled there was no conspiracy and that her judgment had been clouded by her feminist and anti-racist views. A case of racial discrimination by Dr Rovenska, a doctor born in Czechoslovakia, was taken against the General Medical Council. A tribunal originally ruled against her. But a court of appeal said that a requirement to take a test in English, which a smaller proportion of a racial group could pass and which was not justified, was 'continuing' discrimination. This means that a case can be brought at any time during a worker's employment.

Opportunity 2000, a business led initiative in the 1990s to improve the position of women in work, set goals for hospitals to increase their percentages of women. John Radcliffe in Oxford, a hospital with a woman Dean, had achieved its targets in 1998. However, in many hospitals there is neither the time nor money to recruit more women. One method that could be used is to introduce flexible part time training schemes.

Ultimately, patients, taxpayers and perhaps even hospitals themselves suffer if women leave the profession or are discouraged because of discrimination. The cost of training a doctor is £200,000. Choice will also be severely restricted. Addenbrooke's hospital appointed two male consultants in 1998. This meant that no women with breast cancer would be able to consult a female surgeon until the male consultants retired.

Source: adapted from *The Sunday Times*, 27.7.1997, *The Times*, 2.6.1998, *Labour Research*, May 1998.

(a) **Give an example of:**
   (i) **sex discrimination;**
   (ii) **racial discrimination;**
   in the Health Service mentioned in the article.
(b) **Explain the possible effects of discrimination on:**
   (i) **employees in the Health Service;**
   (ii) **NHS hospitals;**
   (iii) **consumers of health services;**
   (iv) **the general public.**
(c) (i) **Identify evidence of positive action by employers in the medical profession.**
   (ii) **Explain the likely benefits of positive action for the Health Service.**
(d) (i) **Suggest, using examples, two other types of discrimination that may take place in the Health Service.**
   (ii) **Advise employers on how they might prevent the discrimination you have suggested.**
(e) **Comment on how effective methods to prevent discrimination have been in the Health Service.**

Why is protection needed?

Why might a business protect its employees? There are certain laws protecting people in the workplace. Legislation has laid down rules about:

- health and safety;
- employment protection (dismissal and redundancy);
- wage protection;
- recruitment, selection and training (☞ unit 76-79).

This legislation provides guidelines and acts as a constraint on how a business makes decisions. In addition, from a purely practical point of view, it makes sense for a firm to protect its workers. Satisfied employees are far more likely to help a business achieve its goals. A business may also feel it has a moral obligation to protect employees. As their employer, it should look after their interests in the workplace.

Health and safety at work

Providing a healthy and safe environment can mean many things. It could include some of the following.

- Providing and maintaining safety equipment and clothing.
- Maintaining workplace temperatures.
- Ensuring adequate work space.
- Ensuring adequate washing and toilet facilities.
- Guaranteeing hygienic and safe conditions.
- Providing breaks in the work timetable.
- Providing protection for the use of hazardous substances.

It is likely that the conditions for a healthy and safe environment will vary depending on the nature of the task carried out. Ensuring the health and safety of a mine worker will require different decisions by a business to protecting an office worker. Although both must be protected from adverse effects of equipment, for example, protection is likely to be different.

Businesses must protect people outside the workplace who might be affected by activities within it, eg those living near a chemical or industrial plant. They must also protect visitors or customers to shops or premises.

It is in the interest of a business to protect its workforce. A healthy and safe work environment should prevent accidents, injury and illness amongst workers. Any one of these may result in staff absence and lost production for the firm. The percentage of working days lost due to sickness or injury per week in different occupations and industries is shown in Figure 81.1. In extreme cases, the business may even be taken to court for failing to provide protection. The court may order the business to pay compensation to the employee and perhaps a fine. Also, loss of employees may require costly recruitment of full or part time workers. Furthermore, it has been argued that high or low temperatures and lack of workspace may lead to a fall in production by employees.

In 1998 it was estimated that 23.9 million work days were lost due to workplace injury. In 1996 just over 1 million employed people a year suffered a workplace injury in Great Britain. The number of reportable injuries which resulted in more than 3 days absence fell from 2,480 per thousand employees in 1990 to 1,640 per thousand employees in 1996. This was a 34 per cent reduction.

Health and safety legislation

In the areas of health and safety at work, laws have been passed to protect employees for well over 100 years. Increasingly, regulations have been based on EU directives, covering such factors as noise control and the manual

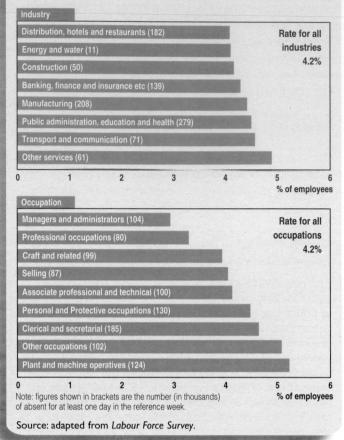

Figure 81.1 *Percentage of employees absent from work for at least one day in the reference week due to sickness or injury, by occupation and industry, United Kingdom, summer 1998, not seasonally adjusted*

Note: figures shown in brackets are the number (in thousands) of absent for at least one day in the reference week.

Source: adapted from *Labour Force Survey*.

handling of heavy loads. There is also a number of **codes of practice** which act as 'guides' for a business.

There are thousands of UK and EU regulations concerning health and safety at work. They are updated from time to time as work conditions change. What are the main laws protecting the health and safety of employees?

The Factories Act, 1961 This Act applies to all premises where two or more people are employed in manual labour. This includes garages to engineering works. The act sets out to ensure that minimum standards of cleanliness, space for people to work, temperature and ventilation, lighting, conveniences, clothing, accommodation and first-aid facilities are maintained.

The Offices, Shops and Railway Premises Act, 1963 This was introduced to extend protection for factories to other buildings. The provisions are similar to those of the Factories Act, and deal with cleanliness, lighting, ventilation etc.

The Fire Precautions Act, 1971 This Act lists premises for which a fire certificate is required. The list includes premises being used as a place of work. When issuing a certificate a fire

authority can impose requirements on the holder. These may concern such things as the means of escape from the building, instruction and training for employees on what to do in the event of fire and limits to the number of people on the premises.

The Health and Safety at Work Act, 1974 The aim of this Act is to raise the standard of safety and health for all individuals at work, and to protect the public whose safety may be put at risk by the activities of people at work.

Every employer is required to prepare a written statement of their general policy on health and safety. Employees must be advised of what the policy is. Management have the main responsibility for carrying out the policy. In the case of negligence, proceedings can be taken against an individual manager as well as against the business. The Act also places a duty on employees while they are at work to take reasonable care for the safety of themselves and others. The employee is legally obliged to comply with the safety rules drawn up by management. Employers or employees who fail to comply can be taken to court and fined. Part of the Act requires a business to give training, information, instruction and supervision to ensure the health and safety at work of employees.

The Act is backed up by the Health and Safety Executive, which has the responsibility of seeing that the Act is carried out. Health and Safety inspectors are appointed by the Commission to make sure the law is being carried out. They have the power to enter employers' premises, carry out examinations and investigations, take measurements, photographs and recordings, take equipment and materials and examine books and documents. The Commission also has the power to issue codes of practice to protect people in various situations, for example:

● the protection of individuals against ionising radiation;
● the control of lead pollution at work;
● time off for training of safety representatives;
● control of substances hazardous to health (various).

Control of Substances Hazardous to Health Regulations, 1988 These regulations, which came into force on 1 October 1989, were made under the Health and Safety at Work Act, 1974. They comprise nineteen regulations, plus four approved codes of practice. The legislation protects all employees who work with any substance hazardous to their health. Employers must take into account the way and extent that such substances are handled, used and controlled. This is particularly important for workers in the nuclear fuel, chemical and asbestos industries.

The Workplace (Health, Safety and Welfare) Regulations (WHSWR) 1992 These implemented EU regulations regarding health and safety. They also set out an Approved Code of Practice (ACOP) for employers. Other regulations introduced at that time included:

● the Management of Health and Safety at Work Regulations (MHSWR) 1992, which relates to the implementation of

health and safety arrangements;
● the Provision and Use of Work Equipment Regulations (PUWER) 1992, which relate to the safe use of equipment and machinery;
● the Personal Protective Equipment at Work Regulations (PPEWR) 1992, which relates to protective clothing and equipment;
● the Health and Safety (Display Screen Equipment) Regulations 1992, which relate to workers using computer screens and technical requirements of workstations;
● the Manual Handling Operations Regulations (MHOR) 1992, which relate to the transport and handling of loads by hand.

The Working Time Regulations, 1998 The new Working Time Regulations, 1998 took effect in the UK on 1 October 1998. They provided the following new rights for workers:
● three week's annual paid leave, rising to four weeks in 1999;
● eleven consecutive hours' rest in any twenty four hour period;
● a day's rest in a week;
● a twenty minute rest break after six hours' work;
● a limit of an average of forty eight hours in a week in which a worker can be required to work;
● a limit of an average of eight hours' work in any twenty four hours for night workers.

There were provisions for even more and longer breaks for younger workers. These regulations were based on the view that excessive work is bad for employees' health. Previously there had been no laws on the numbers of working hours.

Employment protection

Unit 78 showed that employees are entitled to a contract of employment when they are first appointed to a job. The contract of employment is an agreement between the employer and the employee on the terms and conditions under which the employee will work. An employee may be able to claim for a breach of contract by the employer. Employees are also protected by legislation against discrimination (☞ unit 80).

The **Employment Protection (Consolidation) Act, 1978** stated that employees who have worked for an employer continuously for two years had a right not to be unfairly dismissed. Some EU countries such as Denmark have no qualification period. The **Employment Relations Bill, 1999** (☞ unit 78) reduced the qualifying period to one year. It also aimed to introduce 'family friendly policies', such as parental leave for people adopting a child, and to remove limits on awards for unfair dismissal. Certain people cannot claim unfair dismissal, such as an independent contractor or freelance agent, who are not employees.

There is a number of reasons why employees might be dismissed which may be **unfair** dismissal under the

Question 2

In the mid-1990s Frank Davies, chair of the Health and Safety Commission, argued that the penalties for companies putting people at risk were 'ridiculously low'. Mr Davies reported a surge in the number of fatalities at work. They had increased from 258 to 302 in the period 1994/95. Fatalities were mainly in the construction and agricultural industries. One construction company, for example, which was refurbishing flats, sent a new employee to the second floor. He fell to his death over an unprotected edge. The business was fined only £345 with £50 costs. Serious accidents at work were also a cause of concern. Despite advice from the Health and Safety Executive, a manufacturer of paper sacks was fined £45 when an employee's hand was crushed in an unguarded printing machine.

Source: adapted from *The Independent*, 13.12.1997.

(a) Identify the health and safety dangers for employees in the article.
(b) Using two examples, explain how UK or EU legislation might affect a construction business.
(c) Explain how health and safety might be improved in the construction industry.

conditions of the Act (and its amendments).
● Because they were trying to become or were a member of a trade union. Alternatively, because they refused to join or make payments to a union.
● On the grounds of pregnancy, even though she was able to do the job.
● Making workers redundant without following the correct procedure. This is dealt with later.
● As a result of a transfer of a business, such as when one business is bought by another. However, if the business can prove it was for economic, technical or organisational reasons, it may be considered fair.
● For refusing to work on a Sunday. The **Sunday Trading Act, 1994** gives shop workers the right not to be dismissed for refusing to work on Sundays.

There are reasons why dismissal may be **fair**. The employer must have a valid reason and must act 'reasonably' when dealing with this reason.
● The employee is incapable of doing the job or unqualified.
● 'Misconduct' of the employee, such as persistent lateness (minor) or theft (major).
● The employer is unable to employ the worker. For example, a lorry driver may no longer be employed if he has lost his driving licence.
● Any other substantial reason. For example, false

details may have been given on the job application form.
● Redundancy can take place if the employer needs to reduce the workforce. This could be because a factory has closed or there is not enough work to do. The job must have **disappeared**. In other words, it is not redundancy if another worker is hired as a replacement. Certain procedures must be followed by employers. They must consult with trade unions over any proposed redundancy. If the union feels the employer has not met requirements, it can complain to a tribunal. Employees are entitled to a period of notice, as well as a redundancy payment based on how long they have been in continuous employment.

If a worker feels that he has been unfairly dismissed, he can take his case to an **industrial tribunal**. This is dealt with in the next section. For example, a tribunal may decide that an employee who resigns as a result of the employer's actions has been **constructively** dismissed. To do this the employer must have acted in a way that is a substantial breach of the employment contract. An example might be where the employer demoted a worker to a lower rank or lower paid position for no reason.

Unfair dismissal - what to do

If an employee feels that he has been unfairly dismissed, what can he do about it? It may be possible for a worker and a business to settle the dispute voluntarily. If not, the employee may decide to complain to an industrial tribunal. Figure 81.2 shows the stages involved in this.

The complaint must be received within 3 months of the end of contract. A notice of application is sent to the employer asking if they wish to contest the case. Details of the case are then sent to the **Advisory, Conciliation and Arbitration Service** (ACAS) (☞ unit 86). Its role is to help settle the dispute before it reaches a tribunal through a conciliation.

Before the complaint does reach a tribunal, there may be a pre-hearing assessment. If either party has a case that is not likely to succeed, they can be told and also informed that they may be liable for costs. The aim of this stage is to 'weed out' hopeless cases.

Once a complaint goes to a hearing at a tribunal, the employee is entitled to legal advice. After the hearing the tribunal will make a decision. If this is in favour of the employee then the tribunal can order:
● the employee to be reinstated in the same job;
● the employee to be re-engaged in another job;
● compensation to be paid.

It is possible to appeal against a tribunal's decision. This will be heard by the Employment Appeal Tribunal. An employee who disagrees with the decisions of an industrial tribunal and an appeal tribunal may take his or her case to the European Court of Justice (ECJ). This is the highest court of appeal under EU law. If a case is upheld, then UK businesses must comply with its decision as the UK is an EU member.

Question 3

It is unlawful to dismiss a woman who is pregnant or on maternity leave for any reason connected with her maternity. So says the European Court of Justice. Mary Brown worked as a service driver for Rentokill, the pest control company. She regarded the work as heavy. Mary became pregnant in 1990, but had difficulties in August of that year. She took time off work, submitting certificates showing pregnancy-related illnesses, such as backache. In November her manager told her that if she could not return to work by February, her employment would end. Mary was not able to return to work and so the company dismissed her on the basis of their sickness procedure, which stated that anyone off sick for more than six months would be dismissed.

Mary took her case to an industrial tribunal, but it was rejected. The tribunal argued that there was no sex discrimination as it was legitimate for an employer to treat a woman in exactly the same way as a man who had been off sick. When she took her case to the European Court of Justice she was successful. It ruled that dismissal of a worker on account of pregnancy could only affect women, and therefore was discrimination. The court also pointed out that an employer could not dress up a pregnancy dismissal by suggesting that it arose not because of pregnancy, but because a woman was unable to do the job.

Source: adapted from *Labour Research*, August 1998.

(a) Identify reasons for: (i) fair; and (ii) unfair; dismissal mentioned in the article.
(b) Why did the European Court give a different judgment to the UK tribunal?
(c) Using examples, explain two other reasons why an employee who delivered, installed and serviced pest control equipment in shops may be fairly dismissed.

Question 4

John Smart was employed by Jones and Harcourt, a paper merchant in Oxford. The company buys paper in bulk from foreign mills and distributes it to users in the UK. In the early 1990s, trade and paper prices began to fall. The company was looking for ways of cutting costs. John had been employed as warehouse manager to control the arrival and delivery of paper. With no prior consultation, one Monday in early 1993, a director informed John that his services were no longer required. John was told that he was to be made redundant at the end of the week. The following week the company employed a younger man to do John's job, at a far lower salary.

(a) Comment on the fairness of John's dismissal.
(b) What advice would you give John about his next course of action?

Wage protection

The main legislation relating to pay in the UK is the **Wages Act, 1986**. This sets out conditions for payments to workers and deductions from wages. Wages are defined as any sum paid to the worker by the employer in connection with the job. This includes fees, bonuses, commission, sick pay, gift tokens or vouchers. Certain payments, such as redundancy payments, expenses or loans are not included.

Deductions made from wages that are covered by the Act include:
- those that must be taken or are agreed upon, such as income tax or National Insurance;
- those shown in the contract of employment;
- those agreed by the worker in writing, such as trade union payments;

providing that these are the agreed amounts. If the employer deliberately decides not to pay part of a worker's wages, then employees can complain to a tribunal. This is a similar process to complaints about dismissal. Wage protection is also covered by the **Equal Pay Act, 1970** (☞ unit 80).

Before 1993, some workers had minimum wages set by Wages Councils. Their role was set out in the Wages Act, 1986. Councils had the power to fix a basic minimum hourly rate of pay, fix overtime rates and decide the number of hours a week worked before overtime was paid. It was illegal to pay adults less than these rates. Wages Councils were found in industries with traditionally low paid workers. These included:
- retailing (sale of books, clothing, stationery, toys, groceries, magazines etc.);
- licensed establishments (public houses, inns, clubs, restaurants, hotels, holiday camps etc.);
- clothing manufacture;
- unlicensed refreshment (restaurants, cafes, snackbars etc.);
- hairdressing;
- laundry.

The minimum wage

In 1997 the government published a **National Minimum Wage Bill**. It aimed to introduce a minimum wage for workers. Other countries such as France and the USA have minimum wages. It is unlawful to pay a worker below the rate set for the minimum wage. For example, in Portugal the minimum wage was equivalent to £2.10 per hour. In Canada it was £3.80 and in Belgium it was as high as £4.56. In 1999 the UK government introduced a minimum wage of £3.60 an hour for adults, £3.00 an hour for 18-21 year olds, but excluded 16-17 year olds completely.

Why did the government want to introduce a minimum wage?
- To prevent poverty. It would prevent workers being paid very low wages by employers.
- To reduce inequality between the pay of men and women.

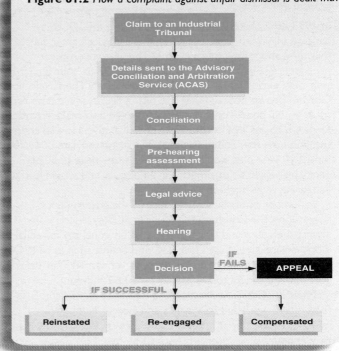

Figure 81.2 How a complaint against unfair dismissal is dealt with

Women often work in low paid full time or part time jobs.
- To benefit businesses. Greater equality and fairness should motivate employees, reduce staff turnover and improve workers' productivity.

Some businesses argue that raising the wages of low paid workers increases their costs. To pay the higher wages, a business may need to make other workers unemployed or take on fewer new workers, particularly younger workers or people just starting work.

The Social Chapter

The European Union's Social Chapter is an attempt to encourage minimum wages and conditions of work in member countries. It was argued that a business may attempt to respond to falling profits or greater competition by cutting costs. This could lead to poor pay and work conditions for employees. To prevent this, member countries outlined an agreement which covered such areas as:
- a limit on hours of work;
- 'fair and reasonable' rewards;
- minimum wages;
- free collective bargaining;
- access to training;
- workers' involvement in company decision making;
- health and safety;
- union recognition;
- equal opportunities.

The Conservative government in the 1990s refused to sign the Social Chapter. It argued that the conditions:
- restricted a business's ability to reduce wages when necessary;

Question 5

In 1997 the Labour government committed the UK to a national minimum wage. However, there was still great debate at that time about how much it should be. The government proposed £3.60 an hour for adults and £3.00 an hour for 18-21 year olds, excluding 16-17 year olds completely. The Chancellor, Gordon Brown, believed that too high a figure would push too many young people onto the dole. It would also make it harder for them to get jobs on the New Deal initiative. He also argued that the Low Pay Commission's (LPC) suggested rate of £3.20 for 18-20 year olds would give average wage rises of 50 per cent. This would be too much for employers and would lead to increasing wage costs and inflation.

A number of organisations criticised the government's suggestions. The British Youth Council said they discriminated against the young and that there should be 'equal pay for equal work, irrespective of age'. The TUC and unions such as UNISON wanted rates of over £4.50 for people over age 18. They defied government leaders to live happily on £3.60 an hour.

Most businesses welcomed the new rate as realistic. Fast food chains, such as McDonald's and Burger King, have minimum adult pay at around £3.60 anyway. But the lower rate may encourage younger workers to be taken on. 75 per cent of Burger King's workers, for example, were aged 16-21 at the time. Some low paying industries were likely to see their costs increase. An LPC report suggested a 3 per cent increase in the wage bills of cleaning companies. But employers in these areas argued that the minimum wage could still be of benefit, encouraging a better quality of employee and allowing them to shed their low pay image. Major retailers like Boots and catering firms like Compass said that there would be little or

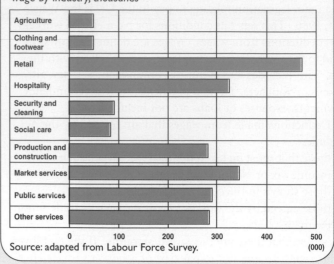

Figure 81.3 *Number of employees paid less than the minimum wage by industry, thousands*

Source: adapted from Labour Force Survey.

no impact on their wage bills of a minimum wage.

Source: adapted from The *Observer*, 21.6.1998; *Labour Research*, July 1998.

(a) What were the: (i) positive views; and (ii) negative views; of the government's proposal for a minimum wage of £3.60 an hour for adults and £3.00 an hour for 18-21 year olds?

(b) (i) Look at Figure 81.3. Which industries are likely to be affected most by a minimum wage? Explain your answer.
   (ii) Explain why a large businesses like Boots or Compass might not be affected by a minimum wage?

(c) Analyse the possible effects of a minimum wage of above £4.50 on: (i) businesses; (ii) the economy.

● did not allow a business to be flexible when employing workers and making them redundant;
● would increase costs.

In 1997, under a Labour government, the UK signed up to the EU's Social Chapter. This meant that its laws would have to be changed to comply with the conditions of the Social

Chapter. For example, the number of hours to be worked by most employees must be limited to 48 hours, part time and full time workers would be given equal rights, and employees would have a right to paid holidays each year. Other changes would include the introduction of **European works councils** (☞ unit 85), to negotiate workers' wages with employers, and the setting of a minimum wage as discussed in the previous section.

Question 6

The signing of the EU's Social Chapter in 1997 would mean new powers for employees in EU based businesses. European works councils will become a reality for any company with more than 1,500 employees in total and with more than 150 employees in two member countries. A European works council is a committee of elected employee representatives which managers must 'inform and consult' on significant issues affecting the business, such as mergers, takeovers, large scale redundancies and new working methods. The CBI issued warnings that such councils would mean that workers across Europe could hold multinationals to ransom and dictate company policy. However, the councils have no powers to veto company decisions. They must, however, be consulted on certain decisions. Renault, for example, closed its Vilvoorde assembly plant in Belgium without consulting its council. Despite facing legal action for a lack of consultation, it still closed the plant.

Those supporting the introduction of councils argue that they give employees statutory backing to gain key management information from businesses for the first time. They also prevent multinational businesses 'playing off' employees in different countries as managers have to deal with employees from its whole European workforce in one council. UK companies such as NatWest, British Telecom and ICI already have European works councils as they employ large workforces on the Continent. They describe them as a useful tool for employee consultation.

Source: adapted from The *Observer*, 11.5.1997.

(a) How might a European works council help to improve the conditions of workers in European businesses?

(b) Explain the possible effects of the introduction of a European works council into a UK business.

Summary

1. Why might it be in a business's interest to protect its workers?
2. State 5 types of health and safety dangers that may exist in business.
3. Briefly explain 3 pieces of legislation regarding health and safety at work.
4. Under what circumstances might dismissal be:
   (a) fair;
   (b) unfair?
5. What is the role of an industrial tribunal in protecting the employee at work?
6. 'An employee without a strong case for unfair dismissal may face problems if a tribunal finds against them.' Explain this statement.
7. State 2 pieces of legislation affecting the wages of employees in UK businesses.
8. What does the European Social Chapter aim to achieve?
9. Discuss 2 effects that signing the Social Chapter may have on the business of a country that signed the agreement.

Case study

Marconi Electronic Systems

Marconi Electronic Systems is a business that is aware of the potential health and safety dangers at work and the implications for the business. It has launched a range of initiatives over the last five years, designed to provide treatment and therapy that goes beyond those offered by the basic occupational health service.

Its back care programme initially involves stretching and relaxing and then more strenuous exercises. One member of its staff to benefit has been Dave Smith, as senior design engineer. After a slipped disc, he found it hard to sit at his desk for any period of time. He often spends much of the day walking around the office to relieve the pain. An exercise therapist carried out treatment after work and also made suggestions about how his furniture could be rearranged at home to reduce the strain on his back. At the moment the business pays around 25 per cent of the fees for the programme. Staff pay the remainder, £60 for 10 weekly sessions that last 75 minutes. Heather Kenzie, Marconi's occupational health nurse adviser, says that employees feel more committed if they have to pay something towards their own treatment.

Other treatments include reflexology and massage. These have been found to relieve stress amongst the workforce. Reflexology, the application of pressure on the feet and other parts of the body, has also benefited people with foot and body pain. Karen Jay, an accounts clerk, saw a reflexologist to relieve pain in her left leg, foot and back. She argues that it relieves pain and stress, although: 'stress builds up as soon as I get back in my office'. Staff pay £12 per 45 minute session which takes place every two weeks in work time. They argue that they would be unlikely to visit a reflexologist out of work time because of the hassle involved in making a special trip. The massage sessions were suspended in early 1998 because of lack of attendance. Staff felt that they could not commit themselves to attend all sessions because they took place in work time.

In late 1998 the company carried out a survey to profile the health of its entire workforce. Employees filled in a questionnaire asking about their health. They then attended a ten minute session carried out by BUPA to check their cholesterol levels and general health. Each employee was given a health profile, with hints on how to become healthier. By December 600 people had attended a session. 'It's free, confidential, and gives people the message and the ability to put change into place', says Kenzie. Four years earlier the company totally banned smoking in offices and other buildings. The occupational health department still runs initiatives to help people stop smoking. These include acupuncture and hypnotherapy as well as more traditional methods.

In 1998 Marconi's personnel department began its People Achieving Together initiative. This included improvements in working conditions and greater access to training.

Overall the company is placing greater emphasis on preventative health care. Screening for osteoporosis (brittle bone disease) showed that site manager Brian Drew's bone density had reduced as a result of steroids he was taking for arthritis. He was taken off the drugs as a result. Marconi hopes that its initiatives will encourage its employees to take greater care of their own bodies.

Source: adapted from *People Management*, 24.12.1998.

(a) What types of health and safety problems might exist at Marconi Electronic Systems?

(b) How has Marconi Electronic Systems attempted to solve these problems?

(c) Using examples, suggest how health and safety legislation may act as a constraint on the business.

(d) What difficulties may result for: (i) employees; and (ii) businesses; from the health and safety problems suggested in the article?

(e) Discuss the implications for: (i) employees; and (ii) the business; of the introduction of health and safety initiatives at Marconi.

What is communication?

Communication is about sending and receiving information. Employees, managers and departments communicate with each other every day in business. For example, in a sole trader organisation, the owner may inform the workers verbally that an order for goods has to be sent out in the next two days. In a company, the personnel manager might send a 'memo' to all departments informing them about training courses that are available.

Good communication is vital for the efficient running of a business. A company exporting goods abroad is likely to have major problems if it fails to give the exact time of departure to its despatch department. Similarly, problems will also arise if instructions are not clear and goods are delivered to the wrong address.

Effective communication will only happen if information is sent, received and then understood. Some examples of information and methods of communicating in business might be:

● information on how to fill out expenses claims forms in a memo sent from the accounts department;
● verbal comments made by a manager to an employee informing them that continued lateness is likely to result in disciplinary action by the company;
● employment details given to a new employee on a written contract of employment (☞ unit 78);
● information on sales figures sent from the sales manager to the chief executive by e-mail or saved as a spreadsheet on computer disc;
● face-to-face negotiations between management and employee representatives over possible rewards for agreeing to changes in work practice;
● a group meeting taking place to discuss how quality could be improved in a work section;
● an order for 20 books faxed to a publisher from a bookshop;
● an advertisement for a salesperson placed on a company website on the internet.

The communication process

Communication within business can take many forms. There are, however, some common features of all communications that take place in the workplace. Figure 82.1 shows an example.

Who sends and receives information? Information must be received and understood by the person or group to whom it was sent. Communication can take place between managers and employees, as well as between representative bodies, such as trade unions. Information is also passed to people and organisations outside the company. For example, company newspapers such as *Ford News* not only inform employees about the firm, but presents a picture to the outside world of its operations.

What message is being communicated? For communication to be effective the correct **message** must be sent and received. Messages can be sent for a number of reasons.
● To provide information about the company. Management might inform the workforce about production levels achieved during the previous year. Some information is required by law. For example, the business has to tell employees about their conditions of employment.
● To give instructions, for example to instruct market research to be carried out.
● To persuade people to change attitudes or behaviour, for example, to warn an employee who is consistently late of the likely action.

What channel is being used? Communication can be along different routes or CHANNELS in the organisation. Sometimes this can be between a manager and a subordinate (**vertical**) or between two departments (**horizontal**). As well as this **formal** type of communication, information is often passed **informally** between departments and employees.

What medium is being used? Information can be

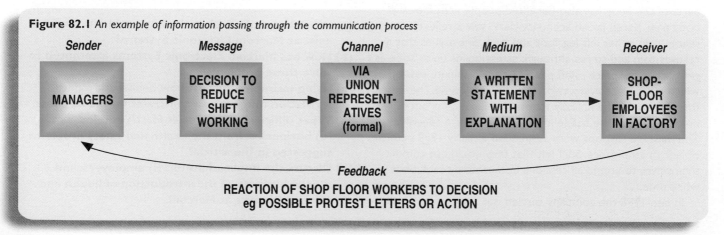

Figure 82.1 *An example of information passing through the communication process*

Sender	Message	Channel	Medium	Receiver
MANAGERS	DECISION TO REDUCE SHIFT WORKING	VIA UNION REPRESENT-ATIVES (formal)	A WRITTEN STATEMENT WITH EXPLANATION	SHOP-FLOOR EMPLOYEES IN FACTORY

Feedback
REACTION OF SHOP FLOOR WORKERS TO DECISION
eg POSSIBLE PROTEST LETTERS OR ACTION

communicated in a variety of ways or through different COMMUNICATION MEDIA. These vary from written methods, such as annual reports, to oral methods such as discussions, to the use of **information and communication (ICT) technology**, such as a fax machine, e-mail or the internet.

Feedback Communication is not complete until the message is received and the receiver confirms that it is understood through feedback of some sort, for example written or verbal confirmation.

Formal/informal communication

Within a business there are both formal and informal channels of communication. Formal channels are recognised and approved by employers and employee representatives. An example of a formal channel would be a personnel department giving 'notice' to an employee about redundancy.

Informal communication channels can both help and hinder formal communications. Information that is communicated through the **grapevine** (☞ unit 84) may become distorted. This might, in extreme situations, cause industrial relations disputes. However, the grapevine can be acknowledged by management and actively approved of. Some firms issue a 'leak' along the grapevine to see what reaction it might provoke, making changes based on the reaction of employees to proposals, before issuing final instructions. Rumours, such as of a launch of a new product by a competitor, can be useful to a business.

Research has shown that effective communication requires both formal and informal channels. Formal statements can then be supported by informal explanations. A business might inform employees that it is introducing new machinery and then management may discuss this with employees and their representatives to find the best way to do it.

It is also possible to make the distinction between **line** and **staff** communication (☞ unit 70). Line communication has

Question 1

The personnel manager of an electrical components company has to communicate two pieces of information to employees. The first is the good news that the company has won a new contract to supply electrical components to a local manufacturer. However, the personnel manager also has to communicate some bad news to 20 operators on the shop floor. Due to increased levels of automation, their employment will no longer be required next month. They are to leave their work at the end of the week, will be paid in full until the end of the month and receive statutory redundancy payments.

For each message:
(a) identify who is sending and receiving the message;
(b) state what message is being communicated;
(c) suggest whether a formal or informal channel would be most suitable and explain your answer.

authority behind it. Staff communication does not. An example of staff communication may be where a manager attempts to persuade a worker that it is a 'good idea' to do something.

Vertical and lateral communication

Information can be communicated downwards, upwards and laterally. These different channels of communication are shown in Figure 82.2. **Downwards** communication has, in the past, been used to tell employees about decisions that have already been made. It may be important as it:
● allows decisions by managers to be carried out by employees;
● ensures that action is consistent and co-ordinated;
● reduces costs because fewer mistakes should be made;
● should lead to greater effectiveness and profitability as a result of the above.

There is evidence, however, that the flow of information

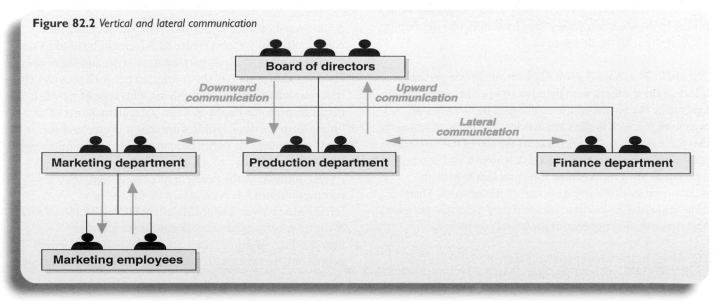

Figure 82.2 *Vertical and lateral communication*

upwards can also help in decision making.

● It helps managers to understand employees' views and concerns.

● It helps managers to keep more in touch with employees' attitudes and values.

● It can alert managers to potential problems.

● It can provide managers with the information that they need for decision making and gives feedback on the effects of previous decisions.

● It helps employees to feel that they are participating and can encourage motivation.

● It provides feedback on the effectiveness of downwards communication and how it can be improved.

Lateral communication takes place when people at the same level within an organisation pass information. An example might be a member of the finance department telling the marketing department about funds available for a sales promotion. One problem that firms sometimes face is that departments may become hostile towards each other if they don't understand the problems that each face. The marketing department may want these funds, but this might adversely affect the firm's cash flow.

Communication networks

Communication takes place within different individuals and parts of a business and between a business and outside bodies. There are advantages and disadvantages to a business of using different types of communication NETWORK.

The circle In a circle, sections, departments etc. can communicate with only two others, as shown Figure 82.3a. This type of communication may occur between middle managers from different departments at the same level of the organisation. The main problem with this type of network is that decision making can be slow or poor because of a lack of co-ordination. If middle managers from different departments had been given the task of increasing sales and profits in the short term, they may have difficulty developing a strategy that all would agree on.

The chain The chain (Figure 82.3b) is where one person passes information to others, who then pass it on. This approach tends to be the formal approach adopted by hierarchical organisations, such as the Civil Service. The main advantage is that there is a leader/co-ordinator at the top of the hierarchy who can oversee communications downwards and upwards to different areas of the business. One problem may be the isolation felt by those at the bottom of the network. Their motivation may be less than others if they feel at the periphery. This network does not encourage lateral communication.

The wheel In the wheel pattern (Figure 82.3c) there is a person, group or department that occupies a central

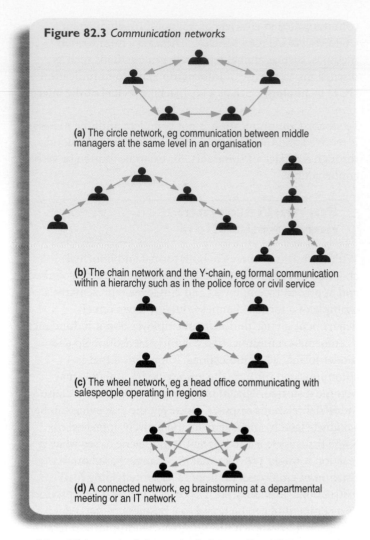

Figure 82.3 *Communication networks*

(a) The circle network, eg communication between middle managers at the same level in an organisation

(b) The chain network and the Y-chain, eg formal communication within a hierarchy such as in the police force or civil service

(c) The wheel network, eg a head office communicating with salespeople operating in regions

(d) A connected network, eg brainstorming at a departmental meeting or an IT network

position. This network is particularly good at solving problems. If, for example, the North West region of an insurance company had been asked to increase sales by central office, then the North West regional manager would be at the centre of policy initiative communicating with local managers about the best way forward. The leader in this network is the regional manager.

A connected or 'all channel' network The 'all channel' communication system (Figure 82.3d) might be used in small group workings. With its participatory style, and more open communication system, the connected network provides the best solutions to complex problems. This type of network might be used, for example, when a department needs to 'brainstorm'. Its disadvantages are that it is slow and that it tends to disintegrate under time pressure to get results when operated in a group.

One solution to the problem of passing complex communications has been solved by the use of INFORMATION and COMMUNICATION TECHNOLOGY. A complex connected network can be set up where instructions and information are passed between many people or departments, or even parts of a business overseas.

Question 2

Which communication network may be most suitable for the following types of message?
(a) An instruction to despatch an order by a certain date.
(b) Discussions about possible extension strategies for a mature product.
(c) A message from head office to local building societies to change mortgage interest rates.
(d) Reacting to a bomb alert in an office block.
(e) Imposing budget cuts in a local authority.
(f) Organising a retirement party.
(g) Developing a brand identity for a consumer product.
Explain your answer in each case.

Communication media

There is a number of methods or media that can be used to communicate information in businesses. Many of these methods can be delivered via electronic media. These are explained in the next section.

Written communication The **letter** is a flexible method which provides a written record. It is often used for communications with others outside the organisation. It can also be used internally where a confidential written record is needed, eg to urge employees against strike action, to announce a redundancy etc.

A **memorandum** is the same as a letter, but is only used for internal communications. It is sent via the internal mail system. Memoranda are useful for many sorts of message, particularly for confirming telephone conversations. Sometimes they are used instead of a telephone. One criticism often made of firms is that they have too many 'memos', when short written notes would do the same job. Some businesses send 'memos' via electronic mail. This allows a person to send a message to another person's computer, which stores it in an electronic mailbox. The memo can then be called up and read by the person receiving it.

Reports allow a large number of people to see complex facts and arguments about issues on which they have to make a decision. A written report does not allow discussion or immediate feedback, as does a meeting, and it can be time-consuming and expensive to produce. However, it does have advantages for passing messages to groups. First, people can study the material in their own time, rather than attending a meeting. Second, time that is often wasted at meetings can be better used. Third, the report is presented in an impartial way, so conflict can be avoided.

Routine information can be communicated through the use of **forms**. A well designed form can be filled in quickly and easily. They are simple to file and information is quickly retrieved and confirmed. Examples of forms used in business include expense forms, timesheets, insurance forms, and stock request forms.

The **noticeboard** is a method which cheaply passes information to a large number of people. The drawbacks to noticeboards are that they can become untidy or irrelevant. In addition, they rely on people reading them, which does not always happen.

Larger companies often print an internal **magazine** or **newspaper** to inform employees about a variety of things. These may include staff appointments and retirements, meetings, sports and social events, results and successes, customer feedback, new products or machinery and motivating competitions, eg safety suggestions. The journal usually avoids being controversial. It may not deal with sensitive issues such as industrial relations (☞ unit 85) or pollution of the environment (☞ unit 35), and may stop short of criticising management policy or products. It is designed to improve communication and morale, and it may be seen by outsiders (especially customers) who might get a favourable impression of the business.

Face-to-face communication Face-to-face communication involves an oral message being passed between people talking to each other. Examples might be:
● a message passed between two workers about how long is left before lunch;
● an instruction given to an employee to change jobs in a job rotation scheme (☞ unit 73);
● a warning given by a health and safety officer to a worker.

Group meetings involve face-to-face communication. Meetings can take a number of forms. They may be formal meetings which are legally required, such as the Annual General Meeting of a limited company. They might also be meetings of groups within the business to discuss problems, such as collective bargaining negotiations (☞ unit 86) or meetings of quality circles (☞ unit 73). Team briefings are also a common method of face-to-face communication in business. Many meetings, however, are simply informal discussions taking place to pass information between employees or managers, such as a 'chat' over lunch.

Face-to-face communication has several advantages. It:
● allows new ideas to be generated;
● allows 'on the spot' feedback, constructive criticism and an exchange of views;
● encourages co-operation;
● allows information to be spread quickly among people.

However, face-to-face communication, such as meetings, can have problems, especially if:
● the terms of reference (defining the purpose and power of the meeting) are not clear;
● the people attending are unskilled or unwilling to communicate;
● there is insufficient guidance or leadership to control the meeting;
● body language creates a barrier.

Oral communication Oral communication can take place

other than in face-to-face situations in a business. The **telephone** is a common method of oral communication between individuals in remote locations or even within an organisation's premises. It provides some of the interactive advantages of face-to-face communication, while saving the time involved in travelling from one place to another. It is, however, more 'distant' and impersonal than an interview for the discussion of sensitive matters and does not provide written 'evidence'. This disadvantage can be overcome by written confirmation.

Sometimes messages can be communicated to groups of employees through a **public address system**. This might operate through loudspeakers placed at strategic points, eg in workshops or yards, where staff cannot be located or reached by telephone.

Information and communication technology

Rapid developments in technology have greatly changed the way businesses communicate with each other. It is now possible to deliver messages instantly, over great distances and to a number of people at the same time via a variety of electronic media.

Mobile phones Many companies and individuals now have mobile phones. These are portable telephones which can be carried around by the user. Telephone calls can be made and received from most areas, often in different countries. They are particularly useful for employees who work outside the office or factory and who move around. Urgent messages can be sent and received immediately. Companies such as Cellnet, Orange, Vodafone and One-to-One offer a variety of services, including receiving and storing messages.

Answerphones Answerphones record messages when the receiver is unable to answer the telephone. They allow important messages to be stored and received if, for example, an employee is away from her desk. They also allow messages to be sent from one company or person to another outside normal office hours. The information will be received when work starts the next day. This is particularly useful when there are time differences between countries. Some people find answerphones impersonal and may not leave a message.

Paging devices These are devices which are useful for people who work outside a business and move around a lot, such as sales representatives. They may also be used by workers in a large organisation, such as a doctor in a hospital. A 'bleeper' alerts the receiver to a message waiting for him on a prearranged telephone number.

Videoconferencing and teleconferencing Videoconferencing is a method of communication which allows individuals in different locations to interact as if they were in the same

Question 3

The amount of business conducted out of office hours is increasing. Clients' parties are sometimes seen as a chore or a social event. However, they can be a useful source of new contacts for business people, a means of cementing existing relationships and a way of raising company profile. Advice given by the Aziz Corporation to business people which attend its 'Working the room workshops' include:
● plan for an event - try to get a guest list and identify who you want to talk to;
● think about who you want to meet at an event;
● prepare a description of your business and ask others about their own;
● don't be scared of small talk;
● have business cards 'at the ready';
● avoid spending too much time with people you know, but try to develop new contacts;
● adapt what you want to say to fit in with the conversation of a group;
● send the host a thank you note after;
● follow up contacts within 10 days of the event.

Source: adapted from *People Management*, 24.12.1998.

(a) Identify the: (i) written; and (ii) oral methods of communication in the article.
(b) Explain why face-to-face communication at clients' parties may be an effective means of communication.
(c) Examine possible methods of communication that a business person may use to 'follow up' contacts made at the parties.

room. Individuals can see each other on monitors with the use of cameras and talk to each other via telephone lines. This is particularly useful when employees need face-to-face interaction, but work in locations that are distant from each other. It also saves the time taken to get to a central meeting place. Teleconferencing is where many people are linked together via telephone lines. Each person can talk to all others as if they were in the same location.

Lap top computers The development of portable computers

means that business people can work in different locations to their office. They allow people to continue working during train journeys, for example, and to e-mail text and images to others via satellite link. They prevent working time from being wasted. They also have the advantage of immediate sending and receiving of information at a variety of locations. Some lap top computers have to be plugged into a telephone terminal to receive e-mail, which can be a problem.

Multi-media communications Businesses are now able to communicate information through a mixture of media. They combine visual images, written text and audio transmissions. This is known as multi-media. Many multi-media programmes are interactive, so that an individual can enter into dialogue with the information that is contained in the programme. The use of multi-media as a business communication tool is particularly useful in the area of training. Individual employees can interact with ideas and concepts developed in the multi-media training package at their own pace.

Electronic noticeboards Businesses are making more use of electronic noticeboards. These communicate the latest information to employees via visual display units located in public places around the business, such as in reception. Their advantage over normal noticeboards is that they can be kept up to date. The main disadvantages are that they are limited to particular locations in the business and the information may not be relevant to everyone who sees it.

E- mail Many businesses now have e-mail addresses. They allow businesses and individuals to communicate immediately with others via word processed text or images that are contained on a computer. Information sent from one e-mail address, via a computer, modem and telephone to another address is stored by the 'server' - a computer dedicated to storage and network facilities. It stays in that address until it is picked up by the receiver. The advantage of e-mail is that long documents can be immediately sent to other people anywhere in the world without them being there.

Fax machines Faxes are similar to e-mail, but the information is already on paper in the form of text or images. This information is read by a fax machine, converted into audio signals, and sent down a telephone line to another fax machine. The machine then reconverts the signals into text and graphics. The advantages of fax machines are that they send messages instantly and that the receiver does not have to be there to receive the message. A disadvantage compared to e-mail is that it can take a long time to process a large document via the fax. The information also has to be printed out or written before it can be sent.

The internet and the intranet The internet, and privately run intranets, look set to challenge the telephone and mail as

Question 4

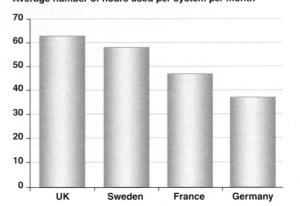

Figure 82.4 *Use of videoconferencing*
Average number of hours used per system per month

A survey by Sony Broadcast & Professional Europe on the use of videoconferencing in four European countries highlighted different rates of use. The results of the survey of 69 user and non-user business are shown in Figure 82.4. The most intensive use was in the UK, followed by Sweden, France and Germany. Attitudes also differed. Travel reduction was the main reason for using videoconferencing, although in Sweden it was seen more as a business tool. These factors were considered highly in the UK, but not in France. This could be because the French prefer personal networking and business lunches. Current users felt that videoconferencing helped to make savings on travel. Companies considering investing in future felt improved communication was the most important benefit.

There are three types of videoconferencing system - fixed equipment in a fitted-out room, group or 'rollabout' systems that can be moved around on wheels and used anywhere, and software on personal computers (PC). The dedicated room systems that cost between £60,000-100,000 are losing ground, particularly in the UK and France, to cheaper, more flexible rollabout systems. The question is how the PC based videoconferencing develops. The UK and Sweden are installing large numbers of PC systems. However, they have not yet replaced group systems, partly because the quality of the audio and video is not as good. Also, a PC-based system cannot really be used as a shared resource. The prices for rollabout systems have fallen sharply, while functionality has increased. A Sony manager says: 'Until the market enters the stage of heavy inter-company usage, and the telephone companies start publishing a videoconferencing directory, enabling users to find out easily who has a unit and dial, group systems will remain a significant portion of the systems installed'.

Source: adapted from the *Financial Times*, 26.3.1997.

(a) Suggest four ways in which a message from a manager in the UK could be sent instantly to a manager in a European country.
(b) Explain the advantages of videoconferencing over face-to-face meetings.
(c) Examine some of the problems for a business introducing videoconferencing for meetings.

main methods of business communications in future. They are a much cheaper way of sending complex, large scale communications. They also ensure that most messages get through to the right person and allow large amounts of data to be quickly and easily delivered. A report in 1997 stated that the volume of internet and intranet messages was expected to exceed telephone calls within five years.

The internet is now used by more than 40 million people. The number of information or 'web sites' grew from 19,000 in 1995 to 250,000 by 1997. Some sites carry information about companies. Others sell products directly to customers. By the year 2000 it was estimated that £50 billion worth of business would be carried out over the 'net'. Examples include Lay & Wheeler, a wine merchant selling high quality wines and Tesco, which offers delivery of wine, flowers and chocolates anywhere in Britain. A leading motor manufacturer in the UK uses the internet to support its 'just-in-time' manufacturing process (☞ unit 92). Suppliers have direct access to a central stock system over the Internet.

Information on the internet is available to the public. This makes it impossible to send confidential messages. An intranet is under the control of the company using it so information sent can be controlled. For example, a company with 150 administration staff may all be linked by a company intranet. Staff can send messages and access common information. It is suggested that the biggest savings from the intranet will come from the distribution of standard information throughout an organisation. For example, information such as the internal phone numbers, diaries and timetables quickly become out of date. In electronic format, however, they could be revised as soon as a change occurs and made available to all staff through a 'browser'. Intranets may also be extended into 'extranets'. These could include customers and suppliers as well as staff of a business.

Barriers to communication

We have seen that effective communication will take place if the message is received and understood by the receiver. There is a number of factors that might prevent this from happening.

The skills of the sender and receiver The ability of the sender to explain a message and the receiver to understand it are important in communication. If an order must be sent out by a certain date, but the sender simply asks for it to be sent as early as possible, communication would not have been effective. If the receiver does not understand what stocks to take the order from, incorrect goods may be sent.

Jargon A word or phrase which has a technical or specialised meaning is known as jargon. The terms understood by a certain group of people may be meaningless to those who don't have this knowledge. One example of this was in Schools of Motoring, where for many years drivers were given the instruction 'clutch in' or 'clutch out', which nearly always

confused the trainee. Later the instruction was changed to 'clutch down' and 'clutch up'. Technical information about a product which is not understood by the marketing department may result in misleading advertising and poor sales.

Choice of communication channel or medium Sometimes the channel or medium chosen to send the message may not communicate the information effectively. An example of this might be where a manager attempts to pass a message to an employee, but would have been more successful if the message had gone through a representative. Another example is that safety campaigns are sometimes unsuccessful because slogans and posters are used to persuade individual employees about the importance of safe working practices rather than changes being discussed.

Perceptions and attitudes How employees perceive other people can affect how they interpret the message that is sent. Employees are more likely to have confidence in people they trust, because of past experience of their reliability. On the other hand, if an employee has learned to distrust someone, then what she says will be either ignored or treated with caution. The way employees view things can be affected by being part of a group.

Form of the message If the message is unclear or unexpected the receiver is unlikely to understand it or remember it. The rate at which we forget is considerable. We have probably forgotten half of what we hear within a few hours of hearing it, and no more than 10 per cent will remain after two or three days.
The sender of the message must make sure it:
● does not contain too much information;
● is not poorly written;
● is not presented too quickly;
● is not presented in a way that the receiver does not expect;
● conveys the information that he actually wants to communicate;
● is written in a way that the receiver will understand.

Stereotypes People can often have beliefs about others. This may result in a **stereotype** (☞ unit 83) of some people. It is possible that, if one person has a stereotype of another, this may affect how they interpret a message. So, for example, if a male manager has a certain stereotype of women being less rational and able than men, his first reaction might be to ignore a female manager's communication because he believes she does not understand the information.

Length of chain of command or distance If information is passed down by word of mouth through a number of receivers, it is possible for the message to be distorted. This may result in the wrong emphasis or wrong information being received by the individual or group at the end of the communication chain. Industrial relations problems in business have sometimes been a result of a long chain of command (☞ unit 70).

Wrong target for the message Businesses sometimes send the wrong information to the wrong person. This can result in costly delays and errors and perhaps a poor image in the eyes of the public.

Breakdown of the channel This could be due to technical problems. For example, a business may rely on its management information system on the computerised network. If this breaks down, businesses might have problems dealing with enquiries. Banks, for example, are unable to tell customers what their balances are if computer terminals are not working.

Different countries and different cultures A business may have a problem sending a message from one country to another because of time differences. This is particularly a difficulty if an urgent decision is needed. Individual national traits can sometimes affect communication. A study of North and South American business people found that they each had different 'conversation distances'. In meetings, problems developed as South American business people came towards people they were talking to, whilst North Americans retreated.

Problems with information and communication technology Although new technologies can help communication, there are problems both with the amount of information sent and the use of the new technology.

● Information overload. Large amounts of information can be sent instantly by such media as fax, e-mail and the internet. This may result in information overload. Individuals and organisations may not be able to fully process all of the information that is sent. As a result, effective communication may not take place.

● Introduction. Electronic media can sometimes create problems when it is first introduced. Staff need training, which is time consuming. Mistakes can be made if information is not stored, as there may be no written record. There may also need to be a change in work methods and employees may work at a slower pace as they get use to the new methods and equipment.

● Misuse of new technology. There is evidence to suggest that employees spend more time using the internet and e-mail facilities than is necessary. 'Browsing' the internet and constantly checking e-mail for new messages can waste time. Employees may also use the technology for non-business messages.

● Confidentiality. Electronic media often send messages that can be seen by people other than the intended receiver. This can be a problem if the sender wants the message to remain confidential.

Question 5

E-mail is being used as a fast, efficient method of sending messages throughout the world. However, companies are now having to face up to e-mail-related problems. One is that staff often waste time during the day checking their e-mail. Messages may also be sent with abandon. Every member of staff in one international company received the message: 'Would the owner of a red Biro left by the second floor coffee machine like to come and collect it?' Important messages risk going unnoticed when too much is sent. A financial officer in a Silicon Valley company once found 2,000 e-mails waiting after he had been away for a week. He deleted the whole list, without looking at a single message.

Old e-mail messages are sometimes hoarded by employees as a record of what has happened for protection. For example, if a manager tells an employee to order stock and later claims he didn't when there is overstocking, the e-mail can be used as proof. This type of activity may lead to poor relations and also takes up valuable computer memory. Companies can have legal difficulties if old messages, assumed deleted, are saved and discovered by a lawyer pursuing a discrimination or unfair dismissal case.

A report by Gartner Group, a US-based research company, says: 'People who would never become emotional in an open business meeting will sometimes express their feelings with great frankness when typing a message on the computer'. The risk that employees' e-mail could give rise to litigation means that companies may reserve the right to read their staff's e-mail. However, many staff view this as an invasion of their privacy, particularly since most companies allow some personal use of e-mail. Information can get into the wrong hands through carelessness. E-mail can be mis-addressed. It is also easy to copy, circulate and forward. In other cases, leaks are not accidental. Hackers from both inside and outside the organisation can be a problem. In one US high street bank, a senior manager would ask one of his IT specialists to hack into the system if he wanted to know what was happening in the human resources department.

So how does a business deal with such problems? A variety of solutions have been used, including restrictions on use, monitoring and technical controls.

Source: adapted from the *Financial Times*, 17.3.1997.

(a) What problems of using e-mail are highlighted in the article?
(b) For each problem you have identified discuss possible rules, practices or safeguards that a business might introduce to prevent them taking place.

Factors affecting choice of medium

There is a number of factors that affect which medium a business will use in any situation.

● Direction of communication. Some methods may only be suitable for downward communication, such as films and posters. Other methods are useful for upwards communication only, such as suggestion schemes. Many methods are useful for both.

● Nature of the communication. The choice of communication method may depend on the nature of the message being sent. For example, a comment from a manager to a subordinate about unsatisfactory work may need to be confidential. It is important for the manager to choose a method which does this.

● Many messages are best sent by the use of more than one communication medium. Company rules, for example, might most effectively be communicated verbally on an induction course and as a written summary for employees to take away as a reminder.

● Costs. Films, videos and some tapeslides can be expensive. A business must decide whether the message could be sent just as well by other media.

● Variety. If, for example, a company tries to communicate too many messages by means of a noticeboard, then employees may stop reading it. To make sure messages are sent effectively, a variety of media should be used.

● Speed. If something needs communicating immediately then verbal or electronic communications tend to be quickest.

● Is a record needed? If it is, there is no point in verbally passing on the information. If it is communicated verbally, it may need written confirmation.

● Length of message. If the message is long, verbal communication may mean the receiver does not remember everything that has been said. If a simple yes or no answer is needed, written communication might not be suitable.

● Who will receive the message? The sender must consider how many people will receive the message. She must also take into account where the receiver will be and whether there is access to a means of communication.

Management information systems

A management information system (MIS) in a business is an ICT system that supplies information and communication services. It usually takes the form of integrated programmes and applications that deal with:

● order transactions;
● project planning;
● co-operative work support, such as networked schedules and diaries;
● personnel and customer databases;
● programmes to assist decision making, which pull together key performance indicators of the organisation.

The applications use both automated and manual procedures. In a well designed MIS, the different applications are not independent. They are interconnected subsystems that form a coherent, overall, integrated structure for information and communication services. An effective MIS system can help an organisation improve productivity. It should increase the amount and speed of information that can be communicated and also help to improve the quality and scope of management decisions.

Key terms

Channel of communication - the route by which a message is communicated from sender to receiver.
Communication media - the written, oral or technological methods used to communicate a message.
Information and communication technology - the use of technology to deliver messages and data from groups, individuals or businesses to others.
Network - the links that allow a message to be communicated between a number of people.

Summary

1. Why is good communication important for a business?
2. Why might a business want feedback in the communication process?
3. Explain the difference between:
   (a) formal and informal communication;
   (b) lateral and vertical communication.
4. How might upward communication be useful to a business?
5. Give an example of a message that might be sent using the following communication networks.
   (a) The circle.
   (b) The chain.
   (c) The wheel.
   (d) A connected network.
6. State 5 methods of written communication that a business might use.
7. When might face-to-face communication be more useful than written communication?
8. What is (a) videoconferencing; (b) teleconferencing; (c) e-mail?
9. Suggest two ways in which a business may use the internet.
10. State 5 factors that might affect the choice of communication.
11. State 5 barriers to communication.

Case study

Pearson's Brewery Distribution Depot

'If there's something wrong, I was usually the last person to know about it; messages from the pubs never seemed to be getting through to the right people.' This was one of the first comments Jerome Rogers heard when he took over as distribution manager of Pearson's Brewery, a medium sized business located in Essex, which served the East Anglia region.

The comment was made by one of the local planners in the large distribution depot of the brewery. Jerome was carrying out a series of interviews with his staff to find out both his own workforce's and the publicans' views about how the depot was operating.

The present system was that when the telephone rang in the office with an order any one of the 4 assistants would answer it. The load planners would then try to group orders together, but there were no regular delivery rounds. The supervisor prided himself on getting orders out quickly - he would give them out on a random basis to the delivery workers who, therefore, rarely made regular visits to one set of pubs.

Through his interviews, Jerome detected a number of problems with the system. He had previously worked in a small brewery where everyone was on first name terms and where good communications with customers was a major objective. He was surprised with the contrast between Pearson's and his old company.

Jerome felt that some way of informing all employees in the depot about its operation may help to develop a corporate culture of unity. He was also looking for ways to keep in more regular contact with head office so that he might advise them of progress and perhaps receive some help with problems.

Jerome Rogers has decided to recommend changes to the operation of Pearson's Brewery Distribution Depot. Write a report from Jerome to the management recommending solutions to the communication problems. In the report:

Depot organisation

The depot's organisation was divided into 3 sections.

● In the office were 4 clerical assistants who took incoming calls from the publicans whom the brewery supplied. The publicans usually phoned in their weekly orders, but would also phone if deliveries were late or incomplete.
● Also in the office, but in a sectioned off area, were 4 load planners who worked at computer terminals, sorting and organising the delivery loads between pubs.
● In the rest of the depot there were 65 delivery employees who carried out the deliveries to the pubs. They communicated with the office via their supervisor, who collected the delivery plans at the start of the day and gave them to the employees making the deliveries.

Results from interviews

● Deliveries were often late. The delivery workers were not very motivated by the work and would 'spin out' a delivery in order to earn overtime.
● Communication between the office and the delivery workers was poor, resulting in poor relations between the two groups.
● Within the office the 2 groups appeared to work in isolation. Each did not know what the other group was doing.
● Publicans felt that there was a lack of interest in their problems. If publicans phoned in on Friday with a rush order, or to find out why a delivery had not been made, they got the impression that no one wanted to help them.
● If there was a problem it was impossible to contact the delivery employees. For example, if someone in the depot noticed stock was left behind, he or she could not contact the driver to return to make up the incomplete order.
● There was often no written record of the orders that were phoned in by the publicans.

● **identify communication problems that exist;**
● **suggest reasons why these problems exist;**
● **outline solutions to the problems that have been identified;**
● **explain why the solutions chosen are more suitable than other methods;**
● **discuss the likely effects on the business of the proposed solutions;**
● **suggest ways in which the solutions could be communicated to the workforce and to publicans.**

Individuals, groups and organisations

A business is made up of individuals. Individual production workers, office workers or managers etc. belong to groups or teams within the firm (☞ unit 84). Many tasks in modern business are technically complex, such as the production of a vehicle, and can only be carried out in groups using the combined skills of individuals. Other tasks, such as marketing research, may require people to work together as a co-ordinated 'team'. As well as these formal groups, individuals will also belong to informal groups, for example a group of workers who become friends after joining a company at the same time. Individuals and the groups they belong to make up the business **organisation** (☞ unit 70).

No two individuals are the same. They have different characteristics, attitudes, needs and personalities. Why does a business need to know something about these differences? It will help a business to:

● make sure it has chosen the most suitable person for a job from a number of applicants;
● make certain employees' skills are used effectively;
● ensure workers are satisfied and motivated;
● tell how individuals in the workforce will react when faced with a decision or a situation at work.

Physical differences

It is very rare indeed for two individuals physically to be the same in all respects. It is possible, however, to group people based on their shape, size, hair colour etc. Sometimes certain groups are more suitable for a job than others and this may be part of the job description (☞ unit 76). For example, people wanting to join the police force must be over a minimum height and an applicant to the fire service must have a certain chest expansion. A business, however, must be careful not to restrict physically demanding jobs to men as this type of discrimination is unlawful (☞ unit 80).

Personality differences

An individual could be described by the way they behave, such as 'happy-go-lucky' or 'quiet'. These give an indication of that person's personality. Psychologists call these words TRAITS. They form the basis of important theories of personality, some of which are used by businesses to make decisions about individuals at work.

Cattell In 1965 Raymond Cattell suggested that people have 16 main traits. To measure these traits he developed a test known as 16 Personality Factor (16PF). Figure 83.1 shows the 16 traits or factors that are measured in the test. Each one has

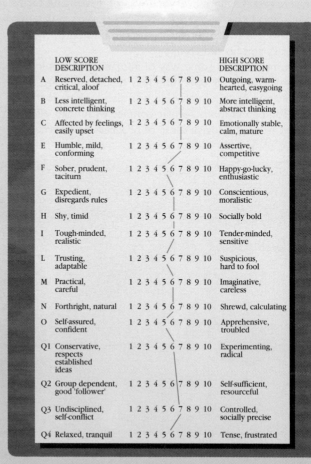

Figure 83.1 *Cattell's 16 Personality Factor questionnaire showing managing directors' average personality profile*

a scale of 1-10. For example, factor 'A' could be reserved (1), outgoing (10) or somewhere in between. People taking the test choose a point on each scale which reflects their personality. Linking together the 'scores' will give a personality profile.

The 16PF has been widely used in the selection of business managers. Kellogg's the cereal manufacturer, has used it successfully in the past. By looking at the profiles of successful managers a firm is able to build up a 'suitable' personality profile. When interviewing candidates in future, the business could ask them to fill in a 16PF test and compare their results with the 'ideal profile' to see if the candidate is suitable. Figure 83.1 shows the results of a study by Makin, Cooper and Cox. The line linking the scores shows the average personality profile of managing directors.

Eysenck In 1975 Hans Eysenck reduced the number of scales upon which personality traits could be measured to two:
● stable-unstable;
● extroverted-introverted.

The stable-unstable scale showed emotional stability. Stable people tended to be calm and reliable, whilst those with low stability tended to be anxious or reserved. The extroverted-introverted scale described people who were either passive, quiet and withdrawn (introverted) or changeable, outgoing and impulsive (extroverted).

Using these traits, Eysenck built a matrix of an individual's personality. This is shown in Figure 83.2. Individuals can be placed in one of the four quarters. A stable-introverted person may be calm and reliable, and perhaps suited to a job such as librarian. However, if the library needed an injection of new ideas a 'stable-extrovert' may be more suitable.

The matrix can have a number of uses for a business. For example, it could help judge how an employee might deal with a new situation or indicate how well a candidate might suit a particular job. A business may also use the information to build up a team of workers whose personalities complement each other to carry out a task.

Costa and McRae In the early 1990s Eysenck's work was developed by a number of theorists, such as Paul Costa and Robert McRae (1992). They outlined what have come to be known as the **'big five'**. The big five are broad personality types or trait clusters. In research studies they have been found consistently to capture the traits that we use to describe ourselves and other people. They are shown in Table 83.1. Research seems to have reproduced these dimensions, in many different settings, with different people, with different forms of data collection and in different languages.

There are, however, limits to how theories can be. They do not precisely predict what a person will do in any situation, only indicate what a person is likely to do given their personality. Behaviour might, for example, change when faced with stress. Also, people with different personalities may still be able to do a 'good' job when faced with the same situation. Another problem is that they assume an individual will give an honest response. But often it is easy to pick out the acceptable answer or the one that is best in terms of the job. For these reasons, the theories are usually used only for selection and internal promotion (☞ unit 77).

Personality and stress

Personality and health may be linked in a way that is relevant to business. In 1974, M. Friedman and R. Rosenman claimed to have identified two extreme personality patterns or 'behaviour syndromes', Type A and Type B, as shown in

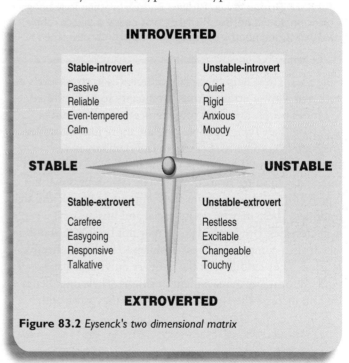

Figure 83.2 *Eysenck's two dimensional matrix*

Table 83.1			
Definitions			
extroversion	gregarious, warm, positive	versus	quiet, reserved, shy
agreeableness	straightforward, compliant, sympathetic	versus	quarrelsome, oppositional, unfeeling
conscientiousness	achievement-orientated, dutiful, self-disciplined	versus	frivolous, irresponsible, disorganised
neuroticism	anxious, depressed, self-conscious	versus	calm, contented, self-assured
openness	creative, open-minded, intellectual	versus	unimaginative, disinterested, narrow-minded

Philip Green In 1998 Philip Green was suggested as a buyer for Sears, the catalogue group. In 1999 he bought it for £549 million. His name crops up whenever any struggling retailer is mentioned. His list of deals is impressive. In 1985 he bought the struggling Jean Jeannie chain and sold it 5 months later to Lee Cooper for £3 million. In 1998 he earned an estimated £38 million after buying the previously loss making Olympus sports shops in 1995, bringing in Sports Division as a partner, and selling it to JJB Sports. It is argued that you either love or hate him, or both. He can be charming or brutal, generous or penny pinching, as the mood takes him. He is described as a high living entrepreneur and the consummate opportunist. He is undoubtedly a risk taker and he doesn't care much about those who criticise him in the City. He made his name from Amber Day Holdings, a struggling menswear company. He invested first in 1989, bought and sold two menswear chains, before buying the discount shops, What Everyone Wants, in 1990. When he fell out with WEW's founders, he quit in 1992, earning £8 million from the sale of his shares. An acquaintance said: 'no one gets on with him in management for very long'.

Source: adapted from *The Observer*, 20.12.1998.

Richard Budge When Richard Budge's brother Tony bought a mansion, so did he. But Richard's was nearly a pile of rubble. Within three months the mansion had been transformed at break neck speed by a team of workers. This sums up Budge - competitiveness with a desire to get things done in a no nonsense way. Indeed, the word fuss does not enter into his vocabulary. Budge's company RJB Mining has controlled most of the UK's coal industry since 1994. He tends to shun interviews and stays out of the limelight, possibly because of past criticism. In the 1980s and 1990s he was said to have exhibited all the trademarks of the Conservative superhero. 'Ebullient, decisive and a bloody good contractor' are how friends and enemies describe him. He has earned a reputation as a man who gets things done. An acquaintance says: 'if he sees a corner, he can't help go around it on two wheels, or even better, one'. He is heavily involved with a couple of miners' welfare groups and sponsors a pit band. In 1993 he was chairperson of the Coal Trade Benevolent Association and he works with the Coal Industry and Social Welfare Organisation.

Source: adapted from *The Observer*, 1997.

(a) What definitions from the 'big five' might be used to adequately describe the personality traits of Richard Budge?
(b) Applying Eysenck's Matrix, categorise Philip Green's personality.
(c) To what extent would you describe Richard Budge as more Type A or Type B?

Table 83.2. These help to explain differences in stress levels at work and allow a 'stress-prone' personality to be identified.

Type A people are more impatient, competitive and aggressive than Type B people, and are more likely to suffer stress-related problems. For example, Friedman and Rosenman found that Type A personalities were three times more likely to suffer heart disease than Type B personalities. Type As thrive on long hours, large amounts of work and tight deadlines. These may be useful social and business characteristics. However, Type As may not be able to stand back from a complex business problem to make an effective decision. They tend to lack the patience and relaxed style required for many management positions. Their impatience can also increase the stress levels of those they work with.

Table 83.2

Type A personality characteristics	Type B personality characteristics
Competitive	Able to take time out to enjoy leisure
High need for achievement	Not preoccupied with achievement
Aggressive	Easygoing
Works fast	Works at a steady pace
Impatient	Seldom impatient
Restless	Not easily frustrated
Extremely alert	Relaxed
Tense facial muscles	Moves and speaks slowly
Constant feeling of time pressure	Seldom lacks enough time

Assessing personality in practice

The work of Cattell and Eysenck tries to 'measure' personality. In business, however, people judge the personality of others in less formal ways, and often fairly quickly. The decision may be based on what they themselves think is important. It could also be influenced by a 'stereotype' (☞ unit 80), where personality is linked to race, sex or age. For example, it may be claimed that female managers are more emotional than male.

It is argued that people get an impression of someone from the first piece of information they receive about that person's characteristics. In an interview, for example, recruiters often make up their minds in the first four minutes and rarely change them. A candidate that did not seem prepared, looked untidy or was abrupt may well have lost the job straight away. People make these decisions because they do not like being uncertain about others. A decision based on first impressions may make the interviewer feel more secure, even if it is wrong. It may take time and further contact before people are seen 'as they really are'. Employers and employees must be prepared to change their minds about people they meet and work with. Only then will they be able to make an 'accurate' assessment of someone's personality.

Differences in intelligence

As well as differing in personality, people differ in intelligence or IQ. There is considerable debate about what intelligence is. One definition, by American psychologist Arthur Jensen, is that it is the ability to discover rules, patterns and principles, and apply these to problems.

Intelligence is usually measured by using **IQ tests.** They test an individual's ability to reason. A simple IQ test question may ask for the next number in the sequence 1,3,6,10. This tests the ability to find a sequence and to apply it. An IQ 'score' is usually given at the end of the test. A high score is supposed to indicate a higher level of intelligence. Such tests are often criticised, particularly when comparing the intelligence of people in different social groups.

There is a number of factors which are thought to influence an individual's IQ although there is little agreement on exactly how they affect the IQ.

● Culture and class. Many researchers argue that IQ tests are biased in favour of the middle classes, since tests are largely constructed by members of this group. Working class people tend to do less well on tests, so comparisons of intelligence between people in these groups are not really valid. It has also been shown that 'Western' IQ tests are not suitable for non-Western people. Cultural differences can mean they often approach and carry out the tests in an inappropriate way.

● Genes. There is general agreement that intelligence can be inherited. Some psychologists, such as Hans Eysenck in Britain, suggest that some 80 per cent of intelligence is inherited from parents. The rest is influenced by environmental factors such as the environment where we live and grow up, diet, quality of housing and family size.

● Environment. Some argue that differences in IQ are largely due to environmental factors. Research has shown that IQ test results can be affected by the education, motivation and physical health of the person taking the test. They can also be influenced by the person's rapport with whoever is carrying out the test and the language the test is set in.

Businesses today are now less likely to use IQ tests as a means of assessing an individual. Evidence suggests there is little connection between a person's IQ and how well he might do a job. It may be more important for a business to find out about an individual's knowledge and skills (which may include elements of IQ) as this could give a greater understanding of how a person might contribute to the organisation.

Question 3

Today's candidate for most famous knowledge worker might be Bill Gates, the founder of Microsoft. The information revolution has made the management of knowledge vitally important for businesses. Some companies believe that the answer to creating knowledge workers is to recruit the brightest people. This may make sense. A 1995 study in 3,100 US workplaces looked at the relationship between education and productivity. The research showed that, on average, a 10 per cent increase in the workforce's education level led to an 8.6 per cent gain in productivity. This could be compared with a 10 per cent rise in plant and equipment values, which increased productivity by 3.4 per cent.

Another example showing the financial value of people who might be called knowledge workers was the move by institutional investors to have Maurice Saatchi dismissed from Cordiant, the advertising agency (formerly Saatchi & Saatchi). When he left, several directors left in protest and customers such as Mars and BA also defected, leading to a halving of the company's share price. This answers the question often asked by Charles Handy, a management specialist: 'What happens when your assets walk out of the door?' In effect the institutional shareholders thought they owned Saatchi & Saatchi. In fact, they owned less than half of it. Most of the value could be attributed to the human capital of the knowledge workers.

But employing bright people is not a guarantee of success. You might have the best brains, but they must be working for you. Some 150,000 of what might be called 'the brightest workers in the world' left IBM. The problem had been, as IBM later admitted, that many of them were working to their own agenda. Another problem is that some companies believe you can be too intelligent for the job. The most brilliant people are not always easy to manage. However, if the job demands a brilliant mind, then it seems logical to seek out the best.

Source: adapted from the *Financial Times*, 11.6.1997.

(a) What are the potential problems of knowledge workers for a business?

(b) Why might it make sense to recruit the 'brightest' people to be knowledge workers?

(c) Using evidence from the article, discuss the importance of knowledge workers as assets to the business.

Differences in knowledge and skills

A business needs to know what knowledge and skills an employee has so that she can be given a position in the business where she will be of most use.

Knowledge can be technical, job specific, vocational or general. To be a plumber, a worker would need the technical knowledge of the trade, eg what types of materials and techniques are used for certain jobs. Also, the plumber would need to have knowledge about the way tasks should be carried out and a thorough knowledge of what is involved in the trade - the vocational aspects of being a plumber. In addition, the plumber may need to have more general knowledge, such as the ability to do simple mathematics.

As well as having knowledge, an employee will also need skills. These are the abilities needed to complete a task. The skills required at work can be job specific, communication skills, IT skills, numeracy and literacy skills or problem solving skills. A plumber would not only need to know how to complete a task, but have the appropriate skills to carry it out. The ability to communicate with customers may also be a useful skill.

Businesses in the 1990s want a more qualified and more skilled workforce. They expect workers to update their skills through training, and to develop new and different skills. This makes employees more adaptable and flexible. In the 1990s it has been suggested that **knowledge work** and **knowledge workers** are critical to business success in a changing business environment. Knowledge work requires employees who can:

● use their own existing knowledge;
● acquire new information;
● combine and process information to produce and communicate new information;
● learn continuously from their experiences.

Management theorists such as Peter Drucker and Michael Porter have suggested that knowledge is an important resource for businesses (☞ unit 85) and a source of competitive advantage (☞ unit 16). They argue that work increasingly involves the processing and production of ideas, images, thoughts, concepts and symbols rather than physical materials. Knowledge workers are most suitable to carry out this sort of work. Knowledge workers are sometimes combined to make knowledge teams (☞ unit 84).

Problem solving and decision making

Businesses are not only interested in the abilities of their employees, but in the way they use them to solve problems. The way in which an employee prefers to work may cause problems if it differs from the way colleagues work or from what the business expects.

In 1984, Michael Kirton studied the way management initiatives in a business might succeed or fail. He suggested that success may depend on how **problem solving** was tackled and identified two approaches. ADAPTORS tend to solve problems by using existing or slightly modified approaches. They do not make rapid changes in the way problems are solved. INNOVATORS, however, try to find exciting and possibly unexpected ways of solving problems. Take the example of a small business having problems finding information quickly and easily when it is stored in files. The adaptor might suggest a better method of organising the files. An innovator, however, may feel that replacing the paper filing system with a computer system will be a better solution. These are two extremes. It is likely in business that people will have a combination of the two appproaches.

Both these approaches have their strengths and weaknesses. The adaptor can effectively work within the present system, but does not find it easy to seek new solutions. For example, an 'adaptor' working in marketing might look for new product developments using existing products. The innovator, on the other hand, may produce ideas for new products. This approach often means that the innovator finds it difficult to get ideas accepted. Innovators may be seen as extroverts, generating lists of new ideas, but ignoring the needs of the business. Their attitude can often mean that an adaptor feels uncomfortable working with them. The adaptor, however, may appear conservative and always willing to agree with a superior.

What can managers do to minimise clashes? A study in 1991 by Makin, Cooper and Cox argued that the solution lies in understanding, together with an acceptance of the other person's position. Knowing someone else's style allows a manager to predict what they are likely to do in any situation.

Differences in emotional intelligence

In 1995 Goleman, an American Harvard Management specialist, coined the term **emotional intelligence**. It is the ability of a person to sense and understand their own and others' emotions and to apply that understanding to achieve an outcome, for example in a business situation. Successful businesses are able to harness emotional intelligence. Goleman argues that the 'business intelligence' of employees is affected by emotions rather than technical expertise, because emotions drive thinking.

Different individuals will have different emotional intelligence. A study of four year old children found that those who controlled their emotions, and resisted the temptation to eat a marshmallow, performed better on college entry tests fourteen years later. The theory may explain why some employees have problems after early career success. Problems arise because of their inability to understand their impact on others rather than to a lack of expertise. A study by the US company 3M found 90 per cent of the problems which affected its employees' performance were unmeasured. This was because they related to a lack of interpersonal skills, stress, emotional conflicts and personal health, rather than technical failure, absenteeism or poor training.

Question 4

Everything in Texas is big except perhaps Don Carty's ego. Modest Carty took over as chief executive of the world's biggest airline, American Airlines, in 1998. He was understudy to the world's most famous airline ego, Bob Crandell, for many years. Crandell was famous for fire, brimstone and big ideas. He terrified rivals and fellow executives. He introduced the very first frequent flyer programme and the powerful Sabre computer reservations system into the airline industry. He fought death defying fares wars. On two occasions in the 1990s President Clinton had to intervene to settle bitter pay disputes.

But Carty has risen to the top with a reputation as a 'nice guy'. He believes in evolution rather than radical ideas, collaborative decision making and a strong focus on profit. A proposed global alliance deal with British Airways has been on the table for two years, but he is patient and prepared to wait. He is prepared to admit his mistakes. He lobbied against BA's previous link with US Airways as uncompetitive, but now wants links with both. He opposed code sharing, where two or more airlines marketed themselves as one, but joined in once everyone else was doing it. He is no Crandell, but then he would never have been chosen to succeed him if he was.

Source: adapted from The Observer, 28.6.1998.

(a) Contrast the two approaches to decision making of the two chief executives of American Airlines.
(b) Using examples from the article, examine possible advantages and disadvantages for American Airlines of these approaches.

Summary

1. State 3 reasons why businesses need to know about the different characteristics of individuals.
2. What is meant by the 16 Personality Factor?
3. Explain the terms:
   (a) stable;
   (b) unstable;
   (c) extrovert;
   (d) introvert;
   in relation to the work of Eysenck.
4. What characteristics might an unstable-extrovert have?
5. How might Eysenck's analysis of personality traits be used by business?
6. State 3 factors which are thought to influence an individual's intelligence.
7. What are the problems a business might face in using IQ tests?
8. State 5 differences in skills and knowledge that one employee might have from another.
9. What is meant by the term knowledge worker?
10. Explain the difference between an innovator's and adaptor's approach to problem solving.
11. What might cause a clash between an innovator and an adaptor in the work setting?
12. Why might understanding emotional intelligence be important for a business?

Key terms

Adaptors - individuals who tend to solve problems by using existing or slightly modified approaches already used by the business.
Innovators - individuals who tend to solve problems by finding new, exciting and unexpected solutions to problems in a business.
Traits - words used in identifying an individual's personality.

Case study

A woman with ideas

Jane is a personnel officer in a large advertising agency. She has achieved rapid promotion in the company from her role as a secretary in the sales department to personnel officer with responsibility for recruitment. She did this by completing the Institute of Personnel Management qualifications through evening and weekend courses over a four year period. She was determined to do it and had the intelligence and perseverance finally to achieve her goal.

She has been in personnel for 2 years and has developed skills and knowledge in many different areas of the profession - in employee legislation, industrial relations issues and in her main interest of recruitment. Jane is outgoing (she had been tested and categorised as stable and extrovert using Eysenck's typology of personality) and popular with her peers. She has always believed in finding new ways to solve particular problems.

The latest problem she faced was the shortage of well qualified administrative staff who were competent in using the newly-installed computer system. The training given by the company was extremely comprehensive and it was difficult to replace lost employees with the same level of expertise.

Jane recognised that the problem consisted of two main elements. First, not enough men were attracted to this area of work and, second, some of the women who had been trained were leaving to start a family. Due to poor local nursery provision, these women tended to stay at home rather than return to work after having children.

Her plan of action encompassed both aspects of the problem. She devised an educational campaign for the company aimed at men, in order that they might review their own ideas about the suitability of administrative work for males. In it she wanted to emphasise the promotion opportunities in administration work and how it was possible to achieve management status through the administrative route. She showed how administrative work had changed from traditionally repetitive office tasks to ones where high technology and problem solving skills were vital. She targeted the male sector by demonstrating that administrative work required types of skills that were often associated with men. At the same time, she planned to introduce creche facilities for the female employees of the company that would cost them far less than a private nursery and would also be cost effective for the organisation.

She drew up her plans and costed them out. The campaign materials and accompanying workshop sessions would be £5,000 for the year. The creche facilities would need capital expenditure of approximately £15,000. The ongoing costs would be met by the employees willing to make use of the service. At present it was costing them £35,000 to recruit and train the staff required for the administration vacancies in the company. She presented her findings to the executive board in a confident and assertive way.

The plan was rejected by senior management as too expensive in the short term and too far fetched. She was told to improve her selection procedures so that she recruited people that would stay. She was also told not to involve herself in other aspects of personnel work that were not her reponsibility.

Jane felt saddened and disillusioned by this experience.

(a) **How would you describe Jane's personality from the information?**

(b) **Identify the characteristics that have gained Jane rapid promotion in the business.**

(c) **What would be her approach to problem solving? Explain your answer using examples from the passage.**

(d) **What potential problems might her decision making approach cause for the business?**

(e) **Why do you think Jane's ideas were rejected by senior management?**

(f) **Suggest an alternative approach that Jane might have used when putting forward her plan.**

Working in groups

Working with other people in groups or teams is something that many employees do in business. An employee in a marketing consultancy business may be part of a team developing TV adverts for a client, part of a group set up to think of ideas to improve working methods and may meet with friends for lunch. Only in a small number of cases will individual employees work on their own, as in the case of a freelance journalist. Even an employee delivering goods on his own from a van will interact with staff and management when he returns to the office or factory.

Individuals may behave differently when working in a group than if they were working on their own. For example, an employee on a building site might want to work at a leisurely pace or find ways to avoid carrying out a task immediately. Group pressure could persuade or embarrass the employee into working harder than he would have wished. The group may want to finish the job early or earn any bonus that is available. In this case the employee's behaviour has changed as a result of being a group member. He is behaving in a way that conforms to the GROUP NORM. In other words, he is behaving in a way that is 'normal' for that group.

There is a certain amount of evidence to support the idea that individual behaviour is influenced by the group. The Hawthorne Studies (☞ unit 71) showed that group behaviour can influence workers' motivation. It is possible to identify certain common features of groups that exist in businesses.

● The behaviour of the group influences all members, eg if a decision is made to take industrial action (☞ unit 87).
● Members of the group have some common interests and objectives, eg a production team may want to increase its level of overtime payments.
● Members meet and discuss common interests, eg assembly line workers might discuss the latest changes to working conditions.
● There are rules or norms influencing members' behaviour, eg members of the finance committee of a business are expected to report back to the managing director after each meeting.

It could be argued that, given the emphasis on team work in many modern organisations, it is essential for businesses to understand how people work in groups. If employees in a group do not work 'well' together, this may reduce productivity and make decision making more difficult.

Types of group

It is possible to distinguish different groups that exist in business. One common method is to divide them into FORMAL and INFORMAL groups.

Formal groups These are groups which are set up by a business specifically to carry out tasks. Formal groups are an actual part of the organisation, with arranged meetings and rules determining their behaviour and actions. Examples of formal groups might be management teams that control one aspect of a business, such as the finance department.

Other examples of formal groups might be groups which are set up to deal with certain problems. For example, a unit might be set up by a business to monitor the introduction of new

Question

Allied Corporation is a multinational. Part of the company is an engine manufacturing division, which became the focus of an investigation. A researcher spent time working in this factory as a participant observer. He observed the following about how groups, made up of operators, schedule co-ordinators and crib attendants, worked on the shop floor.

At the beginning of the shift, operators assembled outside the time office on the shop floor to collect their production cards, punch in and set up for the first task. Usually operators know from talking to their counterparts, before the beginning of the shift, which task they are likely to receive. Knowing what is available on the shop floor for their machine, operators are sometimes able to bargain with the scheduling man, who is distributing the tasks.

After receiving their first tasks, operators have to find the blueprint and tooling for the operation. These are usually in the crib, although they may be already out on the floor. The crib attendant is therefore a strategic person whose co-operation an operator must secure. If the crib attendant chooses to be unco-operative in dispensing tools, blueprints, fixtures etc. and particularly in the grinding of tools, operators can be held up for considerable lengths of time.

Occasionally, operators who have managed to gain the confidence of the crib attendant will enter the crib themselves to speed up the process. Since, unlike the scheduling man, the crib attendant has no real interest in whether operators achieve output targets his co-operation has to be gained by other means. An employee commented, 'For the first five months of my employment my relations with the crib attendant on second shift were very poor, but at Christmas things changed dramatically. Every year the local union distributes a Christmas ham to all its members. I told Harry, the crib attendant, that I couldn't be bothered picking up mine from the union hall and that he could have it for himself. He was delighted and after that, I received good service.'

Source: adapted from *Manufacturing Consent*, M.Burawoy, University of Chicago Press.

(a) Explain how being a member of a group in the above example has affected the workers' behaviour.
(b) Why might this be important for the business?
(c) What common interests might the groups of workers in the factory have?

machinery. The group may include the production manager, an engineer, a supervisor and a number of operators. Its task may be to make sure the changeover is as efficient as possible and it would meet to discuss ways in which this could be achieved.

Formal groups can be **temporary** or **permanent**. A temporary group might be a working party to investigate a computerised information system. Permanent groups include standing committees, such as health and safety committees or a trade union, which is a formal group, but not one created by management. The type of group depends on whether the task involved is recurrent or a 'one-off'.

Informal groups Informal groups are made up of employees with similar interests. They are not a formal part of the business itself. They do not have any formal 'rules', although there are often unofficial norms which influence members' behaviour. An example of an informal group might be a casual meeting over lunch between managers in the production, marketing and finance departments to discuss a new product launch. It could also be a group of hospital workers discussing possible job cuts in their rest room.

There are certain reasons why informal groups exist. It is argued that these groups meet the psychological needs (☞ unit 83) of employees. These might be some of the following.

● The need to be with other people.
● Status is determined by membership of various groups. This will also influence the view people have of their personal value and self-esteem.
● Groups offer a feeling of security and mutual support. By doing so, they reduce uncertainty and anxiety.
● The group may act as a problem solver for its members.

The informal groups that develop will be determined, to a large extent, by the physical layout required for work. Distance has a powerful influence on who will interact with whom. In general, the more frequent the interactions, the more likely informal groups are to be formed. Informal groups can have considerable influence on group members and the norms and values that a group develops may or may not support those of the organisation.

It may appear that formal and informal groups are separate. This is not the case. Groups that start off as formal often develop powerful informal relations. Part of a company, as well as being a department, may be a department of friends. Japanese organisations, such as Sony, deliberately encourage this. Informal groupings, such as friendships outside work, can provide useful channels of communication for the organisation. The **grapevine** is a term used for such channels (☞ unit 82).

It is also possible to divide groups into primary and secondary groups.

● Primary groups are small groups where people can have regular contact, eg a small department or office, or a youth club.
● Secondary groups are large groups where people have less regular contact, eg a large open-plan office or a large meeting.

Question 2

(a) Identify the possible:
  (i) formal;
  (ii) informal;
  groups that the successful candidate might belong to using information in the advertisement.
(b) Explain how belonging to informal groups might help:
  (i) the new employee when settling into the job;
  (ii) the business in its relations with the new employee.

Estate Officer

£15,525 - £16,937 p.a. inc.

Aldenham Country Park is managed by the Environmental Management Group of Hertfordshire County Council's Environment Department. Located in the south of the county it serves a broad catchment area including north London. As a member of the Park team you will help to maintain the Park as a quiet, safe countryside experience for its many visitors. You will have excellent communication skills to cope with a high degree of public contact. Experience of leading volunteer and education groups is also essential, as is the ability to complete practical estate tasks to a high standard, with little supervision. The Park includes a Rare Breeds farm so knowledge of animal husbandry would be an advantage.

You will have a broad knowledge of environmental issues and the flexibility and enthusiasm to tackle the numerous and varied challenges presented to the Park team.

You will work every Saturday and Sunday as well as three midweek days. The post does require a basic level of fitness and mobility.

Informal enquiries can be made to Simon Aries, on (01992) 555255. For an application pack please contact Jackie Platten, Personnel, Environment Department, County Hall, Pegs Lane, Hertford, Herts SG13 8DN. Tel: (01992) 556038 (24 hour answerphone). Minicom: (01992) 555224. Please quote ref: E262. Closing date: 25.6.99. Interviews: w/c 5.7.99

Information available on tape, in Braille or large print on request.

Hertfordshire COUNTY COUNCIL

POSITIVE ABOUT DISABLED PEOPLE

An Equal Opportunity Employer

A **team** is a particular type of group. Teams are usually put together for a purpose. For example, a business may have team meetings of workers to discuss production problems or have a team of designers developing a new product. Teams are dealt with later in this unit.

Group decision making

The aims of businesses are to try and create groups that are effective and efficient. If the business can motivate the group to work harder in order to achieve goals, the sense of pride in the group's own competence might create job satisfaction. There is a number of factors that can help group decision making.

Group members The characteristics and goals of the individual members of the group will help to determine the group's characteristics and goals. An individual is likely to be influenced more strongly by a small group than by a large group. In a large group the person may feel overwhelmed and, therefore, unable to participate effectively in team decisions.

It has been suggested that the effectiveness of a group depends on the blend of the individual skills and abilities of its members. A group might be most effective if it contains:
● a person of originality and ideas;
● a 'get-up-and-go' person with considerable energy, enthusiasm and drive;
● a quiet, logical thinker, who ponders carefully and criticises

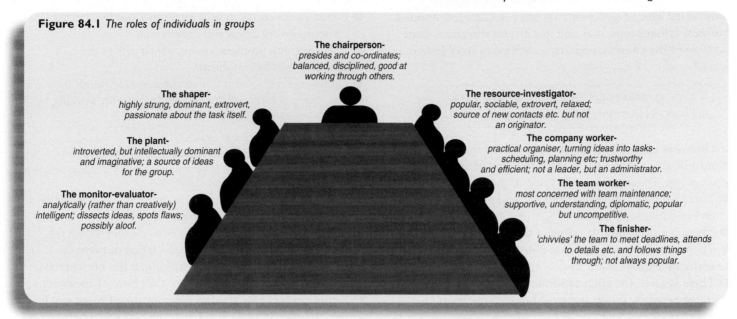

Figure 84.1 *The roles of individuals in groups*

The chairperson-
presides and co-ordinates;
balanced, disciplined, good at
working through others.

The shaper-
highly strung, dominant, extrovert,
passionate about the task itself.

The resource-investigator-
popular, sociable, extrovert, relaxed;
source of new contacts etc. but not
an originator.

The plant-
introverted, but intellectually dominant
and imaginative; a source of ideas
for the group.

The company worker-
practical organiser, turning ideas into tasks-
scheduling, planning etc; trustworthy
and efficient; not a leader, but an administrator.

The monitor-evaluator-
analytically (rather than creatively)
intelligent; dissects ideas, spots flaws;
possibly aloof.

The team worker-
most concerned with team maintenance;
supportive, understanding, diplomatic, popular
but uncompetitive.

The finisher-
'chivvies' the team to meet deadlines, attends
to details etc. and follows things
through; not always popular.

the ideas of others.

This is why groups set up to consider new products often draw members from a number of different departments in the business. This means the group will have a wide range of skills and abilities.

Group roles The most comprehensive study of group roles within a work setting is most probably that of **Meredith Belbin** (1981). He found that successful teams consisted of a mix of individuals, each of whom performed a different role. A summary of these roles is shown in Figure 84.1.

According to Belbin each person has a preferred role and for a group to be effective all the roles need to be filled. So a business might select people to ensure that they fill one or more of the roles which a group lacks. This is not always possible. Most formal groups within business are predetermined by who has the technical expertise to carry out the task.

How then can a knowledge of these roles help?

- For a group to work efficiently the business must be aware of the roles people prefer. These may become apparent through observation. People should be given tasks which allow them to operate in their preferred roles, whether in a sporting team or in a team of medical staff in a casualty department.

- There should be an understanding of which roles are missing that may cause inefficiency. For example, some researchers conducted a study into why some quality circles (☞ unit 73) continued to meet, while others ceased to. They found that all the groups that failed lacked someone who preferred the 'finisher' role. Apparently these groups were good at problem solving and finding solutions but never carried their ideas through.

The group's task The nature of the task may affect how a group is managed. If a job must be done urgently, it is often necessary to dictate how things should be done, rather than to encourage participation in decision making. Jobs which are routine and undemanding are unlikely to motivate individuals or the group as a whole. If individuals want authoritarian leadership, they are also likely to want clearly defined targets.

Group development Groups do not come into existence fully formed. B.Tuckman and N. Jensen (1977) suggested that groups pass through five stages of development. Progress through all stages may be slow, but is necessary for the group to be effective. Some groups get stuck in the middle and remain inefficient.

- **Forming** is when individuals in the group start to find out about each other and are keen to impress other group members. They usually require guidance from a leader about the nature of the group's task.

- **Storming** is a conflict stage. Members bargain with each other and try to sort out what each of them wants individually and as a group. Individuals reveal their personal goals. Hostility may develop if people's goals are different. Individuals may resist the control of other members.

- **Norming** is where group members develop ways of working together. The question of who will do what and how it will be done is addressed. Rules are established. There is greater cohesion and information is passed between group members.

- **Performing** is where the group has developed cohesion. It is concerned with getting the job done and accomplishing its objectives. There is a feeling of interdependence and a commitment to problem solving.

- **Adjourning** is where the group disbands because the task had been achieved or because the members have left.

A group may be ineffective if it has failed to sort out certain issues at earlier stages. For example, problems may result if the issue of leadership has not been decided. Another problem is that people may pull in different directions if the purpose of the group has not been clarified or its objectives agreed.

The characteristics of an effective work group

If a business is to try and improve the effectiveness of groups it must be able to identify the characteristics of an effective work group. These may include some of the following.

● There is a high commitment to the achievement of targets and organisational goals.
● There is a clear understanding of the group's work.
● There is a clear understanding of the role of each person within the group.
● There is a free and open communication between members of the group and trust between members.
● There is idea sharing.
● The group is good at generating new ideas.

Question 3

The Waterfront is a hotel in Bournemouth. It considers that its staff are effective because they operate as a team. It has recently been awarded Investors in People status because of its commitment to its employees. Employees are flexible. Staff absences are covered by other staff, so shortages do not lead to a reduced quality of service. Employees have made a number of suggestions that have solved problems in the hotel. For example, in busy periods some bookings were not taken up. This left empty rooms which could have been filled. One member of staff suggested a reminder be sent in busy periods and this reduced unfilled rooms by 50 per cent.

The hotel had recently promoted its services as a 'wedding centre'. It offered accommodation and a room for the wedding, and provided food for guests. At one reception, however, the owners were on holiday. Staff were unsure who was responsible for ordering flowers. Two sets of flowers were ordered as a result, which raised the costs of the wedding to the hotel. Two of the more senior members of staff also disagreed on the time at which the food would be served.

(a) What might have been the characteristics that made the group at the hotel operate effectively?
(b) Explain the problems that were faced by the group when the new service was introduced.
(c) Examine ways in which the group operation might be improved in future.

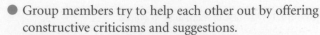

● Group members try to help each other out by offering constructive criticisms and suggestions.
● There is group problem solving which gets to the root causes of the work problem.
● Group members seek a united consensus of opinion.
● The group is motivated to be able to carry on working in the absence of its leader.

Factors influencing group decision making

There is a number of factors which determine how effective groups are when making decisions.

Size of the group Research has been carried out into the effects of group size on decision making. It has been argued that groups become ineffective once they have 21 members. Other researchers have tried to measure an optimum size for groups. It is felt, in many cases, that the best size is between 3-7 members, with 5 often being quoted as an ideal number.

Why might groups containing these numbers be effective? Larger groups often have communication problems, as more and more people wish to contribute to group discussions. In a small group, the chairperson's role may be fairly informal. When groups get large, however, more formal management may be needed. To address all remarks through the chair in a meeting of 4 people is perhaps being over-formal. To do so in a meeting of 20 may be a necessity.

The size of the task can determine group size. A group designing and building a motor racing car may require many people, with a variety of skills. Each member is likely to make some contribution to the task of the group. But a group which decides who is to drive the car in a Grand Prix may be small in order to reach a clear decision.

Communication Communication in groups can influence how group decisions are made. A distinction is often made between two types of group.

● Centralised groups are groups where individuals can only communicate with other group members via a central member.
● Decentralised groups are groups where every member can communicate directly with every other member.

Communication in groups can take place in a number of ways.

● The wheel. This is where a person at the centre of the group can communicate with all the other members. They, on the other hand, can only communicate with him or her. If they wish to communicate to other members they can only do so through the same central person. This might be the case in a formal meeting.
● The chain. Information is passed from one individual to the next before it reaches the last person in the group. Any individual only ever communicates with one other person. This might be the case in a police operation, for example.

- The circle. Communication is circular, in other words, messages pass between certain people, who pass it on to others, such as in a large office.
- The all-channel. Every member of the group can communicate directly with every other member, as in an open discussion on where an 'awards' evening should be held.

The degree of centrality is highest in the wheel and is less in the chain and circle. The all-channel has no centre; decisions are made by reaching an agreement. The degree of centralisation can affect the group's efficiency, but this also depends on the complexity of the task. When the task is simple, eg deciding on the recruitment policy for a particular job, centralised groups like the wheel are faster and make fewer errors. When the task is more complicated, eg organising and putting into practice a recruitment policy for a particular job, decentralised groups may be more suitable.

Unit 82 explains the methods and problems of communication for the business in more detail.

Leadership It is likely that a group will have a 'leader' to control or guide it (☞ unit 74). Leadership may be informal, in the sense that one person 'dominates' a group because of their personality, position or access to information. Leaders can also be elected or nominated by the group, such as chairperson.

There is a number of different leadership styles.

- Autocratic. This involves one-way communication between the leader and others in the group. The leader makes all the decisions and gives out instructions, expecting them to be obeyed by other group members without question. An example might be a powerful head of a large business like Rupert Murdoch.
- Persuasive. The leader makes all the decisions, but believes that other group members need to be motivated to accept them before they will do what she wants them to. She therefore tries to explain her decisions in order to convince them of her point of view, as a teacher or lecturer in a class might.
- Consultative. This involves discussion between the leader and the other group members involved in making a decision, but the leader retains the right to make the decision herself. By consulting with her group members before making any decision, the leader will take into account their advice and feelings. A council leader might have to operate in this way.
- Democratic. This is an approach where the leader makes a decision based on consensus and agreement within the group. Group members with the greatest knowledge of a problem will have greater influence over the decision. A trade union representative is likely to adopt this style.

Skills used in groups For individuals to work well in groups, they need to have a variety of skills. These skills can be categorised into three general areas.

- Contribution. Individuals need to communicate their ideas effectively, informing group members of their thoughts, views and motives. They also need to be able to initiate ideas and evaluate both their own contribution and those of others.
- Co-operation. Individuals need to support other group members so that everyone is involved. This is more likely if individuals share their ideas and listen to others. They should also be able to negotiate and consult, so that everyone feels part of the group's activities.
- Production. Group members need to gather information, materials and ideas, and share them with other group members. They need to show the skills of perseverance and reliability especially if the group is struggling with a problem.

Advantages and problems of group decisions

To what extent are groups more effective in making decisions than individuals? There is a number of advantages in groups making decisions for a business and for the members themselves.

- Groups can pool ideas and draw on a variety of expertise. This makes them particularly good at finding errors. For example, in the design and construction of nuclear reactors, a whole variety of groups working on safety aspects are more likely to ensure that all safety measures are thought of and solutions found to safety problems.
- Groups can handle a great deal of information and involved tasks in a shorter period of time than an individual would take. An example might be the design and writing of a computerised information program.
- Group members may support, motivate and help other members when making decisions.
- Groups provide a basis for accountability within a firm. They can also be used as the basis for a bonus system to increase productivity.

Despite these advantages, there are sometimes problems in group decision making.

- Group decisions may take time. When a decision needs to be made quickly, such as a decision to re-order stock, an individual may be more effective from a business point of view. There will be no debate, which will delay any decision that is made.
- Where one person is an obvious expert in the field, that person may make a more accurate and effective decision, for example, a personnel manager in deciding how best to train certain employees.
- There could be conflicting views and personalities within groups. This can lead to a lack of cohesion, with no shared aims or objectives. The result is that the group becomes inefficient in carrying out a task.
- There may be a possibility of 'risky-shift' decisions. Groups may make riskier decisions than individuals

would, due to too much group cohesion. For example, a board of directors might decide as a group to take over a potentially profitable, but inefficient, firm. An individual entrepreneur might have considered this decision too risky to take.

Inter-group relations and conflict

One problem that may result for the business from group activity is a conflict between groups. Many managers would agree that some inter-group competition is inevitable and perhaps useful. If there was no competition the business may become stagnant, with few pressures to make changes. This could lead to inefficiency. The other extreme, of very high levels of competition and conflict, may also cause problems. It could lead to anxiety and tension in the workforce which are counter-productive.

Why might conflict result between groups?

● Groups are often in competition with each other over resources. One example might be where the sports and leisure department in a local council needs funds for a swimming pool, but this may result in another group such as the social services department having less. Another example would be where an employee who is an integral part of a production team may have to leave the team at a vital time to attend a health and safety meeting. Conflict results from the groups' competition for the employee's time.

● There may be conflict between groups at different levels in the business organisation. For example, non-graduate entrants to a bank may be restricted because of the promotion or higher pay of graduate entrants.

● Conflict can result when groups have different goals. Unit 3 showed that when there is a divorce of **ownership and control** managers may attempt to satisfy their own aims, such as market leadership by a series of price cuts. At the same time they would attempt to make a satisfactory profit for shareholders, who may have wanted the business to maximise profits.

● There are certain psychological factors which can often lead to conflict between groups. When groups are in competition, each will tend to underplay its weaknesses, overestimate its strengths and degrade the other group. The other group may also be seen as hostile or aggressive. As a result it becomes the enemy - 'them' against 'us'. Because of these two factors, interactions between the two groups become strained and decline.

How can conflict either be avoided or, if it already exists, defused? One method that involves low levels of risk is by getting members of one group to work with the other group. This can be achieved by organising joint projects or by some form of exchange. The leaders of the group could initially either work together or exchange roles for this approach to be effective. It can be further developed by communication and

swapping of group members. This technique is often used when one organisation takes over another (☞ unit 101) and there is a need to avoid conflict at all levels within the 'new' business. Another possibility is for a business to rotate membership of groups to prevent divisions taking place.

Question 4

IceCool, a major ice cream manufacturer, is concerned with two business problems - reduced profitability due to rising costs and a lack of appeal among the youth market. It has asked the production and marketing departments for their diagnosis of the problem. Both departments are keen to impress, as it could mean greater resources being dedicated to them if they won the argument.

The marketing department managed to have funds allocated to it so that it could carry out marketing research on the development of a new ice-cream snack. The results of its work suggest that a market segment of 16-19 year olds would particularly like a dynamic, sports and fitness orientated ice-cream snack - a 'Lucozade Sports' ice cream. The price for this product would have to be in the 80p-90p bracket and the packaging would have to be bright, young and dynamic. The advertising approach would be a nationwide television campaign backed up by national billboard displays. It forecast that the payback period will be 2 years, but that high profit margins will then be generated for a further 2 years before going into decline. It has presented its plans to the board of directors.

The production department was far more concerned with the lack of productivity caused by poor capital investment over the last two years. Without any extra allocation of funds, it presented a paper to the board of directors that suggested attacking the problem of poor productivity first so that it might compete more effectively using the product range that was already tried, tested and successful. It was particularly scathing about introducing a new product without solving the underlying problems. Likewise, the marketing department was amazed at the lack of vision from the production department.

(a) Why did conflict arise between the production and marketing departments at IceCool?
(b) What benefits might there be for the company in this conflict?
(c) Discuss how IceCool might ensure that the two departments work together when a final decision is made.

Team building

Businesses often try to improve the productivity and motivation of people working in groups. The 'planned, systematic process designed to improve the efforts of people who work together to achieve goals' is known as TEAM BUILDING.

Team building is based on the idea that before organisations can improve performance, group members must be able to work together effectively. They were first introduced in UK business in the 1970s. Exercises were used to help group members develop trust, open up communication channels, make sure everyone understood the goals of the group, help individuals make decisions with the commitment of all members, prevent the leader from dominating the group, examine and resolve conflicts, and to review work activities. Team building exercises often involve taking groups to outdoor locations and setting them problems to solve. Examples include the pension department at Siemens training in outdoor exercises in Finland and operators at DuPont carrying out charity work such as constructing a play group for disabled children.

A study by W.Dyer (1994) found that many companies said they believed in team building. However, only 22 per cent actually carried out any team building activities. The main reasons suggested for this were that:
● managers did not know how to do team building.
● managers did not understand the benefits of spending time on team building and thought it would take too much time;
● team building efforts were not really rewarded in the company;
● people felt their teams were all right;
● people felt it was not supported by their superiors.

Question 5

Senior managers are discovering new management and team building insights from yacht races. Alan Rudge, deputy chief executive of BT and Humphrey Walters, chief executive of MaST, an international training company, competed in the BT Global Challenge. This is a round-the-world yacht race pitting 14 amateur crews against each other. Both learned a lot from working in a team sailing a yacht in the race. Walters said that: 'it's a hostile environment at sea. The risks and the downside are too great to screw up. Yet there is no blame culture on the boat. We blew a spinnaker and the conversation about why it happened was 30 seconds. In business it's very different. You spend hours, days, analysing what went wrong and who's to blame.' Rudge says he found that the greatest motivator at sea was the fear of letting down his crewmates. 'It is probably the biggest pressure of all. It is not stretching it to say your life is in their hands.'

Source: adapted from the *Financial Times*, 11.4.1997.

(a) Explain the lessons that were learned from working in a team sailing a yacht that may be used in business.
(b) Discuss how using these lessons may help teams operate more effectively in business.

Decision teams and work teams

A distinction can be made between **decision teams** and **work**

teams in business. A decision team might be a management executive committee, a university academic department or a collection of doctors or lawyers in a clinic. The main function of the team is to make decisions. The team members do not rely on each other to carry out individual tasks. However, they do make decisions about the operation of a department or a business.

In contrast a work team must work together to accomplish a goal. It must coordinate its efforts constantly. Examples might be a hospital operating unit or a police SWAT team. Some businesses today organise workers into autonomous work groups. These are groups of employees with a variety of skills who carry out whole tasks, such as manufacturing a complete product. The group exercises a high level of control and makes its own decisions over the work that it carries out.

Knowledge teams

Knowledge teams can be both work teams and decision teams. They are teams of **knowledge workers** (☞ unit 83) who are collectively responsible for a product or service. Knowledge work requires employees who can:
● use their own knowledge;
● acquire new information;
● combine and process information to produce and communicate new information;
● learn continuously from their experiences.

Knowledge teams are often made up of specialist workers from a variety of areas or disciplines. The team integrates the work of the specialists. Specialists may only have a small amount of common values, information and skills, so it is important that they communicate and work together. Examples of knowledge teams may be a team responsible for new product development, a management team made up from managers across the business that develops strategic directions (☞ unit 10) or a process improvement team that examines and makes changes to a business's work methods. The advantage of a knowledge team is that a problem can be examined from a variety of perspectives. For example, a business that is trying to cut production costs can have suggestions from finance, marketing and administration staff as well as technical staff.

Key terms

Formal groups - groups specifically set up by a business to carry out tasks. They have certain formal rules of behaviour.
Group norm - the usual characteristics of behaviour of a group.
Informal groups - groups made up of individuals in business with similar interests. They are not part of the formal business organisation.
Team building - the process designed to improve the effectiveness and motivation of people working together in groups.

Summary

1. 'Group behaviour is different from individual behaviour.' To what extent is this statement likely to be true in business?
2. State 4 common features that groups in business organisations have.
3. Why might a business set up a temporary formal group rather than making it permanent?
4. Give 4 advantages for employees of informal group membership.
5. Give 6 characteristics of effective groups.
6. Briefly explain why optimal group size may be between 3-7 members.
7. What is likely to influence the size of a group?
8. Explain the difference between centralised and decentralised group decision making.
9. What are the advantages to the business of group decision making?
10. In what circumstances might individual decision making be more beneficial to a business?
11. What factors within a business might lead to inter-group conflict?
12. What are knowledge teams?

Case study

ICL

Companies are increasingly becoming interested in knowledge management. Acquiring knowledge quickly and putting it to good use is one way of gaining a competitive advantage over rivals. ICL was originally a computer designer and manufacturer. It gradually transformed itself into a service-led organisation, providing advice to businesses on the use of technology to improve productivity for example. It considers its knowledge of technology to be a major asset.

By 1994 the company was becoming increasingly aware that knowledge was not being used as effectively as possible. For example, in some cases several ICL businesses were attempting to develop the same services. Passing knowledge effectively within the company would have helped to solve this problem. If all parts of the business had knowledge of all services being developed then there would not have been this duplication.

At the time an interested group of people at ICL came together to discuss the problems. A network of people developed from a variety of areas of ICL business. Because of their diversity they were able to identify problems such as duplication of services. They also found that people were carrying out tasks that could be better done by others because they had more time and experience.

In 1996 the business set up Project Vik (Valuing ICL knowledge). It decided to appoint a small 'catalyst' team. The team would be made up of people with 'cross-functional skills'. Its objective was to influence employees in the business, the business culture and business processes to make greater use of the knowledge that ICL had. The members appointed to the five person team needed to be good communicators, effective influencers and agents of change.

Making use of communications technology, Project Vik set up an information service for ICL called Cafe Vik using the company's intranet service. This took the form of a web site on the intranet. It was designed to reduce the time that people spent searching for company information. The Cafe is managed by an information services team. They are

responsible for collecting and updating the web site.

To find out the information that would be included on the intranet, a number of focus groups were run. They asked front line employees about the information they needed to do their job more effectively. The groups included consultants, project managers and salespeople from different ICL businesses. Despite this, they tended to ask for similar information, such as the range of ICL services and products, and expertise across the company that was available to them from different departments.

Management education was felt to be the next step in effective knowledge management. In 1998 the company held a series of workshops for key ICL department management teams. Each team would attempt to develop an action plan for using and enhancing knowledge.

Source: adapted from *People Management*, 19.2.1998.

(a) **Identify the different: (i) informal; and (ii) formal groups; that exist at ICL.**
(b) **Explain the possible benefits to ICL of the groups mentioned in the article.**
(c) **Examine the factors that may have influenced the choice of the 'catalyst' team at ICL.**
(d) **To what extent is the catalyst team likely to be a knowledge team?**
(e) **Discuss the possible problems of team operation that department management teams may have when devising action plans for using and enhancing knowledge at ICL.**

How are groups represented?

There are many different organisations which represent employees and employers in business. Although they are not part of actual businesses themselves, they influence how firms operate.

Trade unions These are perhaps the best known of the representative bodies. A TRADE UNION is an organisation of workers who join together to further their own interests. Trade unions have existed in the UK for over 200 years. Early unions were made up of workers with similar skills and interests, for example the General Union of Operative Spinners set up in 1829. Today unions vary from UNISON, the public services union, with over one million members, to the Iron and Steel Trades Confederation (ISTC), with around 50,000 members, to smaller unions such as the Oswaldtwistle Power Loom Workers Overlookers with 13 members and the Harrods Staff Union with 9 members.

What features are trade unions likely to have? It is possible that a trade union would:
- register itself as a union;
- become affiliated to the Trades Union Congress (although not all do);
- be independent of employers in negotiations;
- regard collective bargaining (☞ unit 86) and the protection of its members' interests as its main functions;
- be prepared to use industrial action (☞ unit 87) to further its members' interests;

although the make-up and role of unions has changed over the last two decades. This is dealt with later in this unit.

The Transport and General Workers Union (T&GWU), the Rail, Maritime and Transport Union (RMT) and the Communication Workers Union (CWU) are large, well established unions with many or all of these features. There are other representative bodies, some of which may not be unions, that also have some of these features.

Staff associations Staff associations represent workers, but perform only some of those functions carried out by trade unions. These might include consultation and bargaining with management. Their members are often made up of workers in a particular business. Examples of staff associations include the staff association at Parc jail in South Wales, a high-tech jail run by Securicor. In some cases staff associations develop into trade unions. A number of unions, including the National Union of Teachers (NUT) and the Banking, Insurance and Finance Union (BIFU) started as staff associations. Some associations, such as The Abbey National Staff Association and the Guinness Staff Association, are affiliated to the TUC, as discussed later in this unit.

Professional associations Professional associations perform similar functions to trade unions and are sometimes even referred to as unions. They represent 'professional' occupations. Examples include the Police Federation, the Institute of Qualified Personal Secretaries (IQPS), The National Association of Head Teachers (NAHT) and the Professional Footballers Association. Some associations, such as the British Medical Association (BMA), represent their members in collective bargaining with employers. They are also responsible for the setting and maintaining of standards. For example, the BMA insists on certain qualifications before admitting employees to its membership. For this reason professional associations tend to be associated with 'white collar' workers and higher paid groups of employees.

Employers' organisations Just as certain bodies represent workers, there are organisations which help and support employers. They are often useful for small firms that may be negotiating with a large union. These organisations give advice to employers about collective bargaining and help with technical problems and overseas trade. They may also provide research and training facilities and act as a pressure group (☞ unit 27) for industries. Examples include the Newspaper Society (NS) and the Engineering Employers' Federation (EEF).

All of the groups mentioned above will aim to protect or further their members' interests. The rest of this unit will concentrate mainly on the role of trade unions, although many of the points dealt with apply to other representative bodies.

The functions of trade unions

What is the role of a union in a business situation? We have already seen that unions are an example of a representative body that aims to further its members' interests. It could be argued that this includes some of the following.
- Obtaining satisfactory rates of pay.
- Securing adequate work facilities.
- Ensuring satisfactory work conditions, such as the number of hours worked or the number of breaks in any period of work.
- Negotiating bonuses for achieving targets.
- Obtaining job security for members.
- Negotiating employment conditions, such as contracts of employment or rights relating to redundancy and dismissal.
- Negotiating grievance procedures.
- Negotiating job descriptions and job specifications (☞ unit 76).

Trade unions are responsible for **collective bargaining** in the workplace. They bargain on behalf of their total membership with employers and attempt to obtain the best possible conditions. It is argued that unions are in a far better position to negotiate with management than an individual employee, who will have little bargaining 'power'.

Trade unions are also responsible, along with management, for **industrial relations**. They communicate their members' wishes to employers and try to negotiate the most favourable conditions. However, successful industrial relations means that each party must take into account the wishes of the other when bargaining. It may not be in members' interests for a union to push for a longer work break if this reduces the efficiency of the business, perhaps resulting in job losses in future. However, it may not be in employers' interests to reduce breaks, even if this cuts costs, if it results in worker dissatisfaction.

The ability of trade unions to carry out these functions may depend on the union membership and UNION DENSITY. A small union, with few members for instance, is unlikely to have as much influence as the Union of Shop Distributive and Allied Workers (USDAW) with its 300,000 plus membership. Union density is expressed as:

$$\frac{\text{actual union membership}}{\text{potential union membership}} \times 100$$

If unions only represent a small percentage of all workers in an industry, they might be less likely to have influence. In public utilities such as electricity, water and gas, union density is 63 per cent. In construction it is 22 per cent and in the hotel industry it is only 7 per cent. This might suggest that unions' influence on the hotel trade is fairly weak.

Types of union

There is a number of ways in which unions can be classified. A traditional method has been to place unions into one of three categories.

- Craft unions are the oldest type of union, developed directly from traditional crafts. Workers with common skills often joined together to form unions. Examples today might be the musicians union (MU) or the bakers union (BFAWU).
- Industrial unions. In the past a number of unions have been formed by employees of particular industries, such as coalminers, railway or gas workers. An example of an industrial union is the National Union of Mineworkers (NUM). It is made up of employees with different skills in the mining industry.
- General unions. These unions are made up of workers with a wide range of skills in many different industries. Examples today might be the General Municipal Boilermakers and Allied Trade Union (GMB) or the

Question 1

What if unions disappeared? Would it matter? Some argue that if trade unions did not exist they would have to be invented. Is it likely, for example, that managers faced with freedom from union involvement would rush out to empower and inform workers? Or would they use the freedom to reduce consultation and participation, making their life easier? A Workplace Industrial Survey said: 'Britain is approaching the position where few employees have any mechanism through which they can contribute to the operation of their workplace in a broader context than their own job'. The Employment Policy Institute argued that: 'we are witnessing the emergence of a tired old world of unrepresented labour, characterised by backward employment practices and reliance on performance related pay'. In 1996/7 wage inequality was at a record high, one in eight workers had a work grievance and workers, fearful for their jobs, were working longer hours and taking more responsibility.

Research suggests that unions, far from stopping them, help managers to manage. They give advice on work issues and training. They 'keep managers on their toes', making them see workers as a resource that needs to be trained and developed. Unions air important issues that may affect the workplace. Business would perform better if they had to justify their actions. Unions also help to negotiate flexible deals over pay, hours and teamworking, as shown in companies such as Rover, Blue Circle and Scottish Power.

Source: adapted from *The Observer*, 7.9.1997.

Using examples from the article, discuss the case for the benefit of trade unions representing employees for: (a) the workers themselves; (b) businesses.

Manufacturing, Science and Finance Union (MSF). Although this division appears straightforward, it does have problems.

- It forces unions into one category, whereas many unions often have features common to all classes. The Amalgamated Electrical Engineering Union (AEEU), for example, has a large number of engineering craftworkers as members, but also recruits foundry workers and unskilled employees.
- Very few unions actually fall into the 'craft' category.
- Mergers of unions in recent years have blurred many of these distinctions. This is dealt with later in this unit.

Another way of dividing unions might be into those with more **open** and those with **restricted** recruitment policies. Those with restricted recruitment policies may recruit their membership from employees with certain skills. For example, only musicians tend to join the Musician's Union. Some unions recruit mainly from specific industries, occupations or businesses. Examples might be Equity, the actors' union, the Association of Teachers and Lecturers (ATC), the ceramic workers union (CATU) or the Union for Bradford and Bingley Staff with its 2,700 members in 1999. This can mean that their membership expands and contracts according to the changing levels of human resource needs in the industry.

More open membership policies tend to be associated with the larger unions. They often seek membership regardless of their members' jobs or industries, such as the T&G, or recruit from a wide variety of related or unrelated industries, such as UNISON, which recruits from public services industries. Such unions organise themselves to deal with different membership needs. This can sometimes lead to conflict, as unions are accused of 'poaching' members from other areas. Many of the larger unions have been formed by the merger of smaller unions with more restricted membership.

Unions and pay

One criticism often made of unions is that if they negotiate very high wage increases, this can lead to redundancies. Unit 17 explained that unions can force up wages by:
- negotiating a minimum wage;
- restricting the supply of workers.

In a free market for labour, it is argued that a business can only pay for these higher wages and maintain profits by making workers unemployed.

Against this it could be argued that:
- if there is an increase in productivity by employees, this should pay for higher wages, without the need for job losses;
- other countries have had similar unit costs of production to the UK, and paid skilled workers relatively high wages, and yet have not had such high unemployment rates;
- there is evidence in the UK that unemployment still exists even if wages are held down or cut (☞ unit 24).

Trade unions and legislation

Much of the legislation that existed in the UK in the 1980s and the early 1990s was the result of the then Conservative government's view of unions. It believed that:
- trade union power was excessive, particularly in wage negotiations;
- unions were often disruptive in preventing changing work practices or the introduction of new machinery;
- unions were increasingly creating industrial stoppages;
- unofficial picketing was disrupting business;
- SHOP STEWARDS were disrupting industry by calling unofficial strikes - strikes not supported by the unions (sometimes called 'wildcat strikes');
- there was undemocratic decision making within unions, especially about industrial action;
- closed shops restricted the rights of employees not to belong to a union;

and that these factors were harming the efficiency of British industry and its ability to compete. Others argued that it had not been trade union power that made British business uncompetitive, but a lack of good management (☞ unit 74) and poor levels of education and training within the

workforce. They suggested that union legislation does not address the long standing causes of UK businesses - the lack of capital investment and the 'laissez-faire' approach of management. The Labour government, elected in 1997, signed the **European Social Chapter** (☞ unit 81). This meant that employees were to be given new rights in the workplace. Businesses would also have to take into account new regulations and legislation on working practices and union activities. The government believed that a greater 'partnership' with more cooperation between business and unions would develop. This would involve more union consultation and unity in the workplace.

The effects of legislation

Trade union activities in the UK are regulated by a variety of legislation. Legislation between 1980-96 was designed to restrict union power, give employees choice and protect employers. After 1997 much of this legislation remained. However, the government aimed to give employees more protection in the workplace and to encourage the partnership between unions and business. Legislation has focussed on a number of areas.

Legal immunity Certain Acts have dealt with whether unions can be sued by a business or individuals as a result of damages caused by their actions. **The 1974 Trade Union and Labour Relations Act** prevented employers from taking civil action in court for damages resulting from industrial action by unions. The Act covered disputes as a result of terms and conditions of employment, suspension or termination of employment, allocation of work duties between workers or groups of employees, matters of discipline, membership or non-membership of a trade union, trade union recognition, and disputes arising from negotiation and consultation.

The **1982 Employment Act**, however, made unions liable for any action which was not in 'furtherance' of an industrial dispute. In other words, unions taking action that was not covered by conditions in the 1974 Act were liable to pay civil damages to businesses.

One result was that courts became willing to grant injunctions, preventing unions taking action not covered in the Acts. Injunctions are court orders instructing unions to refrain from action while a court hearing over a dispute is taking place. Judges might grant the injunction if they feel a business would suffer if the action continued.

Since the **1990 Employment Act,** unions have also been liable for damages to customers or suppliers as a result of action which is not covered in the conditions of legislation.

Picketing PICKETING involves the rights of workers on strike to assemble and persuade others to help or join them. **Official pickets** (those nominated by unions) can stand outside a workplace to inform the public, employees, suppliers and managers that a strike is taking place. A code of practice is set out governing their conduct when dealing with such people.

Picketing has changed greatly since the 1970s. During that period, mass picketing of employers' premises and flying pickets (members of one union or factory picketing another's premises) were common features of strike action.

The two national coalmining strikes in the early 1970s saw the picketing of power stations and coal and coke depots to prevent the generation of electricity and the delivery of fuel to consumers. At the same time, the use of mass picketing by thousands of people, the majority of whom were sympathisers not directly involved in the dispute, led to problems for the police. The 1974 Act above made SECONDARY PICKETING unlawful, but it was difficult to enforce. The police could only act under criminal law if picketing ceased to be peaceful.

The **1980 Employment Act,** however, made it possible for civil action to be taken against secondary picketing. It also limited peaceful picketing for employees to at or near their place of work, and the number of pickets at any one time.

The closed shop A CLOSED SHOP (or union membership agreement) is an agreement between an employer and a trade union that makes it a condition of employment for each employee to be a member of that trade union. It could be argued that such a union membership agreement is sensible as it allows a union to represent all employees. This removes the possibility of conflict or bad feeling between members of the union and non-members. However, a closed shop may make employees join a union against their will. **The 1980 and 1982 Employment Acts** changed the regulations in relation to closed shops. Previously employees were obliged to be a member of the union if a closed shop agreement existed. Anyone refusing to join had no defence against unfair dismissal by the employer for that reason.

Any closed shop agreement coming into existence after August 1980 had to be approved by an 80 per cent vote in a secret ballot. Dismissal for non-membership of a union was made unfair if this 80 per cent vote was not achieved.

Members', business's and consumers' rights Certain legislation has been passed to make the unions more democratic and to protect the rights of workers belonging to unions. The **1984 Trade Union Act** forced unions to conduct secret ballots before industrial action took place if action was to be legal. **The 1988 Employment Act** gave union members the right not to strike if they wished.

The **1993 Trade Union Reform and Employment Rights Act** further attempted to support employees' and consumers' rights and protect business from union action with the following measures.

● The right for workers to have a postal ballot on union action and the right not to have union subscriptions deducted without consent.

● The right for workers not to be expelled or excluded from a union other than for certain reasons, such as not belonging to a certain trade as stated in union rules.
● The right for employers to have 7 days' notice of industrial action.
● The right for customers deprived of public services by 'unlawful' industrial action to take action to prevent it happening.

Trade union recognition **The Employment Relations Bill, 1999** set out a process to enable employees to have a trade union recognised by their employer. The government wanted to encourage voluntary agreement between employers and employees. However, a legal process was set in place in case of disagreement. In some cases trade unions would be automatically recognised. In others, a ballot would take place. In these cases, for a union to be recognised it must win a majority of the ballot and get a 'yes' vote from at least 40 per cent of those eligible to vote. The Bill also made it unlawful for dismissal on grounds of trade union membership or activities and gave a right of complaint if dismissal took place.

The ban on unions at Government Communication Headquarters (GCHQ) was lifted in 1997. The Conservative government had banned unions because industrial action was seen as a security risk given the sensitivity of information dealt with at GCHQ.

Question

In 1998 members of the broadcast union (BECTU), the journalists' union (NUJ) and the AEEU were set to vote on industrial action. The workers, who worked for BBC Worldwide, were responding to management's 3.5 per cent pay offer (following the imposition of a 4 per cent offer on the rest of BBC staff). BECTU members at the BBC had already voted by 2,667 to 889 to reject the 4 per cent offer. They were particularly angered by the disparity between directors' and employees' pay offers.

Source: adapted from *Labour Research,* October 1998.

(a) Explain three reasons why unions may have rejected the pay offer.
(b) Discuss how legislation might affect:
   (i) the unions' ballot on industrial action;
   (ii) the activities of unions taking industrial action;
   (iii) the BBC's response to industrial action.

The changing face of trade unions

Since 1980 a number of important changes which have taken place have affected trade unions.

Membership It has already been suggested that the numbers of members a union has and union density can influence the ability of a union to perform its functions. Figure 85.1 shows that union membership grew in the 1970s, but since then there has been a steady decline. In 1997 there were estimated to be 7.1 million members, the lowest total since 1954. A Labour Force Survey predicted a fall to around 6.8 million members by 2000, but that the decline may be bottoming out. Union density has also fallen, from 39 per cent of all employees in 1989 to 30.2 per cent in 1997, as shown in Figure 85.2. Between 1989 and 1997 union density fell for both males and females, whether full time or part time, in production or service industries and in manual or non-manual jobs. However, the fall has been far slower for certain groups than for others. In 1998, for the first time, union density was higher in services (31.1 per cent) than in production (30.9 per cent).

In the late 1990s, the TUC's New Unionism project was geared at increasing recruitment. It aimed to train union members to organise recruitment meetings in businesses. In 1998 trainee organisers were working in GPMU the print union and BIFU the finance union.

What factors are likely to influence union membership?

● Government. As explained earlier, government passed various Acts in the 1980s and 1990s which made it easier for employees to 'opt out' of union membership. Restrictions on union activity and influence may also have affected workers' willingness to join a union. In the late 1990s, the encouragement of union participation in business and the growth of legislation to protect workers rights, such as the minimum wage or the length of the working week may persuade workers to join unions.

● The economy. It is argued that in periods of recession and high unemployment union membership falls, as people become unemployed and allow their membership to lapse. The opposite should be true in periods of growth. The recession in the early 1990s may have contributed to the fall in membership. It has been suggested that when the economy grew in the mid-1990s unemployment was slow to fall, so membership may not have risen as a result. In periods of inflation, people may join unions to protect their living standards. They hope that unions can negotiate higher wages to keep pace with inflation. The relatively low rates of inflation in the UK in the 1990s has perhaps made this less important for employees and so membership has suffered.

● Economic, technological and labour market changes. Certain industries in the UK, such as shipbuilding and steel, have declined over a number of years. Workers in these and other manufacturing industries have tended to belong to unions. Their decline may have led to a fall in membership. Other industries, particularly in the service sector, have grown relatively. This may mean that individual unions may have seen their membership grow.

● Union amalgamation. When unions join together, the new union has the combined membership of the smaller unions that existed previously. Sometimes new, larger unions may gain membership because of the greater benefits offered to workers.

● It could be argued that the growth of smaller independent businesses has affected union membership. Many employ less than 10 workers and are not affected by certain employee protection legislation. Such employees are less likely to belong to unions.

● The growing use of flexible workers (☞ unit 88). Businesses have tended in recent years to develop a flexible workforce made up of part time workers, temporary staff or teleworkers. These workers have been less likely to be covered by employee legislation. They may also feel that the costs and time involved in joining a union are of little benefit, so fewer tend to be union members.

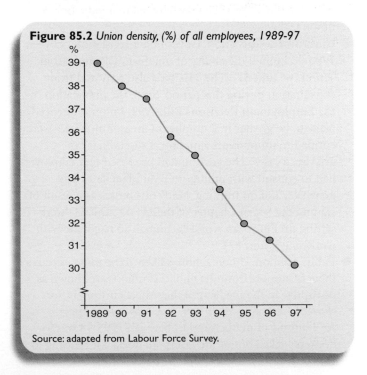

Figure 85.1 *Number of trade unions and union membership, GB, 1976-97*

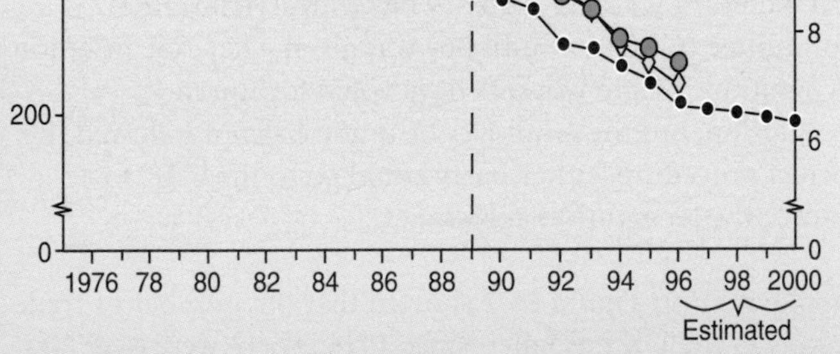

Source: adapted from Certification Officer; Labour Force Survey.

Figure 85.2 *Union density, (%) of all employees, 1989-97*

Source: adapted from Labour Force Survey.

- There has been a fall in **collective bargaining agreements** (☞ unit 86), where unions agree deals for numbers of workers in an industry. More deals have been agreed between the individual employee and management based on the contract of employment. This may have discouraged membership. However, any rise in collective agreements may lead to increasing membership in future.
- Privatisation. The privatisation of the transport and power industries (eg rail and gas) may have affected membership. These industries tended to have large numbers of union members and strong union representation. Splitting them after privatisation is likely to have reduced union influence and may have led to a fall in membership.
- It has been suggested that non-TUC affiliated unions, such as The Royal College of Nursing and the National Association of Head Teachers, have seen their membership grow. One reason for this may have been fear of redundancy in health and education sectors.
- Leadership. Dynamic leaders that are seen by potential members as furthering their interests may encourage them to join a union.
- Demographic trends. The UK faces a 'demographic timebomb' with falling numbers of school leavers and an ageing population. This is likely to mean that fewer new recruits will be available as union members, although this might be offset to some extent by women returning to work in greater numbers.

Trade union power Has trade union influence diminished? How might it change in future? There is a number of factors that might affect the ability of a union to influence businesses for the benefit of their members.

- Membership. As discussed above, union membership and union density can affect a union's power. Falling membership since 1980 may have led to a reduction in union influence.
- Government legislation. Government legislation between 1980-96 limited the ability of unions to take industrial action (☞ unit 87). The TUC was also removed from consultation during this period. Since the publication of the **Employment Relations Bill, 1999,** union influence was likely to be greater in a number of areas. Employees were entitled to union representation at disciplinary or grievance cases. The government proposed that employers had to consult with unions on redundancies or pay penalties, and on training. Many businesses as a result of signing the Social Chapter of the EU (☞ unit 81) were setting up European workers councils to negotiate with workers (☞ unit 87).
- Public opinion. Union action is likely to be more effective if there is support from the public. If unions are shown as disruptive in the media or if they affect customers, for example by transport strikes, they may lose support. An example of public support between 1995-98 was for dockers locked out of the Liverpool docks for refusing to

cross a picket line. Sports people wore T-shirts on television and fundraising took place in theatres and from concerts.
- Managers', employers' and employees' views. It has been suggested that human resource management techniques (☞ unit 88) require management to deal directly with employees. This marginalises the role of unions. Employers may also have developed an aggressive attitude towards unions as a result of legislation and union action. However, in the late 1990s critics of this view argued that the most effective businesses worked in partnership with unions to manage the workforce and to solve problems.
- Organisation. When unions are well organised and have a clear objective they can still be effective in influencing businesses. For example, in 1998 threatened action by 2,000 members of the GMB, T&G, UCATT, AEEU and MSF at the Devonport Royal Dockyard led to the removal of productivity 'strings' from a pay deal and the restoration of union recognition for new workers.
- The economic and political climate. In periods of low inflation unions are less likely to be able to argue that wages need to increase to keep pace with rising prices. Low inflation in the 1990s was reflected in low wage settlements.

Non-union businesses, union recognition and derecognition
In the UK **non-union** firms tend to be small, private sector businesses. Exceptions in the 1990s were Marks & Spencer and the John Lewis Partnership. There was a trend in that period for union **derecognition**. This is where a business refuses to negotiate with certain unions over workers' conditions. If only one union is recognised, it avoids problems of many different pay negotiations for a business. It means that restrictions placed on a business by many different unions are reduced. If a business does not recognise any union, this allows negotiations with individuals, which may be more flexible. The proportion of UK businesses recognising unions fell from 66 per cent to 44 per cent in the period 1984-97.

In 1998 there were 50 cases of union recognition but only 8 cases of derecognition. For example, Webtech, a packaging company, recognised the print and paper union GPMU after a three month union campaign. Over 50 of its 70 workers were union members. One of the reasons for recognition was in response to the **Employment Relations Bill, 1999,** which encouraged union recognition and partnership with business, and increased workers' rights. The Central Arbitration Committee (CAC) (☞ unit 86) was given a key role in union recognition. Where workers have voted for union recognition, but the employer or union has not followed the correct procedure, either party could go to the CAC to enforce the recognition agreement.

Amalgamation Figure 85.1 showed that the number of trade unions in the UK has fallen since 1976. There were over 600 unions in the 1960s. In 1997 there were 245. This fall is largely the result of union mergers. In 1993 the public services unions NALGO, NUPE and COHSE merged to form today's largest union UNISON, with around 1.4 million members. In 1998 the civil service unions CPSA and PTC merged to form the Public and Commercial Services Union (PCS).

Why do unions merge? The fall in membership in some unions may have led to mergers. However, some unions have joined to become larger bodies which represent more workers in an industry. This would place them in a far stronger bargaining position with employers. These larger unions will also have more finance to offer the range of services that today's members demand. This is dealt with in the next section.

Question 3

In the late 1990s, a number of businesses were signing union recognition agreements. A deal was struck between the GMB and the double glazing firm BAC Ltd. The company employed 700 workers, half of which were hourly paid staff covered by the agreement. Previously the business had refused to recognise the union for three years, despite over 200 of the 350 hourly paid staff being workers. This was well over the 50 per cent required for recognition under proposed legislation. A change in managing director, numerous accident claims and a number of tribunal cases changed the climate at the company according to GMB regional organiser Ray Boosey. 'The Fairness at Work White Paper (which became The Employment Relations Bill, 1999) was the final nail in the coffin' he said.

Source: adapted from *Labour Research*, September, 1998.

(a) Discuss the factors that may have influenced union power at BAC.
(b) Suggest the possible effects of union recognition at the business.

The changing role of trade unions

In the 1980s and 1990s it could be argued that the 'traditional' role of unions changed. A number of new practices became part of union activities.

Single union and no strike agreements Businesses began to negotiate single union and no strike agreements with unions. Single union agreements enable a business to recognise and negotiate with one union over pay and conditions. A union may agree not to strike in return for wage increases, improved conditions or limited redundancies. The first such agreement was between Toshiba and the EEPTU (later to become part of the AEEU) in 1981. There are certain features of these agreements that benefit employers.

● Single union recognition. This reduces the time,

complexity, conflict and administration costs of negotiation.
● Single job status for 'white' (non-manual) and 'blue' (manual) collar workers. This removes differentials in salaries, conditions, uniforms, car parking etc.
● Job flexibility. For example, this may mean workers agreeing to annualised hours (☞ unit 72) rather than a fixed number of hours a week. Job flexibility is dealt with in detail in unit 88.
● Union acceptance of training or retraining of employees. This improves the flexibility and the quality of the workforce.
● The use of negotiation or arbitration rather than industrial action. This prevents damaging strikes, for example, taking place.

There may be problems with such deals. In 1998 the AEEU signed a single union agreement with British Airways' budget airline Go. This created tension as the main air transport union, the T&G, had also been recruiting among the 180 staff and would be excluded from negotiations by the deal.

Business and union partnerships There has been growing evidence of businesses and unions working together in **partnership.** Although employers and unions have different interests at times, they work together to achieve common goals. The main attraction is that unions have a 'stake' in the business. Businesses benefit because unions help support improvements and improve competitiveness. Unions benefit because they are able to influence the business in areas such as job security and training. It is suggested that partnership companies have a competitive edge in terms of profit, sales, productivity and employment relations.

Examples of partnerships have included:
● an agreement between Tesco and USDAW, the shop workers union, which allows consultation through workplace, regional and national forums and improved facilities for recruitment;
● a three year no compulsory redundancy policy between the Co-op and BIFU, with improvements in pay and conditions, designed to help the management of change;
● an agreement between cement manufacturer Blue Circle and the AEEU, GMB and T&G unions in which job security was agreed in return for steps towards harmonisation of conditions;
● an agreement between unions and management on new working practices at Rover kept the firm in business;
● the learning centre developed by the GMB and BICC cable company, where workers get up to three hours extra pay a week for brushing up on communication or IT skills.

An agreement between the MSF and Legal and General identified a number of features which they felt were important for the success of any partnership.
● A tradition of stable industrial relations.
● A campaigning and socially aware union.
● Well trained and committed union representatives.

- A union with regular 'people friendly communications' in the workplace and recruitment that is supported by management.
- Management and unions taking time and effort to make it work.
- A desire on both sides to listen to each other.
- Recognising that both sides win by the partnership's success.

However, some have criticised partnerships in business and suggest a number of factors could lead to the end of the partnership. Faced with difficulties, unions and business may not be as committed to the partnership as they were at the start. They may also 'see' the partnership differently, so that there is conflict over decisions. The gains from the partnership may also be too one sided. Unions may also be cut out from key decisions and managers may prefer to communicate directly with employees.

Negotiations The nature of negotiated agreements between unions and employers has changed in recent years. Unions are far more likely to negotiate on aspects other than pay. These may include facilities for women members or for older or disabled workers, reflecting the changing nature of the workforce.

The 1990s saw the beginning of a number of agreements:
- at plant or local level rather than national level to take into account the needs of a particular business activity (mainly in the private manufacturing sector);
- over a larger fixed period, so that a business has knowledge of its future costs and can build these into its budgets.

The numbers of workers covered by collective bargaining agreements fell from 71 per cent to 36 per cent over the period 1984-97 (☞ unit 86). This meant more agreements have taken place without unions being involved.

Services Unions increasingly offer a wide range of services to employees. These may include:
- insurance schemes;
- pension schemes;
- financial and legal advice;
- discounts on travel and goods;
- education courses;
- mortgage discounts;
- welfare and sickness benefits.

The TUC

The Trades Union Congress (TUC) is an organisation which represent trade unions in the UK. In the late 1990s, its 74 affiliated unions had 6.6 million members. There were also 181 unions outside the TUC.

Each year a conference is held and TUC policy is decided. Member unions send delegates to the conference, the number sent depending on the size of the union. The conference also elects the General Council of the TUC. This is responsible for carrying out policy and running TUC affairs in between

Question 4

In 1998 an agreement between Dixons and the AEEU, the engineers' union, was hailed as the first signed since publication of the Fairness at Work White Paper, 1998 (which became The Employment Relations Bill, 1999). The partnership deal covered 1,600 engineers working in shops and service centres. Features of the agreement were that:
- it was a 'no strike' deal;
- it set up a representative forum for union and non-union members;
- no recognition ballot needed to be held before an agreement starts; if union membership is 51 per cent of the eligible workforce then collective bargaining rights are at the discretion of the employer.

The AEEU general secretary Ken Jackson praised the deal, particularly the agreement's commitment to training. In 1996 an ACAS run ballot of 380 in-store engineers resulted in 60 per cent of them backing AEEU recognition.

Source: adapted from *Labour Research*, July 1998.

(a) Identify three factors that might influence the success of the partnership.
(b) Explain the factors that may have influenced the recognition of the AEEU by Dixons.
(c) Discuss the impact of the deal on: (i) management at Dixons; and: (ii) the AEEU and its members.

conferences. A General Secretary is elected, who is often seen as the mouthpiece of the TUC and is directly involved in TUC negotiations with member unions and government. The TUC has a permanent staff which deals with the day to day issues in between the annual Congress.

The main activities of the TUC are to:
- act as a pressure group to influence government policy on labour and union issues;
- decide on the rules and regulations for member unions, but not to interfere with their everyday running.

In the 1980s and early 1990s the TUC's role diminished as it was excluded from consultation by government. It continued to be represented on bodies such as the The Advisory Conciliation and Arbitration Service (ACAS). In the 1990s the TUC introduced a number of new initiatives to raise its profile. It has changed its policies so that it is easier for unions to become affiliated. Between 1995 and 1998 13 new unions joined. The TUC's New Unionism policy is designed to train union sponsored members at its Organising Academy in recruitment methods. The TUC has adopted a positive approach to the European Union. It opened its own office in Brussels in 1993. It has attempted to influence European bodies such as the European Trade Union Confederation (ETUC). Examples of the **social partnerships** encouraged by the Labour government are the TUC and the CBI working together on ways to improve health and safety at work and the TUC campaign to raise awareness of the importance of training.

Question 5

Many unions offer a variety of benefits in addition to their core services linked to collective organisation. In 1998 the Labour Research Department of the TUC carried out a survey of 41 unions that made up over 90 per cent of union membership. Over 40 extra services were identified. In particular, unions in the 1990s were taking advantage of technology by using web sites. Helplines were also increasingly offered to union members.

Table 85.1 *Benefits provided by more than half of unions*

Benefit (percentage of unions providing it)	No of members with access
1 Free legal help (on employment issues)(95%)	6,122,100
2 Members' newspaper/magazine (88%)	6,117,749
3 Free legal help (non-employment related)(83%)	5,393,356
4 Financial/tax advice (78%)	5,456,462
5 Discount motor services (inc. breakdown services)(73%)	5,623,130
6 Discount holidays/travel (71%)	5,946,116
7 Discount loans (63%)	4,978,338
8 Death benefit (61%)	4,561,929
9 Union credit card (59%)	3,333,119
10 Discount mortgages (59%)	4,607,947
11 Discount wills (59%)	5,090,264
12 Accident benefit (56%)	5,652,408
13 Web site (54%)	4,894,707
14 Helplines (54%)	3,035,348
15 Discount conveyancing (51%)	3,621,741

Source: adapted from *Labour Research*, August, 1998.

(a) What is likely to be meant by the phrase: 'in addition to their core services linked to collective organisation'?
(b) Explain how unions might make use of: (i) web sites; (ii) helplines; to benefit members.
(c) Choose two other benefits offered by trade unions and explain how they might help members.

The CBI

The Confederation of British Industry (CBI) was formed in 1965. It has a similar role to the TUC, but voices the opinions of employers rather than union members. CBI membership is drawn from private sector industry, service and commercial enterprises, public sector employers and some employers' associations, trade associations and Chambers of Commerce.

The internal organisation of the CBI is complex. It has a ruling council which decides on policy. It also employs permanent staff, headed by the Director General. Detailed policy proposals are examined by standing committees. The CBI is organised to deal with local and area issues through its regional councils. These aim to keep in touch with the needs of small firms and local employers and help them solve their day to day problems. The membership services of the CBI are wide ranging, both nationally and locally, and are backed up by skilled professional advice from lawyers, accountants and tax specialists.

What role does the CBI have? It attempts to represent its members' interests in a number of ways.

● Government policy. Just like the TUC, it attempts to influence government policy.
● Services. It provides legal, financial and economic advice to its members.
● Local businesses. It provides support and advice to local businesses through its regional offices.
● Through its office in Brussels, the CBI acts in the interests of British industry in the European Union.
● Trade unions. The CBI works with the TUC on consultative bodies such as ACAS (☞ unit 86).
● Other groups. The CBI provides information for a variety of other organisations and the public in general.

Key terms

Closed shop - a practice which prevents workers from being employed in a business unless they belong to a trade union.
Picketing - involves the rights of workers on strike to assemble and persuade others to help or join them.
Secondary picketing - where union members from one place of work picket an unrelated place of work.
Shop steward - an elected union official who represents workers' interests in the place in which the shop steward works.
Trade union - an organisation of workers that join together to further their own interests.
Union density - the actual membership of a trade union as a percentage of the total possible membership.

Summary

1. Explain the difference between a trade union and an employers' organisation.
2. State 6 functions of trade unions.
3. Why are good industrial relations important to a business?
4. What is meant by an 'open' union recruitment policy?
5. Explain 3 reasons why union legislation has taken place.
6. Briefly discuss 3 effects that legislation has had on union activity in business.
7. State 4 factors that have contributed to changes in the organisation and role of trade unions in the UK.
8. What is meant by:
   (a) single union agreements;
   (b) no strike deals;
   (c) union derecognition?
9. What are the main functions of:
   (a) the TUC;
   (b) The CBI?

Case study

Unions in the financial services industry

Union merger

In 1998-99 a three sided merger between finance unions was being discussed. The Banking, Insurance and Finance Union (BIFU), the union of Barclays Bank employees (UNiFI) and the non-TUC affiliated NatWest staff association (NWSA) were discussing the possibility of forming a super union made up of the combined unions' membership. All three unions had backed the plans for a merger, which it was argued could end years of rivalry. A combined statement by the general secretaries of the three unions said: 'Our members increasingly face job insecurity and attacks on their pay. The clear message from our members is to end divided staff representation and reclaim an agenda that is increasingly driven by management to create a genuine partnership.'

It was suggested, despite the different sizes, that there would be a merger of equal partners and TUC affiliation. The unions involved believed that the new union could attract workers from other financial areas, such as building societies. Other staff associations might also be asked to join in the merger. They also argued that one union would prevent the problems that arose by having two unions negotiating in one business. In 1996, for example, Barclays negotiated separately with BIFU and UNiFI. If one union accepted its proposals, the business imposed the settlement on the other union. Another problem in 1997 was that BIFU endorsed strike action in response to pay proposals, but UNiFI did not. One problem might be the different cultures of the unions involved. A suggested merger in 1985 between UNiFI and the NWSA did not take place because the NWSA still thought of itself as an association rather than a union.

Source: adapted from *Labour Research,* November 1997, January 1998; *The Times,* 27.9.1997.

Table 85.3 *Union representation in the banking, insurance and finance industry*

Company	Number of employees in the business	Business	Unions represented
Lloyds-TSB	82,000	Banking and finance	BIFU, LBU
National Westminster	66,000	Banking and finance	BIFU, NWSA
Barclays	60,800	Banking and finance	BIFU, UNiFI
HSBC Holdings	50,000	Banking and finance	BIFU
Halifax	36,000	Banking and finance	IUHS
Royal and Sun Alliance	27,800	Insurance	MSF
Co-operative Retail Society	*	Banking, insurance	BIFU, MSF

Source: adapted from *Labour Research,* September 1997.

* No figure available

TUC unions
BIFU - Banking, Insurance and Finance Union
MSF- Manufacturing, Science and Finance union
UNiFI - Barclays Bank Staff
IUHS - Independent Union of Halifax Staff

Non-TUC unions
LBU - Lloyds Bank Union
NWSA - NatWest Staff Association

Table 85.2 *Union membership*

Union membership	No of members
1 UNISON (public services)	1,300,451
2 T&G (general)	881,357
3 AEEU (engineers and electricians)	720,296
4 GMB (general)	709,708
5 MSF (technical and finance)	416,000
6 USDAW (shopworkers)	293,470
7 CWU (communications)	273,814
8 PCS (public and commercial services)	265,902
9 GPMU (print and paper)	204,822
10 NUT (teachers)	191,828
11 NASUWT (teachers)	172,852
12 UCATT (building)	113,555
13 BIFU (finance)	112,972
14 IPMS (professionals and managers)	74,581
15 NATFHE (lecturers)	65,065
16 FBU (firefighters)	56,943
17 RMT (rail and maritime)	56,337
18 EIS (Scottish teachers)	50,807
19 ISTC (iron and steel)	50,001
20 UNiFI (Barclays bank)	42,729
NWSA (finance)	38,000 approx.

Source: adapted from *Labour Research,* August 1998.

Problems in banking

The traditional paternalistic relations between management and staff in banking were eroded in the period 1980-97. Long standing staff benefits such as cheap mortgages, loans and relocation allowances were removed. Technology, deregulation and increased competition among high street banks led to a closure of 3,000 bank and building society branches between 1990 and 1998. 130,000 jobs were lost. Business mergers in the finance industry were also likely in future with further job losses. The merger, for example, of NatWest, Barclays and the Prudential would create a super finance services business designed to take advantage of globalised markets.

In 1998 Barclaycard, Britain's oldest credit card operator said that 1,100 jobs would be cut by 2002 because of increasing competition and new technology. Its market share had been cut from 35 per cent to 25 per cent over a six year period. It was hoped to absorb the job losses through redeployment and voluntary redundancies, although some compulsory redundancies were inevitable. The scale of the job losses shocked BIFU and UNiFI officers, who said that they would be pushing for redeployment and retraining.

Source: adapted from *Labour Research,* November 1997, January 1998; *The Times,* 27.9.1997, 23.9.1998

You have been asked to write a report for union leaders at BIFU on the proposed merger between the three banking unions. In your report discuss:

● **the factors that may affect the relationships between unions and businesses in the financial services industry;**
● **the arguments for and against the merger;**
● **the impact of the merger on businesses, unions and employees;**
● **whether the merger should take place.**

Employer and employee conflict

Conflict can exist between different groups and individuals working in business. One type of conflict which may lead to major problems is between the objectives of employers and employees. Conflict between these two groups may result from a number of factors.

- Rates of pay. Employers could attempt to keep wage costs down to remain competitive, whereas unions could try to maximise employees' rewards.
- The introduction of machinery. For example, a business may want to introduce machinery which requires workers to learn new production techniques. Employees, however, may feel that this extra responsibility is an unwanted burden.
- Flexible working (☞ unit 102). Businesses often require a more flexible workforce. A printing works might decide to operate a 24 hour shift, for example, to cope with extra work. Employees may be unwilling to work at night.
- Work conditions. Workers may feel that better canteen facilities are needed, but employers could see this as

an unnecessary increase in costs.

The aim of **industrial relations** procedures (☞ unit 85) is to make sure that each party finds an acceptable solution to any conflict that may exist. Successful industrial relations should prevent the need for industrial action (☞ unit 87) by employers' or employees' groups.

Collective bargaining

COLLECTIVE BARGAINING is one way of minimising conflict in the workplace. It involves determining conditions of work and terms of employment through **negotiations** between employers and employee representatives, such as trade unions. These bodies represent the views of all their members and try to negotiate in their interests. One individual employee working for a large company would have little or no influence in setting their wages or conditions. The representative body has more strength and influence and can negotiate for its membership. Without such a bargaining process, employers and managers would be able to set wages and conditions without taking into account employees' interests.

For collective bargaining to take place:
- employees must be free to join representative bodies, such as trade unions;
- employers must recognise such bodies as representative of workers and agree to negotiate with them;
- such bodies must be independent of employers and the state;
- bodies should negotiate in good faith, in their members' interests;
- employers and employees should agree to be bound by agreements without having to use the law to enforce them.

The result of collective bargaining is a COLLECTIVE AGREEMENT. These agreements are usually written and are signed by the parties and will be binding. Collective agreements can either be **substantive agreements** or **procedural agreements**. Substantive agreements are concerned with terms and conditions of employment. They include pay, work conditions and fringe benefits. Procedural agreements set out how the parties in the bargaining should relate to each other on certain issues. They include negotiating, redundancy, dismissal, recruitment and promotion procedures.

In the 1990s fewer and fewer workers had their pay and conditions determined by unions negotiating with management. The proportion of workers covered by collective bargaining agreements fell from 54 per cent in 1990 to just 35.5 per cent in 1997. Pay was increasingly determined at local or regional level, as explained in the next section. The recognition of unions when workers vote for it, consultation over collective redundancies and the Social Chapter

---

Question

In 1998 Yorkshire Water's employees were considering industrial action. There was to be a ballot on strike action following the company's attempt to impose a performance-related pay scheme on staff. The introduction of the scheme had already been rejected twice in ballots by workers. Staff that signed up before July 7 1998 were to be given a £400 bonus. Unions at the company, UNISON and GMB, recommended that employees rejected the company's offer. David Mitchell of Unison said: 'This dispute is not just about pay, it's about the future of collective bargaining in Yorkshire. We cannot accept a situation where the company goes behind our backs to the workforce whenever we disagree with them'. The views of employees are unlikely to be helped by the 30 per cent bonus payments that directors awarded themselves. This was in spite of the Chancellor of the Exchequer's plea for pay restraint, especially from privatised utilities. A company statement said: 'We believe that we have to have a remuneration policy which will enable the company to attract, retain and motivate people with the skills and experience to manage a business of the size and complexity of Yorkshire Water.

Source: adapted from *The Times*, 29.6.1998.

(a) Identify three possible sources of conflict between employers and employees/employee representatives at Yorkshire Water.
(b) Explain why the business might have justified its actions in each case.

(☞ unit 81) may all influence collective agreements after the year 2000.

Levels of negotiation

Negotiations can take place at a number of different levels.

International bargaining Large multinational companies (☞ unit 32) operate in many different countries. Some have considered the possibility of negotiating the same conditions for all employees in the business, no matter what country or factory they work in. This has the advantages that conditions can be standardised and workers in one country will not feel envious of those in another. The major problem of this approach is the inflexibility it causes.

National level Employers and employees may agree a deal which applies to all employees. Negotiations may take place to set wage or salary scales, or to discuss national conditions of work. For example, an agreement could be reached on the number of hours that teachers or lecturers should work a year, or their length of holidays, between teachers' unions and the government. A private sector example might be negotiations over a pay increase between GEC and AEEU, the engineers' union.

Local level Discussions may take place at a local level, so that any settlement can reflect local conditions. An example of local negotiations might be wages or salaries based on the area of operation. From time to time the weightings given to local authority workers for working in the London or surrounding areas are revised. These weightings are added to workers' salaries to take into account the higher cost of living in the area. A locally based engineering company may negotiate with regional union representatives about the need to reduce the workforce because of falling sales. Again, this is likely to take place at local level.

Factory or plant-wide level Negotiations at factory or plant-wide level can take place over a variety of aspects of work. They may involve the personnel department, departmental managers, shop stewards and employee representatives.

Examples of matters that might be agreed upon could be:
- productivity targets;
- the introduction of new machinery;
- hours of work and flexibility within the plant;
- health and safety conditions.

In the 1990s businesses argued that negotiations should take place at factory or local level. National negotiations over pay do not take the 'local' situation into account. A business that wants flexibility to react to changes in the market is better able to do this if each plant can negotiate based on the individual conditions it faces. Such an argument was strongly put forward by former public sector operations which 'opted out', such as NHS trusts.

Individualised bargaining In the 1980s and 1990s there was a trend to individualised bargaining. This is where the result of negotiations is the agreement between the employee and the employer in the contract of employment. Union representatives are not involved in negotiations. This means that the employee does not receive advice and does not have the backing of an influential group when discussing terms and conditions. However, it may mean that both sides in the negotiations have greater flexibility.

The negotiation process

For negotiation to be successful in collective bargaining, an agreement must be reached which satisfies all parties. This is far more likely to be achieved if a pattern is followed during negotiation.

The agenda A meeting between all parties involved in negotiation needs an agenda. This will outline what is to be discussed and all parties must agree to it. The order of items on the agenda may influence the outcome of negotiations. If, for instance, all the employees' claims come first and all the management's points come later, then anything that is agreed at the beginning of the meeting cannot be accepted until the management side is given. An agenda that places management and employee items in alternate and logical order can make negotiations easier.

Information Both parties need 'facts' to support their arguments. Negotiators have to collect the information they need, analyse it and make sure that each member of the negotiating team has a say in its interpretation. Often managers make information about a company's financial position available to representatives before meetings. This ensures that both parties have the correct information on which to base discussions.

Strategy It is important for each side in the negotiations to prepare a strategy. This will help them to achieve their objectives. Developing a strategy could include the following stages.
- Agreeing objectives. What do negotiators seek to achieve? The objectives set by employers or unions should, if achieved, lead to improvements. For example, a change in employment rules might improve efficiency or motivation. Negative objectives that emphasise not 'losing ground' are not usually helpful.
- Allocating roles. Who will do what in the negotiations? Negotiators need specific roles. For example, there may be a chairperson to lead the discussion, someone to put the case and a specialist to provide advice. The roles of group members are discussed in unit 84.
- Predict what the other side might do. Strategies are unlikely to remain the same during negotiations. Their chances of success are improved if the negotiators have tried to predict

Korvac and James is a manufacturer of chemicals. It operates from a factory in Newcastle. Despite a number of years of falling sales in the 1990s, it has recently had 2 good years of orders.

This year's pay negotiations are due to take place, and the management has offered a 2 per cent pay increase, which it feels is a good offer given the need to grow in future and the current rate of inflation. The union representative at the factory thinks this is poor given the work by employees to pull the business around. He has suggested to two local union officials who will be involved in negotiations that a 6 per cent increase should be bargained for or strike action should be considered. He feels certain that the company can afford this, although no figures are yet available on this year's profits. The local officials are not so sure. They suggest that other options are available before calling for a vote on strike action. In particular, they are concerned that higher wages will result in redundancies, although they feel in a strong position to argue that increased productivity by workers will pay for any wage increases.

Another unknown factor is the likely installation of new machinery for the next year, which could lead to new grades for certain workers, but also redundancies in some areas.

(a) Write a letter from one of the union officials to the factory representative outlining the steps that should be taken and the strategy that should be adopted before they enter negotiations with management.

what they will hear from the opposition. Negotiators must be prepared not only to put forward their own arguments, but also to respond to arguments put to them.

Unity Because negotiation involves different sets of interests, each team must work out a united position before negotiations begin. If the group's position changes, all members must agree. It is important that a group shows unity at all times during negotiations or its position may become weaker.

Size of the group The number of people representing each side will influence the negotiations. The larger the group the greater the problem of managing communications between group members (☞ unit 84). When asked to suggest a number, most experienced negotiators opt for three or four in each group. Meetings of fewer people may be accused of 'fixing' an outcome.

Stages of the negotiation Negotiators begin by making it

clear that they are representing the interests of others. They often emphasise the strength of their case and start by saying they are unwilling to move from that position. The displays of strength are necessary to convince themselves and the 'opposition' that they are willing to fight for their position. By the time this part of the negotiations starts, both sides should be very clear on the matters that divide them. After the differences have been explored, the next stage is for negotiators to look for solutions that might be more acceptable to each party. Each party will sound out possibilities, float ideas, ask questions and make suggestions. No firm commitments are made at this stage. Negotiations are likely to be more successful if each group is willing to change its position.

Decision making The next stage is to come to some agreement. The management may make an offer. The decision about what to offer is the most difficult and important task in the whole process. The offer may be revised, but eventually it will be accepted or rejected. Agreement is usual in all but a small minority of situations. Employees do not really wish to disrupt an organisation. Even if they take strike action, they will eventually return to the firm. The management need the employees to work for them. They have to reach an agreement no matter how long it takes.

Written statement Producing a brief written statement before the negotiation has ended will make it clear what both parties have decided, if agreement has been reached.

Commitment of the parties So far, agreement has been reached between negotiators only. This is of no value unless the groups represented by the negotiators accept it and make it work.

Employee representatives have to report back to their members and persuade them to accept the agreement. Management representatives may also have to do the same thing. Once the terms have been agreed by both employees and employers, the negotiating process is complete. It is the joint responsibility of both parties to carry out and monitor the agreement.

Consultation

Negotiation, as we have seen, is an activity by which the two parties make agreements which may cover pay and conditions at work and relations between management and employees. JOINT CONSULTATION, by contrast, is the process where management representatives discuss matters of common interest with employee representatives before negotiating or making a decision. There are three types of consultation.

Pseudo-consultation Pseudo-consultation is where management makes a decision and informs employees of that decision through their representatives. Employees have no power to influence these decisions. Some have suggested that it would be more accurately described as information-giving.

Classical consultation Classical consultation is a way of involving employees, through their representatives, in discussions on matters which affect them. This allows employees to have an influence on management decisions. Unions may be involved, for example, in restructuring (☞ unit 102).

Integrative consultation Pseudo and classical consultation do not directly involve employees in decisions which affect them. Integrative consultation is a more democratic method of decision making. Arguably it is neither consultation nor negotiation. Management and unions discuss and explore matters which are of common concern, such as ways of increasing productivity or methods of changing work practices. The two groups come to a joint decision having used, in many cases, problem solving techniques (☞ units 11, 103 and 104). An example of an integrative approach to consultation might be the use of quality circles (☞ unit 73) in a number of UK businesses and in foreign firms setting up in the UK.

Factors affecting consultation

The extent to which consultation takes place in business may depend on a number of factors.

Legislation UK government legislation and rulings by European bodies on European law are likely to affect consultation. The **Employment Relations Bill, 1999**, for example, stated that employers must consult with unions on training plans. UK law also states that employers have to consult with employee representatives over collective redundancies.

Consultative bodies It was suggested that the introduction of **European works councils,** as a result of the UK signing the Social Chapter of the EU, was also likely to increase consultation after the year 2000. 146 multinationals in the UK would be affected. These councils are bodies which bring together employee representatives from across the EU in multinational companies. In the late 1990s around 515 councils had been set up in Europe. They were consulted by employers on matters such as restructuring and mergers.

Corporate culture Some businesses have developed a culture that recognises the importance of consultation when decisions are made (☞ unit 14). They value the contribution that employees can make to effective decision making. Businesses that make use of knowledge teams (☞ unit 102) are likely to see consultation as important. An example of an

integrated approach to consultation might be the use of quality circles, which have been set up in a number of UK businesses and in foreign firms setting up in the UK.

Tradition In some of the state owned industries, before privatisation, consultation often took place. For example, in the nationalised British Rail train drivers and guards were consulted on training, heath and safety and work rosters at regional level. It was perhaps felt that they would have local knowledge and experience which could help decision making.

Representation and power In certain parts of the private sector, where unions are weak, or collective bargaining does not take place, pseudo-consultation is more likely. An example might be where the owner of a small, non-unionised business decides to move premises and informs the workers that this will take place.

Communication and information technology The introduction of company intranets and other communication technologies (☞ unit 82) has helped to speed up and extend the process of consultation.

Quality standards Organisations may seek a quality award, such as **Investors in People** (☞ unit 79), for the way in which they work with employees. Consultation, the passing of information and involvement in decision making are standards that businesses have to maintain to keep this award. Such an award may attract customers and good quality candidates.

The advantages of consultation

Consultation with employees and representative groups is likely to have a number of advantages for a business.
- It may avoid damaging industrial action.
- It may motivate employees more as they feel part of the decision making process.
- It may lead to an input of new or different ideas which could, for example, make any changes easier to carry out.
- It may help to develop a more open organisational culture in the business (☞ unit 14) and allow a firm to achieve its objectives. Workers in the business might feel their opinions are valued and be prepared to put forward ideas, for example in suggestion boxes.
- It may encourage worker representatives to take a long term view and adopt similar strategies to management, by making them better informed about the reasons behind decisions.
- It might make management more sympathetic to workers' needs. This might put them in a better position to decide if changes in work organisation will be accepted or not by employees.

In 1997 the UK signed the EU's Social Chapter. One of the directives of EU social policy relates to the setting up of European works councils. In 1998 Stagecoach, the bus and rail group, announced the first European works council in the public transport sector. Representatives on the council included Graham Steveson, the T&G's national secretary and Anders Westin, national secretary of the main Swedish bus workers' union. Mike Kinski, chief executive at Stagecoach, said:' I think that for a business to move forward it needs a partnership with its employees and its unions'.

In 1998, in response to judgments by the European Court of Justice, the government suggested that UK provision did not meet the requirements on how employees are consulted about redundancies and mergers affecting their organisation. In February the DTI published a document which set out to clarify the way in which employees should be informed and consulted over company acquisitions and redundancies. It proposed an elected body (which may already exist if there was a works council) to deal with consultation and negotiation. Where no union existed, the employer would be responsible for forming such a body.

Source: adapted from *People Management*, 28.5.1998.

(a) Suggest possible benefits for: (i) the business; and (ii) employees as a result of the introduction of European works councils.
(b) Why might a business oppose the changes proposed by the DTI?

The Advisory, Conciliation and Arbitration Service (ACAS)

Sometimes parties fail to reach agreements after consultation and negotiation. In these situations the Advisory, Conciliation and Arbitration Service (ACAS) can be of great value to both sides.

During the period of industrial action in the 1970s, groups of employers and employees called for the setting up of a conciliation and arbitration service, independent of government control and of civil service influence. The result was ACAS, which took up its formal duties in September 1974. The governing body of ACAS is made up of trade union representatives, for example the general secretary of a union such as the T&G, academics, such as university professors, and members with a business background. ACAS was given the role of improving industrial relations and

encouraging reform of collective bargaining procedures. ACAS provides a wide range of services to employers and employees in business.

Industrial disputes ACAS has conciliation duties. It can intervene in industrial disputes (☞ unit 87) at the request of either management or unions. Its role is to try and encourage a settlement that all parties may agree to, using procedures that both parties accept.

Arbitration and mediation Arbitration is where both parties in a dispute put forward their case to ACAS. ACAS then independently assesses each case and recommends a final decision. Mediation is where ACAS makes recommendations about a possible solution and leaves the parties to find a settlement.

Advisory work ACAS carries out advisory work with employers, trade unions and employers' associations. This can be short visits to answer specific questions or long term, in-depth, projects and surveys. The questions ACAS deal with are wide ranging and can include issues such as contracts of employment, industrial relations legislation, payment systems and personnel policies.

Codes of practice ACAS issues codes of practice. These contain practical guidance on how to improve industrial relations between employers and employees.

Enquiries ACAS has carried out enquiries into the flexible use of labour, appraisal systems, labour turnover, employee involvement, handling redundancy and the use of quality circles (☞ unit 73). Much of this research is published by ACAS as advisory booklets. Employers use them to help improve industrial relations and personnel management practices.

Individual cases ACAS investigates individual cases of unfair discrimination (☞ unit 80) and unfair dismissal (☞ unit 81). The number of cases dealt with has increased from around 4,100 in 1987 to over 72,000 in 1992 to over 100,000 in 1999.

Tribunals Industrial tribunals hear a wide range of employment disputes, including unfair dismissal and discrimination (☞ unit 80). ACAS operates independently from the tribunals. Its role is to offer conciliation on disputes, with the aim of settling the matter without a tribunal hearing. This is known as alternative dispute resolution (ADR). The **Employment Rights (Dispute Resolution) Act, 1998** outlined a new ACAS arbitration scheme designed to find other methods than the courts for solving disputes.

During the 1990s, ACAS developed its services to meet the needs of a changing industrial relations climate. While the bulk of its work continues to be conciliation, mediation and

Question 4

After October 1, 1998, the Employment Rights (Disputes Resolution) Act, 1998 conferred a duty on ACAS to conciliate if someone puts in an application to an employment tribunal concerning redundancy pay entitlement. An ACAS conciliator would make contact with the interested parties to see if the matter could be resolved without the need for a tribunal hearing. Before 1998, ACAS had no authority to conciliate in redundancy payment cases. There were 4,770 such cases registered in 1997/98, some six per cent of the case load for that period.

The 1998 ACAS Annual Report showed that nearly 107,000 claims on individual rights issues were received by ACAS in the previous year. Although this was 6.5 per cent up on 1996, it compared with rises of 10-15 per cent in the preceding two years. The 1997 total was more than double the figure for 1990.

There was a growing tendency for cases to include two or more claims under different jurisdictions (eg unfair dismissal and breach of contract). The number of actual cases brought by individuals rose by only 2 per cent. Two out of every five claims alleged unfair dismissal. The other major jurisdictions covered protection of wages and breach of contract, which between them accounted for a further two out of five cases. The number of discrimination cases received during the year continued at a relatively low level - 6,600 for sex discrimination, 2,900 for race discrimination and, in its first full year, 1,400 for disability discrimination. ACAS had great success in individual conciliation, with only 30 per cent of cases progressing to a tribunal hearing. The success rate was particularly high for the new Disability Discrimination Act cases - only 18 per cent of the 568 completed cases going to a tribunal.

John Hougham, chair of ACAS, commented: 'The signs are that employment relations are taking a turn for the better. After a year in which the number of working days lost through industrial action reached an all-time low, it is encouraging to see that the steep upward trend in individual employment rights disputes has started to flatten out. Nevertheless, ACAS is busier than ever and I am proud to say that our success rate in settling disputes is as high as ever. Despite the reduction in the strike figures, there has been no significant fall in collective disputes (down less than 2 per cent on 1996) and the 1997 figure is almost exactly the same as the average figure over the past five years. Within this total, however, there has been a slight shift away from disputes over redundancy issues to disputes about pay and terms and conditions of employment.

Our Annual Report draws attention to a number of management-workforce partnership arrangements that were concluded during the year. ACAS has long advocated this joint working approach and it is encouraging to see it being taken up by major organisations and unions, with support from the government. In 1998 we shall be placing increased emphasis on providing guidance on good practice, especially among small firms, and we are also looking forward to developing a new service to provide publicly funded arbitration in unfair dismissal cases as a voluntary alternative to having them heard by an industrial tribunal.'

Source: adapted from ACAS website, www.acas.org.uk.

(a) Identify the services provided by ACAS in the article.
(b) Suggest reasons for the changing trends in ACAS services.
(c) How might the success of ACAS's services be evaluated?

---

arbitration, it has steadily developed advisory and training services. ACAS has also become more involved in helping business to improve personnel and management practices. These include:

● effective recruitment and selection of employees;
● setting up and operating equal opportunities policies;
● improving communications and joint consultation;
● developing the skills of managers to help them introduce changes in work organisation.

The Central Arbitration Committee

After 1999, unions had to be recognised where the majority of the relevant workforce voted for it (☞ unit 85). The government wanted to encourage voluntary arrangements between employers and employee representatives. If agreement could not be reached, unions could go to the CENTRAL ARBITRATION COMMITTEE (CAC). This is a statutory government body designed to have responsibility for union recognition. It would first encourage parties to settle the matter

themselves. If this failed it could award recognition or the union could hold a ballot. The CAC has the power to instruct the employer to co-operate with the ballot or risk a fine. It can also widen or narrow the workforce to be covered by recognition.

Key terms

ACAS - a body which mediates where conflict exists in business.
CAC - the government body responsible for union recognition.
Collective agreements - the agreements reached through the process of collective bargaining.
Collective bargaining - a method of determining conditions of work and terms of employment through negotiations between employers and employee representatives.
Joint consultation - discussion between management and employee representatives before a decision is taken.

Summary

1. What factors may lead to conflict between employers and employees?
2. Why is collective bargaining important to employees?
3. What are likely to be the results of collective bargaining?
4. Explain the difference between:
   (a) collective bargaining at national and plant level;
   (b) collective bargaining and individualised bargaining.
5. Briefly explain the stages in negotiation that may help to lead to a satisfactory outcome.
6. Explain the different types of consultation.
7. What are the advantages of consultation for a business?
8. Briefly explain the main areas of activity that ACAS is involved in.

Case study

ISS

In the late 1990s ISS, the worldwide cleaning company, established a global policy for employee relations. It was hailed as a significant international union-company partnership. Working with Fiet, the international trade union federation, it has devised a policy to ensure a standard approach to pay and working conditions across the 140 countries in which it operated. The agreement guaranteed the right to enjoy 'core' standards of pay, training and conditions for its 126,000 employees.

In 1995 ISS was the first service sector company to set up a European works council. The new agreement attempted to strengthen the work of the council and extend its principles beyond Europe. It was suggested that: 'an open dialogue on equal terms between employees and management is a prerequisite for the continuing success of ISS'.

A corporate review of human resource strategies on training, work time and salaries concluded that there was a need for a global approach. The company rejected the policy used by other companies of undercutting competitors to win contracts through low pay and working conditions. It argued that the policy would improve the public perception and esteem of workers and that 'our experience is that well run unions and organised labour can be a guarantor of benefits for both the company and its employees'.

There was still some debate in the late 1990s about the effectiveness of works councils. Some employers were said to be bypassing councils in order to speed up the pace of restructuring and mergers. The European Trade Union Confederation (ETUC) argued that they were simply seen as a 'PR exercise in which things are sold to the workforce'. Officials, representatives and employers also suggested that a lack of training was leading to problems for the growing complexity of issues that works councils were being asked to consider. Problems such as technical jargon and the use of different languages too often caused difficulties. On the other hand it was argued that there was a broad agreement amongst European firms about the benefits of works councils, 'particularly for firms that are restructuring', said Benoit Melet, head of public relations at Renault. The ETUC argued that there was a slow learning process and works councils would be effective if time, money and effort were put into them. They said: 'so far we are far from seeing true consultation'.

Source: adapted from *Labour Research*, 29.10. 1998; *People Management*, 20.5.1999.

(a) Identify the changes made to bargaining by ISS.
(b) What factors might have affected the changes in negotiation and consultation at ISS?
(c) Analyse how changes made in the 1990s by ISS and other European companies may have affected consultation.
(d) Evaluate the extent to which these changes are likely to benefit European businesses and their employees.

Industrial action in the UK

Conflict between employees and employers can lead to **industrial action**. Industrial action can be taken by both employers against employees (such as close supervision of work, or a lock out) and by employees against employers (ranging from an overtime ban to strike action). It is in the interests of both groups to reconcile differences through negotiation and consultation (☞ unit 86) before taking action, although this is not always possible.

The number of stoppages and the working days lost through stoppages in the UK fell greatly over the period 1977-97. This is shown in Figure 87.1 and 87.2. In part this is due to legislation which has made union action more difficult to take (☞ unit 85). It is also, perhaps, due to a movement away from the 'hostile' attitudes taken by employers and trade unions towards industrial relations. In the 1990s, unions appeared more willing to discuss and solve disputes. Management might also have become more interested in the

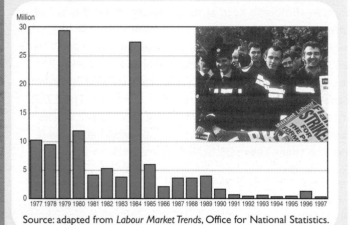

Figure 87.1 *Working days lost in the UK due to stoppages, 1977-97*

Source: adapted from *Labour Market Trends*, Office for National Statistics.

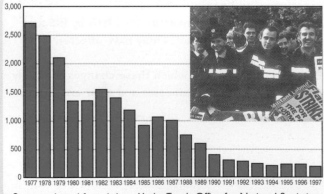

Figure 87.2 *Stoppages in progress, UK, 1977-97*

Source: adapted from *Labour Market Trends*, Office for National Statistics.

area of human resource management, with its emphasis on employee involvement and direct communication.

Employers' industrial action

Action by management against employees can take a number of forms. Sometimes sanctions can be imposed by individual managers. Some may include, for example, close supervision of employees' work, tight work discipline, discrimination against certain groups, lay offs, demoting workers or speeding up work practices. These actions are usually taken by one member of the management team and will not be repeated in other departments in the company. They might lead to individuals or groups of workers starting grievance proceedings against the manager concerned.

Sanctions can also be organised and carried out throughout the business. Management may use some of the following actions when dealing with trade unions.

Withdrawal of overtime and suspension Withdrawing overtime (☞ unit 72) or suspension are sometimes used by management to impress upon unions that they will be standing firm during negotiations over pay and conditions.

Lock-outs A LOCK-OUT by employers involves closing the factory for a period of time. Employees' wages may not be paid during this period. This action might adversely affect the image that the public have of the company. Also, the business is able to achieve the same ends by other, less drastic means.

Changing standards and piecework rates Management may change work standards or alter piecework rates when in dispute with employees. This can have the effect of making the employees' task more difficult or reducing the earnings of employees unless they work a lot harder.

Sometimes a management tactic may be to use a strategy of increasing work standards so that unions will call a strike. This might happen when order books are low and stocks are high. By causing a strike, management do not need to lay anyone off or pay redundancy money. At the same time further stockpiling is reduced. This type of action is only used in extreme cases.

Closure The closing down of factories and offices, or the threat by management to remove plant and machinery from their premises, is a much more likely managerial tactic in modern business. Some people would not even view such activities as industrial action. They would see them as the normal rights of management to shut down uneconomic enterprises or force uncooperative workers to comply with employers' needs in the workplace. Managerial action of this sort can lead to SIT-INS or WORK-INS by employees in an

Question 1

In September 1998 Essex firefighters were due to start their twenty sixth strike in a series which began on 8 June in response to job cuts. The strike was planned to run from 5.30am to 6.30am on 25 August. However, the employer's lockout policy meant that the strike would effectively run from 6.00pm on 24 August to 9.00am on 25 August. This was to be followed by a further two hour per day strike, which would again be extended by the lockout. The firefighters' union (FBU) calculated that the cost of industrial action to the fire authority at the time was around £2 million. This was mainly in charges from the police to cover services. The union estimated that this amount was in excess of the savings that would have been made from the job cuts. On 8 September a pile up of 20 lorries and 12 cars on the M25 resulted in the death of a lorry driver and injuries to some other drivers. The accident was attended by RAF firefighters, as Essex firefighters were on strike. In October 1998 the dispute ended when the unions accepted a new offer following branch consultation which voted by 22 branches to 8 for acceptance.

Source: adapted from *Labour Research*, September, October 1998, January 1999; *The Times*, 9.9.1998.

(a) Why might the employers of Essex firefighters have decided to use a lock out policy?
(b) Examine how the action taken by employers may have affected: (i) the businesses involved; (ii) other businesses.
(c) Suggest another form of action that the employer may have taken and explain possible constraints on this action.

attempt to prevent closure. These are discussed in the next section.

Dismissal Under certain circumstances an employer may dismiss an employee taking industrial action. **The Employment Relations Bill, 1999** proposed that employees were protected against dismissal for taking industrial action for the first eight weeks of a strike. After that, a dismissal would be fair if the Central Arbitration Committee (☞ unit 86) judges that all reasonable action has been taken by the employer to end the strike.

Employees' industrial action

Industrial action used by employees can be wide ranging. It is possible to distinguish between **unorganised** action and **organised** action. R Hyman in his book *Strikes*, wrote that: '... in unorganised conflict the worker typically responds to the oppressive situation in the only way open to him as an individual ... Such reaction rarely derives from any calculative strategy ... Organised conflict, on the other hand, is far more likely to form part of a conscious strategy to change the situation which is identified as the source of discontent.'

Unorganised (or unofficial) action by employees can come in a number of forms.
● High labour turnover (☞ unit 75).
● Poor time keeping.
● High levels of absenteeism.
● Low levels of effort.
● Inefficient work.
● Deliberate time wasting.
● Unofficial strikes not backed by the employees' union.

These are often taken when workers 'down tools' immediately in reaction to employers' actions.

Such action can be disruptive for a business if it continues for a long period of time. The business, however, can use disciplinary procedures against employees and may even be able to terminate contracts in some cases (☞ unit 78). However, unofficial action may lead to organised action backed by the union. Organised action can take a number of different forms.

Work to rule or go slow Organised and group industrial action by trade unions against management can take the form of working to rule or going slow. A work to rule means employees do not carry out duties which are not in their employment contract. They may also carry out management orders to the letter. This can result in workers strictly observing the safety and work rules which are normally disregarded. Working to rule does not mean that employees are in breach of contract, simply that they carry out tasks exactly according to their contract. This means that tasks are not carried out efficiently. The impact of train drivers working to rule, for example, could mean that trains are late arriving or are cancelled. Drivers may delay taking trains out until rigorous checks are carried out. A go slow is where employees deliberately attempt to slow down production, whilst still working within the terms of their contract.

Overtime ban An overtime ban limits workers' hours to the agreed contract of employment for normal hours. Overtime bans are usually used by trade unions to demonstrate to management that the workforce is determined to take further collective action if their demands are not met. An overtime ban does have a disadvantage for workers as it results in lost earnings. It can lead to a reduction in costs for the business, but may also lead to lost production. It can be especially effective where production takes place overnight, eg coal mines, large production lines.

Sit-ins and work-ins Sit-ins and work-ins are mass occupations of premises by workers. A work-in is where employees continue production with the aim of demonstrating that the factory is a viable concern. It is sometimes used when there is a threat of closure. In a sit-in, production does not continue. The aim is to protest against management decisions and, in the case of factory closure, prevent the transfer of machinery to other factories. A

redundancy sit-in or work-in is a protest against the closure of a plant or company. A **collective bargaining sit-in** may be used instead of other forms of industrial action such as working to rule, overtime bans, and all out strikes, to give employees a position of strength in negotiations.

Sit-ins and work-ins mean the illegal occupation of premises by workers. They also allow workers to gain control over the factory. Why are these tactics used? First, they offer some degree of control over the factory or plant being occupied, which is obviously important in redundancy situations where the removal of plant and machinery to other locations is being threatened. Also by working-in or sitting-in, employees are better able to maintain their group solidarity.

Strikes The ultimate sanction used by trade unions against employers is the strike or industrial stoppage. Stoppages at work are normally connected with terms and conditions of employment. Strikes can be **official** or **unofficial**. Official strikes are where a union officially supports its members in accordance with union rules during a dispute after a ballot for action has been carried out and agreed by union members. Unofficial strikes have no union backing or support. They have, in the past, been called by shop stewards in particular factories, often in response to a particular incident. Such strikes are likely to be short term, local, unpredictable and disruptive for a business.

There is no single reason that explains the trend in stoppages in Britain. A study of strikes in Britain over an extensive time period was carried out by researchers for the Department of Employment. They discovered that:
- strikes appear to be over major issues;
- strikes are concentrated in a very small proportion of plants - often the larger ones in certain industries and in

Question 2

According to research for the TUC, there were indications in the latter part of the 1990s of a growing willingness of unions to consider strike action. Most of the action recorded was official, but there there was a 'not insignificant incidence of unofficial action'. For example, unofficial action took place in the Post Office, against changes in work practices, and at companies like Neil and Cooper, the sewing machinists.

The most common form of action tends to be strike action. However, for the first time the survey finds that nearly one in three industrial actions used an overtime ban, including the T&G at Stagecoach West. Most of the action involved relatively small groups of workers, such as 40 GMB members at Tyners Turkeys, but larger groups, such as BIFU the bank union, were also involved in action. There was an increasing use of industrial action ballots. Unions, on average, organised five ballots a month. Eight in every ten ballots, the survey found, result in a yes vote for action. Of course, not every ballot results in strike action. The teaching union NASUWT stated that despite ballots, many issues had been settled prior to action. This confirms that unions use ballots selectively and that employers may settle when they are aware of unions' feelings. However, unions must be careful because the average cost of a ballot is £455 and can be as high as £3,000.

Strike action tends to be called when there are issues of discrimination or victimisation. For example, contractors on the extension of the Jubilee Line of London's underground were accused by the AEEU of victimising 'vocal' workers who raised safety concerns about fire alarms that did not work. Unofficial strike action was taken, but the dispute was resolved after a 2 week strike when the company agreed not to transfer the workers. The strike had spread to other sites and involved 600 workers.

Source: adapted from *Labour Research*, October 1997; January 1999.

(a) Identify the types of industrial action that employees might take.
(b) Analyse the trends and characteristics of industrial action indicated in the article and the data.

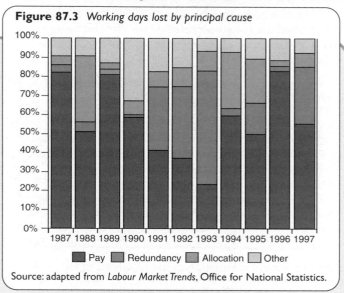

Figure 87.3 *Working days lost by principal cause*

Legend: ■ Pay ■ Redundancy ■ Allocation □ Other

Source: adapted from *Labour Market Trends*, Office for National Statistics.

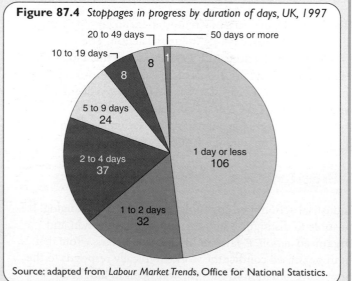

Figure 87.4 *Stoppages in progress by duration of days, UK, 1997*

20 to 49 days — 8
50 days or more — 1
10 to 19 days — 8
5 to 9 days — 24
2 to 4 days — 37
1 to 2 days — 32
1 day or less — 106

Source: adapted from *Labour Market Trends*, Office for National Statistics.

(c) Why might these trends have taken place?

certain areas of the country;
- industries and regions that have large factories, on average, tend to experience relatively high numbers of strikes. These strikes occur fairly often.

Factors influencing the success of employees' industrial action

Whether industrial action by workers and unions is successful in helping them achieve their aims depends on a number of factors.

Nature and strength of the union A large union negotiating with a small business is more likely to be able to influence the employer. Where large unions are negotiating with large multinational companies or with the government, action may not always be successful.

It has also been argued that unions are less influential if representation in the industry is split. This was perhaps the case when some mine workers left the NUM to form the Union of Democratic Mineworkers. It may also have been a reason for the merger of NALGO, NUPE and COHSE to form the UK's largest union, Unison.

Smaller unions tend to have less influence. The Musicians Union, for example, whilst having rates per hour for performers is unlikely to be able to force club owners to pay the 'going rate' for performances.

Location and organisation of the workforce It has been suggested that unions are in a stronger bargaining position if a number of their members are employed in the same 'place'. Farm workers, for example, have traditionally been in a weak bargaining position with employers, as few are employed on any one farm. Also, their places of employment are geographically dispersed. This makes meetings and support difficult.

Public support and union views Public support for a dispute may strengthen a union's position. This may be particularly true of public sector workers, such as nurses, where the public often 'feel' workers deserve higher wages or not to be made redundant. However, public opinion may change once industrial action begins. This may also be the case in industrial action by railway workers, for example, especially in commuter belts around London.

Health unions have in the past refused to strike because of the damaging effects on patients. The Royal College of Nursing is one example. In recent years, however, members of other unions have been prepared to take industrial action within hospitals.

Management tactics Union action is likely to be less effective if management action can reduce the problems for business. In the car industry, a strike by employees may not affect a producer if there are stocks of cars and orders can still be met.

Management may encourage non-union workers or even union members to cross the picket line, or even be prepared to 'bus in' workers from other areas. The government has, in the past, been prepared to use army vehicles and members of the armed forces when fire service workers have taken industrial action.

Legislation and economic climate The **1984 Trade Union Act** (☞ unit 85) forced unions to conduct secret ballots before strike action took place. Ballot rules remained unchanged in the **Employment Relations Bill, 1999**. It could be argued that this reduced the strength of unions. It had the effect of delaying any action, giving members a chance to consider whether they want to take action, and allowed businesses to prepare for the outcome. Legislation that has restricted picketing has also reduced union power.

The economic climate is also likely to influence union membership and strength. In a period of growth or boom (☞ unit 21), more people are employed, have an income, and are more likely to belong to a union.

Question 3

Industrial action at the BBC threatened to disrupt coverage of the World Cup, Wimbledon and Royal Ascot in 1998. A 24 hour stoppage on 4 June resulted in the cancellation of live television and radio broadcasts such as BBC's Breakfast News. The BBC was planning to transfer 4,000 staff from its technical wing to the BBC resources subsidiary. The broadcasting union BECTU said it was the thin edge of full privatisation of the BBC and wanted no changes to terms and conditions and no compulsory redundancies. The BBC refused.

BECTU appealed to Harriet Harmon, the then Social Security Secretary, not to appear on Question Time in support. A DSS spokesperson said that the programme was made by an independent company and so she would not have to cross the picket line. Another strike was proposed, on the day Scotland played Norway in the World Cup, although discussions were taking place with ACAS. Contingency plans were drawn up by the BBC to bring in freelance staff and to move news and live programmes to different locations.

BECTU said it had the support of six French broadcasting unions which could technically pull the plug on England and Scotland matches. ITV said it could not contractually show any of the matches that the BBC was due to show. Tony Lennon, BECTU president, said that members were unable to strike on the day of the Scotland vs Brazil match because the law required them to give 7 days' notice.

Source: adapted from *The Times*, 5.6.1998.

(a) Discuss the factors that might influence the success of industrial action by BECTU members.

Problems of industrial action

There are certain problems which result from industrial action, both for employers and employees.

Employers' problems

- Industrial action can lead to lost production for the business. A go slow or work to rule may reduce output. Strike action could mean that orders are unfulfilled and revenue and profits could fall.
- If industrial action results in production being stopped, then machinery and other resources will be lying idle. A business will have many fixed costs (☞ unit 52) which have to be covered, even if production is not taking place. If output ceases, revenue will not be earned to pay for these costs.
- Industrial action may lead to poor future relationships in a business. Sometimes grievances can carry on after a dispute. This could result in poor motivation and communication.
- Industrial disputes divert managers' attention away from planning. If a business is concerned with solving a dispute that exists now, it may neglect plans for the future.
- Loss of output and delays in production or deliveries caused by action can harm the firm's reputation. This may lead to lost business in future.

Employees' problems

- A work to rule, go slow or strike can lead to a reduction or a loss of earnings.
- Prolonged industrial action may, in some cases, lead to the closure of the business. Employees would then be made redundant.
- Action is likely to place stress on the workforce. It can also cause friction between levels of the hierarchy (☞ unit 70). For example, managers on the other 'side' in a dispute are unlikely to find their employees motivated.

- If action is unsuccessful, the employees' position may be weaker in future. Members may also leave a union if they feel that it is unable to support their interests.
- Public support may suffer if the action affects people's everyday lives.
- Strike action must conform to current legislation (☞ unit 85) or unions may be liable for damages and employees may be disciplined or dismissed.

Benefits of industrial action

Industrial action is often used as a 'final' measure by unions and employers because of the disruption it causes. There are, however, some benefits for both groups.

- It 'clears the air'. Employers and employees may have grievances. Industrial action can bring these out into the open and, once the dispute is solved, this could improve the 'atmosphere' in the business.
- Introducing new rules. How groups operate in businesses is influenced by rules, such as rates of pay or what is meant by unfair dismissal. Conflict is often about disagreement over these rules. When industrial action has been resolved, this often leads to new rules which each group agrees upon.
- Changing management goals. Management often change their goals and the ways they are achieved after industrial action. For example, a business may have attempted to introduce new working practices without consulting unions, which led to industrial action. In future it may consult with unions before changing work practices.
- Understanding the position of each group. Industrial action often makes the position of employers and employees very clear. It allows each group to hear the grievances of the other, consider them and decide to what extent they agree.

Summary

1. Why might the number of days lost through stoppages in the UK have fallen over the last decade?
2. Explain 4 types of industrial action that employers can take.
3. State 6 types of employee action.
4. Why might employees be reluctant to use strike action?
5. Explain the difference between a sit-in and a go slow.
6. What factors might influence the success of employees' industrial action?
7. State 3 problems of industrial action for:
   (a) employees;
   (b) employers.
8. How might industrial action benefit a business?

Question 4

In 1998 strike action was being proposed in the prison service, averted at a travel group business and ending at a retail group.

After two suicides and numerous disturbances, strike action was proposed for staff at Parc prison, the high tech jail near Bridgend, South Wales. The normally moderate Prison Service Union said that the imposition of new shift patterns had been the final straw. It planned to ballot its members over strike action just three weeks after persuading them not to walk out in protest at the way the jail was run. Phillip Hornsby, the union national officer, said that many staff had already left the jail, some were working 16 hour days and that the changes had been imposed arbitrarily. A spokesperson for the jail said that the jail had a staff association and that a consultative negotiating committee had been set up and that consultation on the changes was ongoing.

A proposed strike by members of the pilots' union, BALPA, was averted when it agreed a deal with the Thomson Travel Group which owned Britannia Airways. BALPA wanted an agreement over pay and conditions, and had called for the employee share scheme to be more generous. The union was considering industrial action to put pressure on the company before its stock market flotation in May 1998. The action would have been taken to coincide with the peak summer season, when tour operators make most of their profits.

The 20 month dispute between Magnet and 300 plus employees sacked for taking strike action ended. The dispute began when 370 workers walked out of the factory in Darlington in protest against pay and conditions in the factory. Over the period of the dispute the business had brought in labour to fill the posts. The contracts given to the new workers were at reduced rates of pay, pensions and sick pay. The settlement was agreed by 47 to 34 votes. It would give £8,500 to those still on strike. £850,000 was to be divided amongst all workers originally involved based on how long they had been on strike.

Source: adapted from *The Guardian*, 4.9.1996, *Labour Research*, June, 1997, September 1997, June 1998; *The Times*, 29.4.1998, 28.5.1998.

(a) Identify the reasons for the actual or proposed action in each of the above cases.
(b) Examine the possible: (i) problems; and (ii) benefits; for the employers and employees in each case.

Key terms

Go slow - the reduction of output by workers whilst still carrying on tasks in their contract of employment.
Lock-out - action by employers which prevents employees entering the factory to work.

Sit-in/Work-in - the illegal occupation of premises by workers, which allows workers to gain control of the factory.
Work to rule - when employees do not carry out duties which are not in their employment contract.

Case study

Industrial unrest at British Airways

Cabin crew at BA had long argued for increases in basic pay. BA put forward a complex deal which gave some cabin crew up to a 24 per cent increase and agreed to make up the difference if anyone was made worse off as a result of the loss allowances. One union, Cabin Crew 89, accepted. The T&G affiliated union BASSA did not and called a strike ballot. BA refused to negotiate with T&G representatives (the T&G represents the majority of the workforce) on the cabin crew dispute and closed offices used by the union's cabin crew at Heathrow and Gatwick airports. It argued that negotiating with each section separately, changing work practices and a two year pay freeze would allow it to reduce costs and continue making expected profits.

Before the ballot on strike action by cabin crew, BA sent

out letters warning staff that they may be sued through the courts for loss of business. It also warned the staff that BA would be within its rights to sack staff or take away their promotion rights or chance of early retirement. In June 1997 T&G cabin crew voted 3:1 in favour of strike action and the union rejected the company's claims stating that: 'BA either does not understand the law or is trying to undermine people.' The industrial action was to take the form of a series of 72 hour stoppages. These stoppages would affect all inter-continental flights from Heathrow and Gatwick, but not internal flights.

In July the T&G authorised a three day strike after BA refused to reopen negotiations and refused to renegotiate pay and conditions. The TUC warned that it would call for a consumer boycott of BA if the strikes went ahead. The company responded that: 'Our managers are now working on the basis of running the airline without the help of the T&G.' It was suggested in the media that threatened strike action by pilots in 1996 cost the company £15 million in lost bookings as customers switched to other operators and that lost bookings were running at a similar level. Overall the costs of action to BA could amount to £100 million. Analysts criticised BA chief executive Bob Ayling's approach. They suggested previous executives were committed to cost cutting, but avoided confrontation.

After talks broke down on July 6 industrial action took place. 1,200 cabin crew reported sick in advance of the strike, causing the cancellation of 31 flights. The company said this proved workers did not want to strike. Unions argued much of the sickness was due to stress caused by management tactics. It was expected that action would cancel 146 of the 200 departures from Heathrow, the worst affected airport, on the first day of action. BA said that it aimed to keep as many flights as possible available using members of the Cabin Crew 89 union and cost-cutting labour. It also threatened to lock out employees who took action.

On 10 July BA claimed that the strike was unlawful due to a procedural flaw in the ballot. It threatened to sue the union for damages. On 11 July, after catering staff had rejected concessions on the selling of the meals service, BA offered to discuss renegotiating cabin crew pay and conditions with the T&G. But on 12 July the union said that BA had started 'suspending' cabin crew who had joined the strike. The company argued that it was not suspending staff, but that anyone who had taken part in the stoppage would have to give a commitment to work normally and then wait at home. Richard Branson was considering offering jobs at Virgin Airlines to any BA cabin crew sacked for striking. In August BA estimated the cost of the strike at £125 million. 1,000 domestic and European flights and 220 long haul flights had been cancelled. BA also suggested that over the three days of the strike only 275 cabin crew took action and that the rest were off sick. However, there were still many who went sick who had not returned to work.

In September, after extensive talks between unions and BA, the dispute was settled which saved the £42 million that BA wanted, but guaranteed the earnings of existing cabin staff. Sanctions, such as the removal of travel entitlements, were withdrawn. The union offices were also reopened. BA chief executive Bob Ayling said that the agreement signalled: 'a new beginning in the spirit of cooperation.' Bill Morris of the T&G pledged support for a 'constructive long term relationship in the spirit of partnership.'

The BA position

- Wanted to save £1 billion by 2000 so that the airline could cut prices and remain competitive.
- Cuts would allow £6 billion investment plan in new service, aircraft and staff training.
- Basic pay with incorporation of overtime and allowances into basic salaries would raise staff wages by 14-24 per cent.
- Basic pay of new recruits would drop, but would rise with incorporation of allowances.
- Cabin Crew 89 accepted the deal and deals have been struck with individuals. BA's world cargo staff had accepted a pay freeze, voluntary redundancy and redeployment.

The union position

- Accused BA of bullying tactics.
- Said new pay and conditions would lead to a 19 per cent cut in basic pay for recruits.
- Apparent rises for existing staff achieved by incorporating overtime and allowances into pay.
- Three year pledge not to cut wages amounted to a pay freeze. Pay guaranteed in the short term, but not the long term.
- Angry that the company still spent £60 million on new corporate image, despite pay restraint.
- The 3 day strike would cost BA £200 million with passengers switching, cancelled bookings and compensation for refunds. There would be a knock on effect on many other businesses, estimated at £31 million. For example, the business centre hosting meetings at Heathrow would lose 80 per cent of its trade.

Source: adapted from *Labour Research*, June, July, September, October 1997; *The Guardian*, various, June-August 1997, *The Times*, various, June-November 1997, 15.6.1998.

(a) Suggest possible reasons for industrial action.

(b) Explain the main forms of industrial action used by both employers and employees.

(c) Examine the factors that may have affected the relative strength of the two sides in the dispute.

(d) Analyse the possible problems and benefits of action from both sides.

(e) Evaluate whether either side achieved its objective by taking industrial action.

The importance of human resources

Unit 75 explained how the role of the personnel department was to plan HUMAN RESOURCES. Many business have shown a renewed interest in the management of human resources on recent years. They have come to realise the importance of employees and their knowledge and skills as a asset of the business. For example, in 1999 every one of Shell's 105,000 employees around the world were asked for their opinions, which were to be used as an 'agenda for change' in the company. Companies such as ICL have come to recognise the importance of retaining and using workers' knowledge. Siemens, the electronics company, has developed its pension department's team building skills in freezing Arctic Circle conditions. It has also used personality tests to evaluate staff. Companies such as Jaguar and Peugeot have made use of psychological testing of managers.

Businesses also seem to be placing greater emphasis on motivation, customer care and training. In the late 1990s BT's'... for a better life' programme encouraged staff to make their own decisions to benefit the customer. In 1998 Galliford, the construction business, received a National Training Award for training its workforce to run 'partnerships' with clients and suppliers to improve cooperation. After 1998 there were a growing number of employer and union partnerships and workers councils in business aimed at improving industrial relations (☞ unit 86). Many businesses were also moving towards a **flexible workforce**. This is discussed later in this unit.

Human resources management

One of the most important tasks that involves the personnel department in a business is HUMAN RESOURCES MANAGEMENT (HRM). A business is only likely to achieve its objectives if its employees are used effectively. Planning how best to use human resources will help a business to do this. Human resources management has **strategic** implications. It must be integrated into the strategic and corporate planning of the business (☞ units 15 and 16). It means constantly looking for better ways of using employees to benefit the organisation.

What is involved in the management of human resources? It is often said that it has a 'soft' side and a 'hard' side. This is shown in Figure 88.1.

The soft side of human resources management

This is mainly concerned with the way in which people are managed. It may include:

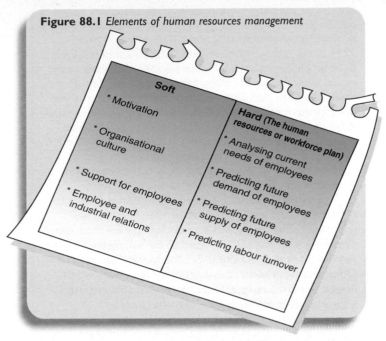

Figure 88.1 *Elements of human resources management*

Soft
* Motivation
* Organisational culture
* Support for employees
* Employee and industrial relations

Hard (The human resources or workforce plan)
* Analysing current needs of employees
* Predicting future demand of employees
* Predicting future supply of employees
* Predicting labour turnover

● how to motivate and satisfy workers;
● how to develop an organisational culture (☞ unit 14) or approach in employees, for example good relations with customers, flexibility, or quality at all stages of production (see TQM unit 95);
● how to support and develop employees, for example by training or by improving health and safety;
● the most suitable relationships between employer and the employees or their representatives;
● evaluating alternative policies and their likely costs.

There are various methods that a business could use when managing human resources. Take the example of a hotel with a variety of staff working in different jobs.

Changing business aims into employee goals The hotel may have decided that its main aim was to provide an excellent service to customers. To achieve this aim, goals would have to be set for the behaviour of employees of the hotel, such as always being polite to the customer. It is likely that staff training in customer care would be used to help employees.

Examining the environment There are factors 'outside' a business that could affect human resources management. The hotel would aim to gather as much information as possible to predict the effects of changes in these factors. For example, if health and safety regulations changed that affected the working of the kitchen, staff would need to be aware of these changes and may need training or support to carry them out. Information about external factors can be found from many sources, ranging from industrial journals to competitors' annual reports.

British Gas used to be responsible for the supply of gas to all households in Britain. After privatisation, companies would be allowed to compete to supply gas. Transco was formed in 1994 to take charge of more than 250,000 km of pipeline. It faced an enormous task. It had to organise the system that would allow dozens of companies to supply gas through the pipelines and to deal with their customers. Transco realised the important role the workforce had to play in this. It would affect all of its 17,000 workers. Procedures needed to be changed. A huge computer system was set up to deal with 4 million transactions. Common aims and objectives, collaboration, team work and personal commitment were all essential if the new system was to work.

The correct corporate culture was essential. People had to communicate with others, rather than having a 'silo' mentality, seeing themselves as working only for their own department. Employees also need to be empowered and to work in a blame-free culture. Feedback was also important. Opinion surveys generated suggestions from staff, which helped to introduce new ideas. More than 100 external support staff, consultants and contractors were commissioned to work alongside Transco staff to coach and support them. 600 agency staff, supervisors and team leaders were recruited on fixed term contracts at a dedicated centre in Stoke. A shortage of analysts and system developers was made up by recruiting 100 contractors from India.

Source: adapted from *People Management*, 12 .11.1998.

(a) Explain the different aspects of:
  (i) the soft side of human resources management;
  (ii) the hard side of human resources management at Transco.
(b) Examine reasons why human resources management was so important for Transco when setting up the new system.

Analysing the current situation It is important for the hotel to be aware of current staff needs. It could do this by using:
- questionnaires to staff and customers;
- interviews with staff;
- discussions with managers;
- performance data;
- recruitment or promotion information.

A questionnaire given to staff and customers at a hotel, for example, might find that customer service is not as good as it could be at the checkout desk because staff are too concerned about getting the paperwork right. A solution might be to simplify the checkout system or use extra staff at busy times. This would help to motivate employees and improve the chances of meeting the goal of improved customer service.

The hard side of human resource management

The hard side of human resource management is concerned

with quantifying the number and type of employees that a business will need, deciding whether they are available and planning how to get them. It is often known as the **human resources** or **workforce plan** (☞ unit 75). The human resources plan will:
- anticipate the likely future demand for workers;
- analyse current employees and their skills;
- anticipate future supply of workers from inside the business or outside. It will take into account factors such as promotion and labour turnover - the extent to which people leave the business;
- plan how to make up any shortfall of workers or reduce an excess of workers.

The quality of the human resources plan depends on the data on which it is based. A business must have accurate and relevant details for the human resources plan to be effective. For example, details about anticipated future business and the volume of production and sales may be needed. It will then be possible to predict the likely numbers and types of employees that are needed. The human resources plan must also make allowance for changes, such as improvements in technology or new products which might increase or reduce the number of employees needed. The information a business would require to develop an effective human resources plan might include:
- the implications for human resources of changes in corporate strategy, eg a possible reduction in the workforce as a result of removing layers of the organisation or deciding to concentrate on core activities of the business;
- the assumptions on which decisions about the workforce have been made, eg that there is likely to be growing competition in future;
- all other relevant data that may affect human resources plans, eg planned spending on new plant or machinery;
- the timing of changes, eg when new products might be introduced;
- anticipated issues in future, eg renegotiation of conditions at work;
- a detailed analysis of the current workforce.

Factors affecting human resources management

There are many factors that could affect the management of human resources in a business.

Changing goals of a business If a chemical company, for example, decided that the most effective way to increase profits or turnover was to become more **market orientated** (☞ unit 36), this is likely to change the personnel the business needs. There would be a need perhaps for employees with marketing research skills or training in how to promote products. The move in recent years by British Rail to close down unprofitable lines has meant fewer workers are required as a result. This is an example of how changing goals can affect the demand for labour.

Changes in the market Changes in purchasing patterns of consumers may mean that the demand for labour or labour skills have to change. One example might be redundancies in the coal industry as a result of demand for cheaper forms of power. Another might be the need to develop good customer relations in fast food retail outlets or financial services as competition has increased.

Changes in the economy can also affect human resource planning. In a recession, a business is likely to reduce its workforce as demand for its products falls.

Technology The introduction of new technology may lead to retraining or a need to recruit workers with specialist skills. For example, many former typists have become computer operators with the introduction of computer systems for storage, retrieval and presentation of information. The business may also have to consider the effect that new technology could have on the motivation of its employees and how to deal with this.

Competition Competition by other firms for workers may affect the supply of labour available to a business. If competitors offer high wages to workers with specialist skills then a business may have to raise its wage levels to recruit the staff it needs.

Competition for customers may also affect a human resource plan. Many firms are now aiming to meet the ISO 9000 quality standard, as customers refuse to use their services without this. An example might be in the electronics industry, where if one firm does not have approval it may lose business to another supplier. A business that obtains the quality standard must employ workers with specialist skills to check the standard is maintained. This can be costly for some small firms.

Population As well as the total population size, the distribution of population in a country can affect the supply of workers available. It is argued that Britain, after the year 2000, faces a number of changes in population distribution (☞ unit 20) that are likely to affect the management of human resource in many businesses.

● Activity rates. These are the percentage of any population in the labour force. There has been a growing number of women seeking employment in the 1990s. The activity rates of women of working age (16-59) is predicted to rise between 1997 and 2011 but for men over 25 it is predicted to fall slightly. A growing number of women seeking employment is likely to affect many aspects of human resources management, including how a business recruits workers, work conditions and employee relations.

● An ageing of the population. This means that older people are predicted to be a larger percentage of the population. There are also likely to be relatively fewer school leavers and

younger workers. A rise of 2.4 million people over the age of 35 in the labour force is predicted between 1997 and 2011, but a fall of 0.7 million people below the age of 35. A greater proportion of older workers means that more employees may be looking to retire. Older employees may also be less flexible than younger workers and motivated by factors other than money.

An older population may affect the demand for certain goods. Businesses might switch their products to appeal to a more mature consumer. Examples include the revival of 1960s and 1970s music on compact disc and the growth in residential care homes. Fewer school leavers mean that employers will have less choice of younger people. Businesses may have to set up apprenticeships to train school leavers (☞ unit 79) as they become relatively scarce. They may also look to fill jobs by recruiting from older workers that may not have previously been considered. The John Lewis Partnership and B&Q are examples of businesses that have had a policy of recruiting older workers.

Corporate culture and structure The corporate culture of the organisation (☞ unit 14) is likely to influence human resources management. If a business sees its employees as an asset that need to be trained, developed and motivated then it is likely to regard the management of human resources as important. It would be prepared to spend money and time on developing workers for the benefit of the business. Changes in the hierarchy of a business may affect human resources planning. A removal of a layer of management, may mean that fewer employees at this level are required.

Trade unions The relationship between a business and trade unions is likely to affect the management of human resources. In the 1980s and early 1990s unions were unlikely to have been involved greatly in planning. In some businesses unions were derecognised and businesses often negotiated with individuals on terms and conditions of work. The growth of business and union partnerships, union consultation and union recognition in the late 1990s is likely to result in greater flexibility in human resources management (☞ unit 85).

Government legislation Government legislation will affect human resources management. Changes in the late 1990s to the conditions of part time workers, the maximum number of hours that can be worked in a week and the minimum wage are all likely to influence the number and type of workers that businesses hire and the way in which labour is used. Government legislation on equal opportunities or a minimum wage has affected the wage costs of businesses and their recruitment and selection procedures. Businesses may also operate a policy where they guarantee disabled workers or ethnic minorities a proportion of jobs. This is dealt with in unit 80.

Finance The finance available to employ, reward or train workers will depend on many factors, such as the overall performance of the business, cash flow (☞ unit 59) and the liquidity of the company. A small business that is building a new factory is unlikely to have funds available to hire new employees, pay large bonuses or carry out extensive training.

The implications of a strategic approach to human resources management

Businesses are increasingly regarding their human resources as an important asset. Developing a human resources management policy is likely to have a number of effects on a business.

- A strategic approach is needed. This means that a business must integrate human resources considerations into its overall corporate planning and strategy (☞ unit 15 and 16). For example, a business that decides to merge with another company must take into account how the workforce needs to change, whether staff need training and assess how motivation may be affected. Alternatively, the hierarchy of the business could be redesigned to suit the needs of employees.
- The business must develop an organisational culture (☞ unit 14) that sees employees as an important part of the company. Managers who are unprepared to listen to employees' views on improvements will prevent the policy from working effectively.
- Motivation, training and support must be given to staff. Staff must be encouraged in the workplace. Businesses may make use of incentives such as bonuses or non-monetary benefits such as job redesign. Training and support must also be given. Marks and Spencer, for example, employs counsellors to give advice to single parents on coping with children and work.
- Group involvement and participation. Employees must be made to feel part of the business and be committed to its objectives. They must also be prepared to contribute to improvements in quality and productivity.
- Coordination with other functions. The management of human resources must be built into all parts of the business, including production, marketing and the finance department, and at all levels in the hierarchy.
- Flexible practices and thinking must be encouraged. Workers must be prepared to change jobs, accept new working methods and conditions. This is dealt with in the next section.
- Recruitment, redundancy and redeployment. Businesses must be able to reduce staff if necessary. Cuts in staff may be achieved in a number of ways. Staff may be allowed to leave without being replaced, known as **natural wastage**. A business may ask for **voluntary redundancies**, where workers agree to leave in return for redundancy payments (☞ unit 78). The company may also offer **early retirement**

to workers close to the compulsory retirement age (65 for men, 60 for women until after 2010). If there is no longer enough work, workers may be made redundant. It may also be possible to **redeploy** staff within a business. Training should help workers adapt to working in a different job in a business. Moving to another part of the country may be more difficult.

Advantages of human resources management

There are certain advantages to a business in taking a strategic approach to managing human resources.

- It may allow a business to gain a competitive advantage over rivals (☞ unit 16). A business which has a well trained, motivated and planned workforce and a human resources policy may be more efficient than competitors.
- It can solve human resources problems that occur in the business such as high rates of turnover and absenteeism.
- Effective human resources management will make the most efficient use of workers and reduce the potential costs of the business.
- A business will be able to anticipate changes to its workforce requirements and plan for these. It will also be able to manage change more effectively (☞ unit 89).
- Industrial relations problems may be prevented if employers and employees are working towards the same goals.
- Human resources management aims to provide long term benefits for the business. Employing part time workers in a crisis may solve a short term problem. But a planned, flexible workforce will give benefits to the business over a longer period.

The problems of human resources management

There is a number of problems a business will face when managing its employees.

- Problems with predicting the behaviour of people. A business may have filled a position, but after being appointed the individual may decide he does not want the job. This could mean another costly and time consuming series of interviews for the firm.
- Problems with predicting external events. Sometimes it is difficult to predict exactly how many employees are required. We have seen that many factors can affect human resource planning. For example, the opening up of former communist countries to trade from the West in the 1990s would have meant changing plans for businesses aiming to break into these markets. It is likely that employees with knowledge of the business and language of these countries would have been in demand.
- Planning has to be constantly monitored. It is unwise for a business to plan its human resource needs and not alter

Question 2

MD Foods is a Danish company set up in 1990 in the UK which produces milk and dairy products. Six months before it introduced a new product a pasteurised milk with a long shelf life, management and unions talked about how this would affect employees. In the past discussions at this stage would have been unthinkable. But it was part of changes in the corporate culture of the company designed to compete in a difficult market. The personnel department put forward a new 'greenfield' human resources policy. It was designed to ensure human resources management and trade union relationships were 'moved forward into a "single company", modern forward looking culture'.

Faced with stiff competition, many competitors had gone to the wall. Restructuring had taken place which involved the introduction of strategic units set up to deal with particular customers, such as Asda. £55 million was spent on new machinery. But a well motivated and skilled workforce were also needed. As a result, a new human resources strategy was introduced. One element involved staff being paid on annualised hours to increase flexibility. Previously if extra work was needed, expensive overtime payments were made to 'get things done'. Hours that were not worked were 'banked up' to be used if needed. The company said it might not use all the hours for work, but might call staff in for training.

At first employees and their unions were concerned that the annualised hours scheme was merely a method to cut costs. However, an agreement was reached which gave basic pay well above the minimum wage, job security and increased holidays. Initially there had been teething problems. Many concerned the interpretation of the annualised hours scheme, notably the idea of 'banking'. It was also difficult to say whether the benefits of the changes would last. Other companies had found that similar changes had not been so successful.

Source: adapted from *People Management*, 12.11.1998.

(a) Explain the likely implications on MD Foods of its human resources strategy.
(b) Examine the possible problems that the business may have faced as a result of its human resources strategy.

them in the light of changing events. Planning has to be checked, revised and updated as other factors change.

● Human resources management must be well thought out or it is likely to lead to industrial relations problems. Cuts in the workforce or wage reductions that are not negotiated could affect workers' motivation and may even lead to industrial action (☞ unit 87).

Evaluating human resources management

A business might evaluate the effectiveness of human resource management by considering some of the following. Similar methods can be used to evaluate the management of

change (☞ unit 89) .

Labour turnover One of the most important tasks in the management of employees is to make sure that labour turnover is minimised and that all vacancies that exist are filled. Labour turnover is a measure of the number of people that **leave** a business in a given period of time as a percentage of the average number of people employed during that period (☞ unit 75). If labour turnover is high, how will this affect a business? There are likely to be costs as a result. These include:
● the cost of advertising, interviewing and training a new employee;
● a loss of production while the place is filled;
● low morale amongst other employees;
● reorganisation before the place is filled and perhaps after a new worker is hired.

The business will need to identify groups that are likely to leave and be ready to fill any vacancies that occur. Employees may leave because they are ill, retiring or having children. In some cases, they may be dismissed.

These are all unavoidable. However, some workers leave voluntarily because they are not satisfied with the job. It is these workers that a business should be most concerned about. Evidence suggests that those workers who leave voluntarily tend to be younger employees, who are often new recruits. They may be looking for promotion and better pay. To prevent dissatisfaction, a firm may:
● set up an internal promotion system;
● develop a staff training programme;
● make sure there is good communication between management and workers to avoid grievances and ensure that employees' views are taken into account;
● increase levels of pay.

Absenteeism High levels of staff absence may lead to a number of problems for a business. The output and productivity of the business may fall. The business will still have the costs of paying workers who are absent even though they are not working. Constant staff absence may also affect the motivation of other workers in the business. The reputation of the business may suffer if staff absence leads to unfulfilled orders or late deliveries.

A reduction in the number of days that employees are absent may be an indication that human resource management is effective. The motivation of staff may be better. Improved work conditions may have reduced stress and other factors which may lead to absence. Staff may feel more committed to the organisation and more likely to work, when they may have taken time off.

Labour productivity and turnover per employee The management of human resources may improve **labour productivity** (☞ unit 96). Labour productivity is a measure of the output per employee over a period of time. For example, if 20 workers in an engineering company produce 1,000 components in a period of time, their productivity is 50 components (1,000 ÷ 20). If work schedules were changed to create more flexibility and motivation improved so that output increased to 1,200, labour productivity would rise to 60 components (1,200 ÷ 20).

If a large multinational company employs 26,000 staff and has a turnover of £2,000 million a year, the **turnover per head** is nearly £77,000 (£2,000 million ÷ 26,000). However, if changes to the workforce meant that the company had the same turnover next year with only 22,000 workers, turnover per head would be nearly £91,000 (£2,000 million ÷ 22,000).

Industrial relations The management of human resources may also improve industrial relations (☞ unit 87). A business may consider that a reduction in the number of:
● industrial disputes;
● days lost through industrial action;
● grievances against the business by employees;
might indicate effective management. Improvements in staff motivation indicated in appraisal questionnaires, attitude surveys or in meetings may also be an indication of the success of the business's policy.

Relations with stakeholders Stakeholders are all the people with an interest in the business (☞ unit 3). They include employees of the business, such as workers and managers, shareholders who may or may not work for the business. They also include people who are affected by the activities of the business, such as clients, customers, suppliers and the general public. An indication of the success of HRM might be found in improved relations with suppliers. It may also be indicated in the views of customers about how the workforce is treated.

Profitability The main aim of most private sector businesses is to make profit. Modern approaches to HRM suggest that the management of human resources should be geared towards improving productivity of workers, reducing costs, raising revenue and increasing profit. It is a vital part of the overall strategy of the company rather than a series of processes, such as recruitment, selection and training. Increasing profit may be a result of improvements in HRM.

One model that has been suggested to evaluate the human resources management is the '4Cs model' of the Harvard Business School. This suggests that HRM should be evaluated under four headings as shown in Table 88.1.

The flexible workforce

Employers have always wanted workers to be as flexible as possible. In the past this has meant paying overtime for extra hours worked, or higher rates for 'shift' work. Faced with competition, businesses attempted to use their existing

---

Question 3

DuPont (UK) designed a plant to manufacture polyester film packaging called Line 53 in Dumfries. The whole operation was staffed by six shifts, each with seven people. It was designed to be ultra-efficient, but a new breed of employee was needed and a different culture of work and training. The company wanted people who were analytical and could bring ideas to manufacturing.

DuPont was committed to training. Each member of the seven person team was trained in an operational skill and also in how to train others. They then taught the operational skill to all other team members. Eventually each member was multi-skilled. This allowed jobs to be rotated. DuPont estimated it had saved £200,000 through this type of training. It was important to make staff as flexible as possible. The company had a low labour turnover. If employees were going to be with the business for the next 10 years, they needed to be able to adapt to changing conditions.

Having completed the training and other areas of development, such as team building, management and budgeting, the teams needed no supervision. DuPont estimated this had saved another £300,000. Many of the training modules for staff have been written by team members themselves. People volunteered for extra training in areas such as IT. But the business said that IT training could only be given to all team members if they could find a cheaper supplier that would provide the service within the existing budget. They succeeded.

The teams also wrote their own guidelines on behaviour, responsibilities and objectives. Members gave and received written feedback on their own performance by other team members. They even amended decisions made by managers for the benefit of the business. For example, they suggested a change from an 8 hour to a 12 hour shift would be more suitable.

Source: adapted from *People Management*, 28.1.1999.

(a) Evaluate the management of human resources at Line 53 DuPont using the 4Cs model.

Table 88.1 *Evaluation of human resources management*

● Commitment - employees' loyalty and motivation, assessed by surveys, labour turnover and absenteeism.
● Competence - employees' skills and training - assessed through appraisal systems and skills inventories.
● Congruence - employees and managers sharing the same values, assessed by absence of grievances and conflict.
● Cost effectiveness - employees' efficiency, assessed by cost, output and profit figures.

---

employees more effectively. Sometimes this could benefit the employee. A single woman with a child may be able to work between the hours of 9am to 3pm each day while her child is at school. Working flexible hours could mean an employee may take time off for personal reasons and still work their required number of hours a week.

Training was also be given to workers so they become **multi-skilled** - able to switch from one job to another if needed. This example of job rotation may perhaps lead to the employee being more motivated. From a firm's point of view, an employee that can change jobs may prevent the need to have temporary workers to cover for illness etc. and so reduce labour costs. An example of this is the 'workstyle' initiative at Birds Eye/Walls, where team working has been introduced so that workers can change from one process to another and do the work of others in the team if necessary.

In 1985 John Atkinson and The Institute of Manpower Studies developed the idea of the **flexible firm**. They suggested that businesses have a 'core' and a 'periphery', as in Figure 88.2. As a result of increasing competition, firms have attempted to make the workforce as flexible as possible, to increase productivity, reduce costs and react more quickly to change. The business would try to motivate core workers, giving them job security, and employ periphery workers only when needed.

Increasingly employers looked to make plans that allow a business to respond to changes. For example, if a large unexpected order arrives, a business will need workers that can 'get it out on time'. Using a FLEXIBLE WORKFORCE enables a business to react effectively to changes that take place outside the business. Examples of workers that are used by a business include:

● part time employees, such as cleaners, who only work a few hours a day;
● temporary employees to deal with increases in demand, such as agricultural workers;
● workers on **zero hours contracts** who are employed by the business but only work and are paid when both the business and the employee agree;
● workers who work to annualised hours contracts, where they work a certain number of hours over a year rather than in a week (☞ unit 72);
● workers who 'bank time', by not working when demand is

slack but being asked to work that time at a later date;
● office temporary workers to cover for illness or sickness;
● self-employed workers, such as management consultants, for specialist tasks;
● job sharing, where two workers are employed to do a full time job that may in the past have been carried out by one person (☞ unit 78).

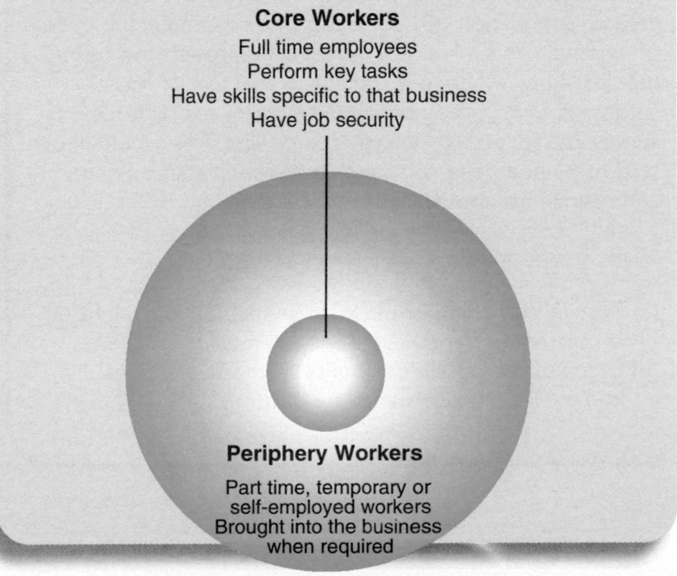

Question 4

In December 1998 Rover struck a deal which at the time kept the plant at Longbridge from closing. The number of hours worked each week would be geared to production. They would be allowed to vary to meet peaks and troughs in demand. A 35 hour week would be worked, but employees could be asked to bank up to 200 hours, either in credit or debit. Employees may be asked to flex their lunch breaks. Instead of everyone taking lunch at the same time, individuals would be relieved by others. This would add five extra working hours per week. Employees may also be asked to start half an hour earlier.

In 1997 Peugeot workers have been contracted to work 1,755 hours a year. They can work up to 200 hours a year more or less than this without it affecting their pay. Extra hours when required are worked on Fridays.

Eli-Lilley, the pharmaceuticals firm, has a family friendly culture. They encourage term time working, reduced hours and career breaks. This was particularly helpful to single parents. However, certain departments operated the policies differently. It was suggested by Randall Tobias, the chief executive, that: 'This is a matter of changing the culture, not only the policy. There are still barriers for women trying to convince management of their commitment and career goals.'

The North East Wales Institute of Higher Education (Newi) employed a pool of workers on zero hours contracts to combat problems of a lack of commitment amongst agency temps. Workers were not guaranteed work, but they have to be available at times that suit the business and the individual. Workers had a right to refuse work and look for another job. Newi argued that this approach was important as it expected poll members to be flexible, so it was only fair that it was also flexible.

Source: adapted from *People Management* 14.5.1998 and 24.12.1998, *Labour Research*, February 1999.

(a) Comment on the extent to which the practices of the businesses in the cases have: (i) increased flexibility; and (ii) benefited the businesses.

Figure 88.2 *Organisation of a flexible workforce*

Core Workers
Full time employees
Perform key tasks
Have skills specific to that business
Have job security

Periphery Workers
Part time, temporary or
self-employed workers
Brought into the business
when required

It has been argued that there are both benefits and disadvantages for these types of employee. On the one hand, a single parent may be able to find work at a convenient time, and job sharing could mean employment for two people, instead of unemployment for one of them. However, the position of flexible staff has often been a source of industrial relations problems for businesses and has led to conflict with trade unions.

In the 1990s individual bargaining increasingly took place. Conditions were negotiated without union involvement and based on the contract of employment. Union recognition and union partnerships with business after the year 2000 are likely to change industrial relations, although some argue that flexibility will still be encouraged by both sides.

There has been a number of criticisms of both Atkinson's model and the approach used by business towards human resources in the 1990s. Pollert (1991) argued that part time workers, contract work and the self employed can not be placed into a single category called ' peripheral work'. Part time workers, for example, may have secure contracts of employment and could be part of the 'core'. It has also been suggested that growth of a flexible workforce has been exaggerated and much has been due to the expansion of the service sector where such employment is common. It has also been suggested that most of the benefits are in favour of the business at the expense of employees. Employees see it as a means of getting them to work harder for less. Although workers have more involvement, management makes all the important decisions. Workers as individuals are ignored as a corporate culture develops and employees feel that they are being manipulated. It is also argued that human resources management takes a lower priority when a business is in difficulty.

Knowledge management

Many businesses today see knowledge management (☞ unit 89) as important to their operation. It involves:
- identifying the knowledge of a business, such as the knowledge of employees;
- assessing how the knowledge can be used and planning how to use it effectively;
- ensuring that knowledge is shared by all people in the organisation.

The management of knowledge can have a number of benefits for a business. The speed at which a business gains knowledge and puts it to good use is one way in which it can gain an advantage over its rivals. For example, Sky was the first company to launch digital television in the UK. It could be argued that this will give it an advantage in future as many customers will have 'signed up' and be unwilling to change to another supplier.

It may also prevent a duplication of services. For example,

ICL found that several of its businesses were bidding for the same project at the same time without each knowing about the others' activities. It also found 23 different uncoordinated information services for employees, often providing the same information. Knowledge management could have prevented this waste of resources.

Sometimes people leave a business and take years of knowledge and experience with them. It often exists 'in the head' of the employee, who has found the best way to carry out a task or the most suitable skills to use. Making sure that this knowledge is collected and passed on may prevent problems for new employees to the job. It will also reduce time and costs for the business.

Unit 89 examines how knowledge management is important in the management of change.

Key terms

Flexible workforce - a workforce that can respond (in quantity and type) to changes in demand a business may face.

Human resources - the employees or personnel in a business that help it to achieve its goals.

Human resources management - an integrated approach which ensures the efficient management of human resources. It is part of the overall business plan.

Question 5

Bristol & West is typical of many businesses in the highly competitive market for financial services. It cannot afford to miss anything that might give it a competitive edge over its rivals. The bank employs 2,800 people.

Up until 1999, access to information stored on its personnel system had been largely restricted to the human resources department. But with new computer software, managers will soon be able to get information themselves. This will free time for the personnel department to concentrate on strategic issues. It will also allow the greater correlation of information. For example, the effect of expenditure on training on revenue growth can be monitored to evaluate if training is effective. It was also suggested that in the near future employees' attitude survey results would be included on line. This would allow staff to pinpoint the relationship between staff turnover and morale on absence levels, for example.

Source: adapted from *People Management*, 28.1.1999.

(a) Explain why changes made at Bristol & West might be an example of knowledge management.
(b) Examine the possible benefits to the business of knowledge management.

Summary

1. Explain the difference between the soft and hard side of human resources management.
2. Briefly describe 5 factors that might affect the managing of human resources by a business.
3. 'A business that does not manage its human resources effectively may face industrial relations problems.' Explain this statement.
4. State:
   (a) 5 implications of taking a strategic approach to HRM;
   (b) 4 advantages of human resource management;
   (c) 4 problems of human resource management;
      for a business.
5. Briefly explain how a business may evaluate its management of human resources.
6. Suggest 3 ways in which a business might reduce labour turnover.
7. State 3 examples of;
   (a) flexible work practices;
   (b) flexible workers.
8. Suggest 3 advantages of:
   (a) a flexible workforce;
   (b) knowledge management.

Case study

Flexible working

The increasing emphasis on part time and temporary work has changed the job market beyond recognition. But while this trend has improved the productivity and flexibility of many businesses, it has raised difficult issues for managers. How do companies find high calibre staff prepared to work unconventional hours, often for relatively low pay? And how do they combat the widespread perception that these workers, who often have an important role in dealing with customers, are poorly trained and undervalued?

Recent research by the Roffey Park Management Institute in Sussex concluded that businesses that are successful at managing part time and temporary employees have put more effort into meeting their needs. Burton Group, which replaced 1,000 full time staff with 3,000 part time jobs in 1993, has responded to recruitment problems by allowing store managers to write contracts to suit individual employees. At one Topshop outlet a job is shared by a student who works in the vacation and a woman who works during the school term. Asda, the retail group where 80 per cent of the workforce work part time, has also felt the need to be more flexible towards part time workers.

Consultations showed that one reason for staff turnover reaching 30 per cent a year was that many wanted a longer working week. 'Employees who work very short hours, below the National Insurance threshold, are very cheap employees,' says David Smith, employee relations manager of Asda. 'But we found people were leaving. So we are going against the trend and offering longer hours.' With the help of longer contracts and other measures, such as improved maternity leave, career breaks and the ability to swap shifts, staff turnover fell by 2 percentage points.

The issues concerning flexible workers are nothing new for Oxfordshire County Council, where more than two-thirds of the 16,000 strong workforce work part time. That partly reflects the need to cover round-the-clock services, such as in residential homes and fire fighting, but offering flexible working is also a way to attract professional employees, such as legal staff, who might be paid more in the private sector. Valued staff may want time off for childcare, further education and other part time jobs or may want to continue part time after taking early retirement. But much of the debate about flexible working concerns the other end of the spectrum, the poorly paid and lowly valued employees who do not qualify for National Insurance, for employment protection or for statutory benefits. Attention has particularly focused on zero-hour contracts, introduced by companies such as Burger King, in which individuals are only paid when dealing with customers. More than half the part timers interviewed in a 1995 TUC study said employers regarded them as 'second class staff'.

The tendency to treat flexible workers as poor relations is creating a dilemma for employers, according to Christina Evans, a research associate at Roffey Park Management Institute. 'In many organisations, it is those who work "flexibly" who have the most responsibility for customer service, at peak trading periods. In other words it is the 'flexible' employees who are the ones who have the most impact on sales,' she says. She says better use of flexible workforces would bring benefits including 'better customer service, lower staff turnover and a more motivated workforce'. Her research uncovered many positive aspects of flexible working. Companies often commented that part time workers were more disciplined in their time management and so more productive.

Nonetheless, the research highlighted a number of barriers to making the best use of flexible employees. Managers are often unenthusiastic about supervising them since it complicates scheduling and rota arrangements. The assumption that part time employees are less career-minded can be self-fulfilling.

Unless companies examine their promotion policies, there may be unintended barriers to the promotion of part-time workers. For example, at First Direct, the telephone banking service, the Roffey Park study noted an assumption that an employee could not be rated 'very good' unless they worked a full shift and were exposed to all the trading activities. Training is a particularly vexed issue for flexible workers. Most companies would agree that part time staff need at least as much training as full time staff, yet few provide that. The training of 80 per cent of those in full time employment is funded by their employer, compared with 36 per cent of those working part time, according to the *Labour Market Quarterly Report*.

The widespread practice of offering flexible workers worse pay, training and conditions than the full time workforce could backfire, says the Institute of Management. It warns that the current attitude towards flexible workers could 'lead to the development of two-tier workforces - with all of the difficulties inherent in managing them.' More effort is needed to integrate flexible employees with the company's core workforce. 'What is needed is a new approach to managing flexible workers, which acknowledges the needs of

this group of employees to be valued, included and invested in,' Christina Evans says. It is the 'flexible' employees who are the ones who have the most impact on sales.

Source: adapted from the *Financial Times*, 29.1.1997.

(a) Identify the:
   (i) hard human resource planning issues;
   (ii) soft human resource planning issues;
       highlighted in the article.
(b) Examine the factors that may have affected the choice of businesses in the article to use flexible staff?
(c) Explain the possible: (i) advantages; and
   (ii) disadvantages; of using flexible staff.
(d) (i) Explain the ways in which the businesses in the article may have dealt with high labour turnover.
   (ii) Examine the possible problems of each method.
(e) Explore the implications for:
   (i) full time;
   (ii) part time staff of the business they work for attempting to make its staff more flexible.
(f) Using evidence from the article, evaluate the management of flexible workforces.

What causes change in business?

Businesses today have to operate in rapidly changing markets and conditions. They can no longer rely on a constant stream of customers, the same production process or the same product over a long period of time. They must constantly be aware of, and be prepared to respond to, changes in a number of areas.

Developments in technology Unit 98 shows that the introduction of new technology can affect a business in many ways. There have, for example, been rapid changes in communications technology, production techniques and electronic components in recent years.

Market changes Businesses must respond to changes in the markets in which they sell. There may be competition from new businesses. This has been the case in the energy supply market. Former public sector owned gas and electricity suppliers were privatised and markets opened up to competition. New markets may open up, such as the mobile phone market for companies such as BT. Competition may also come from new businesses entering a market, such as the offering of financial services by supermarkets. Other factors such as the Single European Market, the globalisation of

markets and the use of the Euro (☞ units 30 and 32) are all likely to change how businesses operate.

Consumer tastes Businesses must also be prepared for changes in the tastes of consumers. Examples might be the purchase of environmentally friendly products, the desire for greater knowledge about products or the need for more efficient methods of shopping, such as purchasing by means of interactive digital television.

Legislation Government legislation can force changes in business activity. Taxation of pollution (☞ unit 35) would affect the production methods of many firms. Safety standards, such as EU regulations for VDU users, are also likely to affect how employees operate. Government aid or subsidies may affect the possible location of a business (☞ unit 100). Legislation on the number of hours employees can work may change work practices.

Changes in the workforce Population changes will affect the age and make-up of the workforce. The 'demographic timebomb' (☞ unit 41) in the UK in the 1990s and the early part of the twenty first century is likely to result in changing recruitment policies for businesses. A falling population is also likely to change how a business plans its human resources.

Question 1

In the mid-1990s 'the big five' record companies dismissed the idea of large sales of music via the internet as sensationalism. By 1998 they were taking part in trials to find pirate-proof ways of selling music on the internet. Music can be sold in two ways. CDs can be advertised on the internet and then ordered via e-mail or telephone, just like mail order. Alternatively, music can be bought and downloaded straight to computers. The growth in internet sales is likely to see greater competition for record stores from online companies such as Amazon. Large record companies can use the internet as another distribution method. Independent stores can broaden their customer bases. Lower costs of selling via the internet may reduce the price of music. The growth of direct sales by downloading may affect manufacturers of CDs. But will the big five dominate the internet market as they now dominate CD sales? There are fewer barriers to entry and greater ease of promotion for the independent company, with even the sole trader selling his or her own music via the internet. Some superstars are negotiating to handle their own long term distribution via the internet rather than renewing record deals. The big five have tried to prevent this by building internet rights into new contracts.

Source: adapted from the *Financial Times*, 13.1.1999.

(a) Outline the changes which are forecast to take place in the sales of music in future.
(b) Examine the possible effects of these changes on all the different businesses involved in the music industry.

Figure 89.1 US music sales, $m and percentages

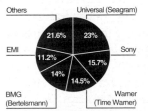

Others 21.6%
Universal (Seagram) 23%
EMI 11.2%
Sony 15.7%
BMG (Bertelsmann) 14%
Warner (Time Warner) 14.5%

	1998	99*	2000*	01*	02*	07*
Traditional sales	12,366	12,622	12,927	13,041	12,805	12,051
Internet mail order	117	445	731	1,155	1,654	3,239
Digital delivery revenues	0	13	41	165	588	3,717
Total industry revenues	12,483	13,080	13,705	14,361	15,047	19,007

* Forecast

Source: adapted from IFPI, NMPA, RIAA, IUMA.

The effects of rapid change

The rapid changes illustrated in the last section can have a number of effects on business.

● Product life cycles (☞ unit 41) could become shorter. This means that businesses must constantly be looking to develop new and profitable products or services.

● The role of marketing research is likely to increase. A business must not be 'surprised' by sudden changes in the market. Research and forecasting techniques should help a firm to predict more accurately the situation in future.

● Research and development (☞ unit 99) will be essential in industries where rapid change is taking place. As well as anticipating market changes, a business must be prepared to respond to the needs of the market with new products, which can compete with those of competitors.

● Retraining of managers and 'shop floor' workers might be necessary. This may be to learn skills associated with new technology or to develop skills to meet changing consumer tastes. Examples may be the education of office staff in communications technology, such as e-mail or videoconferencing (☞ unit 82) or the learning of foreign languages by UK business people wishing to enter foreign markets.

● Businesses must take account of changes in their human resource planning (☞ units 75 and 88). This could mean employing a more flexible workforce that could be changed quickly to meet the needs of the business, for example part time workers or the use of job sharing.

● A business must develop a culture and organisation which is prepared to respond to change (☞ unit 14).

● Businesses must be aware of competitors' actions and be prepared to react to them. Businesses now benchmark (☞ unit 95) their activities against those of rivals or other companies.

● Quality is likely to become more important as consumer awareness develops and competition increases. Firms must consider the quality of their products and also their after sales service and customer relations. An example in the 1990s was the drive by many businesses to achieve the international IS0 9000 quality standard.

● Changes in equipment. Rapid change often makes equipment redundant. Businesses may find problems from the inability to read computer disks because software has been updated to the need for new systems to cope with just in time requests. These changes could involve a large amount of spending if businesses do not wish to become outdated. One problem facing all businesses at the turn of the century is the so-called '**millennium bug**'. This is the inability of some computer software to cope with the date 2000, because certain software operated only on two digits. 1998 was displayed as 98, but the year 2000 would be displayed as 00, which would not be recognised by the computer.

Question 2

Many office environments are changing to meet the demands of the creative age rather than the industrial age. Staff at St Luke's advertising agency have no desks of their own. They hot desk, finding a place to work at any one of a number of shared computer stations. Telephones are mobile and radio based, small enough to fit into a pocket. There's a chill out room for staff to relax between meetings. Pearl Assurance, a former traditional office organisation, has redesigned its workplace. It has themed meeting rooms, including the living room and the garden room. Workers 'romp' from one workspace to another.

Some see this as simply a means of cutting costs. But more sophisticated companies see it as a way of changing the organisation's operations and culture. They recognise employee's needs to meet informally. They see it as a way of offering employees chances to be creative and to work in a non-linear way. But there is a downside. Managers find it difficult to adjust. They miss chatting to subordinates. They find it difficult to 'pick up vibes' from e-mail. Controlling employees can also be a problem. According to Pearl Assurance's MD Richard Surface, faced with change there are three types of people - high flyers, anxious people and cynics. One way of helping to introduce the changes is to make sure the company is serious about change and to ensure employees are rewarded for the new behaviours.

Source: adapted from *The Times*, 20.7.1998.

(a) What advantages of change are suggested in the article?
(b) Why might: (i) employees; and (ii) managers; be resistant to the changes taking place?
(c) An insurance company is considering introducing hot desking into its head office. Discuss how the change might be introduced to avoid resistance from office staff.

Why manage change?

The management of change in business has grown in importance in recent years. Under pressure from competitors, higher costs and economic conditions, many firms in the UK developed company-wide change programmes. Companies such as BT, British Airways and ICI have 'turned around' their organisations through managed change.

There are some examples of firms that have made only minor changes to their business operations and remained successful. The Morgan Car Company still retains many of the original production methods and design features that have been part of its operation since the 1930s. It argues that it is exactly these 'original' features that attract consumers. However, many firms have refused to change or did not respond and went out of business, such as the British motorcycle industry and certain holiday firms. In the face of rapid change and competition, it is likely that firms must respond or go out of business.

Criticisms of management

Some (eg T. Nichols, 1986) have argued that, historically, the problems of British business in managing change and increasing productivity have resulted from the ineffectiveness of management. It has been suggested that British managers in the past have not:

● scored highly in their ability to plan and organise production compared to management in Germany and Japan;
● been as market orientated as those in America and Japan, often producing goods which were uncompetitive;
● been as highly qualified as managers in other countries;
● invested in skilled workers;
● been concerned with long term growth generated by major investment, but only in short term profits.

Today it could be argued that British management are far more aware of what is required for businesses to achieve success in markets. The ways in which they manage change are dealt with in the sections that follow.

The role of the personnel department

Unit 75 explained the role of the personnel department. Traditionally, personnel managers enforced rules and procedures, and were less concerned with change. It has been suggested that if they became human resources managers, and more concerned with the following, then change would take place more effectively in business.

● A move away from job evaluation and fixed grades towards appraisal and performance related pay.
● Pay and conditions negotiated with individuals rather than collectively.
● An emphasis on team work rather than individual job design.
● A flexible workforce trained in a variety of skills.
● Encouraging employees that are **empowered** (☞ unit 73) and self-motivating rather than needing to be 'controlled'.

Resistance to change

Businesses are likely to face some resistance to change from parts of the workforce. Workers and certain levels of management sometimes fear the unknown. They feel safe with work practices, conditions and relationships that they have been used to for a period of time. Employees and managers may fear that they will be unable to carry out new tasks, may become unemployed or many face a fall in earnings. Individual workers might be concerned that they will no longer work with 'friends', or may be moved to a job which they dislike. If change is to be carried out effectively, the business must make certain that these fears are taken into account. Only if employees feel that they can cope with change, will the business be operating to its potential.

Resistance may also be found in the **culture** of the organisation (see next section). Custom and practice are embedded in systems which reflect the norms, values and beliefs of the organisation. While this may give stability, it presents problems of rigidity when a business needs to change. In order to deal with resistance to change there are many theorists who suggest the need for a multi-step approach. Psychologist Kurt Lewin emphasised a three step process.

● Introducing an innovation with information aimed to satisfy a need.
● Overcoming resistance by group discussion and decision-making.
● Establishing a new practice.

It is also argued that those likely to be affected by change should be informed and have a stake in the process of shaping change.

Developing an organisational culture for change

An **organisational culture** (☞ unit 14) includes the beliefs, norms and values of a business. It is a generally held view about how people should behave, the nature of working relationships and attitudes. Many companies, especially Japanese firms such as Honda, Toyota and Sony, place great emphasis on all employees understanding the company's 'culture'.

It has been suggested that a business which creates a culture of change is likely to manage it far more effectively. Management at the top must have a clear idea of how they expect the business to change. Structures, methods of training, management styles etc. must then alter to reflect this. Finally a culture must be established where all employed are aware of the new relationship and methods of working.

One model that has been used to implement change is total quality management (TQM) (☞ unit 95). A feature of TQM is that everyone in the business is responsible for maintaining and improving quality, including the quality of the product, production methods and the supply to the customer. TQM's motto is 'getting it right the first time' and this is applied to external customers and what are known as 'internal customers' - the people employees work with. This approach helps develop a culture where all employees, managers etc. are trying to achieve the same goal, which should motivate, develop teamwork and improve communication, accountability and rewards.

There are those, however, who suggest that organisational culture is not something that can be easily manipulated. They argue that culture depends on human interaction and is continuously being recreated. Hence, to believe that a senior management team can unilaterally change an existing culture according to some blueprint is mistaken. Organisational culture, according to this view, does change, but often slowly and in unpredictable ways. There is also a danger of thinking of organisational culture as a single over-arching idea to which all members of the business subscribe. Organisations, however, may have sub-cultures linked to particular groups. There may be conflict between these subcultures. In addition, even if new culture is established, there is no evidence that simply having a new culture improves performance.

Different approaches to managing change

Research by John Storey has suggested that the way businesses manage change can be classified into four different approaches.

A total imposed package One approach to managing change is for people at the 'top' of the business to plan out major restructuring programmes without consultation with workers or worker representatives. The main advantage of this method is that a company can have a 'vision' of where it is going. It can compare where it is 'now' with where it was 'then'. It is possible, using this approach, to prepare departmental action plans, set timetables and measure how far change has been achieved. The business can also make changes without having to take into account the wishes of other groups. The disadvantage of planning change from the top is that middle managers, supervisors and employees may not feel involved.

Imposed piecemeal initiatives A different approach is to have unplanned or piecemeal initiatives designed to bring about change. Initiatives might be introduced by employers to solve particular problems or only at times when they are needed in the business. Examples of initiatives that might take place are:

- the introduction of team meetings or quality circles (☞ unit 73);
- improvements in technology or channels of communication;
- improvements in incentive payments or rewards;
- improvements in the flexibility of work practices;
- changes in the workforce, such as teleworkers or subcontracting;
- the introduction of performance appraisal (see unit 00).

A problem with piecemeal initiatives is that they sometimes have different objectives. One might be trying to improve management leadership. The other might to trying to encourage greater participation. Another difficulty is that piecemeal initiatives tend to be short lived. In difficult times businesses may decide to drop costly changes.

Negotiated piecemeal initiatives Productivity agreements (☞ unit 72) are often used to help change take place. Unions agree to changes in work practices, usually in exchange for extra payments or improved conditions for workers. These negotiated changes tend to be ad-hoc, without any coordinated policy by the business.

Negotiated total packages This is where a 'total package' for change is put together. It is negotiated by employers and union representatives. It may be in the form of a 'national deal', which involves changes in work practices for all employees in every plant or office in exchange for increased rewards or improved conditions. In practice this method of managing change was rarely used in Britain before the 1990s. However, the changing roles of trade unions and the likelihood of partnerships between business and unions after 1998 may see this type of negotiation taking place ore often.

Evaluating the management of change

Managers will have a clear idea of the improvements to performance that they want from change in business. They may want productivity gains as a result of the use of multi-skilled teams or improved response times to customer demands due to new communication technologies. These are sometimes referred to as **performance indicators**. Performance indicators can be used to evaluate the management of change. Any evaluation strategy will have quantitative and qualitative methods of analysing changes in working practices.

Question 3

Flexible hour deals are the 'inevitable future' according to Rover's personnel director David Bowyer. In December 1998 workers voted by 18,000 to 7,000 to accept a deal hammered out by unions and management. The deal included a phased reduction in the working week to 35 hours based on four shifts. Overtime, attendance allowances and other bonuses were to be abolished and the number of hours worked each week geared to the demands of the production line. Pay rises over the following two years were also set and there would be no shutdowns of the factory, so workers' holidays would be spread over the year. In exchange there would be no redundancies and BMW, Rover's parent company, would invest £2 billion in new plant and equipment. The joint management and union campaign to sell the deal included Rover hiring the NEC in Birmingham to stage presentations outlining the changes to the staff. It was argued that the new deal would save workers' jobs and the whole future of Rover. Tony Woodley, chief T&GWU negotiator, said he had spent days and nights thrashing out the deal.

Source: adapted from *The Observer*, 6.12.1998 and *People Management*, 24.12.1998.

(a) Identify and explain the approach to managing change at Rover in 1998.
(b) Explain the possible benefits for: (i) the business; and (ii) employees; of this method of managing change.

● A rise in output from 10,000 to 15,000 as a result of change or an improvement in average delivery time from two days to 24 hours would be measurable, quantitative improvements.
● Employees' responses to a questionnaire, stating that change had improved their motivation, could be a qualitative method of evaluating the management of change.

Learning organisations and change

In recent years there has been a growing interest in learning organisations. A LEARNING ORGANISATION (☞ unit 102) is a business which absorbs knowledge, acquires skills and changes its attitudes. Solutions that are found to problems become the 'knowledge' of the business. They then become part of the firm's 'memory' and are used when reacting to future events. For example, a business may find that setting up a graduate training programme is more effective than trying to headhunt managers from other organisations. It may use this approach when setting up a branch of the business overseas.

There is a number of implications for a business that wants to be a learning organisation.
● Human resource development strategy must be central to business policy.
● A business must constantly change its decision making in the light of new events.

● Employees must be regularly retrained in new working methods. Managers must develop coaching skills.
● Current practices must be questioned and workers must experiment with new solutions.
● Rewards must be geared to finding new solutions and workers must be allowed to manage themselves in work groups.
● There must be communication between all areas of the business.

There are certain advantages of this approach. Such businesses are more likely to grow and develop naturally to meet new demands because learning is integral to the way they operate. The business will not be using outdated plans and procedures to solve problems. Decision making may therefore be more effective. A business may also be better able to cope with change because it can take into account unpredictable events. Because businesses are constantly adapting their approaches to problems there should be less resistance to change from employees. However, an organisation can quickly go back to 'old ways of doing things' unless it constantly makes use of new knowledge. There may also be resistance from some managers, who see their control diluted, or workers who do not want to or are not able to learn.

Key terms

Learning organisation - a business in a changing environment that constantly revises its working methods.

Question 4

In 1990 British Telecom (BT) employed 250,00 people. In 1998 its 110,000 workforce achieved higher standards and the business's performance was better. Staff cuts had been necessary to remain competitive. But staff attitude surveys in the 1990s began to show concerns about staff morale and motivation.

In 1993 BT formed a new consumer division to deal directly with customers. To be effective the new managing director, Stafford Taylor, realised there had to be a consumer-focussed and motivated workforce. So BT introduced a new way of working called 'for a better life'. This would involve communicating with staff, giving them a sense of how the business was doing and encouraging them to stretch themselves. The new way of working would change how staff operated and instil them with a sense of excitement and belonging. Previously the company had staff manuals for every eventuality, even telling staff exactly what phrases to say. The new system ('own, decide, do') encouraged staff to:
● know instinctively how to contribute to the success of BT;
● take personal accountability for customers' requirements;
● take decisive action on behalf of the customer;
● take considered risks on behalf of the customer.

Staff and managers had to change the way they worked. Managers were required to take on more of a coaching role. A new management team was appointed, with those getting jobs being selected for their ability to coach rather than to supervise. Staff were expected to be more creative, assertive and to take 'considered risks'. One member of staff, for example, working in a BT shop, found that a phone a customer wanted was out of stock. The assistant tracked the model to another shop and delivered it to the customer on the way home from work. Overall the exercise has been quite expensive, but retraining over 20,000 employees was bound to be. And to what extent has this change in the company's culture been effective? Staff attitude surveys have shown that employees are far more willing to take important decisions and even risks.

Source: adapted from *People Management*, 29 .10.1998.

(a) What performance indicators might be used by BT to assess the effectiveness of change?
(b) Examine the possible effects of changes at BT on:
(i) employees; and (ii) the business.
(c) Discuss whether the new corporate culture at BT would help the management of change.

Summary

1. State 5 factors that may cause change in a business.
2. How might change affect:
   (a) market research;
   (b) research and development;
   in a business?
3. Why is it important for businesses to manage change?

4. Explain 4 ways in which the personnel department can plan human resources to deal with change.
5. What is meant by 'developing an organisational culture for change'?
6. Briefly explain 4 approaches to change.

Case study

English Welsh & Scottish Railway

In 1994 British Rail's heavy freight operations were split into four separate companies, ready for privatisation. By 1996 they had been bought by an American rail operator, Wisconsin Central Transportation, which formed the English Welsh & Scottish Railway (EWS) company. The rail freight industry was a dying industry, suffering years of neglect, poor industrial relations, inefficient work practices, bad publicity and under investment. The new American owners realised that replacing old rolling stock and lobbying for freight to be transported by rail rather than road was not likely to be enough. The whole culture of the organisation, built around years of control and command needed turning on its head.

Managing director, Ian Braybrook, says: 'The thing I notice when I go around depots is that I can see people's teeth - because they're smiling. Now they seem to enjoy work a lot more.' But success requires more than happy workers. EWS's customer base has increased by 20 per cent, the number of trains it runs has risen by 25 per cent and the company has made a profit in each of the last two years. He also argues: 'The only thing that can stop us is people's attitudes'.

The new owners took a two pronged approach to the problems. Restructuring terms and conditions, and work practices, were accompanied by a programme designed to change the attitudes of employees. After sorting management jobs and structures the company turned to the problems of poor productivity and inflexible work practices that were synonymous with the UK rail industry. Many staff, particularly train drivers, identified with the union first, then the industry, but rarely the company that employed them. They expected a job for life and overtime payments. Also there were wide variations in regional conditions and how they were applied. Another problem was that, in the run up to privatisation, staff had begun to develop loyalties to the four companies formed by British Rail's break-up.

New terms and conditions were negotiated. Overtime and top up pay was scrapped. Annualised hours were introduced and teams managed by team leaders were set up. Half of the company's administration and support staff were made redundant and this cut the number of layers in the hierarchy from 15 to 5. The company also wished to deal directly with employees so a company council was set up to meet two or three times a year to act as a forum for communication. Pay

and conditions were more or less standard across the company by 1998.

A three year cultural change programme was introduced. Initially 80 team leaders from engineering were trained for a hands-on role to motivate people in the company. They were also trained in how to foster a more customer-orientated, 'can-do' attitude. One team leader asked workers in a questionnaire what they thought of him as a manager. Employees felt motivated and wanted to be part of his team, and productivity increased tenfold. Senior managers visiting factories organised meetings and spoke to staff. As a result of the programme, individuals in the business felt that they were being listened to.

The changes made at the business have not been without problems. Under the old system drivers were paid a basic salary, but only received extra payments, eg overtime, if they turned up. The new system had a higher annual salary than the basic wage plus top ups, but the incentive to attend was taken away. Absenteeism resulted. Getting across the business message and getting people to understand that there are implications if they don't do their job properly was still a problem. Another worry was that the reduced workforce would have more work to do and spend time 'fire fighting' problems, rather than using the new freedom to improve the way things are done. Roy Taylor, development advisor at EWS, said: 'Some people expect us to change the culture overnight. That just doesn't happen. Unless you reinforce it, people go back to where they feel comfortable.

Source: adapted from *People Management*, 12.12.1998.

(a) **Identify the factors that may have led to change at EWS.**
(b) **Explain the factors at EWS that may have led to resistance to change.**
(c) **Examine: (i) the positive effects; and (ii) the problems; that changes at EWS have had on the business.**
(d) (i) **How would you categorise the approach to managing change at EWS? Explain your answer.**
    (ii) **Explain the possible advantages and disadvantages of this approach.**
(e) **Evaluate the management of change at EWS using quantitative and qualitative methods.**

What is production?

PRODUCTION takes place when resources, such as raw materials or components, are changed into 'products'. Land, labour, capital and enterprise - the factors of production (☞ unit 1) - are used in the production process. The use of land and a tractor to grow cabbages is an example of production in **primary industry.** An example of **secondary industry** would be the use of wood, plastic, glue, screws, labour, drilling and cutting equipment to manufacture furniture.

Today production is often referred to more generally as those activities that 'bring a product into being'. Activities which are part of **tertiary industry,** such as services, would be included in this definition. A bank might talk about providing a 'product' in the same way as a carpet manufacturer. Examples of products in a bank's product portfolio (☞ unit 41) might include mortgages, current accounts, house insurance and foreign currency. Direct services from the producer to the consumer, such as car repairs or decorating, can also be regarded as production in this sense.

Features of production

Production takes place when a business takes INPUTS, carries out a PROCESS and produces an OUTPUT or product. Production by a jewellery manufacturer may include the following.
- Inputs are the raw materials and components used by a business. These may include gold, silver and precious stones.
- Processes are the methods used to convert raw materials and components into products. Processes might include designing, cutting, bending, soldering and polishing. Such processes are often performed using machines and tools. For example, metal cutters, specialist jeweller's tools, a soldering iron and a small polishing machine might be used.
- Outputs are the products or services produced when inputs are converted. They might include rings, brooches, bangles, bracelets and necklaces.

Planning and controlling production

For production to be effective, it needs to be planned and controlled.

Planning All businesses, whether small or large, need to plan production. Some large firms employ production planners for this task. A number of factors can influence the plan.
- Demand from customers. Businesses get orders from

different customers, for different products, with different specifications, at different times. A business must plan which orders should go out first and which can wait.
- The design of a product might affect planning. For example, the design specifications of a product might state that certain materials must be used or certain processes, like high quality finishing, must be carried out.
- Planning must make sure that there are enough resources available. Many businesses purchase stocks (☞ unit 94) of raw materials and components and keep them until they are needed. Others order 'just in time'.

Loading This involves deciding which 'work centres' will carry out which tasks. A work centre may be an employee, a machine or a process such as welding.

Sequencing Production usually involves arranging tasks and processes in a sequence. For many products the order of tasks will rarely change, such as in the production of bread. This is often the case when fairly large numbers of the same product

Sales of wedding dresses

Pulling cotton into shape after it has been dyed

Harvesting of cotton bolls

The photographs show activities involved in the production of clothing.
(a) Which of the above activities are examples of:
   (i) primary; (ii) secondary; (iii) tertiary production?
(b) In each of the above cases describe why the activities are examples of production.
(c) Explain, using examples from the photographs, how inputs are changed into outputs using a process.

are produced. However, when non-standard or customised products (☞ unit 91) are made, the order in which tasks and processes are arranged may need to change.

W.H Brakspear & Sons has brewed beer in its Henley brewery, Oxfordshire, since 1799. The brewer markets about six brands of real ale (cask conditioned beer) including XXX Mild, Bitter, Regatta Gold and Old Ale. It owns about 300 tied houses and has used much the same brewing processes since it began.

Figure 90.1 *Production of beer in the brewery*
Source: adapted from the *Good Beer Guide*, 1998.

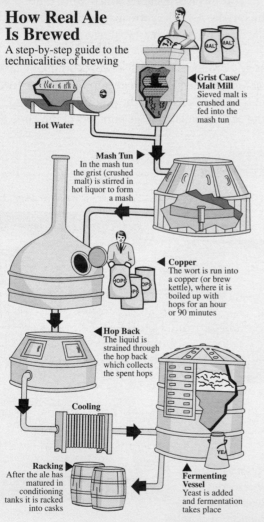

How Real Ale Is Brewed
A step-by-step guide to the technicalities of brewing

Hot Water

Grist Case/ Malt Mill
Sieved malt is crushed and fed into the mash tun

Mash Tun
In the mash tun the grist (crushed malt) is stirred in hot liquor to form a mash

Copper
The wort is run into a copper (or brew kettle), where it is boiled up with hops for an hour or 90 minutes

Hop Back
The liquid is strained through the hop back which collects the spent hops

Cooling

Racking
After the ale has matured in conditioning tanks it is racked into casks

Fermenting Vessel
Yeast is added and fermentation takes place

(a) State two examples of inputs used by Brakspear.
(b) Describe two planning activities Brakspear might undertake when brewing beer.
(c) Would it be possible to change the sequencing of the processes illustrated in the diagram? Explain your answer.

Scheduling The production schedule will show times when particular tasks and processes should start and finish. This is particularly important when large production projects are being undertaken, such as the construction of a large building. The aim of scheduling is to ensure that resources, such as workers, are not idle whilst waiting for someone else to finish a job before starting their own. **Gantt charts** can be used to help scheduling. A Gantt chart is a visual display showing how tasks might be sequenced over time. The Gantt chart in Figure 90.2 shows the tasks required to produce a batch of 1,000 brackets by an engineering company. The chart shows that:

● cutting begins on Monday and takes two days;
● bending, the longest task, begins on Tuesday. It takes three days and can begin before the entire batch has been cut;
● on Thursday welding begins before the entire batch has finished the bending process. Welding takes two days;
● painting begins on Friday even though the whole batch has not been welded and painting the whole batch takes two days;
● packing, which takes only half a day, cannot begin until Tuesday, when the whole batch has been painted.

Dispatching This involves giving instructions about the tasks to be carried out for a particular period. Instructions may be given verbally or in written form.

Progressing This is an ongoing monitoring process. It requires supervisors, teams or managers reporting on the progress of jobs. Managers or teams may have to identify problems and help solve them. They should also try to eliminate bottlenecks and encourage workers, when necessary, to speed up the job.

Task	M	Tu	W	Th	F	M	Tu
Cutting	■	■					
Bending		■	■	■			
Welding				■	■		
Painting					■	■	
Packing							■

Figure 90.2 *Gantt chart showing the sequence of tasks required to produce a batch of 1,000 metal brackets by an engineering company*

Added value

A business adds value to raw materials which it uses in the production process. ADDED VALUE can be found in the difference between the cost of purchasing raw materials and the price which the finished goods are sold for. In Figure 90.3 the builder will use inputs such as land, bricks, wood, tiles, frames, glass and other materials to build a house. The total cost of all the inputs is £31,000. The centre of the diagram shows the various processes required in the construction of the house. These include digging, bricklaying, roofing, tiling, plumbing, joining, painting and other tasks. As a result of these processes an output is produced. In this example the output is a house, which is sold by the builder for £89,000. The **value added** in this case is £58,000 (£89,000 - £31,000).

£58,000 is not the **profit** made by the builder. Part of the £58,000 will be used to pay the wages of employees and business overheads such as insurance, motor expenses and tax. So the profit figure will be lower than the value added figure. Value added is the difference between the price at which goods or services are sold and the cost of raw materials. Profit is the difference between the price at which goods or services are sold and all costs of production.

For services, it is sometimes more difficult to see how value is added. A supermarket will buy in a product from a producer or wholesaler. It will sell the product for a higher price to customers than it has paid for it. The difference in price is added value. The retailer is adding value because it is providing a service (making the products available in a convenient location) to the customer.

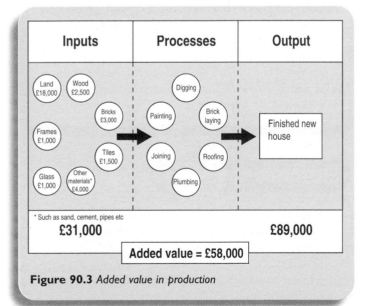

Figure 90.3 *Added value in production*

Production decisions

Businesses make a number of important production decisions. A clothing manufacturer, for example, might decide to produce a new range of casual trousers. This could

Question 3

Stan Ivanov produces bedding plants for the retail market in his Cheshire-based greenhouse complex. One of his most popular lines in the early summer are Salvias. These are sold in seed boxes containing two dozen small plants. Each box is sold for £1.85. The costs incurred by Stan for this product are shown in Figure 90.4.

Figure 90.4 *Costs incurred by Stan Ivanov*

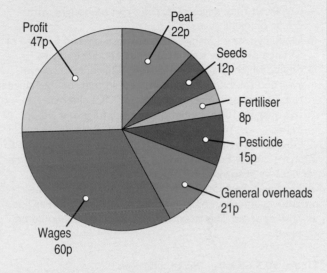

(a) Describe how Stan adds value in the above case.
(b) Calculate the added value by the business.
(c) How might the added value be affected if Stan raises his price to £2.00 per box?

involve using a new type of cloth, changing the layout of the factory, increasing the size of its warehouse, employing more labour and introducing a new quality control system. One production decision will often lead to other decisions having to be made. Decisions made by businesses might include some of the following.

What to produce A business must decide what product it wants to produce. The product may be a new product, that no other business has produced, or an adaptation of its own or a competitor's products. For example, 'Little Feet' are foot shaped plastic moulds which keeps two socks together in the wash. The creator, Andrea Marks, based the design on grips used to hold tea towels in kitchens. Many supermarkets now offer financial services such as savings accounts similar to those of banks.

What production method should be used Businesses choose how best to make their products (☞ unit 71). Different businesses might use different production methods, even when they make the same products. For example, TVR and Nissan both manufacture cars. TVR hand-builds its cars in a small factory in Blackpool. Its production techniques make

Question 4

Orange is one of the country's leading mobile telecommunications companies. In the UK in 1997 the number of mobile phone users had more than doubled since Orange was launched in 1994. One in seven people used a mobile phone at the time. During 1997 Orange introduced a number of product initiatives.

● Talkshare plus, which allows groups of up to 50 people to use shared time and receive one bill.

● Just Talk, which allows users to buy a phone and only pay when they make calls. Time can be bought with credit or debit cards.

● Opening more Orange stores. These offered a range of Orange products such as phones and accessories.

● Equity, which is a reward system where points were awarded for calls made. Points could then be exchanged for Orange accessories, passes for UCI cinemas, champagne, 100 minutes of free call time and other items.

During the year Orange took a number of measures to improve quality. For example, it tried to improve customer services by resolving customer problems immediately when they called. One customer information system introduced, Merlin, could 'blacklist' a stolen phone as soon as it is reported. This means that outgoing calls could be stopped.

Figure 90.5 *Growth in Orange subscribers*

Source: adapted from Orange, *Annual Summary,* 1997.

Group subscriber growth (000's)

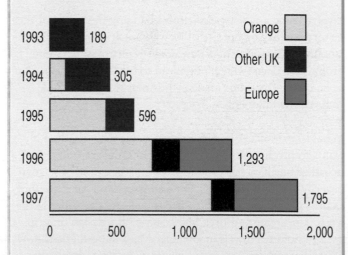

(a) Explain the production decisions that Orange took in 1997.

(b) (i) What has happened to the number of Orange subscribers over the period 1993-97?

(ii) Examine how this might affect production decisions at Orange.

more use of skilled workers than Nissan's and the car bodies are made from fibre glass. Nissan mass produces cars in factories around the world. It relies more on robots, computers and other machines than TVR and uses metal for the car bodies.

Where production should be located Business owners have to decide where best to locate their premises (☞ unit 100). Generally, they will find locations where costs will be lowest. Small business owners may locate near to where they live. Large multinationals (☞ unit 32) may locate production in countries where the government gives them subsidies and grants.

How large the business should be Most businesses start off small and then grow. There are many advantages of growing. One is that costs are likely to fall due to economies of scale (☞ unit 93). However, some business owners are content to remain relatively small, to avoid the extra responsibilities growth brings for instance.

How to ensure quality Businesses are more likely to be successful if they can produce high quality products. Businesses have to decide how they might improve quality (☞ unit 95). This might involve using more expensive raw materials, training staff to higher levels or introducing a quality system, such as total quality management (TQM).

Key terms

Input - the raw materials used in production.
Output - the goods or services resulting from production.
Process - the method used to convert inputs to final goods or services.
Production - the transformation of resources into goods or services.
Value added - the difference between the cost of raw materials and the selling price.

Summary

1. State 3 examples of production in the: (a) primary; (b) secondary and (c) tertiary industries.
2. State 5 features of planning and controlling production.
3. Explain how a cereal manufacturer adds value to production.
4. 'The retailer marked up the wholesale price by 10 per cent.' Explain why this is an example of calculating value added.
5. Why is value added not the same as profit?
6. State 5 questions about production that a business may consider.

Case study

Pilkington Glass

Pilkington Glass, based in St. Helens, Merseyside, is one of the most well known glass producers in the world. One of Pilkington's main products is Float glass. Float glass is distortion free, flat glass with a fire polished finish. This type of glass has a number of advantages. It provides flat surfaces and allows a wide range of thicknesses to be made. Sizes can be cut to order. It can also be toughened or laminated, coloured and silvered to produce mirrors.

A number of years ago, Pilkington Glass developed a unique production method to produce Float glass. The method is highly automated. It involves the use of one of several mile long plants in St Helens. Figure 90.6 shows the different processes used in the production of Float glass.

● Raw materials, such as sand, soda ash, limestone, dolomite and alumina, are weighed, blended and fed continuously into the furnace. Recycled broken glass is also fed into the furnace to avoid waste and keep costs down.

● Inside a furnace heated to 1,600°C, raw materials are melted. The molten glass moves through the tank, stirred by water cooled stirrers.

● The molten glass undertakes a forming process on a bed of molten tin. The glass floats on top of the tin because it is less dense. It spreads out to form a ribbon and cools to about 600°C as it travels along inside the chamber. As it passes over the molten tin, imperfections are melted out and the glass becomes an even thickness. It is this part of the process which gives the glass its high quality.

● An annealing process is used to cool the glass. This removes the stress from the glass so that it can be cut.

● At the end of the annealing process the glass is cool enough to cut. Pilkington uses a computer-controlled automatic warehousing facility. Customers' orders are fed into the computer which works out cutting sizes. The computer then instructs the cutting heads which cut the glass according to customer size.

● Panes are stacked automatically. The stacks can then be automatically or manually loaded onto lorries for distribution.

The whole production process is automated, controlled and monitored by computers. The number of staff involved in production is minimal. For much of time the factory floor is deserted. There is only a maintenance team on duty. The computer room has the highest number of staff in the production area.

Source: adapted from materials supplied by Pilkington Glass; *Annual Report and Acccounts.*

(a) Describe two planning tasks the production planners at Pilkington might have to undertake.
(b) Explain why the manufacturing of glass is an example of secondary production.
(c) Using the example of production at Pilkington, explain what is meant by: (i) inputs; (ii) processes; and (iii) outputs.
(d) Explain how Pilkington adds value in its production process.
(e) Examine two production decisions which Pilkington may have made and how they could have affected production.

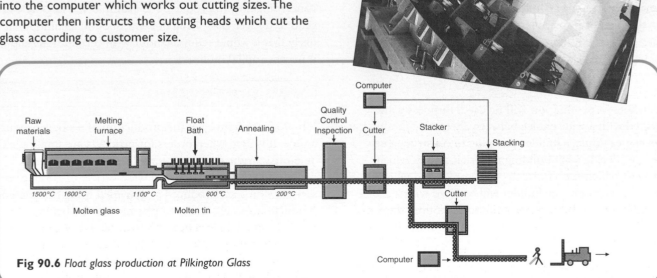

Fig 90.6 *Float glass production at Pilkington Glass*

Deciding how to produce

A business must decide on the most suitable method to manufacture its goods or to provide services. It is likely that products which are different will be produced differently. For example, a plastic drinks bottle may be produced using automated machinery, but a wrist watch may be assembled by hand. Products that are similar can also be produced in different ways. The Ford Motor Company and Morgan Cars both produce cars, but different processes are used. Ford builds cars using a production line and semi-skilled labour, but Morgan cars are hand built by skilled workers. There are three important decisions that businesses must make when choosing how to produce. These are shown in Figure 91.1, along with the factors which influence these decisions. In the diagram it is assumed that the firm has already decided 'what' to produce. When deciding how to produce, the objective of the firm will be to minimise the cost per unit of output, ie PRODUCTIVE EFFICIENCY.

What production method will be used? Production is sometimes divided into one of three methods. JOB PRODUCTION is where one job is completed at a time before moving on to another. An example might be a costume made for a television play set in the nineteenth century. BATCH PRODUCTION involves dividing the work into a number of different operations. An example would be bread production, where each batch goes through several different baking stages before it is completed. FLOW PRODUCTION involves work being completed continuously without stopping. The production of cars on a production line might be one example.

Some industries may combine different methods of production. For example, a large brewery may produce 'batches' of beer, but then send them to a bottling line for packaging, where flow production is used. Such combinations are particularly common in the food industry.

What factors of production will be used? Businesses are often faced with a wide choice between alternative production factors. For example, a builder planning to construct a new house must decide what building materials to buy, which tools to use, which sub-contractors to employ and whether to hire any extra labour. The builder will be faced with a choice in all of these cases. If he decides to hire a labourer, there may be hundreds or even thousands of people to choose from in the area.

How will the factors of production be combined? A third production decision concerns the way in which the available production factors should be combined. For example, should an assembly plant invest in a highly automated assembly

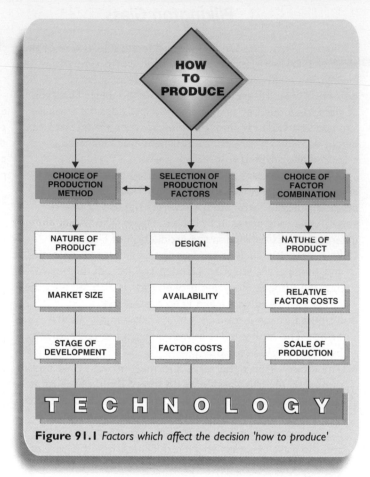

Figure 91.1 *Factors which affect the decision 'how to produce'*

operation, or employ a large semi-skilled labour force to undertake the work?

There is a relationship between the three decisions concerning how to produce. For example, if a large UK firm produced sheet glass using flow production techniques, it is likely that it would require labour with certain skills and that it may be capital intensive.

Job production

Job production involves the production of a single product at a time. It is used when orders for products are small, such as 'one-offs'. Production is organised so that one 'job' is completed at a time. There is a wide variety of goods and services which are produced or provided using this method of production. Small scale examples include the baking of a child's birthday cake, a dentist's treatment session or the construction of an extension to a house. On a large scale, examples could include the building of a ship, the construction of the Channel Tunnel or the manufacture of specialised machinery. Job production is found both in manufacturing and the service industries. Because the numbers of units produced is small, the production process tends to be labour intensive. The workforce is usually skilled craftsmen or specialists and the possibility of using labour saving machinery is limited. Many businesses adopt this method of production when they are 'starting up'.

Advantages of job production What are the benefits to businesses?

- Firms can produce unique or 'one-off' orders according to customer needs. For example, a wedding dress may be designed and produced for the individual taste of a client. It is also possible to change the specifications of a job at the last minute even if the work has actually begun.
- Workers are more likely to be motivated. The tasks employees carry out often require a variety of skills, knowledge and expertise. Their work will be more demanding and interesting. They will also see the end result of their efforts and be able to take pride in their work. Jobs may be carried out by a team of workers aiming to achieve the same objectives. This should help raise the level of job satisfaction.
- The organisation of job production is fairly simple. Because only one job is done at a time, co-ordination, communication, supervision and inspection can be regularly carried out. Also, it is easier to identify and deal with problems, such as a defective damp proof course in a house or a poorly cooked meal in a restaurant.

Disadvantages of job production There are, however, some disadvantages with job production.

- Labour costs will be high because production tends to be labour intensive. The workforce is likely to be skilled and more versatile. Such employees will be more expensive. The amount of time each employee spends on a particular job will also be long.
- Because there is a variety of work, to many specifications, the business would need a wide range of tools, machines and equipment. This can prove expensive. Also, it may not be possible to achieve economies of scale (☞ unit 93) because only one 'job' is produced at a time.
- Lead times can be lengthy. When building a house the business has to incur costs which cannot be recovered until the house is sold. Sometimes the sale of a house can take a long time.
- Selling costs may also be high. This is likely if the product is highly complex and technical. The sales team will need to be well qualified, able to cope with questions and deal with problems concerning sales and installation. Some firms employ agencies to help reduce their selling costs.

Once the demand for a firm's product rises, job production may become costly. Firms may prefer to use a method more suited to producing larger quantities. This is not always the case. Even if demand is high, each customer may require a unique order. In addition, many firms believe that the 'personal touch' they can offer in job production is important. As a result they may choose not to change to other production methods. Other production methods require some degree of product standardisation. This may result in more efficient production, but a loss of 'individuality'.

Batch production

Batch production may be used when demand for a firm's product or service is regular rather than a 'one off'. An example might be furniture where a batch of armchairs is made to a particular design. Production is divided into a number of operations. A particular operation is carried out on all products in a batch. The batch then moves to the next operation.

A baker uses batch production when baking bread. The operations in the baking process are broken down in Table 91.1.

Question **1**

Mark Steinberg and his daughter Tracy Tolkien run a vintage and designer clothes shop called Steinberg and Tolkien. It is located in the Kings Road, Chelsea and has been visited by a number of famous film stars and celebrities such as Kim Basinger, Helena Christensen, Kate Moss and Dolce and Gabbana. The shop currently has in the past had three priceless Fortuny gowns and jackets and an original Erte costume in stock. In addition, there have been original Diors, Balenciagas, Balmains and Puccis coats worn by Elton John, and evening dresses that once filled the wardrobe of seventies nightclub queen, Regine.

It was jewellery that got the business started. Ten years ago Tracy came to London from the US to study mediaeval art and history at the Courtauld Institute. To help her finances, she started selling her mother's old costume jewellery at Camden Lock market. Tolkien discovered that a lot of the Forties and Fifties fake gems were made by master craftsmen who had come from Europe to the States during the Second World War. Her interest in jewellery spread into vintage clothing. The business which began as a stall in Chenil Galleries grew, and four years ago, with the help of her father, the current shop in the Kings Road was opened. If people can't make it to the shop, they can run through Evita and Batman videos and look closely at the jewellery and some of the costumes, or rewind the Oscars. Items are bought from Steinberg and Tolkien because they are usually one-offs and the wearer knows there won't be another like it in Hollywood that night.

Source: adapted from *The Times, Times Magazine*, 4.7.1998.

(a) What evidence is there in the case to suggest that the products sold by Steinberg and Tolkien are made using job production?

(b) Explain why non-standardisation of the products sold in the shop is important to clients.

(c) Explain the possible disadvantage to some clients of products produced in this way.

> **Table 91.1** *Operations involved in the production of a batch of bread*
>
> 1. Blend ingredients in a mixing container until a dough is formed.
> 2. Knead the dough for a period of time.
> 3. Leave the dough to rise for a period of time.
> 4. Divide the dough into suitable units (loaves) for baking.
> 5. Bake the loaves.
> 6. Allow loaves to cool.

These operations would be performed on every batch of bread. There is some standardisation because each loaf in the batch will be the same. However, it may be possible to vary each batch. The ingredients could be changed to produce brown bread or the style of baking tin could be changed for different shaped loaves.

A great number of products are produced using this method, particularly in manufacturing, such as the production of components and food processing. For example, in a canning plant, a firm may can several different batches of soup, each batch being a different recipe. Products can be produced in very large or very small batches depending on the level of demand. Larger production runs tend to lower the **unit** or **average cost** (☞ unit 52) of production. New technology (☞ unit 98) is increasingly being introduced to make batch production more efficient.

Advantages of batch production. What benefits will this method have for a business?

● Even though larger quantities are produced than in job production, there is still flexibility. Each batch can be changed to meet customers' wishes. It is particularly suitable for a wide range of similar products. The settings on machines can be changed according to specifications, such as different clothes sizes.
● Employees can concentrate on one operation rather than the whole task. This reduces the need for costly, skilled employees.
● Less variety of machinery would be needed than in job production because the products are standardised. Also, it is possible to use more standardised machinery.
● It often results in stocks of partly finished goods which have to be stored. This means firms can respond more quickly to an urgent order by processing a batch quickly through the final stages of production.

Disadvantages of batch production. There are also disadvantages with batch production.

● Careful planning and co-ordination are needed, or machines and workers may be idle, waiting for a whole batch to finish its previous operation. There is often a need to clean and adjust machinery before the next batch can be produced. This can mean delays. In brewing, one day of the week is used to clean equipment before the next batch begins.

Chris Dee set up a small business operation in 1976 making underskirts and other basic lingerie at home. She sold the garments at a local market on Saturdays. In 1984 her husband Dave joined her and the business began to expand. By 1997, they employed nine staff and sold a much wider range of products in four local markets.

The working week at Chris's workshop is divided into two. In the first part of the week everyone is employed making clothes in one colour, white for example. In the second half of the week garments are made in another colour, black say.

During the first half of the week the machines might be used to make white bras, briefs, underskirts and bodices. Whilst bras are being made everyone in the workshop makes a contribution to their production. Each worker specialises in a particular task. For example, one person might overlock the seams, another might sew on straps, a third secures the wire and so on.

On average 12 bras of a particular size and design are produced at any one time. The production plan is to ensure that there are enough of each design and size to sell at the market stalls, and if possible, to have a few left over for stock. When production targets for bras have been reached, production switches to another product, such as cami tops.

Source: adapted from company information.

(a) What evidence is there in the case to suggest that Chris Dee uses batch production at her workshop?
(b) What changes might be necessary when switching production from one batch to another?
(c) Explain three advantages of batch production to Chris's business.
(d) Discuss whether the business would be better off producing batches of 500 rather than 12.

● Some machinery may have to be more complex to compensate for the lower skill levels required from the labour force. This may lead to higher costs.
● The workforce may be less motivated, since they have to repeat operations on every single unit in the batch. In addition, they are unlikely to be involved with production from start to finish.

● If batches are small then unit costs will remain relatively high.
● Money will be tied up in work-in-progress (☞ unit 94) since an order cannot be dispatched until the whole batch has been finished.

Flow production

Most people will have some idea of flow production from pictures of motor car factories. Production is organised so that different operations can be carried out, one after the other, in a **continuous** sequence. Vehicles move from one operation to the next, often on a conveyer belt. The main features of flow production are:
● large quantities are produced;
● a simplified or standardised product;
● a semi-skilled workforce, specialising in one operation only;
● large amounts of machinery and equipment;
● large stocks of raw materials and components.

Flow production is used in the manufacture of products as varied as newspapers, food and cement. It is sometimes called **mass production,** as it tends to be used for the production of large numbers of standard products, such as cars or breakfast cereals. Certain types of flow production are known as **continual flow production,** because products such as clothing material pass continually through a series of processes. **Repetitive flow production** is the manufacture of large numbers of the same product, such as plastic toy parts or metal cans. **Process production** is a form of flow production which is used in the oil or chemical industry. Materials pass through a plant where a series of processes are carried out in order to change the product. An example might be the refining of crude oil into petrol.

Flow production relies on the use of computers (☞ unit 98). Computers send instructions to machines, control production speeds and conditions, and monitor quality. They allow large numbers of products to be produced continuously to exact standards or control continuous production which requires many processes.

Food products can be manufactured in batches or using flow production techniques.

Advantages of flow production Why might a business use flow production?
● Unit costs are reduced as firms gain from economies of scale (☞ unit 93).
● In many industries the process is highly automated. Production is controlled by computers. Many of the operations are performed by robots and other types of machinery. Once the production line is set up and running, products can flow off the end non stop for lengthy periods of time. This can reduce the need for labour, as only machine supervisors are needed.
● The need to stockpile finished goods is reduced. The production line can respond to short term changes in demand. For example, if demand falls the line can be shut down for a period of time. If it rises then the line can be opened.

Disadvantages of flow production What are the disadvantages of flow production?
● The set up costs are very high. An enormous investment in plant and equipment is needed. Firms must therefore be confident that demand for the product is sufficient over a period of time to make the investment pay.
● The product will be standardised. It is not possible to offer a wide product range and meet different customers' needs.
● For a number of reasons, worker motivation can be a serious problem. Most of the manual operations required on the production line will be repetitive and boring. Factories with production lines tend to be very noisy. Each worker will only be involved in a very small part of the job cycle. As a result of these problems worker morale may be low and labour turnover (☞ unit 75) and absenteeism high.
● Breakdowns can prove costly. The whole production system is interdependent. If one part of the supply or production line fails the whole system may break down.

In the 1990s flow production processes have been changed in an attempt to solve some of these problems. Japanese manufacturers setting up businesses in the UK introduced methods to improve efficiency. Just in time manufacturing (☞ unit 92) for example, helped to reduce the cost of holding stocks. Some vehicle manufacturers attempted to introduce an element of job production into flow processes by **customising** products for clients. For example, a range of different cars were produced on the same production line. Cars in the same model range differed in colour, engine size, trim and interior design.

Choice of production method

The method of production chosen might depend on a number of factors.
● The nature of the product. Many products require a specific method of production. For example, in the construction industry, projects such as bridges, roads, office blocks and sewers must be produced using job production. Cereal farming involves batch production.

Question 3

McCain Foods produces pizzas using the system shown in Figure 91.2. Pizzas are manufactured on a production line. They pass through different stages in the process. At each stage something is added. Once a variety of pizza has been developed, it is manufactured according to strict specifications. This is to ensure that every single pizza is exactly the same. In order to ensure that quality is consistent there is a number of control systems in operation.

● Ingredients. All the ingredients used by McCain in its production process are checked to strict specifications for quality and are analysed microbiologically to ensure that they are safe.

● Temperature and time. Certain stages in the production process require specific temperatures and humidity conditions. Both the temperature and the amount of time required for different processes are controlled by computer. For example, the temperature of the ovens for the baking process is critical. So is the amount of time pizza bases spend in the oven. Both of these are computer controlled.

● Line rate. This is the speed with which the pizzas move along the line. It is determined by the length of time pizzas need to spend at each stage. The topping line moves at a different speeds depending on the variety of pizza. The object is to keep the lines moving as fast as possible, but at the same time maintaining high quality.

● Quality control. A number of checks are necessary to ensure quality. For example, bases are checked for size and weight. Sauces are checked for viscosity and taste. Every hour samples are taken from the line, cooked and analysed microbiologically.

Source: adapted from company information.

Figure 91.2 *Pizza production at McCain Foods*

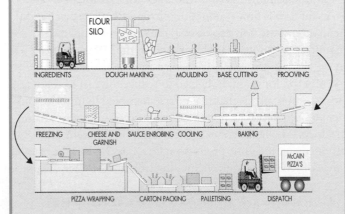

(a) How might the production of pizzas at McCain Foods be categorised? Explain your answer.
(b) Explain three: (i) advantages and (ii) disadvantages to McCain Foods of this type of production method.
(c) Why do you think so many checks and controls are necessary when using such production methods?

A plot of land undergoes several processes before it 'produces' a crop.

● The size of the market. Fast moving consumer goods like soap, confectionery and canned drinks are normally produced using flow production because the market is so big. When the market is small, flow production techniques are not cost effective.

● The stage of development a business has reached. When firms are first set up, they often produce small levels of output and employ job or batch production methods. As they grow and enjoy higher sales levels they may switch to flow production.

● Technology. The current state of technology will affect all decisions concerning how to produce. As technology

Question 4

Provinder and Imran Latif have been running their own fabric business for 9 years. They have a manufacturing unit on a small industrial estate in Leicester. They have experimented with a range of products in the past but now specialise in the production of curtains. They produce made-to-measure curtains and related products for customers who respond to their adverts in the local newspaper. They opened up a shop two years ago which is now run by their eldest son Rajid. The shop stocks a variety of ready made curtains but also displays fabrics and takes orders for made-to-measure curtains. In the first year the shop made a loss, possibly because it was not widely known that it existed. In the second year it just broke even.

In 1999 they began to receive a few orders for batches of curtains, perhaps 8 or 9 of the same size, style and fabric. Imran noticed that the profit margins on these batches were considerably higher than those for individual sets of curtains. In May 1999 they were approached by a national company and offered a contract to produce quite large batches of curtains for hotels.

The contract was very attractive indeed. It would provide enough work for at least 3 years. However, Provinder and Imran acknowledged that there would be problems. There would have to be an investment in new machinery and more skilled staff would have to be recruited. They would have to reduce their customer base substantially and switch production methods. They would also have to borrow quite a large sum of money from the bank and they were not sure whether to continue with the shop.

(a) Explain how Provinder and Imran changed production methods.
(b) Examine the factors that may have influenced Provinder and Imran in deciding whether to switch production methods.
(c) Explain why the profit margins rose when production methods were changed.
(d) Discuss whether the advantages of switching production methods outweighed the disadvantages.

advances, new materials and machinery become available. Changes in technology often result in firms adopting new methods of production. For example, the development of computers and robotic welders has radically changed the way in which cars are manufactured. Also, car manufacturers are now able to produce different models on the same production line at the same time.

Choosing factors of production

A firm has to choose materials, tools, equipment, machinery and labour before production can begin. The more complex the product, the more difficult this will be. There is often a variety of materials and equipment to choose from. For example, a small manufacturer of jeans has to consider which type of cloth, cotton, stud, zip, sewing machine and labour to use. What influences the factors of production a business chooses?

● The actual design itself may specify which materials to use. For example, a new savoury snack will be made to a strict list of ingredients.

● There may be limited amounts of labour, capital or materials. A company recruiting people with a specialist skill may find that supply 'runs out'. It may then have to recruit unskilled workers and train them.

● Businesses will aim to use the cheapest factors, assuming that there is no difference in quality. If there is a difference in quality then the firm must decide which factor most suits its needs and budget. For example, when a company buys a new computer there is a wide range of models to choose from, at a range of different prices. They will have to select a model which suits their needs, and also one which they can afford.

Combining factors of production

Businesses must also decide what combination of factors of production they will use. The firm can adopt one of two approaches. LABOUR INTENSIVE techniques involve using a larger proportion of labour than capital. CAPITAL INTENSIVE techniques involve employing more machinery relative to labour. For example, chemical production is capital intensive with only a relatively small workforce to oversee the process. The postal service is labour intensive with a considerable amount of sorting and delivery done by hand.

The approach that is chosen depends on a number of factors.

● The nature of the product. Everyday products with high demand, like newspapers, are mass produced in huge plants using large quantities of machinery.

● The relative prices of the two factors. If labour costs are rising then it may be worth the company employing more capital instead.

● The size of the firm. As a firm grows and the scale of production increases, it tends to employ more capital relative to labour.

Table 91.2 *The effect on output as more workers are employed, given a fixed amount of capital*

							(Units)	
Capital	40	40	40	40	40	40	40	40
No. of workers	1	2	3	4	5	6	7	8
Total output	4	10	18	30	45	52	55	56

Combining different amounts of labour and capital can affect the **productivity** of these factors in the short run (☞ unit 52). As more units of labour are added to a fixed amount of capital, the output of the extra workers will rise at first and then fall. This is shown in Table 91.2, where the amount of capital is fixed at 40 units. For example, when the second worker is hired the total amount produced (**total output**) rises by 6 units (10-4). When the third worker is employed, output rises by 8 units (18-10), ie a higher amount.

The amount added by each extra worker (the **marginal output**) continues to rise until the sixth worker is employed. Then output rises by a smaller amount (7 units = 52-45). This is called the **law of diminishing returns** (☞ unit 65). Output rises at first because workers are able to specialise in particular tasks, which improves the productivity of extra workers. However, there reaches a point where workers are not able to specialise any more and the productivity of the extra worker begins to fall.

Question 5

Vimco Ltd is a small company which makes electrical engines. In the short run, the amount of capital is fixed at 10 units, but the size of the workforce can be varied. Table 91.3 shows the total output of Vimco Ltd in relation to the number of workers employed.

Table 91.3 *The total output for Vimco Ltd resulting from different combinations of labour and capital*

		(Units)
Capital	Labour	Total output
10	1	20
10	2	54
10	3	100
10	4	151
10	5	197
10	6	230
10	7	251
10	8	234

(a) Calculate the marginal output for each worker employed.
(b) Explain what is happening when
  (i) the fifth worker is employed;
  (ii) the eighth worker is employed.
(c) How might Vimco Ltd make use of the information contained in the table?

Key terms

Batch production - a method which involves completing one operation at a time on all units before performing the next.

Capital intensive - production methods which employ a large amount of machinery relative to labour.

Flow production - very large scale production of a standardised product, where each operation on a unit is performed continuously one after the other, usually on a production line.

Job production - a method of production which involves employing all factors to complete one unit of output at a time.

Labour intensive - production methods which rely on a large workforce relative to the amount of machinery.

Productive efficiency - production methods which minimise unit costs.

Summary

1. What are the 3 main decisions which have to be made regarding the method of production?
2. Under what circumstances might a business become more capital intensive?
3. State 3 types of products which may be manufactured using job production.
4. Describe the advantages and disadvantages of job production.
5. State 3 products that are generally manufactured using batch production.
6. Describe the advantages and disadvantages of batch production.
7. Describe 4 features of flow production.
8. What factors might affect the way a business chooses to combine factors of production?

Case study

CAICE (UK)

Caice (UK) was founded in 1993 and makes air-conditioning units. The company operates from Reading and is run by Martyn Cashmore and Ken Amott. Caice began by selling its design services to architects and developers planning noise-reduction systems. It also supplied and installed finished systems. The manufacturing of units, however, was subcontracted out. It has been successful in the 1990s, raising turnover to £1.3 million and profits to £54,000.

In May 1998 the company made a radical change. It opened a factory in Basingstoke to make acoustic fan units and steel ducts. This would reduce the reliance on sub-contractors, which made significant contributions to production. It would also help to raise profit margins by moving from costly 'one-off special-project work' to 'reproducible standard products'.

Cashmore identified problems with special one-off projects. They often involved research, design and installation costs that do not carry over to another project. For example, one job, for Burton the menswear group, involved a lot of design work. In addition, the key parts had to be commissioned from a manufacturer. The job was one-off with no benefits for the next job. Cashmore said: 'It's not that you don't make a profit on these jobs. But you do a lot of work for a small margin. If you spend your energies on reproducible work the costs per contract will diminish'.

Caice reduced the proportion of sales from special-project work from 50 per cent to 10 per cent, filling the gap by selling standard products. Standardised production would cut costs and allow Caice to be more competitive in the market place. The switch from job to batch production required a significant amount of investment. A feasibility study cost £12,000, leasing finance of £100,000 was needed for new machinery and a £150,000 overdraft facility was obtained. Caice was also very committed to investment in

information technology in production. It allocated around 10 per cent of sales revenue each year to expenditure on IT.

The Basingstoke factory was run by Mark MacDonald. He spotted that the workforce was saddled with the 'culture of the jobbing shop'. Staff were used to working on one job for a while until a crucial component wasn't available, then they would go off and work on something else. MacDonald wanted an assembly line, where work did not begin on a product until all the components were available. A single item would pass down the line accompanied by a trolley of components. All hands would be employed at all times and work would not be interrupted by any bottlenecks or missing components.

Caice did not immediately achieve its ambitious production targets. There were bottlenecks on the press-break machine and an erratic supply of components caused interruptions. Mark was keen to introduce new working practices and production techniques but it would all take time. The factory did well, making a small profit in less than one year. This was largely down to a £300,000 order for 83 acoustic fans, 82 of which were the same design. In the following year Caice's new duct would come on stream, capable of 60,000 variations. This would give Caice more flexibility in production.

Source: adapted from *The Sunday Times*, 6.12.1998.

(a) What is meant by the phrase: 'the culture of the jobbing-shop'?
(b) Explain the difficulties encountered when switching production methods.
(c) Examine the factors which may have influenced Caice to change production methods.
(d) Discuss the implications on the business of producing more standardised products.

LEAN PRODUCTION is an approach to production developed in Japan. Toyota, the Japanese car manufacturer, was the first company to adopt this approach. Its aim is to reduce the quantity of resources used up in production. Lean producers use less of everything, including factory space, materials, stocks, suppliers, labour, capital and time. As a result, lean production raises productivity and reduces costs. The number of defective products is reduced, lead times (☞ unit 94) are cut and reliability improves. Lean producers are also able to design new products more quickly and can offer customers a wider range of products to choose from. Lean production involves using a range of practices designed to reduce waste and to improve productivity and quality.

KAIZEN is perhaps the most important concept in Japanese management. It means continuous improvement. Every aspect of life, including social life, working life and home life, is constantly improved. Everyone in the business is involved.There is a number of features of Kaizen which affect a business.

Continuous improvement Kaizen has been the main difference between the Japanese and the Western approaches to management in the past. The attempts of Western Businesses to improve efficiency and quality have tended to be 'one-offs'. In Figure 92.1 the solid line illustrates the Western approach. Productivity remains the same for long periods of time, then suddenly rises. The increase is followed by another period of stability, before another rise. Increases in productivity may result from new working practices or new

technology. The dotted line shows the Japanese approach. Improvements are continuous. They result from changes in production techniques which are introduced gradually.

Eliminating waste The elimination of waste (called *muda* in Japan) in business practices is an important part of Kaizen. Waste is any activity which raises costs without adding value to a product. Examples may be:
● time wasted while staff wait around before starting tasks, such as waiting for materials to arrive;
● time wasted when workers move unnecessarily in the workplace, such as walking to a central point in the factory to get tools;
● the irregular use of a machine, such as a machine which is only used once a month for a special order;
● excessive demands upon machines or workers, such as staff working overtime seven days a week which causes them to be tired and work poorly.
Firms that adopt the Kaizen approach train and reward workers to continually search for waste and to suggest how it might be eliminated.

The Kaizen umbrella Kaizen is said to be an 'umbrella concept'. A wide range of different production techniques and working practices must be carried out for it to be effective. Figure 92.2 shows examples of the techniques, principles and practices. They should result in ongoing improvements. This approach argues that a day should not pass without some kind of improvement being made somewhere in the business.

Implementing continuous improvement It is often difficult for workers in a business to look for continuous improvement all the time. Japanese businesses tried to solve this problem by introducing the PDCA (Plan, Do, Check, Action) cycle. It is a series of activities that lead to improvement.
● Plan. Businesses must identify where improvement is needed.

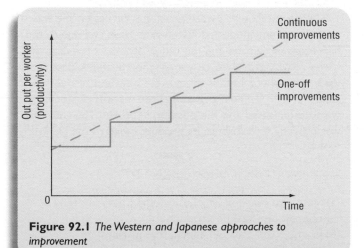

Figure 92.1 *The Western and Japanese approaches to improvement*

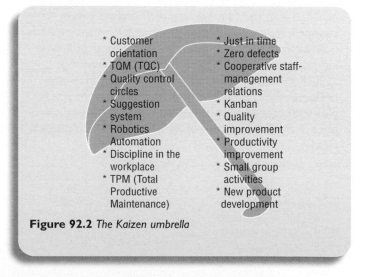

Figure 92.2 *The Kaizen umbrella*

Data must be gathered and used to develop a plan which will result in improvement.
- Do. Once the plan has been finalised it must be carried out. The plan is likely to be implemented by workers, on the production line perhaps.
- Check. The next stage in the cycle is to check whether or not there has been an improvement. This task may be carried out by inspectors.
- Action. If the plan has been successful, it must be introduced in all parts of the business.

Just-in-time manufacturing

JUST-IN-TIME (JIT) manufacturing is an important part of lean production and the kaizen approach. It was developed in the Japanese shipbuilding industry in the 1950s and 1960s. The industry recognised that a great deal of money was tied up in stocks. Traditionally, one month's supply of steel was held by a shipyard. However, as the industry became more competitive, shipbuilders insisted that steel suppliers deliver orders 'just-in-time', ie a few hours or less before the steel was needed. This reduced the need for high levels of working capital and improved the financial performance of the business. JIT was extended to every stage of production. For example, raw materials were delivered JIT to be made into parts, parts were delivered JIT to be made into goods and goods were produced and delivered JIT to be sold.

JIT was introduced in other Japanese industries, such as the car industry, and then spread to other parts of the world, such as the USA and Europe. In the UK, Stoves the Liverpool cooker manufacturer, adopted JIT in the early 1990s. It aimed to 'produce instantaneously with perfect quality and minimum waste'. JCB also uses JIT in its Rochester plant. When JCB excavators are manufactured, every machine on the production line has already been sold. Supplies of components, such as engines from Perkins, and raw materials, such as steel plate, arrive on the day they are needed. JIT manufacturing requires high levels of organisational skills and reliable suppliers. Table 92.1 shows the advantages and disadvantages of JIT manufacturing.

Question

Julian Richer is a disciple of Kaizen. He heads the hi-fi retailing chain, Richer Sounds, which he set up with just one shop in 1979. In recent years he has earned a reputation for 'wacky' but very effective management ideas. Richer places great emphasis on establishing a rapport with every new member of staff. He invites new employees to his house for three days where they 'work hard and play hard'. They undergo an intensive training course, but also enjoy tennis, badminton, snooker, swimming, dance and films.

Every Richer store offers free coffee and mints to customers and has a mirror which says 'you are looking at the most important person in this shop'. If it is raining when a customer buys a new hi-fi system they are given a free umbrella. Customer's opinions are monitored and staff bonuses are linked to customer satisfaction.

Staff are encouraged to express their ideas. They are given £5 each once a month to visit the pub together and talk about new ideas. Staff with the best customer service records are given the use of four classic cars - Jaguars and Bentleys. There are also five holiday homes which they can book free of charge. Absenteeism is between 1 and 2 per cent less than the national average. If staff are caught stealing from the store they are dismissed instantly. He has a fanatical attention for detail, working from a cardboard worksheet that lists his tasks in minute handwriting.

Richer has a policy of slow growth, arising from past mistakes when he tried to over-reach himself. His policies, plus highly competitive pricing, have earned the business a place in the *Guinness Book of Records* as the world's busiest retailer.

Source: adapted from the Financial Times, 27.3.1997.

(a) Identify Kaizen business techniques or practices which Julian Richer adopts at Richer Sounds. In each case explain your answer.
(b) Explain the possible benefits to Richer Sounds of the Kaizen approach.

Question

Lesley and Nicky Clarke run a £20 million a year haircare products company and salon. They began in 1991 with an 'up-market' salon in Berkeley Square, London. The business grew rapidly after Lesley visited her local supermarket. She noticed that the range of shampoos on offer was feeble. She borrowed £60,000 from the NatWest bank under the government's small firms loan guarantee scheme and launched the 'Hairomatherapy' range of products. She took a 'small margin, high volume' approach to sales and secured a contract to supply Tesco. Nine months later she was selling to eight supermarket chains across the country and forecasts were being exceeded by 200 per cent.

Unfortunately, there were problems for Lesley. She was operating production on a just-in-time basis and due to the high levels of demand she ran out of stocks. This meant that Lesley had to 'grovel' to customers. Fortunately customers were sympathetic because they were new and accounts were not lost. Gradually, two or three months of stocks were accumulated and the position improved. The company was planning to distribute its product range to the US in future.

Source: adapted from the *Financial Times*, 27.5.1997.

(a) State two reasons why Lesley might have chosen to operate just-in-time production.
(b) Examine the possible effects that just-in-time production had on Lesley's business.

Table 92.1

Advantages

● It improves cash flow since money is not tied up in stocks.
● The system reduces waste, obsolete and damaged stock.
● More factory space is made available for productive use.
● The costs of stockholding are reduced significantly.
● Links with and the control of suppliers are improved.
● The supplier base is reduced significantly.
● More scope for integration within the factory's computer system.
● The motivation of workers is improved. They are given more responsibility and encouraged to work in teams.

Disadvantages

● A lot of faith is placed in the reliability and flexibility of suppliers.
● Increased ordering and administration costs.
● Advantages of bulk buying may be lost.
● Vulnerable to a break in supply and machinery breakdowns.
● Difficult to cope with sharp increases in demand.
● Possible loss of reputation if customers are let down by late deliveries.

The 'Kanban' system

KANBAN is a Japanese term which means signboards or cards. The Kanban system is a method used to control the transfer of materials between different stages of production. The kanban might be a solid plastic marker or coloured ping-pong ball. They might be used to:
● inform employees in the previous stage of production that a particular part must be taken from stocks and sent to a specific destination (conveyance kanbans);
● tell employees involved in a particular operation that they can begin production and add their output to stock (production kanbans);
● instruct external suppliers to send parts to a destination (vendor kanbans).

Kanbans are used to trigger the movement or production of resources. Used properly, they will be the only means of authorising movement. Kanbans are an important part of JIT manufacturing as they prevent the build up of stock or parts in a factory.

Time-based management

TIME-BASED MANAGEMENT involves reducing the amount of time businesses take carrying out certain tasks, such as launching new products or cutting lead times in production. Time-based management is a feature of lean production because it involves eliminating a type of waste, ie time. Time in business is a valuable resource. Productivity can

be improved if tasks are carried out more quickly. Time-based management has a number of effects on a business.

● Manufacturers focus on customer needs. Customers are given a wide range of products to choose from, ie different models with different specifications. For example, the Rover car plant in Oxford produces a number of different models, such as the MGF and the Rover 600 on the same production line. The same model car can be produced according to different specifications, such as different colours, engine sizes and trims. Manufacturers can achieve this by reducing the length of production runs. Shorter production runs will also allow a firm to cut customer lead times, so customers are not kept waiting.
● Manufacturers use other lean production methods, such as JIT and cellular manufacturing, and total quality management (☞ unit 95). These methods prevent delays on production lines, reduce stock levels and improve scheduling. This means employees are not waiting around for work to arrive.
● Machines must be versatile. They must be able to produce a variety of products and be adjusted to a range of settings. Settings must be changed quickly and easily to deal with shorter production runs.
● Manufacturers speed up the design process by carrying out a number of design tasks simultaneously. The traditional approach to design is to carry out one task after another. However, time can be saved if design tasks can be completed at the same time. Such an approach needs co-ordination and communication between each design team. This approach has been called **lean design.**

Mass producers (☞ unit 91) argue that economics of scale will only be achieved and costs cut if products are standardised and production runs are long. Producing a variety of different models will lead to shorter production runs and higher average costs. Time-based management challenges this view. It may be possible to produce smaller quantities, because costs can be reduced by time savings.

There may be certain advantages for a business using a time-based management system.
● Customers will benefit. A wider range of products will be available and there will be faster delivery times. This might result in higher sales levels for the firm.
● Lean design will result in shorter lead times. This means that resources will be used more effectively and product development will be faster. This will give the business a competitive edge in the market.
● Other lean production techniques will increase efficiency, the quality of products will be improved and waste will be minimised.
● The time spent on a range of production tasks is reduced. This helps to improve productivity and reduce unit costs. As a result manufacturers may offer their products at lower prices or enjoy higher profit margins.

However, it could be argued that some costs might rise as a result of using time-based management. The versatile machinery which this method requires may be more expensive. Staff may also need to be trained in a wider range of skills and tasks to cope with the flexibility in production. Shorter production runs may result in the loss of some economies of scale.

Empowerment

Empowerment (☞ unit 73) involves giving employees the power to make decisions in a business. The aim of empowerment is to give employees more control over their own work conditions. Workers in the past have tended to follow the instructions of managers. They were rarely required to think, make decisions, solve problems or work creatively. There was often conflict between management and workers, and little cooperation and team-spirit.

In recent years many businesses have learned that efficiency will improve if workers are given the opportunity to involve themselves in decision making. Workers will be better motivated and the business may gain from the creativity of its workers. Workers may also be more flexible and adaptable. For example, a worker may speak directly to a customer about changes in an order. For empowerment to be successful, managers must have faith in their workforce. They must also trust them and work in partnership without conflict.

Empowerment is not without difficulties. Some workers may not be able to make their own decisions and training may be required to teach them such skills. Managers may resent giving up authority. Some staff may even abuse their power to make decisions.

Teamworking

A growing number of businesses are introducing teamworking (☞ unit 84) in their organisations. This involves dividing the workforce into fairly small groups. Each team will focus on a particular area of production and team members will have the same common aims. Teamworking probably works best in businesses that do not have a hierarchical structure (☞ unit 70) and which have an organisational culture which supports group work. Effective teamworking requires co-operation between workers and management, training for staff and workers being given responsibility to make decisions.

Both the business and employees might benefit from teamwork. Workers should develop relationships with colleagues and a 'team spirit' which may improve motivation and productivity. Flexibility might improve. For example, team members might be more willing to cover for an absent colleague. Teams might plan their own work schedules, share out tasks, choose their methods of work and solve their own problems. This should lead to quicker decision making and the generation of more ideas. It is also suggested that communication and labour relations may improve as a result of teamworking. However, there may be conflict between team

Question 3

British Steel employs more than 40,000 workers in the UK. Of these, around 28,000 are blue collar workers and 15,000 are white collar workers. In March 1997 the company outlined plans to offer its blue collar, manual workers the same employment conditions as white collar staff. Under the proposals manual workers may not be required to 'clock-on', they would be paid monthly salaries instead of weekly wages, and would be given more holidays and better sick pay. The proposals were expected to cost British Steel £175 million over five years.

In return workers would be asked to adopt more flexible working practices. For example, they would be asked to abolish 'old-fashioned' job demarcation and adopt a teamworking approach. British Steel also said that jobs would be cut and this would include managers. Indeed, they planned to remove one tier of management.

British Steel argued that the introduction of new working practices, such as teamworking, and the significant cuts in the size of the workforce, were needed to improve efficiency and help compensate for the loss in revenues caused by the recent strength of the pound.

Source: adapted from the *Financial Times*, 22.3.1997.

(a) Explain the ways in which teamworking might help British Steel to improve efficiency.
(b) Why do you think the distinctions between white collar workers and blue collar workers are being removed by British Steel?
(c) Discuss why the 'removal of one tier of management' might be compatible with the establishment of teamworking.

members and managers may resent the responsibility delegated to teams. Teamwork also results to some extent in a loss of specialisation amongst workers, which is often found in flow or mass production techniques (☞ unit 91).

Question **4**

Amtico, the Coventry based manufacturer of vinyl floor coverings, were the winners of the Best Small Company award in 1996. Amtico excels at the production of base vinyls, many of which closely resemble natural materials like wood and marble. These are cleverly incorporated into complex designs to produce mosaic-effect floors, complete with borders and motifs. Because of the high quality of their designs and the flexibility which they offer to their customers, they are able to charge a 30 per cent price premium.

A large part of Amtico's success in gaining a competitive edge in the market has been the result of changes made in the factory. One of these changes involved a switch from flow production to cellular manufacturing. The production of one product called Arden was reorganised along classic JIT lines and the use of cells was employed. Instead of being produced in stages in a flow of materials - beginning in a separate stores area and then embracing manufacturing resources in both of their factories - all the materials and resources required to produce Arden were located in a single cell.

Cellular manufacturing was also used for another product called 'Stripwood'. Amtico called for the production flow to be consolidated into a single cell, rather than adopting the leisurely ramble through the manufacturing resources of separate factories that had previously been the case.

Source: adapted from *Management Today's Guide to Britain's Best Factories*, DTI, 1997.

(a) Describe the changes that have been made at Amtico as a result of cellular production.
(b) Examine the effects of cellular manufacturing on:
  (i) Amtico;
  (ii) Amtico's customers.

Table 92.2

The Arden Cell

	Before	After
Movement	4.5 miles	yards
Overdue orders	12 weeks	nil
Lead times	>2 weeks	1 day
Quality		Greatly improved
Work-in-progress	5,000 square yards	50 square yards

The Stripwood Cell

- Robotic handling eliminated
- 11 pallet handling operations eliminated.
- Lead time cut from 5 days to 30 minutes.
- Improved quality.
- Considerably fewer rejects.
- Work-in-progress virtually nil
- Materials movement distance cut from 2 miles to 100 yards.

Cellular manufacturing

Flow production (☞ unit 91) involves mass producing a standard product on a production line. The product undergoes a series of operations in sequence on a continuous basis until a finished product rolls off the 'end of the line'.

CELLULAR MANUFACTURING adopts a different approach and involves dividing the workplace into 'cells'. Each cell occupies an area on the factory floor and focuses on the production of a 'product family'. A 'product family' is a group of products which requires a sequence of similar operations. For example, the metal body part of a machine might require the operations cut, punch, fold, spot weld, dispatch. This could all be carried out in one cell. Inside a cell, machines are grouped together and a team of workers sees the production of a good from start to finish.

Take the example of a furniture manufacturer making parts for a kitchen range in a cell. The raw material, such as wood, would be brought into the cell. Tasks such as turning on a lathe or shaping by routing would be carried out at workstations. The part would then be assembled and passed on to stock. The cell may also be responsible for tasks such as designing, schedule planning, maintenance and problem solving, as well as the manufacturing tasks which are shared by the team.

The advantages of cellular manufacturing include:
- floor space is released because cells use less space than a linear production line;
- product flexibility is improved;
- lead times are cut;
- movement of resources and handling time is reduced;
- there is less work-in-progress;
- teamworking is encouraged;
- there may be a safer working environment and more efficient maintenance.

Key terms

Cellular manufacturing - involves producing a 'family of products' in a small self-contained unit (a cell) within a factory.

Just-in-time manufacturing - a production technique which is highly responsive to customer orders and uses very little stock holding.

Kanban - a card which acts as a signal to move or provide resources in a factory.

Kaizen - a Japanese term which means continuous improvement.

Lean production - an approach to operations management aimed at reducing the quantity of resources used up in production.

Time-based-management - involves setting strict time limits in which tasks must be completed.

Summary

1. What are the aims of lean production?
2. What is meant by the Kaizen umbrella?
3. Explain the purpose of the PDCA cycle.
4. Describe 4 advantages of JIT manufacturing.
5. What is the purpose of the Kanban system?

6. Describe the 3 principles of time-based manufacturing.
7. What are the advantages of time-based manufacturing?
8. Give 2 advantages and 2 disadvantages of empowerment.
9. Why is teamworking a growing trend in businesses?
10. Describe how cellular manufacturing works.

Case study

Dek Printing Machines

On the outside there is nothing to suggest anything special about a blue box-shaped factory on an industrial estate in Weymouth. But once entering the premises of Dek Printing Machines it is evident that it is far from a regular manufacturing plant. A notice at reception asks visitors not to be offended by the casual dress. None of the managers has an office or a secretary. It is unusual to hear anyone refer to a job title. DEK's mission statement states that it wants to be the best, to delight customers, and has commitment to total quality and training.

About 14 years ago Dek changed its products to manufacture machines that apply solder paste to printed circuit boards used in computers and other electronic products. It also changed the way it operated. The company adopted lean production techniques. It took components from suppliers just-in-time. It also used Japanese-style kanbans, where requirement slips are posted with trays so that components can be supplied as and when they are needed. According to John Knowles, managing director, the new approach to production required trust and openness. There is very little supervision of individuals. He said: 'people are just encouraged to get on and do things. If it doesn't work, do something else and if it still doesn't work do something else, but for Christ's sake don't do nothing. We have principally moved from a climate where change was only made out of necessity to one where change happens routinely, daily, hourly, and where it is not seen as a threat'.

There is a recognition that 'just-in-time' places strains on suppliers. So annual and revised weekly forecasts of demand are sent out. Instead of buying single items from a series of suppliers, the company has two year agreements to buy supplies from approved suppliers and it pays them on a seven-day basis.

DEK has improved the flexibility of its operation, particularly in the assembly area. One machine takes 15 days to build from scratch, but the standard models are not customised for their specialist application until day 11. This means that lead times are reduced to just 4 days. Production specialists designed the assembly area so that workers rarely needed to leave their work place. All the

tools that they require are kept on mobile trolleys. Components such as screws, washers and fasteners are placed in compartmentalised trays. A card on the lid indicates the name, size and quantity of parts for each assembly operation. The boxes are filled by suppliers with the exact number of parts required. This provides a checking system because if there are any parts left at the end, the assembler knows that something has been missed.

Many of the workbenches have stickers on the side saying 'Zero the Hero'. If an employee completes a month's assembly work error free, a bronze 'Zero the Hero' sticker is awarded, silver for two months and a gold for three consecutive months. Workers also receive a £50 voucher. After this, if there are a further two error free months, a worker is entitled to a merit review. This review might then result in a £400 addition to annual base pay. This incentive scheme, which has now been extended to a team award, encourages staff to check each other's work and has also led to an improvement in productivity.

DEK's turnover has increased fivefold since the introduction of these practices and the workforce has risen from 200 to 650. In the same period competition in the market has intensified, much of it from Japan. The company planned to open another plant in the near future.

Source: adapted from the *Financial Times*, 17.3.1998.

(a) Using evidence from the article, describe how Dek has adopted: (i) empowerment; (ii) kaizen; (iii) teamworking.
(b) Describe two features of the kanban system at Dek.
(c) Explain the effects of 'just-in-time' production on: (i) Dek: (ii) its suppliers.
(d) Explain the possible benefits of Dek's incentive scheme for: (i) employers; (ii) employees.
(e) Examine two ways in which Dek reduced time wasted in production.
(f) Evaluate the success of the introduction of lean production at Dek.

Defining size

In the UK there are nearly four million businesses. Their sizes vary. A company like BP Amoco has operations around the world, employs thousands of people and has a turnover of billions of pounds. A self-employed joiner may operate in a small workshop, employ one other person and have sales of just a few thousand pounds. Most businesses begin on a small scale and then grow. However, in the UK firms employing less than 20 staff make up 97 per cent of all businesses. What is the difference between a large firm and a small firm? When does a small firm become large? How might size be measured?

Turnover Sales revenue that a business earns could be used to measure size. For example, Zeneca, the pharmaceuticals group, might be classed as a large business. Its turnover in 1998 was £5,510 million.

The number of employees A business with thousands of employees may be considered large. Unilever, for example, employed over 300,000 people a year on average in all its activities in the late 1990s. The Department of Trade and Industry (DTI) uses the term Small, Medium-sized Enterprises (SMEs) when talking about relatively small firms. The following criteria are used by the DTI to measure firm size:
- micro firm: 0-9 employees;
- small firm: 0-49 employees (includes micro);
- medium firm: 50-249 employees;
- large firm: over 250 employees.

The amount of capital employed This measure is based on the amount of money invested in the business. The more money invested the larger the business. For example, in 1998 Northern Foods had capital employed of £883 million. Pizza Express, in comparison, had capital employed of only £82 million.

Profit Businesses which have higher profits than others may be classed as larger businesses. For example, in 1998 Thames Water made a pre-tax profit of £419 million. Capital Radio on the other hand made a pre-tax profit of £26 million.

Table 93.1 *The largest 5 UK firms (market capitalisation), 1999*

Company	Market capitalisation (£bn)	Industry
1 BP Amoco	£94.711	Oil (integrated)
2 Glaxo Wellcome	£70.530	Pharmaceuticals
3 British Telecom	£70.103	Telecommunications
4 Lloyds TSB	£53.860	Banking
5 HSBC	£51.571	Banking

Source: adapted from *The Sunday Times*, 14.3.1999.

Question 1

JJB Sports plc is one of the leading independent sports retailers in the UK. The company operates more than 160 stores supplying sport products such as footwear, replica kits, clothing, equipment and accessories. Its key corporate aims are:
- to further strengthen and expand the business by a controlled increase in the number of stores and to continue the emphasis on developing a chain of superstores;
- to continue to provide excellent service and value for money to customers by supplying the highest quality branded products at the most competitive prices covering a wide range of sports;
- to generate real growth in earnings and dividends per share at a higher rate than the retail sector, which is in the long term interest of shareholders and employees.

Figure 93.1 *JJB Sports turnover, profit and number of stores, 1993-1997*

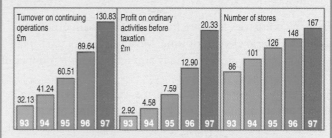

Turnover on continuing operations £m					Profit on ordinary activities before taxation £m					Number of stores				
32.13	41.24	60.51	89.64	130.83	2.92	4.58	7.59	12.90	20.33	86	101	126	148	167
93	94	95	96	97	93	94	95	96	97	93	94	95	96	97

Source: adapted from JJB Sports, *Annual Report and Accounts*, 1997.

(a) What evidence is there to suggest that: (i) JJB has a growth objective; (ii) JJB is achieving its objective?
(b) Why might JJB be said to be a large company?
(c) Calculate the percentage increase in turnover between 1993 and 1997. Comment on the size of this increase.

Market share It could be argued that a business with a 43 per cent market share (☞ unit 39), is larger than one which has a 9 per cent market share in the same industry. Coca-Cola, for example sells over 50 per cent of all cola drinks worldwide.

Market capitalisation This is the current share price multiplied by the number of shares. Table 93.1 shows the largest 5 companies in the UK according to this measure.

According to the **Companies Act, 1985**, a firm is considered to be:
- 'small' if it has a turnover of not more than £2.8 million, a balance sheet total of not more than £1.4 million (ie capital

employed) and not more than 50 employees;
● medium-sized if it has a turnover of not more than £11.2 million, a balance sheet total of not more than £5.6 million and not more than 250 employees;
● large if it exceeds the criteria above.

Problems with measuring size

In practice, measuring the size of a business may not be easy. A highly automated chemical plant may only employ 45 people, but have a turnover of £15 million. According to the number of employees, the DTI and the Companies Act would class it as a small business. However, according to the level of turnover it could be classed as a large business.

Using the level of profit may also be misleading. A large company may have problems and make only a small profit over a period of time and yet still stay in business. One of the problems of using market capitalisation is that share prices change constantly. This means company size is fluctuating all the time. It is the size of the business relative to its particular sector in an industry that is important. Is it large enough to enjoy the benefits of size in the market? Is it too large or too small in relation to other organisational needs of the business?

Reasons for growth

In many industries it is rare for a firm to remain exactly the same size for any length of time. Most businesses start small and then grow in size. They may aim to grow for a number of reasons.
● Survival. In some industries firms will not survive if they remain small. Staying small might mean that costs are too high because the firm is too small to exploit economies of scale. In addition, small firms, even if they are profitable,

may face a takeover bid from a larger firm.
● Gaining economies of scale. As firms grow in size they will begin to enjoy the benefits of ECONOMIES OF SCALE. This means that unit production costs will fall and efficiency and profits will improve. This is dealt with later in the unit.
● To increase future profitability. By growing and selling larger volumes, a firm will hope to raise profits in the future.
● Gaining market share. This can have a number of benefits. If a firm can develop a degree of monopoly power (☞ unit 18) through growth, it might be able to raise price or control part of the market. Some personnel also enjoy the status and power associated with a high market share. For example, it could be argued that Richard Branson enjoys the publicity which goes with leading a large company like Virgin.
● To reduce risk. Risk can be reduced through diversification. Branching into new markets and new products means that if one project fails success in others can keep the company going. For example, tobacco companies have diversified into breweries to guard against a fall in demand for cigarettes.

Methods of growth

There is a number of ways in which a company might grow. **Internal growth** is when a firm expands without involving other businesses. ORGANIC GROWTH means that the firm expands by selling more of its existing products. This could be achieved by selling to a wider market, either at home or abroad. It is likely that internal growth will take a long time for many businesses, but will provide a sound base for development. A quicker alternative is **external growth.** This can be by ACQUISITION or TAKEOVER of other businesses or by MERGING with them. A takeover is when one company buys control of another. A merger usually means that two companies have agreed to join together and create a new third company. In practice these terms are often used interchangeably. In recent decades merger activity has increased greatly leading to a concentration of ownership in many industries. Mergers and takeovers are discussed in unit 101.

It has also been suggested that in the 1980s and 1990s companies attempted to grow in one of three ways. Companies such as Polly Peck and Ratners grew rapidly by **acquisitions.** However, some companies growing in this way collapsed, perhaps by becoming bigger rather than better. Some companies grew by **innovating** and providing new products. Examples may be Microsoft and Intel. A problem for such companies is that rivals start to copy their ideas, which may slow growth. Companies that grew by **robust growth** included Coca Cola and Proctor & Gamble. They had long term growth as an objective, took consumers' needs into account, were prepared to invest in information technology and valued the skills of their workforce.

Question

Bristol Boat Builders currently builds 30 small cruisers per annum. The accountants have investigated the effect on long run costs of locating its production in bigger boat yards. The results are shown in Table 93.2.

Table 93.2 *Long run average costs for Bristol Boat Builders*

Output (cruisers)	10	20	30	40	50	60	70	80
Long run average cost (£000)		40	30	20	15	10	15	25	45

(a) Plot the long run average cost curve for Bristol Boat Builders on graph paper.
(b) How many cruisers should be built by the company? Give reasons for your answer.
(c) Over what range of output can the firm exploit economies of scale?

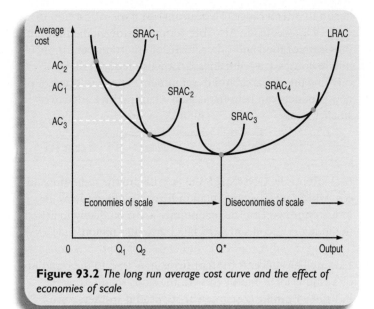

Figure 93.2 *The long run average cost curve and the effect of economies of scale*

Benefits of growth

Earlier in this unit it was argued that firms grow to achieve economies of scale. Economies of scale are the reductions in costs gained by businesses as they increase in size. Unit 52 showed that, in the long run, a firm can build another factory or purchase more machinery. This can cause the average cost of production to fall. In Figure 93.2 a firm is currently producing in a small plant and its short run costs are $SRAC_1$. When it produces an output equal to Q_1 its average cost will be AC_1. If it raises production to Q_2 average costs rise to AC_2. The rise in average costs is a result of **diminishing returns** (☞ unit 65).

If the firm expands the scale of its operations (which it can do in the long run) the same level of output can be produced more efficiently. With a bigger plant, represented by $SRAC_2$, Q_2 can be produced at an average cost of just AC_3. Long run average costs fall due to economies of scale and will continue to do so until the firm has built a plant which minimises long run average costs. In the diagram this occurs when a plant shown by $SRAC_3$ is built. This is sometimes called the MINIMUM EFFICIENT SCALE of plant. When output reaches Q^* in this plant, long run average costs cannot be reduced any further through expansion. Indeed, if the firm continues to grow it will experience rising average costs due to DISECONOMIES OF SCALE, as in $SRAC_4$ in Figure 93.2. This is dealt with later in the unit.

Internal economies of scale

What are the different economies of scale a firm can gain? INTERNAL ECONOMIES OF SCALE are the benefits of growth that arise within the firm. They occur for a number of reasons.

Technical economies Technical economies arise because

larger plants are often more efficient. The capital costs and the running costs of plants do not rise in proportion to their size. For example, the capital cost of a double decker bus will not be twice that of a single decker bus. This is because the main cost (engine and chassis) does not double when the capacity of the bus doubles. Increased size may mean a doubling of output but not cost. The average cost will therefore fall. This is sometimes called the principle of **increased dimensions.** In addition, the cost of the crew and fuel will not increase in proportion to its size.

Another technical economy is that of **indivisibility.** Many firms need a particular item of equipment or machinery, but fail to make full use of it. A small business may pay £400 for a word processor. The cost will be the same whether it is used twice a week by a part time clerical worker or every day. As the business expands, more use will be made of it and so the **average cost** of the machine will fall.

As the scale of operations expands the firm may switch to mass production techniques. Flow production (☞ unit 91), which involves breaking down the production process into a very large number of small operations, allows greater use of highly specialised machinery. This results in large improvements in efficiency as labour is replaced by capital.

Firms often employ a variety of machines which have different capacities. A slow machine may increase production time. As the firm expands and produces more output, it can employ more of the slower machines in order to match the capacity of the faster machines. This is called the **law of multiples.** It involves firms finding a balanced team of machines so that when they operate together they are all running at full capacity.

Managerial economies As the firm grows it can afford to employ specialist managers. In a small business one general manager may be responsible for finance, marketing, production and personnel. The manager may find her role demanding. If a business employs specialists in these fields, efficiency may improve and average costs fall. If specialists were employed in a small firm they would be an indivisibility.

Financial economies Large firms have advantages when they try to raise finance. They will have a wider variety of sources from which to choose. For example, sole traders cannot sell more shares to raise extra funds but large public limited companies can. Very large firms will often find it easier to persuade institutions to lend them money since they will have large assets to offer as security. Finally, large firms borrowing very large amounts of money can often gain better interest rates.

In the past the government has recognised the problems facing small firms. A number of schemes have been designed to help small firms raise funds (☞ unit 2).

Purchasing and marketing economies Large firms are likely to get better rates when buying raw materials and components in bulk. In addition, the administration costs involved do not rise in proportion to the size of the order. The cost of processing an order for 10,000 tonnes of coal does not treble when 30,000 tonnes are ordered.

A number of marketing economies exist. A large company may find it cost effective to acquire its own fleet of vans and lorries, for example. The cost to the sales force of selling 30 product lines is not double that of selling 15 lines. Again, the administration costs of selling do not rise in proportion to the size of the sale.

Risk bearing economies As a firm grows it may well diversify to reduce risk. For example, many sixth form colleges have

Question 3

In the late 1990s American Express, the credit card and travel company, was negotiating a deal with Virgin Atlantic and Continental Airlines aimed at lowering airfares. American Express planned to bulk-buy seats on transatlantic routes from the airlines and then sell them on to customers. This was the first time a travel agent had acted as a wholesaler. At wholesale prices, tickets were up to 30 per cent cheaper. In the past travel agents had been reluctant to bulk-buy in case they were left with expiring tickets.

In 1997 the boards of Yorkshire-Tyne-Tees (YTT) and Granada confirmed that they had joined in talks to discuss a merger. This would bring together two powerful programme makers. YTT had recently produced three top drama series in A Touch of Frost, Heartbeat and the Catherine Cookson specials. Granada, including LWT, produced 40 per cent of ITV's original drama, including Cracker and Prime Suspect. The attraction of the merger was mainly in economies of scale. The two companies already shared a sales operation. However, merging would allow them to sell advertising airtime in the North as a single region.

Source: adapted from *The Guardian*, 10.6.97 and *The Times*, 1998.

(a) Describe the marketing economies the TV companies might enjoy.
(b) Suggest some possible technical economies which the two TV companies might enjoy if they merged.
(c) Using the example in the case, explain why bulk-buying airline seats is an economy of scale.
(d) Why might Virgin Atlantic and Continental Airlines be prepared to sell tickets to American Express for a 30 per cent discount?

begun to offer a range of vocational courses in addition to their 'A' level courses. Also, breweries have diversified into the provision of food and other forms of entertainment in their public houses. Large businesses can also reduce risk by carrying out research and development. The development of new products can help firms gain a competitive edge over smaller rivals.

External economies of scale

EXTERNAL ECONOMIES OF SCALE are the reductions in cost which any business in an industry might enjoy as the industry grows. External economies are more likely to arise if the industry is concentrated in a particular region.

Labour The concentration of firms may lead to the build up of a labour force equipped with the skills required by the industry. Training costs may be reduced if workers have gained skills at another firm in the same industry. Local schools and colleges, or even local government, may offer training courses which are aimed at the needs of the local industry.

Ancillary and commercial services An established industry, particularly if it is growing, tends to attract smaller firms trying to serve its needs. A wide range of commercial and support services can be offered. Specialist banking, insurance, marketing, waste disposal, maintenance, cleaning, components and distribution services are just some examples.

Co-operation Firms in the same industry are more likely to cooperate if they are concentrated in the same region. They might join forces to fund a research and development centre for the industry. An industry journal might be published, so that information can be shared.

Disintegration Disintegration occurs when production is broken up so that more specialisation can take place. When an industry is concentrated in an area firms might specialise in the production of one component and then transport it to a main assembly car plant. In the West Midlands a few large car assembly plants exist whilst there are many supporting firms, such as Lucas, manufacturing components ready for assembly.

The limits to growth

There is a number of factors which might limit the growth of business. If a firm expands the scale of its operations beyond the minimum efficient scale DISECONOMIES OF SCALE may result, leading to rising long run average costs.

Most **internal diseconomies** are caused by the problem of managing large businesses. Communication becomes more complicated and co-ordination more difficult because a large firm is divided into departments. The control of large businesses is also demanding. Thousands of employees, billions of pounds and dozens of plants all mean added responsibility and more supervision. Morale may suffer as individual workers become a minor part of the total workforce. This can cause poor relations between management and the workforce. As shown in Figure 93.2, long run average costs start to rise once a business reaches a certain size. Technical diseconomies also arise. In the chemical industry, construction problems often mean that two smaller plants are more cost effective than one very large one. Also, if a firm employs one huge plant and a breakdown occurs, production will stop. With two smaller plants, production can continue even if one breaks down.

External diseconomies might also arise. These may occur from overcrowding in industrial areas. The price of land, labour, services and materials might rise as firms compete for a limited amount. Congestion might lead to inefficiency, as travelling workers and deliveries are delayed.

There are other constraints on the growth of firms.

● Market limitations. The market for high performance power boats is limited due to their high market price, for example. Also, unless a firm is a monopoly, growth will tend to be restricted due to the existence of competitors in the market.

● Lack of funds. Many small firms would like to grow, but are not able to attract enough investors or lenders.

● Geographical limitations. Some products are low value and bulky. High transport costs may discourage the firm from distributing to customers far away. This means it cannot grow. Bread, beer and crisps may fall into this category. However, with improved communication networks, national distributors of these products have entered the market. Also, the provision of services is often limited to local markets. For example, people are not likely to travel very far to have their hair cut.

Reasons for the survival of small firms

Despite the advantages of large scale production, many firms choose to remain small. Also, small firms sometimes have advantages over larger ones.

Personal service As a firm expands it becomes increasingly difficult to deal with individuals. Many people prefer to do business with the owner of the company directly and are prepared to pay higher prices for the privilege. For example, people may prefer to deal directly with one of the partners in an accountancy practice.

Owner's preference Some entrepreneurs may be content with the current level of profits. Some will want to avoid the added responsibilities that growth brings. Others will want to remain below the VAT threshold or will not want to risk losing control of their business.

Flexibility and efficiency Small firms are more often flexible and innovative. They may be able to react more quickly to changes in market conditions or technology. Management can make decisions quickly, without following lengthy procedures.

Lower costs In some cases small firms might have lower costs than larger producers in the same market. For example, large firms often have to pay their employees nationally agreed wage rates. A small firm may be able to pay lower wages to non-union workers.

Low barriers to entry In some types of business activity like grocery, painting and decorating, gardening services and window cleaning, the set up costs are relatively low. There is little to stop competitors setting up in business.

Small firms can be monopolists Many small firms survive because they supply a service to members of the local community which no other business does. People often use their local shop because it provides a convenient, nearby service, saving them the trouble of travelling.

The popularity of small firms in the economy

During the 1980s and 1990s there was a growth in the number of small businesses in the UK. Self employment also grew, from less than 2 million in 1979 to over 3 million in 1998. What factors have led to these trends?

● Rising unemployment has had an important impact. People with redundancy payments have had the capital to set up in business. In some cases unemployed workers saw self-employment as the only means of support.

● The government and local authorities introduced a number of measures to encourage the development of small businesses. **Business start-up schemes** (☞ unit 2) provided funds for small businesses for an initial period. Tecs and Business Links provided advice on running businesses and obtaining finance. European initiatives have included loans from the European Investment Fund and finance for training from the European Social Fund.

● There have been changes in the structure of the economy The expansion of the tertiary sector has contributed to the growth in small businesses. Many services can be undertaken more effectively on a small scale.

The growth in the number of small firms has had several effects on the economy.

● Increased flexibility. Smaller firms can adapt to change more quickly because the owners, who tend to be the key decision makers, are close at hand to react to change. For example, a customer may insist that the extension to her house is finished one week before the agreed time. The business owner can put in the extra hours required and perhaps encourage employees to help out. Business owners

Question 4

Figure 93.3 *Share of employment in SMEs in the UK 1980-96 by industry*

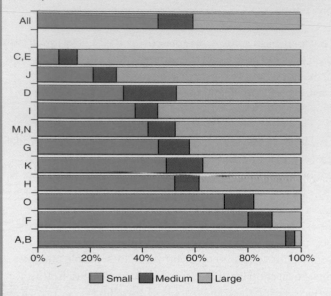

A,B: Agriculture, forestry & fishing
C: Mining/quarrying
D: Manufacturing
E: Electricity, gas, water supply
F: Construction
G: Wholesale, retail & repairs
H: Hotels & restaurants
I: Transport, storage and communication
J: Financial intermediation
K: Real estate, renting & business activities
M: Education
N: Health/Social work
O: Other community, social/personal

Source: adapted from the DTI, *Statistical Press Release*, 17.7.1997.

(a) Identify the industries with the: (i) largest ; and
  (ii) smallest proportion of SMEs.
(b) Suggest reasons to explain why there are so many or so few SMEs in these industries.

may also react quickly when some new technology becomes available. This increased flexibility might help the UK economy win more orders from abroad.

● It could be argued that wage levels might fall as a result of more smaller firms. Employees in small businesses often negotiate their own wage rates with the owner. Since they are not in a powerful position on a one to one basis, there may be a tendency for initial wage rates and future wage increases to be relatively lower. This will help to keep business costs down.

● More casual and part time work may have been created. Small firms are often reluctant to employ full time staff because it is more expensive. For example, part time workers may not be entitled to the same level of holiday pay as full time workers. Casual and part time staff also help to improve flexibility. When a business is quiet it can lay off casual staff to reduce costs.

● Staff loyalty may have been improved. In small businesses, relationships between the owners and other staff may be quite good because they are dealing with each other at a personal level. This might improve motivation and productivity as well as staff loyalty.

● Trade union membership may have declined. In small businesses where relatively fewer workers are employed, trade union membership tends to be lower. This might have implications for the rights of workers in small businesses. It might lead to claims that in some cases, staff are being exploited by small business owners.

● Consumers might benefit from the growth in the number

of small firms. More small firms often results in more competition and a wider choice in the market. For example, there has been a growth in the number of computer software producers in recent years. This has led to a variety of 'games' and programs for business and personal use.

Summary

1. How can the size of a firm be measured?
2. State 5 reasons for growth.
3. What is the difference between internal and external growth?
4. Buying firms to grow quickly can sometimes be a problem. Explain this statement.
5. What are the main sources of: (a) internal economies; (b) external economies; (c) diseconomies; of scale?
6. Explain 5 reasons why small firms survive.
7. Describe 5 limitations to growth.
8. Why has there been a growth in the number of small firms in recent years?
9. What effect will the growth in the small firms sector have on the flexibility of employers?

Key terms

Diseconomies of scale - rising long run average costs as a firm expands beyond its minimum efficient scale.

Economies of scale - the reductions in cost gained by firms as they grow.

External economies of scale - the cost reductions available to all firms as the industry grows.

Internal economies of scale - the cost reductions enjoyed by a single firm as it grows.

Merger - the joining together of two businesses, usually to create a third new company.

Minimum efficient scale (MES) - the output which minimises long run average costs.

Organic growth - growth achieved through the expansion of current business activities.

Takeover/acquisition - the purchase of one business by another.

Case study

Size in the DIY sector

It has been argued that size is important in the DIY market. During the 1980s the sector was troubled by a bitter price war. However, since then the competitive environment had been stable and good returns had been enjoyed by the companies dominating the market. However, in October 1998 Kingfisher, the owner of market leader B&Q, made an announcement. It said that it would invest £750 million in B&Q Warehouse, a subsidiary of B&Q, by increasing the number of stores from 30 to 125 by 2003. To appreciate the scale of the planned expansion by B&Q, imagine a shop the size of Wembley Stadium on the outskirts of every medium-sized town in the UK. Kingfisher's plans included creating another 20,000 jobs.

According to city analysts the expansion plans made a lot of sense. The company had bought 50 per cent of Castorama, the French building products group. Purely on economies of scale advantages, a joint B&Q and Castorama could generate enough buying economies to cut prices without the need to reduce margins. 'Warehouse is an incredibly powerful format which will crush everything else in its path', said one analyst. Richard Perks, of retail consultancy Verdict Research, said larger stores are more efficient and a company of Kingfisher's size can afford to take a long term view of its investment. Even some of B&Q's close rivals admitted that it made sense.

However, not everyone agreed that the plans were appropriate. Bill Archer, chairman of Do-It-All, which had 212 stores in the UK, believed that plans to open 125 B&Q Warehouse stores were over-ambitious. He suggested that planning laws were very restrictive and the UK market just wouldn't stand it. He also said that for every Warehouse store that opened, B&Q cannibalised two of its existing stores. He saw B&Q's plans as part of a consolidation process that would reduce the number of players in the DIY market to just three.

B&Q's new Warehouse format, which was launched in 1994, was formidable. Its size was its key. Existing out-of-town stores were about 40,000 sq ft in size. A Warehouse could be between 100,000 to 150,000 sq ft. B&Q's original plan was for 70 of these stores. But their success prompted the plan to be expanded. According to Kingfisher's chairman, Sir Geoff Mulcahy, doubling the planned rate of opening would ensure that B&Q maintained its record of growth and was able to consistently out-perform its competitors.

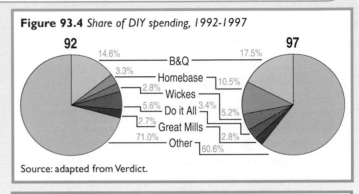

Figure 93.4 *Share of DIY spending, 1992-1997*

	92	97
B&Q	14.6%	17.5%
Homebase	3.3%	10.5%
Wickes	2.8%	3.4%
Do it All	5.6%	5.2%
Great Mills	2.7%	2.8%
Other	71.0%	60.6%

Source: adapted from Verdict.

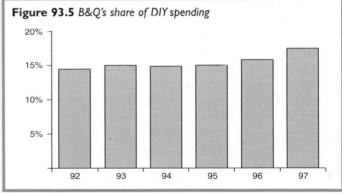

Figure 93.5 *B&Q's share of DIY spending*

Source: adapted from *The Independent*, 28.10.1998.

(a) **What are the motives for B&Q's growth plans?**

(b) **Describe some of the possible barriers to the growth planned by B&Q.**

(c) **Explain why B&Q's growth plans are likely to be organic.**

(d) **Explain the sentence in the article: '... can generate enough buying economies to cut prices without the need to reduce margins ...'.**

(e) (i) **Describe the trends taking place in the DIY market.**

(ii) **Account for the position of small firms in the market.**

(f) **Examine how some of B&Q's rivals might react to its growth plans.**

(g) **Discuss the scope there is for growth in the market for the big companies.**

Managing materials

Businesses purchase raw materials, semi-finished goods and components (☞ unit 90). A washing machine manufacturer, for example, may buy electric motors, circuit boards, rubber drive belts, nuts, bolts, sheet metal and a variety of metal and plastic components. These stocks of materials and components are used to produce products which are then sold to consumers and other businesses. Managing the materials is an important part of any business. Materials management involves:

- the purchasing of stocks and their delivery;
- the storing and control of stocks;
- the issue and handling of stocks;
- the disposal of surpluses;
- providing information about stocks.

Purchasing

Purchasing involves the buying of materials, components, fuel, tools, machinery, equipment, stationery and services by the business. It also includes any method that allows the firm to obtain the goods and services it needs, such as hiring.

The various stages in the purchasing process are shown in Figure 94.1. Purchasing usually begins when the purchasing department is notified of a particular need. For example, a firm's stores or a particular department may send a **requisition form** asking for more stationery. The purchasing department will then act on this. Most purchases are repeat purchases from regular suppliers. Orders are placed with the supplier at previously agreed prices and delivery accepted under previously arranged terms. New products may need different materials and new suppliers. This will involve a period of search and negotiation, as the buyer tries to find the best deal. If there is a delay in delivery, it is the purchasing department's responsibility to find out why and speed up delivery. Once the goods have arrived the invoice is checked and then payment can be made.

In manufacturing the purchasing department works closely with the production and finance departments. Most purchasing is carried out on behalf of the production department. The finance department needs information about purchases to make payments and record the transactions.

Figure 94.1 *Stages in the purchasing process*

REQUISITION → NEGOTIATION → PLACE ORDER → CHASE DELIVERY → CLEAR INVOICE

The importance of purchasing

The importance of purchasing is likely to vary according to the nature and size of the business. In many service industries purchasing is not very important. This is because materials are only a small fraction of the total cost of the final product. For example, hairdressing involves very little purchasing, as production involves a skill and uses few materials. However, a large manufacturer requires a large amount of materials, components etc. and so the firm will employ a purchasing department made up of specialists. In order for the firm to remain competitive the department must obtain the best quality materials, at least cost, and the quickest delivery. Failure to do so may lead to increased cost. The objectives of the purchasing department are:

- to obtain the quality and quantity of goods and materials that the firm requires;
- to purchase goods and materials at the most competitive prices;
- to ensure speedy delivery;
- to arrange delivery at the appropriate site, gate or location;
- to choose reliable suppliers and maintain good relations with them.

Centralised and decentralised purchasing

In some businesses, **centralised purchasing** is used. This is

Question

The Croydon Furniture Centre manufactures a variety of household furniture and supplies small retailers in the South East. It has established a reputation for speedy delivery and favourable prices. The company is about to begin manufacturing a new line of sofas and requires some fabric for covering. The purchasing manager has identified three possible suppliers. Details of their terms are shown in Table 94.1.

Table 94.1 *Prices and terms of delivery from three fabric suppliers*

Supplier	Delivery time	Cost per metre	Delivery charge per 200 metres
Crawfords (Bradford)	2wks	£2.00	£100
Batemans (Oldham)	3wks	£1.80	£80
Jones (London)	3days	£2.10	£30

(a) Calculate the total cost of purchasing 200 metres per month, for one year, from each supplier.
(b) Using your answers in (a), which supplier would you choose if your aim was to minimise cost?
(c) How might your answer in (b) be different if you take into account non-financial factors?

where the purchasing for the whole business is carried out by one department. The advantage of this method is that **economies of scale** can be gained as large scale buyers enjoy lower rates and market power. Also, the same quality and standard of materials can be set throughout the business. The distribution and warehousing of supplies can also be better planned.

Decentralised purchasing may reduce the cost and burden of administration. Purchasing officers in each department may be more in touch with the needs of that department. In retailing, if purchasing is undertaken by each store manager, the needs of each store can be better catered for. The added responsibility might also motivate store managers.

Vendor rating

It is important for a business to evaluate suppliers. A poor supplier may delay production, which can be costly. The measurement of suppliers' performance is called VENDOR RATING. A business must choose **criteria** which could be used to measure the performance of a supplier.

A simple vendor rating system is shown in Table 94.2. The supplier is awarded a mark for performance based on five criteria. For example, the supplier has a good price record, scoring 18 out of a possible 20. Adding the scores gives a total vendor rating of 71/100. When deciding which supplier to chose from alternatives, a firm is likely to pick the one with the highest rating. If a business feels that some criteria are more important than others, it may give them more value using a weighting system (☞ unit 12). One problem with this system is how to judge a supplier's performance against

criteria. It may be possible to use records. But sometimes evaluation may simply be the subjective opinion of a manager.

Table 94.2 *A simple vendor rating system*

Criteria	Max. score	Actual score
Quality	20	17
Price	20	18
Delivery	20	10
Communication	20	12
Flexibility	20	14
Total	100	71

Make or buy?

Another decision which a business often faces is whether to make a component itself or buy it from a supplier. There are reasons for both making a product and buying it in, as shown in Table 94.3. In recent years businesses have tried to improve their flexibility. One method of doing this is to outsource production (☞ unit 102). This is where a business uses the services of another firm, to produce its components for example. A business that aims to outsource production will buy in components rather than make its own.

Table 94.3

Motives for making	*Motives for buying*
● Making is cheaper.	● Buying is cheaper.
● There are no suitable suppliers.	● To increase specialisation.
● Delivery times cannot be met by suppliers.	● Uneconomical to make small quantities.
● Quality standards cannot be met by suppliers.	● Lack of capacity.
● Spare capacity exists in the factory.	● Transfer risk to the vendor.
● To maintain secrecy.	● Avoid investment in specialist plant or labour.
● To ensure continuity of supply.	
● To retain labour during a slack period of trading.	

The nature of stocks

Businesses prefer to minimise stock holding because it is costly. In practice a variety of stocks are held, for different reasons.

● Raw materials and components. These are purchased from suppliers before production. They are stored by firms to cope with changes in production levels. Delays in production can be avoided if materials and components can be supplied from stores rather than waiting for a new delivery to arrive. Also, if a company is let down by suppliers it can use stocks to carry on production.

● Work-in-progress. These are partly finished goods. In a TV assembly plant, WORK IN PROGRESS would be TVs on the assembly line, which are only partly built.

● Finished goods. The main reason for keeping finished goods is to cope with changes in demand and stock. If there is a sudden rise in demand, a firm can meet urgent orders by supplying customers from stock holdings. This

Question 2

McPhersons Ltd is a chain of twenty butchers operating in Scotland and the North of England. Its head office is attached to the shop located in Leeds. All the purchasing is currently undertaken at head office and the meat is delivered in bulk to a warehouse in Leeds. The firm employs a driver to distribute orders to the various shops twice a week. The board of directors is considering the decentralisation of the purchasing function, since the discounts from bulk buying are not particularly significant. If decentralisation takes place each shop manager will receive a £2,000 p.a. salary increase. The discounts lost from bulk buying are expected to total £20,000 p.a. Cold storage, handling and distribution costs are expected to fall by £50,000 in total and administration costs will be £5,000 lower in total. It is expected that the quality of the meat will improve when purchasing is the responsibility of the shop managers.

(a) Advise the company whether or not decentralisation is a worthwhile change in operational policy, in purely financial terms.

(b) Explain the non-financial advantages and disadvantages to McPhersons of decentralising purchasing.

avoids the need to step up production rates quickly.

Stocks are listed as current assets (☞ unit 56) in the firm's balance sheet. Stocks are fairly liquid business resources and the firm would normally expect to convert them into cash within one year. They are also part of working capital (☞ unit 60).

Normally, at least once every year, a business will perform a **stock take**. This involves recording the amount and value of stocks which the firm is holding. The stock take is necessary to help determine the value of total purchases during the year for a firm's accounts. A physical stock take can be done manually by identifying every item of stock on the premises. Many firms have details of stock levels recorded on computer. **Stock valuation** is discussed in unit 63.

The cost of holding stocks

In recent years stock management has become more important for many firms. Careful control of stock levels can improve business performance. Having too much stock may mean that money is tied up unproductively, but inadequate stock can lead to delays in production and late deliveries. Efficient stock control involves finding the right balance. One of the reasons why control is so important is because the costs of holding stocks can be very high.

● There may be an **opportunity cost** (☞ unit 8) in holding stocks. Capital tied up in stocks earns no rewards. The money used to purchase stocks could have been put to other uses, such as new machinery. This might have earned the business money.

● Storage can also prove costly. Stocks of raw materials, components and finished goods occupy space in buildings. A firm may also have to pay heating, lighting and labour costs if, for example, a night watchman is employed to safeguard stores when the business is closed. Some products require very special storage conditions. Food items, may need expensive refrigerated storage facilities. A firm may have to insure against fire, theft and other damages.

● Spoilage costs. The quality of some stock may deteriorate over time, for example, perishable goods. In addition, if some finished goods are held too long they may become outdated and difficult to sell.

● Administrative and financial costs. These include the cost of placing and processing orders, handling costs and the costs of failing to anticipate price increases.

● Out-of-stock costs. These are the costs of lost revenue, when sales are lost because customers cannot be supplied from stocks. There may also be a loss of goodwill if customers are let down.

Stock levels

One of the most important tasks in stock control is to maintain the right level of stocks. This involves keeping stock levels as low as possible, so that the costs of holding stocks are minimised. At the same time stocks must not be allowed to

run out, so that production is halted and customers are let down. A number of factors influence stock levels.

● Demand. Sufficient stocks need to be kept to satisfy normal demand. Firms must also carry enough stock to cover growth in sales and unexpected demand. The term BUFFER STOCK is used to describe stock held for unforeseen rises in demand or breaks in supply.

● Some firms **stockpile** goods. For example, toy manufacturers build up stocks in the few months up to December ready for the Christmas period. Electricity generating stations build up stocks of coal in the summer. During the summer, demand for electricity is low so less coal is needed. At the same time, prices of coal during the summer months are lower, so savings can be made.

● The costs of stock holding. The costs of holding stock were described earlier. If stock is expensive to hold then only a small quantity will be held. Furniture retailers may keep low stock levels because the cost of stock is high and sales levels are uncertain.

● The amount of working capital available. A business that is short of working capital will not be able to purchase more stock, even if it is needed.

● The type of stock. Businesses can only hold small stocks of perishable products. The stock levels of cakes or bread will be very small. Almost the entire stock of finished goods will be sold in one day. The 'life' of stock, however, does not solely depend on its 'perishability'. Stocks can become out of date when they are replaced by new models, for example.

● LEAD TIME. This is the amount of time it takes for a stock purchase to be placed, received, inspected and made ready for use. The longer the lead time, the higher the minimum level of stock needed.

Question 3

Table 94.4 *Manufacturer lead times*

BMW	8 series	8-12 weeks	Factory order (FO) (Special build only)
Daewoo	Leganza	3-4 weeks	Availability good
Ford	Mondeo	FO 12 weeks	Availability good
Jeep	Cherokee Petrol 2.5 Sport	7-8 weeks	Factory order
Mazda	All models	4-6 weeks	General availability good
Renault	Megane	6-8 weeks	General availability good
Volvo	V40	6 weeks	Factory order
Volkswagen	New Golf Gti	16 weeks	Factory order

Source: adapted from *Solutions*, ARRIVA Automotive Solutions, February, 1999.

Table 94.4 shows some lead times for motor car manufacturers for delivery to retailers.

(a) Which products have: (i) relatively short lead times; (ii) relatively long lead times?

(b) Explain two possible reasons for different lead times in the car industry.

(c) Examine the effect that long lead times might have on car retailers.

● External factors. Fear of future shortages may prompt firms to hold higher levels of raw materials in stock as a precaution.

Stock control

It is necessary to control the flow of stocks in the business. This ensures that firms hold the right amount. Several methods of stock control exist. They focus on the RE-ORDER QUANTITY (how much stock is ordered when a new order is placed) and the RE-ORDER LEVEL (the level of stock when an order is placed).

● Economic order quantity (EOQ). It is possible to calculate the level of stocks which minimises costs. This is called the **economic order quantity** (☞ unit 103). It takes into account the costs of holding stock, which rises with the amount of stock held, and the average costs of ordering stock, which fall as the size of the order is increased. A business must calculate the EOQ to balance these costs.

● Fixed re-order interval. Orders of various sizes are placed at fixed time intervals. This method ignores the economic order quantity, but ensures that stocks are 'topped up' on a regular basis. This method may result in fluctuating stock levels.

● Fixed re-order level. This method involves setting a fixed order level, perhaps using the EOQ. The order is then repeated at varying time intervals.

● Two bin system. This simple method involves dividing stock into two bins. When one bin is empty a new order is placed. When the order arrives it is placed into the first bin and stocks are used from the second bin. When the second bin is empty stocks are re-ordered again.

A stock control system is shown in Figure 94.2. It is assumed that:

● 50,000 units are used every two months (25,000 each month);
● the maximum stock level, above which stocks never rise, is 70,000 units;
● the minimum stock level, below which stocks never fall, is 20,000 units, so there is a buffer against delays in delivery;
● stock is re-ordered when it reaches a level of 40,000 units (the re-order level);
● the re-order quantity is 50,000 units - the same quantity as is used up every two months;
● the lead time is just under one month. This is the time between the order being placed and the date it arrives in stock.

This is a hypothetical model which would be the ideal for a business. In practice deliveries are sometimes late, so there is a delay in stocks arriving. Firms may also need to use their buffer stocks in this case. It is likely that re-order quantities will need to be reviewed from time to time. Suppliers might offer discounts for ordering larger quantities. The quantities of stocks used in each time period are unlikely to be constant. This might be because production levels fluctuate according to demand.

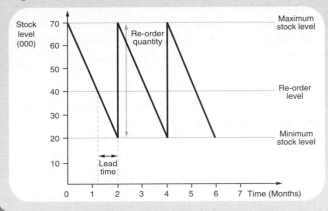
Figure 94.2 *Stock control*

Too much or too little stock

Why might having too much or too little stock be bad business practice?

Too much stock
● Storage, insurance, lighting and handling costs will all be high if too much stock is held.
● Large stock levels will occupy space in the premises. There may be more productive ways of using this space, such as improving the layout of the factory.
● The opportunity cost will be high. Money tied up in stocks could be used to buy fixed assets, for example.
● Large stock levels might result in unsold stock. If there is

Question 4

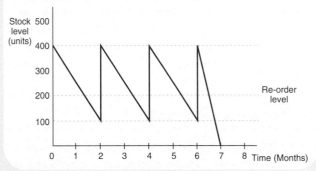

Figure 94.3 shows the usage of a component, 5000XTD, for Bromley Ltd, over a seven month period. Bromley Ltd assembles electric lawn mowers using five main components. It found a new and cheaper supplier for the 5000XTD just two months ago.

Figure 94.3 *Stocks of 5000XTDs at Bromley Ltd*

(a) Identify the: (i) lead time; (ii) minimum stock level; (iii) re-order level; (iv) re-order quantity for the 5000XTD.
(b) Explain the reason for the change in the stock level after the sixth month.
(c) What might be the consequences of this change for the business?

an unexpected change in demand, the firm may be left with stocks that it cannot sell.

● Very large stocks might result in an increase in theft by employees. They may feel the business would not miss a small amount of stock relative to the total stock.

Too little stock

● The business may not be able to cope with unexpected increases in demand if its stocks are too low. This might result in lost customers if they are let down too often.

● If deliveries are delayed the firm may run out of stock and have to halt production. This might lead to idle labour and machinery while the firm waits for delivery.

● The firm is less able to cope with unexpected shortages of materials. Again, this could result in lost production.

● A firm which holds very low stocks may have to place more orders. This will raise total ordering costs. Also, it may be unable to take advantage of discounts for bulk buying.

Computerised stock control

Stock control has been improved by the use of computers. Many businesses hold details of their entire stock on computer databases (☞ unit 9). All additions to and issues from stocks are recorded and up to date stock levels can be found instantly. Actual levels of stock should be the same as shown in the computer printout. A prudent firm will carry out regular **stock checks** to identify differences.

Some systems are programmed to automatically order stock when the re-order level is reached. In some supermarkets, computerised checkout systems record every item of stock purchased by customers and automatically subtract items from total stock levels. The packaging on each item contains a **bar code**. When this is passed over a laser at the checkout, the sale is recorded by the system. This allows a store manager to check stock levels, total stock values and the store's takings at any time of the day. Again, the system can indicate when the re-order level is reached for any particular item of stock.

Access to stock levels is useful when manufacturers are dealing with large orders. The firm might need to find out whether there are enough materials in stock to complete the order. If this information is available, then the firm can give a more accurate delivery date.

JIT and stock rotation

In recent years many businesses have changed their approach to stock management. To reduce costs, firms have held low levels of stocks. In some cases holdings of both finished goods and raw materials have been reduced to zero. This approach to stock control is the key feature of **just-in-time manufacturing** (JIT)(☞ unit 92).

Businesses often use systems to control the flow of stocks in and out of their store areas. This flow of stock is sometimes called STOCK ROTATION. One system used to rotate stock

Question 5

S & A Foods is one of Britain's largest producers of Indian, Chinese, Thai and Malaysian ready-made meals. It sends out 1 million chilled and frozen meals a week from its two factories in Derby. The meals are prepared to order daily and distributed to supermarkets, such as Morrison and Safeway. S & A automated many of its operations, including customer ordering. The supermarket customer places an order electronically, having been alerted by information from its electronic tills that stocks are low and an order is required. This order then passes through S & A's purchase ordering, production, testing and packaging systems. Five hours later, a lorry full of meals leaves the factory gate, its load heading for supermarket shelves.

At no point in the operation is a piece of paper generated and materials are kept to a minimum. This is crucial for supermarkets, which are driven by the need to promote sales by offering consumers ever more choice on limited shelf space. Perween Warsi, who founded the company 12 years ago, said: 'There is simply no way we could handle the volumes and complexity of business we are handling without automation. In producing quality meals for supermarkets consistency is of the essence'. However, while the automated system eliminates the possibility of human error, it increases the vulnerability of the business to systems failure.

Source: adapted from *The Sunday Times*, 18.10.1998.

(a) Using examples from the case, explain three advantages to supermarkets of their computerised stock-control.
(c) Examine the possible problems of electronic ordering systems for: (i) supermarkets; (ii) S & A Foods.

is called **First In First Out** (FIFO) (☞ unit 63). This means that those stocks which are delivered first are the first ones to be issued. This method is useful if stocks are perishable or if they are likely to become obsolete in the near future. A second method of stock rotation is called **Last-In-First-Out** (LIFO). This system involves issuing stock from the latest rather than the earliest deliveries. This method might be used if the stocks are difficult to handle and it is physically easier to issue the more recent deliveries. However, when using this method it is important that stocks are not perishable. 'Old' stock could remain in store for long periods before it is finally used.

Key terms

Buffer stocks - stocks held as a precaution to cope with unforeseen demand.
Lead time - the time between the order and the delivery of goods.
Re-order level - the level of stock when new orders are placed.
Re-order quantity - the amount of stock ordered when an order is placed.
Stock rotation - the flow of stock into and out of stores.
Vendor rating - a method of measuring and evaluating the performance of suppliers.
Work-in-progress - partly finished goods.

Summary

1. What are the activities involved in materials management?
2. What is meant by purchasing in business?
3. Describe the various stages in the purchasing process.
4. What are the objectives of the purchasing department?
5. What effect can poor purchasing have on a business?
6. What are the advantages of centralised purchasing?
7. What is meant by:
   (a) components;
   (b) finished goods?
8. What are the costs of holding stocks?
9. Why are buffer stocks held by firms?
10. Why do some firms stockpile?
11. Describe the advantages of computerised stock control.

Case study

Lukic Holdings

Lukic Holdings manufactures electric heaters which it sells in the European market. One component used in production is a motorised fan. This is currently bought from an Italian company, Amaratti. The fan is the most expensive component which the company has to buy, currently £28. Amaratti has supplied the component for nearly 10 years as a result of its competitive price. Use of the component, which is uniform because production is constant at Lukic Holdings, is shown in Figure 94.4. Unfortunately, although Amaratti provides a good quality product at a competitive price, its increasing inability to meet delivery times is becoming a problem. Amaratti has suffered from industrial relations difficulties and this has threatened supply. Initially, Lukic Holdings reacted to this by raising its minimum stock level of the component.

(a) Using Figure 94.4 state the:
   (i) re-order quantity in the first 6 months;
   (ii) minimum stock level in the first 6 months;
   (iii) lead time in the first 6 months;
   (iv) the number of fans used each year based on the re-order quantity in (a).

(b) **State two disadvantages to Lukic Holdings of having to raise the minimum stock level of the motorised fans.**

(c) **Explain what happened to stocks and deliveries of fans after the sixth month.**

The company decided that a new supplier should be found for the component. Two firms, Intact Ltd, a French supplier and Electro, a local company were both suitable. It was decided to give both a six month trial and review their performances, along with Amaratti's, before awarding a final contract. A simple vendor rating system was used to review performance. The results at the end of the trial are shown in Table 94.5.

(d) **According to the vendor rating system which company should be awarded the contract to supply the fans? Explain your answer.**

(e) **Discuss whether Lukic Holdings should make the fan itself.**

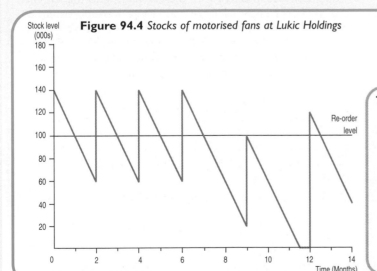

Figure 94.4 *Stocks of motorised fans at Lukic Holdings*

Stock level (000s) / Time (Months)

Re-order level

Table 94.5 *A vendor rating system for Lukic Holdings*

Criteria	Max. score	Actual score Intact	Electro	Amaratti
Price	25	17	18	20
Delivery	25	20	25	10
Quality	25	20	22	20
Flexibility	25	25	20	15

What is quality?

Consumers, faced with many goods or services at similar prices, are likely to consider QUALITY when making choices. Quality could be described as those features of a product or service that allow it to satisfy customers' wants. Take an example of a family buying a television. They may consider some of the following features:

● physical appearance - they may want a certain style;
● reliability and durability - will it last for 10 years?
● special features - does it have stereo sound?
● suitability - they may want a portable television;
● parts - are spare parts available?
● repairs - does the shop carry out maintenance?
● after sales service - how prompt is delivery?

They may also consider features which they perceive as important, such as:

● image - is the manufacturer's name widely recognised?
● reputation - what do other consumers think of the business or product?

The importance of quality has grown in recent years. Consumers are more aware. They get information through magazines such as *Which?* that contain reports on the quality of certain products. They also have more disposable income and higher expectations than ever before. Legislation and competition have also forced firms to improve the quality of their products.

Businesses, faced with competition, are also concerned about the quality of their:

● design - the ideas and plans for the product or service;
● production processes - the methods used to manufacture the goods or provide the services.

Poor designs may lead to problems with the materials and the functions of the finished good or service. It costs time and money to redesign poor products. Clients are unlikely to use businesses with poor designs again. Problems also occur with poor quality production processes. Faulty products are costly for a business. Machinery that breaks down or constantly needs to be repaired will also be expensive. Late delivery and productivity that results from poor quality in production can harm a business's reputation.

Quality in production

Traditionally, in manufacturing, production departments have been responsible for ensuring quality. Their objectives might have been to make sure that products:

● satisfy consumers' needs;
● work under conditions they will face;
● operate in the way they should;
● can be produced cost effectively;
● can be repaired easily;
● conform to safety standards set down by legislation and independent bodies.

At Kellogg's the cereal manufacturers, for example, samples of breakfast cereal were taken from the production line every half hour and tested. The testing took place in a food review room twice a day and was undertaken by a

Question

A car quality survey undertaken by consultants JD Power in 1996 placed Land Rover bottom out of 37 manufacturers. BMW, the owners of Land Rover, immediately drafted in extra engineers and quality controllers at the Solihull plant in Birmingham. Reports from dealers, owners and mechanics seem to support data in the survey. For example, one owner of the Discovery model said: 'This is the worst model I have

ever known. It started with a noisy gear box, then the front suspension was lopsided with the car veering to the left, then the windscreen kept falling out and there were persistent oil leaks.' In addition, the high profile Range Rover, which was gaining a reputation for unreliability, had to be recalled twice in its short life, once for problems with the air conditioning and once for rear suspension faults. One owner of a two year old Range Rover said: 'this was the third Range Rover I've had and stupid things keep going wrong constantly. The central locking plays up all the time, the front wheels seem to wobble when I go round bends, I don't think its even been in for a service without masses of warranty work. Worst of all, my 48,000 mile service cost £940. I had a jeep before this and it never went wrong.'

Source: adapted from *The Independent*, 20.8.1996.

(a) What: (i) actual; and (ii) perceived features might a consumer consider important when buying a Land Rover product?
(b) Explain how the faults described above affect Land Rover in: (i) the short term; (ii) the long term?

small group of staff. Each sample, about 50 in total, was compared with a 'perfect' Kellogg's sample and given a grade between 1 and 10. 10 was perfect but 9,8 and 7, although noticeable to the trained eye, was acceptable to the customer. Below 7 the consumer would notice the reduction in quality. The cereals were tested for appearance, texture, colour, taste etc. More sophisticated tests were carried out in a laboratory where the nutritional value of a sample, for example, was measured.

Quality control in UK organisations, in the past, often meant inspecting other people's work and the product itself after production had taken place. By today's standards this is not quality control, but a method of finding a poor quality product (or a problem) before it is sold to the consumer. Today businesses are less concerned about 'Has the job been done properly?' than 'Are we able to do the job properly?' In other words inspection is carried out during the production process. This means that problems and poor quality products can be prevented before final production. Such a preventative approach has been used by Japanese businesses and is known as TOTAL QUALITY MANAGEMENT (TQM). It is now being adopted by many companies in the UK.

Quality assurance

Businesses are increasingly taking into account the needs of customers. QUALITY ASSURANCE is a method of ensuring quality that takes into account customers' views. This can affect the business in a number of ways. For example, customers may be consulted about their views through marketing research (☞ unit 37) before a product is manufactured or a service provided. They may also be part of a consultation group involved at the design and manufacturing stage.

Businesses also work to quality assurance **codes of practice.** These tell a customer that a production process has been carried out to a certain standard and to the required specification. Once a business has been assessed and has achieved a certain standard, it is regularly checked by the awarding organisation to make sure standards are maintained. ISO 9000 is an international standard which businesses seek to achieve. This is discussed later in this unit.

Businesses also include signs and **symbols** on their products which tell a customer about the product's standards. Examples of such quality symbols include:

Question

Hydrapower Dynamics of Birmingham produces and services hydraulic hoses and fittings for use in agriculture, construction, shipping and aerospace. In the early 1990s a Total Quality Management programme was introduced. The company had already attained some industry standard awards, such as the BS 5750 and ISO 9002. It saw TQM as the next step to ensuring better performance and satisfied staff and customers. The company began by briefing all staff on the concepts of TQM and quality circles. It also involved the National Society for Quality Through Teamwork and the Birmingham Economic Development Unit. This combination of industrial and academic expertise made the quality programme proactive. Representatives from the two organisations provided tutoring for shopfloor workers and management in good quality management procedures. The training consisted of video material, problem solving and brainstorming sessions. All this helped to change the corporate culture of the company. As the TQM programme became clear, suggestions for improvements began to emerge from the shopfloor.

One problem which Hydrapower had was that most of the literature and video material was aimed at large multinationals. Hydrapower was a very small firm and became pioneers in implementing TQM on this scale. However, commitment to the programme came right from the top and the MD was involved in one-to-one sessions with all staff. Hydrapower were not able to use traditional quality circles because it only had 18 staff. Instead, it invented 'quality bubbles', with lots of small circles joined together. Meetings took place, but they tended to be out of working hours. The company formed 'action teams' who could draw on their experience for instant problem solving without having to consult other departments. This saved time. So did having a manager on each action team.

It meant that decisions could be made immediately. For example, one idea was to use a suggestion scheme with financial rewards. The idea was endorsed by a manager by the end of the meeting.

The benefits of introducing their TQM programme have been numerous.
● Managers are more aware of the need to involve staff in problem solving and decision making.
● Staff are more participatory and enthusiastic about their work.
● New benches were designed to make working easier.
● New safety test procedures have been introduced to test hoses.
● A new, more efficient telephone system has been installed.
● Quality Action Team research resulted in shorter lead times.
● Hydrapower's trade counter has improved customer service.
● BSI inspectors have reduced their visits by 50 per cent.

Source: adapted from *Quality Circles*, DTI.

(a) Describe two features of TQM which Hydrapower has adopted.
(b) Using examples from the article, suggest why TQM was successful at Hydrapower.
(c) Examine the possible problems of TQM, using examples at Hydrapower.
(d) Choose any three of the above benefits resulting from the implementation of TQM and explain how they might influence the performance of Hydrapower.

- safety goggles which are awarded the BSI kitemark, telling the customer that the product has been independently tested to a specific standard;
- inflatable arm bands which are awarded the CE mark, an EU award. This tells the customer that they have been tested not to deflate during use and carry a safety warning about supervision;
- the Lion Mark, awarded by the British Toy and Hobby Association (BTHA), which shows that manufacturers have a strict code of practice on toy safety, advertising and counterfeiting.

Some businesses support such guarantees with WARRANTIES. If goods are warranted, it means that the manufacturer will undertake any work necessary arising from a defect in the product, 'free of charge'. Warranties are popular with products such as cars and a wide range of electrical appliances.

Total quality management

Errors are costly for business. It is estimated that about one-third of all the effort of British business is wasted in correcting errors. There are benefits if something is done right the first time. Total quality management (TQM) is a method designed to prevent errors, such as poor quality products, from happening. The business is organised so that the manufacturing process is investigated at every stage. It is argued that the success of Japanese companies is based on their superior organisation. Every department, activity and individual is organised to take into account quality at all times. What are the features of TQM?

Quality chains Great stress is placed on the operation of QUALITY CHAINS. In any business a series of suppliers and customers exists. For example, a secretary is a supplier to a manager, who is the customer. The secretarial duties must be carried out to the satisfaction of the manager. The chain also includes customers and suppliers outside the business. The chain remains intact if the supplier satisfies the customer. It is broken if a person or item of equipment does not satisfy the needs of the customer. Failure to meet the requirements in any part of the quality chain creates problems, such as delays in the next stage of production.

Company policy and accountability There will only be improvements in quality if there is a company-wide quality policy. TQM must start from the top with the most senior executive and spread throughout the business to every employee. People must be totally committed and take a 'pride in the job'. This might be considered as an example of job enrichment (☞ unit 73). Lack of commitment, particularly at the top, causes problems. For example, if the managing director lacks commitment, employees lower down are unlikely to commit themselves. TQM stresses the role of the individual and aims to make everyone accountable for their

own performance. For example, a machine operator may be accountable to a workshop supervisor for his work.

Control Consumers' needs will only be satisfied if the business has control of the factors that affect a product's quality. These may be human, administrative or technical factors. This is shown in Figure 95.1. The process is only under control if materials, equipment and tasks are used in the same way every time. Take an example of a firm making biscuits. Only by cooking in the same way can the quality be consistent every time. These methods can be documented and used to assess operations. Regular audits must be carried out by the firm to check quality.

Information is then fed back from the customer to the 'operator' or producer, and from the operator to the supplier of inputs, such as raw materials. For example, a retailer may return a batch of vehicles to the manufacturer because the gears were faulty. The manufacturer might then identify the person responsible for fitting the gears. An investigation might reveal that the faulty gears were the responsibility of a component supplier. The supplier can then be contacted and the problem resolved. Quality audits and reviews may lead to suggestions for improvements - a different material, perhaps, or a new piece of equipment.

Monitoring the process TQM relies on monitoring the business process to find possible improvements. Methods have been developed to help achieve this. STATISTICAL PROCESS CONTROL (SPC) involves collecting data relating to the performance of a process. Data is presented in diagrams, charts and graphs (☞ unit 9). The information is then passed to all those concerned.

SPC can be used to reduce variability, which is the cause of most quality problems. Variations in products, delivery times, methods, materials, people's attitudes and staff performance

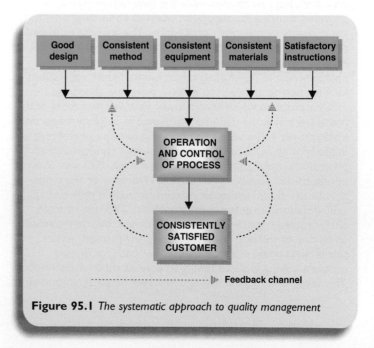

Figure 95.1 *The systematic approach to quality management*

often occur. For example, statistical data may show that worker attitudes may have led to variations in output late on Friday afternoon. Discussion might result in a change in the 'clocking on' and 'clocking off' times to solve the problem.

Teamwork TQM stresses that teamwork is the most effective way of solving problems. The main advantages are:
● a greater range of skills, knowledge and experience can be used to solve the problem;
● employee morale is often improved;
● problems across departments are better dealt with;
● a greater variety of problems can be tackled;
● team 'ideas' are more likely to be used than individual ones.
    TQM strongly favours teamwork throughout the business. It builds trust and morale, improves communications and cooperation and develops interdependence. Many UK firms in the past have suffered due to lack of sharing of information and ideas. Such approaches have often led to division between sections of the workforce.

Consumer views Firms using TQM must be committed to their customers. They must be responsive to changes in people's needs and expectations. To do this, information must be gathered on a regular basis and there must be clear communication channels for customers to express their views. Consumers are often influential in setting quality standards. For example, holiday companies issue questionnaires to their customers on the way back from a package holiday. The information can be used to identify the strengths and weaknesses of their operations. Such information can be used to monitor and upgrade quality standards.

Zero defects Many business quality systems have a zero defects policy. This aims to ensure that every product that is manufactured is free from defects. A business that is able to guarantee zero defects in customers' orders is likely to gain a good reputation. This could lead to new clients and improved sales.

Using TQM

TQM helps companies to:
● focus clearly on the needs of customers and relationships between suppliers and customers;
● achieve quality in all aspects of business, not just product or service quality;
● critically analyse all processes to remove waste and inefficiencies:
● find improvements and develop measures of performance;
● develop a team approach to problem solving;
● develop effective procedures for communication and acknowledgement of work (☞ unit 82);
● continually review the processes to develop a strategy of constant improvement.
There are however, some problems.

● There will be training and development costs of the new system.
● TQM will only work if there is commitment from the entire business.
● There will be a great deal of bureaucracy and documents and regular audits are needed. This may be a problem for small firms.
● Stress is placed on the process and not the product.

Quality circles

TQM stresses the importance of teamwork in a business. Many businesses have introduced quality circles (☞ unit 73) into their operations. Quality circles are small groups of staff, usually from the same work area, who meet on a regular and voluntary basis. They meet in the employer's time and attempt to solve problems and make suggestions about how to improve various aspects of the business. Issues such as pay and conditions are normally excluded. After discussions, the team will present its ideas and solutions to management. Teams are also involved in implementing and monitoring the effectiveness of solutions. In order for quality circles to be successful certain conditions must exist.
● A steering committee should be set up to oversee the whole quality circle programme.
● A senior manager should ideally chair the committee. Managers must show commitment to the principle of quality circles.
● At least one person on the committee should be accountable for the programme.
● Team leaders should be properly trained.

Costs of ensuring quality

Firms will want to monitor the costs of quality control carefully. All businesses are likely to face costs when trying to **maintain** or **improve** the quality of their products and services.
● The cost of designing and setting up a quality control system. This might include the time used to 'think through' a system and the training of staff to use it.
● The cost of monitoring the system. This could be the salary of a supervisor or the cost of an electronic sensor.
● There will be costs if products do not come up to standard. Faulty goods may have to be scrapped or reworked. Product failures might also result in claims against a company, bad publicity and a possible loss of goodwill.
● The cost of improving the actual quality. This may be the cost of new machinery or training staff in new working practices.
● If the whole quality system fails, there may be costs in setting it up again. Time may be needed to 'rethink' or adjust the system. Retraining might also be necessary. It has been suggested that between 10-20 per cent of the

revenue of a business is accounted for by quality related costs. This means that billions of pounds could be saved by UK businesses by cutting such costs. The vast majority of these costs is spent on appraisal and failure, which add very little to the quality of the product. Eliminating failure will also help to reduce appraisal and failure costs.

Although quality systems are costly, it is argued that their benefits outweigh the costs. The actual quality of the product should be improved, so customers are more likely to purchase the product. Business costs may be cut if faults in products are identified before the product reaches the market. The costs of failure once the product has reached the market are likely to be much higher than those during manufacture.

Best practice benchmarking

BEST PRACTICE BENCHMARKING (BPB) is a technique used by some businesses to help them discover the 'best' methods of production available and then adopt them. BPB involves:

● finding out what makes the difference, in the customer's eyes, between an ordinary supplier and an excellent supplier;
● setting standards for business operations based on the best practice that can be found;
● finding out how these best companies meet those standards;
● applying both competitors' standards and their own to meet the new standards and, if possible, exceed them.

Figure 95.2 illustrates the five main steps in BPB. The first step is to **identify** exactly what the company intends to benchmark. Benchmarks that are important for customer satisfaction might include consistency of product, correct invoices, shorter delivery times, shorter lead times and improved after sales service. For example, Motorola, the communications company, has benchmarked the yield and product characteristics of a range of its activities including its

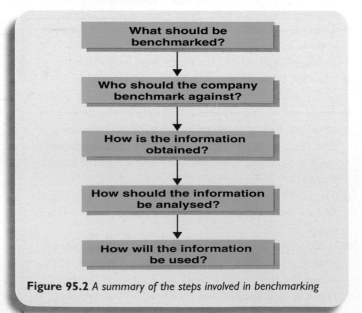

Figure 95.2 A summary of the steps involved in benchmarking

PowerGen, Britain's second biggest electricity generating company, has enjoyed considerable benefits from best practice benchmarking. It believes it is the lowest cost generator in the world, for the class and age of coal-fired generators it operates. The pursuit for efficiency began shortly after the company's separation from the Central Electricity Generating Board in the late 1980s. By 1992-93 the company had made major productivity gains, but felt it could be the 'best in the world' through benchmarking.

Powergen looked to the US, where generators had low operating costs, good technical performance and a good 'people culture'. Also, US operators could be evaluated because performance and operating data had to be published by law. From the data, PowerGen identified the top 17 operators and contacted them. In 1994-95 there was a great deal of co-operation between electricity companies and US generators were happy to expose business practices. Since privatisation such camaraderie disappeared. When comparisons were made, the differences between PowerGen and the US companies were astonishing. It was revealed that PowerGen would have to improve by 100 per cent in order to match its American counterparts. Visits to US plants were also revealing. For example, there was no permanent scaffolding to ease maintenance in plants and there were no cleaners. PowerGen used to spend £1 million on scaffolding, whilst US plants use harnesses and mobile plant. PowerGen employed between 40-80 cleaning staff. In the US everyone was expected to clean up after themselves.

Powergen's response was to redesign jobs, introduce multi-skilling and organise staff into 'multi-disciplined process teams'. They also learnt lessons from the Americans regarding contracting out. US operators have 'right-first-time contracts' with their suppliers which PowerGen decided to adopt. In addition, the two parties agreed to a target price for the work with both parties sharing the gains or losses of cost over and under-runs. The benefits of this benchmarking exercise were staggering. At one power station, Fiddlers Ferry in Cheshire, improvements included:

● a staff reduction from 1,100 to 226;
● better jobs for those remaining;
● maintenance costs cut by 66 per cent;
● the development of a multi-skilled workforce.

Source: adapted from the *Financial Times*, 2.7.1997.

(a) Explain the benefits of benchmarking for PowerGen.
(b) Examine two possible reasons why PowerGen used US companies for its benchmarking exercise.
(c) An Australian power generator has expressed an interest in using PowerGen as a benchmark. Discuss the steps that might need to be taken to carry this out.

assembly, warehousing and purchasing performance.

The second step involves **choosing a company** to set the benchmark against. This may be done by asking customers who they feel is the best in the field. Business analysts, journalists, stockbrokers or industrialists may also be used. Rank Xerox and Centreparc, the leisure group, have used other parts of their own organisations which have developed a reputation for excellence.

In the third step, information can be **gathered** from a number of sources, such as magazines, newspapers, trade association reports, specialist databases, customers and suppliers. Companies in the same industry often share information. An example may be businesses supplying local markets, such as garden centres. The benefits of this are that the worst performers can get advice from the best and perhaps visit their premises.

The **analysis** of information is best done with quantitative techniques (☞ unit 12). For example, a firm might compare numerical data relating to delivery times.

The final stage involves **using** the information. Once standards have been found and set, they must be communicated throughout the business. Improvements must be funded, introduced and monitored. Once a company becomes the best in the field others will begin to benchmark against them. This means the company must continue to benchmark their own process.

Independent bodies and trade organisations

Certain bodies and associations exist that promote quality which are independent of government or businesses seeking to gain quality standards.

The British Standards Institution The British Standards Institution (BSI) is an independent organisation that attempts to set quality standards in industry. It performs a number of functions.
- Any business can apply to the BSI for an inspection of its product. Those that achieve and maintain a standard can carry the BSI kitemark. The kitemark tells the customer that the product has been tested to destruction, to ensure that it meets with certain safety standards. Products that carry a **kitemark** include some cricket helmets, kitchen units, child car safety seats, door locks, curtains, and sofa and duvet covers. This is shown in Figure 95.3
- The BSI also issues a number of other product standards. These include BSI 4224 for yachts, which shows the product conforms to standards used in yachting and ensures the tensile strength of yarns and BS 2724, which sets performance levels for the amount of UV light through sunglasses. BS7131 grades the pile of carpets according to quality and durability. There are four grades used in the UK - light, medium, heavy and extra heavy.
- The BSI and other independent bodies, such as Lloyds,

offer BS EN ISO 9000 registration. The title reflects the European (EN) and international (ISO) recognition for this series. BS EN ISO 9001 gives quality assurance in design, development, production, installation and servicing and is suitable for businesses which have a large element of design in their operations. BS EN ISO 9002 gives quality assurance in production, installation and servicing, for businesses which produce fairly standard products with little or no design. BS EN ISO 9003 gives quality assurance in final inspection and testing. This standard is suitable for small firms or where customers can check quality themselves through inspection.

Question 4

The Treasury held a secret meeting with leading financial and trade bodies at the beginning of 1998 to discuss the government's plans to introduce 'kite marking' for financial products. Since the possibility of a scheme was announced there has been little action by the government and regulators to develop and implement a system. This prompted a consortium of Britain's most reputable financial companies, including Virgin Direct, Direct Line and First Direct, to draft their own Kite mark programme in an effort to hurry the government along.

One of the problems is finding a creditable body or suitable government department to sanction the scheme. A great deal of money will be required to employ a team of experts with necessary qualifications and experience to decide whether or not financial products should be awarded a Kite mark. One possible candidate at the moment is the Consumers Association which has expressed an interest in the scheme if it is cheap enough to run.

One of the main reasons for introducing a Kite mark for financial products is to restore consumer confidence in products such as pensions where the public's trust has been damaged. It is understood that with the new 'stakeholder pensions' it will be the companies that are Kite marked. However, the consortium believe it would be better to Kite mark products themselves rather than the company which sells them. Most current regulation is focused on the selling of such products. Adrian Webb of Direct Line says that 'If we raise the quality benchmark of the products themselves, then mis-selling becomes a secondary issue'.

Source: adapted from the *Sunday Times*, 15.2.1998.

(a) Explain two possible reasons why financial companies might be keen to introduce a Kite mark for financial products.
(b) Explain why there might be problems when Kite marking financial products.
(c) Suggest why the Consumers Association might be an appropriate body to award the financial Kite mark.
(d) Discuss why it might be more appropriate to Kite mark products rather than the companies which sell them.

Firms seeking certification have to show that their methods and procedures meet the recognised standards and comply with requirements. They are inspected on a regular basis to make sure that standards are being maintained. BS EN ISO 9000 certification can help a business to:

- examine and improve systems, methods and procedures to lower costs;
- motivate staff and encourage them to get things right first time;
- define key roles, responsibilities and authorities;
- assure orders are consistently delivered on time;
- highlight product or design problems and develop improvements;
- record and investigate all quality failure and customer complaints and make sure that they do not reoccur;
- give a clear signal to customers that they are taking measures to improve quality;
- produce a documented system for recording and satisfying the training needs of new and existing staff regarding quality.

The British Electrotechnical Approvals Board This is a body which inspects domestic electrical equipment. Manufacturers of domestic electrical appliances will be keen for the BEAB to approve their products. Approval can serve as a recognition of quality that customers will recognise.

The Consumers Association This is a body which follows up complaints by people about faulty products or services. They also make recommendations about products and services to customers. This takes into account such things as quality, reliability and value for money. Often survey results appear in their *Which?* magazines.

The Institute of Quality Assurance (IQA) The Institute of Quality Assurance is the only professional body in the UK whose sole purpose is the promotion and advancement of quality practices. The IQA has three main objectives.

- To seek the advancement of quality management and practices and help the exchange of related information and ideas.
- To promote the education, training, qualification and development of people involved in quality assurance and the management for quality.
- To provide a range of services to members and, where appropriate, to the community at large.

The Association of British Travel Agents (ABTA) The Association of British Travel Agents is a trade association which has drawn up a code of practice for its members. The code aims to improve the trading standards of activities related to the sale of holidays. Travel agents are allowed to register with ABTA if they agree to follow their code of practice. Their logo is shown in Figure 95.3.

The Wool Marketing Board This allows manufacturers to

carry the label shown in Figure 95.3 if their garments are made entirely of pure new wool. Obtaining a trademark is a way for a firm to give quality assurance to customers. If customers know that the quality of a product is guaranteed, they are more likely to buy the product. Also, there is less need to inspect the product, and returns and re-ordering are reduced.

The British Toy and Hobby Association (BTHA) developed the Lion Mark as a symbol of toy safety to be displayed on toy packaging. Toy manufacturers that want to include the Lion Mark must take out a licence with the BTHA. The manufacturer must sign a strict code of practice which sets standards relating to toy safety and advertising, as well as counterfeiting and markings on toy guns. The Lion Mark was adapted by the BTHA and the British Association of Toy Retailers (BATR) for shops. If the symbol is displayed in a shop it indicates that the retailer has agreed to a strict code of practice. They agree only to offer safe toys for sale and to ensure staff are briefed on toy safety matters such as age warnings.

A number of laws exist which protect consumers (☞ unit 22) from poor trading practices. They have tended to focus on safety aspects and consumer exploitation. However, increasingly UK laws and EU regulations are taking into account product quality. The laws are enforced by local inspectors, called **Trading Standards** Officers.

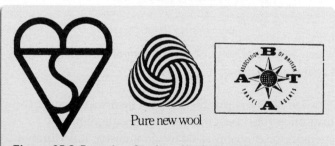

Pure new wool

Figure 95.3 *Examples of trademarks which signify quality assurance*

Summary

1. What is meant by the quality of a product?
2. Explain the difference between actual and perceived quality.
3. Explain the difference between quality control and quality assurance.
4. State 5 implications of TQM for a business.
5. Why is teamwork so important in TQM?
6. What are the costs of ensuring quality?
7. Describe the steps in best practice benchmarking.
8. What is the role of the British Standards Institution?
9. Explain the advantage of manufacturing trademarks to a business.

Key terms

Best practice benchmarking - imitating the standards of an established leader in quality and attempting to better them.
Quality - features of a product that allow it to satisfy customers' needs. It may refer to some standard of excellence.
Quality assurance - a method of working for businesses that takes into account customers' wants when standardising quality. It often involves guaranteeing that quality standards are met.
Quality chains - when employees form a series of links between customers and suppliers in business, both internally and externally.
Statistical process control - the collection of data about the performance of a particular process in a business.
Total quality management - a managerial approach which focusses on quality and aims to improve the effectiveness, flexibility, and competitiveness of the business.
Warranty - a guarantee that faulty products will be repaired or replaced within a period of time.

Case study

Macpak

Macpak designs, manufactures, installs and maintains machines which are used in wrapping and packaging. It employs over 980 staff and operates from a factory in Belfast. Most of Macpak's customers are food processors and the machines it produces have to meet very strict hygiene standards. In the last few years Macpak has seen its financial performance dwindle. Profit fell over the last three years. In 1998, it was unable to pay a dividend.

At the end of 1997 the board decided to make some radical changes in the way the company operated. It was responding, not only to poor financial performance, but also to some data on quality in the organisation which they had spent some time gathering. Figure 95.4 shows data on a number of quality issues at Macpak. The board was particularly worried about the trend in staff turnover. Indeed, they saw a link between this trend and the decline in quality. At a recent board meeting the production manager had suggested that morale in the factory was very low due to poor pay, cramped working conditions and dated tools and equipment. Macpak had never really introduced a formal quality system. It had established the business by being one of the first ever in the market. The board knew positive action was needed and suggested a number of courses of action.

Introduce TQM One of the newly appointed board members believed that a TQM approach was needed. A range of new working practices were required to change the whole culture in the organisation. Staff would need to be trained thoroughly in the importance of quality, how to achieve quality and how to monitor quality. Staff would have to change their whole approach to work. They would need to work in teams, take responsibility for the quality of their own work, be better equipped and enjoy improved working conditions with higher pay. The cost of implementing TQM at Macpak was estimated to be near £80 million.

Best practice benchmarking The board felt that over the years the company had 'lost its way'. They thought that Macpak would benefit from taking a close look at the way another machine producer operates. If a suitable company could be persuaded to act as benchmark the board agreed that they would go ahead with this option.

Introduce BS EN ISO 9000 It was thought that the introduction of a recognised quality standard would help restore customer confidence in Macpak. It was also felt that some external pressure to maintain quality might be helpful.

(a) Describe the nature of Macpak's quality problems.
(b) State 3 features of its performance that Macpak could benchmark.
(c) Explain why the Macpak board thought that there was a link between poor quality and rising staff turnover.
(d) Why might the success of the above measures depend on staff co-operation?
(e) Explain the advantages and disadvantages of introducing TQM at Macpak.
(f) Discuss the implications for Macpak of attempting to gain and maintain BS EN ISO 9000 certification.

Figure 95.4 *Macpak data*

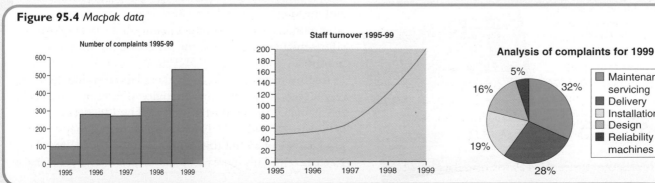

What is efficiency?

The objective of a business might be to be profitable (☞ unit 4). One way of doing this is to increase efficiency. EFFICIENCY is to do with how well resources, such as raw materials, labour and capital can be used to produce a product or service. Businesses often use costs as an indicator of efficiency. A manufacturer, for example, that finds its **average costs** (☞ unit 52) falling may well be improving efficiency as long as the quality of goods or services does not fall. Generally, as efficiency improves firms become more profitable. However firms may still be profitable without being efficient. This may perhaps be the case with firms that have a great deal of market power. BT (British Telecom), for

example, operated profitably in a market free from competition for many years. This does not necessarily mean that increased profits came from being more efficient. Why might businesses want to measure efficiency?

● To improve control of the business. Information about the efficiency of different parts of a business will allow managers to find strengths and weaknesses.
● To make comparisons. The efficiency of different plants can be compared, for example. The efficiency of the business compared to one of its competitors may also be useful.
● To help negotiations. Efficiency indicators can help a business when discussing wage rates, levels of staff and working practices with trade unions, for example.

How might efficiency be measured? Lower average costs or rising profitability are only **indicators** of efficiency. It is difficult to measure efficient business practice as many factors influence it. It is possible, however, to measure the efficiency of a process or an input such as labour or capital.

Measuring efficiency

How might a business measure the efficiency of a production process or its capital or employees?

Measuring labour productivity Labour PRODUCTIVITY can be found by dividing the output over a certain period by the number of workers employed:

$$\text{Labour productivity} = \frac{\text{Output (per period)}}{\text{Number of employees (per period)}}$$

If a small market garden employs 20 pickers who pick 40,000 lettuces a day, their productivity is 2,000 lettuces per worker each day.

This ratio measures the output per employee and is a useful indication of the efficiency of the labour force. There are, however, problems when calculating the ratio. For example, which workers should be counted? Should the maintenance crew, management, and clerical staff be counted, or should the ratio concentrate on direct labour only, ie shopfloor workers? How should part time workers and the long term sick be treated? How can the ratio accommodate a multi-product plant, where an employee's efforts might contribute to the production of more than one product?

Improvements have been made in labour productivity in recent years. The labour productivity of full time workers in the manufacturing industry increased by 13.6 per cent between 1990 and 1997. Over the same period the productivity of all full time workers in the UK increased by 15.6 per cent. This increase in labour productivity may have

---

Question 1

Seddon Greene is a manufacturer of pharmaceuticals. In the last few years it has enjoyed booming profits. In 1994 a new management team was appointed by the company's owners. The company then:
● invested in new technology;
● reduced the workforce;
● acquired several competitors in the market.

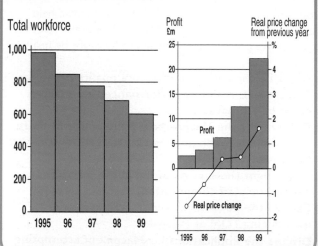

Figure 96.1 *Total workforce, profit and real price increases for Seddon Greene, 1995 to 1999*

(a) What evidence is there in the case which suggests that Seddon Greene has improved its efficiency?
(b) How might the above information be useful for: (i) shareholders of the business; (ii) employee representatives such as trade unions?

been the result of a number of factors.

● There may have been a change in the amount or quality of another input. For example, tools and equipment may have been replaced by more up to date and effective ones.
● The way in which labour and shifts are organised could have been improved.
● Inefficient businesses with low labour productivity may have been closed. This would obviously help improve the figure.
● It is likely that some of the improvement will have resulted from increased effort from the workforce.
● The number of workers may have been cut.

Measuring capital productivity A business may be interested in the productivity of its capital. This is becoming increasingly likely as more and more firms become capital intensive (☞ unit 91). A capital productivity ratio can be calculated by dividing output by the amount of capital employed in a given time period.

$$\text{Capital productivity} = \frac{\text{Output}}{\text{Capital employed}}$$

If a factory employed 10 sewing machinists and the total number of garments sewn in a day was 900, the productivity of capital would be 90 garments per machine each day.

Again, improvements in the productivity of capital may not be the result of more efficient capital alone. For example, the performance of an engine can be improved if it is serviced regularly and used carefully.

The labour and capital productivity ratios above are 'partial factor' productivity ratios. They measure the efficiency of just one input. A firm might want to measure the efficiency of the combined inputs it uses.

$$\text{Multi-factor productivity} = \frac{\text{Output}}{\text{Labour + materials + capital + etc.}}$$

This ratio takes into account that efficiency can be influenced by the quality and effectiveness of all inputs.

Measuring utilisation Managers may wish to measure the efficiency of certain activities. The utilisation of particular machines, or even the whole production process could be measured. This can be done by comparing the actual rate of utilisation with what is physically possible. For example, a food processing plant may be capable of 20 hours per day with two 8 hour shifts. In one working day, the processing line was in operation for 14 hours. So:

$$\text{Actual utilisation} = \frac{\text{Number of hours actually worked}}{\text{Total possible hours per day}} \times 100$$

$$= \frac{14}{20} \times 100$$

$$= 70\%$$

This 70 per cent rate needs to be compared with the rate which would be possible under standard operation. This can be calculated (assuming that two 8 hour shifts are worked) as:

$$\text{Possible utilisation} = \frac{16}{20} \times 100$$

$$= 80\%$$

The results show that the production line is being under-utilised. This could be due to a machine breakdown caused by poorly trained staff or poor maintenance.

Measuring Value Added In recent years some firms have calculated the value added by the business where:

$$\text{Value added = Sales revenue - external expenditure}$$

This is a measure of overall company performance and shows the money available for reinvestment in the business and distribution to shareholders.

Question

Table 96.1 *The productivity of selected European plants, 1996*

	Plant	Location	Vehicles produced	No. of workers
Nissan	Sunderland	UK	231,000	3,156
GM[1]	Eisenach	Germany	161,900	2,391
Toyota	Burnaston	UK	117,000	1,749
Honda	Swindon	UK	105,919	1,650
Ford	Valencia	Spain	296,928	5,340
Ford	Saarlouis	Germany	267,000	4,890
GM[1]	Zaragoza	Spain	436,400	8,052
PSA[2]	Mulhouse	France	349,600	6,762
Fiat	Melfi	Italy	350,000	7,000
SEAT	Martorell	Spain	393,283	8,262

[1] OPEL; [2] Peugeot Citroën

Source: adapted from Economist Intelligence Unit.

(a) Calculate the labour productivity of each plant.
(b) Suggest two reasons which might account for the differences in productivity.

Assessing business efficiency is a complicated task. A whole variety of measures are required and there is no single indicator which reflects accurately the overall efficiency of a business. A range of financial ratios (☞ unit 68) may also be used to help assess the performance of a business.

Work study

WORK STUDY is an attempt to find the 'best' or most 'efficient' way of using labour, machines and materials. The work of FW Taylor (☞ unit 71) is said to have formed the basis of work study methods.

Work study uses two techniques - method study and work measurement. Method study involves identifying all the specific activities in a job, analysing them, and finding the best way to do the job. This could be an existing job or a new one. Method study will allow a firm to:

● identify an optimum way to carry out a task;
● improve the layout of the factory or the workplace;
● minimise effort and reduce fatigue;
● improve the effectiveness of processes;
● improve the use of labour, machines and materials;
● establish the costs of particular activities to help with accounting;
● achieve results in the least time.

Once the best work method has been found, work measurement can be used to find the effort needed to carry out a task to an acceptable standard. The results can be used to design incentive schemes and determine staffing levels.

How is work measurement carried out? One example might be a worker being observed by a work-study assessor. The assessor might watch a worker set up a cutting machine, cut 10 patterns, reset the machine for a different pattern, cut 10 more patterns, and record the findings. The performance might be rated against a scale of, say, 0 - 100, such as the British Standard Rating Scale (where 100 is the standard performance of an average, experienced, motivated worker). It is possible for an efficient and motivated worker to exceed 100 on this scale. Work-study assessors are often disliked by employees. Some regard these time and motion officers with suspicion and feel threatened. Workers are sometimes expected to work harder in the future as a result of their observations.

Ergonomics is also an important feature in work study. Machines and the environment should be adapted so that the individual can achieve the best performance. A study of the working area might concentrate on such things as air temperature, humidity, radiation, noise levels and lighting. A study of the positioning of dials might be used when studying machines. EC legislation has laid down a set of rules relating to the use of VDUs by employees, for example.

Improving efficiency

There is a variety of methods that a business might choose which could improve efficiency. Some of the main methods are explained in the sections that follow. The aim of the business when introducing changes to improve efficiency is to increase the productivity of factors of production, reduce costs and raise profits. Increasingly businesses are adopting company-wide approaches which involve the whole business in improving efficiency. These strategies are dealt with in unit 102.

Changes to the workforce

Improvements in efficiency can be made by making labour more productive and reducing labour costs. How can a business make labour more productive?

● Division of labour. If all the tasks involved in constructing a housing estate were carried out by one worker this would be highly inefficient. If tasks are divided between workers, this allows each worker to specialise in the job they do best, such as joinery or plastering (☞ unit 1).
● Incentives. Incentives may motivate workers to be more productive (☞ units 72 and 73). They may be a reward, such as a bonus, or a threat of punishment.
● Changes in hours and payments. Employees may be asked to work shifts which allow equipment to be run for 24 hours. Flexitime systems allow staff to choose what days they wish to work within limits. Annualised hours (☞ unit 78) mean that workers can be asked to stay at home during slack periods, but work when trading picks up.
● Employing different types of workers may reduce labour costs and increase productivity (☞ unit 78). Workers who work from home, such as teleworkers who communicate with a business by e-mail or fax are often hired by business. They save on office costs. Part time workers or temporary employees may also reduce costs. Workers who job share might allow a job to be filled by two part time employees.
● Teamwork. This involves employees working closely together in teams when carrying out tasks. For example, quality circles (☞ unit 73) are groups of workers who meet to analyse and solve problems, and then pass on their findings to management. Cell production, where a product is manufactured from start to finish when operations are closely linked, is also more effective if teams carry out the work (☞ unit 84).
● Training. It is generally agreed that the efficiency of the workforce is linked to the amount and quality of education and training that it receives (☞ unit 79). Some businesses have their own training schemes, such as health and safety training, graduate training programmes or Modern Apprenticeships. Some employees follow training courses leading to NVQs.
● Multi-skilling. Multi-skilling (☞ unit 73) is where employees are trained in a variety of operations. It may allow a business to reduce its workforce, as more tasks are carried out by fewer workers.

Question 3

MD Foods, part of the Danish MD Foods Group, made a deliberate effort to improve efficiency. Most of the efficiency gains arose from changes in working practices. Changes were needed badly. Employee relations in the mid-1990s were characterised by union suspicion and a confusing variety of different pay rates across the company's plants. Employees had been used to working long hours for low pay. Overtime at premium rates was paid to meet fluctuations in demand. The result was high absenteeism and inefficient production as employees slowed down machines to make up their wages in overtime.

The company decided to streamline pay systems. It introduced an annualised hours scheme. Work rosters were based on 2,000 hours a year, leaving 180 hours placed in the 'work bank'. The banked hours were paid whether or not employees worked them. Staff worked those hours when the company needed them to work longer. Another feature of the system was that employees often worked out their hours between themselves. The new system meant that hourly pay rates rose from £4.32 to £5.20. Also, before the agreement, some staff were contracted to work for 55 to 60 hours per week. Indeed, it was not unknown for some to 'clock-up' 90 hours to earn overtime payments. After the changes no one worked more than 48 hours per week. Other improvements included better pension entitlements and holidays. As a result of the deal efficiency improved, absenteeism halved from 9-10 per cent to 3.5-5 per cent and relations between workers and management also improved.

Source: adapted from the *Financial Times*, 17.12.1998.

(a) Describe how MD Foods was suffering from poor efficiency.
(b) Explain how the changes were designed to improve efficiency.
(c) Examine the possible reasons why staff agreed to adopt the new practices designed to improve efficiency.

● Empowerment. This involves giving workers responsibility to make their own decisions and making them feel valued (☞ unit 73). Empowered workers are likely to be better motivated and to make better decisions, which could increase productivity.
● Employees may be involved in job rotation, job enrichment or job rotation (☞ unit 73). These methods allow individual workers to undertake more tasks than they might otherwise have carried out.

Standardisation

STANDARDISATION involves using uniform resources and activities or producing a uniform product. It can be applied to tools, components, equipment, procedures and business documents.

Changing systems can be very expensive, although there are benefits. A construction firm that builds a range of flats, for example, would benefit if all were fitted with standard cupboards. Savings are made in a number of ways. Bulk purchases can be made, the same tools and procedures could be used for fitting and training time could be reduced. This is an example of internal standardisation. Standardisation can also be more general. For example, efficiency will improve if there are standard components like nuts, bolts, pipe, screws and wire or standard measurements terminology, procedures and equipment.

The creation of the Single European Market in 1992 aimed to standardise regulations, procedures and specifications about quality, health and safety. This has benefited all businesses in member countries (☞ unit 30).

The main disadvantage is that the designers are constrained. They can not change production easily to suit the individual consumer. Designers may also face a more demanding job if they have to design products which must contain certain standard components and dimensions. Standardisation may also lead to inflexibility, which could result in a slower reaction to change.

Factory and office layout

The way in which a factory or office is set out can affect efficiency. The machinery and work stations should be set out so that effort and cost are minimised and output is maximised. This will be achieved if:
● the area is safe and secure;
● handling and movement are minimised;
● good visibility and accessibility is maintained;
● flexibility is maximised;
● managers are co-ordinated.

There is no standard method of factory layout because different products need different techniques. Also, different companies producing the same product might choose different methods. For example, both Bass Charrington and Brakspears produce beer, but the layouts of their breweries are very different. Brakspears uses very traditional brewing techniques. Bass uses more up to date methods. What are the common types of factory layout?

Process layout This system involves performing similar operations on all products in one area or at one work station. For example, the manufacture of wellington boots involves a mixing process where PVC resin and stabiliser are mixed, a moulding process which takes place on a moulding machine, a trimming operation where the boots have unwanted material cut off, and packaging ready for distribution. Each of these processes is undertaken on all boots at each work station, and work stations are located in different parts of the factory.

This type of layout is often used with batch (☞ unit 91)

or cell production (☞ unit 92) because of its flexibility. Planning is needed to avoid machines being overloaded or remaining idle.

Product layout With this method, machinery and tasks are set out in the order required to make the product. The products 'flow' from one machine or task to another. Flow production techniques (☞ unit 91) use this method. It is popular because handling time is reduced and there is greater control. However, it can only be used if there is large demand for the product.

Fixed position layout This involves performing operations on the work-in-progress and then returning it to a fixed location after each process. Alternatively, resources are taken to a site at which production occurs. An example would be the construction of a bridge.

It is not just factories which may change their layout to improve efficiency. For example, some businesses have given more thought to the way their offices should be laid out. Some favour 'open plan' offices. This is where large numbers of employees all work in the same area with no walls or partitions. This could help to improve communication and lead to a 'team spirit' in the organisation. Businesses such as supermarket chains also consider very carefully the best way to lay out their stores. One of their objectives is to ensure that parts of the store do not become congested when the store is busy.

Quality of the production process

It may be possible to improve efficiency by introducing measures to improve the quality of the product or the production process.

- Total Quality Management (TQM) (☞ unit 95) is an approach which aims to reduce the number of errors made in a business. It also encourages staff to continually review and check their work. Fewer errors should improve efficiency because there will be less waste and less repeat work.
- Benchmarking involves a business identifying another organisation which is the very best in a particular field (☞ unit 95). For example, a business may recognise that a company has a low rate of absenteeism. It could identify the reasons why its absenteeism record is so low and adopt its methods.
- Some businesses adopt recognised quality standards in their operations (☞ unit 95), such as the BS EN ISO 9000. Once this standard has been awarded, regular checks are made to ensure standards are maintained. Such high standards will tend to pressurise businesses into being efficient.

Reorganisation of the business

Many businesses have reorganised themselves to improve efficiency. This usually involves changing the structure of the organisation.

- Delayering involves reducing the number of layers in the managerial hierarchy (☞ unit 70 and 102). By stripping out layers of management, for example, businesses may save money. There may be other benefits too if businesses empower (☞ unit 73) the rest of the workforce.
- Downsizing (☞ unit 102) is where the size of the business is reduced. This could mean closing down some unprofitable operations. Downsizing usually results in cutting the size of the workforce. This could save money and improve productivity.
- Outsourcing (☞ unit 102) is where a firm allows a sub-contractor to undertake some work which was done by the business. This could improve efficiency if the sub-contractor can do the work at a lower cost.

Question **4**

Andrew Laing, consultant with DEGW International consultants, believes it is time to redesign the law office. His research found that the individual private office, preferably with a view, remains the main type of office for law firms. This design suggests that:

- every lawyer is the same, doing the same work within the same kind of space;
- the legal work process is individual and isolated and teamwork, face-to-face interaction, informal group work and collaboration are not important;
- the individual lawyer works in a hierarchy;
- the work process is paper based and IT is a fixed and immobile resource;
- occupancy of a private office is full time and little activity occurs outside it.

Laing argues that up to 50 per cent of the day private offices are empty or temporarily unoccupied. He suggests that the modern law office should abandon privately owned individual space. Instead, it should have a series of spaces which include technology. They would be suitable for private or collaborative teamwork and situated close together. He suggests that space used in this way would allow 30 per cent more people to be employed.

Source: adapted from the *Financial Times*, September, 1997.

(a) Explain why the traditional law office may now be out of date.
(b) Explain two ways in which efficiency might improve with the new office design.

Changes in business size

Some businesses believe that they can improve efficiency by growing. This is because larger businesses can exploit **economies of scale** (☞ unit 93). By exploiting economics of scale businesses will enjoy lower costs. Some mergers and takeovers are motivated by this objective.

Technological improvements

Investment in new technology will often improve efficiency (☞ unit 98). New machinery may be quicker, more accurate, be able to carry out more tasks, and work in more extreme conditions than older equipment or labour. Many machines are controlled by computers and can undertake very complex tasks.

● In the primary industry, technology has raised productivity dramatically. The main reason for this is because, in agriculture for example, machinery has replaced people.

● In secondary industry, robots, lasers, CNC machines and automated plants have been increasingly introduced. This has resulted in large increases in efficiency and a reduction in costs.

● Even in the tertiary sector, which tends to be labour intensive, the scope for using technology has increased. For example, a French leisure company has opened a small chain of hotels which are unmanned for most of the day. People check in using their credit cards and make no contact at all with staff. A small team of staff visit the hotels for a short time each day to clean and service the rooms. Information and communication technology has improved the ability communicate over large distances (☞ unit 82).

The benefits of improving efficiency

Improvements in efficiency can benefit a number of business stakeholders.

● Shareholders. Improved efficiency will tend to lower costs and raise profits. With greater profits shareholders may be paid higher dividends and higher share prices. Businesses will also have more profit to reinvest. This could help to protect the long term future of the business.

● Customers. If greater efficiency reduces costs businesses may offer products at lower prices. Customers might benefit if the quality of products are improved. Delivery times and customer service might also be better.

● Employees and managers. A more efficient workforce may be better motivated and enjoy more job satisfaction. They may be valued more by employers, get better training, be given opportunities to use their talents and enjoy better working relationships with managers. Employees may also benefit from higher wages and better working conditions.

● Suppliers. Suppliers may benefit from better relationships with businesses and prompter payment. Measures such as just-in-time manufacturing rely heavily on good relationships with suppliers.

● Community. Better efficiency might reduce waste and lower social costs such as pollution (☞ unit 27).

● Government. If greater efficiency leads to higher profits, the government will gain more tax revenues.

 Question 5

Van de Bergh Foods manufactures margarine at its factory in Purfleet, Essex. The company belongs to Unilever and supplies it with brands such as Flora, Stork and Blue Band. In the middle of the 1980s the management realised that changes were needed to improve efficiency.

● New packaging lines were installed, capable of filling 240 tubs per minute.

● Changes in the margarine-making process helped raise the plant's capacity from 3 tonnes per hour to 7 tonnes per hour.

● A computer-based monitoring system was installed to check the production line.

● The entire warehousing and distribution function was outsourced.

● Palletising was automated, replacing the palletising of cartons by hand.

● The company invested in a training programme. For example, workers were shown how to clean and routinely maintain machinery, identify malfunctions, solve technical problems, share information and offer suggestions for improvements.

● Annualised hours were introduced, resulting in the elimination of overtime, new shift patterns and the end of demarcation.

Source: adapted from *Britain's Best Factories*, Dti 1997

Examine the possible benefits of Van de Burgh's efficiency improvements to the following stakeholders:
(a) shareholders; (b) employees; (c) customers.

Key terms

Efficiency - how well inputs, such as raw materials, labour or capital can be changed into outputs, such as goods or services.

Productivity - the ratio of outputs to inputs in a production process, such as the output of a given amount of labour or capital.

Standardisation - the use of uniform resources and activities.

Work study - a process which investigates the best possible way to use business resources.

Summary

1. Why might businesses wish to measure efficiency?
2. How might: (a) labour productivity; (b) capital productivity be measured?
3. What is meant by multi-factor productivity?
4. What does 'value added' measure?
5. What are the benefits of work study for a business?
6. Describe 4 methods of improving labour productivity.
7. What are the advantages and disadvantages of standardisation?
8. Explain the difference between process and product factory layout.
9. State 3 ways in which a business may be reorganised to improve efficiency.
10. State 5 benefits to a business of improving efficiency.

Case study

Nissan

Nissan, the Japanese car manufacturer, operates a factory in Sunderland and employs 4,200 people. In the early 1990s it had earned a reputation for being the most productive car plant in Europe. Output of its Micra small car and Primera medium-sized saloon was forecast to rise from 179,000 in 1992 to 270,000 in 1993. This was close to the factory's capacity of 300,000 cars a year. However, the recession in Europe reduced sales of Nissan cars from 246,000 in 1993 to 205,000 in 1994. In addition, the value of the Yen rose. This forced Nissan and other car makers into drastic efficiency reforms. Although the Sunderland plant was perhaps the most productive in Europe, it lagged well behind plants in Japan. As a result the company launched NX96, a four year programme to transform Nissan's performance in manufacturing, people management, development and care and supplier base.

Man-hours per car were cut by 10 per cent in each year between 1993-95, and 8 per cent in 1996. In 1997-8, the Micra took about 8 man-hours to produce. The European average was about twice this. The productivity surge also helped to improve Nissan's quality. A company representative said: 'productivity and quality go hand in hand. You can't be good at one and bad at the other'. Nissan was also pursuing the goal of 'no touch' manufacturing. This is where the car which comes off the end of the production line is so perfect that it requires no rectification work.

NX96 recognised that people were crucial if Nissan was to maintain its workforce and attract new employees. Manufacturing staff turnover was less than 3 per cent, well below the manufacturing norm in 1997. In addition, absenteeism was about 2 per cent, a third of the British average. It was suggested that these figures were the result of Nissan's reaction to a staff survey carried out at the start of NX96. The survey revealed that career development needed improving and job rotation should be expanded. Also, considerable work went into making people's jobs easier. For example, there was investment in low-cost automation such as levers and cradles to help fit wheels and simple beams to assist sun-roof installation.

As a result of NX96, the quality of components from Nissan's 199 suppliers improved, as did delivery times and costs. The biggest problem area was product development. This was because European suppliers, unlike their Japanese counterparts, were not used to being asked to initiate component design and development. Nissan set up a programme to promote supplier self-sufficiency in design and right-first-time development. The scheme has helped to cut the time from design to market from 40 months to 30 months.

The management at the Sunderland plant believed that NX96 helped clinch the third model which will boost output to over 300,000 cars per year. Having attained Japanese performance standards in many areas Nissan launched Next21, an improvement programme to put the whole Nissan operation up with the best Nissan practice in Japan early in the 21st century.

Source: adapted from *The Sunday Times*, 6.4.1997 and the *Financial Times*, 25.11.1998.

(a) **What factors led to Nissan trying to improve productivity at its Sunderland plant?**
(b) **Describe two ways in which Nissan might measure improvements in productivity.**
(c) **Explain how Nissan attempted to improve productivity at its Sunderland plant.**
(d) **Explain how efficiency gains might benefit the long term future of the Sunderland plant.**
(e) **Examine how changes in productivity might have affected stakeholders in the business.**
(f) **Evaluate to what extent productivity was improved at Nissan's Sunderland plant by the changes that took place.**

What are resources?

Unit 1 explained that businesses use resources in production. These are the factors of production in business activity - land, labour, capital and enterprise. This unit deals with land and the materials and resources used by businesses. There are many different materials used in business products. Some are manufactured into other materials or components, which are then used to make different products.

● Silk, a natural resource, is used in the textile industry. Silk fibres are made by caterpillars and are used to make a silk yarn. The yarn is then woven into a fabric. This fabric can be dyed or printed on and used in the manufacture of scarves or shirts, for example.

● Lycra is a SYNTHETIC fibre made from chemicals. It is usually combined with other materials such as wool, nylon, cotton or silk to produce clothes, for example. It allows clothing to stretch and recover its shape.

● Sugar is made by a variety of processes from the natural materials sugar cane or beet. It can be added as a sweetener to products such as jam. When sugar is processed it produces BY-PRODUCTS. These are materials which are created as a 'side effect' of the process. For example, raw sugar is separated from syrup, called molasses, in sugar production. This molasses is used in the food industry and as animal feed.

● Pine is a natural wood used in the production of many items, including tables and chairs, beds, toilet roll holders, children's toys and CD racks.

● Medium density fibreboard (MDF) is produced from waste of wood, such as pine or spruce, left over after wooden products are made. Cuttings are combined with water, wax and resin to produce MDF boards. The boards are then used to make products such as furniture, shelving, toys, display stands and flooring.

● Plastics are manufactured from chemicals. Pigments can be added to change their colour and plasticisers make them more bendy. Plastics include polythene (made into bottles, crates and carrier bags), ABS (kettles and telephone bodies), polystyrene (packaging and model kits) and acrylic (as a glass substitute in baths, spectacles and street signs).

● Metals may be natural materials found in rocks, such as iron, copper or tin. Carrying out processes can change metal. Heating iron while blowing oxygen on it produces steel. Joining metals into alloys gives the new metal the combined advantages of the original metals. Brass is an alloy of copper, which conducts electricity, and zinc, which is hard but brittle. An alloy of aluminium and copper resists corrosion and is used for outdoor window frames and motor car parts, as it is lightweight and can be shaped.

Waste

In the production of many goods or services some materials are wasted. WASTE also results from production processes. Waste is any material which is no longer useful in a particular production process and has to be disposed of. The **Special Waste Regulations, 1996** classifies different types of waste.

Inert waste This includes materials which will not cause environmental pollution and will not have physical, chemical or biological reactions. Examples include stone, brick, most mining waste or subsoil from road widening schemes.

Biodegradable waste Biodegradable waste such as wood, waste food and garden waste, rots away by the action of living micro-organisms. It can lead to unpleasant smells. Biological reaction may also take place. This can result in landfill gases containing methane and carbon dioxide. Landfill gases are thought to be a major factor affecting global warming (unit 35).

Question 1

Unigate plc is a European food and distribution group. The group includes a number of businesses.

● Malton Foods makes products for the pork, bacon and cooked meat markets. In the UK its products are sold mainly under retailers' own brand names, although it also sells under the Harris brand name.

● St Ivel UK manufactures fresh foods and dairy products. These include brand names, such as Utterly Butterly, Gold and Vitalite, and retailers' own names. Products include yellow fat spreads, yogurt, fromage frais, desserts, cream, savoury dips and fruit juices.

● St Ivel Foods, Europe includes French and Italian businesses. The product range includes margarines, spreads, yogurt and desserts. Le Fleurier, Prima and Tournolive are popular brands.

● Unigate Dairies is a processor and distributor of fresh milk in the UK. It provides daily doorstep deliveries of milk and other products to 1.4 million homes. Unigate Chill Chain supplies fresh milk and cream and a range of branded fresh products to convenience stores, shops, forecourts, caterers, schools and hospitals.

Source: adapted from Unigate, *Annual Report and Accounts*.

(a) State six examples of natural raw materials which Unigate might use in production.

(b) Explain how the business might make use of synthetic products.

Hazardous waste Hazardous waste can damage health.
Clinical waste is materials from hospitals and vets, which
maybe contaminated with blood. It must be disposed of by
being burned. **Special wastes** are wastes that appear on an EU
list of hazardous wastes and include:

● toxic (poisonous) materials such as lead, rat poison and
cyanide;
● materials which cause health risks if inhaled, swallowed or
absorbed by the skin, such as asbestos;
● corrosive materials, such as acid, which can burn the skin,
eyes and lungs;
● flammable wastes, such as gas cylinders which may ignite.

Businesses must treat some special wastes, such as acids,
engine oils and industrial materials, in treatment plants before
disposal. Special wastes such as solvents must be disposed of
in high temperature incinerators.

Waste management

In the UK around 140 million tonnes of waste is produced
every year. WASTE MANAGEMENT describes how businesses

deal with waste material. In a small hotel or bookshop, it may
just involve making sure that waste material is collected
regularly by the local authority. In a chemical processing plant
toxic waste may be produced, which must be treated and then
disposed of safely. This task might use up a great deal of
resources and need continuous monitoring.

Why is waste a problem for a business and for society? For
a business, unnecessary waste is expensive. It will raise costs
and reduce profit. A firm may try to raise its price to pay for
these extra costs, which might deter customers. For society,
some waste is hazardous. If not treated properly it can harm
people or the environment. Radioactive waste may kill people
if not disposed of carefully. Some resources that are wasted
may be non-renewable, such as oil. If waste is reduced, this
will mean that such resources will last longer.

Methods of dealing with waste

Waste minimisation Perhaps the best way to reduce business
waste is to avoid producing it in the first place. Government
measures, such as a landfill tax, to make sure businesses meet
the cost of waste disposal and environmental effects, have
encouraged firms to minimise waste. The government has
also helped by setting up special schemes to reduce industrial
waste. The Environmental Technology Best Practice
Programme (ETBPP), set up in 1994, aimed to encourage
practices that would reduce costs by £320 million per annum
by the year 2015. In 1998 total savings by industry were £28
million and waste had been cut by 131,000 tonnes. These
savings were the result of businesses:

● using information from benchmarking publications
(☞ unit 95) and case studies and guides on good practice;
● asking advice from an environmental helpline;
● establishing regional waste minimisation projects to reduce
costs.

Re-use One way of minimising waste is to re-use materials
and products which would otherwise be disposed of. Milk
bottles, for example, are collected daily and reused. Plastic
containers can be reused for different liquids. Pallets are used
again and again by businesses when transporting goods.
Charity shops sell second hand clothing. Voluntary groups
such as Waste Watch and Going for Green have helped to
promote this practice.

Recycling Recycling involves the collection of a waste material
such as paper, plastic, glass, aluminium or steel, and
producing a new raw material from that waste. For example,
Plysu makes containers to hold liquids such as detergents
from recycled plastic. It is possible to collect material for
recycling in a number of ways.

● Bring systems, where people take materials to collection
points, such as bottle banks or clothes banks.
● Collect systems, where households separate certain materials
and put them outside the house for collection by voluntary

Question

(a) Describe some: (i) biodegradable; (ii) inert waste;
(iii) hazardous waste which the businesses in the
photographs might generate.
(b) Comment on the difficulty of disposing of waste for
each business.

groups, the council and organisations such as the Scout movement. These groups sell the waste collected to businesses for processing.

● Central processing is carried out by or on behalf of the council. It involves sorting mixed waste at a central processing plant where household refuse is collected. Such plants not only recycle materials but also generate energy.

Although recycling is used in the UK, there is still scope for improvement. Figure 97.1 shows that the UK lags behind both France and Germany in the recycling of waste.

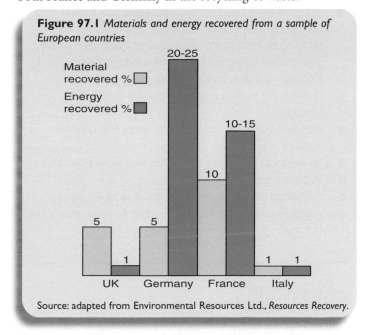

Figure 97.1 *Materials and energy recovered from a sample of European countries*

Material recovered %

Energy recovered %

Source: adapted from Environmental Resources Ltd., *Resources Recovery.*

Incineration This involves burning waste materials at very high temperatures. It reduces the volume of waste by turning about 70 per cent of it into carbon dioxide gas, other gases and water vapour. The ash that results from burning the waste is often used in the construction industry or taken to landfill sites. Some gases are poisonous and must be prevented from entering the atmosphere by special pollution control equipment. Although new incinerators are expensive, interest in them is gaining because of the rising costs of other methods of disposal.

Landfill Around 90 per cent of all solid waste in Britain is LANDFILLED. This is a fairly safe way of disposing of waste which involves burying it in the ground. This is not without problems. In the past gas has escaped leading to explosions. Today landfill sites contain 'liners', such as clay or polythene to prevent escape. Pipes and pumps are used to release the gas. In some cases landfill gas is cleaned and used to provide energy for nearby factories or to generate electricity. When a site is full, a top is constructed, which is covered in clay and layers of soil so rain water can drain off. It is then planted with crops or plants.

Composting Composting involves collecting organic waste such as potato peelings, kitchen scraps, grass cuttings and

In 1988 two research scientists from UMIST developed a technique for recycling unwanted biodegradable compost into oil. The project, called Manoil, was mothballed when oil prices fell and funding for continuation did not materialise. However, it seems now that the project might be revived. Arguably, the environmental value of the project is now more important than ever. Greater Manchester Waste Disposal Authority, which took over the scheme, is facing serious difficulties as landfill space is becoming more scarce and expensive. Colin Vaughan, the authority's client services officer, explained that waste disposal costs, including the landfill tax, were becoming a serious burden - and that is without the environmental factors. As a result, the Manoil project was resurrected.

The recycling method transforms a roomful of cellulosic material into a dustbinful of oil. The oil left behind is only about 40 per cent of the waste, but by volume it is only between 10-15 per cent. This means a landfill site would last for 100 years instead of 20 years. The project has also attracted interest from Taiwanese investors who were keen to buy the rights to the technology.

Source: adapted from the *Manchester Evening News*, 1997.

(a) What types of waste management methods are mentioned in the article?
(b) Explain why the Manoil project may solve some of the problems of existing methods of waste control.
(c) Examine one other way in which the production of biodegradable waste could be reduced.

other garden waste and allowing it to decompose. It can then be returned to the soil, where it will act as a natural fertiliser. Composting tends to be carried out in people's gardens rather than as a business activity because compost can vary in standard and there is a problem finding markets for it.

Design Increasingly businesses are considering the impact of waste when designing products and processes. Design teams are developing products and processes which minimise waste in a number of ways.

● Production processes can reduce waste. For example, JIT and kaizen methods (☞ unit 92) have helped to reduce waste in production.
● Firms are using less packaging. For example, single portion yogurt pots now use 5 grams of plastic instead of 12 grams.
● Manufacturers are designing cars which use less fuel. Cars are now more aerodynamic. Components are made from plastic rather than metal, or aluminium rather than steel, which makes them lighter.
● The development of concentrated products. For example, in the detergent industry producers sell concentrated fabric conditioner in pouches rather than plastic bottles. A 1 litre bottle of conditioner weighs 70 grams. However, a 12 gram

plastic pouch holds 1 litre of conditioner concentrate.
- In the electronics industry designers are continually trying to reduce the size of many products such as computers, mobile phones, hi-fi systems and TVs. Smaller versions use fewer resources.

Benefits and problems of waste management

Businesses which carry out waste management measures may enjoy certain benefits

- Waste management can help businesses reduce their costs. For example, by minimising waste a business may use fewer resources. In addition, if less waste is generated the cost of disposal will be lower.
- If businesses reduce waste they may be able to offer products at lower prices to consumers. This may give the business a competitive edge.
- By spending money on research and development in waste management a business may be able to find ways of using their waste productively. For example, they may produce a material from waste which they might be able to sell.
- If a business has a well developed waste management policy, designed to protect employees and the environment from hazardous waste, its image may be improved.
- By reducing certain wastes businesses might be able to reduce the amount of tax they pay. Business that use landfill sites to dispose of waste must pay landfill tax.
- An effective waste management policy should help a business to avoid breaking the law regarding waste disposal, and thus avoid paying fines.
  There are also some disadvantages of waste management.
- Some aspects of waste management are very expensive and contribute to higher business costs. The proper disposal of hazardous waste, such as nuclear waste, can be very expensive.
- Higher business costs resulting from waste management activities may raise the prices of products to customers. This may be a problem if a business is trying to sell goods in overseas markets where foreign laws regarding waste disposal are less restrictive.
- Small businesses might be at a disadvantage. They may not have the resources to spend on waste management which larger companies have.

Factors affecting waste management

Needs of stakeholders Waste management decisions may be complicated. Different business stakeholders can have needs which may conflict (☞ unit 3). For example, shareholders are keen to maximise returns. They may want a business to maximise profits, which may mean spending less on waste management. However, the local community may want a business to devote more resources to waste management in order to improve the environment. But this could reduce profits. Employees will also be concerned about waste management for health and safety reasons.

There may even be conflict within groups. Some consumers might prefer businesses to keep waste management costs to the minimum, so that prices are kept low. Others may prefer businesses to spend on waste

---

Table 97.1 *Government action regarding waste management*

- Using the landfill tax to encourage sustainable waste management. The landfill tax was £7 per tonne for the dumping of active waste in a controlled landfill site in 1998. This was set to rise to £10 per tonne in April 1999.
- Considering how to improve packaging regulations.
- Investigating ways of improving markets for recycled products.
- Help to increase the composting of waste that results in 'smells'.
- Working with industry on producers' responsibility initiatives.
- Published guidance on recycling plans.
- Encourage the sharing of best practice by local councils.
- Accepted recommendations of Review of Local Authority Role in Recycling, including municipal waste strategies.

Question

Walkers Snack Foods Ltd, famous for its Walkers Crisps, undertook a thorough review of its manufacturing processes to identify ways of reducing waste. As a result the management introduced a series of initiatives to develop a self-sustaining waste minimisation culture in the organisation. Initiatives, which involved all staff, included staff training and empowerment, setting targets for waste reduction and monitoring performance against targets and waste segregation, so that waste could be sold to recycling companies. Some of the benefits of the initiatives included:
- cost savings of about £960,000 in the first year;
- the costs of the initiatives were recovered in only 10 months;
- water consumption reduced by 165,000m³ per year;
- significantly reduced chemical oxygen demand of effluent;
- less solid waste to landfill leading to reduced disposal charges;
- a 6 per cent reduction of carbon dioxide emissions;
- improved motivation of staff and management to improve efficiency.

Source: adapted from *Less Waste More Value* (a government consultation paper on waste strategy in England and Wales), 1998.

What might be the benefits of the waste reduction initiatives to: (a) Walkers; (b) customers; (c) other businesses; (d) the environment?

management activities, even if it means paying higher prices, because of the impact on the environment.

Legislation There is a growing body of UK and EU legislation regarding the disposal and treatment of waste. Complying with the various Acts of Parliament will affect the way businesses handle waste. For example, in the late 1990s the government raised the cost to businesses of using landfill as a method of waste disposal. As a result, some businesses may have decided to find other methods of disposal or tried to reduce the amount of waste they generated. Government action regarding waste management in the late 1990s is shown in Table 97.1.

Costs As already shown, the disposal and treatment of waste is becoming a highly commercialised activity. Businesses need to consider the costs of different methods of waste management and charges made by different businesses in the industry.

Ethical stance As the importance of image and social responsibility (☞ unit 27) grows, businesses are likely to pay more consideration to waste management. Firms must operate within the law when managing waste. But they may go further. For example, a business might incur extra costs by using recycled materials in production or ensure that the

liquid waste discharged into rivers was actually cleaner than the minimum legal standard. This type of ethical behaviour might help to improve their image.

Local initiatives In some regions support groups have been established which encourage businesses in their area to reduce waste. For example, the West Midlands Waste Minimisation Club provides support and advice on waste minimisation in the West Midlands area. The existence of such groups is likely to encourage firms to adopt waste minimisation programmes.

Key terms

By-products - materials which are produced as a result of a process designed to produce a different material.
Synthetic materials - materials which are produced artificially, for example by chemical process, rather than naturally.
Landfill - a way of disposing of waste which involves burying it in the ground.
Waste - any material which is no longer of use to the system that produced it and which has to be disposed of.
Waste management - the way in which businesses deal with the problem of waste materials.

Question 5

Biffa Waste, a subsidiary of Severn Trent Water, is one of the largest providers of waste management services in the UK. One of their waste management activities is the provision of a fluorescent tube recycling service. Most fluorescent tubes are disposed of by businesses in bins and skips where they will often shatter. This is potentially dangerous, as the tubes contain highly toxic mercury powder which can harm the environment.

In addition, mercury is a valuable natural resource which could be recovered, along with other materials, and reused. Recycling tubes can also help protect employees. It avoids the risks of staff inhaling mercury powder or cutting themselves on splinters of glass if the tubes smash on disposal.

Biffa's fluorescent tube recycling service enables businesses to dispose of their spent light tubes and sodium lamps safely and securely. They provide customers with specially designed containers to hold tubes and lamps of varying lengths of up to eight feet. When containers are full, Biffa will empty them on request.

Source: adapted from Severn Trent, *Annual Report and Accounts*.

(a) What type of waste management is mentioned in the article?
(b) Examine the factors that may have influenced businesses to use the services of Biffa Waste.

Summary

1. State 3 materials used in:
   (a) the clothing industry;
   (b) the construction industry;
   (c) the car industry;
   (d) the food industry.
2. Give 2 examples of: (a) inert waste; (b) biodegradable waste; (c) hazardous waste.
3. Why is waste a problem for: (a) a business; (b) society?
4. Why might waste minimisation be the best way to reduce the impact of waste?
5. What is the difference between re-use and recycling?
6. Why is design important in waste management?
7. Suggest 4 advantages and 4 disadvantage of waste management.
8. Explain how the needs of stakeholders can affect waste management decisions.
9. State 4 measures taken by the government to reduce waste.

Table 98.1 *Agriculture statistics*

Rates of reportable, non fatal injury	1995/96 2,180	Change since 1989/90 -33%	
Total gross output	1996 £18,050 million	Change since 1986 +48%	

Source: adapted from *Annual Abstract of Statistics*, Office for National Statistics; HSE website, http://www.open.gov.uk/hse/hsesatas.htm

Examine the possible effects on: (a) farm owners; (b) farm workers; (c) consumers of farm products of the advances in technology.

industries, such as mining, cutting, lifting and tunnelling machines have all led to increased output. There have also been improvements in safety equipment and mining conditions for workers. The extraction of oil now takes place on large oil rigs with computer controlled drilling equipment. This improves the speed and accuracy of production. In fishing, the introduction of refrigerated boats has helped to improve productivity. Forestry has benefited from cutting, lifting and haulage equipment.

One problem with the use of more efficient technology is that resources are used up more quickly. It may be possible to control this in the case of **renewable resources**, such as timber by replanting and managed forestry. However, unless new forms of power can be developed, there are likely to be problems in future with extracting large amounts of the world's finite resources of materials such as coal and oil. There have also been criticisms of genetically modified food and its possible effects on humans.

Applications in the secondary sector

New technology has led to major changes in manufacturing. Many factories and production lines employ complex mechanical, electrical and electronic systems. Even smaller manufacturing businesses have benefited from the introduction of new equipment and processes. Examples of new technology can be found in a number of areas.

Robots Robots are increasingly used on assembly and production lines. They have some form of arm, which moves to instructions given by a computer. Repetitive tasks, such as installing components, can be carried out many times with great accuracy. Such tasks may lead to boredom, lack of motivation, tiredness and human error if undertaken by employees. Robots may also increase the flexibility of a business. For example, in 1998 small robots, each with its own set of paint cans, were installed in the paint shop of the Volkswagen-Audi car plant in Germany. The robot could be activated at a few minutes' notice when a customer wants a

colour which is not included in the current program. Using the robot means that customer demand for less popular colours can be satisfied without having to clean out the pipes of the main painting apparatus, which would be costly.

Computer aided design COMPUTER AIDED DESIGN (CAD) is now used by businesses in the design process, before a product is manufactured (☞ unit 99). Examples of products designed using CAD include vehicle bodies, plastic containers to hold milk and oil, furniture and clothing. Designing on computer allows a business to produce accurate drawings, which can be viewed in 3D and altered cheaply and quickly for a client. Designs can be accurately measured and tested on computer for faults, such as unsuitable components or dimensions, which might have caused problems during manufacture.

Computer numerically controlled machines Products can be manufactured using COMPUTER NUMERICALLY CONTROLLED (CNC) machines. Instructions are given to the CNC machine by the operator. The machine then carries out its instructions, controlled by a computer. An example might be a CNC milling machine which is used to cut out a mould of a mouse in plastic. The computer controls the cutting to produce the shape of a mould. In the textile industry computer controlled sewing, cutting and printing machines are used. Some CNC machines make use of probes and **coordinate measuring machines** (CMM). These are designed to make simple or complex measurements, check batches or components one at a time and inspect geometric or irregular shapes. CMMs are accurate to within a few microns. CNC machines can produce shapes and cut quickly and accurately. They can also carry out repetitive tasks without human error. The instructions can be changed easily to carry out different tasks. For example, JCB uses CNC machines to cut a wide range of patterns from metal plates for its mechanical diggers.

Computer aided manufacture (CAM) In many factories

computers are used to design products and the information is then fed into CNC machines. This automated operation is known as COMPUTER AIDED MANUFACTURE (CAM). For example, a manufacturer of telephones may design a new shape using a CAD software program on computer. The instructions may be taken from the CAD program and inputted into CNC machines. These machines will reproduce the shapes, guided by the information contained in the computer. Other examples of CAM include computer controlled manufacture of plastic bricks at Lego, computer controlled assembly lines at Sony and computer controlled temperatures, flow rates and ingredients for pizza production at McCain Foods. The computer controlled weaving system produced by Bonas stores designs on computer in one part of a factory and sends production information to looms in other parts of the factory. These then weave the designed fabric.

Computer integrated manufacture Some businesses have integrated the entire design and production process. Computers are used to guide and control the production of a good. Employees supervise the manufacturing part of the operation, checking that it is working effectively and repairing faults. This system is known as COMPUTER INTEGRATED MANUFACTURE (CIM). There is a number of stages in the operation. They are shown in Figure 98.1

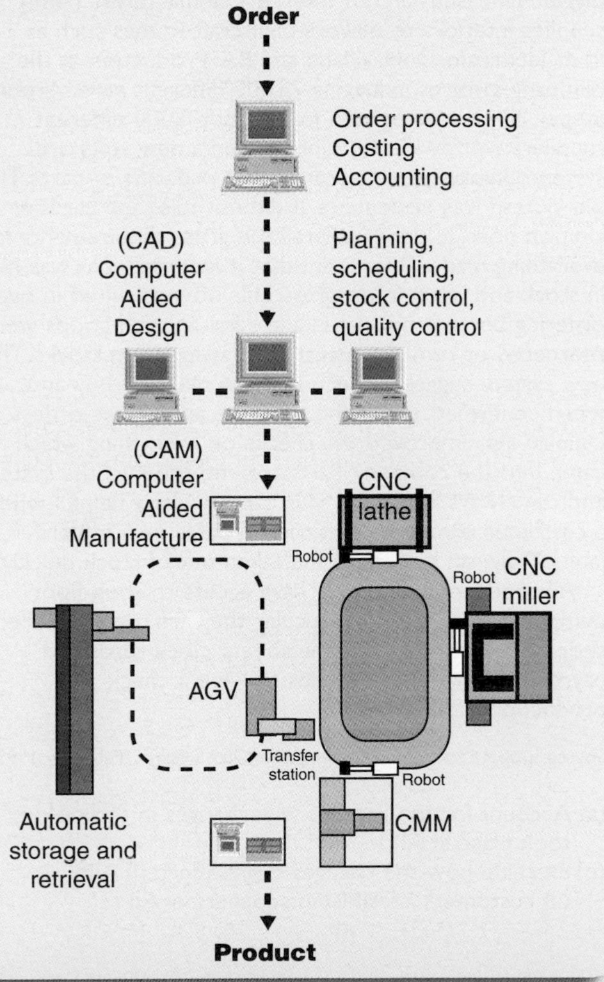

- Orders are received via e-mail, fax or letter and inputted into the system. Costings are carried out on computer using **spreadsheet** programs (☞ unit 9). Customers are stored on **databases**. Accounts are kept on computer and regularly updated. Orders which are received are processed and invoiced at a later date.
- The design department uses CAD packages to design the product for a client, making changes on computer. The instructions to manufacture the design are produced and fed through to the production part of the system.
- Production is planned and scheduled. Parts and materials are ordered as required by the computer, which monitors stock and automatically reorders where necessary.
- The instructions for production are passed to CNC machines which manufacture the product. CMM machines monitor the quality of the work.
- Robots are used to transfer products from one CNC machine to another.
- **Automatically guided vehicles** take components to the machines.
- Finished products are taken to the stores or for dispatch.

Applications in tertiary industry

The supply of services has tended to be relatively more labour intensive (☞ unit 91) in the primary and secondary sectors. This is because supplying services often requires direct and personal contact with customers. However, the use of technology in the tertiary industry is becoming more widespread in a number of areas.

Government and private services There is a range of services provided by government or private alternatives. New technology used in health care and dental care has improved services considerably. Developments in new vaccines and drugs have reduced suffering and cured diseases that not long ago may have led to deaths. Surgeons can carry out exact operations using lasers, viewing them on television screen with the use of fibre optics. Replacement teeth can be produced for patients which exactly fit jaw shapes from materials which will last for years.

Financial services Businesses selling financial services match customers with appropriate financial products. For example, client information can be fed into a computer to identify the most suitable insurance policy or savings plan. The sale of financial products such as ISAs, pensions and insurance policies is increasingly carried out over the telephone. Many financial organisations now have cash dispensers outside their premises. These can be used by customers who want to take out cash with a minimum of fuss or out of normal working hours. Some banks have cash dispensers inside, and

Figure 98.1 Computer integrated manufacture

Order

Order processing
Costing
Accounting

(CAD)
Computer
Aided
Design

Planning,
scheduling,
stock control,
quality control

(CAM)
Computer
Aided
Manufacture

CNC
lathe

Robot

Robot

CNC
miller

AGV

Transfer
station

Robot

Automatic
storage and
retrieval

CMM

Product

customers can enter the bank in non-business hours using 'swipe cards' to open doors. This gives extra security to customers using the facilities.

Distribution The introduction of containers has made the handling of freight quick and easy. They can be hauled onto trailers and locked in position. This prevents movement during transport and possible damage and theft. At port or rail terminals, containers can be loaded safely and quickly onto trains or ships using cranes. Refrigerated containers allow perishable goods to be transported long distances without deteriorating.

Personal services Dating agencies use computers to match couples using personal information held on databases about clients' characteristics and preferences. Agencies also make use of video technology to record messages from clients.

Post and communication Technology has helped to improve the speed and efficiency of postal and packaging delivery. Many businesses have franking machines which weigh and record the required postage. Bar codes allow a free post or business service to be provided by firms. A customer can return a leaflet or envelope without charge to a business. Machines at the post office will read the bar code and bill the business providing the service. Post offices make use of video and televisions to advertise their services.

Hotels, restaurants and transport In the travel industry technology allows customers to travel without a ticket. They can book a flight over the telephone using a credit card. The same card is then used to pick up a boarding pass from an airport machine or a check-in counter. Travellers to Australia can now obtain an 'electronic visa'. Entry can be organised over the telephone by giving passport details to a travel agent. These details are sent electronically to the appropriate port of entry. Booking for hotels or theatre tickets can also be made by credit card. Meals at restaurants can be paid for by a 'swipe or switch' card. The transaction is recorded by a machine and the money is automatically transferred from the current account of the customer.

Advertising In advertising, television makes increasing use of advances in filming technology and special effects to make adverts more sophisticated and entertaining. There is also a growing selection of advertising media. For example, advertisers have used rotating messages on the 'touchlines' of sporting events, or in city centres on the sides of buildings.

Retailing Retailing has benefited in many ways from new technology (☞ unit 46).

● The packaging of goods has changed greatly in recent years. New materials such as polystyrene and strong plastic wrap have improved the way in which goods are packaged. The materials have been lighter and stronger, have

provided better protection, and have been easier to handle. Many firms have redesigned the packaging of goods to increase sales. In some cases new technology has helped. For example, Lucozade and other soft drinks have been packaged in flexible bags instead of cans and bottles.

● There has been a growth in home shopping. Computers and televisions have been linked together to enable shoppers to browse at home and then place orders by telephone or through a link (☞ unit 46). The internet is a growing means of direct selling to customers at home.

● Payment has been made easier. Bar codes and hand held recorders allow customers to register the prices of goods as they shop. This saves time and queues at the checkout. Goods can be paid for by credit or 'swipe cards', increasing security as the customer does not have to carry cash.

Information technology

INFORMATION TECHNOLOGY (IT) is the recording and use of information by electronic means. Some of the uses of IT have already been explained in the previous sections.

Question 3

Biggin Hill-based Aircraft Interior Manufacturers (AIM) supplies interiors to makers of aircraft frames such as Saab, Jetstream, DeHavilland and BA. Production at the company involves managing 78,000 different parts. Around 60 per cent are bought in from about 2,000 different suppliers worldwide. AIM introduced a new software system, Uniplan-plus, to manage the ordering of parts. The old system was inadequate. It did not raise job cards as Uniplan does. It just calculated the gross requirements for everything made. This meant that it ignored what was held in stock and work-in-progress. This often resulted in over-ordering because bought-in and semi-finished goods were reordered or remade instead of drawing from stocks. The new system suggests which parts to make or buy and, when confirmed, raises the purchase and works orders. Uniplan also improved the checks on everything which came into the company. Parts are entered into the system and can always be traced. This is particularly helpful when a customer complains that certain parts on a job are faulty. They can be traced and taken out of stock quickly.

All production staff now have access to shop floor computer terminals. In particular they are used to collect shop floor data, such as time sheets, clock cards and payroll information. This helps to keep a check on production costs.

Source: adapted from *Manufacturing Computer Solutions*, February 1999.

(a) Account for the reasons why changes in technology took place at AIM
(b) Examine how the changes might affect: (i) AIM; (ii) customers of AIM; (iii) suppliers of AIM.

However, there are some common uses of IT which may apply to businesses operating in primary, secondary or tertiary industry.

● Administration. Many routine tasks can be carried out quickly by computer. These may include customer invoicing or billing. Standard letters or memos may be produced which can be easily changed if necessary. Large amounts of information about customers may be stored on databases.

● Personnel. Personnel files are now easily kept on databases. They can be regularly updated. Spreadsheets also allow calculations of salaries and deductions.

● R&D. Computer aided design can be used to research new materials or new product ideas. For example, tests may be carried out on the endurance of materials using a CAD simulation. Recording, monitoring, regulating, forecasting and analysing data are all tasks that can be carried out more easily.

● Finance. Many firms record all financial transactions on spreadsheets. Some allow instant production of financial information such as profit and loss accounts, cash flow forecasts, budgets and financial ratios. It is also possible to make checks on outstanding payments that are due from customers so that credit control will be effective.

● Communications. Developments in information and communications technology (ICT) (☞ unit 82) means that information can be collected, stored and sent electronically in a fraction of a second. This saves money and makes sure information is passed correctly. Mobile telephones, faxes and e-mail mean that people can work from a variety of locations. Information can be sent over great distances and at any time.

● Production information. Information may be stored on the terms of suppliers. Production costs may be calculated on spreadsheets. The ordering of stocks or components may be carried out by computer.

● Information and sales. Many businesses now have their own website on the internet, providing company information. Some are using sites to provide information or to sell products to customers. A reader's survey by *Marketing Technique* about use of the internet by businesses found 75 per cent of respondents worked for companies with their own site. Interestingly, two-thirds of respondents used the internet to monitor competitors' activities.

Data protection

The rapid development in the use of information and communication technology has led to legislation about the collection, storage, processing and distribution of personal data. The **1984 UK Data Protection Act** stated that people or businesses who use personal data must register with the Data Protection Registrar. They must also state the reasons why they hold the data. For example, it may be information held about loans that a person has taken out as a check on their

credit rating. Individuals were also given rights to find information about themselves, challenge the data and claim compensation.

The Act set down 8 conditions with which users must comply.

● Personal data should be obtained and processed fairly and lawfully.

● Personal data can only be held for specified and lawful purposes.

● Personal data cannot be used or disclosed in any manner which is incompatible with the purpose for which it is held.

● The amount of data held should be adequate, relevant and not excessive.

● Personal data should be accurate and kept up to date.

● Personal data should not be kept for longer than is necessary.

● An individual shall be entitled to:
  (a) be informed by any data user if he or she is the subject of personal data and also have access to that data;
  (b) where appropriate, have data corrected or erased.

● Security measures must be taken by data users to prevent unlawful access, alteration, disclosure, destruction, or loss of personal data.

The **1990 Computer Misuse Act** identified certain offences relating to use of computers.

● A person causing a computer to perform a function with intent to secure access.

● Unauthorised access to a computer with the intent to commit a further offence.

● Unauthorised and intentional modification of computer memory or storage media.

An offence is committed if access is unauthorised or if the person knows it is unauthorised. Many codes of practice state that employees may only access information held on a computer which is a relevant part of their work.

Benefits of new technology

There is a number of benefits to business of using new technology.

Increased productivity More can be produced with less and, as a result, businesses may gain higher profits. In addition, fewer of the environment's resources may be used up.

Reducing waste Introducing new technology often results in time being saved and fewer materials being used. For example, technology has created printing machines which waste less paper when printing books or magazines. How resources are used has attracted a great deal of attention in recent years. As the world's population continues to grow it will be necessary to improve resource use even further.

Improving the working environment Statistics on accidents

at work show that the working environment is safer as result of new technology. Mining and manufacturing in particular have benefited. Modern equipment has made work easier and more tolerable. For example, fork lift trucks mean workers no longer need to load goods by hand. These improvements also help to remove workers' dissatisfaction.

Benefits to society Many new products have come onto the market in recent years. Personal stereo systems, video recorders, satellite and digital television, high performance cars and microwave ovens are some examples. New products mean wider consumer choice and possibly higher living standards. Other developments have helped to make our lives easier, such as automatic cash dispensers and mobile telephones.

Improvements in communications Faster means of transport (such as the jet aircraft), answerphones, e-mail computer network links and fax machines are all examples of inventions which have helped to improve the speed of communications.

Higher incomes If firms enjoy greater profits they can afford to pay higher dividends to shareholders and higher wages to employees. Also, if efficiency is improved then products may be sold at lower prices. As the country's income increases the government collects more tax revenue. This could be used to improve the quality of public services or alternatively to reduce the overall level of taxation or government borrowing (☞ unit 26).

Problems with new technology

The introduction of new technology can also cause problems for both business and society.

Cost Development, installation and maintenance can often prove costly. Also, businesses may have to lay off and retrain staff, leading to redundancy payments and retraining costs. If firms borrow to meet these costs, they will have to pay interest. Reorganisation may also be needed. Production may be changed from batch to flow production (☞ unit 91), job descriptions may be changed (☞ unit 76) and in some cases a larger or smaller plant may be needed.

Labour relations In the past, trade unions have resisted the introduction of some new technology because of the threat to their members' jobs. The growth of union and business partnerships in the late 1990s and after the year 2000 may make the introduction of new technology easier.

Job skills New technology creates jobs which require new, technical skills, but replaces manual jobs. These new jobs cannot be done by the existing workforce unless they can be retrained. Often, this is not possible.

Breakdowns Automated production lines are interdependent. If one part of the line breaks down the whole process may stop. There may also be teething problems. Breakdowns occur when technology is first installed. For example, it is argued that the Stock Exchange Automatic Quotation (SEAQ) share dealing system was partially to blame for the 1987 Stock Exchange crash. The system automatically triggered selling instructions, causing big falls in some share prices.

Motivation Some staff may dislike working only with machines. This may affect their motivation (☞ unit 71).

Management The management of technological change is considered very difficult. One reason is due to the rapid pace of the change. When new technology becomes available business managers have to decide whether or not to purchase it, or wait for the next important breakthrough. Deciding when to invest in new technology is very difficult. The management of the human resources leading up to the change, and during the change, requires great skill. People are often unhappy about change in their lives.

Unemployment and employment Much new technology is labour saving. Tasks once carried out by people will be done by machines. As a result people may become unemployed. For example, in automated production lines tasks such as assembly and quality checks are done by robots and CMMs. One or two employees may act as supervisors. On the other hand technology has to be designed, manufactured, installed, programmed, operated, serviced and replaced, which may create new jobs.

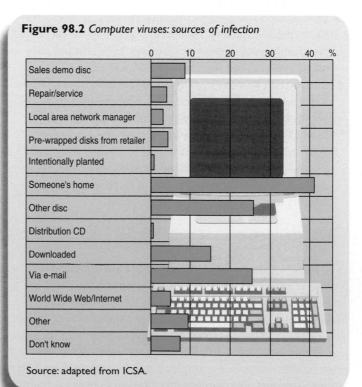

Figure 98.2 *Computer viruses: sources of infection*

Source: adapted from ICSA.

IT problems It is possible for computer software to become infected by viruses. A computer virus is a programme written to deliberately damage or destroy software and files. There are about 18,000 known viruses. One example is the 'Wazu' virus. This randomly swaps words in a document and often puts its title in the text. In the late 1990s writing a virus was not a crime. To be convicted, the writer must have sent a virus with the malicious intent of damaging another person's computer. Such viruses are very damaging and tracing the source is extremely difficult. Sources of viruses are shown in Figure 98.2. It is possible for businesses to use software to check the existence of viruses.

Computer software has other problems which can affect a business. They may have to constantly buy the latest software to be compatible with clients or suppliers who use more modern versions. Modern machines may not run older software. New software may not be able to convert older programs. The **millennium bug** was a major problem for businesses in 1999 as certain computers would not recognise the year 2000.

Leisure time People have gained more leisure time as a result of new technology. They need to learn how to use this extra time in a constructive way. Businesses are taking advantage of this. For example, it is argued that there is enough demand in the UK for many more golf courses.

An ageing population Medicine has benefited greatly from new technology. One effect of this is that the population of many countries is now 'ageing'. As a result the pressure has increased on those in work to support the aged. Demands on public funds will also increase and the government will have to find money for facilities which are needed for the elderly.

Key terms

Computer aided design - the use of computers when designing products.
Computer aided manufacture - the use of computers in the manufacture of products.
Computer numerically controlled machines - machines which have their operations controlled by a computer program.
Computer integrated manufacture - the use of computers to control the entire production process.
Information technology - the recording and use of information by electronic means.
Technology - a creative process which uses human, scientific and material resources to solve problems and improve efficiency.

Question

Sony US's internet site has been likened to an online record store. Splashed across the home page is a logo for the store. A sub-site allows consumers to buy hundreds of albums. Customer orders and credit card details are e-mailed and Sony sends goods through the postal system. US record labels had been reluctant to sell directly to consumers through the internet for fear of upsetting record retailers. Other labels were expected to follow Sony's lead.

The use of the internet as a sales channel by record companies threatened to destabilise the music industry by creating competition between record companies and their retail customers. The online market was small, but growing rapidly in the late 1990s. Consumers appeared to be comfortable buying expensive products such as CDs on the net. One attraction was the opportunity to listen to albums before a purchase was made. Older customers and those in rural areas, who were not used to shopping for albums in stores, were beginning to use the facility.

Record companies were keen to exploit the online sales channel because of its huge profit potential. However, they remained cautious because of the risk of upsetting retailers. Two other record companies, Warner and BMG, had set up their own online sales operations but had used a more subtle approach than Sony to attract customers. Their sub-site advertising was less blatant, offering just a limited range of albums and charging the full listed price.

Source: adapted from the *Financial Times*, 11.8.1997.

(a) Explain the possible advantages to Sony of using the internet as a sales channel?
(b) Explain two possible problems to consumers of buying products on the internet.
(c) Discuss three other ways in which Sony might make use of the internet.

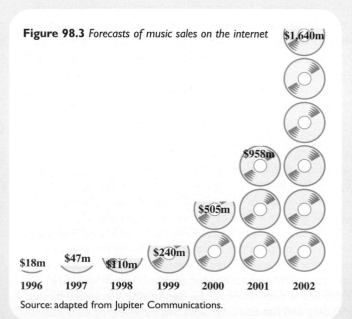

Figure 98.3 *Forecasts of music sales on the internet*

$18m $47m $110m $240m $505m $958m $1,640m
1996 1997 1998 1999 2000 2001 2002

Source: adapted from Jupiter Communications.

Summary

1. What is meant by technology?
2. What is the difference between invention and innovation?
3. State 4 areas of a business that might benefit from new technology.
4. How has new technology been used in marketing?
5. How might a business exporting products abroad make use of new technology?
6. How has information technology been incorporated in production?
7. How has business security used information technology?
8. Why was the Data Protection Act (1984) introduced?
9. In what ways has new technology benefited
   (a) business owners;
   (b) management?
10. Briefly explain problems that:
    (a) workers;
    (b) management;
    may face with the introduction of new technology.
11. How might business exploit the internet?

Case study

Innovation in Motorsport

Motorsport is one of the few areas in which British engineering can claim world leadership. In a typical season Formula One spends around £2 billion. UK component supply and machine tool sectors supply the requirements of the industry. Many machine tool builders have supplier agreements with Formula One teams. There is great pressure on Formula One teams. The sponsors, global car manufacturers, want instant results. Such is the pressure that parts are often taken to a Grand Prix at the last minute as 'hand baggage'. This requirement for high quality and on-time deliveries at short notice also increases the pressure on sub-contractors.

Despite the number of high quality sub-contractors in the industry, some leading Formula One teams have set up their own manufacturing centres. They now have machine shops that feature the latest metal cutting technology, from machining centres to electro-discharge machines (EDM). Many machine shops resemble showrooms due to the high standard of 'housekeeping'. For example, Stewart Grand Prix recently moved to a new state-of-the-art facility at Milton Keynes. The factory is fitted with a wide range of hi-tech machinery. This means that Stewart can manufacture any part to order, day or night, to maintain the car's performance and reliability.

Stewart plans to carry on investing in its own machines and build up capacity. However, it says that sub-contractors will still play an important role, but only if they can achieve high quality, respond to demanding lead times and guarantee total reliability in delivery. Colin McGrory, Stewart's engineering manager, also points out that further investment in new technology may be constrained by capital costs and floor space. He says: 'it is expensive to set up and expand a manufacturing facility, so we will always have a reliance on our better suppliers'.

One supplier is Primrose Engineering of Hemel Hempstead which has supplied the motorsport industry for years. Its managing director, George Speakes, said: 'Motorsport is the most innovative and advanced sector in which we work'. Primrose is committed to the high quality demanded by the industry and has demonstrated this by investing £2.5 million in new technology in the last 5 years. It has purchased new

machine tools and production aids such as EdgeCAM software, co-ordinate measuring equipment, CNC lathes and vertical machining centres. Such investment is necessary to offer the flexibility required by Formula One companies.

The company now has more machines than people. This allows Primrose to react quickly to urgent requirements. According to Speakes the Primrose philosophy is: 'if we need to invest in new machines to stay ahead of technology and to be able to provide a service, we will do so'.

Primrose has also branched out. It invested in heat treatment plant along with non-destructive crack detecting and surface treatment equipment. This would allow it to make suggestions about design changes to Formula One customers, to help in manufacture.

Source: adapted from *Machinery and Production Engineering*, 19.2.1999.

(a) **Identify new technology in: (i) production; (ii) design mentioned in the article.**
(b) **Suggest two constraints on the introduction of new technology.**
(c) (i) **Explain two reasons why Primrose Engineering has invested so heavily in new technology.**
   (ii) **Examine the problems it might encounter as a result of this commitment to heavy investment in technology.**
(d) **Explain how: (i) consumers in the motor car market; (ii) employees at Stewart; might be affected by the commitment to the introduction of new technology.**
(e) **Discuss the need for new technology in the motor racing industry.**

Product choice

New businesses have to decide what product to manufacture or what service to provide (☞ unit 2). Once a business is established, it is unlikely to supply exactly the same product or service indefinitely. Over time businesses modify products, withdraw declining products and introduce new ones. They tend to extend product lines and may even diversify into completely different product areas. Decisions to launch new products or adapt existing ones are often complex and can be uncertain. Most businesses will carry out marketing research before making these decisions. This will help to evaluate the likely success of a new product before production begins.

What influences the products a firm chooses to produce?

The approach of the business Some businesses could be said to be **product orientated**. The nature of the product itself (what it could do and its quality) would be enough to make sure that it sold. For example, when cars were first produced they were unique and a novelty and so the product sold itself. Many firms recognise the need to design products that meet consumers' wishes. These are **market orientated** firms. Increasingly businesses are becoming **asset-led**. They are launching products based on the strengths of the business. For example, a company with a strong brand name for a product may develop other related products (☞ unit 36).

Competitors' behaviour In order to survive in a competitive market, businesses must supply products which customers prefer at the expense of those supplied by competitors. This may mean developing products which are not available, or copying rivals' ideas and improving them.

Technology New inventions and innovations often result in new products. For example, research has resulted in mobile telephones, satellite television, with pay per view options, and digital television with improved picture quality. New materials have been created which have led to improved products. Kevlar is a fibre which is used in the manufacture of bullet proof vests because of its resistance to impact. Carbon fibre racing cycles have been created which are lighter and faster than traditional cycles. Totally new products may be created. Digital video disc (DVD) and laser disc players play films stored on discs similar to CDs. However, they contain far more information.

Management The choice of product is often made by senior management. It is a crucial decision because it may decide the fate of a company. The decision by the Rover Company in the 1990s not to drop the 'Mini' was deemed a success as it subsequently enjoyed strong sales growth abroad.

Question 1

James Dyson earned a reputation over the years as a man who likes to make things work better. Together with his research team he has developed products that have achieved global sales of over £1 billion. His first product in 1970 was the sea truck. Then came the award winning Ballbarrow. Perhaps his most famous product is the Dyson Dual Cyclone vacuum cleaner. In 1979 he noticed that the air filter in the Ballbarrow spray-finishing room was constantly clogging with powder particles (just like a vacuum cleaner bag clogs with dust). This prompted him to design an industrial cyclone tower which removed powder particles by centrifugal force, spinning the extracted air at the speed of sound. The same technology was then adapted to help produce the first bagless vacuum cleaner. This took 5 years and involved making 5,127 prototypes. However, in 1987 a large US manufacturer copied Dyson's design and began manufacturing his invention under their name. After a court battle lasting 5 years, Dyson won back the sole producer rights to the machine.

He then set about his next challenge. Dyson opened a research centre in Chippenham and designed a new model for the UK market. The new model, the Dyson Dual Cyclone, collected much finer particles of dust (microscopic particles which can cause allergies). This system was the first breakthrough in technology since the invention of the vacuum cleaner in 1901. The traditional bag has been replaced by two cyclone chambers which cannot clog. Within them, air circulates at 800mph, generating centrifugal forces that extract dust particles as small as particles of cigarette smoke. The cleaners sell for around £200 each and guarantee maximum suction 100 per cent of the time.

Source: adapted from *The Story of the Dyson Dual Cyclone*.

(a) Explain why Dyson's products are likely to be financially viable.
(b) Examine two factors that may influence the choice of products for Dyson in the future.
(c) To what extent is Dyson's business product or market orientated?

Financial viability Do the benefits of new or adapted goods or services outweigh the costs? The benefit to the firm might be the revenue it gains from selling the product. Accountants often act as a **constraint** on production decisions. They are unlikely to approve funds for products which will make long term losses.

Approaches to product development

Businesses may prefer to develop a new product which is

unique. In practice this is difficult. New product development is expensive and highly risky. As a result most 'new' products tend to be adapted from those which already exist. Product ideas can come from a number of sources.

Ideas from customers Successful firms will be those which provide products which match the wants of customers. Thus it makes sense to listen to the views of customers when forming ideas for new products. The marketing department is likely to play an important role. Questionnaires and interviews can be used to gather data from customers (☞ unit 37). However, it is often argued that less structured methods are more appropriate for collecting new ideas. The use of **focus groups**, where 7 to 10 participants sit to discuss and share ideas about new products, is one approach. Another is to analyse all customer communications, such as complaints and suggestions. It is important for all staff who are in contact with customers to pass on such comments.

Ideas from competitors Companies sometimes rely on copying the products of competitors. This avoids the cost and risk of new product development. It is also difficult to be original. A firm will gain an advantage if it can develop a brand new product and be the first in the market. However, a large number of firms wait for competitors to launch new products and then bring out their own versions. Supermarkets often copy famous brand names when launching their own-label brands of goods. In some cases the copying extends to closely imitating packaging as well as the product. TV companies are quick to bring out their own versions of new quiz games, cookery programmes and other popular TV shows which rival broadcasters launch. Some companies undertake REVERSE ENGINEERING. This process involves taking apart a product to understand how a competitor has made it. A business will closely analyse the product's design and how it has been produced, and identify those key features which are worth copying.

Ideas from staff Businesses may rely on the ideas of their staff for new products. Some staff will work closely with customers and might pass on suggestions for new products as a result of their conversations. Suggestion schemes, where staff might be rewarded for offering new product ideas, are often used.

Ideas from research and development (R&D) Many organisations have research and development facilities. Money is allocated specifically for the invention, experimentation and exploration of new product ideas. This is probably the most expensive source of new ideas. However, the money invested can generate huge returns if a unique product is developed. R&D is discussed in more detail later in this unit.

Ideas from other products Businesses may adapt their own products into new goods or services. They tend to concentrate on best selling brands. Examples might be the development of

Question 2

In 1995, the Rover car company opened a new £30 million product design and development centre in Warwickshire. Around 1,000 staff are employed in the centre, which includes a large showroom where top level discussions and decisions take place based on concept models of cars. Outside is a 'viewing garden', where Rovers' and rival products can be observed in daylight from up to 100 yards. The purpose of this is so that executives never lose contact with how the public sees vehicles. The main building has a central thoroughfare, known as The Street. This includes a number of specialist areas, such as clay model-making, woodmill, trim development, fibreglass styling and a workshop where competitors models are stripped to reveal their secrets.

Two of the specialist research areas have innovative facilities unmatched in the car industry. To tackle tough regulations on noise emitted by passing vehicles, and to overcome effects of the British weather, Rover has built indoor testing facilities. A large chamber is used, where a stationary vehicle is revved on rollers and a computer runs the sound through microphones to reproduce exactly the effect of a moving vehicle. In the Crest facility (combined road and environment simulation test), a vehicle on a suspension-pummelling test rig may also be subject to varying degrees of sunlight, temperature and humidity.

Source: adapted from *The Times*, 12.4.1997.

(a) Using examples from the article, explain how Rover gets ideas for new product development.
(b) What evidence is there to suggest that Rover uses 'reverse engineering'?
(c) Discuss the importance of customer views in new product development at Rover.

ice cream versions of successful chocolate bars, such as the Mars Bar or Bounty.

Product design

In practice, once a business has identified a need for a product, a **design brief** can be written. This will contain features about a product which the designers can use. For example, a firm aiming to produce a new travel iron may write a design brief such as 'a new travel iron is needed which is compact and possesses all the features of a full-sized model'. Designers can work from this design brief. When designing the new travel iron they may take into account:

● the shape and appearance of the iron;
● whether it fits the intended need;
● how easily and cost effectively it can be produced from the design;
● the dimensions and preferred materials to be used;
● the image it gives when displayed;
● whether the design should create a 'corporate identity', saying something about the image of the company.

Well designed products are crucial for businesses. According to the Design Council in 1997, 92 per cent of small businesses believe design provides a competitive edge. Yet 50 per cent still think it is a waste of money. This prompted the council to organise a Design in Business Week to help emphasise that better design means better profits. A 1 per cent investment in design can lead to a 3 or 4 per cent increase in profits. Larger businesses appear to understand this. The British design industry is worth more than £12 billion and employs more than 300,000 people. In manufacturing around £10 billion is spent on product development and design. Examples of well designed products may be Volvo cars, which are recognised for safety, or IKEA furniture, which is well known for its durability, simplicity and usefulness.

The design process

The design process has a number of stages which take the design from an initial idea to a final product. These stages are shown in Figure 99.1.

The design process usually begins when a need is found for a new, adapted or redesigned product. Needs may be identified by the marketing department in a **design brief** for the design team, like the one described for the travel iron above.

The next stage is to produce a **design specification** and **analysis**. One way of achieving this is for the design team, market researchers and the client to meet and discuss their ideas. The design specification and analysis will give a clear description of the purpose of the product, state any functions the product must have and mention constraints, such as cost, size or quality.

Several techniques can be used to produce specifications. One way is to note down all the essential features of a product and be less interested in those which are only desirable. A pair of walking boots might have essential features such as durability, being waterproof, made of leather and comfortable, and desirable features such as attractiveness, lightness and economy in manufacture. Another technique is to 'brainstorm'. This involves listing all possible alternatives or solutions, even

Figure 99.1 *Steps in the design process*

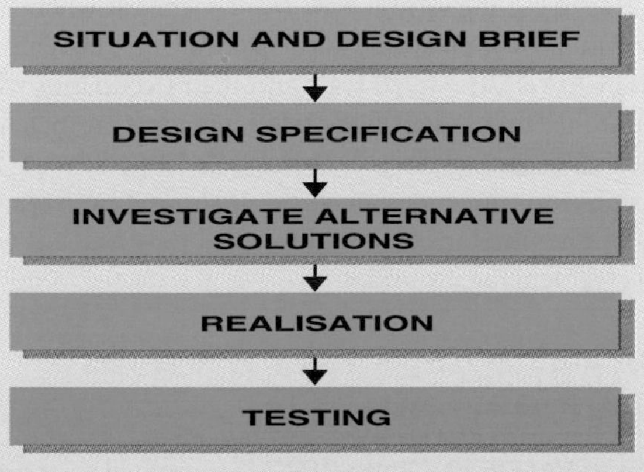

- SITUATION AND DESIGN BRIEF
- DESIGN SPECIFICATION
- INVESTIGATE ALTERNATIVE SOLUTIONS
- REALISATION
- TESTING

those which initially might be considered unlikely.

Next it is necessary to find some practical **solutions** to the design brief. Solutions which the design team have suggested should be assessed. Sketches and working examples will help the evaluation. Finally, the team must decide which model or prototype is the most suitable solution to the problem.

The firm can then **realise** the design solution by making the product. The first production run is likely to be very small because the total design process is not yet complete.

The final stage in the design process is **testing**. Most designs are tested to check that they satisfy the customer. It is often necessary to refine or modify the product. Sometimes new ideas might be generated once the design solution is in a working situation.

Design features

When designing any product a number of features have to be considered by the designer or design team.

Commercial viability Businesses must be able to produce and sell a product at a profit. Thought must be given to the choice of materials and the production techniques that are used so that production costs can be kept down. If the costs are likely to be too high, the design may well be dropped.

Reliability Designers must ensure their designs satisfy customers' expectations about the reliability of the product. Unreliable products may harm the company's image in the eyes of the consumer. The business will also incur costs if products are frequently returned.

Safety Designers must ensure that their design solutions are safe. Safety is particularly important if products are used by children, the elderly, pregnant women and people with injuries. Safety issues which might be important could include:
- ensuring that products do not contain poisons or dangerous materials such as toxic paint;
- designing products which do not have sharp edges or spikes or providing adequate protection if such features are necessary;
- ensuring that products are finished properly so that edges and faces are smooth and clean;
- incorporating safety features such as child proof caps on bottles;
- ensuring that products are durable because a product which breaks could be dangerous.

Maintenance Technical and mechanical products often need maintenance. Products should be designed so that this can be easily carried out. It is particularly important in the design of machinery. The design of the Mini car has been criticised by motor mechanics. They complain that access to parts of the engine is made very difficult by the design. As a result, routine maintenance tasks take much longer and are more expensive for the owner.

Environment In recent years consumers have begun to question the effect certain products have on the environment. Designers now have to take this into account. One example is the use of 'roll on' deodorants instead of sprays which cause CFCs to be emitted.

Convenience and efficiency Products should be designed so that they are convenient and practical to use. For example, some tin openers are 'hand held' whilst others are electrically operated. Consumers are increasingly prepared to pay for products which are easier to use. Businesses also look for machinery and equipment that will lead to a more efficient workforce. Products which are well designed ERGONOMICALLY should increase efficiency and operator safety and also involve less effort for the user.

Manufacture Designers must ensure that their designs are not expensive or technically difficult to make. For example, they may suggest a cheaper material for lining the inside of a suitcase.

Market The designer must consider the marketing mix (☞ unit 40) when designing products. Products are very difficult to market if they are unattractive, clumsy to store and display, expensive to distribute and overpriced.

Aesthetics Designers must consider the colour, size, appearance, shape, smell and taste of products. Many consumers would not wish to be seen wearing poorly designed clothes, for example.

Legal The product should be designed so that it is legally 'fit for purpose'. For example, if a manufacturer claims that a new type of paint is designed to dry within two hours after application, then legally it must.

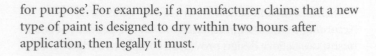

Computer aided design

Computer aided design (CAD) (☞ unit 98) is an interactive computer system which is capable of generating, storing and using geometric and computer graphics. It helps design engineers to solve design problems. CAD is used in many industries today. What benefits does CAD offer to a designer?

● CAD has meant huge cuts in **lead time** (☞ unit 94), ie the length of time between the initial design and actual production. Long lead times result in lower profits as firms lose out to competitors in the race to launch new products.

● A wide range of designs can be shown on the computer screen. Two and three dimensional engineering drawings, wire-framed models, electronic circuit board designs and architectural drawings are examples.

● CAD systems handle repetitive work, allowing the designer more time to concentrate on 'creating' the design. The need for specialists is also reduced, which helps keep down costs.

● Modifications and changes are easily made. The size or shape of a design can be changed in seconds, for example.

● Problems are often more quickly identified. This sometimes prevents the need for expensive reworking later on. Also, the final design, once manufactured, is more likely to be right.

Increasing use is being made of CAD by businesses. In America, customers entering the Digitoe shoe store in Seattle sit in a seat which has a scanner attached to a computer. The equipment takes detailed pictures of their feet. It sends them to a factory where a shoe mould is made and a pair of custom made leather shoes are produced. The first pair are ready in two weeks, but the moulds can be reused and further pairs can be produced within hours of a new order. This sort of individualised production line, called **mass customisation** (☞ unit 91), is a direct result of improvements in CAD and manufacturing software.

CAD was used to allocate tickets in the 1998 World Cup finals in France. The system used allocated tickets to 'virtual stadiums'. The CAD system was also used by the organising committee to see the virtual view from each seat when selecting their own positions in the stadium. CAD helped organisers to visualise filled seats and their occupants, which they found useful in identifying troublemakers at matches. The idea of designing stadia by computer helped the organising committee to plan ahead. It showed how many seats could be fitted inside a stadium and how much it would cost to erect fencing around it.

Value analysis and value engineering

The aim of VALUE ENGINEERING is to reduce costs and

avoid unnecessary costs before production begins. This technique is used by most manufacturers in Japan. It aims to eliminate any costs which do not add value to, or improve the performance of, products and services. VALUE ANALYSIS is a similar process, but is concerned with cost reduction after a product has been introduced.

Value engineering helps businesses to design products at the lowest cost. It is usually carried out by cross departmental teams. Team members might include designers, operations managers, purchasing specialists and cost accountants. The process involves carefully checking components of a product to find ways to reduce their costs. The team will analyse the function and cost of each element and investigate ways to reduce the number of separate components, using cheaper materials and simplifying processes.

The success of value engineering will often depend on how departments work together. Value engineering cannot be undertaken by an individual. Costs can only be reduced if departments take into account each other's needs. For example, in an effort to cut costs, the quality of a product may suffer to such an extent that the marketing department may find it impossible to sell it. The advantages of value engineering include:
- lower costs, resulting in lower prices for consumers;
- more straightforward methods of manufacture;
- fewer components in products, resulting in lower maintenance and repair costs;
- improved co-operation and communication across departments;
- possible 'spin-offs' for other products.

In the late 1990s value engineering was used by Unilever in its capital investment projects. These included plants making products from ice cream to washing powders and speciality chemicals. This helped to reduce the amount of capital needed for a project.

Value analysis has been used by the government to help improve efficiency in some of its departments. For example, the Edinburgh Healthcare NHS trust set up value analysis groups to look at catering services, portering services and laundry. As a result around £400,000 of savings were made on a budget of £5 million. In addition, the quality of services was also improved in some cases.

The nature of research and development

There is a constant need for invention and innovation in business. Businesses must be able to develop new products and improve existing ones in order to grow and to survive. Today, the pace of technological change, coupled with the rising wants and spending power of consumers, has forced firms to respond by investing in research and development (R&D).
- RESEARCH involves the inquiry and discovery of new ideas in order to solve a problem or create an opportunity. Methods used to generate new ideas include laboratory

research, product evaluation of a business's own and its competitors' products and brainstorming.
- DEVELOPMENT involves changing ideas into commercial products. Quite often a business will identify a number of possible ideas which have scope for development. The first stage is to select the idea which shows the most promise. One of the problems with development is the time scale involved. Some projects take many years to complete and success cannot be guaranteed.

The benefits of research and development

Not all businesses can afford to invest in R&D. Those that do may enjoy a number of benefits.

New products R&D leads to the development of new products. Firms which are able to develop new products ahead of their rivals will enjoy a **competitive advantage** (☞ unit 16) in the market. If they can obtain a **patent**, they will be able to sell the product without competition from other business for a period. During this time they may be able to raise price and make higher profits. Examples of businesses benefiting from new products include Dyson, the bagless vacuum cleaner manufacturer, and Microsoft, the creators of the world's main operating system for computers.

New materials Some R&D projects develop new materials. Synthetic materials have helped to reduce the use of natural resources. New materials often have features and characteristics which make them better than natural ones. They might be more durable, heat resistant or malleable, cheaper or lighter. DuPont, for example, created Tactel, a lightweight fabric with great strength. Two years after its invention it had captured 50 per cent of the skiwear market. In addition, the development of new materials often results in the creation of new products.

New production techniques In some industries, such as mechanical and electrical engineering, research projects are designed to develop new types of machines. Computer controlled machines, for example, have been introduced into many component and textile manufacturers and assembly plants (☞ unit 91). New technology is capable of cutting costs and raising productivity. In addition, new machinery is often safer, cleaner and more ergonomically designed. This helps to make the working environment better for employees.

Image It is often argued that expenditure on R&D helps to enhance a firm's image. Consumers may be impressed by businesses which are committed to R&D. This is because consumers themselves appreciate the benefits of R&D and often recognise that such expenditure is risky. Also, breakthroughs in R&D can be highly prestigious. For example, a pharmaceuticals company developing an effective vaccination to combat Aids would receive a huge amount of positive publicity.

Motivation Investment in R&D creates opportunities for creativity and invention. Many employment positions in the R&D department will help staff to satisfy their higher order needs, such as esteem and self-actualisation (☞ unit 71). A successful R&D department might also generate a mood of optimism and anticipation in the organisation. This is likely to have a positive effect on the motivation of staff.

Consumer benefits Consumers enjoy an increasing variety of goods and services as new products come on to the market. They are likely to pay lower prices for products because new technology lowers costs. They may also enjoy better quality products resulting from higher grade materials and more effective production methods. New medicines and drugs will improve health.

The research and development budget

The amount of money allocated to R&D by different businesses varies greatly. The size of the R&D budget may depend on a number of factors.

- It is common for firms to vary their investment according to the funds available in any year. If profits fall for a period of time, R&D spending might fall. Also a business might be criticised by shareholders if too much profit is allocated to R&D at the expense of dividends.
- Certain industries, such as pharmaceuticals, chemicals, motor cars, computers and defence, tend to have high levels of spending on R&D. This is due to the nature of the industry. For example, new drugs are constantly needed to prevent or cure new or existing illnesses.
- Larger public limited companies tend to be more committed to R&D. They are better able to meet the cost and bear the risk involved than smaller businesses.
- Some businesses are committed to high levels of R&D spending because it is part of their corporate objectives and culture (☞ units 4 and 14).
- In some industries businesses are forced to invest in R&D to compete. Failure to keep pace with the investment of rivals may mean that a business struggles to survive in the market.
- Businesses are more likely to invest in R&D when the economy is booming. During a recession R&D funding might be cut or frozen.

Setting a budget for R&D expenditure can be difficult. R&D departments often spend more than they are allocated. Businesses may have to raise funds externally to finance R&D projects. In recent years a number of pharmaceuticals companies have had to use rights issues (☞ unit 57), to raise extra finance to fund research in medicines and drugs. There are several reasons why setting an R&D budget might be difficult.

- The cost of a scientific research project may be difficult to estimate accurately. This is because researchers will not know when a breakthrough is going to occur. Some research, such as for cancer and aids cures, has been ongoing for many years.
- During an R&D project, there may be unforeseen spending. For example, a business might have to unexpectedly recruit staff with specialist knowledge and experience to further the programme.
- Some R&D programmes run for many years. Therefore

Question 4

Swiss-owned textile machine companies produced nearly one third of all textile machinery in the world in 1997. This was quite unusual for such a small country. The market share had risen from about 15 per cent nearly 10 years ago. To achieve the increase Swiss companies extended their production operations around the world and came up with numerous technical innovations. The Swiss textile machine industry employed about 25,000 people, with 15,000 of these outside the country. Most of the 50 or so companies in the industry were privately owned. This might help to account for their commitment to R&D. A spokesman for the textile machine industry in Switzerland said that Swiss companies had consolidated their position by maintaining R&D spending. Swiss companies typically spent 5-8 per cent of their turnover on R&D, while companies in other countries had cut back.

Source: adapted from the *Financial Times*, March 1998.

Figure 99.2 *Production of textile machinery by Swiss manufacturers*

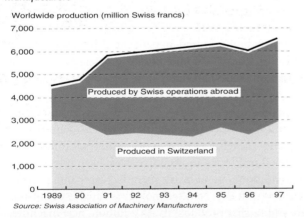

Source: adapted from Swiss Association of Machinery Manufacturers.

(a) Using information from the article, explain the relationship between R&D expenditure and business success.
(b) Examine other possible benefits to Swiss machine makers as a result of their commitment to R&D.
(c) Discuss how the legal status of Swiss textile machine companies may have influenced their policy on R&D investment.

their costs tend to rise with inflation (☞ unit 23). There is a tendency to underestimate inflation and businesses then have to obtain further funding to meet rising costs.

Question 5

(a) Using the information in Table 99.1, discuss which types of industries are committed to heavy expenditure in R&D.
(b) Suggest reasons why pharmaceuticals companies invest so heavily in R&D.
(c) Using examples, explain what types of business might spend relatively little on R&D.

Table 99.1 *Ranking of UK companies by R&D expenditure (Top 20)*

Company	Rank	1996 R&D spend £000	Annual % change
All companies composite		**9,597,041**	**6.0**
Glaxo Wellcome	1	1,161,000	-3
SmithKline Beecham	2	764,000	17
Zeneca	3	602,000	10
Unilever	4	600,000	3
Shell Transport & Trading	5	449,000	-7
General Electric	6	432,000	5
Ford Motor	7	320,000	118
British Telecom	8	282,000	4
Reuters	9	202,000	6
Rolls-Royce	10	199,000	-3
ICI	11	191,000	3
British Aerospace	12	156,000	31
Siebe	13	145,000	29
Siemens	14	133,000	1
British Petroleum	15	127,000	3
BTR	15	127,000	11
IBM	17	112,000	11
Lucas Varity	18	106,800	-1
ICL	19	101,300	-32
BOC	20	98,500	8

Source: adapted from *UK R&D Scoreboard*, Dti, 1997.

Patents

A PATENT aims to protect the inventor of a new product or manufacturing process. It allows a business to design, produce and sell a new invention and prevents competitors from copying it. New inventions can be protected for up to fifteen years. The developer must make details of the invention available to the Patent Office.

Obtaining a patent can be a lengthy process. To qualify for a patent the invention must be brand new. Checks are then made to ensure it is authentic. The patent is published eighteen months after its application and signed and sealed some time after this. The developer must pay annual fees to the Patent Office which become more expensive after the first four years. This is to encourage production of the new idea. Both the inventor and the consumer can benefit from patents. Some benefits to businesses of patents are:
● a higher level of sales;
● reduced competition;

● legal protection that encourages continued research;
● higher profits which can be ploughed back into further research and development;
● the industry benefits from the technical information as a result of the patent;
● high risk research and development is encouraged.

Consumers also benefit. New products mean more variety and perhaps a better standard of living. New, more efficient, productive techniques mean lower costs and lower prices.

There is a number of criticisms of the patent system. The granting of sole production and distribution rights to one firm creates a legal monopoly (☞ unit 18). If this monopoly power is abused then consumers may be exploited. Figure 99.3 illustrates some examples of ideas which have been patented in the past and the extent of their financial success.

Figure 99.3 *Examples of patented ideas*

Catseye patent March '35
Financial benefit:
£2,340,776

Polaroid patent June '46
Financial benefit:
$603,000,000

Ring-pull patent June '65
Financial benefit:
£49,000,000

No FM patent -
Financial benefit:
£0.00

Source: adapted from The Patent Office.

Key terms

Development - the changing of new ideas into commercial propositions.
Ergonomics - the study of people in their working environment and the adaptation of machines and conditions to improve efficiency.
Patent - a licence which prevents the copying of an idea.
Research - an investigation involving the process of enquiry and discovery used to generate new business ideas.
Reverse engineering - a method of analysing a product's design by taking apart the product.
Value analysis - a procedure to evaluate a product after manufacture to see how costs may be reduced.
Value engineering - a procedure designed to reduce and avoid unnecessary costs before production begins.

Summary

1. How can the behaviour of competitors and the state of technology affect the product a firm chooses to produce?
2. How might a business find out if there is a need for a product?
3. What is meant by a design brief?
4. Describe the stages in the design process.
5. What is meant by a design feature?
6. State 6 design features that a firm might consider important when designing a product.
7. How does CAD improve business efficiency?
8. How will value analysis benefit consumers?
9. What is the difference between value analysis and value engineering?
10. State 3 benefits of R&D to businesses.
11. State 2 industries where R&D expenditure tends to be high.
12. What are the benefits of patents to a business?

Case study

BOC

BOC is a large UK-based plc which began trading over 100 years ago as Brin's Oxygen Company. The company was incorporated in 1886 and began producing oxygen in a factory in Westminster, London. The oxygen was used in theatres to intensify limelight and in hospitals to help patients breathe after surgery. Technological developments then allowed BOC to separate all of its major components - nitrogen, oxygen and argon. The business grew as new uses and markets were found for these gases.

In the 1960s BOC embarked on a period of diversification. This was prompted by limited growth potential in the distribution of gases. In particular, BOC acquired Edwards High Vacuum. This formed the basis of what turned out to be a very significant business interest.

In the late 1990s the company had four main business areas - gases and related products, vacuum technology, distribution services and healthcare. Its customer base is drawn from a wide range of industries and includes electronics, food, water treatment, chemicals, pharmaceuticals, hospitals, clothes, distribution and glass coatings.

The management of BOC is committed to investment in R&D. It believes that the development of new technology is crucial to the continuing growth of the company and its ability to remain competitive. BOC's gases business has flourished as a result of its ability to provide technical solutions to customer problems relating to their production costs, product quality, operational productivity and environmental performance.

BOC is committed to the development of technology which reduces its own operating costs. It has already been successful in reducing the consumption of electricity in its plants, the biggest single operating expense. BOC is also developing technology which cleans air before entering its plants and improving and simplifying the complex systems for cooling, liquefying, and separating the air into its constituent gases. More than 90 per cent of BOC's plants installed in 1997 included some new technology to reduce power consumption and capital cost.

New technology has helped BOC to supply the electronics industry with higher purity gases, more efficient plants, and complete systems for controlling gases from the point of production to the point of use in microchip production.

For BOC, business strategies determine technological priorities. Those who run BOC's business operations influence the choice of R&D projects, how urgent they are and where they should be centred. BOC has 20 R&D programmes ongoing around the world, mainly in Europe and the US. Total R&D expenditure fell in 1997 by 18 per cent to £80.6 million. This was after an 8 per cent rise in the previous year and was due to the disposal of Delta Biotechnology, which carried a significant commitment to R&D.

(a) Using examples from the article, explain the benefits of R&D to BOC.
(b) Examine the factors that are likely to affect BOC's R&D budget in future.
(c) (i) Using the data in Figure 99.4, estimate the R&D/sales ratio for each year. (ii) Comment on the changes in R&D expenditure and the R&D/sales ratio over the time period.
(d) To what extent are patents important for a business such as BOC?
(e) Many businesses have chosen to 'outsource' R&D, to other companies that specialise in research. Discuss whether BOC should undertake this strategy.

Figure 99.4 Turnover, R&D expenditure and patents granted for BOC, 1994-97

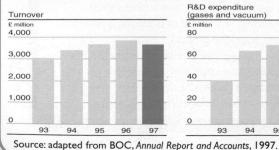
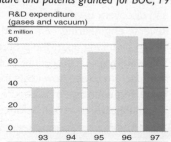
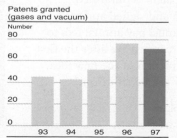

Source: adapted from BOC, Annual Report and Accounts, 1997.

Location decisions

The decision about where to locate is crucial to many businesses. It can affect their sales, costs, profitability and perhaps even their survival.

Why might a company need to make a decision about where to locate?
● New businesses will need to carefully consider where to locate their initial premises.
● Existing businesses may need to expand, but may be unable to do so on their present sites.
● The modernisation of a business may involve moving to more up-to-date premises.
● A business aiming to cut its costs might achieve this by re-locating.
● A multinational company aiming to set up a new plant in another country for the first time may evaluate a variety of possible locations worldwide.

There are many factors which will influence a business's decision about where to locate. It is likely that any location decision will be influenced by a few or many of these factors. When deciding where to locate its premises, a business usually weighs up all potential costs and benefits of setting up in a particular area. This may be carried out with the use of **cost-benefit** analysis (☞ unit 104).

Power and raw materials

Primary industry (☞ unit 1) needs to be located near to raw materials. In the UK, agricultural production has been, and still is, found in areas such as the South, East Anglia, Wales and Scotland. The location of mining and extraction is determined by deposits of raw materials like coal, oil and iron ore. In the UK such deposits in the past have been found in the North. This is also true of offshore oil findings.

After the Industrial Revolution, secondary manufacturing industry largely located close to raw materials and sources of power. This is true of most Western industrialised countries. In the UK industry moved to the North and Midlands, in Germany to the Ruhr region and in the USA to areas such as the Mid-West. One of the reasons for this was that coal was the main source of power for these industries. Also, transport systems were poor by today's standards and raw materials were costly to carry.

It could be argued that these 'traditional factors' are no longer as important as they were. Gas and electricity systems mean that being close to a power source is no longer a constraint for most firms. Also, transport systems now carry goods relatively cheaply and efficiently to manufacturers. Businesses which are still located close to raw materials tend to be ones which have extremely bulky raw materials, which are then reduced to easier-to-transport final products. For

example, timber yards and saw mills might be located close to forests and food caning plants may be located close to agricultural areas.

Markets and transport costs

For some businesses, being close to their market is often the single most important factor in choosing a location. A variety of businesses may be influenced by this factor.
● Businesses that produce products which are more bulky than the raw materials that go into them, such as North Sea oil platforms, are likely to locate close to their market. The components and materials used to assemble North Sea oil platforms are far less bulky than the end product - the platform itself. Therefore, the production of such platforms takes place in locations close to where they will eventually

Question 1

As a centre of business, London can hold its own against similar centres such as Paris and Frankfurt. London has 541 foreign banks, more than any other city in the world. In 1996, 17,429 jobs were created or protected in the South East. The capital itself attracted 22 new firms. £4 billion was invested in the capital's leisure industries alone in the run-up to Millennium 2000. The decision to site the millennium celebrations in London appeared to have given the economy a boost. For example, 9,500 hotel bedrooms were to be built between 1995 and 2000. In 1996 only 7 firms moved out of London, a record low according to Jones Lang Wootton, the estate agents. A survey by Black Horse Relocation Services found that, for the first time, the capital was the favoured place for relocation within the UK. Aggressive marketing helped to attract 27 major relocations over two years.

Nikko Securities, Japan's third largest broker, reorganised, giving London, rather than Tokyo, responsibility for its international operations. The company decided to base its global operations in London, ahead of New York, because the UK was more convenient for dealing with Asia and the US. Nikko is also planning to appoint two non-Japanese directors to its board.

Source: adapted from *The Times* and the *Financial Times*, 1997.

(a) Using examples from the article, suggest types of business that may benefit from location in London.
(b) Explain the possible reasons for the location of these businesses in London.
(c) Examine two possible implications for Nikko securities of its decision to locate in London rather than in New York.

be used - the North Sea coast - in cities such as Aberdeen. If production was located elsewhere transport costs may be very high. There may also be problems transporting the product to its final destination.

● Suppliers of components and intermediate goods may set up close to their main customers. For example, a number of firms emerged in the Liverpool area supplying shipping companies with packing cases for transportation. After the dock industry declined in Liverpool, some of these companies still existed.

● Many financial service businesses locate their premises in London. Some would argue that London is the 'financial centre' of the world.

● The growth of the tertiary sector and the decline in 'heavy' industry has resulted in many FOOTLOOSE secondary and tertiary industries. Businesses in these industries are able to locate premises where they wish. Given this freedom many have chosen to locate by their markets. The South East of the UK developed a service economy as a result, made up of retailing, financial services, leisure industries and a small amount of 'light' manufacturing.

● Most service industries tend to be located near to markets. Businesses providing the general public with services like dentistry, dry cleaning and car maintenance must locate their premises in areas which are accessible to people.

Closeness to the market can also be a **site factor** affecting the location of a business. Site factors affect the choice of one plot of land or one premises rather than another after the business has decided to locate in a particular area. For example, WH Smith originally located its outlets in railway stations because its main market was railway passengers buying newspapers and magazines. When it moved out of railway stations, it located its outlets in the nearest available premises. Small retailers supply the needs of local communities. The 'corner shop', for example, relies mainly on customers from a very small local catchment area.

Communications

The ease of communications can be important in a firm's location decision. Access to motorways, rail networks, ports and airports may all be important. By reducing travel time, motorways may encourage firms to locate premises in areas which might have been regarded as remote from markets or costly in terms of transport. The building of the M4 between London and South Wales has encouraged location along the 'M4 corridor'.

The accessibility of ports and airports might also be important. This is often true of firms which export their goods. For firms which produce light, low bulk, but high value products, air transport might be the best means of reaching both overseas and domestic markets. More bulky and heavy goods might be transported by sea. Businesses which use a great deal of imported raw materials might also locate close to a port.

Question 2

In June 1996 the new Severn bridge was officially opened. The bridge, which is the longest bridge in the UK, spans the River Severn linking South Wales and England. It was built because the original bridge, constructed 30 years ago, could not handle the current traffic volume (19 million vehicles per year). This had resulted in congestion and delays for traffic. In addition the old bridge was dangerous during high winds and often had to be closed. The new bridge had a windshield to prevent this. The reduced risk of delays is hoped to prevent commercial traffic finding alternative routes using unsuitable roads through Gloucestershire.

For Cardiff Bay, the ambitious government-funded scheme to revitalise the City's Victorian docks area, the opening of the new bridge could not have been timed more perfectly. At the same time new road links to Cardiff Bay were also due to be completed. The number of annual visitors to Cardiff was expected to rise from 1.5 million to 2 million by the year 2000.

Figure 100.1 *The new Severn Bridge*

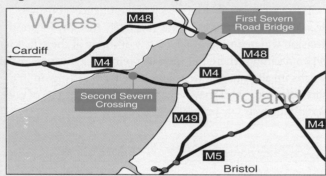

Source: adapted from the *Financial Times*, 1997.

(a) State three advantages to businesses of the new Severn Bridge.
(b) Explain how the construction of the bridge might affect:
  (i) relocating businesses from other areas;
  (ii) site location in Cardiff.
(c) Do you think that Cardiff or Bristol will benefit most from the construction of the new bridge?

The building of the Channel Tunnel improved trade links to the Continent when it was opened. It allowed UK businesses to distribute goods easily and effectively to Europe. It also encouraged firms to locate in the South East if they have markets in Europe. The Channel Tunnel became even more important when trading restrictions with Europe were lifted in 1992. Other regions in the UK may well benefit from increased trade with Europe via rail links. However, with increasing congestion on all motorways, firms with European interests are likely to favour the South East.

Good communications can also be a factor influencing the choice of site. For example, a business locating in Leeds may choose to build a factory close to the M62/M1 junction rather than north west of the city. In many towns and cities, industrial estates tend to be located close to motorways or railway stations.

Land

When choosing where to locate or re-locate premises, firms need to select the 'right' piece of land. This might be a newly completed factory unit, a derelict inner city site, an old factory in need of modernisation or a piece of land never previously used for a business development. When choosing an appropriate piece of land, firms are likely to take into account some combination of the following site factors.

● The cost relative to other potential sites. A firm must compare purchase prices of alternative sites, consider whether or not renting would be more cost effective and compare the level of business rates in each location.
● Certain businesses may need to locate near to rivers or in coastal areas to dispose of waste. Examples might be chemical plants or coal fired power stations.
● The amount of space available for current needs. Some businesses require large areas of land. For example, car manufacturers need sites of several hundred acres.
● Potential for expansion. It is important that firms look into the future when locating premises. When Kellogg's acquired a new cornflake manufacturing plant in Northern Italy, one of the reasons why it favoured Brescia was

because of the large amount of adjacent land which they hoped to use in the future for expansion.
● The availability of planning permission. This is particularly important if a firm is going to change the use of some land or premises, or construct new buildings. Local authorities will not always grant planning permission allowing land development, for example in GREEN BELT areas.
● Geological suitability. Some businesses require particular geological features. A nuclear power station must be sited on a geologically stable site.
● Good infrastructure. Facilities such as good road links, appropriate waste disposal facilities and other public utilities are often an important influence.
● Environmental considerations. Today, firms may face pressure from public opinion when locating premises. There can be opposition from pressure groups if they attempt to locate in environmentally sensitive areas.

Some firms in recent years have opted to move their premises out of traditional industrial areas to GREEN FIELD sites. These are, literally, rural locations generally found on the outskirts of towns and cities. Here the land tends to be cheaper and more plentiful. However, there may be opposition from environmentalists and green field sites can only be developed if there is adequate access. These sites are becoming more popular and are particularly suitable for hi-tech industries. An example was the new location for the *Lancashire Evening Post*. It moved from the centre of Preston to a greenfield site adjacent to junction 32 on the M6 on the outskirts of the town. Brand new premises costing £28 million were built on a plot of land which was previously used for non-commercial purposes.

The use of BROWNFIELD sites for business location is also increasing. According to the government, a brownfield site is an area of land which was previously used for urban development. Some brownfield sites in the UK have been derelict for many years. One such site is the Greenwich peninsular in London. The site used to house a huge gasworks, but became a rubbish dump and scrapyard for much of southeast London. In the late 1990s it was chosen as the location for the Millennium Dome and a number of businesses competed for contracts to build on the land.

Labour

Firms re-locating from one part of the country to another will aim to take most of their staff with them. This should cut down on disruption and avoid the need to recruit and train large numbers of new staff. Sometimes, businesses try not to move very far so that staff can travel from their existing homes. For example, the Woolwich Building Society, when re-locating from North London, chose Bexley Heath in North Kent - already the home of a large number of their employees.

However, if re-location is a long way from the original position, persuading existing staff to move can be difficult.

Question 3

In March 1999 Wembley Stadium was sold for £106 million to the National Stadium Development Company. The sale paved the way for a £250 million rebuilding into a 90,000 seater sports arena on the same site. It was suggested that the new stadium would help the bid for the 2006 World Cup because of the worldwide respect for Wembley.

The area of the River Trent between Lincolnshire and Nottinghamshire contains a series of coal fuelled power stations. Such stations need to dispose of large quantities of hot water which comes from steam turbines that drive the generators.

(a) Contrast the land related factors that may affect the location decisions of the businesses above.
(b) Examine other factors that might affect the location decisions.

During the late 1990s employment in manufacturing in the UK was declining. However, Wales managed to buck this trend. In the mid-1980s unemployment in Wales was around 13 per cent, compared with the UK average of 10 per cent. In 1997 unemployment in Wales was down to 7.5 per cent compared with 6.9 per cent in the UK. Wales benefited from heavy investment in the region by overseas manufacturing companies. Around 400 overseas-owned businesses employed 157,000 people in Wales. In addition these companies had invested more than £10.2 billion in capital projects. The two main areas of development in Wales, electronics and automotive components, experienced huge expansion. The growth, according to Professor Garel Rhys of Cardiff Business School, was because of Wales's low unit labour costs. 'That does not mean low wages', he insisted. He argued that wages paid by foreign employers in Wales are higher than those paid by domestic companies. The unit wage costs are lower because the productivity of Welsh workers is higher. In addition, the flexible nature of the Welsh workforce was noted as important by 50 of the country's top overseas employers, according to a survey by the accountancy firm, Coopers & Lybrand.

The Welsh Development Agency set up a management training programme for businesses introducing Japanese ideas on shop-floor efficiency, communications and relationships with suppliers. This helped managers in the region to come to terms with working practices which foreign investors might want to enforce. In addition, a training centre in semi-conductor electronics has been set up by a local Tec and Imperial College. This was to ensure that skill shortages do not occur.

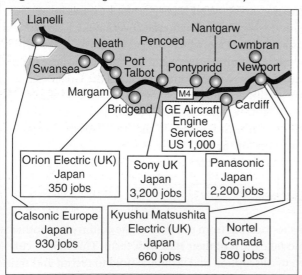

Figure 100.2 *Foreign investment in South Wales by 1997*

Source: adapted from *The Times*, January 1997.

(a) Explain the phrase 'unit wage costs are lower because the productivity of Welsh workers is higher'.
(b) Explain the features of the Welsh labour market which might be attractive to overseas employers.

Selling existing homes, buying new homes, disrupting childrens' education and removal costs can be real obstacles. When choosing a site, firms need to find out whether existing employees can be persuaded to move and whether other sources of labour with the right skills can be recruited locally. Factors that existing staff may feel are important may be the cost of housing, the quality of the local environment, the quality of local schools and perhaps the number of traffic jams in the area.

Labour skills are not evenly distributed throughout the country. If a firm needs a particular type of skilled labour there may be regions which are especially suitable. For example, a firm which is contemplating a new venture in carpet manufacturing might choose Kidderminster as a possible location. Kidderminster is famous for carpet manufacturing and could offer a firm new to the industry a ready supply of appropriately skilled and semi-skilled workers. Other examples of these regional advantages include car workers in the West Midlands, pottery workers in Stoke-on-Trent and steel workers in Sheffield. Where an industry is concentrated in a particular region advantages, such as expertise in local schools and colleges, research facilities in nearby universities and sympathetic and supportive local government agencies often exist. These are known as **external economies of scale** (☞ unit 93).

Information and communication technology

An increasingly important factor in location is access to telecommunications links (☞ unit 82). Telecommunications networks, such as BT's integrated services data network (ISDN), have the capacity to send and receive voices, data and pictures at great speed. The information technology revolution has meant that firms can link separate branches or sections of their operations by computer. Large firms with a Head Office in London, for example, are able to place personnel in locations hundreds of miles from the Capital. Businesses no longer need to concentrate their office staff or production in one location because of communication problems. They can also employ people working at home and contact them via e-mail or fax machine.

Company intranets now allow large numbers of employees to have easy access to the same information. For example, information collected by a member of the marketing department on customers' characteristics will be available to other members of other areas of the business such as R&D.

UK government influence

The UK government has influenced the location of business for many decades, probably since the 1920s. There has been a need to revitalise certain areas where key industries have declined. For example, the North East was hit when the shipbuilding industry declined. The North West region suffered when the textile industry collapsed. The main reasons for government intervention in business location are to:

● control development where there is 'business congestion' and adequate employment;
● encourage firms to locate their operations in regions where unemployment is high and business activity is lacking;
● attract foreign businesses to the UK.

The government has attempted to help areas with particular problems in the UK through REGIONAL POLICY (☞ unit 26). This has involved the use of incentives to attract businesses to regions in need of revitalisation. Incentives have included investment grants, tax breaks, employment subsidies and rent free factory space. In the late 1990s a number of areas in the UK were eligible for help. The Department of trade and industry defined these ASSISTED AREAS as: 'locations of considerable development potential. They all have an available workforce, competitive labour costs and high labour flexibility. They share the benefits which Britain as a whole has for the investor in terms of market proximity, good communications, low taxes, the language of business, a deregulated business environment and a government attitude which welcomes investment and enterprise'.

Assisted areas are divided into DEVELOPMENT AREAS and INTERMEDIATE AREAS. Development areas are regions which are the most severe in terms of decline and need. They include areas such as Merseyside and the Wirral, Tyneside, parts of the West Midlands, Glasgow and the surrounding area and South Yorkshire. Intermediate areas still qualify for help, but do not enjoy the same benefits as development areas. Examples of help available to businesses locating in assisted areas include the following.

Regional Selective Assistance (RSA) This is a grant available for investment projects that would create or safeguard jobs in assisted areas. Grants can be up to £2 million. Projects which create overcapacity and just displace jobs elsewhere in the UK do not qualify.

Regional Enterprise Grants These are either investment grants or innovation grants. Investment grants are available to businesses with no more than 25 employees for projects in Development Areas and locations affected by colliery closure, up to a maximum of £15,000. Innovation grants are available to firms with no more than 50 employees for innovative R&D projects which lead to the introduction of new products or processes. Under this scheme grants of up to 50 per cent of the cost of projects are available to a maximum of £25,000.

European Investment Bank (EIB) The EIB grants loans to SMEs anywhere in the UK for investment projects in most industrial sectors. Loans are available from a range of financial institutions for projects up to £20 million. The EIB also provides large loans for capital investment projects in

industry or infrastructure. Examples of sectors eligible for EIB loans include advanced technology, environmental protection, transport, telecommunications and energy.

Enterprise zones The government attempts to encourage business activity in designated ENTERPRISE ZONES. These are small geographical areas, perhaps a few hundred acres of land, located in urban areas. Areas are given enterprise zone status for 10 year periods. Location in these zones can be attractive. Businesses may be exempt from tax and statutory and administrative controls can be relaxed or speeded up.

Training and Enterprise Councils (Tecs) and Business Links Tecs in England and Wales (☞ unit 2), and Local Enterprise Councils in Scotland, are responsible for allocating government funding for training and vocational education. Business Links have been the first point of contact for smaller businesses or SMEs looking for help. They provide advice, for example, on how to apply for RSA.

Government offices (GOs) Government offices in English regions try to integrate the approaches of the DTI and DfEE and Transport Department. A Single Regeneration Budget (SRB) combines 20 programmes into one budget. It aims to develop partnerships for local development between regional organisations.

Regional Development Areas (RDAs) In the 1990s partnerships between private businesses and local government were encouraged. They worked together to obtain EU funding and encourage regional development. The Scottish Enterprise and Welsh Development Agency did the same. For example, in 1997 the WDA encouraged Lucky Goldstar, a Korean microchip manufacturer, to locate in Newport with a package reported to be worth £200 million. The business would eventually employ 6,000 workers. In 1999 the Labour government developed the partnerships in English regions into **Regional Development Areas** (RDAs). Their tasks were to:
● promote the region and represent its interests in UK central government and in the EU;
● encourage local and regional development strategies;
● monitor and report on trends taking place in the region;
● help to attract inward investment to the region and to the UK.

Public sector businesses Another way in which the government could influence business location is by locating public sector business in depressed regions. For example, the government moved around 4,000 Ministry of Defence Procurement Executive staff from London to Abbey Wood, Bristol in 1996. Eventually, Abbey Wood would employ around 5,000 staff, with new employees being recruited locally.

EU influence

The EU provides a range of funds for businesses which locate in assisted areas. Most are **structural funds**. Between 1994-99 the EU allocated about £120 billion to these funds. Structural funds include the following.

● The European Social Fund (ESF) provides money for the development of human resources. The money can be used to fund training schemes and is designed to solve labour market problems. For example, a Horizon project in Bristol designed to train childcare workers was funded from this source. Since 1994 Merseyside has received £630 million from the ESF.

● The European Regional Development Fund (ERDF) provides money in the most disadvantaged regions for the development of infrastructure. Examples might be the building of roads and improvements in telecommunications.

● The Agricultural Guidance and Guarantee Fund provides money for the creation and protection of jobs in rural areas.

● The Financial Instrument for Fisheries Guidance helps the development of the fisheries industry.

The **Cohesion Fund** was set up in the 1990s to help the preparations for economic and monetary union in Greece, Ireland, Spain and Portugal. The EIB also provides loans to support social cohesion.

Industrial inertia

When businesses in the same industry locate in an area with similar firms, this is called INDUSTRIAL INERTIA. Even when the original advantages cease to exist, new firms might be attracted to the area. The textile industry, although much smaller, persists in the North West. The original attractions, coal and water, have been replaced by other power sources and the natural humidity of the area can be imitated by mechanical means. In addition, natural fibres have been replaced by synthetic materials. Firms continue to locate because of other advantages. These include a supply of skilled labour, specialist marketing and support services and a range of amenities aimed at the textile industry.

Industrial inertia does have disadvantages. When a region relies heavily on one industry it will suffer if that industry declines. One example is the demise of steel producing plants in the 1980s, which devastated areas like Consett in Durham and many parts of South Wales. Throughout the 1990s many UK coal mines were closed down in areas where the local pit was the main employer.

International location

Increasingly businesses are looking to locate parts of their operations in different countries around the world. In the 1990s, for example, Asian companies such as Honda, Nissan,

Question 5

Merseyside is one area in the country which has suffered particularly from a reduction in business activity and a rise in unemployment in the last 20 years. As a result of the decline in GDP per head, it has fallen well below the EU average and the area qualifies for EU funding. Since 1994 Merseyside has benefited from around £1 billion of support. Much has been used to set up industrial estates and business parks which provide attractive locations for a wide range of businesses.

Knowsley is one location which has enjoyed a great deal of success in attracting businesses from all over the world. Companies producing a wide range of products and services, such as Kodak, News International, Liverpool Football Club, Direct Line, QVC (the US shopping channel), Telewest and Delco Electronics, have been attracted to Knowsley's business and industrial parks. With over 2000 companies based in the area Knowsley boasts a diverse and varied economic base. Figure 100.3 shows a breakdown of companies in Knowsley by SIC classification.

Knowsley has a team of staff to help potential investors. A business will be allocated a personal Investment Executive to create a tailor made solution from locating a building or developing land, to packaging grants and assisting with the creation of a suitable workforce. Knowsley is also in partnership with Merseyside Tec, English Partnership and Government Office for Merseyside. The area offers the most competitive financial packages in the world. Location in the area qualifies for the following funding opportunities.

● ERDF to help with land and building costs.

● Regional Selective Assistance for commercial projects.

● Merseyside Special Investment Fund which is aimed at SMEs in Merseyside. This fund offers loans/equity investment up to £500,000 as part of a package usually in conjunction with financial institutions.

● English Partnerships, the national Urban Regeneration Agency, helps to reclaim and develop vacant, derelict, underused and contaminated land and buildings. The partnership often provides funding.

Source: adapted from Knowsley's Business Resource Centre brochure, 1998.

A rapidly expanding manufacturer of large air conditioning units with markets in the UK and America is considering relocation in Knowsley. Evaluate the part that:
(i) government;
(ii) other factors; are likely to play in the decision.

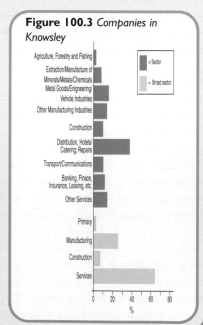

Figure 100.3 *Companies in Knowsley*

Daewoo and QPL located production in Europe. Businesses will aim to locate their operations where costs are minimised and customers can be best served.

A number of factors may influence the decision of a business to locate its operations in another country. Some of the factors influencing the location of businesses in other countries may be the same as those affecting location in a different region of a particular country.

● Protectionism. When a business **exports** to another country (☞ unit 26), the country receiving the product may raise its price by placing a tariff or tax on the good. It might also restrict the number of goods entering the country by quotas. One way to avoid these restrictions is to produce and sell products in the country which imposes the restriction. These goods are then classified as domestic output and avoid tariffs or quotas. Many Japanese companies have located in the EU because it imposes tariffs on products entering the EU from foreign countries. In recent years it could be argued that protectionism has declined. Countries such as India, Japan and Russia have allowed foreign products to enter their countries.

● Legislation and bureaucracy. Businesses want to avoid countries which impose restrictive laws and time consuming bureaucracy when locating operations. They are more likely to locate in countries where there is a liberal approach to issues like health and safety, the environment and employment legislation. For example, some multinationals may have located in the UK rather than other European countries before 1997 because the UK opted out of the Social Chapter (☞ unit 81). They argued that the rights given to workers by the Social Chapter raised the labour costs of businesses.

● Political stability. Businesses will tend to reduce risk by avoiding the location of plants in countries where the political system is unstable. Countries such as Yugoslavia, Lebanon, Algeria, Sri Lanka and Columbia may not be attractive because of political instability or possible military action. In addition, certain countries still operate fairly closed economies and foreign businesses are not welcome.

● The labour force. The cost of labour in different countries may affect the location decision of a business. Multinationals have set up production operations in Asia, where wages in countries like China and South Korea are comparatively very low. More recently countries such as the UK have been able to offer competitive wage rates. The quality of the workforce is also a key factor. Companies will locate plants in countries where the workforce is flexible, cooperative, highly motivated, well trained and talented.

● Market opportunities and transport costs. Some businesses locate plants in countries where they see selling opportunities. When trying to enter a new market, it may be more cost effective to supply the market from within. In particular, if the products are bulky like motor cars, shipping costs from one side of the globe to markets on the other side can reduce profit margins.

● Financial incentives. Businesses may be attracted to a particular country or area if cash or other financial incentives are offered if they locate there. Some of the regional aid available in parts of Europe may have influenced the location of Asian multinationals in the 1990s.

● Globalisation. It has been suggested that businesses are facing globalised markets (☞ unit 32). Selling into a global market, rather than a single country or area, is likely to be more effective if a business produces and sells in many different countries. For example, it may be able to take into account regional characteristics in its products or establish a corporate brand image.

● Corporate image. Some multinationals (☞ unit 32) set up parts of their business in other countries, but keep their head offices and take back profits to the home country. Others have head offices and operations in many different countries. They use labour from the country in which they operate. They reinvest profits in that country and develop infrastructure. This approach could allow a business to improve its corporate image (☞ unit 14), as it is seen as providing benefits to the countries in which it operates.

● The introduction of the single European currency (☞ unit 30) may influence business location after the year 2000. Multinational companies may locate inside Europe to gain the benefits of simplified accounting, pricing and marketing.

Inward investment

INWARD INVESTMENT is the flow of foreign funds into a country for the purposes of setting up business operations. In the 1990s the UK attracted billions of pounds of inward investment from foreign companies setting up production plants in the country. The success of the UK in attracting this investment is largely the work of national, regional and local agencies. Examples include English Partnerships, the Commission for the New Towns, The Mersey Partnership and the West Midlands Development Agency. These play vital roles in attracting overseas investment in new factories and decisions by foreign firms to invest in existing operations. For example, English Partnerships played a key role in attracting Samsung Electronics, the Korean firm, to invest in a £450 million multi-product complex in Teeside.

Inward investment can have a number of benefits to UK industry.

● Foreign businesses which locate in the UK will need supplies, perhaps from UK suppliers of components and specialist commercial services.

● Businesses will recruit workers. Retailers, cinemas, restaurants and other local businesses will gain from the

extra spending.
- Some UK businesses may already supply the overseas business. If production is switched to the UK then transport costs may fall and profits rise.
- UK businesses may learn about new production methods and working practices.
- If UK businesses make a good impression with overseas investors, this might generate publicity which could lead to further investment in the UK.

Question 6

In the late 1990s, the UK government made a special effort to attract inward investment. According to the Prime Minister in 1997: 'Britain has a great deal to offer - fast, easy access to the EU single market, a workforce which is skilled and adaptable, and an environment which allows businesses to prosper. We are committed to maintaining a business environment which gives every incentive for companies to grow, innovate, and gain competitive advantage in the world. We will promote strongly a dynamic, open and competitive market economy with government providing the platform of stability for the long term so that companies can plan and invest.'

Source: adapted from *Invest in Britain*, DTI, 1998; *Labour Market Trends*, Office for National Statistics.

(a) Suggest two possible reasons why the government should want to attract foreign businesses to the UK.
(b) Using information from the data, examine the possible benefits to foreign business of locating in the UK.

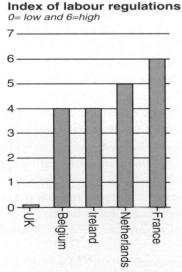

Figure 100.4 *The UK labour force*

Index of labour regulations
0= low and 6=high

Source adapted from: OECD (reflects regulations on working time, fixed-term contracts, employment protection, minimum wages and employee representation).

Summary

1. What factors influenced business location during the Industrial Revolution?
2. Under what circumstances will transport costs be particularly influential in business location?
3. State 3 types of business that will benefit from locating close to the market.
4. Give 4 methods of communication that may influence a location decision.
5. For what type of business activity is land an important factor in influencing location ?
6. Why might it be important to transfer existing employees when re-locating?
7. Give 3 problems that a business might have in transferring its existing labour force to a new location.
8. How might the geographical distribution of labour affect location?
9. Describe the help which the EU gives to businesses when locating in assisted areas in the UK.
10. What is the main disadvantage of industrial inertia?
11. Describe 6 factors which might be important when locating a business operation overseas.
12. State 3 examples of inward investment.

Key terms

Assisted areas - areas that are designated as having problems by the UK or EU and are eligible for support in a variety of forms.

Brownfield site - areas of land which were once used for urban development.

Development areas - regions with high unemployment which qualify for government help aimed at attracting business.

Enterprise zones - small inner city areas designated by the government which qualify for financial assistance.

Footloose industries - those industries which are neither influenced by their market or the source of raw materials when deciding where to locate.

Green belt - areas designated by government, usually in rural areas, where the development of business is prohibited.

Green field sites - areas of land, usually on the outskirts of towns and cities, where businesses develop for the first time.

Industrial inertia - the tendency for firms in the same industry to locate in the same region even when the original locational advantages have disappeared.

Intermediate areas - similar to development areas, but not as 'economically deprived'.

Inward investment - the setting up of business, or investment in business, by a company from another country.

Regional policy - measures used by central and local government to attract businesses to 'depressed' areas.

Case study

The location of call centres

There has been a huge growth in the last few years in the sale of goods and services over the telephone. A wide range of businesses, from those selling kitchenware to life insurance policies, has located call centres in office blocks all over the country. Call centres are said to be the most remarkable employment phenomenon of the 1990s. Large numbers of staff are housed in offices and equipped with headphones and a computer to sell over the telephone.

Corporations are setting up new call centres at an astonishing rate. In 1998 Prudential, the insurance group, planned to locate a call centre in Derby creating around 1,500 jobs while Barclays will create 2,000 jobs at Sunderland. New technology is partly the reason for their popularity. Automated call distribution (ACD) switching allows incoming calls to be sent out in orderly queues to waiting operators, and if necessary transferred to less busy centres in other cities or continents. Computer telephony integration (CTI) allows customers' records to be called up on screen as their calls are answered. Many of the big centres are located outside London to take advantage of plentiful relatively skilled staff and lower wages. For example, London Electricity's billing operation is now carried out in the north-east. The north-west though is fast becoming the most popular area with Scotland and the north east of England now being considered as a serious location by operators.

Location factors which are considered important to operators when choosing locations include the quality of the labour force, the local business network, financial incentives, availability of property and telecommunications expertise. They rarely mention accents in speech. A clear and confident telephone manner is important, but most regional accents are acceptable.

Source: adapted from the *Financial Times*, 23.4.1998 and *The Independent*, 2.6.1998.

Table 100.1 *Location factors for operators*
- Evidence of existing call centre success
- Labour force (sufficient numbers and skill level)
- Provision of good quality business network, human resource and training suppliers can be critical
- Financial incentives
- Good quality location/property. Premises ready to occupy
- Good place to live (quality of life/amenities particularly important for attracting and retaining foreign nationals)
- Telecoms support
- Marketing/promotion by the local national/development agency

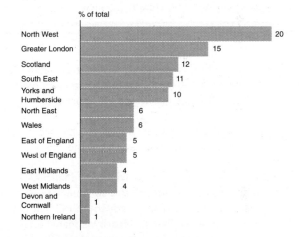

Figure 100.6 *Where the call centre jobs are*

% of total

North West	20
Greater London	15
Scotland	12
South East	11
Yorks and Humberside	10
North East	6
Wales	6
East of England	5
West of England	5
East Midlands	4
West Midlands	4
Devon and Cornwall	1
Northern Ireland	1

Source: adapted from Mitial Group, Datamonitor.

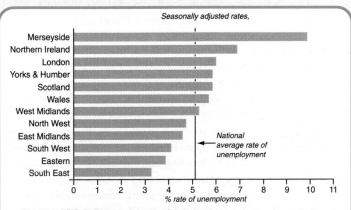

Seasonally adjusted rates,

Merseyside	
Northern Ireland	
London	
Yorks & Humber	
Scotland	
Wales	
West Midlands	
North West	
East Midlands	
South West	
Eastern	
South East	

National average rate of unemployment

% rate of unemployment

Figure 100.5 *Regional unemployment*

Source: adapted from Mitial Group, Datamonitor.

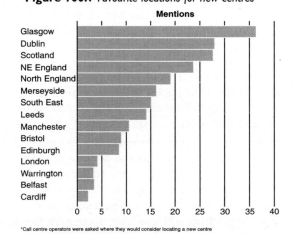

Figure 100.7 *Favourite locations for new centres**

Mentions

Glasgow	
Dublin	
Scotland	
NE England	
North England	
Merseyside	
South East	
Leeds	
Manchester	
Bristol	
Edinburgh	
London	
Warrington	
Belfast	
Cardiff	

*Call centre operators were asked where they would consider locating a new centre

Source: adapted from Mitial Group, Datamonitor.

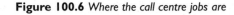

Longbenton

- **Location:** Longbenton is situated in the North East region of England, just north of the conurbations of Tyne and Wear and Teesside.
- **Transportation Services:** Longbenton is well served by a modern transportation network. The main north-south road links are provided by the A1(M) motorway. There are two international airports in the area, at Newcastle and Teesside. The main ports are Tyne, Tees and Sunderland. They offer roll-on, roll-off services to the rest of Europe, including Scandinavia, and other container services to the rest of Europe, the Middle East, Africa and India. Newcastle lies on the main east coast railway line to London.
- **In an assisted area:** Yes - companies locating in Longbenton have access to Regional Selective Assistance, the most generous kind of grant on offer in the UK.
- **Other kinds of financial assistance on offer:** The Council can offer incoming companies grants to help offset such costs as property taxes (or rates) and site improvements, among other costs. Financial support to help pay for training is also available from the Tyne and Wear Training and Enterprises Council.

- **Available sites:** There is a wide range of serviced sites in sizes from one acre up to about 170 acres. All are within easy reach of major highways.
- **Prices:** Average price per acre vacant serviced land £50,000. Rent per sq ft existing factories £3.00.
- **Weekly earnings:** men £330 (89% of national average); women £243 (90% national average)
- **Unemployment rate:** 10.5%
- **Major industries in the area:** Electronics, electrical components, plastics, automotive components, and clothing.
- **Major companies in the area:** 3M, Black & Decker, Caterpillar from the US; Fujitsu Microelectronics, Sanyo, NSK from Japan; Philips Components, Electrolux from mainland Europe; Thorn Lighting from the UK.
- **Local universities:** Durham, Newcastle, Northumbria and Sunderland.
- **Advice and assistance:** Companies interested in locating in Tyne and Wear can use the free services of the Council, which include a 'one-stop shop' covering advice on property, housing, education, meeting local suppliers, etc.

Bolton

- **Location:** Bolton is located in the metropolitan area of Greater Manchester. It is a major centre in its own right. It lies about 12 miles northwest of Manchester city centre.
- **Transportation services:** Bolton has excellent road connections. A dual carriageway from the town centre provides a direct link with the M61, M62, M63, and M6 motorways. Because of its proximity to Manchester, Bolton also has excellent rail and air connections. It is, for example, close to the main north-south rail line that runs up the west coast of Britain. Nearby is Manchester's International Airport - used by more than 50 airlines serving some 180 destinations in the UK, the rest of Europe and elsewhere around the world. In addition, the Royal Seaforth container terminal is only one hour away. East coast ports are easily reached via the M62. And there is a terminal serving the the Channel Tunnel at nearby Trafford Park.
- **In an assisted area:** Yes. Companies locating in Bolton can apply for some of the UK's best grants.
- **Other kinds of financial assistance on offer:** In addition to Regional Selective assistance, companies locating in Bolton have access to training and employment

grants. They can also receive enterprise grants for building work refurbishment, security and environmental works.
- **Available sites:** Wingates Industrial Park, The Valley, Platinum Park, Rivington Parkway, Red Moss and Chequerbent. Two sites over 150 acres are available.
- **Prices:** Average price per acre vacant serviced land £90,000. Rent per sq ft existing factories £4.00.
- **Weekly earnings:** men £352 (94% of national average); women £252 (94% national average)
- **Unemployment rate:** 7.5%
- **Major Industries in the area:** Textiles, food, all types of engineering, plastics, warehousing and distribution.
- **Major companies in the area:** Warburtons Bakery, Robert Watson Constructional Steelworks, Riva, British Aerospace, Vernacare, Bernsteins, Fort Sterling, Ingersoll Rand, Edbro Metal Box, Sanderson Fabrics, Vantona.
- **Local universities:** Manchester, Manchester Metropolitan, Salford, UMIST.
- **Advice and assistance:** Bolton Metropolitan Council can help incoming companies in all major areas including finding key-worker housing and obtaining introductions to local suppliers. It also offers an 'after-care' service for companies once they have invested in Bolton.

A major commercial bank is in the process of closing high street branches to cut costs. It aims to set up a call centre in the UK, creating 2,500 jobs in the area in which it locates. A large plot of land is expected to be needed for the building, which will also have a car park for staff. The bank anticipates growth in the future.

Two possible locations have been identified, in Bolton and Longbenton. You are a member of a special project team that has been asked to investigate the two sites. Write a report analysing the advantages and disadvantages of both sites. Evaluate these factors and recommend which site would be most suitable for a call centre using the data provided.

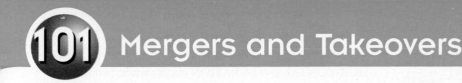

101 Mergers and Takeovers

Reasons for mergers and takeovers

Mergers and takeovers take place when businesses join together and operate as one organisation. Why do some businesses act in this way?

● It is a quick and easy way to expand the business (☞ unit 93). For example, if a supermarket chain wanted to open another twenty stores in the UK, it could find sites and build new premises. A quicker way could be to buy a company that already owns some stores and convert them.

● Buying a business is often cheaper than growing internally. A firm may calculate that the cost of internal growth is £80 million. However, it might be possible to buy another company for £55 million on the stock market. The process of buying the company might inflate its price, but it could still work out much cheaper.

● Some businesses have cash available which they want to use. Buying another business is one way of doing this.

● Mergers have taken place for defensive reasons. A business might buy another to consolidate its position in the market. Also, if a firm can increase its size through merging, it may avoid being the victim of a takeover itself.

● In response to economic changes. For example, some businesses may have merged in the years just before 1992 to prepare for the Single European Market which removed barriers to trade between EU countries (☞ unit 30). This may also have been the case before the introduction of the Euro in 1999.

● Merging with a business in a different country is one way in which a business can gain entry into foreign markets. It may also avoid restrictions that prevent them from locating in a country or avoid paying tariffs on goods sold in that country (☞ unit 26).

● The globalisation of markets (☞ unit 32) has encouraged mergers between foreign businesses. This could allow a company to operate and sell worldwide, rather than in particular countries or regions.

● A business may want to gain economies of scale (☞ unit 93). Firms can often lower their costs by joining with another firm. This is dealt with later in this unit.

● Some firms are asset strippers. They buy a company, sell off profitable parts, close down unprofitable sections and perhaps integrate other activities into the existing business. (see later in this unit).

● Management may want to increase the size of the company. This is because the growth of the business is their main objective (☞ unit 4).

Merger activity

In the late 1990s, both the number and value of mergers

Question 1

In February 1998 it was announced that two UK insurance companies, Commercial Union (CU) and General Accident (GA), would merge to form CGU. The new company would be Britain's second largest insurer, responsible for around £100 billion of funds. Insurance companies had been under pressure and some consolidation in the industry looked likely. A flood of new entrants and the exploitation of telephone sales techniques, which cut out intermediaries and offered insurance more cheaply, had sent premium rates plunging and had squeezed profit margins.

Cost cutting through mergers is one way of competing. CU and GA aimed to cut costs by £225 million. Much of this would be achieved through job losses and integrating information technology systems. Analysts also believed that the merger would provide a better business spread and stronger positions in many areas. In the US, for example, where neither company had a significant market presence, the combined group would be the fifteenth largest general insurer. Each company would also benefit from the types of business and areas of the world where the other was strong.

Source: adapted from the *Financial Times*, 26.2.1998.

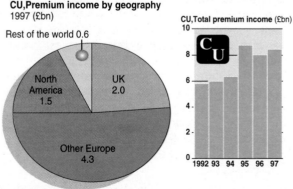

Figure 101.1 *Turnover and income by area, GA and CU.*

Source: adapted from company information.

(a) What is meant by the phrase 'consolidation in the industry'?
(b) Discuss the motives for the merger between the two companies.

reached record levels. What might have been the reasons for this 'merger boom'?

- There was growth in the UK economy and a buoyant stock market. Higher profits attracted companies to buy shares in or take over other businesses. Companies were also prepared to pay higher prices, which raised the value of mergers and takeovers.

- Faced with greater competition in providing services, there was a number of mergers between financial institutions. Examples of mergers in the financial sector include Lloyds Bank and the TSB, and The Royal and Sun Alliance insurance companies.

- Deregulation and liberalisation freed markets. For example, deregulation of the communications industry in the USA allowed an 'alliance' between AT&T and British Telecom. Deregulation of electricity in the UK led to the creation of 14 electricity companies in 1990. By 1998, 12 had either merged together or been bought by outside businesses, mainly because the merged companies would be better able to compete.

- Improvements in information and communication technology (☞ unit 82) meant that it was far easier for businesses to deal with each other. Before, companies in different parts of the country, or in different countries, may have been reluctant to merge because of problems with passing information. Private company **intranets** greatly reduced this problem.

- A growing number of large businesses merged. For example, BP's takeover of Amoco in 1998 was the UK's largest industrial takeover. It was suggested that the merger would lead to cost savings of 6 per cent.

- Many firms adopted a company strategy of 'going global'. They wanted operations in many countries and many markets.

- Companies were 'bargain hunting' by taking over companies in Asia. Economic problems in that part of the world meant that companies could be bought relatively cheaply.

Types of merger or integration

As Figure 101.2 shows, mergers can be classed in a number of

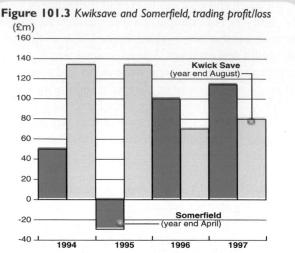

Figure 101.2 A summary of the methods of integration

ways. Not all mergers fit neatly into these categories, however. HORIZONTAL INTEGRATION occurs when two firms which are in exactly the same line of business and the same stage of production join together. The merger between BP and Amoco, the two oil companies is an example of a horizontal merger. The benefits of mergers between firms at the same

Question

Figure 101.3 Kwiksave and Somerfield, trading profit/loss

(£m)

Kwick Save (year end August)

Somerfield (year end April)

1994   1995   1996   1997

Source: adapted from Verdict Analysis, Datastream/ICV.

In February 1998 it was announced that the two supermarket chains, Somerfield and Kwiksave, would merge. Both chains had been struggling to maintain sales levels and market share in the face of competition from Tesco, Sainsbury's, Safeway and Asda and the low price continental discounters such as Aldi and Netto. A merger would give the new organisation about 7 per cent of the total market. This would make them the fifth largest supermarket in the UK. The two companies had also suffered because of the growing trend in out of town shopping. Most Somerfield and Kwiksave stores were located in the high street. It was suggested that high street stores would continue to suffer given the price advantages enjoyed by the larger operators, with their greater buying power.

It was expected that the merger would result in cost savings of between £50-100 million. These savings would result from bulk-buying, head office reductions and pooling distribution and information systems. Some store closures and job losses were expected due to the overlap of about 200 stores. Despite these savings, City analysts said that it would only delay the problems of the two companies. 'There may be some short term benefits, but the longer term growth potential is still difficult to identify', said Frank Davidson, food retail analyst at ABN Amro. Indeed, the merger was described as a nil-premium merger, with no real value being added for shareholders.

Source: adapted from the Financial Times and The Independent ,17.2.1998.

(a) What type of merger is taking place in the article? Explain your answer.

(b) Why might the merger have been proposed?

(c) Examine the possible benefits of the merger to:
   (i) Kwiksave and Somerfield shareholders; (ii) consumers.

stage of operation include:
- a 'common' knowledge of the markets in which they operate;
- less likelihood of failure by moving into a totally new area;
- similar skills of employees;
- less disruption.

VERTICAL INTEGRATION can be FORWARD VERTICAL INTEGRATION or BACKWARD VERTICAL INTEGRATION. Consider a firm which manufactures and assembles mountain bikes. If it were to acquire a firm which was a supplier of tyres for the bikes, this would be an example of backward vertical integration. The two firms are at different stages of production. The main motives for such a merger are to guarantee and control the supply of components and raw materials and to remove the profit margin the supplier would demand. Forward vertical integration involves merging with a firm which is in the next stage of production rather than the previous stage. For example, the mountain bike manufacturer may merge with a retail outlet selling bikes. Again this eliminates the profit margin expected by the firm in the next stage of production. It also gives the manufacturer confidence when planning production, knowing that there are retail outlets in which to sell. Vertical mergers are rare. Some vertical integration has taken place in the electricity industry, where power generators have merged with distributors.

LATERAL INTEGRATION involves the merging of two firms with related goods which do not compete directly with each other. Production technique or perhaps the distribution channels may be similar. Cadbury-Schweppes is perhaps an example. The two companies used similar raw materials and had similar markets, but did not compete with each other.

There are some motives for firms in completely different lines of business to join together. This type of merger is called a CONGLOMERATE or DIVERSIFYING MERGER. A firm might fear a loss of market share due to greater competition. As a result it may try to explore new and different opportunities.

Takeovers

Takeovers amongst public limited companies (☞ unit 5) can occur because their shares are traded openly and anyone can buy them. One business can acquire another by buying 51 per cent of the shares. Some of these can be bought on the stock market and others might be bought directly from existing shareholders. When a takeover is complete, the company that has been 'bought' loses its identity and becomes part of the **predator** company. Private limited companies, however, cannot be taken over unless the majority shareholders 'invite' others to buy their shares.

In practice, a firm can take control of another company by buying less than 51 per cent of the shares. This may happen when share ownership is widely spread and little communication takes place between shareholders. In some cases a predator can take control of a company by purchasing

as little as 15 per cent of the total share issue. Once a company has bought 3 per cent of another company it must make a declaration to the stock market. This is a legal requirement designed to ensure that the existing shareholders are aware of the situation.

Takeovers or mergers can result in situations which may be against consumers' interests. As a result the Department of Trade and Industry might instruct the Competition Commission to investigate the merger (☞ unit 22). This may result in the government allowing the merger to take place provided certain conditions are met. In extreme cases a merger may be completely blocked. For example in 1997 the President of the Board of Trade blocked the proposed merger between the two giant brewers Bass and Carlsberg-Tetley. Had the deal gone ahead the new group would have dominated 40 per cent of the market.

Takeovers of public limited companies often result in sudden increases in their share price. This is due to the volume of buying by the predator and also speculation by investors. Once it is known that a takeover is likely, investors scramble to buy shares, anticipating a quick, sharp price rise. Sometimes more than one firm might attempt to take over a company. This can result in very sharp increases in the share price as the two buyers bid up the price. In 1997 Redland, the UK aggregates and roofing specialist, was taken over by Lafarge, a French building supplies company. Lafarge paid £1.8 billion for Redland. During the bid, Redland's share price rose from just over £2 to £3.45

Hostile and friendly takeovers

Takeovers can be **hostile** or **friendly**. A hostile takeover means that the victim tries to resist the bid. Resistance is usually co-ordinated by the board of directors. They attempt to persuade the shareholders that their interests would be best protected if the company remains under the control of the existing board of directors. Shareholders then have to weigh up the advantages and disadvantages of a new 'owner'.

A takeover may be invited. A firm might be struggling because it has cash flow problems (☞ unit 59), for example. It might want the current business activity to continue, but under the control of another, stronger company. The new company would inject some cash in exchange for control. Such a company is sometimes referred to as a 'white knight'.

The mergers and takeovers described above all refer to public limited companies. It is possible for private limited companies to be taken over. However, an unwanted takeover cannot take place since the shares in private limited companies are not widely available.

Asset stripping

Some takeovers in recent years have resulted in ASSET STRIPPING. The asset stripper aims to buy another company at a market price which is lower than the value of the firm's

Question 3

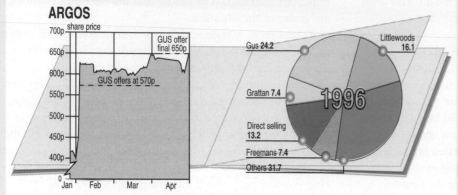

Figure 101.4 *Argos share price and home shopping market shares*

ARGOS

Source: adapted from Verdict analysis, Datastream/ICV.

In February 1998 Great Universal Stores (GUS), the largest UK mail order company, made a surprise £1.68 billion hostile bid for Argos, the high street catalogue retailer. The bid surprised the City and immediately the approach was described as 'opportunistic' by Sir Richard Lloyd, the non-executive chairman of Argos. Lord Wolfson, GUS chairman, suggested that he decided to move for Argos when the company announced that it was to set up a home shopping network. He stated that: 'The whole point of this offer is that they have a catalogue and we have a national delivery service. For us to carry another ten million deliveries would not be a major step'.

Sir Richard Lloyd argued that the bid fundamentally failed to recognise the unique nature and strengths of Argos's business. In addition, GUS's home shopping apparatus was not suitable for the company's own plans, which he defined as 'off-store shopping'. The two are different because Argos does not offer credit and has no plans to use agents. Sir Richard also said: 'We are in two very different things. Their business involves the use of agents to distribute catalogues, and ours does not.' Lord Wolfson complimented Argos's overall strategy, but hinted that GUS would halt its plans to open another 200 more shops. He also said that GUS would not shut down many of Argos's 400 shops and strip the business down to a stand alone catalogue retailer. The success of the bid became apparent when it was disclosed that 58 per cent of Argos's shareholders had accepted the bid even before counting had finished.

Source: adapted from the *Financial Times*, 4.2.1998 and the *Sunday Business*, 26.4.1998.

(a) What evidence is there to suggest that the GUS bid was hostile?
(b) Explain two advantages to GUS of acquiring Argos.
(c) Explain the effect on Argos's share price of the hostile bid.
(d) Discuss the potential, if any, for asset stripping Argos.

total assets. It then sells off the profitable parts of the business and closes down those which are unprofitable. Such activity has often been criticised since it leads to unemployment in those sections which are closed down and generates a degree of uncertainty. Hanson Trust were allegedly criticised for their activity following the £3.3 billion purchase of Consolidated Gold in 1989. Within one year of the acquisition Hanson had sold off £1.03 billion worth of profitable assets.

Reverse takeovers

REVERSE TAKEOVERS usually occur when a smaller company takes over a larger company. They tend to be friendly takeovers because a small company is unlikely to have sufficient financial resources to take over a much larger company against its will. The larger company may allow the takeover because it feels that the smaller company has a lot to offer in the way of expertise or future potential. Alternatively the larger company may be part of a larger organisation and is up for sale. One example of a reverse takeover in 1997 was the acquisition of BDDP, the French advertising agency, by CGT the UK advertising agency famous for its Holsten Pils advertisements. The larger BDDP was owned by a small group of French banks which took control of the company when it went into receivership in 1994. CGT paid £96 million for the company.

Another motive for a reverse takeover is to obtain a stock market listing. A large unquoted company might allow a smaller quoted company to 'reverse into it' so that the new company can trade as a plc. For example, Bolton Wanderers Football Club allowed a reverse takeover by Mosaic Investments, the bar and catering products company, in 1997. After the takeover a new company, Burnden Leisure, was formed. However, Bolton shareholders retained control of 67 per cent of the new company.

Mergers and economies of scale

One of the motives for merging is that costs will be lower if two firms join together. This is because when firms increase their size they gain **economies of scale** (☞ unit 93). It is possible that horizontal mergers may benefit most from economies of scale. For example, two banks with similar operations may each have a branch in a high street. If they merge together, costs may be reduced by closing one of the branches.

In 1980 Professor Dennis Mueller studied the effects on efficiency of 800 mergers in seven countries. He found that they were unlikely to lead to economies of scale. He also suggested that small firms would be the main gainers from mergers. A study by Professor Keith Cowling in 1980 supported this view. He investigated the performance over 7 years of companies involved in horizontal mergers. The results showed that efficiency gains were no greater than in non-merged businesses, and in some cases were worse. This may have been because of a fall in turnover as the merged company 'rationalised' its factory and cut output. Also profits of the combined company may have been lower than what they would have been without the merger.

Many of the businesses involved in mergers and takeovers in the late 1990s, however, suggested that costs savings were the main reason for joining together. Some even produced figures to indicate the costs savings they would make. Examples of the economies of scale to be gained were:

● the elimination of duplicated resources. For example, costs savings from the merger between BP and Amoco in 1998 were to be gained from not duplicating oil exploration. The takeover of Amersham in the UK by Nycomed, a Norwegian biotechnical firm, resulted in savings of £9 million one year later;

● the reduction of risk. A small company may be reluctant to operate in a politically unstable country. The BP-Amoco merger may be willing to do so, because it will have other projects which may be profitable if it has problems in certain countries;

● the spreading of the fixed costs of promotion. For example, the design of an advert or promotion is a fixed cost. An advert may cost £200,000 to make. If it reaches 1 million in the UK, the average cost is 20p (£200,000 ÷ 1,000,000). If it is shown to 10 million in the US the average cost falls to 2p;

● the ability to sell a wider range of products because of a wider sales network. This is known as ONE STOP SHOPPING or **cross selling**. Selling more products from the same distribution network will again reduce the average fixed cost of the sales network;

● that merged companies which become global operators may find that their suppliers also set up in the many countries in which they operate;

● that larger businesses are in a stronger position to negotiate with suppliers and can negotiate to reduce prices;

● that merged businesses may have COMPLEMENTARY ASSETS. John Kay (1996) suggested that businesses may only be able to operate in certain markets if they have certain assets. For example, a business may advertise nationally to create a brand name. This is unlikely to be successful if it only has shops in Newcastle. It needs a complementary asset, such as a chain of national shops.

Joint ventures and alliances

A JOINT VENTURE is where two or more companies share the cost, responsibility and profits of a business venture. The financial arrangements between the companies involved will

Question 4

In 1997 Tesco, the supermarket chain, launched an in-store service to provide both a credit card and a range of financial services, including mortgages, in a joint venture with the Royal Bank of Scotland. Customers of Tesco will be able to obtain online insurance and other financial products at special outlets in selected stores at the same time as they buy their groceries. Ownership of the joint venture was broadly equal, with the partners investing around £20 million each in the first year. Other products, including life assurance and general insurance, offered in conjunction with Scottish Widows and RBS's Direct Line, were thought to be following. The launch followed Safeway's decision to offer its own debit card and the awarding of a banking licence to Sainsbury. It is thought that Tesco's new card would allow customers to buy goods on credit and pay interest on balances.

Source: adapted from The *Times*, 13.2.1997.

(a) Explain the advantages of the joint venture to:
  (i) Tesco; and (ii) RBS.
(b) Examine the reasons why a merger between the two companies may not be appropriate.
(c) Discuss how the profits from the joint venture might be split between the two companies.

tend to differ, although many joint ventures between two firms involve a 50:50 share of costs and profits. There are many examples of joint ventures. In 1997, Unilever formed a joint venture with Helados Helanda, a Mexican ice-cream business. The purpose of this venture was to give Unilever a foothold into a new market. In the same year Mersey Docks and Harbour Company set up a joint venture with Capespan International and Fresh Fruit Services. The venture, Fresh Fruit Terminal (Sheerness) Ltd, involved an investment of £35 million in a new development at Sheerness in Medway to boost the port's fruit imports. The venture was owned equally between the two companies.

There is a number of advantages of joint ventures.

● They allow companies to enjoy some of the advantages of mergers, such as growth of turnover, without having to lose their identity.

● Businesses can specialise in a particular aspect of the venture in which they have experience.

● Takeovers are expensive. Heavy legal and administrative costs are often incurred. Also, the amount of money required to take over another company is sometimes unknown.

● Mergers and takeovers are often unfriendly. Most joint ventures are friendly. The companies commit their funds and share responsibility. Such an attitude may help to improve the success of the venture.

● Competition may be eliminated. If companies co-operate in a joint venture they are less likely to compete with each other. However, the venture must not restrict competition to such an extent that consumers' interests are harmed.

Question 5

Courtaulds, the chemicals group, announced in February 1998 that it planned a three-way demerger. Five years before it had sold off its textiles arm. Since then the performance of the group's coatings and polymers businesses had been hindered by difficulties in fibres. Following a boom in synthetic fibres in the 1960s and 1970s the market has declined. Wild fluctuations in raw material prices and overcapacity in the market also accelerated the deterioration.

The company planned to sell its coatings arm as International Coatings and sell its polymers business for between £200-300 million. Analysts believed that the break-up would increase the value of the group by a third or more. The remaining business would look to develop a new market in Tencel, a new branded fibre. Courtaulds had already invested £350 million in the product and only recently has it begun to return a profit. However, there appeared to be a great deal of potential in this market and Courtaulds believed it could dominate it in the next 15 years. Courtaulds had hoped that the three businesses would grow simultaneously. But as a result of its difficulties gearing had risen to 60 per cent. The sale of polymers was likely to help reduce debt and provide resources for the launch of Tencel.

Source: adapted from the *Financial Times*, 26.2.1998.

(a) Explain how the company is being split up and sold off.
(b) Examine the possible motives for the demerger of Courtaulds.
(c) Discuss whether the shareholders would benefit from the break-up.

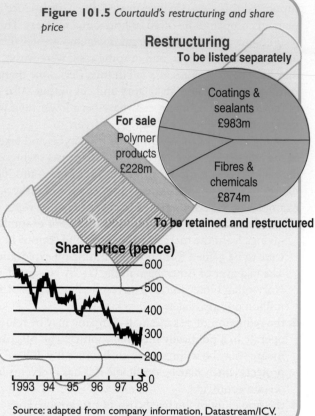

Figure 101.5 *Courtauld's restructuring and share price*

Source: adapted from company information, Datastream/ICV.

There are some disadvantages to joint ventures.

● Some joint ventures fail to achieve the desired results. They are often compromises when an all-out takeover would be better. There may be control struggles. For example, who should have the final say in a 50:50 joint venture?

● It is possible for disagreements to occur about the management of the joint venture. As with any partnership, sometimes there are different views on which course of action to take.

● The profit from the venture is obviously split between the investors. A company might regret this if it became evident at a later date that a particular venture could have been set up by itself.

Alliances may take looser forms than joint ventures. They are usually carried out for three reasons.

● Marketing. For example, McDonald's and Disney have promoted each others products.

● R&D (☞ unit 99), where businesses work together in developing a new product. Each business will be able to contribute its individual expertise.

● Information. Supermarkets gather information on customers' buying habits which they share with food manufacturers. This is perhaps a form of **forward vertical integration**.

Demerging

A DEMERGER is where a company sells off a significant part of its existing operations. A company might choose to break up to:

● raise cash to invest in remaining sections;
● concentrate its efforts on a narrower range of activities;
● avoid rising costs and inefficiency through being too large:
● take advantage of the fact that the company has a higher share valuation when split into two components than it does when operating as one.

In 1996 Hanson, the well known holding company, split into four parts. The process began as early as 1995 when the group sold off around 30 different US businesses. In 1996 the organisation was split into four distinctive groups - Millennium Chemicals (chemicals), Imperial Tobacco (cigarettes and tobacco), Energy Group (electricity and coal) and Hanson (building and construction). The purpose of the demerger was to help management focus more sharply. It was also expected that shareholders would get more value.

In 1998 Sears, the retailing group, said it would demerge both the Selfridges department store and Freemans, the mail order company. One of the motives for the demerger was to allow Sears to concentrate on the launch of a direct sales business similar to the Next Directory.

Summary

1. Why might firms choose to join together?
2. What factors gave rise to the significant increase in takeovers and mergers in the 1980s?
3. Why might external growth be quicker than internal growth?
4. Give 2 examples of:
   (a) horizontal integration;
   (b) vertical integration;
   (c) lateral integration.
5. Why might a firm diversify?
6. Briefly explain how an acquisition is carried out.
7. Why is asset stripping often criticised?
8. What might be a motive for a reverse takeover?
9. Explain why mergers might not result in an improvement in efficiency.
10. What is the difference between a joint venture and a merger?
11. What might be the advantages of demergers?

Key terms

Asset stripping - the selling off of profitable sections and closing down of loss making sections of a business following an acquisition.

Backward vertical integration - merging with a firm involved with the previous stage of production.

Complementary assets - assets that a business requires together to be successful.

Conglomerate or diversifying merger - the merging of firms involved in completely different business activities.

Demerger - where a business splits into two separate organisations.

Forward vertical integration - merging with a firm involved with the next stage of production.

Horizontal integration - the merging of firms which are in exactly the same line of business.

Joint venture - two firms sharing the cost, responsibility and profits of a business venture.

Lateral integration - the merging of firms involved in the production of similar goods, but not in competition with each other.

One stop shopping - the opportunity to purchase a variety of products from a single location.

Reverse takeover - where a company takes over a larger company than itself.

Case study

BP Amoco - Arco takeover

At the end of March in 1999, the former BP announced its intention to take over Atlantic Richfield, the Los Angeles-based oil company known as Arco. The timing of the takeover looked ambitious according to some City analysts. It came just 2 months after BP had concluded one of the world's biggest ever industrial mergers with Amoco, the US oil company. BP Amoco offered $25 billion in stock for Arco. The deal raised questions about 'mega-mergers' in the oil industry. Was BP Amoco in danger of falling into a size-for-size-sake trap? Could it manage the integration of two big companies at the same time?

On the one hand, the takeover of Arco helped BP Amoco to establish itself in the 'oil super league', along with Exxon Mobil and Royal Dutch Shell. However, it was also suggested that the takeover would fill gaps in BP Amoco's existing operations. Arco gives BP access to parts of the US market that it was not in. But it did not, as Amoco did, transform BP into a US oil major. The deal, at $25 billion, was modest. This was just as well

because Sir John Browne, chief executive of BP Amoco, was concerned that BP's rapid expansion could undermine its reputation for high quality. 'Being big can make you look cold, bureaucratic, bungling and less human', he admitted.

The increased concentration in the oil industry did not go unnoticed by the US regulatory authorities. They were particularly concerned about the concentration in refining and marketing. However, unlike Exxon Mobil, there were no overlaps in those areas in the Arco takeover. Arco's two refineries and 1,700 service stations were on the west coast. BP Amoco's refining and retail presence was east of the Rocky Mountains. It was suggested, though, that BP Amoco might have a problem in Alaska. The enlarged group would have full control of the Prudhoe Bay oil and gas field. This is the biggest in the US and a major source of revenues and jobs for the Alaskan State. Hence the Alaskan State government was concerned. Browne was expected to argue that the cost savings and operational efficiencies resulting from complete ownership of the bay would make the Alaskan oil industry more competitive and protect jobs in the area. He was also expected to promise more investment to convert Arco's vast reserves of natural gas in Prudhoe Bay into synthetic fuels.

The major worry regarding the takeover is whether BP could integrate two businesses at the same time. It is argued that many of the benefits of mergers are lost in the integration process. If the takeover went ahead, it was expected that a small team of BP Amoco senior managers would work alongside Arco's managers in LA. However, to date, the BP Amoco merger had gone well. In addition, BP had experience in back-to-back acquisitions. During the 1980s it swallowed Sohio of the US and Britoil of the UK in quick succession. Sir John Browne was extremely keen for this to succeed. His aim was to build an asset base to rival that of Shell, which has the most impressive array of international assets in the industry.

Source: adapted from the *Financial Times*, 31.4.1999.

(a) Using BP, Amoco and Arco as an example, explain the difference between a merger and a takeover.

(b) What regulatory obstacles might have prevented the takeover?

(c) Explain whether you think the Arco takeover was friendly or hostile.

(d) Using the data in the above case, examine reasons why Arco might have been vulnerable to a takeover.

(e) Evaluate the possible advantages and disadvantages to BP Amoco of the takeover of Arco and discuss whether BP Amoco should go ahead with the takeover.

Figure 101.6 *Financial data for BP Amoco and Arco and comparative company size of oil industry leaders*

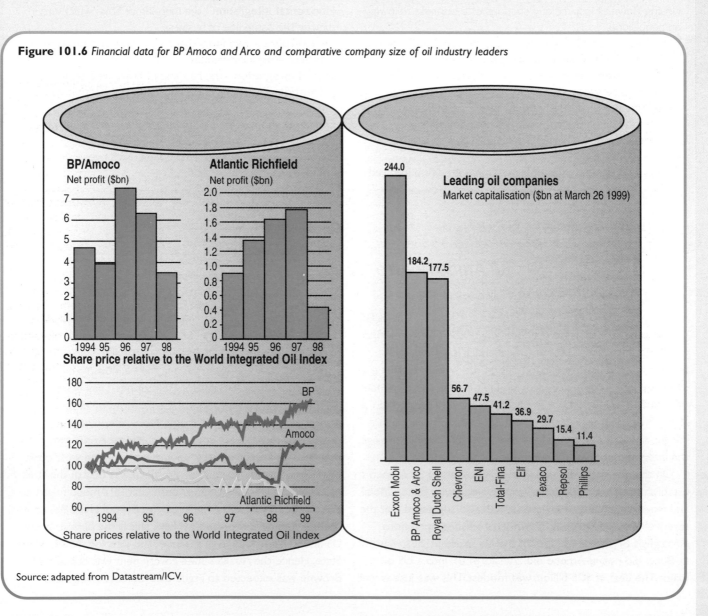

Source: adapted from Datastream/ICV.

Efficiency and business

Unit 96 explained the methods a business may use to measure and improve efficiency. A food manufacturer producing large numbers of pizzas may find that the average cost of each pizza could have fallen over a year. This might **indicate** an improvement in efficiency. The reasons for the fall in costs may be because workers are producing more products. It may also be because operations have been changed so that machines can run for longer periods.

Increasingly businesses are adopting company-wide or corporate strategies (☞ units 15 and 16) that they believe will lead to improvements in productivity. This will involve the whole organisation. It will only be successful if the business has a corporate culture (☞ unit 14) which supports its attempts to improve efficiency. For example, in 1998 it was reported that Scottish Widows and Xerox had experienced productivity increases of up to 60 per cent as a result of increasing the flexibility of the workforce by employing teleworkers.

Table 102.1 *Characteristics of good performing companies*

- Large firms were too slow when making decisions, particularly launching new products. They spent too much time analysing data. A better approach was to launch new products quickly, correct problems after and then market the improved version. Cutting lead times was also emphasised by certain managers.
- Successful companies were those which listened to consumers. Customers tended to know what they would buy and firms should supply products which customers want.
- The generation of new ideas was a key factor for success. All employees should be encouraged to try out new ideas even if they did not always work. Mistakes were not criticised in organisations where were encouraged, but viewed as 'good tries'. Employees should operate as though they were running their own small business.
- Top companies recognised the qualities and potential of their workforce. Given the opportunity, workers would act creatively and solve their own problems. If workers generated ideas ideas which management took into account, improvements in productivity would occur.
- Successful businesses stressed values such as continuous innovation, good customer service and dependable quality. Leading by example was also considered important for managers.
- Diversification could weaken a company. Expanding through the development of strengths would be more profitable than trying to do something completely different.
- Organisation charts in leading companies tended to be flatter. Flat structures and a simple chain of command are more effective than matrix structures.
- Successful businesses tended to be decentralised.

Tom Peters - 'In Search of Excellence'

Tom Peters and R. Waterman, in their book *In Search of Excellence,* identified eight key characteristics of good performing companies from financial statistics and interviews with managers, as shown in Table 102.1.

Peters later revised his ideas to take into account changes in the business environment.

- Businesses should revolutionise their approach when adapting to external influences on the business environment.
- Businesses should aim to develop new 'stars' in their product portfolio (☞ unit 41). Stars are products with a high market share and a high growth potential.
- Businesses, because they cannot control market events, should try to anticipate changes and continually move forward.

Question 1

IDEO is the largest industrial product design firm in the world. It has been involved in projects such as helping to create the first Apple Computer mouse and the design of the 25 ft mechanical whale in the Free Willy films. Its business, innovation, is very much in demand. The company takes the view that firms must 'innovate or die'. Its European director Tim Brown suggests: 'Above all else innovation requires a willingness to embrace chaos. It means giving people freedom to have opinions and challenge the rules. It demands a loose management structure that does not isolate people in departments or on rungs of the ladder. It needs flexible work spaces that encourage cross-fertilisation of ideas. And requires risk taking'.

Despite intense pressure and tight deadlines, the company maintains an air of creative anarchy, which it believes is the ultimate innovation environment. Staff are encouraged to 'play' and break the rules. All work is organised into project teams, which form and disband in a matter of weeks or months. There are no permanent job assignments or job titles. One diverse group employed by IDEO includes cognitive psychologists and computer scientists as well as industrial designers. Between them they create about 90 new products a year. Staff work wherever they happen to be. Scribbled notes are scattered all around. To the untrained eye, it may look a chaotic mess. Speed is essential to the design process at IDEO, with the most promising ideas being developed and worked into prototypes in just a few days.

Source: adapted from the *Financial Times,* 13.8.1998.

(a) Identify elements of Tom Peters' 8 key characteristics of good performing companies in the IDEO case.
(b) Analyse how they may improve efficiency.

Downsizing

A large number of firms have attempted to improve their efficiency by DOWNSIZING. This term, coined by US management theorist Stephen Roach, has been used to describe the process of reducing capacity, ie laying off workers and closing unprofitable divisions. The advantages of this for businesses may be:

● costs savings and increased profit;
● a leaner, more competitive operation;
● only having efficient, profitable business, with no 'dead horses' to flog;
● profitable businesses not subsidising unprofitable ones.

Between 1990 and 1995, the top 12 companies in the UK cut the size of their workforce by 44 per cent. Even the growing financial services sector suffered. The number of staff employed in banking, insurance and building societies was 1,050,000 in 1990, but fell back to 990,000 in 1997.

In the late 1990s the effects of downsizing on businesses were beginning to emerge. A report in 1997 by the Employers Forum on Age (EFA) based on 80 of its members suggested there were few real gains from downsizing. In addition, businesses lost the skills, experience and knowledge of employees. Some companies even hired back redundant staff as consultants.

Delayering

DELAYERING also involves a business reducing its staff. The cuts are directed at particular levels of a business, such as managerial posts. Many traditional organisational charts (☞ unit 70) are hierarchical, with many layers of management. Delayering involves removing some of these layers. This gives a flatter structure. In the late 1980s the average number of layers in a typical organisational structure was 7, although some were as high as 14. By the late 1990s this was reduced to less than 5. The main advantage of delayering is the savings made from laying off expensive managers. It may also lead to better communication and a better motivated staff if they are **empowered** (☞ unit 73) and allowed to make their own decisions.

However, remaining managers may become demoralised after delayering. Also staff may become overburdened as they have to do more work. Fewer layers may also mean less chance of promotion.

Reengineering

REENGINEERING was defined by Michael Hammer and James Champy (1993) in their book *Reengineering the Corporation* as: 'the fundamental rethinking and radical redesign of business processes to achieve dramatic improvements in critical contemporary measures of performance such as cost, quality, service and speed'.

Question 2

In 1997 staff at British Steel (BS) were becoming increasingly anxious. This anxiety was triggered by reports that Europe's largest steel maker was planning to accelerate its redundancy programme, which was running at between 500 to 1,000 job cuts per year. Since 1993, BS had been working hard to ensure that its efficiency was the very best in Europe. However, due to the continued strength of the pound in 1997/98, pressure mounted on the company to accelerate efficiency improvements. BS proposed to do this by benchmarking practices in American mini-mills which have helped to raise productivity significantly in recent years. Its approach has been to cut out several management layers and eliminate demarcations which used to exist. The American mini-mills typically had 3 layers of management compared with British Steel's 5.

BS wanted to develop a single shop floor class of well-educated and highly trained 'operating technicians'. They would be multi-skilled workers who would be indistinguishable in employment terms from white-collar or managerial staff. Sir Brian Moffat, chairman of BS, was aiming for single status among employees. Indeed, management hours had been raised so that their hourly pay rates were the same as other staff. In addition, the company was hoping to build shopfloor teams with skills in operating, maintenance and diagnostic tasks.

Source: adapted from *The Times*, 1997.

(a) Using examples from the article, explain the difference between downsizing and delayering.
(b) Examine the possible: (i) benefits; and (ii) problems to British Steel of its delayering strategy.

Features Reengineering has a number of features as shown in Table 102.2.

What processes are redesigned? These might be processes which are no longer working, for example, a quality assurance system that results in high levels of faulty products, processes which affect customers, such as lead times, and processes which are relatively easy and cheap to redesign.

Table 102.1 *Reengineering*

- Businesses should organise their work around processes. Examples of processes that might be redesigned include assembly or purchasing of stocks.
- Traditional methods of improving efficiency involve small changes to existing practices. Reengineering involves radically changing processes or introducing new ones. A business should discard old practices and 'start from scratch'.
- Reengineered processes operate without assembly lines. This allows several jobs to be combined. For example, jobs such as quality checker, paint sprayer and stock orderer may be combined.
- Workers make decisions and are empowered. This should reduce delays in decision making and shorten processes.
- In traditional production, tasks are completed one after the other in a strict sequence. Reengineered processes allow tasks to be completed in a 'natural order', which could be out of sequence.
- Traditional processes produce standardised products, which limits choice. Reengineering allows multiple designs or products, without the loss of scale economies.
- Most large businesses are divided into departments, which have a function. Reengineered processes cross boundaries. For example, the production department might market its own products.
- In traditional processes there is too much checking. Sometimes controls and checks cost more than the money they save. Reengineered processes only employ cost-effective controls and checks.
- Reengineering cuts down on the external contact points. For example, a supplier chasing payment will only have one point of contact. This prevents different people in the business giving out different information.
- Reengineered processes are able to gain the advantages of centralisation and decentralisation.

How might reengineering of processes affect a business?

- Process teams, such as an assembly team, will take the place of functional departments, such as the production department.
- Jobs change from simple tasks to multi-dimensional work. Repetitive assembly line work disappears. It is replaced by individuals working in process teams, responsible for results.
- Workers will be empowered and no longer follow a set of rules laid down by management. They have to think, interact, use judgment and make decisions. Reengineered processes require workers to have an understanding of their jobs.
- Employees will not be promoted because they have a good performance record, but because they have the ability to do another job. Good performance is rewarded by bonuses.
- Employees must believe that they are working for customers and not their bosses.
- Managers no longer issue instructions and monitor the work of subordinates. They assist, guide and help staff to develop.
- Organisational hierarchies become flatter. Staff make decisions for themselves so there is less need for managers. Flatter organisations bring executives closer to customers and workers. Success depends on the attitudes and efforts of empowered workers rather than the actions of task orientated managers. Executives must be leaders who can influence and reinforce employees' values and beliefs.

Question 3

Measurement Technology Limited (MTL), based in Luton, makes industrial process control instruments. In the mid-1990s, new competition meant the company was forced to face serious challenges. At that time it was still organised along functional lines, with departments and multiple layers of management. Responsibilities were confused and the company's procedures were disjointed and did not reflect how employees really worked. As a result it took a lot longer than it should have done to get products to customers. It was clear that the organisation needed to identify key internal processes and 'reengineer' them to become more efficient. This meant stripping out unnecessary tasks and streamlining operations.

Graeme Philp, the chief executive, gave full support for the reengineering initiative which began in mid-1995. Wendy Bowden, the head of human resources, championed the use of the IDEF model, a tool developed by NASA and used widely in industry. It uses flow diagrams to map out processes. With the cooperation of the whole workforce, MTL developed new processes for strategy, design, manufacturing sales and resources. These were integrated with the company's quality systems.

Some other changes were required to support the new ways of working. With design, for example, the role of project leader was created to lead the newly established multidisciplinary teams. At the same time there was a shift away from functional departments towards processes. As a result the company was more flexible and structured.

The management structure was flattened and a new salary structure introduced. This means technical experts could be rewarded without going into management. This was achieved with no redundancies. Ms Bowden said: 'we're now doing more with the same number of people'. Reengineering allowed us to get costs down and be more competitive'. Scrap and re-work was reduced by 44 per cent in 1997 and labour efficiency was increased by 10 per cent.

Source: adapted from *The Times*, 5.11.1998.

(a) Why was reengineering used at MTL?
(b) Explain how: (i) promotion criteria; (ii) the organisational structure; (iii) work units; have changed as a result of reengineering at MTL.
(c) Examine how reengineering has improved efficiency at MTL.

Agile manufacturing

Some have suggested that businesses need an approach to cope with turbulent markets, competition, changing tastes, fast growth in technology and increasing consumer expectations. Today, customers want to buy products which are custom made and tailored to individual needs. All these trends have led to the development of AGILE MANUFACTURING.

The main aim of agile manufacturing is for a business to be able to perform effectively in a changing market. It will allow customised products to be made with short lead times and without rising costs. Agile manufacturers will be able to adopt new technologies more quickly and have a high degree of flexibility. This will allow large and rapid changes in output, product mixes and delivery dates.

How will a business be able to do this? An agile manufacturer will need flexible people, a reduction in rigid structural hierarchies, broader-based training, flexible production technologies and computer-integrated manufacturing (☞ unit 98). Radical changes in organisation will also be needed. Figure 102.1 shows the differences in approach of three production methods. Agile manufacturers need short term relationships with suppliers. This will allow supply contracts to be set up and ended quickly to cope with changes in technology and demand. There is evidence of this happening already, with a growing number of joint ventures across industries. They will also make greater use of OUTSOURCING. This involves finding a contractor to supply components or to carry out processes that a business may have undertaken. Car manufacturers often outsource production. Brakes, brakepads, electronics, mirrors, windows and seats are all produced by outside suppliers. It leaves the business able to concentrate on its 'core' areas. This growth in outsourcing will require quick and effective communication with suppliers and workers. Improved communications technology (☞ unit 82) will allow this.

These ideas have led to the term the VIRTUAL COMPANY. It refers to a group of closely linked separate 'entities' which can quickly disband and reform to cope with a turbulent environment.

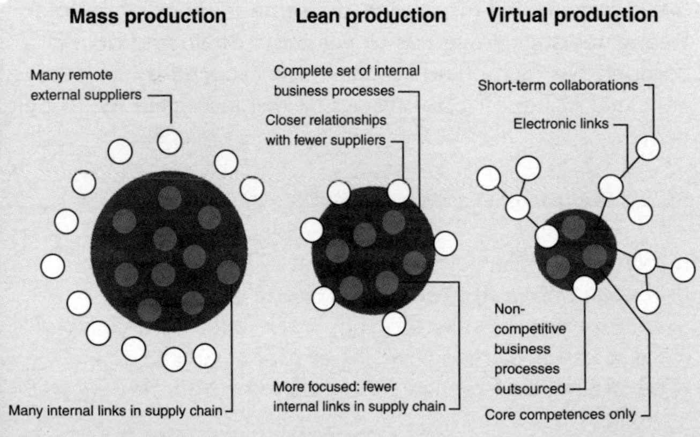

The learning organisation

In his book *The Fifth Disciple*, Peter Senge put forward the idea of the LEARNING ORGANISATION. According to a definition in the IRS Management Review, a learning organisation is one 'that facilitates the learning of all its members and thus continually transforms itself'. It has been argued that to compete in the uncertain and changing conditions of the global market place, a business needs to be able to learn.

Question

In 1996 Roche, one of the world's largest pharmaceuticals companies, set up a subsidiary company called Protodigm. The company had responsibility for taking three drugs for Alzheimer's disease, traumatic shock and cancer through clinical trials. Roche felt that this strategy could reduce the cost of developing the drug by 40 per cent. The company subcontracts its work out to more than 20 different suppliers for each drug. This is supervised by just 8 directors and 1 administrator. Once the drugs have been approved by the regulators they will be handed back to the parent company. Protodigm has been able to cut costs by striking hard bargains with suppliers and keeping overheads and bureaucracy to a minimum.

These ideas are not new. For example, property development has always operated by putting together small teams of contractors, surveyors and architects for individual projects. In a survey by Anderson Consulting and the Economic Intelligence Unit last year, 42 per cent of the 350 respondents predicted that, in the future, their companies would operate in a wide network of alliances and relationships with other organisations.

The driving force behind this trend is the growing awareness that companies cannot do everything for themselves. This is especially when they are faced with greater competition, growing cost pressures, faster technological change and the need to market goods internationally. They also believe that small, nimble suppliers save time and money by cutting out unnecessary bureaucracy. Advances in information and communications technology have made it far easier for a network of autonomous companies to work together. The availability of high quality suppliers has increased as job losses in large organisations encourage experienced staff to leave and set up as independent suppliers.

Source: adapted from the *Financial Times*, 12.1.1998.

(a) Using Protodigm as an example, explain what is meant by a virtual company.
(b) Explain why there is a growing trend in the use of the virtual model.
(c) Why have developments in IT contributed to the growth in 'virtual companies'?

Mass production **Lean production** **Virtual production**

Many remote external suppliers

Many internal links in supply chain

Complete set of internal business processes

Closer relationships with fewer suppliers

More focused: fewer internal links in supply chain

Short-term collaborations

Electronic links

Non-competitive business processes outsourced

Core competences only

Figure 102.1 *The organisation of three production methods*

There are two types of learning. **Learning how** involves processes designed to transfer and improve skills that will improve performance. **Learning why** involves looking at how things are happening using diagnostic skills.

An example of its operation took place in 1998 when Reed Elsevier, the publishing group, began to prepare for the 'age of the internet'. The Reed Elsevier Technology Group (RETG) was set up to educate other parts of the group about new technologies. The aim was to ensure that Reed Elsevier's different business units acquired technological expertise themselves. When part of the company acquired some new technological knowledge RETG passed it around the whole organisation. This ensured that something was only learnt once and time is not wasted.

Other methods

There is a number of other strategies and approaches that a business may take to improve efficiency.

Knowledge management The aim of knowledge management (☞ unit 88) is to unlock the information held by individual members of the workforce and share it throughout the company. If this can be done, efficiency should improve. For example, the marketing department may find that customers are unhappy with the stitching on a shirt. If this knowledge was passed to the production department, it may help to reduce returns. Information and communication technology has a vital role to play in the storage, manipulation and presentation of information to all staff in the organisation.

Kaizen Kaizen means continuous improvement (☞ unit 92). It is a company wide strategy designed to eliminate waste in business and lead to continual improvement in all aspects of a firm's operations. All staff in the organisation are trained to be on the lookout, all of the time, for ways of making improvements. If small improvements are made continually, their impact over long periods of time will be great. In addition, the company will always be moving forward.

Kaizen includes a wide range of different production techniques and working practices, such as quality circles, suggestion schemes, automation, discipline in the workplace, just-in-time manufacturing and zero defects. Businesses which have adopted Kaizen in the UK have enjoyed enormous efficiency gains. For example, GSM Graphic Arts of Thirsk, which makes metal and plastic labels for the motor and electronics industries, operates Kaizen in its factory. In 10 years, GSM improved many aspects of its operations, attracted high profile customers, such as Nissan, GM and Ford, and saw employment grow from 17 to 200.

Michael Porter- competitive advantage Michael Porter suggested that businesses could achieve a competitive advantage over rivals by following one of three generic

strategies (☞ unit 14). One of these strategies is cost leadership. A cost leader will be the firm with the lowest unit costs. Low costs may be achieved through the mass production of a fairly standardised product, exploiting economies of scale, automating and reducing overheads.

The flexible labour force Throughout the 1980s and 1990s many UK businesses felt that their workforces were too inflexible. Labour productivity in many industries was significantly lower than in other countries. Workforces were uncooperative, resistant to change and lacking in motivation. In order to compete with overseas competition firms needed to improve the flexibility of the workforce (☞ unit 88). Methods of improving flexibility included:
- training workers in a number of tasks so that they can be switched around at short notice;
- allowing staff to choose their hours of work between certain limits;
- using temporary staff to cope with seasonal demand;
- using part time staff or workers on zero hours contracts

Question 5

Perkins Engines, the UK based diesel engine maker which became owned by Caterpillar of the US, benefited considerably from changes made to its operations. In one area of the factory, where the Perkins 4-litre engine range was built, sweeping changes were made. Much of the process plant was moved around, with parts of the assembly made to fall more easily to hand by opening up both sides of the assembly line and reducing radically the number of movements required of the operators. As a result of this:
- operator productivity rose by 41 per cent;
- inventory was reduced by 79.5 per cent;
- floor space was reduced by 45 per cent;
- cycle time was reduced by 25 per cent;
- the distance travelled by employees between process functions for a complete cycle fell from 350 metres to 50 metres.

The changes did not meet any resistance from staff at Perkins. Indeed, many of the several thousand employees said they have found the involvement stimulating and surprising. However, part of the ground rules set down by the consulting group, which oversaw the changes was that employees received pledges of no redundancies arising from the exercise. Perkins allowed other groups, such as representatives from customers, financial services and accountants, to participate in the suggestion programme for improvements.

Source: adapted from the *Financial Times*, 23.2.1998.

(a) Discuss the extent to which the strategy taken by Perkins may be a Kaizen approach.

(☞ unit 88) to cope with fluctuations in demand;
- encouraging staff to solve their own work problems;
- allowing staff to plan their own work schedules;
- encouraging staff to share information, help each other and check each other's work;
- the use of annualised hours schemes (☞ unit 72).

It was argued that a business with a flexible workforce would be more efficient in a number of ways. They could operate more freely if workers can be switched from one task to another. Fluctuations in demand could be dealt with more comfortably. The use of overtime payments could almost be eliminated. Stores, offices and other premises could also stay open for longer hours.

Criticisms

In the 1990s some of the modern production and management theories were criticised.

- After implementing strategies such as downsizing, delayering, reengineering and outsourcing, a number of businesses found problems. For example, two thirds of the companies identified by Tom Peters as standard-bearers of excellence in 1982 were in trouble five years later. Michael Hammer admitted that 70 per cent of the firms that claimed to have 'reengineered' themselves failed to improve their market position. In 1996, a survey by the American Management Association found fewer than half of the companies that had downsized since 1990 recorded higher profits in following years. Fewer reported higher productivity.

- Hammer admitted that a flaw existed in his own theory. In an article published in the Wall Street Journal in November 1996, he reported that he had forgotten about one factor - people. He said: 'I was reflecting my engineering background and was insufficiently appreciative of the human dimension. I've learned that is critical'.

- Reengineering in many businesses has simply meant downsizing. Businesses have tried to cut jobs without appreciating the long term effect of their actions. Job cuts have led to a stressed out, insecure and demotivated workforce.

- Peter Drucker and other management theorists emphasise the role of people as a firm's main asset and the corporation as a social as well as a commercial institution. Approaches which seek to remove employees with important business knowledge may have an adverse effect on the business. This is perhaps why knowledge management was said to be important for businesses in the late 1990s.

- Many new management theories have been described as 'fads' or 'bandwagons'. They have failed to deliver improvements in profit or positive change. Businesses may simply use whatever theory happens to be in fashion at the time.

Summary

1. What is meant by a companywide strategy to improve efficiency?
2. Describe 4 of Tom Peters', characteristics of good performing companies.
3. State 4 benefits of downsizing.
4. State 2 (a) advantages; (b) disadvantages: of delayering.
5. State 4 possible effects on businesses of reengineering.
6. Suggest 2 ways in which a business may become more agile in manufacturing.
7. Give 4 examples of labour flexibility.
8. What is the aim of Kaizen?
9. What is the difference between knowledge management and the learning organisation?
10. Suggest 2 criticisms of modern management theories to improve efficiency.

Key terms

Agile manufacturing - a strategy which allows a business to react to rapidly changing conditions.

Delayering - the removal of managerial layers in the hierarchical structure.

Downsizing - the process of reducing capacity, usually by laying off staff.

Learning organisation -a business which facilitates the learning of its members and benefits competitively as a result.

Outsourcing - the contracting out of work to other businesses that might otherwise have been performed within the organisation.

Reengineering - redesigning business processes, such as product design, to improve efficiency in the organisation.

Virtual company - a company which has outsourced every business activity.

Case study

Efficiency in the car industry

Rover

Rover, the BMW owned car manufacturer, made losses of £647 million in 1997. The productivity gap between Rover and other BMW car plants was around 30 per cent. In November 1998, BMW chairman, Bernd Pischetsrieder, said the Longbridge plant would be closed unless certain conditions were met. Perhaps the most important was the introduction of new working practices. Within two years, they would:

- change the individual's working week from five shifts totalling 37 hours to a four-shift, 35 hour week;
- offer optional Saturday morning working at standard pay rates (not overtime rates);
- result in reduced pay increases (less than 1 per cent);
- reduce overtime payments by launching an annual 'working-time account'. Any extra time worked, up to 200 hours, was credited to the worker and could be taken off later;
- mean that the threat of lay-offs for workers on low pay was limited. Up to 200 hours could be debited from the worker, to be made up at a later time when demand picked up.

In exchange for acceptance of these new flexible practices, unions were told that there would be no compulsory redundancies, although around 4,000 jobs would go almost immediately. The deal would allow BMW to keep Rover factories running for 102 hours per week, instead of 74. Productivity gains were expected to be highly significant.

Source: adapted from *The Sunday Times*, 6.12.1998, the *Financial Times*, 3.12.1998 and *The Guardian*, 22.3.1999.

Ford

The Ford Motor Company changed its purchasing process in an attempt to improve efficiency. Before the changes the purchasing department sent an order form to the supplier and a copy of this order form was passed to the 'accounts payable' section. When the goods were received from the supplier, a form describing the goods was sent to 'accounts payable'. The supplier then sent an invoice to 'accounts payable'. At the end of this process 'accounts payable' had three documents. If all three matched, a clerk in 'accounts payable' would pay the supplier. This is usually what happened. But when the documents did not match, time was wasted checking them.

After the changes, accounts clerks no longer needed to match the three different documents. The invoice was eliminated completely. With the new process, when an order was placed, a description of the order was entered into a database. When the goods were received from the supplier an employee checked the shipment with the description on the database. Only two possibilities existed. Either it did or did not match. If the goods matched the description then the employee indicated this on the computer and payment was made. If there was a discrepancy, the goods were returned to the supplier. This reengineering of the process had a huge effect on efficiency. Ford also cut the number of people working in 'accounts payable' from 500 to 125.

Source: adapted from *Reengineering the Corporation*, M. Hammer and J. Champy, 1993, Nicholas Brealey.

A study by the Institute of Work Psychology at Sheffield University of 564 manufacturers revealed that, of 12 new work practices surveyed, none was felt to be very effective. Figure 102.2 shows that in about 50-60 per cent of cases, the methods were only moderately effective or were not effective at all. The most commonly used techniques were supply-chain partnership (developing strategic alliances and long term relations with suppliers and customers), TQM, JIT, teamwork and integrated computer technology. It was argued that in future the most favoured techniques would be those which focused on the customer. Those in decline would be manufacturing cells, concurrent engineering (simultaneously designing and manufacturing products) and outsourcing. Another report, published by the research unit Business Intelligence, suggested that businesses will adopt knowledge management in the future. Around three-quarters of big companies expressed an interest. The BI report stated that 86 per cent of the firms surveyed believed that they were knowledge-intensive, but most used their knowledge poorly. They suggested that they did not capitalise on knowledge and good ideas, lost knowledge through downsizing and staff turnover and had knowledge assets which they fail to exploit.

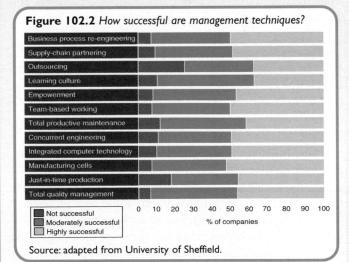

Figure 102.2 *How successful are management techniques?*

Source: adapted from University of Sheffield.

A car manufacturer that is experiencing difficulties has commisioned an independent team to evaluate the use of management and production techniques to improve efficiency. Write a report advising the manufacturer on the most suitable methods of improving efficiency in future.

Operational research

Businesses constantly make decisions. The production department may have to find the cheapest way to carry out a task. The marketing department may have to choose between two advertising campaigns. Unit 10 explained the steps involved in decision making. Businesses can use a number of **quantitative techniques** to help them make decisions and to solve problems that arise. These OPERATIONAL RESEARCH (OR) methods were developed by American scientists in the 1960s. They were based on problem solving methods used in Second World War operations, such as the most effective way to destroy submarines. OR methods use models (or simplified real world situations) to investigate solutions to the problems businesses may face. However, such models are only aids to decision making - the decision itself will still need to be taken and might involve other quantitative and qualitative data which is not included in the model. The types of decision where such models might be used include the following.

● Where should a new plant be sited?
● In what order should a new product be assembled?
● Which method of distribution has the cheapest transport costs?
● How should resources be allocated in production?
● How should the launch of a new product be organised?
● How can customer waiting time be reduced in busy retail outlets?
● How can a building project be timetabled?

This unit deals with linear programming and stock control, while the next looks at network and cost-benefit analysis, and simulation.

Blending

BLENDING is a technique which shows a firm how 'best' to allocate its resources, given a number of constraints. Firms usually aim to allocate resources in a profitable and cost effective way. Blending is one example of LINEAR PROGRAMMING. This method sets out a business problem as a series of linear or mathematical expressions. A linear expression is an equation which links two variables such that their behaviour, if plotted on a graph, would be represented by a straight line. These expressions are then used to find the **optimal** or best solution. How can firms use blending? It may be used when they are making decisions about production. Take, for example, a firm producing two products, denim jeans and denim jackets with a number of constraints:
● the same resources are used for each product;
● the three main operations in their manufacture are cutting, sewing and studding;
● the time taken for each operation is shown in Table 103.1;

Table 103.1

	Cutting	Sewing	Studding	Minutes
Jeans (jn)	3	2	1	
Jackets (jk)	1	2	2	

● in a working day there are 900 minutes of cutting time, 800 minutes of sewing time and 700 minutes of studding time;
● the denim used in jeans costs £5 and in jackets £8;
● jeans sell at £7 per pair and jackets at £11 each.

The firm has to decide what combination of jackets and jeans should be produced to maximise profits, given these constraints.

The cutting constraint The first step when using this technique is to show the information on constraints as a set of **inequalities** where ≤ means less than or equal to and ≥ means greater than or equal to. The firm knows that the amount of cutting time needed for jeans is three minutes and for jackets one minute. So the total cutting time is:

$$3jn + 1jk$$

There is also a constraint. The amount of cutting time must be no more than 900 minutes. So:

$$3jn + 1jk \leq £900$$

We can show this on a graph. If the firm used **all** its time for cutting to make jeans (and no jackets were made), it could make:

$$\frac{900 \text{ minutes}}{3 \text{ minutes}} = 300 \text{ jeans}$$

If all the time was used to make jackets (and no jeans were made), it could produce:

$$\frac{900 \text{ minutes}}{1 \text{ minute}} = 900 \text{ jackets}$$

The cutting constraint is shown in Figure 103.1. The line shows combinations of jeans and jackets that could be cut if all available cutting time is used. So, for example, the firm could make 300 jackets and 200 pairs of jeans. The area inside the line is called the **feasible region**. It shows all combinations of jackets and jeans that could be cut in the time available, ie when 3jn + 1jk ≤ 900.

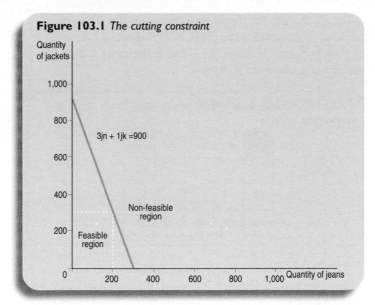

Figure 103.1 *The cutting constraint*

Sewing and studding constraints The time available for sewing is 800 minutes. Sewing jeans and jackets takes 2 minutes each. So:

$$2jn + 2jk \leq £800$$

Similarly, the constraint for studding is 700 minutes. Studding jeans takes 1 minute and jackets 2 minutes. So:

$$1jn + 2jk \leq £700$$

Again we can illustrate these lines on a graph. If all sewing time available was used on jeans or on jackets, the firm could make 400 jeans **or** 400 jackets. If all the time available for studding was used on jeans **or** jackets the firm could make 700 jeans **or** 350 jackets. These two lines are added to the other constraint and are shown in Figure 103.2. All constraints are now illustrated on the graph. The shaded area represents the feasible region taking all these constraints into account. This shows all the combinations of jeans and jackets that **could** be made.

Deciding on a solution How will a firm allocate its resources to maximise profits? This depends on the profit level a firm chooses. The firm knows that the profit made from the sale of a pair of jeans is £7 - £5 = £2. From the sale of a jacket it is £11 - £8 = £3. So the total profit from both is:

$$2jn + 3jk$$

This line can be plotted on the graph. Say that the firm wants to make a profit of £300. This could be gained if the firm produced 150 pairs of jeans and no jackets:

$$£300 = (150 \times 2) + (0 \times 3)$$

or no jeans and 100 jackets:

$$£300 = (0 \times 2) + (100 \times 3)$$

This profit line is shown in Figure 103.3 (which shows the feasible region PQRS of Figure 103.2). A higher level of profit can be shown by moving the line parallel and to the right, eg £600. The optimal or best solution for the firm is at Q. If the profit line is moved away from the origin, this is the last point in the feasible region that the profit line would touch. The firm would produce 300 jackets and 100 pairs of jeans. The profit would be £1,100 (300 x £3 + 100 x £2). There is no other combination of jackets and jeans in the feasible region that will earn more profit. Profit will always be maximised on the edge of the feasible region.

Blending can be very useful when firms are deciding how to make best use of their resources. Businesses might use this method to allocate factors of production between different products so that profits are maximised or costs minimised. However, it does have problems. It is a production technique which does not take the demand for products into account. The example used here only uses two products. In practice, firms produce many different products. The **Simplex Method** is used to cope with this, but requires detailed calculations and the use of computers by business.

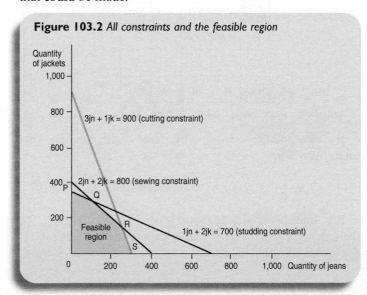

Figure 103.2 *All constraints and the feasible region*

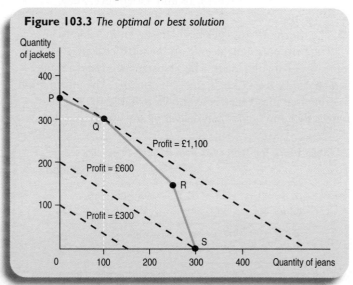

Figure 103.3 *The optimal or best solution*

Question 1

Stonewold Brewery produce two types of ale, best bitter (BB) and strong ale (SA). Three brewing processes are required; malting, mashing and fermenting. The amount of time each process takes and the capacity available is summarised in Table 103.2. The profit made on a barrel of best bitter and strong ale is £24 and £30 respectively.

Table 103.2 *Time constraints for the three brewing processes*

		Malting	Mashing	Fermenting
Hours needed to	(BB)	4	8	2
produce 1,000 barrels	(SA)	6	4	3
Capacity, total hours available		240	240	150

(a) Write out the problem as three equations showing the constraints.
(b) Draw the constraints on a graph.
(c) On the graph, plot a point that shows the allocation of resources that will maximise profit.
(d) Calculate the profit that will be earned at this point.

Transportation

TRANSPORTATION is another linear programming method. It is useful when firms have the problem of transporting items from a number of different origins to various destinations. For example, distribution companies have to decide the most cost effective way to distribute goods from their warehouses to a number of customers. Take an example, where two factories, F1 and F2, supply three warehouses, W1, W2, and W3.

● The output of each factory is constant at 14 and 23 loads per day respectively.
● The warehouses need 16, 18 and 3 loads every day respectively.
● The transport costs per load are shown in Table 103.3.

The firm must now decide on the most cost effective way of transporting the loads. The first step is to build a model which can be used to help decision making. The information is organised into a matrix as shown in Table 103.4. This shows that any factory can deliver to any warehouse. The

Table 103.3 *Transport costs from factories to warehouses*

			£00s per load
		Warehouses	
Factory	W1	W2	W3
F1	3	4	2
F2	1	1	5

small numbers at the top of each box show the transport cost per load in hundreds of pounds. Notice that the total output of both factories, 37 loads (14 + 23), is the same as the warehouses' demand (16 + 18 + 3).

Table 103.4 *A matrix showing transport costs, factory output and warehousing capacities*

	W1	W2	W3	Output
F1	[3]	[4]	[2]	14
F2	[1]	[1]	[5]	23
Demand	16	18	3	37

The firm must now decide which factories will supply which warehouses. One way of doing this is to start in the top left hand corner. Say that 14 loads are transported from F_1 to W_1. This is shown in the top left hand corner in Table 103.5. This represents the whole of F1's output. If W_1, W_2 and W_3 need supplying, they must be supplied from F_2.

Table 103.5 *The start of the solution*

	W1	W2	W3	Output
F1	[3] 14	[4]	[2]	14
F2	[1]	[1]	[5]	23
Demand	16	18	3	37

Now assume that F_2 sends 2 loads to W_1, 18 loads to W_2 and 3 loads to W_3. All output has been delivered to the warehouses. Also, the warehouses' demand for goods has been satisfied. This is known as a **feasible solution** and is shown in Table 103.6.

Table 103.6 *A feasible solution*

	W1	W2	W3	Output
F1	[3] 14	[4]	[2]	14
F2	[1] 2	[1] 18	[5] 3	23
Demand	16	18	3	37

It is now possible to work out the cost of this solution. The total cost will be:

(14 x £300) + (2 x £100) + (18 x £100) + (3 x £500) = £7,700

It is unlikely that this arbitrary method of deciding on deliveries will give the **least cost solution**. The solution for the firm is shown in Table 103.7.

Table 103.7 *The least cost solution*

	W₁	W₂	W₃	Output
F₁	11 [3]	[4]	3 [2]	14
F₂	5 [1]	18 [1]	[5]	23
Demand	16	18	3	37

The cost of this solution would be:

(11 x £300) + (3 x £200) + (5 x £100) + (18 x £100) = £6,200

An alternative method used to find this optimal solution involves the use of **shadow costs** and **opportunity costs**. However, if the figures are simple it may be easier to use trial and error - keep manipulating the data until any further attempt to move the loads around would either increase the total cost or leave it unchanged. In business, a computer would be used to look at all possible combinations and choose the least cost solution.

Question 2

Two warehouses W1 and W2 supply three retailers R1, R2 and R3. The supply capacity of the warehouses is 20 and 40 loads per week respectively. The demands of the retailers are 14, 20 and 26 loads per week respectively. The transport costs between the warehouses and retailers are summarised in Table 103.8.

Table 103.8

(£00s)

	Retailers		
Warehouse	R1	R2	R3
W1	1	3	6
W2	4	10	3

(a) Set up a transportation model by constructing a suitable matrix showing costs, demands, and supply capacities.
(b) Determine the least cost solution for the distribution of loads from warehouses to retailers using your answer to (a) and calculate the cost. (Use trial and error.)

The economic order quantity (EOQ)

Businesses use a number of quantitative techniques to make decisions about their purchases and stock levels (☞ unit 94). It is possible, for example, for a business to calculate the **order size** of its stocks, materials or components, which minimises total costs. This is called the ECONOMIC ORDER QUANTITY. Total costs are made up of the costs of acquiring stock and the costs of holding stock. Acquisition costs include costs involved with the choice of vendor (☞ unit 94), negotiation, administration and the inspection of incoming goods.

Acquisition costs, holding costs and total costs are shown in Figure 103.4. Holding costs rise as order sizes get larger. Holding costs are zero when there are no orders. The larger the order size, the greater the costs of holding it in stock. Acquisition costs fall as order sizes get larger. For example, there are likely to be lower costs in negotiating a few large orders than constantly negotiating many small orders. The order size which minimises total costs will always be at the point where the acquisition cost and the holding cost curves cross each other. This is shown at point EOQ on the diagram.

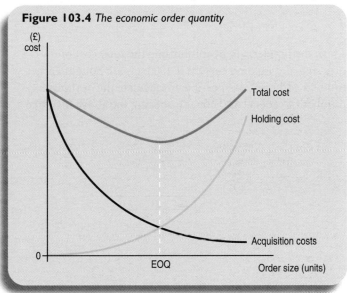

Figure 103.4 *The economic order quantity*

Calculation Say that a builder wants to know what order size of bags of cement will minimise its costs. How can the business calculate this? One method used to calculate the EOQ makes the following assumptions.
- Demand for stocks is uniform and does not vary a great deal.
- Store capacity is unlimited.
- Acquisition costs and stock holding costs are not related to the order quantity.
- Material prices are stable.
- Order and delivery quantities are equal.
- Stocks do not fall in value due to deterioration or obsolescence.

The economic order quantity (Q) can be found using the formula:

$$Q = \sqrt{\frac{2CA}{HP}}$$

where C is the acquisition cost per order, A is the total number of units used each year, H is the holding costs as a percentage of the average stock value and P is the price of each unit.

The building contractor uses 5,000 bags of cement each year which cost £10 each. The holding cost of the cement is 5 per cent of average stock value and acquisition costs are £8. The economic order quantity for cement purchases will be:

$$Q = \sqrt{\frac{2 \times £8 \times 5,000}{0.05 \times £10}}$$

$$Q = \sqrt{\frac{80,000}{0.5}}$$

$$Q = \sqrt{160,000}$$

$$Q = 400 \text{ bags}$$

Thus, the builder will be minimising the total cost of ordering and holding cement if 400 bags are bought each time. In addition, it is possible to calculate the optimum number of orders (A/Q) by transposing the above formula:

$$\frac{A}{Q} = \sqrt{\frac{HPA}{2C}}$$

$$= \sqrt{\frac{0.05 \times £10 \times 5,000}{2 \times £8}}$$

$$= 12.5 \text{ orders per year}$$

Limitations The assumptions on which the economic order quantity formula is based may be unrealistic in practice. The price of many materials, particularly commodities like oil, copper, coffee and cotton, tends to fluctuate with changing market conditions. Businesses are unlikely to have unlimited storage space. Materials, such as perishable goods, may deteriorate if left for a period of time. Changes in these assumptions may lead to different costs for a business, which might affect the EOQ. On the other hand, it could be argued that assumptions are not important, as long as a business realises the limitations and finds the predictions of the model useful.

Question 3

Moss Peters Ltd assembles domestic drying machines. It buys components from all over Europe and is keen to minimise storage costs. One component, the drum, is bought from Northern Spain. Moss Peters has just acquired a new warehouse where it hopes to hold larger quantities of certain key components. The drum is one of these components. The purchasing manager has been asked to review the economic order quantity now that there is almost unlimited space for its storage. The drums cost £40 to buy and Moss Peters uses 40,000 of them each year. The acquisition costs are £50 and the holding cost is 8 per cent of the average stock value.

(a) Calculate the economic order quantity for the drums.
(b) Calculate the total cost of holding and acquiring the drums for one year (do not include the cost of the actual drums).
(c) What would happen to the economic order quantity if the price of the drums rose to £45?

Summary

1. State 5 problems that operational research methods could be used to investigate.
2. Why are blending and transportation examples of linear programming?
3. Explain briefly two problems that businesses might have when using blending.
4. What does the use of blending show a firm?
5. What types of problem does the transportation technique help to solve?
6. What does the use of transportation show a firm?
7. Why might a business want to calculate its economic order quantity?
8. State 2 problems with calculating the economic order quantity.

Key terms

Blending - a graphical approach to linear programming which deals with resource allocation subject to constraints.
Economic order quantity (EOQ) - the level of stock order which minimises ordering and stock holding costs.
Linear programming - a technique which shows practical problems as a series of mathematical equations which can then be manipulated to find the optimum or best solution.

Operational research - a logical and scientific approach to decision making which uses calculations.
Transportation - a method designed to solve problems where there are a number of different points of supply and demand, such as a number of manufacturers distributing their products to a number of different wholesalers.

Case study

Westmoore Metal Products

Westmoore Metal Products (WMP) is a medium sized engineering company. It employs 45 staff and operates cell production in its factory. Each cell concentrates on a particular family of products. One such cell, the metal rod cell, makes two of the most popular products. These are high precision steel rods for an Austrian customer which makes machine tools. Their component codes are MK and MG.

The metal rod cell contains three machines and employs five staff. The staff organise their own work patterns, but must keep the cell operating for 15 hours per day, 6 days per week. The three machines include, a CNC lathe, a CNC milling machine and a vertical profile projector (an inspection machine). To manufacture the MK and MG three key processes are required - turning, milling and inspection. The vertical profile projector is used by other cells for some of the week. The amount of time each process takes and the capacity available is summarised in Table 103.9. The profit made by each component is £100 for the MK and £80 for the MG.

Westmoore introduced cell production about 5 years ago. One of the problems it had in the factory was a lack of space. In the past the company tended to hold quite high levels of stocks. Westmoore imported most of its steel from northern Spain. Although it is some of the cheapest steel in the world, lead times are long and delivery very unreliable. Thus, the high stock holdings occupy a lot of factory space. At the moment WMP orders about 80 tonnes of steel at a time from its Spanish supplier.

In order to keep stock holding costs to a minimum at WMP, a newly recruited cost accountant has suggested using the economic order quantity (EOQ) to determine the amount of stock to purchase when placing a new order. This takes into account the acquisition cost per order (C), the total number of tonnes used each year (A), the holding cost as a percentage of the average stock value (H) and the price of each tonne (P).

(e) Assuming that C = £100, A = 500 tonnes, H = 20 per cent and P = £200, calculate (i) the EOQ; (ii) the number of orders to be placed during the year.

(f) Using the information in (e), evaluate whether WMP's current ordering policy is cost effective.

Table 103.9 *Time constraints for the three engineering processes*

		Turning	Milling	Inspection
Hours needed to produce one unit	MK	1.5	4	2
	MG	4.5	2	2
Total hours per week available		90	80	50

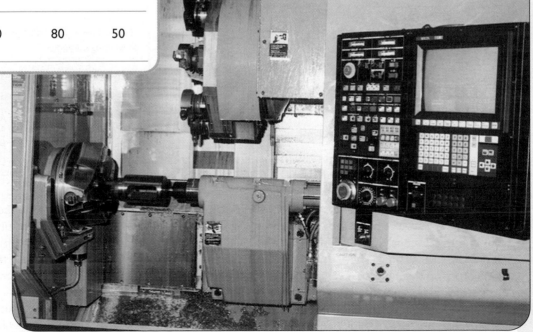

(a) Write out the problem above as three equations showing the constraints.

(b) Draw the constraints on a graph.

(c) (i) On the graph identify the point which maximises profit.

(ii) State how many of each component should be produced to maximise profit.

(d) Calculate the weekly profit made from the two components at the profit maximising point.

Network analysis

Unit 103 showed that a variety of techniques can be used in a business to make more effective decisions. Some operations in business are carried out by large numbers of people, using a large amount of resources. Others are more straightforward.

NETWORK or CRITICAL PATH ANALYSIS is a technique which allows a business to:
- estimate the minimum time that could be taken to complete a possibly complex operation;
- identify whether resources are being used efficiently;
- anticipate any tasks that may or may not cause delays in the operation.

Critical path analysis is used in many industries, particularly manufacturing and construction. For example, a builder may consider the use of network analysis when planning the sequence of tasks to build a new house. In such industries the time and resources used are vital to the project.

Take a simple operation, such as painting a window frame, that a builder might carry out. This could involve many different tasks, for example:
- preparing the woodwork;
- applying the undercoat;
- waiting for the undercoat to dry;
- applying the gloss.

This is shown in Figure 104.1 as a network diagram.

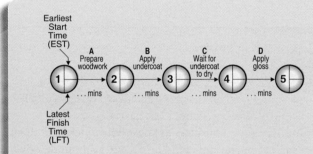

Figure 104.1 *A network diagram showing the sequence of activities in painting a window frame*

There are certain features in Figure 104.1 that are important when constructing any network.
- The circles are called **nodes.** They show the start or finish of a task. The arrows show the tasks involved in painting the window. They use up resources as they are carried out. For example, even waiting for paint to dry uses up resources, such as time. The activities are **dependent** on each other. So the undercoat cannot be applied until the woodwork has been prepared.
- Nodes contain information. Figure 104.1 shows that nodes are divided into three sections. In the left hand semi-circle the **node number** is written. This makes it possible to follow tasks more easily through the network. The number

in the top right is the earliest **starting time** (EST). This shows the earliest time that the next task can begin. The number in the bottom right is the **latest finishing time** (LFT). This shows the latest time that the previous task can finish without delaying the next task.
- Arrows show the **order** in which the tasks take place. They often have letters next to them to show what the order is. The length of time each task takes is placed below the arrow.

Constructing a network

Figure 104.1 is a rather simple example of a network. In practice operations in business may be more complex with many different tasks, some of which can be carried out at the same time as others. For example, the tasks involved in producing an advertising campaign for a company could be:
- A - plan the advertising campaign;
- B - make a TV video;
- C - make a poster;
- D - test market the TV video;
- E - test suitability of poster;
- F - present campaign to the board of directors;
- G - communicate the campaign to all company personnel.

The estimated length of time for each task and the order, ie the tasks that **depend** upon others being completed, are shown in Table 104.1. The total estimated time is 49 hours, but this is not important because activities B and C, and D and E can be done at the same time by different employees.

Figure 104.2 shows the network for the marketing campaign summarised in Table 104.1. The tasks, node numbers and time durations are all included.

Table 104.1 *The order and times of tasks when producing an advertising campaign*

Tasks	Order/dependency	Estimated time (hours)
A	Must be done first	4
B	Can only start when A is complete	6
C	Can only start when A is complete	7
D	Can only start when B is complete	8
E	Can only start when C is complete	10
F	Can only start when D and E is complete	9
G	Must wait for D, E and F to be completed	5

Once the network has been constructed it is possible to 'fill-in' the earliest start times and latest finishing times, and then show the critical path. This will tell the business how long it will take to launch the advertising campaign, and indicate where delays could take place.

Earliest start time Assuming that the **earliest time** task A can be started is hour 0 then tasks B and C cannot start for 4 hours (0 + 4), ie until task A has been completed. These are shown in the top right of nodes 1 and 2.

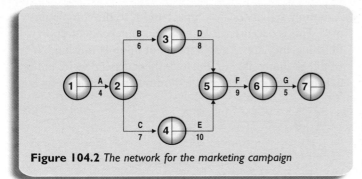

Figure 104.2 *The network for the marketing campaign*

Task D cannot start until A and B have been completed, this takes 10 hours (0+4+6) which is shown in node 3. Task E cannot start for 11 hours (0+4+7) and is shown in node 4. Task F cannot start until E and D are complete. The EST for task F is 21 (0 + 4 + 7 + 10). It is important to choose the longest route when calculating the ESTs. The route A,B,D is only 18 (0 + 4 + 6 + 8). The EST of the longer route (21) is shown in node 5. The EST in the final node also shows the time it takes to complete the whole marketing campaign. It is 35 hours (0 + 4 + 7 + 10 + 9 + 5) and is shown in node 7. All this information is shown in Figure 104.3.

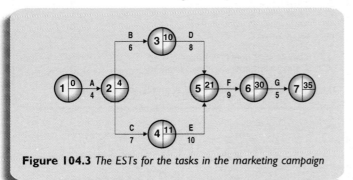

Figure 104.3 *The ESTs for the tasks in the marketing campaign*

Latest finish time The next step is to identify the **latest finish time** (LFT) of each task without extending the project duration. We must start at node 7 and work back. Task G must be completed by the 35th hour. This LFT is shown in the bottom right of node 7. To calculate the LFT for task F, we subtract the time it takes to perform task F from the previous LFT, ie 30 (35 - 5). This LFT is shown in node 6. The LFTs for tasks D and E are 21 (30 - 9), as shown in node 5. For task B the LFT is 13 (21 - 8) and for task C 11 (21 - 10). The LFT for task A is 4, following the route that will give the earliest time, ie C (11-7=4) rather than B which would give (13-6=7). The LFTs for all tasks are shown in Figure 104.4.

The critical path Once all the LFTs have been identified it is possible to outline the CRITICAL PATH. This can be drawn through the nodes where the ESTs and the LFTs are the **same.** This means that there can be no delays between completing the preceding tasks and starting the next ones on this path without prolonging the total time of the marketing campaign. The critical path for the campaign, A, C, E, F, G, is shown by a dotted line in Figure 104.4. It is critical because any task on

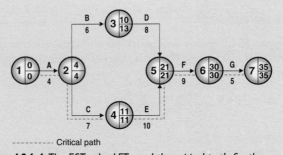

----- Critical path

Figure 104.4 *The ESTs, the LFTs and the critical path for the marketing campaign*

this path which is delayed will delay the whole campaign beyond the 35 hours identified earlier as the minimum time.

The float What about tasks which do not lie on the critical path, ie B and D? B and D together, could be delayed up to 3 hours without prolonging the campaign's completion time. This is called the **float.** We have already seen that the critical path is the longest route through the network. Activities C and E take longer than B and D by 3 hours, so speeding up activities B and D will not help the business to finish earlier.

● The **total float** is found by subtracting the EST and the duration from the LFT. So for task B it would be:

13-6-4=3.

This is the total float up to that activity (B).

● The **free float** is found by subtracting the EST at the start of the task and the duration from the EST at the end. So for task B this would be:

10-6-4=0.

This is the free float for that task. It shows that task B can be delayed, but this will interfere with other tasks, ie D. Table 104.2 shows the total float after each task in the marketing campaign. The tasks without a float (shown by a ⋆) are 'critical' - any delay in these and the whole campaign will be prolonged. Only non-critical tasks have a float.

It is important for a business to know how much float there is. If tasks in the operations could be delayed without delaying the whole job, then resources in these tasks, (such as labour, machinery etc.), could be used more productively elsewhere or shared between tasks. It is also important when tasks may take days or weeks. If an operation is delayed, a business will not be too worried if there is some float, only if the float disappears.

Table 104.2 *The duration, EST, LFT and floats for each task in the marketing campaign*

(Hours)

Task	Duration	EST	LFT	Total Float	Free Float
A	4	0	4	0⋆	0
B	6	4	13	3	0
C	7	4	11	0⋆	0
D	8	10	21	3	3
E	10	11	21	0⋆	0
F	9	21	30	0⋆	0
G	5	30	35	0⋆	0

Question 1

Figure 104.5 shows a network for the installation of a new piece of machinery. The times shown are for the number of days taken.

Figure 104.5

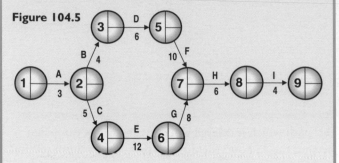

(a) Calculate the earliest start time for each task.
(b) Calculate the latest finish time for each task and the minimum time for the whole project.
(c) Determine the critical path.
(d) Identify the amount of total float and free float in a table.
(e) Determine the critical path if task D took 12 days.

A more complex network

Sometimes it is necessary to include a **dummy activity** or task in a network diagram. Take an example made up of four tasks A, B, C and D. Assume that task C cannot start until tasks A and B have been completed. Task D can only start when B has been completed. The network in Figure 104.6 appears to represent this sequence of tasks. However, the diagram also shows that task D cannot start until A and B have been completed, yet this is not a requirement in our example. In order to show a **dependency** the network can be redrawn using a dummy activity as shown in Figure 104.7. The dummy task is shown by a dotted line and now the diagram shows that task D is only dependent upon the completion of task B. Dummy activities do not use up any time - they always have a time duration of zero.

Let's look at a network which involves a variety of tasks and a dummy activity. Table 104.3 and Figure 104.8 show tasks involved in the assembly of a vehicle engine. The earliest start times and latest finish times have been calculated using the method in Figures 104.3 and 104.4 earlier. There are certain features about this network.

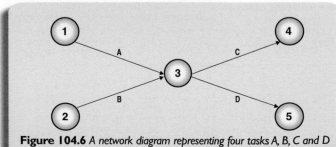

Figure 104.6 *A network diagram representing four tasks A, B, C and D*

● A dummy activity or task links J and K to the completion of C. This is because whilst J and K are dependent upon C finishing, they are also dependent upon H finishing. It would be impossible to illustrate these dependencies in the network without the use of a dummy line, which shows a

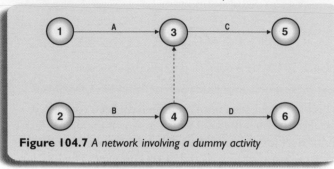

Figure 104.7 *A network involving a dummy activity*

Table 104.3 *Tasks and their estimated time involved in assembling a vehicle engine*

Task	Order/dependency	Estimated time (hours)
A	Can start at the same time as B	2
B	Can start at the same time as A	2
C	Must follow A	6
D	Must follow A	3
E	Must follow B	1
F	Must follow B	8
G	Must follow C	2
H	Must follow D,E	1
J	Cannot start until C,H have finished	3
K	Cannot start until C,H have finished	3
L	Must follow G,J	4

The operation is complete when F, K and L have finished.

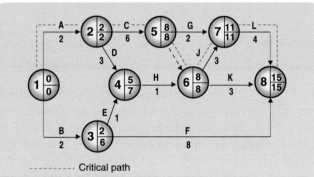

- - - - - - - Critical path

Figure 104.8 *A network involving a dummy activity*

Table 104.4

Task	Duration	EST	LFT	Total Float	Free Float
A	2	0	2	0*	0
B	2	0	6	4	0
C	6	2	8	0*	0
D	3	2	7	2	0
E	1	2	7	4	2
F	8	2	15	5	5
G	2	8	11	1	1
H	1	5	8	2	2
J	3	8	11	0*	0
K	3	8	15	4	4
L	4	11	15	0*	0

logical connection, but does not show any time passing.

- The critical path through the network is shown by a broken (blue) line, linking activities A,C,J and L. Notice that these are the nodes where the ESTs and LFTs are equal. It is also the route with the longest ESTs, as explained earlier in this unit.
- The minimum time to complete the assembly of the engine would be 15 hours.
- The float in the network is shown in Table 104.4.

Advantages of critical path analysis

The major advantage of critical path analysis is that it provides decision makers with a picture of a problem which may be easier to interpret. It can be used to suit a range of circumstances and help solve a variety of business problems.

- Reduce the time lost between tasks, ensuring that projects run smoothly.
- Encourage forward planning. The process ensures that all the tasks in a particular operation have been identified and timed from start to finish. The construction of the network forces decision makers to consider all aspects of a project.
- Improve efficiency in production. The level of working capital can be minimised by ordering and receiving materials and components 'just-in-time'. By identifying float and critical activities, resources such as labour and capital can be used more effectively.
- Control cash flow. This is achieved by not ordering supplies too early and only making purchases when they are required.

Disadvantages of critical path analysis

Despite the advantages of critical path analysis, there are drawbacks.

- The construction of a network alone will not guarantee the smooth completion of a project. The co-operation and commitment of the entire team of staff is needed to ensure that each task is completed according to the estimated duration. Staff should also be consulted when management decides how long tasks will take.
- Some projects are immense. Network diagrams may become complex and unmanageable. Computers may be used to manage information more effectively .
- Network analysis will only be helpful if the data used to construct diagrams is reliable. If the task durations are inaccurate or the order of tasks is wrong, then the EST's, LFT's and the critical path will all be misleading.

Queueing and simulation

SIMULATIONS are models which try to reproduce in a dynamic way what is going on in reality. Business simulations, such as business games, have become common

Question 2

A toy manufacturer has designed a new wooden toy. The construction of the toy involves 9 activities A to J. The order and the duration of tasks are shown in the network diagram illustrated in Figure 104.9. The time durations shown are in minutes.

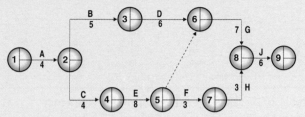

Figure 104.9 *Network diagram for the construction of a new wooden toy*

(a) What is the minimum construction time for the new toy?
(b) What is the critical path?
(c) If task D and task H were each delayed by one minute what would be the effect on:
    (i) the minimum construction time;
    (ii) the critical path?
(d) Explain how critical path analysis might benefit the toy manufacturer.

tools in management training and Business Studies teaching. But simulations can also be used to look at a very specific problem, such as queueing. People who are kept waiting in queues may look for a different place to buy goods and services. Queues also waste resources, such as time spent dealing with customer complaints.

Such problems often result when customers arrive at random. Examples may be people using a cashpoint or a public telephone, patients arriving at casualty or cars arriving at a toll booth. It is the random element which causes the problem. If people used these items regularly it would be easy to decide on the number of staff required to deal with customers without causing delay. This assumes, however, that the service time is constant. This is not always the case. Where the service time is variable, such as at a supermarket checkout, a problem will exist.

Take an example of how a simulation can be used to reduce queuing at checkouts in a supermarket. A number of variables need to be considered:

- The number of customers arriving at the checkouts.
- The number of checkouts in operation.
- The frequency of arrival at checkouts.
- The length of time each customer takes at the checkout.

A simulation will allow a business to work out the number of checkouts it must operate at different times of the day to keep queues at a minimum.

The first stage is to collect information about how the system operates at present. The supermarket collected information about 100 customers who 'checked out' between 5.00pm and 5.30pm. Table 104.5 shows this information.

Table 104.5 *Information relating to customers arriving at a supermarket checkout*

Time between arrivals at checkout (mins)	Frequency (per cent)	Cumulative frequency	Time at check out (mins)	Frequency (per cent)	Cumulative frequency
0	8	8	1	7	7
1	20	28	2	25	32
2	32	60	3	32	64
3	21	81	4	16	80
4	9	90	5	12	92
5	10	100	6	8	100

Table 104.5 also shows the **cumulative frequency** (☞ unit 12) of people at the checkout. The information forms the basis of a model which will try to simulate the arrival of customers at checkouts. Random numbers are used to indicate the time between arrivals and the length of time spent at the checkout. Random numbers are obtained from computers and have no pattern provided they are used in a random way. For example a random series of 50 numbers may be:

20 84 27 38 66 19 60 10 51 20
35 16 74 58 72 79 98 09 47 07
98 82 69 63 23 70 80 88 86 23
94 67 94 34 03 77 89 30 49 51
04 54 32 55 94 82 08 19 20 73

Table 104.6 *Cumulative frequencies and allocated random numbers*

Time between arrivals (mins)	Cumulative frequency	Random numbers	Time at check out (mins)	Cumulative frequency	Random numbers
0	8	01 - 08	1	7	01 - 07
1	28	09 - 28	2	32	08 - 32
2	60	29 - 60	3	64	35 - 64
3	81	61 - 81	4	80	65 - 80
4	90	82 - 90	5	92	81 - 92
5	100	91 -100	6	100	93 -100

The random numbers are allocated to the 'Time between arrivals' and the 'Time spent at the checkout', according to the cumulative frequencies as shown in Table 104.6. The simulation can now begin, using the random numbers in the order they are shown above:

Random number 20 - customer 1 arrives after 1 minute
Random number 84 - customer 1 takes 5 minutes to be served

Random number 27 - customer 2 arrives 1 minute after customer 1
Random number 38 - customer 2 takes 3 minutes to be served

Random number 66 - customer 3 arrives 3 minutes after customer 2
Random number 19 - customer 3 takes 2 minutes to be served

The simulation can be recorded as shown in Table 104.7. It is assumed that there is just one checkout in operation to start with.

Table 104.7 *The results of the simulation showing the arrival times, waiting times, service times, and the leaving times of customers*

Customer	Random number Arrival	Random number Service time	Simulated times Between arrival (mins)	Simulated times Service time (mins)	Arrived at	Served at	Leaves at	Cust wait (mins)	Checkout wait (mins)
1	20	84	1	5	5.01	5.01	5.06	0	1
2	27	38	1	3	5.02	5.06	5.09	4	0
3	66	19	3	2	5.05	5.09	5.11	4	0
4	60	10	2	2	5.07	5.11	5.13	4	0
5	51	20	2	2	5.09	5.13	5.15	4	0
6	35	16	2	2	5.11	5.15	5.17	4	0
7	74	58	3	3	5.14	5.17	5.20	3	0
8	72	79	3	4	5.17	5.20	5.24	3	0
9	98	09	5	2	5.22	5.24	5.26	2	0
10	47	07	2	1	5.24	5.26	5.27	2	0

With just one checkout in operation, the average customer waiting time is about three minutes - this might be considered acceptable. Also, the checkout has been working constantly. Let us now run the simulation with two checkouts in operation. The results are shown in Table 104.8.

Table 104.8 *Results from simulation with two checkouts employed (the random numbers are excluded)*

Customer	Simulated times Between arrival (mins)	Simulated times Service time (mins)	Arrived at	Checkout number	Served at	Leaves at	Cust. wait (mins)	Checkout wait (mins)
1	1	5	5.01	1	5.01	5.06	0	1
2	1	3	5.02	2	5.02	5.05	0	2
3	3	2	5.05	2	5.05	5.07	0	0
4	2	2	5.07	1	5.07	5.09	0	1
5	2	2	5.09	1	5.09	5.11	0	0
6	2	2	5.11	2	5.11	5.13	0	4
7	3	3	5.14	1	5.14	5.17	0	3
8	3	4	5.17	2	5.17	5.21	0	4
9	5	2	5.22	1	5.22	5.24	0	5
10	2	1	5.24	2	5.24	5.25	0	3

With two checkouts in operation, customers are never kept waiting. However, both checkouts are waiting for customers on many occasions. The results from this simulation can help the supermarket decide whether it wants to operate one or two checkouts. The final decision will also depend on its policy towards customer queueing and staff productivity. For example, if its policy is to keep staff fully employed then it will use just one checkout. Simulations like this may appear cumbersome, but the use of a computer will help speed up the process. They are used quite commonly in business. Other OR techniques are too complex to deal with problems like queueing and congestion. However, simulations are only as good as the data upon which they are based. Inaccurate data could lead to incorrect conclusions being drawn. Also, the data may be expensive to collect in the first place.

Question 3

A warehouse receives lorry loads of corn from local farmers. It currently operates one tipping facility. Table 104.9 shows the arrival intervals of successive lorries and the times taken to tip their loads.

Table 104.9 *Information regarding the arrival of lorries at a warehouse and the time it takes to tip their loads*

Time between arrivals (mins)	Frequency (per cent)	Cumulative frequency	Tipping time (mins)	Frequency (per cent)	Cumulative Frequency
3	5	5	10	12	12
4	10	15	11	20	32
7	45	60	12	30	62
10	30	90	13	28	90
13	10	100	14	10	100

(a) Use a simulation to show the: (i) arrival time; (ii) waiting time; of 10 lorries which begin arriving at 9.00am. Use the random numbers in the text on the previous page.

(b) Using another simulation, show the effect of operating two tipping facilities.

(c) Do you think a second tipping facility would be a worthwhile investment? Explain your answer.

(d) Explain one possible disadvantage of using simulation in this case.

Cost - benefit analysis

Many decisions in business are 'financial' decisions. When considering different courses of action decision makers often weigh up the financial costs against the financial benefits. Normally, a business will choose the course of action which generates the greatest net financial benefit. Recently, some firms have begun to consider the costs and benefits of their decisions to the rest of society. Take an example of a chemical company. It is likely to face the 'private' costs of machinery etc., but may also generate pollution into the atmosphere. Pollution is one example of negative externalities (☞ unit 35) or external costs. Similarly, the business will aim to sell its product to earn revenue (a private benefit), but may build a factory and a new road which eases traffic congestion in the area (an external benefit). We can say:

Social costs = private/financial costs + external costs.
Social benefit = private/financial benefit + external benefit.

COST-BENEFIT ANALYSIS is a method used to take into account social costs and benefits when making decisions. A business must place a monetary value on any social costs and benefits which a particular course of action might lead to. For example, consider a business calculating the cost of locating a new factory in a rural area. Part of the external cost might be the potential loss of wildlife. The business must find a way of evaluating this cost in monetary terms. Quite obviously this would be difficult and this is one of the problems with cost-benefit analysis.

Cost-benefit analysis is more commonly used in the public sector. Government investment projects have often been the subject of cost-benefit analysis. For example, the decision whether or not to build a bypass would look at external costs, such as the loss of custom to local businesses when the traffic is diverted. These would be compared with the possible external benefits, such as less congestion and fewer accidents on the local roads. The overall decision would depend on both the external costs and benefits, and the financial costs of constructing the bypass. The abandoning of a Thames crossing at Oxleas Wood because of the impact it would have had on the environment is an example of a project that took social costs and benefits into account.

Question 4

Motorcorp plc builds roads and motorways for the Highways Agency in the UK. In 1997 it won a contract to build a bypass around a small town in East Anglia. The new dual carriageway was expected to cost £47 million and would re-route the main 'A' road. Local residents were in favour of the bypass because traffic through the town had become intolerable. Congestion at the small roundabout in the centre of the town raised journey times for locals and had created a serious hazard for pedestrians. Figure 104.10 shows road accidents in the village between 1992 and 1999. However, the construction of the bypass destroyed an area of outstanding natural beauty. Following the announcement of the starting date for work on the construction, 300 environmental protesters moved into the area. They dug a complex network of tunnels under a forest and stated their intention to occupy them when constructors arrived. Motorcorp had dealt with the occupation of sites in the past, but underestimated the commitment of these protesters. Evicting them took three months longer than anticipated and cost Motorcorp an extra £2.1 million.

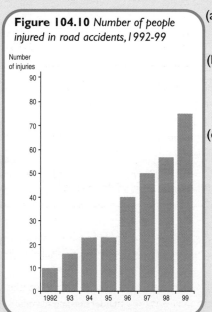

Figure 104.10 *Number of people injured in road accidents, 1992-99*

(a) What is the private cost of the new bypass?

(b) Explain two possible: (i) social benefits; (ii) social costs of building the bypass.

(c) Assuming that social costs and social benefits were taken into account when the Highways Agency was deciding whether or not to build the bypass, discuss how the social costs might have been evaluated.

Key terms

Cost-benefit analysis - a technique which involves taking into account all social costs and benefits, when deciding on a course of action.

Critical path - in an operation which consists of a sequence of activities, this is the one sequence which cannot afford any delays without prolonging the operation.

Network analysis or Critical path analysis - a technique used to find the cheapest or fastest way to complete an operation.

Simulation - a technique which imitates what might happen in reality by using random numbers.

Summary

1. What is meant by a network?
2. What does the critical path show a firm?
3. What is meant by a float in a network and what does it tell a business?
4. Briefly explain 3 uses of critical path analysis to a firm.
5. State 3 problems of critical path analysis
6. State 3 situations where a simulation might be used.
7. Explain what is meant by:
   (a) private costs and private benefits;
   (b) external costs and external benefits.
8. 'The private costs of building a new motorway through a rural area are not the only costs that must be taken into consideration.' Briefly explain this statement.

Case study

Precision Electronics plc

Precision Electronics plc has won a contract to design and install a new traffic control system for a large city in the North of England which is introducing trams as part of the transport network. Trams had been introduced in towns such as Sheffield and Manchester. The contract covers both the design and manufacture of the electronic control system (the console) and the construction of a control building attached to the existing central bus station. For the construction work Precision would need to use outside contractors.

The tasks involved in designing and equipping the new control units are shown in Table 104.10. In their planning for

the construction, Precision had to draw up the network in Figure 104.11 in order to establish the time the contract would take and the likely bid it would put in.

(a) For these activities, calculate the:
  (i) earliest start time;
  (ii) latest finishing time;
  (iii) total float;
  (iv) free float.
(b) What would be the minimum time between Precision receiving this contract and the control building being fully operational?
(c) Which tasks lie on the critical path for the operation? Explain why.
(d) What would be the effect of a delay in making the console of 2 weeks?
(e) The outside contractors would be employed at the stage when the foundations of the building needed constructing. What would be the latest time at which they could start doing this without delaying the whole project?
(f) What are the limitations for Precision in using such an analysis in deciding their likely bid for the contract?

Table 104.10

Task	Weeks
Design console	2
Make console	15
Deliver console	1
Install console	2
Test console	4
Design control building	4
Order and deliver foundation material	2
Construct foundations	1
Order and deliver control building material	2
Construct central building	8
Decorate and equip building	3

Figure 104.11

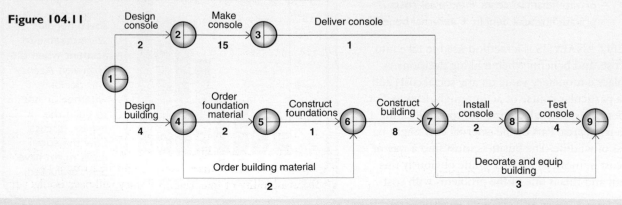

Studying and assessment

Study skills are the skills that a student needs to plan, organise and carry out their work effectively. They also help a student to answer questions and carry out tasks which are designed to test their abilities. Units 105 and 106 are set out like a manual. They provide guidance and examples to help students when working in term time or when taking examinations. Examples are shown in italics. The units could be used:

● at the start of the course to get ideas on the best way to study;
● constantly throughout the course when studying;
● before examinations during revision preparation.

Action planning

Studying is more effective if there is a **plan** or **strategy**. An action plan can be formally written out, but it does not have to be. For any piece of work, it is important for a student to plan:

● how long it will take, bearing in mind any deadline;
● where the student will work;
● when the student will work;
● in what order tasks will be carried out;
● factors likely to affect the work, such as unforeseen occurrences.

A plan can be made for an individual piece of work, work over a term, coursework or project work, revision or a entire scheme of work. It is important for a student to develop a **routine** of work that is effective. It is also important for students to be **committed** to complete the plan. Figure 105.1 shows a possible action plan that may be used for study, work or revision.

Figure 105.1

Title and nature of work	What needs to be done? What is the focus? How will it be judged?
Start and finish date	What is the deadline? How long will it take?
Collecting information	Where from? How can it be obtained? What help is needed? How long will it take? How will it be used?
Carry out the work	Where? When? How long? Who with? What order? Continuous or broken down? Help needed? What factors might affect the work? Possible changes?
Review	Did the plan work? Was the outcome successful? How could it have been done better? Was everything covered?

Time management

An important part of the action plan is planning how long to study or work. Certain factors must be considered when deciding how much time to take when studying.

When to start and when to finish There is a deadline for most pieces of work. This is the date by which it has to be completed. It is important to start early enough and to leave enough time to finish the work. Some people work faster than others. This will affect the time they allocate.

How long the work will take Some pieces of work will take longer than others. Short answer questions will perhaps take less time than an essay. A piece of coursework or project work may take months. So will revision. Some people work quicker than others, which may reduce the time taken.

How long to work The length of time spent on work can affect its quality.

● Spending a greater amount of time preparing and planning may improve a piece of work.
● The time spent writing may also improve work.
● Working for too long can be tiring and work may suffer. Sometimes it is better to take a short break.
● Some work, such as coursework and revision, can not be done all at once and must be broken up.
● It is useful to try to break up revision, by learning as you go along. There is likely to be too much to learn in one session at the end. Spreading the work also allows practice.

When to study This will depend on the time available. Some people have a free choice of time. They could work in free time in the day, at lunchtime, in the evening or at weekends. People with part time jobs or with great commitments may find it more difficult. They may have to work when they can. Sometimes there may be free time which could be usefully used, such as travelling to school or college on a bus or train. Students should also consider that it may not be useful to work:

● late at night because they are tired;
● after strenuous exercise because it may be difficult to concentrate;
● when they are doing lots of other things.

Where to study

It is important to consider where to work. Some students will work better in certain environments than others. Should you work at home or in a different place such as school, a library or another person's house? Issues to consider might be:

● the availability of materials. A library will have books you can use. It may also have a facility to find book titles, newspapers and magazines, perhaps on CD Rom, and access to the internet. If you keep all your materials at home, it may be better to work there;

● ease of access. Working at home allows easy access to drinks and food. Some people may also want to take a break to watch television or do something else;

● comfortable or not? Working in a familiar environment, such as home, can make work easier. Other people prefer to work in a more 'academic' atmosphere;

● alone or in a group? Some people prefer to work alone. Others like to work with someone else, even if they are doing their own work. Sometimes group activities demand that people work together.

● silent or not? Some people prefer to work in silence as they concentrate better. Working in a library would allow this. Others prefer things to be happening around them.

Other learning considerations

There are other factors that students may want to take into consideration when working.

● Some people prefer to sit on a hard chair. Some prefer to be more comfortable and sit on a soft or relaxing chair.

● Some people like to listen to music whilst they are working. Others prefer silence.

● Some people prefer bright lighting so that everything is clear. Others work better in dimmed lighting.

● Some people prefer to carry out several tasks or activities at once. Others prefer to do one task and then move on to another.

● Some people prefer to eat or chew while they are working as it helps them to concentrate. Others don't.

● Some people learn better by moving around from time to time and some by standing up.

Learning and memory strategies

Different people learn in different ways. Some people learn and remember more easily when they hear something. Others prefer to see it written down and to read it. Some prefer a diagram or picture. Each of these styles of learning may be useful in different circumstances. If a student finds learning something difficult in one way, he or she might try another.

Written methods In many cases students will have to read information and take notes. This is often the most common form of learning on a course at advanced level.
A possible technique used to read information is to:

● choose a section of written material that you will read and quickly scan through it to get the overall idea;

● read the material more slowly;

● put the written material aside and recite the key ideas or points that you have read;

● check that you have covered the main points;

● if you have missed anything, re-read the information.

Often in work or for revision students have to condense large amounts of information into shorter note form. This makes it easier to remember. Steps to note taking may involve the following:

● reading the information and making sure that you understand it first;

● dividing up the information into topic headings and subheadings;

● making suitable notes that are clear and easy to read, and are in a logical order;

● underlining or highlighting important words or key phrases that will trigger memory of the point;

● using page references to the written material;

● leaving space for additions;

● creating an index for your notes, either using a card system or a computer package and updating the order.

Once you have a set of notes you can use the reading technique above to make sure you understand them or for revision.

Example

The European Commission is poised to open an investigation into BP Amoco's proposed $26bn merger with Atlantic Richfield (Arco). EU sources said the merger, which would further tighten the oligopolistic structure of the oil market, had to be examined in the context of other anti-trust investigations involving the sector - notably the Exxon-Mobil project. Competition authorities in Brussels and the US are worried that these and other deals will enhance the power of a small number of oil companies in the exploration and production of oil and gas worldwide. If the two mergers go through, the top three oil majors - including the Anglo Dutch group Shell - will account for close to 50 per cent of crude oil production by publicly quoted western companies, bankers estimate.

EU officials had serious doubts about the BP Amoco-Arco merger. One problem involves the high joint share BP Amoco-Arco would have in pipeline transportation of natural gas in the UK sector of the North Sea. The potential blocks to the approval of Exxon-Mobil are greater. As well as its doubts about the global structure of the industry, Brussels has identified numerous problems affecting Europe as a whole, as well as the EU member states. One is that the deal could harm competition in the onshore production and distribution of low calorific gas in Netherlands and Germany, where the two companies jointly have a high market share. The Commission said that it was determined not to let the merger damage the consumer benefits expected to flow from the recent liberalisation of the European gas market.

Source: adapted from the *Financial Times*, 11.6.1999.

Oil mergers
● *Possible investigation by European Commission of BP Amoco -Arco and Exxon-Mobil mergers.*

(a) Mind maps

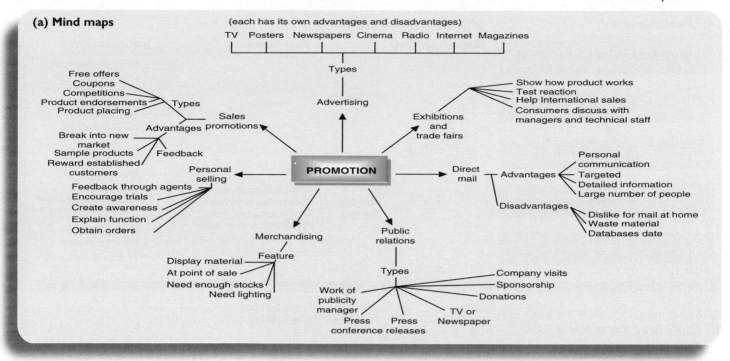

- *Concern that the mergers will increase <u>oligopolistic</u> nature of oil market. If mergers go through, BP Amoco-Arco, Exxon-Mobil and Shell would have nearly 50 per cent of crude oil production.*
- *Problem of BP Amoco/Arco merger. Domination of natural gas pipelines.*
- *Problems of Exxon-Mobil merger. Harm to competition transport of low caloric gas in Holland and Germany and possible benefits of market liberalisation (lower prices, better choice etc.)*

Oral methods It is sometimes easier to remember or understand something if you hear it. When you meet people do you remember their name? If so you may have a strong oral memory. Strategies for learning might include:

- answering questions asked by another person;
- making oral notes onto a tape recorder which are played back regularly;
- constantly repeating phrases or key words, perhaps in an order;
- make up a **mnemonic**, rhyme or phrase which can be repeated. For example, PEST analysis stands for the Political, Economic, Social and Technological factors that affect a business.

Pictorial/visual When you meet people do you remember their face? If so you may have a strong visual memory. Visual material can provide an instant 'picture' of information. Sometimes it is easier to see relationships by visual representation. Visual information may make use of some of the note taking techniques explained above. They may also make use of photographs. Examples of visual presentation include the following.

(b) Family trees

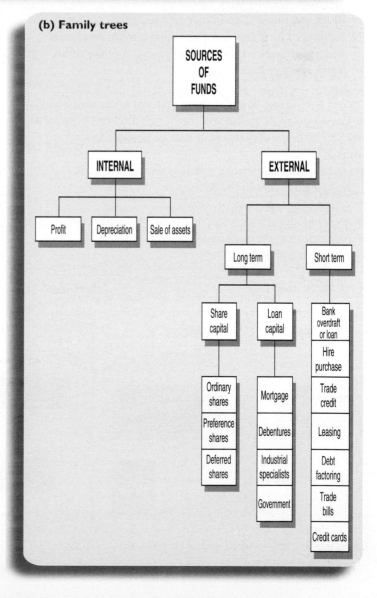

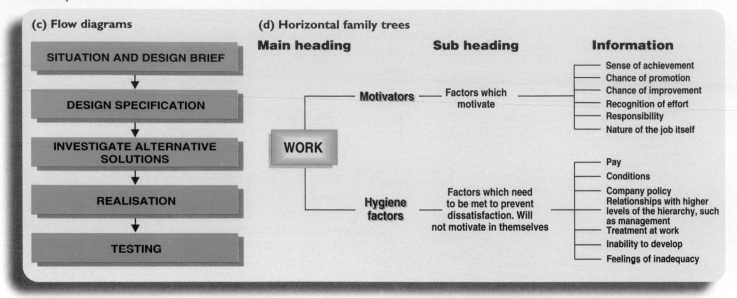

(c) Flow diagrams

SITUATION AND DESIGN BRIEF

↓

DESIGN SPECIFICATION

↓

INVESTIGATE ALTERNATIVE SOLUTIONS

↓

REALISATION

↓

TESTING

(d) Horizontal family trees

Main heading	Sub heading	Information

WORK

Motivators — Factors which motivate —
- Sense of achievement
- Chance of promotion
- Chance of improvement
- Recognition of effort
- Responsibility
- Nature of the job itself

Hygiene factors — Factors which need to be met to prevent dissatisfaction. Will not motivate in themselves —
- Pay
- Conditions
- Company policy
- Relationships with higher levels of the hierarchy, such as management
- Treatment at work
- Inability to develop
- Feelings of inadequacy

(a) Mind maps. *Promotion methods.*

(b) Family trees. *The sources of funds.*

(c) Flow diagrams. *The stages in the design process.*

(d) Horizontal family trees. *Hertzberg's two-factor theory.*

(e) Block diagrams. *Calculating profit and loss.*

(f) Method of loci. This involves taking a room you know and imagining certain key words in parts of the room. *Types of integration.*

Learning by doing You may think that you know something or know how to do it. But you might only find out if you test yourself by doing something. It may be possible to test yourself by using:

- classroom or homework activities you have already completed earlier in the course;
- activities in textbooks or workbooks;
- applying ideas in a project or a piece of coursework;
- past examination questions;
- your own activities.

Key skills

Key skills allow a student to learn, select and apply important competences. Key skills at advanced level may include communication, application of number, information technology, working with others, improving own learning and performance, and problem solving. All of these skills can be developed by a student taking a course in Business Studies. Some examples of each key skill are shown below.

Communication

- Debates. *The extent to which business ethics should influence profit.*
- Role play. *An interview scenario or a meeting with a pressure group.*
- Group discussions. *How a business might promote a new product.*
- Interviews. *A one-to-one interview with a manager about a business problem.*

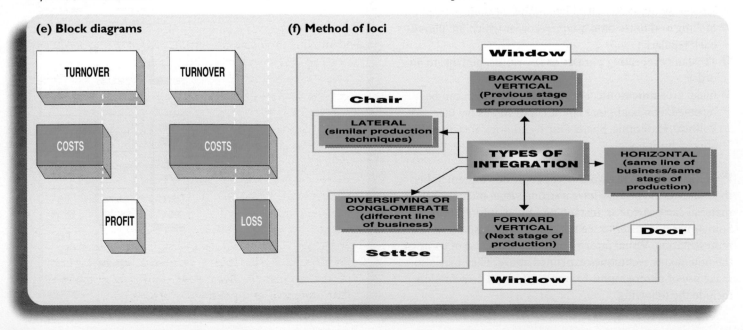

(e) Block diagrams

TURNOVER   TURNOVER

COSTS   COSTS

PROFIT   LOSS

(f) Method of loci

Window

Chair

BACKWARD VERTICAL (Previous stage of production)

LATERAL (similar production techniques)

TYPES OF INTEGRATION

HORIZONTAL (same line of business/same stage of production)

DIVERSIFYING OR CONGLOMERATE (different line of business)

FORWARD VERTICAL (Next stage of production)

Door

Settee

Window

- Oral presentations. *The results of marketing research.*
- Passing information. *A memo to staff about reorganisation following the introduction of new technology.*
- Written analysis. *A report recommending action to solve problems identified in the profit and loss account and a balance sheet or strategy to deal with entry into foreign markets.*
- Written and visual presentations. *Producing a business plan or charts showing the market share of businesses in an industry.*
- Summarising information. *Producing a business organisational chart or a summary of performance from financial ratio data.*
- Written responses. *A letter to a dissatisfied customer.*
- Communication using technology. *An e-mail to the manager showing sales figures on a spreadsheet.*

Application of number

- Numerical calculations. *Calculating the depreciation of assets using different methods or calculating labour turnover.*
- Planning information. *Preparing information for a sales revenue budget.*
- Interpreting results. *Identifying gearing problems from ratios.*
- Numerical analysis. *Investment appraisal using various methods.*
- Graphical analysis. *Identifying stock problems from a chart.*
- Construction of graphs. *Constructing a break-even chart.*
- Construction of tables. *Constructing a balance sheet.*
- Collection and presentation of data. *Sales figures used to produce product life cycle diagrams or market research information showing customers' responses.*
- Forecasting. *Estimating future sales figures from a trend.*

Information technology

- Searching for information. *Finding information on a CD Rom or an internet website.*
- Reviewing and selecting information. *Selecting appropriate information from the internet to show accidents at work.*
- Written presentation and manipulation of information. *Writing a report using appropriate software on the impact on a business of the euro.*
- Visual presentation of information. *Illustrating the number of full time, part time and outworkers in a business as percentages in a pie chart.*
- Calculation using data. *Calculating cash flow using a spreadsheet.*
- Collection of data. *Marketing research information on a database.*
- Manipulation and management of data. *Updating stock figures over time on a spreadsheet to show stock balances.*
- Transfer of data. *Storing cost information on disk so that it can be used for financial calculations by someone else.*
- Communication technology. *Sending an e-mail containing ideas for a new product.*

Working with others

- Discussions. *To discuss the possible effects on a business of lean production methods.*
- Group debates. *Should multinational businesses take their profits back to the 'home' country or spend it in foreign countries in which they operate?*
- Searching for information. *When dealing with a great deal of information such as changes in government legislation over a period.*
- Collecting information. *When dealing with a great deal of information such as the effects of government policy on a business over a year.*
- Summarising. *When a great deal of information has to be summarised, each group member could take one aspect. For example, when looking at changes in a business, summaries of marketing, production and approaches to human resources could be made.*
- Question practice and cross checking. *Using another person to ask questions or to check your answers.*
- Brainstorming. *Developing possible promotional methods using brainstorming sessions.*
- Using outside sources of information. *Discussing the effects of pedestrianisation of a town on a local retailer.*

Improving own learning performance

- Identifying areas to improve. *Knowledge, memory, time management, work and resource management, such as where to find information and what resources to use, interpreting questions, answering questions, working with others, the work environment, motivation.*
- Evaluating work. *Own evaluation, others' opinions, evaluation against criteria, past experience of problems.*
- Identifying methods of improvement. *More practice, changing the method of learning, identifying strengths and applying to other areas, reorganisation of environment such as changing the place or time of work, changing attitudes, changing resources.*
- Identifying help. *Resources, other people, self-help.*

Problem solving

- Identifying problems. *Identify the need to change operations or strategy as a result of variance analysis.*
- Identifying the possible solutions to a problem. *Identifying the different strategies that a business might use to effectively manage change.*
- Choosing solutions from alternatives. *Choosing the most effective advertising campaign using decision trees or the most effective method of work using critical path analysis.*
- Evaluating solutions. *Evaluate the reorganisation of a business to improve productivity using mean and standard deviation calculations.*
- Using IT. *Using spreadsheet calculations to solve problems by identifying the most cost effective or profitable solution.*
- Problem solving in students' own work. *Identifying and solving problems involved in coursework, such as collection of data, storage of data, presentation of data.*

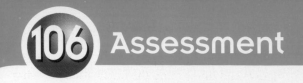

Command, directive or key words

When presented with a task or question as part of internally assessed work or externally assessed examinations:
- how do you know what the question is asking?
- how do you know what the assessor or examiner wants you to do?

In many forms of assessment certain **command, directive or key words** in a question will tell the student what is expected of them. Sometimes two or more words appear together in a question. They must all be taken into account when giving the answer.

Information and knowledge Certain command words are designed to find out what a student knows about the subject.
- Define - to state the exact meaning of a term or a phrase. *Define what is meant by marketing research.*
- Describe - to give an account or a portrayal of something. *Describe the hierarchy and span of control of the business.*
- Give - to write down or say something. Sometimes followed by 'an example' or 'an account of'. *Give an example of a private limited company.* May also be followed by 'reasons for' which may involve greater analysis.
- How - to present an account of something. *How has the business raised funds to buy new machinery?*
- Identify - to pick from a variety of information. *Identify three reasons for the merger.*
- Illustrate - to show clearly, often with the use of an example. *Illustrate the main methods used to promote the product.*
- Outline - to give a short description of the main aspects or features. *Outline the view of workers by management.*
- State - to write down or say something. Sometimes followed by what that 'something should be'. *State 3 features of an effective leader.*
- Summarise - to provide a brief account covering the main points. *Summarise the approach to quality at the business.*
- What - to clarify something. *What is meant by a stakeholder?*
- Which - to select from certain options or to indicate a choice. *Which location did the business find most suitable?*

Application, justification and explanation Certain command words are designed to allow the student to apply knowledge to a given situation, to work out why something has happened and to give reasons for something that has happened.
- Account for - to give reasons for. *Account for the growth in part time workers over the period.*
- Analyse - to examine in detail, showing relationships, the

importance of certain things and criticisms if applicable. *Analyse the approach to lean production of the organisation.*
- Apply - to bring knowledge to bear on a situation. Note that sometimes the word does not appear in the question. For example, 'Using examples from the article, explain how the business might promote its product' requires an application of knowledge to a particular situation. *Apply the Boston Matrix to the product mix of the company.*
- Calculate - to work out mathematically, usually numerically, but sometimes from a graph for example. *Calculate the return on net assets for the business.*
- Compare and contrast - to show the similarities and differences between two or more things. *Compare and contrast the approaches to recruitment of the two companies.*
- Distinguish - to show the differences between two or more things. *Distinguish between job and batch production.*
- Examine - to investigate closely to find out the 'truth' of the situation as if carrying out an inquiry. *Examine the factors that may have led to cash flow problems.*
- Explain - to make clear a concept, idea or viewpoint. It may involve giving an illustration of the meaning or examples. Note that it is sometimes followed by the word 'why' (see below). *Explain the pricing strategies used by the business.*
- Explore - to investigate or examine in detail, as explained above. *Explore the ways in which a business is affected by changes in interest rates.*
- Investigate - to carry out a detailed examination. *Investigate the factors that may have led the business to go into liquidation.*
- Suggest or give reasons for - to explain why giving a justification. *Suggest reasons why the business chose to reduce its workforce.*
- Why - to present reasons for something. *Explain why labour turnover has increased.*

Evaluation Certain command words are designed to allow students to make a judgment or to evaluate a judgment that has taken place.
- Assess - an invitation to measure or place a value on the importance of something. *Assess whether the change to just in time manufacturing is likely to be successful.*
- Comment on - to give an opinion about the extent to which something has occurred. *Comment on the environmental policy of the organisation.*
- Criticise or critically analyse - to pass judgment on a debatable area. *Critically analyse the growing globalisation of business.*
- Determine - to settle, decide, or find out the nature of. *Determine the most suitable new location for the business.*

- Do you think - to comment on or give an opinion on the basis of evidence. *Do you think the decision of the business to expand was a suitable strategy in the circumstances?*
- Discuss - to consider a contentious statement or to review an area which might have two or more views. *Discuss whether the business should have introduced group decision making.*
- Evaluate - to make an appraisal of something and to find out how important it is. *Evaluate the strategy used by the business over the period.*
- To what extent (does/do) - to make a judgment or to measure. *To what extent has the change in corporate culture been successful?*

Assessment criteria

It is possible to use a range of **criteria** when assessing the performance of students. This means that examiners or assessors want students to demonstrate a range of different skills. In order to be successful students must:
- understand the skills required by examiners or assessors;
- recognise the skill that is being assessed in a particular question;
- demonstrate all of the skills assessed by the examiner;
- practice skills before the examination.

The criteria used by examiners may fall into the following categories.

Knowledge Students have to demonstrate that they:
- understand business theories and concepts;
- recognise and understand business terms;
- interpret information given in a business context.

Students can recognise questions which test knowledge by looking at the command words in the question. Such words are explained in the section above. An example of a question assessing knowledge might be: *What is meant by best practice benchmarking?*

Application and understanding This assessment criterion requires students to apply theories and concepts in both familiar and unfamiliar situations. This might involve:
- using a business formula in appropriate circumstances, for example, calculating the current ratio for a business;
- using a theory to explain why a business has chosen a particular course of action, for example, using McGregor's Y theory to explain why a business has introduced quality circles;
- using a business theory to suggest a suitable course of action for a business, for example, suggesting a chainstore uses loyalty cards to increase repeat sales.

Questions requiring application can again be recognised by looking at the command word. An example of a question requiring application might be: *Explain why the business has cut its research and development budget.*

Analysis Students have to demonstrate that they can break down information and understand the implications of what they have been presented with. Students will encounter both qualitative and quantitative information and will need to:
- identify causes and effects and interrelationships, for example, recognise from a graph that sales are falling and could be a result of a new competition in the market;
- break down information to identify specific causes or problems, for example, realise that a business is suffering from inefficiency because according to the information staff motivation has fallen, equipment is worn and working practices are outdated;
- use appropriate techniques to analyse data, for example, use ratio analysis to assess the solvency of a business;
- use appropriate theories, business cases/practices to investigate the question, for example, use elasticity theory to show that raising price may be ineffective.

Questions requiring analysis can be recognised by looking at the command word. An example of a question requiring analysis might be: *Examine the factors which have influenced the firm's decision to close its Cardiff factory.*

Evaluation Evaluation involves making a judgment. Evaluation questions are often used to award the highest grades in examinations. Students might be expected to:
- show judgment in weighing up the relative importance of different points or sides of an argument, in order to reach a conclusion;
- comment on the reliability of information or evidence;
- distinguish between fact and opinion;
- distinguish between relevant and irrelevant information;
- draw conclusions from the evidence presented;
- show judgment on the wider issues and implications.

Questions requiring evaluation can be identified by looking at the command word. For example, *To what extent has the decision to re-engineer the business been successful?*

When evaluating it is often possible for a student to draw a number of different conclusions. Examiners may be less concerned with the particular conclusion drawn. Very often in business studies there is no 'right' answer. They are more interested in whether students have actually made a judgment and also the quality of their argument in support of the judgment.

Synthesis Opportunities to demonstrate this particular skill may be limited. Synthesis is required in long written answers such as essays, project work or report writing. It involves bringing together a wide range of information in a clear and meaningful way. In particular students must:
- develop points and themes in a way which builds on previous material and ends with a rounded conclusion;
- produce an argument in a logical sequence;

- provide a clear summarised argument which draws on all the individual elements.

Examiners will tend to look for evidence of synthesis in essays and report writing questions. The sections below on essay writing and report writing will explain how students can demonstrate synthesis.

Quality of language Codes of Practice may require the assessment of candidates' quality of language wherever they are required to write in continuous prose. In these circumstances students are required to:

- avoid errors in grammar, punctuation and spelling;
- provide well structured arguments which are consistently relevant;
- write in sentences and paragraphs which follow on from one another smoothly and logically;
- express complex ideas clearly and fluently.

This criterion may be used in all questions, but is especially important in essay and report writing, and project or coursework.

Levels of response

Examiners and assessors may award marks according to the levels of response demonstrated by the student in the answer. The higher the level of response the more marks are awarded to students. An example of different levels that might be identified is shown below.

Level 4 This is the most sophisticated of responses and attracts the most marks. At this level students must provide good evidence of the appropriate skill. Responses must be accurate, extensive, balanced and logical. For example, in evaluation, judgments must be well made and supported by logical arguments. Students must draw original conclusions from the evidence and show awareness of underlying and related themes or issues.

Level 3 At this level student responses are classified as good but with some weaknesses. For example, with regard to knowledge of the subject, to attain level 3 a student must demonstrate that his or her knowledge is satisfactory or better. However, there may be some weaknesses or perhaps the focus is too narrow.

Level 2 If students show that they have clearly used a particular skill, but evidence is limited and there are obvious weaknesses, the response may be classified as level 2. For example, a level 2 response in evaluation would mean that a student has made judgments but they are not well supported by arguments. The evidence will be generally too limited and often below average.

Level 1 This is the most basic of student responses. Some marks will be awarded if a student can demonstrate that they

have at least tried to provide some evidence of a particular skill. For example, in analysis a level 1 response would involve some attempt at analysis of data, but lacking in insight and depth.

This approach may be used by examiners when assessing performance in all of the above criteria, even quality of language. However, examiners do not expect students to offer level 4 responses in all of their answers. It depends on the type of question being asked. For example, level 4 responses may only be required in essays, report writing questions and parts of structured questions in decision making case studies. Some examination questions may only require level 1 or level 2 responses. If this is the case, the answers required at level 1 and level 2 may be slightly different from the descriptions above. For example, a question which offers just 4 marks in an examination may require the responses described below.

- Level 2. Students must develop in detail at least one of the relevant factors identified and show some clarity in their explanation.
- Level 1. Students must identify at least one relevant factor and demonstrate some limited attempt at development.

The levels of response required are not normally shown on examination papers. However, students will understand that those questions which carry more marks will require higher levels of response.

Structured questions

In Business Studies examiners often use structured questions when assessing students' performance. The main features of structured questions are as follows.

- They contain several parts.
- The parts normally follow a sequence or pattern.
- Some of the parts may be linked in some way.
- They are generally accompanied by some data to provide students with a stimulus.
- The whole question may require students to demonstrate all skills covered by the assessment criteria, but only one part may be testing a particular skill.
- The parts of the question generally get more demanding as students work through it.
- Different parts may be assessed by different levels of response.

Structured questions are broken down into 'parts'.

First part The first part of the structured question is usually the easiest. This may help students to 'settle' into a question and perhaps give them some confidence. The first part of a structured question:

- is usually designed to test knowledge of a business concept or business term;
- may require a student to perform a simple skill, eg a calculation;

- may require a student to give a straightforward explanation or definition;
- usually requires students to provide a basic level response, eg level 1 or 2 ;
- would carry only a few marks.

Examples

(a) Explain the term 'working capital'.

(a) Distinguish between job analysis and job evaluation.

Middle part The middle part of structured questions may vary. There is no set pattern and this gives examiners and assessors some flexibility when setting structured questions. However, the middle part of structured questions:

- may contain two or more parts;
- usually test knowledge, application and analysis;
- may require students to perform simple or more difficult calculations;
- may require a mixture of straightforward explanation and more complex analysis;
- may require up to level 3 responses;
- may carry more marks than the first part.

Examples

(b)(i) Calculate the gross profit margin and the net profit margin for the business.

(ii) Comment on your findings in (i).

(b)(i) Explain the meaning of the term price inelastic.

(ii) To what extent is the concept of price elasticity helpful to a business?

(c) Analyse the possible reasons why increasing numbers of companies are introducing flexible working practices.

(c) Examine the possible implications of the data for:

(i) employees;

(ii) a large manufacturer planning to export for the first time.

Final part This part of the question is usually the most demanding part. The final part of the structured question:

- will nearly always require a higher level response;
- will usually test application, analysis and evaluation;
- will usually carry a higher mark allocation;
- may not be broken down into smaller parts.

Examples

(d) Assess the view that business advertising practices should be more heavily regulated.

(d) Evaluate the non-financial factors which might influence the firm's decision to relocate its operations.

(d) Discuss the factors that have influenced

the business to change its marketing strategy.

Data response questions

Data response or case study questions are very common in Business Studies. They are used by examiners to test student skills in unfamiliar circumstances. The key features of data response questions include:

- the provision of qualitative or quantitative data, or both, to provide a stimulus for students;
- hypothetical or real case study data;
- the use of structured questions;
- opportunities for students to demonstrate knowledge, application, analysis and evaluation.

Hints

- Always read the data at least twice.
- Use a felt pen to highlight important words, sentences or key numerical information.
- Read the structured questions very carefully, perhaps highlighting command words and other key terms.
- Some of your answers **must** be related to the data provided.
- Some of your answers **must** use ideas, concepts and theories not mentioned in the data.
- Answer the parts of the question in order.
- Allocate your time according to the number of marks offered for each part.
- Show all your working out when performing calculations.
- Always attempt all parts of the questions.
- **Do not** use bullet points when writing your answers.

Answering the first part The information below contains data from a case study question. The data is just a small extract from the question.

The directors are recommending a final dividend of 18p, making a full year dividend of 27p, an increase of 8 per cent over the previous year. The Directors will consider further limited reductions of dividend cover in the medium-term, allowing real dividend growth to be maintained.

Source: adapted from National Power, *Annual Report and Accounts*, 1998.

(a) Explain the term 'dividend cover'.

- To begin with it is helpful to highlight the key words in the question and the key words in the data as shown above. This might help students to focus.
- The question may carry only a few marks and it is likely that a level 2 response is required.
- To pick up all marks in this case it would be necessary to use a couple of sentences to explain the term and then give the formula which is used to calculate the dividend cover.

- The explanation needs to be crisp, clear and uncomplicated. Students need to demonstrate in their answer that they understand the term. The formula can be added at the end.
- A student could give a numerical illustration here. *For example, if a business made a total dividend payment of £300m and net profit for the year was £500m, dividend cover would be given by:*

$$\frac{Net\ profit}{Dividends} = \frac{£500m}{£300m} = 1.67\ times$$

- In this case it is not necessary to make reference to National Power, the business to which the data relates.

Answering the middle part The data below is from another case study.

There are many factors which will influence the group's future performance. These include the growth of mobile telecommunications markets, the group's market share, revenue per customer, the costs of providing and selling existing services and start up costs of new businesses. In many of the international markets where the group operates, cellular penetration continues to be low, which should enable the businesses to grow more rapidly than in the UK and make a larger contribution to group profits.

Potential for growth

	Population million	Market penetration %	Penetration added in 97/98 %
UK	58.4	15.5	3.4
Australia	18.5	28.5	3.0
Fiji	0.8	0.6	0.1
France	58.6	11.3	6.5
Germany	81.7	11.3	4.1
Greece	10.5	10.2	4.1
Malta	0.4	5.1	1.0
Netherlands	15.6	13.0	5.8
South Africa	38.6	4.6	2.4
Sweden	8.9	37.6	8.7
Uganda	22.6	0.1	-

Source: adapted from Vodafone, *Annual Report and Accounts*, 1998.

(b) (i) Explain which markets have the most potential for growth for Vodafone.
(ii) Analyse two factors which might influence Vodafone's ability to achieve a greater market share.

- Again the first step is to highlight the key words in the question as shown above.
- The question **cannot** be answered without reference to the data. This question requires students to interpret numerical data and understand some business terms.

- Students need to understand that markets with the most potential for growth will be those with large populations **and/or** low market penetration.
- A level 2 response is likely to be required.
- To earn all the marks in this question students first need to identify some countries with high populations and or low market penetration, Germany and South Africa for example.
- Students then need to explain why these countries provide the most potential for growth, ie because they have large populations and at the moment only a relatively small number of the population have mobile phones.

The second part of this question requires students to write in more depth. This will be evident from the higher mark allocation which may be given and the command words used in the question.

- Again, begin by highlighting the key words in the question and the data as above.
- Because the mark allocation may be higher, and the command word is analyse, it is likely that a level 3 response is required.
- Before writing an answer it is helpful to jot down the two factors which are to be analysed. One is suggested in the data, ie the fact that cellular penetration continues to be low. Others need to be identified by the student. They could be the strength of competition or the effectiveness of Vodafone's marketing activities. By jotting down a few alternatives students can spend a few seconds deciding which they prefer to analyse.
- A few marks would be allocated for identifying two appropriate factors.
- The remaining marks may be awarded for demonstrating analysis. Students need to use a few sentences explaining, for example, how very strong competition from rivals such as Orange would reduce Vodafone's ability to raise their own market share. Students could also explain how rivals might compete through the use of advertising or promotions, giving appropriate examples.

Answering the final part As a rule this part carries the most marks so it is important that students leave enough time to answer it properly. The data below contains an extract from another case study.

The Institute of Directors is forecasting that the economy will grow by 0.75 per cent this year, which is close to the market consensus of 0.7 per cent growth. The Treasury continues to forecast a range as low as 1 per cent. Even the most pessimistic forecasts expect only a brief recession, with growth stagnant or negative during the fourth quarter of last year and the first quarter of this year. The growth that is forecast is expected to be seen in the second half of the year.

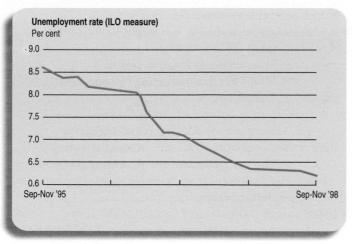

Unemployment rate (ILO measure)
Per cent

Sep-Nov '95 — Sep-Nov '98

Source: adapted from the *Financial Times*, 14.1.1999.

(d) To what extent do external factors, such as those mentioned in the case, influence the performance of a business?

- Answering this final part requires more planning and thought because there is more to say and a level 3 or 4 response may be required.
- Students will need to introduce a lot of their own material into their answer.
- Before writing, students should jot down a plan. A plan for this question might appear as follows.
  1. *Explain how external factors, eg recession, affect businesses.*
  2. *Identify 2 other factors which might affect businesses, eg effectiveness of marketing, competition and efficiency.*
  3. *Analyse the 2 factors.*
  4. *Evaluate by saying that external factors have a great influence because they are beyond the control of businesses. However, a good business will include their effect in their forecasting.*
- If the above plan is executed effectively the student will demonstrate all the skills required and achieve a level 4 response.
- Students should remember that it is not necessary to identify and list lots of factors. Listing is a low order skill and more marks are awarded for analysis and evaluation.

Decision making and problem solving case studies (unseen)

Features These are often in the form of extended case studies. They can be demanding and require a slightly different approach to answering than shorter data response questions.
- The case material tends to be hypothetical but usually based on a real life situation.
- The case material tends to focus on a single business.
- The volume of material given is much greater.
- There tends to be some financial information in the case material.

- The case often emphasises analysis and evaluation skills and will require more level 3 and level 4 responses.
- Many of the case questions require an integrated approach when answering. This means that students will need to embrace the full range of syllabus areas in their answers. A single answer may need to address issues such as marketing, production, human resources, finance and external factors all at the same time.
- Questions set usually require students to make decisions or solve problems. For example, a question may require students to suggest a suitable future strategy for a business.
- One question will often require students to use a quantitative technique when answering.

Hints
- Skim read the case material to get a feel for the business, its people, its circumstances and its objectives (see section below on things to think about).
- Read again thoroughly highlighting key information.
- Look at the numerical information and analyse it briefly, without performing any calculations.
- Make brief notes on the key objectives and key themes.
- Read the questions highlighting command words and other key terms.
- Identify some business theories you might consider discussing in your answers. Questions will probably not request specific theories. The onus is on students to introduce relevant theories.
- Reread hints on answering data response questions above.

Issues to think about when planning answers
- People. Business is about people and your answers need to reflect this. Consider the age, family circumstances, the attitudes and personal interests of the people involved in the case material. What motivates them? What is their background? What are their objectives? What are their strengths and weaknesses? These are some of the people issues which students need to consider when shaping their answers.
- Situation. It is important to think about the context in which the business is set. Examples of issues to consider include the type of business organisation (Ltd, plc or sole trader), the prevailing culture, the type of industry, the nature of competition, the size, its financial position, its age, history and potential. It is often helpful to liken the case material to a business which actually exists in a similar context. However, this may not always be possible.
- Objectives. Answers to questions are bound to be linked to what the business is trying to achieve in its given context. A business may be trying to survive following a recession, it may be trying to break into new markets, it may be trying to raise finance for a big investment

project, it may be trying to change its culture or take over another business. It is often useful to consider, and distinguish between, short term and long term objectives.

● Theories. Students should introduce business theories into their answers. There may be little or no guidance as to what theories are required. Students need to be on the lookout for opportunities to introduce some business theory in every answer they write. For example, if a business is considering a price change, price elasticity theory could be introduced. If a business is merging with another, economies of scale may be discussed. If a business is downsizing the effect on staff might be discussed, in which case motivational theories such as Herzberg or Maslow might be applied.

Example 1
Most of the structured questions in decision making/problem solving case studies usually require lengthy answers with analysis and evaluation. Therefore it is important to plan before writing an answer. Below is an extract from part of an extended case study. The case study is about Henshaws Ltd, a components manufacturer for the computer industry. It has faced difficulties in recent years due to escalating costs. It is considering ways of improving efficiency and reducing costs.

One option currently being considered by Henshaws Ltd is to outsource its marketing activities. The directors of the company have not been impressed with the performance of this department. Their expenditure has consistently exceeded their budget and they seem to get new business and then lose it. In addition, communications between the department and others in the organisation have not been good. Two of the four company directors have long claimed that the company's strength is manufacturing high quality components, although the other two directors argue that the company must avoid clinging to 'past glories' and move forward with the times. A number of marketing agencies have given presentations to the board of directors and a decision whether to outsource marketing is imminent.

(b) Assess the likely advantages and disadvantages to Henshaws Ltd of outsourcing its marketing function.

● To answer this question it is necessary to identify and analyse 2 or 3 advantages, identify and analyse 2 or 3 disadvantages and then evaluate by making a judgment about whether Henshaws should outsource marketing or not.
● Although the question does not specifically ask for a judgment examiners are probably expecting one. This is because the mark allocation may be quite high, perhaps as high as 9 or 10 marks. This would indicate a possible

level 3 or level 4 response.
● A plan should be drafted which might look like this:
Adv. 1. Costs fall
  2. More focus on manufacturing
  3. More effective marketing by specialists
Disadv. 1. Redundancies
  2. Loss of control of a vital function
  3. Long term marketing costs might rise.
Eval. Yes - outsource because current marketing is expensive, ineffective and is causing problems. Henshaws will then be more focused and able to exploit its strengths.

● In the answer it is necessary to analyse the above advantages and disadvantages in detail explaining their relevance.
● In the evaluation some students may suggest that Henshaws should not outsource its marketing function. This does not matter. Examiners just want students to make a judgment and support it with a coherent and plausible argument. Remember that these case studies are decision making case studies and therefore a decision must be made!

Example 2
Some quantitative analysis is usually required in extended case studies. It may be quite complex and students often make the mistake of spending too long on this section. The data below contains an extract from an extended case study about a business which is considering a new investment. Arpan Shrinath & Co manufactures training shoes and Arpan is deciding which investment project to go ahead with.

Project 1. *Arpan has considered buying a large delivery van and undertaking his own distribute. At the moment he pays a local company to distribution training shoes to his customers. This has proved expensive and often ineffective.*

Project 2. *A new moulding machine has just been launched on the market by a German machine manufacturer. It is computer numerically controlled and would help to improve the quality of Arpan's products. It would also be more productive than his existing machine.*

Project 3. *Arpan is becoming increasingly concerned that his office staff are working in conditions which are too cramped. Staff frequently complain and he is aware of inefficiencies due to a lack of space. He is considering the construction of a purpose built annex to the factory where office staff can work more effectively.*

The table below shows the costs and expected returns for each of these projects over a 6 year period.

Expected returns

	Cost	Year 1	Year 2	Year 3	Year 4	Year 5	Year 6	Total
Project 1	£15,000	£4,000	£4,000	£4,000	£4,000	£4,000	£4,000	£24,000
Project 2	£40,000	£12,000	£10,000	£10,000	£9,000	£9,000	£9,000	£59,000
Project 3	£30,000	£7,000	£7,000	£7,000	£7,000	£7,000	£7,000	£42,000

(c) Calculate the (i)payback; (ii)average rate of return; for the 3 investment projects and decide which project is the most attractive. Take into account your results from the calculations and any other information you feel is appropriate.

● This question requires knowledge and understanding of investment appraisal techniques. Provided students have revised the quantitative techniques required they just need to apply the appropriate formulae.

● It is often helpful to produce calculations (or the results of calculations) in tables. One way in which the answers to the above question might be presented is:

	Project 1	Project 2	Project 3
Cost	£15,000	£40,000	£30,000
Total return	£24,000	£59,000	£42,000
Total profit	£9,000	£19,000	£12,000
Profit p.a.	£1,500	£3,167	£2,000
ARR	10%	7.9%	6.6%
Payback	3.75 years	3.88 years	4.29 years

● According to the calculations above project 1 appears the most attractive. It has the highest ARR and also the shortest payback period.

● There is likely to be other information in the case which will influence the decision here. For example, if customers are complaining about the quality of products, Arpan might decide to buy the new machine to improve quality, even though the projected financial returns are slightly lower.

● This question is likely to offer a high mark allocation. The calculations alone would not generate all the marks. Students must bring in other information from the case, use their own ideas and also evaluate.

● Some thought must be given to setting out of numerical answers. Good presentation is important. Avoid deletions and sprawling calculations. Space answers generously and underline final answers.

Example 3

The final question in an extended case study often requires students to suggest a strategy or give an overall view. This is likely to require a level 4 response where synthesis becomes

important. The question might also carry higher marks. A possible question might be:

(d) Taking the whole case into account, do you consider that the board of directors should discontinue production at the Newport factory?

● Again, planning is very important here. A lengthy answer is required with relevant points being identified, thorough analysis, evaluation and synthesis. Students need to bring together a range of relevant points and make a decision.

● Timing is also crucial. Students must ensure that they leave sufficient time to plan and write the answer to this final, and important, question properly.

● Students may use some of the material generated in other answers in the case. But obviously repetition must be avoided.

● Again, it probably does not matter in this question whether students suggest that production is discontinued or not. Examiners want to see a well structured, logical argument with a meaningful conclusion drawn.

● Remember to consider the people, the situation, the objectives and to introduce theories.

Pre-seen case studies

A pre-seen case study is a method of assessment which involves giving students case study material before the day of the examination. This allows students to prepare more thoroughly for the examination by analysing the information and forming ideas in advance.

● Case study material may be issued a number of weeks before the day of the examination.

● The structured questions relating to the case study will not be known until the day of the examination.

● Additional information regarding the case may also be supplied within the question structure.

● The nature of the material provided in the case is likely to be the same as any other case study, but perhaps in more detail. Students should read the previous sections on data response and decision making questions.

Hints

● The general approach to pre-seen case studies is little different from those which are not pre-seen. The only important difference is that students have a great deal of time to study the data. Again, the hints in previous sections on answering data questions should be read.

● There is much more time to read the material so more time can be spent highlighting key words and terms. Students could also note theories, issues or themes which are relevant.

● Any words, terms or theories which are unfamiliar or forgotten can be looked up in the text book. For example, if the case contains an extract from a balance sheet, it might

be helpful to consult the balance sheet unit to reinforce understanding of balance sheet terms and structure.
- It is helpful to try and predict possible questions which the examiner might set. This will allow students to prepare answers.
- Try to identify trends, patterns and links in the data and account for them.
- Get help from friends and parents.
- When answering the questions in the examination it is very important to answer the ones set. Students should not try to reproduce their own 'model answers'.
- Level 3 and level 4 responses are likely to be required.

Essay writing

An essay is an assessment method used to find out how students can respond in depth to an open question. It involves writing in continuous prose and provides an opportunity to explain something in detail.
- It will probably be marked using all levels of response.
- The quality of grammar, vocabulary, sentence construction and spelling is particularly important.
- A strong emphasis is usually placed on analysis, evaluation and synthesis.
- Essay questions may be integrated and synoptic. This means that students must consider the full range of syllabus or specification areas when writing answers. Essays based on one section of a specification or syllabus, such as marketing, may draw on all areas within it.
- The length will vary depending on the time allocated.
- They require a great deal of thought and planning before writing begins.
- The use of real world examples to illustrate points is essential.
- The use of diagrams, such as the Boston Matrix, is encouraged.
- There is rarely a 'right' answer. It is possible for two students to put forward opposing arguments and both be awarded high marks. It is the quality of the argument which is important, not the nature of it.

Planning
- Read the question very carefully.
- Highlight the command words and other key words to help provide focus.
- Planning could be in two stages. Stage one might involve a 2 or 3 minute brainstorming session where students jot down an explosion of points and issues they think might be relevant.
- Stage two would then involve sorting points into an appropriate order and planning out a structure which will accommodate an argument.

Introduction
- It is common to begin with a short introduction where key

terms are defined and the question is put into context. Some general information may also be given. An introduction should be no more than a third of a side long, for example.

The main body
- When writing the main body of an answer it is important to follow the plan and write in detail, ensuring that evidence of analysis and evaluation is provided.
- It is vital to answer the question. It is better to write one side of relevant material than five sides of 'waffle'.
- Never use bullet points in essays.
- Never use subheadings in essays.
- Never write lists in essays. Extra marks are not awarded for identifying a large number of relevant points.
- Remember to include real world examples where appropriate.
- It is inadvisable to switch emphasis during the essay. It is best to stick to the plan.
- Diagrams, graphs and other illustrative material may be used but make sure it is clearly labelled and explained in the text.

Conclusion
- It is important to write a conclusion. It may be a statement which answers the question 'in a nutshell', drawing on the points analysed in the main body.
- Conclusions should not repeat material used elsewhere.
- The best conclusions are those which demonstrate evaluation and synthesis.
- Students are often required to make a judgment or give an opinion. Do not 'sit on the fence'.

Example
It has been argued that the productivity of UK businesses falls well behind that of its overseas rivals. Suggest possible reasons why this might be the case and examine the measures which might be taken by UK businesses to improve productivity?

- Essay questions can carry a relatively high number of marks.
- The words highlighted in the title are productivity, UK businesses, overseas rivals, suggest possible reasons, examine, measures and improve productivity.
- Brainstorming might deliver the following responses.
    Define productivity, labour, capital, Rover productivity poor, Nissan good, lack of investment, lack of funds, lack of R & D, dividends too high, too short termist. Standardisation, reengineering, kaizen, JIT, outsourcing, virtual companies, TQM, benchmarking, work study, culture, trade unions, weak management, quality circles, technology, training, labour flexibility, delayering, downsizing.

- Brainstorming will generate ideas but not in any particular order. The focus in the above responses appear to be production and ways of improving efficiency.
- Another 2 or 3 minutes spent planning might deliver the following essay structure.

Introduction
➤ *Define productivity - output in relation to inputs.*
➤ *An example of evidence which might support the statement is the low productivity of Rover compared with, say, Japanese car makers.*
➤ *Suggest that there are a number of approaches to improving productivity, some specific and some strategic.*

Main body
➤ *Analyse three possible reasons why productivity is lower in UK.*
➤ *Low investment, therefore, inadequate and dated technology.*
➤ *Lack of R & D because the City wants higher dividends NOW.*
➤ *Trade unions may have resisted changes which might improve productivity.*
➤ *Explain that measures designed to improve efficiency might be specific or strategic.*
➤ *Analyse 3 specific measures - JIT, benchmarking and new technology.*
➤ *Analyse 3 strategic measures - kaizen, reengineering and TQM.*

Conclusion
➤ *Argue that the statement is probably right for the reasons given. Evaluate by saying that one particular reason may be more important eg lack of investment.*
➤ *Argue that the methods employed to improve efficiency depend on the individual firm and their needs.*
➤ *Evaluate by suggesting that particular methods may be more suitable, if, for example, a business has dated machinery new technology may have a very significant impact on productivity.*
➤ *Argue that all measures will require cooperation of staff if they are to be successful.*
- When the essay is finished it is important to read through it and check for errors such as spelling, grammar and punctuation. However, avoid frantic crossing out at the last minute because this tends to have a negative effect on presentation.

Report writing

A business report is a formal method of communication. It is a written document designed to convey information in a concise but detailed way. A report is written in a structured way so that information is broken down into manageable parts. The end section of the report is very important. It will contain recommendations for action that a business should take.
- A report begins with a formal section showing who the report is for, who has written it, the date it was written and the title.
- A report is broken into a series of sections. Each section might address a particular issue.

- Each new section should begin with a clear heading and each section could be numbered.
- Each section can be broken down into sub-sections, which again can be numbered. Each sub-section may be a single paragraph.
- Information should be written in sentences and not in note form. Sections will require analysis and evaluation.
- Numerical information such as tables, graphs and charts should be shown in an appendix. Similarly, calculations should be shown in an appendix.
- The conclusion is very important and should aim at bringing together points raised and analysed in previous sections. No new material should be introduced at this stage. A conclusion is often an action plan or a series of recommendations.

Features Sometimes examiners require a report in a data response question. Students may be required to write reports based on a wide range of numerical data presented to them in tables or charts. It is this latter style which is the focus of attention here. It is sometimes called the numerical report. In a numerical report:
- information is presented in a number of tables or charts, perhaps 5 or 6 distinct pieces of data;
- the data will relate to a particular business and its market, there may also be some general economic data;
- students are required to interpret and analyse the data;
- some data may not be very helpful and should therefore be ignored, examiners deliberately give more information than is required to force students to be selective;
- the report question will normally be very specific and require students to make a decision, ie make recommendations;
- level 3 and level 4 responses are required therefore students must analyse, evaluate and use synthesis;
- students are often allocated a role when writing the report;
- the structure of the report will often be indicated in the question.

Hints
- Read the introduction and become familiar with the type of business, its market and circumstances.
- Read the tables of data and begin to form views about what they show.
- Make brief notes and comments adjacent to tables and graphs relating to trends and patterns shown by the data.
- Decide whether any data is irrelevant.
- Try to spot links between the different tables of data.
- Start to plan the report structure by identifying some appropriate section headings, **but do not use a heading for each piece of data.** Identify 4 or 5 key issues.
- Identify the points to be raised in each section.
- Decide what your conclusions and recommendations will be. Remember that there is not likely to be a right or wrong answer, but you must make a judgment.

● Write the report using the structure outlined above and remembering that the student is playing a role.
● Remember to analyse and evaluate throughout, and also, that the conclusion requires synthesis.

Example
Moa Kuk Ltd is a family business which imports a wide range of oriental soft furnishings and household artifacts. The business has two large stores in London. The second store was opened two years ago and has very quickly returned a profit. Moa Kuk, the managing director, believes that the company could grow very quickly and become a successful franchising operation.

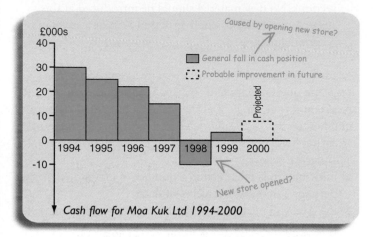

Cash flow for Moa Kuk Ltd 1994-2000

Extracts from Moa Kuk's balance sheet 1994-1999

	1994	1995	1996	1997	1998	1999
Share capital	£25,000	£25,000	£25,000	£25,000	£25,000	£25,000
Long term borrowing	£10,000	£12,000	£13,500	£15,000	£24,500	£27,000
Current assets	£17,500	£18,900	£21,400	£21,000	£36,700	£39,900

No new capital from owners

Big increase in borrowing - more highly geared

Not relevant. Increase due to more stock?

You are employed by a firm of business consultants. You have been asked to write a report to assess whether or not Moa Kuk should set up a franchising operation or grow independently.

● The question is likely to carry a relatively high number of marks.
● Begin to think of suitable section headings for the report structure. We only have an extract from a question here, but the limited information does provide some guidance for appropriate headings. For example:
  ➤ *The financial position of Moa Kuk Ltd*
  ➤ *The advantages of franchising*
  ➤ *The disadvantages of franchising*
  ➤ *Recommendations*
● Write brief notes by each data box. These are shown in the graph and the table.
● A plan can be drawn up for the first section.
  ➤ *Cash flow has deteriorated over the period particularly in the last two years when the new store was opened.*
  ➤ *The owners have not contributed any more capital to the business over the period.*
  ➤ *The development of the business has been funded by increased borrowing.*
  ➤ *Borrowing has increased steadily over the period making the company more highly geared.*
● A plan should be drawn up for the other sections in the answer. For example, the information may lead to a conclusion that: *Moa Kuk Ltd is not really in a financial position to fund independent growth. Therefore setting up a franchising operation may well be an effective strategy.*
● There will obviously be other points to consider based on other data which is not provided here.

Project / Coursework

A project is now a common feature of Business Studies, forming the coursework element of the examination. A project usually involves:
● extended research carried out over a period of time within a real business setting;
● the investigation of a problem or decision that the business is facing;
● the use of both qualitative and quantitative data and analysis in researching and analysing the problem or decision;
● the application of a range of business knowledge, skills and methods to the problem or decision;
● the identification of a number of feasible strategies that the business might pursue;
● evaluation of these strategies and making recommendations about which strategy should be pursued and why;
● the production of an extended report which presents the research and findings and use of a range of methods of presentation to enhance the quality of the report.

Unlike other elements of Business Studies examinations, this work is carried out over a period of time during the course. There will be a deadline by which time the project has to be completed, but it is largely the student's responsibility to set up and carry out the investigation and to produce the report by that deadline. The required length of the report is laid down by the awarding body.

Assessment The teacher is the first assessor for project work. He or she will mark the project as a whole and award marks based upon the assessment criteria set by the awarding body.

This will vary between different examinations, but typically covers the following skills:

- the way the problem or decision has been explained and objectives for the project set;
- the use made of relevant business knowledge, ideas and concepts in tackling the problem;
- applying appropriate research methods;
- carrying out relevant analysis using both qualitative and quantitative information;
- evaluating evidence to draw conclusions and make recommendations;
- presentation of evidence in a structured way that shows a logical development of ideas;
- employing a good quality of language including spelling, punctuation and grammar.

There may then be some internal moderation of your teacher's marking by another teacher or lecturer in the school or college to check that all the teachers are marking in a consistent way. Finally a sample of projects will be sent to an external moderator, employed by the awarding body, who will check that the marking has been carried out to the criteria set by the examining body.

Hints

- Choose an organisation for your project with which you have contact, perhaps through family or friends and which will allow you access to the information you require. Your teacher may also have established initial contact with a number of organisations which will provide appropriate projects.
- Don't be too ambitious with your choice of problem. *How might Marks & Spencer improve its profitability?* would be too much of a challenge, whereas *How might Marks & Spencer's Wilmslow branch increase its sales of microwave meals* might be a more realistic title.
- Produce a project/coursework action plan before you start your research - *what are your objectives? what information do you want to collect? what will be the sources of information? who do you want to talk to? when will you collect the information? what analysis will you carry out? when does the report have to be completed?*
- When carrying out your research within an organisation you will need to collect background information about the organisation as well as information specific to your project.
- Listen carefully and give yourself time each day to write up your notes - you will find that you will collect much more data than you will need, but you won't know which is relevant until you write up the project.
- When you come to the analysis of the data, use the concepts and techniques that you have been learning in your lessons and explain in the project why you are using a particular technique as a means of analysis
- Try to use both quantitative as well as qualitative analysis if the project lends itself to both.

- There are always alternative strategies for solving a problem - one alternative is always for an organisation to do nothing. You must present alternatives and evaluate their strengths and weaknesses.
- Make your recommendations and relate these back to your project objectives. It does not matter if the organisation would not necessarily follow your advice; but your recommendation should be firmly backed by evidence from your analysis.
- There will always be more that you could have done, but keep to the time deadline and keep to the word limit

Example
What is the feasibility of extending a 9-hole golf course to 18 holes?

This is an example of a project title that a student has negotiated with the local golf club where she plays as a junior member.

Objectives For this particular project the student, in discussion with the organisation, might set the following objectives:

- to identify the potential demand for an 18-hole course;
- to explore the local competition for the golf club;
- to examine the financial feasibility of building an 18- hole extension;
- to identify possible sources of finance for the extension to 18 holes;
- to make recommendations to the club on whether they should go ahead.

This is a piece of coursework that provides a reasonable problem for the student to tackle; it has scope for both qualitative and quantitative research and analysis and allows the student to make a clear choice at the end. By negotiating the objectives with the club, the student can hope to receive good access to the necessary people to talk to and the club's financial information. Access to accurate financial data is often the major constraint the students face when carrying out project research.

The scope of the project does not require the student to explore the legal background to expanding the golf course. This is a reasonable limitation that makes the project more manageable and the student would not be penalised for this provided the objectives and limitations of the project are made clear at the start.

Collecting information The student might plan to collect a range of data from primary and secondary sources. **Primary research** might include:

- a survey of existing members to establish their demand for an 18-hole course;
- a survey of potential members who might use the course if it had 18-holes;

● interviews with club officials who would be responsible for carrying out the extension;
● identifying the costs of building an extension;
● identifying the costs and availability of different sources of finance;

Secondary research might include:

● identification of the demand for golf through national statistics;
● identification of the location, size and facilities of other golf courses in the area;
● looking at the club's existing financial position through its published income and expenditure statements;
● looking at economic trends that might affect the future costs and revenue for a golf club;
● making use of any previous data that the club had collected if this problem had been considered previously.

Analysis Once the above research has taken place, the student would be in a position to carry out the following analyses of the information collected:

● a forecast of likely demand for the 18-hole course and thereby of the revenue that the club might generate;
● a forecast of the likely flow of expenditures on the project in order to set up and maintain the extended course;
● a cash flow for the project over the next 5/10 years;
● using the pay-back method or discounted cash flow method, an analysis of the financial benefit of the project when compared to other possible investments;
● a comparison of the costs and benefits of different sources

of funding for the extension of the course.

Evaluation Before making his/her final recommendation, the student would need to consider the following questions, making use of evidence drawn from the information and analyses presented in the report.

● Does the decision to expand the course fit into the overall strategy of the club?
● On purely financial grounds, is the expansion a viable option? Are there better financial options for the club, eg leaving the money in a high interest bearing account?
● Can the club raise the necessary finance for the expansion? Would the costs of increased borrowing outweigh the benefits?
● How reliable are the forecasts of the demand and revenue figures and the cost and expenditure figures? How accurate is the research on demand? What might change to increase the cost estimates?
● What other external and internal factors would the club need to take into account before making a final decision?

This evaluation would help to provide the basis upon which the student is making their final recommendation as well as pointing forward to other areas that might be considered in a longer report. It should not be seen as a sign of weakness that the report writer asks such questions of their own work. It shows that he or she understands both the strengths and weaknesses of their final decision. It is important to remember that there is no correct answer in report or coursework writing.

Index